GUNS
ILLUSTRATED 2001
33rd Annual Edition

Edited by
Ken Ramage

Manuscripts, contributions and inquiries, including first class return postage, should be sent to the GUNS ILLUSTRATED Editorial Offices, Krause Publications, 700 E. State Street, Iola, WI 54990-0001. All materials received will receive reasonable care, but we will not be responsible for their safe return. Material accepted is subject to our requirements for editing and revisions. Author payment covers all rights and title to the accepted material, including photos, drawings and other illustrations. Payment is at our current rates.

CAUTION: Technical data presented here, particularly technical data on the handloading and on firearms adjustment and alteration, inevitably reflects individual experience with particular equipment and components under specific circumstances the reader cannot duplicate exactly. Such data presentations therefore should be used for guidance only and with caution. Krause Publications, Inc., accepts no responsibility for results obtained using this data.

Published by

krause publications

700 E. State Street • Iola, WI 54990-0001
Telephone: 715/445-2214
Web: www.krause.com

Please call or write for our free catalog.

Our toll-free number to place an order or obtain a free catalog is 800-258-0929 or please use our regular business telephone 715-445-2214 for editorial comment and further information.

Library of Congress Catalog Number: 69-11342
ISBN: 0-87341-926-X

—GUNS ILLUSTRATED STAFF—

EDITOR
Ken Ramage

ASSOCIATE EDITOR
Ross Bielema

CONTRIBUTING EDITORS

Holt Bodinson   Robert Hausman
Doc Carlson   John Malloy
Bill Hanus   Hal Swiggett

Editorial Comments and Suggestions

We're always looking for feedback on our books. Please let us know what you like about this edition. If you have suggestions for articles you'd like to see in future editions, please contact.

Ken Ramage/Guns Illustrated
700 East State St.
Iola, WI 54990
email: ramagek@krause.com

About Our Covers...

A new firearms company was born early this year–American Western Arms, of Delray Beach, Florida. A new name, true, but the formerly separate businesses which now comprise the new company are well-known.

Classic Old West Styles, perhaps the most prominent purveyor of authentic period clothing, leather goods and accessories to the growing ranks of cowboy action shooters, has acquired the well-known Italian manufacturer of replica firearms, Armi San Marco, SA, which will now be known as American Western Arms Italy. The new entity is marketing an interesting line of rifles, cartridge-conversion c&b revolvers and reproductions of the first generation Colt single-action revolver in different models and chamberings. We have two of their guns displayed on our covers.

Front and Back: The Model 1892 lever-action rifle is arguably one of the most desirable of the old Winchester/Browning designs. This particular specimen is beautifully finished and chambered for the 45 Colt cartridge. The 1892 action is derived from the 1886 action and thus strengthened by the pair of vertically sliding bars which rise to intercept the bolt as the action is closed, locking the bolt securely. A handy, well-liked rifle resulted, with slightly over a million units made

(Flayderman's Guide to Antique American Firearms and their Values, 7th Edition), including all variations and chamberings.

The Model 1892 is well-known to John Wayne fans as the rifle he carried in most of his Westerns, including *True Grit*.

The single-action revolver on the front cover is the Longhorn model, available in a range of barrel lengths from 3 inches out to 12 inches. A variety of chamberings are also offered: 32-20, 38/357 Magnum, 38-40, 44 Special and 45 Colt. Subtleties of interest to experienced shooters, not discernible in the photograph, include the desirable .452-inch cylinder mouth diameter and 11-degree barrel forcing cone for cast bullet accuracy. Interested in authenticity? The Longhorn carries two-line patent dates and has the correct trigger guard configuration. There are two options on the frame style as well - your choice of the early blackpowder frame or the later version which retained the cylinder pin with a spring-loaded cross-bolt. A nice touch is the one-piece walnut grip.

For more information, contact American Western Arms, Inc., 1450 S.W. 10th Street, Ste. 3B, Delray Beach, FL 33444/800-595-2697. Website: www.awaguns.com

Guns Illustrated 2001

The Standard Reference for Today's Firearms

CONTENTS

Page 8

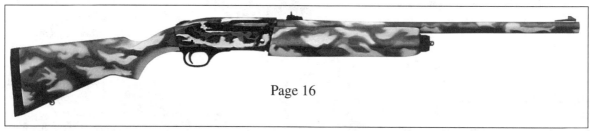

Page 16

Page 43

Page 86

CATALOG OF TODAY'S FIREARMS

Exclusive New Section!
Semi-Custom Arms
Handguns — Rifles — Shotguns

Page 123

Page 196

Page 288

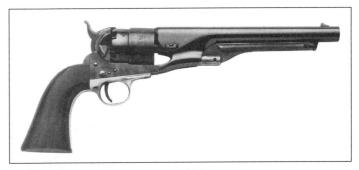

Page 294

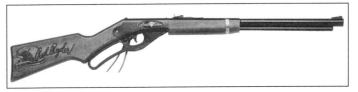

Page 324

Remington
Etron X

by Ralph Lermayer

Like it or not, the EtronX represents the future. Remington has taken a bold step from which there is no turning back.

TRACE THE HISTORY of the modern rifle's development, and it is apparent a few key events dramatically impacted the rifle's evolution from the first primitive hand-held pipe gun to the highly accurate, reliable rifles we use today. The inexpensive flintlock placed rifles into the hands of the masses, and that lock style reigned supreme for over 200 years. The compact percussion cap heralded the next significant change and, although it was around for less than 60 years, it made rifles faster to reload and reliable in any weather. The introduction of cased cartridges brought convenience, faster reloading–and gave birth to a

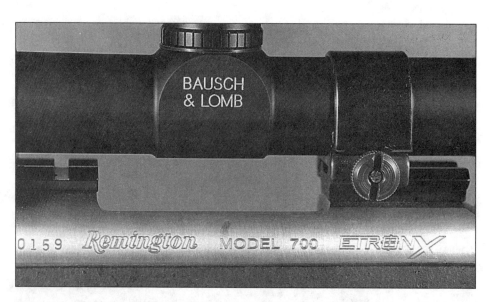

The EtronX looks and handles like the standard Model 700, but the toggle switch safety is the first giveaway. Author mounted a particularly accurate Bausch & Lomb Elite scope for testing.

lock style that is today's standard for reliability and accuracy in sporting rifles.

Since Paul Mauser first developed his bolt action in the 1800s, that basic design has been refined, improved and perfected to deliver levels of accuracy and reliability that many felt were unsurpassable.

We now blueprint actions for total concentricity, pillar- and glass-bed the action to the stock for a perfect match-up and shot-to-shot repeatability. Cartridge cases and loads are fine-tuned by weighing and trimming cases, carefully selecting components and building ammunition that delivers precise, consistent performance.

Bolts, sears and triggers are honed and polished to reduce the unavoidable friction that is part of a mechanically linked trigger in order to reduce the time it takes for the firing pin to travel to the primer (lock time). Two areas that, in spite of refinement, place an element of time delay between a perfect sight picture and ignition.

We are about to experience the next major development in rifle evolution. Remington has introduced the electronic EtronX rifle and line of electronically-fired cartridges, providing a commercially available, cost-effective rifle with an electronic ignition system, which removes the disadvantage of a mechanical trigger and spring-loaded firing pin. Rifle performance and safety have just taken another quantum leap forward.

Rumors about an exciting new technology being worked on at Remington have been bouncing around the industry since early '95, but facts were scarce. Remington was very tight-lipped. At the '99 Writer's Seminar, held at the Rough Creek Lodge in central Texas, they introduced the product to a group of writers and editors who were then given the opportunity to handle and shoot the new rifle. The EtronX looks, at first glance, like most other higher end Model 700s. The ergonomics and handling are the same as you would find on the Model 700 Sendero or VS (Varmint/Synthetic), but a closer inspection reveals features not found on any 700 you've ever seen.

All components in the firing sequence (trigger, safety, and firing pin), are electronic. Trigger movement is minimal. For practical comparisons, when you squeeze the trigger on an EtronX, nothing moves–and the gun fires. The mechanical linkage between trigger, sear, bolt and firing pin prior to primer contact is gone.

The safety, located where you would find the safety on a Model 700, is now a quiet toggle switch. With the switch to the rear, the rifle is totally disabled. Move it forward, and the rifle goes into fire mode but, unlike conventional safeties, this one has a brain.

Remington's objective was not only to develop electronic ignition. That technology is not new; the military has been using different forms of electronic ignition for years. Remington's concept adds patented new improvements to enhance both accuracy and, as importantly, safety. While it is not, by any means, what some would call a "smart gun", the EtronX won't let the rifle fire if certain potentially dangerous conditions exist. Mechanical safeties can fail, but the EtronX system greatly increases the safety factor.

The heart of the system is an eight-bit, on-board computer built on a single circuit board housed completely inside the butt-stock. A common 9-volt alkaline battery, the same battery you would use in a smoke detector or range finder, powers it. The battery is located behind the recoil pad and easily accessed by removing two screws in the pad. Changeover is simple even if it has to be done in the field, but that shouldn't be necessary, as battery life is good for approximately 1,500 rounds. The 9-volt battery supplies the 150-volt surge required to fire the round by amplifying the voltage in the circuit board. This surge is delivered to the special cartridge primer only when, and if, a series of safety conditions are met. We will detail the safety status checks later, but assuming all conditions are 'go', tracing this pulse helps us understand the unique working of the EtronX system.

The EtronX trigger is, in fact, a switch. Squeezing it as you would a trigger allows it to move to the rear. Although it is billed as a non-moving trigger, it does travel a short distance before it makes contact and starts the process of sending that 150-volt pulse on its way. The pressure it takes to reach that contact is adjustable down to as low as two pounds and, unlike the company's policy with standard Model 700s, Remington

fully endorses the customer making this adjustment. Adjustment of a simple screw, accessible from the front, is all it takes to adjust the pressure. Trigger travel is also minimal, fully 36% less than found in a standard trigger.

Once contact is made, the pulse travels through the safety switch, through a 10-pin connector plug that ties the receiver to the stock assembly

Author in field

and heads to the bolt assembly where it is fed directly to the firing pin.

The EtronX firing pin is completely insulated from contacting any metal surface in the bolt. A series of bushings hold it away from the bolt body, and the firing pin itself is coated with a non-conductive, ceramic material. That patented material is one of the key elements to reliable operation, and is projected to last for up to 7,500 rounds, twice the expected barrel life. I don't understand how this pin can ever wear out since it doesn't move. In fact, it is in constant contact with the primer when a round is loaded in the chamber. Having a constant contact between the firing pin and the cartridge primer takes some getting used to for those of us who think mechanically holding the firing pin away from the primer is the first rule of safety. The bare, exposed metal tip of the firing pin, with its 150-volt pulse at the ready, is always in firm contact with the primer in the cartridge, but no reasonable amount of mechanical impact can ever set off the unique priming compound found in the special EtronX primer.

Standard primers are filled with a compound that is impact sensitive. Like the old paper caps you played with as a kid, you impact this material by striking it with the firing pin and it goes off, igniting the powder and firing the round. Not so with the specially formulated lead styphnate found in the EtronX primers.

To ignite the special priming compound takes a substantial electrical charge. Close inspection shows this primer is really two primers in one. In the very center is a small primer with an indent in the middle that the firing pin sits in. Around that central primer, a small ring of polymer insulation separates and protects it from the rest of the primer—which is filled with more material to add power. That polymer ring insulates it from the metal surfaces, which could contact or prematurely short the pulse through the case to the rest of the metal surfaces of the rifle. Eventually the pulse will go through this case to the metal of the receiver. This small ring forces it to travel through the priming compound first, before it gets to the receiver.

From the origin of the pulse in the circuit board in the stock, through the insulated firing pin, and further insulated center of the special primer, the charge is fully separated from any metal anywhere in the rifle until it is sent through the center of the primer.

EtronX bolt, on right, showing firing pin permanently protruding to make constant contact with the cartridge primer.

The rest of the EtronX cartridge—the case, powder and bullet, are standard components all the way. The only difference is the primer. Handloaders will be able to purchase these primers in bulk, as you would any primers, and reload on normal equipment with conventional components in standard cases. The electronic primers don't alter or change ballistic performance. As of this writing, the U.S. Department of Transportation (D.O.T.) had not yet issued a permit for shipping these bulk primers. Loaded ammunition has been approved for shipment, but not primers. The results in the chart are Remington's factory comparisons testing electronic vs. standard primers in the 22-250 Remington and 220 Swift. I'm comfortable the results will be the same with the 243 Winchester chambering used for this review.

The entire firing process sounds complicated but, in fact, it is nearly instantaneous. From the moment you exert pressure on the trigger until the cartridge is ignited takes less than 27 microseconds—a whopping 99% reduction in lock time from the finest-tuned standard Model 700 found anywhere. With the EtronX, lock time is so fast that the bullet has exited the bore before the firing pin has struck the primer in a standard bolt action. Not only has it left faster, it has done

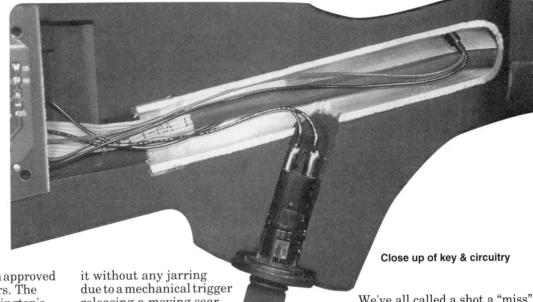

Close up of key & circuitry

▼ **Close up of circuit board inside EtronX stock.**

it without any jarring due to a mechanical trigger releasing a moving sear, and subsequently releasing a spring-loaded firing pin. Pull the trigger on the EtronX and it instantly fires. It is fast, it is impressive, it is eerie! For those of us who have spent decades living

With the EtronX, lock time is so fast that the bullet has exited the bore before the firing pin has struck the primer in a standard bolt action.

with standard triggers, the benefits of this new trigger and firing mechanism are immediately apparent. Once your brain says the sight picture is correct, the rifle fires!

How this will translate to performance in the field is obvious.

We've all called a shot a "miss" because we "pulled", or more commonly, "jerked" the trigger in the heat of the moment. A smooth trigger squeeze is vital to good marksmanship, but no one is perfect. With the EtronX the detrimental effect of a less-than-perfect trigger squeeze is greatly minimized, which will result in better performance on game. When, and if, it's ever allowed for competition, this system is destined to set new standards of accuracy in the benchrest community.

Overall, the quality of the ammunition, the quality of the barrel and the effects of bedding between the barrel and the stock will still limit the accuracy potential of the commercial EtronX rifles. The EtronX won't be a 1/4-minute shooter just because of the ignition system, but field performance will be greatly improved by

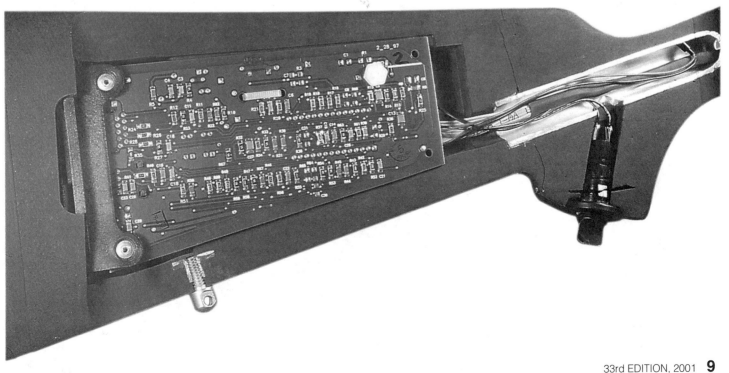

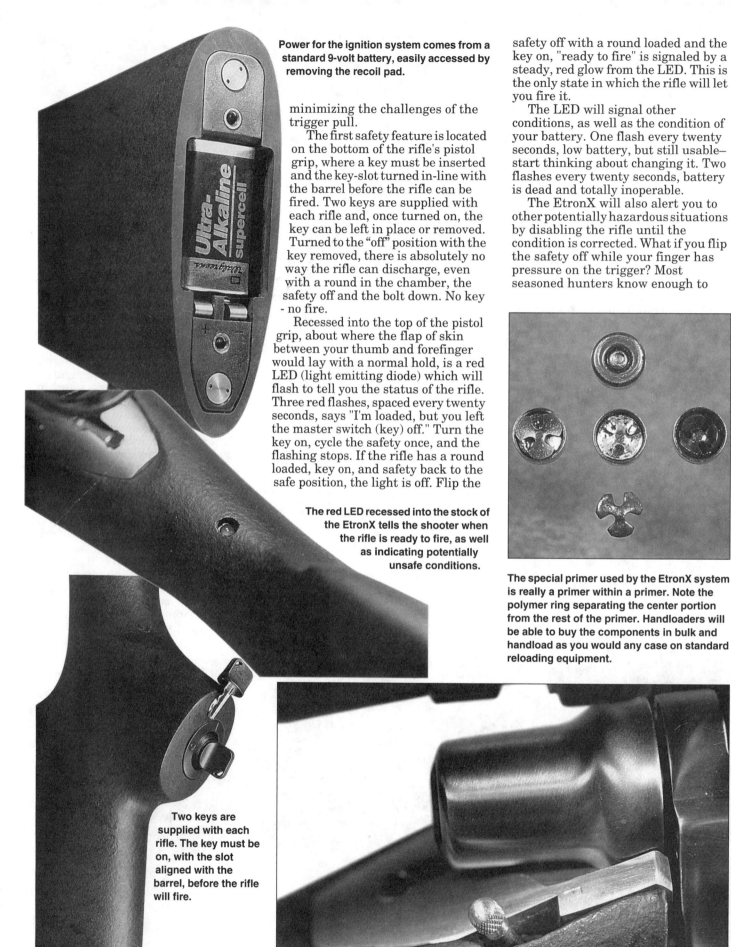

Power for the ignition system comes from a standard 9-volt battery, easily accessed by removing the recoil pad.

minimizing the challenges of the trigger pull.

The first safety feature is located on the bottom of the rifle's pistol grip, where a key must be inserted and the key-slot turned in-line with the barrel before the rifle can be fired. Two keys are supplied with each rifle and, once turned on, the key can be left in place or removed. Turned to the "off" position with the key removed, there is absolutely no way the rifle can discharge, even with a round in the chamber, the safety off and the bolt down. No key - no fire.

Recessed into the top of the pistol grip, about where the flap of skin between your thumb and forefinger would lay with a normal hold, is a red LED (light emitting diode) which will flash to tell you the status of the rifle. Three red flashes, spaced every twenty seconds, says "I'm loaded, but you left the master switch (key) off." Turn the key on, cycle the safety once, and the flashing stops. If the rifle has a round loaded, key on, and safety back to the safe position, the light is off. Flip the

The red LED recessed into the stock of the EtronX tells the shooter when the rifle is ready to fire, as well as indicating potentially unsafe conditions.

safety off with a round loaded and the key on, "ready to fire" is signaled by a steady, red glow from the LED. This is the only state in which the rifle will let you fire it.

The LED will signal other conditions, as well as the condition of your battery. One flash every twenty seconds, low battery, but still usable–start thinking about changing it. Two flashes every twenty seconds, battery is dead and totally inoperable.

The EtronX will also alert you to other potentially hazardous situations by disabling the rifle until the condition is corrected. What if you flip the safety off while your finger has pressure on the trigger? Most seasoned hunters know enough to

The special primer used by the EtronX system is really a primer within a primer. Note the polymer ring separating the center portion from the rest of the primer. Handloaders will be able to buy the components in bulk and handload as you would any case on standard reloading equipment.

Two keys are supplied with each rifle. The key must be on, with the slot aligned with the barrel, before the rifle will fire.

The safety on the EtronX is a toggle switch located where a standard safety would be found on any Model 700.

keep the trigger finger clear of the trigger until they're ready to fire, but it's conceivable that in the heat of the moment, an over-excited hunter could flip off the mechanical safety while there's pressure on the trigger.

I've guided a few hunters who have had their rifle mysteriously go off before they were ready. Can't happen with the EtronX. Flip the safety "off" while there's any pressure on the trigger, and the gun shuts down until you correct the situation by taking your finger off the trigger and cycling the safety. That situation is signaled by a series of four fast flashes.

Leave the rifle cocked and loaded while you are changing a battery: rifle shuts down, signals five flashes, and won't go back to ready until–you guessed it–you cycle the safety and are aware of its status. It's like a having a hunting buddy watching what you're doing - reminiscent of my early days afield as a youngster with Dad watching my technique. I could almost hear the words "Is your safety on?" or "We're over the fence, reload now."

The EtronX will also shut itself down after long periods of inactivity, forcing you to check it out in case it was inadvertently put away loaded. Being monitored like this takes a little getting used to but, after a session or two, you learn to adjust to the new level of communication between you and the rifle…and it becomes perfectly natural.

The test rifle sent for review was chambered in 243 Winchester. It has a heavy 26-inch fluted stainless barrel and is housed in the Sendero-style stock. The Sendero stock is Kevlar-reinforced, with an aluminum bedding block molded into it, from the pistol grip to the forend, for rigidity. That stock was chosen to house the EtronX because the aluminum block can be machined to hold the stock "half" of the 10-pin connector in perfect alignment with its counterpart on the receiver. That machining would not have been as consistent cut into hollow fiberglass.

Without scope, unloaded, the rifle weighed in at 8 7/8 pounds. With it came several boxes of factory 243 Winchester loaded with 90-grain Nosler Ballistic Tips. Pulling several bullets and checking the charge showed an average of 42 grains of extruded powder that looked much

The special coated firing pin is completely shielded from any contact with any metal other than the primer.

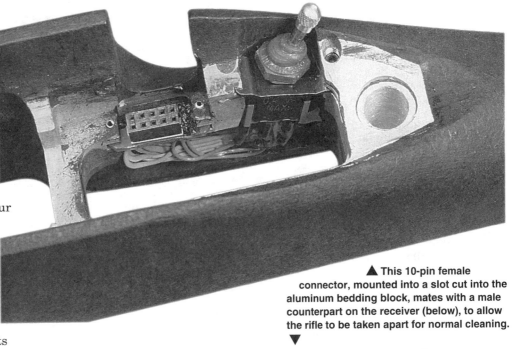

▲ This 10-pin female connector, mounted into a slot cut into the aluminum bedding block, mates with a male counterpart on the receiver (below), to allow the rifle to be taken apart for normal cleaning.

▼

like H4350. That approximates one of my pet loads for my 243s and 6mm Remington.

I mounted a particularly clear and accurate Bausch & Lomb 2-10X Elite 4000 that I reserve for serious accuracy testing. This scope has proven totally reliable, and I was confident that any inaccuracy wouldn't be the scope's fault. (B&L has discontinued this great scope, but they tell me it will be reintroduced in the Bushnell line.) With scope and rings the rifle weighed 9 3/4 pounds.

After bore-sighting and firing three rounds at 25 yards to impact dead-center, I fired the balance of the two boxes at 100 yards, off a rest. I must admit I was fully prepared to witness the smallest groups I had ever seen, and immediately enter myself and the new wonder rifle in every local contest I could find as I prepared myself for national and international greatness, but it was not to be.

The rifle simply shot very well, turning in groups that varied from a "best" of 1/2 inch to the largest of 1 1/2 inches, depending on the wind and my skill. Precisely the same performance I expect from my best hunting rifles. And then it dawned on me. The EtronX is just a hunting rifle. With a standard barrel and factory-loaded ammo, that performance is as good as it gets for those components, and probably a good deal better than most. I experienced no flyers, no erratic performance, no delayed firing–or problems of any kind. The rifle consistently shot average one inch to sub-one inch groups at 100 yards, with boring regularity. Velocity averaged 3,115 fps, and deviated only 33 fps, for the average of twenty rounds

The ceramic-coated firing pin is kept from contacting any metal in the bolt by the coating and a series of non-conductive bushing. Note the polymer insert the pin goes through in the bolt face.

fired through the chronograph screens, indicating excellent uniformity in primer performance as well as load.

Remington will initially offer two other chamberings in the EtronX, primarily for the varmint shooter - a 22-250 shooting a 50-grain Hornady V-

max bullet at a muzzle velocity of 3,725 fps, and a 220 Swift launching that same bullet at 3,780 fps, according to factory-published data. That seems a little hot for the 22-250, and about right for the Swift. Handloaders will no doubt tweak both these hot-stepping 224s to the limits for long range varmint performance and accuracy.

The review rifle was only here for a few days before it had to move on to another writer, so there wasn't a chance for any super cold weather, big-game testing. I did have the opportunity to fire a series of groups on a typical New Mexico winter day where the temperatures ranged from 27 degrees in the early (pre-dawn) a.m. and climbed to 68 degrees by noon. Groups fired at 27, 40 and 68 degrees were consistent, although not the rifle's best due to the very dim early morning and late

I was prepared to dislike the whole notion of electronic ignition, but after our short session, its merits were apparent.

evening light. Remington claims the rifle will function from sub-freezing temperatures to scorching desert conditions with no difference in performance, due to the electronic system. Battery life, however, will have to be watched in extreme cold and fresh batteries should be kept handy.

A local prairie dog town and a couple of low IQ coyotes gave me the opportunity to wring out the EtronX in the hills. Whether I was shooting from a sitting position, prone, off of shooting sticks, or on an impromptu rest, the rifle accounted for a dozen dirt dogs and those two unfortunate coyotes at ranges from 100 yards to a maximum of 275 yards. I had a limited supply of ammo, and no primers to reload, so I was careful about the shots I took. After the initial "newness" of dealing with the messages of the flashing red LED wore off, we both settled in, and I was soon comfortable enough with the system to forget that it was any different than any of my other rifles. Actually, once you get used to it, it kind of grows on you...as you find yourself constantly glancing at the LED to make sure all is well.

The special primer used by the EtronX system is really a primer within a primer. Note the polymer ring separating the center portion from the rest of the primer. Handloaders will be able to buy the components in bulk and handload as you would any case on standard reloading equipment.

Remington claims the system is also weatherproof, with all the components safely protected from the elements. I couldn't see any way for normal, or even hard-driving, rain or snow moisture to get to anything important, but as much as I wanted to, I couldn't bring myself to subject this prototype rifle to the garden hose test. When I get my hands on a production unit, it will be so baptized. Other than dropping this rifle overboard, or perhaps setting it in the bottom of a leaky boat or canoe, normal foul weather conditions won't adversely affect the EtronX system.

I was prepared to dislike the whole notion of electronic ignition, but after our short session, its merits were apparent. A return to my conventional rifles made the benefits of the EtronX obvious. Custom triggers that I always thought were superb, suddenly seemed archaic by comparison. Like it or not, the EtronX represents things to come. Remington has taken a bold step from which there is no turning back. Other manufacturers will follow suit. Circuit boards will get smaller and, no doubt, smarter. Battery life will be extended, and operating systems will be standardized in the interest of safety.

As with anything new, especially a radical departure from the long-familiar standards, some will condemn and fight the change while others embrace it. Some feel threatened, thinking the use of electronics will bring us a step closer to total control from Big Brother, while those in pursuit of that elusive one-hole group see it as a step closer to that goal.

In either case, electronics are here to stay. Can a double-action handgun that recognizes and only shoots for its owner be far off? ●

SHOTGUNS

by Larry Sterett

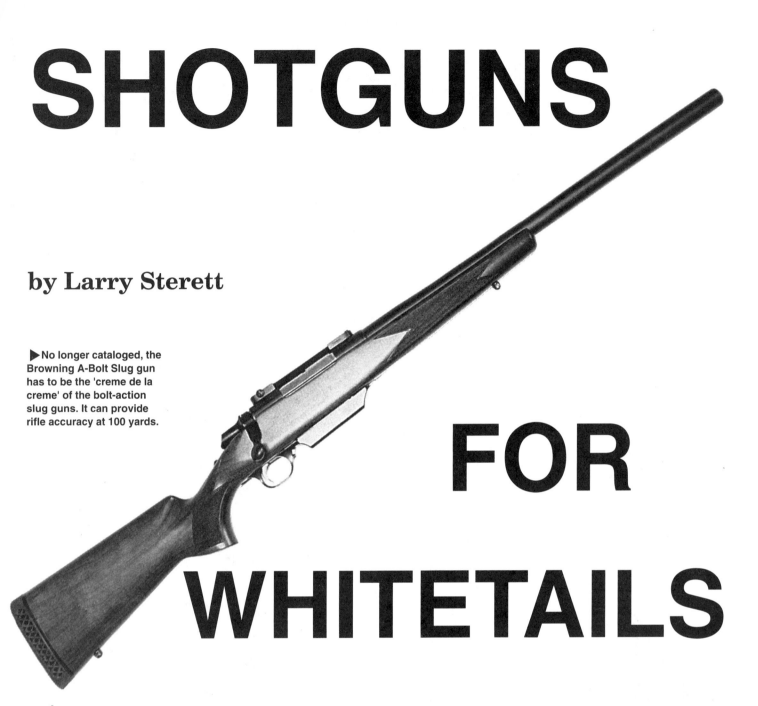

▶No longer cataloged, the Browning A-Bolt Slug gun has to be the 'creme de la creme' of the bolt-action slug guns. It can provide rifle accuracy at 100 yards.

FOR

WHITETAILS

A CENTURY AGO the whitetail deer population in the continental United States numbered under 500,000 animals. In some states, particularly in the Midwest and East, several generations never observed a native whitetail during their lifetime.

Today, the whitetail population in the continental U.S. is estimated at nearly 30,000,000 animals, making it the most popular big-game species for hunting. This remarkable comeback is due in part to the use of Pittman-Robinson funds and the live trapping of animals in states with plentiful whitetail herds. One of the leading sources of whitetails for restocking into states with few or no deer populations was the heavily forested

Keystone state—Pennsylvania. (Pennsylvania's whitetail annual roadkill is larger than some states' annual harvest by hunters.)

Many states–such as Illinois, whose hunters have enjoyed whitetail seasons for the past four decades after a fifty-year lapse–do not allow deer hunting with centerfire rifles. Hunters are limited to hunting with bow and arrows, percussion (muzzleloading) rifles, shotguns using rifled or sabot slugs, or handguns. Further limitations are placed on the calibers and gauges with which whitetails may be hunted. These limitations vary with the state, but usually the muzzleloaders must be .45-caliber or larger; the handguns, revolvers or

single-shot pistols of .40-caliber or larger. Shotguns–in the majority of states requiring their use for the taking of deer–may have smoothbore or rifled barrels in gauges of 20 or larger.

Rifled barrels for shotguns became popular slightly over a decade ago, but custom barrels were available prior to the many current commercial models. Today, the hunter having need of a suitable shotgun for hunting whitetail deer, or similar size game, is faced with a wide variety of suitable models from which to choose. The following report covers the latest models.

Benelli USA has the most unique new slug gun available. The Nova Pump Slug features a one-piece, receiver/buttstock assembly molded

▶The new 12 gauge Benelli Nova Pump Slug gun features an 18 1/2-inch smoothbore barrel with rifle-type sights. It will handle 3 1/2-inch shells.

▶The Benelli Super Black Eagle Slug autoloader features a 24-inch fully rifled 12-gauge barrel and rifle-type sights. The receiver is drilled and tapped for scope mounting.

◀ Benelli's Ml Field Slug autoloader features a fully rifled 24-inch barrel, rifle-type sights and a receiver drilled and tapped for scope mounts. It will handle 3-inch shells. The Ml Tactical M model is similar, but with synthetic pistol grip stock, 'Ghost Ring' sights and a smoothbore 18 1/2-inch 12-gauge barrel with interchangeable choke tubes. The Ml Practical features a 26-inch barrel with muzzle brake, plus a Picatinny rail on the receiver, along with additional IPSC features.

together using glass-reinforced techno-polymers. (An embedded steel cage serves as the connection for the barrel and magazine tube assemblies; the receiver can be drilled and tapped for scope mounting.) The Nova weighs over seven pounds, but to help tame the effects of repeated use with 3 1/2-inch shells, an optional recoil assembly can be installed in the buttstock cavity; this is accomplished by pulling the heavy duty recoil pad off the stock butt, exposing the hollow. Other features of the new Nova Pump Slug, which is also available in six

field grades, include double action bars, the proven Montefeltro rotating breech bolt design which locks into the barrel extension, a magazine cap which can be used as a disassembly tool for the trigger assembly group, a chrome-lined 18 1/2-inch smoothbore barrel, adjustable rifle-type sights, a two-shell free-floating carrier and a 'mag-stop' button on the forearm to serve as a magazine cut-off. (This last feature permits the chamber to be emptied

while keeping the shells in the magazine in reserve. Magazine capacity is four rounds. (A rifled bore barrel version may be introduced later.)

Other Benelli slug guns include the Super Black Eagle Slug and the Ml Field Slug guns featuring 24-inch rifled barrels having rifle-type sights and receivers drilled and tapped for scope mounting. The Super Black Eagle is available with a choice of walnut or synthetic stock and forearm, while the Ml comes only with a black synthetic stock and forearm and a three-round magazine capacity. Three additional models, the Ml Tactical, Ml Tactical M, and M3 Convertible can

▶Heckler & Koch's new 12-gauge FP6 features a 20-inch barrel with flip-up front sight and a Picatinny rail on the receiver to accept a host of optical sights.

▶The new Ithaca Gun Model 37 Deerslayer Hardwoods 20/2000 12-gauge pump features the Realtree camo pattern finish, a receiver drilled and tapped for scope mounting and 'TruGlo' optical sights. Like all smoothbore Deerslayer Model 37s, it has a bore specifically reduced in diameter to handle Foster-type rifled slugs.

◀Marlin Firearms' new 12 gauge Model 512P features a ported 21-inch fully rifled barrel with 'Fire Sights'. The black synthetic stock features molded-in checkering, and the receiver is drilled and tapped for easy scope mounting.

▶H&K's Camo Turkey is chambered for 3 1/2-inch 12 gauge shells. It features a Picatinny rail on the over-barrel; fitted with rifled choke tubes, it would make a great over/under slug gun.

Benelli's M3 Convertible (pump/autoloader) 12 gauge features a smoothbore 19 3/4-inch barrel, 'Ghost Ring' sights.

Benelli's M3 Convertible (pump/autoloader) is also available with standard rifle-type sights.

make great deer guns, and even the Ml Practical could be used, although it was designed for IPSC events. (The Practical, being specifically designed for competition shooting, has such features as an oversized safety, speedloader, muzzle brake and Picatinny rail.) The Tactical and Tactical M feature 18 1/2-inch barrels and interchangeable choke tubes, while the M3 has a 19 1/4-inch cylinder bore barrel. The M3, Ml Tactical M and Practical feature excellent ghost ring sights, while the Ml Tactical has regular barrel-mounted rifle-type sights.

Beretta USA has two new autoloaders, the ES100 Rifled Slug and the 1201FP "Ghost Ring," suitable for deer hunting. Both models, available in 12 gauge only, feature black synthetic stocks and forearms and non-glare matte black finish on the barrel and receiver. The ES100 has a 24-inch fully rifled barrel with rifle-type sights, while the 1201FP features an 18-inch barrel with a tritium-insert blade front sight and receiver-mounted adjustable "Ghost Ring." (The receiver of the ES-100 is drilled and tapped for a scope mount.) Both models are inertia-operated,

chambered for 3-inch shells and come with sling swivel studs.

Browning no longer catalogs their excellent A-Bolt 12 gauge bolt-action shotgun. But joining the BPS Deer Special and Cantilever Game Guns and the autoloading Gold Deer Hunter are the new Gold Deer Stalker and Mossy Oak Gold Deer guns. The guns are similar except for one having the Mossy Oak Breakup finish on most exterior parts, and the other having a matte black finish. The 22-inch barrel is fully rifled, chambered for 3-inch shells, and fitted with a special cantilever scope mount. Magazine

Mossberg's Model 695 bolt-action 12-gauge slug gun now has 'TruGlo' optical fiber sights on its ported 22-inch rifled barrel. The receiver is drilled and tapped for scope mounting.

The 12 gauge Mossberg Model 9200 is available with a choice Woodlands (shown) or Mossy Oak Shadow camo finish with 24-inch vent rib barrel fitted with 'TruGlo' optic sights, or as part of a combo featuring a 24-inch rifled barrel with rifle-type sights (shown) plus a 28-inch Accu-choke vent rib barrel.

Mossberg's Model 835 Ulti-Magnum, with Realtree X-tra Brown camo finish, features a ported 24-inch vent rib barrel fitted with 'Tru-Glo' optical fiber sights. It will handle all 12 gauge shells up to 3 1/2-inches, and accepts screw-in Ulti-choke tubes.

This Mossberg Model 500 Slugster features a ported, fully-rifled 20 gauge barrel, cantilever scope mount and interchangeable stock comb.

capacity is four rounds and overall weight is approximately 7-3/4 pounds. Otherwise, the new Browning has all the great features of the regular Gold line of autoloaders including speed loading and the self-cleaning, self-adjusting gas system.

European American Armory Corporation exhibited a "Baker's Dozen" new Russian shotguns at last year's SHOT Show, but only one has suitable features for a slug gun. This was the autoloading Saiga model based on the time-tested Kalashnikov design. Featuring a detachable 5-round box magazine, the Saiga–used by Russian hunters–in either 12 or 20 gauges could be used to bag big game. Available with black or camo finish, the shotgun can be obtained with detachable or fixed chokes, and a choice of 12, 24, 26, or 28-inch barrel length. Rifle-type sights are standard, but a scope with side mount is optional.

Harrington & Richardson introduced their break-action single-shot Ultra Slug Gun in 12 gauge in 1995 and in 20 gauge a year later. The Ultras feature fully rifled heavy 24- and 22-inch barrels, respectively. Two additional versions are now available, differing only in having a hand-checkered, laminated, camo Monte Carlo stock and semi-beavertail forearm in place of walnut-stained American hardwood. Scope mount bases, sling swivels and slings are standard accessories, but no sights.

H & R also has a Topper Deluxe Slug Gun in 12 gauge. Featuring a black Monte Carlo stock and forearm, this Topper has rifle-type sights, and weighs in the 5- to 6-pound range; the Ultra models weigh from 7 to 9 pounds, depending on the model and gauge. Available only in 12 gauge, chambered for 3-inch shells, the Topper has a 24-

inch fully rifled barrel with integral compensator, five slots on each side of the front sight. Under the New England Firearms label the Tracker and Tracker II models are similar to the Topper, but with walnut-stained hardwood stock and forearm in place

Shotguns–in the majority of states requiring their use for the taking of deer–may have smoothbore or rifled barrels in gauges of 20 or larger.

of black; color case-hardened receiver finish in place of satin-nickel, and a choice of smooth-bore or rifled 24-inch non-compensated barrel. (the Tracker II models feature the rifled barrels.) Both Tracker models are available in a choice of 20 or 12 gauge, chambered for 3-inch shells, and weigh approximately 5-1/4 pounds.

The Clay Center, Kansas, firm of Hastings does not import or manufacture shotguns, but does distribute after-market shotgun barrels, smoothbore and rifled, in 12 and 20 gauge that shotgun owners can install on their own shotguns. Manufactured by Verney-Carron of France, the barrels range in length from 20 to 26 inches, and include versions with rifle-type sights or scope mount bases. Currently barrels are available to fit popular Beretta,

Browning, Ithaca Model 37 and Remington autoloading and pump shotguns, having 2 - or 3-inch chambers. (The regular rifled barrel, the Paradox, will handle all lead Foster and Brenneke-type rifled slugs, but Hastings does not recommend the use of Remington's Solid Sabot ammunition in earlier Hastings Paradox barrels.)

The newest Hastings rifled barrel, available in 12 gauge only, is the CSD (Controlled Sabot Discard), which features a dozen radially-milled exhaust ports at the muzzle. A tapered exit bore allows uniform sabot separation for increased accuracy. (CSD barrels are available only for the Ithaca Model 37, and some Remington Models 870/1100/11-87 in 1999.)

Heckler & Koch is known the world over for their handguns and rifle designs, but the firm also distributes the Fabarm line of pump-action and over/under shotguns. One 12 gauge model of each type is ideal for use with slugs. Both are smoothbores with screw-in choke tubes capable of handling a rifled tube.

The FP6 pump features twin action bars, a 20-inch barrel chambered for 3-inch shells, a flip-up post front sight and a receiver-mounted Picatinny rail having an integral rear sight. (The rail allows the use of a scope, red dot optical sight or other optional sights.) The magazine capacity is five rounds, the weight under seven pounds, and the polymer forearm and stock compliment the anti-corrosion black finish on the receiver and barrel. (A sling attachment point is recessed into the base of the pistol grip.)

The Camo Turkey Magnum features 20-inch TriBore barrels, chambered for 3 1/2-inch shells, and screw-in choke tubes. (All exterior surfaces have a Xtra Brown

Camouflage finish.) A single selective trigger is standard, as is a blade front sight and quick-detachable Picatinny rail scope mount base. (The Picatinny rail can be used for scope or other optical sights and, by pushing its locking latch and removing it forward, its grooved track can be used as an expedient rear sight.) Fitted with a pair of rifled slug tubes, the Camo Turkey Mag would serve as a 12 gauge double rifle.

Ithaca Gun introduced the Model 37 more than six decades ago after

▶ Savage's new Model 210F Slug Gun features a 24-inch rifled 12 gauge barrel, and receiver-mounted scope mount bases.

Remington Arms discontinued their Model 17 on which the 37 is based. Over 35 years ago Ithaca introduced the Model 37 Deerslayer, designed with an undersized bore to fit the Foster-type rifled slugs then available. Using a scope, mounted on a rear sight base designed for the purpose, the smoothbore Deerslayer was capable of producing pie-plate (6-inch) groups at 75 yards. The new Deerslayer II features a fully rifled, non-takedown, free-floating barrel capable of 3-inch groups at 100 yards, using sabot-type slugs. Available in both 12 and 20 gauge versions, with 20 or 25-inch barrel chambered for 3-inch shells, it features an American walnut Monte Carlo stock and forearm with cut checkering, and a receiver drilled and tapped for scope mounting.

The regular Model 37 Deerslayer is available in the new RealTree Hardwoods 20/200 camo pattern. It features a synthetic stock and forearm having the new camo pattern, a 'TruGlo' fiber optic sighting system, and a receiver drilled and tapped for easy scope mounting. All steel—except for the stock, forearm, and optic sight—the latest Model 37 is hand-assembled from U.S. components, just as it was in 1937.

Marlin Firearms introduced their bolt-action 12 gauge Model 512 Slugmaster shotgun with 21-inch fully rifled barrel earlier in the 1990s. In 1999 they added the 512P featuring a

black fiberglass-filled synthetic stock with molded-in checkering, and a ported barrel fitted with 'Fire Sights'. The receiver is drilled and tapped for a scope mount base, included with the shotgun. Both the 512 and 512P feature detachable two-round box magazines, and will handle all 12 gauge shells up to the 3-inch length.

O.F. Mossberg & Sons has added eight new grades to their already extensive shotgun line–plus upgrading some of the older versions. All have standard or optic fiber 'TruGlo' rifle-type sights, with receivers drilled and tapped for scope mounts. The Model 9200 autoloader is available in a choice of Woodlands or Mossy Oak Shadow Brand camo finish, and features a 24-inch vent rib barrel with 'TruGlo' fiber optic sights; the rear adjustable for windage and elevation and the front adjustable for windage. (Three versions of the Model 9200 are available as Combos, with 28-inch vent rib Accu-II barrel and 24-inch fully rifled slug barrel having rifle-type sights.) Suitable for use with slugs, with or without a rifled choke tube, all eight new grades feature synthetic stocks and forearms. Seven models are available in 12 gauge with 24-inch barrels while the 20 gauge Model 500

Crown Grade Bantam features a 22-inch vent rib barrel.

There are four new versions of the Model 835 3 1/2-inch Ultra Mag, differing mainly in the type of finish: Woodlands Mossy Oak Shadow Branch or Realtree X-tra Brown camo. One version, the Combo, available only with Woodlands Camo finish, features a 24-inch vent rib barrel with 'Tru-Glo' sights, plus an extra 24-inch fully-rifled barrel with 'TruGlo' sights. All barrels are ported and will handle all 12 gauge shells up to 3 1/2 inches in length.

The Model 695 bolt action shotgun is now available with 'TruGlo' fiber optic rifle sights, in addition to the standard rifle sights, and the version with the Bushnell 1.5-4.5X scope mounted. The Model 695 versions feature 22-inch barrels, while the pump-action Model 500 Slugster Crown Grade versions in 12 and 20 gauge have 24-inch barrels. The barrels on both the 695 and Slugster models are ported.

Mossberg has two other 12 gauge models–the 500 Persuader/ Cruiser with 18 1/2-inch barrel and the 590 Special Purpose with 20-inch barrel– that could serve as handy short-range slug guns. Both models feature excellent 'Ghost Ring' sights, smoothbore barrels and synthetic stocks. They can handle Foster-type rifled slug loads but an after-market screw-in rifled choke tube would definitely improve performance with sabot loads.

Remington Arms has more versions (16!) of their popular models, 870/

The magazine on the Savage is an integral part of the stock, just as it is on the Mossberg Model 695.

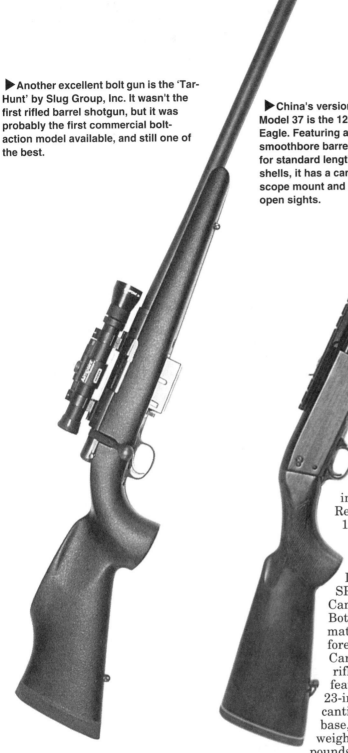

▶Another excellent bolt gun is the 'Tar-Hunt' by Slug Group, Inc. It wasn't the first rifled barrel shotgun, but it was probably the first commercial bolt-action model available, and still one of the best.

▶China's version of the Ithaca Model 37 is the 12-gauge YL-12 Eagle. Featuring a 20-inch smoothbore barrel chambered for standard length (2 3/4-inch) shells, it has a cantilever scope mount and rifle-type open sights.

1100/11-87, specially designed for use with deer slugs than any other manufacturer. Five of the models feature the cantilever scope mounts, while the other feature rifle-type sights on the barrel. All but one version of the autoloaders are available only in 12 gauge; several versions of the Model 870 pump are available in 20 gauge, including a couple of youth versions. Remington also has after-market rifled barrels available to fit their various models,

in addition to rifled Rem-Choke tubes in 12 gauge only. There are two recent Model 870s: the Express Synthetic Deer Gun and the SPS "Super Slug" Cantilever Deer Gun. Both versions feature matte black synthetic forearms and Monte Carlo stocks, and fully rifled barrels. The SPS features a new contour 23-inch barrel with cantilever scope mount base, and an overall weight of about eight pounds. The Express version features a 20-inch barrel with rifle-type open sights, and an overall weight of around seven pounds. Both versions have a four-round magazine capacity and a black matte-finish on metal surfaces.

Once a leading U.S. manufacturer of shotguns–including single shot, side/side, over/under, autoloading, pump and bolt-action models–Savage Arms now produces only a bolt-action model in two grades, plus a combination gun. The Mastershot

Model 210F bolt-action "Slug Gun" is based on a modified, time-tested Model 110 rifle action fitted with a 24-inch rifled (8-groove) 12 gauge barrel chambered for 3-inch shells. The 210F features no sights, but comes ready for scope mounting with a one-piece mount base. Overall weight of the 210F is approximately 7-1/2 pounds and it features a black synthetic stock with integral box magazine, for a capacity of three rounds.

Under the Winchester label, U.S. Repeating Arms offers three pump-action Model 1300 deer guns, plus a new Camp Defender model that will do the job when fitted with a rifled choke tube. The new Camp gun features a 22-inch smoothbore 12 gauge barrel chambered for 3-inch shells and fitted with rifle-type sights. The stock and forearm are synthetic, the magazine capacity is eight rounds, and the cylinder Winchoke tube is interchangeable with an after-market rifled tube for use with slugs. Featuring a completely black finish, the Camp Defender is similar to the Black Shadow Deer version which is available with a choice of smoothbore or rifled barrel, a five-round shell capacity and a receiver drilled and tapped for scope mounting.

The Winchester Model 1300 Deer gun is similar to the Black Shadow Deer except for having a walnut stock and forearm and a rifled barrel only. A similar version–but with walnut-stained hardwood stock and forearm, a choice of 22-inch rifled or smoothbore barrel with rifle-type sights, and an extra 28-inch ventilated rib Winchoke barrel–becomes the Ranger Deer Combo.

There are a number of other shotguns on the market suitable for use with rifled slugs. Some models, such as Tar-Hunt's rifled-barrel bolt action have been on the market for a number of years while others, such as the pump-action Norinco YL-12 Eagle, feature a smoothbore barrel. Regardless, the latest crop of shotguns designed for use with slugs is way beyond what shotgunners could even have dreamed of four decades ago. In place of the old smoothbore smokepole with a muzzle bead and possible after-market receiver sight, today's best feature a choice of ported, rifled or smoothbore barrel with screw-in rifled choke tube, rifle-type sights, scope mounts, black or camo finish and synthetic or hardwood stocks. And, you just read about them in this report. ●

THE SPACE-AGE 22 MAGNUM

by John Lachuk

THE EMERGENCE OF next-generation high-tech cartridges delivering target accuracy, with extended reach and more explosive results at the target, has been a major engine propelling renewed interest in the 22 Magnum.

After decades of wearily waiting in the wings, the 22 Winchester Magnum Rimfire is finally achieving some well-deserved popularity! The 22 WMR—or simply 22 Magnum—was introduced by the Winchester Division of Olin Corporation in 1959, combining the low cost and throw-away brass of the 22 Long Rifle with roughly double the range of its smaller sibling. Certainly not a plinking cartridge, the 22 Magnum eventually became the small game hunter's best friend.

The "outskirts" of town, once minutes away, may now be hours distant, often along clogged freeways. Even then, you're looking at privately owned land, often posted "NO HUNTING". The good news is that a polite request from a neatly dressed hunter to a farmer or rancher often elicits permission to shoot. He's happy to have you terminate ground squirrels that weave a labyrinth of tunnels, raise destructive mounds and create gaping holes to trap unwary cattle and horses.

To assure a continued welcome, you can use the muted-voice 22 Magnum, that won't alarm stock—or the farmer's wife! And "leave nothing but your tracks"—that is, no bullet holes in signs, fence posts, irrigation piping or barns!

Why the 22 Magnum instead of a 22 LR rifle? A 22 Long Rifle may work for awhile, especially early in the season. However, after the ground squirrels become educated, those nearby duck and run at first sight of hunters, that's when the added reach of a 22 Magnum becomes indispensable. The 22 Magnum also has the killing power to anchor larger prey, such as rockchucks and badgers, or even bobcats and coyotes within the range at which

◄ The 22 Magnum not only greatly increased rimfire range over the high velocity 22 Long Rifle, it offered greater stopping power on predators such as this bobcat, taken with a scoped Anschütz Model 141M.

you're able to make positive hits in vital areas to result in humane kills.

Among centerfire smallbore rifles, the 22 Hornet or the 222 come to mind with similar assets. However, the cost factor is compelling in favor of the 22 Magnum! Recommended retail from Lew Horton Distributing is just $7.55 for 50-round boxes of Remington 22 Win. Mag., compared to $30.75 for 50 rounds of 22 Hornet, and $16.71 for only 20 rounds of hollow-point "Triple Deuce."

Admittedly, reloading can cut the centerfire cost substantially, but the weary hours spent cleaning and sorting brass and pumping the press handle could be better used out hunting. Just setting up to reload costs enough to buy a couple of cases of 22 Magnum ammo. Then, just think of how long it would take to load 10,000 rounds of ammo!

When Winchester introduced the 22 WMR, it used a 40-grain true jacketed hollow-point with a section of the lead exposed ahead of the thin copper jacket, creating a bullet obviously designed for hunting small game. Tissue damage was so extensive that meat hunters, especially tree squirrel fans, elected to return to the 22 Long Rifle, despite its limited range. Winchester responded with a full metal-jacketed bullet, flat-nosed to retain ample stopping effect, but yielding greatly reduced tissue damage.

Winchester's 22 WMR wasn't their first effort at "magnumizing" the smallbore rimfire. In 1890 they introduced the 22 Winchester Rim Fire (22 WRF), featuring a cannelured case, longer and larger in diameter than the then-popular 22 Long. The inside-lubricated 45-grain flat-nosed lead bullet was seated deep instead of sharing the heel-crimped outside-lubricated bullets common to other 22 rimfires of the time. Surprisingly, the 22 WRF actually predated the 22 Long Rifle. The latter evolved as a happy combination of the 22 Long case and the 40-grain bullet of the ill-starred 22 Extra Long, introduced in 1880.

Winchester chambered the 22 WRF into their slender-barreled top-ejecting Model 90 pump-action rifle with under-barrel tubular magazine. In 22 Short chambering, the lightweight fast-firing rifle was the darling of the thousands of shooting galleries in the States around that time, and a popular field rifle in 22 Long Rifle caliber, but the thin-barreled rifle lacked the accuracy to take full advantage of 22 WRF, and the more powerful rimfire drifted into obscurity and finally, abandonment.

Winchester makes periodic runs of 22 WRF ammunition to accommodate owners of discontinued rifles of that

caliber. The last was produced in 1994, with a muzzle velocity of 1320 fps. The 22 WRF can be fired in a 22 WMR chamber, albeit with poor accuracy, but Winchester made the new case .092-inch longer to contain 7 1/2 grains of Olin ball powder, and prevent the new magnum (with a chamber pressure of 30,000 psi/CUP) from seating in old 22 WRF rifles.

Winchester waited almost a year to produce a 22 WMR rifle, the Model 61, another soda straw-barreled pump action. It would be hard to find a more inappropriate rifle for this wonderful new cartridge! Two twin rifles, the

The 22 WMR (right) survived its only serious challenge in the form of the bottle-necked rimfire 5mm Remington Magnum (center), which failed because of extraction problems with Remington's bolt action Model 591/592, caused by chamber pressures of 33,000 psi/cup.

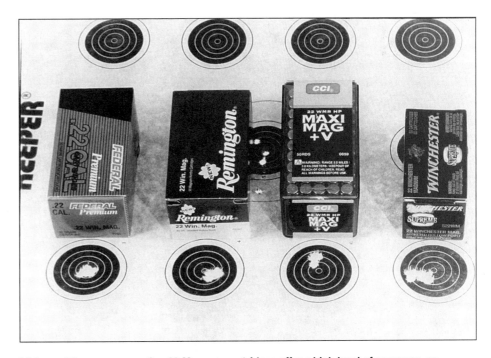

All four of the new-generation 22 Magnum cartridges offer a high level of accuracy, as demonstrated by these bench-rest 10-round groups, fired at 50 yards with the author's veteran Anschutz Model 54.

Model 255 lever action and Model 275 slide action, were Winchester's next choice for the 22 WMR. They shared dovetailed alloy receivers and 11-shot under-barrel tubular actions. Although acceptable as field rifles, the 5 pound lightweights couldn't provide the accuracy required to take advantage of the added range the 22 WMR could offer.

Other gun companies treated the 22 Magnum with greater respect. Anschutz chambered the potent rimfire into their Model 141M, and later the 6 3/4-pound Model 54 Custom Sporter, with 24-inch tapered barrel and Monte Carlo Schnabel-tipped European walnut stock, featuring the 54 Target bolt action that for decades dominated the German Championships and the Olympics. Currently, Anschutz offers their look-alike–but updated–Model 1720-D in 22 Magnum.

Eventually, Winchester came up with an accurate 22 WMR rifle. In 1972 they introduced the 20-inch barreled lever-action Model 9422, twin to the ubiquitous 30-30 deer rifle, in both 22 LR and the 22 WMR. The magnum version holds eleven rounds in the under-barrel tubular magazine.

The 6 1/4-pound all-steel carbine, with checkered walnut stock and forend, was designed to handle the high-pressure magnum rimfire with strength to spare.

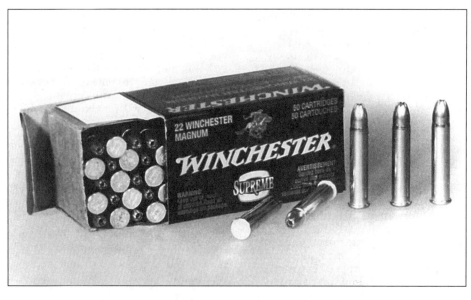

The 22 Winchester Magnum Rimfire Supreme, the latest high-tech offering from the inventor of the 22 Magnum, delivers ultimate power and accuracy in an extremely effective 34-grain jacketed hollow point bullet.

Remington challenged the 22 WMR in 1968, with their 5mm Remington Magnum, a bottle-necked sharp-shouldered rimfire, launching an electroplated 38-grain 20-caliber hollow-point bullet at 2100 fps. Unfortunately, Remington elected to chamber their new rimfire in a lightweight field rifle suitable only for medium range small game hunting, instead of creating an accurate long range rifle. The magazine-fed bolt-action Model 591 and tubular magazine Model 592 were doomed in any case. The 33,000 psi/CUP chamber pressure swelled the cases so that they stuck in the chamber. Even Remington's receiver-mounted Rube Goldberg extractor failed to solve the problem, so the rifles and cartridge were summarily dropped.

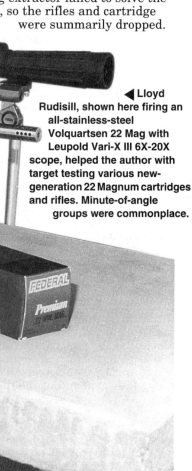

◄ Lloyd Rudisill, shown here firing an all-stainless-steel Volquartsen 22 Mag with Leupold Vari-X III 6X-20X scope, helped the author with target testing various new-generation 22 Magnum cartridges and rifles. Minute-of-angle groups were commonplace.

Recognizing the growing demand for accurate rifles chambered for the 22 Magnum, today gun companies are producing a parade of fine guns. Marlin makes the 6 1/2-pound 22 Magnum Model 922 7-shot magazine-fed autoloading carbine, with a 20 1/2-inch Micro-Groove blued steel barrel topped by open sights. The square 7075-T6 alloy receiver tapers abruptly down into the pistol grip, somewhat reminiscent of a Browning autoloading shotgun. The genuine American black walnut Monte Carlo stock is cut-checkered fore and aft, with sling swivel studs standard.

The same 7-shot detachable magazine is fitted to Marlin's Model 882SS stainless steel bolt action rifle, with a scope-grooved receiver and medium-weight Micro-Grooved 22-inch, open-sighted barrel. Rounding out the weatherproof package is a checkered black fiberglass-filled polycarbonate stock, with nickel-plated swivel studs. The Model 882SSV is as above, but with a 22-inch heavy barrel, sans sights.

Marlin's 22 Magnum Model 882 echoes the lines of the stainless model, but in blued steel, with a cut-checkered genuine walnut Monte Carlo stock. The magazine-fed Model 882L features a eye-catching laminated hardwood stock, which is shared by the Model 883SS, with 12-shot under-barrel tubular magazine. The Model 883 is blued steel, with the tubular magazine and a genuine walnut stock. The blued steel Marlin Model 25MN comes in a walnut-finished birch stock, with pressed checkering.

In 1996 Savage introduced a budget-priced 22 Magnum, their 5-pound Model 93FSS 5-shot magazine-fed stainless steel "All Weather" bolt action rifle, with button-rifled free-floating 20 3/4-inch barrel, topped by open sights. The black graphite/polymer-filled stock features a fluted classic comb and positive checkering. The Model 93FVSS is as above, but with a heavy barrel and no open sights. The Model 93F is identical to the 93FSS, but in blued steel. The blued steel Savage Model 93G comes with a Monte Carlo walnut-stained American hardwood stock.

Since Czechoslovakia emerged from behind the Iron Curtain, we've had access to their fine precision firearms. The 6-shot magazine-fed semi-automatic 22 Magnum ZKM-611 all-steel rifle is an example of Czech engineering and craftsmanship at its best. The two-piece European walnut stock is hand-checkered and finished to perfection, with sling swivels standard. The scope-grooved slab-sided blued steel receiver, along with the hammer-forged 20-inch field-

The 22 Magnum clearly stands at the top of the rimfire family of cartridges, that led off with the 22 BB Cap, followed by the 22 CB Cap, the 22 Short, the 22 Long, the 22 Long Rifle, the now-obsolete 22 WRF and, finally, the 22 WMR.

Some of the test rifles included the Marlin Model 883SS, the new Ruger 10/22 RBM 22 Magnum, the Volquartsen 22 MAG, and the all-steel 22 Magnum ZKM-611 from Czechoslovakia.

Some of the ground squirrels taken in an afternoon by the author, using a Marlin Model 883, when they still had tubular magazines.

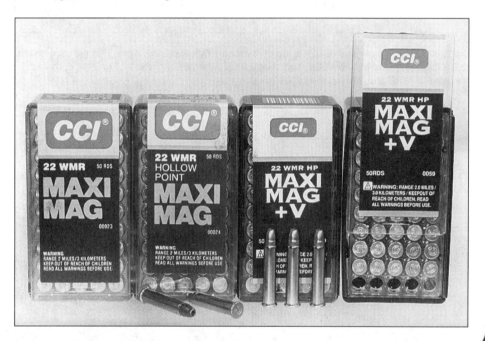

CCI was the first to develop an alternative 22 Magnum ammo, in their Maxi-Mag with 40-grain electro-plated Bonded Jacket hollow-point and solid-point cartridges. The Maxi-Mag +V came later, with its 30-grain hollowpoint at 2200 fps.

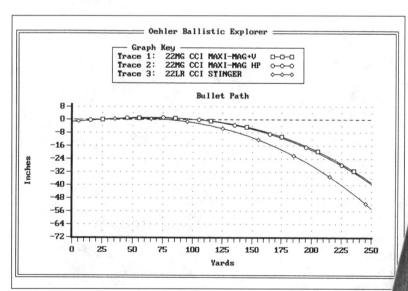

This Oehler Ballistic Explorer chart demonstrates the differences in the bullet paths of the CCI 22 Magnum Maxi-Mag +V with a 30-grain HP at 2200 fps, the Maxi-Mag 40-grain hollowpoint at 1910 fps, and the CCI 22 LR Stinger—the fastest of all 22 LRs—with a 32-grain HP at 1640 fps.

weight barrel, separate from the butt with the removal of a single knurled thumbscrew on the left side. At six pounds, two ounces, the rifle is deceptively solid, and it performs accordingly, delivering minute-of-angle groups at 100 yards. Currently, Lew Horton Distributing Co. is sold out of the BRNO ZKM-611, but your local dealer may still have one in stock, and more are expected. This high-dollar rifle is worth the price.

Introduced in 1964, the Ruger 10/22 was originally conceived merely as a rimfire companion to the 44 Magnum carbine, now deceased. The 10/22 took on a life of its own, and far outlived its big-bore brother, to become one of the most

◀ At the outset, the 22 WMR was burdened with a reputation for poor accuracy. The problem was more a poor choice of rifles by Winchester than deficiencies in the cartridge itself. The slide-action Model 61 was too light to realize the inherent accuracy of the new round.

popular autoloading rimfire rifles of all time. Now the 22 Long Rifle version has spawned a new more robust sibling, the Ruger 10/22 RBM 22 Magnum.

To contain the more powerful cartridge, Ruger designed a longer receiver of steel, rather than alloy, with two dovetailed lumps on top to accept 1-inch scope rings supplied with the rifle. To handle the greater chamber pressure of the 22 Magnum in a blowback action based upon the 22 LR 10/22, Ruger resorted to a tungsten heavy metal bolt, double the weight of the standard steel 22 LR bolt. The new bolt is created by heat-fusing alloy powder into specially formed blanks. The 18 1/2-inch tapered barrel is AISI 1137 blued steel, 6-groove, 1-turn in 14-inch twist, topped with open

▼The 5mm Remington was an excellent cartridge that didn't deserve to die! It was accurate and highly effective on small game.

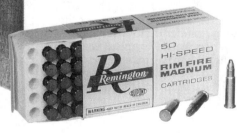

The author's veteran Model 54 Anschütz ekes out the last millimeter of accuracy from every 22 Magnum cartridge. Based upon the Olympics champion Anschütz Match 54 action, it was one of the first rifles to demonstrate the inherent accuracy of the 22 Magnum.

The author's favorite small game hunting rifle is the Volquartsen 22 Mag. Accuracy equals or exceeds that of bolt-action rifles, and it allows quick follow-up shots to correct errors in holdover or windage.

sights. The trigger assembly is identical to the standard 10/22, and the 9-round rotary magazine is taken from the bolt-action Ruger 77/22 Magnum. The America hardwood stock, with 13 1/2-inch length of pull, is adapted from the standard 10/22, complete with its familiar front barrel band and smooth curved butt plate.

Currently Ruger is having trouble keeping up with demand for the 10/22 RBM. Butler Creek, Hogue and Magnum Research are already making target barrels for the new Ruger autoloading 22 Magnum. Butler Creek and Hogue are already making stocks to handle the bull barrels. Surely others will follow!

The 20-inch-barreled 6-pound bolt-action Ruger 77/22 also comes in 22 Magnum, with a 9-shot detachable rotary box magazine, stocked with checkered genuine walnut, wood laminate or black Zytel. Scope rings to fit the grooved steel receiver are included. The lever-action Ruger Model 96 pre-dated the new autoloader but looks identical, save for the manual action.

Tom Volquartsen, noted for his innovative aftermarket target barrels and trigger pull components for the Ruger 10/22 22 LR, introduced his 7 1/2-pound autoloading "22 MAG" rifle a couple of years ago, with a receiver fully machined from a non-magnetic stainless steel, topped by an integral full-length Weaver-type scope dovetail with numerous cross-slots to position the scope for optimum eye relief. The Volquartsen 22 MAG bolt is made of an alloy twice the weight of normal steel. Trigger components are CNC-machined of high-tech stainless steel, held to

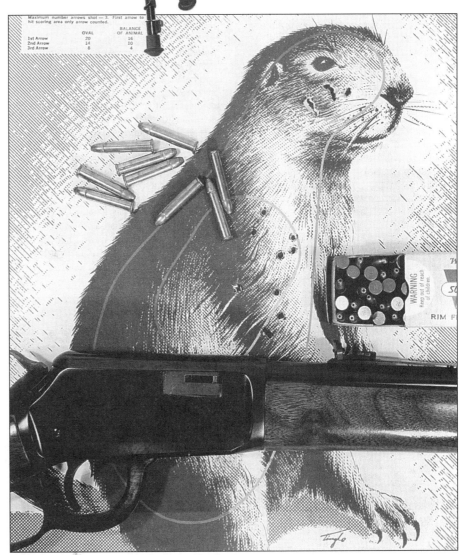

The author fired his Winchester Model 9422M at 50 yards, aiming at the head, followed by five shots–fired both at 75 and 100 yards–aiming at the shoulder of this animal effigy. Not bad for iron sights!

Marlin's stainless steel Model 882SSV offers target accuracy from a 22-inch heavy barrel, cradled in a checkered black fiberglass-filled polycarbonate stock.

The blued steel Marlin 25N offers an excellent 22 Magnum medium-weight field rifle at modest cost, with a press-checkered walnut-finished birch stock.

precision .0001-inch tolerance. A polymer-tipped adjustment screw in the rear of the trigger guard eliminates backlash, resulting in a crisp 2 1/2-pound pull. The 9-shot rotary magazine has an easy-access release. A manual bolt-hold lever releases with a tug on the bolt handle. Stainless steel .920-inch diameter bull barrels with mirror-polished bores, are offered in standard 18 1/2-inch or deluxe 20-inch, with 32-hole compensator, fluted for added stiffness and lighter weight. Stock options include McMillan Sporter and Thumbhole styles, plus Hogue semi-soft rubber-surfaced Overmolded Classic style, as well as laminated hardwood or checkered walnut Monte Carlo styles.

Accuracy with my Volquartsen test rifle is outstanding and functioning flawless, making this a premier small game hunting/target rifle, and my own

favorite in the field! New from Volquartsen is a 22 LR version, virtually identical, but with the receiver shortened by 1/2-inch. Volquartsen is also currently producing a rear-grip pistol version of the 22 MAG, with a 10-inch bull barrel, either in fluted stainless steel or lightweight carbon fiber.

The 22 WMR took a bad rap from the beginning, labeled by the gun press as inaccurate and redundant. I never joined that chorus because I knew better. I still have a Mossberg Model 640KD Chuckster that I bought several decades ago. One of the least costly smallbore rifles of its day, it grouped right at minute-of-angle with Winchester's original Super-X ammo. One of my readers once sent a 100-yard Mossberg 22 Magnum target to me with a 10-shot group just over half an inch. Add to that my Anschütz Model 141M and Anschütz Model 54, both of which

still maintain 1-inch groups at 100 yards with Super-X, and you have a powerful argument in favor of the first 22 Winchester Magnum Rimfire ammo!

Given that the original Winchester Super-X 22 Magnum ammo was no slouch, CCI was the first to offer an edge in both power and velocity, combined with outstanding accuracy, in their 22 Maxi-Mag, with a 40-grain electro-plated bonded jacket hollowpoint and a full-metal jacketed load both at 1910 fps. To prevent excessive expansion or blown case heads, CCI added a reinforcing belt of double-thick brass near the rim. Later, they introduced their 30-grain hollowpoint 22 Maxi-Mag+V at 2200 fps, and the shotshell with its unique plastic capsule containing 52 grains of fine lead shot. I've found that the shotshell is capable of dispatching small vermin, such as rats, out to about 30 feet.

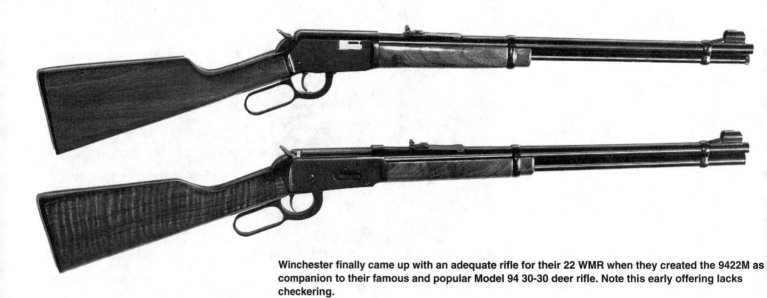

Winchester finally came up with an adequate rifle for their 22 WMR when they created the 9422M as companion to their famous and popular Model 94 30-30 deer rifle. Note this early offering lacks checkering.

In 1998, Remington created a sensation with their new autoloading Model 597 22 LR, quickly followed by a 22 Magnum version. This man-sized rimfire offers such features as a staggered 10-shot magazine and automatic bolt hold-open after the last shot.

The Savage Model 93FSS 22 Magnum is a budget-priced 5-pound 5-shot magazine-fed stainless steel bolt action, featuring a free-floating 20 3/4-inch button-rifled barrel, in a black graphite/polymer-filled stock.

The 22 Magnum ZKM-611 is an all-steel magazine-fed autoloader imported from Czechoslovakia. Despite the slender barrel, it proved to be quite accurate. The two-piece checkered walnut stock exhibits the familiar European down-curved butt.

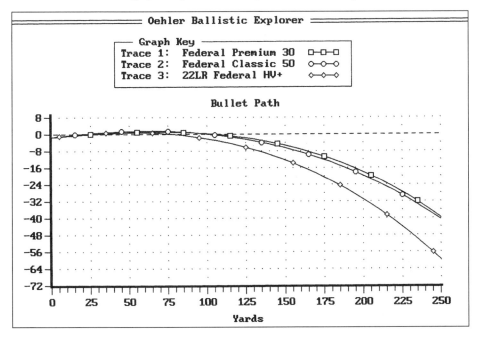

Federal introduced their 22 Magnum Premium cartridge, with a jacketed hollowpoint, custom-made for them to exacting specs by Sierra Bullets, launched at 2200 fps.

Oehler Ballistic Explorer

Graph Key
Trace 1:	Federal Premium 30	□—□—□
Trace 2:	Federal Classic 50	○—○—○
Trace 3:	22LR Federal HV+	◇—◇—◇

Bullet Path

The Oehler Ballistic Explorer chart shows the bullet paths for the Federal Premium .22 Magnum with a 30-grain hollowpoint at 2200 fps, the Federal 50-grain Classic at 1650 fps, and the Federal 31-grain HP 22 LR HV+ at 1550 fps.

On the target range, my Oehler 35P Proof Chronograph recently confirmed CCI's advertised velocities as honest, with the Maxi-Mag 40-grain hollow points clocking 1910 fps, and 40-grain solids reading 1906 fps, while the 30-grain Maxi-Mag+V tached 2188 fps.

A major engine propelling renewed interest in the 22 Magnum has been the emergence of a bevy of next-generation high-tech cartridges that deliver target accuracy combined with extended reach and more explosive results at the target.

Federal was first in line with their Premium 22 Win. Mag. cartridge. Federal began their quest for 22 rimfire accuracy with a three-year R&D program that resulted in the Gold Medal 22 Long Rifle target ammo that, in the hands of lovely and talented Launi Meili, set a new world's record, and won the first Women's Three-Position Small Bore Rifle Competition Gold Medal for the United States at the 1992 Olympics in Barcelona, Spain. Using the same ammo, and also shouldering an Anschütz rifle, Bob Foth brought America a Silver Medal, missing gold by less than a one-point margin in the Men's Match.

High-tech production methods developed in the making 22 LR Gold Medal ammo carried over into Federal's new Premium 22 Win. Mag. One lesson really sank in—all else being equal, it's the bullet that determines group size at long range! Federal turned to Sierra for a custom 30-grain true jacketed hollow-point bullet. To meet the demanding specs set by Federal, Sierra jackets are

blanked and drawn to exact wall thickness, from copper alloy manufactured with three times the quality control required by industry standards.

I knew the three boys who started Sierra Bullets in a war-surplus galvanized steel Quonset hut in Santa Fe Springs, California. Just after WWII, when America was just beginning to recover from wartime shortages, and bullets were still hard to get, I watched their first– then only– bullet-stamping machine pumping tiny 22-caliber slugs into five-gallon paint buckets. They set top standards for quality in the beginning that are still maintained by the present Sierra management.

The Sierra bullet configuration for Federal's 30-grain true jacketed

Remington came late to the 22 Magnum arena, with their 40-grain JHP 22 Win. Mag. at 1910 fps.

▲ ▶ The bolt-action Ruger 77/22 exhibits the same styling and quality as the centerfire Ruger Model 77, providing small game hunters with an accurate 22 Magnum field rifle at relatively modest cost. A major feature is the 9-round rotary magazine that has been adapted to other 22 Magnum Ruger rifles.

Premium 22 Win. Mag. results in an improved ballistic coefficient, compared to Federal's 30-grain Classic 22 Win. Mag., copper-coated by electrolysis. Although both have the same muzzle velocity of 2200 fps, at 150 yards, the 30-grain Premium bullet is still clocking 1240 fps, while the 30-grain Classic bullet only retains 1120 fps.

A gaping hollow point in the 30-grain Premium bullet, combined with a thin, highly frangible jacket, delivers an atom-bomb effect to any critter in its path. Minute-of-angle accuracy

◀ A major target for the longer reach of the 22 Magnum is the lowly ground squirrel that ruins pastures and farm lands alike.

▶ The Ruger 96/22M with 9-shot rotary magazine, offers a valid 22 Magnum option for lovers of lever action rifles, in a gun that echoes the lines of the popular 10/22 autoloader.

◀ The blockbuster hit Ruger 10/22 RBM 22 Magnum is breaking sales records at Ruger. The 5 1/2-pound rifle promises to fuel the flames of emerging 22 Magnum popularity. It uses the same 9-shot rotary magazine as the 77/22 and 96/22M.

holds to extreme range. Bench rest groups at 200 yards hover around two inches—sometimes under!

Federal has an exclusive in their heavyweight Classic 22 Win. Mag. 50-grain hollow point with a relatively modest muzzle velocity of 1650 fps. However, the added penetration promised by the added momentum makes it a premier choice for hunters after larger predators such as coyotes and bobcats.

At 200 yards all three Federal bullets level off at about 1000 fps, and little is lost after that. Given equal velocity, the heaviest bullet has a distinct advantage in terms of remaining energy—read that "killing power!"

Obviously, ground squirrels won't know the difference. However, bigger targets such as rockchucks and groundhogs will go down more convincingly at long range with the heavier bullets. Ballistically, Federal's Classic 50-grain bullet has a remaining energy at 200 yards of 124.2 foot pounds, compared to 92.59 for the 40-grain, and just 76.21 for the 30-grain slug.

Witnessing the popularity of CCI and Federal ultra-high velocity 22 Magnum ammo, Winchester countered with their Winchester Supreme 22 WMR, launching a 34-grain jacketed serrated-nose hollow point at 2120 fps. Overall high-tech design components resulted in significantly improved accuracy as well as explosive terminal effect on game.

During bench-rest testing of the new rounds, I fired 10-shot groups at ranges from 50 to 200 yards. At the extreme range, I found the drop from a 100-yard zero was 16 inches. Using my Volquartsen 22 Mag with a Leupold Vari-X III 6.5X-20X with Mil-Dot reticle, I discovered that the third dot from the top was dead center, providing a positive holdover that spelled sudden death for several rockchucks sunning themselves on distant piles of boulders.

Remington entered the 22 Magnum market late, with their new 22 Win. Mag. 40-grain PSP (Pointed Soft Point) and 40-grain JHP (Jacketed Hollow Point), both at 1910 fps muzzle velocity. Their Premier 22 Win. Mag. with a 33-grain polymer-tipped jacketed bullet at 2000 fps looks like a winner, both in terms of accuracy and terminal effect.

Modern high-tech ammo has brought the 22 Magnum into a new millennium well ahead of Y2K. As a result, it's almost impossible to make a bad choice from among the battery of excellent modern medium-to-heavy-weight rifles offered by various makers today. Small game hunters, pick one and enjoy! ●

Handgun News
Autoloading Pistols

by John Malloy

"It WAS THE best of times, it was the worst of times ... This introduction from Dickens' TALE OF TWO CITIES seems somehow appropriate for a discussion of autoloading handguns.

On one hand, handguns have been made and sold in record numbers. On the other, semiautomatic pistols have been under attack as never before.

Several factors contributed to the reported record sales of handguns. Reaction of some politicians to the Columbine school shootings of April, 1999 was to "do something" to demonstrate their concern. Much of this "something" was to introduce anti-gun legislation. Gun shows came under legislative attack in many places. Many people, fearing that some firearms--or some rights--might no longer be available, bought guns in record numbers.

Added to this was growing concern in 1999 of potential Year 2000 (Y2K) computer problems. Prudent people reasoned that if Y2K problems caused disruptions in basic services, then social unrest (riots and assaults) could ensue. Firearms were purchased as protection against such problems, many by first-time gunowners. As we now know, civilization did not collapse on January 1, 2000. Many new gunowners found they liked the fun and the self-discipline of shooting and became dedicated members of the shooting sports community.

Along with the agitation for legislation, litigation by city governments against manufacturers of autoloading handguns was initiated as a weapon. Small companies, in particular, could not bear the cost of defending themselves against multiple lawsuits. By late 1999, it was rumored that several companies--among them Lorcin and Davis--had gone bankrupt. The good news, as we shall see, is that this is only partially true. The bad news is that this is partially true.

Many manufacturers are offering key locks to disable the mechanism of the pistols they offer. Many shooters feel that this concept seems to have some merit, as it can be used or not used at the option of the owner.

With woeful deception involved in the misnaming, so-called "smart guns" are also being developed. The favored concept seems to be an electronic device that would not allow the trigger to be pulled unless the gun received a signal from a transmitter worn by an

Petite Kathy Gilliam displays the small Accu-Tek XL-9 subcompact pistol, a stainless-steel double-action in 9mm.

authorized person. The concept has received more attention following the tragic school shootings, but apparently was originally developed to keep police officers from being shot with their own guns. Some officers, however, contend that training is preferable to complex gadgetry.

Still, not all the news is related to the political situation and, very definitely, not all of it is bad.

True, some manufacturers are gone, and a surprising number of models of semiautomatic handguns have been discontinued within the past year.

However, new manufacturers have entered the autoloading handgun field, and interesting new ideas and new models from existing manufacturers are being introduced. Importers are bringing in new models from abroad.

The effect of expanding, lawful concealed carry is evident as more people in our country choose to exercise their right to bear arms. The autoloading handgun lines of many companies have grown smaller and lighter. Polymer frames grow in popularity, and several manufacturers have introduced new pistols with such frames. Titanium, introduced for revolvers within the past few years, is now being used for autoloaders.

Several powerful new centerfire cartridges have been introduced for big-bore semiautomatics. At the same time, conversion kits to adapt centerfire autoloaders to use the 22 Long Rifle (22 LR) cartridge are in demand; several new ones are offered by pistol manufacturers and aftermarket suppliers.

The 1911 Colt/Browning pistol design remains a favorite. New variations of models made by traditional manufacturers are offered. Also, new manufacturers have

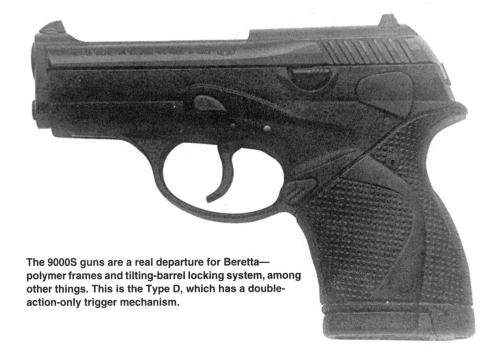

Alchemy Arms has introduced a new pistol, the Spectre, with a very short double-action straight-line trigger pull.

appeared on the handgun scene to offer their versions of the 1911.

To celebrate their company anniversaries or the anniversary of a particular pistol's introduction, several manufacturers have introduced new models recently. Other manufacturers seem to have timed new models to coincide with the turnover of the calendar. Note how many models bear the designation "Millennium" or the number "2000."

Indeed, the current autoloading handgun scene is an active one, with much going on.

Let's take a look at what the companies are doing:

ACCU-TEK

Excel Industries, the manufacturer of Accu-Tek firearms, is offering a new 9mm double-action only (DAO) pistol. The stainless-steel pistol, dubbed the XL-9, measures only 3.6x5.6 inches, easily placing it in the subcompact category. With its 3-inch barrel, weight is 24 ounces and capacity is 5+1. It comes with two magazines, one flush and one with a finger-rest extension.

New compact single-action Accu-Tek pistols in 9mm, 40 and 45 calibers are

presently in development. The new stainless-steel All-Star pistols will be the company's largest-caliber offerings. Scheduled availability for the new guns was set for mid-2000.

ALCHEMY ARMS

Shown for the first time at the January 2000 SHOT Show was the Alchemy Arms Spectre pistol. Looking a little bit like a 1911, the Spectre can be considered a full-size pistol, and comes with a 4 1/2-inch barrel. The frame is aluminum alloy, and slides in both carbon steel and stainless are offered. The locking system is of a conventional tilting-barrel type. The gun has a beavertail tang grip safety and a frame-mounted thumb safety.

What makes the new pistol stand out is the trigger mechanism. The striker-fired pistol is double-action only (DAO) yet it has a straight-line trigger pull, like a 1911, with only .155-inch of travel. If your decimals are rusty, .155-inch is right between 1/8 and 3/16-inch.

The pistol is offered in 9mm, 40 S&W and 45 ACP. Three versions are planned—a standard 32-ounce black (SI) model with a carbon-steel slide, a two-tone (SG) model with a stainless-steel slide and a 27-ounce titanium (TI) model. Production of these three models was scheduled to begin in February 2000. A compact variant with a 3-inch barrel will come later.

Alchemy began about 12 years ago as a supplier of aftermarket pistol parts, and now the new firearms manufacturer offers this new pistol design. The company feels that the Spectre offers the straight trigger movement and the feel of a 1911, combined with the striker fire and trigger action that Glock has made popular.

The 9000S guns are a real departure for Beretta— polymer frames and tilting-barrel locking system, among other things. This is the Type D, which has a double-action-only trigger mechanism.

Century International Arms is now the importer of the South African Republic Arms pistols. Century's Steve Kehaya shows the latest model, the 40-caliber RAP 440.

BERETTA

Beretta has introduced a new 9000S pistol. This is a new look and a new concept for Beretta, as the pistol is a polymer-frame compact. Available in 9mm and 40 S&W calibers, it is hammer-fired and retains the traditional Beretta open-top slide. However, the slide opening is relatively narrow and has a definite ejection "scallop" and the locking system is of the tilting-barrel type, with the locking surfaces toward the sides instead of on the top. The 9000S measures 4.8x6.6 inches and weighs about 27 ounces. Two variants will be made. The type F is a conventional double-action (DA) and the Type D is DAO.

To commemorate the millennium, Beretta has introduced the Elite 2000 pistol as a limited-production item. Based on the Model 92 pistol, the new gun has a matte black finish and laminated rosewood grips with a Beretta logo medallion inset. Serial numbers will be Y2K-0001 to Y2K-2000.

With little fanfare, Beretta has added a titanium version to its Bobcat 32 ACP pistol line. Although it is a catalog item, it has been reported that only a limited run will be made.

CENTURY INTERNATIONAL

Century International Arms is now the importer of the South African Republic Arms pistols. New in that line is the 40 S&W caliber RAP 440. The steel pistol is 6 inches long and weighs 31 ounces. It has a 3 1/2-inch barrel, and a capacity of 8+1.

Century also is offering the new compact Hungarian pistol, the FEG P9RZ. This scaled-down 9mm FEG has a bobbed hammer, a 3.6-inch barrel and is 7 inches long. It weighs about 30 ounces and has 10+1 capacity.

CHARLES DALY

The Charles Daly name was first applied to handguns only a short time ago, when a 1911-type pistol was introduced in 1998. Now, the pistol offerings have been expanded.

Completely new pistols of new design have polymer frames and are conventional DA. The designation is DDA, for Daly Double Action. The guns are made by Bul Transmark of Israel and are similar to, but not the same as, ones that Bul now markets elsewhere. The internal mechanism is similar to that of the CZ-75. Calibers are 40 S&W and 45 ACP.

Two DDA variants are offered. A compact version has a 3 5/8-inch barrel, and is 7 3/8 inches long, weighing 26 ounces. The full-size model has a 4 1/2-inch barrel, with an overall length of 8 1/4 inches. It weighs 28.5 ounces. Both variants have 10+1 capacity.

Actually, a number of other variants could be said to exist, as the polymer frames are available in several different colors.

CIENER

A new 22 Long Rifle (22 LR) conversion kit for the Glock pistols has been introduced by Jonathan Arthur Ciener. The new conversion unit has the exact dimensions and appearance of the original Glocks. That factor alone is important to some people. However, converted pistols can also use holsters and some other accessories that work with the Glock, a nice plus. The Ciener conversions are offered in two different sizes, and will work with most of Glock's 9mm and 40-caliber pistols.

COLT

There were rampant Colt rumors in the air prior to the 2000 SHOT Show. At that time, Colt spokesmen verified that most of the guns in the previous handgun line, including all the new models introduced last year, have been discontinued. This means that all double-action (DA) revolvers are gone, including the new multi-caliber models. All the Mustang/Pony 380 semiautos are gone. The new 9mm DAO autoloaders introduced just last year are also gone.

Still in the line are the single-action revolvers and the 1911-style 45s. The

Begun in 1968, the Dan Wesson firm offered interchangeable-barrel revolvers, such as this early DII used by Malloy. Now, the reorganized company offers 1911-type semiautomatics as well as revolvers.

"Absolute confidence."

Chris Thurston, North American Sheep Hunter

Chris' choice: The A-Bolt Stainless Stalker.

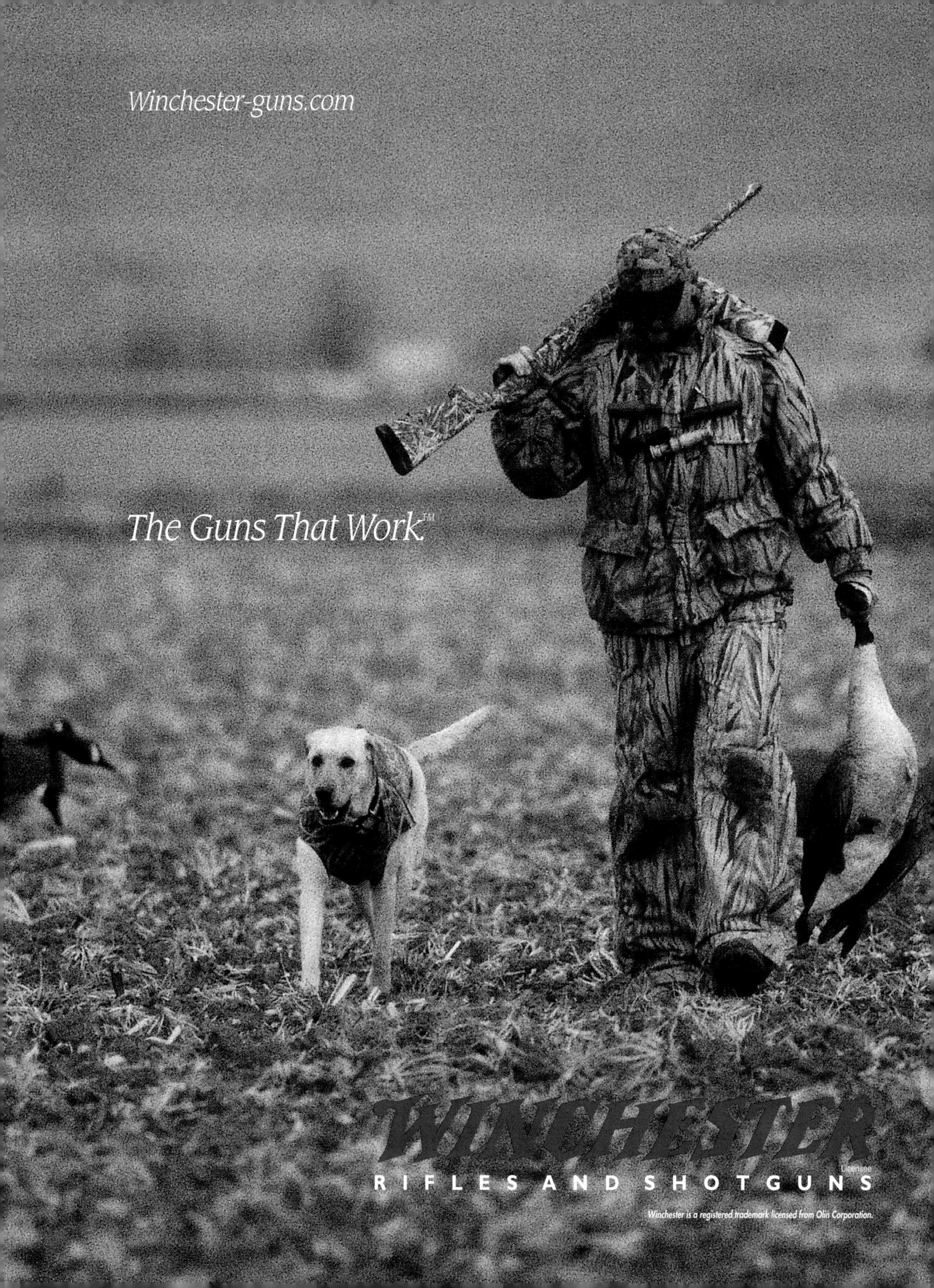
Winchester-guns.com
The Guns That Work™
WINCHESTER
Licensee
RIFLES AND SHOTGUNS
Winchester is a registered trademark licensed from Olin Corporation.

Jim Davis (right) and his son Aaron Davis were at the 2000 SHOT Show to prove that rumors of the company's demise were false. Davis Industries displayed their line of affordable derringers and semiautomatic pistols.

1911s, however, are pretty much limited to Government- and Commander-size pistols, and only in 45 ACP caliber. The smaller Officers variant is gone, but the recently-introduced Defender is still in the catalog. The 1991-series 45s are also still listed.

The Colt Custom Shop is still making custom guns.

There has been another reorganization of Colt's leadership. Colt now has a new CEO, Lt. Gen. William Keys. Keys replaces Stephen Sliwa, who briefly headed up iColt, a now-defunct subsidiary formed to develop "smart gun" technology.

CZ

A new DAO version of the CZ-75 has been introduced. The new variant has a bobbed hammer. The trigger mechanism is such that the hammer can be activated again in case of a misfire. The new CZ will be available in 9mm and 40 calibers.

CZ is going the other way, too. Also offered is a new single-action-only version of the CZ-75. This one can be carried cocked-and-locked, and is designed to appeal to those who use such pistols in competition. It has a distinctive appearance because of its straight trigger.

The CZ-75 PCR model is being offered in the U. S. now. PCR stands for "Police of the Czech Republic", and the pistol is of the same type as designed for that law-enforcement group. It is an alloy-frame compact, with a decocking lever and rubber grips.

To commemorate the CZ-75's 25th anniversary (and a total of over 2 million pistols made), CZ is introducing a special 25th Anniversary model. It is a high-polish pistol with walnut grips and special markings. Only 1000 will be made, with 500 allotted for the United States market.

A 22LR conversion kit is now available for the CZ-75 from the company.

DAN WESSON

Known for its interchangeable-barrel revolver design since 1968, Dan Wesson has been under new ownership since 1996, and the company is now in the autoloading pistol business. Based on the 1911 design, Dan Wesson's new "PointMan" pistols will be offered in Government and Commander sizes. A variety of features will make the variants suitable for Bullseye, IDPA, IPSC or other types of pistol shooting in which revolvers seem to be playing second fiddle to semiautos.

DAVIS

Davis is still in business! The Davis display at the 2000 SHOT Show was welcome proof that rumors of the company's demise were greatly exaggerated. Davis quietly continues to make their affordable line of derringers and semiautomatic 32 and 380 pistols. In business since 1982, Davis offers a lifetime warranty on its products, so Davis customers certainly want the company to remain in business.

EAA

European American Armory is now offering a 22LR conversion kit for their Witness series of pistols.

Also, the company has introduced the Tanfoglio-developed F.A.R. system for semiautomatic pistols. (F.A.R. stands for "Fast, Accurate, Reliable" in company literature). Essentially, this system uses a Witness pistol redesigned to be blowback operated, with a fixed barrel. Chamber pressure is controlled by using a much-longer cartridge case of an as-yet unnamed cartridge. The case is slightly longer than that of a 38 Super, but has the smaller internal capacity of a 9mm Luger case. Thus, the rear of the case has a very large solid section. So, as the case moves rearward out of the chamber, the solid rear portion leaves first, and is unaffected by the pressure in the chamber. By the time the thin case walls move out of the

FireStorm is a new name in the autoloading pistol field. Several different types will be offered, this one a full-size 45-caliber Government style.

chamber, the bullet has exited from the barrel and pressure has dropped.

EAA claims that the advantages of the system are a straight-line, fixed barrel for better potential accuracy, faster cycle time without a locking system, and the ability to use a longer, gentler ramp into the chamber for more reliable feeding.

FIRESTORM

A new line of imported semiautomatic pistols was introduced at the January 2000 SHOT Show. Although the first ones will probably be 1911-style 45s, the Firestorm pistols fall into three general categories.

The Firestorm 380 is a conventional DA blowback of the pocket pistol type. With a 3 1/2-inch barrel and 23-ounce weight, its size of about 6 1/2x4 3/4 inches places it in the compact class. It has a slide-mounted safety that blocks the firing pin. Capacity is 7+1.

The Mini-Firestorm 9mm and 40 pistols are locked-breech pistols. Trigger mechanism is conventional DA, and the thumb safety is frame-mounted. A barrel length of 3 1/2 inches gives dimensions of 7x4 1/2 inches. Although larger than the 380, the Mini is still in the compact class. Weight is 24.5 ounces, and capacity is 10+1.

The Firestorm 45s are steel-frame 1911-style pistols, in three sizes. The full-size Government pistols have 5 1/8-inch barrels and weigh 36 ounces. Similar to the 1911 design, they have grip safeties and frame-mounted thumb safeties. Capacity is 7+1. The Compact 45 has a 4 1/4-inch barrel, reducing the length and cutting weight to 34 ounces. The 45 Mini-Compact is a smaller pistol

Glock's new slimline Model 36--the company's first pistol with a single-column magazine--is now in production.

The Griffon 1911A1 Combat pistol is being imported from South Africa. The Commander-size pistol is offered in 45 ACP.

with a double-column magazine. Barrel length is 3 1/8 inches. Weight is 31 ounces and capacity goes up to 10+1.

Firestorm pistols are imported by SGS Importers of Wanamassa, New Jersey.

GALENA/AMT

Recall that Galena Industries took over production of the AMT firearms line last year. Galena now makes the line of Backups, Automags and 1911-style pistols previously manufactured by AMT. In mid-1999, production of those guns was moved from Irwindale, California to Sturgis, South Dakota.

Since the move, the company has been retooling for all the product lines, a process they anticipated to last into late 2000. The company believes this retooling will result in better reliability and better accuracy for all the Galena guns.

Galena points out that all their firearms carry a lifetime warranty.

Heckler & Koch's Jennifer Golisch holds the cased Number 1 of 1000 commemorative USP pistol. The series of 1000 guns will recognize the company's 50th anniversary.

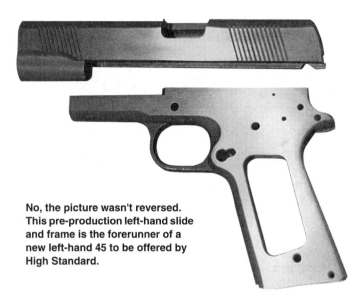

No, the picture wasn't reversed. This pre-production left-hand slide and frame is the forerunner of a new left-hand 45 to be offered by High Standard.

Bob Shea helped man the High Standard booth at the 2000 SHOT Show. Shea, who started his working career with High Standard in 1942, now works part-time for the company, and still works on the 22 semiautomatics.

GLOCK

Glock's single-column compact 45, the Model 36, introduced last year, is now in production. First shipment of the slimline production pistols was scheduled for the Spring of 2000.

Noticeably thinner than the Glock 30, (its double-column counterpart), the 36 has a 3 3/4" barrel, measures 6.7x4.7 inches, and weighs 22.5 ounces. It has 6+1 capacity.

GRIFFON

Griffon USA, the importer of the South African Griffon pistols, is offering the Griffon 1911A1 Combat model, a designation which leaves little doubt as to the origin of the design. For now at least, all Griffon pistols are Commander-size 45s. They have 4 1/8-inch barrels, and weigh 36.5 ounces. Capacity is 7+1. The Griffon pistols have distinctive portholes on the front of the slide.

The Griffon 9mm pistol, based on a modified Tokarev design, was originally scheduled to come in along with the 45, but will not be imported.

HECKLER & KOCH

The year 2000 marked HK's 50th anniversary. To commemorate the event, a special series of 1000 USP Compact 45-caliber pistols have been made. The pistols have the HK 50th Anniversary logo on the slide and are numbered "- of 1000". They come cased with a commemorative coin and an extra magazine and a key for the lockout device. Number 1 of 1000 was displayed at the January 2000 SHOT Show.

Rumors were circulating prior to the SHOT Show that Colt was planning to buy Heckler & Koch. At the show, an HK spokesman reported that HK's

Firearms designer Robert Pauza displays his new P51 pistol and the 50-caliber cartridge it shoots.

Two new cartridges for semiautomatic pistols were recently introduced. The 50 Pauza, for the Pauza P51 pistol, is at left. In the center is the high-velocity 40 Super cartridge. A 45 ACP is shown at the right for comparison.

Kahr has introduced a polymer-frame pistol. The new Kahr P9 is a double-action-only 9mm with a capacity of 7+1.

Charles Brown (left) explains features of the new Hi-Point pistols to Malloy. The first factory offering of pistols with aperture sights is being made by Hi-Point.

parent company had signed a letter of intent with Colt, and that negotiations were under way. Later information, however, indicated that the arrangements were being made with one of Colt's principal owners, and not with the Colt company.

HIGH STANDARD

Lots of things are going on at High Standard.

A joint venture has been established between High Standard, Firearms International (FI) and Olympic Arms. A number of new things are being offered. Even more are being planned.

The High Standard line of 22-caliber target pistols remains a mainstay, and the guns continue to use the familiar High Standard names from the past. The target 22s now feature Herrett grips.

New is a full line of 1911-style 45 pistols, and the company has resurrected the "Crusader" name for their custom series 45s, with 4- or 5-inch barrels. Match versions will be made with 5- or 6-inch barrels, and there will be military-style variants offered also. A 5-inch barrel, 26-ounce titanium variant will also be made. "Sharpshooter" conversion kits to convert the 45s to use 22 LR ammunition are also offered.

The Olympic name will now be used primarily on guns made for export—the High Standard name will be phased in on all the new 45s.

By mid-2000, the company also planned to introduce a left-hand 1911-type 45. Olympic had bought the tooling for the departed Randall pistols, including the left-hand models, and the time may be right to offer pistols for the southpaws among us again.

Sure to catch attention is the new P51 50-caliber pistol designed by Robert Pauza. Pauza's big rifle chambered for the 50 BMG (50 Browning Machine Gun) cartridge is a prominent item in the FI catalog. A prototype of the 1911-style, tilting-barrel pistol was demonstrated at the January 2000 SHOT Show. Pauza points out that the new 50 has 24% more frontal area than a 45. The prototype pistol is said to be controllable while pushing a 300-grain bullet out at 1250 feet per second. High Standard hoped to have the P51 in production during the year 2000.

HI-POINT

The Hi-Point 9mm Comp pistol, announced last year, is now in production. It is available from the company with an optional laser.

Hi-Point has a tradition of introducing new features into the line without much fanfare. For 2000, all models will have a trigger lock and adjustable sights. Of special interest, all models will also come with an additional aperture rear sight. Aperture sights, also called "peep" sights or "ghost rings," have been installed on custom handguns before, but the new Hi-Points may be the first factory offering of pistols so equipped. The notch and aperture sights can be easily switched by the owner.

HS AMERICA

A new company, HS America, has been formed to market a new pistol from Croatia. The 2000 SHOT Show was its first public showing. The new HS 2000 has a polymer frame with steel

The new HS2000 pistol, available initially in 9mm and 40 S&W, features a polymer frame and a Glock-type trigger safety. It also has a grip safety.

Kel-Tec's light little 32-caliber polymer-frame P-32, introduced last year, is now in full production.

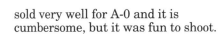

Kimber now claims to be first in the number of 1911-type pistols made and sold. Among its new offerings is the CDP series, designed for concealed carry and personal protection. This one is the Ultra, with 3-inch barrel and 6+1 capacity. 45 ACP, of course.

rails. The pistol, now available in 9mm and 40, locks by means of a cam-operated tilting-barrel system. Trigger action is similar to that of the Glock.

With a 4-inch barrel, the pistol measures 5.7x7.2 inches (just outside our arbitrary 5x7 "compact" category) and weighs only 23 ounces. It can be supplied with a 15-round magazine for law enforcement or a standard 10-round magazine for the common folk. The magazine is of Beretta dimensions; although the catch hole is in a different position, pre-ban Beretta magazines can be adapted.

The HS 2000 has a true ambidextrous magazine release, a grip safety as well as trigger safety and internal firing pin block, and an external slide release. Planned for the future are versions in 357 SIG and 45 ACP. A smaller compact variant is also in the works.

HS 2000 pistols are imported by Intrac Arms of Knoxville, Tennessee.

KAHR

Kahr, one of the early leaders in the small 9mm pistol field, has now introduced a polymer-frame model. The new P9 is a 9mm DAO pistol with a 3 1/2-inch barrel, weighs about 16 ounces and measures 4 1/2x6 inches. Capacity is 7+1. Only a single polymer version is available, but everyone who handled it at the SHOT Show seemed to like it, so perhaps Kahr will offer variants in the future.

Recall that Kahr acquired Auto-Ordnance (A-0) last year. Kahr plans to make 45-caliber Auto-Ordnance/Thompson 1911A1 pistols standardized on the appearance of the World War II GI model, complete with brown plastic grips and lanyard loop on the butt. Previous A-0 pistols used parts from different suppliers, and

sold very well for A-0 and it is cumbersome, but it was fun to shoot.

KEL-TEC

The new 6 1/2-ounce 32-caliber P-32 reached full production in November of 1999, and by January 2000, Kel-Tec had shipped over 10,000 pistols.

In the near future, the company plans to offer hard chrome and Parkerized versions. In addition, the polymer frames may be offered in a rainbow of colors.

KIMBER

Kimber's Dwight van Brunt reports that the company, in sheer numbers of pistols sold, has become the number one maker of 1911-style pistols. There should be something in their line that should suit most shooters--they offer 54 different variations.

New for 2000 was a line of custom shop-pistols designed for concealed carry. These guns are designated "CDP" for "Custom Defense Package." Assembly is of matte black aluminum frames and stainless-steel slides. Chambering is 45 ACP.

They feature the rounding of all edges and corners, 3-dot Tritium night sights, checkered front strap, aluminum match trigger, ambidextrous safety and special "double diamond" rosewood grips.

CDP pistols come in three sizes. The Ultra, at 25 ounces, has a 3-inch barrel and 6+1 capacity. The Compact, with a longer slide, goes 28 ounces, has a 4-inch barrel and also has 6+1 capacity. The Pro, also with a 4-inch barrel, has the longer grip frame, giving it 7+1 capacity.

features varied from lot to lot. In addition to the military model, Thompson 1911A1 offerings include Standard and Deluxe models, with no lanyard loop and different finishes and grips.

The Thompson 1927A1 and M1 semiautomatic "Tommy Gun" carbines are in Kahr's lineup, but the 1927A5 Thompson semiautomatic pistol was not in the new catalog. That model never

Les Baer Custom has introduced their new Monolith pistol. Based on the 1911 design, the Monolith has an extended forward frame section and full-length frame/slide rails.

LES BAER

New from Les Baer is the Monolith, a 1911-type competition pistol with a 5-inch barrel. The new pistol has a

Magnum Research's new 45-caliber Baby Eagle pistol is offered with a full-size grip frame and a short slide to match its 3.7-inch barrel.

1999, it was available in 9mm and 40, with a 45 scheduled for later. Now the promised 45 has arrived. The new 45 has a full-size frame and a shorter 3.7 inch barrel. Overall length is 7.75 inches. Although the frame will hold the larger law-enforcement magazine, capacity for ordinary people is 10+1.

NORTH AMERICAN ARMS

NAA now has a custom shop. This means that their little 32-caliber Guardian, normally available in stainless with flat black grips, can now be had in a number of different finishes and grips. They also offer alternate sights, porting and other modifications.

Two magazines are now furnished with each NAA Guardian pistol. One has the original flat base, while the second has a finger rest, giving the owner a choice. As another incentive to buy one, North American has reduced the retail price of the Guardian.

NORTHWEST ARMS

A new company, Northwest Arms, recently purchased the factory operation formerly known as Wilkinson Arms. Designer Ray Wilkinson had named his guns after his daughters, and the guns made by Northwest carry those same names.

The Linda was a large tubular-receiver 9mm pistol with an extended magazine. Northwest has finished the remaining receivers as carbines with 16 3/16-inch barrels which, with BATF approval, come with pre-ban 31-round magazines.

The Sherry was a little 22 LR-caliber pocket pistol.

Northwest has revised the design somewhat with a new magazine and a redesigned firing pin. While the original pistols used top ejection, the new version features ejection angled to the right.

special frame with the forward section, generally called the dust cover, lengthened to the front of the special matching slide. Rail contact is therefore along the entire length of the slide and frame, in a fashion similar to that of the early pre-1911 Colt 38 autos. The Monolith's extended frame puts more weight forward, reducing muzzle rise. Les Baer guarantees 3-inch groups at 50 yards. Calibers offered are 45 ACP and 400 Cor-Bon, and also 40, 9mm and 38 Super.

LORCIN

Lorcin Engineering Company, of Mira Loma, California, has gone out of business. In the company's twelve years of business, it reportedly became the largest maker of 380-caliber pistols in the United States.

Numrich Gun Parts Corporation has bought all the existing Lorcin parts.

MAGNUM RESEARCH

New for 2000 was the Baby Eagle in 45 ACP caliber. The Baby Eagle pistols are made by Israeli Military Industries (IMI). Recall that the Baby Eagle was gone from the Magnum Research line for several years. When it returned in

North American Arms' little Guardian 32 now comes with two magazines—the original version, which is flat on the bottom, and the new finger-rest version shown.

Originally offered by Wilkinson Arms, the little 22-caliber Sherry pistol is now available again, in slightly redesigned form, from Northwest Arms.

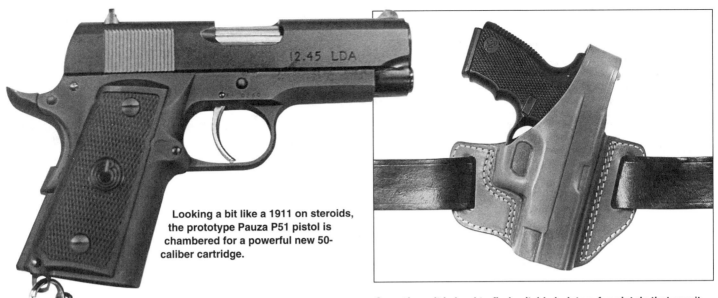

Looking a bit like a 1911 on steroids, the prototype Pauza P51 pistol is chambered for a powerful new 50-caliber cartridge.

Sometimes it is hard to find suitable holsters for pistols that aren't 1911s. Republic Arms of Chino, CA has addressed the problem by offering a line of holsters for the company's 45-caliber Patriot pistol.

The little Sherry weighs 9 1/4 ounces, has a 2 1/2-inch barrel, and measures 3x4 3/8 inches, hiding easily under a 3x5 note card. It comes with an 8-round magazine.

Northwest says that, for a limited time, a free Sherry 22 pistol will be included with the purchase of a Linda carbine.

PARA-ORDNANCE

Para-Ordnance proudly points out that their new double-action LDA (Light Double Action) pistol, introduced last year, was named "Gun of the Year" by Guns & Ammo magazine.

A new variant of that system, the P12 LDA, has now been introduced. It features the same light DAO trigger, but is made with a spurless hammer, in the small "Officer's" size, with a 3 1/2-inch barrel. At this time, it is available in 45 ACP only. An interesting feature is that the slide will not open if the grip safety is not activated. Availability was planned for the Spring of 2000.

Something different coming up. A new departure for Para-Ordnance, which began with and gained fame for its high-capacity double-column pistol frames, is its planned first-ever single-column-magazine pistol. This slimmer variant will be called the 745 LDA.

PHOENIX

Phoenix has introduced a neat little pistol kit. Called the Deluxe Rangemaster Target Kit, it contains an impressive group of items in a lockable plastic case.

Included are the Phoenix HP 22 pistol with 3-inch barrel and flush magazine, and also a 5-inch barrel and extended grip magazine to convert the

compact pistol into an informal target pistol. Also included are a basic cleaning kit, a cable lanyard to fasten the gun to a fixed object, and a magazine well lock that disables the pistol when installed. As a nice touch, the magazine well lock and the carrying case are keyed alike.

The pistol lock/cable lanyard are shipped with all new Phoenix pistols. Phoenix also offers them to owners of older pistols simply for the cost of the shipping charge.

REPUBLIC ARMS (U.S.)

Republic Arms, of Chino, California, has made note of their customers' requests for a holster specifically

designed for their Patriot pistol. Republic now offers such a line of holsters. The holsters are made by Gould & Goodrich, and are available in belt and paddle varieties.

At the 2000 SHOT Show, Republic displayed some pistols made up with express-type sights--a large bead front sight, and a shallow V-notch rear--that may be considered as an option later.

REPUBLIC ARMS (South Africa)

The South African Republic Arms line of steel-frame 9mm and 40 pistols is now being imported by Century International Arms of St. Albans, Vermont.

The introduction of SIG's new EPLS (Electronic Personal Locking System) pistol—the first to have a built-in composite electronic/mechanical locking system—has created considerable discussion.

RUGER

Sturm, Ruger & Co., having made a big splash during its 50th anniversary in 1999, had no new offerings in the semiautomatic pistol field for 2000.

However, the company made the news. Ruger sent out a memo that was the subject of a January 2000 Associated Press (AP) news story. A Denver Post reporter became aware of a December 1999 instruction from Ruger to its distributors. It stated that guns be shipped only to Federal Firearms License (FFL) dealers "selling exclusively from their regular place of business." This instruction was interpreted as banning sales of Ruger guns at gun shows.

The resulting flap caused Ruger to issue, in late January, a clarification. It stated that Ruger policy since 1985 has been to instruct distributors to sell only to dealers who sell from retail stores. It explained that the word "exclusively" was added in December 1999 only to stop mail-order sales to individual FFL holders. The company has no objection to Ruger firearms being legally sold at a gun show by a stocking retail dealer. The letter concluded that gun shows "occupy a special and legitimate niche in the lawful enjoyment of firearms."

SIG

Last year SIG Arms introduced their Trailside 22 pistol, basically a Hammerli dressed down for use as a field or plinking pistol. Now, the Trailside itself has been dressed up, and the result is the Trailside Competition pistol. The new match pistol has adjustable sights, adjustable grips and a steel weight balance system. To prove that they are good shooters, SIG includes a factory target center in a medallion that comes with each pistol.

Also new is the SIG E.P.L.S. pistol, which will begin limited shipments during 2000. The initials stand for Electronic Personal Locking System. The pistol has an electronic/mechanical device that locks the trigger. It is powered by a small lithium battery to operate a tiny electric servo motor that can lock or unlock the trigger. The device sits forward of the trigger guard and has buttons that allow the owner to program the system, assigning his own code. The E.P.L.S. can also be preprogrammed in unlocked or locked modes, or with time delays of one hour or eight hours, after which, the gun will revert to a locked condition. The pistol itself is a modified P229 and is available in 9mm, 357 SIG and 40 S&W.

Something old gone: The beautifully-made SIG P210, the single-action 9mm that has been in only limited production in recent

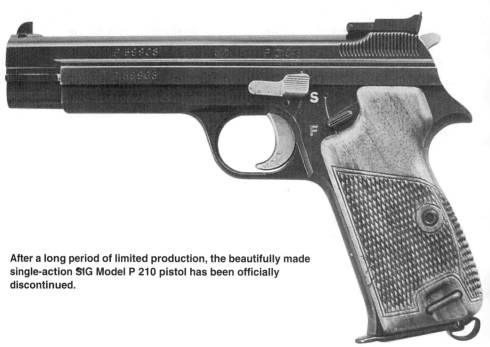

After a long period of limited production, the beautifully made single-action SIG Model P 210 pistol has been officially discontinued.

years, is now dropped from the line and gone for good.

Something new: SIG of Switzerland reportedly has purchased the Mauser trade name and SIG Arms will handle the importing of a new Mauser M2 pistol, made in Germany. It is a DAO, with a rotating barrel locking system, and will be chambered for 357 SIG, 40 S&W and 45 ACP.

SMITH & WESSON

S&W and Walther have an arrangement, and one of the results is the SW99 pistol offered by the American company. The polymer frame is made in Germany by Walther, and the slide and barrel are made in the U. S. by S&W. Although at first glance it is difficult to distinguish between the SW99 and the Walther P99, there are subtle differences. The SW99's trigger guard is rounded, not squared. The S&W slide is contoured differently and has slide serrations front and rear. Features such as the interchangeable backstrap system and the flush decocking control are included in the SW99. It is a conventional DA pistol, offered in 9mm

The S&W Model 4586TSW pistol demonstrates the features of the new Tactical pistol line. Noticeable is the new accessory or equipment rail on the forward dust cover of the frame. This version is an 8+1 stainless-steel 45 with a 4 1/4-inch barrel.

S&W's Performance Center offers non-catalog items such as the 945, a single-action 45 with a 3.75-inch barrel and a weight of 28 ounces. Unlike most S&W autos, the 945 can be carried cocked-and-locked.

is available.

Springfield offers a Parkerized 1911A1 that essentially recreates a military-specification '11A1. All other Springfield 1911-type pistols now come, in the company's term, "loaded." They have beavertail grip safeties, extended thumb safeties, front and rear slide serrations, special sights and other niceties that are currently popular.

STANDARD ARMS

A new company, Standard Arms of Nevada, had the first showing of its new SA-9 9mm pistol at the 2000 SHOT Show. The DAO pistol has a polymer frame and 4140 steel slide. It has a pronounced projection on the front of the trigger guard for those who favor placing a finger there in a two-handed hold. The pistol's size of 4.3x6 inches squeezes it into the subcompact class. Capacity is 10+1.

However, the grip can accommodate a 13-round magazine, which is available for law enforcement.

A 380-caliber Standard pistol was scheduled for availability in mid-2000. A 40-caliber variant was anticipated by the beginning of 2001.

STEYR

Steyr made a splash with its interesting polymer-frame M9 and M40 pistols last year. For 2000, they introduced S-series (small size) variants. The new S9 and S40 pistols are about 1/2-inch shorter in both directions, measuring 4.6x6.5 inches.

and 40, with about a 4-inch barrel. The length is 7 1/4 inches and the weight is about 25 ounces.

The TSW (Tactical Smith & Wesson) series of pistols has been expanded, and the pistols have some new features, including an accessory rail on the frame's forward extension, often called the dust cover. The other remaining pistols now in the line are all in the Sigma, Chiefs Special or Value series. Long-time standby full-size guns, such as the 4506, have been discontinued. The longest barrel cataloged for an S&W centerfire autoloader now is 4 1/4 inches.

Special pistols are still available from the S&W Performance Center.

SPRINGFIELD

Compact 45s with 10-shot magazines caught the attention of the shooting world in the last couple of years. Springfield, claiming to have the greatest selection of 1911-type pistols has one, of course, in their line. Actually, the pistol can use a 12-shot magazine, but is sold with a 10-rounder except to law enforcement and sales outside the U. S. The diminutive 1911-style 45 has a 3.5-inch barrel and weighs 31 ounces. It is available in stainless or Parkerized finish, and a V-10 ported version

The SW99 pistol is Smith & Wesson's slightly-revised version of the Walther P99. The double-action SW99 is offered in 9mm and 40 S&W calibers.

The big Smith & Wesson 4506, here being shot by Malloy, and other full-size pistols have been dropped from the S&W line, replaced by an extended line of TSW, Value, Sigma and Chiefs Special pistols.

The new Standard Arms SA-9 is a compact polymer-frame pistol, offered in 9mm. The trigger mechanism is double-action-only. A new gun from a new company.

Lots of people like high-capacity compact 45s. Vickie Lawrence demonstrates Springfield Armory's offering in that category.

The Steyr M-series pistol, introduced last year, now has a shortened variant available. The new S-series pistols have barrels about 3-1/2 inches long, and are offered in 9mm and 40 S&W chamberings.

They weigh about 22.5 ounces. Barrel length in either caliber is about 3 1/2 inches, also about 1/2-inch shorter. The new S-series pistols were scheduled for full production by mid-2000.

Also, a new M-series pistol in 357 SIG was planned for introduction by the end of 2000.

STI

STI International has introduced a new Xcaliber 450 pistol with a single-column frame and the Xcaliber 450+ with a double-column frame. The guns have 6-inch bull barrels with V-10 porting. The barrels are bored and rifled for 45 caliber. A change of recoil springs allows the use of cartridges of different power levels--45 ACP, +P and +P+ loads, and 45 Super.

STI also introduced pistols chambered for the new 40 Super cartridge. Developmental work for this cartridge began by necking down the 45 Super and then the 45 Winchester Magnum (45 WM) cartridge. The final form is a bottleneck case of 45 ACP base diameter and the .992-inch length of the 10mm Auto cartridge case. Overall length is 1.25 inches, so that the 40 Super will work through a standard 45 magazine. STI offers a combo pistol with barrels for both 45 and 40 Super. 40 Super ammunition is available from Triton. In testing, 135-grain bullets were pushed to about 1800 feet per second—pretty zippy. (As an aside, it is rumored that the CZ97B will be offered in 40 Super next year.)

Also of interest in the STI line is the LS pistol in 9mm and 40 S&W. The pistol takes the 1911 design and squeezes it down until the dimensions are suited to the 9mm and 40 S&W cartridges. The thickness is .765-inch across the metal, 1-inch across the grips. With a 3.4-inch barrel, dimensions are 4.25x7 inches. Capacity is 6+1 in 40, 7+1 in 9mm. A longer-grip variant, the BLS, which increases the capacity to 8+1 and 9+1, is also available.

STI's new Xcaliber 450 can handle 45-caliber cartridges of various power levels by changing the recoil springs.

TAURUS

Taurus was in the forefront of the recent introduction of Titanium revolvers. Now, the company is offering its Millennium PT-111 as a titanium-slide autoloader. The frame is the original polymer, but the lighter slide

The new 40-caliber Vektor CP2 is styled in the futuristic styling of the CP1, but the internal mechanism may be different. This is a functional prototype, with different trigger, safety and locking mechanism.

reduces weight to 16 ounces. The Titanium Millennium remains a 10+1 9mm and, although it is a DAO, has a frame-mounted thumb safety.

The Millennium series, previously 9mm, 40 and 380, now has added 45 ACP to its chamberings. As the Taurus catalog cutely puts it, it took "only a few fractions of an inch here and there" to make the Millennium into a 45. Actually, the overall length of the PT-145, as the new 45 is designated, is given as an even 6 inches--actually 1/8-inch shorter than the original 9mm. The PT-145 has standard Millennium features, including the thumb safety.

During 2000, Taurus began to phase in a key-locking system for its semiautomatic pistols. Similar to the system used successfully on its revolvers the key lock, once locked, would make the pistol inoperable until manually unlocked again. Two keys will come with each gun. This is a nice extra, so that your wife can unlock the gun when you're away and things go bump in the night.

One gun is back in the Taurus lineup. The 40-caliber versions of the PT-92 and PT-99 had been previously dropped from the line. Now, the redesigned 40 is back as the PT-100. Several finish options are offered.

VEKTOR

Last year, Vektor USA created some sensation with its futuristic-looking 9mm CPl polymer pistol. Recall that the sleek-looking compact pistol was a South African design, using a gas-delay blowback system.

The January 2000 SHOT Show marked the debut of the 40-caliber CP2. At first glance, it looks similar to the CP1. However, the pistol displayed was a functional prototype, and

Disassembled, the Vektor CP2 prototype can be seen to have a cam-actuated tilting-barrel locking system, a system very different from that of the CP1.

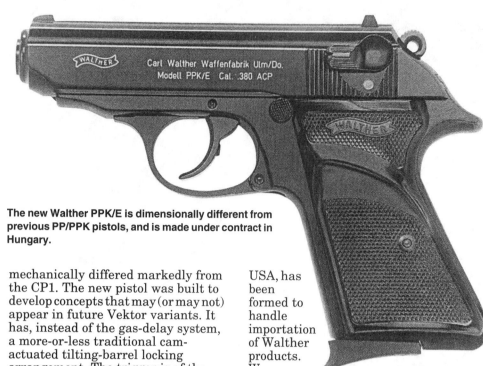

The new Walther PPK/E is dimensionally different from previous PP/PPK pistols, and is made under contract in Hungary.

mechanically differed markedly from the CP1. The new pistol was built to develop concepts that may (or may not) appear in future Vektor variants. It has, instead of the gas-delay system, a more-or-less traditional cam-actuated tilting-barrel locking arrangement. The trigger is of the pivoting, rather than the sliding, type. It has an external slide release and a frame-mounted manual safety.

Whatever final form the new CP2 takes, it will probably be ready for production in 2001.

Vektor has also expanded its line of full-size 9mm and 40 S&W service pistols to include variants suitable for many types of sport and competition, including some designed for IPSC open class.

WALTHER

The previous importer of Walther pistols, Interarms, is no longer in business. A new company, Walther USA, has been formed to handle importation of Walther products. We are reminded of the previously-discussed relationship with Smith & Wesson, for Walther USA uses the same corporate mailing address.

The Walther line coming in is much smaller, but has some interesting offerings. The original conventional-DA P99 has been changed to the P99QA ("Quick Action"). Described as a single-action trigger mechanism, it is actually a Glock-type trigger. The striker is partially cocked by the movement of the slide, then the cocking is completed by the action of the trigger. To accomplish this, the trigger moves about 1/4-inch. Some customers require the trigger pressure to be of certain specifications for all shots, so Walther has phased out the original P99 and P990 in favor of the P99QA.

One special version of the outgoing standard P99 was scheduled for availability during the year 2000. A Year 2000 commemorative version was planned, engraved with Year 2000 markings and special serial numbers. Each pistol came with a case, a special certificate and a fascinating 150-minute videotape of the history of the Walther firm.

Also only available as commemoratives are the last 500 PP and PPK pistols made. The design dates back to 1929, and after 70 years the PP/PPK series was retired. The 500 "Last Edition" guns were engraved and cased, each with a certificate and the Walther video.

One would hope that the PPK/S would still be in the line, but that little pistol is also gone, replaced by a similar, but not the same, new model, the PPK/E. Parts are not necessarily interchangeable with the earlier models, as the PPK/E is made by a different European manufacturer (FEG) to slightly different dimensions. The most noticeable difference is the larger grip, which gives a capacity of 7+1 for the 380 and 8+1 for the 32. The 32 and 380 versions were planned for March 2000 availability, while a 22LR variant was scheduled for September 2000. The PPK/E is offered in blued finish only.

WILSON

New for the year 2000, Wilson Combat offers a 1911-style 45 called the Millennium Protector. With its black Parkerized finish, it is Wilson's lowest-price custom pistol. Yet it comes with features such as a high-ride beavertail grip safety, speed hammer, front and rear slide serrations, beveled magazine well and other things currently in vogue. The black rubber grips have a large-diamond checkering pattern. The Millennium Protector is guaranteed to shoot groups of 1 1/2 inches or less at 25 yards.

Wilson makes a 22 LR conversion unit for 1911-type pistols and, also offers a complete 22 pistol built on a Wilson frame. It also is guaranteed to shoot within 1 1/2 inches at 25 yards. ●

POSTSCRIPT

Today, our entire firearms industry is facing challenges.

It is vital to continue our fight against those who would deprive us of our rights. But this is never-ending work. Every now and then, take a break and enjoy yourself. Buy a new gun. Go shooting.

After seven decades of production (1929-1999), all models of the original Walther PP and PPK pistols, such as this 22-caliber PPK, have been discontinued.

HANDGUN NEWS
REVOLVERS, SINGLE SHOTS AND OTHERS
by HAL SWIGGETT

THE ANNUAL SHOT Show is the "biggie" as far as the shooting sports market is concerned. Each year, thousands of firearms dealers walk the aisles to inspect — and order — the latest in firearms, optics, ammunition and such. This year, the show was held in Las Vegas and enjoyed record attendance. Happily, there is plenty of handgun news to report.

I'll begin my review with the oldest handgun manufacturing company in the United States. A company founded in 1857 and still going strong today in the same location. That company is…

SMITH & WESSON

Their new catalog lists thirty-two (32) models of double-action revolvers with barrel lengths from 1 7/8-inch to 8 3/8-inches. Here's the rundown:

Models 317/317LS, in 22LR, are made of aluminum alloy and stainless steel, have an 8-round capacity and 1 7/8-inch barrels. The Model 317 Kit Gun wears a 3-inch barrel and an adjustable rear sight. Same capacity and construction as above.

On page 12 of the new S&W catalog is a model I have owned for many, many years — and used extensively — the K-22. Mine is engraved by Charlie Price, an engraver who was shot down during WWII and survived. He very fancifully engraved the back portion of the frame and, on the right side, inlaid a gold coiled ready-to-strike rattlesnake. S&W's "modern" K-22 is machined

from stainless steel, offered with barrel lengths of 4-,6- or 8 3/8-inches and your choice of 6- or 10-shot cylinders.

Models 331 and 332 have fixed sights, 6-round cylinders chambered for the 32 H&R Magnum and 1 7/8-inch barrels. Their only difference: M331 is single- or double-action and M332 double-action-only. Weight: M331 - 11.9 ounces; M332 - a full 12 ounces.

S&W offers eight models chambered in 38 Special. Barrel lengths range from 1 7/8-inches to 3.2-inches, with three models in double-action-only. Weights vary from 10.8 ounces to 20 ounces. Their only common feature is cylinder capacity - all are 5 rounds.

Model 60/60LS is chambered 38 Special/357 Magnum with choice of 2 1/8- or 3-inch barrels. Model 640 likewise, but DAO (double-action-only).

S&W's catalog lists eight more double-action revolvers chambered 38 Special/357 Magnum.

Model 610 is stainless steel (S/S), chambered for the 10mm; Model 657, chambered 41 Magnum and Model 625, 45 ACP. This model is among my "acquirements not for sale"! It belonged to a San Antonio police officer who was into competitive shooting and won a lot of matches. When he retired, he wouldn't sell it but, one afternoon, he drove by my home and gave it to me.

COLT

This Hartford, CT-based company offers a pair of single action revolvers.

First is the Cowboy, chambered for the 45 Colt, with a barrel length of 5 1/2-inches and six-round capacity. The new lockwork design includes a transfer bar safety, meaning the revolver can safely utilize all six chambers. Grips are First Generation as is the blued barrel and color-cased frame.

Second is the Single Action Army in blue & color-case or nickel finish, chambered in your choice of 44-40 or 45 Colt. Barrel lengths are 4 3/4- or 5 1/2-inch, your choice. One of my all-time favorite six-guns is a 7 1/2-inch Colt SAA with blued barrel and cylinder, color-cased frame and stag grips. Plus, I'd best add, an adjustable rear sight. The barrel reads, left side, "COLT NEW FRONTIER S.A.A. .45".

Two more Colt favorites — make that three — no longer in production, all double-action: a stainless steel ANACONDA chambered for the 45 Colt, a 7 1/2-inch New Service in 45 Colt and, third, a blued 6-inch Officers Model Match marked "CAL. 22 MAGNUM CTG". I was told by one of Colt's top executives, during an NSGA Show held in Chicago's McCormick Place (before the SHOT Show came into existence), that 500 of these had been manufactured but only 88 ever left the factory.

RUGER

Would you believe a double-action six-shooter chambered for the 454 Casull? On the right side of the barrel, in big capital letters, is "SUPER

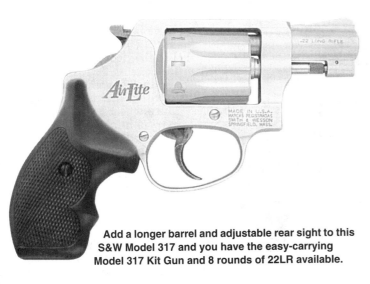

Add a longer barrel and adjustable rear sight to this S&W Model 317 and you have the easy-carrying Model 317 Kit Gun and 8 rounds of 22LR available.

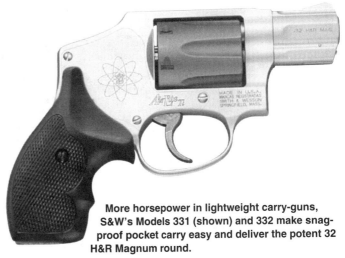

More horsepower in lightweight carry-guns, S&W's Models 331 (shown) and 332 make snag-proof pocket carry easy and deliver the potent 32 H&R Magnum round.

This 7 1/2-inch 45 Colt Single Action drops its hammer with only 4 1/4 pounds of pressure. It is one of Hal's all-time favorites.

Winchester's 454 Casull cartridges do in fact "fill" this Ruger's six chambers.

way I can describe it is simply "gray". *Ruger calls the finish 'Target Grey'/Ed.* Trigger pull on my evaluation sample is surprisingly crisp for a straight-from-the-factory revolver and breaks, consistently, at 4 3/4 pounds. Weight? With Leupold's 2-8x scope aboard in Ruger's rings, the rig weighs 4 pounds, 2 1/2 ounces. How does it shoot? At 50 yards my five-shot groups consistently measured 1 3/4- to 2 1/2-inches with Winchester ammunition (the only manufacturer of 454 Casull factory ammunition I know about). I couldn't see any difference, in accuracy, between their 250-grain JHPs and 260-grain Partition Gold cartridges. I did try two full cylinders of Winchester's 225-grain Silvertip Hollow Point 45 Colt ammo but, honestly, can't imagine anyone underpowering a 454 Casull revolver to this extent.

As most of my readers know, I am a dedicated single-action shooter and, although a double-action, this Ruger Super Redhawk 45 Colt/454 Casull just may have found a home.

THOMPSON/CENTER ARMS

T/C's Encore single shot pistol is delivered in more barrel lengths, finishes and chamberings than you would believe possible - plus an Encore package.

These pistols come in your choice of blued or stainless steel. There is another decision to make - solid American walnut or rubber finger-grooved grips. Barrel lengths are 10, 12 and 15 inches. Chamberings offered: 223 Remington, 22-250 Remington, 243 Winchester, 260 Remington, 270 Winchester, 7mm-08 Remington, 308 Winchester, 30-06 Springfield, 44 Remington Magnum, 454 Casull, 45/70 Govt. and 45 Colt/.410-bore (3" chamber). My Thompson/Center Encore pistol - as described below - weighs an even five pounds on my postal scale.

I used an Encore chambered in 308 Winchester, with T/C's 2.5-7x scope on a 15-inch barrel, and one of Peter Pi's Cor-Bon cartridges to tag the most unusual deer I've ever killed in my 72 years of hunting.

Why so unusual? By the taxidermist's estimate, the buck had between 200 and 300 yards of electric fence wire around his antlers, pinning his ears tight — plus 21 strands around his neck. A single round of Cor-Bon's 150-grain Bonded Spitzer SP took off the top of his heart, at 99 yards according to Bushnell's newest rangefinder.

REDHAWK". Ruger's chambering specification is stamped on the frame's right side and that same "designation" is on its cylinder - two lines, in two places: ".45 COLT CAL. "(top line) then ".454 CASULL CAL."

Barrel length is 7 1/2 inches. The rear sight has a white-outlined notch and is fully adjustable.

The front sight is a field ramp design, with a red insert. This Super Redhawk is designed with integral scope bases and delivered with 1-inch rings. This Super Redhawk's finish is, for lack of a better way to put it, unusual. The best

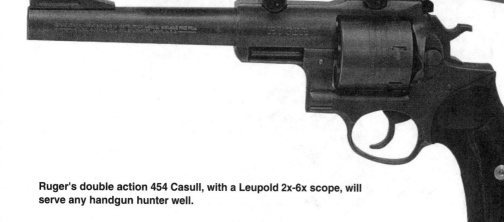

Ruger's double action 454 Casull, with a Leupold 2x-6x scope, will serve any handgun hunter well.

Thompson/Center's "ENCORE", chambered 308 Win., with T/Cs 2.5-7x scope took, with a single shot, a mighty unusual deer this past season - in Wyoming.

Sighting-in with Cor-Bon's 308 Winchester 150-grain cartridges before I left Texas, I was able to put two, 3-shot groups 2 1/2 inches high at 100 yards into, believe it or not, 1 3/4- and 1 1/2-inches. Now you know why I am so high on T/C's 308 Winchester-chambered Encore pistol and Peter Pi's Single Shot Hunter hunting pistol ammunition. Cor-Bon lists muzzle velocity for this particular load at 2625 fps with the warning: Not for use in lever-action rifles.

FREEDOM ARMS, INC.

FA now offers two versions of their Model 83: Premier Grade and Field Grade; both with adjustable sights. Both five-shot, single-action revolvers are available in 50 Action Express, 475 Linebaugh, 454 Casull, 44 Remington Magnum, 41 Remington Magnum and 357 Remington Magnum.

Barrel lengths of the 50, 454, 44 RM and 41 RM are 4 3/4-, 6-7 1/2- and 10-inches. The 475 lists only 4 3/4-, 6- and 7 1/2-inch barrels; their 357 Magnum, those same lengths, plus 9-inch. FA also catalogs a Model 97 (a five- or six-shot revolver), listed as a five-shot when chambered in 45 Colt and 41 Remington Magnum; a six-shot in 357 Magnum.

Also from Freedom Arms: Two models chambered in 22 Long Rifle - one with a 10-inch barrel called "Silhouette Class" wearing silhouette competition sights, black micarta grips and trigger over-travel screw. The "Varmint Class" 22 LR offers a choice of 5 1/8- or 7 1/2-inch barrel, express sights, black and green laminated hardwood grips and a trigger over-travel screw. Both of these 22s are matte-finish stainless steel, as are all of FA's single-actions.

I have been shooting, for many years, a Freedom Arms 454 Casull with a 9 1/4-inch barrel (including SSK Industries' muzzle brake - fitted so perfectly even a trained eye cannot distinguish where the brake starts and the original barrel ends), topped with a Simmons 1.5-4x scope in SSK's 4-ring mount. This one will be back in South Africa with me in June. I believe the customs agents at Johannesburg's Jan Smuts International Airport have its serial number memorized; they actually smile every time they see it.

In South Africa (I've been there many times) my Freedom Arms 454 Casull with 4 3/4-inch barrel is always on my right hip - fully loaded - in a holster made for me years ago with cartridge loops on the outside. Never have needed it but sure as I don't wear it I will need it — badly.

COMPETITOR CORP.

Al Straitiff continues on with his cannon-breech single-shot pistol, available in a wide array of chamberings. The one I have been shooting for a good many years is chambered 284 Winchester with a Leupold 2.5-8x scope on top. With its one-piece stock and 14-inch barrel (including muzzle brake) my Competitor's overall length is 16 inches and it weighs - scope, mount and all - 5 1/4 pounds.

How does it work? Twist its "breech" to the right to open - insert a cartridge - back to the left to close - then gently, very gently touch the trigger. Why so gently? There is an "insert" in Competitor's trigger. Mine breaks at 1 1/4-pounds of "touch" - not, really, a "pull".

True, with its cannon-breech, it looks a bit strange. Also true, once the shooter has become accustomed to firing the Competitor a second, or even a third, shot can be fired muy pronto when extra cartridges are held in a wrist band. Mine will be in South Africa with me, again, in June. It is zeroed 3 inches high at 100 yards. This means any "critter" within 200 yards is in serious trouble.

M.O.A. Corporation

Richard Mertz takes his single-shot pistol business mighty serious. He will chamber almost any cartridge you can dream up and put it into your choice of 8 3/4, 10 1/2- or 14-inch barrels. Special barrel lengths are available at extra charge and must be approved by Richard Mertz himself. And, I'd best add, his Maximum barrels are free-floated.

The product literature reports 1/2-minute-of-angle accuracy from the 22-250, 6PPC and 250 Savage chamberings. The Maximum pistol is widely used in IHMSA silhouette and has won championships every year since 1986. Of interest to handgun hunters, there are nine color photographs in his catalog showing "critters" from wild hogs to elk — even Greater Kudu — taken by hunters.

The Maximum is available in either blued or stainless steel. Options include a muzzle brake, fluted barrel (stainless only) and most any chambering you might desire. Delivery time averages three to four months.

TAURUS

This Florida-based company extols, for all the shooting world to hear, TITANIUM. New for 2000, they offer their Model 627 Tracker, a 7-shot 357 Magnum or 5-shot 41 Magnum, with 4-inch barrel, in their "Total Titanium Shadow Gray" finish.

Taurus' new Police Model 85 is a 5-shooter, hammerless (meaning double-action-only), weighing 13 ounces and chambered 38 Special. Model 617 is 357 Magnum, 7-shot,

Freedom Arms "pair"—their 4 5/8-inch and 9 1/2-inch, both chambered 454 Casull. These have become one of this writer's all-time favorites for hunting - both stateside and in South Africa.

Wherever Hal's scoped 454 Casull goes hunting, his iron-sighted 4 5/8-inch FA rig is always on his hip to better handle close encounters.

double-action (as are all of these next offerings). Model 415 is chambered 41 Magnum and, like all of these except Model 617, a 5-shooter.

Model 450 is chambered 45 Colt (for reasons unknown - Taurus added the word "LONG" before Colt). There is no such cartridge listed in *Cartridges of the World*.

Model 445 is chambered 44 Special. Models 85 MULTI and 85 CHULT are chambered 38 Special with the latter (CHULT) listed as double-action-only (DAO).

All of the above carry two-inch barrels and are made of "Total Titanium".

Taurus lists, on page six of their new catalog, eight 22 Short/Long/Long Rifle-chambered, double-action 9-shot revolvers. Plus, eight models offering 22 Magnum (WMR) as eight-shooters. Page seven lists sixteen models of two- and three-inch 38 Special double-action revolvers, with four of those sixteen as DAO (double action only).

Page eight and nine details a 7-shot +P 38 Special as well as five- and seven-shot 357 Magnum double action revolvers.

Page 10 and 11 are back on twenty (20) models of Total Titanium double action revolvers chambered 357 Magnum, 44 Special, 41 Magnum and 45 Colt.

Pages 12 through 14 are, by far, most interesting to big-bore shooters. Here are displayed b-i-g 6 1/2-inch to 8 3/8-inch double-action revolvers chambered 44 Magnum, 45 Colt and 454 Casull.

Page 15 will interest more than a few handgunners. Why?

Taurus starts off the page with b-i-g black letters reading "VARMINTS BEWARE". This one is 8-shot with 10-inch heavy vent-rib barrel, designed to accept 22 Hornet cartridges. It is delivered with a scope mounting base installed and, yes, the shooter will have to pull the trigger eight times before it has to be reloaded. Recoil? There should be very little, if any, because this Raging Hornet weighs 50 ounces (minus scope).

There is no way, on these pages, their entire catalog be properly described, so see your nearest firearms dealer, or order your own copy.

SAVAGE ARMS

This company is far better known for its excellent, reasonably priced rifles. However, they do turn out some mighty fine bolt-action pistols, with the bolt on the proper side for right-handed shooters (meaning left-side), with right-side ejection. I have been shooting one chambered 22-250 Remington, topped with a Burris 3-9x scope. This rig did, in fact, cause the demise of more than a few Kansas prairie dogs a few months back. Trigger pull, from their factory, is clean as breaking glass - at 2 1/8 pounds. Their new catalog lists six models:

516SAK is chambered 22-250 Remington, 243 Winchester, 7mm-O8 Remington, 260 Remington and 308 Winchester, all with a 12-inch barrel AND their very efficient muzzle brake.

Model 516FSS carries a 14-inch barrel with no muzzle brake, chambered 223 Remington, 22-250 Remington, 243 Winchester, 7mm-08 Remington, 260 Remington and 308 Winchester. Both of the foregoing have stainless-steel barrels.

Model 510F is blued and chambered for 223 Remington, 22-250 Remington, 243 Winchester, 7mm-08 Remington, 260 Remington and 308 Winchester.

Sport Striker carries 10 inches of barrel with choice of two chamberings: 501F - 22 Long Rifle; 502F - 22 WMR.

Still more: Super Striker is offered in two models - 516BSAK, with 12 inches of fluted stainless steel barrel, with muzzle brake, chambered to accept 223 Remington, 22-250 Rem., 243 Win., 7mm-08 Rem., 260 Remington and 308 Winchester. Model

▲ The Competitor is a bit "unusual" with its "cannon-like" breech - but - once understood.....

◄ ..... it is mighty fast to eject the empty and get a fresh cartridge chambered.

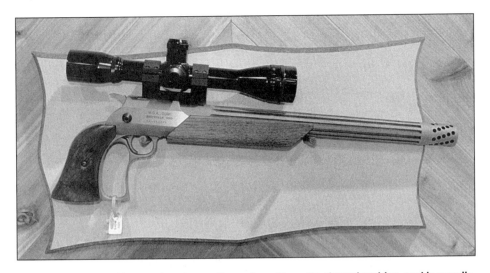

M.O.A.'s "Maximum" has captured more than a few silhouette championships, and is equally successful in the hunting field.

516BSS is 14 inches of fluted stainless steel barrel, minus the muzzle brake. Chamberings are same as listed above.

These last two wear thumb-hole laminated stocks with dual pillar-bedding. And, I'd best add, all are drilled and tapped for scope mounting.

HARRINGTON & RICHARDSON / NEW ENGLAND FIREARMS

Harrington & Richardson and New England Firearms have decided to sit out this year in terms of handgun manufacturing. Neither company will manufacture handguns during 2000. However, I'm told both plan to resume production of their revolvers next year - 2001.

CHARTER ARMS

Charter Arms is offering two double-action revolvers - both with 5-round cylinders and stainless steel construction. Undercover is chambered 38 Special and weighs 19 1/2 ounces; Bulldog is chambered for the 44 Special and is a bit heavier at 21 ounces. Each with 2-inch barrels. Both lock up in three places: at the hand, cylinder stop and ejector-rod collar.

I've often carried an earlier model, no longer manufactured, called Bulldog Pug, chambered for the 44 Special. Its hammer is "bobbed", meaning double-action-only. Charter also offers the Compact with a standard hammer and the Super Compact hammerless (like mine).

AMERICAN DERRINGER

This company has been around for many, many years. My very own stainless steel derringer – 45 Colt, three-inch barrels; weight: (both

barrels filled with 255-grain SWC cartridges) 1pound, 1/2-ounce, is here on my desk as these words are typed.

BOND ARMS

Greg Bond manufactures single-action, high-quality derringers with interchangeable barrels. Chamberings are 9mm, 357 Magnum/38 Special, 40, 44 Magnum/44 Special, 45 Colt/.410-bore and 45 ACP. Bond Arms is a fairly young company but does manufacture a very fine product. If that was not the case, the company would not be mentioned here.

MANURHIN

A few years back I visited the Manurhin plant in Mulhouse, France. In fact - I spent 8 1/2 hours in their facility - about half with the international sale manager and an interpreter.

The interpreter took me through their manufacturing department then to the range, in a basement, where all Manurhin handguns were test-fired before shipping. The rangemaster asked if I would like to shoot one of their guns and handed me one of their 357 Magnum DAs and a box of ammunition. Loading five in its 6-shot cylinder I, carefully as I could, fired them at the 25-yard target. He looked, very closely, then asked, "Sir, would you do that again?" I placed another five in the cylinder then touched them off. He watched every one - then turned to me and said, "Sir, you shoot better than our guns!" All of you reading this know that to be totally impossible.

Once back in the United States I received a Manurhin MR 73 double-action revolver, with excellent target sights, chambered 32 Long. These are, by far, the best-finished handguns I've seen anyplace in the world. Immaculate might be a better description. The entire metal finish is polished and deeply blued to perfection.

The factory trigger pull is 3 1/4 pounds. Another desirable feature not commonly offered by American manufacturers is the trigger stop screw which adjusts so that no trigger over-travel is felt. Actual trigger movement is the tiniest fraction of an inch - barely visible to even a practiced eye.

SSK INDUSTRIES

J.D. Jones, founder of SSK Industries, is a long, long-time friend. How long? His youngest daughter still calls me "My Pal Hal" and she is now a schoolteacher with children of her own.

All that to say this: I have a Ruger Super Redhawk 44 Magnum that he rebuilt. Its octagon barrel reads: "Custom Crafted For Hal Swiggett By J.D. Jones". On that same side, the frame reads (over Super Redhawk) "SSK Custom". Over .44 MAGNUM

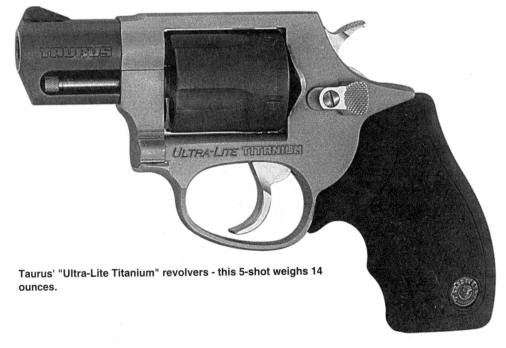

Taurus' "Ultra-Lite Titanium" revolvers - this 5-shot weighs 14 ounces.

Taurus' big Raging Bull 454 Casull is still doing its more-than-creditable job.

CAL. on that same portion of the frame, it reads: "Beauty and the Beast". Beast's barrel is 6 1/8-inches long but only 3 1/2-inches protrudes from the frame - with a cavernous hole beneath its red front sight.

J.D. - and his SSK Industries - can and will build anything within semi-reason should you have custom-work desires.

DAVIS DERRINGERS

This California-based company offers three versions of their derringers: Standard D-Series is chambered 22 LR, 22 WMR, 25 Auto or 32 Auto. Barrel length is 2.4 inches. Weight empty, 9.5 ounces. Grips unbreakable pearl on their 22 LR and 25 Auto.

The Big Bore Series is chambered 22 WMR, 32 H&R Magnum, 9mm or 38 Special. Barrel length is 2.75 inches and weight empty, is 14 ounces. Grips are molded black synthetic, laminated oak or laminated rosewood. Metal finish is your choice of chrome or black Teflon.

The Long Bore Series is chambered 22 WMR, 9mm or 38 Special. Barrel length is 3.5 inches and it weighs, empty, 16 ounces. Grips are molded black synthetic, laminated oak or laminated rosewood. Metal finish is your choice of chrome or black Teflon.

DAN WESSON

On my desk, as these words are typed, are two DWs I've hung onto for years: one is a very heavy 45 Colt, with a 6-inch barrel and immaculately blued

finish. It weighs, on my postal scale, 3 1/2 pounds. Trigger pull is 2 1/2 pounds. The other is a stainless steel 6-inch, chambered 22 Winchester Magnum. Trigger pull is exactly 3 pounds. Both are fitted with adjustable rear sights. The 45 has a yellow insert up front and my 22 Winchester Magnum has a red insert.

ANSCHUTZ

Anschütz bolt-action pistols are known world-wide. Dieter Anschutz' two newest offerings are: the Model 64 P chambered 22 Long Rifle (5 round capacity) and the Model 64 P Magnum for the larger 22 WMR cartridge (4 round capacity).

The well-proven barreled actions of these two are seated in a black – ergonomic, weather-proof and non-slip – synthetic stock. Both weigh 3 1/2 pounds, have two-stage triggers and are drilled and tapped for scope mounting.

BOWEN CLASSIC ARMS CORP.

I have two examples of Hamilton Bowen's expertise on my desk. One a rechambered stainless steel Smith & Wesson 5-inch that started life chambered 10mm. The other is built on a Ruger 44 Magnum New Model Super Blackhawk frame - but no longer feeds on those little 44 Magnum "cattiges", as one of my gunsmith friends called them.

First, the S&W: It started life as the Model 610, chambered 10mm, with S&W's full lug barrel. Approximately 5,000 were manufactured in 1990 only, then the model was reintroduced in 1998.

Stamped on the right side its barrel, where 10mm used to be, now appears 38-40. I showed this to Ross Seyfried at one of Winchester's meetings. He sort of ho-hummed and, more than likely, wondered

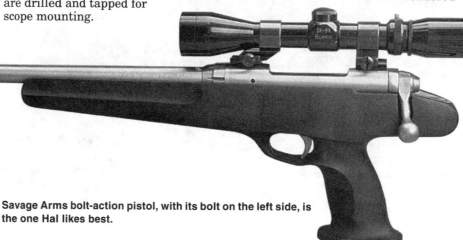

Savage Arms bolt-action pistol, with its bolt on the left side, is the one Hal likes best.

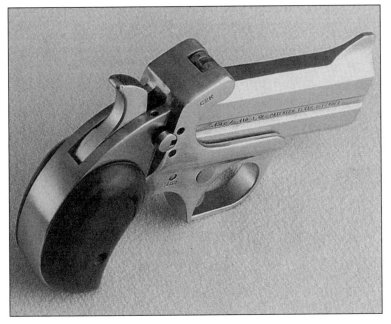

Bond Arms is one of the newer, but very successful, manufacturers of pocket pistols. Shown here is their newest 45 Colt/.410 3-inch pistol.

all Cowboy revolvers. Barrel length is 5 1/2-inches and, quoting their literature, "Great Attention Has Been Given to Every Detail to insure That it Truly is Identical to the Original Colt Single Action Revolver in Authenticity as Well as Quality. All Parts are Interchangeable with the Original 1st and 2nd Generation Colts." All those "capital letters" are theirs - not mine.

1873 Sixshooter - This 4 3/4-inch barrel single-action is listed as "The New Hartford Model Revolver", available with either the Old Model or New Model frames. And yes, there is more. Old Model frames are chambered 45 Colt, 38-40, 32-20 and 44-40. New Model frames are chambered 45 Colt, 357 Magnum and 44 Special. They offer engraved models with what they call "Class 'A' Engraving and Custom Blue Finish".

E.M.F. also lists a Cavalry Model (7 1/2-inch) and Artillery Model (5 1/2-inch) - both chambered for what they call 45 Long Colt (it is still, correctly, the 45 Colt cartridge). There are more - a lot more - including Lightning or Express models with 4-, 4 3/4- and 5 1/2-inch barrels. You really will need their catalog.

why I was wasting his time. I suggested turning it over and looking at its "other" side. Soon as he saw ".38-40 CAL." he looked me in the eye and said, "Hal, I think you have something here!" I already knew I did.

Hamilton's "other" work of gunsmithing art started life as a Ruger 44 Magnum New Model Super Blackhawk. It now wears a 7 1/2-inch octagon barrel that reads "BOWEN CLASSIC ARMS CORP." on its left side and ".500 MAGNUM CAL." on that opposite side, and measures .745-inches across the "flats".

My rather heavy single-action Ruger weighs, on my postal scale, 3 pounds, 1 ounce. Trigger pull on this highly customized single action is a mighty crisp 3 1/2 pounds, with no take-up slack.

The load Hamilton gave me uses H110 under a 420-grain cast .512-inch bullet launched by one of Winchester's

Large Rifle primers. The case, originally 348 Winchester, is shortened to 1.39-inches, making a loaded cartridge measure 1.8-inches overall. The loaded cartridge weight is a fraction short of 1 1/2 ounces.

E.M.F.

This California-based importer lists more than a few single-action revolvers. You will need their catalog to see them all - but - I'll do my best to describe a few - the rest will be up to you. All are listed as "HARTFORD MODEL".

1873 Single Action Army - Their 1873 Single Action Army's barrel length is 7 1/2-inches and is chambered for six cartridges: 45 Colt, 357 Magnum and 44-40 as standard, plus "special" chamberings of 38-40, 32-20 and 44 Special.

1873 Frontier - The Hartford Single Action Revolver is the most prized of

I A R

This California-based importer of Italian-manufactured single-action revolvers offers three versions - the 1873 Six Shooter (22 Long Rifle/22 WMR combo) with a 5 1/2-inch barrel, the 1873 Frontier Marshall (357 Magnum or 45 Colt) with 7 1/2-inch barrel and the 1873 Frontier 22 (22 Long Rifle only), with a 4 1/2-inch barrel. I had reason to work with their 22 LR-chambered single-actions a few months back and they performed right well.

HERITAGE MANUFACTURING

Manufactured here in good ol' USA, this Florida-based company turns out (in the revolver category) only 22 Long Rifle and 22 WMR single-action revolvers with two grip configurations - bird head and traditional. Two finishes also - blue or nickel - with barrel lengths 3 1/2-, 4 3/4-, 6- and 9-inches.

I've said it before - but here it is again - for honest-to-goodness fun with any handgun, it has to be - must be - a rimfire single action.

EUROPEAN AMERICAN ARMORY

This Florida-based importer offers one double-action revolver and three single-action revolvers manufactured in Germany.

"Windicator" is their 38 Special/357 Magnum 6-shot

Manurhin revolvers are manufactured in France. Though offered in several chamberings, the one shown here is chambered for the 32 Long.

One of my favorite revolvers is this stainless Dan Wesson chambered 22 WMR.

double-action revolver. Barrel lengths are 2 or 4 inches. Finish is blue with a choice of fixed or adjustable sights.

Two of EAA's single-actions are chambered 357 Magnum, 44-40, 44 Remington Magnum or 45 Colt. Barrel lengths are 4 1/2 or 7 1/2 inches with fixed sights, 6-shot cylinders and deep bluing with color case frames, or nickel finish. Weight of their shorter version is 2.45 pounds and 2.7 pounds for their longer-barreled six-gun. New to EAA's line is a 6- or 8-shot 22 Long Rifle/ 22 WMR single-action in two barrel lengths: 4 3/4- or 6 3/4 inches. Your choice of deep blue or nickel finish. Grips on all three are European walnut and sights are fixed.

CIMARRON ARMS

Cimarron imports replicas any of you would be hard-pressed to differentiate from an original, except for the finish. Elderly, original six-guns would be well-worn. Should you be interested I can fully recommend your looking into Cimarron's line of brand-spankin' new "Oldtimers".

Not a gun, but a fine book about...single action revolvers. Three hundred twenty pages filled with information about single-action revolvers. Devoted - entirely - to *Action Shooting Cowboy Style* (the title). Written by John Taffin and published by Krause Publications, the book goes into detail about Cowboy Action Shooting and the guns and loads used - including cap-and-ball six-guns. Though I have never become involved in this sort of shooting I will support anything that speaks favorably about my all-time favorite hunting firearm. As most of you know - I hunt over a lot of the world and only with handguns!

How long have I been shooting handguns? My grandfather started me with a Colt's Single Action revolver on my sixth birthday - July 22, 1927. And I am still at it!

PHELPS MFG. CO.

I have owned, for many years, one of Gene Phelps' humongous six-guns - chambered for the 45-70 Government. Barrel length is 8 inches - weight an even six pounds on my Remington Game Scale. Cylinder length is 2 1/4 inches with 6-shot capacity. Yes! With adjustable sights, too. The one here on my desk (which came from Gene himself) reads, on its right-side frame below the cylinder, "Heritage 1". Trigger pull is 3 1/2 pounds.

Phelps first manufactured his b-i-g single actions in 1978 - all chambered 45-70. Later he added 444 Marlin, 375 Winchester and, last, 50-70 Government. These six-guns are no longer manufactured so you'll have to watch the classified ads and check the gun shows to find one.

CLASSIC OLD WEST STYLES

Based in El Paso, Texas this company offers anything any of you "Westerners" might think of concerning how, and where, to carry your single- and double-action revolvers.

Their catalog offers more gunleather styles than you might imagine. In other words "nothing has been left out". That includes clothing, etc.

This includes gun inlays (A) United States Marshall, (B) Texas Ranger, (C) Rattlesnake, (D) Tombstone Marshall, (E) Deputy Sheriff, (F) Wyatt Earp and (G) Texas Star. Plus imitation ivory grips with Mexican Eagle, Liberty Cap, Liberty Eagle, Checkered, Checkered with Star, Steer Skull, Schofield, Navy Eagle, Ruger Vaquero Plain and Ruger Vaquero Bull. There is more, much more - so - send for their catalog.

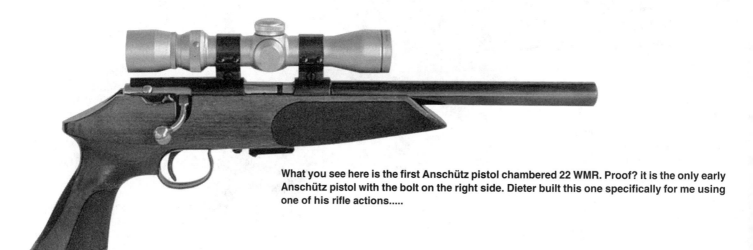

What you see here is the first Anschütz pistol chambered 22 WMR. Proof? it is the only early Anschütz pistol with the bolt on the right side. Dieter built this one specifically for me using one of his rifle actions.....

Hamilton Bowen built this octagon-barreled 500 Magnum on a Ruger frame.

COR-BON

Peter Pi's Cor-Bon ammunition company turns out, by far, the best specialty ammunition offered today. I say "specialty" because his company does not load for every caliber/cartridge. His company also turns out what he calls "Bee Safe Pre-Fragmented Safety Ammunition" in eight different chamberings.

I used his 308 Super Mag in my Thompson/Center Encore pistol to take the most unusual deer I've ever tagged. He has two loadings for the 308 Winchester cartridge: 165-grain SPBT and 180-grain SPBT. The cartridge that "tagged" my trophy was one of his 165-grainers. A one-shot kill, top of the heart shot at, according to Bushnell's new rangefinder, 99 yards.

LASERGRIPS

I have these on one of my Smith & Wesson stainless steel double-actions. Other than the tiny "hump" on the right grip, topside, no one would ever notice anything different until the red laser beam hits them right where a bullet could instantly follow.

C-MORE SYSTEMS

I have one of these sights on an 8 1/2-inch Mag-na-Ported STALKER 44 Magnum Ruger New Model SUPER BLACKHAWK and it is, by far, the "fastest" sight on any of my handguns. Simply put the red dot on where you want your bullet to go, then touch it off! A bit bulky - but it does everything C-More says it will.

GARRETT CARTRIDGES

Though Randy Garrett does not manufacture "Sixguns and Others" firearms, he does load the finest ammunition for 44 Remington Magnum-chambered Ruger Redhawk and Super Redhawk double-action revolvers. By "finest" I mean "most powerful" - designed specifically for Ruger's b-i-g double-action six-guns.

Gene Phelps' 45-70 six-shooter is not really intended for quick-draw competition. Why? It weighs an even six pounds.

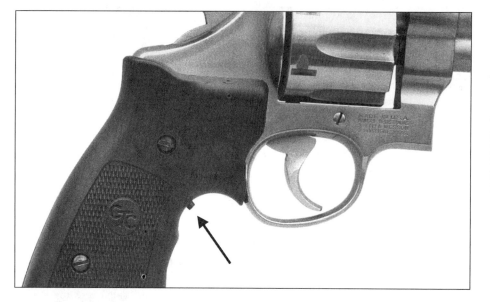

Lasergrips are black, nicely checkered for a firm grip and look like any other handgun grip except for a tiny, almost invisible, protrusion on the upper right side. Gripping the revolver automatically activates a red laser beam, which indicates exactly where a bullet will go.

Kirkpatrick Leather's "Hal Swiggett" shoulder holster for big hunting handguns. This one was built for Hal's 454 Casull Freedom Arms single action with its 1.5-4x Simmons scope.

KIRKPATRICK LEATHER

I found this Laredo (Texas)-based company many years back. He designed a shoulder holster specifically for my Freedom Arms 454 Casull single-action with its 9 1/4-inch barrel (including muzzle brake) and its 1.5-4x Simmons scope on top. He made another to fit my Thompson/Center Encore 308 Winchester - with its 15-inch barrel and T/C's 2.5-7x scope. My name is stamped on each and every shoulder holster he has sold.

Should you have one of the above handgun models, he can build a holster for you, too. Or you can lay your handgun (scoped or not) on a large sheet of paper, draw an outline around it - mail it to him - and he will tell you exactly what the cost will be before he starts his expert leather workers on it.

MICHAELS OF OREGON

Home of the "World's Fastest Gun Bore Cleaner". Mine measures 22 inches and includes an end-weighted cord to get it through the barrel. It does what it says in the literature - "Cleans Gun Bores in 10 Seconds". For 44/45-caliber pistol, 30-caliber rifle or 12 gauge.   ●

Rifle Report

by Robert M. Hausman

GUNMAKERS ARE PRODUCING a mix of the old and the new to appeal to the tastes of rifleman everywhere. There are replicas of 19th century designs for the growing numbers of cowboy action shooters, traditional hunting arms, sporterized military rifles–as well as innovative products making use of cutting-edge arms manufacturing technology. Here is a company-by-company look at some of the most noteworthy rifles being produced today.

American Arms offers a variety of Old West rifles imported from the Aldo Uberti Co. of Italy. One example is the 1860 Henry, the first true repeating rifle to become both practical and reliable. The two models offered by American Arms are available in either 44-40 or 45 Colt, and feature a tubular steel magazine, straight-grip walnut buttstock and a brass frame, elevator, magazine follower and buttplate.

American Arms also offers replicas of the Winchester Models 1866, 1873 and 1885. All come in 44-40 or 45 Colt and have a steel tubular magazine, walnut buttstock and forend. The 1866 models have a brass frame, elevator and buttplate.

The 1873 models feature a color case-hardened steel frame with a brass elevator and a steel buttplate.

The 1885 Winchester single shot was originally designed to compete with the Sharps rifle of the period. American Arms' version has a forged steel case-hardened frame and lever, and a European walnut stock and forend.

Sharps rifle replicas are also available from American Arms. The Cavalry and Frontier models sport 22-inch barrels, for an overall length just under 40 inches and are chambered for the 45-70 cartridge. The 1874 Sporting Rifle and 1874 Deluxe Sporting Rifle versions of the Sharps have 28-inch barrels, an overall length of just under 46 inches and are offered in 45-70 and 45-120 chamberings.

For the lovers of really big boomers, a new 50-caliber rifle is available from **ArmaLite, Inc**. The AR-50, chambered for the 50 Browning Machine Gun cartridge, is an innovative single-shot, bolt-action rifle built around a unique octagonal receiver bedded into an aluminum stock. Features include a multi-flute recoil check at the muzzle, modified M16-type vertical pistol grip and removable buttstock for ease of transport. Recoil of this 42-pound rifle is described by the manufacturer as "very moderate."

The long-awaited **Beretta Mato** (the Dakota Indian word for "bear"), based on the Mauser 98 action, is being produced. The claw extractor provides controlled round feeding and enables cartridges to be run through the magazine and ejected without having to first close the bolt completely on the round in the chamber. The trigger is adjustable for both overtravel and weight-of-pull, while the stock is of Claro walnut with hand-rubbed, satin oil finish. The Mato is chambered for the 270 Winchester, 280 Remington, 30-06 Springfield, 7mm Remington Magnum, 300 Winchester Magnum, 338 Winchester Magnum and 375 H&H Magnum.

Beretta's S689 Sable family of double-barrel express rifles are built on a 20 gauge boxlock shotgun frame with double triggers, rifle-type firing pins and breech faces toughened to handle large centerfire cartridges. Barrels are rotary-forged with a blade front sight and a V-notch rear. The stock is made from select walnut with cheek rest and Schnabel forend with sling swivels as standard. Chamberings include 30-06 Springfield, 9.3x74R, and 444 Marlin. For added versatility, 20 gauge shotgun barrels may also be fitted.

In a move that will increase its presence in the rifle market, Beretta Holding of Italy, has purchased Sako

Beretta Mato

Beretta S689 Sable Express Rifle

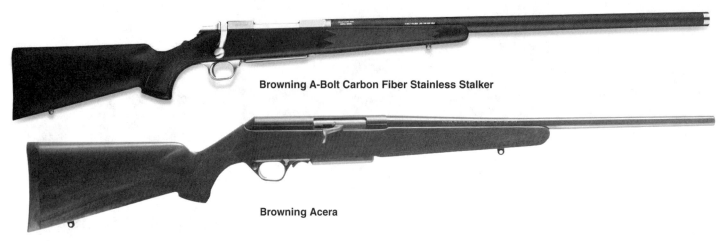

Browning A-Bolt Carbon Fiber Stainless Stalker

Browning Acera

Ltd., the manufacturer of hunting and sports rifles. As part of Beretta, Sako will gain access to a strong sales and distribution network and to the other resources of the nearly 500-year old Beretta operation.

Browning has partnered with **Christensen Arms** to offer carbon fiber barrels on the A-Bolt rifle. These strong fibers surround a stainless steel inner sleeve on the new A-Bolt Carbon Fiber Stainless Stalker rifle. The material is stronger than steel, yet 80% lighter and dissipates heat ten times faster. Overall, carbon fiber technology offers weather resistance, accuracy, light weight and shot-after-shot stability.

Two chamberings are available in the A-Bolt Carbon Fiber Stainless Stalker: the 22-250 Remington, perhaps creating the ultimate long-range varmint rifle; the 300 Winchester Magnum, a hard-hitting, long-range nail driver.

Browning has also introduced the Acera straight-pull rifle utilizing an action requiring only two movements, unlike the four needed to cycle a conventional bolt-action rifle. With the Acera it is a simple *pull*, to eject a spent case, and a *push* to feed the next live round into the chamber.

The Acera uses the seven-lug bolt design of the proven BAR, contributing to quick cycling, the ability to handle magnum calibers and the accuracy of a bolt action. Other features include a detachable box magazine, Teflon-coated breech block, American walnut stock and the option of the Browning-exclusive BOSS recoil-reducing system. The Acera is available in 30-06 and 300 Winchester Magnum.

Cimarron Arms has debuted a three-quarter scale version of the old Sharps Model 1874 rifle, ideal for smaller-statured aficionados of cowboy action shooting.

The Cimarron Model 1892 rifle is manufactured faithfully to the specifications of John Browning's patents of 1884, the same patents covering the Model 1886 rifle. The 1892 was made in popular calibers introduced by Winchester and proven in the Model 1873. The Model 1892 rifle later gained fame as the lever gun John Wayne carried in many of his western films.

Cimarron also produces the Model 1873 in Saddle Ring Carbine and Short Rifle versions. The Cimarron Saddle Ring Carbine comes with or without the saddle ring, and a case-colored frame is available on charcoal-blue models. As with all Cimarron models, both the carbine and short rifle are authentically marked with the original patent and caliber designations. The Model 1873 Short Rifle, with tapered octagon barrel, is one of the best-balanced of all the 1873s. Chamberings available for the pair are 45 Colt, 44 WCF, 357 Magnum and 32 WCF.

Gibbs Rifle Co. specializes in collectible military rifles. The firm's M98K rifles came from the Haganah Jewish defense forces, which used the rifles for over 20 years while protecting border settlements and farms. The Israeli arsenal, Ha'as, rebarreled these rifles to 7.62x51 NATO (308 Winchester). Gibbs' M98K rifles come from a variety of makers.

An updated design based on the battle-proven No. 5 Enfield Jungle Carbine, the Gibbs Quest Extreme Carbine is a modern version of this

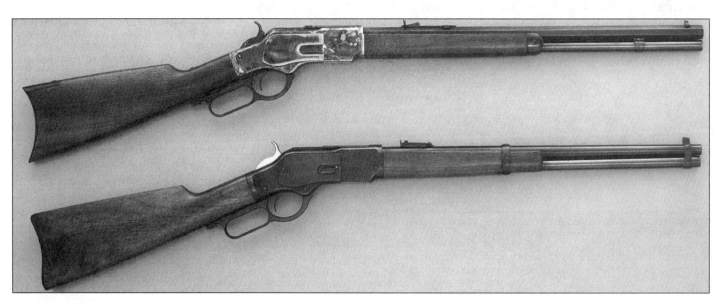

Cimarron Model 1873 "Short" Rifle 20-inch octagon barrel (top). Cimarron Model 1873 "Saddle Ring" carbine 19-inch barrel (bottom).

Henry Repeating Arms is using new tooling to produce a version of the famous AR-7 survival 22 rifle.

The Henry Repeating Arms 22 Magnum lever action is intended to bring out the "west" in you!

popular and rugged little carbine. Each Quest is electroless-nickel finished and fitted with a new hardwood stock. The unique compensator/flash hider reduces muzzle jump and flash and provides rugged front sight protection. The solid brass butt trap houses a survival kit with Brunton liquid-filled compass, waterproof matches with striker, firestarter, snare wire, twine and fishing hooks. At only 7 3/4 pounds, the Quest is ideal for trail, camp, cabin or hunting vehicle.

The Henry Repeating Arms Co. has purchased new tooling to manufacture a new and improved version of the famous U.S. Air Force AR-7 22 rifle. The piece is ultra-light at 2 1/2 pounds and breaks down for

storage: the barrel, action and magazine fit into the waterproof floating stock and the resultant package is just 16 1/2 inches long. The steel barrel and receiver are coated with Teflon for corrosion resistance.

Henry's 22 Magnum lever action, ideal for small game and varmints, has a deluxe checkered American walnut stock, a grooved receiver for scope mounting and a 19 1/4-inch barrel. The tubular magazine holds 11 rounds, the rifle weighs 5 1/2 pounds and the overall length is 37 1/2 inches.

The Henry pump-action, external hammer 22 rimfire rifle is a modern rendering of the traditional gallery rifle with a walnut stock and forend; sights consist of a square-notch Patridge-type rear and square-topped

front sight. The alloy receiver is grooved to accept scope mounts. The tubular magazine holds 15 rounds of 22 Long Rifle cartridges, barrel length is 17 1/2 inches, overall length 35 1/2 inches and the weight is just 5 1/2 pounds, making it perfect as a kid's first 22 rifle.

A staple in the Japanese arms manufacturing industry, **Howa** products are now available through a new entity, **Legacy Sports International**. The Howa M-1500 Lightning and M-15 Hunter rifles are well-made bolt action rifles designed for strength, simplicity, smoothness and accuracy—all at a moderate price.

Both models are available in blue or stainless steel; the Lightning is equipped with a Butler Creek polymer

Howa M1500 Hunter

Howa M1500 Lightning

The classic Marlin Model 336 deer rifle is now available in a stainless steel version dubbed the Model 336M.

The new Marlin Model 1894P is the shortest model in the gunmaker's popular "Guide Gun" series.

stock, in chamberings from 223 Remington up to 338 Winchester Magnum. The M-1500 Hunter features a walnut-finished hardwood stock in the same caliber range. Both come with a solid rubber buttpad and are drilled and tapped for scope mounts.

The Howa M-1500 Varmint, available in 223 Remington and 22-250 Remington, carries a heavy hammer-forged 24-inch barrel and is stocked with either checkered polymer or walnut-finished hardwood; both versions include solid rubber recoil pad and sling swivel studs.

For the serious rifleman, the Howa M-1500 PCS (Police Counter Sniper), available in 308 Winchester, will be of interest. The heart of the rifle is the proven M-1500 action in blued or stainless steel. The grooved trigger is factory preset at 4 pounds.

In addition to complete rifles, the Howa M-1500 is available as a heavy-barreled action-only in three sizes: short, long and Magnum Long Action variations, in a wide range of chamberings.

The **Lazzeroni** rifle is carved from a solid block of 17R stainless steel utilizing the latest CNC machining equipment.

The helically-fluted bolt, with its two massive locking lugs and heavy-duty extractor, contains both spring-loaded and mechanical ejectors. The Lazzeroni match-grade 416R stainless fluted barrels are hand-lapped and cryogenic-treated. Both the conventional and thumbhole stock designs involve hand-bedding with aluminum pillar blocks. The triggers are fully-adjustable, stainless steel benchrest-style and the floorplate/ trigger guard assembly is machined of steel. All parts are then finished in gray matte electroless nickel for corrosion protection. Chamberings include: 6.53 (.257) Scramjet, 7.82

The new Marlin Model 1895M is the most powerful "Guide Gun" yet, chambered for the ultra-powerful new 450 Marlin cartridge.

The Marlin Model 25NC is an economical 22 bolt action fitted with a Mossy Oak Break-Up stock.

The Marlin Model 60C, one of the world's most popular self-loading 22s, is now available with a Mossy Oak Break-Up stock.

(.308) Warbird, 7.21 (.284) Firebird, 8.59 (.338) Titan and 10.57 (.416) Meteor.

A new high-tech graphite barrel, called the "Magnum Lite," is now available for the Mountain Eagle rifle from **Magnum Research**. The graphite barrel is 75% lighter than a conventional bull barrel, but it doesn't twist, walk or whip.

Standard Mountain Eagle rifle specifications still apply: Sako action with adjustable trigger, high-comb Kevlar-graphite stock, five-shot magazine capacity in the long action version; four rounds in the magnum action. For traditionalists, the 4140 blued steel version is still available.

For decades a deer hunter's favorite, **Marlin's** Model 336CS 30/30 lever action, has been considered the ultimate deer rifle–until now. The first stainless steel lever action to carry the Marlin name, the new Model 336M is ready for all the rain and snow deer season can dish out. Almost all of the major parts of this rifle are stainless steel, the rest are nickel-plated.

The Model 336M's 20-inch stainless barrel is fitted to a stainless receiver tapped for a receiver sight or scope mounts. Other stainless parts are the lever, trigger guard plate, six-shot magazine tube and loading gate. The American black walnut pistol-grip stock is protected with the Mar-Shield finish and carries nickel-plated swivel studs and a rubber buttpad.

The shortest and lightest of the Marlin "Guide Guns" is the new Model 1894P with a 16 1/4-inch ported barrel and an overall length of just 33 1/4 inches. Lightweight (at only 5 3/4 pounds), it is chambered for the 44 Magnum/44 Special cartridges, making it suitable for taking both deer and black bear. An eight-shot tubular magazine, squared finger lever, deep-cut

▲ The SSi-ONE single-shot rifle with interchangeable barrels, from O.F. Mossberg, is a versatile new hunting companion from this noted gunmaking firm.

Ballard-type rifling, hammer block safety, offset hammer spur for scope use, and deeply blued metal surfaces are just a few of the new rifle's many features.

With 3,427 foot-pounds of muzzle energy, the new Marlin Model 1895M delivers the most knock-down power of any in the "Guide Gun" series. It is chambered for the belted magnum 450 Marlin, a new cartridge by Hornady especially for this rifle. Ideal for the needs of the big game hunter and guide, it weighs 7 pounds with a 37-inch overall length and contains an 18 1/2-inch ported barrel with Ballard-type cut rifling. The receiver top is sandblasted to prevent glare and is tapped for scope mounts or a receiver sight. Supplied sights are a hooded front ramp with brass bead and an adjustable, folding semi-buckhorn sight mounted at the rear.

The new Marlin Model 60C combines the features of one of the most popular 22s in the world with the effectiveness of Mossy Oak Break-Up camouflage on the stock. The tubular magazine holds fourteen 22 Long Rifle cartridges.

An originator of the replica arms field, **Navy Arms Co.** offers one of the largest varieties of 19th century firearms.

Navy Arms' 1866 "Yellow Boy" rifle is a replica of Oliver Winchester's improved version of the Henry rifle, with a side loading port and wooden forearm. It features an octagonal barrel, polished brass receiver (thus the name "Yellow Boy") with walnut stock. It is chambered for 38 Special., 44-40 and 45 Colt.

Navy Arms' 1873 Winchester-style rifle is a replica of "The Gun that Won the West." The '73, and the Colt single-action revolver, were among the two favorite arms of the Western pioneers. "Buffalo Bill" Cody was so impressed with the rifle he wrote, *"...and for general hunting or Indian fighting, I pronounce the improved Winchester the 'boss'."* This replica has a case-hardened receiver, full-octagon 24 1/4-inch barrel, and

walnut stocks. Chamberings are 357 Magnum, 44-40 WCF and 45 Colt.

Navy Arms also offers replicas of the Model 1892 Winchester rifle. Originally designed by John Browning to replace the Model 1873, the 1892 Winchester rifle became one of the most popular lever actions of all time. Simplification of the elevator and feeding system gave the 1892 a much

Navy Arms 1874 Sharps

smoother action than previous models. Calibers available are 357 Magnum, 44-40 WCF and 45 Colt.

Navy Arms' replicas of the 1874 Sharps rifles recreate one of the most popular sporting rifles of the Old West, known for its long range and knockdown power. Hunters, frontier scouts, settlers and Indians all respected and coveted this classic breechloader. Manufactured by Pedersoli of Italy, Navy Arms' Sharps rifles are available in several variations, chambered for the 45-70 Gov't. and 45-90 cartridges.

A series of rolling block rifles is marketed by Navy Arms, including a replica of the Remington Rolling Block with a heavy, full-octagon barrel chambered for the 45-70 Gov't., color case-hardened receiver, trigger guard, barrel band and buttplate. The buttstock and forend are walnut, the sights consist of a "Rocky Mountain" front blade and an open notch rear. The tang is drilled and tapped to accept an optional Creedmoor sight.

Navy Arms offers iron and brass frame Henry rifle replicas. The Iron Frame models are a reproduction of B. Tyler Henry's original model 1860 rifle. The receiver of this 44-40 rifle is made of high quality steel and the walnut stock is oil-finished. The forerunner of all Winchester lever actions, the Henry was known as *"the rifle that you loaded on Sunday and fired all week."* The Navy Arms brass frame replicas feature blue steel barrels, walnut stocks, and highly polished brass receivers and buttplates.

O.F. Mossberg & Sons, Inc., an industry leader in pump-action security and sporting shotgun manufacturing, has begun a new chapter in its company history with the introduction of the SSi-ONE single-shot rifle. The Ssi, or *"single shot interchangeable"* rifle, is a lever-opening, break-action design with a crisp single-stage trigger, ambidextrous top-tang safety and an internal eject/extract selector. Other features include a firing pin cocking indicator, black rubber buttpad, recessed muzzle crown, black walnut stock, swivel studs and scope base.

The SSi-ONE's interchangeable barrel/caliber system allows a choice of six different chamberings in 223 Remington, 22-250 Remington, 243 Winchester, 270 Winchester, 308 Winchester and 30-06 Springfield. There is also a rifled 12 gauge slug barrel available.

The Professional Ordnance
Carbon 15 rifle (Type 20), chambered in 223 Remington, has both its upper and lower receivers constructed of high-tech carbon fiber, for a remarkable unloaded weight of only 3.9 pounds. Features include a

Professional Ordnance Carbon 15 Rifle

stainless steel match-grade barrel, hard-chromed bolt and bolt carrier, carbon fiber buttstock and foregrip and an optics mounting base. An optional recoil compensator is available.

The biggest news to come out of **Remington Arms Co.** this year is the company's introduction of the EtronX, an electronic ignition rifle with the look and feel of the Remington Model 700. While this product is covered more extensively elsewhere in this issue, a brief review of the product follows.

The electronic ignition system of the EtronX delivers near-zero lock time to aid in better accuracy. A

standard 9-volt battery–contained in the stock–sends current through a contact in the bolt face to the cartridge's electronic primer, practically eliminating lock time. The electronic trigger offers significantly less travel than the standard Model 700 mechanical trigger and eliminates all creep.

The EtronX rifle contains a light-emitting diode (LED) on top of the grip which indicates system status (*fire* or *safe* modes), chamber status (*loaded* or *unloaded*), a low-battery indicator and malfunction indicators. The 26-inch heavy, stainless steel barrel is fluted to

Remington EtronX Rifle

Remington 700 BDL SS

Remington Model 7 Youth

The Scout rifle by Savage Arms is designed to be a practical yet tactical rifle.

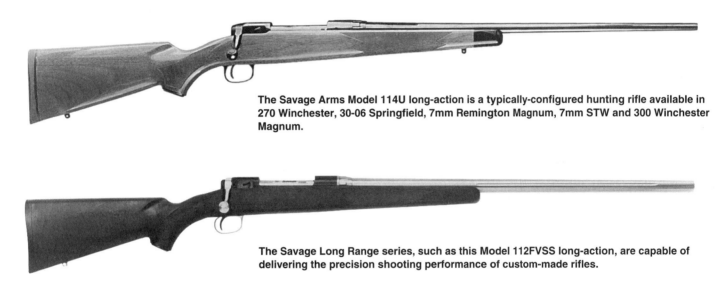

The Savage Arms Model 114U long-action is a typically-configured hunting rifle available in 270 Winchester, 30-06 Springfield, 7mm Remington Magnum, 7mm STW and 300 Winchester Magnum.

The Savage Long Range series, such as this Model 112FVSS long-action, are capable of delivering the precision shooting performance of custom-made rifles.

help dissipate heat and an aircraft-grade aluminum bedding block runs the entire length of the stainless steel receiver. The composite stock is constructed of fiberglass and graphite reinforced with DuPont Kevlar. Initial chamberings are 220 Swift, 22-250 Remington and 243 Winchester. A line of Remington ammunition is available with special electronic primers. The ammunition's case, propellant and bullet consist of conventional components.

In other Remington news, the company has brought out the newest member of the Ultra Mag family of beltless magnum calibers: the 338 Remington Ultra Mag. For hunters of truly big–or dangerous–game, the 338 delivers maximum stopping power at medium to long ranges. Remington now chambers eight rifles for this cartridge.

The Model 700 BDL offers all the BDL features, with the added brawn of the new 338 beltless magnum. Additionally, the Model 700 BDL SS adds the durability of a synthetic stock and a stainless steel barreled action. The Model 700 LSS, with gray-laminated stock and stainless steel barreled action, is available in 338 Ultra Mag. Both left- and right-hand models are available.

To utilize the long-distance performance abilities of the 338 Ultra Mag, Remington introduces their ultimate long-range rifle: the Model 700 Sendero SF, with stainless steel barrel and weight-reducing longitudinal barrel flutes.

From the Remington Custom Shop, four 338 Ultra Mags are available: the Model 700 African Plains Rifle with laminated stock and the Model 700

Alaskan Wilderness Rifle with Kevlar stock and Teflon-coated stainless steel barrel and receiver. Also offered is the Model 700 Custom Kevlar Stock and the Model 700 Custom KS Stainless Mountain Rifle. All of the 338 Ultra Mag rifles in the series have 26-inch barrels.

Another new cartridge, the non-belted 300 Remington Ultra Mag, has a new rifle chambered for it, the left-handed Model 700 BDL. Complete with a high-gloss American walnut stock, polished blue carbon steel barrel and hinged floor plate with three-round magazine, the rifle provides another choice for lefties at a price-point well below that of a custom rifle.

For the varmint hunter, back by popular demand is the Remington Model 700 VS (Varmint Synthetic) rifle in three chamberings: 223 Remington,

The author is a fan of SIG Arms' rifles as they are known for quality construction and extreme accuracy.

The new SIG Arms STR 970 precision long range rifle delivers better than one minute-of-angle accuracy–right out of the box.

22-250 Remington and 308 Winchester. The rifle comes with a Kevlar-reinforced composite stock, full-length aircraft-grade aluminum bedding block and matte-finished, heavy-contour 26-inch barrel and receiver.

There are three new variations on the famous short-action Model Seven: The Model Seven LSS with satin-finished laminated stock, four-round magazine and hinged floor plate is available in 22-250 Remington, 243 Winchester and 7mm-08 Remington. The Model Seven LS has the same brown laminated stock, a carbon steel barrel and is offered in five chamberings: 223 Remington, 243 Winchester, 260 Remington, 7mm-08 Remington and 308 Winchester. The Model Seven Youth has a walnut-toned hardwood stock, carbon steel barrel and action and is available in 223 Remington, 243 Winchester, 260 Remington and 7mm-08 Remington. All have 20-inch barrels for use by close-cover hunters.

For the rimfire shooter, Remington introduces the Model 597 Stainless Sporter with hardwood stock and 20-inch satin-finished, stainless steel barrel. It is furnished with fully adjustable rifle sights, is drilled and tapped to accommodate the Remington scope rail, has a grooved receiver for tip-off scope mounts and

feeds from a staggered 10-shot magazine. The barrel is mated to the receiver with a wedge-shaped lug designed to tighten the barrel-receiver connection with each shot fired.

Remington is now producing rifle scope bases. With multiple cross slots for secure lock-down, scalloped sides for easy action access and tapered ends for cosmetic appeal. The bases are contoured to fit these specific centerfire rifles: Models 7400TM, 700TM Long Action (blued and stainless), 700 Short Action (blued and stainless), and the Model Seven.

Sako, Ltd., the Finland-based manufacturer of world-class hunting rifles, has introduced an innovative concept in hunting rifle safety-the Sako Key Concept, a built-in locking mechanism for the Sako 75 hunting rifle. The locking mechanism is built into the rifle's bolt action and is activated by a key unique to each rifle. The key blends into the rifle contours when the lock is open and the gun is operational. When the key is removed, the lock takes effect and the hunting rifle is completely safe and inoperative.

Savage Arms has built its business and reputation by providing feature-packed rifles at competitive prices; its latest offerings are no exception. Incorporating many of the features

recommended to students by noted arms instructor, Col. "Jeff" Cooper, the Savage Scout short action has a 20-inch barrel, large bolt handle, removable ghost ring rear sight with gold bead front sight and a mount for a long eye relief scope. It is chambered for 7mm-08 Remington and the 308 Winchester.

The Savage Model 114U long action is a traditional bolt-action hunting rifle featuring a high luster blued finish, high gloss American walnut stock with ebony tip and custom checkering. Approximate weight is seven pounds.

With a 22-inch barrel, it is available in 270 Winchester and 30-06 Springfield. The 24-inch barrel version comes in a choice of 7mm Magnum, 7mm STW and 300 Winchester Magnum.

The Savage Long Range series of rifles are designed to deliver the shooting performance of custom-made rifles, according to the manufacturer. Features include 26-inch heavy barrels with recessed target-style barrel crowns, composite or laminated wood stocks. The six rifles in the series are offered in top-loading, 5-shot capacity models and 4-shot magnum versions, as well as single shots with rigid solid-bottom receivers. All are drilled and tapped for scope mounting

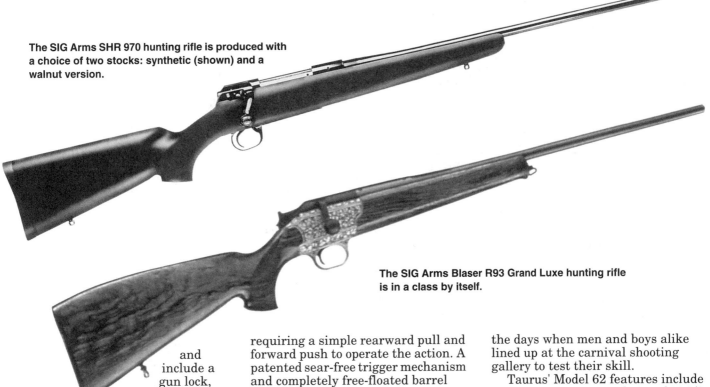

The SIG Arms SHR 970 hunting rifle is produced with a choice of two stocks: synthetic (shown) and a walnut version.

The SIG Arms Blaser R93 Grand Luxe hunting rifle is in a class by itself.

and include a gun lock, factory-fired test target and ear plugs. Chambering choices range from 223 Remington to 300 Winchester.

The new **SIG Arms** STR 970 precision long range rifle utilizes a bolt that locks directly into the barrel, rather than the receiver, to allow the system to be caliber-interchangeable while controlling headspace from one barrel to the next. Designed to deliver better than minute-of-angle accuracy right out of the box, the rifle has a McMillan stock with custom bedding blocks, full non-reflective coating for corrosion resistance, fluted heavy-contour barrel, integral muzzle brake and is chambered in both the 308 Winchester and 338 Winchester Magnum.

The Blaser R93 Grand Luxe rifle delivers elegance with its full coverage hand-engraved receiver combined with a high grade walnut stock. Yet, the Blaser is also a rifle of the future, incorporating a versatile modular barrel system in chamberings from 22-250 to 375 H&H.

The Grand Luxe also features a fast, straight no-lift bolt movement,

requiring a simple rearward pull and forward push to operate the action. A patented sear-free trigger mechanism and completely free-floated barrel promote accuracy.

SIG Arms' SHR 970 bolt-action rifle is available in a choice of two stocking configurations: a durable synthetic stock and a newly introduced satin-finished European walnut stock. This new SHR 970 combines function, precision and durability with the timeless qualities of natural wood at a surprisingly affordable price.

The world famous small arms manufacturer, *Mauser-Werke Oberndorf Waffensysteme GmbH* of Oberndorf, Germany was recently acquired by SIG Arms. With the acquisition, SIG assumes the rights to the renowned Mauser name and is integrating the Mauser line into SIG Arms' current product offering. Riflemen the world over are looking for good things to come from this acquisition.

Taurus has come out with an American shooting classic–the Model 62 series, a 22 Long Rifle-chambered slide-action carbine and rifle available in blued or stainless steel. The design is faithful in most respects to the legendary product developed by John Browning. The rifle hearkens back to

the days when men and boys alike lined up at the carnival shooting gallery to test their skill.

Taurus' Model 62 features include all-steel construction, choice of 16 1/2-inch round-barrel carbine model with 12-round tubular magazine or 23-inch barrel rifle with 13-round magazine. Standard features include a walnut-finished hardwood buttstock and flattened forend slide, hard rubber buttplate, adjustable rear sight and bead front sight. The safety systems include a manual firing pin block on top of the receiver bolt and the integral Taurus Security System key lock on the hammer.

Thompson/Center (T/C) departs from its well-established role as a leading manufacturer of single-shot modern firearms and muzzleloaders to offer the small-bore shooter a premium semi-automatic, the T/C 22 LR Classic. Using traditional styling and materials, the rifle is reminiscent of the way 22s used to be built. It has a full-size, deluxe American walnut stock with Monte Carlo cheekpiece and satin finish, with a 22-inch match-grade barrel (with target crown) threaded into the blued, all-steel receiver. Unlike many 22s with press-fit and pinned barrels, the T/C 22 LR Classic's precise barrel lockup results

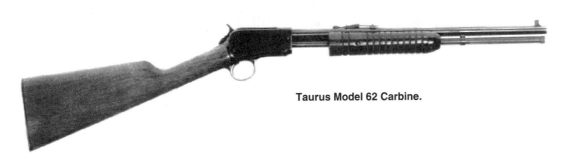

Taurus Model 62 Carbine.

Thompson/Center has come out with a classically-styled 22 semi-auto rifle with premium features for the discriminating shooter.

in consistent accuracy from shot to shot. The rifle loads from a detachable 8-shot magazine.

Mention the word **"Weatherby"** to the average hunter and chances are they'll conjure up images of the Mark V Deluxe. Still being produced, it's the quintessential Weatherby and perhaps the most widely-recognized rifle in the world. The hand-selected American walnut stock has a traditional rosewood forend tip and pistol grip cap with maple wood spacers and diamond inlay. Fineline diamond point checkering provides an additional custom touch to this uncompromising rifle. It is available in the following Weatherby Magnum chamberings: 257, 270, 7mm, 300, 340, 378, 416 and 460.

The new Weatherby Mark V Super VarmintMaster raises the performance bar to a new level. The heavy contour .823-inch muzzle diameter, 26-inch button-rifled fluted barrel is cryogenically treated to -300 degrees F. to reduce stress and harden the bore. The bore is then hand-lapped to reduce fouling. An 11-degree, parabolic target crown promotes even gas dispersion.

The VarmintMaster's Mark V barreled action is fitted to a CNC-machined aluminum bedding block, which is then bedded in a tan hand-laminated, raised-comb Monte Carlo stock with a widened, flat beavertail forearm. The factory-tuned, fully-adjustable trigger breaks at four pounds. The VarmintMaster is available in 223 Remington, 22-250 Remington, 220 Swift, 243 Winchester, 7mm-08 Remington and 308 Winchester.

Winchester licensee **U.S. Repeating Arms Co.** has introduced two new historic rifles – the Model 1886 Extra Light Rifle and the Model 1895 405 Winchester.

The Model 1886 has a 22-inch round tapered barrel, solid frame, shotgun-style steel buttplate, half-magazine and is chambered for 45-70. Grade I and High Grade versions are available. The High Grade features an extra-fancy checkered walnut stock and engraved game scenes of elk and whitetail deer on a blue receiver.

The Model 1895 is available in the most sought-after caliber: 405 Winchester. This gun was described by Teddy Roosevelt as *"big medicine"* and his *"beloved Winchester."* He took three of these rifles on his historic African safari. High grades have engraved elk and whitetail scenes on a polished white receiver. Grade I is deeply blued.

Winchester also introduces the Model 94 Pack Rifle, a specialized 'deer-getter' for hunting the hard-to-get-to places. The 18-inch barrel makes it compact and maneuverable; the pistol grip stock and full forend with nose-cap promote control. Other features include three-quarter magazine, hooded front sight and sling studs. It is available in 44 Remington Magnum and 30-30 Winchester.

For hunters who need the carrying ease and pointability of a sporter-style rifle, combined with the long range accuracy of a varminter, Winchester has designed the Model 70 Coyote. It features a medium-heavy stainless steel 24-inch sporter barrel and rugged, laminated stock with reverse-taper forend. The Coyote uses the proven push feed bolt design and is available in 223 Remington, 22-250 Remington and 243 Winchester. ●

Winchester 1895 in 405 Winchester

"A gun is a tool."

Alan Ladd in "Shane", Paramount Pictures, 1953

SL8-1 RIFLE
Caliber .223

USC CARBINE
Caliber .45 ACP

Power tools for a new century.

Man is a tool using being. And for centuries firearms have been one of his most important tools. Whether for hunting, defense, or sport—a truly modern utilitarian firearm gives shooters the power to use and control advanced technology. The highest level of that advanced technology is found in the design and materials used on the HK USC carbine and SL8-1 rifle.

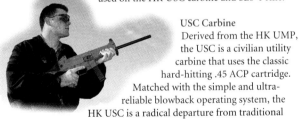

USC Carbine

Derived from the HK UMP, the USC is a civilian utility carbine that uses the classic hard-hitting .45 ACP cartridge. Matched with the simple and ultra-reliable blowback operating system, the HK USC is a radical departure from traditional firearms designs.

Extensive use of the same durable, reinforced polymers used on HK's new line of military and police arms ensures light weight and durability. And the highest grade of weapons steel is used where it matters—in the cold hammer forged target barrel and the solidly-constructed bolt mechanism.

User ergonomics are not sacrificed. The skeletonized buttstock is topped with a comfortable rubber cheek rest and recoil pad. The web of the pistol grip is open for a comfortable shooting handhold. Hard points located on the top and front of the receiver make attachment of optional Picatinny rails easy, allowing almost any kind of sighting system or accessory to be mounted. If you're looking for a .45 ACP carbine designed and engineered for the tasks of a new age, choose the HK USC.

SL8-1 Rifle

The caliber .223 companion to the USC—the HK SL8-1 is also constructed almost entirely of reinforced carbon-fiber polymer. Based on the current combat-tested German Army G36 rifle, the SL8-1 uses a proven short stroke, piston-actuated gas operating system, well known for simplicity and reliability.

Designed and engineered to deliver exceptional shooting performance, the SL8-1 is already a favorite among European rifle shooters, due in large part to the many modular sighting systems available. These modular systems include extended and short rail mounts with open sights, a 1.5x scope with an integral carry handle, and a dual optical system that combines a 3x scope with an electronic red dot sight.

The sleek and clean lines of the HK SL8-1 and the USC are functional and modern—they have the look, the feel, and the performance that shooters demand. And like the best kind of tools, they're guaranteed for life. To put a USC or SL8-1 in your hands, see your local authorized HK dealer. In a world of compromise, some don't.

HK HECKLER & KOCH, INC.
21480 Pacific Boulevard
Sterling, Virginia 20166 U.S.A.
Tel. (703) 450-1900 • Fax (703) 450-8160 • www.hecklerkoch-usa.com

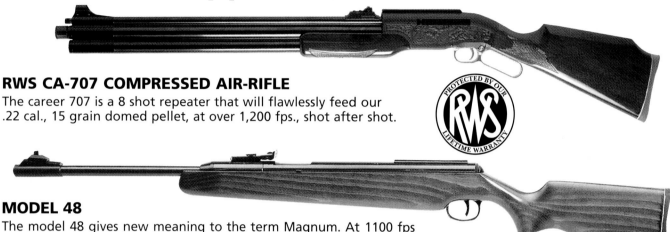

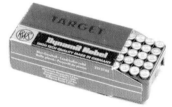

"SWAROVSKI AV SCOPES... ACCURACY FIRST."

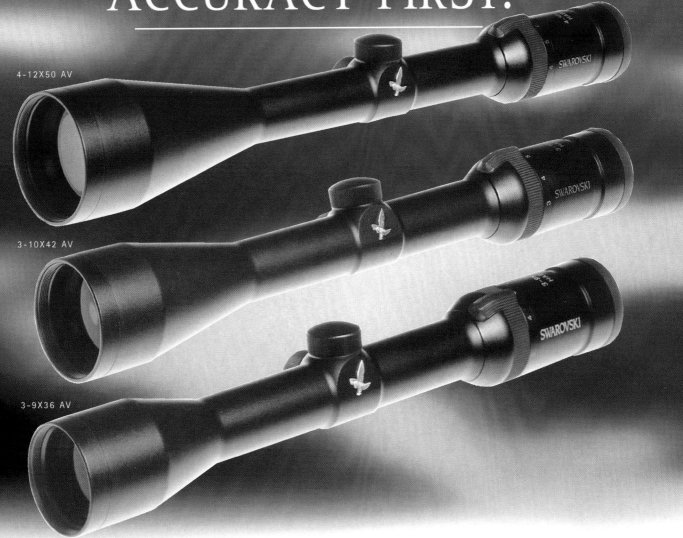

4-12X50 AV

3-10X42 AV

3-9X36 AV

SHOTGUN UPDATE

by Bill Hanus

IF LAST YEAR was designated as the "Year of the Magnum", then 2K has to be built around the theme of letting the good times roll. As the baby boom generation quick-marches toward its peak spending years, they have become increasingly aware of shotgun deficiencies in their gun cabinets.

It did not take a mint to fall on some of the shotgun makers for them to figure out the that there is a market for shootable art - "shoulder candy" in the parlance of the day - among the boomers. These five-figure confections will, no doubt, be chronicled in the coffee table magazines designed to whet the appetites of this new class of shotgun "collector/investor."

Among those who feel the best return on a shotgun investment is not missing a bird off point all season - equally nifty and exciting things are happening in shotgunning. So lean back, take a deep breath and prepare to join shotgun makers, dealers, shooters and collectors in another chorus of: "Happy Days Are Here Again!"

Start this year's taste-testing with these three dandies:

"Cutting edge, outside the box" and "pushing the envelope" are hardly cliches that one would think of applying to the shotgun industry. Indeed, in a business where a coat of camouflage paint on a goose gun can be passed off as a "new" turkey gun; and some of the nicest birdgun doubles on today's market are reproductions of designs that have since celebrated their Diamond Jubilee anniversaries - the technology that FABARM puts into its doubles, over/ unders and semi- automatics makes them the most technically advanced shotguns on the market. The 12 gauge FABARM Classic Lion Grade 11 side-by-side has all the usual amenities that you'd expect - a single

FABARM Classic Lion Grade II, $2,249 cased.

selective trigger, 3-inch chambers, chrome-lined bores, screw-in chokes, etc. But it's what you get that you didn't expect that explain why it deserves your special attention this year.

The FABARM TriBore Barrel System has all the advantages of back-boring—something competition target shooters have been doing for years. It's benefits? Softer recoil, increased velocity and optimum patterning. The first over-bored region, just ahead of the chamber and lengthened forcing cones has an internal diameter of 18.8mm. This softens recoil without sacrificing velocity. In the middle of the barrel the "first choking" area begins with an internal bore diameter of 18.4 mm, increasing velocity. About 6 inches from the end of the muzzle the bore tapers into the screw-in choke. The final choke constriction takes place about 1 1/2 inches from the muzzle, with the selected choke dimensions consistent to the muzzle – ensuring uniform distribution and patterning.

Five standard chokes (C, IC, M, IM, F) are standard with a rifled choke, which functions as a "spreader", available that would be perfect for bobwhite, woodcock and station 8 on the skeet field. The gun is steel shot-friendly (in the open chokes).

The Grade II Classic Lion has so many other "nice touches" in addition to the palm swell grip that it's hard to know where to begin. It has nicely upgraded dark wood that contrasts with the white metal finish. Good wood-to-metal fit. The sideplates are engraved and detachable (and you'll discover coiled hammer springs inside). It has a checkered trigger. A pierced opening lever. The screw-in chokes are inletted so that there is a built-in stop, making it hard to over-tighten the chokes. It comes in a deluxe, fitted case. And, rarest of all - a Lifetime Warranty backed by Heckler & Koch, the importer of this line of fine guns.

You might expect to pay $4,000 for a side-by-side of this quality, but the Year 2000 price is only $2,249!

Sturm, Ruger seems to have this knack of inventing the obvious. The idea of adding the option of .410 barrel inserts to their 28-gauge gun is a wonderful one.

As luck would have it, I had borrowed a 50th Anniversary (1949-1999) Limited Edition of Ruger's Red Label 28-gauge for review when Ruger announced the availability of .410 barrel inserts. It took only a phone call to be allowed to have all the fun I wanted in .41 0 on top of the joy of 28 gauge!

The insert tubes themselves are made of red anodized aircraft aluminum alloy, NOT STEEL. The chambers are made from grade 6 titanium alloy. They weigh about 10 ounces - but the added weight on the front end of this gun does nothing but enhance the swing on the skeet field.

These .410 conversion sets are available in either 26- or 28-inch lengths with 2 stainless steel Skeet choke tubes and a suggested retail price of $525 from the Product Service Department of Sturm, Ruger & Co., Inc. Newport, NH 603/865-2442.

Baschieri & Pellagri Shotgun Shells

In the period between World War I and World War II live pigeon shooting emerged as a high-stakes spectator sport for the rich and famous. Shotgun manufacturers developed special models (AYA's heavy frame Model 56, for example) that set new standards for accuracy, reliability and excellence. Price was no object. Performance was everything. "Pigeon Grade" described the best of the best.

In 1940, Baschieri & Pellagri shotshells were used to win the first of 22 World Live Pigeon Championships. Plus five Olympic Gold Medals, including Atlanta in 1996. It's clear that B&P makes superb shotgun shells - "Pigeon Grade" ammunition, you might say.

After discovering their 29-gram, 1,325 fps 16-gauge load (think of lightning striking), which I was pleased to recommend last year, I learned that Bob Brister (who literally wrote the book: *Shotgunning*) had asked Mike Dotson of B&P America to make up some shells that would reliably break sporting clays targets out to 60 yards. I can confirm Larry Nailon's (ace shotshell ballistician and writer on the

Benelli Nova Pump Rifled Slug Model expands Benelli's superb Nova Pump line introduced last year.

Benelli Montefeltro Short Stock 20-gauge with 12 1/2-inch length of pull with 24- or 26-inch barrel and weighing under 5-1/2 pounds.

subject) findings: they work just as Bob Brister wanted.

The secret: it's a 28-gram (1 oz.) load, in a Gordon System case using B&P components to exit at 1,409 fps, measured one meter from the muzzle. The best 5% antimony pellets in the world are polished super-smooth (they look like they are nickel-plated) and dry-lubricated.

New for the millennium from B&P:

*The 28-gram load described above, designated F2 Ultra Velocity Sporting Clay, will be a stock item;

*Photodegradeable wads will be used in all versions of the F2 Sporting Clays shotshells;

*The Gordon System case will also be used on all 16-and 20-gauge shotshells instead of just 12-gauge loads. Briefly, the Gordon case with its collapsible base wad cushions felt recoil by spreading out the recoil over about a 20% longer time period.

*A 28-gauge shotshell based on the Fiocchi (reloadable) case. First call on this newcomer to the lineup is 3/4 oz. @ 1,230 fps in No. 7-1/2 and No. 8 shot of polished shot - the same used in the Ultra Velocity load - delivered with an amazingly low pressure of 8550 P.S.I.

Call Mike Dotson, B&P America, at 972/726-9073 and identify yourself "as a friend of Bill Hanus" and put yourself in touch with the good stuff.

Like the appetizers? Here comes the meat-and-potatos!

Benelli

For decades, autoloading shotguns have used one of four operating systems. Long-recoil guns were the first,

beginning with Browning's 1903 invention. Short-recoil guns appeared in the 1950s, followed by short- and long-stroke piston gas operation in the 1960s. All these systems have been successful, with millions of guns using them.

The Benelli uses a unique inertia recoil system - with only seven moving parts, entirely contained in the receiver of the gun - and will operate with all sorts of ammunition interchangeably, without adjustment. Benelli's 20-gauge semi-automatics are among the lightest 20-gauge guns on the market — all weighing under 6 pounds. All sporting models come with a set of shims to adjust the amount of drop and/or the length of pull to a limited degree.

Benelli Limited Edition Legacy in 12 and 20-gauge (250 of each) with game scene engraving and gold accents and upgraded fancy walnut.

Beretta

As one of the Honors Graduates from the "if it ain't broke, don't fix it" School of Life, it boggled my mind when Beretta announced they were replacing their AL-390 with the Model AL-391. What they've added is well worth noting. The improvements include:

Most important - a system of shims and spacers that allows the shooter to adjust the drop and cast, while interchangeable recoil pads allow for adjustment in length of pull. This may be old stuff to competitive shooters, but this is big news to hunters.

Significant others - the AL-391 has a little plastic bumper in the back of the receiver that helps soak up recoil and vibration when the bolt slams into the

receiver—a "no-brainer" kind of idea; a larger opening in the trigger guard making it easier to get at the trigger wearing a glove; plus a weatherproof coating that provides protection against humidity and harsh weather conditions. I count over 30 different models of the AL-391, about a third of which are 20-gauge guns.

On top of the AL-391 Urika, about which paeans are yet to be writ, comes the all-new DT 10 Trident, which they describe as "the technology of victory." The "DT" in the model description stands for Detachable Trigger - which quickly conveys the message that what we are looking at is another phrase they use in describing this gun - "professional perfection."

Bill Hanus Birdguns by AYA

These elegant small gauge doubles duplicate the style and handling characteristics of traditional, ejector-grade English game guns. Made only in 16, 20 and 28 gauge with each mounted on frames proportionate to the gauge. Standard stock dimensions are 1 1/2 x 2 3/8 x 14 3/8 inches with about 3/16-inch cast-off. Stocks set with 3/16-inch cast-on for left-handed shooters may be ordered at no extra charge.

These guns have longer barrels, open chokes, English grips, splinter forends, upgraded wood, fit and finish, and come with an English leather-covered hand-guard.

Briley

Long known for their excellence with screw-chokes and small gauge

Beretta AL391 Urika Gold Field is available in both 12 and 20-gauge with a variety of barrel lengths with screw-in chokes.

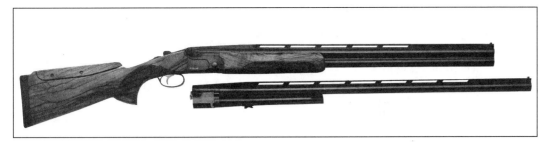

Beretta DT 10 Trident, the new top-of-the-line 12-gauge competition gun from Beretta

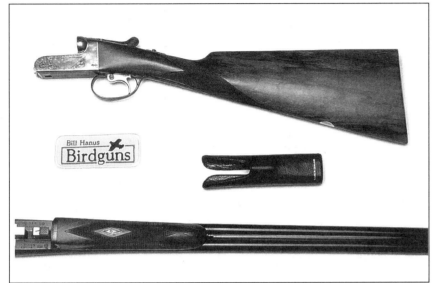

Bill Hanus Birdgun by AYA - new single selective trigger model in 16, 20, or 28 gauge with select wood, leather hand-guard and available stocked for left-handers.

conversion tubes for 12 gauge skeet guns, Briley has expanded big-time into the small gauge area with such offerings as: 28 gauge and .410 conversion sets for 20 gauge guns; 28 gauge and .410 inserts for 16 gauge and .410 tubes for 28 gauge guns. Give your old side-by-side or over/under new life with a set of small gauge tubes. Available in both standard and "Ultralite" weights, prices per pair start at $350 for the standard tubes and include 4 choke tubes per set. 800/331-5718 (outside Texas) or 713/932-6996 in the Lone Star.

Browning

Browning introduced some new high grade Citoris with Privilege, BG, VI and BG, III nameplates, which vie with one another for beauty. The Citori Ultra XS/XT and Citori Feather XS skeet and sporting clays guns, like all Browning target guns (but with the exception of 28 gauge and .410 bores) are ported, to reduce recoil and muzzle jump. Gauge for gauge the Feather models

Browning Citori Privilege. Browning's first side plate in over a decade, lavishly engraved with high-grade walnut. 12 gauge only.

Browning Auto-5 Final Tribute special edition of 1000 guns with distinctive white, engraved receiver, high-grade select walnut. 12 gauge only.

Browning BPS 12 Gauge Stalker Combo. The 3 1/2-inch Stalker is available in a combo that includes a 22-inch rifled barrel or 20.5-inch standard barrel with an Extra-Full Turkey choke tube.

appear to be lighter than the Ultras by about 10 ounces in the 28 gauges. One of Browning's nice touches is their Triple Trigger system that comes standard on all sporting clays guns. This consists of three interchangeable trigger shoes (wide-smooth, wide-checkered and narrow-smooth) each of which is adjustable to three positions for length of pull or, more accurately, adjusting the radius of the pistol grip to the length of the shooter's finger.

Browning's Gold guns — except for the rifled slug barrel guns — are backbored. This reduces the friction of the shot charge against the barrel wall, which reduces the pressure or constriction of the barrel walls on the shot charge. This means fewer deformed shot pellets, resulting in more shot pellets in the target zone.

Charles Daly

What the world needs is a good .410 double that doesn't cost an arm and a leg. Well, Charles Daly has found a small Italian maker that produces an underlever over/under and side-by-side, both of which are a joy to hold and behold. Slim English grips, nice wood, a red rubber pad with case color receiver and opening lever/trigger guards. These are extractor guns with gold-plated double triggers and priced in the $700 range.

F.A.I.R./I.Rizzini

There are several members of the Rizzini family who make shotguns, so confusion comes easily when referring to a "Rizzini" shotgun.

F.A.I.R. is the acronym for *Fabbrica Armi Isidoro Rizzini*. The hot item in this line is a 16 gauge over/under with screw-in chokes, available with a half-pistol grip or English grip, in four trim lines.

The 16 gauge is built on a true 16-gauge frame, not 16-gauge barrels on a 12-gauge frame. Higher grades offer more gold accents, better wood, fitted cases.

A 28 gauge over/under built on a true 28-gauge frame with screw-in chokes has been announced for year 2000. It will be available in all four grades and priced slightly higher than the 16 gauge guns.

Fausti Stefano

Makes a pretty complete line of side-by-side and over/under shotguns that are imported by **Traditions Performance Firearms**. The over/unders come in three grades, all of which have single selective triggers, mechanical triggers and recoil pads. The Field I has fixed chokes and extractors and is available in 12, 20, 28 and .410. Field II adds screw-in chokes and automatic ejectors. Field III is the top-of-the-line with some gold appointments, but is available in 12 gauge only.

Charles Daly Country Squire Over & Under built from the ground up as a .410 with 26-inch barrels, fixed Full/Full chokes and raised ventilated rib.

Charles Daly Country Squire Side by Side sculpted to .410 dimensions with Chrome-Moly steel barrels, internally honed and chromed. 26-inch barrels, fixed F/F chokes.

The Elite side-by-side series has two models, each of which is offered in 12, 20, 28 and .410. Elite ST is a single trigger model with pistol grip and beavertail forend. The Elite DT has double triggers, pistol grip and splinter forend.

Federal Ammunition

Several new shotshell products of interest at Federal this year: (1) A Federal Gold Medal Spreader Load in 12 gauge with 1-1/8 ounce of #8 or #8-1/2 shot which promises wide, even patterns as close as 15 yards; (2) new Tungsten-Polymer loads in 3 1/2-inch for 10 and 12 gauge, plus a 3- and 2 3/4-inch for 20 gauge, all in #4 and #6 shot; (3) new high-velocity - 1,500 fps - steel loads in 12 and 20 gauge; and (4) a non-toxic shell which combines tungsten-iron and steel pellets — two sizes of shot with two different metals — recommended as an upgrade from all-steel loads.

Franchi

Now owned by Benelli, Franchi is operated as a separate division and continues to offer its line of Alcione Field and Light Field over/unders and long-recoil AL 48 semi-autos built on the John Browning design, now almost a century old. New this year is the AL 48 Deluxe with high-polish blued finish

Fausti Stefano Field II moderately priced, full-featured over/under available in all four popular gauges.

Fausti Stefano Elite ST moderately priced side-by-sides in all popular gauges and available in both single and double trigger models.

and upgraded walnut on butt stock and forend. All AL 48 models come with a set of shims to add cast-on, cast-off as well as move the butt stock up and down. All AL 48 models are available in 12, 20 and 28 gauge.

The Alcione Field has, new this year, a left-hand model 12 gauge with 26- or 28-inch barrels.

H&R 1871

They've introduced the Trigger Guardian Trigger Locking System for their long guns. This device is not simply a trigger lock but a lockable trigger-immobilizing device.

Owners of New England Firearms-, Harrington & Richardson-, Wesson & Harrington- or H&H 1871-brand guns shipped before 12/l/99, may buy Trigger Guard units for $5.95 each from: Trigger Guard Offer, H&R 1871R, Inc., 60 Industrial Rowe, Gardner, MA 01440.

HK/FABARMS

Heckler & Koch, a well-known military and police firearms manufacturer, joined forces with FABARM — *Fabbrica Bresciana Armi S.p.A.* — a direct descendant of the Galesi family, a 100-year-old gunsmithing dynasty. Although well-known in Europe,

they are virtually unknown in the U.S. They bring innovative technology to the American marketplace — like their patented TriBore Barrel System — and they offer the industry's only Lifetime Warranty.

In addition to TriBore barrels, FABARM makes extensive use of palm swell grips, barrel porting, double sets of locking lugs on over/under and side-by-side shotguns, inertial single selective triggers, carbon fiber protective coating on some models, better-than-average polished oil-finished walnut, diamond fine-hand-checkering, fitted cases and moderate prices. They are full-line shotgun makers, offering semi-automatic, pump (although thse are primarily police/

▼Franchi 612 Sporting in 12 gauge with 5 extended choke tubes, select walnut and 30-inch barrels.

◄ Franchi AL 48 Deluxe special treatment is available only on their 5.6-pound 20 gauge and 5.4-pound 28 gauge semi-autos, both with C, IC and M choke tubes.

military types), over/under and side-by-side models.

Several innovative examples stand out and are illustrated in this article.

FABARM Max Lion Light 12 or 20 Gauge feature 24-inch TriBore ported barrels (this includes 20 gauge models), adjustable trigger, palm swell grip, C-IC-M-IM-F choke tubes, manual safety, leather-faced rubber recoil pad. The 20 gauge model tested weighed under six pounds!

Kent Cartridge America

Kent Cartridge claims their IMPACT Tungsten MatriX non-toxic waterfowl loads have been field-tested and proven the most effective shot shell you can buy. They say that you can put 90% of the pellets in a 30-inch circle at 40 yards - and that "it is solidly lethal at 65 yards."

FABARM Monotrap 12 Gauge - built on a 20 gauge frame (for quick handling) with adjustable comb, adjustable trigger, palm swell grip, TriBore ported 30-inch barrel with M-IM-F choke tubes.

FABARM Sporting Clays Extra 12 Gauge 28-inch ported (30-inch available), recoil deduction system installed, adjustable comb, carbon fiber finish, eight competition tubes, palm swell grip, olive wood grip cap and leather-faced recoil pad.

FABARM Sporting Clays Competition Lion Extra competition buttstock with adjustable comb, durable carbon fiber finish, set of eight competition choke tubes and 30-inch TriBore ported barrels.

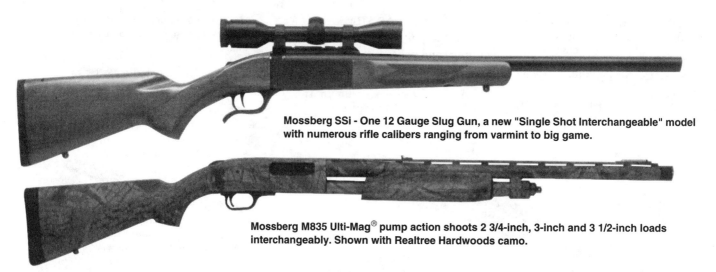

Mossberg SSi - One 12 Gauge Slug Gun, a new "Single Shot Interchangeable" model with numerous rifle calibers ranging from varmint to big game.

Mossberg M835 Ulti-Mag® pump action shoots 2 3/4-inch, 3-inch and 3 1/2-inch loads interchangeably. Shown with Realtree Hardwoods camo.

These Waterfowl loads in 12 and 20 gauge are mostly between 1,350 and 1,400 fps with #1, #3 and #5 shot sizes. There's a new 3 1/3-inch 12 gauge 2 1/4 oz. version with #1 or #3 shot. The IMPACT Pheasant/Game loads in 12, 16 and 20 gauge range from 1,200 to 1,350 fps with #5 and #6 shot sizes offered.

Non-toxic IMPACT Tungsten MatriX shotshells satisfy environmental and conservation requirements and can be used in any nitro-proofed shotgun with the same chokes one would normally use for lead shot.

Mossberg

Factory porting and over-bored barrels are standard on Mossberg's Model 835 Ulti-Mag 12 gauge 3 1/2-inch repeater shotgun. M835 barrels are overbored to .775-inch, which compares to .731-inch for their standard M500, hence require oversized choke tubes to accommodate the larger bore diameter at the muzzle. Mossberg claims the ported barrels and over-bored barrels significantly reduce recoil in the 3 1/2-inch magnum loads and reduce muzzle jump and make for faster target acquisition on repeat shots.

Merkel

Merkel is enhancing their fine line of side-by-side shotgun and over/under

shotguns with Luxury Grade Wood and fitted cases. The well-known model 147E, for example, becomes Model 147EL with luxury grade wood - a $1,000 option for all gauges.

New models this year are the M280EL in 28 gauge, M360EL in .410 bore (built on the 28-gauge frame) and the M280/360EL two-barrel set, all with luxury grade wood and fitted cases. Similarly, the M280SL, M360SL and M280/360SL two-barrel 28/410 sets have silver-greyed sidelocks, with luxury grade wood in fitted cases.

Merkel does not have a bottom-of-the-line over/under. Every model offered has luxury grade wood and comes with a fitted case and are priced from about $5,200 to $20,000 and available in 12, 20, and 28 gauge.

Left-hand stocking is offered as an $895 option and guns stocked to customer's specifications add $1,395.

Perazzi

Perazzi introduced a MX5 model in 20 and 28 gauge, as well as a two-gauge MX5/20-28 set. These are available in four different barrel lengths, from 26 3/4-inch to 29 1/2-inch, fixed or screw-in chokes and single selective trigger. These guns extend Perazzi's offerings in the MX5

game gun line, which last year saw the introduction of a 16 gauge over/under.

Poly-Wad

Jay Menefee of Spred-R Wad fame has introduced a line of low pressure 12 and 16 gauge 2 1/2-inch loads — called "The Vintager" — for people who shoot older model guns. These are 7/8 oz. loads of #6 or #7-1/2 magnum shot with pressure readings of 6,300 and 7,000 P.S.I. Low recoil with just enough oomph to get the job done. 800/998-0669.

Remington

Lots of new and exciting things at Remington this year. The Model 300 Ideal heads the list - a new 12 gauge over/under chambered for 2 3/4- and 3-inch shells and available in 26-, 28- and 30-inch barrel lengths, pistol grip, Rem Chokes, single mechanical trigger and automatic ejectors. This gun has a straight comb and a drop at heel of 2 inches, "to keep recoil in a straighter line."

The Model 11-87 Super Magnum autoloader handles all 12 gauge loads up to the 3 1/2-inch and is available with either a cut-checkered walnut stock or a tough black synthetic model. The Model 11-87 Premier includes a variety of options including cantilever

◀ **Merkel Model 147SL side-by-side H&H style sidelocks with cocking indicators, side clips and double triggers in 12, 16, 20 or 28 gauge with luxury wood.**

▲ **Merkel Model 2001 EL Sporter boxlock, single or double triggers, English or pistol grip, ventilated forend, luxury wood in 12, 20 or 28 gauge.**

▼Remington Model 300 Ideal Over/Under - a new 12 gauge chambered for 2 3/4- and 3-inch shells.

▼Remington SP-10 Synthetic - the 10 gauge semi-auto designed to function under adverse weather conditions.

▼Remington Model 11-87 Upland Special - a quick-handling upland game gun available in either 12 or 20 gauge.

◄Remington Model 1100 Sporting 12 with a 28-inch target barrel and four extended Rem Choke constrictions.

scope mount, which may be used to convert the Model 11-87 to a deer gun. These scope mounts are also made for M870 and M1100 shotguns. The Model 11-87 Premier handles 2 3/4- and 3-inch shells interchangeably. Upland Special Model 11-87 has English grips, a 23-inch barrel and is available in both 12 and 20 gauge.

The Model 1100 line appears to be more focused on competitive shooting with two new models introduced - the Model 1100 Sporting 12 and the Classic Trap. The Model 1100 .410 semi-auto is not cataloged by Remington this year.

Remington's Special Purpose Waterfowl Guns include both 10 and 12 gauge guns with the 10 gauge on Remington's proven SP-10 model and the 12 gauge on the 11-87.

The 870 Express Super Magnum heads Remington's line-up for pump action fans. This is the 3 1/2-inch model and available in a variety of finishes for both turkey, waterfowl and upland game plus a model with an extra rifled barrel for deer. A new Model 870 Classic Trap is introduced this year, while the Model 870 Express continues to offer a wide variety of turkey, deer, waterfowl, upland game, youth, left-hand and self-defense models in 12 and 20 gauge. Model 870 Wingmaster pumps are offered in Super Magnum (3 1/2-inch chamber) and in regular 12, 20, 28 and .410 models.

Ruger

Ruger has taken a bold new step into the world of competitive shooting with their new Ruger Trap Model for competitive trap shooters. The new gun features a fully adjustable rib for pattern position (with 3/8-inch height adjustment) and a select walnut checkered stock, adjustable for length of pull from 13 1/2 to 15 1/2 inches. The comb of the stock is adjustable for height and cast for right-hand or left-handed shooters. The target trigger is adjustable for weight of pull and the pattern-control barrel is manufactured with straight grooves running the full length to prevent the wad from rotating in its passage down the barrel. The chrome-molybdenum monoblock is mated to the stainless steel receiver and 34" stainless steel barrel. Full and modified tubes are provided with the gun.

The engraved series of Ruger Red Labels introduced for Ruger's 50th

Ruger Model KTS-1 234-BRE Trap Model - Ruger's all-new trap gun for competitive shooters.

▲ SIG Apollo TR-40 Gold with case-colored sideplates and discreet gold game scenes.

▶SIG Apollo TR-40 Silver with polished chrome receiver and gold accents.

◀ SIG Apollo TR-30 with case-colored sideplates.

◀SIG Apollo TT-25 Competition Shotgun dimensioned and balanced for the American sporting clays shooter.

Anniversary in 1999 proved so popular that the line is now available with special scroll engraving and a 24-carat gold game bird appropriate to each gauge.

S. I. A. C. E.

A modern-day 20 gauge side-by-side hammer gun emulating a "Best" grade English gun of a by-gone era. This gun has a top-mounted safety so that the gun may be carried with the hammers fully cocked, and fired only when the safety is released.

S.I.A.C.E. "Vintager" 20 gauge hammer gun available with extractors, English grip and fixed chokes.

SKB

SKB makes very nice side-by-side and over/under shotguns. The side-by-side models are on the 12 gauge production cycle, so 20 gauge guns and the smaller gauges based on the 20 gauge side-by-side frame are in limited supply this year.

In their 12 gauge over/under line, SKB has been a pioneer in over-bored barrels, longer forcing cones and, more recently in their target models, competition chokes and porting by Pro-port.

SIG Arms

SIG Arms has joined with the Italian maker B. Rizzini to produce the Apollo line of over/under shotguns in two distinct product groups: Apollo TR Field Shotguns - Nice shotguns made in two frame weights and four forend sizes to accommodate 12, 20, 28 and .410 barrel sizes. There are five trim levels in all four gauges. These are full-feature guns, with single selective triggers, full set of chokes tubes (in 12 and 20 gauge), select Turkish walnut, 20-line checkering and a rubber recoil pad. This pad is of the non-skid variety and the length of pull is 14 3/4 inches, which hung up on my sweater every time I tried to shoulder the gun, so try before you buy. The small

Weatherby SAS Superflauge features M.L. Lynch Superflauge camo, the ultimate camo concealment pattern.

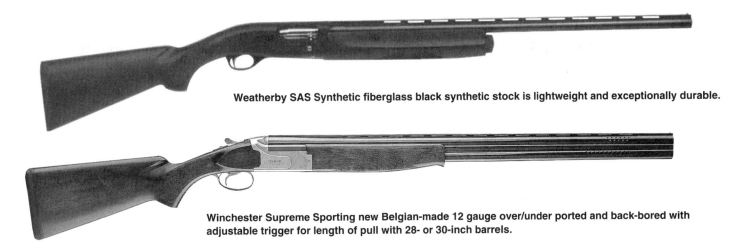

Weatherby SAS Synthetic fiberglass black synthetic stock is lightweight and exceptionally durable.

Winchester Supreme Sporting new Belgian-made 12 gauge over/under ported and back-bored with adjustable trigger for length of pull with 28- or 30-inch barrels.

gauge guns have fixed chokes and the radius of the 28 gauge forend is smaller than the 20 and the .410 forend is smaller than the 28 — an illusion that fools your left hand into thinking you are shooting a smaller gun than one mounted on a 20 gauge frame.

The Apollo TT 25 Competition shotguns are offered in 12 and 20 gauge, 28-, 30- and 32-inch barrels in 12 gauge; 28- and 30-inch in 20 gauge. Four interchange-able chokes are provides - F-M-IC-SK - and five-inch forcing cones are standard.

Weatherby

The big news at Weatherby this year is the introduction of their SAS - semiautomatic shotgun. It comes in four basic sub-models - Field, SAS Shadow Grass, SAS Superflauge and SAS Synthetic. It is chambered for 2 3/4- and 3-inch 12 gauge shells and comes with five standard Briley chokes.

Weatherby's well-established over/ under line all come with Briley choke tubes as standard. Forcing cones have been lengthened and the Orion Sporting Clays SSC Model has ported barrels, comes with cast-off and has an adjustable trigger to accommodate different finger lengths.

Winchester

Finding an encore for their introduction of the 3 1/2-inch Super X2 last year would be a daunting task for any maker - but Winchester is up to the job. This year they've come back with a Belgian-made 12 gauge over/ under called the Supreme that's available in two models - Field and Sporting. Both models back-bored but the Sporting model is also ported and comes with an adjustable trigger shoe to customize the length of pull. Winchester also back-bored their new-last-year Super X2 line 3- and 3 1/2-inch semi-automatics.

The Model 1300R Speed Pump deserves some comment. Winchester shotguns have been equipped with rotary bolts for years. Winchester says it is the key to its tight lockup and uncommon strength and — they say — it's the reason you get inertia-assisted pumping for faster second and third shots.

Winchester Model 1300 Speed Pump now available in 12 or 20 gauge, 3-inch chambers, English grip and WinChoke tubes.   ●

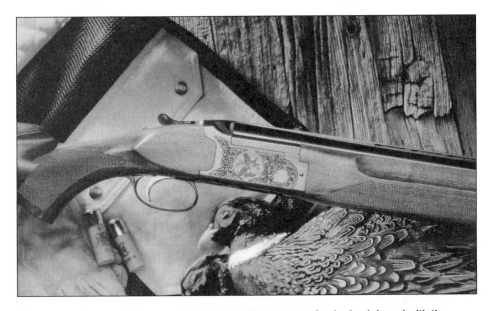

Winchester Supreme Field new Belgian-made 12 gauge over/under back-bored with the Invector Plus choke system and 28-inch barrels.

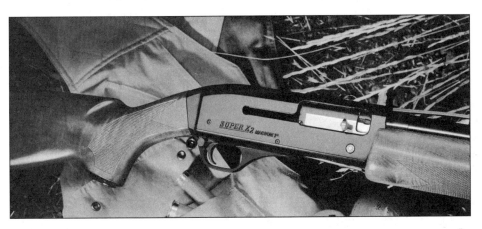

Winchester Super 2X Field 3-inch with traditional satin walnut stock and low luster barrel and receiver this gun goes from pheasant to clay birds without a hitch.

Muzzleloader News

by Doc Carlson

IT WAS NOT very many years ago when the selection of newly made firearms and accessories of interest to the blackpowder shooter was pretty slim. One or two companies were either importing or making a very few replicas of the old time guns. As a result, there was very little interest in the blackpowder-oriented shooting sports. Interest lived in re-enactors, a few target shooters and the die-hard muzzleloading hunter. I guess I qualified for all three categories. Then, in the 1960s, the Civil War Centennial came along and interest picked up—at least among the Civil War re-enactor groups. The average citizen became aware of the fun and challenge of shooting and hunting with the guns of our ancestors. More companies got into the market and several states set up primitive weapon seasons. Suddenly, muzzleloading guns were back.

Today, the blackpowder shooter has a plethora of guns and accessories available. Many companies, old and new, are supplying the varied interests and activities of the muzzleloader: hunting, reenacting, target shooting, black powder cartridge silhouette, cowboy action shooting — or just plinking with a gun that's fun to load and shoot.

The tremendous interest in the in-line muzzleloader over the past few years seems to have slowed, although there are many models out there in all sizes and shapes. There is still plenty of interest in this area and upgrading and improving the breed continues. But, there does seem to be more traditional blackpowder firearms being introduced. Some hunters and casual shooters who started with the in-lines are now getting into the traditional sidehammer gun. We'll see where this goes in the next couple of years.

Modern Muzzleloading Inc., the maker of the well-known **Knight Muzzleloading** line of in-line guns, has upgraded their very successful Disc Rifle by adding a laminated thumbhole Monte Carlo stock with palm swell grip and fluted stainless barrel. Called the Master Hunter, the rifle has a jeweled bolt, gold-plated trigger and a satin-finished metal ramrod added to make this a very nice-looking rifle. Too nice to take into the woods and risk scratching the stock? Knight has the answer. They include a black thumbhole synthetic stock so the hunter can change stocks before he takes to the woods and save the fancy stock for display in the home gun rack or at the range, where the environment is a little more controllable. A nice idea.

Knight's entire rifle line is available with Realtree camouflage over hardwood or with black synthetic stocks. All their rifles now come with a Magnum Cross Fire breech plug. This plug has a cross machined in its face to direct the fire in four directions around the bottom of the powder charge to ensure good ignition. This design is aimed at eliminating misfires when using Pyrodex or the newer Pyrodex pellets. Also, many of the Knight guns are available with Tru-Glo fiber-optic sights, including the Master Hunter series of Disc Rifle.

White Rifles, another well-known in-line manufacturer, has added a 41-caliber to their line for this year. The company that makes these fine rifles, Muzzleloading Technologies, has designed the rifle in line with the bore axis to improve pointing and recoil management, important in a rifle intended to launch bullets weighing up to 600 grains.

The White system uses an easy-loading undersize bullet. On firing, inertia causes the bullet to shorten and fill the rifling along its entire length for superb accuracy. They also now are offering sabot loads. These are not pistol bullets but a harder lead bullet that carries a great deal of weight and, due to its hardness, penetrates well in large and/or dangerous game. The patented sabot features two grooves that can be filled with lubricant to keep fouling soft and facilitate loading.

For 2000, Modern Muzzleloading has expanded their DISC rifle line with this Master Hunter model featuring a laminated thumbhole stock, fluted stainless steel barrel and other trimmings.

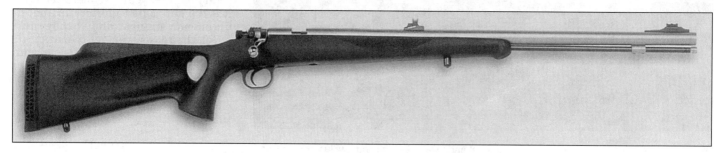

DISC rifles are now available with synthetic thumbhole stock, stainless steel action and barrel.

The Magnum Cross-Fire Breech Plug, designed to ignite Pyrodex pellets reliably, now standard on all rifles from Modern Muzzleloading.

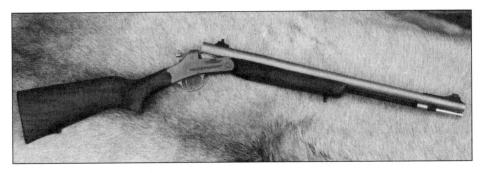

The Buckwacka percussion rifle or shotgun, from Millennium-Designed Muzzleloaders.

This system was developed by Dr. Gary White during a lifetime of hunting all over the world. It's a good system and worth a look by any serious hunter.

Millennium-Designed Muzzleloaders is relatively new to the muzzleloading marketplace, having been making in-line guns for about three years, if memory serves. They have a new muzzleloading firearm this year that is a bit different — but will be very familiar to many shooters. They have taken the familiar single barrel shotgun and adapted it to muzzleloading use. The result is a break-open, center-hammer muzzleloader offered in 50-caliber and 12 gauge. It features a transfer bar system that blocks firing of the gun unless the trigger is held back. This precludes firing by a blow on the hammer in its at-rest position. The gun cannot be opened with the hammer cocked, nor can the hammer be cocked if the breech is open, to prevent inadvertent discharge.

The gun uses #209 shotgun primers but can also use #11 or musket caps, if desired. The breech is a closed system but the guns are also available with a modified breech for those states requiring an exposed ignition system. Easily used by right- or left-handers, the gun retails for under $300. Certainly a familiar feel for those of us who learned to shoot using the venerable single-shot shotgun.

Austin and Halleck makes possibly the best-looking in-line bolt action on the market. Their top-of-the-line gun features high gloss blue, gloss-finished Exhibition-grade wood stock with cut checkering and a half-octagon to round barrel. These are very nice-looking rifles. They look custom — top quality all the way. The guns can also be had with hand-selected wood, only slightly less-figured than the Exhibition grade. They have now added Fancy and Standard rifle grades, at lower prices. The difference is the grade of wood used. The Standard stock is straight-grained, while the Fancy shows a bit more figure but not in the realm of the Exhibition or Hand-Select grades. I did a test-fire report of these guns some time back and they shoot as good as they look. Also new this year is a Monte Carlo-style stock that is intended for use with scopes. Along with the classic style of the other rifles, this makes a pretty complete line.

Another new product this year is the classic style in synthetic stocks. These guns are the same Austin and Halleck action and barrel as their higher-priced offerings but are stocked with the very

practical synthetic gun handle. Actions and barrels of these rifles are octagon to round and available in either blued or stainless steel. These new offerings will come in well under $400 retail. A good, practical hunting gun at a good price.

Along with the in-line rifles, the Austin and Halleck folks are bringing out a very traditional half-stock rifle with styling similar to the Hatfield rifle of a few years back. This Kentucky-style rifle uses all iron hardware with a browned barrel. Sights are traditional rear notch and blade front. Caliber is 50 with either a 1-in-66-inch twist for round ball or 1-in-28 for slug shooting. Stocks can be had in either Standard or Select wood, with the Select being very nicely figured. Ignition is by either caplock or flintlock, your choice. The triggerguard and forend tip are reminiscent of the Hawken rifles of yesteryear but the overall style is half-stock Kentucky. The lock, in either flint or percussion, features a fly on the tumbler for use with the standard double-set triggers. I can't wait to get my hands on one of these.

Traditions Performance Firearms, a company that has been in the muzzleloading business for some time, has added to their Buckhunter series of in-line guns. This gun is now available with a black synthetic stock and a C-Nickel action and barrel. The C-Nickel is their name for a matte-finish nickel plate that imitates the more expensive stainless steel. Supplied in 50-caliber with a stainless steel breech plug and adjustable sights,

Austin & Halleck's new halfstock traditional rifle, in 50-caliber, percussion or flint and several grades of wood.

this is a solid, plain Jane, no-nonsense gun. Priced at under 160 bucks, it is an ideal first-time in-line rifle for the muzzleloading hunter, or a youth starter gun.

Traditions also expanded their bolt action in-line guns with the addition of the Lightning Lightweight series. These guns use a synthetic stock with a spiderweb pattern and a 22-inch fluted barrel in blue, stainless or nickel plate. Tru-Glo fiber-optic sights and an ignition system that can use either standard #11 caps or the hotter musket caps, along with a built-in weather shroud, make this a serious hunting gun. The gun is rated for up to three Pyrodex pellets or 150 grains of powder behind a pistol bullet/sabot combination.

Of interest to the Cowboy Action shooters is the addition of a carbine version to the popular 1892 Lever Action line of rifles. These guns look good with their color case-hardened receivers, crescent butt plate and barrels that are octagon on the 24-inch rifle and round on the 20-inch carbine. These rifles compliment Tradition's line of 1873 single-action cartridge revolvers and the 38 Special cartridge conversions based on the Colt and Remington Army and Navy cap and ball guns.

Also new this year for the Cowboy Action shooters, **Smith and Wesson** is reintroducing the Model 3 Schofield revolver. Designed by Brevet Lieutenant Colonel George W.

Schofield and accepted by the U. S. Military in 1874, Smith and Wesson produced nearly 9,000 of the guns before production ceased in 1879. Now, after 125 years, the Smith and Wesson Schofield is back. Chambered in 45 S&W, the blued steel revolver features walnut grips and case-hardened hammer, trigger and latch. The 7-inch barrel is the same length as was standard on the Cavalry Model of 1875. The gun is a top-break design that was, and still is, an ideal system for fast reloading by a mounted man. Horse soldiers of the time could reload the Schofield seven times while the competing Colt 1873 single-action was reloaded once. This Smith and Wesson single-action revolver was considered by many to be the best available on the American frontier.

The new gun, called the Schofield 2000 by S&W, uses better steel than the original and incorporates a couple of safety features to make the gun compatible with our litigious society, something the original designers of the revolver didn't have to deal with. Every one of that simpler time was expected to know how to use their possessions correctly. At any rate, instead of the fixed firing pin on the hammer, the newly designed gun uses a spring-loaded, frame-mounted, rebounding firing pin. It also incorporates a hammer block safety that will not allow the gun to fire unless the trigger is held full back.

Interestingly, the S&W folks say the decision to reintroduce this classic

The Buckhunter, from Traditions, is an affordable first in-line muzzleloader.

Tradition's new in-line rifle series, the Lightning Lightweight, is designed for the serious hunter.

firearm came from the clamoring of the Cowboy Action shooters and aficionados. Nice to know that the major companies still listen to their customers. It's good to see this old classic back.

Connecticut Valley Arms has added a three-way breech plug to their in-line guns that will allow the hunter to use #11 caps, musket caps or #209 shotgun primers. This allows the shooter to use whatever igniter he feels is best for the prevailing conditions. It also allows one to try the different primers when working up a load. This seems to be a trend among the in-line makers, probably brought on by field reports of misfires. They are also selling the breech plug separately so that owners of older CVA guns may update their rifles.

CVA is now marketing a bore-diameter lead bullet, with a snap-on plastic skirt. These are similar to the Black Belt bullets that may be familiar to some. The idea is that the bullet loads easily, even after several shots, and the skirt effectively seals the bore behind the bullet to ensure best accuracy. I have used the Black Belt bullet for some time and find them to be very accurate and effective on game, due to the heavyweight bullet. These should produce much the same results. These bullets, legal in Colorado by the way, are available in

Rounding out Tradition's growing line of cartridge guns, the Model 1892 lever-action is now also available in carbine form.

Smith & Wesson's new Schofield 2000 revolver is for the cowboy action shooter.

50- and 54-caliber and either copper-coated for deeper penetration, or pure lead.

For the youth or petite woman shooter or hunter, CVA has their Youth Hunter Rifle. With an overall length of 38 inches, a shorter length of pull and a 24-inch barrel with a 1-in-48-inch twist, this is a light, handy rifle for the smaller person. It will handle either conical bullets or patched roundball with equal aplomb. This is a traditional style, sidelock rifle for those who prefer them to the in-lines. The hardwood stock has a recoil pad softer than the usual ones. A synthetic ramrod, very resistant to breaking, completes the unit. This is a good beginner rifle that is equally at home plinking, target shooting or hunting. At a price of less than $130.00 retail, I suspect these will be very popular.

Thompson/Center Arms is an outfit that never ceases to amaze me with their continual innovation. Their latest is a traditional flintlock rifle that will shoot Pyrodex pellets as well as standard blackpowder and even loose Pyrodex. What makes this gun work is an innovative breech plug that has a cone-shape at the front that holds the pellet slightly above the breech plug. This allows the priming powder to ignite all around the base of the pellet for good ignition. The touch hole is large

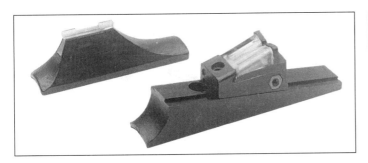

CVA US Illuminator II Sight System.

CVA copper-plated 50-caliber PowerBelt Bullets, 295- or 348-grains.

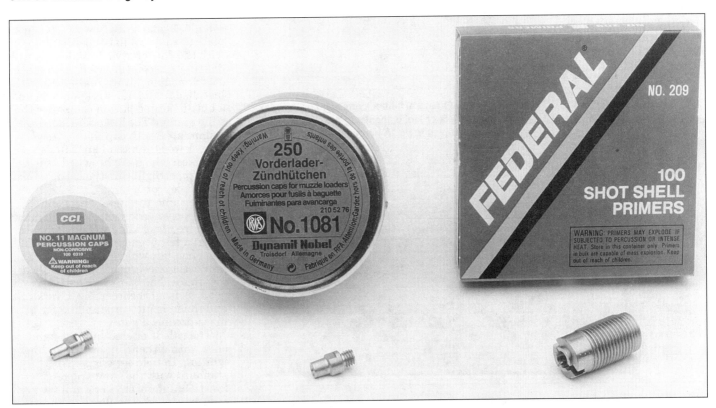

CVA MusketMag 3-Way Ignition System.

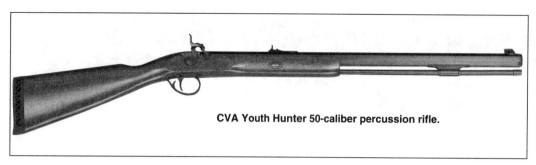

CVA Youth Hunter 50-caliber percussion rifle.

ignition — is the barrel uses a 1-in-28-inch twist for conicals and sabot loads. Both guns are fitted with fully adjustable fiber-optic sights, appreciated by hunters in bad light situations. The percussion rifle is also recommended for use with 150 grain magnum loadings. Both guns feature a heavy recoil lug welded under the barrel for solid and consistent barrel-to-stock fit, which contributes to uniform accuracy.

There is very good news for the traditional gun lovers out there. **Dixie Gun Works**, well known for traditional reproductions as well as parts and accessories for those guns, has a new Early American Jaeger Rifle. Patterned after the early forerunners to the graceful Kentucky Rifle, this Germanic rifle is a delight for those who are oriented toward a more historically correct firearm.

The first impression of this Italian-made replica is that one is looking at a custom-made firearm. It has the custom look and feel. The walnut stock

enough that 4Fg priming powder will infiltrate around the edge of the breech plug cone making, in effect, a small booster charge that helps ignite the pellets or loose Pyrodex. Pyrodex must be under pressure to burn well and simultaneous ignition of the pellet raises this pressure quickly and it then delivers velocities that are similar to a percussion gun. My testing with one of the guns showed that, if one is careful to get some of the priming powder worked through the touch hole as the pan is primed, ignition is instantaneous and accuracy is good. This rifle is very good news for those who shoot flintlocks, either from preference or because of law, and have trouble buying blackpowder. Pyrodex is carried almost universally by dealers who carry muzzleloading supplies whereas blackpowder is difficult to find in many areas, due to regulations on the local level and shipping difficulties.

The new rifle is called the Firestorm. It is offered in 50-caliber with a 1-turn-in-48-inch barrel to handle either conical bullets, sabot bullets or patched roundball with equal accuracy. The 26-inch barrel has the

popular QLA loading system; a counterbore extending about an inch inside the muzzle. This makes it much easier to center and load both slugs and sabots. The stock is a black synthetic with a black recoil pad. The lock is, of course, a typical sidelock flintlock fired by a single trigger and the ramrod is aluminum. Overall, a no-nonsense hunting rifle conforming to the law in those states that require flintlocks firing patched roundball for hunting. The gun is recommended for use with heavy magnum 150 grain loads.

A companion rifle in percussion is also available. This gun has a special breech that uses #209 shotgun primers instead of caps for surer ignition. Called the Firestorm 209 Caplock, the major difference between this and the flintlock rifle — other than the percussion

carries what looks like a satin oil finish that sets off the browned steel furniture. The 54-caliber, 1-inch octagon barrel is just under 28 inches long. The twist is 1-in-24-inches. This gun is obviously intended for use with conicals or sabot loads but, I'm told by the Dixie folks, it shoots patched roundball surprisingly well. The butt plate is a typical flat-type that, along with the Jaeger-style butt design, will distribute recoil very well. A U-shape attachment for an original-type sling is installed in the full stock forearm and a butt-mounted button completes the sling system. The forend is tipped with a simulated horn cap that looks very nice. A wood ramrod hangs in two thimbles, which are browned as is the entry pipe. Sights are typical open rear and blade front.

The thing that really gets one's attention when viewing this gun is the presence of a sliding wood patch box cover, a feature many of the original guns had but which is never seen on production firearms. This is really a nice touch. The fit of the wood lid is very good, as is all the inletting. Overall fit and finish is just outstanding for a mass-produced gun.

The rifle is offered in right-hand only, with either flint or percussion ignition. Double-set triggers are standard with the front trigger functional if unset. Lock and trigger quality is good. The flintlock throws good sparks and should be a reliable

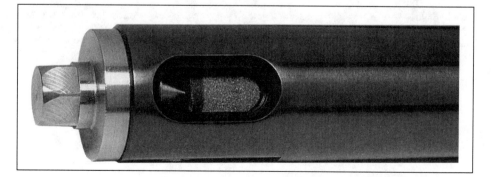

T/C's new Firestorm flintlock rifle handles Pyrodex, either pellets or loose, thanks to the newly-designed breechplug. A percussion model is also available.

This new breechplug design from T/C delivers even ignition to the base of Pyrodex pellets.

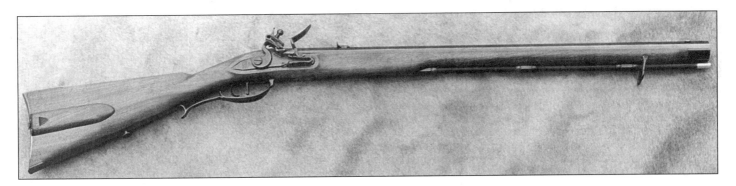

Early American Jaeger flintlock rifle, from Dixie Gunworks.

shooter. Priced at about half what a basic custom rifle would cost, this hunting rifle should find many friends out there. I'm told that the Jaeger may be available with traditional carving on the stock later. This is going to be a winner, in my opinion.

A new cartridge reproduction gun is on the horizon for the Cowboy Action shooters and the Civil War re-enactors. **Taylor's and Company** will have a reproduction of the Spencer Carbine out by mid-year, I'm told. Having seen the prototype action, it appears this will be a top-quality gun. Calibers planned are 45 Schofield, 44 Russian and 56/50.

Also new this year, from the Taylor's people, is the reproduction Starr revolver of Civil War fame. These 44-caliber revolvers will be offered in both double- and single-action.

These additions will fit nicely in their very complete line of Civil War-era reproductions and their line of Sharps rifles and sights, early Winchester lever guns and single-action Colt repros for the Cowboy Action crowd.

Goex, Inc. is making a new non-fouling, non-corrosive blackpowder replica propellant that is intended as a Pyrodex-type replacement powder. It

can be loaded on a weight or volume basis to replace blackpowder loadings and produces consistent shot-to-shot ballistics. It leaves very little residue and can be cleaned up with tap water. Called Clear Shot, it is a ball-type powder and is available in 2Fg and 3Fg granulations.

Also, along the propellant line, **Elephant Brand** blackpowder continues to improve their already top quality product. It is giving very consistent burn rates and somewhat higher velocities, load for load. This powder is well known for very little velocity variation shot-to-shot and is considered to be a top quality propellant for blackpowder firearms.

Petro-Explo Company, the importer of Elephant Black Powder, is also bringing in Swiss blackpowder. This powder gets high ratings from the blackpowder cartridge shooters, especially those shooting the long range competitions such as Black Powder Cartridge Silhouette. It looks as if powder supplies for shooters who glory in clouds of white smoke will be in good shape for the future.

The fiber-optic sight is increasingly seen on muzzle-loading hunting arms in the past couple of years. **Tru-Glo**, **HiViz**, **Williams** and others have

these sights available to install on most any muzzle loader, as well as modern firearms. The more fragile plastic sights are being replaced by metal sights, which stand the rigors of the hunting field much better. Fiber-optic sights give a much better sight picture in poor light or for those of us whose "over 40" eyes do not see open sights as well as we used to. It really helps those folks hunting in states that do not allow anything but open sights on muzzle-loaders. Many of the muzzleloader manufacturers are installing these sights as standard equipment on their hunting guns also.

While on the subject of sights, aperture sights have long been an answer when focusing over the open sights becomes a problem. Until now, most aperture sights looked too modern to blend in on traditional muzzleloading guns. **Ashley Outdoors** has cured that problem. They make a line of small good-looking aperture sights that are unobtrusive on traditional guns. They closely resemble sights that I have seen on 15th century cross-bows in the Tower of London collections. That should be authentic enough for anybody. They also make a ramrod with a folding "T" handle that fits in the ferrules of a ML gun and is indistinguishable from the standard rod, but gives the shooter a steel ramrod with a "T" handle for loading and cleaning. Really a very innovative and handy accessory in the hunting field or at the range. They also make the same ramrod in a threaded take-down version that can be carried in your possibles bag or, certainly, in your luggage when you go on a hunting trip, it being only 6 1/2-inches long and 1-inch in diameter when broken down in its carrying bag with all tips, etc.

With all the new stuff coming onto the market, a trip to your local blackpowder shooters supply store is certainly in order. If he isn't carrying some of the aforementioned products, tell him to contact the manufacturer or importer and get them in stock. It sure looks as this blackpowder game is here to stay. ●

Aperture rear sight, from Ashley Outdoors.

Ammo Update

by Holt Bodinson

MAYBE IT'S THE wealth effect or maybe it's the growing sophistication of a more demanding group of shooters, but what's been impressive in the ammunition field is the expansion of premium lines featuring higher quality custom bullets and harder shot at faster and faster velocities. As innovation goes, Remington stole the show with their introduction of electronically primed ammunition; Winchester with its totally redesigned "AA" case; Hornady/Marlin with their belted levergun cartridge, the 450 Magnum; and SSK with their .50-caliber Peacekeeper. And where's "moly" going when Nosler brings out a new line of completely "Moly-Free" bullets? Then there's FN's new 5.7x28mm military small arms cartridge propelling a wee 31-grain projectile at 2346 fps and rumored to have tremendous terminal ballistics. If that whets one's interest, see the new 5mm-centerfire cartridge description under "Schroeder" and the .12-caliber under "Eichelberger" in our text. From all points of view, it's been a busy and fascinating year in the wonderful world of ammunition, ballistics and components.

AFSCO Ammunition

Advertising as a one-stop source for "American, foreign, obsolete and African" ammunition, Anthony Sailer of AFSCO is just that. I haven't stumped him yet. Try him for everything from 17 BumbleBee to 500 Jeffery. If he doesn't stock it, he will create it overnight.

Tel: (715) 229-2516

Ammo Depot

This is a general supply company for ammunition, components and reloading tools that is impressive because of its diverse offerings, including Pyrodex loaded ammunition for all of the cowboy and obsolete Winchester rifle calibers. Well worth knowing. www.ammodepot.com

Ballard Rifle & Cartridge

Need cases for the 25-20 Single Shot, 25-21 Stevens, 577 Snider, 577-450 Martini Henry, 50 Rem Pistol, or most other obsolete cases? Check Ballard. This unique firm that is manufacturing classic, and I might add, stunning, Ballard rifles and original replacement parts, also offers a very complete line of lathe-turned cases. I've used their 577-450 cases. Quality products. Nice to deal with. www.ballardrifles.com

Ballistic Products, Inc.

When I go looking for the most technologically advanced and diverse selection of shotshell components and reloading data, Ballistic Products is where I head. Their catalogs and extensive offering of proprietary reloading manuals are mind-bending. The quality of their products and service is superior. Four updated reloading manuals are rolling off the press— *Status of Steel 2001; Handloading Bismuth 2001*; the *Sixteen-Gauge*; and the *Powder Manual*. Special attention is being given this year to expanding their lines of wads for the smaller bores including 20-gauge steel shot, spreader and trap wads; and two, new .410 wads--the "Stump" brush wad and the "Stretch" mid-to-long range wad. If you need to make a 2- 2 1/2-inch shell for one of those fine European doubles, Ballistic Products has introduced a neat hand-operated trimmer—the Trim Doctor— that will do just that. This house is also a good source for Kent Tungsten Matrix and FASTEEL and the Bismuth lines of non-toxic ammunition. www.ballisticproducts.com

Barnes

Barnes' baked-on, high-tech, dry film bullet lubricant is proving increasingly popular as an alternative to moly, so they're applying it to a variety of existing X-Bullets this year in calibers .224, .308, .375, .416, .470 and .500. With renewed interest in the 45/70 and this year's introduction of the 450 Magnum from Hornady, Barnes' latest 250- and 300-grain FNSP X-Bullets are right on target. www.barnesbullet.com

Beartooth Bullets

Offering an extensive selection of LBT bullet designs in calibers from .22 to .600 Nitro that are cast and sized specifically to the customer's requirements, Beartooth Bullets also offers a *"Technical Manual"* on the loading and performance of cast bullets. Bullet prices are reasonable; quality is exceptional; and Beartooth's website is first rate. www.beartoothbullets.com

Bell Brass

Advertising as "The toughest brass in the business," Bell isn't kidding if my experience with their Lazzeroni magnum cases is any indication. New this year for British fans are the 450/ 400 3 1/4" and 450 Basic cases. In the black powder category, new cases include the 44 Sharps Basic, 43 Mauser, 43 Spanish, and 50 Sharps

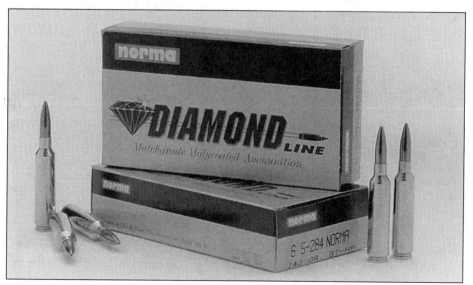

Norma's popular 6.5-284 match cartridge is being loaded by Black Hills.

Cylindrical 3-inch. Rounding out the 2001 offerings are the 458 Lott and the 416 Remington with a company promise to draw the 505 Gibbs, 405 Win., and 500/465 NE sometime in the near future. Finally, as a builder and re-builder of arsenal-quality loading machinery, Bell is offering production-style gauges for the serious handloader. www.bellammo.com

Black Hills Ammunition

If you see boxes of Norma Diamond Line ammunition in 6.5-284 Norma, 6mm Norma BR or 338 Lapua on your dealer's shelves, be advised that it's being loaded this year right here in the USA by Black Hills Ammunition. Black Hills already loads the .223/69-grain BTHP and .308/ 168-grain BTHP in the Norma Diamond Line, and the latest Norma contract follows on the heels of Black Hills' continuing contracts to supply our US military shooting teams with a variety of high quality match ammunition. Also new in the Black Hill lineup this year are a 32 H&R Magnum load featuring Hornady's 85-grain XTP bullet at 1100 fps; two 357 SIG loads with either the Speer 125-grain TMJ or Gold Dot bullet at 1350 fps; a heavy 223 match loading featuring the 77- grain Sierra MatchKing at 2750 fps; and a new 308 Winchester loading with the 165-grain Nosler Ballistic Tip at 2650 fps. By all means, order Black Hills' year 2000 catalog. It's informative, graphically stunning and refreshingly humorous. www.black-hills.com

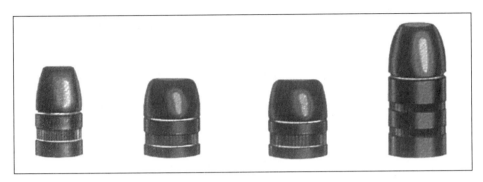

Given the popularity of cowboy action shooting, Speer has introduced a complete line of authentic looking, Old West-type bullets.

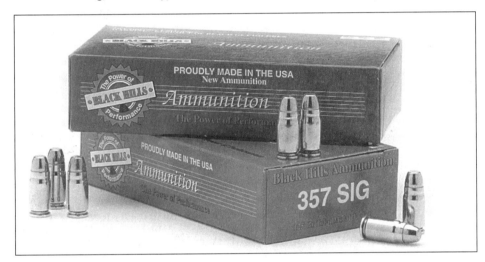

The hot and sensational 357 SIG has been added to the Black Hills line this year.

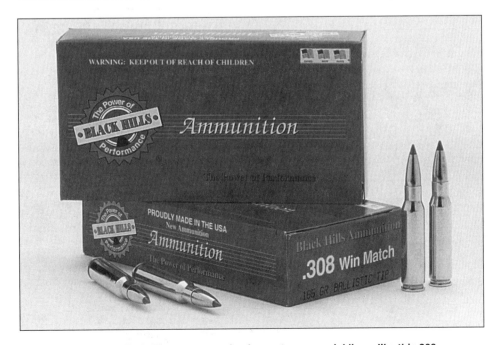

Nosler's accurate Ballistic Tips are appearing in most commercial lines, like this 308 Winchester match load by Black Hills.

Buffalo Bore Ammunition

Here is a fairly new company that has focused on assembling high velocity, high performance, hunting ammunition for modern rifles and revolvers. Loading jacketed and hard cast lead bullets, Buffalo Bore has pushed velocities to the max. For example, in the 45/70 lever gun category, they offer a 405-grain Remington bullet at 2000 fps; a 350-grain Speer at 2100 fps; and a 430-grain lead load at 1925 fps. The company has a complete selection of heavy hunting loads for the 475 and 500 Linebaugh, 45 Colt, 454 Casull and 44 Magnum while a new line of +P tactical/defensive ammunition has been added this year for calibers from 32 ACP through 45 ACP. Two unusual loadings being offered are the 38/55 Winchester with bullets properly sized to fit those generous, old Winchester Model '94 bores and a heavy 348 Winchester load consisting of a 250-grain JFN at 2250 fps. Buffalo Bore also catalogs a complete selection of hard cast bullets for sale featuring many of the excellent LBT designs. www.sixgunner.com

James Calhoon

Covered in detail last year, one of Calhoon's proprietary cartridges, the 19 Calhoon, a .19-caliber wildcat based on an improved Hornet case, received quite a bit of attention by some of the "majors" at the last SHOT Show. This wee cartridge propels a 27-grain bullet at 3600 fps and a 32-grain at 3400 fps with a miserly 12-15 grains of powder. Stay tuned. It may be coming to your dealer's shelves. www.jamescalhoon.com

Cast Performance Bullet Company

As a measure of their quality, this company provides the heat-treated LBT designs that are loaded by both Federal and Cor-Bon in their premium handgun ammunition lines. Fortunately for the handloader, the company offers a very complete and economical retail selection of LBT bullets in .38, .41, .44, .458(rifle), .475 and .500 (Linebaugh) calibers. Their

spec sheets also contain recommended loading data. Check 'em out at www.castperformance.com

CCI/Speer

The 22 Magnum is certainly on the comeback trail, and CCI has added a 5th loading to their 22 Win.Mag. line. The new loading labeled the "TNT" features a 30-grain bullet with a cavernous hollowpoint at a velocity of 2200 fps. Missing from the handgun shotshell line has been the old 45 Colt. This year CCI has corrected that with a load of one hundred and fifty #9 shot at 1000 fps. In response to the need for lead-free, non-toxic range loads, Speer has introduced Lawman RHT ammunition for the 9mm, 40 S&W and 45 ACP. The new loading consists of a sintered copper bullet that breaks up into small particles when it impacts the backstop. Comes with lead-free primers, too. The nose of the RHT bullet carries a raised cruciform brand that signals to the range master that it's

◄ Speer's new sintered copper bullet for indoor ranges fragments upon impact into a pile of copper dust.
▼

O.K. ammo and to the police officer that it's not regular duty ammunition. To please the handgun hunting community, Speer is introducing a 240-grain Gold Dot 44 Magnum load at 1400 fps. Added to the Speer jacketed bullet component line are the 400-grain .475 Linebaugh Gold Dot; 85-grain .32 JHP; 225-grain .338 Grand Slam SP; 300-grain .375 African Grand Slam SP; 90-grain 6.5mm TNT HP; and 130-grain 7-30 Waters FNSP. And to keep the cowboys and cowgirls shooting, a new line of swaged lead bullets in 38, 44, 45 and 45/70 caliber has been introduced that features a revolutionary lubricant that virtually eliminates leading. www.cci-ammunition.com and www.speer-bullets.com

Clean Shot Powder

A volume-to-volume replacement for black powder without the latter's fouling and sulfur corrosion, Clean Shot powder can now be obtained in pellet form for the 44/45 cap-and-ball revolver and 50/54-caliber rifles. www.cleanshot.com

Cole Distributing

A major importer and distributor of the IMI and Aguila brands plus a good deal of surplus military ammunition, Cole has announced that they will be importing non-corrosive, boxer-primed, 7.5 MAS and 7.5 Swiss ammunition from FNM in Portugal. This will be the best of news to all of the owners of the 1000s of French MAS rifles that have been imported into the USA during the last few years. Surplus French military ball has been scarce, expensive and corrosive. www.cole distributing.com

Eichelberger

If sub-sub calibers like the .12 and .14 sound intriguing, W.A. Eichelberger is man who keeps them shooting. Eichelberger is THE source for .12-,.14-, and .20-caliber bullets, cases, cleaning rods and loading manuals. Even if you never intend to shoot these tiny bores, you may be interested in one of his many cartridge collector sets, including one consisting of the Long Rifle case formed and loaded with bullets from .12-to-.20-caliber. His brochure is also an excellent reference source for sub-caliber barrels, reamers, dies, rifles and journals. Address: 158 Crossfield Rd., King of Prussia,PA 19406

Estate Cartridge

Known for their high quality and custom shotgun ammunition, Estate Cartridge is adding a Buffered Magnum Hunting load in 12- and 20-gauge with extra-hard #4 or #6 shot as well as a new 3 1/2-inch High Velocity Magnum Steel loading with 1 1/2

Federal has a new hunting bullet—the Deep-Shok—providing improved penetration and expansion on big game.

Combining steel and tungsten-iron shot gives the duck hunter an added edge over decoys.

Federal's new 20-gauge steel loads are a welcome response to increased lead shot restrictions for upland game.

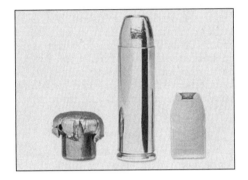

Federal's 454 Casull load features a tough 300-grain Trophy Bonded Bear Claw bullet for the largest game.

ounces of BBB,BB,1,2,3,4,6 shot at 1400 fps. Tel: 409-856-7277

Federal

Federal has designed a new rifle bullet. Called the "Deep-Shok," this spitzer boattail features a core that is mechanically locked into the jacket, providing 85% weight retention upon impact and reliable expansion at velocities from 1800-to-3000 fps. The Deep-Shok will be loaded in most popular hunting calibers from the 243 to the 300 Win. Mag. Added this year to the Premium Safari Rifle line is the 300 Rem. Ultra Mag. loaded with a 180-grain Trophy Bonded Bear Claw. Featuring a 300-grain Trophy Bonded HP, the 454 Casull cartridge its appearance in the Premium Handgun Hunting line. Combining #4 Tungsten-Iron and #2 steel pellets in the same shot column, Federal has designed a 12-gauge 3 1/2-inch non-toxic shell that costs less than Tungsten-Iron and Tungsten-Polymer and provides excellent patterning performance for near or far targets. New also to Federal's shotgun ammunition line are a 12-gauge spreader load with #8 or #8 1/2 shot; 12- and 20-gauge high velocity upland game steel loads for areas mandating the use of non-toxic shot; high velocity turkey loads for the 3-inch and 3 1/2-inch 10- and 12-gauges with buffered #4,5 and 6 copper-plated shot. In the handgun ammunition area, Federal has added to their American Eagle line reduced-lead target loads for the 9mm, 40 S&W and 45 Auto. www.federalcartridge.com

Fiocchi

Fiocchi is well known for their hard nickel-plated shot loads that deliver exceptional patterns. This year Fiocchi is expanding the line with a three-inch 20-gauge 1 1/4 ounce load of #4,5 and 6; a Live Pigeon/FITASC 12-gauge load with 1 1/4 ounce of #7 1/2 or 8's at 1225 fps as well as a high velocity hunting load with 1 1/4 ounce of #4,5,6 and 7 at 1330. The steel shot line has been expanded greatly, and particularly intriguing are the 20-gauge loadings that include in the 3-inch case, 7/8-ounce of #2,3 and 4 steel at a sizzling 1500 fps.

www.fiocchiusa.com

Garrett Cartridges

Like to hunt with the 45/70 or 44 Magnum? Randy Garrett's custom ammunition for both calibers is legendary in big game circles for its ability to penetrate bone-and-body through-and-through. His latest 45/70 loading consists of a super-hard-cast, gas-checked, 530-grain bullet with a .360-inch meplat that moves out at 1550 fps from a 22" barrel. Normal accuracy for 3-shot groups at 100 yards from a lever gun is 1-1.5 inches. Complementing the 45/70 load is a new +P loading for the 44 Mag. featuring a 330-grain hard cast Hammerhead bullet at 1385 fps. Because of its length and chamber pressure, the new 44 Mag. loading is suitable only for Ruger Redhawks and Super Redhawks. www.garrettcartridge.com

Hi-Tech Ammunition

Simply the best source I know of for surplus .223, .30, and .50 military bullets, brass, and powder. They have it all—FMJ, tracer, APIT—even military reference manuals on loading data and performance. www.hi-techammo.com

Hodgdon Powder Co., Inc.

The Powder Meisters have done it again--two new powders for the reloading bench. LONGSHOT, a spherical shotgun powder, will definitely turn some heads. Due to its slow burning rate and long peak time, LONGSHOT is capable of propelling 1 1/8 ounces of lead shot to 1585 fps from a 2 3/4-inch 12-gauge hull. Suitable for all gauges other than the .410, it establishes a new benchmark for high performance shotgun propellants. And speaking

Fiocchi is expanding it's line of hard nickel-plated shot loads for the coming hunting season.

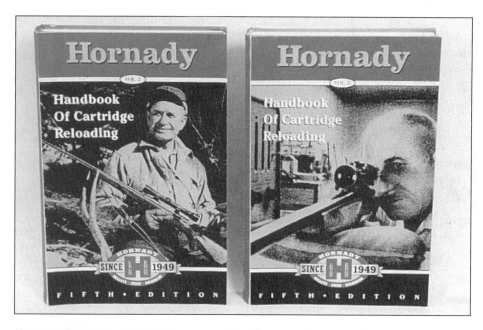

Hornady's fifth edition of its loading manual has been completely updated.

about benchmarks, Hodgdon's other new powder is BENCHMARK—a small-grained, temperature-tolerant propellant for accurate little cases like the 22 PPC, 6mm BR, 222 and 223. BENCHMARK also turns in sterling performance in the 308 with 147-155-grain bullets. Hodgdon reports excellent results in the 7mm-08, 7x57, 30-30 and 35 Rem as well. To tailor their reloading data to the needs of computer fans, Hodgdon has released a new computer reloading program titled, BLAST ELECTRONIC MANUAL VERSION TWO. The program contains updated data from Hodgdon's #27 *Data Manual*, extensive shotshell and cowboy action data plus a condensed version of the Barnes external ballistics program. I found the shotshell portion of the program especially useful. For those without a computer, Hodgdon has also issued the *Basic Reloading Manual 2000* in printed form that covers 1,100 loads for 105 metallic cartridges and more than 1,400 of the latest shotshell recipes. www.hodgdon.com

Hornady

Hornady and Marlin joined together to bring shooters a new belted .45-caliber cartridge, the 450 Marlin. Chambered in Marlin's fast-handling 1895M Guide Gun, the 450 Marlin case launches a 350-grain FP bullet at 2100 fps from a 24 inch barrel. While many handloaders reach that level of performance with the 45/70 cartridge in modern rifles, the 450 Marlin permits ammunition companies to load and market what amounts to a +P 45/70 load without the concern that it will be accidentally fired in one of the many older and weaker 45/70s still in circulation. This is a banner year for Hornady and new cartridges with the

introduction of loadings and new component bullets for the 376 Steyr, 475 Linebaugh, and 454 Casull. For slug gunners, there is a hot new factory load consisting of a 300-grain XTP bullet loaded to 2000 fps in a 2 3/4-inch case. Even Hornady's "Light Magnum" series has been expanded with the addition of 150-grain Super Shock Tip (SST) bullets in the 308 Win. and 30-06. Finally, Hornady's excellent two-volume reloading manual has been completely updated and should be available by the time you read this. www.hornady.com

Lazzeroni

What may be the ultimate 7mm long-range hunting cartridge, John Lazzeroni has introduced the 7.21 Firebird. Basically the large capacity 7.82(.308) Warbird case necked down to 7mm, the Firebird delivers a scorching 3,724 fps with a plated 140-grain Nosler Partition bullet. www.lazzeroni.com

Mountain State Muzzleloading Supplies, Inc.

Here's the one-stop shop for muzzleloading projectiles and components par excellence. If they don't have it, they can probably get it. Their massive new catalog sells for $4.00 and the price is refundable. www.mtnstatesmuzzle loading.com

Noble Sport

Imported by ADCO of Woburn, Massachusetts, Noble Sport now offers a complete line of 16 Vectan propellants for rifle, pistol and shotgun cartridges. More importantly, Nobel Sport has issued a comprehensive handloading manual in English that covers both

U.S. and European calibers in depth. The manual is well written and includes valuable data that does not typically appear in U.S. manuals. The U.S. importer, ADCO, can be reached at (781) 935-1799. www.snpe.com

Norma

Remember Norma's Magnum Rifle Powder(MRP)? Well, this year Norma's given us a new blend called MRP-2 that is even slower and designed specifically for the big boomers—like the 30-387 Weatherby and 7mm STW. Norma reports MRP-2 is also ideal for extracting the utmost velocity from their new 6.5-284 case. www.norma.cc

Northern Precision

If you own one of Marlin's 45/70 or 450 Guide Guns, Northern Precision, working with Ken Waters, has developed a 400-grain, flat point, bonded-core bullet designed specifically for these great big game cartridges. Also new this year are a bonded-core, fast-expanding, 30-caliber White-Tail bullet in weights from 150-220-grains made with J-4 jackets treated with Fastex to minimize fouling, and a series of bonded-core .375 pistol and rifle bullets in a variety of weights and tip forms. Tel: 315-493-1711

Nosler

Whether you agree with it or not, a lot of deer and antelope are successfully taken each year with high velocity .224 varmint rifles. A few years ago, Winchester introduced its 64-grain "deer" bullet in the 223, and this year, Nosler has introduced its smallest Partition bullet yet—a 60-grain .224-inch pill designed specifically for taking light big game with rifles in the 22-250 and 220 Swift class. At the other caliber extreme, Nosler has introduced a .416/400-grain Partition designed for heavy North American and African big game. In a very interesting move, Nosler has fielded "Moly-Free" Partition Gold bullets in .270/150-grain; 7mm/160-

Nosler's .224-caliber 60-grain Partition is designed specifically for hunting deer and antelope with high velocity .224s.

European and African hunters who shoot a lot of 9.3s now have a modern Ballistic Tip to work with.

grain; .308/150- and 180-grain, and .338/250-grain. Moly has not been found to be a cure-all. Many members of the benchrest fraternity have stopped using moly-coated match bullets entirely while some custom barrel makers will not guarantee their products if used with moly-coated bullets. Expanding their J4 Competition line, Nosler has fielded a 30-caliber 155-grain HPBT. New Ballistic Tip offerings this year include a 9.3mm/250-grain; 8mm/180-grain; 6mm/80-grain; and a .224/55-grain Ballistic Silvertip varmint bullet. www.nosler.com

Old Western Scrounger

Entering the millennium with the slogan "The impossible comes off the shelf; the miracle takes a bit longer," the OWS is at it again. With the reintroduction of the Model 1895 Winchester in 405 Winchester, everyone has been asking, "Who will be making the ammunition?" The Scrounger already does, of course, but this year he is introducing a loading featuring Woodleigh's terrific 300-grain, bonded-core SP/RN in Bertram brass headstamped "O.W.S. 405 Win." Just in time for the African big game season! And the good news continues. Also new this year are 2 7/8-inch 10-gauge smokeless and blackpowder shells plus some new 8-gauge loads from GameBore. And if you have a gun but no ammunition, the OWS is bringing back the 41 Remington derringer cartridge, the 221 Fireball, 222 Rem. Mag., 7.92x33 Kurz, 350 Rem. Mag., 357 Maximum, 401 Herter's Power Mag., and is importing S&B's 22 Savage H.P., 25-35 Win, and 7.62x25 Tokarev ammunition. Bullet casters, need pure tin? The OWS has it in 1-lb. blocks. Finally, the OWS has taken on the whole Kynoch line of big bore ammunition. www.snowcrest.net/oldwest

PMC Ammunition

PMC has greatly expanded its shotshell line with low recoil 12-gauge loads for cowboy action shooting;

PMC has integrated the famous Brenneke slug into its shotgun ammunition line.

PMC's low recoil buckshot load is a favorite for tactical and home defense use.

The 22 Winchester Magnum is undergoing a sensational revival and PMC is offering their new SP and FMJ loads this year.

J. D. Jones' new 50 Peacekeeper cartridge provides 88% of the ballistics of the 50 BMG in a 13-pound rifle.

heavy field loads for the 16-, 28- and .410-bores; clay target loads for the 28-gauge and .410; a 3-inch 12-gauge turkey load pushing #4 or #6 shot at 1210 fps; a 1 ounce Brenneke slug load for the 12-gauge doing 1600 fps; high velocity 00 and #4 buck, and low recoil OO buck shells for the 12-gauge. In the rifle line, there's two new 22 Mag. loadings featuring either a 40- grain SP or FMJ at 1910 fps; a 180-grain SP and 174-grain FMJ load for the grand old 303 British; and a 170-grain SP

loading for the 7x64 Brenneke. Finally, PMC is offering the increasingly popular 357 SIG with either a Starfire or FMJ 124-grain bullet at 1350 fps.
www.pmcammo.com

Precision Reloading, Inc.

Simply a great source for reloading components with a particular bent toward smoothbores. Beautiful catalog.
www.precisionreloading.com

Ramshot

The Western Powders company of Miles City, Montana has come on line with nine handloading propellants for rifle, pistol and shotgun.

They're not widely distributed yet so see their data at:
www.westernpowders.com

RCBS

For the owners of 310 Cadet Martinis or 310s that have been rechambered to 32/20—owners who have been frustrated in their search for accurate bullets— RCBS brings great news. They have catalogued a mould that was formerly supplied only to N.D.F.S. in England. The actual specifications for the new 310 Cadet mould are .323-inch nose and .312-inch heel—not the .310-inch diameter as reflected in the new catalog.
www.rcbs.com

Remington

The millennium innovation award in components has to go to Remington for the commercial introduction of their large rifle electronic primer—the EtronX. We've seen electronic primers in caseless sporting ammunition but not as reloading components. Better yet, the EtronX primer provides the handloader with the same performance and pressure level achieved with standard 9 1/2s. It was only a matter of time until Big Green necked its Ultra Mag case up and down. This year it's UP as the 338 Ultra Mag loaded with

SSK's complete lineup of .50-caliber offerings, from the diminutive 50 American Eagle to the 50 Sharps 3 1/4-inch.

Remington is already loading Swift's bonded-core, polymer-tipped Scirocco bullet.

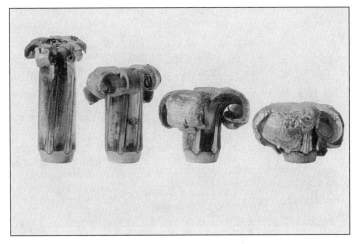

Swift's Scirocco bullet exhibits excellent expansion over a wide range of velocities while maintaining jacket/core integrity.

a 250-grain Swift A-Frame bullet at 2900 fps. There are two new loadings for the 300 Utra Mag—a 200-grain Nosler Partition at 3075 and a 180-grain Swift Scirocco at 3250 fps. The little green-tipped 22 Win. Mag. load featuring a 33-grain Hornady V-Max boat-tail bullet at 2000 fps is here--it's good-looking and accurate. Speaking about rimfire, Remington and Eley, Ltd. are partnering to provide three grades of target 22 rimfire ammunition for serious competitors. Finally, Remington is fielding a much needed 20-gauge Copper Solid Sabot Slug weighing 5/8-ounce and driven at a velocity of 1500 fps. www.remington.com

Schroeder

For the owners of Model 591/592 Remingtons chambered for the utterly obsolete 5mm Remington rimfire cartridge, there is hope. Steve Schroeder is offering a simple conversion kit, cases and three bullet types to convert those rimfires into delightful 5mm centerfires. I've done the conversion, and it works perfectly. Taking only 4.5-5.0 grains of Win. 296 powder, the new little 5mm centerfire at 2000 fps is a real hoot--the perfect suburban varmint cartridge. Schroeder also offers a complete selection of obsolete jacketed bullet forms for oddballs like the 7mm and 8mm Nambu's and 351 Win. Tel: (619) 423-8124

Sierra

Combining their MatchKing jackets with an explosive acetyl resin tip, Sierra has expanded its BlitzKing varmint bullet line to include a 6mm 55-grain flat base; a 6mm 70-grain boattail; and in .224-caliber, boattail BlitzKings in 50-grain and 55-grain and a 40-grain flat base. Available in bulk boxes of 100 and 500, the BlitzKings can be ordered with a moly-coating in the 500 bulk pack. Speaking of bulk packs, the whole range of Sierra MatchKings can now be ordered in boxes of 500 with many of the more popular bullets available with moly-coating. To clarify a vital issue, the new catalog clearly indicates the best barrel twists required to stabilize Sierra's superb long-range specialty bullets. www.sierrabullets.com

SSK Industries

J.D. Jones has been as creative as ever during the last twelve months. His latest brainchild is the 50 Peacekeeper—the 460 Weatherby opened up to .50-caliber and set-up for .50-caliber BMG and hunting bullets. Performance of this new cartridge is sensational in a 13-pound gun with a 23-inch barrel giving fully 88% of the velocity normally obtained in a full 50 BMG chambering; for example, 2400 fps with a 650-grain bullet and 2206 fps with a 750-grain. SSK currently offers a complete selection of .50-caliber cartridges from the diminutive 50 American Eagle through the 50x3 1/4-inch Sharps, and for big things that need killing, the 700 JDJ and the 950 JDJ--the latter slinging a 3200-grain bullet. Great new web site at www.sskindustries.com

Winchester's component bullets and brass are now bulk-packed for added convenience and cost savings to the handloader.

Winchester's redesigned "AA" hull, featured in loads like these Super Handicaps, will give extended life at the reloading bench.

Winchester's Supreme surface coating technology delivers superior ballistic performance and higher velocities in its Power Point Plus ammunition.

Swift Bullet Company

Combining a pure copper jacket, a bonded lead core, a polymer tip, a 15-degree boattail and a secant ogive, Swift's new Scirocco bullet is being offered in a .30-caliber 180- and 165-grain form; a .270-caliber 130-grain; 7mm 150-grain; and a .338-caliber weight that is yet to be determined. Swift plans on offering the Scirocco line in every caliber from .224 through .338, and as we've seen Remington is already

loading the new bullet in their .300 Ultra Mag. Tel: (785) 754-3959

VihtaVuori/Lapua

Imported by Kaltron/Pettibone of Bensenville, Illinois, VihtaVuori has just released the 3rd edition of its reloading manual. The manual has been thoroughly updated and includes data for newer cartridges like the 30-378 Weatherby, 357 SIG and 50 AE. The manual is an entertaining and informative read with information about Scandinavian wildcat cartridges unavailable elsewhere. Lapua has some interesting new "extra-long range shooting cartridges" that include the 6mm BR Norma, the 308 Win, and the 338 Lapua Mag. Reach Kaltron/Pettibone at ((630) 350-1116. VihtaVuori-www.nammo.fi and Lapua www.lapua.com

Winchester

Labeling the line, the "Official Ammunition of the New Millennium," Winchester has been busy. The justifiably famous "AA" hull just got a face-lift. No longer is it "compression-formed." Searching for a way to improve its durability as a highly prized case for reloading, the new "AA 2000" is made from an extruded tube of super high strength plastic and a separate polymer base wad and head. The internal volume of the new AA hull is identical to the old so identical reloading data can be used. Most importantly, Winchester claims the new hull will stand up to more sizing and reloading than any hull currently on the market. There are some surprises not even reflected in the current catalog. The AA Super-Handicap load has been souped up to 1290 fps featuring hard shot with a 6% antimony content. The AA Super-Sport sporting clays loads have been given a shot of adrenaline with the 12-gauge one ounce #7 1/2 and #8 loads doing 1350 fps and the 20-gauge one ounce loads achieving 1165 fps. Gone from the line is the "Upland Game" loads that this year are replaced by the return of the "Super-X" brand. The shells are improved, too, featuring AA wads and base wads. Winchester and Bismuth have split the blanket, so Bismuth will disappear from the line. In the Supreme rifle area, Power-Point Plus loads for the 270 Winchester and 7mm-08 Remington have been added as well as a 168-grain match load for the 308 Winchester. Lots of interesting new handgun ammunition including WinClean loads for the 380 Auto and 357 Mag. Bowing to the wishes of the handloading community, Winchester is marketing bulk "consumer packs" (read "plastic bags") full of handgun and rifle bullets as well as a complete selection of unprimed handgun and rifle brass. Finally, the component powder line has been streamlined to include only Win. 231, 296, Super-Target, Super-Field, 748, 760 and WXR(replacing Magnum Rifle powder). If you load Action Pistol, AA Plus, Super-Lite, 540 or Magnum Rifle powder, you better stock-up now. ●

2001
GUNS ILLUSTRATED
Complete Compact
CATALOG

GUNDEX

SEMI-CUSTOM

HANDGUNS

RIFLES

SHOTGUNS

BLACKPOWDER

AIRGUNS

MANUFACTURERS DIRECTORY

GUNDEX

GUNDEX

GUNDEX

Slim is in!

With the new "Slimline" GLOCK 36

6+1 rounds of potent .45 Auto... in a package that fits the hand of almost any shooter.

Renowned for its safety, accuracy, reliability, durability, and ease of use, GLOCK's proven "Safe Action" technology has now been applied to the grip-slimming single-stack magazine concept. The result should come as no surprise: The GLOCK system makes shooting the high-performance .45 Auto a pleasure, while the reduced width of the finger-grooved grip frame, ambidextrous thumb rests and extended magazine floor plate make handling the G36 a breeze!

GLOCK has slimmed the width of the G36 to an incredible 1.13 inches, making it the slimmest GLOCK yet.

GLOCK® PERFECTION

Rule #1: Handle all firearms as if they were loaded.

Nominated as
Shooting Industry's Academy of Excellence
Handgun of the Year 2000

GUNDEX

GUNDEX

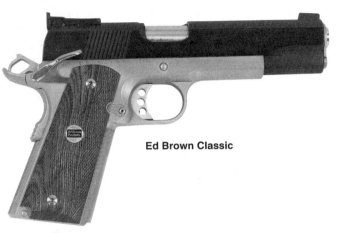

Ed Brown Classic

Ed Brown Classic Class A

BRILEY 1911-STYLE AUTO PISTOLS

Caliber: 9mm Para., 38 Super, 40 S&W, 10-shot magazine; 45 ACP, 8-shot magazine. **Barrel:** 3.6" or 5". **Weight:** NA. **Length:** NA. **Grips:** rosewood or rubber. **Sights:** Bo-Mar adjustable rear, Briley dovetail blade front. **Features:** Modular or Caspian alloy, carbon steel or stainless steel frame; match barrel and trigger group; lowered and flared ejection port; front and rear serrations on slide; beavertail grip safety; hot blue, hard chrome or stainless steel finish. Introduced 2000. Made in U.S. From Briley Manufacturing Inc.

Price: Fantom (3.6" bbl., fixed low-mount rear sight, armor coated lower receiver) . . . . from **$1,795.00**
Price: Fantom with two-port compensator . . . . from **$2,145.00**
Price: Advantage (5" bbl., adj. low-mount rear sight, checkered mainspring housing) . . . . from **$1,495.00**
Price: Versatility Plus (5" bbl., adj. low-mount rear sight, modular or Caspian frame) . . . . from **$1,695.00**
Price: Signature Series (5" bbl., adj. low-mount rear sight, 40 S&W only) . . . . from **$1,995.00**
Price: Plate Master (5" bbl. with compensator, lightened slide, Briley scope mount) . . . . from **$1,795.00**
Price: El Presidente (5" bbl. with Briley quad compensator, Briley scope mount) . . . . from **$2,195.00**

ED BROWN CLASSIC CUSTOM
AND CLASS A LIMITED 1911-STYLE AUTO PISTOLS

Caliber: 45 ACP; 7-shot magazine; 40 S&W, 400 Cor-Bon, 38 Super, 9x23, 9mm Para. **Barrel:** 4.25", 5", 6". **Weight:** NA. **Length:** NA. **Grips:** Hogue exotic checkered wood. **Sights:** Bo-Mar or Novak rear, blade front. **Features:** Blued or stainless steel frame; ambidextrous safety; beavertail grip safety; checkered forestrap and mainspring housing; match-grade barrel; slotted hammer; long lightweight or Videki short steel trigger. Many options offered. Made in U.S. by Ed Brown Products.

Price: Classic Custom (45 ACP, 5" barrel) . . . . from **$2,499.00**
Price: Class A Limited (all calibers; several bbl. lengths in competition and carry forms) . . . . from **$1,999.00**

EUROPEAN AMERICAN ARMORY WITNESS AUTO PISTOLS

Caliber: 9mm Para., 9x21, 38 Super, 40 S&W, 45 ACP, 10mm; 10-shot magazine. **Barrel:** 3.55", 3.66", 4.25", 4.5", 4.75", 5.25". **Weight:** 26 to 38 oz. **Length:** 7.25" to 10.5" overall. **Grips:** Black rubber, smooth walnut, checkered walnut, ivory polymer. **Sights:** three-dot, windage-adjustable or fully adjustable rear, blade front. **Features:** Single and double action; polymer or forged steel frame; forged steel slide; field strips without tools; ergonomic grip angle; front and rear serrations on slide; matte blue and stainless steel finish. Frame can be converted to other calibers. Imported from Italy by European American Armory.

Price: Witness Full Size (4.5" bbl., three-dot sights, 8.1" overall) . . . . from **$399.00**
Price: Witness Compact (3.66" bbl., three-dot sights, 7.25" overall) . . . . from **$399.00**

Kimber Custom Compact CDP

Price: Carry-Comp (4.25" bbl. with compensator, three-dot sights, 8.1" overall) . . . . from **$439.00**
Price: Gold Team (5.25" bbl. with compensator, adjustable sights, 10.5" overall) . . . . from **$2,195.00**
Price: Silver Team (5.25" bbl. with compensator, adjustable sights, 9.75" overall) . . . . from **$999.00**
Price: Limited Class (4.75" barrel, adj. sights and trigger, drilled for scope mount) . . . . from **$999.00**
Price: P-Series (4.55" bbl., polymer frame in four colors, many porting and sight options) . . . . from **$379.00**

KIMBER CUSTOM 1911-STYLE AUTO PISTOLS

Caliber: 9mm Para., 38 Super, 9-shot magazines; 40 S&W, 8-shot magazine; 45 ACP, 7-shot magazine. **Barrel:** 5". **Weight:** 38 oz. **Length:** 8.7" overall. **Grips:** Black synthetic, smooth or double-diamond checkered rosewood, or double-diamond checkered walnut. **Sights:** McCormick low profile or Kimber adjustable rear, blade front. **Features:** Machined steel slide, frame and barrel; front and rear beveled slide serrations; cut and button-rifled, match-grade barrel; adjustable aluminum trigger; full-length guide rod; Commander-style hammer; high-ride beavertail safety; beveled magazine well. Other models available. Made in U.S. by Kimber Mfg. Inc.

Price: Custom (black matte finish) **$723.00**
Price: Custom Royal (polished blue finish, checkered rosewood grips) **$745.00**
Price: Custom Stainless (satin-finished stainless steel frame and slide) **$825.00**
Price: Custom Target (matte black or stainless finish, Kimber adj. sight) **$935.00**

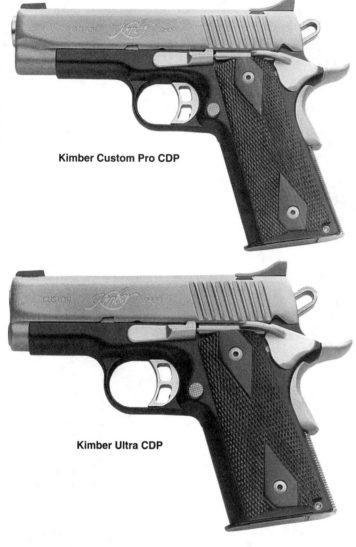

Kimber Custom Pro CDP

Kimber Ultra CDP

**North American
Arms Guardian
with gold accents**

Price: Custom Compact CDP (4" bbl., alum. frame, tritium
three-dot sights, 28 oz.) **$1,109.00**
Price: Custom Pro CDP (4" bbl., alum. frame, tritium sights,
full-length grip, 28 oz.) **$1,109.00**
Price: Ultra CDP (3" bbl., aluminum frame, tritium sights,
25 oz.). **$1,109.00**
Price: Gold Match (polished blue finish, hand-fitted barrel,
ambid. safety) **$1,135.00**
Price: Stainless Gold Match (stainless steel frame and slide,
hand-fitted bbl., amb. safety) **$1,277.00**
Price: Gold Combat (hand-fitted, stainless barrel; KimPro
black finish, tritium sights) **$1,633.00**
Price: Gold Combat Stainless (stainless frame and slide,
satin silver finish, tritium sights) **$1,576.00**
Price: Super Match (satin stainless frame, KimPro black finished,
stainless slide) **$1,871.00**

LES BAER CUSTOM 1911-STYLE AUTO PISTOLS
Caliber: 9mm Para., 38 Super, 40 S&W, 45 ACP, 400 Cor-Bon; 7- or 8-shot
magazine. **Barrel:** 4-1/4", 5", 6". **Weight:** 28 to 40 oz. **Length:** NA.
Grips: Checkered cocobolo. **Sights:** Low-mount combat fixed, combat
fixed with tritium inserts or low-mount adjustable rear, dovetail front. **Features:** Forged steel or aluminum frame; slide serrated front and rear; lowered and flared ejection port; beveled magazine well; speed trigger with

4-pound pull; beavertail grip safety; ambidextrous safety. Other models
available. Made in U.S. by Les Baer Custom.
Price: Baer 1911 Premier II 5" Model (5" bbl., optional stainless steel frame
and slide) . . . . from **$1,428.00**
Price: Premier II 6" Model (6" barrel) . . . . from **$1,595.00**
Price: Premier II LW1 (forged aluminum frame,
steel slide and barrel) . . . . from **$1,740.00**
Price: Custom Carry (4" or 5" barrel, steel frame) . . . . . . from **$1,640.00**
Price: Custom Carry (4" barrel, aluminum frame) . . . . from **$1,923.00**
Price: Swift Response Pistol (fixed tritium sights,
Bear Coat finish). . . . . from **$2,495.00**
Price: Monolith (5" barrel and slide with extra-long dust cover)
. . . . from **$1,599.00**
Price: Stinger (4-1/4" barrel, steel or aluminum frame) . . . from **$1,491.00**
Price: Thunder Ranch Special (tritium fixed combat sight,
Thunder Ranch logo) . . . . from **$1,620.00**
Price: National Match Hardball (low-mount adj. sight;
meets DCM rules). . . . . from **$1,335.00**
Price: Bullseye Wadcutter Pistol (Bo-Mar rib w/ adj. sight,
guar. 2-1/2" groups) . . . . from **$1,495.00**
Price: Ultimate Master Combat (5" or 6" bbl., adj. sights,
checkered front strap). . . . . from **$2,376.00**
Price: Ultimate Master Combat Compensated (four-port
compensator, adj. sights) . . . . from **$2,476.00**

NORTH AMERICAN ARMS GUARDIAN AUTO PISTOL
Caliber: 32 ACP, 6-shot magazine. **Barrel:** 2.18". **Weight:** 13.57 oz.
Length: 4.36" overall. **Grips:** Checkered or smooth; cocobolo, kingwood,
winewood, goncalo alves, pau ferro, white or black simulated mother of
pearl. **Sights:** White dot, fiber optics or tritium (nine models). **Features:**
Double action only; stainless steel frame and slide; barrel porting; frame
stippling; forward striped or scalloped slide serrations; meltdown (rounded
edges) treatment; slide/frame finishes available in combinations that include black titanium, stainless steel, gold titanium and highly polished or
matte choices. From North American Arms Custom Shop.
Price: NAA-32 Guardian. **$359.00**
Price: Gold or black titanium finish . . . . add **$120.00**
Price: High-polish finish . . . . add **$150.00**
Price: Ported barrel . . . . add **$90.00**

North American Arms Guardian with high polish finish

North American Arms Guardian with matte finish

Rock River Arms Elite Commando

Rock River Arms Standard Match

Rock River Arms National Match Hardball

ROCK RIVER ARMS 1911-STYLE AUTO PISTOLS

Caliber: 9mm Para., 38 Super, 40 S&W, 45 ACP. **Barrel:** 4" or 5". **Weight:** NA. **Length:** NA. **Grips:** Double-diamond, checkered cocobolo or black synthetic. **Sights:** Bo-Mar low-mount adjustable, Novak fixed with tritium inserts, Heine fixed or Rock River scope mount; dovetail front blade. **Features:** Chrome-moly, machined steel frame and slide; slide serrated front and rear; aluminum speed trigger with 3.5-4 lb. pull; national match KART barrel; lowered and flared ejection port; tuned and polished extractor; beavertail grip safety; beveled mag. well. Other frames offered. Made in U.S. by Rock River Arms Inc.

Price: Elite Commando (4" barrel, Novak tritium sights) . . from **$1,175.00**
Price: Standard Match (5" barrel, Heine fixed sights). . . . . from **$1,025.00**
Price: National Match Hardball (5" barrel, Bo-Mar adj. sights)
. . . . from **$1,275.00**
Price: Bullseye Wadcutter (5" barrel, Rock River slide scope
mount) . . . . from **$1,380.00**
Price: Basic Limited Match (5" barrel, Bo-Mar adj. sights)
. . . . from **$1,395.00**
Price: Limited Match (5" barrel, guaranteed 1-1/2" groups
at 50 yards). . . . . from **$1,795.00**
Price: Hi-Cap Basic Limited (5" barrel, four frame choices)
. . . . from **$1,895.00**
Price: Ultimate Match Achiever (5" bbl. with compensator,
mount and Aimpoint) . . . . from **$2,255.00**
Price: Match Master Steel (5" bbl. with compensator,
mount and Aimpoint) . . . . from **$2,355.00**

Rock River Arms
Bullseye Wadcutter

Rock River Arms
Ultimate Match Achiever

Rock River Arms
Basic Limited Match

Rock River Arms
Limited Match

Rock River Arms
Match Master Steel

Springfield Pro

Vektor SP1 Target

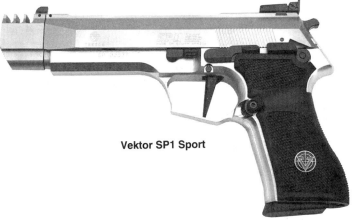

Vektor SP1 Sport

SPRINGFIELD ARMORY 1911-STYLE AUTO PISTOLS

Caliber: 9mm Para., 8- or 9-shot magazine; 45 ACP, 6-, 7-, 8- or 10-shot magazine; 45 Super, 7-shot magazine. **Barrel:** 3.5", 3.9", 5", 6". **Weight:** 25 to 41 oz. **Length:** 7" to 9.5" overall. **Grips:** Checkered cocobolo or synthetic. **Sights:** Novak low-profile, Novak tritium or adjustable target rear; blade front. **Features:** Parkerized, blued, stainless steel or bi-tone frame and slide; lightweight Delta hammer; match trigger; front and rear slide serrations; hammer-forged, air-gauged barrel; beavertail grip safety; extended thumb safety; beveled magazine well. Made in U.S. From Springfield Inc.

Price: Mil-Spec 1911-A1 (5" barrel, fixed three-dot sights, parkerized finish) **$610.00**

Price: Full-Size 1911-A1 (5" bbl., Novak fixed or adj. sights, steel or alum. frame). from **$648.00**

Price: Champion 1911-A1 (3.9" bbl., Novak fixed sights, steel or alum. frame). from **$669.00**

Price: Compact 1911-A1 (3.9" bbl., Novak fixed sights, alum. frame) . . . . from **$678.00**

Price: Ultra-Compact 1911-A1 (3.5" bbl., Novak fixed sights, steel or alum. frame). . . . . from **$669.00**

Price: Trophy Match 1911-A1 (5" or 6" bbl., adj. sights, blued or stainless) . . . . from **$1,089.00**

Price: Long Slide 1911-A1 (6" bbl., adj. sights, stainless, 45 ACP or 45 Super) . . . . from **$849.00**

Price: Full Size High Capacity (5" bbl., Novak fixed sights, two 10-shot magazines) . . . . from **$733.00**

Price: Ultra Compact High Capacity (3.5" bbl., Novak fixed sights, 10-shot mag.) . . . . from **$759.00**

Price: Tactical Response Pistol (3.9" or 5", Novak fixed sights, Teflon or stain.). . . . . from **$1,289.00**

Price: Professional Model (5" bbl., Novak three-dot tritium sights, Black-T finish). . . . . from **$2,395.00**

STI 2011 AUTO PISTOLS

Caliber: 9mm Para., 9x23, 38 Super, 40 S&W, 40 Super, 10mm, 45 ACP. **Barrel:** 3.4", 5", 5.5", 6". **Weight:** 28 to 44 oz. **Length:** 7" to 9-5/8" overall. **Grips:** Checkered, double-diamond rosewood or glass-filled nylon polymer (six colors). **Sights:** STI, Novak or Heine adjustable rear, blade front. **Features:** Updated version of 1911-style auto pistol; serrated slide, front and rear; STI skeletonized trigger; ambidextrous or single-sided thumb safety; blue or hard-chrome finish; etched logo and model name. From STI International.

Price: Competitor (38 Super, 5.5" barrel, C-More Rail Scope and mount) . . . . from **$2,499.00**

Price: Trojan (9mm, 45 ACP, 40 Super, 40 S&W; 5" or 6" barrel) . . . . from **$970.00**

Price: Edge 5.0" (40 S&W or 45 ACP; 5" barrel) . . . . from **$1,776.00**

Price: Eagle 5.0" (9mm, 9x23, 38 Super, 40 S&W, 10mm, 40 Super, 45 ACP; 5" bbl.) . . . . from **$1,699.00**

Price: Eagle 6.0" (9mm, 38 Super, 40 S&W, 10mm, 40 Super, 45 ACP; 6" bbl.) . . . . from **$1,795.40**

Price: BLS9/BLS40 (9mm, 40 S&W; 3.4" barrel, full-length grip) . . . . from **$843.70**

STI COMPACT AUTO PISTOLS

Caliber: 9mm Para., 40 S&W. **Barrel:** 3.4". **Weight:** 28 oz. **Length:** 7" overall. **Grips:** Checkered double-diamond rosewood. **Sights:** Heine Low Mount fixed rear, slide integral front. **Features:** Similar to STI 2011 models except has compact frame, 7-shot magazine in 9mm (6-shot in 40 cal.), single-sided thumb safety, linkless barrel lockup system, matte blue finish. From STI International.

Price: (9mm Para. or 40 S&W) . . . . from **$746.50**

VEKTOR SP1/SP2 AUTO PISTOLS

Caliber: 9mm Para., 40 S&W; 10-shot magazine. **Barrel:** 4", 4-5/8", 5", 5-7/8". **Weight:** 31.5 to 42 oz. **Length:** 7-1/2" to 11" overall. **Grips:** Black synthetic. **Sights:** Fixed, three-dot adjustable or scope mount; blade front. **Features:** Cold forged, polygon-rifled barrel; Aluminum alloy frame with machined steel slide; blued, anodized or nickel finish. Imported from South Africa by Vektor USA.

Price: SP1 Service Pistol (9mm Para., 4-5/8" barrel, fixed sights) . . . . from **$619.95**

Price: SP2 Service Pistol (40 S&W, 4-5/8" barrel, fixed sights) . . . . from **$649.95**

Price: SP1 Sport Pistol (9mm, 5" bbl. with compensator, combat sight, trigger stop) . . . . from **$849.95**

Price: SP1 Target Pistol (9mm, 5-7/8" bbl. with compensator, three-dot sights, adj. trigger) **$1,199.95**

Price: SP1 Ultra Sport (9mm, 5-7/8" bbl. with comp., integral Weaver rail, polymer mount) **$1,949.95**

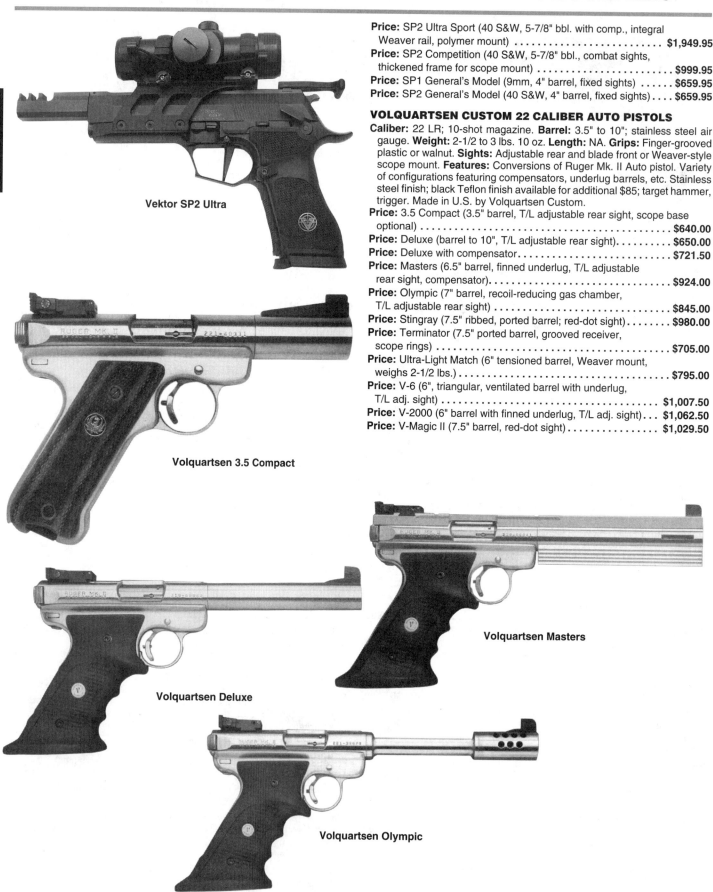

Price: SP2 Ultra Sport (40 S&W, 5-7/8" bbl. with comp., integral Weaver rail, polymer mount) **$1,949.95**
Price: SP2 Competition (40 S&W, 5-7/8" bbl., combat sights, thickened frame for scope mount) **$999.95**
Price: SP1 General's Model (9mm, 4" barrel, fixed sights) **$659.95**
Price: SP2 General's Model (40 S&W, 4" barrel, fixed sights) **$659.95**

VOLQUARTSEN CUSTOM 22 CALIBER AUTO PISTOLS

Caliber: 22 LR; 10-shot magazine. **Barrel:** 3.5" to 10"; stainless steel air gauge. **Weight:** 2-1/2 to 3 lbs. 10 oz. **Length:** NA. **Grips:** Finger-grooved plastic or walnut. **Sights:** Adjustable rear and blade front or Weaver-style scope mount. **Features:** Conversions of Ruger Mk. II Auto pistol. Variety of configurations featuring compensators, underlug barrels, etc. Stainless steel finish; black Teflon finish available for additional $85; target hammer, trigger. Made in U.S. by Volquartsen Custom.
Price: 3.5 Compact (3.5" barrel, T/L adjustable rear sight, scope base optional) **$640.00**
Price: Deluxe (barrel to 10", T/L adjustable rear sight) **$650.00**
Price: Deluxe with compensator **$721.50**
Price: Masters (6.5" barrel, finned underlug, T/L adjustable rear sight, compensator) **$924.00**
Price: Olympic (7" barrel, recoil-reducing gas chamber, T/L adjustable rear sight) **$845.00**
Price: Stingray (7.5" ribbed, ported barrel; red-dot sight) **$980.00**
Price: Terminator (7.5" ported barrel, grooved receiver, scope rings) **$705.00**
Price: Ultra-Light Match (6" tensioned barrel, Weaver mount, weighs 2-1/2 lbs.) **$795.00**
Price: V-6 (6", triangular, ventilated barrel with underlug, T/L adj. sight) **$1,007.50**
Price: V-2000 (6" barrel with finned underlug, T/L adj. sight) ... **$1,062.50**
Price: V-Magic II (7.5" barrel, red-dot sight) **$1,029.50**

Vektor SP2 Ultra

Volquartsen 3.5 Compact

Volquartsen Deluxe

Volquartsen Masters

Volquartsen Olympic

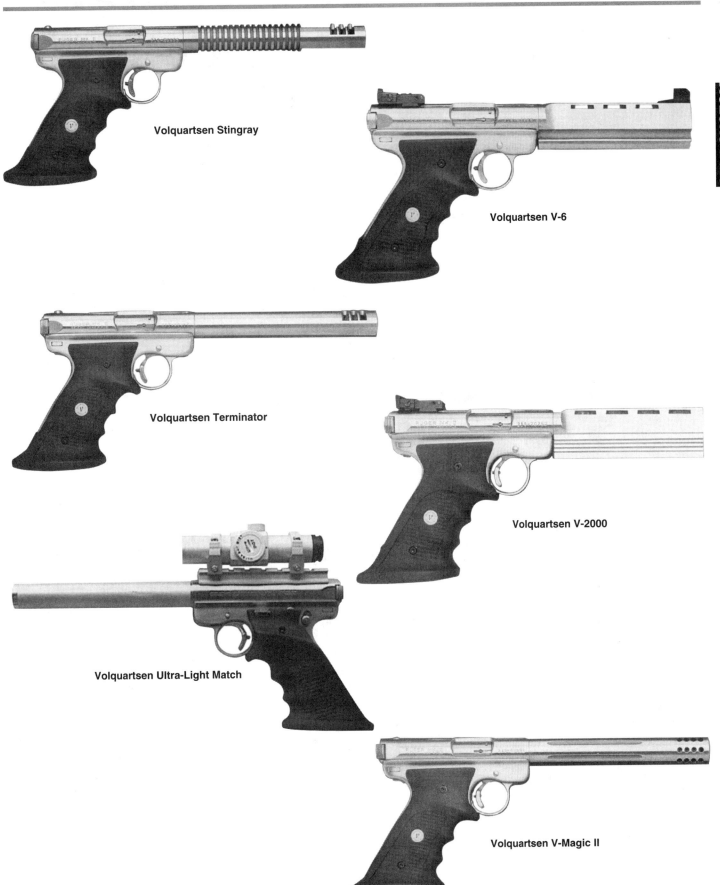

Volquartsen Stingray

Volquartsen V-6

Volquartsen Terminator

Volquartsen V-2000

Volquartsen Ultra-Light Match

Volquartsen V-Magic II

SEMI-CUSTOM

500 Linebaugh

44 Linebaugh Long

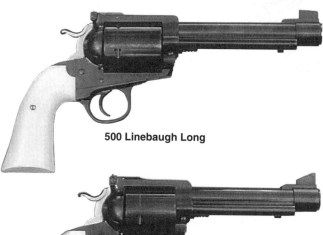

500 Linebaugh Long

500 Linebaugh

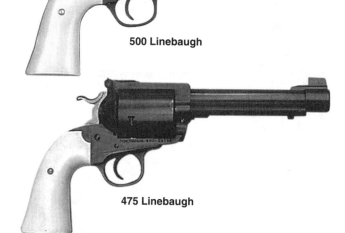

500 Linebaugh

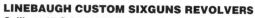

475 Linebaugh

LINEBAUGH CUSTOM SIXGUNS REVOLVERS

Caliber: 45 Colt, 44 Linebaugh Long, 458 Linebaugh, 475 Linebaugh, 500 Linebaugh, 500 Linebaugh Long, 445 Super Mag. **Barrel:** 4-3/4", 5-1/2", 6", 7-1/2"; other lengths available. **Weight:** NA. **Length:** NA. **Grips:** Dustin Linebaugh Custom made to customer's specs. **Sights:** Bowen steel rear or factory Ruger; blade front. **Features:** Conversions using customer's Ruger Blackhawk Bisley and Vaquero Bisley frames. Made in U.S. by Linebaugh Custom Sixguns.
Price: Small 45 Colt conversion (rechambered cyl., new barrel)
. . . . from **$1,000.00**
Price: Large 45 Colt conversion (oversized cyl., new barrel, 5- or 6-shot) . . . . from **$1,500.00**
Price: 475 Linebaugh, 500 Linebaugh conversions . . . . . . from **$1,500.00**
Price: Linebaugh and 445 Super Mag calibers on 357 Maximum frame . . . . from **$2,700.00**

GARY REEDER CUSTOM GUNS REVOLVERS

Caliber: 357 Magnum, 45 Colt, 44-40, 41 Magnum, 44 Magnum, 454 Casull, 475 Linebaugh, 500 Linebaugh. **Barrel:** 2-1/2" to 12". **Weight:** Varies by model. **Length:** Varies by model. **Grips:** Black Cape buffalo horn, laminated walnut, simulated pearl, others. **Sights:** Notch fixed or adjustable rear, blade or ramp front. **Features:** Custom conversions of Ruger Vaquero, Blackhawk Bisley and Super Blackhawk frames. Jeweled hammer and trigger, tuned action, model name engraved on barrel, additional engraving on frame and cylinder, integral muzzle brake, finish available in high-polish or satin stainless steel or black Chromex finish. Also available on customer's gun at reduced cost. Other models available. Made in U.S. by Gary Reeder Custom Guns.
Price: Gamblers Classic (2-1/2" bbl., engraved cards and dice, no ejector rod housing) . . . . from **$995.00**
Price: Tombstone Classic (3-1/2" bbl. with gold bands, notch sight, birdshead grips) . . . . from **$750.00**
Price: Doc Holliday Classic (3-1/2" bbl., engraved cards and dice, white pearl grips) . . . . from **$750.00**
Price: Ultimate Vaquero (engraved barrel, frame and cylinder, made to customer specs) . . . . from **$750.00**
Price: Black Widow (4-5/8" bbl., black Chromex finish, black widow spider engraving) . . . . from **$995.00**
Price: Cowboy Classic (stainless finish, cattle brand engraved, limited to 100 guns) . . . . from **$995.00**
Price: African Hunter (6" bbl., with or without muzzle brake, 475 or 500 Linebaugh) . . . . from **$1,395.00**
Price: Alaskan Survivalist (3" bbl., Redhawk frame, engraved bear, 45 Colt or 44 Magnum) . . . . from **$995.00**
Price: Master Hunter (7-1/2" bbl. with muzzle brake, Super Redhawk frame, scope rings) . . . . from **$995.00**
Price: Ultimate Back-Up (3-1/2" bbl., fixed sights, choice of animal engraving, 454 Casull) . . . . from **$1,995.00**

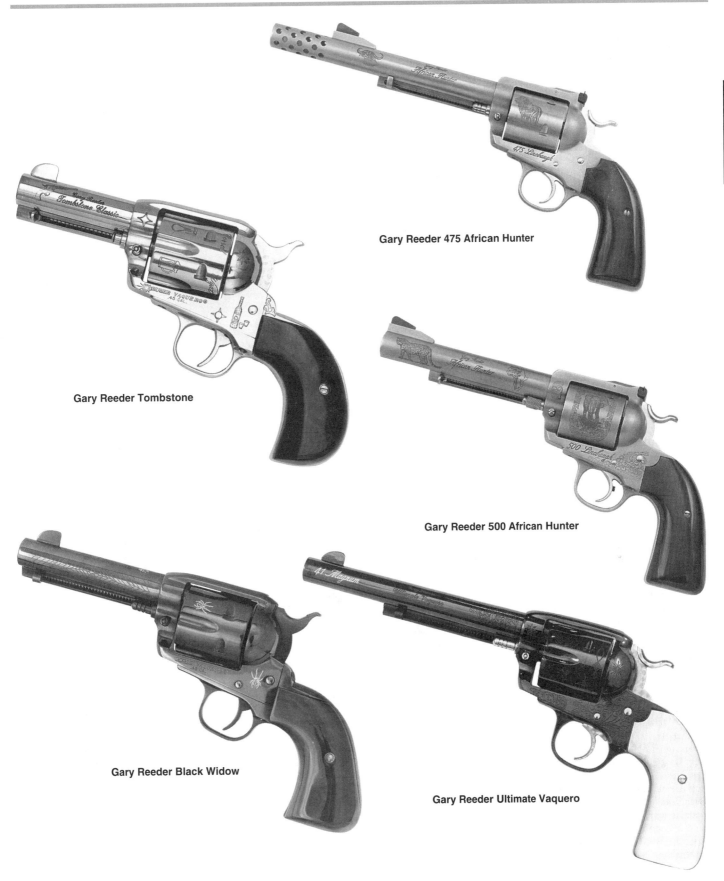

Gary Reeder 475 African Hunter

Gary Reeder Tombstone

Gary Reeder 500 African Hunter

Gary Reeder Black Widow

Gary Reeder Ultimate Vaquero

SEMI-CUSTOM

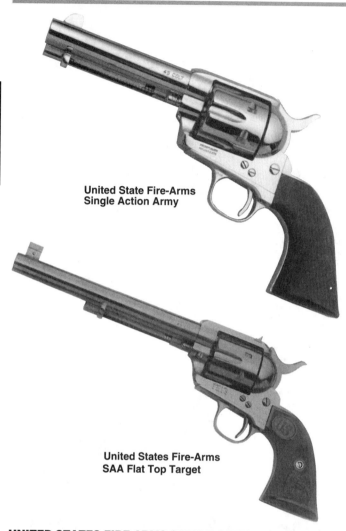

**United State Fire-Arms
Single Action Army**

**United States Fire-Arms
SAA Flat Top Target**

**United States Fire-Arms
SAA Bisley**

**United States Fire-Arms
Omni-Snubnose**

**United States Fire-Arms
Omni-Potent Six Shooter**

UNITED STATES FIRE-ARMS SINGLE-ACTION REVOLVERS

Caliber: 32 WCF, 38 Special, 38 WCF, 41 Colt, 44 WCF, 44 Special, 45 Colt, **Barrel:** 2", 3", 4-3/4", 5-1/2", 7-1/2", 16". **Weight:** NA. **Length:** NA. **Grips:** Hard rubber, rosewood, stag, pearl, ivory, ivory Micarta, smooth walnut, burled walnut and checkered walnut. **Sights:** Notch rear, blade front. **Features:** Hand-fitted replicas of Colt single-action revolvers. Full Dome Blue, Dome Blue, Armory Blue (gray-blue), Old Armory Bone Case (color casehardened) and nickel plate finishes. Carved and scrimshaw grips, engraving and gold inlays offered. Made in U.S. From United States Fire-Arms Mfg. Co.

Price: Single Action Army (32 WCF, 38 Spec., 38 WCF, 41 Colt, 45 Colt, 44 Spec., 44 WCF) **$919.00**

Price: SAA Flat Top Target (extended blade front, drift-adj. rear sights . . . . from **$995.00**

Price: SAA Bisley (Bisley grip and hammer) . . . . from **$995.00**

Price: Omni-Snubnose (2" or 3" barrel, lanyard loop, 45 Colt only) . . . . from **$1,120.00**

Price: Omni-Potent Six Shooter (lanyard loop on grip). . . . from **$1,125.00**

Price: New Buntline Special (16" bbl., skeleton shoulder stock, case, scabbard) . . . . from **$2,199.00**

Price: China Camp Cowboy Action Gun (4-3/4", 5-1/2" or 7-1/2" bbl., Silver Steel finish) . . . . from **$989.00**

Price: Henry Nettleton Cavalry Revolver (5-1/2" or 7-1/2" bbl., 45 Colt only) . . . . from **$1,125.00**

Price: U.S. 1851 Navy Conversion (7-1/2" bbl., color casehardened frame, 38 Spec. only) . . . . from **$1,499.00**

Price: U.S. Pre-War (SAA, Old Armory Bone Case or Armory Blue finish) . . . . from **$1,175.00**

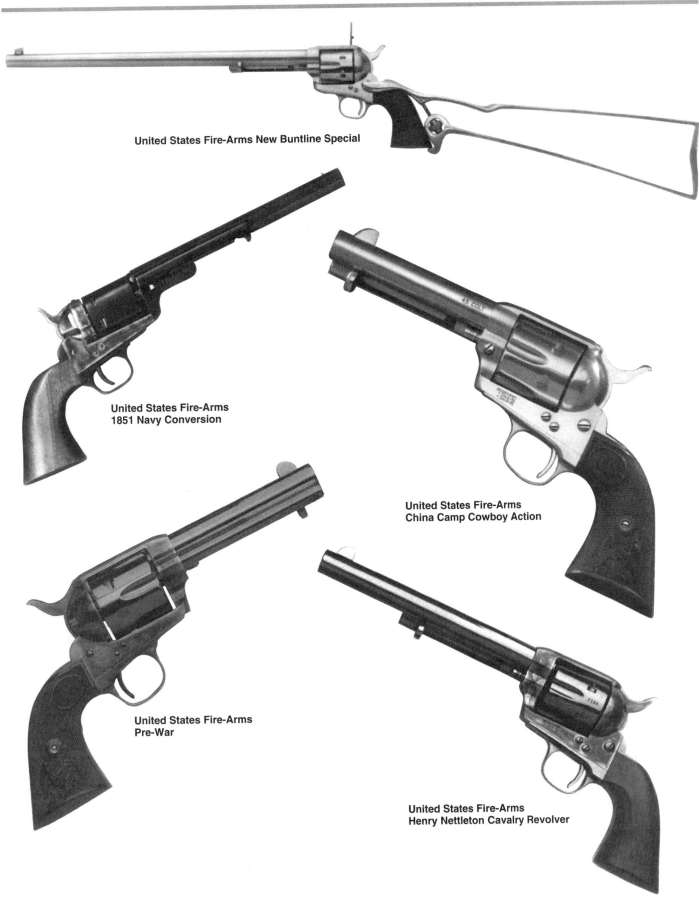

United States Fire-Arms New Buntline Special

United States Fire-Arms
1851 Navy Conversion

United States Fire-Arms
China Camp Cowboy Action

United States Fire-Arms
Pre-War

United States Fire-Arms
Henry Nettleton Cavalry Revolver

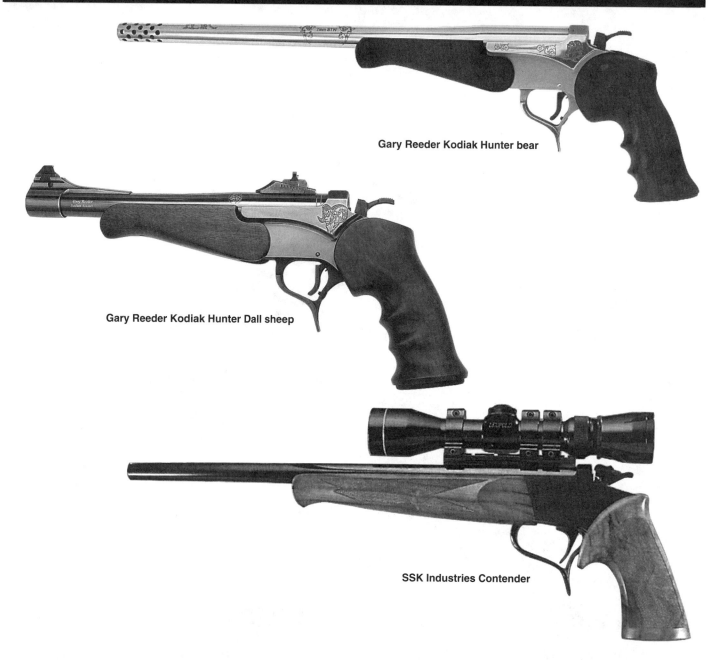

Gary Reeder Kodiak Hunter bear

Gary Reeder Kodiak Hunter Dall sheep

SSK Industries Contender

GARY REEDER CUSTOM GUNS
CONTENDER AND ENCORE PISTOLS

Caliber: 22 Cheetah, 218 Bee, 22 K-Hornet, 22 Hornet, 218 Mashburn Bee, 22-250 Improved, 6mm/284, 7mm STW, 7mm GNR, 30 GNR, 338 GNR, 300 Win. Magnum, 338 Win. Magnum, 350 Rem. Magnum, 358 STA, 375 H&H, 378 GNR, 416 Remington, 416 GNR, 450 GNR, 475 Linebaugh, 500 Linebaugh, 50 Alaskan, 50 AE, 454 Casull; others available. **Barrel:** 8" to 15" (others available). **Weight:** NA. **Length:** Varies with barrel length. **Sights:** Express-style adjustable rear and barrel band front (Kodiak Hunter); none furnished most models. **Features:** Offers complete guns and barrels in the T/C Contender and Encore. Integral muzzle brake, engraved animals and model name, tuned action, high-polish or satin stainless steel or black Chromex finish. Made in U.S. by Gary Reeder Custom Guns.
Price: Kodiak Hunter (50 AE or 454 Casull, Kodiak bear and Dall sheep engravings) . . . . from **$995.00**
Price: Ultimate Encore (15" bbl. with muzzle brake, grizzly bear engraving) . . . . from **$995.00**

SSK INDUSTRIES CONTENDER AND ENCORE PISTOLS

Caliber: More than 200, including most standard pistol and rifle calibers, as well as 226 JDJ, 6mm JDJ, 257 JDJ, 6.5mm JDJ, 7mm JDJ, 6.5mm Mini-Dreadnaught, 30-06 JDJ, 280 JDJ, 375 JDJ, 6mm Whisper, 300 Whisper and 338 Whisper. **Barrel:** 10" to 26"; blued or stainless; variety of configurations. **Weight:** Varies with barrel length and features. **Length:** Varies with barrel length. **Grips:** Pachmayr, wood models available. **Features:** Offers frames, barrels and complete guns in the T/C Contender and Encore. Fluted, diamond, octagon and round barrels; flatside Contender frames; chrome-plating; muzzle brakes; trigger jobs; variety of stocks and forends; sights and optics. Made in U.S. by SSK Industries.
Price: Blued Contender frame . . . . from **$263.00**
Price: Stainless Contender frame . . . . from **$290.00**
Price: Blued Encore frame . . . . from **$290.00**
Price: Stainless Encore frame . . . . from **$318.00**
Price: Contender barrels . . . . from **$315.00**
Price: Encore barrels . . . . from **$340.00**

Ed Brown 702 Savanna

Ed Brown 702 Varmint

ED BROWN CUSTOM BOLT-ACTION RIFLES

Caliber: 222, 223, 22-250, 220 Swift, 243, 243 Ackley Imp., 25-06, 270 Win., 280 Rem., 280 Ackley Imp., 6mm, 6.5/284, 7mm/08, 7mm Rem. Mag., 7STW, 30/06, 308, 300 Win. Mag., 338 Win. Mag., 375 H&H, 404 Jeffery, 416 Rem. Mag., 416 Rigby, 458 Win. Mag. **Barrel:** 21", 24", 26". **Weight:** NA. **Length:** NA. **Stock:** HS Precision, Hi-Tech Specialties or McMillan synthetic; swivel studs; recoil pad. Sights: None furnished (option on Model 76 Bushveld); scope rings and base furnished. **Features:** Machined receiver; hand-fitted bolt with welded handle; M16-type extractor (Mauser-type extractor on Bushveld); three-position safety; trigger adjustable for pull and overtravel; match-quality, hand-lapped barrel with deep countersunk crowning. Made in U.S. by Ed Brown Products.
Price: Model 702 Savanna long-action repeater (lightweight 24" barrel) . . . . from **$2,495.00**
Price: Model 702 Tactical long-action repeater (heavy contour 26" barrel). . . . . from **$2,795.00**
Price: Model 702 Ozark short-action repeater (lightweight 21" barrel) . . . . from **$2,195.00**
Price: Model 702 Varmint short-action single shot (med. 26" or hvy. 24") . . . . from **$2,195.00**
Price: Model 702 Light Tactical short-action repeater (med. 21" barrel) . . . . from **$2,495.00**
Price: Model 76 Bushveld dangerous game rifle (24" med. Or heavy barrel) . . . . from **$3,000.00**

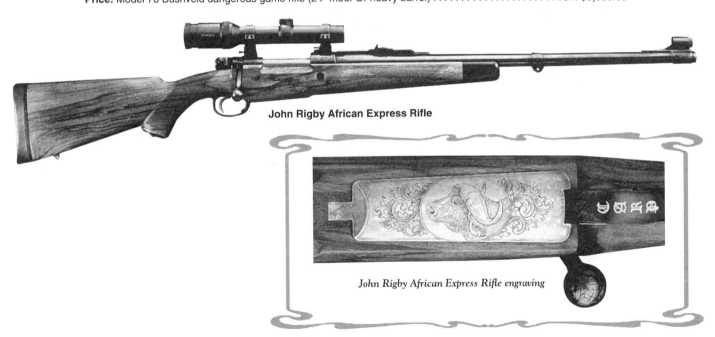

John Rigby African Express Rifle

John Rigby African Express Rifle engraving

JOHN RIGBY CUSTOM AFRICAN EXPRESS RIFLE

Caliber: 375 H&H Magnum, 416 Rigby, 450 Rigby, 458 Winchester, 505 Gibbs. **Barrel:** To customer specs. **Weight:** NA. **Length:** To customer specs. **Stock:** Customer's choice. Sights: Express-type rear, hooded ramp front; scope mounts offered. **Features:** Handcrafted bolt-action rifle built to customer specifications. Variety of engraving and stock wood options available. Imported from England by John Rigby & Co.
Price: African Express Rifle. . . . . from **$15,500.00**

SEMI-CUSTOM

Remington 700 APR

Remington 700 AWR

REMINGTON MODEL 700 CUSTOM SHOP RIFLES

Caliber: 270 Win., 280 Rem., 30-06, 7mm Rem. Mag., 7mm STW, 300 Win. Mag., 300 Wea. Mag., 338 Win. Mag., 8mm Rem. Mag., 35 Whelen, 375 H&H Mag., 416 Rem. Mag., 458 Win. Mag. **Barrel:** 22", 24", 26". **Weight:** 6 lbs. 6 oz. to 9 lbs. **Length:** 44-1/4" to 46-1/2" overall. **Stock:** Laminated hardwood, walnut or Kevlar-reinforced fiberglass. **Sights:** Adjustable rear (Safari models); all receivers drilled and tapped for scope mounts. **Features:** Black matte, satin blue or uncolored stainless steel finish; hand-fitted action is epoxy-bedded to stock; tuned trigger; bolt-supported extractor for sure extraction; fancy wood and other options available. Made in U.S. by Remington Arms Co.
Price: Custom KS Mountain Rifle (24" barrel, synthetic stock, 6-3/4 lbs. in mag. cals.) . . . . from **$1,221.00**
Price: Custom KS Safari Stainless (22" barrel, synthetic stock, 9 lbs.) . . . . from **$1,410.00**
Price: Safari Classic or Monte Carlo (24" barrel, walnut stock, polished blue finish) . . . . from **$1,225.00**
Price: APR (African Plains Rifle — 26" barrel, laminated stock, satin blue finish) . . . . from **$1,593.00**
Price: AWR (Alaskan Wilderness Rifle — 24" barrel, syn. stock, black matte finish) . . . . from **$1,480.00**

REMINGTON MODEL 40-X CUSTOM SHOP TARGET RIFLES

Caliber: 22 LR, 22 BR Rem., 222 Rem., 223 Rem., 22-250, 220 Swift, 6mm BR Rem., 6mm Rem., 243 Win., 25-06, 260 Rem., 7mm BR Rem., 7mm Rem. Mag., 7mm STW, 308 Win., 30-06, 300 Win. Mag. **Barrel:** 24", 27-1/4"; various twist rates offered. **Weight:** 9-3/4 to 11 lbs. **Length:** 40" to 47" overall. **Stock:** Walnut, laminated wood or Kevlar-reinforced fiberglass. **Sights:** None; receiver drilled and tapped for scope mounts. **Features:** Single shot or 5-shot repeater; carbon steel or stainless steel receiver; externally adjustable trigger (1-1/2 to 3-1/2 lbs.); rubber butt pad. From Remington Arms Co.
Price: 40-XB Rangemaster (27-1/4" bbl., walnut stock, forend rail with hand stop) . . . . from **$1,565.00**
Price: 40-XB Rangemaster with laminated thumbhole stock . . . . from **$1,768.00**
Price: 40-XB KS (27-1/4" bbl., black synthetic stock) . . . . from **$1,768.00**
Price: 40-XBBR KS (24" bbl., Remington green synthetic stock with straight comb) . . . . from **$1,742.00**
Price: 40-XC KS (308, 24" bbl., gray synthetic stock with adj. comb) . . . . from **$1,742.00**

REMINGTON MODEL SEVEN CUSTOM SHOP RIFLES

Caliber: 222 Rem., 223 Rem., 22-250 Rem., 243 Win., 6mm Rem., 250 Savage, 257 Roberts, 260 Rem., 308 Win., 7mm-08 Rem., 35 Rem., 350 Rem. Mag. **Barrel:** 20". **Weight:** 5-3/4 to 6-1/2 lbs. **Length:** 39-1/2" overall. **Stock:** Laminated hardwood or Kevlar-reinforced fiberglass. **Sights:** Adjustable ramp rear, hooded blade front. **Features:** Hand-fitted action; epoxy bedded; deep blue or non-reflective black matte finish; drilled and tapped for scope mounts. From Remington Arms Co.
Price: Model Seven MS (Mannlicher stock, deep blue finish) . . . . from **$1,236.00**
Price: Model Seven Custom KS (synthetic stock, matte finish) . . . . from **$1,221.00**

TIME PRECISION BOLT-ACTION RIFLES

Caliber: 22 LR, 222, 223, 308, 378, 300 Win. Mag., 416 Rigby, others. **Barrel:** NA. **Weight:** 10 lbs. and up. **Length:** NA. **Stock:** Fiberglass. **Sights:** None; receiver drilled and tapped for scope mount. **Features:** Thirty different action types offered, including single shots and repeaters for bench rest, varmint and big-game hunting. Machined chrome-moly action; three-position safety; Shilen match trigger (other triggers available); twin cocking cams; dual firing pin. Built to customer specifications. From Time Precision.
Price: 22 LR Bench Rest Rifle (Shilen match-grade stainless steel bbl., fiberglass stock) . . . . from **$2,202.00**
Price: 22 LR Target Rifle . . . . from **$2,220.00**
Price: 22 LR Sporter . . . . from **$1,980.00**
Price: Hunting Rifle (calibers to 30-06) . . . . from **$2,202.00**
Price: Hunting Rifle (7mm Rem. Mag., 300 Win. Mag., 338 Win. Mag.) . . . . from **$2,322.00**

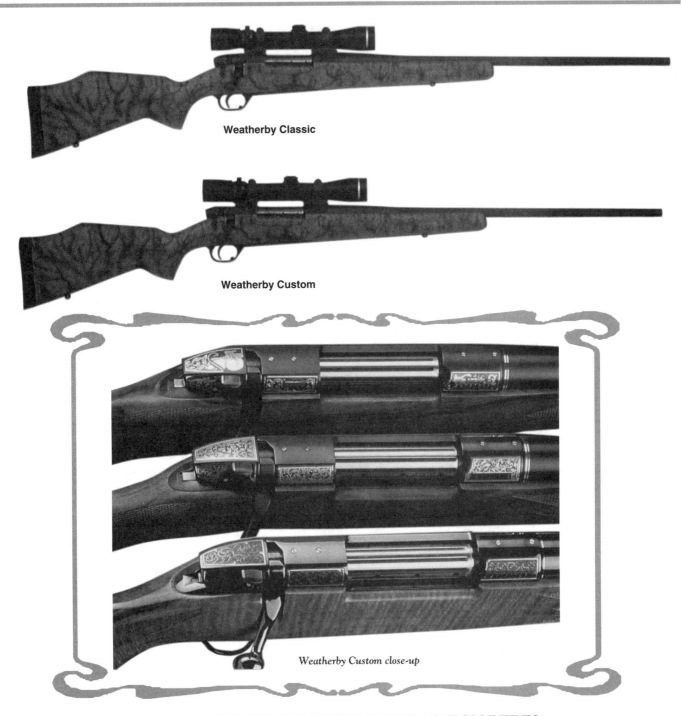

Weatherby Classic

Weatherby Custom

Weatherby Custom close-up

WEATHERBY CUSTOM SHOP BOLT-ACTION RIFLES

Caliber: 257 Wby. Mag., 270 Wby. Mag., 7mm Wby. Mag., 300 Wby. Mag., 340 Wby. Mag., 375 H&H Mag., 378 Wby. Mag., 416 Wby. Mag., 460 Wby. Mag. **Barrel:** 24", 26", 28". **Weight:** NA. **Length:** NA. **Stock:** Monte Carlo, modified Monte Carlo or Classic design in Exhibition- or Exhibition Special Select grades of claro or French walnut; injection-molded synthetic in Snow Camo, Alpine Camo or Dark Timber colors. **Sights:** Quarter-rib rear with one standing and one folding leaf, hooded ramp front (Safari Grade); drilled and tapped for scope mount. **Features:** Rosewood or ebony pistol-grip caps with inlaid diamonds in rosewood, walnut or maple; three grades of engraving patterns for receiver, bolt and handle; gold inlays; wooden inlaid buttstock, forearm and magazine box; three grades of engraved and gold inlaid rings and bases; canvas/leather, solid leather or leather with oak trim case. From the Weatherby Custom Shop.
Price: Classic Custom (bead-blast blue finish, checkered, oil-finished French walnut stock) **$5,099.000**
Price: Safari Grade (engr. floorplate, oil-finished French wal. stock w/fleur-de-lis checkering.) **$5,199.00**
Price: Crown (engr., inlaid floorplate, engr. bbl. and receiver, hand-carved walnut stock) **$6,599.00**
Price: Outfitter Krieger (Krieger stainless steel bbl., Bell and Carlson syn. camo. stock) **$3,499.00**
Price: Outfitter Custom (standard barrel, Bell and Carlson syn. camo stock) . . . . from **$2,149.00**

BUSHMASTER AUTO RIFLES

Caliber: 223. **Barrel:** 16" regular or fluted, 20" regular, heavy or fluted, 24" heavy or fluted. **Weight:** 6.9 to 8.37 lbs. **Length:** 34.5" to 38.25" overall. **Stock:** Polymer. Sights: Fully adjustable dual flip-up aperture rear, blade front or picatinny rail for scope mount. **Features:** Versions of the AR-15 style rifle. Aircraft-quality aluminum receiver; chrome-lined barrel and chamber; chrome-moly-vanadium steel barrel with 1:9" twist; manganese phosphate matte finish; forged front sight; receiver takes down without tools; serrated, finger groove pistol grip. Made in U.S. by Bushmaster Firearms/Quality Parts Co.
Price: DCM Competition Rifle **$1,525.00**

LES BAER AR 223 AUTO RIFLES

Caliber: 223. **Barrel:** 16-1/4", 20", 22" or 24"; cryo-treated, stainless steel bench-rest grade. **Weight:** NA. **Length:** NA. **Stock:** Polymer. Sights: None; picatinny rail for scope mount. **Features:** Forged and machined upper and lower receiver; single- or double-stage adjustable trigger; free-float handguard; Bear Coat protective finish. Made in U.S. by Les Baer Custom.
Price: Ultimate Super Varmint (Jewell two-stage trigger, guar. to shoot 1/2 MOA groups) . . . . from **$1,989.00**
Price: Ultimate M4 Flattop (16-1/4" bbl., Ultra single-stage trigger, shoots 1 MOA groups) . . . . from **$2,195.00**
Price: Ultimate IPSC Action (20" bbl., Jewell two-stage trigger, shoots 1 MOA groups) . . . . from **$2,195.00**

SSK INDUSTRIES AR-15 RIFLES

Caliber: 223, 6mm PPC, 6.5mm PPC, Whisper and other wildcats. **Barrel:** 16-1/2" and longer (to order). **Weight:** NA. **Length:** NA. **Stock:** Black plastic. Sights: Blade front, adjustable rear (scopes and red-dot sights available). **Features:** Variety of designs to full match-grade guns offered. Customer's gun can be rebarreled or accurized. From SSK Industries.
Price: Complete AR-15 . . . . from **$1,500.00**
Price: A2 upper unit (front sight, short handguard **$1,100.00**
Price: Match Grade upper unit (bull barrel, tubular handguard, scope mount) **$1,100.00**

Volquartsen Ultra Light

VOLQUARTSEN CUSTOM 22 CALIBER AUTO RIFLES

Caliber: 22 LR, 22 Magnum. **Barrel:** 16-1/2" to 20"; stainless steel air gauge. **Weight:** 4-3/4 to 5-3/4 lbs. **Length:** NA. **Stock:** Synthetic or laminated. Sights: Not furnished; Weaver base provided. **Features:** Conversions of the Ruger 10/22 rifle. Tuned trigger with 2-1/2 to 3-1/2 lb. pull. Variety of configurations and features. From Volquartsen Custom.
Price: Ultra-Light (22 LR, 16-1/2" tensioned barrel, synthetic stock) . . . . from **$645.00**
Price: Grey Ghost (22 LR, 18-1/2" barrel, laminated wood stock) . . . . from **$665.00**
Price: Deluxe (22 LR, 20" barrel, laminated wood or fiberglass stock) . . . . from **$825.00**
Price: Mossad (22 LR, 20" fluted and ported barrel, fiberglass thumbhole stock) . . . . from **$945.00**
Price: VX-2500 (22 LR, 20" fluted and ported barrel, aluminum/fiberglass stock) . . . . from **$1,019.00**
Price: Volquartsen 22 LR (stainless steel receiver) . . . . from **$895.00**
Price: Volquartsen 22 Mag (22 WMR, stainless steel receiver) . . . . from **$925.00**

SEMI-CUSTOM

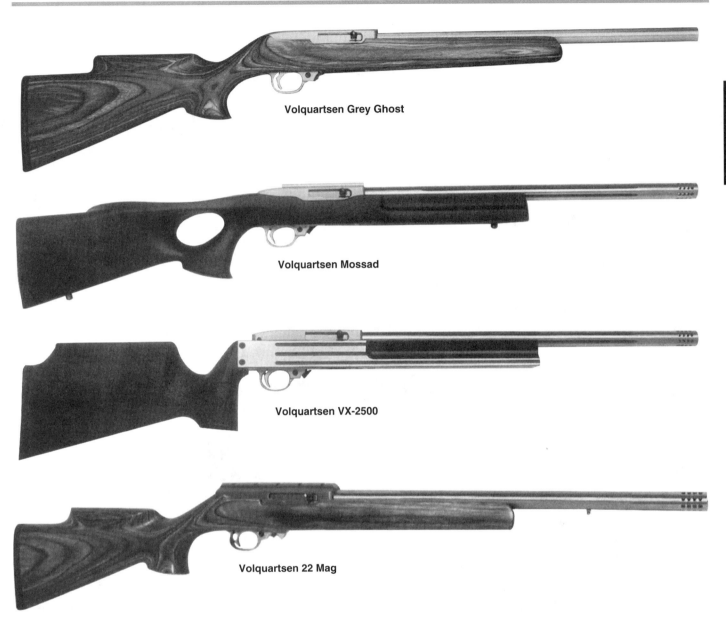

Volquartsen Grey Ghost

Volquartsen Mossad

Volquartsen VX-2500

Volquartsen 22 Mag

WHITE BARN WORKSHOP 22 CALIBER AUTO RIFLES

Caliber: 22 LR, 22 Magnum. **Barrel:** Bull, plain, fluted, tapered or fully compensated. **Weight:** NA. **Length:** NA. **Stock:** Laminated hardwood. Sights: None; Trinity Bridge Weaver base and other scope mounts offered. **Features:** Conversions of the Ruger 10/22 rifle. Tuned trigger; extended magazine release; quick bolt release; jeweled bolt; hand-lapped bore; Chief AJ logo. From White Barn Workshop.
Price: Standard Scout 10/22 (Scout barrel mount with Leupold scope, flash hider) . . . . from **$695.00**
Price: Bull Scout 10/22 (Douglas bull barrel, Scout barrel mount with Leupold scope) . . . . from **$995.00**
Price: Leader 10/22 (Trinity Bridge scope base and scope, laminated stock) . . . . from **$1,200.00**

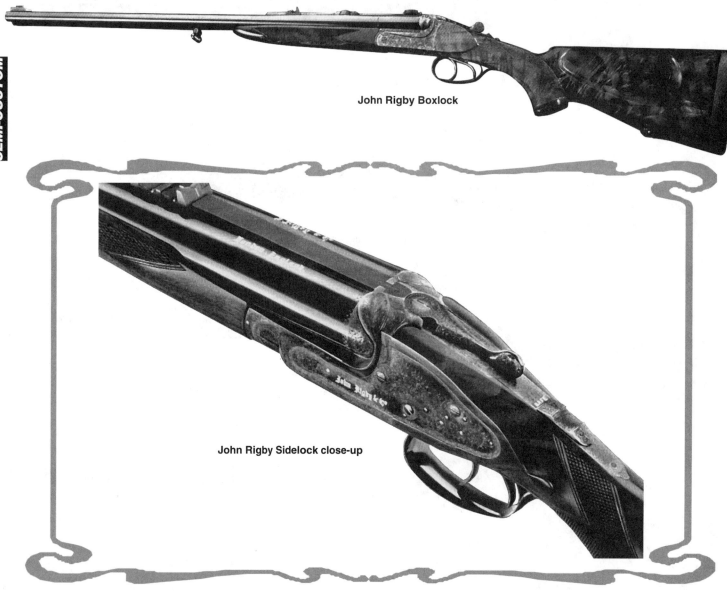

John Rigby Boxlock

John Rigby Sidelock close-up

BERETTA EXPRESS DOUBLE RIFLES

Caliber: 9.3x74R, 375 H&H Mag., 416 Rigby, 458 Win. Mag., 470 Nitro Express, 500 Nitro Express. **Barrel:** 23" to 25". **Weight:** 11 lbs. **Length:** NA. **Stock:** Hand-finished, hand-checkered walnut with cheek rest. Sights: Folding-leaf, Express-type rear, blade front. **Features:** High-strength steel action with reinforced receiver sides; top tang extends to stock comb for strength; double triggers (articulated front trigger and automatic blocking device eliminate chance of simultaneous discharge); hand-cut, stepped rib; engraved receiver; trapdoor compartment in stock for extra cartridges; spare front sights stored in pistol-grip cap. Imported from Italy by Beretta USA.
Price: SSO6 o/u (optional claw mounts for scope) . . . . from **$39,500.00**
Price: SSO6 EELL o/u (engraved game scenes or color case-hardened with gold inlays). . . . . from **$42,500.00**
Price: 455 s/s (color case-hardened action) . . . . from **$53,000.00**
Price: 455 EELL s/s (receiver engraved with big-game animals) . . . . from **$72,500.00**

JOHN RIGBY DOUBLE RIFLES

Caliber: 375 H&H, 500/416, 450 Nitro Express, 470 Nitro Express, 500 Nitro Express, 577 Nitro Express. **Barrel:** To customer specs. **Weight:** NA. **Length:** To customer specs. **Stock:** To customer specs. Sights: Dovetail, express-type sights; claw-foot scope mount available. **Features:** Handcrafted to customer specifications. Boxlock or sidelock action, hand-fitted; variety of engraving and other options offered. Imported from England by John Rigby & Co.
Price: Rigby 4th Century Boxlock . . . . from **$18,950.00**
Price: Rigby 4th Century Sidelock. . . . . from **$34,950.00**

Lone Star Silhouette

C. SHARPS ARMS RIFLES

Caliber: 22 Hornet, 30-40 Krag, 30-30, 348 Win., 40-65, 45-70, 45-90, 50-2-1/2", others. **Barrel:** 22" to 34". **Weight:** NA. **Length:** NA. **Stock:** Extra fancy American walnut. Sights: Buckhorn or tang rear, blade or globe with apertures and spirit level front. **Features:** Authentic replicas of Sharps rifles. Octagon or half-octagon hand-polished barrel; German silver nose cap; straight or pistol grip. Made in U.S. by C. Sharps Arms Co. Inc.
Price: New Model 1885 Highwall (machined steel receiver, mid-range tang sight). . . . . .from **$1,999.92**
Price: New Model 1885 Semi-Custom Highwall (silver-inlay pistol grip, single set trigger). . . . . .from **$2,560.12**
Price: New Model 1885 Custom Grade (silver-inlay pistol grip, extra fancy walnut stock) . . . . .from **$2,760.38**
Price: New Model 1875 Sporting Rifle (round barrel, buckhorn rear sight) . . . . .from **$1,309.29**
Price: New Model 1874 Sporting & Long Range Rifle (octagon bbl., long-range tang sight) . . . . .from **$2,542.80**
Price: New Model 1874 Custom Classic (half-octagon bbl., extra fancy walnut stock). . . . . .from **$3,242.09**
Price: New Model 1874 Custom Hartford (oct. bbl. w/Hartford collar, l.range tang sight) . . . . .from **$3,382,82**
Price: New Model 1874 Custom Long Range (oct. bbl. w/Hartford collar, l. range aper. sights). **$3,707.57**

LONE STAR ROLLING BLOCK RIFLES

Caliber: 30-40 Krag, 30-30, 32-40, 38-55, 40-50 SS, 40-50 BN, 40-65, 40-70 SS, 40-70 BN, 40-82, 40-90 SBN, 40-90 SS, 44-90 Rem. Sp., 45 Colt, 45-110 (3-1/4"), 45-110 (2-7/8"), 45-100, 45-90, 45-70, 50-70, 50-90. **Barrel:** 26" to 34". **Weight:** 6 to 11 lbs. **Length:** NA. **Stock:** American walnut. Sights: Buckhorn rear, blade or dovetail front. **Features:** Authentic replicas of Remington rolling block rifles. Round, tapered round, octagon, tapered octagon or half-octagon barrel; bone-pack, color case hardened action; drilled and tapped for vernier sight; single, single-set or double-set trigger; variety of sight, finish and engraving options. Fires blackpowder or factory ammo. Made in U.S. by Lone Star Rifle Co. Inc.
Price: No. 5 Sporting Rifle (30-30 or 30-40 Krag, 26" barrel, buckhorn rear sight) **$1,495.00**
Price: Cowboy Action Rifle (28" round barrel, buckhorn rear sight) **$1,495.00**
Price: Silhouette Rifle (32" or 34" round barrel, drilled and tapped for vernier sight) **$1,495.00**
Price: Sporting Rifle (straight grip, semi-crescent butt). . . . . .from **$2,200.00**
Price: Target Rifle (pistol grip, shotgun-type butt). . . . . .from **$2,200.00**

REMINGTON CUSTOM SHOP ROLLING BLOCK RIFLES

Caliber: 45-70. **Barrel:** 30". **Weight:** NA. **Length:** NA. **Stock:** American walnut. Sights: Buckhorn rear and blade front (optional tang-mounted vernier rear, globe with spirit level front). **Features:** Satin blue finish with case-colored receiver; single set trigger; steel Schnabel fore end tip; steel butt plate. From Remington Arms Co. Custom Gun Shop.
Price: No. 1 Mid-Range Sporter (round or half-octagon barrel). **$1,348.00**
Price: No. 1 Silhouette (heavy barrel with 1:18" twist; no sights) **$1,448.00**

SEMI-CUSTOM SHOTGUNS

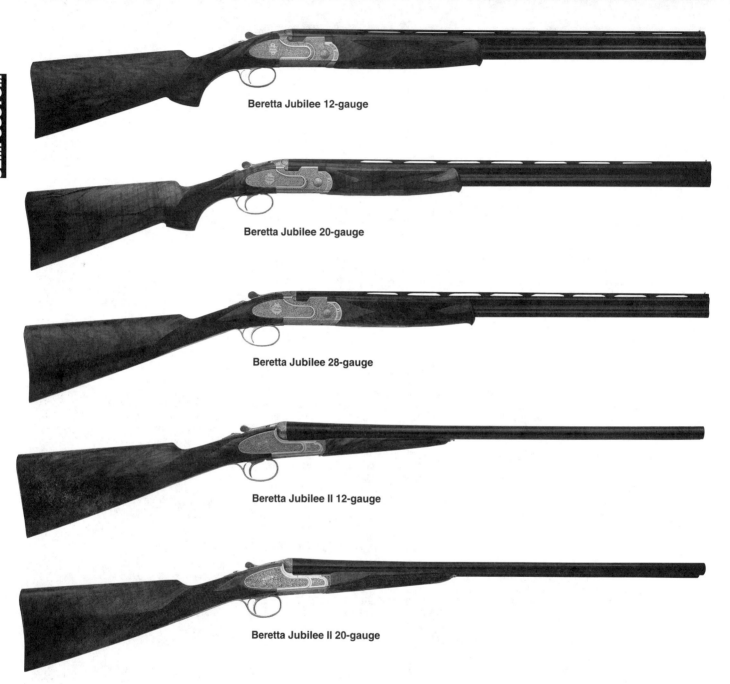

Beretta Jubilee 12-gauge

Beretta Jubilee 20-gauge

Beretta Jubilee 28-gauge

Beretta Jubilee II 12-gauge

Beretta Jubilee II 20-gauge

BERETTA PREMIUM GRADE SHOTGUNS

Gauge: 12, 20, 410, 3" chamber; 28, 2-3/4" chamber. **Barrel:** 26", 28", 30", 32". **Weight:** 5 to 7-1/2 lbs. **Length:** NA.
Stock: Highly figured English or American walnut; straight or pistol grip; hand-checkered. **Features:** Machined nickel-chrome-moly action, hand-fitted; cross-bolt breech lock; Boehler Antinit steel barrels with fixed chokes or Mobilchoke tubes; single selective or non-selective or double trigger; numerous stock and engraving options. From Beretta USA.
Price: Giubileo (Jubilee) o/u (engraved sideplates, trigger guard, safety and top lever)............ from **$13,750.00**
Price: Giubileo II (Jubilee II) s/s (English-style stock, engraved sideplates and fixtures)........... from **$13,750.00**
Price: ASE Deluxe o/u (engraved receiver and forend cap)................................. from **$24,000.00**
Price: SO5 Trap (single, non-selective trigger, heavy beavertail fore end, fixed chokes)........... from **$19,500.00**
Price: SO5 Skeet (26" or 28" bbl., heavy beavertail fore end, fixed chokes).................... from **$19,500.00**
Price: SO5 Sporting (single, selective trigger, Mobilchoke tubes)........................... from **$19,500.00**
Price: SO6 EELL o/u (engraved receiver with gold inlays, custom-fit stock)..................... from **$42,700.00**
Price: SO6 EL o/u (light English scroll engravings on receiver) .... from **$25,500.00**
Price: SO6 EESS o/u (enamel-colored receiver in green, red or blue, arabesque engravings) **$51,000.00**
Price: SO9 o/u (single, non-selective trigger, engraved receiver and fixtures) .... from **$44,500.00**

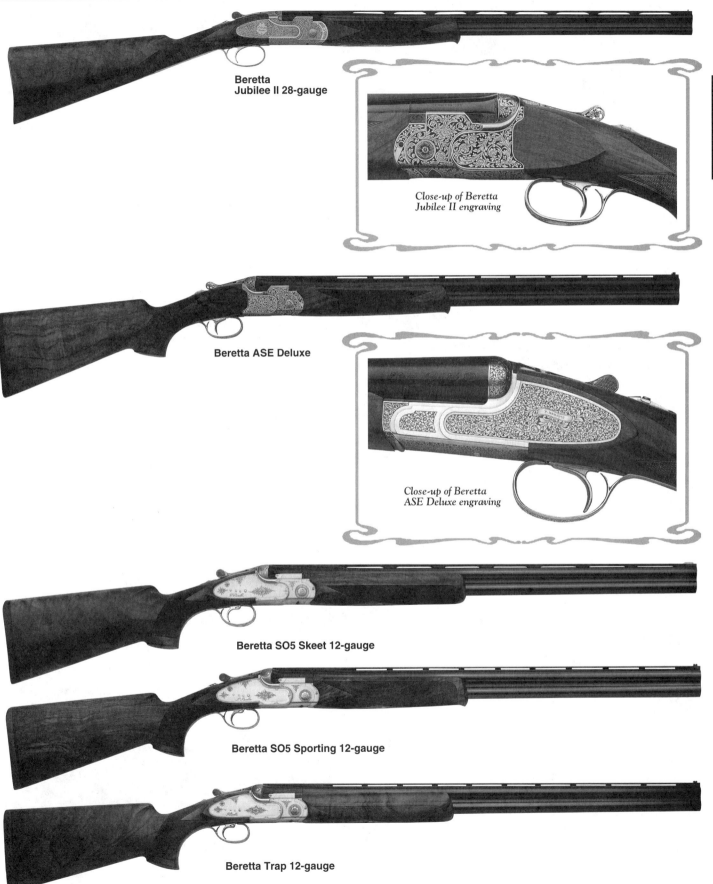

Beretta
Jubilee II 28-gauge

*Close-up of Beretta
Jubilee II engraving*

Beretta ASE Deluxe

*Close-up of Beretta
ASE Deluxe engraving*

Beretta SO5 Skeet 12-gauge

Beretta SO5 Sporting 12-gauge

Beretta Trap 12-gauge

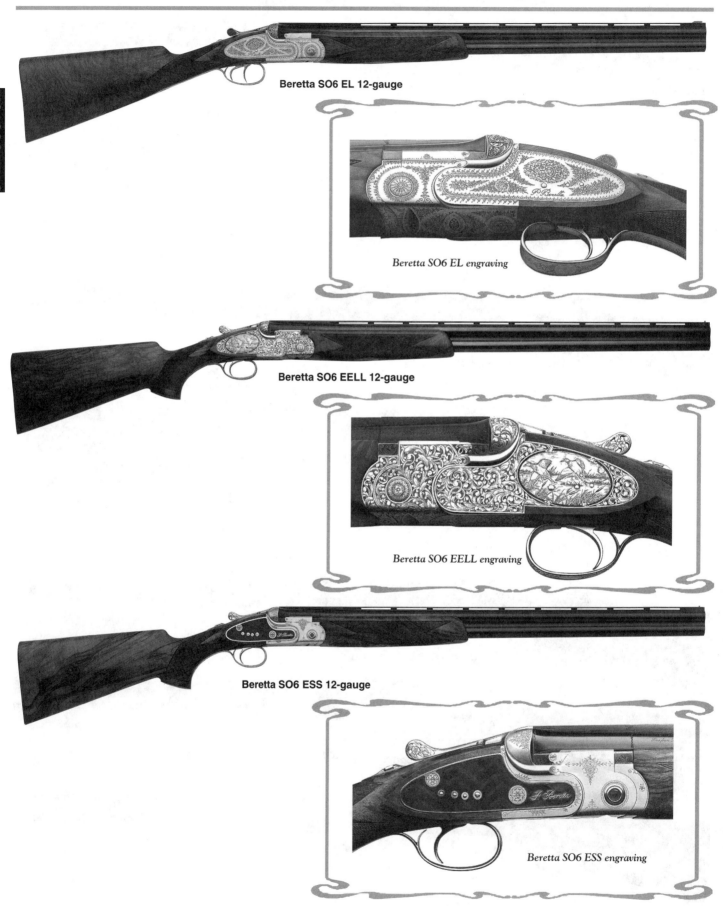

Beretta SO6 EL 12-gauge

Beretta SO6 EL engraving

Beretta SO6 EELL 12-gauge

Beretta SO6 EELL engraving

Beretta SO6 ESS 12-gauge

Beretta SO6 ESS engraving

SEMI-CUSTOM — SHOTGUNS

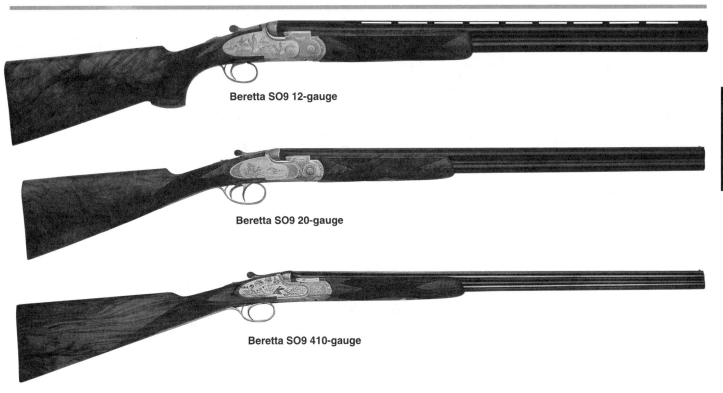

Beretta SO9 12-gauge

Beretta SO9 20-gauge

Beretta SO9 410-gauge

Examples of engraving on Beretta SO9

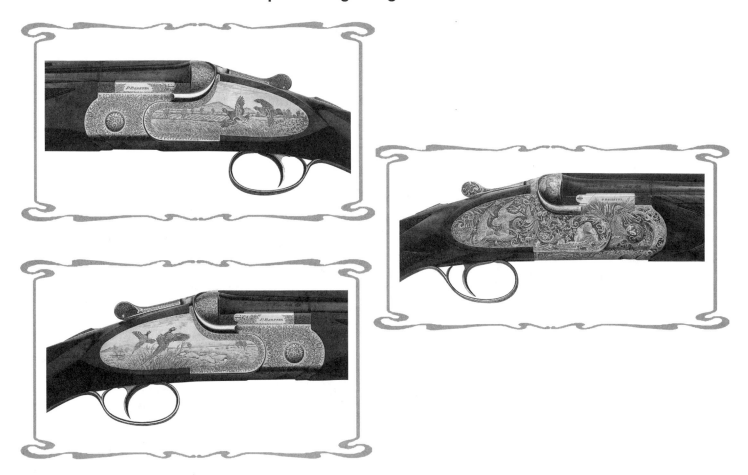

SEMI-CUSTOM — SHOTGUNS

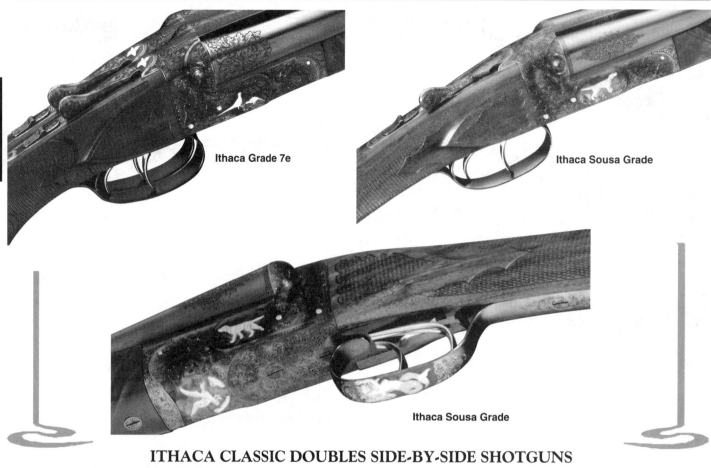

Ithaca Grade 7e

Ithaca Sousa Grade

Ithaca Sousa Grade

ITHACA CLASSIC DOUBLES SIDE-BY-SIDE SHOTGUNS

Gauge: 20, 28, 2-3/4" chamber; 410, 3" chamber. **Barrel:** 26", 28", 30". **Weight:** 5 lbs. 5 oz. (410 ga.) to 5 lbs. 14 oz. (20 ga.). **Length:** NA. **Stock:** Exhibition-grade American black walnut, hand-checkered with hand-rubbed oil finish. **Features:** Updated duplicates of original New Ithaca Double double-barrel shotguns. Hand-fitted boxlock action; splinter or beavertail forend; bone-charcoal color case-hardened receiver; chrome-moly steel rust-blued barrels; ejectors; gold double triggers; fixed chokes; hand-engraved game scenes. Made in U.S. by Ithaca Classic Doubles.
Price: Special Skeet Grade (plain color case-hardened receiver, feather crotch walnut stock) $3,465.00
Price: Grade 4E (gold-plated triggers, jeweled barrel flats, engraved game-bird scene) $4,625.00
Price: Grade 7E (gold-inlaid ducks, pheasants and bald eagle on scroll engraving) $9,200.00
Price: Sousa Grade (gold-inlaid setter, pointer, flying ducks and Sousa mermaid) $11,550.00

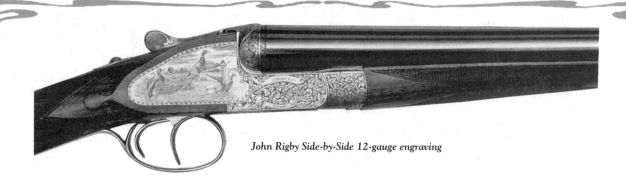

John Rigby Side-by-Side 12-gauge engraving

JOHN RIGBY SHOTGUNS

Gauge: 12, 16, 20, 28 and 410. **Barrel:** To customer specs. **Weight:** NA. **Length:** To customer specs. **Stock:** Customer's choice. **Features:** True sidelock side-by-side and over-under shotguns made to customer's specifications. Hand-fitted actions and stocks; engraved receivers embellished with game scenes; over-under includes removable choke tubes. Imported from England by John Rigby & Co.
Price: Sidelock over-under (single selective, non-selective or double triggers, 12 ga. only) . . . . from **$28,750.00**
Price: Sidelock side-by-side (engraved receiver, choice of stock wood) . . . . from **$34,750.00**

Merkel 47E

Merkel 47SL

Merkel 280EL

Merkel 303EL

Merkel 2001EL

MERKEL EXHIBITION, VINTAGERS EXPO AND CUSTOM ENGRAVED SHOTGUNS

Gauge: 12, 16, 20, 28, 410. **Barrel:** 26-3/4", 28"; others optional. **Weight:** NA. **Length:** NA. **Stock:** Highly figured walnut; English (straight) or pistol grip. **Features:** Highly engraved versions of Merkel over-under and side-by-side shotguns. Imported from Germany by GSI Inc.
Price: .... **NA**

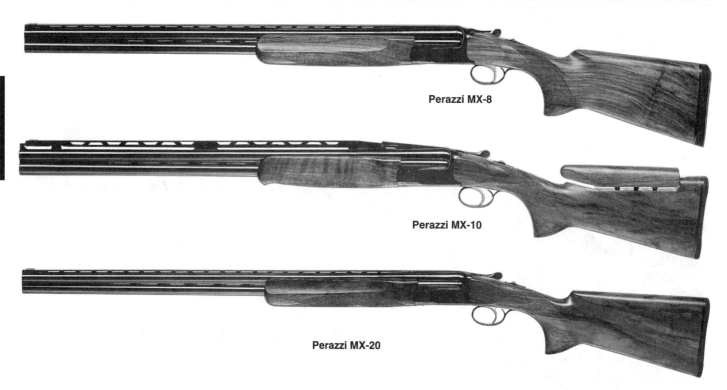

Perazzi MX-8

Perazzi MX-10

Perazzi MX-20

PERAZZI SCO, SCO GOLD, EXTRA AND EXTRA GOLD SHOTGUNS

Gauge: 12, 20, 28, 410. **Barrel:** 23-5/8" to 34". **Weight:** 6 lbs. 3 oz. to 8 lb. 13 oz. **Length:** NA. **Stock:** To customer specs. **Features:** Enhanced, engraved models of game and competition over-under shotguns. Customer may choose from many engraved hunting and wildlife scenes. Imported from Italy by Perazzi USA Inc.
Price: SCO Grade in competition and game o/u guns (fully engraved receiver) . . . . from **$25,500.00**
Price: SCO Gold Grade in comp. and game o/u guns (engraved w/gold inlays) . . . . from **$28,800.00**
Price: Extra Grade in competition and game o/u guns (highly detailed engraving) . . . . from **$72,900.00**
Price: Extra Gold Grade in comp. and game o/u guns (detailed engraving w/ gold inlays) . . . . from **$78,500.00**
Price: SCO Grade with engraved sideplates (extends engraved area) . . . . from **$39,100.00**
Price: SCO Gold Grade with engraved sideplates . . . . from **$45,450.00**

Perazzi SCO Grade engraving

SEMI-CUSTOM — SINGLE-SHOT

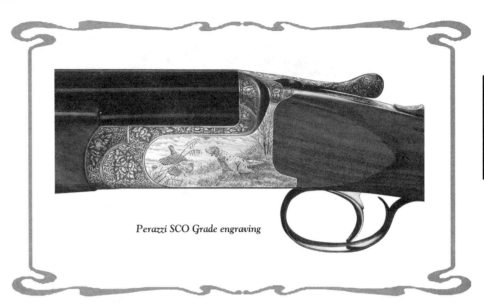

Perazzi SCO Grade engraving

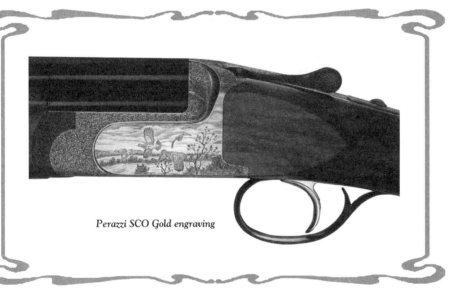

Perazzi SCO Gold engraving

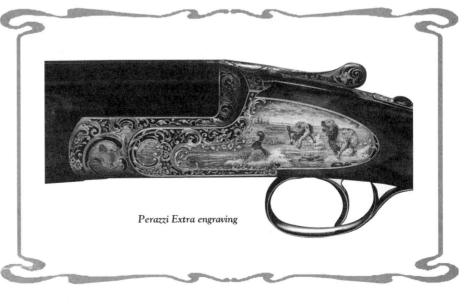

Perazzi Extra engraving

SEMI-CUSTOM — SHOTGUNS

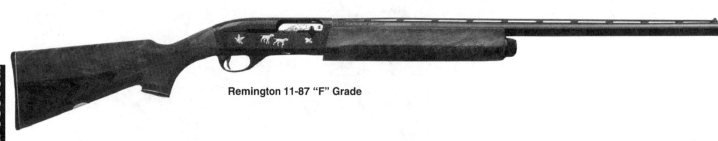

Remington 11-87 "F" Grade

REMINGTON CUSTOM SHOP AUTO SHOTGUNS

Gauge: 10, 12, 20, 28. **Barrel:** 21" to 30". **Weight:** NA. **Length:** NA. **Stock:** Two grades of American walnut. **Features:** Engraved versions of the Model 11-87 and Model 1100 shotgun. "D" or "F" grade fancy walnut, hand-checkered stock; choice of ebony, rosewood, skeleton steel or solid steel grip cap; choice of solid steel, standard, Old English or ventilated recoil pad; optional inletted gold oval with three initials on bottom of stock. From Remington Arms. Co. Custom Gun Shop.
Price: 11-87 and 1100 "D" Grade (English scroll engraving on receiver, breech and trig. guard) **$2,806.00**
Price: 11-87 and 1100 "F" Grade (engraved game scene, "F" Grade walnut stock) **$5,780.00**
Price: 11-87 and 1100 "F" Grade with gold inlay (inlaid three-panel engraved game scene) **$8,665.00**

REMINGTON CUSTOM SHOP PUMP SHOTGUNS

Gauge: 10, 12, 20, 28, 410. **Barrel:** 20" to 30". **Weight:** NA. **Length:** NA. **Stock:** Two grades of American walnut. **Features:** Engraved versions of the Model 870 shotgun. "D" or "F" grade fancy walnut hand-checkered stock; choice of ebony, rosewood, skeleton steel or solid steel grip cap; choice of solid steel, standard, Old English or ventilated recoil pad; optional inletted gold oval with three initials on bottom of stock. From Remington Arms Co. Custom Gun Shop.
Price: 870 "D" Grade (English scroll engraving on receiver, breech and trig. guard) **$2,806.00**
Price: 870 "F" Grade (engraved game scene, "F" grade walnut stock) **$5,780.00**
Price: 870 "F" Grade with gold inlay (inlaid three-panel engraved game scene) **$8,665.00**

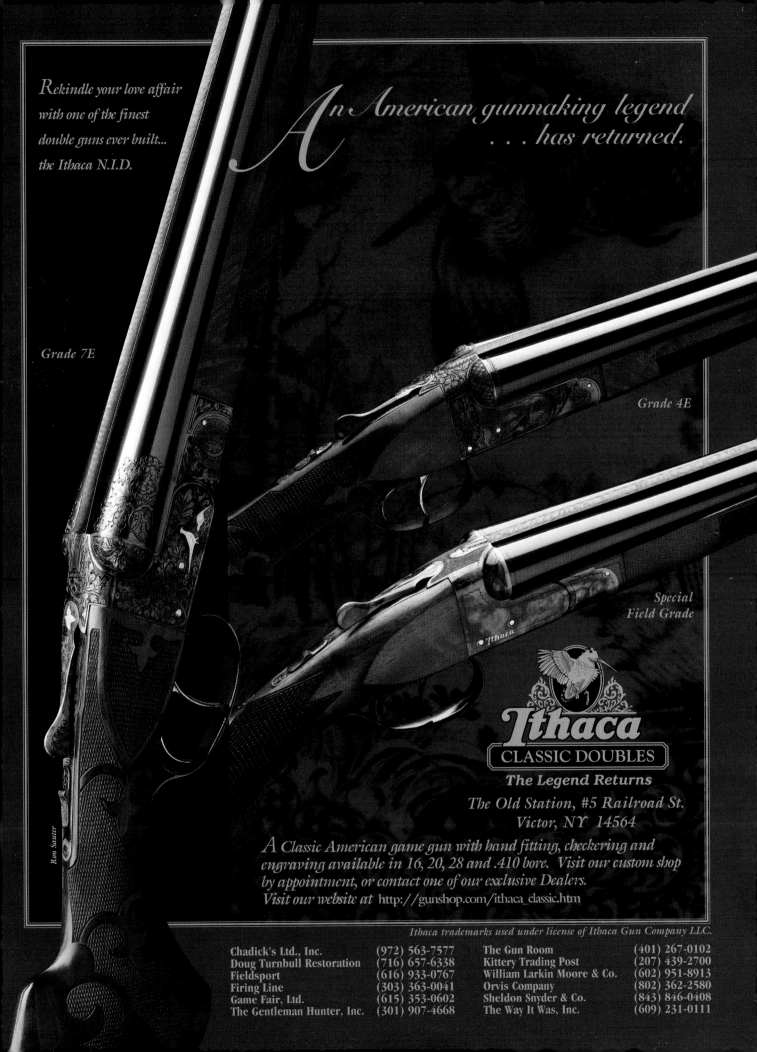

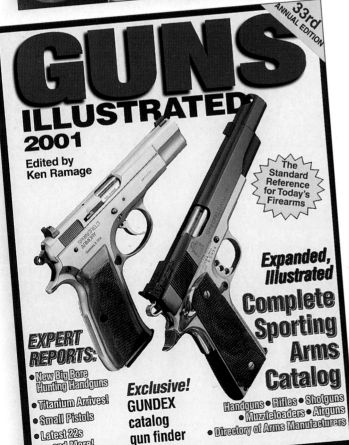

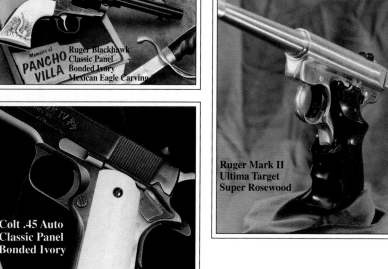
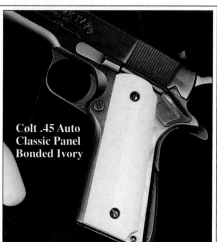

Includes models suitable for several forms of competition and other sporting purposes.

Accu-Tek BL-9

Accu-Tek AT-380

Accu-Tek CP-45

Accu-Tek HC-380

AA ARMS AP9 MINI PISTOL

Caliber: 9mm Para., 10-shot magazine. **Barrel:** 3". **Weight:** 3.5 lbs. **Length:** 12" overall. **Stocks:** Checkered black synthetic. **Sights:** Post front adjustable for elevation, rear adjustable for windage. **Features:** Ventilated barrel shroud; blue or electroless nickel finish. Made in U.S. by AA Arms.
Price: 3" barrel, blue **$239.00**
Price: 3" barrel, electroless nickel **$259.00**
Price: Mini/5, 5" barrel, blue **$259.00**
Price: Mini/5, 5" barrel, electroless nickel **$279.00**

ACCU-TEK BL-9 AUTO PISTOL

Caliber: 9mm Para., 5-shot magazine. **Barrel:** 3". **Weight:** 22 oz. **Length:** 5.6" overall. **Stocks:** Black pebble composition. **Sights:** Fixed. **Features:** Double action only; black finish. Introduced 1997. Price includes cleaning kit and gun lock, two magazines. Made in U.S. by Accu-Tek.
Price: **$232.00**

Accu-Tek Model AT-32SS Auto Pistol

Same as the AT-380SS except chambered for 32 ACP. Introduced 1991. Price includes cleaning kit and gun lock.
Price: Satin stainless **$221.00**

ACCU-TEK MODEL AT-380 AUTO PISTOL

Caliber: 380 ACP, 5-shot magazine. **Barrel:** 2.75". **Weight:** 20 oz. **Length:** 5.6" overall. **Stocks:** Grooved black composition. **Sights:** Blade front, rear adjustable for windage. **Features:** Stainless steel frame and slide. External hammer; manual thumb safety; firing pin block, trigger disconnect. Introduced 1991. Price includes cleaning kit and gun lock. Made in U.S. by Accu-Tek.
Price: Satin stainless **$221.00**

ACCU-TEK CP-45 AUTO PISTOL

Caliber: 45 ACP, 6-shot magazine. **Barrel:** 3-1/4 inches. **Weight:** 31 oz. **Length:** 6-3/8 inches overall. **Grips:** Checkered black nylon. **Sights:** Fully adjustable rear, three-dot; blade front. **Features:** Stainless steel frame and slide; single action with external hammer and firing pin block, manual thumb safety; last-shot hold open. Includes gun lock and cleaning kit. Introduced 2000. Made in U.S. by Excel Industries Inc.
Price: **$425.00**

ACCU-TEK MODEL HC-380 AUTO PISTOL

Caliber: 380 ACP, 10-shot magazine. **Barrel:** 2.75". **Weight:** 26 oz. **Length:** 6" overall. **Stocks:** Checkered black composition. **Sights:** Blade front, rear adjustable for windage. **Features:** External hammer; manual thumb safety with firing pin and trigger disconnect; bottom magazine release. Stainless steel construction. Introduced 1993. Price includes cleaning kit and gun lock. Made in U.S. by Accu-Tek.
Price: Satin stainless **$231.00**

ACCU-TEK XL-9 AUTO PISTOL

Caliber: 9mm Para., 5-shot magazine. **Barrel:** 3". **Weight:** 24 oz. **Length:** 5.6" overall. **Stocks:** Black pebble composition. **Sights:** Three-dot system; rear adjustable for windage. **Features:** Stainless steel construction; double-action-only mechanism. Introduced 1999. Price includes cleaning kit and gun lock, two magazines. Made in U.S. by Accu-Tek.
Price: **$248.00**

Accu-Tek XL9

AMT Backup

Auto-Ordnance 1911A1 Standard

AMERICAN ARMS MATEBA AUTO/REVOLVER

Caliber: 357 Mag., 6-shot. **Barrel:** 4", 6", 8". **Weight:** 2.75 lbs. **Length:** 8.77" overall. **Stocks:** Smooth walnut. **Sights:** Blade on ramp front, adjustable rear. **Features:** Double or single action. Cylinder and slide recoil together upon firing. All-steel construction with polished blue finish. Introduced 1995. Imported from Italy by American Arms, Inc.
Price: **$1,295.00**
Price: 6" **$1,349.00**

AMT AUTOMAG II AUTO PISTOL

Caliber: 22 WMR, 9-shot magazine (7-shot with 3-3/8" barrel). **Barrel:** 3-3/8", 4-1/2", 6". **Weight:** About 32 oz. **Length:** 9-3/8" overall. **Stocks:** Grooved carbon fiber. **Sights:** Blade front, adjustable rear. **Features:** Made of stainless steel. Gas-assisted action. Exposed hammer. Slide flats have brushed finish, rest is sandblast. Squared trigger guard. Introduced 1986. From Galena Industries, Inc.
Price: **$429.00**

AMT AUTOMAG III PISTOL

Caliber: 30 Carbine, 8-shot magazine. **Barrel:** 6-3/8". **Weight:** 43 oz. **Length:** 10-1/2" overall. **Stocks:** Carbon fiber. **Sights:** Blade front, adjustable rear. **Features:** Stainless steel construction. Hammer-drop safety. Slide flats have brushed finish, rest is sandblasted. Introduced 1989. From Galena Industries, Inc.
Price: **$529.00**

AMT AUTOMAG IV PISTOL

Caliber: 45 Winchester Magnum, 6-shot magazine. **Barrel:** 6.5". **Weight:** 46 oz. **Length:** 10.5" overall. **Stocks:** Carbon fiber. **Sights:** Blade front, adjustable rear. **Features:** Made of stainless st3578eel with brushed finish. Introduced 1990. Made in U.S. by Galena Industries, Inc.
Price: **$599.00**

AMT 45 ACP HARDBALLER II

Caliber: 45 ACP. **Barrel:** 5". **Weight:** 39 oz. **Length:** 8-1/2" overall. **Stocks:** Wrap-around rubber. **Sights:** Adjustable. **Features:** Extended combat safety, serrated matte slide rib, loaded chamber indicator, long grip safety, beveled magazine well, adjustable target trigger. All stainless steel. From Galena Industries, Inc.
Price: **$425.00**
Price: Government model (as above except no rib, fixed sights) . **$399.00**
Price: 400 Accelerator (400 Cor-Bon, 7" barrel). **$549.00**
Price: Commando (40 S&W, Government Model frame) **$435.00**

AMT 45 ACP HARDBALLER LONG SLIDE

Caliber: 45 ACP. **Barrel:** 7". **Length:** 10-1/2" overall. **Stocks:** Wrap-around rubber. **Sights:** Fully adjustable rear sight. **Features:** Slide and barrel are 2" longer than the standard 45, giving less recoil, added velocity, longer sight radius. Has extended combat safety, serrated matte rib, loaded chamber indicator, wide adjustable trigger. From Galena Industries, Inc.
Price: **$529.00**

AMT BACKUP PISTOL

Caliber: 357 SIG (5-shot); 38 Super, 9mm Para. (6-shot); 40 S&W, 400 Cor-Bon; 45 ACP (5-shot). **Barrel:** 3". **Weight:** 23 oz. **Length:** 5-3/4" overall. **Stocks:** Checkered black synthetic. **Sights:** None. **Features:** Stainless steel construction; double-action-only trigger; dust cover over the trigger transfer bar; extended magazine; titanium nitride finish. Introduced 1992. Made in U.S. by Galena Industries.
Price: 9mm, 40 S&W, 45 ACP **$319.00**
Price: 38 Super, 357 SIG, 400 Cor-Bon. **$369.00**

AMT 380 DAO Small Frame Backup

Similar to the DAO Backup except has smaller frame, 2-1/2" barrel, weighs 18 oz., and is 5" overall. Has 5-shot magazine, matte/stainless finish. Made in U.S. by Galena Industries.
Price: **$319.00**

AUTO-ORDNANCE 1911A1 AUTOMATIC PISTOL

Caliber: 45 ACP, 7-shot magazine. **Barrel:** 5". **Weight:** 39 oz. **Length:** 8-1/2" overall. **Stocks:** Checkered plastic with medallion. **Sights:** Blade front, rear adjustable for windage. **Features:** Same specs as 1911A1 military guns—parts interchangeable. Frame and slide blued; each radius has non-glare finish. Made in U.S. by Auto-Ordnance Corp.
Price: 45 ACP, blue **$447.00**
Price: 45 ACP, Parkerized **$462.00**
Price: 45 ACP Deluxe (three-dot sights, textured rubber wraparound grips). **$455.00**

Auto-Ordnance 1911A1 Custom High Polish Pistol

Similar to the standard 1911A1 except has a Videki speed trigger, extended thumb safety, flat mainspring housing, Acurod recoil spring guide system, rosewood grips, custom combat hammer, beavertail grip safety. High-polish blue finish. Introduced 1998. Made in U.S. by Auto-Ordnance Corp.
Price: **$585.00**

Auto-Ordnance Deluxe

Baer Custom Carry

Auto-Ordnance Pit Bull

Baer Premium II

Baer 1911 Concept III Auto Pistol

Same as the Concept I except has forged stainless frame with blued steel slide, Bo-Mar rear sight, 30 lpi checkering on front strap. Made in U.S. by Les Baer Custom, Inc.

Price: **$1,520.00**
Price: Concept IV (with Baer adjustable rear sight) **$1,499.00**
Price: Concept V (all stainless, Bo-Mar sight, checkered front strap)
. . . . **$1,558.00**
Price: Concept VI (stainless, Baer adjustable sight, checkered
front strap) **$1,558.00**

BAER 1911 PREMIER II AUTO PISTOL

Caliber: 9x23, 38 Super, 400 Cor-Bon, 45 ACP, 7- or 10-shot magazine. **Barrel:** 5". **Weight:** 37 oz. **Length:** 8.5" overall. **Stocks:** Checkered rosewood, double diamond pattern. **Sights:** Baer dovetailed front, low-mount Bo-Mar rear with hidden leaf. **Features:** Baer NM forged steel frame and barrel with stainless bushing; slide fitted to frame; double serrated slide; lowered, flared ejection port; tuned, polished extractor; Baer extended ejector, checkered slide stop, aluminum speed trigger with 4-lb. pull, deluxe Commander hammer and sear, beavertail grip safety with pad, beveled magazine well, extended ambidextrous safety; flat mainspring housing; polished feed ramp and throated barrel; 30 lpi checkered front strap. Made in U.S. by Les Baer Custom, Inc.

Price: Blued **$1,428.00**
Price: Stainless. **$1,558.00**
Price: 6" model, blued, from **$1,595.00**

BAER 1911 S.R.P. PISTOL

Caliber: 45 ACP. **Barrel:** 5". **Weight:** 37 oz. **Length:** 8.5" overall. **Stocks:** Checkered walnut. **Sights:** Trijicon night sights. **Features:** Similar to the F.B.I. contract gun except uses Baer forged steel frame. Has Baer match barrel with supported chamber, Wolff springs, complete tactical action job. All parts Mag-na-fluxed; deburred for tactical carry. Has Baer Ultra Coat finish. Tuned for reliability. Contact Baer for complete details. Introduced 1996. Made in U.S. by Les Baer Custom, Inc.

Price: Government or Comanche length **$2,990.00**

Auto-Ordnance ZG-51 Pit Bull Auto

Same as the 1911A1 except has 3-1/2" barrel, weighs 36 oz. and has an over-all length of 7-1/4". Available in 45 ACP only; 7-shot magazine. Introduced 1989.

Price: **$470.00**

AUTAUGA 32 AUTO PISTOL

Caliber: 32 ACP, 6-shot magazine. **Barrel:** 2". **Weight:** 11.3 oz. **Length:** 4.3" overall. **Stocks:** Black polymer. **Sights:** Fixed. **Features:** Double-action-only mechanism. Stainless steel construction. Uses Winchester Silver Tip ammunition.

Price: . . . . **NA**

BAER 1911 CUSTOM CARRY AUTO PISTOL

Caliber: 45 ACP, 7- or 10-shot magazine. **Barrel:** 5". **Weight:** 37 oz. **Length:** 8.5" overall. **Stocks:** Checkered walnut. **Sights:** Baer improved ramp-style dovetailed front, Novak low-mount rear. **Features:** Baer forged NM frame, slide and barrel with stainless bushing; fitted slide to frame; double serrated slide (full-size only); Baer speed trigger with 4-lb. pull; Baer deluxe hammer and sear, tactical-style extended ambidextrous safety, beveled magazine well; polished feed ramp and throated barrel; tuned extractor; Baer extended ejector, checkered slide stop; lowered and flared ejection port, full-length recoil guide rod; recoil buff. Made in U.S. by Les Baer Custom, Inc.

Price: Standard size, blued. **$1,620.00**
Price: Standard size, stainless **$1,690.00**
Price: Comanche size, blued **$1,640.00**
Price: Comanche size, stainless. **$1,690.00**
Price: Comanche size, aluminum frame, blued slide **$1,890.00**
Price: Comanche size, aluminum frame, stainless slide **$1,995.00**

BAER 1911 CONCEPT I AUTO PISTOL

Caliber: 45 ACP, 7-shot magazine. **Barrel:** 5". **Weight:** 37 oz. **Length:** 8.5" overall. **Stocks:** Checkered rosewood. **Sights:** Baer dovetail front, Bo-Mar deluxe low-mount rear with hidden leaf. **Features:** Baer forged steel frame, slide and barrel with Baer stainless bushing; slide fitted to frame; double serrated slide; Baer beavertail grip safety, checkered slide stop, tuned extractor, extended ejector, deluxe hammer and sear, match disconnector; lowered and flared ejection port; fitted recoil link; polished feed ramp, throated barrel; Baer fitted speed trigger, flat serrated mainspring housing. Blue finish. Made in U.S. by Les Baer Custom, Inc.

Price: **$1,390.00**
Price: Concept II (with Baer adjustable rear sight) **$1,390.00**

Baer 1911 Concept VII Auto Pistol

Same as the Concept I except reduced Comanche size with 4.25" barrel, weighs 27.5 oz., 7.75" overall. Blue finish, checkered front strap. Made in U.S. by Les Baer Custom, Inc.

Price: **$1,495.00**
Price: Concept VIII (stainless frame and slide, Baer adjustable rear sight) **$1,547.00**

Baer 1911 Concept IX Auto Pistol

Same as the Comanche Concept VII except has Baer lightweight forged aluminum frame, blued steel slide, Baer adjustable rear sight. Chambered for 45 ACP, 7-shot magazine. Made in U.S. by Les Baer Custom, Inc.

Price: **$1,655.00**
Price: Concept X (as above with stainless slide) **$1,675.00**

Baer 1911 Prowler III Auto Pistol

Same as the Premier II except also has full-length guide rod, tapered cone stub weight and reverse recoil plug. Made in U.S. by Les Baer Custom, Inc.

Price: Standard size, blued. **$1,795.00**

BERETTA MODEL 92FS PISTOL

Caliber: 9mm Para., 10-shot magazine. **Barrel:** 4.9". **Weight:** 34 oz. **Length:** 8.5" overall. **Stocks:** Checkered black plastic. **Sights:** Blade front, rear adjustable for windage. Tritium night sights available. **Features:** Double action. Extractor acts as chamber loaded indicator, squared trigger guard, grooved front- and backstraps, inertia firing pin. Matte or blued finish. Introduced 1977. Made in U.S. and imported from Italy by Beretta U.S.A.

Price: With plastic grips **$655.00**
Price: Stainless, rubber grips **$718.00**

Beretta Model 92FS/96 Brigadier Pistols

Similar to the Model 92FS/96 except with a heavier slide to reduce felt recoil and allow mounting removable front sight. Wrap-around rubber grips. Three-dot sights dovetailed to the slide, adjustable for windage. Weighs 35.3 oz. Introduced 1999.

Price: 9mm or 40 S&W, 10-shot. **$702.00**

Beretta Model 92FS 470th Anniversary Limited Edition

Similar to the Model 92FS stainless except has mirror polish finish, smooth walnut grips with inlaid gold-plated medallions. Special and unique gold-filled engraving includes the signature of Beretta's president. The anniversary logo is engraved on the top of the slide and the back of the magazine. Each pistol identified by a "1 of 470" gold-filled number. Special chrome-plated magazine included. Deluxe lockable walnut case with teak inlays and engraving. Only 470 pistols will be sold. Introduced 1999.

Price: **$2,082.00**

Beretta Model 92FS Compact and Compact Type M Pistol

Similar to the Model 92FS except more compact and lighter: overall length 7.8"; 4.3" barrel; weighs 30.9 oz. Has Bruniton finish, chrome-lined bore, combat trigger guard, ambidextrous safety/decock lever. Single column 8-shot magazine (Type M), or double column 10-shot (Compact), 9mm only. Introduced 1998. Imported from Italy by Beretta U.S.A.

Price: Compact (10-shot) **$655.00**
Price: Compact Type M (8-shot). **$655.00**

Beretta 96

Beretta 950 Jetfire

Beretta Model 96 Pistol

Same as the Model 92FS except chambered for 40 S&W. Ambidextrous safety mechanism with passive firing pin catch, slide safety/decocking lever, trigger bar disconnect. Has 10-shot magazine. Available with three-dot sights. Introduced 1992.

Price: Model 96, plastic grips **$655.00**
Price: Stainless, rubber grips **$718.00**

Beretta M9 Special Edition Pistol

Copy of the U.S. M9 military pistol. Similar to the Model 92FS except has special M9 serial number range; one 15-round (pre-ban) magazine; dot-and-post sight system; special M9 military packaging; Army TM 9-1005-317-10 operator's manual; M9 Special Edition patch; certificate of authenticity; Bianchi M12 holster, M1025 magazine pouch, and M1015 web pistol belt. Introduced 1998. From Beretta U.S.A.

Price: **$861.00**

BERETTA MODEL 80 CHEETAH SERIES DA PISTOLS

Caliber: 380 ACP, 10-shot magazine (M84); 8-shot (M85); 22 LR, 7-shot (M87). **Barrel:** 3.82". **Weight:** About 23 oz. (M84/85); 20.8 oz. (M87). **Length:** 6.8" overall. **Stocks:** Glossy black plastic (wood optional at extra cost). **Sights:** Fixed front, drift-adjustable rear. **Features:** Double action, quick takedown, convenient magazine release. Introduced 1977. Imported from Italy by Beretta U.S.A.

Price: Model 84 Cheetah, plastic grips. **$565.00**
Price: Model 84 Cheetah, wood grips **$595.00**
Price: Model 84 Cheetah, wood grips, nickel finish **$639.00**
Price: Model 85 Cheetah, plastic grips, 8-shot. **$533.00**
Price: Model 85 Cheetah, wood grips, 8-shot **$566.00**
Price: Model 85 Cheetah, wood grips, nickel, 8-shot **$596.00**
Price: Model 87 Cheetah, wood, 22 LR, 7-shot **$565.00**

Beretta Model 86 Cheetah

Similar to the 380-caliber Model 85 except has tip-up barrel for first-round loading. Barrel length is 4.4", overall length of 7.33". Has 8-shot magazine, walnut grips. Introduced 1989.

Price: **$566.00**

BERETTA MODEL 950 JETFIRE AUTO PISTOL

Caliber: 25 ACP, 8-shot. **Barrel:** 2.4". **Weight:** 9.9 oz. **Length:** 4.7" overall. **Stocks:** Checkered black plastic or walnut. **Sights:** Fixed. **Features:**

HANDGUNS

Beretta M8000/8040 Cougar

Bersa Thunder 380

Single action, thumb safety; tip-up barrel for direct loading/unloading, cleaning. From Beretta U.S.A.
Price: Jetfire plastic, blue **$220.00**
Price: Jetfire plastic, nickel **$300.00**
Price: Jetfire wood, EL **$337.00**
Price: Jetfire plastic, matte finish **$220.00**

Beretta Model 21 Bobcat Pistol

Similar to the Model 950 BS. Chambered for 22 LR or 25 ACP. Both double action. Has 2.4" barrel, 4.9" overall length; 7-round magazine on 22 cal.; 8 rounds in 25 ACP, 9.9 oz., available in nickel, matte, engraved or blue finish. Plastic or walnut grips. Introduced in 1985.
Price: Bobcat, 22-cal., blue. **$279.00**
Price: Bobcat, nickel, 22-cal. **$322.00**
Price: Bobcat, 25-cal., blue. **$279.00**
Price: Bobcat, nickel, 25-cal. **$322.00**
Price: Bobcat EL, 22 or 25 . . . . **$356.00**
Price: Bobcat plastic matte, 22 or 25 . . . . **$246.00**

BERETTA MODEL 3032 TOMCAT PISTOL

Caliber: 32 ACP, 7-shot magazine. **Barrel:** 2.45". **Weight:** 14.5 oz. **Length:** 5" overall. **Stocks:** Checkered black plastic. **Sights:** Blade front, drift-adjustable rear. **Features:** Double action with exposed hammer; tip-up barrel for direct loading/unloading; thumb safety; polished or matte blue finish. Imported from Italy by Beretta U.S.A. Introduced 1996.
Price: Blue **$362.00**
Price: Matte **$333.00**

BERETTA MODEL 8000/8040/8045 COUGAR PISTOL

Caliber: 9mm Para., 10-shot, 40 S&W, 10-shot magazine; 45 ACP, 8-shot. **Barrel:** 3.6". **Weight:** 33.5 oz. **Length:** 7" overall. **Stocks:** Checkered plastic. **Sights:** Blade front, rear drift adjustable for windage. **Features:** Slide-mounted safety; rotating barrel; exposed hammer. Matte black Bruniton finish. Announced 1994. Imported from Italy by Beretta U.S.A.
Price: **$695.00**
Price: D model, 9mm, 40 S&W. **$672.00**
Price: D model, 45 ACP **$724.00**

BERETTA MODEL 9000S COMPACT PISTOL

Caliber: 9mm Para., 40 S&W; 10-shot magazine. **Barrel:** 3.4". **Weight:** 26.8 oz. **Length:** 6.6". **Grips:** Soft polymer. **Sights:** Windage-adjustable white-dot rear, white-dot blade front. **Features:** Glass-reinforced polymer frame; patented tilt-barrel, open-slide locking system; chrome-lined barrel; external serrated hammer; automatic firing pin and manual safeties. Introduced 2000. Imported from Italy by Beretta USA.
Price: 9000S Type F (single and double action, external
hammer) **$551.00**
Price: 9000S Type D (double-action only, no external
hammer or safety). **$551.00**

Beretta Model 8000/8040/8045 Mini Cougar

Similar to the Model 8000/8040 Cougar except has shorter grip frame and weighs 27.6 oz. Introduced 1998. Imported from Italy by Beretta U.S.A.
Price: 9mm or 40 S&W. **$695.00**
Price: 9mm or 40 S&W, DAO. **$672.00**
Price: 45 ACP, 6-shot. **$724.00**
Price: 45 ACP DAO **$724.00**

BERSA THUNDER 380 AUTO PISTOLS

Caliber: 380 ACP, 7-shot (Thunder 380 Lite), 9-shot magazine (Thunder 380 DLX). **Barrel:** 3.5". **Weight:** 25.75 oz. **Length:** 6.6" overall. **Stocks:** Black polymer. **Sights:** Blade front, notch rear adjustable for windage; three-dot system. **Features:** Double action; firing pin and magazine safeties. Available in blue or nickel. Introduced 1995. Distributed by Eagle Imports, Inc.
Price: Thunder 380, 7-shot, deep blue finish **$234.95**

BROWNING FORTY-NINE AUTOMATIC PISTOL

Caliber: 40 S&W, 10-shot magazine. **Barrel:** 4.25". **Weight:** 26 oz. **Length:** 7.75" overall. **Stocks:** Integral; black nylon with pebble-grain texture. **Sights:** Dovetailed three-dot. **Features:** Has FN's patented RSS (Repeatable Secure Striker) firing system; extended modular slide rails; reversible magazine catch; stainless slide, black nylon frame. Introduced 1999. Imported by Browning.
Price: **$440.00**

BROWNING HI-POWER 9mm AUTOMATIC PISTOL

Caliber: 9mm Para., 40 S&W, 10-shot magazine. **Barrel:** 4-21/32". **Weight:** 32 oz. **Length:** 7-3/4" overall. **Stocks:** Walnut, hand checkered, or black Polyamide. **Sights:** 1/8" blade front; rear screw-adjustable for windage and elevation. Also available with fixed rear (drift-adjustable for windage). **Features:** External hammer with half-cock and thumb safeties. A blow on the hammer cannot discharge a cartridge; cannot be fired with magazine removed. Fixed rear sight model available. Imported from Belgium by Browning.
Price: Fixed sight model, walnut grips **$615.00**
Price: 9mm with rear sight adj. for w. and e., walnut grips **$668.00**
Price: Mark III, standard matte black finish, fixed sight, moulded grips,
ambidextrous safety **$579.00**
Price: Silver chrome, adjustable sight, Pachmayr grips **$684.00**

Browning 40 S&W Hi-Power Mark III Pistol

Similar to the standard Hi-Power except chambered for 40 S&W, 10-shot magazine, weighs 35 oz., and has 4-3/4" barrel. Comes with matte blue finish, low profile front sight blade, drift-adjustable rear sight, ambidextrous safety, moulded polyamide grips with thumb rest. Introduced 1993. Imported from Belgium by Browning.
Price: Mark III **$579.00**

Browning Capitan Hi-Power   Browning Micro Buck Mark Standard   Browning Buck Mark Challenge   Browning Buck Mark Varmint

Browning Capitan Hi-Power Pistol

Similar to the standard Hi-Power except has adjustable tangent rear sight authentic to the early-production model. Also has Commander-style hammer. Checkered walnut grips, polished blue finish. Reintroduced 1993. Imported from Belgium by Browning.

Price: 9mm only $728.00

Browning Hi-Power HP-Practical Pistol

Similar to the standard Hi-Power except has silver-chromed frame with blued slide, wrap-around Pachmayr rubber grips, round-style serrated hammer and removable front sight, fixed rear (drift-adjustable for windage). Available in 9mm Para. or 40 S&W. Introduced 1991.

Price: $662.00
Price: With fully adjustable rear sight $717.00

BROWNING BUCK MARK 22 PISTOL

Caliber: 22 LR, 10-shot magazine. Barrel: 5-1/2". Weight: 32 oz. Length: 9-1/2" overall. Stocks: Black moulded composite with checkering. Sights: Ramp front, Browning Pro Target rear adjustable for windage and elevation. Features: All steel, matte blue finish or nickel, gold-colored trigger. Buck Mark Plus has laminated wood grips. Made in U.S. Introduced 1985. From Browning.

Price: Buck Mark, blue $265.00
Price: Buck Mark, nickel finish with contoured rubber stocks. . . . $312.00
Price: Buck Mark Plus $324.00

Browning Buck Mark Camper

Similar to the Buck Mark except 5-1/2" bull barrel. Weight is 34 oz. Available in matte blue. Introduced 1999. From Browning.

Price: $234.00

Browning Buck Mark Challenge, Challenge Micro

Similar to the Buck Mark except has a lightweight barrel and smaller grip diameter. Barrel length is 5-1/2", weight is 25 oz. Introduced 1999. From Browning.

Price: $296.00
Price: Challenge Micro (4" barrel) $296.00

Calico M-110

Browning Micro Buck Mark

Same as the standard Buck Mark and Buck Mark Plus except has 4" barrel. Available in blue or nickel. Has 16-click Pro Target rear sight. Introduced 1992.

Price: Blue $265.00
Price: Nickel $312.00
Price: Buck Mark Micro Plus $324.00
Price: Buck Mark Micro Plus Nickel $354.00

Browning Buck Mark Varmint

Same as the Buck Mark except has 9-7/8" heavy barrel with .900" diameter and full-length scope base (no open sights); walnut grips with optional forend, or finger-groove walnut. Overall length is 14", weighs 48 oz. Introduced 1987.

Price: $403.00

CALICO M-110 AUTO PISTOL

Caliber: 22 LR. Barrel: 6". Weight: 3.7 lbs. (loaded). Length: 17.9" overall. Stocks: Moulded composition. Sights: Adjustable post front, notch rear. Features: Aluminum alloy frame; compensator; pistol grip compartment; ambidextrous safety. Uses same helical-feed magazine as M-100 Carbine. Introduced 1986. Made in U.S. From Calico.

Price: $570.00

Carbon-15

Colt 1991 Model O Compact

Charles Daly M-1911-A1P

Colt XS Model O Commander

CARBON-15 (Type 97) PISTOL

Caliber: 223, 10-shot magazine. **Barrel:** 7.25". **Weight:** 46 oz. **Length:** 20" overall. **Stock:** Checkered composite. **Sights:** Ghost ring. **Features:** Semi-automatic, gas-operated, rotating bolt action. Carbon fiber upper and lower receiver; chromemoly bolt carrier; fluted stainless match barrel; mil. spec. optics mounting base; uses AR-15-type magazines. Introduced 1992. From Professional Ordnance, Inc.
Price: **$1,600.00**
Price: Type 20 pistol (light-profile barrel, no compensator, weighs
40 oz.). **$1,500.00**

CHARLES DALY M-1911-A1P AUTOLOADING PISTOL

Caliber: 45 ACP, 7- or 10-shot magazine. **Barrel:** 5". **Weight:** 38 oz. **Length:** 8-3/4" overall. **Stocks:** Checkered. **Sights:** Blade front, rear drift adjustable for windage; three-dot system. **Features:** Skeletonized combat hammer and trigger; beavertail grip safety; extended slide release; over-size thumb safety; Parkerized finish. Introduced 1996. Imported from the Philippines by K.B.I., Inc.
Price: **$469.95**

COLT MODEL 1991 MODEL O AUTO PISTOL

Caliber: 45 ACP, 7-shot magazine. **Barrel:** 5". **Weight:** 38 oz. **Length:** 8.5" overall. **Stocks:** Checkered black composition. **Sights:** Ramped blade front, fixed square notch rear, high profile. **Features:** Parkerized finish. Continuation of serial number range used on original G.I. 1911 A1 guns. Comes with one magazine and moulded carrying case. Introduced 1991.
Price: **$573.00**
Price: Stainless. **$628.00**

Colt Model 1991 Model O Compact Auto Pistol

Similar to the Model 1991 A1 except has 3-1/2" barrel. Overall length is 7", and gun is 3/8" shorter in height. Comes with one 6-shot magazine, moulded case. Introduced 1993.
Price: **$556.00**

COLT XS SERIES MODEL O AUTO PISTOLS

Caliber: 45 ACP, 8-shot magazine. **Barrel:** 4.25", 5". **Weight:** N/A. **Length:** N/A. **Grips:** Checkered, double diamond rosewood. **Sights:** Drift-adjustable three-dot combat. **Features:** Brushed stainless finish; adjustable, two-cut aluminum trigger; extended ambidextrous thumb safety; upswept beavertail with palm swell; elongated slot hammer; beveled magazine well. Introduced 1999. From Colt's Manufacturing Co., Inc.
Price: XS Government (5" barrel) **$750.00**
Price: XS Commander (4.25" barrel) **$750.00**

COLT XS LIGHTWEIGHT COMMANDER AUTO PISTOL

Caliber: 45 ACP, 8-shot. **Barrel:** 4-1/4". **Weight:** 26 oz. **Length:** 7-3/4" overall. **Stocks:** Double diamond checkered rosewood. **Sights:** Fixed, glare-proofed blade front, square notch rear; three-dot system. **Features:** Brushed stainless slide, nickeled aluminum frame; McCormick elongated-slot enhanced hammer, McCormick two-cut adjustable aluminum hammer. Made in U.S. by Colt's Mfg. Co., Inc.
Price: 45, stainless **$750.00**

Colt Model 1991 Model O Commander Auto Pistol

Similar to the Model 1991 Model O except has 4-1/4" barrel. Parkerized finish. 7-shot magazine. Comes in moulded case. Introduced 1993.
Price: **$556.00**

Colt XS Lightweight Commander

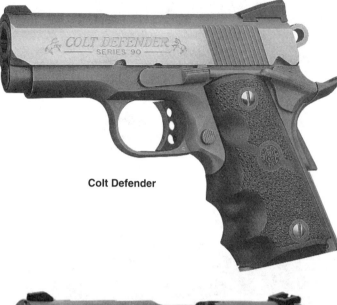

Colt Defender

Colt Lightweight Commander

Coonan 357 Magnum

COLT DEFENDER
Caliber: 40 S&W, 45 ACP, 7-shot magazine. **Barrel:** 3". **Weight:** 22-1/2 oz. **Length:** 6-3/4" overall. **Stocks:** Pebble-finish rubber wraparound with finger grooves. **Sights:** White dot front, snag-free Colt competition rear. **Features:** Stainless finish; aluminum frame; combat-style hammer; Hi Ride grip safety, extended manual safety, disconnect safety. Introduced 1998. Made in U.S. by Colt's Mfg. Co.
Price: **$840.00**

COONAN 357 MAGNUM, 41 MAGNUM PISTOLS
Caliber: 357 Mag., 41 Magnum, 7-shot magazine. **Barrel:** 5". **Weight:** 42 oz. **Length:** 8.3" overall. **Stocks:** Smooth walnut. **Sights:** Interchangeable ramp front, rear adjustable for windage. **Features:** Stainless steel construction. Unique barrel hood improves accuracy and reliability. Linkless barrel. Many parts interchange with Colt autos. Has grip, hammer, half-cock safeties, extended slide latch. Made in U.S. by Coonan Arms, Inc.
Price: 5" barrel, from..................................... **$735.00**
Price: 6" barrel, from..................................... **$768.00**
Price: With 6" compensated barrel........................ **$1,014.00**
Price: Classic model (Teflon black two-tone finish, 8-shot magazine, fully adjustable rear sight, integral compensated barrel) **$1,400.00**
Price: 41 Magnum Model, from **$825.00**

Coonan Compact Cadet 357 Magnum Pistol
Similar to the 357 Magnum full-size gun except has 3.9" barrel, shorter frame, 6-shot magazine. Weight is 39 oz., overall length 7.8". Linkless bull barrel, full-length recoil spring guide rod, extended slide latch. Introduced 1993. Made in U.S. by Coonan Arms, Inc.
Price: **$855.00**

CZ 75B 9mm

CZ 75B AUTO PISTOL
Caliber: 9mm Para., 40 S&W, 10-shot magazine. **Barrel:** 4.7". **Weight:** 34.3 oz. **Length:** 8.1" overall. **Stocks:** High impact checkered plastic. **Sights:** Square post front, rear adjustable for windage; three-dot system. **Features:** Single action/double action design; firing pin block safety; choice of black polymer, matte or high-polish blue finishes. All-steel frame. Imported from the Czech Republic by CZ-USA.

CZ 75B Decocker

CZ 85

CZ 75D Compact

CZ 83B

Price: Black polymer **$472.00**
Price: Glossy blue **$486.00**
Price: Dual tone or satin nickel **$486.00**
Price: 22 LR conversion unit **$279.00**

CZ 75B Decocker

Similar to the CZ 75B except has a decocking lever in place of the safety lever. All other specifications are the same. Introduced 1999. Imported from the Czech Republic by CZ-USA.
Price: 9mm, black polymer **$467.00**

CZ 75B Compact Auto Pistol

Similar to the CZ 75 except has 10-shot magazine, 3.9" barrel and weighs 32 oz. Has removable front sight, non-glare ribbed slide top. Trigger guard is squared and serrated; combat hammer. Introduced 1993. Imported from the Czech Republic by CZ-USA.
Price: 9mm, black polymer **$499.00**
Price: Dual tone or satin nickel **$513.00**
Price: D Compact, black polymer **$526.00**

CZ 85B Auto Pistol

Same gun as the CZ 75 except has ambidextrous slide release and safe-ty-levers; non-glare, ribbed slide top; squared, serrated trigger guard; trig-ger stop to prevent overtravel. Introduced 1986. Imported from the Czech Republic by CZ-USA.

Price: Black polymer **$483.00**
Price: Combat, black polymer **$540.00**
Price: Combat, dual tone **$487.00**
Price: Combat, glossy blue **$499.00**

CZ 85 Combat

Similar to the CZ 85B (9mm only) except has an adjustable rear sight, ad-justable trigger for overtravel, free-fall magazine, extended magazine catch. Does not have the firing pin block safety. Introduced 1999. Import-ed from the Czech Republic by CZ-USA.
Price: 9mm, black polymer **$540.00**
Price: 9mm, glossy blue **$561.00**
Price: 9mm, dual tone or satin nickel **$561.00**

CZ 83B DOUBLE-ACTION PISTOL

Caliber: 9mm Makarov, 32 ACP, 380 ACP, 10-shot magazine. **Barrel:** 3.8". **Weight:** 26.2 oz. **Length:** 6.8" overall. **Stocks:** High impact checkered plastic. **Sights:** Removable square post front, rear adjustable for windage; three-dot system. **Features:** Single action/double action; ambidextrous magazine release and safety. Blue finish; non-glare ribbed slide top. Im-ported from the Czech Republic by CZ-USA.
Price: Blue **$378.00**
Price: Nickel **$378.00**

HANDGUNS

CZ 97B

CZ 100

CZ 75/85 Kadet

Davis P-380

Davis P-32

CZ 97B AUTO PISTOL

Caliber: 45 ACP, 10-shot magazine. **Barrel:** 4.85". **Weight:** 40 oz. **Length:** 8.34" overall. **Stocks:** Checkered walnut. **Sights:** Fixed. **Features:** Single action/double action; full-length slide rails; screw-in barrel bushing; linkless barrel; all-steel construction; chamber loaded indicator; dual transfer bars. Introduced 1999. Imported from the Czech Republic by CZ-USA.
Price: Black polymer.................................... $607.00
Price: Glossy blue..................................... $621.00

CZ 75/85 KADET AUTO PISTOL

Caliber: 22 LR, 10-shot magazine. **Barrel:** 4.88". **Weight:** 36 oz. **Length:** NA. **Stocks:** High impact checkered plastic. **Sights:** Blade front, fully adjustable rear. **Features:** Single action/double action mechanism; all-steel construction. Duplicates weight, balance and function of the CZ 75 pistol. Introduced 1999. Imported from the Czech Republic by CZ-USA.
Price: Black polymer.................................... $486.00

CZ 100 AUTO PISTOL

Caliber: 9mm Para., 40 S&W, 10-shot magazine. **Barrel:** 3.7". **Weight:** 24 oz. **Length:** 6.9" overall. **Stocks:** Grooved polymer. **Sights:** Blade front with dot, white outline rear drift adjustable for windage. **Features:** Double action only with firing pin block; polymer frame, steel slide; has laser sight mount. Introduced 1996. Imported from the Czech Republic by CZ-USA.
Price: 9mm Para...................................... $405.00
Price: 40 S&W $405.00

DAVIS P-380 AUTO PISTOL

Caliber: 380 ACP, 5-shot magazine. **Barrel:** 2.8". **Weight:** 22 oz. **Length:** 5.4" overall. **Stocks:** Black composition. **Sights:** Fixed. **Features:** Choice of chrome or black Teflon finish. Introduced 1991. Made in U.S. by Davis Industries.
Price: $98.00

DAVIS P-32 AUTO PISTOL

Caliber: 32 ACP, 6-shot magazine. **Barrel:** 2.8". **Weight:** 22 oz. **Length:** 5.4" overall. **Stocks:** Laminated wood. **Sights:** Fixed. **Features:** Choice of black Teflon or chrome finish. Announced 1986. Made in U.S. by Davis Industries.
Price: $107.00

Desert Eagle Mark XIX

E.A.A. Witness

Desert Eagle Baby Eagle

Entréprise Elite P500

HANDGUNS

DESERT EAGLE MARK XIX PISTOL

Caliber: 357 Mag., 9-shot; 44 Mag., 8-shot; 50 Magnum, 7-shot. **Barrel:** 6", 10", interchangeable. **Weight:** 357 Mag.—62 oz.; 44 Mag.—69 oz.; 50 Mag.—72 oz. **Length:** 10-1/4" overall (6" bbl.). **Stocks:** Rubber. **Sights:** Blade on ramp front, combat-style rear. Adjustable available. **Features:** Interchangeable barrels; rotating three-lug bolt; ambidextrous safety; adjustable trigger. Military epoxy finish. Satin, bright nickel, hard chrome, polished and blued finishes available. 10" barrel extra. Imported from Israel by Magnum Research, Inc.

Price: 357, 6" bbl., standard pistol	**$1,199.00**
Price: 44 Mag., 6", standard pistol	**$1,199.00**
Price: 50 Magnum, 6" bbl., standard pistol	**$1,199.00**
Price: 440 Cor-Bon, 6" bbl.	**$1,389.00**

DESERT EAGLE BABY EAGLE PISTOLS

Caliber: 9mm Para., 40 S&W, 45 ACP, 10-round magazine. **Barrel:** 3.5", 3.7", 4.72". **Weight:** NA. **Length:** 7.25" to 8.25" overall. **Grips:** Polymer. **Sights:** Drift-adjustable rear, blade front. **Features:** Steel frame and slide; polygonal rifling to reduce barrel wear; slide safety; decocker. Reintroduced in 1999. Imported from Israel by Magnum Research Inc.

Price: Standard (9mm or 40 cal.; 4.72" barrel, 8.25" overall)	**$449.00**
Price: Semi-Compact (9mm, 40 or 45 cal.; 3.7" barrel, 7.75" overall)	**$449.00**
Price: Compact (9mm or 40 cal.; 3.5" barrel, 7.25" overall)	**$449.00**
Price: Polymer (9mm or 40 cal; polymer frame; 3.25" barrel, 7.25" overall)	**$449.00**

E.A.A. WITNESS DA AUTO PISTOL

Caliber: 9mm Para., 10-shot magazine; 38 Super, 40 S&W, 10-shot magazine; 45 ACP, 10-shot magazine. **Barrel:** 4.50". **Weight:** 35.33 oz.

Length: 8.10" overall. **Stocks:** Checkered rubber. **Sights:** Undercut blade front, open rear adjustable for windage. **Features:** Double-action trigger system; round trigger guard; frame-mounted safety. Introduced 1991. Imported from Italy by European American Armory.

Price: 9mm, blue	**$351.00**
Price: 9mm, Wonder finish	**$366.00**
Price: 9mm Compact, blue, 10-shot	**$351.00**
Price: As above, Wonder finish	**$366.60**
Price: 40 S&W, blue	**$366.60**
Price: As above, Wonder finish	**$366.60**
Price: 40 S&W Compact, 9-shot, blue	**$366.60**
Price: As above, Wonder finish	**$366.60**
Price: 45 ACP, blue	**$351.00**
Price: As above, Wonder finish	**$366.60**
Price: 45 ACP Compact, 8-shot, blue	**$351.00**
Price: As above, Wonder finish	**$366.60**

E.A.A. EUROPEAN MODEL AUTO PISTOLS

Caliber: 32 ACP or 380 ACP, 7-shot magazine. **Barrel:** 3.88". **Weight:** 26 oz. **Length:** 7-3/8" overall. **Stocks:** European hardwood. **Sights:** Fixed blade front, rear drift-adjustable for windage. **Features:** Chrome or blue finish; magazine, thumb and firing pin safeties; external hammer; safety-lever takedown. Imported from Italy by European American Armory.

Price: Blue	**$132.60**
Price: Wonder finish	**$163.80**

ENTRÉPRISE ELITE P500 AUTO PISTOL

Caliber: 45 ACP, 10-shot magazine. **Barrel:** 5". **Weight:** 40 oz. **Length:** 8.5" overall. **Stocks:** Black ultra-slim, double diamond, checkered synthetic. **Sights:** Dovetailed blade front, rear adjustable for windage; three-dot system. **Features:** Reinforced dust cover; lowered and flared ejection

Entréprise Boxer P500

Entréprise Tactical 500

FEG PJK-9HP

Felk MTF 450

port; squared trigger guard; adjustable match trigger; bolstered front strap; high grip cut; high ride beavertail grip safety; steel flat mainspring housing; extended thumb lock; skeletonized hammer, match grade sear, disconnector; Wolff springs. Introduced 1998. Made in U.S. by Entréprise Arms.
Price: **$739.90**

Entréprise Boxer P500 Auto Pistol

Similar to the Medalist model except has adjustable Competizione "melded" rear sight with dovetailed Patridge front; high mass chiseled slide with sweep cut; machined slide parallel rails; polished breech face and barrel channel. Introduced 1998. Made in U.S. by Entréprise Arms.
Price: **$1,399.00**

Entréprise Medalist P500 Auto Pistol

Similar to the Elite model except has adjustable Competizione "melded" rear sight with dovetailed Patridge front; machined slide parallel rails with polished breech face and barrel channel; front and rear slide serrations; lowered and flared ejection port; full-length one-piece guide rod with plug; National Match barrel and bushing; stainless firing pin; tuned match extractor; oversize firing pin stop; throated barrel and polished ramp; slide lapped to frame. Introduced 1998. Made in U.S. by Entréprise Arms.
Price: 45 ACP **$979.00**
Price: 40 S&W **$1,099.00**

Entréprise Tactical P500 Auto Pistol

Similar to the Elite model except has Tactical2 Ghost Ring sight or Novak lo- mount sight; ambidextrous thumb safety; front and rear slide serrations; full-length guide rod; throated barrel, polished ramp; tuned match extractor; fitted barrel and bushing; stainless firing pin; slide lapped to frame; dehorned. Introduced 1998. Made in U.S. by Entréprise Arms.
Price: **$979.90**
Price: Tactical Plus (full-size frame, Officer's slide) **$1,049.00**

ERMA KGP68 AUTO PISTOL

Caliber: 32 ACP, 6-shot, 380 ACP, 5-shot. **Barrel:** 4". **Weight:** 22-1/2 oz. **Length:** 7-3/8" overall. **Stocks:** Checkered plastic. **Sights:** Fixed. **Features:** Toggle action similar to original "Luger" pistol. Action stays open after last shot. Has magazine and sear disconnect safety systems.
Price: **$499.95**

FEG PJK-9HP AUTO PISTOL

Caliber: 9mm Para., 10-shot magazine. **Barrel:** 4.75". **Weight:** 32 oz. **Length:** 8" overall. **Stocks:** Hand-checkered walnut. **Sights:** Blade front, rear adjustable for windage; three dot system. **Features:** Single action; polished blue or hard chrome finish; rounded combat-style serrated hammer. Comes with two magazines and cleaning rod. Imported from Hungary by K.B.I., Inc.
Price: Blue **$259.95**
Price: Hard chrome **$259.95**

FEG SMC-380 AUTO PISTOL

Caliber: 380 ACP, 6-shot magazine. **Barrel:** 3.5". **Weight:** 18.5 oz. **Length:** 6.1" overall. **Stocks:** Checkered composition with thumbrest. **Sights:** Blade front, rear adjustable for windage. **Features:** Patterned after the PPK pistol. Alloy frame, steel slide; double action. Blue finish. Comes with two magazines, cleaning rod. Imported from Hungary by K.B.I., Inc.
Price: **$224.95**

FELK MTF 450 AUTO PISTOL

Caliber: 9mm Para. (10-shot); 40 S&W (8-shot); 45 ACP (9-shot magazine). **Barrel:** 3.5". **Weight:** 19.9 oz. **Length:** 6.4" overall. **Stocks:** Checkered. **Sights:** Blade front; adjustable rear. **Features:** Double-action-only trigger, striker fired; polymer frame; trigger safety, firing pin safety, trigger

Glock 17C

Glock 22

Glock 26

bar safety; adjustable trigger weight; fully interchangeable slide/barrel to change calibers. Introduced 1998. Imported by Felk Inc.

Price: **$395.00**
Price: 45 ACP pistol with 9mm and 40 S&W slide/barrel
assemblies **$999.00**

GLOCK 17 AUTO PISTOL

Caliber: 9mm Para., 10-shot magazine. **Barrel:** 4.49". **Weight:** 22.04 oz. (without magazine). **Length:** 7.32" overall. **Stocks:** Black polymer. **Sights:** Dot on front blade, white outline rear adjustable for windage. **Features:** Polymer frame, steel slide; double-action trigger with "Safe Action" system; mechanical firing pin safety, drop safety; simple takedown without tools; locked breech, recoil operated action. Adopted by Austrian armed forces 1983. NATO approved 1984. Imported from Austria by Glock, Inc.

Price: Fixed sight, with extra magazine, magazine loader, cleaning kit
.... **$641.00**
Price: Adjustable sight **$671.00**
Price: Model 17L (6" barrel) **$800.00**
Price: Model 17C, ported barrel (compensated) **$646.00**

Glock 19 Auto Pistol

Similar to the Glock 17 except has a 4" barrel, giving an overall length of 6.85" and weight of 20.99 oz. Magazine capacity is 10 rounds. Fixed or adjustable rear sight. Introduced 1988.

Price: Fixed sight **$641.00**
Price: Adjustable sight **$671.00**
Price: Model 19C, ported barrel **$646.00**

Glock 20 10mm Auto Pistol

Similar to the Glock Model 17 except chambered for 10mm Automatic cartridge. Barrel length is 4.60", overall length is 7.59", and weight is 26.3 oz. (without magazine). Magazine capacity is 10 rounds. Fixed or adjustable rear sight. Comes with an extra magazine, magazine loader, cleaning rod and brush. Introduced 1990. Imported from Austria by Glock, Inc.

Price: Fixed sight **$700.00**
Price: Adjustable sight **$730.00**

Glock 21 Auto Pistol

Similar to the Glock 17 except chambered for 45 ACP, 10-shot magazine. Overall length is 7.59", weight is 25.2 oz. (without magazine). Fixed or adjustable rear sight. Introduced 1991.

Price: Fixed sight **$700.00**
Price: Adjustable sight **$730.00**

Glock 22 Auto Pistol

Similar to the Glock 17 except chambered for 40 S&W, 10-shot magazine. Overall length is 7.28", weight is 22.3 oz. (without magazine). Fixed or adjustable rear sight. Introduced 1990.

Price: Fixed sight **$641.00**
Price: Adjustable sight **$671.00**
Price: Model 22C, ported barrel **$646.00**

Glock 23 Auto Pistol

Similar to the Glock 19 except chambered for 40 S&W, 10-shot magazine. Overall length is 6.85", weight is 20.6 oz. (without magazine). Fixed or adjustable rear sight. Introduced 1990.

Price: Fixed sight **$641.00**
Price: Model 23C, ported barrel **$646.00**
Price: Adjustable sight **$671.00**

GLOCK 26, 27 AUTO PISTOLS

Caliber: 9mm Para. (M26), 10-shot magazine; 40 S&W (M27), 9-shot magazine. **Barrel:** 3.46". **Weight:** 21.75 oz. **Length:** 6.29" overall. **Stocks:** Integral. Stippled polymer. **Sights:** Dot on front blade, fixed or fully adjustable white outline rear. **Features:** Subcompact size. Polymer frame, steel slide; double-action trigger with "Safe Action" system, three safeties. Matte black Tenifer finish. Hammer-forged barrel. Imported from Austria by Glock, Inc. Introduced 1996.

Price: Fixed sight **$641.00**
Price: Adjustable sight **$671.00**

GLOCK 29, 30 AUTO PISTOLS

Caliber: 10mm (M29), 45 ACP (M30), 10-shot magazine. **Barrel:** 3.78". **Weight:** 24 oz. **Length:** 6.7" overall. **Stocks:** Integral. Stippled polymer. **Sights:** Dot on front, fixed or fully adjustable white outline rear. **Features:** Compact size. Polymer frame steel slide; double-recoil spring reduces recoil; Safe Action system with three safeties; Tenifer finish. Two magazines supplied. Introduced 1997. Imported from Austria by Glock, Inc.

Price: Fixed sight **$700.00**
Price: Adjustable sight **$730.00**

Glock 30

Glock 35

Glock 31

Hammerli Trailside PL 22

Glock 31/31C Auto Pistols

Similar to the Glock 17 except chambered for 357 Auto cartridge; 10-shot magazine. Overall length is 7.32", weight is 23.28 oz. (without magazine). Fixed or adjustable sight. Imported from Austria by Glock, Inc.

Price: Fixed sight **$641.00**
Price: Adjustable sight **$671.00**
Price: Model 31C, ported barrel **$646.00**

Glock 32/32C Auto Pistols

Similar to the Glock 19 except chambered for the 357 Auto cartridge; 10-shot magazine. Overall length is 6.85", weight is 21.52 oz. (without magazine). Fixed or adjustable sight. Imported from Austria by Glock, Inc.

Price: Fixed sight **$616.00**
Price: Adjustable sight **$644.00**
Price: Model 32C, ported barrel **$646.00**

Glock 33 Auto Pistol

Similar to the Glock 26 except chambered for the 357 Auto cartridge; 9-shot magazine. Overall length is 6.29", weight is 19.75 oz. (without magazine). Fixed or adjustable sight. Imported from Austria by Glock, Inc.

Price: Fixed sight **$641.00**
Price: Adjustable sight **$671.00**

GLOCK 34, 35 AUTO PISTOLS

Caliber: 9mm Para. (M34), 40 S&W (M35), 10-shot magazine. **Barrel:** 5.32". **Weight:** 22.9 oz. **Length:** 8.15" overall. **Stocks:** Integral. Stippled polymer. **Sights:** Dot on front, fully adjustable white outline rear. **Features:** Polymer frame, steel slide; double-action trigger with "Safe Action" system; three safeties; Tenifer finish. Imported from Austria by Glock, Inc.

Price: Model 34, 9mm. **$770.00**
Price: Model 35, 40 S&W **$770.00**

GLOCK 36 AUTO PISTOL

Caliber: 45 ACP, 6-shot magazine. **Barrel:** 3.78". **Weight:** 20.11 oz. **Length:** 6.77" overall. **Stocks:** Integral. Stippled polymer. **Sights:** Dot on front, fully adjustable white outline rear. **Features:** Polymer frame, steel slide; double-action trigger with "Safe Action" system; three safeties; Tenifer finish. Imported from Austria by Glock, Inc.

Price: Fixed sight **$700.00**
Price: Adj. sight **$730.00**

HAMMERLI TRAILSIDE PL 22 TARGET PISTOL

Caliber: 22 LR, 10-shot magazine. **Barrel:** 4.5", 6". **Weight:** 28 oz. (4.5" barrel). **Length:** 7.75" overall. **Stocks:** Wood target-style. **Sights:** Blade front, rear adjustable for windage. **Features:** One-piece barrel/frame unit; two-stage competition-style trigger; dovetail scope mount rail. Introduced 1999. Imported from Switzerland by SIGARMS, Inc.

Price: . . . . **NA**

HECKLER & KOCH USP AUTO PISTOL

Caliber: 9mm Para., 10-shot magazine, 40 S&W, 10-shot magazine. **Barrel:** 4.25". **Weight:** 28 oz. (USP40). **Length:** 6.9" overall. **Stocks:** Non-slip stippled black polymer. **Sights:** Blade front, rear adjustable for windage. **Features:** New HK design with polymer frame, modified Browning action with recoil reduction system, single control lever. Special "hostile environment" finish on all metal parts. Available in SA/DA, DAO, left- and right-hand versions. Introduced 1993. Imported from Germany by Heckler & Koch, Inc.

Price: Right-hand **$699.00**
Price: Left-hand **$714.00**
Price: Stainless steel, right-hand **$749.00**
Price: Stainless steel, left-hand **$799.00**

Heckler & Koch USP Compact

Heckler & Koch USP45 Tactical

Heckler & Koch USP45

Heckler & Koch USP Expert

Heckler & Koch USP Compact Auto Pistol

Similar to the USP except has 3.58" barrel, measures 6.81" overall, and weighs 1.60 lbs. (9mm). Available in 9mm Para. or 40 S&W with 10-shot magazine. Introduced 1996. Imported from Germany by Heckler & Koch, Inc.

Price: Blue **$719.00**
Price: Blue with control lever on right **$744.00**
Price: Stainless steel **$769.00**
Price: Stainless steel with control lever on right **$794.00**

Heckler & Koch USP45 Auto Pistol

Similar to the 9mm and 40 S&W USP except chambered for 45 ACP, 10-shot magazine. Has 4.13" barrel, overall length of 7.87" and weighs 30.4 oz. Has adjustable three-dot sight system. Available in SA/DA, DAO, left- and right-hand versions. Introduced 1995. Imported from Germany by Heckler & Koch, Inc.

Price: Right-hand **$759.00**
Price: Left-hand **$784.00**
Price: Stainless steel right-hand **$799.00**
Price: Stainless steel left-hand **$724.00**

Heckler & Koch USP45 Compact

Similar to the USP45 except has stainless slide; 8-shot magazine; modified and contoured slide and frame; extended slide release; 3.80" barrel, 7.09" overall length, weighs 1.75 lbs.; adjustable three-dot sights. Introduced 1998. Imported from Germany by Heckler & Koch, Inc.

Price: With control lever on left, stainless **$789.00**
Price: As above, blue **$739.00**
Price: With control lever on right, stainless **$814.00**
Price: As above, blue **$739.00**

HECKLER & KOCH USP45 TACTICAL PISTOL

Caliber: 45 ACP, 10-shot magazine. **Barrel:** 4.92". **Weight:** 2.24 lbs. **Length:** 8.64" overall. **Stocks:** Non-slip stippled polymer. **Sights:** Blade front, fully adjustable target rear. **Features:** Has extended threaded barrel with rubber O-ring; adjustable trigger; extended magazine floorplate; adjustable trigger stop; polymer frame. Introduced 1998. Imported from Germany by Heckler & Koch, Inc.

Price: **$999.00**

HECKLER & KOCH MARK 23 SPECIAL OPERATIONS PISTOL

Caliber: 45 ACP, 10-shot magazine. **Barrel:** 5.87". **Weight:** 43 oz. **Length:** 9.65" overall. **Stocks:** Integral with frame; black polymer. **Sights:** Blade front, rear drift adjustable for windage; three-dot. **Features:** Polymer frame; double action; exposed hammer; short recoil, modified Browning action. Civilian version of the SOCOM pistol. Introduced 1996. Imported from Germany by Heckler & Koch, Inc.

Price: **$2,169.00**

Heckler & Koch USP Expert Pistol

Combines features of the USP Tactical and HK Mark 23 pistols with a new slide design. Chambered for 45 ACP; 10-shot magazine. Has adjustable target sights, 5.20" barrel, 8.74" overall length, weighs 1.87 lbs. Match-grade single- and double-action trigger pull with adjustable stop; ambidextrous control levers; elongated target slide; barrel O-ring that seals and centers barrel. Suited to IPSC competition. Introduced 1999. Imported from Germany by Heckler & Koch, Inc.

Price: **$1,369.00**

HECKLER & KOCH P7M8 AUTO PISTOL

Caliber: 9mm Para., 8-shot magazine. **Barrel:** 4.13". **Weight:** 29 oz. **Length:** 6.73" overall. **Stocks:** Stippled black plastic. **Sights:** Blade front, adjustable rear; three dot system. **Features:** Unique "squeeze cocker" in frontstrap cocks the action. Gas-retarded action. Squared combat-type trigger guard. Blue finish. Compact size. Imported from Germany by Heckler & Koch, Inc.

Price: P7M8, blued **$1,229.00**

Heckler & Koch P7M8

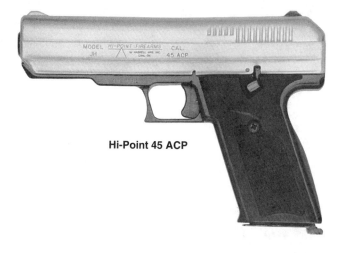

Hi-Point 45 ACP

Heritage Stealth

Hi-Point 9MM Comp

HERITAGE STEALTH AUTO PISTOL

Caliber: 9mm Para., 40 S&W, 10-shot magazine. **Barrel:** 3.9". **Weight:** 20.2 oz. **Length:** 6.3" overall. **Stocks:** Black polymer; integral. **Sights:** Blade front, rear drift adjustable for windage. **Features:** Gas retarded blowback action; polymer frame, 17-4 stainless slide; frame mounted ambidextrous trigger safety, magazine safety. Introduced 1996. Made in U.S. by Heritage Mfg., Inc.

Price: **$289.95**
Price: Stainless or stainless/black **$329.95**

HERITAGE H25S AUTO PISTOL

Caliber: 25 ACP, 6-shot magazine. **Barrel:** 2.25". **Weight:** 13.5 oz. **Length:** 4.5" overall. **Stocks:** Smooth hardwood. **Sights:** Fixed. **Features:** Frame-mounted trigger safety, magazine disconnect safety. Made in U.S. by Heritage Mfg. Inc.

Price: Blue **$149.95**
Price: Nickel **$159.95**

HI-POINT FIREARMS 40 S&W AUTO

Caliber: 40 S&W, 8-shot magazine. **Barrel:** 4.5". **Weight:** 39 oz. **Length:** 7.72" overall. **Stocks:** Checkered acetal resin. **Sights:** Adjustable; low profile. **Features:** Internal drop-safe mechanism; alloy frame. Introduced 1991. From MKS Supply, Inc.

Price: Matte black. **$159.00**

HI-POINT FIREARMS 45 CALIBER PISTOL

Caliber: 45 ACP, 7-shot magazine. **Barrel:** 4.5". **Weight:** 39 oz. **Length:** 7.95" overall. **Stocks:** Checkered acetal resin. **Sights:** Adjustable; low profile. **Features:** Internal drop-safe mechanism; alloy frame. Introduced 1991. From MKS Supply, Inc.

Price: Matte black **$159.00**
Price: Chrome slide, black frame **$169.00**

HI-POINT FIREARMS 9MM COMP PISTOL

Caliber: 9mm, Para., 10-shot magazine. **Barrel:** 4". **Weight:** 39 oz. **Length:** 7.72" overall. **Stocks:** Textured acetal plastic. **Sights:** Adjustable; low profile. **Features:** Single-action design. Scratch-resistant, non-glare blue finish, alloy frame. Muzzle brake/compensator. Compensator is slotted for laser or flashlight mounting. Introduced 1998. From MKS Supply, Inc.

Price: Matte black. **$159.00**

HI-POINT FIREARMS MODEL 9MM COMPACT PISTOL

Caliber: 9mm Para., 8-shot magazine. **Barrel:** 3.5". **Weight:** 29 oz. **Length:** 6.7" overall. **Stocks:** Textured acetal plastic. **Sights:** Combat-style adjustable three-dot system; low profile. **Features:** Single-action design; frame-mounted magazine release; polymer or alloy frame. Scratch-resistant matte finish. Introduced 1993. From MKS Supply, Inc.

Price: Black, alloy frame **$137.00**
Price: With polymer frame (29 oz.), non-slip grips **$137.00**
Price: Aluminum with polymer frame **$137.00**

Hi-Point Firearms Model 380 Polymer Pistol

Similar to the 9mm Compact model except chambered for 380 ACP, 8-shot magazine, adjustable three-dot sights. Weighs 29 oz. Polymer frame. Introduced 1998. Made in U.S. From MKS Supply.

Price: **$99.95**

Kahr MK40

Kel-Tec P-11

Kahr K9

Kel-Tec P-32

HANDGUNS

HS AMERICA HS 2000 PISTOL

Caliber: 9mm Para., 357 SIG, 40 S&W, 10-shot magazine. **Barrel:** 4.08 inches. **Weight:** 22.88 oz. **Length:** 7.2 inches overall. **Grips:** Integral black polymer. **Sights:** Drift-adjustable white dot rear, white dot blade front. **Features:** Incorporates trigger, firing pin, grip and out-of-battery safeties; firing-pin status and loaded chamber indicators; ambidextrous magazine release; dual-tension recoil spring with stand-off device; polymer frame; black finish with chrome-plated magazine. Imported from Croatia by HS America.
Price: **$419.00**

KAHR K9, K40 DA AUTO PISTOLS

Caliber: 9mm Para., 7-shot, 40 S&W, 6-shot magazine. **Barrel:** 3.5". **Weight:** 25 oz. **Length:** 6" overall. **Stocks:** Wrap-around textured soft polymer. **Sights:** Blade front, rear drift adjustable for windage; bar-dot combat style. **Features:** Trigger-cocking double-action mechanism with passive firing pin block. Made of 4140 ordnance steel with matte black finish. Contact maker for complete price list. Introduced 1994. Made in U.S. by Kahr Arms.
Price: E9, black matte finish **$399.00**
Price: Matte black, night sights 9mm **$640.00**
Price: Matte stainless steel, 9mm **$580.00**
Price: 40 S&W, matte black **$550.00**
Price: 40 S&W, matte black, night sights **$640.00**
Price: 40 S&W, matte stainless **$580.00**
Price: K9 Elite 98 (high-polish stainless slide flats, Kahr combat trigger), from **$631.00**
Price: As above, MK9 Elite 98, from **$631.00**
Price: As above, K40 Elite 98, from **$631.00**

Kahr K9 9mm Compact Polymer Pistol

Similar to K9 steel frame pistol except has polymer frame, matte stainless steel slide. Barrel length 3.5"; overall length 6"; weighs 17.9 oz. Includes two 7-shot magazines, hard polymer case, trigger lock. Introduced 2000. Made in U.S. by Kahr Arms.
Price: **$527.00**

Kahr MK9/MK40 Micro Pistol

Similar to the K9/K40 except is 5.5" overall, 4" high, has a 3" barrel. Weighs 22 oz. Has snag-free bar-dot sights, polished feed ramp, dual recoil spring system, DA-only trigger. Comes with 6- and 7-shot magazines. Introduced 1998. Made in U.S. by Kahr Arms.
Price: Matte stainless **$580.00**
Price: Elite 98, polished stainless, tritium night sights **$721.00**

KEL-TEC P-11 AUTO PISTOL

Caliber: 9mm Para., 10-shot magazine. **Barrel:** 3.1". **Weight:** 14 oz. **Length:** 5.6" overall. **Stocks:** Checkered black polymer. **Sights:** Blade front, rear adjustable for windage. **Features:** Ordnance steel slide, aluminum frame. Double-action-only trigger mechanism. Introduced 1995. Made in U.S. by Kel-Tec CNC Industries, Inc.
Price: Blue **$309.00**
Price: Hard chrome **$363.00**
Price: Parkerized **$350.00**

KEL-TEC P-32 AUTO PISTOL

Caliber: 32 ACP, 7-shot magazine. **Barrel:** 2.68". **Weight:** 6.6 oz. **Length:** 5.07" overall. **Stocks:** Checkered composite. **Sights:** Fixed. **Features:** Double-action-only mechanism with 6-lb. pull; internal slide stop. Textured composite grip/frame. Made in U.S. by Kel-Tec CNC Industries, Inc.
Price: **$295.00**

Kimber Custom 45

Kimber Ultra Carry

Kimber Compact Custom

Kimber High Capacity Polymer

KIMBER CUSTOM AUTO PISTOL

Caliber: 45 ACP, 7-shot magazine. **Barrel:** 5", match grade. **Weight:** 38 oz. **Length:** 8.7" overall. **Stocks:** Checkered black rubber (standard), or rosewood. **Sights:** McCormick dovetailed front, low combat rear. **Features:** Slide, frame and barrel machined from steel forgings; match-grade barrel, chamber, trigger; extended thumb safety; beveled magazine well; beveled front and rear slide serrations; high-ride beavertail safety; checkered flat mainspring housing; kidney cut under trigger guard; high cut grip design; match-grade stainless barrel bushing; Commander-style hammer; lowered and flared ejection port; Wolff springs; bead blasted black oxide finish. Made in U.S. by Kimber Mfg., Inc.

Price: Custom $723.00
Price: Custom Walnut (double-diamond walnut grips) $745.00
Price: Custom Stainless $823.00
Price: Custom Stainless 40 S&W $861.00
Price: Custom Stainless Target 45 ACP (stainless, adj. sight) $935.00
Price: Custom Stainless Target 40 S&W $968.00

Kimber Compact Auto Pistol

Similar to the Custom model except has 4" bull barrel fitted directly to the slide without a bushing; full-length guide rod; grip is .400" shorter than full-size gun; no front serrations. Steel frame models weigh 34 oz., aluminum 28 oz. Introduced 1998. Made in U.S. by Kimber Mfg., Inc.

Price: 45 ACP, matte black. $757.00
Price: Compact Stainless 45 ACP $863.00
Price: Compact Stainless 40 S&W $893.00
Price: Compact Stainless Aluminum 45 ACP (aluminum frame,
stainless slide) $829.00
Price: Compact Stainless Aluminum 40 S&W $864.00

Kimber Pro Carry Auto Pistol

Similar to the Compact model except has aluminum frame with full-length grip. Has 4" bull barrel fitted directly to the slide without bushing. Introduced 1998. Made in U.S. by Kimber Mfg., Inc.

Price: 45 ACP $758.00
Price: 40 S&W $792.00
Price: Stainless Pro Carry 45 ACP $829.00
Price: Stainless Pro Carry 40 S&W $864.00

Kimber Ultra Carry Auto Pistol

Similar to the Compact Aluminum model except has 3" balljoint spherical bushingless cone barrel; aluminum frame; beveling at front and rear of ejection port; relieved breech face; tuned ejector; special slide stop; dual captured low-effort spring system. Weighs 25 oz. Introduced 1999. made in U.S. by Kimber Mfg., Inc.

Price: 45 ACP $792.00
Price: 40 S&W $822.00
Price: Stainless, 45 ACP $868.00
Price: Stainless, 40 S&W $904.00

KIMBER HIGH CAPACITY POLYMER PISTOL

Caliber: 45 ACP, 14-shot magazine. **Barrel:** 5". **Weight:** 34 oz. **Length:** 8.7" overall. **Stocks:** Integral; checkered black polymer. **Sights:** McCormick low profile front and rear. **Features:** Polymer frame with steel insert. Comes with pre-ban magazine. Checkered front strap and mainspring housing; polymer trigger; stainless high ride beavertail grip safety; hooked trigger guard. Introduced 1997. Made in U.S. by Kimber Mfg., Inc.

Price: Matte black finish $904.00
Price: Polymer Stainless (satin-finish stainless slide) $973.00
Price: Polymer Pro Carry (compact slide, 4" bull barrel) $924.00
Price: Polymer Pro Carry Stainless $993.00

Kimber Pro CDP

Kimber Ultra CDP

Kimber Gold Match Auto Pistol

Similar to the Custom model except has Kimber adjustable sight with rounded and blended edges; stainless steel match-grade barrel hand-fitted to spherical barrel bushing; premium aluminum trigger; extended ambidextrous thumb safety; hand-checkered double diamond rosewood grips. Hand-fitted by Kimber Custom Shop. Made in U.S. by Kimber Mfg., Inc.

Price: Gold Match 45 ACP **$1,135.00**
Price: Stainless Gold Match 45 ACP (highly polished flats) **$1,277.00**
Price: Stainless Gold Match 40 S&W **$1,306.00**

Kimber Polymer Gold Match Auto Pistol

Similar to the Polymer model except has Kimber adjustable sight with rounded and blended edges; stainless steel match-grade barrel hand-fitted to spherical barrel bushing; premium aluminum trigger; extended ambidextrous thumb safety. Hand-fitted by Kimber Custom Shop. Introduced 1999. Made in U.S. by Kimber Mfg., Inc.

Price: **$1,183.00**
Price: Polymer Stainless Gold Match (polished stainless slide) . **$1,337.00**

Kimber Gold Combat Auto Pistol

Similar to the Gold Match except designed for concealed carry. Has two-piece extended and beveled magazine well, tritium night sights; premium aluminum trigger; 30 lpi front strap checkering; special Custom Shop markings; Kim Pro black finish. Introduced 1999. Made in U.S. by Kimber Mfg., Inc.

Price: 45 ACP **$1,633.00**
Price: Gold Combat Stainless (satin-finished stainless frame
and slide, special Custom Shop markings) **$1,576.00**

KIMBER PRO CDP AUTO PISTOL

Caliber: 45 ACP, 7-shot magazine. **Barrel:** 4". **Weight:** 28 oz. **Length:** 7.7" overall. **Grips:** Hand-checkered. double diamond rosewood. **Sights:** Tritium three-dot. **Features:** Matte black, machined aluminum frame; satin stainless steel slide; match-grade barrel and chamber; beveled magazine well; extended ejector; high-ride beavertail grip safety; match-grade trigger group; ambidextrous safety; checkered frontstrap; meltdown treatment. Introduced 2000. Made in U.S. by Kimber.

Price: **$1,086.00**

KIMBER ULTRA CDP AUTO PISTOL

Caliber: 45 ACP, 6-shot magazine. **Barrel:** 3". **Weight:** 25 oz. **Length:** 6.8" overall. **Grips:** Hand-checkered. double diamond rosewood. **Sights:** Tritium three-dot. **Features:** Matte black, machined aluminum frame; satin stainless steel slide; match-grade barrel and chamber; beveled magazine well and ejection port; dual recoil spring system for reliability and ease of manual slide operation; match-grade barrel, chamber and trigger; ambi-

Llama Micromax

dextrous safety; checkered frontstrap; meltdown treatment. Introduced 2000. Made in U.S. by Kimber.

Price: **$1,086.00**

LLAMA MICROMAX 380 AUTO PISTOL

Caliber: 32 ACP, 8-shot, 380 ACP, 7-shot magazine. **Barrel:** 3-11/16". **Weight:** 23 oz. **Length:** 6-1/2" overall. **Stocks:** Checkered high impact polymer. **Sights:** 3-dot combat. **Features:** Single-action design. Mini custom extended slide release; mini custom extended beavertail grip safety; combat-style hammer. Introduced 1997. Imported from Spain by Import Sports, Inc.

Price: Matte blue **$246.95**
Price: Satin chrome (380 only) **$281.95**

LLAMA MINIMAX SERIES

Caliber: 9mm Para., 8-shot; 40 S&W, 7-shot; 45 ACP, 6-shot magazine. **Barrel:** 3-1/2". **Weight:** 35 oz. **Length:** 7-1/3" overall. **Stocks:** Checkered rubber. **Sights:** Three-dot combat. **Features:** Single action, skeletonized combat-style hammer, extended slide release, cone-style barrel, flared ejection port. Introduced 1996. Imported from Spain by Import Sports, Inc.

Price: Blue **$308.95**
Price: Duo-Tone finish (45 only) **$314.95**
Price: Satin chrome **$314.95**

Llama Minimax

Llama Max-1

Lorcin L9MM

North American
Arms Guardian

Llama Minimax Sub Compact Auto Pistol

Similar to the Minimax except has 3.14" barrel, weighs 31 oz.; 6.8" overall length; has 10-shot magazine with finger extension; beavertail grip safety. Introduced 1999. Imported from Spain by Import Sports, Inc.

Price: 9mm Para., 40 S&W, 45 ACP, matte blue $314.95
Price: As above, satin chrome $324.95
Price: Duo-Tone finish (45 only) $341.95

LLAMA MAX-I AUTO PISTOLS

Caliber: 45 ACP, 7-shot. Barrel: 5-1/8". Weight: 36 oz. Length: 8-1/2" overall. Stocks: Black rubber. Sights: Blade front, rear adjustable for windage; three-dot system. Features: Single-action trigger; skeletonized combat-style hammer; steel frame; extended manual and grip safeties. Introduced 1995. Imported from Spain by Import Sports, Inc.

Price: 45 ACP, 7-shot, Government model $298.95
Price: As above, satin chrome finish $314.95

LORCIN L-22 AUTO PISTOL

Caliber: 22 LR, 9-shot magazine. Barrel: 2.5". Weight: 16 oz. Length: 5.25" overall. Stocks: Black combat, or pink or pearl. Sights: Fixed three-dot system. Features: Available in chrome or black Teflon finish. Introduced 1989. From Lorcin Engineering.

Price: About $89.00

LORCIN L9MM AUTO PISTOL

Caliber: 9mm Para., 10-shot magazine. Barrel: 4.5". Weight: 31 oz. Length: 7.5" overall. Stocks: Grooved black composition. Sights: Fixed; three-dot system. Features: Matte black finish; hooked trigger guard; grip safety. Introduced 1994. Made in U.S. by Lorcin Engineering.

Price: $159.00

LORCIN L-25, LT-25 AUTO PISTOLS

Caliber: 25 ACP, 7-shot magazine. Barrel: 2.4". Weight: 14.5 oz. Length: 4.8" overall. Stocks: Smooth composition. Sights: Fixed. Features: Available in choice of finishes: chrome, black Teflon or camouflage. Introduced 1989. From Lorcin Engineering.

Price: L-25 . . . . $69.00
Price: LT-25 . . . . $79.00

LORCIN L-32, L-380 AUTO PISTOLS

Caliber: 32 ACP, 380 ACP, 7-shot magazine. Barrel: 3.5". Weight: 27 oz. Length: 6.6" overall. Stocks: Grooved composition. Sights: Fixed. Features: Black Teflon or chrome finish with black grips. Introduced 1992. From Lorcin Engineering.

Price: L-32 32 ACP $89.00
Price: L-380 380 ACP $100.00

NORTH AMERICAN ARMS GUARDIAN PISTOL

Caliber: 32 ACP, 6-shot magazine. Barrel: 2.1". Weight: 13.5 oz. Length: 4.36" overall. Stocks: Black polymer. Sights: Fixed. Features: Double-action-only mechanism. All stainless steel construction; snag-free. Introduced 1998. Made in U.S. by North American Arms.

Price: $359.00

OLYMPIC ARMS OA-96 AR PISTOL

Caliber: 223. Barrel: 6", 8", 4140 chrome-moly steel. Weight: 5 lbs. Length: 15-3/4" overall. Stocks: A2 stowaway pistol grip; no buttstock or receiver tube. Sights: Flat-top upper receiver, cut-down front sight base. Features: AR-15-type receivers with special bolt carrier; short aluminum hand guard; Vortex flash hider. Introduced 1996. Made in U.S. by Olympic Arms, Inc.

Price: $858.00

One Pro .45

Para-Ordnance LDA

Para-Ordnance P12.45

Peters Stahl High Capacity

Olympic Arms OA-98 AR Pistol

Similar to the OA-93 except has removable 7-shot magazine, weighs 3 lbs. Introduced 1999. Made in U.S. by Olympic Arms, Inc.

Price: **$990.00**

ONE PRO .45 AUTO PISTOL

Caliber: 45 ACP or 400 Cor-Bon, 10-shot magazine. **Barrel:** 3.75" **Weight:** 31.1 oz. **Length:** 7.04" overall. **Stocks:** Textured composition. **Sights:** Blade front, drift-adjustable rear; three-dot system. **Features:** All-steel construction; decocking lever and automatic firing pin lock; DA or DAO operation. Introduced 1997. Imported from Switzerland by Magnum Research, Inc.

Price: **$649.00**
Price: Conversion kit, 45 ACP/400, 400/45 ACP **$249.00**

ONE PRO 9 AUTO PISTOL

Caliber: 9mm Para., 10-shot magazine. **Barrel:** 3.01". **Weight:** 25.1 oz. **Length:** 6.06" overall. **Stocks:** Smooth wood. **Sights:** Blade front, rear adjustable for windage. **Features:** Rotating barrel; short slide; double recoil springs; double-action mechanism; decocking lever. Introduced 1998. Imported from Switzerland by Magnum Research.

Price: **$649.00**

PARA-ORDNANCE P-SERIES AUTO PISTOLS

Caliber: 9mm Para., 40 S&W, 45 ACP, 10-shot magazine. **Barrel:** 3", 3-1/2", 4-1/4", 5". **Weight:** From 24 oz. (alloy frame). **Length:** 8.5" overall. **Stocks:** Textured composition. **Sights:** Blade front, rear adjustable for windage. High visibility three-dot system. **Features:** Available with alloy, steel or stainless steel frame with black finish (silver or stainless gun). Steel and stainless steel frame guns weigh 40 oz. (P14.45), 36 oz. (P13.45), 34 oz. (P12.45). Grooved match trigger, rounded combat-style hammer. Beveled magazine well. Manual thumb, grip and firing pin lock

safeties. Solid barrel bushing. Contact maker for full details. Introduced 1990. Made in Canada by Para-Ordnance.

Price: P14.45ER (steel frame) **$775.00**
Price: P14.45RR (alloy frame) **$740.00**
Price: P12.45RR (3-1/2" bbl., 24 oz., alloy) **$740.00**
Price: P13.45RR (4-1/4" barrel, 28 oz., alloy) **$740.00**
Price: P12.45ER (steel frame) **$750.00**
Price: P16.40ER (steel frame) **$875.00**
Price: P10-9RR (9mm, alloy frame) **$740.00**

Para-Ordnance Limited Pistols

Similar to the P-Series pistols except with full-length recoil guide system; fully adjustable rear sight; tuned trigger with overtravel stop; beavertail grip safety; competition hammer; front and rear slide serrations; ambidextrous safety; lowered ejection port; ramped match-grade barrel; dovetailed front sight. Introduced 1998. Made in Canada by Para-Ordnance.

Price: 9mm, 40 S&W, 45 ACP .... **$865.00** to **$899.00**

Para-Ordnance LDA Auto Pistols

Similar to the P-series except has double-action trigger mechanism. Steel frame with matte black finish, checkered composition grips. Available in 9mm Para., 40 S&W, 45 ACP. Introduced 1999. Made in Canada by Para-Ordnance.

Price: **$775.00**

PETERS STAHL AUTOLOADING PISTOLS

Caliber: 9mm Para., 45 ACP. **Barrel:** 5" or 6". **Weight:** NA. **Length:** NA. **Grips:** Walnut or walnut with rubber wrap. **Sights:** Fully adjustable, blade front. **Features:** Stainless steel extended slide stop, safety and extended magazine release button; speed trigger with stop and approx. 3-lb. pull; polished ramp. Introduced 2000. Imported from Germany by Phillips & Rogers.

Price: High Capacity (accepts 15-shot magazines in 45 cal.; includes 10-shot magazine) **$1,695.00**

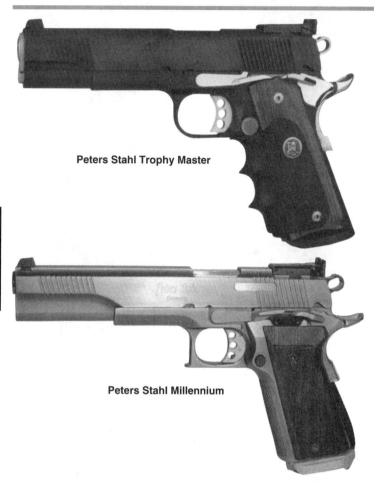

Peters Stahl Trophy Master

Phoenix Arms HP22

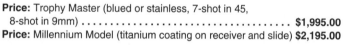

Peters Stahl Millennium

PSA-25 Auto

Republic Patriot

Price: Trophy Master (blued or stainless, 7-shot in 45,
8-shot in 9mm) **$1,995.00**
Price: Millennium Model (titanium coating on receiver and slide) **$2,195.00**

PHOENIX ARMS HP22, HP25 AUTO PISTOLS

Caliber: 22 LR, 10-shot (HP22), 25 ACP, 10-shot (HP25). **Barrel:** 3".
Weight: 20 oz. **Length:** 5-1/2" overall. **Stocks:** Checkered composition.
Sights: Blade front, adjustable rear. **Features:** Single action, exposed
hammer; manual hold-open; button magazine release. Available in satin
nickel, polished blue finish. Introduced 1993. Made in U.S. by Phoenix
Arms.
Price: With gun lock **$116.00**

PSA-25 AUTO POCKET PISTOL

Caliber: 25 ACP, 6-shot magazine. **Barrel:** 2-1/8". **Weight:** 9.5 oz. **Length:**
4-1/8" overall. **Stocks:** Checkered black polymer, ivory, checkered trans-
parent carbon fiber-filled polymer. **Sights:** Fixed. **Features:** All steel construction; striker fired; single action only; magazine disconnector; cocking
indicator. Introduced 1987. Made in U.S. by Precision Small Arms, Inc.
Price: Traditional (polished black oxide) **$269.00**
Price: Nouveau - Satin (brushed nickel) **$269.00**
Price: Nouveau - Mirror (highly polished nickel) **$309.00**
Price: Featherweight (aluminum frame, nickel slide) **$405.00**
Price: Diplomat (black oxide with gold highlights, ivory grips) **$625.00**
Price: Montreaux (gold plated, ivory grips) **$692.00**
Price: Renaissance (hand engraved nickel, ivory grips) **$1,115.00**
Price: Imperiale (inlaid gold filigree over blue, scrimshawed
ivory grips) **$3,600.00**

REPUBLIC PATRIOT PISTOL

Caliber: 45 ACP, 6-shot magazine. **Barrel:** 3". **Weight:** 20 oz. **Length:** 6"
overall. **Stocks:** Checkered. **Sights:** Blade front, drift-adjustable rear.
Features: Black polymer frame, stainless steel slide; double-action-only

trigger system; squared trigger guard. Introduced 1997. Made in U.S. by
Republic Arms, Inc.
Price: About **$325.00**

ROCK RIVER ARMS STANDARD MATCH AUTO PISTOL

Caliber: 45 ACP. **Barrel:** NA. **Weight:** NA. **Length:** NA. **Grips:** Cocobolo,
checkered. **Sights:** Heine fixed rear, blade front. **Features:** Chrome-moly
steel frame and slide; beavertail grip safety with raised pad; checkered
slide stop; ambidextrous safety; polished feed ramp and extractor; aluminum speed trigger with 3.5 lb. pull. Made in U.S. From Rock River Arms.
Price: **$1,025.00**

Rock River Standard Match

Ruger P89

Ruger P93DAO

Ruger P90

ROCKY MOUNTAIN ARMS PATRIOT PISTOL

Caliber: 223, 10-shot magazine. **Barrel:** 7", with muzzle brake. **Weight:** 5 lbs. **Length:** 20.5" overall. **Stocks:** Black composition. **Sights:** None furnished. **Features:** Milled upper receiver with enhanced Weaver base; milled lower receiver from billet plate; machined aluminum National Match handguard. Finished in DuPont Teflon-S matte black or NATO green. Comes with black nylon case, one magazine. Introduced 1993. From Rocky Mountain Arms, Inc.

Price: With A-2 handle top . . . . $2,500.00 to $2,800.00
Price: Flat top model. . . . . $3,000.00 to $3,500.00

RUGER P89 AUTOLOADING PISTOL

Caliber: 9mm Para., 10-shot magazine. **Barrel:** 4.50". **Weight:** 32 oz. **Length:** 7.84" overall. **Stocks:** Grooved black Xenoy composition. **Sights:** Square post front, square notch rear adjustable for windage, both with white dot inserts. **Features:** Double action with ambidextrous slide-mounted safety-levers. Slide is 4140 chrome-moly steel or 400-series stainless steel, frame is a lightweight aluminum alloy. Ambidextrous magazine release. Blue or stainless steel. Introduced 1986; stainless introduced 1990.

Price: P89, blue, with extra magazine and magazine loading tool, plastic case with lock $430.00
Price: KP89, stainless, with extra magazine and magazine loading tool, plastic case with lock $475.00

Ruger P89D Decocker Autoloading Pistol

Similar to the standard P89 except has ambidextrous decocking levers in place of the regular slide-mounted safety. The decocking levers move the firing pin inside the slide where the hammer can not reach it, while simultaneously blocking the firing pin from forward movement—allows shooter to decock a cocked pistol without manipulating the trigger. Conventional thumb decocking procedures are therefore unnecessary. Blue or stainless steel. Introduced 1990.

Price: P89D, blue with extra magazine and loader, plastic case with lock $430.00
Price: KP89D, stainless, with extra magazine, plastic case with lock $475.00

Ruger P89 Double-Action-Only Autoloading Pistol

Same as the KP89 except operates only in the double-action mode. Has a spurless hammer, gripping grooves on each side of the rear of the slide; no external safety or decocking lever. An internal safety prevents forward movement of the firing pin unless the trigger is pulled. Available in 9mm Para., stainless steel only. Introduced 1991.

Price: With lockable case, extra magazine, magazine loading tool $475.00

RUGER P90 MANUAL SAFETY MODEL AUTOLOADING PISTOL

Caliber: 45 ACP, 7-shot magazine. **Barrel:** 4.50". **Weight:** 33.5 oz. **Length:** 7.87" overall. **Stocks:** Grooved black Xenoy composition. **Sights:** Square post front, square notch rear adjustable for windage, both with white dot inserts. **Features:** Double action with ambidextrous slide-mounted safety-levers which move the firing pin inside the slide where the hammer can not reach it, while simultaneously blocking the firing pin from forward movement. Stainless steel only. Introduced 1991.

Price: KP90 with extra magazine, loader, plastic case with lock $513.00
Price: P90 (blue). $476.00

Ruger KP90 Decocker Autoloading Pistol

Similar to the P90 except has a manual decocking system. The ambidextrous decocking levers move the firing pin inside the slide where the ham-

Ruger 22/45

Ruger KP95DAO

Ruger KMK-4

Ruger KP512

mer can not reach it, while simultaneously blocking the firing pin from forward movement—allows shooter to decock a cocked pistol without manipulating the trigger. Available only in stainless steel. Overall length 7.87", weighs 34 oz. Introduced 1991.

Price: KP90D with lockable case, extra magazine, and magazine
loading tool **$513.00**

RUGER P93 COMPACT AUTOLOADING PISTOL

Caliber: 9mm Para., 10-shot magazine. **Barrel:** 3.9". **Weight:** 31 oz. **Length:** 7.3" overall. **Stocks:** Grooved black Xenoy composition. **Sights:** Square post front, square notch rear adjustable for windage. **Features:** Front of slide is crowned with a convex curve; slide has seven finger grooves; trigger guard bow is higher for a better grip; 400-series stainless slide, lightweight alloy frame; also in blue. Decocker-only or DAO-only. Introduced 1993. Made in U.S. by Sturm, Ruger & Co.

Price: KP93DAO, double-action-only **$520.00**
Price: KP93D ambidextrous decocker, stainless **$520.00**
Price: P93D, ambidextrous decocker, blue **$445.00**

Ruger KP94 Autoloading Pistol

Sized midway between the full-size P-Series and the compact P93. Has 4.25" barrel, 7.5" overall length and weighs about 33 oz. KP94 is manual safety model; KP94DAO is double-action-only (both 9mm Para., 10-shot magazine); KP94D is decocker-only in 40-caliber with 10-shot magazine. Slide gripping grooves roll over top of slide. KP94 has ambidextrous safety-levers; KP94DAO has no external safety, full-cock hammer position or decocking lever; KP94D has ambidextrous decocking levers. Matte finish stainless slide, barrel, alloy frame. Also available in blue. Introduced 1994. Made in U.S. by Sturm, Ruger & Co.

Price: P94, P944, blue (manual safety) **$445.00**
Price: KP94 (9mm), KP944 (40-caliber) (manual
safety-stainless) **$520.00**
Price: KP94DAO (9mm), KP944DAO (40-caliber) **$520.00**
Price: KP94D (9mm), KP944D (40-caliber) - decock only **$520.00**

RUGER P95 AUTOLOADING PISTOL

Caliber: 9mm Para., 10-shot magazine. **Barrel:** 3.9". **Weight:** 27 oz. **Length:** 7.3" overall. **Stocks:** Grooved; integral with frame. **Sights:** Blade front, rear drift adjustable for windage; three-dot system. **Features:** Moulded polymer grip frame, stainless steel or chrome-moly slide. Suitable for +P+ ammunition. Decocker or DAO. Introduced 1996. Made in U.S. by Sturm, Ruger & Co. Comes with lockable plastic case, spare magazine, loading tool.

Price: P95 DAO double-action-only **$388.00**
Price: P95D decocker only **$388.00**
Price: KP95 stainless steel **$431.00**
Price: KP95DAO double-action only, stainless steel **$431.00**

RUGER P97 AUTOLOADING PISTOL

Caliber: 45ACP 8-shot magazine. **Barrel:** 4-1/8". **Weight:** 30-1/2 oz. **Length:** 7-1/4" overall. **Grooved:** Integral with frame. **Sights:** Blade front, rear drift adjustable for windage; three dot system. **Features:** Moulded polymer grip frame, stainless steel slide. Decocker or DAO. Introduced 1997. Made in U.S. by Sturm, Ruger & Co. Comes with lockable plastic case, spare magaline, loading tool. .

Price: (KP97D decock-only) **$460.00**
Price: (KP97DAO double-action only) **$460.00**

RUGER MARK II STANDARD AUTOLOADING PISTOL

Caliber: 22 LR, 10-shot magazine. **Barrel:** 4-3/4" or 6". **Weight:** 25 oz. (4-3/4" bbl.). **Length:** 8-5/16" (4-3/4" bbl.). **Stocks:** Checkered plastic. **Sights:** Fixed, wide blade front, fixed rear. **Features:** Updated design of the original Standard Auto. Has new bolt hold-open latch. 10-shot magazine, magazine catch, safety, trigger and new receiver contours. Introduced 1982.

Price: Blued (MK 4, MK 6) **$278.00**
Price: In stainless steel (KMK 4, KMK 6) **$364.00**

Ruger 22/45 Mark II Pistol

Similar to the other 22 Mark II autos except has grip frame of Zytel that matches the angle and magazine latch of the Model 1911 45 ACP pistol. Available in 4", 4-3/4" standard and 5-1/2" bull barrel. Comes with extra magazine, plastic case, lock. Introduced 1992.

Price: P4, 4", adjustable sights **$265.00**
Price: KP 4 (4-3/4" barrel), fixed sights **$294.00**
Price: KP512 (5-1/2" bull barrel), stainless steel, adj. sights **$347.00**
Price: P512 (5-1/2" bull barrel, all blue), adj. sights **$265.00**

HANDGUNS — AUTOLOADERS, SERVICE & SPORT

SAFARI ARMS ENFORCER PISTOL

Caliber: 45 ACP, 6-shot magazine. **Barrel:** 3.8", stainless. **Weight:** 36 oz. **Length:** 7.3" overall. **Stocks:** Smooth walnut with etched black widow spider logo. **Sights:** Ramped blade front, LPA adjustable rear. **Features:** Extended safety, extended slide release; Commander-style hammer; beavertail grip safety; throated, polished, tuned. Parkerized matte black or satin stainless steel finishes. Made in U.S. by Safari Arms.
Price: $630.00

SAFARI ARMS GI SAFARI PISTOL

Caliber: 45 ACP, 7-shot magazine. **Barrel:** 5", 416 stainless. **Weight:** 39.9 oz. **Length:** 8.5" overall. **Stocks:** Checkered walnut. **Sights:** G.I.-style blade front, drift-adjustable rear. **Features:** Beavertail grip safety; extended thumb safety and slide release; Commander-style hammer. Parkerized finish. Reintroduced 1996.
Price: $439.00

SAFARI ARMS CARRIER PISTOL

Caliber: 45 ACP, 7-shot magazine. **Barrel:** 6", 416 stainless steel. **Weight:** 30 oz. **Length:** 9.5" overall. **Stocks:** Wood. **Sights:** Ramped blade front, LPA adjustable rear. **Features:** Beavertail grip safety; extended controls; full-length recoil spring guide; Commander-style hammer. Throated, polished and tuned. Satin stainless steel finish. Introduced 1999. Made in U.S. by Safari Arms, Inc.
Price: $714.00

SAFARI ARMS COHORT PISTOL

Caliber: 45 ACP, 7-shot magazine. **Barrel:** 3.8", 416 stainless. **Weight:** 37 oz. **Length:** 8.5" overall. **Stocks:** Smooth walnut with laser-etched black widow logo. **Sights:** Ramped blade front, LPA adjustable rear. **Features:** Combines the Enforcer model, slide and MatchMaster frame. Beavertail grip safety; extended thumb safety and slide release; Commander-style hammer. Throated, polished and tuned. Satin stainless finish. Introduced 1996. Made in U.S. by Safari Arms, Inc.
Price: $654.00

SAFARI ARMS MATCHMASTER PISTOL

Caliber: 45 ACP, 7-shot. **Barrel:** 5" or 6", 416 stainless steel. **Weight:** 38 oz. (5" barrel). **Length:** 8.5" overall. **Stocks:** Smooth walnut. **Sights:** Ramped blade, LPA adjustable rear. **Features:** Beavertail grip safety; extended controls; Commander-style hammer; throated, polished, tuned. Parkerized matte-black or satin stainless steel. Made in U.S. by Olympic Arms, Inc.
Price: 5" barrel $594.00
Price: 6" barrel $654.00

Safari Arms Carry Comp Pistol

Similar to the Matchmaster except has Wil Schueman-designed hybrid compensator system. Made in U.S. by Olympic Arms, Inc.
Price: $1,067.00

SEECAMP LWS 32 STAINLESS DA AUTO

Caliber: 32 ACP Win. Silvertip, 6-shot magazine. **Barrel:** 2", integral with frame. **Weight:** 10.5 oz. **Length:** 4-1/8" overall. **Stocks:** Glass-filled nylon. **Sights:** Smooth, no-snag, contoured slide and barrel top. **Features:** Aircraft quality 17-4 PH stainless steel. Inertia-operated firing pin. Hammer fired double-action-only. Hammer automatically follows slide down to safety rest position after each shot—no manual safety needed. Magazine safety disconnector. Polished stainless. Introduced 1985. From L.W. Seecamp.
Price: $425.00

SIG SAUER P220 SERVICE AUTO PISTOL

Caliber: 45 ACP, (7- or 8-shot magazine). **Barrel:** 4-3/8". **Weight:** 27.8 oz. **Length:** 7.8" overall. **Stocks:** Checkered black plastic. **Sights:** Blade front, drift adjustable rear for windage. Optional Siglite nightsights. **Features:** Double action. Decocking lever permits lowering hammer onto locked firing pin. Squared combat-type trigger guard. Slide stays open after last shot. Imported from Germany by SIGARMS, Inc.
Price: Blue SA/DA or DAO $790.00
Price: Blue, Siglite night sights $880.00
Price: K-Kote or nickel slide $830.00
Price: K-Kote or nickel slide with Siglite night sights $930.00

SIG Sauer P220

SIG Arms P245 Compact

SIG Sauer P220 Sport Auto Pistol

Similar to the P220 except has 4.9" barrel, ported compensator, all-stainless steel frame and slide, factory-tuned trigger, adjustable sights, extended competition controls. Overall length is 9.9", weighs 43.5 oz. Introduced 1999. From SIGARMS, Inc.
Price: $1,320.00

SIG Sauer P245 Compact Auto Pistol

Similar to the P220 except has 3.9" barrel, shorter grip, 6-shot magazine, 7.28" overall length, and weighs 27.5 oz. Introduced 1999. From SIGARMS, Inc.
Price: Blue $780.00
Price: Blue, with Siglite sights $850.00
Price: Two-tone $830.00
Price: Two-tone with Siglite sights $930.00
Price: With K-Kote finish $830.00
Price: K-Kote with Siglite sights $930.00

SIG Sauer P229 DA Auto Pistol

Similar to the P228 except chambered for 9mm Para., 40 S&W, 357 SIG. Has 3.86" barrel, 7.08" overall length and 3.35" height. Weight is 30.5 oz. Introduced 1991. Frame made in Germany, stainless steel slide assembly made in U.S.; pistol assembled in U.S. From SIGARMS, Inc.
Price: $795.00
Price: With nickel slide $890.00
Price: Nickel slide Siglite night sights $935.00

SIG PRO AUTO PISTOL

Caliber: 9mm Para., 40 S&W, 10-shot magazine. **Barrel:** 3.86". **Weight:** 27.2 oz. **Length:** 7.36" overall. **Stocks:** Composite and rubberized one-piece. **Sights:** Blade front, rear adjustable for windage. Optional Siglite night sights. **Features:** Polymer frame, stainless steel slide; integral frame accessory rail; replaceable steel frame rails; left- or right-handed magazine release. Introduced 1999. From SIGARMS, Inc.

HANDGUNS

SIG Arms Pro 2009

SIG Sauer P229S

SIG Sauer P232

Smith & Wesson 457

Price: SP2340 (40 S&W) $596.00
Price: SP2009 (9mm Para.) $596.00
Price: As above with Siglite night sights.................. $655.00

SIG Sauer P226 Service Pistol

Similar to the P220 pistol except has 4.4" barrel, and weighs 28.3 oz. 357 SIG or 40 S&W. Imported from Germany by SIGARMS, Inc.

Price: Blue SA/DA or DAO $830.00
Price: With Siglite night sights $930.00
Price: Blue, SA/DA or DAO 357 SIG $830.00
Price: With Siglite night sights $930.00
Price: K-Kote finish, 40 S&W only or nickel slide $830.00
Price: K-Kote or nickel slide Siglite night sights $930.00
Price: Nickel slide 357 SIG............................. $875.00
Price: Nickel slide, Siglite night sights $930.00

SIG Sauer P229 Sport Auto Pistol

Similar to the P229 except available in 357 SIG only; 4.8" heavy barrel; 8.6" overall length; weighs 40.6 oz.; vented compensator; adjustable target sights; rubber grips; extended slide latch and magazine release. Made of stainless steel. Introduced 1998. From SIGARMS, Inc.

Price: $1,320.00

SIG SAUER P232 PERSONAL SIZE PISTOL

Caliber: 380 ACP, 7-shot. **Barrel:** 3-3/4". **Weight:** 16 oz. **Length:** 6-1/2" overall. **Stocks:** Checkered black composite. **Sights:** Blade front, rear adjustable for windage. **Features:** Double action/single action or DAO. Blowback operation, stationary barrel. Introduced 1997. Imported from Germany by SIGARMS, Inc.

Price: Blue SA/DA or DAO $505.00
Price: In stainless steel.............................. $545.00
Price: With stainless steel slide, blue frame................ $525.00
Price: Stainless steel, Siglite night sights, Hogue grips $585.00

SIG SAUER P239 PISTOL

Caliber: 9mm Para., 8-shot, 357 SIG 40 S&W, 7-shot magazine. **Barrel:** 3.6". **Weight:** 25.2 oz. **Length:** 6.6" overall. **Stocks:** Checkered black composite. **Sights:** Blade front, rear adjustable for windage. Optional Siglite night sights. **Features:** SA/DA or DAO; blackened stainless steel slide, aluminum alloy frame. Introduced 1996. Made in U.S. by SIGARMS, Inc.

Price: SA/DA or DAO $620.00
Price: SA/DA or DAO with Siglite night sights $720.00
Price: Two-tone finish................................. $665.00
Price: Two-tone finish, Siglite sights...................... $765.00

SMITH & WESSON MODEL 22A SPORT PISTOL

Caliber: 22 LR, 10-shot magazine. **Barrel:** 4", 5-1/2", 7". **Weight:** 29 oz. **Length:** 8" overall. **Stocks:** Two-piece polymer. **Sights:** Patridge front, fully adjustable rear. **Features:** Comes with a sight bridge with Weaver-style integral optics mount; alloy frame; .312" serrated trigger; stainless steel slide and barrel with matte blue finish. Introduced 1997. Made in U.S. by Smith & Wesson.

Price: 4" $230.00
Price: 5-1/2" $255.00
Price: 7" $289.00

SMITH & WESSON MODEL 457 TDA AUTO PISTOL

Caliber: 45 ACP, 7-shot magazine. **Barrel:** 3-3/4". **Weight:** 29 oz. **Length:** 7-1/4" overall. **Stocks:** One-piece Xenoy, wrap-around with straight backstrap. **Sights:** Post front, fixed rear, three-dot system. **Features:** Aluminum alloy frame, matte blue carbon steel slide; bobbed hammer; smooth trigger. Introduced 1996. Made in U.S. by Smith & Wesson.

Price: $563.00

Smith & Wesson 4013 TSW

Smith & Wesson 3913 LadySmith

Smith & Wesson 3913 TSW

SMITH & WESSON MODEL 908 AUTO PISTOL
Caliber: 9mm Para., 8-shot magazine. **Barrel:** 3-1/2". **Weight:** 26 oz. **Length:** 6-13/16". **Stocks:** One-piece Xenoy, wrap-around with straight backstrap. **Sights:** Post front, fixed rear, three-dot system. **Features:** Aluminum alloy frame, matte blue carbon steel slide; bobbed hammer; smooth trigger. Introduced 1996. Made in U.S. by Smith & Wesson.
Price: **$509.00**

SMITH & WESSON 9mm RECON AUTO PISTOL MODEL
Caliber: 9mm Para. **Barrel:** 3-1/2". **Weight:** 27 oz. **Length:** 7" overall. **Stocks:** Hogue wrap-around, finger-groove rubber. **Sights:** Three-dot Novak Low Mount, drift adjustable. **Features:** Traditional double-action mechanism. Tuned action, hand-crowned muzzle, polished feed ramp, hand-lapped slide, spherical barrel bushing. Checkered frontstrap. Introduced 1999. Made by U.S. by Smith & Wesson.
Price: **$1,150.00**

SMITH & WESSON MODEL 2213, 2214 SPORTSMAN AUTOS
Caliber: 22 LR, 8-shot magazine. **Barrel:** 3". **Weight:** 18 oz. **Length:** 6-1/8" overall. **Stocks:** Checkered black polymer. **Sights:** Patridge front, fixed rear; three-dot system. **Features:** Internal hammer; serrated trigger; single action. Model 2213 is stainless with alloy frame, Model 2214 is blued carbon steel with alloy frame. Introduced 1990. Made in U.S. by Smith & Wesson.
Price: Model 2213. . . . . **$340.00**
Price: Model 2214. . . . . **$292.00**

SMITH & WESSON MODEL 4013, 4053 TSW AUTOS
Caliber: 40 S&W, 9-shot magazine. **Barrel:** 3-1/2". **Weight:** 26.4 oz. **Length:** 6-7/8" overall. **Stocks:** Xenoy one-piece wrap-around. **Sights:** Novak three-dot system. **Features:** Traditional double-action system; stainless slide, alloy frame; fixed barrel bushing; ambidextrous decocker; reversible magazine catch. Introduced 1997. Made in U.S. by Smith & Wesson.
Price: Model 4013 TSW **$844.00**
Price: Model 4053 TSW, double-action-only **$844.00**

Smith & Wesson Model 22S Sport Pistols
Similar to the Model 22A Sport except with stainless steel frame. Available only with 5-1/2" or 7" barrel. Introduced 1997. Made in U.S. by Smith & Wesson.
Price: 5-1/2" standard barrel. **$312.00**
Price: 5-1/2" bull barrel, wood target stocks with thumbrest. **$379.00**
Price: 7" standard barrel. **$344.00**
Price: 5-1/2" bull barrel, two-piece target stocks with thumbrest . . **$353.00**

SMITH & WESSON MODEL 410 DA AUTO PISTOL
Caliber: 40 S&W, 10-shot magazine. **Barrel:** 4". **Weight:** 28.5 oz. **Length:** 7.5 oz. **Stocks:** One-piece Xenoy, wrap-around with straight backstrap. **Sights:** Post front, fixed rear; three-dot system. **Features:** Aluminum alloy frame; blued carbon steel slide; traditional double action with left-side slide-mounted decocking lever. Introduced 1996. Made in U.S. by Smith & Wesson.
Price: **$563.00**

SMITH & WESSON MODEL 910 DA AUTO PISTOL
Caliber: 9mm Para., 10-shot magazine. **Barrel:** 4". **Weight:** 28 oz. **Length:** 7-3/8" overall. **Stocks:** One-piece Xenoy, wrap-around with straight backstrap. **Sights:** Post front with white dot, fixed two-dot rear. **Features:** Alloy frame, blue carbon steel slide. Slide-mounted decocking lever. Introduced 1995.
Price: Model 910 . . . . **$509.00**

SMITH & WESSON
MODEL 3913 TRADITIONAL DOUBLE ACTION
Caliber: 9mm Para., 8-shot magazine. **Barrel:** 3-1/2". **Weight:** 26 oz. **Length:** 6-13/16" overall. **Stocks:** One-piece Delrin wrap-around, textured surface. **Sights:** Post front with white dot, Novak LoMount Carry with two dots, adjustable for windage. **Features:** Aluminum alloy frame, stainless slide (M3913) or blue steel slide (M3914). Bobbed hammer with no half-cock notch; smooth .304" trigger with rounded edges. Straight backstrap. Extra magazine included. Introduced 1989.
Price: **$662.00**

Smith & Wesson Model 3913-LS LadySmith Auto
Similar to the standard Model 3913 except has frame that is upswept at the front, rounded trigger guard. Comes in frosted stainless steel with matching gray grips. Grips are ergonomically correct for a woman's hand. Novak LoMount Carry rear sight adjustable for windage, smooth edges for snag resistance. Extra magazine included. Introduced 1990.
Price: **$744.00**

Smith & Wesson 4506

Smith & Wesson 4553 TSW

Smith & Wesson Sigma SW40V

Smith & Wesson Model 3953 DAO Pistol

Same as the Model 3913 except double-action-only. Model 3953 has stainless slide with alloy frame. Overall length 7"; weighs 25.5 oz. Extra magazine included. Introduced 1990.
Price: $724.00

Smith & Wesson Model 3913TSW/3953TSW Auto Pistols

Similar to the Model 3913 and 3953 except TSW guns have tighter tolerances, ambidextrous manual safety/decocking lever, flush-fit magazine, delayed-unlock firing system; magazine disconnector. Compact alloy frame, stainless steel slide. Straight backstrap. Introduced 1998. Made in U.S. by Smith & Wesson.
Price: Single action/double action $724.00
Price: Double action only $724.00

SMITH & WESSON MODEL 4006 TDA AUTO

Caliber: 40 S&W, 10-shot magazine. **Barrel:** 4". **Weight:** 38.5 oz. **Length:** 7-7/8" overall. **Stocks:** Xenoy wrap-around with checkered panels. **Sights:** Replaceable post front with white dot, Novak LoMount Carry fixed rear with two white dots, or micro. click adjustable rear with two white dots. **Features:** Stainless steel construction with non-reflective finish. Straight back-strap. Extra magazine included. Introduced 1990.
Price: With adjustable sights $899.00
Price: With fixed sight................................. $864.00
Price: With fixed night sights $991.00

Smith & Wesson Model 4043, 4046 DA Pistols

Similar to the Model 4006 except is double-action-only. Has a semi-bobbed hammer, smooth trigger, 4" barrel; Novak LoMount Carry rear sight, post front with white dot. Overall length is 7-1/2", weighs 28 oz. Model 4043 has alloy frame. Extra magazine included. Introduced 1991.
Price: Model 4043 (alloy frame) $844.00
Price: Model 4046 (stainless frame)...................... $864.00
Price: Model 4046 with fixed night sights $991.00

SMITH & WESSON MODEL 4500 SERIES AUTOS

Caliber: 45 ACP, 8-shot magazine. **Barrel:** 5" (M4506). **Weight:** 41 oz. (4506). **Length:** 8-1/2" overall. **Stocks:** Xenoy one-piece wrap-around, arched or straight backstrap. **Sights:** Post front with white dot, adjustable or fixed Novak LoMount Carry on M4506. **Features:** M4506 has serrated hammer spur. All have two magazines. Contact Smith & Wesson for complete data. Introduced 1989.
Price: Model 4506, fixed sight $822.00
Price: Model 4506, adjustable sight $855.00
Price: Model 4566 (stainless, 4-1/4", traditional DA, ambidextrous safety, fixed sight)................................... $897.00
Price: Model 4586 (stainless, 4-1/4", DA only).............. $897.00

SMITH & WESSON MODEL 4513TSW/4553TSW PISTOLS

Caliber: 45 ACP, 6-shot magazine. **Barrel:** 3-3/4". **Weight:** 28 oz. (M4513TSW). **Length:** 6-7/8 overall. **Stocks:** Checkered Xenoy; straight

backstrap. **Sights:** White dot front, Novak Lo Mount Carry 2-Dot rear. **Features:** Model 4513TSW is traditional double action, Model 4553TSW is double action only. TSW series has tighter tolerances, ambidextrous manual safety/decocking lever, flush-fit magazine, delayed-unlock firing system; magazine disconnector. Compact alloy frame, stainless steel slide. Introduced 1998. Made in U.S. by Smith & Wesson.
Price: Model 4513TSW $880.00
Price: Model 4553TSW $837.00

SMITH & WESSON MODEL 5900 SERIES AUTO PISTOLS

Caliber: 9mm Para., 10-shot magazine. **Barrel:** 4". **Weight:** 28-1/2 to 37-1/2 oz. (fixed sight); 38 oz. (adjustable sight). **Length:** 7-1/2" overall. **Stocks:** Xenoy wrap-around with curved backstrap. **Sights:** Post front with white dot, fixed or fully adjustable with two white dots. **Features:** All stainless, stainless and alloy or carbon steel and alloy construction. Smooth .304" trigger, .260" serrated hammer. Introduced 1989.
Price: Model 5906 (stainless, traditional DA, adjustable sight, ambidextrous safety) $861.00
Price: As above, fixed sight $822.00
Price: With fixed night sights $948.00
Price: Model 5946 DAO (as above, stainless frame and slide) .. $822.00

SMITH & WESSON ENHANCED SIGMA SERIES PISTOLS

Caliber: 9mm Para., 40 S&W, 10-shot magazine. **Barrel:** 4". **Weight:** 26 oz. **Length:** 7.4" overall. **Stocks:** Integral. **Sights:** White dot front, fixed rear; three-dot system. Tritium night sights available. **Features:** Ergonomic polymer frame; low barrel centerline; internal striker firing system; corrosion-resistant slide; Teflon-filled, electroless-nickel coated magazine. Introduced 1994. Made in U.S. by Smith & Wesson.

Springfield 1911A1 Standard

Springfield Full-Size 1911A1

Springfield N.R.A. PPC

Price: SW9E, 9mm, 4" barrel, black finish, fixed sights **$657.00**
Price: SW9V, 9mm, 4" barrel, satin stainless, fixed night sights . **$447.00**
Price: SW40E, 40 S&W, 4" barrel, black finish, fixed sights. **$657.00**
Price: SW40V, 40 S&W, 4" barrel, black polymer, fixed sights . . **$447.00**

SMITH & WESSON SIGMA SW380 AUTO

Caliber: 380 ACP, 6-shot magazine. **Barrel:** 3". **Weight:** 14 oz. **Length:** 5.8" overall. **Stocks:** Integral. **Sights:** Fixed groove in the slide. **Features:** Polymer frame; double-action-only trigger mechanism; grooved/serrated front and rear straps; two passive safeties. Introduced 1995. Made in U.S. by Smith & Wesson.
Price: **$328.00**

Smith & Wesson Model 6906 Double-Action Auto

Similar to the Model 5906 except with 3-1/2" barrel, 10-shot magazine, fixed rear sight, .260" bobbed hammer. Extra magazine included. Introduced 1989.
Price: Model 6906, stainless. **$720.00**
Price: Model 6906 with fixed night sights **$836.00**
Price: Model 6946 (stainless, DA only, fixed sights). **$720.00**

SMITH & WESSON MODEL CS9 CHIEFS SPECIAL AUTO

Caliber: 9mm Para., 7-shot magazine. **Barrel:** 3". **Weight:** 20.8 oz. **Length:** 6-1/4" overall. **Stocks:** Hogue wrap-around rubber. **Sights:** White dot front, fixed two-dot rear. **Features:** Traditional double-action trigger mechanism. Alloy frame, stainless or blued slide. Introduced 1999. Made in U.S. by Smith & Wesson.
Price: Blue or stainless. **$648.00**

Smith & Wesson Model CS40 Chiefs Special Auto

Similar to the CS9 except chambered for 40 S&W (7-shot magazine), has 3-1/4" barrel, weighs 24.2 oz., and measures 6-1/2" overall. Introduced 1999. Made in U.S. by Smith & Wesson.
Price: Blue or stainless. **$683.00**

Smith & Wesson Model CS45 Chiefs Special Auto

Similar to the CS40 except chambered for 45 ACP, 6-shot magazine, weighs 23.9 oz. Introduced 1999. Made in U.S. by Smith & Wesson.
Price: Blue or stainless. **$683.00**

SPRINGFIELD, INC. FULL-SIZE 1911A1 AUTO PISTOL

Caliber: 9mm Para., 9-shot; 38 Super, 9-shot; 45 ACP, 8-shot. **Barrel:** 5". **Weight:** 35.6 oz. **Length:** 8-5/8" overall. **Stocks:** Checkered plastic or walnut. **Sights:** Fixed three-dot system. **Features:** Beveled magazine well; lowered and flared ejection port. All forged parts, including frame, barrel, slide. All new production. Introduced 1990. From Springfield, Inc.
Price: Mil-Spec 45 ACP, Parkerized. **$610.00**
Price: Standard, 45 ACP, blued **$669.00**
Price: Standard, 45 ACP, stainless **$719.00**
Price: Lightweight (28.6 oz., matte finish). **$695.00**
Price: Standard, 9mm, 38 Super, blued **$549.00**
Price: Standard, 9mm, stainless steel **$599.00**

Springfield, Inc. N.R.A. PPC Pistol

Specifically designed to comply with NRA rules for PPC competition. Has custom slide-to-frame fit; polished feed ramp; throated barrel; total internal honing; tuned extractor; recoil buffer system; fully checkered walnut grips; two fitted magazines; factory test target; custom carrying case. Introduced 1995. From Springfield, Inc.
Price: **$1,469.00**

Springfield, Inc. TRP Pistols

Similar to the 1911A1 except 45 ACP only; has checkered front strap and mainspring housing; Novak combat rear sight and matching dovetailed front sight; tuned, polished extractor; oversize barrel link; lightweight speed trigger and combat action job; match barrel and bushing; extended ambidextrous thumb safety and fitted beavertail grip safety; Carry bevel on entire pistol; checkered cocobolo wood grips; comes with two Wilson 8-shot magazines. Frame is engraved "Tactical," both sides of frame with "TRP." Introduced 1998. From Springfield, Inc.
Price: Standard with Armory Kote finish. **$1,299.00**
Price: Standard, stainless steel **$1,289.00**
Price: Champion, Armory Kote. **$1,349.00**

Springfield, Inc. 1911A1 High Capacity Pistol

Similar to the Standard 1911A1 except available in 45 ACP with 10-shot magazine. Has Commander-style hammer, walnut grips, beveled magazine well, plastic carrying case. Introduced 1993. From Springfield, Inc.
Price: Mil-Spec 45 ACP **$733.00**
Price: 45 ACP Factory Comp. **$1,198.00**
Price: 45 ACP Compact, Ultra **$759.00**
Price: As above, stainless steel **$859.00**

Springfield, Inc. 1911A1 Custom Carry Gun

Similar to the standard 1911A1 except has Novak low-mount sights, Videki speed trigger, match barrel and bushing; extended thumb safety, beavertail grip safety; beveled, polished magazine well, polished feed ramp

Springfield TRP

Stoeger American Eagle Luger

Springfield V10 Ultra Compact

Taurus PT 22

and throated barrel; match Commander hammer and sear, tuned extractor; lowered and flared ejection port; recoil buffer system, full-length spring guide rod; walnut grips. Comes with two magazines with slam pads, plastic carrying case. Available in all popular calibers. Introduced 1992. From Springfield, Inc.
Price: **$1,299.00**

Springfield, Inc. 1911A1 Factory Comp
Similar to the standard 1911A1 except comes with bushing-type dual-port compensator, adjustable rear sight, extended thumb safety, Videki speed trigger, and beveled magazine well. Checkered walnut grips standard. Available in 45 ACP, blue only. Introduced 1992.
Price: 45 ACP....................................... **$1,158.00**

Springfield, Inc. 1911A1 Champion Pistol
Similar to the standard 1911A1 except slide is 4.025". Novak sight system. Comes with Delta hammer and cocogrips. Available in 45 ACP only; Parkerized or stainless. Introduced 1989.
Price: Parkerized **$669.00**
Price: Stainless... **$739.00**

Springfield, Inc. V10 Ultra Compact Pistol
Similar to the 1911A1 Compact except has shorter slide, 3.5" barrel, recoil reducing compensator built into the barrel and slide. Beavertail grip safety, beveled magazine well, "hi-viz" combat sights, Videki speed trigger, flared ejection port, stainless steel frame, blued slide, match grade barrel, walnut grips. Introduced 1996. From Springfield, Inc.
Price: V10 45 ACP **$769.00**
Price: Ultra Compact (no compensator), 45 ACP........... **$1069.00**

STEYR M & S SERIES AUTO PISTOLS
Caliber: 9mm Para., 40 S&W, 357 SIG; 10-shot magazine. **Barrel:** 4" (3.58" for Model S). **Weight:** 28 oz. (22.5 oz. for Model S). **Length:** 7.05" overall (6.53" for Model S). **Grips:** Ultra-rigid polymer. **Sights:** Drift-adjustable, white-outline rear; white-triangle blade front. **Features:** Polymer frame; trigger-drop firing pin, manual and key-lock safeties; loaded chamber indicator; 5.5-lb. trigger pull; 111-degree grip angle enhances natural pointing. Introduced 2000. Imported from Austria by GSI Inc.
Price: Model M (full-sized frame with 4" barrel) **$609.95**
Price: Model S (compact frame with 3.58" barrel) **$609.95**
Price: Extra 10-shot magazines (Model M or S) **$39.00**

STOEGER AMERICAN EAGLE LUGER
Caliber: 9mm Para., 7-shot magazine. **Barrel:** 4", 6". **Weight:** 32 oz. **Length:** 9.6" overall. **Stocks:** Checkered walnut. **Sights:** Blade front, fixed rear. **Features:** Recreation of the American Eagle Luger pistol in stainless steel. Chamber loaded indicator. Introduced 1994. From Stoeger Industries.
Price: 4", or 6" Navy Model **$720.00**
Price: With matte black finish........................... **$798.00**

TAURUS MODEL PT 22/PT 25 AUTO PISTOLS
Caliber: 22 LR, 8-shot (PT 22); 25 ACP, 9-shot (PT 25). **Barrel:** 2.75". **Weight:** 12.3 oz. **Length:** 5.25" overall. **Stocks:** Smooth rosewood. **Sights:** Blade front, fixed rear. **Features:** Double action. Tip-up barrel for loading, cleaning. Blue or stainless. Introduced 1992. Made in U.S. by Taurus International.
Price: 22 LR or 25 ACP, blue, nickel or with duo-tone finish with rosewood grips **$203.00**

Taurus PT92B   **Taurus PT-911**   **Taurus PT-945**   **Taurus PT-957**

Price: 22 LR or 25 ACP, blue with gold trim, rosewood grips. . . . **$219.00**
Price: 22 LR or 25 ACP, blue, nickel or duo-tone finish with checkered wood grips **$180.00**
Price: 22 LR or 25 ACP, blue with gold trim, mother of pearl grips **$219.00**

TAURUS MODEL PT92B AUTO PISTOL

Caliber: 9mm Para., 15-shot magazine. **Barrel:** 5". **Weight:** 34 oz. **Length:** 8.5" overall. **Stocks:** Black rubber. **Sights:** Fixed notch rear. Three-dot sight system. **Features:** Double action, exposed hammer, chamber loaded indicator, ambidextrous safety, inertia firing pin. Imported by Taurus International.
Price: Blue **$508.00**
Price: Stainless steel **$523.00**
Price: Blue with gold trim, rosewood grips **$550.00**
Price: Stainless steel with gold trim, rosewood grips **$570.00**

Taurus Model PT99 Auto Pistol

Similar to the PT92 except has fully adjustable rear sight, smooth Brazilian walnut stocks and is available in stainless steel or polished blue. Introduced 1983.
Price: Blue **$531.00**
Price: Stainless steel **$547.00**

TAURUS MODEL PT-111 MILLENNIUM AUTO PISTOL

Caliber: 9mm Para., 10-shot magazine. **Barrel:** 3.25". **Weight:** 18.7 oz. **Length:** 6.0" overall. **Stocks:** Polymer. **Sights:** Fixed. Low profile, three-dot combat. **Features:** Double action only. Firing pin lock; polymer frame; striker fired; push-button magazine release. Introduced 1998. Imported by Taurus International.
Price: Blue **$367.00**
Price: Stainless. **$383.00**

Taurus Model PT-111 Millennium Titanium Pistol

Similar to the PT-111 except with titanium slide, night sights.
Price: **$547.00**

TAURUS MODEL PT-911 AUTO PISTOL

Caliber: 9mm Para., 10-shot magazine. **Barrel:** 4". **Weight:** 28.2 oz. **Length:** 7" overall. **Stocks:** Black rubber. **Sights:** Fixed. Low profile, three-dot combat. **Features:** Double action, exposed hammer; ambidextrous hammer drop; chamber loaded indicator. Introduced 1997. Imported by Taurus International.
Price: Blue **$453.00**
Price: Stainless. **$469.00**
Price: Blue with gold accents **$504.00**
Price: Stainless with gold accents **$508.00**

Taurus Model PT-138 Auto Pistol

Similar to the PT-911 except chambered for 380 ACP, with 10-shot magazine. Double-action-only mechanism. Has black polymer frame with blue or stainless slide. Introduced 1999. Imported by Taurus International.
Price: Blue **$367.00**
Price: Stainless. **$383.00**

TAURUS MODEL PT-945 AUTO PISTOL

Caliber: 45 ACP, 8-shot magazine. **Barrel:** 4.25". **Weight:** 29.5 oz. **Length:** 7.48" overall. **Stocks:** Black rubber. **Sights:** Drift-adjustable front and rear; three-dot system. **Features:** Double-action mechanism. Has manual ambidextrous hammer drop safety, intercept notch, firing pin block, chamber loaded indicator, last-shot hold-open. Introduced 1995. Imported by Taurus International.
Price: Blue **$484.00**
Price: Stainless. **$500.00**
Price: Blue, ported **$523.00**
Price: Stainless, ported **$539.00**

TAURUS MODEL PT-957 AUTO PISTOL

Caliber: 357 SIG, 10-shot magazine. **Barrel:** 3-5/8". **Weight:** 28 oz. **Length:** 7" overall. **Stocks:** Checkered rubber. **Sights:** Fixed, low profile, three-dot combat. **Features:** Double action mechanism; exposed hammer; ported barrel/slide; three-position safety with decocking lever and ambidextrous safety. Introduced 1999. Imported by Taurus International.
Price: Blue **$508.00**
Price: Stainless. **$523.00**
Price: Blue with gold accents, rosewood grips **$553.00**
Price: Stainless with gold accents, rosewood grips **$568.00**

Taurus PT-938

Taurus PT-940

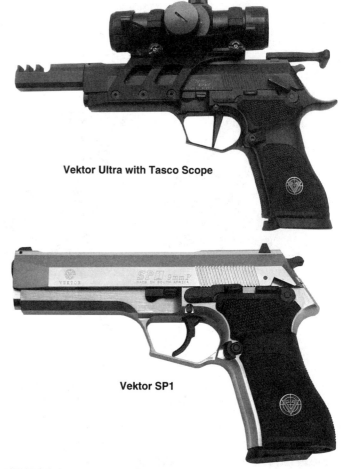

Vektor Ultra with Tasco Scope

Vektor SP1

TAURUS MODEL PT-938 AUTO PISTOL

Caliber: 380 ACP, 10-shot magazine. **Barrel:** 3.72". **Weight:** 27 oz. **Length:** 6.5" overall. **Stocks:** Black rubber. **Sights:** Fixed. Low profile, three-dot combat. **Features:** Double-action only. Chamber loaded indicator; firing pin block; ambidextrous hammer drop. Introduced 1997. Imported by Taurus International.

Price: Blue	**$453.00**
Price: Stainless	**$469.00**

TAURUS MODEL PT-940 AUTO PISTOL

Caliber: 40 S&W, 10-shot magazine. **Barrel:** 3.35". **Weight:** 28.2 oz. **Length:** 7.05" overall. **Stocks:** Black rubber. **Sights:** Drift-adjustable front and rear; three-dot combat. **Features:** Double action, exposed hammer; manual ambidextrous hammer-drop; inertia firing pin; chamber loaded indicator. Introduced 1996. Imported by Taurus International.

Price: Blue	**$469.00**
Price: Stainless steel	**$484.00**
Price: Blue with gold accents, rosewood grips	**$540.00**
Price: Stainless with gold accents, rosewood grips	**$555.00**

VEKTOR SP1 SPORT PISTOL

Caliber: 9mm Para., 10-shot magazine. **Barrel:** 5 ".**Weight:** 38 oz. **Length:** 9-3/8" overall. **Stocks:** Checkered black composition. **Sights:** Combat-type blade front, adjustable rear. **Features:** Single action only with adjustable trigger stop; three-chamber compensator; extended magazine release. Introduced 1999. Imported from South Africa by Vektor USA.

Price:	**$829.95**

Vektor SP1 Tuned Sport Pistol

Similar to the Vektor Sport except has fully adjustable straight trigger, LPA three-dot sight system, and hard nickel finish. Introduced 1999. Imported from South Africa by Vektor USA.

Price:	**$1,199.95**

VEKTOR SP1 Target Pistol

Similar to the Vektor Sport except has 5-7/8" barrel without compensator; weighs 40-1/2 oz.; has fully adjustable straight match trigger; black slide, bright frame. Introduced 1999. Imported from South Africa by Vektor USA.

Price:	**$1,299.95**

Vektor SP1, SP2 Ultra Sport Pistols

Similar to the Vektor Target except has three-chamber compensator with three jet ports; strengthened frame with integral beavertail; lightweight polymer scope mount (Weaver rail). Overall length is 11", weighs 41-1/2 oz. Model SP2 is in 40 S&W. Introduced 1999. Imported from South Africa by Vektor USA.

Price: SP1 (9mm)	**$2,149.95**
Price: SP2 (40 S&W)	**$2,149.95**

VEKTOR SP1 AUTO PISTOL

Caliber: 9mm Para., 40 S&W (SP2), 10-shot magazine. **Barrel:** 4-5/8". **Weight:** 35 oz. **Length:** 8-1/4" overall. **Stocks:** Checkered black composition. **Sights:** Combat-type fixed. **Features:** Alloy frame, steel slide; traditional double-action mechanism; matte black finish. Introduced 1999. Imported from South Africa by Vektor USA.

Price: SP1 (9mm)	**$599.95**
Price: SP1 with nickel finish	**$629.95**
Price: SP2 (40 S&W)	**$649.95**

Vektor SP1, SP2 Compact General's Model Pistol

Similar to the 9mm Para. Vektor SP1 except has 4" barrel, weighs 31-1/2 oz., and is 7-1/2" overall. Recoil operated. Traditional double-action mechanism. SP2 model is chambered for 40 S&W. Introduced 1999. Imported from South Africa by Vektor USA.

Price: SP1 (9mm Para.)	**$649.95**
Price: SP2 (40 S&W)	**$649.95**

Walther PP

Walther PPK/S

Walther PPK

Walther P99

Walther TPH

VEKTOR CP-1 COMPACT PISTOL

Caliber: 9mm Para., 10-shot magazine. **Barrel:** 4". **Weight:** 25.4 oz. **Length:** 7" overall. **Stocks:** Textured polymer. **Sights:** Blade front adjustable for windage, fixed rear; adjustable sight optional. **Features:** Ergonomic grip frame shape; stainless steel barrel; delayed gas-buffered blowback action. Introduced 1999. Imported from South Africa by Vektor USA.

Price: With black slide	**$479.95**
Price: With nickel slide	**$499.95**
Price: With black slide, adjustable sight	**$509.95**
Price: With nickel slide, adjustable sight	**$529.95**

WALTHER PP AUTO PISTOL

Caliber: 380 ACP, 7-shot magazine. **Barrel:** 3.86". **Weight:** 23-1/2 oz. **Length:** 6.7" overall. **Stocks:** Checkered plastic. **Sights:** Fixed, white markings. **Features:** Double action; manual safety blocks firing pin and drops hammer; chamber loaded indicator on 32 and 380; extra finger rest magazine provided. Imported from Germany by Carl Walther USA.

Price: 380 . . . . **$999.00**

Walther PPK/S American Auto Pistol

Similar to Walther PP except made entirely in the United States. Has 3.27" barrel with 6.1" length overall. Introduced 1980.

Price: 380 ACP only, blue **$540.00**
Price: As above, 32 ACP or 380 ACP, stainless **$540.00**

Walther PPK American Auto Pistol

Similar to Walther PPK/S except weighs 21 oz., has 6-shot capacity. Made in the U.S. Introduced 1986.

Price: Stainless, 32 ACP or 380 ACP **$540.00**
Price: Blue, 380 ACP only **$540.00**

WALTHER MODEL TPH AUTO PISTOL

Caliber: 22 LR, 25 ACP, 6-shot magazine. **Barrel:** 2-1/4". **Weight:** 14 oz. **Length:** 5-3/8" overall. **Stocks:** Checkered black composition. **Sights:** Blade front, rear drift-adjustable for windage. **Features:** Made of stainless steel. Scaled-down version of the Walther PP/PPK series. Made in U.S. Introduced 1987. From Carl Walther USA.

Price: Blue or stainless steel, 22 or 25 . . . . **$440.00**

WALTHER P88 COMPACT PISTOL

Caliber: 9mm Para., 10-shot magazine. **Barrel:** 3.93". **Weight:** 28 oz. **Length:** NA. **Stocks:** Checkered black polymer. **Sights:** Blade front, drift adjustable rear. **Features:** Double action with ambidextrous decocking lever and magazine release; alloy frame; loaded chamber indicator; matte blue finish. Imported from Germany by Carl Walther USA.

Price: **$900.00**

WALTHER P99 AUTO PISTOL

Caliber: 9mm Para., 9x21, 40 S&W, 10-shot magazine. **Barrel:** 4". **Weight:** 25 oz. **Length:** 7" overall. **Stocks:** Textured polymer. **Sights:** Blade front (comes with three interchangeable blades for elevation adjustment), micrometer rear adjustable for windage. **Features:** Double-action mechanism with trigger safety, decock safety, internal striker safety; chamber loaded indicator; ambidextrous magazine release levers; polymer frame

Dan Wesson Pointman Major

Dan Wesson Pointman Guardian

Dan Wesson Pointman Seven

Wilkinson Sherry

with interchangeable backstrap inserts. Comes with two magazines. Introduced 1997. Imported from Germany by Carl Walther USA.
Price: **$799.00**

Walther P990 Auto Pistol
Similar to the P99 except is double action only. Available in blue or silver tenifer finish. Introduced 1999. Imported from Germany by Carl Walther USA.
Price: **$749.00**

WALTHER P-5 AUTO PISTOL
Caliber: 9mm Para., 8-shot magazine. **Barrel:** 3.62". **Weight:** 28 oz. **Length:** 7.10" overall. **Stocks:** Checkered plastic. **Sights:** Blade front, adjustable rear. **Features:** Uses the basic Walther P-38 double-action mechanism. Blue finish. Imported from Germany by Carl Walther USA.
Price: **$900.00**

DAN WESSON POINTMAN MAJOR AUTO PISTOL
NEW! **Caliber:** 45 ACP. **Barrel:** 5". **Weight:** NA. **Length:** NA. **Grips:** Rosewood checkered. **Sights: Features:** Stainless steel frame and serrated slide; Chip McCormick match-grade trigger group, sear and disconnect; match-grade barrel; high-ride beavertail safety; checkered slide release; high rib; interchangeable sight system; laser engraved. Introduced 2000. Made in U.S. by Dan Wesson Firearms.
Price: Model PM1 .... **$779.00**

Dan Wesson Pointman Minor Auto Pistol
NEW! Similar to Pointman Major except has blued frame and slide with fixed rear sight. Introduced 2000. Made in U.S. by Dan Wesson Firearms.
Price: Model PM2 .... **$599.00**

Dan Wesson Pointman Seven Auto Pistols
Similar to Pointman Major except has dovetail adjustable target rear sight and dovetail target front sight. Available in blued or stainless finish. Introduced 2000. Made in U.S. by Dan Wesson Firearms.
Price: PM7 (blued frame and slide) **$999.00**
Price: PM7S (stainless finish) **$1,099.00**

Dan Wesson Pointman Guardian Auto Pistols
Similar to Pointman Major except has a more compact frame with 4.25" barrel. Avaiable in blued or stainless finish with fixed or adjustable sights. Introduced 2000. Made in U.S. by Dan Wesson Firearms.
Price: PMG-FS (blued frame and slide, fixed sights) **$769.00**
Price: PMG-AS (blued frame and slide, adjustable sights) **$779.00**
Price: PMGD-FS Guardian Duce (stainless frame and blued slide, fixed sights) **$829.00**
Price: PMGD-AS Guardian Duce (stainless frame and blued slide, adj. sights) **$839.00**

WILKINSON SHERRY AUTO PISTOL
Caliber: 22 LR, 8-shot magazine. **Barrel:** 2-1/8". **Weight:** 9-1/4 oz. **Length:** 4-3/8" overall. **Stocks:** Checkered black plastic. **Sights:** Fixed, groove. **Features:** Cross-bolt safety locks the sear into the hammer. Available in all blue finish or blue slide and trigger with gold frame. Introduced 1985.
Price: **$195.00**

WILKINSON LINDA AUTO PISTOL
Caliber: 9mm Para. **Barrel:** 8-5/16". **Weight:** 4 lbs., 13 oz. **Length:** 12-1/4" overall. **Stocks:** Checkered black plastic pistol grip, walnut forend. **Sights:** Protected blade front, aperture rear. **Features:** Fires from closed bolt. Semi-auto only. Straight blowback action. Cross-bolt safety. Removable barrel. From Wilkinson Arms.
Price: **$533.33**

Includes models suitable for several forms of competition and other sporting purposes.

Baer 1911 Ultimate Master

Baer 1911 Bullseye Wadcutter

Beretta Model 89

Beretta Model 96 Combat

BAER 1911 ULTIMATE MASTER COMBAT PISTOL

Caliber: 9x23, 38 Super, 400 Cor-Bon 45 ACP (others available), 10-shot magazine. **Barrel:** 5", 6"; Baer NM. **Weight:** 37 oz. **Length:** 8.5" overall. **Stocks:** Checkered rosewood. **Sights:** Baer dovetail front, low-mount Bo-Mar rear with hidden leaf. **Features:** Full-house competition gun. Baer forged NM blued steel frame and double serrated slide; Baer triple port, tapered cone compensator; fitted slide to frame; lowered, flared ejection port; Baer reverse recoil plug; full-length guide rod; recoil buff; beveled magazine well; Baer Commander hammer, sear; Baer extended ambidextrous safety, extended ejector, checkered slide stop, beavertail grip safety with pad, extended magazine release button; Baer speed trigger. Made in U.S. by Les Baer Custom, Inc.

Price: Compensated, open sights........................ $2,560.00
Price: 6" Model 400 Cor-Bon $2,590.00
Price: Compensated, with Baer optics mount.............. $3,195.00

Baer 1911 Ultimate Master Steel Special Pistol

Similar to the Ultimate Master except chambered for 38 Super with supported chamber (other calibers available), lighter slide, bushing-type compensator; two-piece guide rod. Designed for maximum 150 power factor. Comes without sights—scope and mount only. Hard chrome finish. Made in U.S. by Les Baer Custom, Inc.

Price: $2,980.00

BAER 1911 NATIONAL MATCH HARDBALL PISTOL

Caliber: 45 ACP, 7-shot magazine. **Barrel:** 5". **Weight:** 37 oz. **Length:** 8.5" overall. **Stocks:** Checkered walnut. **Sights:** Baer dovetail front with undercut post, low-mount Bo-Mar rear with hidden leaf. **Features:** Baer NM forged steel frame, double serrated slide and barrel with stainless bushing; slide fitted to frame; Baer match trigger with 4-lb. pull; polished feed ramp, throated barrel; checkered front strap, arched mainspring housing; Baer beveled magazine well; lowered, flared ejection port; tuned extractor; Baer extended ejector, checkered slide stop; recoil buff. Made in U.S. by Les Baer Custom, Inc.

Price: $1,335.00

Baer 1911 Bullseye Wadcutter Pistol

Similar to the National Match Hardball except designed for wadcutter loads only. Has polished feed ramp and barrel throat; Bo-Mar rib on slide;

full-length recoil rod; Baer speed trigger with 3-1/2-lb. pull; Baer deluxe hammer and sear; Baer beavertail grip safety with pad; flat mainspring housing checkered 20 lpi. Blue finish; checkered walnut grips. Made in U.S. by Les Baer Custom, Inc.

Price: From... $1,495.00
Price: With 6" barrel, from $1,690.00

BENELLI MP90S WORLD CUP PISTOL

Caliber: 22 Long Rifle, 6- or 9-shot magazine. **Barrel:** 4.4" **Weight:** 2.5 lbs. **Length:** 11.75". **Grip:** Walnut. **Sights:** Blade front, fully adjustable rear. **Features:** Single-action target pistol with fully adjustable trigger and adjustable heel rest; integral scope rail mount; attachment system for optional external weights.

Price: $1,190.00

Benelli MP95E Atlanta Pistol

Similar to MP90S World Cup Pistol, but available in blue finish with walnut grip or chrome finish with laminate grip. Overall length 11.25". Trigger overtravel adjustment only.

Price: (blue finish, walnut grip)......................... $740.00
Price: (chrome finish, laminate grip) $810.00

BERETTA MODEL 89 GOLD STANDARD PISTOL

Caliber: 22 LR, 8-shot magazine. **Barrel:** 6". **Weight:** 41 oz. **Length:** 9.5" overall. **Stocks:** Target-type walnut with thumbrest. **Sights:** Interchangeable blade front, fully adjustable rear. **Features:** Single action target pistol. Matte black, Bruniton finish. Imported from Italy by Beretta U.S.A.

Price: $802.00

BERETTA MODEL 96 COMBAT PISTOL

Caliber: 40 S&W, 10-shot magazine. **Barrel:** 4.9" (5.9" with weight). **Weight:** 34.4 oz. **Length:** 8.5" overall. **Stocks:** Checkered black plastic. **Sights:** Blade front, fully adjustable target rear. **Features:** Uses heavier Brigadier slide with front and rear serrations; extended frame-mounted safety; extended, reversible magazine release; single-action-only with competition-tuned trigger with extra-short let-off and over-travel adjust-

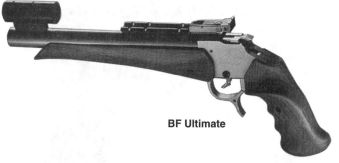

BF Ultimate

Browning Buck Mark Bullseye

Browning Buck Mark Target 5.5

Colt Gold Cup Trophy

ment. Comes with tool kit. Introduced 1997. Imported from Italy by Beretta U.S.A.

Price: **$1,593.00**
Price: 4.9" barrel **$1,341.00**
Price: 5.9" barrel **$1,634.00**
Price: Combo **$1,599.00**

Beretta Model 96 Stock Pistol

Similar to the Model 96 Combat except is single/double action, with half-cock notch. Has front and rear slide serrations, rubber magazine bumper, replaceable accurizing barrel bushing, ultra-thin fine-checkered grips (aluminum optional), checkered front and back straps, radiused back strap, fitted case. Weighs 35 oz., 8.5" overall. Introduced 1997. Imported from Italy by Beretta U.S.A.

Price: **$1,700.00**

BF ULTIMATE SINGLE SHOT PISTOL

Caliber: 7mm U.S., 22 LR Match and 100 other chamberings. **Barrel:** 10.75" Heavy Match Grade with 11"target crown. **Weight:** 3 lbs., 15 oz. **Length:** 16" overall. **Stocks:** Thumbrest target style. **Sights:** Bo-Mar/Bond ScopeRib I Combo with hooded post front adjustable for height and width, rear notch available in .032", .062", .080" and .100" widths; 1/2-MOA clicks. **Features:** Designed to meet maximum rules for IHMSA Production Gun. Falling block action gives rigid barrel-receiver mating. Hand fitted and headspaced. Etched receiver; gold-colored trigger. Introduced 1988. Made in U.S. by E.A. Brown Mfg.

Price: **$895.00**

BROWNING BUCK MARK SILHOUETTE

Caliber: 22 LR, 10-shot magazine. **Barrel:** 9-7/8". **Weight:** 53 oz. **Length:** 14" overall. **Stocks:** Smooth walnut stocks and forend, or finger-groove walnut. **Sights:** Post-type hooded front adjustable for blade width and height; Pro Target rear fully adjustable for windage and elevation. **Features:** Heavy barrel with .900" diameter; 12-1/2" sight radius. Special sighting plane forms scope base. Introduced 1987. Made in U.S. From Browning.

Price: **$448.00**

Browning Buck Mark Target 5.5

Same as the Buck Mark Silhouette except has a 5-1/2" barrel with .900" diameter. Has hooded sights mounted on a scope base that accepts an optical or reflex sight. Rear sight is a Browning fully adjustable Pro Target, front sight is an adjustable post that customizes to different widths, and

can be adjusted for height. Contoured walnut grips with thumbrest, or finger-groove walnut. Matte blue finish. Overall length is 9-5/8", weighs 35-1/2 oz. Has 10-shot magazine. Introduced 1990. From Browning.

Price: **$425.00**
Price: Target 5.5 Gold (as above with gold anodized frame and top rib) **$477.00**
Price: Target 5.5 Nickel (as above with nickel frame and top rib) **$477.00**

Browning Buck Mark Field 5.5

Same as the Target 5.5 except has hoodless ramp-style front sight and low profile rear sight. Matte blue finish, contoured or finger-groove walnut stocks. Introduced 1991.

Price: **$425.00**

Browning Buck Mark Bullseye

Similar to the Buck Mark Silhouette except has 7-1/4" heavy barrel with three flutes per side; trigger is adjustable from 2-1/2 to 5 lbs.; specially designed rosewood target or three-finger-groove stocks with competition-style heel rest, or with contoured rubber grip. Overall length is 11-5/16", weighs 36 oz. Introduced 1996. Made in U.S. From Browning.

Price: With ambidextrous moulded composite stocks **$389.00**
Price: With rosewood stocks, or wrap-around finger groove **$500.00**

COLT GOLD CUP TROPHY MK IV/SERIES 80

Caliber: 45 ACP, 8-shot magazine. **Barrel:** 5", with new design bushing. **Weight:** 39 oz. **Length:** 8-1/2". **Stocks:** Checkered rubber composite with silver-plated medallion. **Sights:** Patridge-style front, Colt-Elliason rear adjustable for windage and elevation, sight radius 6-3/4". **Features:** Arched or flat housing; wide, grooved trigger with adjustable stop; ribbed-top slide, hand fitted, with improved ejection port.

Price: Blue **$1,224.00**
Price: Stainless **$1,300.00**

COLT NATIONAL MATCH PISTOL

Caliber: 45 ACP, 8-shot magazine. **Barrel:** 5". **Weight:** 39 oz. **Length:** 8-1/2" overall. **Stocks:** Double-diamond checkered rosewood. **Sights:** Dovetailed Patridge front, fully adjustable rear; three-dot system. **Features:** Adjustable two-cut aluminum trigger; Defender grip safety; ambidextrous manual safety. Introduced 1999. Made in U.S. by Colt's Mfg., Inc.

Price: . . . . **NA**

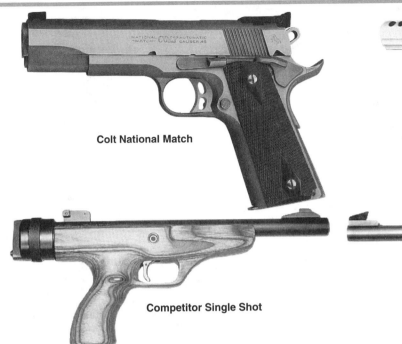

Colt National Match

Competitor Single Shot

E.A.A. Witness Gold Team

Freedom Arms 252 Silhouette

COMPETITOR SINGLE SHOT PISTOL

Caliber: 22 LR through 50 Action Express, including belted magnums. **Barrel:** 14" standard; 10.5" silhouette; 16" optional. **Weight:** About 59 oz. (14" bbl.). **Length:** 15.12" overall. **Stocks:** Ambidextrous; synthetic (standard) or laminated or natural wood. **Sights:** Ramp front, adjustable rear. **Features:** Rotary canon-type action cocks on opening; cammed ejector; interchangeable barrels, ejectors. Adjustable single stage trigger, sliding thumb safety and trigger safety. Matte blue finish. Introduced 1988. From Competitor Corp., Inc.
Price: 14", standard calibers, synthetic grip **$414.95**
Price: Extra barrels, from **$159.95**

CZ 75 CHAMPION COMPETITION PISTOL

Caliber: 9mm Para., 9x21, 40 S&W, 10-shot magazine. **Barrel:** 4.49". **Weight:** 35 oz. **Length:** 9.44" overall. **Stocks:** Black rubber. **Sights:** Blade front, fully adjustable rear. **Features:** Single-action trigger mechanism; three-port compensator (40 S&W, 9mm have two port) full-length guide rod; extended magazine release; ambidextrous safety; flared magazine well; fully adjustable match trigger. Introduced 1999. Imported from the Czech Republic by CZ USA.
Price: 9mm Para., 9x21, 40 S&W, dual-tone finish **$1,484.00**

CZ 75 ST IPSC AUTO PISTOL

Caliber: 40 S&W, 10-shot magazine. **Barrel:** 5.12". **Weight:** 2.9 lbs. **Length:** 8.86" overall. **Stocks:** Checkered walnut. **Sights:** Fully adjustable rear. **Features:** Single-action mechanism; extended slide release and ambidextrous safety; full-length slide rail; double slide serrations. Introduced 1999. Imported from the Czech Republic by CZ-USA.
Price: Dual-tone finish **$1,038.00**

EAA/BAIKAL IZH35 AUTO PISTOL

Caliber: 22 LR, 5-shot magazine. **Barrel:** 6". **Weight:** NA. **Length:** NA. **Grips:** Walnut; fully adjustable right-hand target-style. **Sights:** Fully adjustable rear, blade front; detachable scope mount. **Features:** Hammer-forged target barrel; machined steel receiver; adjustable trigger; manual slide hold back, grip and manual trigger-bar disconnect safeties; cocking indicator. Introduced 2000. Imported from Russia by European American Armory.
Price: Blued finish. **$519.00**

E.A.A. WITNESS GOLD TEAM AUTO

Caliber: 9mm Para., 9x21, 38 Super, 40 S&W, 45 ACP. **Barrel:** 5.1". **Weight:** 41.6 oz. **Length:** 9.6" overall. **Stocks:** Checkered walnut, competition style. **Sights:** Square post front, fully adjustable rear. **Features:**

Triple-chamber cone compensator; competition SA trigger; extended safety and magazine release; competition hammer; beveled magazine well. Hand-fitted major components. Hard chrome finish. Match-grade barrel. From E.A.A. Custom Shop. Introduced 1992. From European American Armory.
Price: **$2,150.00**

E.A.A. Witness Silver Team Auto

Similar to the Witness Gold Team except has double-chamber compensator, oval magazine release, black rubber grips, double-dip blue finish. Comes with Super Sight and drilled and tapped for scope mount. Built for the intermediate competition shooter. Introduced 1992. From European American Armory Custom Shop.
Price: 9mm Para., 9x21, 38 Super, 40 S&W, 45 ACP **$968.00**

ENTRÉPRISE TOURNAMENT SHOOTER MODEL I

Caliber: 45 ACP, 10-shot magazine. **Barrel:** 6". **Weight:** 40 oz. **Length:** 8.5" overall. **Stocks:** Black ultra-slim double diamond checkered synthetic. **Sights:** Dovetailed Patridge front, adjustable Competizione "melded" rear. **Features:** Oversized magazine release button; flared magazine well; fully machined parallel slide rails; front and rear slide serrations; serrated top of slide; stainless ramped bull barrel with fully supported chamber; full-length guide rod with plug; stainless firing pin; match extractor; polished ramp; tuned match extractor; black oxide. Introduced 1998. Made in U.S. by Entréprise Arms.
Price: **$2,300.00**
Price: TSMIII (Satin chrome finish, two-piece guide rod) **$2,700.00**

FREEDOM ARMS CASULL MODEL 252 SILHOUETTE

Caliber: 22 LR, 5-shot cylinder. **Barrel:** 10". **Weight:** 63 oz. **Length:** 15.5" overall. **Stocks:** Black micarta, western style. **Sights:** Adjustable front with bead, Iron Sight Gun Works silhouette rear, click adjustable for windage and elevation. **Features:** Stainless steel. Built on the Model 83. Two-point firing pin, lightened hammer for fast lock time. Trigger pull is 3 to 5 lbs. with pre-set overtravel screw. Introduced 1991. From Freedom Arms.
Price: Silhouette Class **$1,578.00**
Price: Extra fitted 22 WMR cylinder **$264.00**

GAUCHER GP SILHOUETTE PISTOL

Caliber: 22 LR, single shot. **Barrel:** 10". **Weight:** 42.3 oz. **Length:** 15.5" overall. **Stocks:** Stained hardwood. **Sights:** Hooded post on ramp front, open rear adjustable for windage and elevation. **Features:** Matte chrome barrel, blued bolt and sights. Other barrel lengths available on special order. Introduced 1991. Imported by Mandall Shooting Supplies.
Price: **$425.00**

HANDGUNS

Hammerli SP 20

High Standard Victor

High Standard Trophy

HAMMERLI SP 20 TARGET PISTOL

Caliber: 22 LR, 32 S&W. **Barrel:** 4.6". **Weight:** 34.6-41.8 oz. **Length:** 11.8" overall. **Stocks:** Anatomically shaped synthetic Hi-Grip available in five sizes. **Sights:** Integral front in three widths, adjustable rear with changeable notch widths. **Features:** Extremely low-level sight line; anatomically shaped trigger; adjustable JPS buffer system for different recoil characteristics. Receiver available in red, blue, gold, violet or black. Introduced 1998. Imported from Switzerland by SIGARMS, Inc and Hammerli Pistols USA.
Price: . . . . **NA**

HARRIS GUNWORKS SIGNATURE JR. LONG RANGE PISTOL

Caliber: Any suitable caliber. **Barrel:** To customer specs. **Weight:** 5 lbs. **Stock:** Gunworks fiberglass. **Sights:** None furnished; comes with scope rings. **Features:** Right- or left-hand benchrest action of titanium or stainless steel; single shot or repeater. Comes with bipod. Introduced 1992. Made in U.S. by Harris Gunworks, Inc.
Price: **$2,700.00**

HIGH STANDARD TROPHY TARGET PISTOL

Caliber: 22 LR, 10-shot magazine. **Barrel:** 5-1/2" bull or 7-1/4" fluted. **Weight:** 44 oz. **Length:** 9.5" overall. **Stock:** Checkered hardwood with thumbrest. **Sights:** Undercut ramp front, frame-mounted micro-click rear adjustable for windage and elevation; drilled and tapped for scope mounting. **Features:** Gold-plated trigger, slide lock, safety-lever and magazine release; stippled front grip and backstrap; adjustable trigger and sear. Barrel weights optional. From High Standard Manufacturing Co., Inc.
Price: 5-1/2", scope base $510.00
Price: 7.25" $650.00
Price: 7.25", scope base $591.00

HIGH STANDARD VICTOR TARGET PISTOL

Caliber: 22 LR, 10-shot magazine. **Barrel:** 4-1/2" or 5-1/2"; push-button takedown. **Weight:** 46 oz. **Length:** 9.5" overall. **Stock:** Checkered hardwood with thumbrest. **Sights:** Undercut ramp front, micro-click rear adjustable for windage and elevation. Also available with scope mount, rings, no sights. **Features:** Stainless steel construction. Full-length vent rib. Gold-plated trigger, slide lock, safety-lever and magazine release; stippled front grip and backstrap; polished slide; adjustable trigger and sear. Comes with barrel weight. From High Standard Manufacturing Co., Inc.
Price: $591.00
Price: With Weaver rib $532.00

KIMBER SUPER MATCH AUTO PISTOL

Caliber: 45 ACP, 7-shot magazine. **Barrel:** 5". **Weight:** 38 oz. **Length:** 18.7" overall. **Sights:** Blade front, Kimber fully adjustable rear. **Features:**

Guaranteed to have shot 3" group at 50 yards. Stainless steel frame, black KimPro slide; two-piece magazine well; premium aluminum match-grade trigger; 30 lpi front strap checkering; stainless match-grade barrel; ambidextrous safety; special Custom Shop markings. Introduced 1999. Made in U.S. by Kimber Mfg., Inc.
Price: **$1,871.00**

MORINI MODEL 84E FREE PISTOL

Caliber: 22 LR, single shot. **Barrel:** 11.4". **Weight:** 43.7 oz. **Length:** 19.4" overall. **Stocks:** Adjustable match type with stippled surfaces. **Sights:** Interchangeable blade front, match-type fully adjustable rear. **Features:** Fully adjustable electronic trigger. Introduced 1995. Imported from Switzerland by Nygord Precision Products.
Price: **$1,450.00**

PARDINI MODEL SP, HP TARGET PISTOLS

Caliber: 22 LR, 32 S&W, 5-shot magazine. **Barrel:** 4.7". **Weight:** 38.9 oz. **Length:** 11.6" overall. **Stocks:** Adjustable; stippled walnut; match type. **Sights:** Interchangeable blade front, interchangeable, fully adjustable rear. **Features:** Fully adjustable match trigger. Introduced 1995. Imported from Italy by Nygord Precision Products.
Price: Model SP (22 LR) $950.00
Price: Model HP (32 S&W) $1,050.00

PARDINI GP RAPID FIRE MATCH PISTOL

Caliber: 22 Short, 5-shot magazine. **Barrel:** 4.6". **Weight:** 43.3 oz. **Length:** 11.6" overall. **Stocks:** Wrap-around stippled walnut. **Sights:** Interchangeable post front, fully adjustable match rear. **Features:** Model GP Schuman has extended rear sight for longer sight radius. Introduced 1995. Imported from Italy by Nygord Precision Products.
Price: Model GP $1,095.00
Price: Model GP Schuman $1,595.00

PARDINI K22 FREE PISTOL

Caliber: 22 LR, single shot. **Barrel:** 9.8". **Weight:** 34.6 oz. **Length:** 18.7" overall. **Stocks:** Wrap-around walnut; adjustable match type. **Sights:** Interchangeable post front, fully adjustable match open rear. **Features:** Removable, adjustable match trigger. Barrel weights mount above the barrel. New model introduced in 1999. Imported from Italy by Nygord Precision Products.
Price: **$1,295.00**

RUGER MARK II TARGET MODEL AUTOLOADING PISTOL

Caliber: 22 LR, 10-shot magazine. **Barrel:** 6-7/8". **Weight:** 42 oz. **Length:** 11-1/8" overall. **Stocks:** Checkered hard plastic. **Sights:** .125" blade front, micro-click rear, adjustable for windage and elevation. Sight radius 9-3/8". Comes with lockable plastic case with lock.
Features: Introduced 1982.
Price: Blued (MK-678) $326.00
Price: Stainless (KMK-678) $408.00

Ruger Mark II Government Target Model

Same gun as the Mark II Target Model except has 6-7/8" barrel, higher sights and is roll marked "Government Target Model" on the right side of the receiver below the rear sight. Identical in all aspects to the military model used for training U.S. Armed Forces except for markings. Comes with factory test target. Comes with lockable plastic case with lock. Introduced 1987.
Price: Blued (MK-678G) $393.00
Price: Stainless (KMK-678G) $470.00

HANDGUNS

Ruger Mark II Bull Barrel

Safari Arms Big Deuce

Smith & Wesson Model 41

Springfield 1911A1 Trophy Match

Ruger Stainless Competition Model Pistol

Similar to the Mark II Government Target Model stainless pistol except has 6-7/8" slab-sided barrel; the receiver top is fitted with a Ruger scope base of blued, chrome moly steel; comes with Ruger 1" stainless scope rings for mounting a variety of optical sights; has checkered laminated grip panels with right-hand thumbrest. Has blued open sights with 9-1/4" radius. Overall length is 11-1/8", weight 45 oz. Comes with lockable plastic case with lock. Introduced 1991.
Price: KMK-678GC. **$486.00**

Ruger Mark II Bull Barrel

Same gun as the Target Model except has 5-1/2" or 10" heavy barrel (10" meets all IHMSA regulations). Weight with 5-1/2" barrel is 42 oz., with 10" barrel, 51 oz. Comes with lockable plastic case with lock.
Price: Blued (MK-512) **$326.00**
Price: Blued (MK-10) **$330.00**
Price: Stainless (KMK-10) **$413.00**
Price: Stainless (KMK-512) **$408.00**

SAFARI ARMS BIG DEUCE PISTOL

Caliber: 45 ACP, 7-shot magazine. **Barrel:** 6", 416 stainless steel. **Weight:** 40.3 oz. **Length:** 9.5" overall. **Stocks:** Smooth walnut. **Sights:** Ramped blade front, LPA adjustable rear. **Features:** Beavertail grip safety; extended thumb safety and slide release; Commander-style hammer. Throated, polished and tuned. Parkerized matte black slide with satin stainless steel frame. Introduced 1995. Made in U.S. by Safari Arms, Inc.
Price: **$714.00**

SMITH & WESSON MODEL 41 TARGET

Caliber: 22 LR, 10-shot clip. **Barrel:** 5-1/2", 7". **Weight:** 44 oz. (5-1/2" barrel). **Length:** 9" overall (5-1/2" barrel). **Stocks:** Checkered walnut with modified thumbrest, usable with either hand. **Sights:** 1/8" Patridge on ramp base; micro-click rear adjustable for windage and elevation. **Features:** 3/8" wide, grooved trigger; adjustable trigger stop.
Price: S&W Bright Blue, either barrel **$801.00**

SMITH & WESSON MODEL 22A TARGET PISTOL

Caliber: 22 LR, 10-shot magazine. **Barrel:** 5-1/2" bull. **Weight:** 38.5 oz. **Length:** 9-1/2" overall. **Stocks:** Dymondwood with ambidextrous thumbrests and flared bottom or rubber soft touch with thumbrest. **Sights:** Patridge front, fully adjustable rear. **Features:** Sight bridge with Weaver-style integral optics mount; alloy frame, stainless barrel and slide; matte black finish. Introduced 1997. Made in U.S. by Smith & Wesson.
Price: **$320.00**

Smith & Wesson Model 22S Target Pistol

Similar to the Model 22A except has stainless steel frame. Introduced 1997. Made in U.S. by Smith & Wesson.
Price: **$379.00**

Springfield, Inc. 1911A1 Trophy Match Pistol

Similar to the 1911A1 except factory accurized, Videki speed trigger, skeletonized hammer; has 4- to 5-1/2-lb. trigger pull, click adjustable rear sight, match-grade barrel and bushing. Comes with cocobolo grips. Introduced 1994. From Springfield, Inc.
Price: Blue **$1,089.00**
Price: Stainless steel **$1,149.00**
Price: High Capacity (stainless steel, 10-shot magazine, front slide serrations, checkered slide serrations). **$1,118.00**

Springfield, Inc. Expert Pistol

Similar to the Competition Pistol except has triple-chamber tapered cone compensator on match barrel with dovetailed front sight; lowered and flared ejection port; fully tuned for reliability; fitted slide to frame; extended ambidextrous thumb safety, extended magazine release button; beavertail grip safety; Pachmayr wrap-around grips. Comes with two magazines, plastic carrying case. Introduced 1992. From Springfield, Inc.
Price: 45 ACP, Duotone finish **$1,724.00**
Price: Expert Ltd. (non-compensated) **$1,624.00**

Springfield, Inc. Distinguished Pistol

Has all the features of the 1911A1 Expert except is full-house pistol with deluxe Bo-Mar low-mounted adjustable rear sight; full-length recoil spring guide rod and recoil spring retainer; checkered frontstrap; S&A magazine well; walnut grips. Hard chrome finish. Comes with two magazines with slam pads, plastic carrying case. From Springfield, Inc.
Price: 45 ACP. **$2,445.00**
Price: Distinguished Limited (non-compensated). **$2,345.00**

SPRINGFIELD, INC. 1911A1 BULLSEYE WADCUTTER PISTOL

Caliber: 38 Super, 45 ACP. **Barrel:** 5". **Weight:** 45 oz. **Length:** 8.59" overall (5" barrel). **Stocks:** Checkered walnut. **Sights:** Bo-Mar rib with undercut blade front, fully adjustable rear. **Features:** Built for wadcutter loads only. Has full-length recoil spring guide rod, fitted Videki speed trigger with 3.5-lb. pull; match Commander hammer and sear; beavertail grip safety; lowered and flared ejection port; tuned extractor; fitted slide to frame; recoil buffer system; beveled and polished magazine well; checkered front strap and steel mainspring housing (flat housing standard); polished and throated National Match barrel and bushing. Comes with two magazines with slam pads, plastic carrying case, test target. Introduced 1992. From Springfield, Inc.
Price: **$1,499.00**

HANDGUNS

Thompson/Center Super 14 Contender

Unique D.E.S. 69U

Wichita Silhouette

Springfield, Inc. Basic Competition Pistol

Has low-mounted Bo-Mar adjustable rear sight, undercut blade front; match throated barrel and bushing; polished feed ramp; lowered and flared ejection port; fitted Videki speed trigger with tuned 3.5-lb. pull; fitted slide to frame; recoil buffer system; checkered walnut grips; serrated, arched mainspring housing. Comes with two magazines with slam pads, plastic carrying case. Introduced 1992. From Springfield, Inc.
Price: 45 ACP, blue, 5" only $1,295.00

Springfield, Inc. 1911A1 N.M. Hardball Pistol

Has Bo-Mar adjustable rear sight with undercut front blade; fitted match Videki trigger with 4-lb. pull; fitted slide to frame; throated National Match barrel and bushing, polished feed ramp; recoil buffer system; tuned extractor; Herrett walnut grips. Comes with two magazines, plastic carrying case, test target. Introduced 1992. From Springfield, Inc.
Price: 45 ACP, blue $1,336.00

STI EAGLE 5.1 PISTOL

Caliber: 9mm Para., 38 Super, 40 S&W, 45 ACP, 10-ACP, 10-shot magazine. **Barrel:**5", bull. **Weight:** 34 oz. **Length:** 8.62" overall. **Stocks:** Checkered polymer. **Sights:** Bo-Mar blade front, Bo-Mar fully adjustable rear. **Features:** Modular frame design; adjustable match trigger; skeletonized hammer; extended grip safety with locator pad; match-grade fit of all parts. Many options available. Introduced 1994. Made in U.S. by STI International.
Price: $1,792.00

THOMPSON/CENTER SUPER 14 CONTENDER

Caliber: 22 LR, 222 Rem., 223 Rem., 7-30 Waters, 30-30 Win., 357 Rem. Maximum, 44 Mag., single shot. **Barrel:** 14". **Weight:** 45 oz. **Length:** 17-1/4" overall. **Stocks:** T/C "Competitor Grip" (walnut and rubber). **Sights:** Fully adjustable target-type. **Features:** Break-open action with auto safety. Interchangeable barrels for both rimfire and centerfire calibers. Introduced 1978.
Price: Blued $520.24
Price: Stainless steel $578.40
Price: Extra barrels, blued $251.06
Price: Extra barrels, stainless steel $278.68

Thompson/Center Super 16 Contender

Same as the T/C Super 14 Contender except has 16-1/4" barrel. Rear sight can be mounted at mid-barrel position (10-3/4" radius) or moved to the rear (using scope mount position) for 14-3/4" radius. Overall length is 20-1/4". Comes with T/C Competitor Grip of walnut and rubber. Available in, 223 Rem., 45-70 Gov't. Also available with 16" vent rib barrel with internal choke, caliber 45 Colt/410 shotshell.
Price: Blue $525.95
Price: 45-70 Gov't., blue. $531.52
Price: Super 16 Vent Rib, blued. $559.70

Price: Extra 16" barrel, blued $245.61
Price: Extra 45-70 barrel, blued $251.08
Price: Extra Super 16 vent rib barrel, blue $278.73

UNIQUE D.E.S. 32U TARGET PISTOL

Caliber: 32 S&W Long wadcutter. **Barrel:** 5.9". **Weight:** 40.2 oz. **Stocks:** Anatomically shaped, adjustable stippled French walnut. **Sights:** Blade front, micrometer click rear. **Features:** Trigger adjustable for weight and position; dry firing mechanism; slide stop catch. Optional sleeve weights. Introduced 1990. Imported from France by Nygord Precision Products.
Price: Right-hand, about. $1,350.00
Price: Left-hand, about. $1,380.00

UNIQUE D.E.S. 69U TARGET PISTOL

Caliber: 22 LR, 5-shot magazine. **Barrel:** 5.91". **Weight:** 35.3 oz. **Length:** 10.5" overall. **Stocks:** French walnut target-style with thumbrest and adjustable shelf; hand-checkered panels. **Sights:** Ramp front, micro. adjustable rear mounted on frame; 8.66" sight radius. **Features:** Meets U.I.T. standards. Comes with 260-gram barrel weight; 100, 150, 350-gram weights available. Fully adjustable match trigger; dry-firing safety device. Imported from France by Nygord Precision Products.
Price: Right-hand, about. $1,250.00
Price: Left-hand, about. $1,290.00

UNIQUE MODEL 96U TARGET PISTOL

Caliber:22 LR, 5- or 6-shot magazine. **Barrel:** 5.9". **Weight:** 40.2 oz. **Length:** 11.2" overall. **Stocks:** French walnut. Target style with thumbrest and adjustable shelf. **Sights:** Blade front, micrometer rear mounted on frame. **Features:** Designed for Sport Pistol and Standard U.I.T. shooting. External hammer; fully adjustable and movable trigger; dry-firing device. Introduced 1997. Imported from France by Nygord Precision Products.
Price: $1,350.00

WALTHER GSP MATCH PISTOL

Caliber: 22 LR, 32 S&W Long (GSP-C), 5-shot magazine. **Barrel:** 4.22". **Weight:** 44.8 oz. (22 LR), 49.4 oz. (32). **Length:** 11.8" overall. **Stocks:** Walnut. **Sights:** Post front, match rear adjustable for windage and elevation. **Features:** Available with either 2.2-lb. (1000 gm) or 3-lb. (1360 gm) trigger. Spare magazine, barrel weight, tools supplied. Imported from Germany by Nygord Precision Products.
Price: GSP, with case. $1,495.00
Price: GSP-C, with case. $1,595.00

WICHITA SILHOUETTE PISTOL

Caliber: 308 Win. F.L., 7mm IHMSA, 7mm-308. **Barrel:** 14-15/16". **Weight:** 4-1/2 lbs. **Length:** 21-3/8" overall. **Stock:** American walnut with oil finish. Glass bedded. **Sights:** Wichita Multi-Range sight system. **Features:** Comes with left-hand action with right-hand grip. Round receiver and barrel. Fluted bolt, flat bolt handle. Wichita adjustable trigger. Introduced 1979. From Wichita Arms.
Price: Center grip stock $1,800.00
Price: As above except with Rear Position Stock and target-type Lightpull trigger $1,800.00

WICHITA CLASSIC SILHOUETTE PISTOL

Caliber: All standard calibers with maximum overall length of 2.800". **Barrel:** 11-1/4". **Weight:** 3 lbs., 15 oz. **Stocks:** AAA American walnut with oil finish, checkered grip. **Sights:** Hooded post front, open adjustable rear. **Features:** Three locking lug bolt, three gas ports; completely adjustable Wichita trigger. Introduced 1981. From Wichita Arms.
Price: $3,450.00

*Includes models suitable for hunting and
competitive courses of fire, both police and international.*

Armscor M-200DC

Ruger GP161

Medusa Model 47

Ruger KSP-931

ARMSCOR M-200DC REVOLVER

Caliber: 38 Spec., 6-shot cylinder. **Barrel:** 2-1/2", 4". **Weight:** 22 oz. (2-1/2" barrel). **Length:** 7-3/8" overall (2-1/2" barrel). **Stocks:** Checkered rubber. **Sights:** Blade front, fixed notch rear. **Features:** All-steel construction; floating firing pin, transfer bar ignition; shrouded ejector rod; blue finish. Reintroduced 1996. Imported from the Philippines by K.B.I., Inc.
Price: 2-1/2" **$199.99**
Price: 4" **$205.00**

ARMSPORT MODEL 4540 REVOLVER

Caliber: 38 Special. **Barrel:** 4". **Weight:** 32 oz **Length:** 9" overall. **Sights:** Fixed rear, blade front. **Features:** Ventilated rib; blued finish. Imported from Argentina by Armsport Inc.
Price: **$140.00**

E.A.A. STANDARD GRADE REVOLVERS

Caliber: 38 Spec., 6-shot; 357 magnum, 6-shot. **Barrel:** 2", 4". **Weight:** 38 oz. (22 rimfire, 4"). **Length:** 8.8" overall (4" bbl.). **Stocks:** Rubber with finger grooves. **Sights:** Blade front, fixed or adjustable on rimfires; fixed only on 32, 38. **Features:** Swing-out cylinder; hammer block safety; blue finish. Introduced 1991. Imported from Germany by European American Armory.
Price: 38 Special 2" **$180.00**
Price: 38 Special, 4" **$199.00**
Price: 357 Magnum, 2" **$199.00**
Price: 357 Magnum, 4" **$233.00**

MEDUSA MODEL 47 REVOLVER

Caliber: Most 9mm, 38 and 357 caliber cartridges; 6-shot cylinder. **Barrel:** 2-1/2", 3", 4", 5", 6"; fluted. **Weight:** 39 oz. **Length:** 10" overall (4" barrel). **Stocks:** Gripper-style rubber. **Sights:** Changeable front blades, fully adjustable rear. **Features:** Patented extractor allows gun to chamber, fire and extract over 25 different cartridges in the .355- to .357 range, without half-moon clips. Steel frame and cylinder; match quality barrel. Matte blue finish. Introduced 1996. Made in U.S. by Phillips & Rogers, Inc.
Price: **$899.00**

RUGER GP-100 REVOLVERS

Caliber: 38 Spec., 357 Mag., 6-shot. **Barrel:** 3", 3" full shroud, 4", 4" full shroud, 6", 6" full shroud. **Weight:** 3" barrel—35 oz., 3" full shroud—36 oz., 4" barrel—37 oz., 4" full shroud—38 oz. **Sights:** Fixed; adjustable on 4" full shroud and all 6" barrels. **Stocks:** Ruger Santoprene Cushioned Grip with Goncalo Alves inserts. **Features:** Uses action and frame incorporating improvements and features of both the Security-Six and Redhawk revolvers. Full length and short ejector shroud. Satin blue and stainless steel.
Price: GP-141 (357, 4" full shroud, adj. sights, blue) **$462.00**
Price: GP-160 (357, 6", adj. sights, blue) **$462.00**
Price: GP-161 (357, 6" full shroud, adj. sights, blue), 46 oz. **$462.00**
Price: GPF-331 (357, 3" full shroud) **$445.00**
Price: GPF-340 (357, 4") **$445.00**
Price: GPF-341 (357, 4" full shroud) **$445.00**
Price: KGP-141 (357, 4" full shroud, adj. sights, stainless) **$498.00**
Price: KGP-160 (357, 6", adj. sights, stainless), 43 oz. **$498.00**
Price: KGP-161 (357, 6" full shroud, adj. sights, stainless) 46 oz. **$498.00**
Price: KGPF-330 (357, 3", stainless) **$480.00**
Price: KGPF-331 (357, 3" full shroud, stainless) **$480.00**
Price: KGPF-340 (357, 4", stainless), KGPF-840 (38 Spec.).... **$480.00**
Price: KGPF-341 (357, 4" full shroud, stainless) **$480.00**

Ruger SP101 Double-Action-Only Revolver

Similar to the standard SP101 except is double-action-only with no single-action sear notch. Has spurless hammer for snag-free handling, floating firing pin and Ruger's patented transfer bar safety system. Available with 2-1/4" barrel in 357 Magnum. Weighs 25-1/2 oz., overall length 7.06". Natural brushed satin or high-polish stainless steel. Introduced 1993.
Price: KSP321XL (357 Mag.) **$458.00**

RUGER SP101 REVOLVERS

Caliber: 22 LR, 32 H&R Mag., 6-shot; 9mm Para., 38 Spec. +P, 357 Mag., 5-shot. **Barrel:** 2-1/4", 3-1/16", 4". **Weight:** (38 & 357 mag models) 2-1/4"—25 oz.; 3-1/16"—27 oz. **Sights:** Adjustable on 22, 32, fixed on others. **Stocks:** Ruger Santoprene Cushioned Grip with Xenoy inserts. **Features:** Incorporates improvements and features found in the GP-100

Ruger KSRH-7

Smith & Wesson Model 10

Smith & Wesson Model 14

Smith & Wesson Model 19

revolvers into a compact, small frame, double-action revolver. Full-length ejector shroud. Stainless steel only. Introduced 1988.

Price: KSP-821 (2-1/2", 38 Spec.) **$458.00**
Price: KSP-831 (3-1/16", 38 Spec.) **$458.00**
Price: KSP-221 (2-1/4", 22 LR), 32 oz. **$458.00**
Price: KSP-240 (4", 22 LR), 33 oz. **$458.00**
Price: KSP-241 (4" heavy bbl., 22 LR), 34 oz. **$458.00**
Price: KSP-3231 (3-1/16", 32 H&R), 30 oz. **$458.00**
Price: KSP-921 (2-1/4", 9mm Para.) **$458.00**
Price: KSP-931 (3-1/16", 9mm Para.) **$458.00**
Price: KSP-321 (2-1/4", 357 Mag.) **$458.00**
Price: KSP331X (3-1/16", 357 Mag.) **$458.00**

RUGER REDHAWK

Caliber: 44 Rem. Mag., 45 Colt, 6-shot. **Barrel:** 5-1/2", 7-1/2". **Weight:** About 54 oz. (7-1/2" bbl.). **Length:** 13" overall (7-1/2" barrel). **Stocks:** Square butt Goncalo Alves. **Sights:** Interchangeable Patridge-type front, rear adjustable for windage and elevation. **Features:** Stainless steel, brushed satin finish, or blued ordnance steel. Has a 9-1/2" sight radius. Introduced 1979.

Price: Blued, 44 Mag., 5-1/2" RH-445, 7-1/2" RH-44 . . . . **$545.00**
Price: Blued, 44 Mag., 7-1/2" RH44R, with scope mount, rings . . **$578.00**
Price: Stainless, 44 Mag., 5-1/2", 7-1/2" KRH-445 . . . . **$603.00**
Price: Stainless, 44 Mag., 7-1/2", with scope mount, rings
KRH-44 . . . . **$629.00**
Price: Stainless, 45 Colt, 5-1/2", 7-1/2" KRH-455 . . . . **$603.00**
Price: Stainless, 45 Colt, 7-1/2", with scope mount KRH-45 . . . . **$629.00**

Ruger Super Redhawk Revolver

Similar to the standard Redhawk except has a heavy extended frame with the Ruger Integral Scope Mounting System on the wide topstrap. Also available in 454 Casull. The wide hammer spur has been lowered for better scope clearance. Incorporates the mechanical design features and improvements of the GP-100. Choice of 7-1/2" or 9-1/2" barrel, both with ramp front sight base with Redhawk-style Interchangeable Insert sight blades, adjustable rear sight. Comes with Ruger "Cushioned Grip" panels of Santoprene with Goncalo Alves wood panels. Satin stainless steel. Introduced 1987.

Price: KSRH-7 (7-1/2"), KSRH-9 (9-1/2") **$629.00**
Price: KSRH-7454 (7-1/2") 454 Casull **$745.00**

Ruger Super Redhawk 454 Casull Revolver

NEW!

Similar to the Ruger Super Redhawk except chambered for 454 Casull (also accepts 45 Colt cartridges). Unfluted cylinder, 7" barrel, weighs 53 ounces. Comes with 1" stainless scope rings. Introduced 2000.

Price: (satin or target gray stainless steel finishes) **$745.00**

SMITH & WESSON MODEL 10 M&P HB REVOLVER

Caliber: 38 Spec., 6-shot. **Barrel:** 4". **Weight:** 33.5 oz. **Length:** 9-5/16" overall. **Stocks:** Uncle Mike's Combat soft rubber; square butt. **Sights:** Fixed; ramp front, square notch rear.

Price: Blue **$458.00**

SMITH & WESSON MODEL 14 FULL LUG REVOLVER

Caliber: 38 Spec., 6-shot. **Barrel:** 6", full lug. **Weight:** 47 oz. **Length:** 11-1/8" overall. **Stocks:** Hogue soft rubber. **Sights:** Pinned Patridge front,

adjustable micrometer click rear. **Features:** Has .500" target hammer, .312" smooth combat trigger. Polished blue finish. Reintroduced 1991. Limited production.

Price: **$498.00**

SMITH & WESSON MODEL 15 COMBAT MASTERPIECE

Caliber: 38 Spec., 6-shot. **Barrel:** 4". **Weight:** 32 oz. **Length:** 9-5/16" (4" bbl.). **Stocks:** Uncle Mike's Combat soft rubber. **Sights:** Serrated ramp front, micro-click rear adjustable for windage and elevation.

Price: Blued **$450.00**

SMITH & WESSON MODEL 19 COMBAT MAGNUM

Caliber: 357 Mag. and 38 Spec., 6-shot. **Barrel:** 4". **Weight:** 36 oz. **Length:** 9-9/16" (4" bbl.). **Stocks:** Uncle Mike's Combat soft rubber; wood optional. **Sights:** Red ramp front, micro-click rear adjustable for windage and elevation.

Price: 4" **$457.00**

SMITH & WESSON MODEL 629 REVOLVERS

Caliber: 44 Magnum, 6-shot. **Barrel:** 5", 6", 8-3/8". **Weight:** 47 oz. (6" bbl.). **Length:** 11-3/8" overall (6" bbl.). **Stocks:** Soft rubber; wood optional. **Sights:** 1/8" red ramp front, micro-click rear, adjustable for windage and elevation.

Price: Model 629 (stainless steel), 5" **$625.00**
Price: Model 629, 6" **$631.00**
Price: Model 629, 8-3/8" barrel **$646.00**

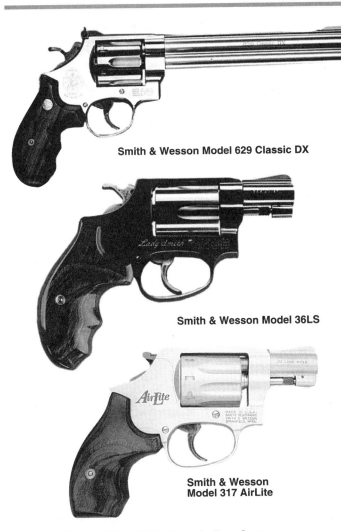

Smith & Wesson Model 629 Classic DX

Smith & Wesson Model 36LS

Smith & Wesson
Model 317 AirLite

Smith & Wesson Model 65LS

Smith & Wesson Model 629 Classic Revolver

Similar to the standard Model 629 except has full-lug 5", 6-1/2" or 8-3/8" barrel; chamfered front of cylinder; interchangeable red ramp front sight with adjustable white outline rear; Hogue grips with S&W monogram; the frame is drilled and tapped for scope mounting. Factory accurizing and endurance packages. Overall length with 5" barrel is 10-1/2"; weighs 51 oz. Introduced 1990.

Price: Model 629 Classic (stainless), 5", 6-1/2" **$670.00**
Price: As above, 8-3/8". **$691.00**

Smith & Wesson Model 629 Classic DX Revolver

Similar to the Model 629 Classic except offered only with 6-1/2" or 8-3/8" full-lug barrel; comes with five front sights: red ramp; black Patridge; black Patridge with gold bead; black ramp; and black Patridge with white dot. Comes with Hogue combat-style and wood round butt grip. Introduced 1991.

Price: Model 629 Classic DX, 6-1/2" **$860.00**
Price: As above, 8-3/8". **$888.00**

SMITH & WESSON
MODEL 36, 37 CHIEFS SPECIAL & AIRWEIGHT

Caliber: 38 Spec.+P, 5-shot. **Barrel:** 1-7/8". **Weight:** 19-1/2 oz. (2" bbl.); 13-1/2 oz. (Airweight). **Length:** 6-1/2" (round butt). **Stocks:** Round butt soft rubber. **Sights:** Fixed, serrated ramp front, square notch rear.

Price: Blue, standard Model 36 . . . . **$406.00**
Price: Blue, Airweight Model 37 . . . . **$483.00**

Smith & Wesson Model 36LS, 60LS LadySmith

Similar to the standard Model 36. Available with 1-7/8" barrel, 38 Special. Comes with smooth, contoured rosewood grips with the S&W monogram.

Has a speedloader cutout. Comes in a fitted carry/storage case. Introduced 1989.

Price: Model 36LS **$478.00**
Price: Model 60LS, as above except in stainless, 357 Magnum . **$539.00**

SMITH & WESSON MODEL 60 357 MAGNUM

Caliber: 357 Magnum, 5-shot. **Barrel:** 2-1/8" or 3". **Weight:** 24 oz. **Length:** 7-1/2 overall (3" barrel). **Stocks:** Uncle Mike's Combat. **Sights:** Fixed, serrated ramp front, square notch rear. **Features:** Stainless steel construction. Made in U.S. by Smith & Wesson.

Price: 2-1/8" barrel **$505.00**
Price: 3" barrel **$536.00**

SMITH & WESSON MODEL 65

Caliber: 357 Mag. and 38 Spec., 6-shot. **Barrel:** 3", 4". **Weight:** 34 oz. **Length:** 9-5/16" overall (4" bbl.). **Stocks:** Uncle Mike's Combat. **Sights:** 1/8" serrated ramp front, fixed square notch rear. **Features:** Heavy barrel. Stainless steel construction.

Price: **$501.00**

SMITH & WESSON
MODEL 317 AIRLITE, 317 LADYSMITH REVOLVERS

Caliber: 22 LR, 8-shot. **Barrel:** 1-7/8" 3". **Weight:** 9.9 oz. **Length:** 6-3/16" overall. **Stocks:** Dymondwood Boot or Uncle Mike's Boot. **Sights:** Serrated ramp front, fixed notch rear. **Features:** Aluminum alloy, carbon and stainless steels, and titanium construction. Short spur hammer, smooth combat trigger. Clear Cote finish. Introduced 1997. Made in U.S. by Smith & Wesson.

Price: With Uncle Mike's Boot grip **$508.00**
Price: With DymondWood Boot grip, 3" barrel **$537.00**
Price: Model 317 LadySmith (DymondWood only, comes
with display case) **$568.00**

Smith & Wesson Model 637 Airweight Revolver

Similar to the Model 37 Airweight except has alloy frame, stainless steel barrel, cylinder and yoke; rated for 38 Spec. +P; Uncle Mike's Boot Grip. Weighs 15 oz. Introduced 1996. Made in U.S. by Smith & Wesson.

Price: **$459.00**

SMITH & WESSON MODEL 64 STAINLESS M&P

Caliber: 38 Spec., 6-shot. **Barrel:** 2", 3", 4". **Weight:** 34 oz. **Length:** 9-5/16" overall. **Stocks:** Soft rubber. **Sights:** Fixed, 1/8" serrated ramp front, square notch rear. **Features:** Satin finished stainless steel, square butt.

Price: 2" **$487.00**
Price: 3", 4" **$496.00**

SMITH & WESSON MODEL 65LS LADYSMITH

Caliber: 357 Magnum, 6-shot. **Barrel:** 3". **Weight:** 31 oz. **Length:** 7.94" overall. **Stocks:** Rosewood, round butt. **Sights:** Serrated ramp front, fixed notch rear. **Features:** Stainless steel with frosted finish. Smooth combat trigger, service hammer, shrouded ejector rod. Comes with case. Introduced 1992.

Price: **$539.00**

Smith & Wesson Model 586,
686 Distinguished Combat

Smith & Wesson Model 625

SMITH & WESSON MODEL 66 STAINLESS COMBAT MAGNUM

Caliber: 357 Mag. and 38 Spec., 6-shot. **Barrel:** 2-1/2", 4", 6". **Weight:** 36 oz. (4" barrel). **Length:** 9-9/16" overall. **Stocks:** Soft rubber. **Sights:** Red ramp front, micro-click rear adjustable for windage and elevation. **Features:** Satin finish stainless steel.
Price: 2-1/2" $545.00
Price: 4", 6" $551.00

SMITH & WESSON MODEL 67 COMBAT MASTERPIECE

Caliber: 38 Special, 6-shot. **Barrel:** 4". **Weight:** 32 oz. **Length:** 9-5/16" overall. **Stocks:** Soft rubber. **Sights:** Red ramp front, micro-click rear adjustable for windage and elevation. **Features:** Stainless steel with satin finish. Smooth combat trigger, semi-target hammer. Introduced 1994.
Price: $546.00

SMITH & WESSON MODEL 242 AIRLITE Ti REVOLVER

Caliber: 38 Special, 7-shot. **Barrel:** 2-1/2". **Weight:** 18.9 oz. **Length:** 7-3/8" overall. **Stocks:** Uncle Mike's Boot grip. **Sights:** Serrated ramp front, fixed notch rear. **Features:** Alloy frame, yoke and barrel shroud; titanium cylinder; stainless barrel insert. Medium L-frame size. Introduced 1999. Made in U.S. by Smith & Wesson.
Price: $658.00

SMITH & WESSON MODEL 296 AIRLITE Ti REVOLVER

Caliber: 44 Spec. **Barrel:** 2-1/2". **Weight:** 18.9 oz. **Length:** 7-3/8" overall. **Stocks:** Uncle Mike's Boot grip. **Sights:** Serrated ramp front, fixed notch rear. **Features:** Alloy frame, yoke and barrel shroud; titanium cylinder; stainless steel barrel insert. Medium, L-frame size. Introduced 1999. Made in U.S. by Smith & Wesson.
Price: $718.00

SMITH & WESSON MODEL 586, 686 DISTINGUISHED COMBAT MAGNUMS

Caliber: 357 Magnum. **Barrel:** 4", 6" (M 586); 2-1/2", 4", 6", 8-3/8" (M 686). **Weight:** 46 oz. (6"), 41 oz. (4"). **Stocks:** Soft rubber. **Sights:** Red ramp front, S&W micrometer click rear. Drilled and tapped for scope mount. **Features:** Uses L-frame, but takes all K-frame grips. Full-length ejector rod shroud. Smooth combat-type trigger, semi-target type hammer. Also available in stainless as Model 686. Introduced 1981.
Price: Model 586, blue, 4", from $494.00
Price: Model 586, blue, 6" $499.00
Price: Model 686, 6", ported barrel $564.00
Price: Model 686, 8-3/8" $550.00
Price: Model 686, 2-1/2" $514.00

Smith & Wesson Model 686 Magnum PLUS Revolver

Similar to the Model 686 except has 7-shot cylinder, 2-1/2", 4" or 6" barrel. Weighs 34-1/2 oz., overall length 7-1/2" (2-1/2" barrel). Hogue rubber grips. Introduced 1996. Made in U.S. by Smith & Wesson.
Price: 2-1/2" barrel $534.00
Price: 4" barrel $542.00
Price: 6" barrel $550.00

SMITH & WESSON MODEL 625 REVOLVER

Caliber: 45 ACP, 6-shot. **Barrel:** 5". **Weight:** 46 oz. **Length:** 11.375" overall. **Stocks:** Soft rubber; wood optional. **Sights:** Patridge front on ramp,

S&W micrometer click rear adjustable for windage and elevation. **Features:** Stainless steel construction with .400" semi-target hammer, .312" smooth combat trigger; full lug barrel. Introduced 1989.
Price: $636.00

SMITH & WESSON MODEL 640 CENTENNIAL

Caliber: 357 Mag., 5-shot. **Barrel:** 2-1/8". **Weight:** 25 oz. **Length:** 6-3/4" overall. **Stocks:** Uncle Mike's Boot Grip. **Sights:** Serrated ramp front, fixed notch rear. **Features:** Stainless steel. Fully concealed hammer, snag-proof smooth edges. Introduced 1995 in 357 Magnum.
Price: $502.00

SMITH & WESSON MODEL 617 FULL LUG REVOLVER

Caliber: 22 LR, 6- or 10-shot. **Barrel:** 4", 6", 8-3/8". **Weight:** 42 oz. (4" barrel). **Length:** NA. **Stocks:** Soft rubber. **Sights:** Patridge front, adjustable rear. Drilled and tapped for scope mount. **Features:** Stainless steel with satin finish; 4" has .312" smooth trigger, .375" semi-target hammer; 6" has either .312" combat or .400" serrated trigger, .375" semi-target or .500" target hammer; 8-3/8" with .400" serrated trigger, .500" target hammer. Introduced 1990.
Price: 4" $534.00
Price: 6", target hammer, target trigger $524.00
Price: 6", 10-shot $566.00
Price: 8-3/8", 10 shot $578.00

SMITH & WESSON MODEL 610 CLASSIC HUNTER REVOLVER

Caliber: 10mm, 6-shot cylinder. **Barrel:** 6-1/2" full lug. **Weight:** 52 oz. **Length:** 12" overall. **Stocks:** Hogue rubber combat. **Sights:** Interchangeable blade front, micro-click rear adjustable for windage and elevation. **Features:** Stainless steel construction; target hammer, target trigger; unfluted cylinder; drilled and tapped for scope mounting. Introduced 1998.
Price: $684.00

SMITH & WESSON MODEL 331, 332 AIRLITE Ti REVOLVERS

Caliber: 32 H&R Mag., 6-shot. **Barrel:** 1-7/8". **Weight:** 11.2 oz. (with wood grip). **Length:** 6-15/16" overall. **Stocks:** Uncle Mike's Boot or Dymondwood Boot. **Sights:** Black serrated ramp front, fixed notch rear. **Features:** Aluminum alloy frame, barrel shroud and yoke; titanium cylinder; stainless steel barrel liner. Matte finish. Introduced 1999. Made in U.S. by Smith & Wesson.
Price: Model 331 Chiefs $682.00
Price: Model 332 . . . . $699.00

SMITH & WESSON MODEL 337 CHIEFS SPECIAL AIRLITE Ti

Caliber: 38 Spec., 5-shot. **Barrel:** 1-7/8". **Weight:** 11.2 oz. (Dymondwood grips). **Length:** 6-5/16" overall. **Stocks:** Uncle Mike's Boot or Dymondwood Boot. **Sights:** Black serrated front, fixed notch rear. **Features:** Aluminum alloy frame, barrel shroud and yoke; titanium cylinder; stainless steel barrel liner. Matte finish. Introduced 1999. Made in U.S. by Smith & Wesson.
Price: $682.00

SMITH & WESSON MODEL 342 CENTENNIAL AIRLITE Ti

Caliber: 38 Spec., 5-shot. **Barrel:** 1-7/8". **Weight:** 11.3 oz. (Dymondwood stocks). **Length:** 6-15/16" overall. **Stocks:** Uncle Mike's Boot or Dymondwood Boot. **Sights:** Black serrated ramp front, fixed notch rear. **Features:**

Smith & Wesson Model 442

Smith & Wesson Model 649

Smith & Wesson Model 696

Taurus Model 82

Aluminum alloy frame, barrel shroud and yoke; titanium cylinder; stainless steel barrel liner. Shrouded hammer. Matte finish. Introduced 1999. Made in U.S. by Smith & Wesson.

Price: **$699.00**

Smith & Wesson Model 442 Centennial Airweight

Similar to the Model 640 Centennial except has alloy frame giving weight of 15.8 oz. Chambered for 38 Special, 1-7/8" carbon steel barrel; carbon steel cylinder; concealed hammer; Uncle Mike's Boot grip. Fixed square notch rear sight, serrated ramp front. Introduced 1993.

Price: Blue **$459.00**

SMITH & WESSON MODEL 638 AIRWEIGHT BODYGUARD

Caliber: 38 Spec., 5-shot. **Barrel:** 1-7/8". **Weight:** 15 oz. **Length:** 6-15/16" overall. **Stocks:** Uncle Mike's Boot grip. **Sights:** Serrated ramp front, fixed notch rear. **Features:** Alloy frame, stainless cylinder and barrel; shrouded hammer. Introduced 1997. Made in U.S. by Smith & Wesson.

Price: With Uncle Mike's Boot grip **$492.00**

Smith & Wesson Model 642 Airweight Revolver

Similar to the Model 442 Centennial Airweight except has stainless steel barrel, cylinder and yoke with matte finish; Uncle Mike's Boot Grip; weighs 15.8 oz. Introduced 1996. Made in U.S. by Smith & Wesson.

Price: **$474.00**

Smith & Wesson Model 642LS LadySmith Revolver

Same as the Model 642 except has smooth combat wood grips, and comes with case; aluminum alloy frame, stainless cylinder, barrel and yoke; frosted matte finish. Weighs 15.8 oz. Introduced 1996. Made in U.S. by Smith & Wesson.

Price: **$505.00**

SMITH & WESSON MODEL 649 BODYGUARD REVOLVER

Caliber: 357 Mag., 5-shot. **Barrel:** 2-1/8". **Weight:** 20 oz. **Length:** 6-5/16" overall. **Stocks:** Uncle Mike's Combat. **Sights:** Black pinned ramp front, fixed notch rear. **Features:** Stainless steel construction; shrouded hammer; smooth combat trigger. Made in U.S. by Smith & Wesson.

Price: **$502.00**

SMITH & WESSON MODEL 657 REVOLVER

Caliber: 41 Mag., 6-shot. **Barrel:** 6". **Weight:** 48 oz. **Length:** 11-3/8" overall. **Stocks:** Soft rubber. **Sights:** Pinned 1/8" red ramp front, micro-click rear adjustable for windage and elevation. **Features:** Stainless steel construction.

Price: **$564.00**

SMITH & WESSON MODEL 696 REVOLVER

Caliber: 44 Spec., 5-shot. **Barrel:** 3". **Weight:** 35.5 oz. **Length:** 8-1/4" overall. **Stocks:** Uncle Mike's Combat. **Sights:** Red ramp front, click adjustable white outline rear. **Features:** Stainless steel construction; round butt frame; satin finish. Introduced 1997. Made in U.S. by Smith & Wesson.

Price: **$525.00**

TAURUS MODEL 65 REVOLVER

Caliber: 357 Mag., 6-shot. **Barrel:** 4". **Weight:** 38 oz. **Length:** 10-1/2" overall. **Stocks:** Soft rubber. **Sights:** Serrated front, notch rear. **Features:** Solid rib barrel; +P rated. Imported by Taurus International.

Price: Blue **$313.00**
Price: Stainless. **$359.00**

Taurus Model 66 Revolver

Same to the Model 65 except with 4" or 6" barrel, 7-shot cylinder, adjustable rear sight. Imported by Taurus International.

Price: Blue **$359.00**
Price: Stainless. **$406.00**

TAURUS MODEL 82 HEAVY BARREL REVOLVER

Caliber: 38 Spec., 6-shot. **Barrel:** 4", heavy. **Weight:** 34 oz. (4" bbl.). **Length:** 9-1/4" overall (4" bbl.). **Stocks:** Soft black rubber. **Sights:** Serrated ramp front, square notch rear. **Features:** Imported by Taurus International.

Price: Blue **$297.00**
Price: Polished, stainless **$344.00**

TAURUS MODEL 85 REVOLVER

Caliber: 38 Spec., 5-shot. **Barrel:** 2", 3". **Weight:** 21 oz. **Stocks:** Black rubber, boot grip. **Sights:** Ramp front, square notch rear. **Features:** Blue finish or stainless steel. Introduced 1980. Imported by Taurus International.

Taurus Model 85   Taurus Model 85Ti/731Ti   Taurus Model 85CH   Taurus Model 94UL

Price: Blue, 2", 3" **$286.00**
Price: Stainless steel **$327.00**
Price: Blue, 2", ported barrel **$305.00**
Price: Stainless, 2", ported barrel **$345.00**
Price: Blue, Ultra-Lite (17 oz.), 2" **$311.00**
Price: Stainless, Ultra-Lite (17 oz.), 2", ported barrel **$342.00**
Price: Blue with gold trim, ported **$350.00**

Taurus Model 85UL/Ti Revolver

Similar to the Model 85 except has titanium cylinder, aluminum alloy frame, and ported aluminum barrel with stainless steel sleeve. Weight is 13.5 oz. International.
Price: **$515.00**

Taurus Model 85Ti, Model 731Ti Revolvers

Similar to the 2" Model 85 except has titanium frame, cylinder and ported barrel with stainless steel liner; yoke detent and extended ejector rod. Weight is 15.4 oz. Comes with soft, ridged Ribber grips. Available in Bright and Matte Spectrum blue, Matte Spectrum gold, and Steel Gray colors. Introduced 1999. Imported by Taurus International.
Price: Model 85Ti **$529.00**
Price: Model 731Ti (32 H&R mag., 6-shot). **$529.00**

Taurus Model 85CH Revolver

Same as the Model 85 except has 2" barrel only and concealed hammer. Double aciton only. Soft rubber boot grip. Introduced 1991. Imported by Taurus International.
Price: Blue **$286.00**
Price: Stainless. **$327.00**
Price: Blue, ported barrel **$305.00**
Price: Stainless, ported barrel **$345.00**

TAURUS MODEL 94 REVOLVER

Caliber: 22 LR, 9-shot cylinder. **Barrel:** 2", 4", 5". **Weight:** 25 oz. **Stocks:** Soft black rubber. **Sights:** Serrated ramp front, click-adjustable rear for windage and elevation. **Features:** Floating firing pin, color case-hardened hammer and trigger. Introduced 1989. Imported by Taurus International.
Price: Blue **$308.00**
Price: Stainless. **$356.00**

Taurus Model 22H Raging Hornet

Price: Model 94 UL, blue, 2", fixed sight, weighs 14 oz. **$342.00**
Price: As above, stainless **$391.00**

TAURUS MODEL 22H RAGING HORNET REVOLVER

Caliber: 22 Hornet, 8-shot cylinder. **Barrel:** 10". **Weight:** 50 oz. **Length:** 6.5" overall. **Stocks:** Soft black rubber. **Sights:** Patridge front, micrometer click adjustable rear. **Features:** Ventilated rib; 1:10 twist rifling; comes with scope base; stainless steel construction with matte finish. Introduced 1999. Imported by Taurus International.
Price: **$898.00**

TAURUS MODEL 44 REVOLVER

Caliber: 44 Mag., 6-shot. **Barrel:** 4", 6-1/2", 8-3/8". **Weight:** 44-3/4 oz. (4" barrel). **Length:** NA. **Stocks:** Soft black rubber. **Sights:** Serrated ramp front, micro-click rear adjustable for windage and elevation. **Features:** Heavy solid rib on 4", vent rib on 6-1/2", 8-3/8". Compensated barrel. Blued model has color case-hardened hammer and trigger. Introduced 1994. Imported by Taurus International.
Price: Blue, 4". **$447.00**
Price: Blue, 6-1/2", 8-3/8". **$466.00**
Price: Stainless, 4" **$508.00**
Price: Stainless, 6-1/2", 8-3/8" **$530.00**

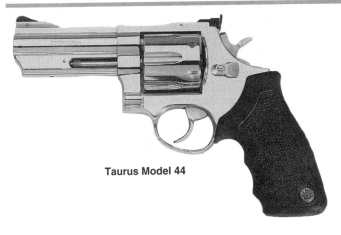

Taurus Model 44

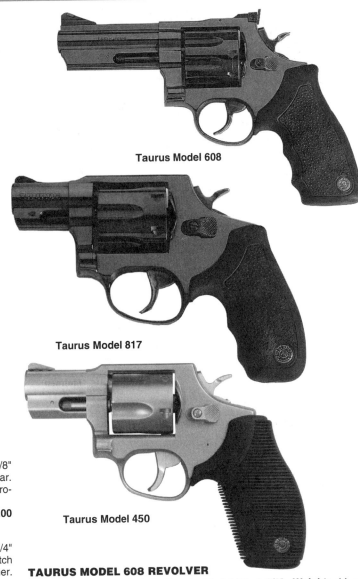

Taurus Model 608

Taurus Model 415

Taurus Model 817

Taurus Model 450

TAURUS MODEL 415 REVOLVER

Caliber: 41 Mag., 5-shot. **Barrel:** 2-1/2". **Weight:** 30 oz. **Length:** 7-1/8" overall. **Stocks:** Soft, ridged Ribber. **Sights:** Serrated front, notch rear. **Features:** Stainless steel construction; matte finish; ported barrel. Introduced 1999. Imported by Taurus International.
Price: **$452.00**

TAURUS MODEL 445, 445CH REVOLVERS

Caliber: 44 Special, 5-shot. **Barrel:** 2". **Weight:** 28.25 oz. **Length:** 6-3/4" overall. **Stocks:** Soft black rubber. **Sights:** Serrated ramp front, notch rear. **Features:** Blue or stainless steel. Standard or concealed hammer. Introduced 1997. Imported by Taurus International.
Price: Blue **$323.00**
Price: Blue, ported **$342.00**
Price: Stainless. **$370.00**
Price: Stainless, ported. **$389.00**
Price: M445CH, concealed hammer, blue, DAO **$323.00**
Price: M445CH, blue, ported **$342.00**
Price: M445CH, stainless **$370.00**
Price: M445CH, stainless, ported. **$389.00**
Price: M445CH, Ultra-Lite, stainless, ported **$483.00**

TAURUS MODEL 605 REVOLVER

Caliber: 357 Mag., 5-shot. **Barrel:** 2-1/4", 3". **Weight:** 24.5 oz. **Length:** NA. **Stocks:** Soft black rubber. **Sights:** Serrated ramp front, fixed notch rear. **Features:** Heavy, solid rib barrel; floating firing pin. Blue or stainless. Introduced 1995. Imported by Taurus International.
Price: Blue **$303.00**
Price: Stainless. **$344.00**
Price: Model 605CH (concealed hammer) 2-1/4", blue, DAO . . . **$303.00**
Price: Model 605CH, stainless, 2-1/4" **$344.00**
Price: Blue, 2-1/4", ported barrel **$322.00**
Price: Stainless, 2-1/4", ported barrel. **$363.00**
Price: Blue, 2-1/4", ported barrel, concealed hammer, DAO **$322.00**
Price: Stainless, 2-1/4", ported barrel, concealed hammer, DAO **$363.00**

TAURUS MODEL 608 REVOLVER

Caliber: 357 Mag., 8-shot. **Barrel:** 4", 6-1/2", 8-3/8". **Weight:** 44 oz. **Length:** 9-3/8" overall. **Stocks:** Soft black rubber. **Sights:** Serrated ramp front, fully adjustable rear. **Features:** Built-in compensator. Available in blue or stainless. Introduced 1995. Imported by Taurus international.
Price: Blue, 4", solid rib **$447.00**
Price: Blue, 6-1/2", 8-3/8", vent rib **$466.00**
Price: Stainless, 4", solid rib **$508.00**
Price: Stainless, 6-1/2", 8-3/8", vent rib **$530.00**

TAURUS MODEL 817 REVOLVER

Caliber: 38 Spec., 7-shot. **Barrel:** 2". **Weight:** 21 oz. **Length:** 6-1/2" overall. **Stocks:** Soft rubber. **Sights:** Serrated front, notch rear. **Features:** Compact alloy frame. Introduced 1999. Imported by Taurus International.
Price: Blue **$350.00**
Price: Blue, ported **$369.00**
Price: Matte, stainless **$389.00**
Price: Matte, stainless, ported **$408.00**

TAURUS MODEL 450 REVOLVER

Caliber: 45 Colt, 5-shot cylinder. **Barrel:** 2". **Weight:** 28 oz. **Length:** 6-5/8" overall. **Stocks:** Soft, ridged rubber. **Sights:** Serrated front, notch rear. **Features:** Stainless steel construction; ported barrel. Introduced 1999. Imported by Taurus International.
Price: **$452.00**
Price: Ultra-Lite (alloy frame) **$483.00**

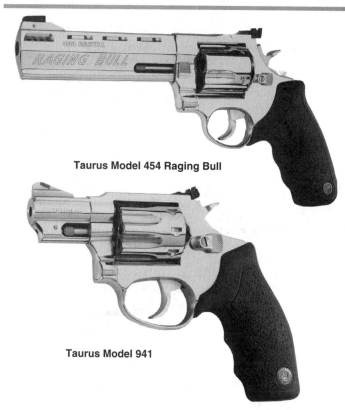

Taurus Model 454 Raging Bull

Taurus Model 941

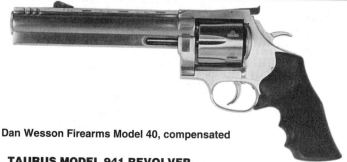

Dan Wesson Firearms Model 40, compensated

TAURUS MODEL 45, 444, 454 RAGING BULL REVOLVER

Caliber: 454 Casull, 5-shot. **Barrel:** 5", 6-1/2", 8-3/8". **Weight:** 53 oz. (6-1/2" barrel). **Length:** 12" overall (6-1/2" barrel). **Stocks:** Soft black rubber. **Sights:** Patridge front, micrometer click adjustable rear. **Features:** Ventilated rib; integral compensating system. Introduced 1997. Imported by Taurus International.

Price: 6-1/2", 8-3/8", blue $750.00
Price: 6-1/2", polished, stainless $820.00
Price: 5", 6-1/2", 8-3/8", matte stainless $820.00
Price: 5", 6-1/2", 8-3/8", color case-hardened frame $845.00
Price: Model 45 (45 Colt), blue, 6-1/2", 8-3/8" $545.00
Price: Model 45, stainless, 6-1/2", 8-3/8" $608.00
Price: Model 444 (44 Mag.), blue, 6-1/2", 8-3/8" $545.00
Price: Model 444, matte, stainless, 6-1/2", 8-3/8" $608.00

TAURUS MODEL 617, 606CH REVOLVER

Caliber: 357 Magnum, 7-shot. **Barrel:** 2". **Weight:** 29 oz. **Length:** 6-3/4" overall. **Stocks:** Soft black rubber. **Sights:** Serrated ramp front, notch rear. **Features:** Heavy, solid barrel rib, ejector shroud. Available with porting, concealed hammer. Introduced 1998. Imported by Taurus International.

Price: Blue, regular or concealed hammer $355.00
Price: Stainless, regular or concealed hammer $402.00
Price: Blue, ported $373.00
Price: Stainless, ported. $420.00
Price: Blue, concealed hammer, ported $373.00
Price: Stainless, concealed hammer, ported $420.00

Taurus Model 415Ti, 445Ti, 450Ti, 617Ti Revolvers

Similar to the Model 617 except has titanium frame, cylinder, and ported barrel with stainless steel liner; yoke detent and extended ejector rod; +P rated; ridged Ribber grips. Available in Bright and Matte Spectrum Blue, Matte Spectrum Gold, and Stealth Gray. Introduced 1999. Imported by Taurus International.

Price: Model 617Ti, (357 Mag., 7-shot, 19.9 oz.) $599.00
Price: Model 415Ti (41 Mag., 5-shot, 20.9 oz.) $599.00
Price: Model 450Ti (45 Colt, 5-shot, 19.2 oz.) $599.00
Price: Model 445Ti (44 Spec., 5-shot, 19.8 oz.) $599.00

TAURUS MODEL 941 REVOLVER

Caliber: 22 WMR, 8-shot. **Barrel:** 2", 4", 5". **Weight:** 27.5 oz. (4" barrel). **Length:** NA. **Stocks:** Soft black rubber. **Sights:** Serrated ramp front, rear adjustable for windage and elevation. **Features:** Solid rib heavy barrel with full-length ejector rod shroud. Blue or stainless steel. Introduced 1992. Imported by Taurus International.

Price: Blue $331.00
Price: Stainless. $384.00
Price: Model 941 Ultra Lite, blue, 2", fixed sight, weighs 8.5 oz. . . $366.00
Price: As above, stainless $419.00

DAN WESSON FIREARMS MODEL 22 SILHOUETTE REVOLVER

Caliber: 22 LR, 6-shot. **Barrel:** 10", regular vent or vent heavy. **Weight:** 53 oz. **Stocks:** Combat style. **Sights:** Patridge-style front, .080" narrow notch rear. **Features:** Single action only. Available in blue or stainless. Reintroduced 1997. Made in U.S. by Dan Wesson Firearms.

Price: Blue, regular vent $474.00
Price: Blue, vent heavy. $492.00
Price: Stainless, regular vent $504.00
Price: Stainless, vent heavy $532.00

DAN WESSON FIREARMS
MODEL 322/7322 TARGET REVOLVER

Caliber: 32-20, 6-shot. **Barrel:** 2.5", 4", 6", 8", standard vent, vent heavy. **Weight:** 43 oz. (6" VH). **Length:** 11.25" overall. **Stocks:** Checkered walnut. **Sights:** Red ramp interchangeable front, fully adjustable rear. **Features:** Bright blue or stainless. Reintroduced 1997. Made in U.S. by Dan Wesson Firearms.

Price: 6", vent heavy, blue $619.00
Price: 6", vent heavy, stainless. $659.00
Price: 8", vent heavy, blue $649.00
Price: 8", vent heavy, stainless. $699.00

DAN WESSON FIREARMS MODEL 40 SILHOUETTE

Caliber: 357 Maximum, 6-shot. **Barrel:** 4", 6", 8", 10". **Weight:** 64 oz. (8" bbl.). **Length:** 14.3" overall (8" bbl.). **Stocks:** Smooth walnut, target-style. **Sights:** 1/8" serrated front, fully adjustable rear. **Features:** Meets criteria for IHMSA competition with 8" slotted barrel. Blue or stainless steel. Made in U.S. by Dan Wesson Firearms.

Price: Blue, 4". $702.00
Price: Blue, 6". $749.00
Price: Blue, 8". $795.00
Price: Blue, 10". $858.00
Price: Stainless, 4" $834.00
Price: Stainless, 6" $892.00
Price: Stainless, 8" slotted $1,024.00
Price: Stainless, 10" $998.00
Price: 4", 6", 8" Compensated, blue . . . . $749.00 to $885.00
Price: As above, stainless . . . . $893.00 to $1,061.00

DAN WESSON FIREARMS MODEL 22 REVOLVER

Caliber: 22 LR, 22 WMR, 6-shot. **Barrel:** 2-1/2", 4", 6", 8"; interchangeable. **Weight:** 36 oz. (2-1/2"), 44 oz. (6"). **Length:** 9-1/4" overall (4" barrel). **Stocks:** Checkered; undercover, service or over-size target. **Sights:** 1/8" serrated, interchangeable front, white outline rear adjustable for windage and elevation. **Features:** Built on the same frame as the Wesson 357; smooth, wide trigger with over-travel adjustment, wide spur hammer, with short double-action travel. Available in Brite blue or stainless steel. Reintroduced 1997. Contact Dan Wesson Firearms for complete price list.

**Dan Wesson Firearms
Model 445 Supermag**

Price: 2-1/2" bbl., blue $489.00
Price: As above, stainless $509.00
Price: With 4", vent heavy, blue $509.00
Price: As above, stainless $539.00
Price: Blue Pistol Pac, 22 LR $1,199.00

Dan Wesson Firearms Model 414, 445 SuperMag Revolvers
Similar size and weight as the Model 40 revolvers. Chambered for the 445 SuperMag cartridge, a longer version of the 44 Magnum and 414 SuperMag. Barrel lengths of 4", 6", 8", 10". Contact maker for complete price list. Reintroduced 1997. Made in the U.S. by Dan Wesson Firearms.
Price: 4", vent heavy, blue $797.00
Price: As above, stainless $829.00
Price: 8", vent heavy, blue $899.00
Price: As above, stainless $929.00
Price: 10", vent heavy, blue $959.00
Price: As above, stainless $995.00
Price: 8", vent slotted, blue $987.00
Price: As above, stainless $1,134.00
Price: 10", vent slotted, blue $1,195.00
Price: As above, stainless $1,285.00
Price: 4", 6", 8" Compensated, blue .... $859.00 to $979.00
Price: As above, stainless .... $899.00 to $995.00

DAN WESSON FIREARMS MODEL 15 & 32 REVOLVERS
Caliber: 32-20, 32 H&R Mag. (Model 32), 357 Mag. (Model 15). **Barrel:** 2-1/2", 4", 6", 8" (M32), 2-1/2", 4", 6", 8", 10" (M15); vent heavy. **Weight:** 36 oz. (2-1/2" barrel). **Length:** 9-1/4" overall (4" barrel). **Stocks:** Checkered, interchangeable. **Sights:** 1/8" serrated front, fully adjustable rear. **Features:** New Generation Series. Interchangeable barrels; wide, smooth trigger, wide hammer spur; short double-action travel. Available in blue or stainless. Reintroduced 1997. Made in U.S. by Dan Wesson Firearms. Contact maker for full list of models.
Price: Model 15, blue, 2-1/2" $489.00
Price: Model 15, blue, 8" $569.00
Price: Model 15, stainless, 4" $539.00
Price: Model 15, stainless, 6" $569.00
Price: Model 15, blue, compensated .... $579.00 to $699.00
Price: Model 15, stainless, compensated ...... $619.00 to $759.00
Price: Model 32, blue, 4" $589.00
Price: Model 32, blue, 8" $649.00
Price: Model 32, stainless, 2-1/2" $589.00
Price: Model 32, stainless, 6" $659.00

DAN WESSON FIREARMS MODEL 41V, 44V, 45V REVOLVERS
Caliber: 41 Mag., 44 Mag., 45 Colt, 6-shot. **Barrel:** 4", 6", 8", 10"; interchangeable; 4", 6", 8" Compensated. **Weight:** 48 oz. (4"). **Length:** 12" overall (6" bbl.) **Stocks:** Smooth. **Sights:** 1/8" serrated front, white outline rear adjustable for windage and elevation. **Features:** Available in blue or stainless steel. Smooth, wide trigger with adjustable over-travel; wide hammer spur. Available in Pistol Pac set also. Reintroduced 1997. Contact Dan Wesson Firearms for complete price list.
Price: 41 Mag., 4", vent heavy $579.00
Price: As above except in stainless $599.00
Price: 44 Mag., 4", blue $579.00
Price: As above except in stainless $599.00
Price: 45 Colt, 4", vent heavy $599.00

Dan Wesson Firearms Silhouette

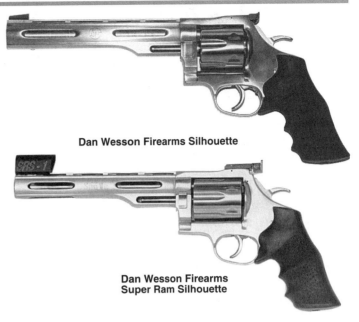

**Dan Wesson Firearms
Super Ram Silhouette**

Price: As above except in stainless $619.00
Price: Model 41, 44, 45, blue, 4", 6", 8" compensated . $633.00 to $727.00
Price: As above in stainless .... $752.00 to $868.00

DAN WESSON FIREARMS MODEL 360 REVOLVER
Caliber: 357 Mag. **Barrel:** 4", 6", 8", 10"; vent heavy. **Weight:** 64 oz. (8" barrel). **Length:** NA. **Stocks:** Hogue rubber finger groove. **Sights:** Interchangeable ramp or Patridge front, fully adjustable rear. **Features:** New Generation Large Frame Series. Interchangeable barrels and grips; smooth trigger, wide hammer spur. Blue or stainless. Introduced 1999. Made in U.S. by Dan Wesson Firearms.
Price: Blue, from $639.00
Price: Stainless, from $669.00

DAN WESSON FIREARMS MODEL 460 REVOLVER
Caliber: 45 ACP and 460 Rowland. **Barrel:** 4", 6", 8", 10"; vent heavy. **Weight:** 49 oz. (4" barrel). **Length:** NA. **Stocks:** Hogue rubber finger groove; interchangeable. **Sights:** Interchangeable ramp or Patridge front, fully adjustable rear. **Features:** New Generation Large Frame Series. Shoots 45 ACP and 460 Rowland. Interchangeable barrels and grips. Available with non-fluted cylinder and Slotted Lightweight barrel shroud. Introduced 1999. Made in U.S. by Dan Wesson Firearms.
Price: .... NA

DAN WESSON FIREARMS STANDARD SILHOUETTE REVOLVER
Caliber: 357 SuperMag/Maxi, 41 Mag., 414 SuperMag, 445 SuperMag. **Barrel:** 8", 10" **Weight:** 64 oz. (8" barrel). **Length:** 14.3" overall (8" barrel). **Stocks:** Hogue rubber finger groove; interchangeable. **Sights:** Patridge front, fully adjustable rear. **Features:** Interchangeable barrels and grips; fluted or non-fluted cylinder; blue or stainless. Introduced 1999. Made in U.S. by Dan Wesson Firearms.
Price: 357 SuperMag/Maxi, 8", blue or stainless $949.00
Price: 41 Mag., 10", blue or stainless $929.00
Price: 414 SuperMag., 8", blue or stainless $949.00
Price: 445 SuperMag., 8", blue or stainless $949.00

Dan Wesson Firearms Super Ram Silhouette Revolver
Similar to the Standard Silhouette except has 10 land and groove Laser Coat barrel, Bo-Mar target sights with hooded front, and special laser engraving. Fluted or non-fluted cylinder. Introduced 1999. Made in U.S. by Dan Wesson Firearms.
Price: 357 SuperMag/Maxi, 414 SuperMag., 445 SuperMag., 8", blue or stainless $1,195.00
Price: 41 Magnum, 44 Magnum, 8", blue or stainless $1,099.00
Price: 41 Magnum, 44 Magnum, 10", blue or stainless $1,139.00

Both classic six-shooters and modern adaptations for hunting and sport.

American Frontier 1871-1872 Open-Top

American Frontier 1851 Mason

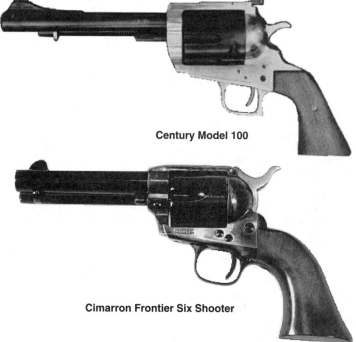

Century Model 100

Cimarron Frontier Six Shooter

AMERICAN FRONTIER 1851 NAVY CONVERSION

Caliber: 38, 44. **Barrel:** 5-1/2", 7-1/2", octagon. **Weight:** NA. **Length:** NA. **Stocks:** Varnished walnut, Navy size. **Sights:** Blade front, fixed rear. **Features:** Shoots metallic cartridge ammunition. Non-rebated cylinder; blued steel backstrap and trigger guard; color case-hardened hammer, trigger, ramrod, plunger; no ejector rod assembly. Introduced 1996.
Price: **$795.00**

AMERICAN FRONTIER 1871-1872 OPEN-TOP REVOLVERS

Caliber: 38, 44. **Barrel:** 5-1/2", 7-1/2", 8" round. **Weight:** NA. **Length:** NA. **Stocks:** Varnished walnut. **Sights:** Blade front, fixed rear. **Features:** Reproduction of the early cartridge conversions from percussion. Made for metallic cartridges. High polish blued steel, silver-plated brass backstrap and trigger guard, color case-hardened hammer; straight non-rebated cylinder with naval engagement engraving; stamped with original patent dates. Does not have conversion breechplate.
Price: **$795.00**

AMERICAN FRONTIER RICHARDS 1860 ARMY

Caliber: 38, 44. **Barrel:** 5-1/2", 7-1/2", round. **Weight:** NA. **Length:** NA. **Stocks:** Varnished walnut, Army size. **Sights:** Blade front, fixed rear. **Features:** Shoots metallic cartridge ammunition. Rebated cylinder; available with or without ejector assembly; high-polish blue including backstrap; silver-plated trigger guard; color case-hardened hammer and trigger. Introduced 1996.
Price: **$795.00**

American Frontier 1851 Navy Richards & Mason Conversion

Similar to the 1851 Navy Conversion except has Mason ejector assembly. Introduced 1996. Imported from Italy by American Frontier Firearms Mfg.
Price: **$695.00**

CENTURY GUN DIST. MODEL 100 SINGLE-ACTION

Caliber: 30-30, 375 Win., 444 Marlin, 45-70, 50-70. **Barrel:** 6-1/2" (standard), 8", 10". **Weight:** 6 lbs. (loaded). **Length:** 15" overall (8" bbl.). **Stocks:** Smooth walnut. **Sights:** Ramp front, Millett adjustable square notch rear. **Features:** Highly polished high tensile strength manganese bronze frame, blue cylinder and barrel; coil spring trigger mechanism. Contact maker for full price information. Introduced 1975. Made in U.S. From Century Gun Dist., Inc.
Price: 6-1/2" barrel, 45-70 .... **$2,000.00**

CIMARRON U.S. CAVALRY MODEL SINGLE-ACTION

Caliber: 45 Colt. **Barrel:** 7-1/2". **Weight:** 42 oz. **Length:** 13-1/2" overall. **Stocks:** Walnut. **Sights:** Fixed. **Features:** Has "A.P. Casey" markings; "U.S." plus patent dates on frame, serial number on backstrap, trigger guard, frame and cylinder, "APC" cartouche on left grip; color case-hardened frame and hammer, rest charcoal blue. Exact copy of the original. Imported by Cimarron F.A. Co.
Price: **$499.00**

Cimarron Rough Rider Artillery Model Single-Action

Similar to the U.S. Cavalry model except has 5-1/2" barrel, weighs 39 oz., and is 11-1/2" overall. U.S. markings and cartouche, case-hardened frame and hammer; 45 Colt only.
Price: **$499.00**

CIMARRON 1873 FRONTIER SIX SHOOTER

Caliber: 38 WCF, 357 Mag., 44 WCF, 44 Spec., 45 Colt. **Barrel:** 4-3/4", 5-1/2", 7-1/2". **Weight:** 39 oz. **Length:** 10" overall (4" barrel). **Stocks:** Walnut. **Sights:** Blade front, fixed or adjustable rear. **Features:** Uses "old model" blackpowder frame with "Bullseye" ejector or New Model frame. Imported by Cimarron F.A. Co.
Price: 4-3/4" barrel **$469.00**
Price: 5-1/2" barrel **$469.00**
Price: 7-1/2" barrel **$469.00**

Cimarron Bisley Model Single-Action Revolvers

Similar to the 1873 Frontier Six Shooter except has special grip frame and trigger guard, knurled wide-spur hammer, curved trigger. Available in 357 Mag., 44 WCF, 45 Schofield, 45 Colt. Introduced 1999. Imported by Cimarron F.A. Co.
Price: **$499.00**

Cimarron Flat Top Single-Action Revolvers

Similar to the 1873 Frontier Six Shooter except has flat top strap with windage-adjustable rear sight, elevation-adjustable front sight. Available in 357 Mag., 44 WCF, 45 Schofield, 45 Colt; 4-3/4", 5-1/2", 7-1/2" barrel. Introduced 1999. Imported by Cimarron F.A. Co.
Price: **$479.00**

Cimarron Bisley Flat Top Revolver

Similar to the Flat Top revolver except has special grip frame and trigger guard, wide spur hammer, curved trigger. Introduced 1999. Imported by Cimarron F.A. Co.
Price: **$509.00**

CIMARRON THUNDERER REVOLVER

Caliber: 357 Mag., 44 WCF, 44 Spec., 45 Colt, 6-shot. **Barrel:** 3-1/2", 4-3/4", 5-1/2", 7-1/2", with ejector. **Weight:** 38 oz. (3-1/2" barrel). **Length:** NA. **Stocks:** Smooth walnut. **Sights:** Blade front, notch rear. **Features:**

HANDGUNS

Colt Cowboy

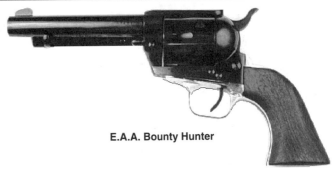

E.A.A. Bounty Hunter

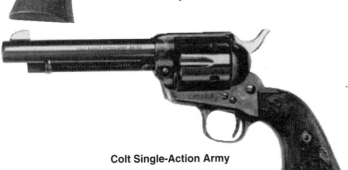

Colt Single-Action Army

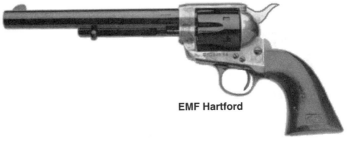

EMF Hartford

EMF 1894 Bisley

Thunderer grip; color case-hardened frame with balance blued. Introduced 1993. Imported by Cimarron F.A. Co.

Price: 3-1/2", 4-3/4", smooth grips	**$489.00**
Price: As above, checkered grips	**$524.00**
Price: 5-1/2", 7-1/2", smooth grips	**$529.00**
Price: As above, checkered grips	**$564.00**

CIMARRON 1872 OPEN-TOP REVOLVER

Caliber: 38 Spec., 38 Colt, 44 Spec., 44 Colt, 44 Russian, 45 Schofield. **Barrel:** 7-1/2". **Weight:** NA. **Length:** NA. **Stocks:** Smooth walnut. **Sights:** Blade front, fixed rear. **Features:** Replica of the original production. Color case-hardened frame, rest blued, including grip frame. Introduced 1999. Imported from Italy by Cimarron F.A. Co.
Price: **$579.00**

COLT COWBOY SINGLE-ACTION REVOLVER

Caliber: 45 Colt, 6-shot. **Barrel:** 5-1/2". **Weight:** 42 oz. **Stocks:** Black composition, first generation style. **Sights:** Blade front, notch rear. **Features:** Dimensional replica of Colt's original Peacemaker with medium-size color case-hardened frame; transfer bar safety system; half-cock loading. Introduced 1998. Made in U.S. by Colt's Mfg. Co.
Price: About **$599.00**

COLT SINGLE-ACTION ARMY REVOLVER

Caliber: 44-40, 45 Colt, 6-shot. **Barrel:** 4-3/4", 5-1/2", 7-1/2". **Weight:** 40 oz. (4-3/4" barrel). **Length:** 10-1/4" overall (4-3/4" barrel). **Stocks:** Black Eagle composite. **Sights:** Blade front, notch rear. **Features:** Available in full nickel finish with nickel grip medallions, or Royal Blue with color case-hardened frame, gold grip medallions. Reintroduced 1992.
Price: **$1,900.00**

E.A.A. BOUNTY HUNTER SA REVOLVERS

Caliber: 22 LR/22 WMR, 357 Mag., 44 Mag., 45 Colt, 6-shot. **Barrel:** 4-1/2", 7-1/2". **Weight:** 2.5 lbs. **Length:** 11" overall (4-5/8" barrel). **Stocks:** Smooth walnut. **Sights:** Blade front, grooved topstrap rear. **Features:** Transfer bar safety; three position hammer; hammer forged barrel. Introduced 1992. Imported by European American Armory.

Price: Blue or case-hardened	**$280.00**
Price: Nickel	**$298.00**
Price: 22LR/22WMR, blue	**$187.20**
Price: As above, nickel	**$204.36**

EMF HARTFORD SINGLE-ACTION REVOLVERS

Caliber: 22 LR, 357 Mag., 32-20, 38-40, 44-40, 44 Spec., 45 Colt. **Barrel:** 4-3/4", 5-1/2", 7-1/2". **Weight:** 45 oz. **Length:** 13" overall (7-1/2" barrel).

Stocks: Smooth walnut. **Sights:** Blade front, fixed rear. **Features:** Identical to the original Colts with inspector cartouche on left grip, original patent dates and U.S. markings. All major parts serial numbered using original Colt-style lettering, numbering. Bullseye ejector head and color case-hardening on frame and hammer. Introduced 1990. From E.M.F.

Price:	**$600.00**
Price: Cavalry or Artillery	**$655.00**
Price: Nickel plated	**$725.00**
Price: Engraved, nickel plated	**$840.00**

EMF 1894 Bisley Revolver

Similar to the Hartford single-action revolver except has special grip frame and trigger guard, wide spur hammer; available in 45 Colt only, 5-1/2" or 7-1/2" barrel. Introduced 1995. Imported by E.M.F.

Price: Blue	**$680.00**
Price: Nickel	**$805.00**

EMF Hartford Pinkerton Single-Action Revolver

Same as the regular Hartford except has 4" barrel with ejector tube and birds head grip. Calibers 32-20, 38-40, 44-40, 44 Special, 45 Colt. Introduced 1997. Imported by E.M.F.
Price: **$475.00**

EMF Hartford Express Single-Action Revolver

Same as the regular Hartford model except uses grip of the Colt Lightning revolver. Barrel lengths of 4", 4-3/4", 5-1/2". Introduced 1997. Imported by E.M.F.
Price: **$475.00**

HANDGUNS — SINGLE ACTION REVOLVERS

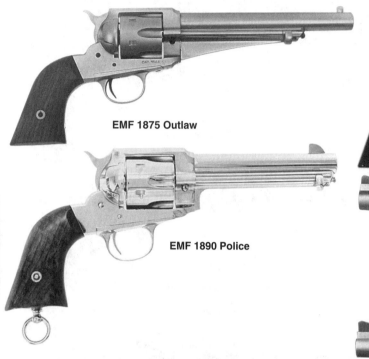

EMF 1875 Outlaw

EMF 1890 Police

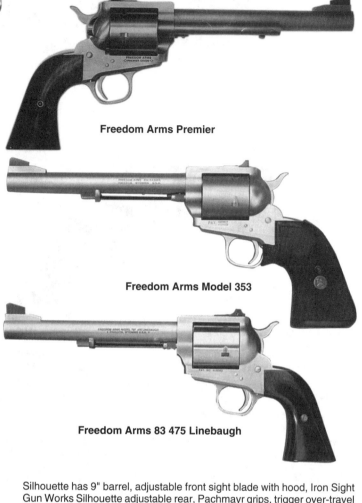

Freedom Arms Premier

Freedom Arms Model 353

Freedom Arms 83 475 Linebaugh

EMF 1875 OUTLAW REVOLVER

Caliber: 357 Mag., 44-40, 45 Colt. **Barrel:** 7-1/2". **Weight:** 46 oz. **Length:** 13-1/2" overall. **Stocks:** Smooth walnut. **Sights:** Blade front, fixed groove rear. **Features:** Authentic copy of 1875 Remington with firing pin in hammer; color case-hardened frame, blue cylinder, barrel, steel backstrap and brass trigger guard. Also available in nickel, factory engraved. Imported by E.M.F.

Price: All calibers **$465.00**
Price: Nickel **$550.00**
Price: Engraved **$600.00**
Price: Engraved nickel **$710.00**

EMF 1890 Police Revolver

Similar to the 1875 Outlaw except has 5-1/2" barrel, weighs 40 oz., with 12-1/2" overall length. Has lanyard ring in butt. No web under barrel. Calibers 357, 44-40, 45 Colt. Imported by E.M.F.

Price: All calibers **$470.00**
Price: Nickel **$560.00**
Price: Engraved **$620.00**
Price: Engraved nickel **$725.00**

FREEDOM ARMS MODEL 83 454 SINGLE-ACTION REVOLVER

Caliber: 357 Mag., 41 Rem. Mag., 44 Rem. Mag., 454 Casull, 50 AE, 5-shot. **Barrel:** 4-3/4", 6", 7-1/2", 10". **Weight:** 50 oz. **Length:** 14" overall (7-1/2" bbl.). **Stocks:** Impregnated hardwood (Premier grade), or Pachmayr (Field Grade). **Sights:** Blade front, notch or adjustable rear. **Features:** All stainless steel construction; sliding bar safety system. Lifetime warranty. Made in U.S. by Freedom Arms, Inc.

Price: Premier Grade, 454 Casull, 50 AE, adj. sight **$1,958.00**
Price: Premier Grade, 454 Casull, fixed sight. **$1,894.00**
Price: Field Grade, 454 Casull, 50 AE, adj. sight **$1,519.00**
Price: Field Grade, 454 Casull, fixed sight **$1,484.00**
Price: Premier Grade, 357 Mag., 41 Rem. Mag., 44 Rem. Mag.,
adj. sight **$1,882.00**
Price: Premier Grade, 44 Rem. Mag., fixed sight. **$1,816.00**
Price: Field Grade, 357 Mag., 41 Rem. Mag., 44 Rem. Mag.,
adj. sight **$1,442.00**

Freedom Arms Model 83 353 Revolver

Made on the Model 83 frame. Chambered for 357 Magnum with 5-shot cylinder; 4-3/4", 6", 7-1/2" or 9" barrel. Weighs 59 oz. with 7-1/2" barrel. Field grade model has adjustable sights, matte finish, Pachmayr grips.

Silhouette has 9" barrel, adjustable front sight blade with hood, Iron Sight Gun Works Silhouette adjustable rear, Pachmayr grips, trigger over-travel adjustment screw. All stainless steel. Introduced 1992.

Price: Field Grade **$1,340.00**
Price: Premier Grade (brushed finish, impregnated hardwood grips,
Premier Grade sights) **$1,760.00**
Price: Silhouette (9", 357 Mag., 10", 44 Mag.) **$1,448.00**

Freedom Arms Model 83 654 Revolver

Made on the Model 83 frame. Chambered for 41 Magnum with 5-shot cylinder. Introduced 1998. Made in U.S. by Freedom Arms.

Price: Field Grade, adjustable sights **$1,400.00**
Price: Premier Grade, adjustable sights **$1,820.00**
Price: Silhouette **$1,448.00**

FREEDOM ARMS MODEL 83 475 LINEBAUGH REVOLVER

Caliber: 475 Linebaugh, 5-shot. **Barrel:** 4.75", 6", 7.5". **Weight:** NA. **Length:** NA. **Stocks:** Impregnated hardwood (Premier Grade) or Pachmayr (Field Grade). **Sights:** Removable ramp front, fully adjustable notch rear. **Features:** All stainless steel construction with brushed finish (Premier Grade) or matte finish (Field Grade); patented slide bar safety. Introduced 1999. Made in U.S. by Freedom Arms.

Price: Premier Grade **$1,958.00**
Price: Field Grade **$1,519.00**

Freedom Arms Model 83 555 Revolver

Made on the Model 83 frame. Chambered for the 50 A.E. (Action Express) cartridge. Offered in Premier and Field Grades with adjustable sights, 4-3/4", 6", 7-1/2" or 10" barrel. Introduced 1994. Made in U.S. by Freedom Arms, Inc.

Price: Premier Grade **$1,820.00**
Price: Field Grade **$1,400.00**

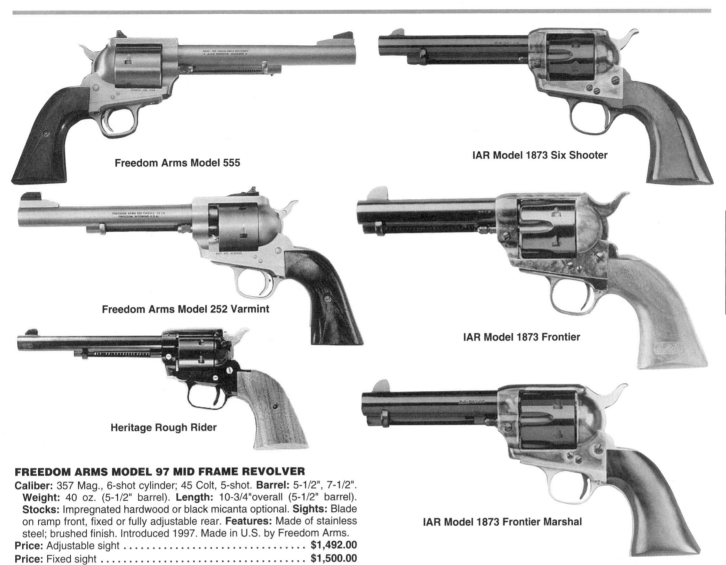

Freedom Arms Model 555

IAR Model 1873 Six Shooter

Freedom Arms Model 252 Varmint

IAR Model 1873 Frontier

Heritage Rough Rider

IAR Model 1873 Frontier Marshal

FREEDOM ARMS MODEL 97 MID FRAME REVOLVER
Caliber: 357 Mag., 6-shot cylinder; 45 Colt, 5-shot. **Barrel:** 5-1/2", 7-1/2". **Weight:** 40 oz. (5-1/2" barrel). **Length:** 10-3/4"overall (5-1/2" barrel). **Stocks:** Impregnated hardwood or black micanta optional. **Sights:** Blade on ramp front, fixed or fully adjustable rear. **Features:** Made of stainless steel; brushed finish. Introduced 1997. Made in U.S. by Freedom Arms.
Price: Adjustable sight **$1,492.00**
Price: Fixed sight **$1,500.00**

FREEDOM ARMS MODEL 252 VARMINT CLASS REVOLVER
Caliber: 22 LR, 5-shot. **Barrel:** 5.125", 7.5". **Weight:** 58 oz. (7.5" barrel). **Length:** NA. **Stocks:** Black and green laminated hardwood. **Sights:** Brass bead express front, express rear with shallow V-notch. **Features:** All stainless steel construction. Dual firing pins; lightened hammer; pre-set trigger stop. Built on Model 83 frame and accepts Model 83 Freedom Arms sights and/or scope mounts. Introduced 1991. Made in U.S. by Freedom Arms.
Price: **$1,527.00**
Price: Extra fitted 22 WMR cylinder **$264.00**

HERITAGE ROUGH RIDER REVOLVER
Caliber: 22 LR, 22 LR/22 WMR combo, 6-shot. **Barrel:** 2-3/4", 3-1/2", 4-3/4", 6-1/2", 9". **Weight:** 31 to 38 oz. **Length:** NA. **Stocks:** Exotic hardwood. **Sights:** Blade front, fixed rear. Adjustable sight on 6-1/2" only. **Features:** Hammer block safety. High polish blue or nickel finish. Introduced 1993. Made in U.S. by Heritage Mfg., Inc.
Price: . . . . **$119.95** to **$174.95**
Price: 2-3/4", 3-1/2", 4-3/4" bird's-head grip . . . . **$139.95** to **$174.95**

IAR MODEL 1873 SIX SHOOTER
Caliber: 22 LR/22 WMR combo. **Barrel:** 5-1/2". **Weight:** 36-1/2" oz. **Length:** 11-3/8" overall. **Stocks:** One-piece walnut. **Sights:** Blade front, notch rear. **Features:** A 3/4-scale reproduction. Color case-hardened frame, blued barrel. All-steel construction. Made by Uberti. Imported from Italy by IAR, Inc.
Price: **$360.00**

IAR MODEL 1873 FRONTIER REVOLVER
Caliber: 22 RL, 22 LR/22 WMR. **Barrel:** 4-3/4". **Weight:** 45 oz. **Length:** 10-1/2" overall. **Stocks:** One-piece walnut with inspector's cartouche. **Sights:** Blade front, notch rear. **Features:** Color case-hardened frame, blued barrel, black nickel-plated brass trigger guard and backstrap. Bright nickel and engraved versions available. Introduced 1997. Imported from Italy by IAR, Inc.
Price: **$395.00**
Price: Nickel-plated **$485.00**
Price: 22 LR/22WMR combo **$425.00**

IAR MODEL 1873 FRONTIER MARSHAL
Caliber: 357 Mag., 45 Colt. **Barrel:** 4-3/4", 5-1/2, 7-1/2". **Weight:** 39 oz. **Length:** 10-1/2" overall. **Stocks:** One-piece walnut. **Sights:** Blade front, notch rear. **Features:** Bright brass trigger guard and backstrap, color case-hardened frame, blued barrel and cylinder. Introduced 1998. Imported from Italy by IAR, Inc.
Price: **$395.00**

MAGNUM RESEARCH BFR SINGLE-ACTION REVOLVER
Caliber: 22 Hornet, 45 Colt +P, 454 Casull, 50 A.E. (Little Max, standard cylinder). **Barrel:** 7-1/2", 10". **Weight:** 4 lbs. **Length:** 11" overall with 7-1/2" barrel. **Stocks:** Uncle Mike's checkered rubber. **Sights:** Orange blade on ramp front, fully adjustable rear. **Features:** Stainless steel construction. Optional pearl and finger-groove grips available. Introduced 1997. Made in U.S. From Magnum Research, Inc.
Price: **$999.00**

HANDGUNS

Navy Arms Flat Top · Navy Arms Pinched Frame · Navy Arms Bisley · Navy Arms 1873 · Navy Arms Schofield

MAGNUM RESEARCH LITTLE MAX REVOLVER

Caliber: 22 Hornet, 45 Colt, 454 Casull, 50 A.E. **Barrel:** 6-1/2", 7-1/2", 10". **Weight:** 45 oz. **Length:** 13" overall (7-1/2" barrel). **Stocks:** Rubber. **Sights:** Ramp front, adjustable rear. **Features:** Single action; stainless steel construction. Announced 1998. Made in U.S. From Magnum Research.
Price: $999.00
Price: Maxline model (7-1/2", 10", 45 Colt, 45-70, 444 Marlin)... $999.00

NAVY ARMS FLAT TOP TARGET MODEL REVOLVER

Caliber: 45 Colt, 6-shot cylinder. **Barrel:** 7-1/2". **Weight:** 40 oz. **Length:** 13-1/4" overall. **Stocks:** Smooth walnut. **Sights:** Spring-loaded German silver front, rear adjustable for windage. **Features:** Replica of Colt's Flat Top Frontier target revolver made from 1888 to 1896. Blue with color case-hardened frame. Introduced 1997. Imported by Navy Arms.
Price: $425.00

NAVY ARMS "PINCHED FRAME" SINGLE-ACTION REVOLVER

Caliber: 45 Colt, 6-shot. **Barrel:** 7-1/2". **Weight:** 37 oz. **Length:** 13" overall. **Stocks:** Smooth walnut **Sights:** German silver blade, notch rear. **Features:** Replica of Colt's original Peacemaker. Color case-hardened frame, hammer, rest charcoal blued. Introduced 1997. Imported by Navy Arms.
Price: $415.00

NAVY ARMS BISLEY MODEL SINGLE-ACTION REVOLVER

Caliber: 44-40 or 45 Colt, 6-shot cylinder. **Barrel:** 4-3/4", 5-1/2", 7-1/2". **Weight:** 40 oz. **Length:** 12-1/2" overall (7-1/2" barrel). **Stocks:** Smooth walnut. **Sights:** Blade front, notch rear. **Features:** Replica of Colt's Bisley Model. Polished blue finish, color case-hardened frame. Introduced 1997. Imported by Navy Arms.
Price: $405.00

Navy Arms Bisley Model Flat Top Target Revolver

Similar to the standard Bisley model except with flat top strap, 7-1/2" barrel only, and a spring-loaded German silver front sight blade, standing leaf rear sight adjustable for windage. Polished blue finish, color case-hardened frame. Introduced 1998. Imported by Navy Arms.
Price: $435.00

NAVY ARMS 1872 OPEN TOP REVOLVER

Caliber: 38 Spec., 6-shot. **Barrel:** 5-1/2" or 7-1/2". **Weight:** 2 lbs., 12 oz. **Length:** 11" or 13". **Stocks:** Smooth walnut. **Sights:** Blade front, notch rear. **Features:** Replica of Colt's first production cartridge "six shooter." Polished blue finish with color case hardened frame, silver plated trigger guard and backstrap Introduced 2000. Imported by Navy Arms.
Price: $390.00

NAVY ARMS 1873 SINGLE-ACTION REVOLVER

Caliber: 357 Mag., 44-40, 45 Colt, 6-shot cylinder. **Barrel:** 4-3/4", 5-1/2", 7-1/2". **Weight:** 36 oz. **Length:** 10-3/4" overall (5-1/2" barrel). **Stocks:** Smooth walnut. **Sights:** Blade front, notch rear. **Features:** Blue with color case-hardened frame. Introduced 1991. Imported by Navy Arms.
Price: $385.00
Price: 1873 U.S. Cavalry Model (7-1/2", 45 Colt, arsenal markings) $455.00
Price: 1895 U.S. Artillery Model (as above, 5-1/2" barrel) $455.00

NAVY ARMS SHOOTIST MODEL SINGLE-ACTION REVOLVER

Caliber: 357 Mag., 44-40, 45 Colt, 6-shot cylinder. **Barrel:** 4-3/4", 5-1/2", 7-1/2". **Weight:** 36 oz. **Length:** 11-1/4" overall (5-1/2" barrel). **Stocks:** Smooth walnut. **Sights:** Blade front, notch rear. **Features:** Replica of Colt's Single Action Army. Parts interchange with first and second generation Colts. Polished blue, color case-hardened frame. Introduced 1999. Imported by Navy Arms.
Price: $385.00

NAVY ARMS 1875 SCHOFIELD REVOLVER

Caliber: 44-40, 45 Colt, 6-shot cylinder. **Barrel:** 3-1/2", 5", 7". **Weight:** 39 oz. **Length:** 10-3/4" overall (5" barrel). **Stocks:** Smooth walnut. **Sights:** Blade front, notch rear. **Features:** Replica of Smith & Wesson Model 3 Schofield. Single-action, top-break with automatic ejection. Polished blue finish. Introduced 1994. Imported by Navy Arms.
Price: Hideout Model, 3-1/2" barrel $695.00
Price: Wells Fargo, 5" barrel. $695.00
Price: U.S. Cavalry model, 7" barrel, military markings $695.00

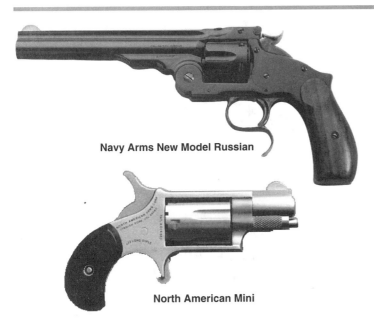

Navy Arms New Model Russian

North American Mini

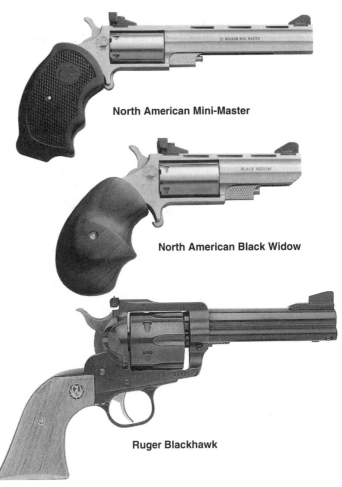

North American Mini-Master

North American Black Widow

Ruger Blackhawk

Navy Arms Deluxe 1875 Schofield Revolver

Similar to standard Schofield except has hand-cut "A" engraving and gold inlays, charcoal blue finish. Available in either Wells Fargo (5" barrel) or Cavalry (7" barrel) model. Introduced 1999. Imported by Navy Arms.
Price: **$1,875.00**

NAVY ARMS NEW MODEL RUSSIAN REVOLVER

Caliber: 44 Russian, 6-shot cylinder. **Barrel:** 6-1/2". **Weight:** 40 oz. **Length:** 12" overall. **Stocks:** Smooth walnut. **Sights:** Blade front, notch rear. **Features:** Replica of the S&W Model 3 Russian Third Model revolver. Spur trigger guard, polished blue finish. Introduced 1999. Imported by Navy Arms.
Price: **$745.00**

NAVY ARMS 1851 NAVY CONVERSION REVOLVER

Caliber: 38 Spec., 38 Long Colt. **Barrel:** 5-1/2", 7-1/2". **Weight:** 44 oz. **Length:** 14" overall (7-1/2" barrel). **Stocks:** Smooth walnut. **Sights:** Bead front, notch rear. **Features:** Replica of Colt's cartridge conversion revolver. Polished blue finish with color case-hardened frame, silver plated trigger guard and backstrap. Introduced 1999. Imported by Navy Arms.
Price: **$365.00**

NAVY ARMS 1860 ARMY CONVERSION REVOLVER

Caliber: 38 Spec., 38 Long Colt. **Barrel:** 5-1/2", 7-1/2". **Weight:** 44 oz. **Length:** 13-1/2" overall (7-1/2" barrel). **Stocks:** Smooth walnut. **Sights:** Blade front, notch rear. **Features:** Replica of Colt's conversion revolver. Polished blue finish with color case-hardened frame, full-size 1860 Army grip with blued steel backstrap. Introduced 1999. Imported by Navy Arms.
Price: **$365.00**

NAVY ARMS 1861 NAVY CONVERSION REVOLVER

Caliber: 38 Spec., 38 Long Colt. **Barrel:** 5-1/2", 7-1/2". **Weight:** 44 oz. **Length:** 13-1/2" overall (7-1/2" barrel). **Stocks:** Smooth walnut. **Sights:** Blade front, notch rear. **Features:** Replica of Colt's cartridge conversion. Polished blue finish with color case-hardened frame, silver plated trigger guard and backstrap. Introduced 1999. Imported by Navy Arms.
Price: **$365.00**

NORTH AMERICAN MINI-REVOLVERS

Caliber: 22 Short, 22 LR, 22 WMR, 5-shot. **Barrel:** 1-1/8", 1-5/8". **Weight:** 4 to 6.6 oz. **Length:** 3-5/8" to 6-1/8" overall. **Stocks:** Laminated wood. **Sights:** Blade front, notch fixed rear. **Features:** All stainless steel construction. Polished satin and matte finish. Engraved models available. From North American Arms.
Price: 22 Short, 22 LR **$176.00**
Price: 22 WMR, 1-5/8" bbl. **$194.00**
Price: 22 WMR, 1-1/8" or 1-5/8" bbl. with extra 22 LR cylinder .. **$231.00**

NORTH AMERICAN MINI-MASTER

Caliber: 22 LR, 22 WMR, 5-shot cylinder. **Barrel:** 4". **Weight:** 10.7 oz. **Length:** 7.75" overall. **Stocks:** Checkered hard black rubber. **Sights:** Blade front, white outline rear adjustable for elevation, or fixed. **Features:** Heavy vent barrel; full-size grips. Non-fluted cylinder. Introduced 1989.
Price: Adjustable sight, 22 WMR or 22 LR **$299.00**
Price: As above with extra WMR/LR cylinder **$336.00**
Price: Fixed sight, 22 WMR or 22 LR **$281.00**
Price: As above with extra WMR/LR cylinder **$318.00**

North American Black Widow Revolver

Similar to the Mini-Master except has 2" heavy vent barrel. Built on the 22 WMR frame. Non-fluted cylinder, black rubber grips. Available with either Millett Low Profile fixed sights or Millett sight adjustable for elevation only. Overall length 5-7/8", weighs 8.8 oz. From North American Arms.
Price: Adjustable sight, 22 LR or 22 WMR **$269.00**
Price: As above with extra WMR/LR cylinder **$306.00**
Price: Fixed sight, 22 LR or 22 WMR **$251.00**
Price: As above with extra WMR/LR cylinder **$288.00**

RUGER NEW MODEL BLACKHAWK REVOLVER

Caliber: 30 Carbine, 357 Mag./38 Spec., 41 Mag., 45 Colt, 6-shot. **Barrel:** 4-5/8" or 5-1/2", either caliber; 7-1/2" (30 Carbine and 45 Colt). **Weight:** 42 oz. (6-1/2" bbl.). **Length:** 12-1/4" overall (5-1/2" bbl.). **Stocks:** American walnut. **Sights:** 1/8" ramp front, micro-click rear adjustable for windage and elevation. **Features:** Ruger transfer bar safety system, independent firing pin, hardened chrome-moly steel frame, music wire springs throughout. Comes with plastic lockable case and lock.
Price: Blue 30 Carbine, 7-1/2" (BN31) **$399.00**
Price: Blue, 357 Mag., 4-5/8", 6-1/2" (BN34, BN36).......... **$399.00**
Price: As above, stainless (KBN34, KBN36) **$489.00**

Ruger Super Blackhawk

Ruger New Bearcat

Ruger Vaquero

Ruger Super Single-Six

Ruger Bisley Single-Action

Price: 357 Mag. KBNV34 (4-5/8"), KBNV35 (5-1/2") stainless . . . **$498.00**
Price: BNV44 (4-5/8"), BNV445 (5-1/2"), BNV45 (7-1/2"), blue . . **$498.00**
Price: KBNV44 (4-5/8"), KBNV455 (5-1/2"), KBNV45 (7-1/2"),
 stainless **$498.00**
Price: 45 Colt BNV455, all blue finish, 4-5/8" or 5-1/2" **$498.00**
Price: 45 Colt KBNV455, stainless, 5-1/2" **$498.00**

RUGER BISLEY-VAQUERO SINGLE-ACTION REVOLVER
Similar to the Vaquero except has Bisley-style hammer, grip and trigger and is available in 357 Magnum, 44 Magnum and 45 Colt only, with 4-5/8" or 5-1/2" barrel. Has smooth rosewood grips with Ruger medallion. Roll-engraved, unfluted cylinder. Introduced 1997. From Sturm, Ruger & Co.
Price: Color case-hardened frame, blue grip frame, barrel and cylinder,
 RBNV-475, RBNV-455 . . . . **$498.00**
Price: High-gloss stainless steel, KRBNV-475, KRBNV-455 . . . . . **$529.00**
Price: For simulated ivory grips add **$36.00**
Price: 44-40 BNV40 (4-5/8"), BNV405 (5-1/2"), BNV407 (7-1/2") . **$498.00**
Price: 44-40 KBNV40 (4-5/8"), KBNV405 (5-1/2"), KBNV407 (7-1/2")
 stainless **$498.00**

Price: Blue, 357 Mag./9mm Convertible, 4-5/8", 6-1/2" (BN34X,
 BN36X) **$449.00**
Price: Blue, 41 Mag., 4-5/8", 6-1/2" (BN41, BN42) **$399.00**
Price: Blue, 45 Colt, 4-5/8", 5-1/2", 7-1/2" (BN44, BN455, BN45) **$399.00**
Price: Stainless, 45 Colt, 4-5/8", 7-1/2" (KBN44, KBN45) **$489.00**
Price: Blue, 45 Colt/45 ACP Convertible, 4-5/8", 5-1/2" (BN44X, BN455X)
 . . . . **$449.00**

RUGER NEW MODEL SUPER BLACKHAWK
Caliber: 44 Mag., 6-shot. Also fires 44 Spec. **Barrel:** 4-5/8", 5-1/2", 7-1/2", 10-1/2" bull. **Weight:** 48 oz. (7-1/2" bbl.), 51 oz. (10-1/2" bbl.). **Length:** 13-3/8" overall (7-1/2" bbl.). **Stocks:** American walnut. **Sights:** 1/8" ramp front, micro-click rear adjustable for windage and elevation. **Features:** Ruger transfer bar safety system, fluted or un-fluted cylinder, steel grip and cylinder frame, round or square back trigger guard, wide serrated trigger and wide spur hammer. Comes with plastic lockable case and lock.
Price: Blue, 4-5/8", 5-1/2", 7-1/2" (S458N, S45N, S47N) **$478.00**
Price: Blue, 10-1/2" bull barrel (S411N) **$485.00**
Price: Stainless, 4-5/8", 5-1/2", 7-1/2" (KS458N, KS45N, KS47N). **$499.00**
Price: Stainless, 10-1/2" bull barrel (KS411N) **$505.00**

RUGER VAQUERO SINGLE-ACTION REVOLVER
Caliber: 357 Mag., 44-40, 44 Mag., 45 Colt, 6-shot. **Barrel:** 4-5/8", 5-1/2", 7-1/2". **Weight:** 41 oz. **Length:** 13-1/8" overall (7-1/2" barrel). **Stocks:** Smooth rosewood with Ruger medallion. **Sights:** Blade front, fixed notch rear. **Features:** Uses Ruger's patented transfer bar safety system and loading gate interlock with classic styling. Blued model has color case-hardened finish on the frame, the rest polished and blued. Stainless model has high-gloss polish. Introduced 1993. From Sturm, Ruger & Co.
Price: 357 Mag. BNV34 (4-5/8"), BNV35 (5-1/2") **$498.00**

RUGER NEW BEARCAT SINGLE-ACTION
Caliber: 22 LR, 6-shot. **Barrel:** 4". **Weight:** 24 oz. **Length:** 8-7/8" overall. **Stocks:** Smooth rosewood with Ruger medallion. **Sights:** Blade front, fixed notch rear. **Features:** Reintroduction of the Ruger Bearcat with slightly lengthened frame, Ruger patented transfer bar safety system. Available in blue only. Introduced 1993. Comes with plastic lockable case and lock. From Sturm, Ruger & Co.
Price: SBC4, blue **$347.00**

RUGER SINGLE-SIX AND SUPER SINGLE-SIX CONVERTIBLE
Caliber: 22 LR, 6-shot; 22 WMR in extra cylinder. **Barrel:** 4-5/8", 5-1/2", 6-1/2", 9-1/2" (6-groove). **Weight:** 35 oz. (6-1/2" bbl.). **Length:** 11-13/16" overall (6-1/2" bbl.). **Stocks:** Smooth American walnut. **Sights:** Improved Patridge front on ramp, fully adjustable rear protected by integral frame ribs (super single-six); or fixed sight 9single six). **Features:** Ruger transfer bar safety system, loading gate interlock, hardened chrome-moly steel frame, wide trigger, music wire springs throughout, independent firing pin.
Price: 4-5/8", 5-1/2", 6-1/2", 9-1/2" barrel, blue, adjustable sight NR4, NR6, NR9, NR5 . . . . **$352.00**
Price: 5-1/2", 6-1/2" bbl. only, stainless steel, adjustable sight KNR5, KNR6 . . . . **$436.00**
Price: 5-1/2", 6-1/2" barrel, blue fixed sights **$347.00**

Traditions 1851 Navy

Traditions 1861 Navy

Traditions 1873

Traditions Sheriffs

Traditions 1875 Schofield

Ruger Bisley Small Frame Revolver

Similar to the Single-Six except frame is styled after the classic Bisley "flat-top." Most mechanical parts are unchanged. Hammer is lower and smoothly curved with a deeply checkered spur. Trigger is strongly curved with a wide smooth surface. Longer grip frame designed with a hand-filling shape, and the trigger guard is a large oval. Adjustable dovetail rear sight; front sight base accepts interchangeable square blades of various heights and styles. Has an unfluted cylinder and roll engraving. Weighs 41 oz. Chambered for 22 LR, 6-1/2" barrel only. Comes with plastic lockable case and lock. Introduced 1985.
Price: RB-22AW **$402.00**

Ruger Bisley Single-Action Revolver

Similar to standard Blackhawk except the hammer is lower with a smoothly curved, deeply checkered wide spur. The trigger is strongly curved with a wide smooth surface. Longer grip frame has a hand-filling shape. Adjustable rear sight, ramp-style front. Has an unfluted cylinder and roll engraving, adjustable sights. Chambered for 357, 44 Mags. and 45 Colt; 7-1/2" barrel; overall length of 13"; weighs 48 oz. Comes with plastic lockable case and lock. Introduced 1985.
Price: RB-35W, 357Mag, R3-44W, 44Mag, RB-45W, 45 Colt . . . **$498.00**

TRADITIONS 1851 NAVY CONVERSION REVOLVER

Caliber: 38 Spec. **Barrel:** 7-1/2". **Weight:** 40 oz. **Length:** 14-1/2" overall. **Stocks:** Smooth walnut. **Sights:** Post front, hammer-notch rear. **Features:** Steel frame, brass trigger guard. Introduced 1998. From Traditions.
Price: **$395.00**

TRADITIONS 1858 REMINGTON CONVERSION REVOLVER

Caliber: 38 Spec. **Barrel:** 7-1/2". **Weight:** 2 lbs., 8 oz. **Length:** 14-1/2" overall. **Stocks:** Smooth walnut. **Sights:** Post front, notch rear. **Features:** Replica of converted Remington. Blued steel grip frame and trigger guard. Introduced 1999. Imported by Traditions.
Price: **$425.00**

TRADITIONS 1860 ARMY CONVERSION REVOLVER

Caliber: 38 Spec. **Barrel:** 7-1/2". **Weight:** 44 oz. **Length:** 14-1/2" overall. **Stocks:** Smooth walnut. **Sights:** Blade front, notch rear. **Features:** Replica of Colt's conversion revolver. Polished blue finish with color case-hardened frame, full-size 1860 Army grip with blued steel backstrap. Introduced 1999. Imported by Traditions.
Price: **$410.00**

TRADITIONS 1861 NAVY CONVERSION REVOLVER

Caliber: 38 Spec. **Barrel:** 7-1/2". **Weight:** 44 oz. **Length:** 14-1/2" overall. **Stocks:** Smooth walnut. **Sights:** Blade front, notch rear. **Features:** Replica of Colt's cartridge conversion. Polished blue finish with color case-hardened frame, brass trigger guard and backstrap. Introduced 1999. Imported by Traditions.
Price: **$410.00**

TRADITIONS 1872 OPEN-TOP CONVERSION REVOLVER

Caliber: 38 Spec. **Barrel:** 8". **Weight:** 2 lbs. 8 oz. **Length:** 14-1/2" overall. **Stocks:** Smooth walnut. **Sights:** Blade front, fixed rear. **Features:** Replica of the original production. Color case-hardened frame, rest blued, including grip frame. Introduced 1999. Imported from Italy by Traditions.
Price: **$410.00**

TRADITIONS 1873 SINGLE-ACTION REVOLVER

Caliber: 22 LR, 357 Mag., 44-40, 45 Colt, 6-shot cylinder. **Barrel:** 4-3/4", 5-1/2", 7-1/2". **Weight:** 44 oz. **Length:** 10-3/4" overall (5-1/2" barrel). **Stocks:** Walnut. **Sights:** Blade front, groove in topstrap rear. **Features:** Blued barrel, cylinder, color case-hardened frame, blue or brass trigger guard. Nickel-plated frame with polished brass trigger guard available in 357 Mag., 44-40, 45 Colt. Introduced 1998. From Traditions.
Price: . . . . **$300.00 to $395.00**

Traditions Sheriffs Revolver

Similar to the 1873 single-action revolver except has special birds-head grip with spur, and smooth or checkered walnut grips. Introduced 1998. From Traditions.
Price: With smooth walnut grips **$370.00**

TRADITIONS 1875 SCHOFIELD REVOLVER

Caliber: 44-40, 45 Schofield, 45 Colt, 6-shot cylinder. **Barrel:** 5-1/2". **Weight:** 40 oz. **Length:** 11-1/4" overall. **Stocks:** Walnut. **Sights:** Blade front, notch rear. **Features:** Blue finish, case-hardened frame, hammer, trigger. Introduced 1998. From Traditions.
Price: **$659.00**

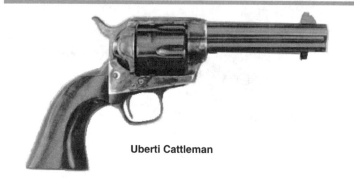

Uberti Cattleman

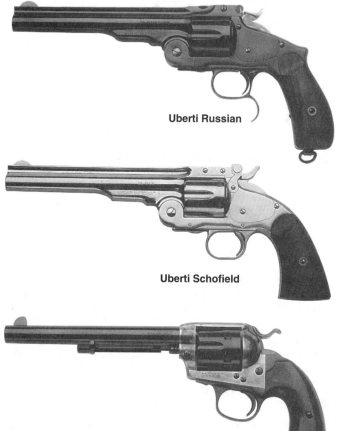

Uberti Russian

Uberti 1875 Army

Uberti Schofield

Uberti 1890 Army

Uberti Bisley

UBERTI 1873 CATTLEMAN SINGLE-ACTION

Caliber: 22 LR/22 WMR, 38 Spec., 357 Mag., 44 Spec., 44-40, 45 Colt/45 ACP, 6-shot. **Barrel:** 4-3/4", 5-1/2", 7-1/2"; 44-40, 45 Colt also with 3", 3-1/2", 4". **Weight:** 38 oz. (5-1/2" bbl.). **Length:** 10-3/4" overall (5-1/2" bbl.). **Stocks:** One-piece smooth walnut. **Sights:** Blade front, groove rear; fully adjustable rear available. **Features:** Steel or brass backstrap, trigger guard; color case-hardened frame, blued barrel, cylinder. Imported from Italy by Uberti U.S.A.
Price: Steel backstrap, trigger guard, fixed sights **$435.00**
Price: Brass backstrap, trigger guard, fixed sights **$365.00**
Price: Bisley model **$435.00**

Uberti 1873 Buckhorn Single-Action

A slightly larger version of the Cattleman revolver. Available in 44 Magnum or 44 Magnum/44-40 convertible, otherwise has same specs.
Price: Steel backstrap, trigger guard, fixed sights **$410.00**
Price: Convertible (two cylinders) **$475.00**

UBERTI 1875 SA ARMY OUTLAW REVOLVER

Caliber: 357 Mag., 44-40, 45 Colt, 45 Colt/45 ACP convertible, 6-shot. **Barrel:** 5-1/2", 7-1/2". **Weight:** 44 oz. **Length:** 13-3/4" overall. **Stocks:** Smooth walnut. **Sights:** Blade front, notch rear. **Features:** Replica of the 1875 Remington S.A. Army revolver. Brass trigger guard, color case-hardened frame, rest blued. Imported by Uberti U.S.A.
Price: **$435.00**
Price: 45 Colt/45 ACP convertible **$475.00**

UBERTI 1890 ARMY OUTLAW REVOLVER

Caliber: 357 Mag., 44-40, 45 Colt, 45 Colt/45 ACP convertible, 6-shot. **Barrel:** 5-1/2", 7-1/2". **Weight:** 37 oz. **Length:** 12-1/2" overall. **Stocks:** American walnut. **Sights:** Blade front, groove rear. **Features:** Replica of the 1890 Remington single-action. Brass trigger guard, rest is blued. Imported by Uberti U.S.A.
Price: **$435.00**
Price: 45 Colt/45 ACP convertible **$475.00**

UBERTI NEW MODEL RUSSIAN REVOLVER

Caliber: 44 Russian, 6-shot cylinder. **Barrel:** 6-1/2". **Weight:** 40 oz. **Length:** 12" overall. **Stocks:** Smooth walnut. **Sights:** Blade front, notch rear. **Features:** Repica of the S&W Model 3 Russian Third Model revolver. Spur trigger guard, polished blue finish. Introduced 1999. Imported by Uberti USA.
Price: **$775.00**

UBERTI 1875 SCHOFIELD REVOLVER

Caliber: 44-40, 45 Colt, 6-shot cylinder. **Barrel:** 5", 7". **Weight:** 39 oz. **Length:** 10-3/4" overall (5" barrel). **Stocks:** Smooth walnut. **Sights:** Blade front, notch rear. **Features:** Replica of Smith & Wesson Model 3 Schofield. Single-action, top-break with automatic ejection. Polished blue finish. Introduced 1994. Imported by Uberti USA.
Price: **$700.00**

UBERTI BISLEY MODEL SINGLE-ACTION REVOLVER

Caliber: 38-40, 357 Mag., 44 Spec., 44-40 or 45 Colt, 6-shot cylinder. **Barrel:** 4-3/4", 5-1/2", 7-1/2". **Weight:** 40 oz. **Length:** 12-1/2" overall (7-1/2" barrel). **Stocks:** Smooth walnut. **Sights:** Blade front, notch rear. **Features:** Replica of Colt's Bisley Model. Polished blue finish, color case-hardened frame. Introduced 1997. Imported by Uberti USA.
Price: **435.00**

Uberti Bisley Flat Top

Uberti Bisley Model Flat Top Target Revolver

Similar to the standard Bisley model except with flat top strap, 7-1/2" barrel only, and a spring-loaded German silver front sight blade, standing leaf rear sight adjustable for windage. Polished blue finish, color case-hardened frame. Introduced 1998. Imported by Uberti USA.

Price: **$455.00**

U.S. PATENT FIRE-ARMS SINGLE ACTION ARMY REVOLVER

Caliber: 22 LR, 22 WMR, 357 Mag., 44 Russian, 38-40, 44-40, 45 Colt, 6-shot cylinder. **Barrel:** 3", 4", 4-3/4", 5-1/2", 7-1/2", 10". **Weight:** 37 oz. **Length:** NA. **Stocks:** Smooth walnut. **Sights:** Blade front, notch rear. **Features:** Recreation of original guns; 3" and 4" have no ejector. Available with all-blue, blue with color case-hardening, or full nickel-plate finish. Made in Italy; available from United States Patent Fire-Arms Mfg. Co.

Price: 3" blue **$600.00**
Price: 4-3/4", blue/cased-colors **$732.00**
Price: 7-1/2", blue/case-colors **$739.00**
Price: 10", nickel..................................... **$847.50**

U.S. Patent Fire-Arms Nettleton Cavalry Revolver

Similar to the Single Action Army, except in 45 Colt only, with 7-1/2" barrel, color case-hardened/blue finish, and has old-style hand numbering, exact cartouche branding and correct inspector hand-stamp markings. Made in Italy; available from United States Patent Fire-Arms Mfg. Co.

Price: **$950.00**
Price: Artillery Model, 5-1/2" barrel....................... **$950.00**

U.S. Patent Fire-Arms Bird Head Model Revolver

Similar to the Single Action Army except has bird's-head grip and comes with 3-1/2", 4" or 4-1/2" barrel. Made in Italy; available from United States Patent Fire-Arms Mfg. Co.

Price: 3-1/2", blue..................................... **$635.50**
Price: 4", blue with color case-hardening.................... **$735.00**
Price: 4-1/2", nickel-plated **$795.50**

U.S. Patent Fire-Arms Flattop Target Revolver

Similar to the Single Action Army except 4-3/4", 5-1/2" or 7-1/2" barrel, two-piece hard rubber stocks, flat top frame, adjustable rear sight. Made in Italy; available from United States Patent Fire-Arms Mfg. Co.

Price: 4-3/4", blue, polished hammer **$690.00**
Price: 4-3/4", blue, case-colored hammer **$813.00**
Price: 5-1/2", blue, case-colored hammer **$816.00**
Price: 5-1/2", nickel-plated **$765.00**
Price: 7-1/2", blue, polished hammer **$717.00**
Price: 7-1/2", blue, case-colored hammer **$822.00**

U.S. PATENT FIRE-ARMS BISLEY MODEL REVOLVER

Caliber: 4 Colt, 6-shot cylinder. **Barrel:** 4-3/4", 5-1/2", 7-1/2", 10". **Weight:** 38 oz. (5-1/2" barrel). **Length:** NA. **Stocks:** Smooth walnut. **Sights:** Blade front, notch rear. **Features:** Available in all-blue, blue with color case-hardening, or full nickel plate finish. Made in Italy; available from United States Patent Fire-Arms Mfg. Co.

Price: 4-3/4", blue..................................... **$652.00**
Price: 5-1/2", blue/case-colors **$750.50**
Price: 7-1/2", blue/case-colors **$756.00**
Price: 10", nickel..................................... **$862.50**

HANDGUNS

Specially adapted single-shot and multi-barrel arms.

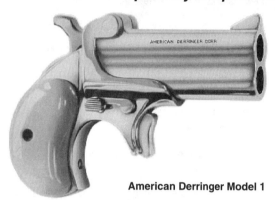

American Derringer Model 1

Bond Arms C2K Defender

AMERICAN DERRINGER MODEL 1

Caliber: 22 LR, 22 WMR, 30 Carbine, 30 Luger, 30-30 Win., 32 H&R Mag., 32-20, 380 ACP, 38 Super, 38 Spec., 38 Spec. shotshell, 38 Spec. +P, 9mm Para., 357 Mag., 357 Mag./45/410, 357 Maximum, 10mm, 40 S&W, 41 Mag., 38-40, 44-40 Win., 44 Spec., 44 Mag., 45 Colt, 45 Win. Mag., 45 ACP, 45 Colt/410, 45-70 single shot. **Barrel:** 3". **Weight:** 15-1/2 oz. (38 Spec.). **Length:** 4.82" overall. **Stocks:** Rosewood, Zebra wood. **Sights:** Blade front. **Features:** Made of stainless steel with high-polish or satin finish. Two-shot capacity. Manual hammer block safety. Introduced 1980. Available in almost any pistol caliber. Contact the factory for complete list of available calibers and prices. From American Derringer Corp.

Price: 22 LR	$260.00
Price: 38 Spec.	$285.00
Price: 357 Maximum	$310.00
Price: 357 Mag.	$300.00
Price: 9mm, 380	$285.00
Price: 40 S&W	$300.00
Price: 44 Spec.	$363.00
Price: 44-40 Win.	$363.00
Price: 45 Colt	$350.00
Price: 30-30, 45 Win. Mag.	$425.00
Price: 41, 44 Mags.	$400.00
Price: 45-70, single shot	$352.00
Price: 45 Colt, 410, 2-1/2"	$363.00
Price: 45 ACP, 10mm Auto	$300.00

American Derringer Model 4

Similar to the Model 1 except has 4.1" barrel, overall length of 6", and weighs 16-1/2 oz.; chambered for 357 Mag., 357 Maximum, 45-70, 3" 410-bore shotshells or 45 Colt or 44 Mag. Made of stainless steel. Manual hammer block safety. Introduced 1985.

Price: 3" 410/45 Colt	$390.00
Price: 45-70 (Alaskan Survival model)	$440.00
Price: 44 Mag. with oversize grips	$480.00
Price: Alaskan Survival model (45-70 upper barrel, 410 or 45 Colt lower)	$400.00

American Derringer Model 6

Similar to the Model 1 except has 6" barrel chambered for 3" 410 shotshells or 22 WMR, 357 Mag., 45 ACP, 45 Colt; rosewood stocks; 8.2" o.a.l. and weighs 21 oz. Shoots either round for each barrel. Manual hammer block safety. Introduced 1986.

Price: 22 WMR	$405.00
Price: 357 Mag.	$405.00
Price: 45 Colt/410	$415.00
Price: 45 ACP	$405.00

American Derringer Model 7 Ultra Lightweight

Similar to Model 1 except made of high strength aircraft aluminum. Weighs 7-1/2 oz., 4.82" o.a.l., rosewood stocks. Available in 22 LR, 22 WMR, 32 H&R Mag., 380 ACP, 38 Spec., 44 Spec. Introduced 1986.

Price: 22 LR, WMR	$290.00

Price: 38 Spec.	$290.00
Price: 380 ACP	$290.00
Price: 32 H&R Mag/32 S&W Long	$290.00
Price: 44 Spec.	$530.00

American Derringer Model 10 Lightweight

Similar to the Model 1 except frame is of aluminum, giving weight of 10 oz. Stainless barrels. Available in 38 Spec., 45 Colt or 45 ACP only. Matte gray finish. Introduced 1989.

Price: 45 Colt	$350.00
Price: 45 ACP	$295.00
Price: 38 Spec.	$270.00

American Derringer Lady Derringer

Same as the Model 1 except has tuned action, is fitted with scrimshawed synthetic ivory grips; chambered for 32 H&R Mag. and 38 Spec.; 357 Mag., 45 Colt, 45/410. Deluxe Grade is highly polished; Deluxe Engraved is engraved in a pattern similar to that used on 1880s derringers. All come in a French fitted jewelry box. Introduced 1991.

Price: 32 H&R Mag.	$340.00
Price: 357 Mag.	$370.00
Price: 38 Spec.	$325.00
Price: 45 Colt, 45/410	$400.00

American Derringer Texas Commemorative

A Model 1 Derringer with solid brass frame, stainless steel barrel and rosewood grips. Available in 38 Spec., 44-40 Win., or 45 Colt. Introduced 1987.

Price: 38 Spec.	$330.00
Price: 44-40	$385.00
Price: Brass frame, 45 Colt	$415.00

AMERICAN DERRINGER DA 38 MODEL

Caliber: 22 LR, 9mm Para., 38 Spec., 357 Mag., 40 S&W. **Barrel:** 3". **Weight:** 14.5 oz. **Length:** 4.8" overall. **Stocks:** Rosewood, walnut or other hardwoods. **Sights:** Fixed. **Features:** Double-action only; two-shots. Manual safety. Made of satin-finished stainless steel and aluminum. Introduced 1989. From American Derringer Corp.

Price: 22 LR, 38 Spec.	$400.00
Price: 9mm Para.	$410.00
Price: 357 Mag.	$415.00
Price: 40 S&W	$440.00

ANSCHUTZ MODEL 64P SPORT/TARGET PISTOL

Caliber: 22 LR, 22 WMR, 5-shot magazine. **Barrel:** 10". **Weight:** 3 lbs., 8 oz. **Length:** 18-1/2" overall. **Stock:** Choate Rynite. **Sights:** None furnished; grooved for scope mounting. **Features:** Right-hand bolt; polished blue finish. Introduced 1998. Imported from Germany by AcuSport.

Price: 22 LR	$455.95
Price: 22 WMR	$479.95

BOND ARMS TEXAS DEFENDER DERRINGER

Caliber: 9mm Para, 38 Spec./357 Mag., 40 S&W, 44 Spec./44 Mag., 45 Colt/410 shotshell. **Barrel:** 3", 3-1/2". **Weight:** 21 oz. **Length:** 5" overall.

HANDGUNS — MISCELLANEOUS

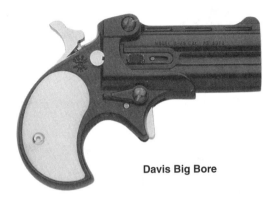

Davis Big Bore

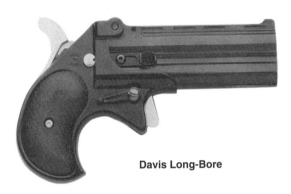

Davis Long-Bore

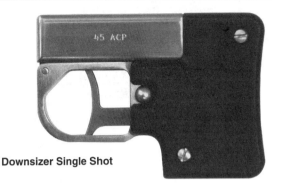

Downsizer Single Shot

Gaucher GN1 Silhouette

IAR Model 1872 Derringer

Stocks: Laminated black ash or rosewood. **Sights:** Blade front, fixed rear. **Features:** Interchangeable barrels; retracting firing pins; rebounding firing pins; cross-bolt safety; removable trigger guard; automatic extractor for rimmed calibers. Stainless steel construction with blasted/polished and ground combination finish. Introduced 1997. Made in U.S. by Bond Arms, Inc.
Price: **$349.00**
Price: Century 2000 Defender (410-bore, 3-1/2" barrels) **$369.00**

BROWN CLASSIC SINGLE SHOT PISTOL
Caliber: 17 Ackley Hornet through 45-70 Govt. **Barrel:** 15" airgauged match grade. **Weight:** About 3 lbs., 7 oz. **Stocks:** Walnut; thumbrest target style. **Sights:** None furnished; drilled and tapped for scope mounting. **Features:** Falling block action gives rigid barrel-receiver mating; hand-fitted and headspaced. Introduced 1998. Made in U.S. by E.A. Brown Mfg.
Price: **$499.00**

DAVIS BIG BORE DERRINGERS
Caliber: 22 WMR, 38 Spec., 9mm Para. **Barrel:** 2.75". **Weight:** 11.5 oz. **Length:** 4.65" overall. **Stocks:** Textured black synthetic. **Sights:** Blade front, fixed notch rear. **Features:** Alloy frame, steel-lined barrels, steel breech block. Plunger-type safety with integral hammer block. Chrome or black Teflon finish. Introduced 1992. Made in U.S. by Davis Industries.
Price: **$98.00**
Price: 9mm Para. **$104.00**

DAVIS LONG-BORE DERRINGERS
Caliber: 22 WMR, 38 Spec., 9mm Para. **Barrel:** 3.5". **Weight:** 13 oz. **Length:** 5.65" overall. **Stocks:** Textured black synthetic. **Sights:** Fixed. **Features:** Chrome or black Teflon finish. Larger than Davis D-Series models. Introduced 1995. Made in U.S. by Davis Industries.
Price: **$104.00**
Price: 9mm Para. **$110.00**
Price: Big-Bore models (same calibers, 3/4" shorter barrels) **$98.00**

DAVIS D-SERIES DERRINGERS
Caliber: 22 LR, 22 WMR, 25 ACP, 32 ACP. **Barrel:** 2.4". **Weight:** 9.5 oz. **Length:** 4" overall. **Stocks:** Laminated wood or pearl. **Sights:** Blade front,

fixed notch rear. **Features:** Choice of black Teflon or chrome finish; spur trigger. Introduced 1986. Made in U.S. by Davis Industries.
Price: **$99.50**

DOWNSIZER WSP SINGLE SHOT PISTOL
Caliber: 9mm Para, 357 Magnum, 40 S&W, 45 ACP. **Barrel:** 2.10". **Weight:** 11 oz. **Length:** 3.25" overall. **Stocks:** Black polymer. **Sights:** None. **Features:** Single shot, tip-up barrel. Double action only. Stainless steel construction. Measures .900" thick. Introduced 1997. From Downsizer Corp.
Price: **$354.00**

GAUCHER GN1 SILHOUETTE PISTOL
Caliber: 22 LR, single shot. **Barrel:** 10". **Weight:** 2.4 lbs. **Length:** 15.5" overall. **Stocks:** European hardwood. **Sights:** Blade front, open adjustable rear. **Features:** Bolt action, adjustable trigger. Introduced 1990. Imported from France by Mandall Shooting Supplies.
Price: About **$525.00**
Price: Model GP Silhouette **$425.00**

IAR MODEL 1872 DERRINGER
Caliber: 22 Short. **Barrel:** 2-3/8". **Weight:** 7 oz. **Length:** 5-1/8" overall. **Stocks:** Smooth walnut. **Sights:** Blade front, notch rear. **Features:** Gold or nickel frame with blue barrel. Reintroduced 1996 using original Colt designs and tooling for the Colt Model 4 Derringer. Made in U.S. by IAR, Inc.
Price: **$99.00**
Price: Single cased gun **$125.00**
Price: Double cased set **$215.00**

IAR MODEL 1888 DOUBLE DERRINGER
Caliber: 38 Special. **Barrel:** 2-3/4". **Weight:** 16 oz. **Length:** NA. **Stocks:** Smooth walnut. **Sights:** Blade front, notch rear. **Features:** All steel con-

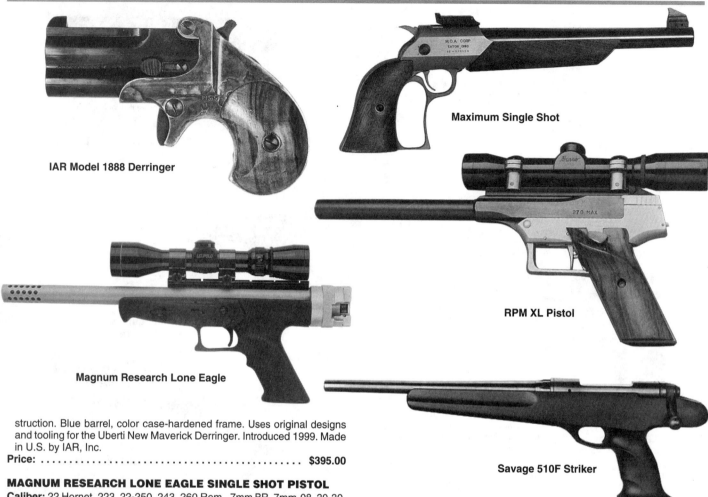

IAR Model 1888 Derringer

Maximum Single Shot

RPM XL Pistol

Magnum Research Lone Eagle

Savage 510F Striker

struction. Blue barrel, color case-hardened frame. Uses original designs and tooling for the Uberti New Maverick Derringer. Introduced 1999. Made in U.S. by IAR, Inc.

Price: **$395.00**

MAGNUM RESEARCH LONE EAGLE SINGLE SHOT PISTOL

Caliber: 22 Hornet, 223, 22-250, 243, 260 Rem., 7mm BR, 7mm-08, 30-30, 7.62x39, 308, 30-06, 357 Max., 35 Rem., 358 Win., 44 Mag., 444 Marlin, 440 Cor-Bon. **Barrel:** 14", interchangeable. **Weight:** 4 lbs., 3 oz. to 4 lbs., 7 oz. **Length:** 15" overall. **Stocks:** Ambidextrous. **Sights:** None furnished; drilled and tapped for scope mounting and open sights. Open sights optional. **Features:** Cannon-type rotating breech with spring-activated ejector. Ordnance steel with matte blue finish. Cross-bolt safety. External cocking lever on left side of gun. Muzzle brake optional. Introduced 1991. Available from Magnum Research, Inc.

Price: Complete pistol, black **$438.00**
Price: Barreled action only, black **$319.00**
Price: Complete pistol, chrome. **$478.00**
Price: Barreled action, chrome **$359.00**
Price: Scope base **$14.00**
Price: Adjustable open sights **$35.00**

MAXIMUM SINGLE SHOT PISTOL

Caliber: 22 LR, 22 Hornet, 22 BR, 22 PPC, 223 Rem., 22-250, 6mm BR, 6mm PPC, 243, 250 Savage, 6.5mm-35M, 270 MAX, 270 Win., 7mm TCU, 7mm BR, 7mm-35, 7mm INT-R, 7mm-08, 7mm Rocket, 7mm Super-Mag., 30 Herrett, 30 Carbine, 30-30, 308 Win., 30x39, 32-20, 350 Rem. Mag., 357 Mag., 357 Maximum, 358 Win., 375 H&H, 44 Mag., 454 Casull. **Barrel:** 8-3/4", 10-1/2", 14". **Weight:** 61 oz. (10-1/2" bbl.); 78 oz. (14" bbl.). **Length:** 15", 18-1/2" overall (with 10-1/2" and 14" bbl., respectively). **Stocks:** Smooth walnut stocks and forend. Also available with 17" finger groove grip. **Sights:** Ramp front, fully adjustable open rear. **Features:** Falling block action; drilled and tapped for M.O.A. scope mounts; integral grip frame/receiver; adjustable trigger; Douglas barrel (interchangeable). Introduced 1983. Made in U.S. by M.O.A. Corp.

Price: Stainless receiver, blue barrel **$799.00**
Price: Stainless receiver, stainless barrel. **$883.00**
Price: Extra blued barrel. **$254.00**

Price: Extra stainless barrel **$317.00**
Price: Scope mount **$60.00**

RPM XL SINGLE SHOT PISTOL

Caliber: 22 LR through 45-70. **Barrel:** 8", 10-3/4", 12", 14". **Weight:** About 60 oz. **Length:** NA. **Stocks:** Smooth Goncalo Alves with thumb and heel rests. **Sights:** Hooded front with interchangeable post, or Patridge; ISGW rear adjustable for windage and elevation. **Features:** Barrel drilled and tapped for scope mount. Visible cocking indicator. Spring-loaded barrel lock, positive hammer-block safety. Trigger adjustable for weight of pull and over-travel. Contact maker for complete price list. Made in U.S. by RPM.

Price: Hunter model (stainless frame, 5/16" underlug, latch lever and
positive extractor) **$1,295.00**
Price: Extra barrel, 8" through 10-3/4" **$387.50**
Price: Extra barrel with positive extractor, add. **$100.00**
Price: Muzzle brake **$100.00**

SAVAGE STRIKER BOLT-ACTION HUNTING HANDGUN

Caliber: 223, 22-250, 243, 260, 7mm-08, 308, 2-shot magazine. **Barrel:** 14". **Weight:** About 5 lbs. **Length:** 22-1/2" overall. **Stock:** Black composite ambidextrous mid-grip; grooved forend; "Dual Pillar" bedding. **Sights:** None furnished; drilled and tapped for scope mounting. **Features:** Short left-hand bolt with right-hand ejection; free-floated barrel; uses Savage Model 110 rifle scope rings/bases. Introduced 1998. Made in U.S. by Savage Arms, Inc.

Price: Model 510F (blued barrel and action) **$425.00**
Price: Model 516FSS (stainless barrel and action) **$462.00**
Price: Model 516FSAK (stainless, adjustable muzzle brake). **$512.00**
Price: Super Striker **$512.00**

T/C Encore

T/C Stainless Contender

Weatherby Mark V CFP

Savage Sport Striker Bolt-Action Hunting Handgun

Similar to the Striker, but chambered in 22 LR and 22 WMR. Detachable, 10-shot magazine (5-shot magazine for 22 WMR). Overall length 19", weighs 4 lbs. Ambidextrous fiberglass/graphite composite rear grip. Drilled and tapped, scope mount installed. Introduced 2000. Made in U.S. by Savage Arms Inc.

Price: Model 501F (blue finish, 22LR) $201.00
Price: Model 502F (blue finish, 22 WMR).................. $221.00

THOMPSON/CENTER ENCORE PISTOL

Caliber: 22-250, 223, 260 Rem., 7mm-08, 243, 308, 270, 30-06, 44 Mag., 454 Casull, 444 Marlin single shot. Barrel: 12", 15", tapered round. Weight: NA. Length: 21" overall with 12" barrel. Stocks: American walnut with finger grooves, walnut forend. Sights: Blade on ramp front, adjustable rear, or none. Features: Interchangeable barrels; action opens by squeezing the trigger guard; drilled and tapped for scope mounting; blue finish. Announced 1996. Made in U.S. by Thompson/Center Arms.

Price: $554.06
Price: Extra 12" barrels................................ $240.68
Price: Extra 15" barrels................................ $248.14
Price: 45 Colt/410 barrel, 12".......................... $263.24
Price: 45 Colt/410 barrel, 15".......................... $280.39

Thompson/Center Stainless Encore Pistol

Similar to the blued Encore except made of stainless steel and available wtih 15" barrel in 223, 22-250 7mm-08, 308. Comes with black rubber grip and forend. Made in U.S. by Thompson/Center Arms.

Price: $620.99

Thompson/Center Stainless Super 14

Same as the standard Super 14 and Super 16 except they are made of stainless steel with blued sights. Both models have black Rynite forend and finger-groove, ambidextrous grip with a built-in rubber recoil cushion that has a sealed-in air pocket. Receiver has a different cougar etching. Available in 22 LR Match, .223 Rem., 30-30 Win., 35 Rem. (Super 14), 45 Colt/410. Introduced 1993.

Price: $578.40
Price: 45 Colt/410, 14" $613.94

Thompson/Center Contender Shooter's Package

Package contains a 14" barrel without iron sights (10" for the 22 LR Match); Weaver-style base and rings; 2.5x-7x Recoil Proof pistol scope; and a soft carrying case. Calibers 22 LR, 223, 7-30 Waters, 30-30. Frame and barrel are blued; grip and forend are black composite. Introduced 1998. Made in U.S. by Thompson/Center Arms.

Price $735.00

THOMPSON/CENTER CONTENDER

Caliber: 7mm TCU, 30-30 Win., 22 LR, 22 WMR, 22 Hornet, 223 Rem., 270 Rem., 7-30 Waters, 32-20 Win., 357 Mag., 357 Rem. Max., 44 Mag., 10mm Auto, 445 SuperMag., 45/410, single shot. Barrel: 10", bull barrel and vent. rib. Weight: 43 oz. (10" bbl.). Length: 13-1/4" (10" bbl.). Stock: T/C "Competitor Grip." Right or left hand. Sights: Under-cut blade ramp front, rear adjustable for windage and elevation. Features: Break-open action with automatic safety. Single-action only. Interchangeable bbls., both caliber (rim & centerfire), and length. Drilled and tapped for scope. Engraved frame. See T/C catalog for exact barrel/caliber availability.

Price: Blued (rimfire cals.) $509.03
Price: Blued (centerfire cals.)........................... $509.03
Price: Extra bbls. $229.02
Price: 45/410, internal choke bbl. $235.11

Thompson/Center Stainless Contender

Same as the standard Contender except made of stainless steel with blued sights, black Rynite forend and ambidextrous finger-groove grip with a built-in rubber recoil cushion that has a sealed-in air pocket. Receiver has a different cougar etching. Available with 10" bull barrel in 22 LR, 22 LR Match, 22 Hornet, 223 Rem., 30-30 Win., 357 Mag., 44 Mag., 45 Colt/410. Introduced 1993.

Price: $566.59
Price: 45 Colt/410..................................... $590.44
Price: With 22 LR match chamber $578.40

UBERTI ROLLING BLOCK TARGET PISTOL

Caliber: 22 LR, 22 WMR, 22 Hornet, 357 Mag., 45 Colt, single shot. Barrel: 9-7/8", half-round, half-octagon. Weight: 44 oz. Length: 14" overall. Stock: Walnut grip and forend. Sights: Blade front, fully adjustable rear. Features: Replica of the 1871 rolling block target pistol. Brass trigger guard, color case-hardened frame, blue barrel. Imported by Uberti U.S.A.

Price: $410.00

WEATHERBY MARK V CFP PISTOL

Caliber: 22-250, 243, 7mm-08, 308. Barrel: 15" fluted stainless. Weight: NA. Length: NA. Stock: Brown laminate with ambidextrous rear grip. Sights: None furnished; drilled and tapped for scope mounting. Features: Uses Mark V lightweight receiver of chrome-moly steel, matte blue finish. Introduced 1998. Made in U.S. From Weatherby.

Price: $1,049.00

WEATHERBY MARK V ACCUMARK CFP PISTOL

Caliber: 223, 22-250, 243, 7mm-08, 308; 3-shot magazine. Barrel: 15"; 1:12" twist (223). Weight: 5 lbs. Length: 26-1/2" overall. Stock: Kevlar-fiberglass composite. Sights: None; drilled and tapped for scope mounting. Features: Molded-in aluminum bedding plate; fluted stainless steel barrel; fully adjustable trigger. Introduced 2000. From Weatherby.

Price: .... NA

Both classic arms and recent designs in American-style repeaters for sport and field shooting.

Armalite M15A2

Armalite AR-10A4

Auto-Ordnance 1927 A-1 Thompson

Barrett Model 82A-1

AA ARMS AR9 SEMI-AUTOMATIC RIFLE

Caliber: 9mm Para., 10-shot magazine. **Barrel:** 16". **Weight:** 6 lbs. **Length:** 31" overall. **Stock:** Fixed **Sights:** Post front adjustable for elevation, open rear for windage. **Features:** Blue or electroless nickel finish. Made in U.S. by AA Arms, Inc.
Price: Blue **$695.00**

ARMALITE M15A2 CARBINE

Caliber: 223, 7-shot magazine. **Barrel:** 16" heavy chrome lined; 1:9" twist. **Weight:** 7 lbs. **Length:** 35-11/16" overall. **Stock:** Green or black composition. **Sights:** Standard A2. **Features:** Upper and lower receivers have push-type pivot pin; hard coat anodized; A2-style forward assist; M16A2-type raised fence around magazine release button. Made in U.S. by ArmaLite, Inc.
Price: Green **$930.00**
Price: Black **$945.00**

ARMALITE AR-10A4 SPECIAL PURPOSE RIFLE

Caliber: 308 Win., 10-shot magazine. **Barrel:** 20" chrome-lined, 1:12" twist. **Weight:** 9.6 lbs. **Length:** 41" overall **Stock:** Green or black composition. **Sights:** Detachable handle, front sight, or scope mount available; comes with international style flattop receiver with Picatinny rail. **Features:** Proprietary recoil check. Forged upper receiver with case deflector. Receivers are hard-coat anodized. Introduced 1995. Made in U.S. by ArmaLite, Inc.
Price: Green **$1,378.00**
Price: Black **$1,393.00**

AUTO-ORDNANCE 1927 A-1 THOMPSON

Caliber: 45 ACP. **Barrel:** 16-1/2". **Weight:** 13 lbs. **Length:** About 41" overall (Deluxe). **Stock:** Walnut stock and vertical forend. **Sights:** Blade front, open rear adjustable for windage. **Features:** Recreation of Thompson Model 1927. Semi-auto only. Deluxe model has finned barrel, adjustable rear sight and compensator; Standard model has plain barrel and military sight. From Auto-Ordnance Corp.
Price: Deluxe **$950.00**
Price: 1927A1C Lightweight model (9-1/2 lbs.) **$950.00**

Auto-Ordnance Thompson M1

Similar to the 1927 A-1 except is in the M-1 configuration with side cocking knob, horizontal forend, smooth unfinned barrel, sling swivels on butt and forend. Matte black finish. Introduced 1985.
Price: **$950.00**

Auto-Ordnance 1927A1 Commando

Similar to the 1927A1 except has Parkerized finish, black-finish wood butt, pistol grip, horizontal forend. Comes with black nylon sling. Introduced 1998. Made in U.S. by Auto-Ordnance Corp.
Price: **$950.00**

BARRETT MODEL 82A-1 SEMI-AUTOMATIC RIFLE

Caliber: 50 BMG, 10-shot detachable box magazine. **Barrel:** 29". **Weight:** 28.5 lbs. **Length:** 57" overall. **Stock:** Composition with energy-absorbing recoil pad. **Sights:** Scope optional. **Features:** Semi-automatic, recoil op-

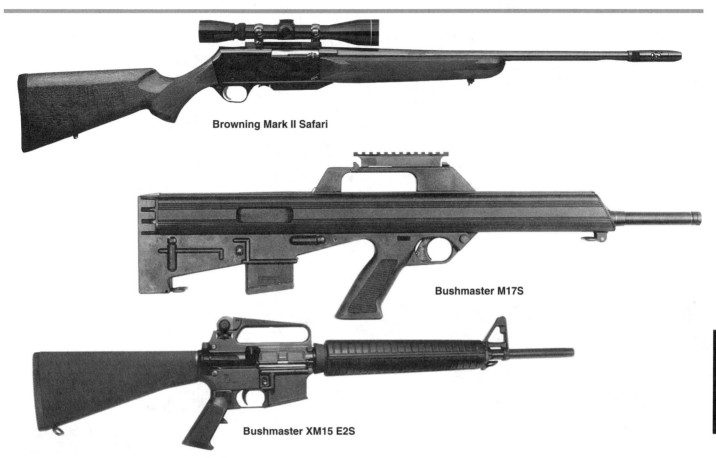

Browning Mark II Safari

Bushmaster M17S

Bushmaster XM15 E2S

erated with recoiling barrel. Three-lug locking bolt; muzzle brake. Adjustable bipod. Introduced 1985. Made in U.S. by Barrett Firearms.
Price: From **$7,200.00**

BROWNING BAR MARK II SAFARI SEMI-AUTO RIFLE
Caliber: 22-250, 243, 25-06, 270, 30-06, 308. **Barrel:** 22" round tapered. **Weight:** 7-3/8 lbs. **Length:** 43" overall. **Stock:** French walnut pistol grip stock and forend, hand checkered. **Sights:** Gold bead on hooded ramp front, click adjustable rear, or no sights. **Features:** Has new bolt release lever; removable trigger assembly with larger trigger guard; redesigned gas and buffer systems. Detachable 4-round box magazine. Scroll-engraved receiver is tapped for scope mounting. BOSS barrel vibration modulator and muzzle brake system available only on models without sights. Mark II Safari introduced 1993. Imported from Belgium by Browning.
Price: Safari, with sights **$760.00**
Price: Safari, no sights **$743.00**
Price: Safari, no sights, 270 Wea. Mag. **$797.00**
Price: Safari, no sights, BOSS **$803.00**

Browning BAR MARK II Lightweight Semi-Auto
Similar to the Mark II Safari except has lighter alloy receiver and 20" barrel. Available in 243, 308, 270, 30-06, 7mm Rem. Mag., 300 Win. Mag., 338 Win. Mag. Weighs 7 lbs., 2 oz.; overall length 41". Has dovetailed, gold bead front sight on hooded ramp, open rear click adjustable for windage and elevation. BOSS system optional. Introduced 1997. Imported from Belgium by Browning.
Price: 243, 308, 30-06 . . . . **$760.00**
Price: 7mm Rem. Mag., 300 Win. Mag., 338 Win. Mag **$814.00**
Price: As above with BOSS **$857.00**

Browning BAR Mark II Safari Magnum Rifle
Same as the standard caliber model, except weighs 8-3/8 lbs., 45" overall, 24" bbl., 3-round mag. Cals. 7mm Mag., 300 Win. Mag., 338 Win. Mag. BOSS barrel vibration modulator and muzzle brake system available only on models without sights. Introduced 1993.

Price: Safari, with sights **$814.00**
Price: Safari, no sights **$797.00**
Price: Safari, no sights, BOSS **$857.00**

BUSHMASTER M17S BULLPUP RIFLE
Caliber: 223, 10-shot magazine. **Barrel:** 21.5", chrome lined; 1:9" twist. **Weight:** 8.2 lbs. **Length:** 30" overall. **Stock:** Fiberglass-filled nylon. **Sights:** Designed for optics—carrying handle incorporates scope mount rail for Weaver-type rings; also includes 25-meter open iron sights. **Features:** Gas-operated, short-stroke piston system; ambidextrous magazine release. Introduced 1993. Made in U.S. by Bushmaster Firearms, Inc./Quality Parts Co.
Price: **$625.00**

BUSHMASTER SHORTY XM15 E2S CARBINE
Caliber: 223, 10-shot magazine. **Barrel:** 16", heavy; 1:9" twist. **Weight:** 7.2 lbs. **Length:** 34.75" overall. **Stock:** A2 type; fixed black composition. **Sights:** Fully adjustable M16A2 sight system. **Features:** Patterned after Colt M-16A2. Chrome-lined barrel with manganese phosphate finish. "Shorty" handguards. Has forged aluminum receivers with push-pin. Made in U.S. by Bushmaster Firearms Inc.
Price: **$780.00**

Bushmaster XM15 E2S Dissipator Carbine
Similar to the XM15 E2S Shorty carbine except has full-length "Dissipator" handguards. Weighs 7.6 lbs.; 34.75" overall; forged aluminum receivers with push-pin style takedown. Made in U.S. by Bushmaster Firearms, Inc.
Price **$790.00**

Bushmaster XM15 E25 AK Shorty Carbine
Similar to the XM15 E2S Shorty except has 14.5" barrel with an AK muzzle brake permanently attached giving 16" barrel length. Weighs 7.3 lbs. Introduced 1999. Made in U.S. by Bushmaster Firearms, Inc.
Price: **$800.00**

RIFLES

CENTERFIRE RIFLES — AUTOLOADERS

Calico Liberty 50

Carbon 15

Colt Match Target Lightweight

Hi-Point Carbine

Kel-Tec Sub-9

CALICO LIBERTY 50, 100 CARBINES

Caliber: 9mm Para. **Barrel:** 16.1". **Weight:** 7 lbs. **Length:** 34.5" overall. **Stock:** Glass-filled, impact resistant polymer. **Sights:** Adjustable front post, fixed notch and aperture flip rear. **Features:** Helical feed magazine; ambidextrous, rotating sear/striker block safety; static cocking handle; retarded blowback action; aluminum alloy receiver. Introduced 1995. Made in U.S. by Calico.
Price: Liberty 50 . . . . **$860.00**
Price: Liberty 100 . . . . **$925.00**

CARBON 15 (TYPE 97) AUTO RIFLE

Caliber: 223. **Barrel:** 16". **Weight:** 3.9 lbs. **Length:** 35" overall. **Stock:** Carbon fiber butt and forend, rubberized pistol grip. **Sights:** None furnished; optics base. **Features:** Carbon fiber upper and lower receivers; stainless steel match-grade barrel; hard-chromed bolt and carrier; quick-detachable compensator. Made in U.S. by Professional Ordnance Inc.
Price: **$1,700.00**
Price: Type 20 (light-profile stainless barrel, compensator
optional) **$1,550.00**

COLT MATCH TARGET LIGHTWEIGHT RIFLE

Caliber: 9mm Para., 223 Rem., 5-shot magazine. **Barrel:** 16". **Weight:** 6.7 lbs. (223); 7.1 lbs. (9mm Para.). **Length:** 34.5" overall. **Stock:** Composition stock, grip, forend. **Sights:** Post front, rear adjustable for windage and elevation. **Features:** 5-round detachable box magazine, flash suppressor, sling swivels. Forward bolt assist included. Introduced 1991.
Price: **$1,111.00**

HI-POINT 9MM CARBINE

Caliber: 9mm Para., 40 S&W, 10-shot magazine. **Barrel:** 16-1/2" (17-1/2" for 40 S&W). **Weight:** 4-1/2 lbs. **Length:** 31-1/2" overall. **Stock:** Black polymer. **Sights:** Protected post front, aperture rear. Integral scope mount. **Features:** Grip-mounted magazine release. Black or chrome finish. Sling swivels. Introduced 1996. Made in U.S. by MKS Supply, Inc.
Price: Black or chrome, 9mm **$199.00**
Price: 40 S&W **$225.00**

KEL-TEC SUB-9 AUTO RIFLE

Caliber: 9mm Para or 40 S&W. **Barrel:** 16.1". **Weight:** 4.6 lbs. **Length:** 30" overall (extended), 15.9" (closed). **Stock:** Metal tube; grooved rubber butt pad. **Sights:** Hooded post front, flip-up rear. Interchangeable grip assemblies allow use of most double-column high capacity pistol magazines. **Features:** Barrel folds back over the butt for transport and storage. Introduced 1997. Made in U.S. by Kel-Tec CNC Industries, Inc.
Price: 9mm **$700.00**
Price: 40 S&W **$725.00**

RIFLES

Remington Model 7400

Ruger PC4GR Carbine

Ruger Mini 14/5R

LR 300 SR LIGHT SPORT RIFLE

Caliber: 223. **Barrel:** 16-1/4"; 1:9" twist. **Weight:** 7.2 lbs. **Length:** 36" overall (extended stock), 26-1/4" (stock folded). **Stock:** Folding, tubular steel, with thumbhold-type grip. **Sights:** Trijicon post front, Trijicon rear. **Features:** Uses AR-15 type upper and lower receivers; flattop receiver with weaver base. Accepts all AR-15/M-16 magazines. Introduced 1996. Made in U.S. from Z-M Weapons.
Price: $2,550.00

OLYMPIC ARMS CAR-97 RIFLES

Caliber: 223, 7-shot; 9mm Para., 45 ACP, 40 S&W, 10mm, 10-shot. **Barrel:** 16". **Weight:** 7 lbs. **Length:** 34.75" overall. **Stock:** A2 stowaway grip, telescoping-look butt. **Sights:** Post front, fully adjustable aperature rear. **Features:** Based on AR-15 rifle. Post-ban version of the CAR-15. Made in U.S. by Olympic Arms, Inc.
Price: 223 .... $780.00
Price: 9mm Para., 45 ACP, 40 S&W, 10mm $840.00
Price: PCR Eliminator (223, full-length handguards) $803.00

OLYMPIC ARMS PCR-4 RIFLE

Caliber: 223, 10-shot magazine. **Barrel:** 20". **Weight:** 8 lbs., 5 oz. **Length:** 38.25" overall. **Stock:** A2 stowaway grip, trapdoor buttstock. **Sights:** Post front, A1 rear adjustable for windage. **Features:** Based on the AR-15 rifle. Barrel is button rifled with 1:9" twist. No bayonet lug. Introduced 1994. Made in U.S. by Olympic Arms, Inc.
Price: $792.00

OLYMPIC ARMS PCR-6 RIFLE

Caliber: 7.62x39mm (PCR-6), 10-shot magazine. **Barrel:** 16". **Weight:** 7 lbs. **Length:** 34" overall. **Stock:** A2 stowaway grip, trapdoor buttstock. **Sights:** Post front, A1 rear adjustable for windage. **Features:** Based on the CAR-15. No bayonet lug. Button-cut rifling. Introduced 1994. Made in U.S. by Olympic Arms, Inc.
Price: $845.00

REMINGTON MODEL 7400 AUTO RIFLE

Caliber: 243 Win., 270 Win., 280 Rem., 308 Win., 30-06, 4-shot magazine. **Barrel:** 22" round tapered. **Weight:** 7-1/2 lbs. **Length:** 42-5/8" overall. **Stock:** Walnut, deluxe cut checkered pistol grip and forend. Satin or high-gloss finish. **Sights:** Gold bead front sight on ramp; step rear sight with windage adjustable. **Features:** Redesigned and improved version of the Model 742. Positive cross-bolt safety. Receiver tapped for scope mount. Introduced 1981.

Price: About $612.00
Price: Carbine (18-1/2" bbl., 30-06 only) $612.00
Price: With black synthetic stock, matte black metal, rifle or carbine $509.00

ROCK RIVER ARMS STANDARD A2 RIFLE

Caliber: 45 ACP. **Barrel:** N/A. **Weight:** 8.2 lbs. **Length:** N/A. **Stock:** Thermoplastic. **Sights:** Standard AR-15 style sights. **Features:** Two-stage, national match trigger; optional muzzle brake. Made in U.S. From River Rock Arms.
Price: $925.00

RUGER PC4, PC9 CARBINES

Caliber: 9mm Para., 40 cal., 10-shot magazine. **Barrel:** 16.25". **Weight:** 6 lbs., 4 oz. **Length:** 34.75" overall. **Stock:** Black DuPont (Zytel) with checkered grip and forend. **Sights:** Blade front, open adjustable rear; integral Ruger scope mounts. **Features:** Delayed blowback action; manualpush-button cross bolt safety and internal firing pin block safety automatic slide lock. Introduced 1997. Made in U.S. by Sturm, Ruger & Co.
Price: PC9, PC4, (9mm, 40 cal.) $575.00
Price: PC9G4, PC4GR (ghost ring sight) $598.00

RUGER MINI-14/5 AUTOLOADING RIFLE

Caliber: 223 Rem., 5-shot detachable box magazine. **Barrel:** 18-1/2". Rifling twist 1:9". **Weight:** 6.4 lbs. **Length:** 37-1/4" overall. **Stock:** American hardwood, steel reinforced. **Sights:** Ramp front, fully adjustable rear. **Features:** Fixed piston gas-operated, positive primary extraction. New buffer system, redesigned ejector system. Ruger S100RH scope rings included.
Price: Mini-14/5R, Ranch Rifle, blued, scope rings $649.00
Price: K-Mini-14/5R, Ranch Rifle, stainless, scope rings $710.00
Price: Mini-14/5, blued, no scope rings $606.00
Price: K-Mini-14/5, stainless, no scope rings $664.00
Price: K-Mini-14/5P, stainless, synthetic stock............... $664.00
Price: K-Mini-14/5RP, Ranch Rifle, stainless, synthetic stock $710.00

Ruger Mini Thirty Rifle

Similar to the Mini-14 Ranch Rifle except modified to chamber the 7.62x39 Russian service round. Weight is about 6-7/8 lbs. Has 6-groove barrel with 1:10" twist, Ruger Integral Scope Mount bases and folding peep rear sight. Detachable 5-shot staggered box magazine. Blued finish. Introduced 1987.
Price: Blue, scope rings $649.00
Price: Stainless, scope rings $710.00

Springfield M1A

Springfield National Match M1A

Springfield Super Match with Camo M1A

SPRINGFIELD, INC. M1A RIFLE

Caliber: 7.62mm NATO (308), 5- or 10-shot box magazine. **Barrel:** 25-1/16" with flash suppressor, 22" without suppressor. **Weight:** 8-3/4 lbs. **Length:** 44-1/4" overall. **Stock:** American walnut with walnut-colored heat-resistant fiberglass handguard. Matching walnut handguard available. Also available with fiberglass stock. **Sights:** Military, square blade front, full click-adjustable aperture rear. **Features:** Commercial equivalent of the U.S. M-14 service rifle with no provision for automatic firing. From Springfield, Inc.

Price: M1A-A1, black fiberglass stock **$1,319.00**
Price: Standard M1A rifle, about. **$1,448.00**
Price: National Match, about **$1,995.00**
Price: Super Match (heavy premium barrel), about **$2,479.00**

STONER SR-15 M-5 RIFLE

Caliber: 223. **Barrel:** 20". **Weight:** 7.6 lbs. **Length:** 38" overall. **Stock:** Black synthetic. **Sights:** Post front, fully adjustable rear. **Features:** Modular weapon system. Black finish. Introduced 1998. Made in U.S. by Knight's Mfg.

Price: **$1,295.00**
Price: M-4 Carbine (16" barrel, 6.8 lbs) **$1,295.00**

STONER SR-25 CARBINE

Caliber: 7.62 NATO, 10-shot steel magazine. **Barrel:** 16" free-floating **Weight:** 7-3/4 lbs. **Length:** 35.75" overall. **Stock:** Black synthetic. **Sights:** Integral Weaver-style rail. Scope rings, iron sights optional. **Features:** Shortened, non-slip handguard; removable carrying handle. Matte black finish. Introduced 1995. Made in U.S. by Knight's Mfg. Co.

Price: **$2,995.00**

STONER SR-50 LONG RANGE PRECISION RIFLE

Caliber: 50 BMG, 10-shot magazine. **Barrel:** 35.5". **Weight:** 31.5 lbs. **Length:** 58.37" overall. **Stock:** Tubular steel. **Sights:** Scope mount. **Features:** Gas-operated semi-automatic action; two-stage target-type trigger; M-16-type safety lever; easily removable barrel. Introduced 1996. Made in U.S. by Knight's Mfg. Co.

Price: **$6,995.00**

RIFLES

Both classic arms and recent designs in American-style repeaters for sport and field shooting.

American Arms/Uberti 1873 Sporting

American Arms/Uberti 1866 Sporting

Browning BPR

Browning Lightning BLR

RIFLES

AMERICAN ARMS/UBERTI 1873 SPORTING RIFLE

Caliber: 44-40, 45 Colt. **Barrel:** 24-1/4", 30", octagonal. **Weight:** 8.1 lbs. **Length:** 43-1/4" overall. **Stock:** Walnut. **Sights:** Blade front adjustable for windage, open rear adjustable for elevation. **Features:** Color case-hardened frame, blued barrel, hammer, lever, buttplate, brass elevator. Imported from Italy by American Arms, Inc.
Price: 24-1/4" barrel $860.00
Price: 30" barrel $940.00

AMERICAN ARMS/UBERTI 1866 SPORTING RIFLE, CARBINE

Caliber: 22 LR, 22 WMR, 38 Spec., 44-40, 45 Colt. **Barrel:** 24-1/4", octagonal. **Weight:** 8.1 lbs. **Length:** 43-1/4" overall. **Stock:** Walnut. **Sights:** Blade front adjustable for windage, rear adjustable for elevation. **Features:** Frame, buttplate, forend cap of polished brass, balance charcoal blued. Imported by American Arms, Inc.
Price: $730.00
Price: Yellowboy Carbine (19" round bbl.) $710.00

AMERICAN ARMS/UBERTI 1860 HENRY RIFLE

Caliber: 44-40, 45 Colt. **Barrel:** 24-1/4", half-octagon. **Weight:** 9.2 lbs. **Length:** 43-3/4" overall. **Stock:** American walnut. **Sights:** Blade front, rear adjustable for elevation. **Features:** Frame, elevator, magazine follower, buttplate are brass, balance blue. Imported by American Arms, Inc.
Price: $940.00
Price: 1860 Henry White (polished steel finish) $990.00

AMERICAN ARMS/UBERTI 1860 HENRY TRAPPER CARBINE

Similar to the 1860 Henry Rifle except has 18-1/2" barrel, measures 37-3/4" overall, and weighs 8 lbs. Introduced 1999. Imported from Italy by American Arms.
Price: Brass frame, blued barrel $940.00
Price: Henry Trapper White (brass frame, polished steel barrel) . . $990.00

BROWNING BPR PUMP RIFLE

Caliber: 243, 308 (short action); 270, 30-06, 7mm Rem. Mag., 300 Win. Mag., 4-shot magazine (3 for magnums). **Barrel:** 22"; 24" for magnum calibers. **Weight:** 7 lbs., 3 oz. **Length:** 43" overall (22" barrel). **Stock:** Select walnut with full pistol grip, high gloss finish. **Sights:** Gold bead on hooded ramp front, open click adjustable rear. **Features:** Slide-action mechanism cams forend down away from the barrel. Seven-lug rotary bolt; cross-bolt safety behind trigger; removable magazine; alloy receiver. Introduced 1997. Imported from Belgium by Browning.
Price: Standard calibers $718.00
Price: Magnum calibers $772.00

BROWNING LIGHTNING BLR LEVER-ACTION RIFLE

Caliber: 223, 22-250, 243, 7mm-08, 308 Win., 4-shot detachable magazine. **Barrel:** 20" round tapered. **Weight:** 6 lbs., 8 oz. **Length:** 39-1/2" overall. **Stock:** Walnut. Checkered grip and forend, high-gloss finish. **Sights:** Gold bead on ramp front; low profile square notch adjustable rear. **Features:** Wide, grooved trigger; half-cock hammer safety; fold-down hammer. Receiver tapped for scope mount. Recoil pad installed. Introduced 1996. Imported from Japan by Browning.
Price: $600.00

Browning Lightning BLR Long Action

Similar to the standard Lightning BLR except has long action to accept 30-06, 270, 7mm Rem. Mag. and 300 Win. Mag. Barrel lengths are 22" for 30-06 and 270, 24" for 7mm Rem. Mag. and 300 Win. Mag. Has six-lug rotary bolt; bolt and receiver are full-length fluted. Fold-down hammer at half-cock. Weighs about 7 lbs., overall length 42-7/8" (22" barrel). Introduced 1996.
Price: $634.00

CENTERFIRE RIFLES — LEVER AND SLIDE

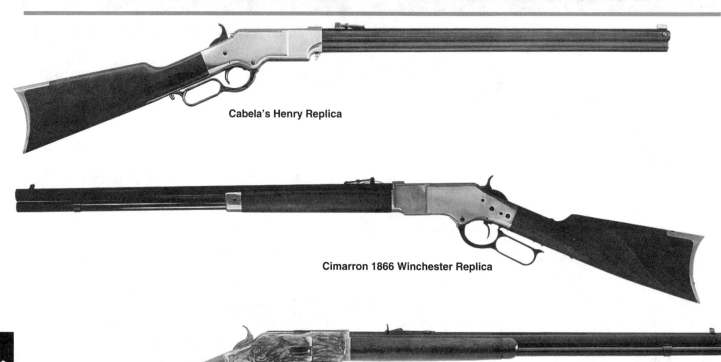

Cabela's Henry Replica

Cimarron 1866 Winchester Replica

Cabela's 1873 Winchester

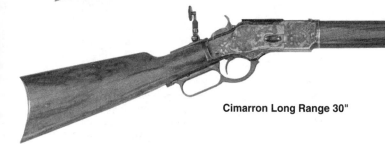

Cimarron Long Range 30"

CABELA'S 1858 HENRY REPLICA
Caliber: 44-40, 45 Colt. **Barrel:** 24-1/4". **Weight:** 9.5 lbs. **Length:** 43" overall. **Stock:** European walnut. **Sights:** Bead front, open adjustable rear. **Features:** Brass receiver and buttplate. Uses original Henry loading system. Faithful to the original rifle. Introduced 1994. Imported by Cabela's.
Price: $749.99

CABELA'S 1866 WINCHESTER REPLICA
Caliber: 44-40, 45 Colt. **Barrel:** 24-1/4". **Weight:** 9 lbs. **Length:** 43" overall. **Stock:** European walnut. **Sights:** Bead front, open adjustable rear. **Features:** Solid brass receiver, buttplate, forend cap. Octagonal barrel. Faithful to the original Winchester '66 rifle. Introduced 1994. Imported by Cabela's.
Price: $619.99

CABELA'S 1873 WINCHESTER REPLICA
Caliber: 44-40, 45 Colt. **Barrel:** 24-1/4", 30". **Weight:** 8.5 lbs. **Length:** 43-1/4" overall. **Stock:** European walnut. **Sights:** Bead front, open adjustable rear; globe front, tang rear. **Features:** Color case-hardened steel receiver. Faithful to the original Model 1873 rifle. Introduced 1994. Imported by Cabela's.
Price: Sporting model, 30" barrel, 44-40, 45 Colt $749.99
Price: Sporting model, 24" or 25" barrel $729.99

CIMARRON 1860 HENRY REPLICA
Caliber: 44 WCF, 13-shot magazine. **Barrel:** 24-1/4" (rifle), 22" (carbine). **Weight:** 9-1/2 lbs. **Length:** 43" overall (rifle). **Stock:** European walnut. **Sights:** Bead front, open adjustable rear. **Features:** Brass receiver and buttplate. Uses original Henry loading system. Faithful to the original rifle. Introduced 1991. Imported by Cimarron F.A. Co.
Price: $1,029.00

CIMARRON 1866 WINCHESTER REPLICAS
Caliber: 22 LR, 22 WMR, 38 Spec., 44 WCF. **Barrel:** 24-1/4" (rifle), 19" (carbine). **Weight:** 9 lbs. **Length:** 43" overall (rifle). **Stock:** European walnut. **Sights:** Bead front, open adjustable rear. **Features:** Solid brass receiver, buttplate, forend cap. Octagonal barrel. Faithful to the original Winchester '66 rifle. Introduced 1991. Imported by Cimarron F.A. Co.
Price: Rifle $839.00
Price: Carbine $829.00

CIMARRON 1873 SHORT RIFLE
Caliber: 22 LR, 22 WMR, 357 Mag., 44-40, 45 Colt. **Barrel:** 20" tapered octagon. **Weight:** 7.5 lbs. **Length:** 39" overall. **Stock:** Walnut. **Sights:** Bead front, adjustable semi-buckhorn rear. **Features:** Has half "button" magazine. Original-type markings, including caliber, on barrel and elevator and "Kings" patent. From Cimarron F.A. Co.
Price: $799.00

CIMARRON 1873 LONG RANGE RIFLE
Caliber: 22 LR, 22 WMR, 357 Mag., 38-40, 44-40, 45 Colt. **Barrel:** 30", octagonal. **Weight:** 8-1/2 lbs. **Length:** 48" overall. **Stock:** Walnut. **Sights:** Blade front, semi-buckhorn ramp rear. Tang sight optional. **Features:** Color case-hardened frame; choice of modern blue-black or charcoal blue for other parts. Barrel marked "Kings Improvement." From Cimarron F.A. Co.
Price: $999.00

Dixie 1873

IAR 1873 Revolver Carbine

Marlin 1894S
Lever-Action

Marlin 1894CS

Cimarron 1873 Sporting Rifle

Similar to the 1873 Long Range except has 24" barrel with half-magazine.
Price: **$949.00**
Price: 1873 Saddle Ring Carbine, 19" barrel **$949.00**

DIXIE ENGRAVED 1873 RIFLE

Caliber: 44-40, 11-shot magazine. **Barrel:** 20", round. **Weight:** 7-3/4 lbs.
Length: 39" overall. **Stock:** Walnut. **Sights:** Blade front, adjustable rear.
Features: Engraved and case-hardened frame. Duplicate of Winchester
1873. Made in Italy. From 21 Gun Works.
Price: **$1,295.00**
Price: Plain, blued carbine **$850.00**

E.M.F. 1860 HENRY RIFLE

Caliber: 44-40 or 44 rimfire. **Barrel:** 24.25". **Weight:** About 9 lbs. **Length:**
About 43.75" overall. **Stock:** Oil-stained American walnut. **Sights:** Blade
front, rear adjustable for elevation. **Features:** Reproduction of the original
Henry rifle with brass frame and buttplate, rest blued. From E.M.F.
Price: Standard.................................... **$,850.00**

E.M.F. 1866 YELLOWBOY LEVER ACTIONS

Caliber: 38 Spec., 44-40. **Barrel:** 19" (carbine), 24" (rifle). **Weight:** 9 lbs.
Length: 43" overall (rifle). **Stock:** European walnut. **Sights:** Bead front,
open adjustable rear. **Features:** Solid brass frame, blued barrel, lever,
hammer, buttplate. Imported from Italy by E.M.F.
Price: Rifle **$690.00**
Price: Carbine...................................... **$675.00**

E.M.F. HARTFORD MODEL 1892 LEVER-ACTION RIFLE

Caliber: 45 Colt. **Barrel:** 24", octagonal. **Weight:** 7-1/2 lbs. **Length:** 43"
overall. **Stock:** European walnut. **Sights:** Blade front, open adjustable
rear. **Features:** Color case-hardened frame, lever, trigger and hammer
with blued barrel, or overall blue finish. Introduced 1998. Imported by
E.M.F.
Price: Standard.................................... **$1,000.00**
Price: Deluxe **$1,085.00**
Price: Premier..................................... **$1,250.00**

E.M.F. MODEL 73 LEVER-ACTION RIFLE

Caliber: 357 Mag., 44-40, 45 Colt. **Barrel:** 24". **Weight:** 8 lbs. **Length:** 43-
1/4" overall. **Stock:** European walnut. **Sights:** Bead front, rear adjustable
for windage and elevation. **Features:** Color case-hardened frame (blue on
carbine). Imported by E.M.F.
Price: Rifle **$865.00**
Price: Carbine, 19" barrel **$865.00**

IAR MODEL 1873 REVOLVER CARBINE

Caliber: 357 Mag., 45 Colt. **Barrel:** 18". **Weight:** 4 lbs., 8 oz. **Length:** 34"
overall. **Stock:** One-piece walnut. **Sights:** Blade front, notch rear. **Features:** Color case-hardened frame, blue barrel, backstrap and trigger-
guard. Introduced 1998. Imported from Italy by IAR, Inc.
Price: Standard...................................... **$490.00**

MARLIN MODEL 1894S LEVER-ACTION CARBINE

Caliber: 44 Spec./44 Mag., 10-shot tubular magazine. **Barrel:** 20" Ballard-
type rifling. **Weight:** 6 lbs. **Length:** 37-1/2" overall. **Stock:** Checkered
American black walnut, straight grip and forend. Mar-Shield® finish. Rubber rifle butt pad; swivel studs. **Sights:** Wide-Scan hooded ramp front,
semi-buckhorn folding rear adjustable for windage and elevation. **Features:** Hammer-block safety. Receiver tapped for scope mount, offset
hammer spur, solid top receiver sand blasted to prevent glare.
Price: **$510.00**

Marlin Model 1894CS Carbine

Similar to the standard Model 1894S except chambered for 38 Spec./357
Mag. with full-length 9-shot magazine, 18-1/2" barrel, hammer-block safe-
ty, hooded front sight. Introduced 1983.
Price: **$510.00**

MARLIN MODEL 1894 COWBOY, COWBOY II

Caliber: 357 Mag., 44 Mag., 44-40, 45 Colt, 10-shot magazine. **Barrel:** 24"
tapered octagon, deep cut rifling. **Weight:** 7-1/2 lbs. **Length:** 41-1/2" overall. **Stock:** Straight grip American black walnut with cut checkering, hard
rubber buttplate, Mar-Shield® finish. **Sights:** Marble carbine front, adjustable Marble semi-buckhorn rear. **Features:** Squared finger lever; straight
grip stock; blued steel forend tip. Designed for Cowboy Shooting events.
Introduced 1996. Made in U.S. by Marlin.
Price: Cowboy I, 45 Colt................................ **$752.00**
Price: Cowboy II, 357 Mag., 44 Mag., 44-40 .... **$752.00**

Marlin 1894 Cowboy II

Marlin 444P Outfitter

Marlin 1895SS

Marlin 336CS

Marlin 336CB Cowboy

MARLIN MODEL 444SS LEVER-ACTION SPORTER

Caliber: 444 Marlin, 5-shot tubular magazine. **Barrel:** 22" deep cut Ballard rifling. **Weight:** 7-1/2 lbs. **Length:** 40-1/2" overall. **Stock:** Checkered American black walnut, capped pistol grip with white line spacers, rubber rifle butt pad. Mar-Shield® finish; swivel studs. **Sights:** Hooded ramp front, folding semi-buckhorn rear adjustable for windage and elevation. **Features:** Hammer-block safety. Receiver tapped for scope mount; offset hammer spur.
Price: **$582.00**

Marlin Model 444P Outfitter Lever-Action

Similar to the 444SS except has a ported 18-1/2" barrel with deep-cut Ballard-type rifling; weighs 6-3/4 lbs.; overall length 37". Available only in 444 Marlin. Introduced 1999. Made in U.S. by Marlin.
Price: **$595.00**

MARLIN MODEL 1895SS LEVER-ACTION RIFLE

Caliber: 45-70, 4-shot tubular magazine. **Barrel:** 22" round. **Weight:** 7-1/2 lbs. **Length:** 40-1/2" overall. **Stock:** Checkered American black walnut, full pistol grip. Mar-Shield® finish; rubber butt pad; quick detachable swivel studs. **Sights:** Bead front with Wide-Scan hood, semi-buckhorn folding rear adjustable for windage and elevation. **Features:** Hammer-block safety. Solid receiver tapped for scope mounts or receiver sights; offset hammer spur.
Price: **$582.00**

Marlin Model 1895G Guide Gun Lever Action

Similar to the Model 1895SS except has 18-1/2" ported barrel with deep-cut Ballard-type rifling; straight-grip walnut stock. Overall length is 37", weighs 6-3/4 lbs. Introduced 1998. Made in U.S. by Marlin.
Price: **$595.00**

MARLIN MODEL 336CS LEVER-ACTION CARBINE

Caliber: 30-30 or 35 Rem., 6-shot tubular magazine. **Barrel:** 20" Micro-Groove®. **Weight:** 7 lbs. **Length:** 38-1/2" overall. **Stock:** Checkered American black walnut, capped pistol grip with white line spacers. Mar-Shield® finish; rubber butt pad; swivel studs. **Sights:** Ramp front with Wide-Scan hood, semi-buckhorn folding rear adjustable for windage and elevation. **Features:** Hammer-block safety. Receiver tapped for scope mount, offset hammer spur; top of receiver sand blasted to prevent glare.
Price: **$493.00**

Marlin Model 336CB Cowboy

Similar to the Model 336CS except chambered for 30-30 and 38-55 Win., 24" tapered octagon barrel with deep-cut Ballard-type rifling; straight-grip walnut stock with hard rubber buttplate; blued steel forend cap; weighs 7-1/2 lbs.; 42-1/2" overall. Introduced 1999. Made in U.S. by Marlin.
Price: **$677.00**

Marlin Model 336AS Lever-Action Carbine

Same as the Marlin 336CS except has cut-checkered, walnut-finished Maine birch pistol grip stock with swivel studs, 30-30 only, 6-shot. Hammer-block safety. Adjustable rear sight, brass bead front.
Price: **$418.00**
Price: With 4x scope and mount **$462.00**

RIFLES

CENTERFIRE RIFLES — LEVER AND SLIDE

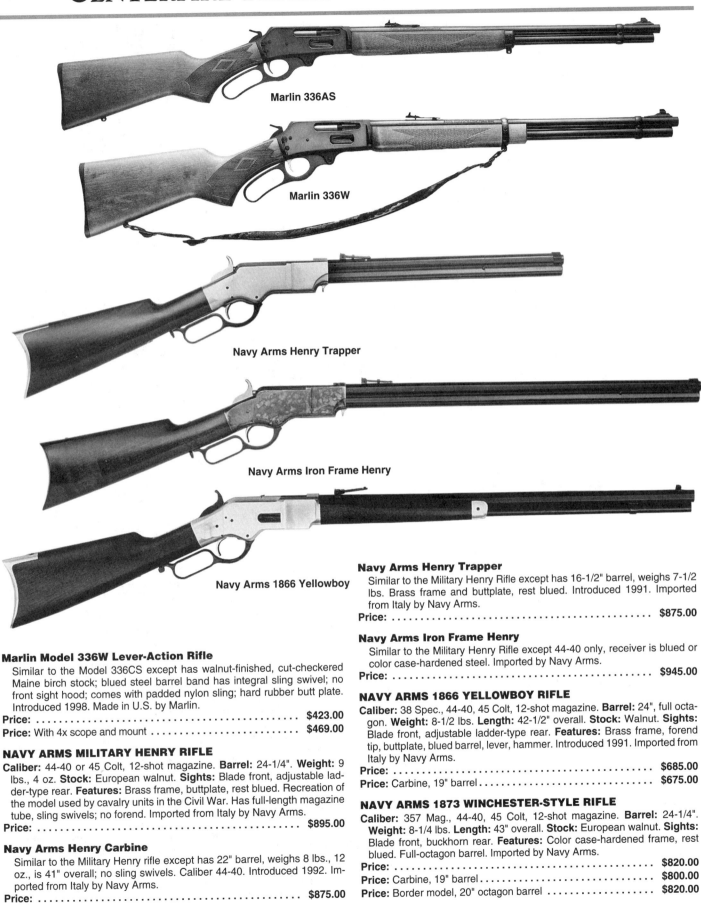

Marlin 336AS

Marlin 336W

Navy Arms Henry Trapper

Navy Arms Iron Frame Henry

Navy Arms 1866 Yellowboy

Marlin Model 336W Lever-Action Rifle
Similar to the Model 336CS except has walnut-finished, cut-checkered Maine birch stock; blued steel barrel band has integral sling swivel; no front sight hood; comes with padded nylon sling; hard rubber butt plate. Introduced 1998. Made in U.S. by Marlin.
Price: $423.00
Price: With 4x scope and mount $469.00

NAVY ARMS MILITARY HENRY RIFLE
Caliber: 44-40 or 45 Colt, 12-shot magazine. **Barrel:** 24-1/4". **Weight:** 9 lbs., 4 oz. **Stock:** European walnut. **Sights:** Blade front, adjustable ladder-type rear. **Features:** Brass frame, buttplate, rest blued. Recreation of the model used by cavalry units in the Civil War. Has full-length magazine tube, sling swivels; no forend. Imported from Italy by Navy Arms.
Price: $895.00

Navy Arms Henry Carbine
Similar to the Military Henry rifle except has 22" barrel, weighs 8 lbs., 12 oz., is 41" overall; no sling swivels. Caliber 44-40. Introduced 1992. Imported from Italy by Navy Arms.
Price: $875.00

Navy Arms Henry Trapper
Similar to the Military Henry Rifle except has 16-1/2" barrel, weighs 7-1/2 lbs. Brass frame and buttplate, rest blued. Introduced 1991. Imported from Italy by Navy Arms.
Price: $875.00

Navy Arms Iron Frame Henry
Similar to the Military Henry Rifle except 44-40 only, receiver is blued or color case-hardened steel. Imported by Navy Arms.
Price: $945.00

NAVY ARMS 1866 YELLOWBOY RIFLE
Caliber: 38 Spec., 44-40, 45 Colt, 12-shot magazine. **Barrel:** 24", full octagon. **Weight:** 8-1/2 lbs. **Length:** 42-1/2" overall. **Stock:** Walnut. **Sights:** Blade front, adjustable ladder-type rear. **Features:** Brass frame, forend tip, buttplate, blued barrel, lever, hammer. Introduced 1991. Imported from Italy by Navy Arms.
Price: $685.00
Price: Carbine, 19" barrel $675.00

NAVY ARMS 1873 WINCHESTER-STYLE RIFLE
Caliber: 357 Mag., 44-40, 45 Colt, 12-shot magazine. **Barrel:** 24-1/4". **Weight:** 8-1/4 lbs. **Length:** 43" overall. **Stock:** European walnut. **Sights:** Blade front, buckhorn rear. **Features:** Color case-hardened frame, rest blued. Full-octagon barrel. Imported by Navy Arms.
Price: $820.00
Price: Carbine, 19" barrel $800.00
Price: Border model, 20" octagon barrel $820.00

Navy Arms 1873 Winchester Style

Navy Arms 1892 Rifle

Navy Arms 1892 Short Rifle

Remington 7600 Rifle

Ruger Model 96/44

Navy Arms 1873 Sporting Rifle

Similar to the 1873 Winchester-Style rifle except has checkered pistol grip stock, 30" octagonal barrel (24-1/4" available). Introduced 1992. Imported by Navy Arms.
Price: 30" barrel **$960.00**
Price: 24-1/4" barrel **$930.00**

NAVY ARMS 1892 RIFLE

Caliber: 357 Mag., 44-40, 45 Colt. **Barrel:** 24-1/4" octagonal. **Weight:** 7 lbs. **Length:** 42" overall. **Stock:** American walnut. **Sights:** Blade front, semi-buckhorn rear. **Features:** Replica of Winchester's early Model 1892 with octagonal barrel, forend cap and crescent buttplate. Blued or color case-hardened receiver. Introduced 1998. Imported by Navy Arms.
Price: **$495.00**

Navy Arms 1892 Carbine

Similar to the 1892 Rifle except has 20" round barrel, weighs 5-3/4 lbs., and is 37-1/2" overall. Introduced 1998. Imported by Navy Arms.
Price: **$465.00**

Navy Arms 1892 Short Rifle

Similar to the 1892 Rifle except has 20" octagonal barrel, weighs 6-1/4 lbs., and is 37-3/4" overall. Replica of the rare, special order 1892 Winchester nicknamed the "Texas Special." Blued or color case-hardened receiver and furniture. Introduced 1998. Imported by Navy Arms.
Price: **$495.00**
Price: (stainless steel, 20" octagon barrel) **$535.00**
Price: Stainless carbine (20"round barrel, saddle ring) **$470.00**

NAVY ARMS 1892 STAINLESS RIFLE

Caliber: 357 Mag., 44-40, 45 Colt. **Barrel:** 24-1/4" octagonal. **Weight:** 7 lbs. **Length:** 42". **Stock:** American walnut. **Sights:** Brass bead front, semi-buckhorn rear. **Features:** Designed for the Cowboy Action Shooter. Stainless steel barrel, receiver and furniture. Introduced 2000. Imported by Navy Arms.
Price: **$535.00**

REMINGTON MODEL 7600 PUMP ACTION

Caliber: 243, 270, 280, 30-06, 308. **Barrel:** 22" round tapered. **Weight:** 7-1/2 lbs. **Length:** 42-5/8" overall. **Stock:** Cut-checkered walnut pistol grip and forend, Monte Carlo with full cheekpiece. Satin or high-gloss finish. **Sights:** Gold bead front sight on matted ramp, open step adjustable sporting rear. **Features:** Redesigned and improved version of the Model 760. Detachable 4-shot clip. Cross-bolt safety. Receiver tapped for scope mount. Introduced 1981.
Price: **$576.00**
Price: Carbine (18-1/2" bbl., 30-06 only) **$576.00**
Price: With black synthetic stock, matte black metal, rifle or carbine **$473.00**

RUGER MODEL 96/44 LEVER-ACTION RIFLE

Caliber: 44 Mag., 4-shot rotary magazine. **Barrel:** 18-1/2". **Weight:** 5-7/8 lbs. **Length:** 37-5/16" overall. **Stock:** American hardwood. **Sights:** Gold bead front, folding leaf rear. **Features:** Solid chrome-moly steel receiver. Manual cross-bolt safety, visible cocking indicator; short-throw lever action; integral scope mount; blued finish; color case-hardened lever. Introduced 1996. Made In U.S. by Sturm, Ruger & Co.
Price: 96/44M, 44 Mag **$470.00**

CENTERFIRE RIFLES — LEVER AND SLIDE

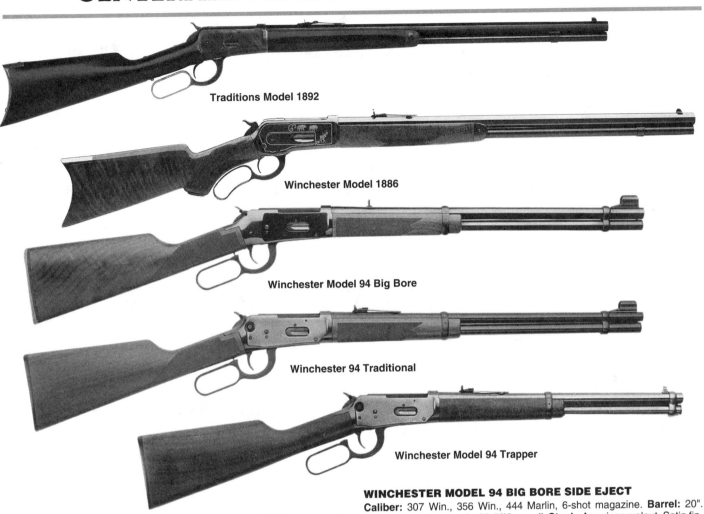

Traditions Model 1892

Winchester Model 1886

Winchester Model 94 Big Bore

Winchester 94 Traditional

Winchester Model 94 Trapper

TRADITIONS MODEL 1892 LEVER-ACTION RIFLE

Caliber: 357 Mag., 44-40, 45 Colt. **Barrel:** 24" octagonal. **Weight:** 7 lbs. **Length:** 42" overall. **Stock:** Walnut. **Sights:** Blade front, semi-buckhorn rear. **Features:** Replica of Winchester's Model 1892 with octagonal barrel, forend cap, crescent buttplate. Antique silver, brass frame, or color case-hardened receiver. Introduced 1999. Imported by Traditions.
Price: Color case-hardened $615.00
Price: Antique silver $660.00
Price: Brass $630.00

Traditions Model 1892 Carbine

Similar to the 1892 Rifle except has 20" round barrel, saddle ring, weighs 6 lbs., and is 38" overall. Introduced 1999. Imported by Traditions.
Price: $615.00

VEKTOR H5 SLIDE-ACTION RIFLE

Caliber: 223 Rem., 5-shot magazine. **Barrel:** 18", 22". **Weight:** 9 lbs., 15 oz. **Length:** 42-1/2" overall (22" barrel). **Stock:** Walnut thumbhole. **Sights:** Comes with 1" 4x32 scope with low-light reticle. **Features:** Rotating bolt mechanism. Matte black finish. Introduced 1999. Imported from South Africa by Vektor USA.
Price: $849.95

WINCHESTER MODEL 1886
EXTRA LIGHT LEVER-ACTION RIFLE

Caliber: 45-70, 8-shot magazine. **Barrel:** 26", full octagon. **Weight:** 9-1/4 lbs. **Length:** 45" overall. **Stock:** Smooth walnut. **Sights:** Bead front, ramp-adjustable buckhorn-style rear. **Features:** Recreation of the Model 1886. Polished blue finish; crescent metal butt plate; metal forend cap; pistol grip stock. Reintroduced 1998. From U.S. Repeating Arms Co., Inc.
Price: Grade I $1,156.00
Price: High Grade $1,447.00

WINCHESTER MODEL 94 BIG BORE SIDE EJECT

Caliber: 307 Win., 356 Win., 444 Marlin, 6-shot magazine. **Barrel:** 20". **Weight:** 7 lbs. **Length:** 38-5/8" overall. **Stock:** American walnut. Satin finish. **Sights:** Hooded ramp front, semi-buckhorn rear adjustable for windage and elevation. **Features:** All external metal parts have Winchester's deep blue finish. Rifling twist 1:12". Rubber recoil pad fitted to buttstock. Introduced 1983. From U.S. Repeating Arms Co., Inc.
Price: $446.00

Winchester Timber Carbine

Similar to the Model 94 Big Bore. Chambered only for 444 Marlin; 17-3/4" barrel is ported; half-pistol grip stock with butt pad; checkered grip and forend. Introduced 1999. Made in U.S. by U.S. Repeating Arms Co., Inc.
Price: $548.00

WINCHESTER MODEL 94 TRADITIONAL

Caliber: 30-30 Win., 44 Mag., 6-shot tubular magazine. **Barrel:** 20". **Weight:** 6-1/2 lbs. **Length:** 37-3/4" overall. **Stock:** Straight grip walnut stock and forend. **Sights:** Hooded blade front, semi-buckhorn rear. Drilled and tapped for scope mount. Post front sight on Trapper model. **Features:** Solid frame, forged steel receiver; side ejection, exposed rebounding hammer with automatic trigger-activated transfer bar. Introduced 1984.
Price: 30-30 .... $430.00
Price: 44 Mag. $452.00
Price: Checkered walnut $404.00
Price: No checkering, walnut, 30-30 only $398.00

Winchester Model 94 Trapper Side Eject

Same as the Model 94 Walnut Side Eject except has 16" barrel, 5-shot magazine in 30-30, 9-shot in 357 Mag., 44 Magnum/44 Special, 45 Colt. Has stainless steel claw extractor, saddle ring, hammer spur extension, walnut wood.
Price: 30-30 .... $337.00
Price: 44 Mag., 357 Mag., 45 Colt $355.00

RIFLES

Winchester Model 94 Trails End

Winchester Model 94 Black Shadow

Winchester Model 94 Legacy

Winchester Model 1895

Winchester Model 94 Trails End

Similar to the Model 94 Walnut except chambered only for 357 Mag., 44-40, 44 Mag., 45 Colt; 11-shot magazine. Available with standard lever loop. Introduced 1997. From U.S. Repeating Arms Co., Inc.
Price: With standard lever loop **$434.00**

Winchester Model 94 Black Shadow Lever-Action Rifle

Similar to the Model 94 Walnut except has black synthetic stock with higher comb for easier scope use, and fuller forend. Non-glare finish; recoil pad. Available in 30-30 with 20" or 24" barrel, 44 Mag. or as Big Bore model in 444 Marlin. Introduced 1998. Made in U.S. by U.S. Repeating Arms Co., Inc.
Price: Black Shadow, 30-30, 44 Mag. . . . . **$381.00 to $394.00**
Price: Black Shadow Big Bore, 444 Marlin **$395.00**

Winchester Model 94 Legacy

Similar to the Model 94 Side Eject except has half-pistol grip walnut stock, checkered grip and forend. Chambered for 30-30, 357 Mag., 44 Mag., 45 Colt; 24" barrel. Introduced 1995. Made in U.S. by U.S. Repeating Arms Co., Inc.
Price: With 24" barrel **$446.00**

Winchester Model 94 Ranger Compact

Similar to the Model 94 Ranger except has 16" barrel and 12-1/2" length of pull, rubber recoil pad, post front sight. Introduced 1998. Made in U.S. by U.S. Repeating Arms Co., Inc.
Price: 357 Mag. **$368.00**
Price: 30-30 . . . . **$347.00**

WINCHESTER MODEL 1895 LEVER-ACTION RIFLE

Caliber: 405 Win, 4-shot magazine. **Barrel:** 24", round. **Weight:** 8 lbs. **Length:** 42" overall. **Stock:** American walnut. **Sights:** Gold bead front, buckhorn rear adjustable for elevation. **Features:** Recreation of the original Model 1895. Polished blue finish with Nimschke-style scroll engraving on receiver. Scalloped receiver, two-piece cocking lever, Schnabel forend, straight-grip stock. Introduced 1995. From U.S. Repeating Arms Co., Inc.
Price: Grade I **$1,050.00**
Price: High Grade **$1,540.00**

RIFLES

Includes models for a wide variety of sporting and competitive purposes and uses.

Anschutz 1733D

Arnold Arms Alaskan

Arnold Arms Safari

RIFLES

ANSCHUTZ 1743D BOLT-ACTION RIFLE

Caliber: 222 Rem., 3-shot magazine. **Barrel:** 19.7". **Weight:** 6.4 lbs. **Length:** 39" overall. **Stock:** European walnut. **Sights:** Hooded blade front, folding leaf rear. **Features:** Receiver grooved for scope mounting; single stage trigger; claw extractor; sling safety; sling swivels. Imported from Germany by AcuSport Corp.

Price: $1,588.95

ANSCHUTZ 1740 MONTE CARLO RIFLE

Caliber: 22 Hornet, 5-shot clip; 222 Rem., 3-shot clip. **Barrel:** 24". **Weight:** 6-1/2 lbs. **Length:** 43.25" overall. **Stock:** Select European walnut. **Sights:** Hooded ramp front, folding leaf rear; drilled and tapped for scope mounting. **Features:** Uses match 54 action. Adjustable single stage trigger. Stock has roll-over Monte Carlo cheekpiece, slim forend with Schnabel tip, Wundhammer palm swell on grip, rosewood gripcap with white diamond insert. Skip-line checkering on grip and forend. Introduced 1997. Imported from Germany by AcuSport Corp.

Price: From $1,439.00

Price: Model 1730 Monte Carlo, as above except in 22 Hornet $1,439.00

Anschutz 1733D Rifle

Similar to the 1740 Monte Carlo except has full-length, walnut, Mannlicher-style stock with skip-line checkering, rosewood Schnabel tip, and is chambered for 22 Hornet. Weighs 6.4 lbs., overall length 39", barrel length 19.7". Imported from Germany by AcuSport Corp.

Price: $1,588.95

ARNOLD ARMS ALASKAN RIFLE

Caliber: 243 to 338 Magnum. **Barrel:** 22" to 26". **Weight:** NA. **Length:** NA. **Stock:** Synthetic; black, woodland or arctic camouflage. **Sights:** Optional; drilled and tapped for scope mounting. **Features:** Uses Apollo, Remington or Winchester action with controlled round feed or push feed; chrome-moly steel or stainless; one-piece bolt, handle, knob; cone head bolt and breech; three-position safety; fully adjustable trigger. Introduced 1996. Made in U.S. by Arnold Arms Co.

Price: From $2,695.00

Arnold Arms Alaskan Guide Rifle

Similar to the Alaskan rifle except chambered for 257 to 338 Magnum; choice of A-grade English walnut or synthetic stock; three-position safety; scope mount only. Introduced 1996. Made in U.S. by Arnold Arms Co.

Price: From $3,249.00

Arnold Arms Grand Alaskan Rifle

Similar to the Alaskan rifle except has AAA fancy select or exhibition-grade English walnut; barrel band swivel; comes with iron sights and scope mount; 24" to 26" barrel; 300 Magnum to 458 Win. Mag. Introduced 1996. Made in U.S. by Arnold Arms Co.

Price: From $7,570.00

Arnold Arms Alaskan Trophy Rifle

Similar to the Alaskan rifle except chambered for 300 Magnum to 458 Win. Mag.; 24" to 26" barrel; black synthetic or laminated stock; comes with barrel band on 375 H&H and larger; scope mount; iron sights. Introduced 1996. Made in U.S. by Arnold Arms Co.

Price: From $3,249.00

ARNOLD ARMS SAFARI RIFLE

Caliber: 243 to 458 Win. Mag. **Barrel:** 22" to 26". **Weight:** NA. **Length:** NA. **Stock:** Grade A and AA Fancy English walnut. **Sights:** Optional; drilled and tapped for scope mounting. **Features:** Uses Apollo, Remington or Winchester action with controlled or push round feed; one-piece bolt, handle, knob; cone head bolt and breech; three-position safety; fully adjustable trigger; chrome-moly steel in matte blue, polished, or bead blasted stainless. Introduced 1996. Made in U.S. by Arnold Arms Co.

Price: From $6,495.00

Arnold Arms African Trophy Rifle

Similar to the Safari rifle except has AAA Extra Fancy English walnut stock with wrap-around checkering; matte blue chrome-moly or polished or bead blasted stainless steel; scope mount standard or optional Express sights. Introduced 1996. Made in U.S. by Arnold Arms Co.

Price: Blued chrome-moly steel $6,921.00

Price: Stainless steel $6,971.00

Arnold Arms Grand African Rifle

Similar to the Safari rifle except has Exhibition Grade stock; polished blue chrome-moly steel or bead-blasted or Teflon-coated stainless; barrel band; scope mount, express sights; calibers 338 Magnum to 458 Win. Mag.; 24" to 26" barrel. Introduced 1996. Made in U.S. by Arnold Arms Co.

Price: Chrome-moly steel $8,172.00

Price: Stainless steel $8,022.00

CENTERFIRE RIFLES — BOLT ACTION

Beretta Mato Deluxe

Barrett Model 95

Beretta Mato Synthetic

Blaser R93 Classic

BARRETT MODEL 95 BOLT-ACTION RIFLE

Caliber: 50 BMG, 5-shot magazine. **Barrel:** 29". **Weight:** 22 lbs. **Length:** 45" overall. **Stock:** Energy-absorbing recoil pad. **Sights:** Scope optional. **Features:** Bolt-action, bullpup design. Disassembles without tools; extendable bipod legs; match-grade barrel; high efficiency muzzle brake. Introduced 1995. Made in U.S. by Barrett Firearms Mfg., Inc.
Price: From **$4,950.00**

BERETTA MATO DELUXE BOLT-ACTION RIFLE

Caliber: 270, 280 Rem., 30-06, 7mm Rem. Mag., 300 Win. Mag., 338 Win. Mag., 375 H&H. **Barrel:** 23.6". **Weight:** 7.9 lbs. **Length:** 44.5" overall. **Stock:** XXX claro walnut with ebony forend tip, hand-rubbed oil finish. **Sights:** Bead on ramp front, open fully adjustable rear; drilled and tapped for scope mounting. **Features:** Mauser-style action with claw extractor; three-position safety; removable box magazine; 375 H&H has muzzle brake. Introduced 1998. From Beretta U.S.A.
Price: **$2,470.00**
Price: 375 H&H. **$2,795.00**

Beretta Mato Synthetic Bolt-Action Rifle

Similar to the Mato except has fiberglass/Kevlar/carbon fiber stock in classic American style with shadow line cheekpiece, aluminum bedding block and checkering. Introduced 1998. From Beretta U.S.A.
Price: **$1,660.00**
Price: 375 H&H. **$2,015.00**

BLASER R93 BOLT-ACTION RIFLE

Caliber: 22-250, 243, 6.5x55, 270, 7x57, 7mm-08, 308, 30-06, 257 Wea. Mag., 7mm Rem. Mag., 300 Win. Mag., 300 Wea. Mag., 338 Win Mag., 375 H&H, 416 Rem. Mag. **Barrel:** 22" (standard calibers), 26" (magnum). **Weight:** 7 lbs. **Length:** 40" overall (22" barrel). **Stock:** Two-piece European walnut. **Sights:** None furnished; drilled and tapped for scope mounting. **Features:** Straight pull-back bolt action with thumb-activated safety slide/cocking mechanism; interchangeable barrels and bolt heads. Introduced 1994. Imported from Germany by SIGARMS.
Price: R93 Classic **$3,680.00**
Price: R93 LX. **$1,895.00**
Price: R93 Synthetic (black synthetic stock) **$1,595.00**
Price: R93 Safari Synthetic (416 Rem. Mag. only). **$1,855.00**
Price: R93 Grand Lux. **$4,915.00**
Price: R93 Attaché **$5,390.00**

BRNO 98 BOLT-ACTION RIFLE

Caliber: 7x64, 243, 270, 308, 30-06, 300 Win. Mag., 9.3x62. **Barrrel:** 23.6". **Weight:** 7.2 lbs. **Length:** 40.9" overall. **Stock:** European walnut. **Sights:** Blade on ramp front, open adjustable rear. **Features:** Uses Mauser 98-type action; polished blue. Announced 1998. Imported from the Czech Republic by Euro-Imports.
Price: Standard calibers **$507.00**
Price: Magnum calibers **$547.00**
Price: With set trigger, standard calibers **$615.00**
Price: As above, magnum calibers. **$655.00**
Price: With full stock, set trigger, standard calibers **$703.00**
Price: As above, magnum calibers. **$743.00**

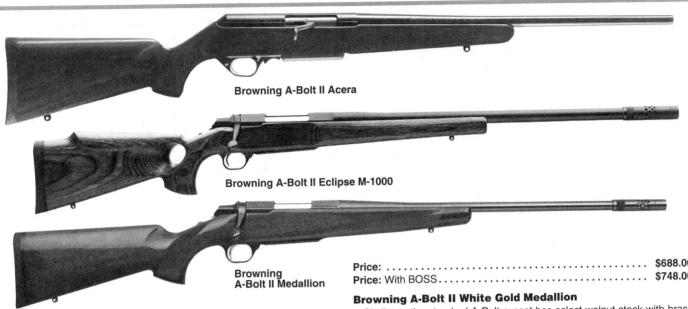

Browning A-Bolt II Acera

Browning A-Bolt II Eclipse M-1000

Browning A-Bolt II Medallion

BROWNING ACERA STRAIGHT-PULL RIFLE

Caliber: 30-06, 300 Win. Mag. **Barrel:** 22"; 24" for magnums. **Weight:** 6 lbs., 9 oz. **Length:** 41-1/4" overall. **Stock:** American walnut with high gloss finish. **Sights:** Blade on ramp front, open adjustable rear. **Features:** Straight-pull action; detachable box magazine; Teflon coated breechblock; drilled and tapped for scope mounting. Introduced 1999. Imported by Browning.

Price: 30-06, no sights $845.00
Price: 300 Win. Mag., no sights $877.00
Price: 30-06 with sights $869.00
Price: 300 Win. Mag., with sights $901.00
Price: 30-06, with BOSS. $901.00
Price: 300 Win. Mag., with BOSS. $933.00

BROWNING A-BOLT II RIFLE

Caliber: 25-06, 270, 30-06, 260 Rem., 280, 7mm Rem. Mag., 300 Win. Mag., 338 Win. Mag., 375 H&H Mag. **Barrel:** 22" medium sporter weight with recessed muzzle; 26" on mag. cals. **Weight:** 6-1/2 to 7-1/2 lbs. **Length:** 44-3/4" overall (magnum and standard); 41-3/4" (short action). **Stock:** Classic style American walnut; recoil pad standard on magnum calibers. **Features:** Short-throw (60") fluted bolt, three locking lugs, plunger-type ejector; adjustable trigger is grooved and gold-plated. Hinged floorplate, detachable box magazine (4 rounds std. cals., 3 for magnums). Slide tang safety. Medallion has glossy stock finish, rosewood grip and forend caps, high polish blue. BOSS barrel vibration modulator and muzzle brake system not available in 375 H&H. Introduced 1985. Imported from Japan by Browning.

Price: Medallion, no sights $662.00
Price: Hunter, no sights $557.00
Price: Medallion, 375 H&H Mag., no sights $767.00
Price: For BOSS add $60.00

Browning A-Bolt II Short Action

Similar to the standard A-Bolt except has short action for 223, 22-250, 243, 257 Roberts, 260 Rem., 7mm-08, 284 Win., 308 chamberings. Available in Hunter or Medallion grades. Weighs 6-1/2 lbs. Other specs essentially the same. BOSS barrel vibration modulator and muzzle brake system optional. Introduced 1985.

Price: Medallion, no sights $662.00
Price: Hunter, no sights $557.00
Price: Composite stalker, no sights $580.00
Price: For BOSS, add. $60.00

Browning A-Bolt II Medallion Left-Hand

Same as the Medallion model A-Bolt except has left-hand action and is available in 25-06, 270, 280, 30-06, 7mm Rem. Mag., 300 Win. Mag., 338 Win. Mag., 375 H&H. Introduced 1987.

Price: $688.00
Price: With BOSS. $748.00

Browning A-Bolt II White Gold Medallion

Similar to the standard A-Bolt except has select walnut stock with brass spacers between rubber recoil pad and between the rosewood gripcap and forend tip; gold-filled barrel inscription; palm-swell pistol grip, Monte Carlo comb, 22 lpi checkering with double borders; engraved receiver flats. In 270, 30-06, 7mm Rem. Mag. only. Introduced 1988.

Price: $949.00
Price: For BOSS, add. $60.00

Browning A-Bolt II Custom Trophy Rifle

Similar to the A-Bolt Medallion except has select American walnut stock with recessed swivel studs, octagon barrel, skeleton pistol gripcap, gold highlights, shadowline cheekpiece. Calibers 270, 30-06, 7mm Rem. Mag., 300 Win. Mag. Introduced 1998. Imported from Japan by Browning.
Price: $1,360.00

Browning A-Bolt II Eclipse

Similar to the A-Bolt II except has gray/black laminated, thumbhole stock, BOSS barrel vibration modulator and muzzle brake. Available in long and short action with standard weight barrel, or short-action Varmint with heavy barrel. Introduced 1996. Imported from Japan by Browning.
Price: Standard barrel, Hunter, with BOSS $941.00
Price: Varmint with BOSS $969.00

Browning A-Bolt II Eclipse M-1000

Similar to the A-Bolt II Eclipse except has long action and heavy target barrel. Chambered only for 300 Win. Mag. Adjustable trigger, bench-style forend, 3-shot magazine; laminated thumbhold stock; BOSS system standard. Introduced 1997. Imported for Japan by Browning.
Price: $969.00

Browning A-Bolt II Varmint Rifle

Same as the A-Bolt II Hunter except has heavy varmint/target barrel, laminated wood stock with special dimensions, flat forend and palm swell grip. Chambered only for 223, 22-250, 308. Comes with BOSS barrel vibration modulator and muzzle brake system. Introduced 1994.
Price: With BOSS, gloss or matte finish. $853.00

Browning A-Bolt II Micro Hunter

Similar to the A-Bolt II Hunter except has 13-5/16" length of pull, 20" barrel, and comes in 260 Rem., 243, 308, 7mm-08, 22-250, 22 Hornet. Weighs 6 lbs., 1 oz. Introduced 1999. Imported by Browning.
Price: $557.00

Browning A-Bolt II Classic Series

Similar to the A-Bolt II Hunter except has low-luster bluing and walnut stock with Monte Carlo comb, pistol grip palm swell, double-border checkering. Available in 270, 30-06, 7mm Rem. Mag., 300 Win. Mag. Introduced 1999. Imported by Browning.
Price: $633.00

RIFLES

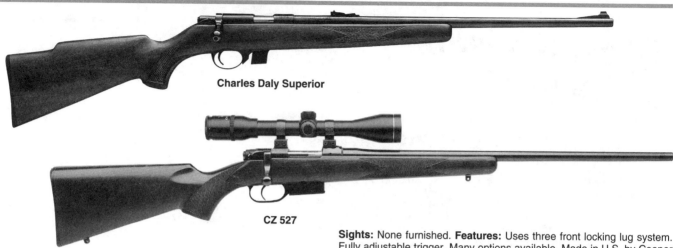

Charles Daly Superior

CZ 527

Browning A-Bolt II Stainless Stalker

Similar to the Hunter model A-Bolt except receiver and barrel are made of stainless steel; the rest of the exposed metal surfaces are finished with a durable matte silver-gray. Graphite-fiberglass composite textured stock. No sights are furnished. Available in 223, 22-250, 243, 308, 7mm-08, 270, 30-06, 7mm Rem. Mag., 375 H&H. Introduced 1987.

Price: **$737.00**
Price: With BOSS **$797.00**
Price: Left-hand, no sights **$760.00**
Price: With BOSS **$820.00**
Price: 375 H&H, with sights **$899.00**
Price: 375 H&H, left-hand, no sights **$865.00**
Price: Carbon-fiber barrel, 22-250, 300 Win. Mag. . . . . **NA**

Browning A-Bolt II Composite Stalker

Similar to the A-Bolt II Hunter except has black graphite-fiberglass stock with textured finish. Matte blue finish on all exposed metal surfaces. Available in 223, 22-250, 243, 7mm-08, 308, 30-06, 270, 280, 25-06, 7mm Rem. Mag., 300 Win. Mag., 338 Win. Mag. BOSS barrel vibration modulator and muzzle brake system offered in all calibers. Introduced 1994.

Price: No sights **$580.00**
Price: No sights, BOSS **$640.00**

CHARLES DALY SUPERIOR BOLT-ACTION RIFLE

Caliber: 22 Hornet, 5-shot magazine. **Barrel:** 22.6". **Weight:** 6.6 lbs. **Length:** 41.25" overall. **Stock:** Walnut-finished hardwood with Monte Carlo comb and cheekpiece. **Sights:** Ramped blade front, fully adjustable open rear. **Features:** Receiver dovetailed for tip-off scope mount. Introduced 1996. Imported by K.B.I., Inc.
Price: **$364.95**

Charles Daly Empire Grade Rifle

Similar to the Superior except has oil-finished American walnut stock with 18 lpi hand checkering; black hardwood gripcap and forend tip; highly polished barreled action; jewelled bolt; recoil pad; swivel studs. Imported by K.B.I., Inc.
Price: **$469.95**

COLT LIGHT RIFLE BOLT ACTION

Caliber: 243, 7x57, 7mm-08, 308 (short action); 25-06, 270, 280, 7mm Rem., Mag., 30-06, 300 Win. Mag. **Barrel:** 24" **Weight:** 5.4 to 6 lbs. **Length:** NA. **Stock:** Black synthetic. **Sights:** None furnished; low, medium, high scope mounts. **Features:** Matte black finish; three-position safety. Introduced 1999. Made in U.S. From Colt's Mfg., Inc.
Price: **$779.00**

COOPER MODEL 22 BOLT-ACTION RIFLE

Caliber: 22 BR, 22-250 Rem., 22-250 Ackley Imp., 243, 25-06, 25-06 Ackley Imp., 220 Swift, 257 Roberts, 257 Roberts Ackley Imp., 6mm Rem., 6mm PPC, 6mm BR, 7mm-08, single shot. **Barrel:** 24" stainless match grade. **Weight:** 7-3/4 to 8 lbs. **Stock:** AA Claro walnut, 20 lpi checkering.

Sights: None furnished. **Features:** Uses three front locking lug system. Fully adjustable trigger. Many options available. Made in U.S. by Cooper Firearms.
Price: Classic **$1,295.00**
Price: Varminter **$1,199.00**
Price: Varmint Extreme **$1,895.00**
Price: Custom Classic **$2,195.00**
Price: Western Classic **$2,495.00**

COOPER MODEL 21, 38 BOLT-ACTION RIFLES

Caliber: 17 Rem., 17 Mach IV, 17 Javelina, 19-223 Calhoon, 20 VarTag, 22 PPC, Model 21, 6mm PPC, 221 Fireball, 222 Rem., 222 Rem. Mag., 223 Rem., 223 Ackley Imp., 6x45, 6x47, single shot; Model 38—17 Squirrel, 17 HeBee, 17 Ackley Hornet, 22 Hornet, 22 K Hornet, 218 Mashburn Bee, 218 Bee, 22 Squirrel, single shot. **Barrel:** 24" stainless match grade. **Weight:** 6-1/2 to 7-1/4 lbs. **Stock:** AA Claro walnut; 20 l.p.i. checkering. **Sights:** None furnished. **Features:** Uses three front locking lug system. Fully adjustable trigger. Many options available. Contact maker for details. Made in U.S. by Cooper Firearms.
Price: Classic **$1,050.00**
Price: Varminter **$995.00**
Price: Varmint Extreme **$1,795.00**
Price: Custom Classic **$1,995.00**
Price: Western Classic **$2,295.00**

COOPER ARMS MODEL 22 PRO VARMINT EXTREME

Caliber: 22-250, 220 Swift, 243, 25-06, 6mm PPC, 308, single shot. **Barrel:** 26"; stainless steel match grade, straight taper; free-floated. **Weight:** NA. **Length:** NA. **Stock:** AAA Claro walnut, oil finish, 22 lpi wrap-around borderless ribbon checkering, beaded cheekpiece, steel gripcap, flared varminter forend, Pachmayr pad. **Sights:** None furnished; drilled and tapped for scope mounting. **Features:** Uses a three front locking lug system. Available with sterling silver inlaid medallion, skeleton gripcap, and French walnut. Introduced 1995. Made in U.S. by Cooper Arms.
Price: **$1,795.00**
Price: Benchrest model with Jewell trigger. **$2,195.00**
Price: Black Jack model (McMillan synthetic stock) **$1,795.00**

CZ 527 LUX BOLT-ACTION RIFLE

Caliber: 22 Hornet, 222 Rem., 223 Rem., detachable 5-shot magazine. **Barrel:** 23-1/2"; standard or heavy barrel. **Weight:** 6 lbs., 1 oz. **Length:** 42-1/2" overall. **Stock:** European walnut with Monte Carlo. **Sights:** Hooded front, open adjustable rear. **Features:** Improved mini-Mauser action with non-rotating claw extractor; single set trigger; grooved receiver. Imported from the Czech Republic by CZ-USA.
Price: **$540.00**
Price: Model FS, full-length stock, cheekpiece. **$607.00**

CZ 527 American Classic Bolt-Action Rifle

Similar to the CZ 527 Lux except has classic-style stock with 18 l.p.i. checkering; free-floating barrel; recessed target crown on barrel. No sights furnished. Introduced 1999. Imported from the Czech Republic by CZ-USA.
Price: 22 Hornet, 222 Rem., 223 Rem. **$540.00**

CZ 550 Lux

CZ 550 American Classic

CZ 550 Magnum

Dakota 76 Classic

CZ 550 LUX BOLT-ACTION RIFLE

Caliber: 22-250, 243, 6.5x55, 7x57, 7x64, 308 Win., 9.3x62, 270 Win., 30-06. **Barrel:** 20.47". **Weight:** 7.5 lbs. **Length:** 44.68" overall. **Stock:** Turkish walnut in Bavarian style or FS (Mannlicher). **Sights:** Hooded front, adjustable rear. **Features:** Improved Mauser-style action with claw extractor, fixed ejector, square bridge dovetailed receiver; single set trigger. Imported from the Czech Republic by CZ-USA.
Price: Lux . . . . **$561.00 to $609.00**
Price: FS (full stock) **$645.00**

CZ 550 American Classic Bolt-Action Rifle

Similar to the CZ 550 Lux except has American classic-style stock with 18 l.p.i. checkering; free-floating barrel; recessed target crown. Has 25.6" barrel; weighs 7.48 lbs. No sights furnished. Introduced 1999. Imported from the Czech Republic by CZ-USA.
Price: . . . . **$576.00 to $609.00**

CZ 550 Magnum Bolt-Action Rifle

Similar to the CZ 550 Lux except has long action for 300 Win. Mag., 375 H&H, 416 Rigby, 458 Win. Mag. Overall length is 46.45"; barrel length 25"; weighs 9.24 lbs. Comes with hooded front sight, express rear with one standing, two folding leaves. Imported from the Czech Republic by CZ-USA.
Price: 300 Win. Mag. **$717.00**
Price: 375 H&H. **$756.00**
Price: 416 Rigby **$796.00**
Price: 458 Win. Mag. **$744.00**

DAKOTA 76 TRAVELER TAKEDOWN RIFLE

Caliber: 257 Roberts, 25-06, 7x57, 270, 280, 30-06, 338-06, 35 Whelen (standard length); 7mm Rem. Mag., 300 Win. Mag., 338 Win. Mag., 416 Taylor, 458 Win. Mag. (short magnums); 7mm, 300, 330, 375 Dakota Magnums. **Barrel:** 23". **Weight:** 7-1/2 lbs. **Length:** 43-1/2" overall. **Stock:** Medium fancy-grade walnut in classic style. Checkered grip and forend; solid butt pad. **Sights:** None furnished; drilled and tapped for scope mounts. **Features:** Threadless disassembly—no threads to wear or

stretch, no interrupted cuts, and headspace remains constant. Uses modified Model 76 design with many features of the Model 70 Winchester. Left-hand model also available. Introduced 1989. Made in U.S. by Dakota Arms, Inc.
Price: Classic **$4,295.00**
Price: Safari **$5,295.00**
Price: Extra barrels. **$1,650.00 to $1,950.00**

DAKOTA 76 CLASSIC BOLT-ACTION RIFLE

Caliber: 257 Roberts, 270, 280, 30-06, 7mm Rem. Mag., 338 Win. Mag., 300 Win. Mag., 375 H&H, 458 Win. Mag. **Barrel:** 23". **Weight:** 7-1/2 lbs. **Length:** 43-1/2" overall. **Stock:** Medium fancy grade walnut in classic style. Checkered pistol grip and forend; solid butt pad. **Sights:** None furnished; drilled and tapped for scope mounts. **Features:** Has many features of the original Model 70 Winchester. One-piece rail trigger guard assembly; steel gripcap. Model 70-style trigger. Many options available. Left-hand rifle available at same price. Introduced 1988. From Dakota Arms, Inc.
Price: **$3,495.00**

Dakota 76 Classic Rifles

A scaled-down version of the standard Model 76. Standard chamberings are 22-250, 243, 6mm Rem., 250-3000, 7mm-08, 308, others on special order. Short Classic Grade has 21" barrel; Alpine Grade is lighter (6-1/2 lbs.), has a blind magazine and slimmer stock. Introduced 1989.
Price: Short Classic **$3,195.00**

DAKOTA 76 SAFARI BOLT-ACTION RIFLE

Caliber: 270 Win., 7x57, 280, 30-06, 7mm Dakota, 7mm Rem. Mag., 300 Dakota, 300 Win. Mag., 330 Dakota, 338 Win. Mag., 375 Dakota, 458 Win. Mag., 300 H&H, 375 H&H, 416 Rem. **Barrel:** 23". **Weight:** 8-1/2 lbs. **Length:** 43-1/2" overall. **Stock:** XXX fancy walnut with ebony forend tip; point-pattern with wrap-around forend checkering. **Sights:** Ramp front, standing leaf rear. **Features:** Has many features of the original Model 70 Winchester. Barrel band front swivel, inletted rear. Cheekpiece with shadow line. Steel gripcap. Introduced 1988. From Dakota Arms, Inc.
Price: Wood stock **$4,495.00**

RIFLES

Dakota 76 Safari

Dakota Longbow

Dakota 97 Lightweight Hunter

Dakota Hunter

Dakota 416 Rigby African

Similar to the 76 Safari except chambered for 404 Jeffery, 416 Rigby, 416 Dakota, 450 Dakota, 4-round magazine, select wood, two stock cross-bolts. Has 24" barrel, weight of 9-10 lbs. Ramp front sight, standing leaf rear. Introduced 1989.
Price: **$4,995.00**

DAKOTA LONGBOW TACTICAL E.R. RIFLE

Caliber: 300 Dakota Magnum, 330 Dakota Magnum, 338 Lapua Magnum. **Barrel:** 28", .950" at muzzle **Weight:** 13.7 lbs. **Length:** 50" to 52" overall. **Stock:** Ambidextrous McMillan A-2 fiberglass, black or olive green color; adjustable cheekpiece and buttplate. **Sights:** None furnished. Comes with Picatinny one-piece optical rail. **Features:** Uses the Dakota 76 action with controlled-round feed; three-position firing pin block safety; claw extractor; Model 70-style trigger. Comes with bipod, case tool kit. Introduced 1997. Made in U.S. by Dakota Arms, Inc.
Price: **$4,250.00**

DAKOTA 97 VARMINT HUNTER

Caliber: 17 Rem., 222 Rem., 223 Rem., 220 Swift, 22-250, 22 BR, 22 PPC, 6mm BR. **Barrel:** 24". **Weight:** 8 lbs. **Length:** NA. **Stock:** X walnut; 13-5/8" length of pull. **Sights:** Optional. **Features:** Round short action; solid-bottom single shot; chrome-moly #4 barrel; adjustable trigger. Introduced 1998. Made in U.S. by Dakota Arms.
Price: **$1,795.00**

DAKOTA 97 LIGHTWEIGHT HUNTER

Caliber: 22-250 to 308. **Barrel:** 22"-24". **Weight:** 6.1-6.5 lbs. **Length:** 43" overall. **Stock:** Fiberglass. **Sights:** Optional. **Features:** Matte blue finish, black stock. Right-hand action only. Introduced 1998. Made in U.S. by Dakota Arms, Inc.
Price: **$1,795.00**

DAKOTA LONG RANGE HUNTER RIFLE

Caliber: 25-06, 257 Roberts, 270 Win., 280 Rem., 7mm Rem. Mag., 7mm Dakota Mag., 30-06, 300 Win. Mag., 300 Dakota Mag., 338 Win. Mag., 330 Dakota Mag., 375 H&H Mag., 375 Dakota Mag. **Barrel:** 24", 26", match-quality; free-floating. **Weight:** 7.7 lbs. **Length:** 45" to 47" overall. **Stock:** H-S Precision black synthetic, with one-piece bedding block system. **Sights:** None furnished. Drilled and tapped for scope mounting. **Features:** Cylindrical machined receiver controlled round feed; Mauser-style extractor; three-position striker blocking safety; fully adjustable match trigger. Right-hand action only. Introduced 1997. Made in U.S. by Dakota Arms, Inc.
Price: **$1,795.00**

HARRIS GUNWORKS SIGNATURE CLASSIC SPORTER

Caliber: 22-250, 243, 6mm Rem., 7mm-08, 284, 308 (short action); 25-06, 270, 280 Rem., 30-06, 7mm Rem. Mag., 300 Win. Mag., 300 Wea. (long action); 338 Win. Mag., 340 Wea., 375 H&H (magnum action). **Barrel:** 22", 24", 26". **Weight:** 7 lbs. (short action). **Stock:** Fiberglass in green, beige, brown or black. Recoil pad and 1" swivels installed. Length of pull up to 14-1/4". **Sights:** None furnished. Comes with 1" rings and bases. **Features:** Uses right- or left-hand action with matte black finish. Trigger pull set at 3 lbs. Four-round magazine for standard calibers; three for magnums. Aluminum floorplate. Wood stock optional. Introduced 1987. From Harris Gunworks, Inc.
Price: **$2,700.00**

Harris Gunworks Alaskan

Harris Gunworks Signature Titanium Mountain

Harris Gunworks Signature Super Varminter

Harris Gunworks Talon Safari

Harris Gunworks Signature Classic Stainless Sporter

Similar to the Signature Classic Sporter except action is made of stainless steel. Same calibers, in addition to 416 Rem. Mag. Comes with fiberglass stock, right- or left-hand action in natural stainless, glass bead or black chrome sulfide finishes. Introduced 1990. From Harris Gunworks, Inc.
Price: **$2,900.00**

Harris Gunworks Signature Alaskan

Similar to the Classic Sporter except has match-grade barrel with single leaf rear sight, barrel band front, 1" detachable rings and mounts, steel floorplate, electroless nickel finish. Has wood Monte Carlo stock with cheekpiece, palm-swell grip, solid butt pad. Chambered for 270, 280 Rem., 30-06, 7mm Rem. Mag., 300 Win. Mag., 300 Wea., 358 Win., 340 Wea., 375 H&H. Introduced 1989.
Price: **$3,800.00**

Harris Gunworks Signature Titanium Mountain Rifle

Similar to the Classic Sporter except action made of titanium alloy, barrel of chrome-moly steel. Stock is of graphite reinforced fiberglass. Weight is 5-1/2 lbs. Chambered for 270, 280 Rem., 30-06, 7mm Rem. Mag., 300 Win. Mag. Fiberglass stock optional. Introduced 1989.
Price: **$3,300.00**
Price: With graphite-steel composite light weight barrel...... **$3,700.00**

Harris Gunworks Signature Varminter

Similar to the Signature Classic Sporter except has heavy contoured barrel, adjustable trigger, field bipod and special hand-bedded fiberglass stock. Chambered for 223, 22-250, 220 Swift, 243, 6mm Rem., 25-06, 7mm-08, 7mm BR, 308, 350 Rem. Mag. Comes with 1" rings and bases. Introduced 1989.
Price: **$2,700.00**

HARRIS GUNWORKS TALON SAFARI RIFLE

Caliber: 300 Win. Mag., 300 Wea. Mag., 300 Phoenix, 338 Win. Mag., 30/378, 338 Lapua, 300 H&H, 340 Wea. Mag., 375 H&H, 404 Jeffery, 416 Rem. Mag., 458 Win. Mag. (Safari Magnum); 378 Wea. Mag., 416 Rigby, 416 Wea. Mag., 460 Wea. Mag. (Safari Super Magnum). **Barrel:** 24". **Weight:** About 9-10 lbs. **Length:** 43" overall. **Stock:** Gunworks fiberglass Safari. **Sights:** Barrel band front ramp, multi-leaf express rear. **Features:** Uses Harris Gunworks Safari action. Has quick detachable 1" scope mounts, positive locking steel floorplate, barrel band sling swivel. Match-grade barrel. Matte black finish standard. Introduced 1989. From Harris Gunworks, Inc.
Price: Talon Safari Magnum........................... **$3,900.00**
Price: Talon Safari Super Magnum **$4,200.00**

HARRIS GUNWORKS TALON SPORTER RIFLE

Caliber: 22-250, 243, 6mm Rem., 6mm BR, 7mm BR, 7mm-08, 25-06, 270, 280 Rem., 284, 308, 30-06, 350 Rem. Mag. (long action); 7mm Rem. Mag., 7mm STW, 300 Win. Mag., 300 Wea. Mag., 300 H&H, 338 Win. Mag., 340 Wea. Mag., 375 H&H, 416 Rem. Mag. **Barrel:** 24" (standard). **Weight:** About 7-1/2 lbs. **Length:** NA. **Stock:** Choice of walnut or fiberglass. **Sights:** None furnished; comes with rings and bases. Open sights optional. **Features:** Uses pre-'64 Model 70-type action with cone breech, controlled feed, claw extractor and three-position safety. Barrel and action are of stainless steel; chrome-moly optional. Introduced 1991. From Harris Gunworks, Inc.
Price: **$2,900.00**

HOWA LIGHTNING BOLT-ACTION RIFLE

Caliber: 223, 22-250, 243, 270, 308, 30-06, 7mm Rem. Mag., 300 Win. Mag., 338 Win. Mag. **Barrel:** 22", 24" magnum calibers. **Weight:** 7-1/2 lbs.

Howa Lightning

Howa M-1500 Hunter

Howa M-1500 PCS Police Counter Sniper

Howa M-1500 Varmint

L.A.R. Grizzly

Length: 42" overall (22" barrel). **Stock:** Black Bell & Carlson Carbelite composite with Monte Carlo comb; checkered grip and forend. **Sights:** None furnished. Drilled and tapped for scope mounting. **Features:** Sliding thumb safety; hinged floorplate; polished blue/black finish. Introduced 1993. From Legacy Sports International.

Price: Blue, standard calibers $435.00
Price: Blue, magnum calibers $455.00
Price: Stainless, standard calibers $485.00
Price: Stainless, magnum calibers $505.00

Howa M-1500 Hunter Bolt-Action Rifle

Similar to the Lightning model except has walnut-finished hardwood stock. Polished blue finish or stainless steel. Introduced 1999. From Legacy Sports International.

Price: Blue, standard calibers $455.00
Price: Stainless, standard calibers $505.00
Price: Blue, magnum calibers $475.00
Price: Stainless, magnum calibers $525.00

Howa M-1500 PCS Police Counter Sniper Rifle

Similar to the M-1500 Lightning except chambered only for 308 Win., 24" hammer-forged heavy barrel. Trigger is factory set at 4 lbs. Available in blue or stainless steel, polymer or hardwood stock. Introduced 1999. Imported from Japan by Legacy Sports International.

Price: Blue, polymer stock $465.00
Price: Stainless, polymer stock $525.00
Price: Blue, wood stock $485.00
Price: Stainless, wood stock $545.00

Howa M-1500 Varmint Rifle

Similar to the M-1500 Lightning except has heavy 24" hammer-forged barrel. Chambered for 223 and 22-250. Weighs 9.3 lbs.; overall length 44.5". Introduced 1999. Imported from Japan by Interarms/Howa.

Price: Blue, polymer stock $465.00
Price: Stainless, polymer stock $525.00
Price: Blue, wood stock $485.00
Price: Stainless, wood stock $545.00

L.A.R. GRIZZLY 50 BIG BOAR RIFLE

Caliber: 50 BMG, single shot. **Barrel:** 36". **Weight:** 28.4 lbs. **Length:** 45.5" overall. **Stock:** Integral. Ventilated rubber recoil pad. **Sights:** None furnished; scope mount. **Features:** Bolt-action bullpup design; thumb safety. All-steel construction. Introduced 1994. Made in U.S. by L.A.R. Mfg., Inc.

Price: $2,570.00

MOUNTAIN EAGLE RIFLE

Caliber: 222 Rem., 223 Rem. (Varmint); 270, 280, 30-06 (long action); 7mm Rem. Mag., 7mm STW, 300 Win. Mag., 338 Win. Mag., 300 Wea. Mag., 375 H&H, 416 Rem. Mag. (magnum action). **Barrel:** 24", 26" (Varmint); match-grade; fluted stainless on Varmint. Free floating. **Weight:** 7 lbs., 13 oz. **Length:** 44" overall (24" barrel). **Stock:** Kevlar-graphite with aluminum bedding block, high comb, recoil pad, swivel studs; made by H-S Precision. **Sights:** None furnished; accepts any Remington 700-type base. **Features:** Special Sako action with one-piece forged bolt, hinged steel floorplate, lengthened receiver ring; adjustable trigger. Krieger cut-rifled benchrest barrel. Introduced 1996. From Magnum Research, Inc.

Price: Right-hand $1,499.00

CENTERFIRE RIFLES — BOLT ACTION

Mountain Eagle Varmint

Raptor Bolt-Action

Remington 700 ADL Synthetic

Remington 700 BDL

Remington 700 BDL Left Hand

Price: Left-hand **$1,549.00**
Price: Varmint Edition. **$1,629.00**
Price: 375 H&H, 416 Rem., add. **$300.00**
Price: Magnum Lite (graphite barrel) **$2,295.00**

RAPTOR BOLT-ACTION RIFLE
Caliber: 270, 30-06, 243, 25-06, 308; 4-shot magazine. **Barrel:** 22".
Weight: 7 lbs., 6 oz. **Length:** 42.5" overall. **Stock:** Black synthetic, fiberglass reinforced; checkered grip and forend; vented recoil pad; Monte Carlo cheekpiece. **Sights:** None furnished; drilled and tapped for scope mounts. **Features:** Rust-resistant "Taloncote" treated barreled action; pillar bedded; stainless bolt with three locking lugs; adjustable trigger. Announced 1997. Made in U.S. by Raptor Arms Co., Inc.
Price: **$249.00**

REMINGTON MODEL 700 CLASSIC RIFLE
Caliber: 223 Rem. **Barrel:** 24". **Weight:** About 7-1/4 lbs. **Length:** 44-1/2" overall. **Stock:** American walnut, 20 lpi checkering on pistol grip and forend. Classic styling. Satin finish. **Sights:** None furnished. Receiver drilled and tapped for scope mounting. **Features:** A "classic" version of the BDL with straight comb stock. Fitted with rubber recoil pad. Sling swivel studs installed. Hinged floorplate. Limited production in 2000 only.
Price: **$633.00**

REMINGTON MODEL 700 ADL DELUXE RIFLE
Caliber: 270, 308, 30-06 and 7mm Rem. Mag. **Barrel:** 22" or 24" round tapered. **Weight:** 7-1/4 to 7-1/2 lbs. **Length:** 41-5/8" to 44-1/2" overall. **Stock:** Walnut. Satin-finished pistol grip stock with fine-line cut checkering, Monte Carlo. **Sights:** Gold bead ramp front; removable, step-adjustable rear with windage screw. **Features:** Side safety, receiver tapped for scope mounts.
Price: From. **$531.00**

Remington Model 700 ADL Synthetic
Similar to the 700 ADL except has a fiberglass-reinforced synthetic stock with straight comb, raised cheekpiece, positive checkering, and black rubber butt pad. Metal has matte finish. Available in 22-250, 223, 243, 270, 308, 30-06 with 22" barrel, 300 Win. Mag., 7mm Rem. Mag. with 24" barrel. Introduced 1996.
Price: From. **$457.00**

Remington Model 700 ADL Synthetic Youth
Similar to the Model 700 ADL Synthetic except has 1" shorter stock, 20" barrel. Chambered for 243, 308. Introduced 1998.
Price: **$484.00**

Remington Model 700 BDL Custom Deluxe Rifle
Same as the 700 ADL except chambered for 222, 223 (short action, 24" barrel), 22-250, 25-06. (short action, 22" barrel), 243, 270, 30-06; skip-line checkering; black forend tip and gripcap with white line spacers. Matted receiver top, fine-line engraving, quick-release floorplate. Hooded ramp front sight; quick detachable swivels. 7mm-08, .280.
Price: **$633.00**
Also available in 17 Rem., 7mm Rem. Mag., 7mm-08, 280, 300 Win. Mag. (long action, 24" barrel); 338 Win. Mag., (long action, 22" barrel); 300 Rem. Ultra Mag. 338 Rem. Ultra Mag. (26" barrel). Overall length 44-1/2", weight about 7-1/2 lbs. 338 Rem Ultra Mag.
Price: **$660.00**

Remington 700 BDL SS DM

Remington 700 BDL SS DM-B

Remington 700 Safari KS

**Remington 700 APR
African Plains**

Remington Model 700 BDL Left Hand Custom Deluxe

Same as 700 BDL except mirror-image left-hand action, stock. Available in 270, 30-06, 7mm Rem. Mag., 300 Rem. Ultra Mag.
Price: **$660.00**
Price: 7mm Rem. Mag., 300 Rem. Ultra Mag. **$687.00**

Remington Model 700 BDL DM Rifle

Same as the 700 BDL except has detachable box magazine (4-shot, standard calibers, 3-shot for magnums). Has glossy stock finish, fine-line engraving, open sights, recoil pad, sling swivels. Available in 270, 30-06, 7mm Rem. Mag., 300 Win. Mag. Introduced 1995.
Price: From **$681.00**

Remington Model 700 BDL SS Rifle

Similar to the 700 BDL rifle except has hinged floorplate, 24" standard weight barrel in all calibers; magnum calibers have magnum-contour barrel. No sights supplied, but comes drilled and tapped. Has corrosion-resistant follower and fire control, stainless BDL-style barreled action with fine matte finish. Synthetic stock has straight comb and cheekpiece, textured finish, positive checkering, plated swivel studs. Calibers—270, 30-06; magnums—7mm Rem. Mag., 300 Rem. Ultra Mag. (26" barrel) 300 Win. Mag., 338 Win. Mag., 338 Rem. Ultra Mag., 375 H&H. Weighs 7-3/8 - 7-1/2 lbs. Introduced 1993.
Price: From **$681.00**

Remington Model 700 BDL SS DM Rifle

Same as the 700 BDL SS except has detachable box magazine. Barrel, receiver and bolt made of #416 stainless steel; black synthetic stock, fine-line engraving. Available in 25-06, 260 Rem., 270, 280, 30-06, 7mm Rem. Mag., 7mm-08, 300 Win. Mag., 300 Wea. Mag. Introduced 1995.
Price: From **$756.00**

Remington Model 700 BDL SS DM-B

Same as the 700 BDL SS DM except has muzzle brake, fine-line engraving. Available only in 7mm STW, 300 Win. Mag. Introduced 1996.
Price: **$845.00**

Remington Model 700 Custom KS Mountain Rifle

Similar to the 700 BDL except custom finished with Kevlar reinforced resin synthetic stock. Available in both left- and right-hand versions. Chambered for 270 Win., 280 Rem., 30-06, 7mm Rem. Mag., 7mm STW, 300 Rem. Ultra Mag., 338 Rem. Ultra Mag., 300 Win. Mag., 300 Wea. Mag., 35 Whelen, 338 Win. Mag., 8mm Rem. Mag., 375 H&H, with 24" barrel (except 300 Rem. Ultra Mag., 26"). Weighs 6 lbs., 6 oz. Introduced 1986.
Price: .338 Ultra **$1,221.00**

Remington Model 700 LSS Mountain Rifle

Similar to Model 700 Custom KS Mountain Rifle except has stainless steel 22" barrel and two-tone laminated stock. Chambered in 260 Rem., 7mm-08, 270 Winchester and 30-06. Overall length 42-1/2", weighs 6-5/8 oz. Introduced 1999. From Remington Arms Co.
Price: **$744.00**

Remington Model 700 Safari Grade

Similar to the 700 BDL except custom finished and tuned. In 8mm Rem. Mag., 375 H&H, 416 Rem. Mag. or 458 Win. Mag. calibers only with heavy barrel. Hand checkered, oil-finished stock in classic or Monte Carlo style with recoil pad installed. Classic available in right- and left-hand versions.
Price: From **$1,225.00**
Price: Safari KS (Kevlar stock), from **$1,410.00**

Remington Model 700 AWR Alaskan Wilderness Rifle

Similar to the Model 700 BDL except has stainless barreled action with satin blue finish; special 24" Custom Shop barrel profile; matte gray stock of fiberglass and graphite, reinforced with DuPont Kevlar, straight comb with raised cheekpiece, magnum-grade black rubber recoil pad. Chambered for 7mm Rem. Mag., 7mm STW, 300 Rem. Ultra Mag., 300 Win. Mag., 300 Wea. Mag., 338 Rem. Ultra Mag., 338 Win. Mag., 375 H&H. Introduced 1994.
Price: From **$1,480.00**

Remington Model 700 APR African Plains Rifle

Similar to the Model 700 BDL except has magnum receiver and specially contoured 26" Custom Shop barrel with satin finish, laminated wood stock with raised cheekpiece, satin finish, black butt pad, 20 lpi cut checkering. Chambered for 7mm Rem. Mag., 300 Rem. Ultra Mag., 300 Win. Mag., 300 Wea. Mag., 338 Win. Mag., 338 Rem. Ultra Mag., 375 H&H. Introduced 1994.
Price: **$1,593.00**

RIFLES

Remington 700 VLS

Remington 700 Varmint Synthetic

Remington 700 VS Composite

Remington 700 VF SF

Remington 700 Sendero SF

Remington Model 700 EtronX Electronic Ignition Rifle

Similar to Model 700 VS SF except features battery-powered ignition system for near-zero lock time and electronic trigger mechanism. Requires ammunition with EtronX electrically fired primers. Aluminum-bedded 26" heavy, stainless steel, fluted barrel; overall length 45-7/8"; weight 8 lbs., 14 oz. Black, Kevlar-reinforced composite stock. Light-emitting diode display on grip top indicates fire or safe mode, loaded or unloaded chamber, battery condition. Introduced 2000. From Remington Arms Co.
Price: 220 Swift, 22-250 or 243 Win. **$1,999.00**

Remington Model 700 LSS Rifle

Similar to the 700 BDL except has stainless steel barreled action, gray laminated wood stock with Monte Carlo comb and cheekpiece. No sights furnished. Available in 7mm Rem. Mag., 300 Rem. Ultra Mag., 300 Win. Mag., and 338 Rem. Ultra Mag. in right-hand, and 270, 7mm Rem. Mag., 30-06, 300 Rem. Ultra Mag., 300 Win. Mag., 338 Rem. Ultra Mag. in left-hand model. Introduced 1996.
Price: From **$771.00**

Remington Model 700 MTN DM Rifle

Similar to the 700 BDL except weighs 6-1/2 to 6-5/8 lbs., has a 22" tapered barrel. Redesigned pistol grip, straight comb, contoured cheekpiece, hand-rubbed oil stock finish, deep cut checkering, hinged floorplate and magazine follower, two-position thumb safety. Chambered for 260 Rem., 270 Win., 7mm-08, 25-06, 280 Rem., 30-06, 4-shot detachable box magazine. Overall length is 41-5/8"-42-1/2". Introduced 1995.
Price: About **$681.00**

Remington Model 700 VLS Varmint Laminated Stock

Similar to the 700 BDL except has 26" heavy barrel without sights, brown laminated stock with beavertail forend, gripcap, rubber butt pad. Available in 223 Rem., 22-250, 6mm, 243, 308. Polished blue finish. Introduced 1995.
Price: From **$675.00**

Remington Model 700 VS Varmint Synthetic Rifles

Similar to the 700 BDL Varmint Laminated except has composite stock reinforced with DuPont Kevlar, fiberglass and graphite. Has aluminum bedding block that runs the full length of the receiver. Free-floating 26" barrel. Metal has black matte finish; stock has textured black and gray finish and swivel studs. Available in 223, 22-250, 308. Right- and left-hand. Introduced 1992.
Price: From **$759.00**

Remington Model 700 VS Composite Rifle

Similar to the Model 700 VS Varmint Synthetic except has a composite varmint-weight barrel, weighs 7-1/8 lbs., and is available in right-hand in 22-250, 223, 308 Win. Introduced 1999.
Price: **$1,912.00**

Remington Model 700 VS SF Rifle

Similar to the Model 700 Varmint Synthetic except has satin-finish stainless barreled action with 26" fluted barrel, spherical concave muzzle crown. Chambered for 223, 220 Swift, 22-250. Introduced 1994.
Price: From **$916.00**

Remington Model 700 Sendero Rifle

Similar to the Model 700 Varmint Synthetic except has long action for magnum calibers. Has 26" heavy varmint barrel with spherical concave crown. Chambered for 25-06, 270, 7mm Rem. Mag., 300 Win. Mag. Introduced 1994.
Price: From **$759.00**

Remington Model Seven

Ruger 77/22 Hornet Varmint

Remington Model 700 Sendero SF Rifle

Similar to the 700 Sendero except has stainless steel action and 26" fluted stainless barrel. Weighs 8-1/2 lbs. Chambered for 25-06, 7mm Rem. Mag., 300 Wea. Mag., 7mm STW, 300 Rem. Ultra Mag., 338 Rem. Ultra Mag., 300 Win. Mag. Introduced 1996.
Price: From $943.00

REMINGTON MODEL SEVEN LSS BOLT-ACTION RIFLE

Caliber: 22-250, 243, 7mm-08. **Barrel:** 20". **Weight:** 6-1/2 lbs. **Length:** 39-1/4" overall. **Stock:** Brown laminated. Cut checkering. **Sights:** Ramp front, adjustable open rear. **Features:** Short-action design; silent side safety; free-floated barrel except for single pressure point at forend tip. Introduced 1983.
Price: $727.00

Remington Model Seven Custom KS

Similar to the Model Seven except has gray Kevlar reinforced stock with 1" black rubber recoil pad and swivel studs. Metal has black matte finish. No sights on 223, 260 Rem., 7mm-08, 308; 35 Rem. and 350 Rem. have iron sights.
Price: $1,221.00

Remington Model Seven LSS

Similar to Model Seven except has satin-finished, brown laminated stock, stainless steel 20" barrel and receiver. Overall length, 39-1/4", weighs 6-1/2 lbs. Chambered for 22-250, 243, 7mm-08 Rem. Introduced 2000.
Price: $633.00

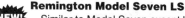

Remington Model Seven LS

Similar to Model Seven except has satin-finished, brown laminated stock with 20" carbon steel barrel. Introduced 2000.
Price: $633.00

Remington Model Seven SS

Similar to the Model Seven except has stainless steel barreled action and black synthetic stock, 20" barrel. Chambered for 223, 243, 260 Rem., 7mm-08, 308. Introduced 1994.
Price: $681.00

Remington Model Seven Custom MS Rifle

Similar to the Model Seven except has full-length Mannlicher-style stock of laminated wood with straight comb, solid black recoil pad, black steel forend tip, cut checkering, gloss finish. Barrel length 20", weighs 6-3/4 lbs. Available in 222 Rem., 223, 22-250, 243, 6mm Rem., 260 Rem., 7mm-08 Rem., 308, 350 Rem. Mag. Calibers 250 Savage, 257 Roberts, 35 Rem. Polished blue finish. Introduced 1993. From Remington Custom Shop.
Price: From $1,236.00

Remington Model Seven Youth Rifle

Similar to the Model Seven except has hardwood stock with 12-3/16" length of pull and chambered for 223, 243, 260 Rem., 7mm-08. Introduced 1993.
Price: $519.00

Ruger M77RSI International Carbine

Same as the standard Model 77 except has 18" barrel, full-length International-style stock, with steel forend cap, loop-type steel sling swivels. Integral-base receiver, open sights, Ruger 1" steel rings. Improved front sight. Available in 243, 270, 308, 30-06. Weighs 7 lbs. Length overall is 38-3/8".
Price: M77RSIMKII $713.00

RUGER M77 MARK II EXPRESS RIFLE

Caliber: 270, 30-06, 7mm Rem. Mag., 300 Win. Mag., 338 Win. Mag., 4-shot magazine (3-shot Magnum calibers). **Barrel:** 22" (std. calibers) or 24" (Magnum calibers), with integral steel rib; barrel-mounted front swivel stud; hammer forged. **Weight:** 7.5 lbs. **Length:** 42.125" overall. **Stock:** Hand-checkered circassian walnut with steel gripcap, black rubber butt pad, swivel studs. **Sights:** Ramp front, V-notch two-leaf express rear adjustable for windage mounted on rib. **Features:** Mark II action with three-position safety, stainless steel bolt, steel trigger guard, hinged steel floorplate. Introduced 1991.
Price: M77RSEXPMKII $1,695.00

RUGER 77/22 HORNET BOLT-ACTION RIFLE

Caliber: 22 Hornet, 6-shot rotary magazine. **Barrel:** 20". **Weight:** About 6 lbs. **Length:** 39-3/4" overall. **Stock:** Checkered American walnut, black rubber butt pad. **Sights:** Brass bead front, open adjustable rear; also available without sights. **Features:** Same basic features as the rimfire model except has slightly lengthened receiver. Uses Ruger rotary magazine. Three-position safety. Comes with 1" Ruger scope rings. Introduced 1994.
Price: 77/22RH (rings only) $525.00
Price: 77/22RSH (with sights) $550.00
Price: K77/22VHZ Varmint, laminated stock, no sights $575.00

RUGER M77 MARK II RIFLE

Caliber: 223, 220 Swift, 22-250, 243, 6mm Rem., 257 Roberts, 25-06, 6.5x55 Swedish, 270, 7x57mm, 260 Rem., 280 Rem., 308, 30-06, 7mm Rem. Mag., 300 Win. Mag., 338 Win. Mag., 4-shot magazine. **Barrel:** 20", 22"; 24" (magnums). **Weight:** About 7 lbs. **Length:** 39-3/4" overall. **Stock:** Hand-checkered American walnut; swivel studs, rubber butt pad. **Sights:** None furnished. Receiver has Ruger integral scope mount base, comes with Ruger 1" rings. Some models have iron sights. **Features:** Short action with new trigger and three-position safety. New trigger guard with redesigned floorplate latch. Left-hand model available. Introduced 1989.
Price: M77RMKII (no sights) $634.00
Price: M77RSMKII (open sights) $713.00
Price: M77LRMKII (left-hand, 270, 30-06, 7mm Rem. Mag.,300 Win. Mag.)
. . . . $634.00

Ruger M77 Mark II All-Weather Stainless Rifle

Similar to the wood-stock M77 Mark II except all metal parts are of stainless steel, and has an injection-moulded, glass-fiber-reinforced Du Pont Zytel stock. Also offered with laminated wood stock. Chambered for 223, 243, 270, 308, 30-06, 7mm Rem. Mag., 300 Win. Mag., 338 Win. Mag. Has the fixed-blade-type ejector, three-position safety, and new trigger guard with patented floorplate latch. Comes with integral Scope Base Receiver and 1" Ruger scope rings, built-in sling swivel loops. Introduced 1990.

RIFLES

Ruger M77 Mark II All-Weather

Ruger 77/44

Ruger M77VT Target

Sako TRG-S

Price: K77RPMKII. **$604.00**
Price: K77RLPMKII Ultra-Light, synthetic stock, rings, no sights . . **$604.00**
Price: K77LRBBZMKII, left-hand bolt, rings, no sights, laminated
stock **$673.00**
Price: K77RSPMKII, synthetic stock, open sights **$672.00**
Price: K77RBZMKII, no sights, laminated wood stock, 223, 22/250, 243,
270, 280 Rem., 7mm Rem. Mag., 30-06, 308, 300 Win. Mag., 338
Win. Mag. **$673.00**
Price: K77RSBZMKII, open sights, laminated wood stock, 243, 270,
7mm Rem. Mag., 30-06, 300 Win. Mag., 338 Win. Mag. **$740.00**

Ruger M77RL Ultra Light

Similar to the standard M77 except weighs only 6 lbs., chambered for
223, 243, 308, 270, 30-06, 257 Roberts; barrel tapped for target scope
blocks; has 20" Ultra Light barrel. Overall length 40". Ruger's steel 1"
scope rings supplied. Introduced 1983.
Price: M77RLMKII **$677.00**

RUGER M77 MARK II MAGNUM RIFLE

Caliber: 375 H&H, 4-shot magazine; 416 Rigby, 3-shot magazine. **Barrel:**
23", with integral steel rib; hammer forged. **Weight:** 9.25 lbs. (375); 9-3/4
lbs. (416, Rigby). **Length:** 40.5" overall. **Stock:** Circassian walnut with
hand-cut checkering, swivel studs, steel gripcap, rubber butt pad. **Sights:**
Ramp front, two leaf express on serrated integral steel rib. Rib also serves
as base for front scope ring. **Features:** Uses an enlarged Mark II action
with three-position safety, stainless bolt, steel trigger guard and hinged
steel floorplate. Controlled feed. Introduced 1989.
Price: M77RSMMKII **$1,695.00**

RUGER 77/44 BOLT-ACTION RIFLE

Caliber: 44 Magnum, 4-shot magazine. **Barrel:** 18-1/2". **Weight:** 6 lbs.
Length: 38-1/4" overall. **Stock:** American walnut with rubber butt pad and
swivel studs or black polymer (stainless only). **Sights:** Gold bead front,
folding leaf rear. Comes with Ruger 1" scope rings. **Features:** Uses same
action as the Ruger 77/22. Short bolt stroke; rotary magazine; three-position safety. Introduced 1997. Made in U.S. by Sturm, Ruger & Co.
Price: Blue, walnut, 77/44RS **$580.00**
Price: Stainless, polymer, stock, K77/44RS **$580.00**

RUGER M77VT TARGET RIFLE

Caliber: 22-250, 220 Swift, 223, 243, 25-06, 308. **Barrel:** 26" heavy stainless steel with target gray finish. **Weight:** 9-3/4 lbs. **Length:** Approx. 44"
overall. **Stock:** Laminated American hardwood with beavertail forend,
steel swivel studs; no checkering or gripcap. **Sights:** Integral scope mount
bases in receiver. **Features:** Ruger diagonal bedding system. Ruger steel
1" scope rings supplied. Fully adjustable trigger. Steel floorplate and trigger guard. New version introduced 1992.
Price: K77VTMKII **$759.00**

SAKO TRG-S BOLT-ACTION RIFLE

Caliber: 243, 7mm-08, 270, 6.5x55, 30-06, 7mm Rem. Mag., 300 Win.
Mag., 338 Win. Mag., 270 Wea. Mag., 7mm Wea. Mag., 340 Wea. Mag.,
375 H&H, 416 Rem. Mag., 5-shot magazine (4-shot for 375 H&H). **Barrel:**
22", 24" (magnum calibers). **Weight:** 7.75 lbs. **Length:** 45.5" overall.
Stock: Reinforced polyurethane with Monte Carlo comb. **Sights:** None
furnished. **Features:** Resistance-free bolt with 60-degree lift. Recoil pad
adjustable for length. Free-floating barrel, detachable magazine, fully adjustable trigger. Matte blue metal. Introduced 1993. Imported from Finland
by Stoeger.
Price: 243, 7mm-08, 270, 30-06 . . . . **$854.00**
Price: Magnum calibers **$894.00**

SAKO 75 HUNTER BOLT-ACTION RIFLE

Caliber: 22-250, 243, 7MM-08, 308 Win., 25-06, 270, 280, 30-06; 270 Wea.
Mag., 7mm Rem. Mag., 7mm STW, 7mm Wea. Mag., 300 Win. Mag., 300
Wea. Mag., 338 Win. Mag., 340 Wea. Mag., 375 H&H, 416 Rem. Mag.
Barrel: 22", standard calibers; 24", 26" magnum calibers. **Weight:** About
6 lbs. **Length:** NA. **Stock:** European walnut with matte lacquer finish.
Sights: None furnished; dovetail scope mount rails. **Features:** New de-
sign with three locking lugs and a mechanical ejector; key locks firing pin
and bolt; cold hammer-forged barrel is free-floating; two-position safety;

CENTERFIRE RIFLES — BOLT ACTION

Sako 75 Hunter

Sako 75 Deluxe

Sako 75 Stainless Hunter

Sako 75 Varmint

hinged floorplate or detachable magazine that can be loaded from the top; short 70 degree bolt lift. Available in five action lengths. Introduced 1997. Imported from Finland by Stoeger Industries.

Price: Standard calibers **$1,184.00**
Price: Magnum Calibers **$1,219.00**

Sako 75 Stainless Synthetic Rifle

Similar to the 75 Hunter except all metal is of stainless steel, and the synthetic stock has soft composite panels moulded into the forend and pistol grip. Available in 22-250, 243, 308 Win., 25-06, 270, 30-06 with 22" barrel, 7mm Rem. Mag., 300 Win. Mag. with 24" barrel. Introduced 1997. Imported from Finland by Stoeger Industries.

Price: Standard calibers **$1,284.00**
Price: Magnum calibers **$1,314.00**

Sako 75 Deluxe Rifle

Similar to the 75 Hunter except has select wood rosewood gripcap and forend tip. Available in 25-06, 270, 280, 30-06; 270 Wea. Mag., 7mm Rem. Mag., 7mm STW, 7mm Wea. Mag., 300 Win. Mag., 300 Wea. Mag., 338 Win. Mag., 340 Wea. Mag., 375 H&H, 416 Rem. Mag. Introduced 1997. Imported from Finland by Stoeger Industries.

Price: Standard calibers **$1,724.00**
Price: Magnum calibers **$1,754.00**

Sako 75 Stainless Hunter Rifle

Similar to the Sako 75 Hunter except all metal is of stainless steel. Comes with walnut stock with matte lacquer finish, rubber butt pad. Introduced 1999. Imported from Finland by Stoeger Industries.

Price: 270, 30-06 . . . . **$1,284.00**
Price: 7mm Rem. Mag., 7mm STW, 300 Win. Mag., 300 Wea. Mag., 338 Win. Mag. **$1,314.00**

Sako 75 Varmint Stainless Laminated Rifle

Similar to the Sako 75 Hunter except chambered only for 222, 223, 22-250, 22 PPC USA, 6 PPC USA; has heavy 24" barrel with recessed crown; all metal is of stainless steel; has laminated wood stock with beavertail forend. Introduced 1999. Imported from Finland by Stoeger Industries.

Price: **$1,459.00**

Sako 75 Varmint Rifle

Similar to the Model 75 Hunter except chambered only for 17 Rem., 222 Rem., 223 Rem., 22-250 Rem.; 24" heavy barrel with recessed crown; beavertail forend. Introduced 1998. Imported from Finland by Stoeger Industries.

Price: **$1,364.00**

SAUER 202 BOLT-ACTION RIFLE

Caliber: Standard—243, 6.5x55, 270 Win., 308 Win., 30-06; magnum— 7mm Rem. Mag., 300 Win. Mag., 300 Wea. Mag., 375 H&H. **Barrel:** 23.6" (standard), 26" (magnum). **Weight:** 7.7 lbs. (standard). **Length:** 44.3" overall (23.6" barrel). **Stock:** Select American Claro walnut with high-gloss epoxy finish, rosewood grip and forend caps; 22 lpi checkering. Synthetic also available. **Sights:** None furnished; drilled and tapped for scope mounting. **Features:** Short 60" bolt throw; detachable box magazine; six-lug bolt; quick-change barrel; tapered bore; adjustable two-stage trigger; firing pin cocking indicator. Introduced 1994. Imported from Germany by Sigarms, Inc.

Price: Standard calibers, right-hand **$1,035.00**
Price: Magnum calibers, right-hand **$1,106.00**
Price: Standard calibers, synthetic stock **$985.00**
Price: Magnum calibers, synthetic stock **$1,056.00**

SAVAGE MODEL 110GXP3, 110GCXP3 PACKAGE GUNS

Caliber: 223, 22-250, 243, 25-06, 270, 300 Sav., 30-06, 308, 7mm Rem. Mag., 7mm-08, 300 Win. Mag. (Model 110GXP3); 270, 30-06, 7mm Rem. Mag., 300 Win. Mag. (Model 110GCXP3). **Barrel:** 22" (standard calibers), 24" (magnum calibers). **Weight:** 7.25-7.5 lbs. **Length:** 43.5" overall (22" barrel). **Stock:** Monte Carlo-style hardwood with walnut finish, rubber butt pad, swivel studs. **Sights:** None furnished. **Features:** Model 110GXP3 has fixed, top-loading magazine, Model 110GCXP3 has detachable box magazine. Rifles come with a factory-mounted and bore-sighted 3-9x32 scope, rings and bases, quick-detachable swivels, sling. Left-hand models available in all calibers. Introduced 1991 (GXP3); 1994 (GCXP3). Made in U.S. by Savage Arms, Inc.

Price: Model 110GXP3, right- or left-hand **$513.00**
Price: Model 110GCXP3, right- or left-hand **$513.00**

Savage Model 111FXP3, 111FCXP3 Package Guns

Similar to the Model 110 Series Package Guns except with lightweight, black graphite/fiberglass composite stock with non-glare finish, positive

Savage Model 10FM

Savage Model 10FP

Savage Model 11F

Savage Model 11G

checkering. Same calibers as Model 110 rifles, plus 338 Win. Mag. Model 111FXP3 has fixed top-loading magazine; Model 111FCXP3 has detachable box. Both come with mounted 3-9x32 scope, quick-detachable swivels, sling. Introduced 1994. Made in U.S. by Savage Arms, Inc.

Price: Model 111FXP3, right- or left-hand **$476.00**
Price: Model 111FCXP3, right- or left-hand **$525.00**

SAVAGE MODEL 110FM SIERRA ULTRA LIGHT WEIGHT RIFLE

Caliber: 243, 270, 308, 30-06. **Barrel:** 20". **Weight:** 6-1/4 lbs. **Length:** 41-1/2" overall. **Stock:** Graphite/fiberglass-filled composite. **Sights:** None furnished; drilled and tapped for scope mounting. **Features:** Comes with black nylon sling and quick-detachable swivels. Introduced 1996. Made in U.S. by Savage Arms, Inc.

Price: **$449.00**

Savage Model 10FM Sierra Ultra Light Rifle

Similar to the Model 110FM Sierra except has a true short action, chambered for 223, 243, 308; weighs 6 lbs. "Dual Pillar" bedding in black synthetic stock with silver medallion in gripcap. Comes with sling and quick-detachable swivels. Introduced 1998. Made in U.S. by Savage Arms, Inc.

Price: **$449.00**

SAVAGE MODEL 110FP TACTICAL RIFLE

Caliber: 223, 25-06, 308, 30-06, 300 Win. Mag., 7mm Rem. Mag., 4-shot magazine. **Barrel:** 24", heavy; recessed target muzzle. **Weight:** 8-1/2 lbs. **Length:** 45.5" overall. **Stock:** Black graphite/fiberglass composition; positive checkering. **Sights:** None furnished. Receiver drilled and tapped for scope mounting. **Features:** Pillar-bedded stock. Black matte finish on all metal parts. Double swivel studs on the forend for sling and/or bipod mount. Right or left-hand. Introduced 1990. From Savage Arms, Inc.

Price: Right- or left-hand **$476.00**

Savage Model 10FP Tactical Rifle

Similar to the Model 110FP except has true short action, chambered for 223, 308; black synthetic stock with "Dual Pillar" bedding. Introduced 1998. Made in U.S. by Savage Arms, Inc.

Price: **$476.00**
Price: Model 10FLP (left-hand) **$476.00**

SAVAGE MODEL 111 CLASSIC HUNTER RIFLES

Caliber: 223, 22-250, 243, 250 Sav., 25-06, 270, 300 Sav., 30-06, 308, 7mm Rem. Mag., 7mm-08, 300 Win. Mag., 338 Win. Mag. (Models 111G, GL, GNS, F, FL, FNS); 270, 30-06, 7mm Rem. Mag., 300 Win. Mag. (Models 111GC, GLC, FAK, FC, FLC). **Barrel:** 22", 24" (magnum calibers). **Weight:** 6.3 to 7 lbs. **Length:** 43.5" overall (22" barrel). **Stock:** Walnut-finished hardwood (M111G, GC); graphite/fiberglass filled composite. **Sights:** Ramp front, open fully adjustable rear; drilled and tapped for scope mounting. **Features:** Three-position top tang safety, double front locking lugs, free-floated button-rifled barrel. Comes with trigger lock, target, ear puffs. Introduced 1994. Made in U.S. by Savage Arms, Inc.

Price: Model 111FC (detachable magazine, composite stock, right- or left-hand) **$445.00**
Price: Model 111F (top-loading magazine, composite stock, right- or left-hand) **$419.00**
Price: Model 111FNS (as above, no sights, right-hand only) **$411.00**
Price: Model 111G (wood stock, top-loading magazine, right- or left-hand) **$395.00**
Price: Model 111GC (as above, detachable magazine), right- or left-hand **$433.00**
Price: Model 111GNS (wood stock, top-loading magzine, no sights, right-hand only) **$389.00**
Price: Model 111FAK Express (blued, composite stock, top loading magazine, Adjustable muzzle brake) . . . . **NA**

Savage Model 11 Hunter Rifles

Similar to the Model 111F except has true short action, chambered for 223, 22-250, 243, 308; black synthetic stock with "Dual Pillar" bedding, positive checkering. Introduced 1998. Made in U.S. by Savage Arms, Inc.

Price: Model 11F **$419.00**
Price: Model 11FL (left-hand) **$419.00**
Price: Model 11FNS (right-hand, no sights) **$411.00**
Price: Model 11G (wood stock) **$395.00**
Price: Model 11GL (as above, left-hand) **$395.00**
Price: Model 11GNS (wood stock, no sights) **$389.00**

RIFLES

Savage Model 10GY

Savage Model 114CE

Savage Model 12FV

Savage Model 10GY, 110GY Rifle

Similar to the Model 111G except weighs 6.3 lbs., is 42-1/2" overall, and the stock is scaled for ladies, small-framed adults and youths. Chambered for 223, 243, 270, 308. Ramp front sight, open adjustable rear; drilled and tapped for scope mounts. Made in U.S. by Savage Arms, Inc.
Price: Model 110GY **$395.00**
Price: Model 10GY (short action, calibers 223, 243, 308) **$395.00**

SAVAGE MODEL 114C CLASSIC RIFLE

Caliber: 270, 30-06, 7mm Rem. Mag., 300 Win. Mag.; 4-shot detachable box magazine in standard calibers, 3-shot for magnums. **Barrel:** 22" for standard calibers, 24" for magnums. **Weight:** 7-1/8 lbs. **Length:** 45-1/2" overall. **Stock:** Oil-finished American walnut; checkered grip and forend. **Sights:** None furnished; drilled and tapped for scope mounting. **Features:** High polish blue on barrel, receiver and bolt handle; Savage logo laser-etched on bolt body; push-button magazine release. Introduced 1996. Made in U.S. by Savage Arms, Inc.
Price: **$556.00**

Savage Model 114CE Classic European

Similar to the Model 114C except the oil-finished walnut stock has a Schnabel forend tip, cheekpiece and skip-line checkering; bead on blade front sight, fully adjustable open rear; solid red butt pad. Chambered for 270, 30-06, 7mm Rem. Mag., 300 Win. Mag. Introduced 1996. Made in U.S. by Savage Arms, Inc.
Price: **$635.00**

Savage Model 114U Ultra Rifle

Similar to the Model 114C except has high-luster blued finish, high-gloss walnut stock with custom cut checkering, ebony tip. No sights; drilled and tapped for scope. Chambered for 270, 30-06, 7mm Rem. Mag., 7mm STW and 300 Win.
Price: **$504.00**

SAVAGE MODEL 112 LONG RANGE RIFLES

Caliber: 22-250, 223, 5-shot magazine. **Barrel:** 26" heavy. **Weight:** 8.8 lbs. **Length:** 47.5" overall. **Stock:** Black graphite/fiberglass filled composite with positive checkering. **Sights:** None furnished; drilled and tapped for scope mounting. **Features:** Pillar-bedded stock. Blued barrel with recessed target-style muzzle. Double front swivel studs for attaching bipod. Introduced 1991. Made in U.S. by Savage Arms, Inc.
Price: Model 112FVSS (cals. 223, 22-250, 25-06, 7mm Rem. Mag., 300 Win. Mag., stainless barrel, bolt handle, trigger guard), right- or left-hand **$549.00**
Price: Model 112FVSS-S (as above, single shot) **$549.00**

Price: Model 112BVSS (heavy-prone laminated stock with high comb, Wundhammer swell, fluted stainless barrel, bolt handle, trigger guard) **$575.00**
Price: Model 112BVSS-S (as above, single shot) **$575.00**

Savage Model 12 Long Range Rifles

Similar to the Model 112 Long Range except with true short action, chambered for 223, 22-250, 308. Models 12FV, 12FVSS have black synthetic stocks with "Dual Pillar" bedding, positive checkering, swivel studs; model 12BVSS has brown laminated stock with beavertail forend, fluted stainless barrel. Introduced 1998. Made in U.S. by Savage Arms, Inc.
Price: Model 12FV (223, 22-250 only, blue) **$455.00**
Price: Model 12FVSS (blue action, fluted stainless barrel) **$549.00**
Price: Model 12FLVSS (as above, left-hand) **$549.00**
Price: Model 12FVSS-S (blue action, fluted stainless barrel, single shot) **$549.00**
Price: Model 12BVSS (laminated stock) **$575.00**
Price: Model 12BVSS-S (as above, single shot) **$575.00**

Savage Model 12VSS Varminter Rifle

Similar to other Model 12s except has blue/stainless steel action, fluted stainless barrel, Choate full pistol-grip, adjustable synthetic stock and Sharp Shooter trigger. Overall length 47-1/2 inches, weighs about 15 pounds. No sights; drilled and tapped for scope mounts. Chambered in 223 and 22-250. Made in U.S. by Savage Arms Inc.
Price: **$852.00**

SAVAGE MODEL 116SE SAFARI EXPRESS RIFLE

Caliber: 300 Win. Mag., 338 Win. Mag., 375 H&H, 458 Win. Mag. **Barrel:** 24". **Weight:** 8.5 lbs. **Length:** 45.5" overall. **Stock:** Classic-style select walnut with ebony forend tip, deluxe cut checkering. Two cross bolts; internally vented recoil pad. **Sights:** Bead on ramp front, three-leaf express rear. **Features:** Controlled-round feed design; adjustable muzzle brake; one-piece barrel band stud. Satin-finished stainless steel barreled action. Introduced 1994. Made in U.S. by Savage Arms, Inc.
Price: **$925.00**

SAVAGE MODEL 116 WEATHER WARRIORS

Caliber: 223, 243, 270, 30-06, 7mm Rem. Mag., 300 Win. Mag., 338 Win. Mag. (Model 116FSS); 270, 30-06, 7mm Rem. Mag., 300 Win. Mag. (Models 116FCSAK, 116FCS); 270, 30-06, 7mm Rem. Mag., 300 Win. Mag., 338 Win. Mag. (Models 116FSAK, 116FSK). **Barrel:** 22", 24" for 7mm Rem. Mag., 300 Win. Mag., 338 Win. Mag. (M116FSS only). **Weight:** 6.25 to 6.5 lbs. **Length:** 43.5" overall (22" barrel). **Stock:** Graphite/fiberglass filled composite. **Sights:** None furnished; drilled and tapped for scope mounting. **Features:** Stainless steel with matte finish; free-floated barrel; quick-detachable swivel studs; laser-etched bolt; scope bases and rings. Left-hand models available in all models, calibers at same price. Models

RIFLES

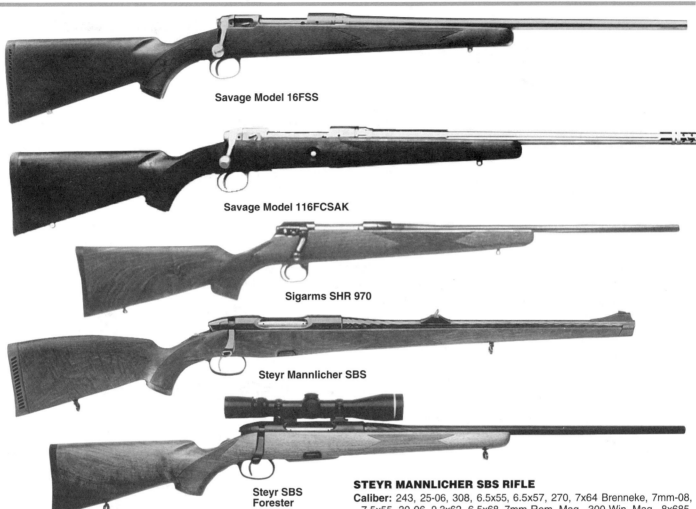

Savage Model 16FSS

Savage Model 116FCSAK

Sigarms SHR 970

Steyr Mannlicher SBS

Steyr SBS Forester

116FCS, 116FSS introduced 1991; Model 116FSK introduced 1993; Model 116FCSAK, 116FSAK introduced 1994. Made in U.S. by Savage Arms, Inc.
Price: Model 116FSS (top-loading magazine) $528.00
Price: Model 116FCS (detachable box magazine) . . . . **NA**
Price: Model 116FCSAK (as above with Savage Adjustable Muzzle Brake
system) **$668.00**
Price: Model 116FSAK (top-loading magazine, Savage Adjustable Muzzle
Brake system) **$602.00**
Price: Model 116FSK Kodiak (as above with 22" Shock-Suppressor
barrel) **$569.00**

Savage Model 16FSS Rifle

Similar to the Model 116FSS except has true short action, chambered for 223, 243, 308; 22" free-floated barrel; black graphite/fiberglass stock with "Dual Pillar" bedding. Introduced 1998. Made in U.S. by Savage Arms, Inc.
Price: $528.00
Price: Model 16FLSS (left-hand) $528.00

SIGARMS SHR 970 SYNTHETIC RIFLE

Caliber: 270, 30-06. **Barrel:** 22". **Weight:** 7.2 lbs. **Length:** 41.9" overall. **Stock:** Textured black fiberglass or walnut. **Sights:** None furnished; drilled and tapped for scope mounting. **Features:** Quick takedown; interchangeable barrels; removable box magazine; cocking indicator; three-position safety. Introduced 1998. Imported by Sigarms, Inc.
Price: Synthetic stock $499.00
Price: Walnut stock $550.00

STEYR MANNLICHER SBS RIFLE

Caliber: 243, 25-06, 308, 6.5x55, 6.5x57, 270, 7x64 Brenneke, 7mm-08, 7.5x55, 30-06, 9.3x62, 6.5x68, 7mm Rem. Mag., 300 Win. Mag., 8x685, 4-shot magazine. **Barrel:** 23.6" standard; 26" magnum; 20" full stock standard calibers. **Weight:** 7 lbs. **Length:** 40.1" overall. **Stock:** Hand-checkered fancy European oiled walnut with standard forend. **Sights:** Ramp front adjustable for elevation, V-notch rear adjustable for windage. **Features:** Single adjustable trigger; 3-position roller safety with "safe-bolt" setting; drilled and tapped for Steyr factory scope mounts. Introduced 1997. Imported from Austria by GSI, Inc.
Price: Half-stock, standard calibers **$2,795.00**
Price: Half-stock, magnum calibers **$2,995.00**
Price: Full-stock, standard calibers **$2,995.00**

STEYR SBS FORESTER RIFLE

Caliber: 243, 25-06, 270, 7mm-08, 308 Win., 30-06, 7mm Rem. Mag., 300 Win. Mag. Detachable 4-shot magazine. **Barrel:** 23.6", standard calibers; 25.6", magnum calibers. **Weight:** 7.5 lbs. **Length:** 44.5" overall (23.6" barrel). **Stock:** Oil-finished American walnut with Monte Carlo cheekpiece. Pachmayr 1" swivels. **Sights:** None furnished. Drilled and tapped for Browning A-Bolt mounts. **Features:** Steyr Safe Bolt systems, three-position ambidextrous roller tang safety, for Safe, Loading Fire. Matte finish on barrel and receiver; adjustable trigger. Rotary cold-hammer forged barrel. Introduced 1997. Imported by GSI, Inc.
Price: Standard calibers **$899.00**
Price: Magnum calibers **$1,045.00**

Steyr SBS Prohunter Rifle

Similar to the SBS Forester except has ABS synthetic stock with adjustable butt spacers, straight comb without cheekpiece, palm swell, Pachmayr 1" swivels. **Features:** Special 10-round magazine conversion kit available. Introduced 1997. Imported by GSI.
Price Standard calibers $799.00
Price Magnum calibers $899.00

RIFLES

Steyr SBS Prohunter

Steyr Scout Rifle

Tikka Whitetail Hunter

Tikka Whitetail Hunter Stainless Synthetic

Tikka Varmint

STEYR SCOUT BOLT-ACTION RIFLE

Caliber: 308 Win., 5-shot magazine. **Barrel:** 19", fluted. **Weight:** NA. **Length:** NA. **Stock:** Gray Zytel. **Sights:** None furnished; comes with Leupold M8 2.5x28 IER scope on Picatinny optic rail with Steyr mounts. **Features:** Comes with luggage case, scout sling, two stock spacers, two magazines. Introduced 1998. From GSI.
Price: From **$2,699.00**

STEYR SSG BOLT-ACTION RIFLE

Caliber: 308 Win., detachable 5-shot rotary magazine. **Barrel:** 26" **Weight:** 8.5 lbs. **Length:** 44.5" overall. **Stock:** Black ABS Cycolac with spacers for length of pull adjustment. **Sights:** Hooded ramp front adjustable for elevation, V-notch rear adjustable for windage. **Features:** Sliding safety; NATO rail for bipod; 1" swivels; Parkerized finish; single or double-set triggers. Imported from Austria by GSI, Inc.
Price: SSG-PI, iron sights. **$1,699.00**
Price: SSG-PII, heavy barrel, no sights **$1,699.00**
Price: SSG-PIIK, 20" heavy barrel, no sights **$1,699.00**
Price: SSG-PIV, 16.75" threaded heavy barrel with flash hider . **$2,659.00**

TIKKA WHITETAIL HUNTER BOLT-ACTION RIFLE

Caliber: 22-250, 223, 243, 7mm-08, 25-06, 270, 308, 30-06, 7mm Rem. Mag., 300 Win. Mag., 338 Win. Mag. **Barrel:** 22-1/2" (std. cals.), 24-1/2" (magnum cals.). **Weight:** 7-1/8 lbs. **Length:** 43" overall (std. cals.). **Stock:** European walnut with Monte Carlo comb, rubber butt pad, checkered grip and forend. **Sights:** None furnished. **Features:** Detachable four-shot magazine (standard calibers), three-shot in magnums. Receiver dovetailed for scope mounting. Reintroduced 1996. Imported from Finland by Stoeger Industries.
Price: Standard calibers **$609.00**
Price: Magnum calibers **$639.00**

Tikka Continental Varmint Rifle

Similar to the standard Tikka rifle except has 26" heavy barrel, extra-wide forend. Chambered for 22-250, 223, 308. Reintroduced 1996. Made in Finland by Sako. Imported by Stoeger.
Price: **$709.00**

Tikka Whitetail Hunter Deluxe Rifle

Similar to the Whitetail Hunter except has select walnut stock with rollover Monte Carlo comb, rosewood grip cap and forend tip. Has adjustable trigger, detachable magazine, free-floating barrel. Same calibers as the Hunter. Introduced 1999. Imported from Finland by Stoeger Industries.
Price: Standard calibers **$734.00**
Price: Magnum calibers **$764.00**

Tikka Whitetail Hunter Synthetic Rifle

Similar to the Whitetail Hunter except has black synthetic stock; calibers 223, 308, 25-06, 270 Win., 30-06, 7mm Rem. Mag., 300 Win. Mag., 338 Win. Mag. Introduced 1996. Imported from Finland by Stoeger.
Price: Standard calibers **$609.00**
Price: Magnum calibers **$639.00**

RIFLES

Weatherby Mark V Lazermark

Weatherby Mark V Euromark

Weatherby Mark V Stainless

Tikka Continental Long Range Hunting Rifle

Similar to the Whitetail Hunter except has 26" heavy barrel. Available in 25-06, 270 Win., 7mm Rem. Mag., 300 Win. Mag. Introduced 1996. Imported from Finland by Stoeger.

Price: 25-06, 270 Win. **$709.00**
Price: 7 Rem. Mag., 300 Win. Mag. **$739.00**

Tikka Whitetail Hunter Stainless Synthetic

Similar to the Whitetail Hunter except all metal is of stainless steel, and it has a black synthetic stock. Available in 22-250, 243, 25-06, 308, 30-06, 7mm Rem. Mag., 300 Win. Mag., 338 Win. Mag. Introduced 1997. Imported from Finland by Stoeger.

Price: Standard calibers **$669.00**
Price: Magnum calibers **$699.00**

VEKTOR BUSHVELD BOLT-ACTION RIFLE

Caliber: 243, 308, 7x57, 7x64 Brenneke, 270 Win., 30-06, 300 Win. Mag., 300 H&H, 9.3x62. **Barrel:** 22"-26". **Weight:** NA. **Length:** NA. **Stock:** Turkish walnut with wrap-around hand checkering. **Sights:** Blade on ramp front, fixed standing leaf rear. **Features:** Combines the best features of the Mauser 98 and Winchester 70 actions. Controlled-round feed; Mauser-type extractor; no cut-away through the bolt locking lug; M70-type three-position safety; Timney-type adjustable trigger. Introduced 1999. Imported from South Africa by Vektor USA.

Price: . . . . **$1,595.00 to $1,695.00**

VEKTOR MODEL 98 BOLT-ACTION RIFLE

Caliber: 243, 308, 7x57, 7x64 Brenneke, 270 Win., 30-06, 300 Win. Mag., 300 H&H, 375 H&H, 9.3x62. **Barrel:** 22"-26". **Weight:** NA. **Length:** NA. **Stock:** Turkish walnut with hand-checkered grip and forend. **Sights:** None furnished; drilled and tapped for scope mounting. **Features:** Bolt has guide rib; non-rotating, long extractor enhances positive feeding; polished blue finish. Updated Mauser 98 action. Introduced 1999. Imported from South Africa by Vektor USA.

Price: . . . . **$1,149.00 to $1,249.00**

WEATHERBY MARK V DELUXE BOLT-ACTION RIFLE

Caliber: All Weatherby calibers plus 22-250, 243, 25-06, 270 Win., 280 Rem., 7mm-08, 308 Win. **Barrel:** 26" round tapered. **Weight:** 8-1/2 to 10-1/2 lbs. **Length:** 46-5/8" to 46-3/4" overall. **Stock:** Walnut, Monte Carlo with cheekpiece; high luster finish; checkered pistol grip and forend; recoil pad. **Sights:** None furnished. **Features:** Cocking indicator; adjustable trigger; hinged floorplate, thumb safety; quick detachable sling swivels. Made in U.S. From Weatherby.

Price: 257, 270, 7mm. 300, 340 Wea. Mags., 26" barrel **$1,649.00**
Price: 416 Wea. Mag. with Accubrake, 26" barrel **$1,931.00**
Price: 460 Wea. Mag. with Accubrake, 26" barrel **$2,259.00**

Weatherby Mark V Lazermark Rifle

Same as Mark V Deluxe except stock has extensive oak leaf pattern laser carving on pistol grip and forend. Introduced 1981.

Price: 257, 270, 7mm Wea. Mag., 300, 340, 26" **$1,799.00**
Price: 378 Wea. Mag., 26" **$2,097.00**
Price: 416 Wea. Mag., 26", Accubrake. **$2,097.00**
Price: 460 Wea. Mag., 26", Accubrake. **$2,464.00**

Weatherby Mark V Sporter Rifle

Same as the Mark V Deluxe without the embellishments. Metal has low-luster blue, stock is Claro walnut with high-gloss epoxy finish, Monte Carlo comb, recoil pad. Introduced 1993.

Price: 257, 270, 7mm, 300, 340 Wea. Mags., 26" **$1,049.00**
Price: 375 H&H, 24" **$1,049.00**
Price: 7mm Rem. Mag., 300 Win. Mag., 338 Win. Mag., 24", . . **$1,049.00**

Weatherby Mark V Euromark Rifle

Similar to the Mark V Deluxe except has raised-comb Monte Carlo stock with hand-rubbed oil finish, fine-line hand-cut checkering, ebony grip and forend tips. All metal has low-luster blue. Right-hand only. Uses Mark V action. Introduced 1995. Made in U.S. From Weatherby.

Price: 257, 270, 7mm, 300, 340 Wea. Mags., 26" barrel **$1,049.00**
Price: 7mm Rem. Mag., 300 Win. Mag., 338 Win. Mag.,
375 H&H, 24" barrel **$1,049.00**

Weatherby Mark V Stainless Rifle

Similar to the Mark V Deluxe except made of 400-series stainless steel. Also available in 30-378 Wea. Mag. Has lightweight injection-moulded synthetic stock with raised Monte Carlo comb, checkered grip and forend, custom floorplate release. Right-hand only. Introduced 1995. Made in U.S. From Weatherby.

Price: 257, 270, 7mm, 300, 340 Wea. Mags., 26" barrel **$999.00**
Price: 7mm Rem. Mag., 300, 338 Win. Mags., 24" barrel **$999.00**
Price: 375 H&H, 24" barrel **$999.00**
Price: 30-378 Wea. Mag. **$1,149.00**

Weatherby
Mark V Synthetic

Weatherby Accumark

Weatherby Accumark Lightweight

Weatherby Mark V SLS Stainless Laminate Sporter

Similar to the Mark V Stainless except all metalwork is 400 series stainless with a corrosion-resistant black oxide bead-blast matte finish. Action is hand-bedded in a laminated stock with a 1" recoil pad. Weighs 8-1/2 lbs. Introduced 1997. Made in U.S. From Weatherby.
Price: 257, 270, 7mm, 300, 340 Wea. Mag., 26" barrel **$1,299.00**
Price: 7mm Rem. Mag., 300 Win. Mag., 338 Win. Mag., 24" barrel
. . . . **$1,299.00**

Weatherby Mark V Eurosport Rifle

Similar to the Mark V Deluxe except has raised-comb Monte Carlo stock with hand-rubbed satin oil finish, low-luster blue metal. No gripcap or forend tip. Right-hand only. Introduced 1995. Made in U.S. From Weatherby.
Price: 257, 270, 7mm, 300, 340 Wea. Mags., 26" barrel **$1,049.00**
Price: 7mm Rem. Mag., 300, 338 Win. Mags., 24" barrel **$1,049.00**
Price: 375 H&H, 24" barrel **$1,049.00**

WEATHERBY MARK V SPORTER BOLT ACTION RIFLE

Caliber: 22-250, 243, 25-06, 270, 7MM-08, 280, 30-06, 308, 240 Wea. Mag. **Barrel:** 24". **Weight:** 6-3/4 lbs. **Length:** 44" overall. **Stock:** Claro walnut. Monte Carlo with cheekpiece; high luster finish, checkered pistol grip and forend, recoil pad. **Sights:** None furnished. Drilled and tapped for scope mounting. **Features:** Cocking indicator; adjustable trigger; hinged floorplate; thumb safety; six locking lugs; quick detachable swivels. Introduced 1997. Made in U.S. from Weatherby.
Price: $999.00

Weatherby Mark V Stainless

Similar to the Sporter except made of 400 series stainless steel; injection moulded synthetic stock with Monte Carlo comb, checkered grip and forend. Weighs 6-1/2 lbs. Introduced 1997. Made in U.S. From Weatherby.
Price: $899.00
Price: Stainless Carbine (as above with 20" barrel, 243 Win.,
7mm-08 Rem., 308 Win.), weighs 6 lbs. $899.00

Weatherby Mark V Synthetic

Similar to the Mark V Stainless except made of matte finished blued steel. Injection moulded synthetic stock. Weighs 6-1/2 lbs., 24" barrel. Available in 22-250, 240 Wea. Mag., 243, 25-06, 270, 7mm-08, 280, 30-06, 308. Introduced 1997. Made in U.S. From Weatherby.
Price: $699.00

Weatherby Mark V Synthetic Rifle

Similar to the Mark V except has synthetic stock with raised Monte Carlo comb, dual-taper checkered forend. Low-luster blued metal. Weighs 8 lbs. Uses Mark V action. Right-hand only. Also available in 30-378 Wea. Mag. Introduced 1995. Made in U.S. From Weatherby.
Price: 257, 270, 7mm, 300, 340 Wea. Mags., 26" barrel **$799.00**
Price: 7mm Rem. Mag., 300, 338 Win. Mags., 24" barrel **$799.00**
Price: 375 H&H, 24" barrel **$799.00**

Weatherby Mark V Carbine

Similar to the Mark V Synthetic except has 20" barrel; injection moulded synthetic stock. Available in 243, 7mm-08, 308. Weighs 6 lbs.; overall length 40". Introduced 1997. Made in U.S. From Weatherby.
Price: **$699.00**

WEATHERBY MARK V SVM RIFLE

Caliber: 223, 22-250, 220 Swift, 243, 7mm-08, 308. **Barrel:** 26" fluted stainless steel. **Weight:** 8 1/2 lbs. **Length:** 46" overall. **Stock:** Free-floated barrel; aluminum bedding block; fully adjustable trigger. Introduced 2000. From Weatherby.
Price: . . . . NA

WEATHERBY MARK V ACCUMARK RIFLE

Caliber: 257, 270, 7mm, 300, 340 Wea. Mags., 338-378 Wea. Mag., 30-378 Wea. Mag., 7mm STW, 7mm Rem. Mag., 300 Win. Mag. **Barrel:** 26". **Weight:** 8-1/2 lbs. **Length:** 46-5/8" overall. **Stock:** H-S Precision Pro-Series synthetic with aluminum bedding plate. **Sights:** None furnished. Drilled and tapped for scope mounting. **Features:** Uses Mark V action with heavy-contour stainless barrel with black oxidized flutes, muzzle diameter of .705". Introduced 1996. Made in U.S. From Weatherby.
Price: $1,549.00
Price: 30-378 Wea. Mag., 338-378 Wea. Mag., 26",
Accubrake. $1,649.00
Price: Accumark Left-Hand 257, 270, 7mm, 300, 340 Wea.
Mag., 7mm Rem. Mag., 7mm STW, 300 Win. Mag. $1,449.00
Price: Accumark Left-Hand 30-378, 333-378 Wea. Mags. $1,649.00

Weatherby Mark V Accumark Ultra Light Weight Rifle

Similar to the Mark V Accumark except weighs 5-3/4 lbs.; free-floated 24" fluted barrel with recessed target crown; hand-laminated stock with CNC-machined aluminum bedding plate and faint gray "spider web" finish. Available in 257, 270, 7mm, 300 Wea. Mags., 243, 240 Wea. Mag., 25-06, 270 Win., 280 Rem., 7mm-08, 7mm Rem. Mag., 30-06, 308, 300 Win. Mag. Introduced 1998. Made in U.S. from Weatherby.
Price: $1,299.00

RIFLES

CENTERFIRE RIFLES — BOLT ACTION

Wilderness Explorer

Winchester Model 70 Classic

Winchester Model 70 Classic Stainless

Winchester Model 70 Classic Laminated

Weatherby Mark V Accumark Rifle

Similar to the Mark V Accumark except chambered for 22-250, 243, 240 Wea. Mag., 25-06, 270, 280 Rem., 7mm-08, 30-06, 308; fluted 24" heavy-contour stainless barrel; hand-laminated Monte Carlo-style stock with aluminum bedding plate. Weighs 7 lbs.; 44" overall. Introduced 1998. Made in U.S. from Weatherby.

Price: **$1,349.00**

WICHITA VARMINT RIFLE

Caliber: 222 Rem., 222 Rem. Mag., 223 Rem., 22 PPC, 6mm PPC, 22-250, 243, 6mm Rem., 308 Win.; other calibers on special order. **Barrel:** 20-1/8". **Weight:** 9 lbs. **Length:** 40-1/8" overall. **Stock:** AAA Fancy American walnut. Hand-rubbed finish, hand checkered, 20 lpi pattern. Hand-inletted, glass bedded, steel gripcap. Pachmayr rubber recoil pad. **Sights:** None. Drilled and tapped for scope mounts. **Features:** Right- or left-hand Wichita action with three locking lugs. Available as a single shot only. Checkered bolt handle. Bolt is hand fitted, lapped and jeweled. Side thumb safety. Firing pin fall is 3/16". Non-glare blue finish. From Wichita Arms.

Price: Single shot **$3,000.00**

WICHITA CLASSIC RIFLE

Caliber: 17-222, 17-222 Mag., 222 Rem., 222 Rem. Mag., 223 Rem., 6x47; other calibers on special order. **Barrel:** 21-1/8". **Weight:** 8 lbs. **Length:** 41" overall. **Stock:** AAA Fancy American walnut. Hand-rubbed and checkered (20 lpi). Hand-inletted, glass bedded, steel gripcap. Pachmayr rubber recoil pad. **Sights:** None. Drilled and tapped for scope mounting. **Features:** Available as single shot only. Octagonal barrel and Wichita action, right- or left-hand. Checkered bolt handle. Bolt is hand-fitted, lapped and jeweled. Adjustable trigger is set at 2 lbs. Side thumb safety. Firing pin fall is 3/16". Non-glare blue finish. From Wichita Arms.

Price: Single shot **$3,495.00**

WILDERNESS EXPLORER MULTI-CALIBER CARBINE

Caliber: 22 Hornet, 218 Bee, 44 Magnum, 50 A.E. (interchangeable). **Barrel:** 18", match grade. **Weight:** 5.5 lbs **Length:** 38-1/2" overall. **Stock:**

Synthetic or wood. **Sights:** None furnished; comes with Weaver-style mount on barrel. **Features:** Quick-change barrel and bolt face for caliber switch. Removable box magazine; adjustable trigger with side safety; detachable swivel studs. Introduced 1997. Made in U.S. by Phillips & Rogers, Inc.

Price: **$995.00**

WINCHESTER MODEL 70 CLASSIC SPORTER LT

Caliber: 25-06, 270 Win., 270 Wea., 30-06, 264 Win. Mag., 7mm STW, 7mm Rem. Mag., 300 Win. Mag., 300 Wea. Mag., 338 Win. Mag., 3-shot magazine; 5-shot for 25-06, 270 Win., 30-06. **Barrel:** 24", 26" for magnums. **Weight:** 7-3/4 lbs. **Length:** 44-3/4" overall. **Stock:** American walnut with cut checkering and satin finish. Classic style with straight comb. **Sights:** Optional hooded ramp front, adjustable folding leaf rear. Drilled and tapped for scope mounting. **Features:** Uses pre-64-type action with controlled round feeding. Three-position safety, stainless steel magazine follower; rubber butt pad; epoxy bedded receiver recoil lug. From U.S. Repeating Arms Co.

Price: Without sights. **$669.00**
Price: Left-hand, 270, 30-06, 7mm Rem. Mag., 7mm STW,
300 Win. Mag., 338 Win. Mag. **$669.00**

Winchester Model 70 Classic Stainless Rifle

Same as the Model 70 Classic Sporter except has stainless steel barrel and pre-64-style action with controlled round feeding and matte gray finish, black composite stock impregnated with fiberglass and graphite, contoured rubber recoil pad. Available in 22-250, 243, 308, 270 Win., 270 Wea. Mag., 30-06, 7mm Rem. Mag., 300 Win. Mag., 300 Wea. Mag., 338 Win. Mag., 375 H&H Mag. (24" barrel), 3- or 5-shot magazine. Weighs 6.75 lbs. Introduced 1994.

Price: Without sights. **$737.00**
Price: 375 H&H Mag., with sights. **$823.00**
Price: Classic Laminated Stainless (gray laminated stock,
270, 30-06, 7mm Rem. Mag., 300 Win. Mag., 338 Win. Mag.) . . **$737.00**

RIFLES

Winchester Model 70 Classic Featherweight

Winchester Model 70 Classic Compact

Winchester Model 70 Ranger

Winchester Model 70 Classic Super Grade

Winchester Model 70 Classic Featherweight

Same as the Model 70 Classic except has claw controlled-round feeding system; action is bedded in a standard-grade walnut stock. Available in 22-250, 243, 6.5x55, 308, 7mm-08, 270 Win., 280 Rem., 30-06. Drilled and tapped for scope mounts. Weighs 7.25 lbs. Introduced 1992.
Price: **$680.00**

Winchester Model 70 Classic Compact

Similar to the Classic Featherweight except scaled down for smaller shooters. Has 20" barrel, 12-1/2" length of pull. Pre-'64-type action. Available in 243, 308 or 7mm-08. Introduced 1998. Made in U.S. by U. S. Repeating Arms Co.
Price: **$680.00**

WINCHESTER RANGER RIFLE

Caliber: 223, 22-250, 243, 270, 30-06, 7mm Rem. Mag. **Barrel:** 22". **Weight:** 7-3/4 lbs. **Length:** 42" overall. **Stock:** Stained hardwood. **Sights:** Hooded blade front, adjustable open rear. **Features:** Three-position safety; push feed bolt with recessed-style bolt face; polished blue finish; drilled and tapped for scope mounting. Introduced 1985. From U.S. Repeating Arms Co.
Price: **$528.00**
Price: Ranger Compact, 22-250, 243, 7mm-08, 308 only,
scaled-down stock **$528.00**

Winchester Model 70 Black Shadow

Similar to the Ranger except has black composite stock, matte blue barrel and action. Push-feed bolt design; hinged floorplate. Available in 270, 30-06, 7mm Rem. Mag., 300 Win. Mag. Made in U.S. by U.S. Repeating Arms Co.
Price: **$491.00**

WINCHESTER MODEL 70 STEALTH RIFLE

Caliber: 223, 22-250, 308 Win. **Barrel:** 26". **Weight:** 10-3/4 lbs. **Length:** 46" overall. **Stock:** Kevlar/fiberglass/graphite Pillar Plus Accu-Block with full-length aluminum bedding block. **Sights:** None furnished. **Features:** Push-feed bolt design; matte finish. Introduced 1999. Made in U. S. by U.S. Repeating Arms Co.
Price: 223 . . . . **$737.00**
Price: 22-250, 308 Win. **$737.00**

WINCHESTER MODEL 70 CLASSIC SUPER GRADE

Caliber: 270, 30-06, 5-shot magazine; 7mm Rem. Mag., 7mm STW, 300 Win. Mag., 338 Win. Mag., 3-shot magazine. **Barrel:** 24", 26" for magnums. **Weight:** About 7-3/4 lbs. to 8 lbs. **Length:** 44-1/2" overall (24" bbl.) **Stock:** Walnut with straight comb, sculptured cheekpiece, wrap-around cut checkering, tapered forend, solid rubber butt pad. **Sights:** None furnished; comes with scope bases and rings. **Features:** Controlled round feeding with stainless steel claw extractor, bolt guide rail, three-position safety; all steel bottom metal, hinged floorplate, stainless magazine follower. Introduced 1994. From U.S. Repeating Arms Co.
Price: **$702.00**

WINCHESTER MODEL 70 CLASSIC SAFARI EXPRESS MAGNUM

Caliber: 375 H&H Mag., 416 Rem. Mag., 458 Win. Mag., 3-shot magazine. **Barrel:** 24". **Weight:** 8-1/4 to 8-1/2 lbs. **Stock:** American walnut with Monte Carlo cheekpiece. Wrap-around checkering and finish. **Sights:** Hooded ramp front, open rear. **Features:** Controlled round feeding. Two steel cross bolts in stock for added strength. Front sling swivel stud mounted on barrel. Contoured rubber butt pad. From U.S. Repeating Arms Co.
Price: **$1,007.00**
Price: Left-hand, 375 H&H only **$1,042.00**

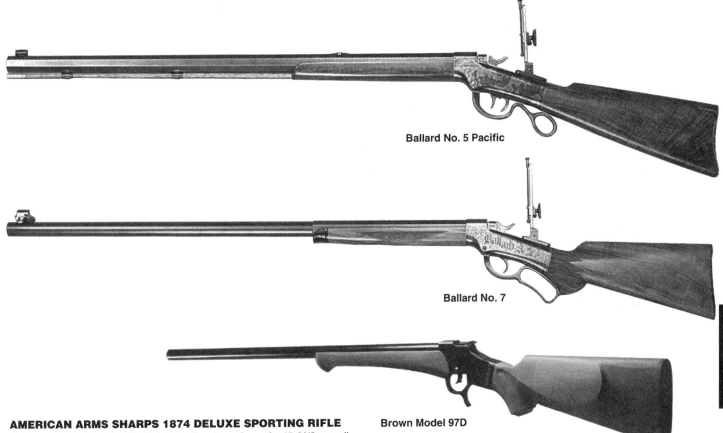

Ballard No. 5 Pacific

Ballard No. 7

Brown Model 97D

AMERICAN ARMS SHARPS 1874 DELUXE SPORTING RIFLE

Caliber: 45-70. **Barrel:** 28". **Weight:** 9 lbs., 3 oz. **Length:** 45-3/4" overall. **Stock:** European walnut; checkered grip and forend. **Sights:** Brass blade front, ladder-type adjustable rear. **Features:** Double-set triggers. Color case-hardened receiver, hammer, lever, browned barrel. Introduced 1999. Imported by American Arms, Inc.
Price: $705.00
Price: With blued barrel $685.00

American Arms Sharps Cavalry, Frontier Carbines

Similar to the 1874 Sporting RIfle except with 22" barrel. The Cavalry Carbine has double-set triggers; single trigger on Frontier, which also has a barrel band. Introduced 1999. Imported by American Arms, Inc.
Price: Cavalry carbine $660.00
Price: Frontier carbine $675.00

AMERICAN ARMS/UBERTI 1885 SINGLE SHOT

Caliber: 45-70. **Barrel:** 28". **Weight:** 8.75 lbs. **Length:** 44.5" overall. **Stock:** European walnut. **Sights:** Bead on blade front, open step-adjustable rear. **Features:** Recreation of the 1885 Winchester. Color case-hardened receiver and lever, blued barrel. Introduced 1998. Imported from Italy by American Arms. Inc.
Price: $810.00

ARMSPORT 1866 SHARPS RIFLE, CARBINE

Caliber: 45-70. **Barrel:** 28", round or octagonal. **Weight:** 8.10 lbs. **Length:** 46" overall. **Stock:** Walnut. **Sights:** Blade front, folding adjustable rear. Tang sight set optionally available. **Features:** Replica of the 1866 Sharps. Color case-hardened frame, rest blued. Imported by Armsport.
Price:: $865.00
Price: With octagonal barrel $900.00
Price: Carbine, 22" round barrel $850.00

BALLARD NO. 5 PACIFIC SINGLE-SHOT RIFLE

Caliber: 32-40, 38-55, 40-65, 40-90, 40-70 SS, 45-70 Govt., 45-110 SS, 50-70 Govt., 50-90 SS. **Barrel:** 30", or 32" octagonal. **Weight:** 10-1/2 lbs. **Length:** NA. **Stock:** High-grade walnut; rifle or shotgun style. **Sights:** Blade front, Rocky Mountain rear. **Features:** Standard or heavy barrel;

double-set triggers; under-barrel wiping rod; ring lever. Introduced 1999. Made in U.S. by Ballard Rifle & Cartridge Co.
Price: $2,575.00

BALLARD NO. 7 LONG RANGE RIFLE

Caliber: 32-40, 38-55, 40-65, 40-70 SS, 45-70 Govt., 45-90, 45-110. **Barrel:** 32", 34" half-octagon. **Weight:** 11-3/4 lbs. **Length:** NA. **Stock:** Fancy walnut; checkered pistol grip, ebony forend cap. **Sights:** Globe front. **Features:** Designed for shooting up to 1000 yards. Standard or heavy barrel; single or double-set trigger; hard rubber or steel buttplate. Introduced 1999. Made in U.S. by Ballard Rifle & Cartridge Co.
Price: From $2,950.00

BALLARD NO. 8 UNION HILL RIFLE

Caliber: 22 LR, 32-40, 38-55, 40-65 Win., 40-70 SS. **Barrel:** 30" half-octagon. **Weight:** About 10-1/2 lbs. **Length:** NA. **Stock:** Fancy walnut; pistol grip butt with cheekpiece. **Sights:** Globe front. **Features:** Designed for 200-yard offhand shooting. Standard or heavy barrel; double-set triggers; full loop lever; hook Schuetzen buttplate. Introduced 1999. Made in U.S. by Ballard Rifle & Cartridge Co.
Price: From $2,850.00

BALLARD MODEL 1885 HIGH WALL SINGLE SHOT RIFLE

Caliber: 17 Bee, 22 Hornet, 218 Bee, 219 Don Wasp, 219 Zipper, 22 Hi-Power, 225 Win., 25-20 WCF, 25-35 WCF, 25 Krag, 7mmx57R, 30-30, 30-40 Krag, 303 British, 33 WCF, 348 WCF, 35 WCF, 35-30/30, 9.3x74R, 405 WCF, 50-110 WCF, 500 Express, 577 Express. **Barrel:** Lengths to 34". **Weight:** N/A. **Length:** N/A. **Stock:** Straight-grain American walnut. **Sights:** buckhorn or flat top rear, blade front. **Features:** Faithful copy of original Model 1885 High Wall; parts interchange with original rifles; variety of options available. Introduced 2000. Made in U.S. by Ballard Rifle & Cartridge LLC.
Price: From $1,850.00
Price: With single set trigger from $2,050.00

Browning Model 1885 Traditional Hunter

Browning Model 1885 Low Wall

Cabela's Sharps

BARRETT MODEL 99 SINGLE SHOT RIFLE

Caliber: 50 BMG. **Barrel:** 33". **Weight:** 25 lbs. **Length:** 50.4" overall. **Stock:** Anodized aluminum with energy-absorbing recoil pad. **Sights:** None furnished; integral M1913 scope rail. **Features:** Bolt action; detachable bipod; match-grade barrel with high-efficiency muzzle brake. Introduced 1999. Made in U.S. by Barrett Firearms.
Price: From **$3,000.00**

BROWN MODEL 97D SINGLE SHOT RIFLE

Caliber: 17 Ackley Hornet through 45-70 Govt. **Barrel:** Up to 26", air gauged match grade. **Weight:** About 5 lbs., 11 oz. **Stock:** Sporter style with pistol grip, cheekpiece and Schnabel forend. **Sights:** None furnished; drilled and tapped for scope mounting. **Features:** Falling block action gives rigid barrel-receiver matting; polished blue/black finish. Hand-fitted action. Made in U.S. by E. A. Brown Mfg.
Price: **$599.00**

BROWNING MODEL 1885 HIGH WALL SINGLE SHOT RIFLE

Caliber: 22-250, 30-06, 270, 7mm Rem. Mag., 454 Casull, 45-70. **Barrel:** 28". **Weight:** About 8-1/2 lbs. **Length:** 43-1/2" overall. **Stock:** Walnut with straight grip, Schnabel forend. **Sights:** None furnished; drilled and tapped for scope mounting. **Features:** Replica of J.M. Browning's high-wall falling block rifle. Octagon barrel with recessed muzzle. Imported from Japan by Browning. Introduced 1985.
Price: **$987.00**

Browning Model 1885 BPCR Rifle

Similar to the 1885 High Wall rifle except the ejector system and shell deflector have been removed; chambered only for 40-65 and 45-70; color case-hardened full-tang receiver, lever, buttplate and gripcap; matte blue 30" part octagon, part round barrel. The Vernier tang sight has indexed elevation, is screw adjustable windage, and has three peep diameters. The hooded front sight has a built-in spirit level and comes with sight interchangeable inserts. Adjustable trigger. Overall length 46-1/8", weighs about 11 lbs. Introduced 1996. Imported from Japan by Browning.
Price: **$1,749.00**
Price: BPCR Creedmoor (45-90, 34" barrel with wind gauge sight) **$1,764.00**

Browning Model 1885 Traditional Hunter

Similar to the Model 1885 High Wall except chambered for 357 Mag., 44 Mag., 45 Colt, 30-30, 38-55 and 45-70 only; steel crescent buttplate; 1/16" gold bead front sight, adjustable buckhorn rear, and tang-mounted peep sight with barrel-type elevation adjuster and knob-type windage adjustments. Barrel is drilled and tapped for a Browning scope base. Oil-finished select walnut stock with swivel studs. Introduced 1997. Imported for Japan by Browning.
Price: High Wall **$1,208.95**
Price: Low Wall **$1,276.00**

Browning Model 1885 Low Wall Rifle

Similar to the Model 1885 High Wall except has trimmer receiver, thinner 24" octagonal barrel. Forend is mounted to the receiver. Adjustable trigger. Walnut pistol grip stock, trim Schnabel forend with high-gloss finish. Available in 22 Hornet, 223 Rem., 243 Win., 260 Rem. Overall length 39-1/2", weighs 6 lbs., 4 oz. Rifling twist rates: 1:16" (22 Hornet); 1:12" (223); 1:10" (243). Polished blue finish. Introduced 1995. Imported from Japan by Browning.
Price: **$987.00**

BRNO ZBK 110 SINGLE SHOT RIFLE

Caliber: 222 Rem., 5.6x52R, 22 Hornet, 5.6x50 Mag., 6.5x57R, 7x57R, 8x57JRS. **Barrel:** 23.6". **Weight:** 5.9 lbs. **Length:** 40.1" overall. **Stock:** European walnut. **Sights:** None furnished; drilled and tapped for scope mounting. **Features:** Top tang opening lever; cross-bolt safety; polished blue finish. Announced 1998. Imported from The Czech Republic by Euro-Imports.
Price: Standard calibers **$223.00**
Price: 7x57R, 8x57JRS **$245.00**
Price: Lux model, standard calibers **$311.00**
Price: Lux model, 7x57R, 8x57JRS **$333.00**

CABELA'S SHARPS SPORTING RIFLE

Caliber: 45-70. **Barrel:** 32", tapered octagon. **Weight:** 9 lbs. **Length:** 47-1/4" overall. **Stock:** Checkered walnut. **Sights:** Blade front, open adjustable rear. **Features:** Color case-hardened receiver and hammer, rest blued. Introduced 1995. Imported by Cabela's.
Price: **$849.99**

CIMARRON BILLY DIXON 1874 SHARPS SPORTING RIFLE

Caliber: 40-65, 45-70. **Barrel:** 32" tapered octagon. **Weight:** NA. **Length:** NA. **Stock:** European walnut. **Sights:** Blade front, Creedmoor rear. **Features:** Color case-hardened frame, blued barrel. Hand-checkered grip and forend; hand-rubbed oil finish. Introduced 1999. Imported by Cimarron F.A. Co.
Price: **$1,495.00**

CIMARRON MODEL 1885 HIGH WALL RIFLE

Caliber: 38-55, 40-65, 45-70, 45-90. **Barrel:** 30" octagonal. **Weight:** NA. **Length:** NA. **Stock:** European walnut. **Sights:** Bead front, semi-buckhorn rear. **Features:** Replica of the Winchester 1885 High Wall rifle. Color case-hardened receiver and lever, blued barrel. Curved buttplate. Introduced 1999. Imported by Cimarron F.A. Co.
Price: **$995.00**

CIMARRON CREEDMOOR ROLLING BLOCK RIFLE

Caliber: 40-65, 45-70. **Barrel:** 30" tapered octagon. **Weight:** NA. **Length:** NA. **Stock:** European walnut. **Sights:** Globe front, fully adjustable rear. **Features:** Color case-hardened receiver, blued barrel. Hand-checkered pistol grip and forend; hand-rubbed oil finish. Introduced 1999. Imported by Cimarron F.A. Co.
Price: **$1,295.00**

Cumberland Mountain Plateau

Dakota Single Shot

Dixie 1874 Sharps Silhouette

H&R Ultra Hunter

CUMBERLAND MOUNTAIN PLATEAU RIFLE

Caliber: 40-65, 45-70. **Barrel:** Up to 32"; round. **Weight:** About 10-1/2 lbs. (32" barrel). **Length:** 48" overall (32" barrel). **Stock:** American walnut. **Sights:** Marble's bead front, Marble's open rear. **Features:** Falling block action with underlever. Blued barrel and receiver. Stock has lacquer finish, crescent buttplate. Introduced 1995. Made in U.S. by Cumberland Mountain Arms, Inc.

Price: **$1,085.00**

DAKOTA SINGLE SHOT RIFLE

Caliber: Most rimmed and rimless commercial calibers. **Barrel:** 23". **Weight:** 6 lbs. **Length:** 39-1/2" overall. **Stock:** Medium fancy grade walnut in classic style. Checkered grip and forend. **Sights:** None furnished. Drilled and tapped for scope mounting. **Features:** Falling block action with under-lever. Top tang safety. Removable trigger plate for conversion to single set trigger. Introduced 1990. Made in U.S. by Dakota Arms.

Price: **$3,495.00**
Price: Barreled action................................. **$2,050.00**
Price: Action only **$1,675.00**
Price: Magnum calibers **$3,595.00**
Price: Magnum barreled action......................... **$2,050.00**
Price: Magnum action only............................. **$1,775.00**

DIXIE 1874 SHARPS BLACKPOWDER SILHOUETTE RIFLE

Caliber: 45-70. **Barrel:** 30"; tapered octagon; blued; 1:18" twist. **Weight:** 10 lbs., 3 oz. **Length:** 47-1/2" overall. **Stock:** Oiled walnut. **Sights:** Blade front, ladder-type hunting rear. **Features:** Replica of the Sharps #1 Sporter. Shotgun-style butt with checkered metal buttplate; color case-hardened receiver, hammer, lever and buttplate. Tang is drilled and tapped for tang sight. Double-set triggers. Meets standards for NRA blackpowder cartridge matches. Introduced 1995. Imported from Italy by Dixie Gun Works.

Price: **$995.00**

Dixie 1874 Sharps Lightweight Hunter/Target Rifle

Same as the Dixie 1874 Sharps Blackpowder Silhouette model except has a straight-grip buttstock with military-style buttplate. Based on the 1874 military model. Introduced 1995. Imported from Italy by Dixie Gun Works.

Price: **$995.00**

E.M.F. SHARPS RIFLE

Caliber: 45-70. **Barrel:** 28", octagon. **Weight:** 10-3/4 lbs. **Length:** NA. **Stock:** Oiled walnut. **Sights:** Blade front, flip-up open rear. **Features:** Replica of the 1874 Sharps Sporting rifle. Color case-hardened lock; double-set trigger; blue finish. Imported by E.M.F.

Price: **$950.00**
Price: With browned finish **$1,000.00**
Price: Carbine (round 22" barrel, barrel band) **$860.00**

HARRINGTON & RICHARDSON ULTRA VARMINT RIFLE

Caliber: 223, 243. **Barrel:** 24", heavy. **Weight:** About 7.5 lbs. **Length:** NA. **Stock:** Hand-checkered laminated birch with Monte Carlo comb. **Sights:** None furnished. Drilled and tapped for scope mounting. **Features:** Break-open action with side-lever release, positive ejection. Comes with scope mount. Blued receiver and barrel. Swivel studs. Introduced 1993. From H&R 1871, Inc.

Price: **$254.95**

Harrington & Richardson Ultra Hunter Rifle

Similar to the Ultra Varmint rifle except chambered for 25-06 with 26" barrel, or 308 Win., 357 Rem. Max. with 22" barrel. Stock and forend are of cinnamon-colored laminate; hand-checkered grip and forend. Introduced 1995. Made in U.S. by H&R 1871, Inc.

Price: **$249.95**

Harrington & Richardson Ultra Comp Rifle

Similar to the Ultra Varmint except chambered for 270 or 30-06; has compensator to reduce recoil; camo-laminate stock and forend; blued, highly polished frame; scope mount. Made in U.S. by H&R 1871, Inc.

Price: **$289.95**

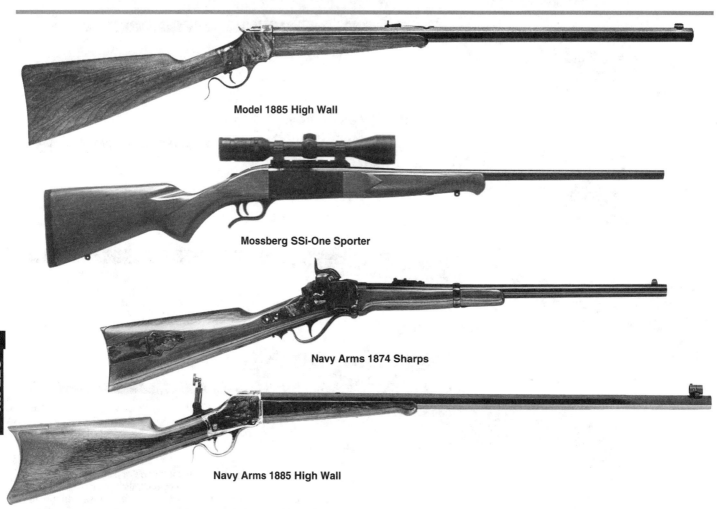

Model 1885 High Wall

Mossberg SSi-One Sporter

Navy Arms 1874 Sharps

Navy Arms 1885 High Wall

HARRIS GUNWORKS ANTIETAM SHARPS RIFLE

Caliber: 40-65, 45-75. **Barrel:** 30", 32", octagon or round, hand-lapped stainless or chrome-moly. **Weight:** 11.25 lbs. **Length:** 47" overall. **Stock:** Choice of straight grip, pistol grip or Creedmoor with Schnabel forend; pewter tip optional. Standard wood is A Fancy; higher grades available. **Sights:** Montana Vintage Arms #111 Low Profile Spirit Level front, #108 mid-range tang rear with windage adjustments. **Features:** Recreation of the 1874 Sharps sidehammer. Action is color case-hardened, barrel satin black. Chrome-moly barrel optionally blued. Optional sights include #112 Spirit Level Globe front with windage, #107 Long Range rear with windage. Introduced 1994. Made in U.S. by Harris Gunworks.
Price: **$2,400.00**

MODEL 1885 HIGH WALL RIFLE

Caliber: 30-40 Krag, 32-40, 38-55, 40-65 WCF, 45-70. **Barrel:** 26" (30-40), 28" all others. Douglas Premium #3 tapered octagon. **Weight:** NA. **Length:** NA. **Stock:** Premium American black walnut. **Sights:** Marble's standard ivory bead front, #66 long blade top rear with reversible notch and elevator. **Features:** Recreation of early octagon top, thick-wall High Wall with Coil spring action. Tang drilled, tapped for High Wall tang sight. Receiver, lever, hammer and breechblock color case-hardened. Introduced 1991. Available from Montana Armory, Inc.
Price: **$1,095.00**

MOSSBERG SSi-ONE SINGLE SHOT RIFLE

NEW! **Caliber:** 223 Rem., 22-250 Rem., 243 Win., 270 Win., 308 Rem., 30-06. **Barrel:** 24". **Weight:** 8 lbs. **Length:** 40". **Stock:** Satin-finished walnut, fluted and checkered; sling-swivel studs. **Sights:** None (scope base furnished). **Features:** Frame accepts interchangeable barrels, including 12-gauge, fully rifled slug barrel. Lever-opening, break-action design; single-stage trigger; ambidextrous, top-tang safety; internal eject/extract selector. Introduced 2000. From Mossberg.

Price: SSi-One Sporter (standard barrel) **$400.00**
Price: SSi-One Varmint (bull barrel, 22-250 Rem. only;
weighs 10 lbs.) **$400.00**
Price: SSi-One 12-gauge Slug (fully rifled barrel, no sights,
scope base) **$400.00**

NAVY ARMS 1874 SHARPS CAVALRY CARBINE

Caliber: 45-70. **Barrel:** 22". **Weight:** 7 lbs., 12 oz. **Length:** 39" overall. **Stock:** Walnut. **Sights:** Blade front, military ladder-type rear. **Features:** Replica of the 1874 Sharps military carbine. Color case-hardened receiver and furniture. Imported by Navy Arms.
Price: **$935.00**

Navy Arms 1874 Sharps Sniper Rifle

Similar to the Navy Arms Sharps Carbine except has 30" barrel, double-set triggers; weighs 8 lbs., 8 oz., overall length 46-3/4". Introduced 1984. Imported by Navy Arms.
Price: $1,115.00
Price: 1874 Sharps Infantry Rifle (three-band). **$1,060.00**

NAVY ARMS 1885 HIGH WALL RIFLE

Caliber: 45-70; others available on special order. **Barrel:** 28" round, 30" octagonal. **Weight:** 9.5 lbs. **Length:** 45-1/2" overall (30" barrel). **Stock:** Walnut. **Sights:** Blade front, buckhorn rear; globe front, Vernier tang-mounted peep rear. **Features:** Replica of Winchester's High Wall designed by Browning. Color case-hardened receiver, blued barrel. Introduced 1998. Imported by Navy Arms.
Price: 28", round barrel, buckhorn sights **$745.00**
Price: As above, target sights. **$845.00**
Price: 30" octagonal barrel, buckhorn sight **$815.00**
Price: As above, target sights. **$915.00**

RIFLES

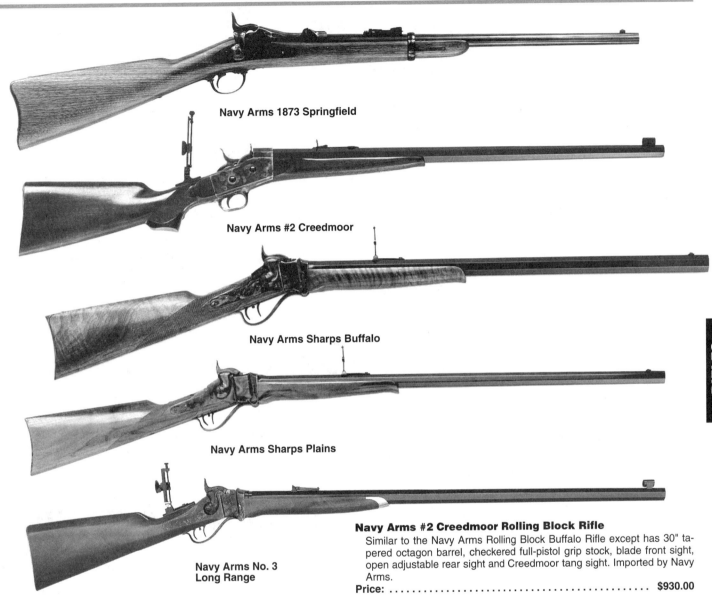

Navy Arms 1873 Springfield

Navy Arms #2 Creedmoor

Navy Arms Sharps Buffalo

Navy Arms Sharps Plains

Navy Arms No. 3 Long Range

RIFLES

NAVY ARMS 1873 SPRINGFIELD CAVALRY CARBINE
Caliber: 45-70. **Barrel:** 22". **Weight:** 7 lbs. **Length:** 40-1/2" overall. **Stock:** Walnut. **Sights:** Blade front, military ladder rear. **Features:** Blued lockplate and barrel; color case-hardened breechblock; saddle ring with bar. Replica of 7th Cavalry gun. Imported by Navy Arms.
Price: $870.00

Navy Arms 1873 Springfield Infantry Rifle
Same action as the 1873 Springfield Cavalry Carbine except in rifle configuration with 32-1/2" barrel, three-band full-length stock. Introduced 1997. Imported by Navy Arms.
Price: $995.00

NAVY ARMS ROLLING BLOCK BUFFALO RIFLE
Caliber: 45-70. **Barrel:** 26", 30". **Stock:** Walnut. **Sights:** Blade front, adjustable rear. **Features:** Reproduction of classic rolling block action. Available with full-octagon or half-octagon-half-round barrel. Color case-hardened action, steel fittings. From Navy Arms.
Price: $765.00

Navy Arms #2 Creedmoor Rolling Block Rifle
Similar to the Navy Arms Rolling Block Buffalo Rifle except has 30" tapered octagon barrel, checkered full-pistol grip stock, blade front sight, open adjustable rear sight and Creedmoor tang sight. Imported by Navy Arms.
Price: $930.00

NAVY ARMS 1874 SHARPS BUFFALO RIFLE
Caliber: 45-70, 45-90. **Barrel:** 28" heavy octagon. **Weight:** 10 lbs., 10 oz. **Length:** 46" overall. **Stock:** Walnut; checkered grip and forend. **Sights:** Blade front, ladder rear; tang sight optional. **Features:** Color case-hardened receiver, blued barrel; double-set triggers. Imported by Navy Arms.
Price: $1,090.00

Navy Arms Sharps Plains Rifle
Similar to the Sharps Buffalo rifle except 45-70 only, has 32" medium-weight barrel, weighs 9 lbs., 8 oz., and is 49" overall. Imported by Navy Arms. **NEW!**
Price: $1,055.00

Navy Arms Sharps Sporting Rifle
Same as the Navy Arms Sharps Plains Rifle except has pistol grip stock. **NEW!** Introduced 1997. Imported by Navy Arms.
Price: 45-70 only $1,090.00

NAVY ARMS SHARPS NO. 3 LONG RANGE RIFLE
Caliber: 45-70, 45-90. **Barrel:** 34" octagon. **Weight:** 10 lbs., 12 oz. **Length:** 51-1/2". **Stock:** Deluxe walnut. **Sights:** Globe target front and match grade rear tang. **Features:** Shotgun buttplate, German silver forend cap, color case hardenend receiver. Imported by Navy Arms.
Price: $1,745.00

CENTERFIRE RIFLES — SINGLE SHOT

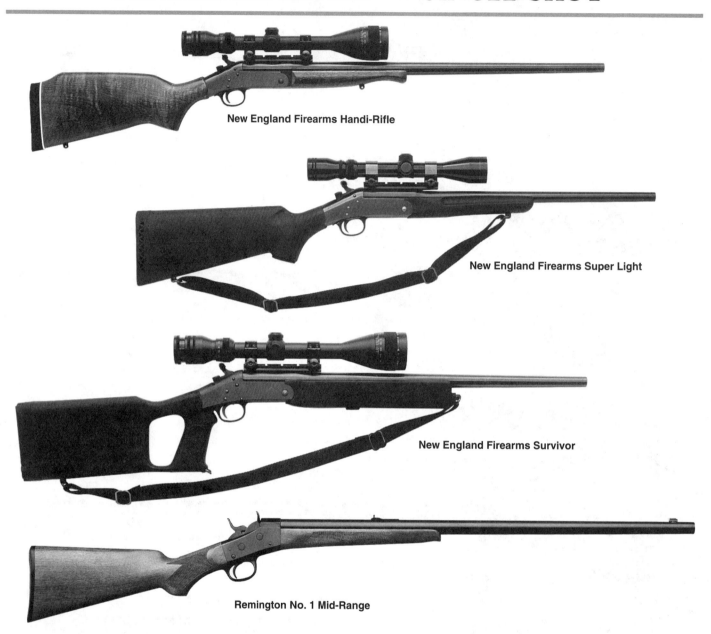

New England Firearms Handi-Rifle

New England Firearms Super Light

New England Firearms Survivor

Remington No. 1 Mid-Range

NEW ENGLAND FIREARMS HANDI-RIFLE

Caliber: 22 Hornet, 223, 243, 7x57, 7x64 Brenneke, 30-30, 270, 280 Rem., 308, 30-06, 44 Mag., 45-70. **Barrel:** 22", 24"; 26" for 280 Rem. **Weight:** 7 lbs. **Stock:** Walnut-finished hardwood; black rubber recoil pad. **Sights:** Ramp front, folding rear (22 Hornet, 30-30, 45-70). Drilled and tapped for scope mount; 223, 243, 270, 280, 30-06 have no open sights, come with scope mounts. **Features:** Break-open action with side-lever release. The 223, 243, 270 and 30-06 have recoil pad and Monte Carlo stock for shooting with scope. Swivel studs on all models. Blue finish. Introduced 1989. From New England Firearms.
Price: **$209.95**
Price: 7x57, 7x64 Brenneke, 24" barrel **$211.95**
Price: 280 Rem., 26" barrel **$214.95**
Price: Synthetic Handi-Rifle (black polymer stock and forend, swivels, recoil pad). **$219.95**
Price: Handi-Rifle Youth (223, 243) **$209.95**

New England Firearms Super Light Rifle

Similar to the Handi-Rifle except has new barrel taper, shorter 20" barrel with recessed muzzle and special lightweight synthetic stock and forend. No sights are furnished on the 223 and 243 versions, but have a factory-mounted scope base and offset hammer spur; Monte Carlo stock; 22 Hornet has ramp front, fully adjustable open rear. Overall length is 36", weight is 5.5 lbs. Introduced 1997. Made in U.S. by New England Firearms.
Price: 22 Hornet, 223 Rem. or 243 Win. **$219.95**

NEW ENGLAND FIREARMS SURVIVOR RIFLE

Caliber: 223, 357 Mag., single shot. **Barrel:** 22". **Weight:** 6 lbs. **Length:** 36" overall. **Stock:** Black polymer, thumbhole design. **Sights:** Blade front, fully adjustable open rear. **Features:** Receiver drilled and tapped for scope mounting. Stock and forend have storage compartments for ammo, etc.; comes with integral swivels and black nylon sling. Introduced 1996. Made in U.S. by New England Firearms.
Price: Blue **$219.95**
Price: Electroless nickel **$234.95**

REMINGTON NO. 1 ROLLING BLOCK MID-RANGE SPORTER

Caliber: 45-70. **Barrel:** 30" round. **Weight:** 8-3/4 lbs. **Length:** 46-1/2" overall. **Stock:** American walnut with checkered pistol grip and forend. **Sights:** Beaded blade front, adjustable center-notch buckhorn rear. **Features:** Recreation of the original. Polished blue metal finish. Many options available. Introduced 1998. Made in U.S. by Remington.
Price: **$1,348.00**

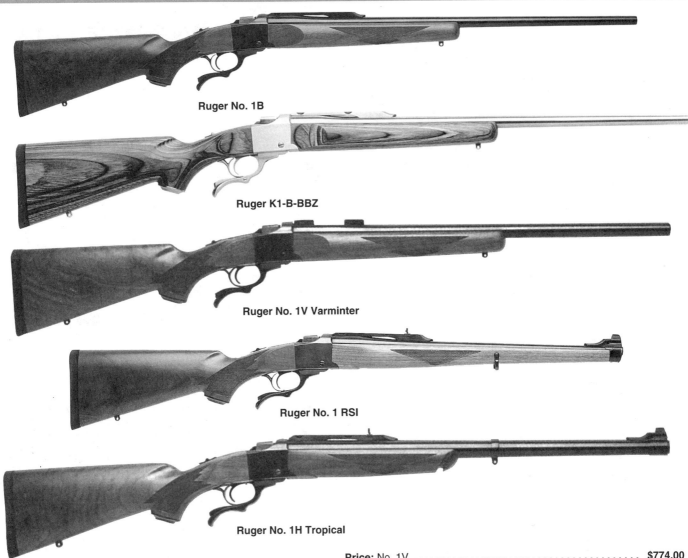

Ruger No. 1B

Ruger K1-B-BBZ

Ruger No. 1V Varminter

Ruger No. 1 RSI

Ruger No. 1H Tropical

RUGER NO. 1B SINGLE SHOT

Caliber: 218 Bee, 22 Hornet, 220 Swift, 22-250, 223, 243, 6mm Rem., 25-06, 257 Roberts, 270, 280, 30-06, 7mm Rem. Mag., 300 Win. Mag., 338 Win. Mag., 270 Wea., 300 Wea. **Barrel:** 26" round tapered with quarter-rib; with Ruger 1" rings. **Weight:** 8 lbs. **Length:** 43-3/8" overall. **Stock:** Walnut, two-piece, checkered pistol grip and semi-beavertail forend. **Sights:** None, 1" scope rings supplied for integral mounts. **Features:** Under-lever, hammerless falling block design has auto ejector, top tang safety.

Price: 1B	$774.00
Price: Barreled action	$555.00
Price: K1-B-BBZ Stainless steel, laminated stock 25-06, 7MM mag, 7MM STW, 300 Win Mag.	$820.00

Ruger No. 1A Light Sporter

Similar to the No. 1B Standard Rifle except has lightweight 22" barrel, Alexander Henry-style forend, adjustable folding leaf rear sight on quarter-rib, dovetailed ramp front with gold bead. Calibers 243, 30-06, 270 and 7x57. Weighs about 7-1/4 lbs.

Price: No. 1A	$774.00
Price: Barreled action	$555.00

Ruger No. 1V Varminter

Similar to the No. 1B Standard Rifle except has 24" heavy barrel. Semi-beavertail forend, barrel ribbed for target scope block, with 1" Ruger scope rings. Calibers 22-250, 220 Swift, 223, 25-06. Weight about 9 lbs.

Price: No. 1V	$774.00
Price: Barreled action	$555.00
Price: K1-U-BBZ stainless steel, laminated stock 22-250	$820.00

Ruger No. 1 RSI International

Similar to the No. 1B Standard Rifle except has lightweight 20" barrel, full-length International-style forend with loop sling swivel, adjustable folding leaf rear sight on quarter-rib, ramp front with gold bead. Calibers 243, 30-06, 270 and 7x57. Weight is about 7-1/4 lbs.

Price: No. 1 RSI	$794.00
Price: Barreled action	$555.00

Ruger No. 1H Tropical Rifle

Similar to the No. 1B Standard Rifle except has Alexander Henry forend, adjustable folding leaf rear sight on quarter-rib, ramp front with dovetail gold bead. 24" heavy barrel. Calibers 375 H&H, 416 Rem. Mag. (weighs about 8-1/4 lbs.), 416 Rigby, and 458 Win. Mag. (weighs about 9 lbs.).

Price: No. 1H	$774.00
Price: Barreled action	$555.00

Ruger No. 1S Medium Sporter

Similar to the No. 1B Standard Rifle except has Alexander Henry-style forend, adjustable folding leaf rear sight on quarter-rib, ramp front sight base and dovetail-type gold bead front sight. Calibers 218 Bee, 7mm Rem. Mag., 338 Win. Mag., 300 Win. Mag. with 26" barrel, 45-70 with 22" barrel. Weighs about 7-1/2 lbs. In 45-70.

Price: No. 1S	$774.00
Price: Barreled action	$555.00

CENTERFIRE RIFLES — SINGLE SHOT

C. Sharps New Model
1875 Old Reliable

C. Sharps New Model 1874

C. Sharps
New Model 1885

RIFLES

Ruger No. 1 Stainless Steel Rifles

NEW! Similar to No. 1 Standard except has stainless steel receiver and barrel, laminated hardwood stock. Calibers 25-06, 7mm Rem. Mag., 7mm STW, 300 Win. Mag. (Standard) or 22-250 (Varminter). Introduced 2000.
Price: No. 1 Stainless Standard (26" barrel, 8 lbs.) **$820.00**
Price: No. 1 Stainless Varminter (24" heavy barrel,
9 lbs.) **$820.00**

C. SHARPS ARMS NEW MODEL 1875 OLD RELIABLE RIFLE

Caliber: 22LR, 32-40 & 38-55 Ballard, 38-56 WCF, 40-65 WCF, 40-90 3-1/4", 40-90 2-5/8", 40-70 2-1/10", 40-70 2-1/4", 40-70 2-1/2", 40-50 1-11/16", 40-50 1-7/8", 45-90, 45-70, 45-100, 45-110, 45-120. Also available on special order only in 50-70, 50-90, 50-140. **Barrel:** 24", 26", 30" (standard), 32", 34" optional. **Weight:** 8-12 lbs. **Stock:** Walnut, straight grip, shotgun butt with checkered steel buttplate. **Sights:** Silver blade front, Rocky Mountain buckhorn rear. **Features:** Recreation of the 1875 Sharps rifle. Production guns will have case colored receiver. Available in Custom Sporting and Target versions upon request. Announced 1986. From C. Sharps Arms Co. and Montana Armory, Inc.
Price: 1875 Carbine (24" tapered round bbl.) **$810.00**
Price: 1875 Saddle Rifle (26" tapered oct. bbl.) **$910.00**
Price: 1875 Sporting Rifle (30" tapered oct. bbl.) **$975.00**
Price: 1875 Business Rifle (28" tapered round bbl.) **$860.00**

C. Sharps Arms 1875 Classic Sharps

Similar to the New Model 1875 Sporting Rifle except has 26", 28" or 30" full octagon barrel, crescent buttplate with toe plate, Hartford-style forend with cast German silver nose cap. Blade front sight, Rocky Mountain buckhorn rear. Weighs 10 lbs. Introduced 1987. From C. Sharps Arms Co. and Montana Armory, Inc.
Price: **$1,185.00**

C. Sharps Arms New Model 1875 Target & Long Range

Similar to the New Model 1875 except available in all listed calibers except 22 LR; 34" tapered octagon barrel; globe with post front sight, Long Range Vernier tang sight with windage adjustments. Pistol grip stock with cheek rest; checkered steel buttplate. Introduced 1991. From C. Sharps Arms Co. and Montana Armory, Inc.
Price: **$1,535.00**

C. SHARPS ARMS NEW MODEL 1874 OLD RELIABLE

Caliber: 40-50, 40-70, 40-90, 45-70, 45-90, 45-100, 45-110, 45-120, 50-70, 50-90, 50-140. **Barrel:** 26", 28", 30" tapered octagon. **Weight:** About 10 lbs. **Length:** NA. **Stock:** American black walnut; shotgun butt with checkered steel buttplate; straight grip, heavy forend with Schnabel tip. **Sights:** Blade front, buckhorn rear. Drilled and tapped for tang sight. **Features:** Recreation of the Model 1874 Old Reliable Sharps Sporting Rifle. Double set triggers. Reintroduced 1991. Made in U.S. by C. Sharps Arms. Available from Montana Armory, Inc.
Price: **$1,175.00**

C. SHARPS ARMS NEW MODEL 1885 HIGHWALL RIFLE

Caliber: 22 LR, 22 Hornet, 219 Zipper, 25-35 WCF, 32-40 WCF, 38-55 WCF, 40-65, 30-40-Krag, 40-50 ST or BN, 40-70 ST or BN, 40-90 ST or BN, 45-70 2-1/10" ST, 45-90 2-4/10" ST, 45-100 2-6/10" ST, 45-110 2-7/8" ST, 45-120 3-1/4" ST. **Barrel:** 26", 28", 30", tapered full octagon. **Weight:** About 9 lbs., 4 oz. **Length:** 47" overall. **Stock:** Oil-finished American walnut; Schnabel-style forend. **Sights:** Blade front, buckhorn rear. Drilled and tapped for optional tang sight. **Features:** Single trigger; octagonal receiver top; checkered steel buttplate; color case-hardened receiver and buttplate, blued barrel. Many options available. Made in U.S. by C. Sharps Arms Co. Available from Montana Armory, Inc.
Price: From **$1,195.00**

SHARPS 1874 RIFLE

Caliber: 45-70. **Barrel:** 28", octagonal. **Weight:** 9-1/4 lbs. **Length:** 46" overall. **Stock:** Checkered walnut. **Sights:** Blade front, adjustable rear. **Features:** Double set triggers on rifle. Color case-hardened receiver and buttplate, blued barrel. Imported from Italy by E.M.F.
Price: Rifle or carbine **$950.00**
Price: Military rifle, carbine **$860.00**
Price: Sporting rifle **$860.00**

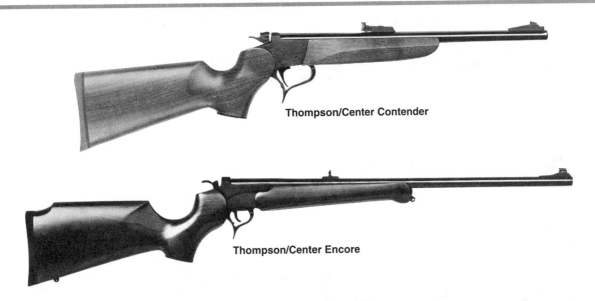

Thompson/Center Contender

Thompson/Center Encore

SHILOH SHARPS 1874 LONG RANGE EXPRESS

Caliber: 40-50 BN, 40-70 BN, 40-90 BN, 45-70 ST, 45-90 ST, 45-110 ST, 50-70 ST, 50-90 ST, 50-110 ST, 32-40, 38-55, 40-70 ST, 40-90 ST. **Barrel:** 34" tapered octagon. **Weight:** 10-1/2 lbs. **Length:** 51" overall. **Stock:** Oil-finished semi-fancy walnut with pistol grip, shotgun-style butt, traditional cheek rest, Schnabel forend. **Sights:** Globe front, sporting tang rear. **Features:** Recreation of the Model 1874 Sharps rifle. Double set triggers. Made in U.S. by Shiloh Rifle Mfg. Co.
Price: $1,796.00
Price: Sporting Rifle No. 1 (similar to above except with 30" bbl., blade front, buckhorn rear sight). $1,706.00
Price: Sporting Rifle No. 3 (similar to No. 1 except straight-grip stock, standard wood) $1,504.00
Price: 1874 Hartford model. $1,702.00

Shiloh Sharps 1874 Montana Roughrider

Similar to the No. 1 Sporting Rifle except available with half-octagon or full-octagon barrel in 24", 26", 28", 30", 34" lengths; standard supreme or semi-fancy wood, shotgun, pistol grip or military-style butt. Weight about 8-1/2 lbs. Calibers 30-40, 30-30, 40-50x1-11/16"BN, 40-70x2-1/10" BN, 45-70x2-1/10"ST. Globe front and tang sight optional.
Price: Standard supreme $1,504.00
Price: Semi-fancy $1,704.00

Shiloh Sharps 1874 Business Rifle

Similar to No. 3 Rifle except has 28" heavy round barrel, military-style buttstock and steel buttplate. Weight about 9-1/2 lbs. Calibers 40-50 BN, 40-70 BN, 40-90 BN, 45-70 ST, 45-90 ST, 50-70 ST, 50-100 ST, 32-40, 38-55, 40-70 ST, 40-90 ST.
Price: $1,604.00
Price: 1874 Saddle Rifle (similar to Carbine except has 26" octagon barrel, semi-fancy shotgun butt) $1,706.00

THOMPSON/CENTER CONTENDER CARBINE

Caliber: 22 LR, 22 Hornet, 223 Rem., 7x30 Waters, 30-30 Win. **Barrel:** 21". **Weight:** 5 lbs., 2 oz. **Length:** 35" overall. **Stock:** Checkered American walnut with rubber butt pad. Also with Rynite stock and forend. **Sights:** Blade front, open adjustable rear. **Features:** Uses the T/C Contender action. Eleven interchangeable barrels available, all with sights, drilled and tapped for scope mounting. Introduced 1985. Offered as a complete Carbine only.
Price: Rifle calibers. $571.38
Price: Extra barrels, rifle calibers, each $251.08

THOMPSON/CENTER ENCORE RIFLE

Caliber: 22-250, 223, 243, 25-06, 270, 7mm-08, 308, 30-06, 7mm Rem. Mag., 300 Win. Mag. **Barrel:** 24", 26". **Weight:** 6 lbs., 12 oz. (24" barrel). **Length:** 38-1/2" (24" barrel). **Stock:** American walnut. Monte Carlo style; Schnabel forend or black composite. **Sights:** Ramp-style white bead front, fully adjustable leaf-type rear. **Features:** Interchangeable barrels; action opens by squeezing trigger guard; drilled and tapped for T/C scope mounts; polished blue finish. Introduced 1996. Made in U.S. by Thompson/Center Arms.
Price: $582.29
Price: Extra barrels. $249.10
Price: With black composite stock and forend $582.29

Thompson/Center Stainless Encore Rifle

Similar to the blued Encore except made of stainless steel with blued sights, and has black composite stock and forend. Available in 22-250, 223, 7mm-08, 30-06, 308. Introduced 1999. Made in U.S. by Thompson/Center Arms.
Price: $650.42

UBERTI ROLLING BLOCK BABY CARBINE

Caliber: 22 LR, 22 WMR, 22 Hornet, 357 Mag., single shot. **Barrel:** 22". **Weight:** 4.8 lbs. **Length:** 35-1/2" overall. **Stock:** Walnut stock and forend. **Sights:** Blade front, fully adjustable open rear. **Features:** Resembles Remington New Model No. 4 carbine. Brass trigger guard and buttplate; color case-hardened frame, blued barrel. Imported by Uberti USA Inc.
Price: $490.00

WESSON & HARRINGTON BUFFALO CLASSIC RIFLE

Caliber: 45-70. **Barrel:** 32" heavy. **Weight:** 9 lbs. **Length:** 52" overall. **Stock:** American black walnut. **Sights:** None furnished; drilled and tapped for peep sight; barrel dovetailed for front sight. **Features:** Color case-hardened Handi-Rifle action with exposed hammer; color case-hardened crescent buttplate; 19th century checkering pattern. Introduced 1995. Made in U.S. by H&R 1871, Inc.
Price: About $349.95

Wesson & Harrington 38-55 Target Rifle

Similar to the Buffalo Classic rifle except chambered for 38-55 Win., has 28" barrel. The barrel and steel furniture, including steel trigger guard and forend spacer, are highly polished and blued. Color case-hardened receiver and buttplate. Barrel is dovetailed for a front sight, and drilled and tapped for receiver sight or scope mount. Introduced 1998. Made in U.S. by H&R 1871, Inc.
Price: $389.95

Designs for sporting and utility purposes worldwide.

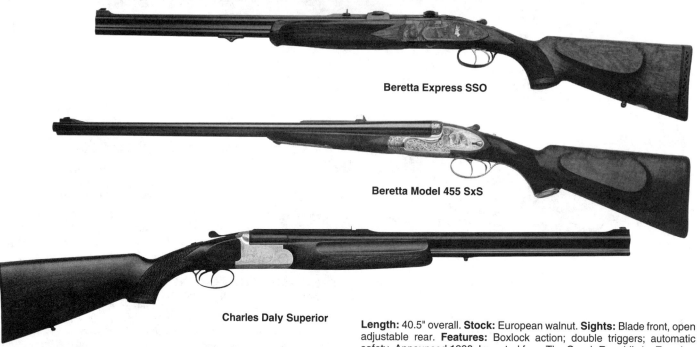

Beretta Express SSO

Beretta Model 455 SxS

Charles Daly Superior

AMERICAN ARMS SILVER EXPRESS O/U DOUBLE RIFLE
Caliber: 8x57 JRS, 9.3x74R. **Barrel:** 24". **Weight:** 7 lbs., 14 oz. **Length:** 41-1/4" overall. **Stock:** European walnut. **Sights:** Ramped high-visibility front, standing leaf rear on rib. **Features:** Boxlock action with single trigger, extractors; engraved, silvered receiver; blued barrels; no barrel center rib. Introduced 1999. Imported by American Arms, Inc.
Price: **$1,949.00**

BERETTA EXPRESS SSO O/U DOUBLE RIFLES
Caliber: 375 H&H, 458 Win. Mag., 9.3x74R. **Barrel:** 25.5". **Weight:** 11 lbs. **Stock:** European walnut with hand-checkered grip and forend. **Sights:** Blade front on ramp, open V-notch rear. **Features:** Sidelock action with color case-hardened receiver (gold inlays on SSO6 Gold). Ejectors, double triggers, recoil pad. Introduced 1990. Imported from Italy by Beretta U.S.A.
Price: SSO6 .... **$21,000.00**
Price: SSO6 Gold **$23,500.00**

BERETTA MODEL 455 SxS EXPRESS RIFLE
Caliber: 375 H&H, 458 Win. Mag., 470 NE, 500 NE 3", 416 Rigby. **Barrel:** 23-1/2" or 25-1/2". **Weight:** 11 lbs. **Stock:** European walnut with hand-checkered grip and forend. **Sights:** Blade front, folding leaf V-notch rear. **Features:** Sidelock action with easily removable sideplates; color case-hardened finish (455), custom big game or floral motif engraving (455EELL). Double triggers, recoil pad. Introduced 1990. Imported from Italy by Beretta U.S.A.
Price: Model 455 .... **$36,000.00**
Price: Model 455EELL **$47,000.00**

BRNO 500 COMBINATION GUNS
Caliber/Gauge: 12 (2-3/4" chamber) over 5.6x52R, 5.6x50R, 222 Rem., 243, 6.x55, 308, 7x57R, 7x65R, 30-06. **Barrel:** 23.6". **Weight:** 7.6 lbs. **Length:** 40.5" overall. **Stock:** European walnut. **Sights:** Bead front, V-notch rear; grooved for scope mounting. **Features:** Boxlock action; double set trigger; blue finish with etched engraving. Announced 1998. Imported from The Czech Republic by Euro-Imports.
Price: **$1,023.00**
Price: O/U double rifle, 7x57R, 7x65R, 8x57JRS ... **$1,125.00**

BRNO ZH 300 COMBINATION GUN
Caliber/Gauge: 22 Hornet, 5.6x50R Mag., 5.6x52R, 7x57R, 7x65R, 8x57JRS over 12, 16 (2-3/4" chamber). **Barrel:** 23.6". **Weight:** 7.9 lbs.

Length: 40.5" overall. **Stock:** European walnut. **Sights:** Blade front, open adjustable rear. **Features:** Boxlock action; double triggers; automatic safety. Announced 1998. Imported from The Czech Republic by Euro-Imports.
Price: **$724.00**

BRNO ZH Double Rifles
Similar to the ZH 300 combination guns except with double rifle barrels. Available in 7x65R, 7x57R and 8x57JRS. Announced 1998. Imported from The Czech Republic by Euro-Imports.
Price: **$1,125.00**

CHARLES DALY SUPERIOR COMBINATION GUN
Caliber/Gauge: 12 ga. over 22 Hornet, 223 Rem., 22-250, 243 Win., 270 Win., 308 Win., 30-06. **Barrel:** 23.5", shotgun choked Imp. Cyl. **Weight:** About 7.5 lbs. **Stock:** Checkered walnut pistol grip buttstock and semi-beavertail forend. **Features:** Silvered, engraved receiver; chrome-moly steel barrels; double triggers; extractors; sling swivels; gold bead front sight. Introduced 1997. Imported from Italy by K.B.I. Inc.
Price: **$1,249.95**

Charles Daly Empire Combination Gun
Same as the Superior grade except has deluxe wood with European-style comb and cheekpiece; slim forend. Introduced 1997. Imported from Italy by K.B.I., Inc.
Price: **$1,789.95**

CZ 584 SOLO COMBINATION GUN
Caliber/Gauge: 7x57R; 12, 2-3/4" chamber. **Barrel:** 24.4". **Weight:** 7.37 lbs. **Length:** 45.25" overall. **Stock:** Circassian walnut. **Sights:** Blade front, open rear adjustable for windage. **Features:** Kersten-style double lump locking system; double-trigger Blitz-type mechanism with drop safety and adjustable set trigger for the rifle barrel; auto safety, dual extractors; receiver dovetailed for scope mounting. Imported from the Czech Republic by CZ-USA.
Price: **$850.00**

EAA/BAIKAL IZH-94 COMBINATION GUN
Caliber/Gauge: 12, 3" chamber; 222 Rem., 223, 5.6x50R, 5.6x55E, 7x57R, 7x65R, 7.62x39, 7.62x51, 308, 7.62x53R, 7.62x54R, 30-06. **Barrel:** 24", 26"; imp., mod. and full choke tubes. **Weight:** 7.28 lbs. **Stock:** Walnut; rubber butt pad. **Sights:** Express style. **Features:** Hammer-forged barrels with chrome-lined bores; machined receiver; single-selective or double triggers. Imported by European American Armory.
Price: Blued finish **$499.00**

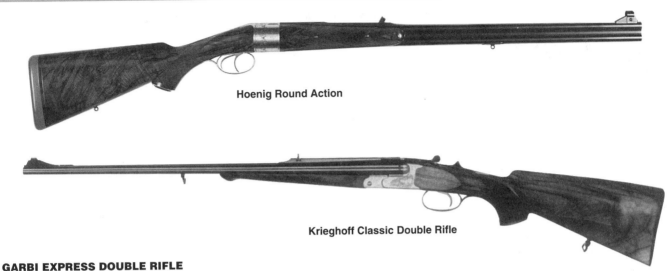

Hoenig Round Action

Krieghoff Classic Double Rifle

GARBI EXPRESS DOUBLE RIFLE

Caliber: 7x65R, 9.3x74R, 375 H&H. **Barrel:** 24-3/4". **Weight:** 7-3/4 to 8-1/2 lbs. **Length:** 41-1/2" overall. **Stock:** Turkish walnut. **Sights:** Quarter-rib with express sight. **Features:** Side-by-side double; H&H-pattern sidelock ejector with reinforced action, chopper lump barrels of Boehler steel; double triggers; fine scroll and rosette engraving, or full coverage ornamental; coin-finished action. Introduced 1997. Imported from Spain by Wm. Larkin Moore.
Price: **$21,800.00**

HOENIG ROTARY ROUND ACTION DOUBLE RIFLE

Caliber: Most popular calibers from 225 Win. to 9.3x74R. **Barrel:** 22"-26". **Weight:** NA. **Length:** NA. **Stock:** English Walnut; to customer specs. **Sights:** Swivel hood front with button release (extra bead stored in trap door gripcap), express-style rear on quarter-rib adjustable for windage and elevation; scope mount. **Features:** Round action opens by rotating barrels, pulling forward. Has inertia extractor system; rotary safety blocks the strikers; single lever quick-detachable scope mount. Simple takedown without removing forend. Introduced 1997. Made in U.S. by George Hoenig.
Price: **$19,980.00**

KRIEGHOFF CLASSIC DOUBLE RIFLE

Caliber: 7x65R, 308 Win., 30-06, 30R Blaser, 8x57 JRS, 8x75RS, 9.3x74R. **Barrel:** 23.5". **Weight:** 7.3 to 8 lbs. **Length:** NA. **Stock:** High grade European walnut. Standard has conventional rounded cheekpiece, Bavaria has Bavarian-style cheekpiece. **Sights:** Bead front with removable, adjustable wedge (375 H&H and below), standing leaf rear on quarter-rib. **Features:** Boxlock action; double triggers; short opening angle for fast loading; quiet extractors; sliding, self-adjusting wedge for secure bolting; Purdey-style barrel extension; horizontal firing pin placement. Many options available. Introduced 1997. Imported from Germany by Krieghoff International.
Price: With small Arabesque engraving **$7,850.00**
Price: With engraved sideplates......................... **$9,800.00**
Price: For extra barrels................................. **$4,500.00**
Price: Extra 20-ga., 28" shotshell barrels **$3,200.00**

Krieghoff Classic Big Five Double Rifle

Similar to the standard Classic excpet available in 375 Flanged Mag. N.E., 500/416 N.E., 470 N.E., 500 N.E. 3". Has hinged front trigger, non-removable muzzle wedge (larger than 375-caliber), Universal Trigger System, Combi Cocking Device, steel trigger guard, specially weighted stock bolt for weight and balance. Many options available. Introduced 1997. Imported from Germany by Krieghoff International.
Price: **$9,450.00**
Price: With engraved sideplates........................ **$11,400.00**

LEBEAU - COURALLY EXPRESS RIFLE SxS

Caliber: 7x65R, 8x57JRS, 9.3x74R, 375 H&H, 470 N.E. **Barrel:** 24" to 26". **Weight:** 7-3/4 to 10-1/2 lbs. **Stock:** Fancy French walnut with cheekpiece. **Sights:** Bead on ramp front, standing left express rear on quarter-rib. **Fea-**

tures: Holland & Holland-type sidelock with automatic ejectors; double triggers. Imported from Belgium by Wm. Larkin Moore.
Price: **$51,000.00**

MERKEL DRILLINGS

Caliber/Gauge: 12, 20, 3" chambers, 16, 2-3/4" chambers; 22 Hornet, 5.6x50R Mag., 5.6x52R, 222 Rem., 243 Win., 6.5x55, 6.5x57R, 7x57R, 7x65R, 308, 30-06, 8x57JRS, 9.3x74R, 375 H&H. **Barrel:** 25.6". **Weight:** 7.9 to 8.4 lbs. depending upon caliber. **Length:** NA. **Stock:** Oil-finished walnut with pistol grip; cheekpiece on 12-, 16-gauge. **Sights:** Blade front, fixed rear. **Features:** Double barrel locking lug with Greener cross-bolt; scroll-engraved, case-hardened receiver; automatic trigger safety; Blitz action; double triggers. Imported from Germany by GSI.
Price: Model 96K (manually cocked rifle system), from **$6,495.00**
Price: Model 96K Engraved (hunting series on receiver) **$7,995.00**

MERKEL OVER/UNDER DOUBLE RIFLES

Caliber: 22 Hornet, 5.6x50R Mag., 5.6x52R, 222 Rem., 243 Win., 6.5x55, 6.5x57R, 7x57R, 7x65R, 308, 30-06, 8x57JRS, 9.3x74R. **Barrel:** 25.6". **Weight:** About 7.7 lbs, depending upon caliber. **Length:** NA. **Stock:** Oil-finished walnut with pistol grip, cheekpiece. **Sights:** Blade front, fixed rear. **Features:** Kersten double cross-bolt lock; scroll-engraved, case-hardened receiver; Blitz action with double triggers. Imported from Germany by GSI.
Price: Model 221 E (silver-grayed receiver finish, hunting scene engraving).. **$10,895.00**

MERKEL MODEL 160 SIDE-BY-SIDE DOUBLE RIFLE

Caliber: 22 Hornet, 5.6x50R Mag., 5.6x52R, 222 Rem., 243 Win., 6.5x55, 6.5x57R, 7x57R, 7x65R, 308, 30-06, 8x57JRS, 9.3x74R, 375 H&H. **Barrel:** 25.6". **Weight:** About 7.7 lbs, depending upon caliber. **Length:** NA. **Stock:** Oil-finished walnut with pistol grip, cheekpiece. **Sights:** Blade front on ramp, fixed rear. **Features:** Sidelock action. Double barrel locking lug with Greener cross-bolt; fine engraved hunting scenes on sideplates; Holland & Holland ejectors; double triggers. Imported from Germany by GSI.
Price: From... **$13,295.00**

Merkel Boxlock Double Rifles

Similar to the Model 160 double rifle except with Anson & Deely boxlock action with cocking indicators, double triggers, engraved color case-hardened receiver. Introduced 1995. Imported from Germany by GSI.
Price: Model 140-1, from **$5,995.00**
Price: Model 140-1.1 (engraved silver-gray receiver), from **$6,995.00**
Price: Model 150-1 (false sideplates, silver-gray receiver, Arabesque engraving), from **$7,495.00**
Price: Model 150-1.1 (as above with English Arabesque engraving), from **$8,995.00**

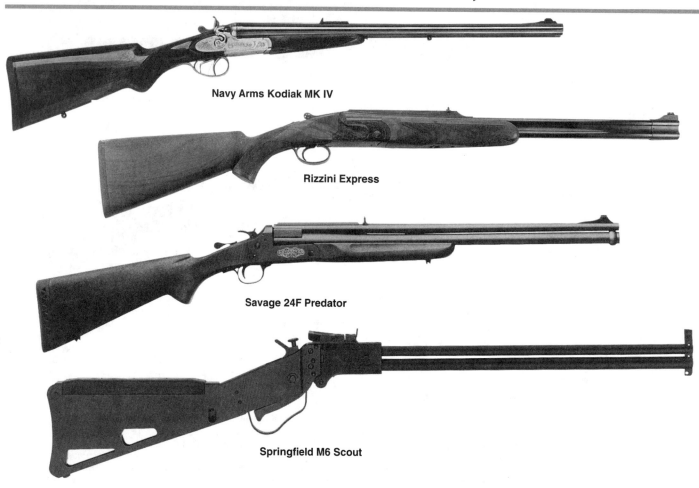

Navy Arms Kodiak MK IV

Rizzini Express

Savage 24F Predator

Springfield M6 Scout

NAVY ARMS KODIAK MK IV DOUBLE RIFLE

Caliber: 45-70. **Barrel:** 24". **Weight:** 10 lbs., 3 oz. **Length:** 39-3/4" overall. **Stock:** Checkered European walnut. **Sights:** Bead front, folding leaf express rear. **Features:** Blued, semi-regulated barrels; color case-hardened receiver and hammers; double triggers. Replica of Colt double rifle 1879-1885. Introduced 1996. Imported by Navy Arms.

Price: **$2,815.00**
Price: Engraved satin-finished receiver, browned barrels **$3,690.00**

RIZZINI EXPRESS 90L DOUBLE RIFLE

Caliber: 30-06, 7x65R, 9.3x74R. **Barrel:** 24". **Weight:** 7-1/2 lbs. **Length:** 40" overall. **Stock:** Select European walnut with satin oil finish; English-style cheekpiece. **Sights:** Ramp front, quarter-rib with express sight. **Features:** Color case-hardened boxlock action; automatic ejectors; single selective trigger; polished blue barrels. Extra 20-gauge shotshell barrels available. Imported for Italy by Wm. Larkin Moore.

Price: With case **$4,500.00**

SAVAGE 24F PREDATOR O/U COMBINATION GUN

Caliber/Gauge: 22 Hornet, 223, 30-30 over 12 (24F-12) or 22 LR, 22 Hornet, 223, 30-30 over 20-ga. (24F-20); 3" chambers. **Action:** Takedown, low rebounding visible hammer. Single trigger, barrel selector spur on hammer. **Barrel:** 24" separated barrels; 12-ga. has Full, Mod., Imp. Cyl. choke tubes, 20-ga. has fixed Mod. choke. **Weight:** 8 lbs. **Length:** 40-1/2" overall. **Stock:** Black Rynite composition. **Sights:** Ramp front, rear open adjustable for elevation. Grooved for tip-off scope mount. **Features:** Removable butt cap for storage and accessories. Introduced 1989.

Price: 24F-12 . . . . **$476.00**
Price: 24F-20 . . . . **$449.00**

Savage 24F-12/410 Combination Gun

Similar to the 24F-12 except comes with "Four-Tenner" adaptor for shooting 410-bore shotshells. Rifle barrel chambered for 22 Hornet, 223 Rem., 30-30 Win. Introduced 1998. Made in U.S. by Savage Arms, Inc.

Price: **$504.00**

SPRINGFIELD, INC. M6 SCOUT RIFLE/SHOTGUN

Caliber/Gauge: 22 LR or 22 Hornet over 410-bore. **Barrel:** 18.25". **Weight:** 4 lbs. **Length:** 32" overall. **Stock:** Folding detachable with storage for 15 22 LR, four 410 shells. **Sights:** Blade front, military aperture for 22; V-notch for 410. **Features:** All-metal construction. Designed for quick disassembly and minimum maintenance. Folds for compact storage. Introduced 1982; reintroduced 1996. Imported from the Czech Republic by Springfield, Inc.

Price: Parkerized **$185.00**
Price: Stainless steel **$219.00**

RIFLES

Designs for hunting, utility and sporting purposes, including training for competition

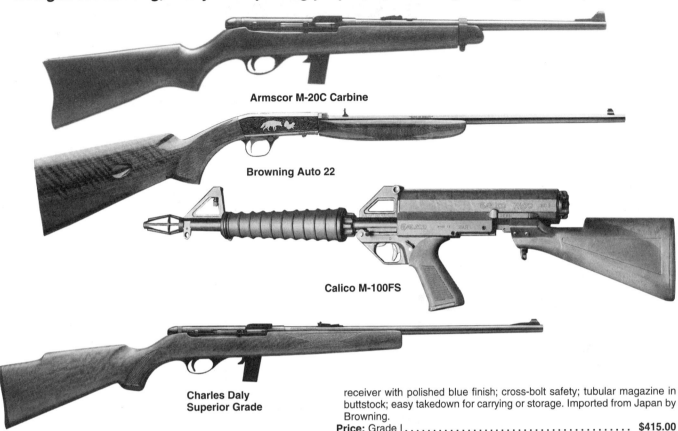

Armscor M-20C Carbine

Browning Auto 22

Calico M-100FS

Charles Daly
Superior Grade

AR-7 EXPLORER CARBINE
Caliber: 22 LR, 8-shot magazine. **Barrel:** 16". **Weight:** 2-1/2 lbs. **Length:** 34-1/2" / 16-1/2" stowed. **Stock:** Moulded Cycolac; snap-on rubber butt pad. **Sights:** Square blade front, aperture rear. **Features:** Takedown design stores barrel and action in hollow stock. Light enough to float. Reintroduced 1999. From AR-7 Industries, LLC.
Price: **$150.00**
Price: AR-20 Explorer (tubular stock, barrel shroud) **$200.00**

ARMSCOR MODEL AK22 AUTO RIFLE
Caliber: 22 LR, 10-shot magazine. **Barrel:** 18.5". **Weight:** 7.5 lbs. **Length:** 38" overall. **Stock:** Plain mahogany. **Sights:** Adjustable post front, leaf rear adjustable for elevation. **Features:** Resembles the AK-47. Matte black finish. Introduced 1987. Imported from the Philippines by K.B.I., Inc.
Price: About **$219.95**

ARMSCOR M-1600 AUTO RIFLE
Caliber: 22 LR, 10-shot magazine. **Barrel:** 18.25". **Weight:** 6.2 lbs. **Length:** 38.5" overall. **Stock:** Black finished mahogany. **Sights:** Post front, aperture rear. **Features:** Resembles Colt AR-15. Matte black finish. Introduced 1987. Imported from the Philippines by K.B.I., Inc.
Price: About **$199.95**

ARMSCOR M-20C AUTO CARBINE
Caliber: 22 LR, 10-shot magazine. **Barrel:** 18.25". **Weight:** 6.5 lbs. **Length:** 38" overall. **Stock:** Walnut-finished mahogany. **Sights:** Hooded front, rear adjustable for elevation. **Features:** Receiver grooved for scope mounting. Blued finish. Introduced 1990. Imported from the Philippines by K.B.I., Inc.
Price: **$154.95**

BROWNING AUTO-22 RIFLE
Caliber: 22 LR, 11-shot. **Barrel:** 19-1/4". **Weight:** 4-3/4 lbs. **Length:** 37" overall. **Stock:** Checkered select walnut with pistol grip and semi-beavertail forend. **Sights:** Gold bead front, folding leaf rear. **Features:** Engraved receiver with polished blue finish; cross-bolt safety; tubular magazine in buttstock; easy takedown for carrying or storage. Imported from Japan by Browning.
Price: Grade I **$415.00**

Browning Auto-22 Grade VI
Same as the Grade I Auto-22 except available with either grayed or blued receiver with extensive engraving with gold-plated animals: right side pictures a fox and squirrel in a woodland scene; left side shows a beagle chasing a rabbit. On top is a portrait of the beagle. Stock and forend are of high-grade walnut with a double-bordered cut checkering design. Introduced 1987.
Price: Grade VI, blue or gray receiver **$860.00**

BRNO ZKM 611 AUTO RIFLE
Caliber: 22 WMR, 6- or 10-shot magazine. **Barrel:** 20.4". **Weight:** 5.9 lbs. **Length:** 38.9" overall. **Stock:** European walnut. **Sights:** Hooded blade front, open adjustable rear. **Features:** Removable box magazine; polished blue finish; cross-bolt safety; grooved receiver for scope mounting; easy takedown for storage. Imported from The Czech Republic by Euro-Imports.
Price: **$475.00**

CALICO M-100FS CARBINE
Caliber: 22 LR. **Barrel:** 16.25". **Weight:** 5 lbs. **Length:** 36" overall. **Stock:** Glass-filled, impact-resistant polymer. **Sights:** Adjustable post front, notch rear. **Features:** Has helical-feed magazine; aluminum receiver; ambidextrous safety. Made in U.S. by Calico.
Price: **$650.00**

CHARLES DALY FIELD GRADE AUTO RIFLE
Caliber: 22 LR, 10-shot magazine. **Barrel:** 20-3/4". **Weight:** 6.5 lbs. **Length:** 40-1/2" overall. **Stock:** Walnut-finished hardwood with Monte Carlo. **Sights:** Hooded front, adjustable open rear. **Features:** Receiver grooved for scope mounting; blue finish; shell deflector. Introduced 1998. Imported by K.B.I.
Price: **$124.00**
Price: Superior Grade (cut checkered stock, fully adjustable sight) **$199.00**

CZ 511 Auto

Henry U.S. Survival

Marlin Model 60

Marlin Model 60 SSK

Marlin Model 70PSS

Charles Daly Empire Grade Auto Rifle

Similar to the Field Grade except has select California walnut stock with 24 l.p.i. hand checkering, contrasting forend and gripcaps, damascened bolt, high-polish blue. Introduced 1998. Imported by K.B.I.

Price: **$369.00**

CZ 511 AUTO RIFLE

Caliber: 22 LR, 8-shot magazine. **Barrel:** 22.2". **Weight:** 5.39 lbs. **Length:** 38.6" overall. **Stock:** Walnut with checkered pistol grip. **Sights:** Hooded front, adjustable rear. **Features:** Polished blue finish; detachable magazine; sling swivel studs. Imported from the Czech Republic by CZ-USA.

Price: **$351.00**

HENRY U.S. SURVIVAL RIFLE .22

Caliber: 22 LR, 8-shot magazine. **Barrel:** 16" steel lined. **Weight:** 2.5 lbs. **Stock:** ABS plastic. **Sights:** Blade front on ramp, aperture rear. **Features:** Takedown design stores barrel and action in hollow stock. Light enough to float. Silver, black or camo finish. Comes with two magazines. Introduced 1998. From Henry Repeating Arms Co.

Price: **$165.00**

MAGTECH MT 7022 AUTO RIFLE

Caliber: 22 LR, 10-shot magazine. **Barrel:** 18". **Weight:** 4.8 lbs. **Length:** 37" overall. **Stock:** Brazilian hardwood. **Sights:** Hooded blade front, fully adjustable open rear. **Features:** Cross-bolt safety; last-shot bolt hold-open; alloy receiver is drilled and tapped for scope mounting. Introduced 1998. Imported from Brazil by Magtech Ammunition Co.

Price: **$100.00**

MARLIN MODEL 60 SELF-LOADING RIFLE

Caliber: 22 LR, 14-shot tubular magazine. **Barrel:** 22" round tapered. **Weight:** About 5-1/2 lbs. **Length:** 40-1/2" overall. **Stock:** Press-checkered, walnut-finished Maine birch with Monte Carlo, full pistol grip; Mar-Shield® finish. **Sights:** Ramp front, open adjustable rear. **Features:** Matted receiver is grooved for scope mount. Manual bolt hold-open; automatic last-shot bolt hold-open.

Price: **$172.00**
Price: With 4x scope. **$179.00**

Marlin Model 60SS Self-Loading Rifle

Same as the Model 60 except breech bolt, barrel and outer magazine tube are made of stainless steel; most other parts are either nickel-plated or coated to match the stainless finish. Monte Carlo stock is of black/gray Maine birch laminate, and has nickel-plated swivel studs, rubber butt pad. Introduced 1993.

Price: **$273.00**
Price: Model 60SSK (black fiberglass-filled stock) **$236.00**
Price: Model 60SSK with 4x scope **$251.00**
Price: Model 60SB (walnut-finished birch stock) **$219.00**
Price: Model 60SB with 4x scope. **$232.00**

MARLIN 70PSS STAINLESS RIFLE

Caliber: 22 LR, 7-shot magazine. **Barrel:** 16-1/4" stainless steel, Micro-Groove® rifling. **Weight:** 3-1/4 lbs. **Length:** 35-1/4" overall. **Stock:** Black fiberglass-filled synthetic with abbreviated forend, nickel-plated swivel studs, moulded-in checkering. **Sights:** Ramp front with orange post, cutaway Wide Scan® hood; adjustable open rear. Receiver grooved for scope mounting. **Features:** Takedown barrel; cross-bolt safety; manual bolt hold-open; last shot bolt hold-open; comes with padded carrying case. Introduced 1986. Made in U.S. by Marlin.

Price: **$278.00**

Marlin Model 922

Marlin 7000

Marlin 795

Remington 597

MARLIN MODEL 922 MAGNUM SELF-LOADING RIFLE

Caliber: 22 WMR, 5-shot magazine. **Barrel:** 20.5". **Weight:** 6.5 lbs. **Length:** 39.75" overall. **Stock:** Now walnut finished hardwood, swivel studs, rubber butt pad. **Sights:** Ramp front with bead and removable Wide-Scan® hood, adjustable folding semi-buckhorn rear. **Features:** Action based on the centerfire Model 9 Carbine. Receiver drilled and tapped for scope mounting. Automatic last-shot bolt hold-open; magazine safety. Introduced 1993.
Price: **$441.00**

MARLIN MODEL 7000 SELF-LOADING RIFLE

Caliber: 22 LR, 10-shot magazine **Barrel:** 18" heavy target with 12-groove Micro-Groove® rifling, recessed muzzle. **Weight:** 5-1/2 lbs. **Length:** 37" overall. **Stock:** Black fiberglass-filled synthetic with Monte Carlo combo, swivel studs, moulded-in checkering. **Sights:** None furnished; comes with ring mounts. **Features:** Automatic last-shot bolt hold-open, manual bolt hold-open; cross-bolt safety; steel charging handle; blue finish, nickel-plated magazine. Introduced 1997. Made in U.S. by Marlin Firearms Co.
Price: **$232.00**

Marlin Model 795 Self-Loading Rifle

Similar to the Model 7000 except has standard-weight 18" barrel with 16-groove Micro-Groove rifling. Comes with ramp front sight with brass bead, screw adjustable open rear. Receiver grooved for scope mount. Introduced 1997. Made in U.S. by Marlin Firearms Co.
Price: **$164.00**
Price: With 4x scope................................. **$171.00**

REMINGTON MODEL 552 BDL DELUXE SPEEDMASTER RIFLE

Caliber: 22 S (20), L (17) or LR (15) tubular mag. **Barrel:** 21" round tapered. **Weight:** 5-3/4 lbs. **Length:** 40" overall. **Stock:** Walnut. Checkered grip and forend. **Sights:** Bead front, step open rear adjustable for windage and elevation. **Features:** Positive cross-bolt safety, receiver grooved for tip-off mount.
Price: **$365.00**

REMINGTON 597 AUTO RIFLE

Caliber: 22 LR, 10-shot clip. **Barrel:** 20". **Weight:** 5-1/2 lbs. **Length:** 40" overall. **Stock:** Gray synthetic. **Sights:** Bead front, fully adjustable rear. **Features:** Matte black finish, nickel-plated bolt. Receiver is grooved and drilled and tapped for scope mounts. Introduced 1997. Made in U.S. by Remington.
Price: **$163.00**
Price: Model 597 Magnum, 22 WMR, 8-shot clip............. **$321.00**
Price: Model 597 Magnum LS (laminated stock) **$377.00**
Price: Model 597 Sporter (22 LR, wood stock)............... **$199.00**
Price: Model 597 SS (22 LR, stainless steel, black synthetic stock) **$217.00**
Price: Model 597 Stainless Sporter / wood stock, SS barrel, 10-shot clip............................... **$239.00**

Remington 597 LSS Auto Rifle

Similar to the Model 597 except has satin-finish stainless barrel, gray-toned alloy receiver with nickel-plated bolt, and laminated wood stock. Receiver is grooved and drilled and tapped for scope mounting. Introduced 1997. Made in U.S. by Remington.
Price: **$272.00**

RIFLES

Ruger 10/22 International

Savage Model 64FV

RIFLES

RUGER 10/22 AUTOLOADING CARBINE

Caliber: 22 LR, 10-shot rotary magazine. **Barrel:** 18-1/2" round tapered. **Weight:** 5 lbs. **Length:** 37-1/4" overall. **Stock:** American hardwood with pistol grip and barrel. band. **Sights:** Brass bead front, folding leaf rear adjustable for elevation. **Features:** Detachable rotary magazine fits flush into stock, cross-bolt safety, receiver tapped and grooved for scope blocks or tip-off mount. Scope base adaptor furnished with each rifle.
Price: Model 10/22 RB (blue) $235.00
Price: Model K10/22RB (bright finish stainless barrel) $273.00
Price: Model 10/22RP (blue, synthetic stock) $230.00

Ruger 10/22 International Carbine

Similar to the Ruger 10/22 Carbine except has full-length International stock of American hardwood, checkered grip and forend; comes with rubber butt pad, sling swivels. Reintroduced 1994.
Price: Blue (10/22RBI) $267.00
Price: Stainless (K10/22RBI) $267.00

Ruger 10/22 Deluxe Sporter

Same as 10/22 Carbine except walnut stock with hand checkered pistol grip and forend; straight buttplate, no barrel band, has sling swivels.
Price: Model 10/22 DSP $279.00

Ruger 10/22T Target Rifle

Similar to the 10/22 except has 20" heavy, hammer-forged barrel with tight chamber dimensions, improved trigger pull, laminated hardwood stock dimensioned for optical sights. No iron sights supplied. Introduced 1996. Made in U.S. by Sturm, Ruger & Co.
Price: 10/22T $397.50
Price: K10/22T, stainless steel $445.00

Ruger K10/22RP All-Weather Rifle

Similar to the stainless K10/22/RP except has black composite stock of thermoplastic polyester resin reinforced with fiberglass; checkered grip and forend. Brushed satin, natural metal finish with clear hardcoat finish. Weighs 5 lbs., measures 36-3/4" overall. Introduced 1997. From Sturm, Ruger & Co.
Price: $273.00

RUGER 10/22 MAGNUM AUTOLOADING CARBINE

Caliber: 22 WMR, 10-shot rotary magazine. **Barrel:** 18-1/2". **Weight:** 6 lbs. **Length:** 37-1/4" overall. **Stock:** Birch. **Sights:** Gold bead front, folding rear. **Features:** All-steel receiver has integral Ruger scope bases for the included 1" rings. Introduced 1999. Made in U.S. by Sturm, Ruger & Co.
Price: $430.00

SAVAGE MODEL 64G AUTO RIFLE

Caliber: 22 LR, 10-shot magazine. **Barrel:** 20". **Weight:** 5-1/2 lbs. **Length:** 40" overall. **Stock:** Walnut-finished hardwood with Monte Carlo-type comb, checkered grip and forend. **Sights:** Bead front, open adjustable rear. Receiver grooved for scope mounting. **Features:** Thumb-operated rotating safety. Blue finish. Side ejection, bolt hold-open device. Introduced 1990. Made in Canada, from Savage Arms.
Price: $134.00
Price: Model 64F, black synthetic stock $124.00
Price: Model 64GXP Package Gun includes 4x15 scope and mounts $140.00
Price: Model 64FXP (black stock, 4x15 scope) $128.00

Savage Model 64FV Auto Rifle

Similar to the Model 64F except has heavy 21" barrel with recessed crown; no sights provided—comes with Weaver-style bases. Introduced 1998. Imported from Canada by Savage Arms, Inc.
Price: $164.00

THOMPSON/CENTER 22 LR CLASSIC RIFLE

Caliber: 22 LR, 8-shot magazine. **Barrel:** 22" match-grade. **Weight:** 5-1/2 pounds. **Length:** 39-1/2" overall. **Stock:** Satin-finished American walnut with Monte Carlo-type comb and pistol grip cap, swivel studs. **Sights:** Ramp-style front and fully adjustable rear, both with fiber optics. **Features:** All-steel receiver drilled and tapped for scope mounting; barrel threaded to receiver; thumb-operated safety; trigger-guard safety lock included.
Price: T/C 22 LR Classic (blue) $335.55

WINCHESTER MODEL 63 AUTO RIFLE

Caliber: 22 LR, 10-shot magazine. **Barrel:** 23". **Weight:** 6-1/4 lbs. **Length:** 39" overall. **Stock:** Walnut. **Sights:** Bead front, open adjustable rear. **Features:** Recreation of the original Model 63. Magazine tube loads through a port in the buttstock; forward cocking knob at front of forend; easy takedown for cleaning, storage; engraved receiver. Reintroduced 1997. From U.S. Repeating Arms Co.
Price: Grade I $678.00
Price: High grade, select walnut, cut checkering, engraved scenes with gold accents on receiver (made in 1997 only) $1,083.00

Classic and modern models for sport and utility, including training.

Browning BL-22

Henry Lever-Action 22

Henry Goldenboy 22

Henry Pump-Action 22

Marlin Model 39AS

RIFLES

BROWNING BL-22 LEVER-ACTION RIFLE

Caliber: 22 S (22), L (17) or LR (15), tubular magazine. **Barrel:** 20" round tapered. **Weight:** 5 lbs. **Length:** 36-3/4" overall. **Stock:** Walnut, two-piece straight grip Western style. **Sights:** Bead post front, folding-leaf rear. **Features:** Short throw lever, half-cock safety, receiver grooved for tip-off scope mounts. Imported from Japan by Browning.
Price: Grade I $360.00
Price: Grade II (engraved receiver, checkered grip and forend) . $412.00

HENRY LEVER-ACTION 22

Caliber: 22 Long Rifle (15-shot). **Barrel:** 18-1/4" round. **Weight:** 5-1/2 lbs. **Length:** 34" overall. **Stock:** Walnut. **Sights:** Hooded blade front, open adjustable rear. **Features:** Polished blue finish; full-length tubular magazine; side ejection; receiver grooved for scope mounting. Introduced 1997. Made in U.S. by Henry Repeating Arms Co.
Price: $239.95
Price: Youth model (33" overall, 11-rounds 22 LR) $229.95

HENRY GOLDENBOY 22 LEVER-ACTION RIFLE

Caliber: 22 LR, 16-shot. **Barrel:** 20" octagonal. **Weight:** 6.25 lbs. **Length:** 38" overall. **Stock:** American walnut. **Sights:** Blade front, open rear. **Features:** Brasslite receiver, brass buttplate, blued barrel and lever. Introduced 1998. Made in U.S. from Henry Repeating Arms Co.
Price: $329.95

HENRY PUMP-ACTION 22 PUMP RIFLE

Caliber: 22 LR, 15-shot. **Barrel:** 18.25". **Weight:** 5.5 lbs. **Length:** NA. **Stock:** American walnut. **Sights:** Bead on ramp front, open adjustable rear. **Features:** Polished blue finish; receiver groved for scope mount; grooved slide handle; two barrel bands. Introduced 1998. Made in U.S. from Henry Repeating Arms Co.
Price: $249.95

MARLIN MODEL 39AS GOLDEN LEVER-ACTION RIFLE

Caliber: 22 S (26), L (21), LR (19), tubular magazine. **Barrel:** 24" Micro-Groove®. **Weight:** 6-1/2 lbs. **Length:** 40" overall. **Stock:** Checkered American black walnut with white line spacers at pistol gripcap and buttplate; Mar-Shield® finish. Swivel studs; rubber butt pad. **Sights:** Bead ramp front with detachable Wide-Scan™ hood, folding rear semi-buckhorn adjustable for windage and elevation. **Features:** Hammer-block safety; rebounding hammer. Takedown action, receiver tapped for scope mount (supplied), offset hammer spur; gold-plated steel trigger.
Price: $509.00

Marlin Model 1897CB Cowboy Lever Action Rifle

Similar to the Model 39AS except it has straight-grip stock with hard rubber buttplate; blued steel forend cap; 24" tapered octagon barrel with Micro-Groove® rifling; adjustable Marble semi-buckhorn rear sight, Marble carbine front with brass bead; overall length 40". Introduced 1999. Made in U.S. by Marlin.
Price: $687.00

Remington Model 572

Ruger Model 96/22

Winchester 9422 Large Loop

Winchester Model 9422 Trapper

REMINGTON 572 BDL DELUXE FIELDMASTER PUMP RIFLE

Caliber: 22 S (20), L (17) or LR (14), tubular magazine. **Barrel:** 21" round tapered. **Weight:** 5-1/2 lbs. **Length:** 40" overall. **Stock:** Walnut with checkered pistol grip and slide handle. **Sights:** Blade ramp front; sliding ramp rear adjustable for windage and elevation. **Features:** Cross-bolt safety; removing inner magazine tube converts rifle to single shot; receiver grooved for tip-off scope mount.
Price: $379.00

RUGER MODEL 96/22 LEVER-ACTION RIFLE

Caliber: 22 LR, 10-shot rotary magazine; 22 WMR, 9-shot rotary magazine. **Barrel:** 18-1/2". **Weight:** 5-1/4 lbs. **Length:** 37-1/4" overall. **Stock:** American hardwood. **Sights:** Gold bead front, folding leaf rear. **Features:** Cross-bolt safety, visible cocking indicator; short-throw lever action. Screw-on dovetail scope base. Introduced 1996. Made in U.S. by Sturm, Ruger & Co.
Price: 96/22 (22 LR) $332.50
Price: 96/22M (22 WMR) $350.00

TAURUS MODEL 62R PUMP RIFLE

Caliber: 22 LR, 13-shot. **Barrel:** 23" round. **Weight:** 5-3/4 lbs. **Length:** 39" overall. **Stock:** Walnut-finished hardwood, straight grip, grooved forend. **Sights:** Fixed front, adjustable rear. **Features:** Blue finish; bolt-mounted safety; quick takedown. Imported from Brazil by Interarms.
Price: $279.00

Taurus Model 62C Pump Carbine

Same as standard model except 22 LR, has 16-1/2" barrel. Magazine holds 12 cartridges.
Price: $279.00

WINCHESTER MODEL 9422 LEVER-ACTION RIFLE

Caliber: 22 LR, 22 WMR, tubular magazine. **Barrel:** 20-1/2". **Weight:** 6-1/4 lbs. **Length:** 37-1/8" overall. **Stock:** American walnut, two-piece, straight grip (no pistol grip). **Sights:** Hooded ramp front, adjustable semi-buckhorn rear. **Features:** Side ejection, receiver grooved for scope mounting, take-down action. From U.S. Repeating Arms Co.
Price: Traditional $437.00
Price: Model 9422 Legacy (semi-pistol grip stock, 22 LR and 22 WMR)
. . . . $467.00

Winchester Model 9422 Magnum Lever-Action Rifle

Same as the 9422 except chambered for 22 WMR cartridge, has 11-round mag. capacity.
Price: Traditional $457.00
Price: Legacy 22 WMR $488.00

Winchester Model 9422 Trapper

Similar to the Model 9422 with walnut stock except has 16-1/2" barrel, overall length of 33-1/8", weighs 5-1/2 lbs. Magazine holds 15 Shorts, 12 Longs, 11 Long Rifles. Introduced 1996.
Price: $437.00
Price: 22 WMR, 8-shot $457.00

WINCHESTER MODEL 1892 SHORT LEVER-ACTION RIFLE

Caliber: 44 Mag.; 11-shot magazine. **Barrel:** 20". **Weight:** 6-1/4 lbs. **Length:** 37-3/4" overall. **Stock:** Smooth walnut. **Sights:** Blade front, buckhorn-style, ramp-adjustable rear. **Features:** Dual, vertical locking lugs; compact design with shorter forearm resembles original design. From U.S. Repeating Co., Inc.
Price: $752.00

WINCHESTER MODEL 1886 EXTRA LIGHT GRADE I

Caliber: 45-70, 4-shot magazine. **Barrel:** 22". **Weight:** 7-1.4 lbs. **Length:** 40-1/2" overall. **Sights:** Blade front, buckhorn-style ramp-adjustable rear. **Features:** Round, tapered barrel; shotgun-style steel buttplate; half-magazine. Limited production. Introduced 2000. From U.S. Repeating Arms Co., Inc.
Price: $1,156.00
Price: High Grade (extra-fancy, checkered walnut stock, engraved elk and deer scenes) $1,447.00

Includes models for a variety of sports, utility and competitive shooting.

Anschutz 1518D Luxus

Anschutz 1710D

Charles Daly Field Grade

ANSCHUTZ 1416D/1516D CLASSIC RIFLES

Caliber: 22 LR (1416D), 5-shot clip; 22 WMR (1516D), 4-shot clip. **Barrel:** 22-1/2". **Weight:** 6 lbs. **Length:** 41" overall. **Stock:** European hardwood with walnut finish; classic style with straight comb, checkered pistol grip and forend. **Sights:** Hooded ramp front, folding leaf rear. **Features:** Uses Match 64 action. Adjustable single stage trigger. Receiver grooved for scope mounting. Imported from Germany by AcuSport Corp.

Price: 1416D, 22 LR	**$755.95**
Price: 1516D, 22 WMR	**$779.95**
Price: 1416D Classic left-hand	**$679.95**

Anschutz 1416D/1516D Walnut Luxus Rifles

Similar to the Classic models except have European walnut stocks with Monte Carlo cheekpiece, slim forend with Schnabel tip, cut checkering on grip and forend. Introduced 1997. Imported from Germany by AcuSport Corp.

Price: 1416D (22 LR)	**$755.95**
Price: 1516D (22 WMR)	**$779.95**

ANSCHUTZ 1518D LUXUS BOLT-ACTION RIFLE

Caliber: 22 WMR, 4-shot magazine. **Barrel:** 19-3/4". **Weight:** 5-1/2 lbs. **Length:** 37-1/2" overall. **Stock:** European walnut. **Sights:** Blade on ramp front, folding leaf rear. **Features:** Receiver grooved for scope mounting; single stage trigger; skip-line checkering; rosewood forend tip; sling swivels. Imported from Germany by AcuSport Corp.

Price: **$1,186.95**

ANSCHUTZ 1710D CUSTOM RIFLE

Caliber: 22 LR, 5-shot clip. **Barrel:** 24-1/4". **Weight:** 7-3/8 lbs. **Length:** 42-1/2" overall. **Stock:** Select European walnut. **Sights:** Hooded ramp front, folding leaf rear; drilled and tapped for scope mounting. **Features:** Match 54 action with adjustable single-stage trigger; roll-over Monte Carlo cheekpiece, slim forend with Schnabel tip, Wundhammer palm swell on pistol grip, rosewood gripcap with white diamond insert; skip-line checkering on grip and forend. Introduced 1988. Imported from Germany by AcuSport Corp.

Price: **$1,289.95**

CABANAS MASTER BOLT-ACTION RIFLE

Caliber: 177, round ball or pellet; single shot. **Barrel:** 19-1/2". **Weight:** 8 lbs. **Length:** 45-1/2" overall. **Stocks:** Walnut target-type with Monte Carlo. **Sights:** Blade front, fully adjustable rear. **Features:** Fires round ball or pellet with 22-cal. blank cartridge. Bolt action. Imported from Mexico by Mandall Shooting Supplies. Introduced 1984.

Price: **$189.95**
Price: Varmint model (has 21-1/2" barrel, 4-1/2 lbs., 41" overall length, varmint-type stock) **$119.95**

Cabanas Leyre Bolt-Action Rifle

Similar to Master model except 44" overall, has sport/target stock.

Price: **$149.95**
Price: Model R83 (17" barrel, hardwood stock, 40" o.a.l.) **$79.95**
Price: Mini 82 Youth (16-1/2" barrel, 33" overall length, 3-1/2 lbs.) . **$69.95**
Price: Pony Youth (16" barrel, 34" overall length, 3.2 lbs.) **$69.95**

Cabanas Espronceda IV Bolt-Action Rifle

Similar to the Leyre model except has full sporter stock, 18-3/4" barrel, 40" overall length, weighs 5-1/2 lbs.

Price: **$134.95**

CABANAS LASER RIFLE

Caliber: 177. **Barrel:** 19". **Weight:** 6 lbs., 12 oz. **Length:** 42" overall. **Stock:** Target-type thumbhole. **Sights:** Blade front, open fully adjustable rear. **Features:** Fires round ball or pellets with 22 blank cartridge. Imported from Mexico by Mandall Shooting Supplies.

Price: **$159.95**

CHARLES DALY SUPERIOR BOLT-ACTION RIFLE

Caliber: 22 LR, 10-shot magazine. **Barrel:** 22-5/8". **Weight:** 6.7 lbs. **Length:** 41.25" overall. **Stock:** Walnut-finished mahogany. **Sights:** Bead front, rear adjustable for elevation. **Features:** Receiver grooved for scope mounting. Blued finish. Introduced 1998. Imported by K.B.I., Inc.

Price: **$189.95**

Charles Daly Field Grade Rifle

Similar to the Superior except has short walnut-finished hardwood stock for small shooters. Introduced 1998. Imported by K.B.I., Inc.

Price: **$134.95**
Price: Field Youth (17.5" barrel) **$144.95**

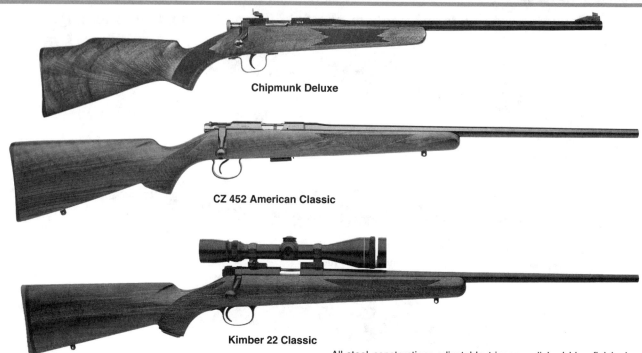

Chipmunk Deluxe

CZ 452 American Classic

Kimber 22 Classic

Charles Daly Superior Magnum Grade Rifle

Similar to the Superior except chambered for 22 WMR. Has 22.6" barrel, double lug bolt, checkered stock, weighs 6.5 lbs. Introduced 1987.
Price: About **$204.95**

Charles Daly Empire Magnum Grade Rifle

Similar to the Superior Magnum except has oil-finished American walnut stock with 18 lpi hand checkering; black hardwood gripcap and forend tip; highly polished barreled action; jewelled bolt; recoil pad; swivel studs. Imported from the Philippines by K.B.I., Inc.
Price: **$364.95**

Charles Daly Empire Grade Rifle

Similar to the Superior except has oil-finished American walnut stock with 18 lpi hand checkering; black hardwood gripcap and forend tip; highly polished barreled action; jewelled bolt; recoil pad; swivel studs. Imported by K.B.I., Inc.
Price: **$329.00**

CHARLES DALY TRUE YOUTH BOLT-ACTION RIFLE

Caliber: 22 LR, single shot. **Barrel:** 16-1/4". **Weight:** About 3 lbs. **Length:** 32" overall. **Stock:** Walnut-finished hardwood. **Sights:** Blade front, adjustable rear. **Features:** Scaled-down stock for small shooters. Blue finish. Introduced 1998. Imported by K.B.I., Inc.
Price: **$154.95**

CHIPMUNK SINGLE SHOT RIFLE

Caliber: 22, S, L, LR, single shot. **Barrel:** 16-1/8". **Weight:** About 2-1/2 lbs. **Length:** 30" overall. **Stocks:** American walnut. **Sights:** Post on ramp front, peep rear adjustable for windage and elevation. **Features:** Drilled and tapped for scope mounting using special Chipmunk base ($13.95). Made in U.S. Introduced 1982. From Rogue Rifle Co., Inc.
Price: Standard. **$194.25**
Price: Deluxe (better wood, checkering). **$246.95**
Price: With black, brown or camouflage laminate stock. **$209.95**
Price: With black polyurethane-coated wood stock **$183.95**
Price: Bull barrel models of above, add **$16.00**

CZ 452 M 2E LUX BOLT-ACTION RIFLE

Caliber: 22 LR, 22 WMR, 5-shot detachable magazine. **Barrel:** 24.8". **Weight:** 6.6 lbs. **Length:** 42.63" overall. **Stock:** Walnut with checkered pistol grip. **Sights:** Hooded front, fully adjustable tangent rear. **Features:**

All-steel construction; adjustable trigger; polished blue finish. Imported from the Czech Republic by CZ-USA.
Price: 22 LR **$351.00**
Price: 22 WMR **$378.00**
Price: Synthetic stock, nickel finish, 22 LR. **$344.00**

CZ 452 M 2E Varmint Rifle

Similar to the Lux model except has heavy 20.8" barrel; stock has beavertail forend; weighs 7 lbs.; no sights furnished. Available only in 22 LR. Imported from the Czech Republic by CZ-USA.
Price: **$369.00**

CZ 452 American Classic Bolt-Action Rifle

Similar to the CZ 452 M 2E Lux except has classic-style stock of Circassian walnut; 22.5" free-floating barrel with recessed target crown; receiver dovetail for scope mounting. No open sights furnished. Introduced 1999. Imported from the Czech Republic by CZ-USA.
Price: 22 LR **$351.00**
Price: 22 WMR **$378.00**

KIMBER 22 CLASSIC BOLT-ACTION RIFLE

Caliber: 22 LR, 5-shot magazine. **Barrel:** 22" Kimber match grade; 11-degree target crown. **Weight:** About 6.5 lbs. **Length:** 40.5" overall. **Stock:** Classic style in Claro walnut with 18 l.p.i. hand-cut checkering; satin finish; steel gripcap; swivel studs. **Sights:** None furnished; Kimber sculpted bases available that accept all rotary dovetail rings. **Features:** All-new action with Mauser-style full-length claw extractor; two-position in M70-type safety; fully adjustable trigger set at 2 lbs.; pillar-bedded action with recoil lug, free-floated barrel. Introduced 1999. Made in U.S. by Kimber Mfg., Inc.
Price: **$919.00**

Kimber 22 SuperAmerica Bolt-Action Rifle

Similar to the 22 Classic except has AAA Claro walnut stock with wraparound 22 l.p.i. hand-cut checkering, ebony forened tip, beaded cheekpiece. Introduced 1999. Made in U.S. by Kimber Mfg., Inc.
Price: **$1,493.00**

Kimber 22 SVT Bolt-Action Rilfe

Similar to the 22 Classic except has 18" stainless steel, fluted bull barrel, gray laminated, high-comb target-style stock with deep pistol grip, high comb, and beavertail forend with bipod stud. Weighs 7.5 lbs., overall length 36.5". Matte finish on action. Introduced 1999. Made in U.S. by Kimber Mfg., Inc.
Price: **$915.00**

Kimber 22 SVT

Kimber 22 HS

Marlin Model 15YN

Marlin Model 880SS

Marlin 880SQ Squirrel

Kimber 22 HS (Hunter Silhouette) Bolt-Action Rifle

Similar to the 22 Classic except has 24" medium sporter match-grade barrel with half-fluting; high comb, walnut, Monte Carlo target stock with 18 l.p.i. checkering; matte blue metal finish. Introduced 1999. Made in U.S. by Kimber Mfg., Inc.

Price: $748.00

MARLIN MODEL 15YN "LITTLE BUCKAROO"

Caliber: 22 S, L, LR, single shot. **Barrel:** 16-1/4" Micro-Groove®. **Weight:** 4-1/4 lbs. **Length:** 33-1/4" overall. **Stock:** One-piece walnut-finished, press-checkered Maine birch with Monte Carlo; Mar-Shield® finish. **Sights:** Ramp front, adjustable open rear. **Features:** Beginner's rifle with thumb safety, easy-load feed throat, red cocking indicator. Receiver grooved for scope mounting. Introduced 1989.

Price: $193.00

MARLIN MODEL 880SS BOLT-ACTION RIFLE

Caliber: 22 LR, 7-shot clip magazine. **Barrel:** 22" Micro-Groove®. **Weight:** 6 lbs. **Length:** 41" overall. **Stock:** Black fiberglass-filled synthetic with nickel-plated swivel studs and moulded-in checkering. **Sights:** Ramp front with orange post and cutaway Wide-Scan™ hood, adjustable semi-buck-

horn folding rear. **Features:** Stainless steel barrel, receiver, front breech bolt and striker; receiver grooved for scope mounting. Introduced 1994. Made in U.S. by Marlin.

Price: $289.00

Marlin Model 81TS Bolt-Action Rifle

Same as the Marlin 880SS except blued steel, tubular magazine, holds 17 Long Rifle cartridges. Weighs 6 lbs.

Price: $196.00
Price: With 4x scope. $203.00

Marlin Model 880SQ Squirrel Rifle

Similar to the Model 880SS except uses the heavy target barrel of Marlin's Model 2000L target rifle. Black synthetic stock with moulded-in checkering; double bedding screws; matte blue finish. Comes without sights, no dovetail or filler screws; receiver grooved for scope mount. Weighs 7 lbs. Introduced 1996. Made in U.S. by Marlin.

Price: $302.00

Marlin Model 25N Bolt-Action Repeater

Similar to Marlin 880, except walnut-finished p.g. stock, adjustable open rear sight, ramp front.

Price: $195.00
Price: With 4x scope. $201.00

Marlin 883SS

Ruger K77/22 Varmint

Ruger 77/22R

Sako Finnfire

Marlin Model 25MN Bolt-Action Rifle

Similar to the Model 25N except chambered for 22 WMR. Has 7-shot clip magazine, 22" Micro-Groove® barrel, checkered walnut-finished Maine birch stock. Introduced 1989.

Price: $223.00
Price: With 4x scope. $229.00

Marlin Model 882 Bolt-Action Rifle

Same as the Marlin 880 except 22 WMR cal. only with 7-shot clip magazine; weight about 6 lbs. Comes with swivel studs.

Price: $296.00
Price: Model 882L (laminated hardwood stock) $313.00

Marlin Model 883 Bolt-Action Rifle

Same as Marlin 882 except tubular magazine holds 12 rounds of 22 WMR ammunition.

Price: $308.00

Marlin Model 882SS Bolt-Action Rifle

Same as the Marlin Model 882 except has stainless steel front breech bolt, barrel, receiver and bolt knob. All other parts are either stainless steel or nickel-plated. Has black Monte Carlo stock of fiberglass-filled polycarbonate with moulded-in checkering, nickel-plated swivel studs. Introduced 1995. Made in U.S. by Marlin Firearms Co.

Price: $314.00

Marlin Model 882SSV Bolt-Action Rifle

Similar to the Model 882SS except has selected heavy 22" stainless steel barrel with recessed muzzle, and comes without sights; receiver is grooved for scope mount and 1" ring mounts are included. Weighs 7 lbs. Introduced 1997. Made in U.S. by Marlin Firearms Co.

Price: $309.00

Marlin Model 883SS Bolt-Action Rifle

Same as the Model 883 except front breech bolt, striker knob, trigger stud, cartridge lifter stud and outer magazine tube are of stainless steel; other parts are nickel-plated. Has two-tone brown laminated Monte Carlo stock with swivel studs, rubber butt pad. Introduced 1993.

Price: $326.00

RUGER K77/22 VARMINT RIFLE

Caliber: 22 LR, 10-shot, 22 WMR, 9-shot detachable rotary magazine. **Barrel:** 24", heavy. **Weight:** 7.25 lbs. **Length:** 43.25" overall. **Stock:** Laminated hardwood with rubber butt pad, quick-detachable swivel studs. No checkering or gripcap. **Sights:** None furnished. Comes with Ruger 1" scope rings. **Features:** Made of stainless steel with target gray finish. Three-position safety, dual extractors. Stock has wide, flat forend. Introduced 1993.

Price: K77/22VBZ, 22 LR $539.00
Price: K77/22VMBZ, 22 WMR $539.00

RUGER 77/22 RIMFIRE BOLT-ACTION RIFLE

Caliber: 22 LR, 10-shot rotary magazine; 22 WMR, 9-shot rotary magazine. **Barrel:** 20". **Weight:** About 5-3/4 lbs. **Length:** 39-3/4" overall. **Stock:** Checkered American walnut or injection-moulded fiberglass-reinforced DuPont Zytel with Xenoy inserts in forend and grip, stainless sling swivels. **Sights:** Brass bead front, adjustable folding leaf rear or plain barrel with 1" Ruger rings. **Features:** Mauser-type action uses Ruger's 10-shot rotary magazine. Three-position safety, simplified bolt stop, patented bolt locking system. Uses the dual-screw barrel attachment system of the 10/22 rifle. Integral scope mounting system with 1" Ruger rings. Blued model introduced in 1983. Stainless steel model and blued model with the synthetic stock introduced in 1989.

Price: 77/22R (no sights, rings, walnut stock) $498.00
Price: 77/22RS (open sights, rings, walnut stock) $506.00
Price: K77/22RP (stainless, no sights, rings, synthetic stock) . . . $498.00
Price: K77/22RSP (stainless, open sights, rings, synthetic stock) . $491.00
Price: 77/22RM (22 WMR, blue, walnut stock). $483.00
Price: K77/22RSMP (22 WMR, stainless, open sights, rings, synthetic stock) $491.00
Price: K77/22RMP (22 WMR, stainless, synthetic stock). $483.00
Price: 77/22RSM (22 WMR, blue, open sights, rings, walnut stock). $491.00

SAKO FINNFIRE HUNTER BOLT-ACTION RIFLE

Caliber: 22 LR, 5-shot magazine. **Barrel:** 22". **Weight:** 5.75 lbs. **Length:** 39-1/2" overall. **Stock:** European walnut with checkered grip and forend. **Sights:** Hooded blade front, open adjustable rear. **Features:** Adjustable single-stage trigger; has 50-degree bolt lift. Introduced 1994. Imported from Finland by Stoeger Industries.

Price: $874.00
Price: Varmint (heavy barrel) $924.00

RIFLES

Savage Mark II-FXP

Savage Model 93G

Winchester Model 52B

SAKO FINNFIRE SPORTER RIFLE

Caliber: 22 LR. **Barrel:** 22"; heavy, free-floating. **Weight:** NA. **Length:** NA. **Stock:** Match style of European walnut; adjustable cheekpiece and butt-plate; stippled pistol grip and forend. **Sights:** None furnished; has 11mm integral dovetail scope mount. **Features:** Based on the Sako P94S action with two bolt locking lugs, 50-degree bolt lift and 30mm throw; adjustable trigger. Introduced 1999. Imported from Finland by Stoeger Industries.
Price: $984.00

SAVAGE MARK I-G BOLT-ACTION RIFLE

Caliber: 22 LR, single shot. **Barrel:** 20-3/4". **Weight:** 5-1/2 lbs. **Length:** 39-1/2" overall. **Stock:** Walnut-finished hardwood with Monte Carlo-type comb, checkered grip and forend. **Sights:** Bead front, open adjustable rear. Receiver grooved for scope mounting. **Features:** Thumb-operated rotating safety. Blue finish. Rifled or smooth bore. Introduced 1990. Made in Canada, from Savage Arms Inc.
Price: Mark I, rifled or smooth bore, right- or left-handed $119.00
Price: Mark I-GY (Youth), 19" barrel, 37" overall, 5 lbs. $127.00

SAVAGE MARK II-G BOLT-ACTION RIFLE

Caliber: 22 LR, 10-shot magazine. **Barrel:** 20-1/2". **Weight:** 5-1/2 lbs. **Length:** 39-1/2" overall. **Stock:** Walnut-finished hardwood with Monte Carlo-type comb, checkered grip and forend. **Sights:** Bead front, open adjustable rear. Receiver grooved for scope mounting. **Features:** Thumb-operated rotating safety. Blue finish. Introduced 1990. Made in Canada, from Savage Arms, Inc.
Price: $140.00
Price: Mark II-GY (youth), 19" barrel, 37" overall, 5 lbs. $140.00
Price: Mark II-GL, left-hand $140.00
Price: Mark II-GLY (youth) left-hand. $140.00
Price: Mark II-GXP Package Gun (comes with 4x15 scope),
right- or left-handed $147.00
Price: Mark II-FXP (as above except with black synthetic
stock) $133.00
Price: Mark II-F (as above, no scope) $127.00

Savage Mark II-LV Heavy Barrel Rifle

Similar to the Mark II-G except has heavy 21" barrel with recessed target-style crown; gray, laminated hardwood stock with cut checkering. No sights furnished, but has dovetailed receiver for scope mounting. Overall length is 39-3/4", weight is 6-1/2 lbs. Comes with 10-shot clip magazine. Introduced 1997. Imported from Canada by Savage Arms, Inc.
Price: $222.00
Price: Mark II-FV, with black graphite/polymer stock $194.00

Savage Mark II-FSS Stainless Rifle

Similar to the Mark II-G except has stainless steel barreled action and graphite/polymer filled stock; free-floated barrel. Weighs 5 lbs. Introduced 1997. Imported from Canada by Savage Arms, Inc.
Price: $169.00

Savage Model 93FVSS Magnum Rifle

Similar to the Model 93FSS Magnum except has 21" heavy barrel with recessed target-style crown; satin-finished stainless barreled action; black graphite/fiberglass stock. Drilled and tapped for scope mounting; comes with Weaver-style bases. Introduced 1998. Imported from Canada by Savage Arms, Inc.
Price: $222.00

SAVAGE MODEL 93G MAGNUM BOLT-ACTION RIFLE

Caliber: 22 WMR, 5-shot magazine. **Barrel:** 20-3/4". **Weight:** 5-3/4 lbs. **Length:** 39-1/2" overall. **Stock:** Walnut-finished hardwood with Monte Carlo-type comb, checkered grip and forend. **Sights:** Bead front, adjustable open rear. Receiver grooved for scope mount. **Features:** Thumb-operated rotary safety. Blue finish. Introduced 1994. Made in Canada, from Savage Arms.
Price: About $160.00
Price: Model 93F (as above with black graphite/fiberglass
stock) $154.00

Savage Model 93FSS Magnum Rifle

Similar to the Model 93G except has stainless steel barreled action and black synthetic stock with positive checkering. Weighs 5-1/2 lbs. Introduced 1997. Imported from Canada by Savage Arms, Inc.
Price: $194.00

WINCHESTER MODEL 52B BOLT-ACTION RIFLE

Caliber: 22 Long Rifle, 5-shot magazine. **Barrel:** 24". **Weight:** 7 lbs. **Length:** 41-3/4" overall. **Stock:** Walnut with checkered grip and forend. **Sights:** None furnished; grooved receiver and drilled and tapped for scope mounting. **Features:** Has Micro Motion trigger adjustable for pull and over-travel; match chamber; detachable magazine. Reintroduced 1997. From U.S. Repeating Arms Co.
Price: $654.00

Includes models for classic American and ISU target competition and other sporting and competitive shooting.

Anschutz 1451 Target

Anschutz 2013

ANSCHUTZ 1451R SPORTER TARGET RIFLE

Caliber: 22 LR, 5-shot magazine. **Barrel:** 22" heavy match. **Weight:** 6.4 lbs. **Length:** 39.75" overall. **Stock:** European hardwood with walnut finish. **Sights:** None furnished. Grooved receiver for scope mounting or Anschutz micrometer rear sight. **Features:** Sliding safety, two-stage trigger. Adjustable buttplate; forend slide rail to accept Anschutz accessories. Imported from Germany by AcuSport Corp.
Price: **$549.00**

ANSCHUTZ 1451 TARGET RIFLE

Caliber: 22 LR. **Barrel:** 22". **Weight:** About 6.5 lbs. **Length:** 40". **Sights:** Optional. Receiver grooved for scope mounting. **Features:** Designed for the beginning junior shooter with adjustable length of pull from 13.25" to 14.25" via removable butt spacers. Two-stage trigger factory set at 2.6 lbs. Introduced 1999. Imported from Germany by Gunsmithing, Inc.
Price: **$347.00**
Price: #6834 Match Sight Set. **$227.10**

ANSCHUTZ 1808D-RT SUPER RUNNING TARGET RIFLE

Caliber: 22 LR, single shot. **Barrel:** 32-1/2". **Weight:** 9 lbs. **Length:** 50" overall. **Stock:** European walnut. Heavy beavertail forend; adjustable cheekpiece and buttplate. Stippled grip and forend. **Sights:** None furnished. Grooved for scope mounting. **Features:** Designed for Running Target competition. Nine-way adjustable single-stage trigger, slide safety. Introduced 1991. Imported from Germany by Accuracy International, Gunsmithing, Inc.
Price: Right-hand **$1,364.10**

ANSCHUTZ 1903 MATCH RIFLE

Caliber: 22 LR, single shot. **Barrel:** 25.5", .75" diameter. **Weight:** 10.1 lbs. **Length:** 43.75" overall. **Stock:** Walnut-finished hardwood with adjustable cheekpiece; stippled grip and forend. **Sights:** None furnished. **Features:** Uses Anschutz Match 64 action and #5098 two-stage trigger. A medium weight rifle for intermediate and advanced Junior Match competition. Introduced 1987. Imported from Germany by Accuracy International, Gunsmithing, Inc.
Price: Right-hand **$720.40**
Price: Left-hand **$757.90**

ANSCHUTZ 64-MSR SILHOUETTE RIFLE

Caliber: 22 LR, 5-shot magazine. **Barrel:** 21-1/2", medium heavy; 7/8" diameter. **Weight:** 8 lbs. **Length:** 39.5" overall. **Stock:** Walnut-finished hardwood, silhouette-type. **Sights:** None furnished. **Features:** Uses Match 64 action. Designed for metallic silhouette competition. Stock has stippled checkering, contoured thumb groove with Wundhammer swell.

Two-stage #5098 trigger. Slide safety locks sear and bolt. Introduced 1980. Imported from Germany by AcuSport Corp., Accuracy International, Gunsmithing, Inc.
Price: 64-MSR **$704.30**

ANSCHUTZ 2013 BENCHREST RIFLE

Caliber: 22 LR, single shot. **Barrel:** 19.6". **Weight:** About 10.3 lbs. **Length:** 37.75" to 42.5" overall. **Stock:** Benchrest style of European hardwood. Stock length adjustable via spacers and buttplate. **Sights:** None furnished. Receiver grooved for mounts. **Features:** Uses the Anschutz 2013 target action, #5018 two-stage adjustable target trigger factory set at 3.9 oz. Introduced 1994. Imported from Germany by Accuracy International, Gunsmithing, Inc.
Price: **$1,757.20**

Anschutz 2007 Match Rifle

Uses same action as the Model 2013, but has a lighter barrel. European walnut stock in right-hand, true left-hand or extra-short models. Sights optional. Available with 19.6" barrel with extension tube, or 26", both in stainless or blue. Introduced 1998. Imported from Germany by Gunsmithing, Inc., Accuracy International.
Price: Right-hand, blue, no sights **$1,766.60**
Price: Right-hand, blue, no sights, extra-short stock **$1,756.60**
Price: Left-hand, blue, no sights. **$1,856.80**

ANSCHUTZ 1827 BIATHLON RIFLE

Caliber: 22 LR, 5-shot magazine. **Barrel:** 21-1/2". **Weight:** 8-1/2 lbs. with sights. **Length:** 42-1/2" overall. **Stock:** European walnut with cheekpiece, stippled pistol grip and forend. **Sights:** Optional globe front specially designed for Biathlon shooting, micrometer rear with hinged snow cap. **Features:** Uses Super Match 54 action and nine-way adjustable trigger; adjustable wooden buttplate, Biathlon butthook, adjustable hand-stop rail. Introduced 1982. Imported from Germany by Accuracy International, Gunsmithing, Inc.
Price: Right-hand, with sights, about . . . . **$1,500.50 to $1,555.00**

Anschutz 1827BT Fortner Biathlon Rifle

Similar to the Anschutz 1827 Biathlon rifle except uses Anschutz/Fortner system straight-pull bolt action, blued or stainless steel barrel. Introduced 1982. Imported from Germany by Accuracy International, Gunsmithing, Inc.
Price: Right-hand, with sights. . . . . **$1,908.00 to $2,210.00**
Price: Left-hand, with sights . . . . **$2,099.20 to $2,395.00**
Price: Right-hand, sights, stainless barrel (Gunsmithing, Inc.) **$2,045.20**

RIFLES

Anschutz 54.18MS REP

Armalite AR-10 (T)

ANSCHUTZ SUPER MATCH SPECIAL MODEL 2013 RIFLE
Caliber: 22 LR, single shot. **Barrel:** 25.9". **Weight:** 13 lbs. **Length:** 41.7-42.9". **Stock:** A thumbhole version made of European walnut, both the cheekpiece and buttplate are highly adjustable. **Sights:** None furnished. **Features:** Developed by Anschütz for women to shoot in the sport rifle category. Stainless or blue. This top of the line rifle was introduced in 1997.
Price: Right-hand, blue, no sights, walnut **$2,219.30**
Price: Right-hand, stainless, no sights, walnut **$2,345.30**
Price: Left-hand, blue, no sights, walnut **$2,319.50**

ANSCHUTZ 2012 SPORT RIFLE
Caliber: 22 LR, 5-shot magazine. **Barrel:** 22.4" match; detachable muzzle tube. **Weight:** 7.9 lbs. **Length:** 40.9" overall. **Stock:** European walnut, thumbhole design. **Sights:** None furnished. **Features:** Uses Anschutz 54.18 barreled action with two-stage match trigger. Introduced 1997. Imported from Germany by Accuracy International, AcuSport Corp.
Price: . . . . $1,425.00 to **$2,219.95**

ANSCHUTZ 1911 PRONE MATCH RIFLE
Caliber: 22 LR, single shot. **Barrel:** 27-1/4". **Weight:** 11 lbs. **Length:** 46" overall. **Stock:** Walnut-finished European hardwood; American prone-style with adjustable cheekpiece, textured pistol grip, forend with swivel rail and adjustable rubber buttplate. **Sights:** None furnished. Receiver grooved for Anschutz sights (extra). **Features:** Two-stage #5018 trigger adjustable from 2.1 to 8.6 oz. Extremely fast lock time. Stainless or blue barrel. Imported from Germany by Accuracy International, Gunsmithing, Inc.
Price: Right-hand, no sights **$1,714.20**

ANSCHUTZ 1912 SPORT RIFLE
Caliber: 22 LR, single shot. **Barrel:** 25.9". **Weight:** About 11.4 lbs. **Length:** 41.7-42.9". **Stock:** European walnut or aluminum. **Sights:** None furnished. **Features:** Light weight sport rifle version. Still uses the 54 match action like the 1913 but weighs 1.5 pounds less. Stainless or blue barrel. Introduced 1997.
Price: Right-hand, blue, no sights, walnut **$1,789.50**
Price: Right-hand, blue, no sights, aluminum **$2,129.80**
Price: Right-hand, stainless, no sights, walnut **$1,910.30**
Price: Left-hand, blue, no sights, walnut **$1,879.00**

ANSCHUTZ 1913 SUPER MATCH RIFLE
Caliber: 22 LR, single shot. **Barrel:** 27.1". **Weight:** About 14.3 lbs. **Length:** 44.8-46". **Stock:** European walnut, color laminate, or aluminum. **Sights:** None furnished. **Features:** Two-stage #5018 trigger. Extremely fast lock time. Stainless or blue barrel.
Price: Right-hand, blue, no sights, walnut stock **$2,262.90**
Price: Right-hand, blue, no sights, color laminate stock **$2,275.10**
Price: Right-hand, blue, no sights, aluminum stock **$2,262.90**
Price: Left-hand, blue, no sights, walnut stock **$2,382.20**

Anschutz 1913 Super Match Rifle
Same as the Model 1911 except European walnut International-type stock with adjustable cheekpiece, or color laminate, both available with straight or lowered forend, adjustable aluminum hook buttplate, adjustable hand stop, weighs 15.5 lbs., 46" overall. Stainless or blue barrel. Imported from Germany by Accuracy International, Gunsmithing, Inc.
Price: Right-hand, blue, no sights, walnut stock. . . **$2,139.00 to $2,175.00**
Price: Right-hand, blue, no sights, color laminate stock. **$2,199.40**
Price: Right-hand, blue, no sights, walnut, lowered forend **$2,181.80**
Price: Right-hand, blue, no sights, color laminate, lowered forend **$2,242.20**
Price: Left-hand, blue, no sights, walnut stock. . . **$2,233.10 to $2,275.00**

Anschutz 54.18MS REP Deluxe Silhouette Rifle
Same basic action and trigger specifications as the Anschutz 1913 Super Match but with removable 5-shot clip magazine, 22.4" barrel extendable to 30" using optional extension and weight set. Weight id 8.1 lbs. Receiver drilled and tapped for scope mounting. Stock is Thumbhole silhouette version or standard silhouette version, both are European walnut. Introduced 1990. Imported from Germany by Accuracy International, Gunsmithing, Inc.
Price: Thumbhole stock **$1,461.40**
Price: Standard stock **$1,212.10**

Anschutz 1907 Standard Match Rifle
Same action as Model 1913 but with 7/8" diameter 26" barrel (stainless or blue). Length is 44.5" overall, weighs 10.5 lbs. Choice of stock configurations. Vented forend. Designed for prone and position shooting ISU requirements; suitable for NRA matches. Also available with walnut flat-forend stock for benchrest shooting. Imported from Germany by Accuracy International, Gunsmithing, Inc.
Price: Right-hand, blue, no sights, hardwood stock . **$1,253.40 to $1,299.00**
Price: Right-hand, blue, no sights, colored laminated stock . . . . $1,316.10 to **$1,375.00**
Price: Right-hand, blue, no sights, walnut stock. **$1,521.10**
Price: Left-hand, blue barrel, no sights, walnut stock. **$1,584.60**

ARMALITE AR-10 (T) RIFLE
Caliber: 308, 10-shot magazine. **Barrel:** 24" target-weight Rock 5R custom. **Weight:** 10.4 lbs. **Length:** 43.5" overall. **Stock:** Green or black compostion; N.M. fiberglass handguard tube. **Sights:** Detachable handle, front sight, or scope mount available. Comes with international-style flat-top receiver with Picatinny rail. **Features:** National Match two-stage trigger. Forged upper receiver. Receivers hard-coat anodized. Introduced 1995. Made in U.S. by ArmaLite, Inc.
Price: Green **$2,075.00**
Price: Black **$2,090.00**

RIFLES

Bushmaster XM15 E2S Target

Bushmaster DCM

Colt Match Target HBAR

Price: AR-10 (T) Carbine, lighter 16" barrel, single stage trigger, weighs 8.8 lbs. Green **$1,970.00**
Price: Black **$1,985.00**

ARMALITE M15A4 (T) EAGLE EYE RIFLE

Caliber: 223, 7-shot magazine. **Barrel:** 24" heavy stainless; 1:8" twist. **Weight:** 9.2 lbs. **Length:** 42-3/8" overall. **Stock:** Green or black butt, N.M. fiberglass handguard tube. **Sights:** One-piece international-style flattop receiver with Weaver-type rail, including case deflector. **Features:** Detachable carry handle, front sight and scope mount (30mm or 1") available. Upper and lower receivers have push-type pivot pin, hard coat anodized. Made in U.S. by ArmaLite, Inc.
Price: Green **$1,378.00**
Price: Black **$1,393.00**

ARMALITE M15A4 ACTION MASTER RIFLE

Caliber: 223, 7-shot magazine. **Barrel:** 20" heavy stainless; 1:9" twist. **Weight:** 9 lbs. **Length:** 40-1/2" overall. **Stock:** Green or black plastic; N.M. fiberglass handguard tube. **Sights:** One-piece international-style flattop receiver with Weaver-type rail. **Features:** Detachable carry handle, front sight and scope mount available. National Match two-stage trigger group; Picatinny rail; upper and lower receivers have push-type pivot pin; hard coat anodized finish. Made in U.S. by ArmaLite, Inc.
Price: **$1,175.00**

BLASER R93 LONG RANGE RIFLE

Caliber: 308 Win., 10-shot detachable box magazine. **Barrel:** 24". **Weight:** 10.4 lbs. **Length:** 44" overall. **Stock:** Aluminum with synthetic lining. **Sights:** None furnished; accepts detachable scope mount. **Features:** Straight-pull bolt action with adjustable trigger; fully adjustable stock; quick takedown; corrosion resistant finish. Introduced 1998. Imported from Germany by Sigarms.
Price: **$2,360.00**

BUSHMASTER XM15 E2S TARGET MODEL RIFLE

Caliber: 223. **Barrel:** 20", 24", 26"; 1:9" twist; heavy. **Weight:** 8.3 lbs. **Length:** 38.25" overall (20" barrel). **Stock:** Black composition; A2 type. **Sights:** Adjustable post front, adjustable aperture rear. **Features:** Patterned after Colt M-16A2. Chrome-lined barrel with manganese phos-

phate exterior. Forged aluminum receivers with push-pin takedown. Made in U.S. by Bushmaster Firearms Co./Quality Parts Co.
Price: 20" match heavy barrel **$960.00**

Bushmaster DCM Competition Rifle

Similar to the XM15 E2S Target Model except has 20" extra-heavy (1" diameter) barrel with 1.8" twist for heavier competition bullets. Weighs about 12 lbs. with balance weights. Has special competition rear sight with interchangeable apertures, extra-fine 1/2- or 1/4-MOA windage and elevation adjustments; specially ground front sight post in choice of three widths. Full-length handguards over free-floater barrel tube. Introduced 1998. Made in U.S. by Bushmaster Firearms, Inc.
Price: **$1,525.00**

BUSHMASTER XM15 E2S V-MATCH RIFLE

Caliber: 223. **Barrel:** 20", 24", 26"; 1:9" twist; heavy. **Weight:** 8.1 lbs. **Length:** 38.25" overall (20" barrel). **Stock:** Black composition. A2 type. **Sights:** None furnished; upper receiver has integral scope mount base. **Features:** Chrome-lined .950" heavy barrel with counter-bored crown, manganese phosphate finish; free-floating aluminum handguard; forged aluminum receivers with push-pin takedown, hard anodized mil-spec finish. Competition trigger optional. Made in U.S. by Bushmaster Firearms, Inc.
Price: 20" Match heavy barrel **$1,025.00**
Price: 24" Match heavy barrel **$1,040.00**
Price: V-Match Carbine (16" barrel) **$1,015.00**

COLT MATCH TARGET MODEL RIFLE

Caliber: 223 Rem., 8-shot magazine. **Barrel:** 20". **Weight:** 7.5 lbs. **Length:** 39" overall. **Stock:** Composition stock, grip, forend. **Sights:** Post front, aperture rear adjustable for windage and elevation. **Features:** Five-round detachable box magazine, standard-weight barrel, sling swivels. Has forward bolt assist. Military matte black finish. Model introduced 1991.
Price: **$1,144.00**
Price: With compensator **$1,150.00**

Colt Accurized Rifle

Similar to the Colt Match Target Model except has 24" stainless steel heavy barrel with 1.9" rifling, flattop receiver with scope mount and 1" rings, weighs 9.25 lbs. Introduced 1998. Made in U.S. by Colt's Mfg. Co., Inc.
Price: **$1,424.00**

Colt Match Target HBAR Rifle

Similar to the Target Model except has heavy barrel, 800-meter rear sight adjustable for windage and elevation. Introduced 1991.
Price: **$1,194.00**

Harris Gunworks Long Range

Harris Gunworks M-86

Marlin Model 2000L

Colt Match Target Competition HBAR Rifle

Similar to the Sporter Target except has flat-top receiver with integral Weaver-type base for scope mounting. Counter-bored muzzle, 1:9" rifling twist. Introduced 1991.
Price: Model R6700 .... **$1,199.00**

Colt Match Target Competition HBAR II Rifle

Similar to the Match Target Competition HBAR except has 16:1" barrel, weighs 7.1 lbs., overall length 34.5"; 1:9" twist barrel. Introduced 1995.
Price: **$1,172.00**

E.A.A./HW 660 MATCH RIFLE

Caliber: 22 LR. **Barrel:** 26". **Weight:** 10.7 lbs. **Length:** 45.3" overall. **Stock:** Match-type walnut with adjustable cheekpiece and buttplate. **Sights:** Globe front, match aperture rear. **Features:** Adjustable match trigger; stippled pistol grip and forend; forend accessory rail. Introduced 1991. Imported from Germany by European American Armory.
Price: About **$999.00**
Price: With laminate stock **$1,159.00**

HARRIS GUNWORKS NATIONAL MATCH RIFLE

Caliber: 7mm-08, 308, 5-shot magazine. **Barrel:** 24", stainless steel. **Weight:** About 11 lbs. (std. bbl.). **Length:** 43" overall. **Stock:** Fiberglass with adjustable buttplate. **Sights:** Barrel band and Tompkins front; no rear sight furnished. **Features:** Gunworks repeating action with clip slot, Canjar trigger. Match-grade barrel. Available in right-hand only. Fiberglass stock, sight installation, special machining and triggers optional. Introduced 1989. From Harris Gunworks, Inc.
Price: **$3,500.00**

HARRIS GUNWORKS LONG RANGE RIFLE

Caliber: 300 Win. Mag., 7mm Rem. Mag., 300 Phoenix, 338 Lapua, single shot. **Barrel:** 26", stainless steel, match-grade. **Weight:** 14 lbs. **Length:** 46-1/2" overall. **Stock:** Fiberglass with adjustable buttplate and cheekpiece. Adjustable for length of pull, drop, cant and cast-off. **Sights:** Barrel band and Tompkins front; no rear sight furnished. **Features:** Uses Gunworks solid bottom single shot action and Canjar trigger. Barrel twist 1:12". Introduced 1989. From Harris Gunworks, Inc.
Price: **$3,620.00**

HARRIS GUNWORKS M-86 SNIPER RIFLE

Caliber: 308, 30-06, 4-shot magazine; 300 Win. Mag., 3-shot magazine. **Barrel:** 24", Gunworks match-grade in heavy contour. **Weight:** 11-1/4 lbs. (308), 11-1/2 lbs. (30-06, 300). **Length:** 43-1/2" overall. **Stock:** Specially designed McHale fiberglass stock with textured grip and forend, recoil pad. **Sights:** None furnished. **Features:** Uses Gunworks repeating action. Comes with bipod. Matte black finish. Sling swivels. Introduced 1989. From Harris Gunworks, Inc.
Price: **$2,700.00**

HARRIS GUNWORKS M-89 SNIPER RIFLE

Caliber: 308 Win., 5-shot magazine. **Barrel:** 28" (with suppressor). **Weight:** 15 lbs., 4 oz. **Stock:** Fiberglass; adjustable for length; recoil pad. **Sights:** None furnished. Drilled and tapped for scope mounting. **Features:** Uses Gunworks repeating action. Comes with bipod. Introduced 1990. From Harris Gunworks, Inc.
Price: Standard (non-suppressed) **$3,200.00**

HARRIS GUNWORKS
COMBO M-87 SERIES 50-CALIBER RIFLES

Caliber: 50 BMG, single shot. **Barrel:** 29, with muzzle brake. **Weight:** About 21-1/2 lbs. **Length:** 53" overall. **Stock:** Gunworks fiberglass. **Sights:** None furnished. **Features:** Right-handed Gunworks stainless steel receiver, chrome-moly barrel with 1:15" twist. Introduced 1987. From Harris Gunworks, Inc.
Price: **$3,885.00**
Price: M87R 5-shot repeater **$4,000.00**
Price: M-87 (5-shot repeater) "Combo" **$4,300.00**
Price: M-92 Bullpup (shortened M-87 single shot with bullpup
stock) **$4,770.00**
Price: M-93 (10-shot repeater with folding stock, detachable
magazine) **$4,150.00**

MARLIN MODEL 2000L TARGET RIFLE

Caliber: 22 LR, single shot. **Barrel:** 22" heavy, Micro-Groove® rifling, match chamber, recessed muzzle. **Weight:** 8 lbs. **Length:** 41" overall. **Stock:** Laminated black/gray with ambidextrous pistol grip. **Sights:** Hooded front with ten aperture inserts, fully adjustable target rear peep. **Features:** Buttplate adjustable for length of pull, height and angle. Aluminum forend rail with stop and quick-detachable swivel. Two-stage target trigger; red cocking indicator. Five-shot adaptor kit available. Introduced 1991. From Marlin.
Price: **$689.00**

Marlin Model 7000T

Savage Model 900TR

Savage Model 112BT

MARLIN MODEL 7000T SELF-LOADING RIFLE

Caliber: 22 LR, 10-shot magazine. **Barrel:** 18" heavy target with Micro-Groove® rifling. **Weight:** 7-1/2 lbs. **Length:** 37" overall. **Stock:** Laminated red, white and blue hardwood with ambidextrous pistol grip, adjustable buttplate, aluminum forend rail. **Sights:** None furnished; grooved receiver for scope mounting. **Features:** Trigger stop; last-shot bolt hold-open; blue finish; scope mounts included. Introduced 1999. Made in U.S. by Marlin.
Price: **$465.00**

OLYMPIC ARMS PCR-SERVICEMATCH RIFLE

Caliber: 223, 10-shot magazine. **Barrel:** 20", broach-cut 416 stainless steel. **Weight:** About 10 lbs. **Length:** 39.5" overall. **Stock:** A2 stowaway grip and trapdoor buttstock. **Sights:** Post front, E2-NM fully adjustable aperture rear. **Features:** Based on the AR-15. Conforms to all DCM standards. Free-floating 1:8.5" or 1:10" barrel; crowned barrel; no bayonet lug. Introduced 1996. Made in U.S. by Olympic Arms, Inc.
Price: **$1,062.00**

OLYMPIC ARMS PCR-1 RIFLE

Caliber: 223, 10-shot magazine. **Barrel:** 20", 24"; 416 stainless steel. **Weight:** 10 lbs., 3 oz. **Length:** 38.25" overall with 20" barrel. **Stock:** A2 stowaway grip and trapdoor butt. **Sights:** None supplied; flattop upper receiver, cut-down front sight base. **Features:** Based on the AR-15 rifle. Broach-cut, free-floating barrel with 1:8.5" or 1:10" twist. No bayonet lug. Crowned barrel; fluting available. Introduced 1994. Made in U.S. by Olympic Arms, Inc.
Price: **$1,038.00**

Olympic Arms PCR-2, PCR-3 Rifles

Similar to the PCR-1 except has 16" barrel, weighs 8 lbs., 2 oz.; has post front sight, fully adjustable aperture rear. Model PCR-3 has flattop upper receiver, cut-down front sight base. Introduced 1994. Made in U.S. by Olympic Arms, Inc.
Price: **$958.00**

REMINGTON 40-XB RANGEMASTER TARGET CENTERFIRE

Caliber: 15 calibers from 220 Swift to 300 Win. Mag. **Barrel:** 27-1/4". **Weight:** 11-1/4 lbs. **Length:** 47" overall. **Stock:** American walnut, laminated thumbhole or Kevlar with high comb and beavertail forend stop. Rubber non-slip buttplate. **Sights:** None. Scope blocks installed. **Features:** Adjustable trigger. Stainless barrel and action. Receiver drilled and tapped for sights.
Price: Standard single shot **$1,565.00**
Price: Repeater **$1,684.00**

REMINGTON 40-XBBR KS

Caliber: Five calibers from 22 BR to 308 Win. **Barrel:** 20" (light varmint class), 24" (heavy varmint class). **Weight:** 7-1/4 lbs. (light varmint class); 12 lbs. (heavy varmint class). **Length:** 38" (20" bbl.), 42" (24" bbl.). **Stock:** Kevlar. **Sights:** None. Supplied with scope blocks. **Features:** Unblued stainless steel barrel, trigger adjustable from 1-1/2 lbs. to 3-1/2 lbs. Special 2-oz. trigger at extra cost. Scope and mounts extra.
Price: With Kevlar stock **$1,742.00**

REMINGTON 40-XC TARGET RIFLE

Caliber: 7.62 NATO, 5-shot. **Barrel:** 24", stainless steel. **Weight:** 11 lbs. without sights. **Length:** 43-1/2" overall. **Stock:** Kevlar, with palm rail. **Sights:** None furnished. **Features:** Designed to meet the needs of competitive shooters. Stainless steel barrel and action.
Price: **$1,742.00**

SAKO TRG-22 BOLT-ACTION RIFLE

Caliber: 308 Win., 10-shot magazine. **Barrel:** 26". **Weight:** 10-1/4 lbs. **Length:** 45-1/4" overall. **Stock:** Reinforced polyurethane with fully adjustable cheekpiece and buttplate. **Sights:** None furnished. Optional quick-detachable, one-piece scope mount base, 1" or 30mm rings. **Features:** Resistance-free bolt, free-floating heavy stainless barrel, 60-degree bolt lift. Two-stage trigger is adjustable for length, pull, horizontal or vertical pitch. Introduced 2000. Imported from Finland by Stoeger Industries.
Price: **$2,699.00**
Price: Model TRG-42, as above except in 338 Lapua Mag or 300 Win. Mag. **$3,099.00**

SAVAGE MODEL 900TR TARGET RIFLE

Caliber: 22 LR, 5-shot magazine. **Barrel:** 25". **Weight:** 8 lbs. **Length:** 43-5/8" overall. **Stock:** Target-type, walnut-finished hardwood. **Sights:** Target front with inserts, peep rear with 1/4-minute click adjustments. **Features:** Comes with shooting rail and hand stop. Introduced 1991. Made in Canada, from Savage Arms Inc.
Price: Right- or left-hand **$440.00**

RIFLES

Springfield, Inc. M1A Super Match

Springfield, Inc. M1A/M-21

SAVAGE MODEL 112BT COMPETITION GRADE RIFLE

Caliber: 223, 308, 5-shot magazine, 300 Win. Mag., single shot. **Barrel:** 26", heavy contour stainless with black finish; 1:9" twist (223), 1:10" (308). **Weight:** 10.8 lbs. **Length:** 47.5" overall. **Stock:** Laminated wood with straight comb, adjustable cheek rest, Wundhammer palm swell, ventilated forend. Recoil pad is adjustable for length of pull. **Sights:** None furnished; drilled and tapped for scope mounting and aperture target-style sights. Recessed target-style muzzle has .812" diameter section for universal target sight base. **Features:** Pillar-bedded stock, matte black alloy receiver. Bolt has black titanium nitride coating, large handle ball. Has alloy accessory rail on forend. Comes with safety gun lock, target and ear puffs. Introduced 1994. Made in U.S. by Savage Arms, Inc.
Price: **$1,028.00**
Price: 300 Win. Mag. (single shot 112BT-S) **$1,028.00**

SPRINGFIELD, INC. M1A SUPER MATCH

Caliber: 308 Win. **Barrel:** 22", heavy Douglas Premium. **Weight:** About 10 lbs. **Length:** 44.31" overall. **Stock:** Heavy walnut competition stock with longer pistol grip, contoured area behind the rear sight, thicker butt and forend, glass bedded. **Sights:** National Match front and rear. **Features:** Has figure-eight-style operating rod guide. Introduced 1987. From Springfield, Inc.
Price: About **$2,479.00**

Springfield, Inc. M1A/M-21 Tactical Model Rifle

Similar to the M1A Super Match except has special sniper stock with adjustable cheekpiece and rubber recoil pad. Weighs 11.2 lbs. From Springfield, Inc.
Price: **$2,975.00**

STONER SR-15 MATCH RIFLE

Caliber: 223. **Barrel:** 20". **Weight:** 7.9 lbs. **Length:** 38" overall. **Stock:** Black synthetic. **Sights:** None furnished; flat-top upper receiver for scope mounting. **Features:** Short Picatinny rail; two-stage match trigger. Introduced 1998. Made in U.S. by Knight's Mfg.Co.
Price: **$1,595.00**

STONER SR-25 MATCH RIFLE

Caliber: 7.62 NATO, 10-shot steel magazine, 5-shot optional. **Barrel:** 24" heavy match; 1:11.25" twist. **Weight:** 10.75 lbs. **Length:** 44" overall. **Stock:** Black synthetic AR-15A2 design. Full floating forend of Mil-spec synthetic attaches to upper receiver at a single point. **Sights:** None furnished. Has integral Weaver-style rail. Rings and iron sights optional. **Features:** Improved AR-15 trigger; AR-15-style seven-lug rotating bolt. Gas block rail mounts detachable front sight. Introduced 1993. Made in U.S. by Knight's Mfg. Co.
Price: **$2,995.00**
Price: SR-25 Lightweight Match (20" medium match target contour barrel, 9.5 lbs., 40" overall) **$2,995.00**

TANNER 50 METER FREE RIFLE

Caliber: 22 LR, single shot. **Barrel:** 27.7". **Weight:** 13.9 lbs. **Length:** 44.4" overall. **Stock:** Seasoned walnut with palm rest, accessory rail, adjustable hook buttplate. **Sights:** Globe front with interchangeable inserts, Tanner micrometer-diopter rear with adjustable aperture. **Features:** Bolt action with externally adjustable set trigger. Supplied with 50-meter test target. Imported from Switzerland by Mandall Shooting Supplies. Introduced 1984.
Price: About **$3,900.00**

TANNER STANDARD UIT RIFLE

Caliber: 308, 7.5mm Swiss, 10-shot. **Barrel:** 25.9". **Weight:** 10.5 lbs. **Length:** 40.6" overall. **Stock:** Match style of seasoned nutwood with accessory rail; coarsely stippled pistol grip; high cheekpiece; vented forend. **Sights:** Globe front with interchangeable inserts, Tanner micrometer-diopter rear with adjustable aperture. **Features:** Two locking lug revolving bolt encloses case head. Trigger adjustable from 1/2 to 6-1/2 lbs.; match trigger optional. Comes with 300-meter test target. Imported from Switzerland by Mandall Shooting Supplies. Introduced 1984.
Price: About **$4,700.00**

TANNER 300 METER FREE RIFLE

Caliber: 308 Win., 7.5 Swiss, single shot. **Barrel:** 27.58". **Weight:** 15 lbs. **Length:** 45.3" overall. **Stock:** Seasoned walnut, thumbhole style, with accessory rail, palm rest, adjustable hook butt. **Sights:** Globe front with interchangeable inserts, Tanner-design micrometer-diopter rear with adjustable aperture. **Features:** Three-lug revolving-lock bolt design; adjustable set trigger; short firing pin travel; supplied with 300-meter test target. Imported from Switzerland by Mandall Shooting Supplies. Introduced 1984.
Price: About **$4,900.00**

TIKKA SPORTER RIFLE

Caliber: 223, 22-250, 308, detachable 5-shot magazine. **Barrel:** 23-1/2" heavy. **Weight:** 9 lbs. **Length:** 43-5/8" overall. **Stock:** European walnut with adjustable comb, adjustable buttplate; stippled grip and forend. **Sights:** None furnished; drilled and tapped for scope mounting. **Features:** Buttplate is adjustable for distance, angle, height and pitch; adjustable trigger; free-floating barrel. Introduced 1998. Imported from Finland by Stoeger Industries.
Price: **$939.00**

Includes a wide variety of sporting guns and guns suitable for various competitions.

Benelli Legacy

Benelli Limited Edition Legacy 12 gauge

Benelli M1 Super 90 Camouflage

Benelli Super Black Eagle

AMERICAN ARMS PHANTOM AUTO SHOTGUNS
Gauge: 12, 3" chamber. **Barrel:** 24", 26", 28" (Imp. Cyl., Mod., Full choke tubes). **Stock:** Walnut or black synthetic. **Features:** Gas-operated action; blued barrel; checkered pistol grip and forend; vent rib barrel. Introduced 1999. Imported by American Arms, Inc.
Price: .... NA

BENELLI LEGACY SHOTGUN
Gauge: 12, 20, 3" chamber. **Barrel:** 26", 28" (Full, Mod., Imp. Cyl., Imp. Mod., Skeet choke tubes). Mid-bead sight. **Weight:** 7.1 to 7.6 lbs. **Length:** 49-5/8" overall (26" barrel). **Stock:** European walnut with high-gloss finish. Special competition stock comes with drop adjustment kit. **Features:** Uses the rotating bolt inertia recoil operating system with a two-piece steel/aluminum etched receiver (bright on lower, blue upper). Drop adjustment kit allows the stock to be custom fitted without modifying the stock. Black lower receiver finish, blued upper. Introduced 1998. Imported from Italy by Heckler & Koch, Inc.
Price: $1,350.00

NEW! Benelli Limited Edition Legacy
Similar to the Legacy model except receiver has gold-filled, etched game scenes and limited to 250 12 gauge (28" barrel) and 250 20 gauge (26" barrel) guns to commemorate the year 2000.
Price $1,600.00

Benelli Sport Shotgun
Similar to the Legacy model except has matte blue receiver, two carbon fiber interchangeable ventilated ribs, adjustable butt pad, adjustable buttstock, and functions with ultra-light target loads. Walnut stock with satin finish. Introduced 1997. Imported from Italy by Benelli U.S.A.
Price: $1,340.00

BENELLI M1 FIELD AUTO SHOTGUN
Gauge: 12, 3" chamber. **Barrel:** 21", 24", 26", 28" (choke tubes). **Weight:** 7 lbs., 4 oz. **Stock:** High impact polymer; wood on 26", 28". **Sights:** Metal bead front. **Features:** Sporting version of the military & police gun. Uses the rotating Montefeltro bolt system. Ventilated rib; blue finish. Comes with set of five choke tubes. Imported from Italy by Benelli U.S.A.
Price: $920.00
Price: Wood stock version $935.00
Price: 24" rifled barrel, polymer stock. $1,000.00
Price: 24" rifled barrel, camo stock $1,100.00
Price: Synthetic stock, left-hand version (24", 26", 28" brls) $935.00
Price: Camo Stock, left-hand version (24", 26", 28" brls.) $1,025.00

Benelli Montefeltro 90 Shotgun
Similar to the M1 Super 90 except has checkered walnut stock with high-gloss finish. Uses the Montefeltro rotating bolt system with a simple inertia recoil design. Full, Imp. Mod., Mod., Imp. Cyl. choke tubes. Weighs 6.8-7.1 lbs. Finish is matte black. Introduced 1987.
Price: 24", 26", 28" $940.00
Price: Left-hand, 26", 28" $960.00

Benelli Montefeltro 20 gauge Shotgun
Similar to the 12 gauge Montefeltro except chambered for 3" 20 gauge, 24" or 26" barrel (choke tubes), weighs 5-1/2 lbs., has drop-adjustable walnut stock with satin or camo finish, blued receiver. Overall length 47.5". Introduced 1993. Imported from Italy by Benelli U.S.A.
Price: 26" barrels $940.00
Price: 26", camouflage finish $1,040.00
Price: Montefeltro Short Stock, 24" and 26" brls. $975.00

BENELLI SUPER BLACK EAGLE SHOTGUN
Gauge: 12, 3-1/2" chamber. **Barrel:** 24", 26", 28" (Cyl. Imp. Cyl., Mod., Imp. Mod., Full choke tubes). **Weight:** 7 lbs., 5 oz. **Length:** 49-5/8" overall (28" barrel). **Stock:** European walnut with satin finish, or polymer. Adjustable for drop. **Sights:** Bead front. **Features:** Uses Montefeltro inertia recoil bolt system. Fires all 12 gauge shells from 2-3/4" to 3-1/2" magnums. Introduced 1991. Imported from Italy by Benelli U.S.A.
Price: With 26" and 28" barrel, wood stock $1,240.00
Price: With 24", 26" and 28" barrel, polymer stock. $1,220.00
Price: Left-hand, 24", 26", 28", polymer stock $1,250.00
Price: Left-hand, 24", 26", 28", camo stock $1,330.00

SHOTGUNS

Beretta Urika Gold Sporting

Beretta Urika Sporting

Beretta Urika Gold Trap

Benelli Super Black Eagle Slug Gun

Similar to the Benelli Super Black Eagle except has 24" rifled barrel with 3" chamber, and drilled and tapped for scope. Uses the inertia recoil bolt system. Matte-finish receiver. Weight is 7.5 lbs., overall length 45.5". Wood or polymer stocks available. Introduced 1992. Imported from Italy by Benelli U.S.A.

Price: With wood stock **$1,280.00**
Price: With polymer stock **$1,270.00**
Price: 26" barrels **$1,390.00**

Benelli Executive Series Shotguns

Similar to the Super Black Eagle except has grayed steel lower receiver, hand-engraved and gold inlaid (Grade III), and has highest grade of walnut stock with drop adjustment kit. Barrel lengths 26" or 28"; 3" chamber. **Special order only.** Introduced 1995. Imported from Italy by Benelli U.S.A.

Price: Grade I (engraved game scenes). **$5,035.00**
Price: Grade II (game scenes with scroll engraving) **$5,720.00**
Price: Grade III (full coverage, gold inlays). **$6,670.00**

BERETTA AL391 URIKA AUTO SHOTGUNS

Gauge: 12, 20 gauge; 3" chamber. **Barrel:** 22", 24", 26", 28", 30"; five Mobilchoke choke tubes. **Weight:** 5.95 to 7.28 lbs. **Length:** Varies by model. **Stock:** Walnut, black or camo synthetic; shims, spacers and interchangeable recoil pads allow custom fit. **Features:** Self-compensating gas operation handles full range of loads; recoil reducer in receiver; enlarged trigger guard; reduced-weight receiver, barrel and forend; hard-chromed bore. Introduced 2000. Imported from Italy by Beretta USA.

Price: AL391 Urika (12 ga., 26", 28", 30" barrels) **$960.00**
Price: AL391 Urika (20 ga., 24", 26", 28" barrels) **$960.00**
Price: AL391 Urika Synthetic (12 ga., 24", 26", 28", 30" barrels) **$960.00**
Price: AL391 Urika Camo. (12 ga., Realtree Hardwoods
or Advantage Wetlands) **$1,055.00**

Beretta AL391 Urika Gold and Gold Sporting Auto Shotguns

Similar to AL391 Urika except features deluxe wood, jeweled bolt and carrier, gold-inlaid receiver with black or silver finish. Introduced 2000. Imported from Italy by Beretta USA.

Price: AL391 Urika Gold (12 or 20 ga., black receiver) **$1,150.00**
Price: AL391 Urika Gold (silver, lightweight receiver). **$1,185.00**
Price: AL391 Urika Gold Sporting (12 or 20, black or silver
receiver, scroll engraving). **$1,195.00**

Beretta AL391 Urika Sporting Auto Shotguns

Similar to AL391 Urika except has competition sporting stock with rounded rubber recoil pad, wide ventilated rib with white front and mid-rib beads, satin-black receiver with silver markings. Available in 12 and 20 gauge. Introduced 2000. Imported from Italy by Beretta USA.

Price: AL391 Urika Sporting. **$1,000.00**

Beretta AL391 Urika Trap and Gold Trap Auto Shotguns

Similar to AL391 Urika except in 12 ga. only, has wide ventilated rib with white front and mid-rib beads, Monte Carlo stock and special trap recoil pad. Gold Trap features highly figured walnut stock and forend, gold-filled Beretta logo and signature on receiver. Introduced 2000. Imported from Italy by Beretta USA.

Price: AL391 Urika Trap **$1,000.00**
Price: AL391 Urika Gold Trap. **$1,195.00**

Beretta AL391 Urika Parallel Target RL and SL Auto Shotguns

Similar to AL391 Urika except has parallel-comb, Monte Carlo stock with tighter grip radius to reduce trigger reach and stepped ventilated rib. SL model has same features but with 13.5" length of pull stock. Introduced 2000. Imported from Italy by Beretta USA.

Price: AL391 Urika Parallel Target RL **$1,000.00**
Price: AL391 Urika Parallel Target SL **$1,000.00**

Beretta AL391 Urika Slug Shotgun

Similar to AL391 except has a 22" barrel with V-shaped rear sight, hooded blade front sight, special rib, receiver designed to accept Weaver scope bases. Introduced 2000. From Beretta USA.

Price: . . . . **NA**

Beretta AL391 Urika Youth Shotgun

Similar to AL391 except has a 24" or 26" barrel with 13.5" stock for youth and smaller shooters. Introduced 2000. From Beretta USA.

Price: **$960.00**

BERETTA ES100 NWTF SPECIAL AUTO SHOTGUN

Gauge: 12, 3" chamber. **Barrel:** 24", MC3 tubes and Briley extended Extra-Full Turkey. **Weight:** 7.3 lbs. **Stock:** Synthetic, checkered. **Sights:** Truglo fiber optic front and rear three-dot system. **Features:** Short recoil inertia operation. Mossy Oak Break-Up camouflage finish on stock and forend, black matte finish on all metal. Comes with camouflage sling. Introduced 1999. Imported from Italy by Beretta U.S.A.

Price: **$945.00**

Browning Gold Deer Hunter

Browning Gold Sporting Golden Clays

Browning Gold Waterfowl

BROWNING GOLD HUNTER AUTO SHOTGUN

Gauge: 12, 20, 3" chamber. **Barrel:** 12 ga.—26", 28", 30", Invector Plus choke tubes; 20 ga.—26", 30", Invector choke tubes. **Weight:** 7 lbs., 9 oz. (12 ga.), 6 lbs., 12 oz. (20 ga.). **Length:** 46-1/4" overall (20 ga., 26" barrel). **Stock:** 14"x1-1/2"x2-1/3"; select walnut with gloss finish; palm swell grip. **Features:** Self-regulating, self-cleaning gas system shoots all loads; lightweight receiver with special non-glare deep black finish; large reversible safety button; large rounded trigger guard, gold trigger. The 20 gauge has slightly smaller dimensions; 12 gauge have back-bored barrels, Invector Plus tube system. Introduced 1994. Imported by Browning.

Price: 12 or 20 gauge $772.00
Price: Extra barrels $290.00

Browning Gold Deer Hunter Auto Shotgun

Similar to the Gold Hunter except 12 gauge only, 22" rifled or smooth Standard Invector barrel with 5" rifled choke tube, cantilever scope mount, extra-thick recoil pad. Weighs 7 lbs., 12 oz., overall length 42-1/2". Sling swivel studs fitted on the magazine cap and butt. Introduced 1997. Imported by Browning.

Price: $839.00
Price: With Mossy Oak Break-up camouflage $909.00

Browning Gold Deer Stalker

Similar to the Gold Deer Hunter except has black composite stock and forend, fully rifled barrel, cantilever scope mount. Introduced 1999. Imported by Browning.

Price: $839.00

Browning Gold Sporting Clays Auto

Similar to the Gold Hunter except 12 gauge only with 28" or 30" barrel; front and center beads on tapered ventilated rib; ported and back-bored Invector Plus barrel; 2-3/4" chamber; satin-finished stock with solid, radiused recoil pad with hard heel insert; non-glare black alloy receiver has "Sporting Clays" inscribed in gold. Introduced 1996. Imported from Japan by Browning.

Price: $798.00

Browning Gold Sporting Golden Clays

Similar to the Sporting Clays except has silvered receiver with gold engraving, high grade wood. Introduced 1999. Imported by Browning.

Price: $1,267.00

Browning Gold Ladies/Youth Sporting Clays Auto

Similar to the Gold Sporting Clays except has stock dimensions of 14-1/4"x1-3/4"x2" for women and younger shooters. Introduced 1999. Imported by Browning.

Price: $798.00

Browning Gold Stalker Auto Shotgun

Similar to the Gold Hunter except has black composite stock and forend. Choice of 3" or 3-1/2" chamber.

Price: With 3" chamber $772.00
Price: With 3-1/2" chamber $929.00

Browning Gold Waterfowl Shotgun

Similar to the Gold Hunter except 12 gauge only, completely covered with Mossy Oak Shadow Grass comouflage. Choice of 3" or 3-1/2" chamber. Introduced 1999. Imported by Browning.

Price: 26", 28" $999.00

Browning Gold Classic Hunter Auto Shotgun

Similar to the Gold Hunter 3" except has semi-hump back receiver, magazine cut-off, adjustable comb, and satin-finish wood. Introduced 1999. Imported by Browning.

Price: 12 gauge $772.00
Price: 20 gauge $772.00
Price: High Grade (silvered, gold engraved receiver, high grade wood) $1,427.00

Browning Gold Classic Stalker

Similar to the Gold Classic Hunter except has adjustable composite stock and forend. Introduced 1999. Imported by Browning.

Price: $772.00

Browning Gold Turkey/Waterfowl Hunter Auto

Similar to the Gold Hunter except available with 3" or 3-1/2" chamber; has 24" barrel with Hi-Viz front sight. Introduced 1999. Imported by Browning.

Price: $929.00

Browning Gold Turkey/Waterfowl Camo Shotgun

Similar to the Gold Turkey/Waterfowl Hunter except 12 gauge only, 3" or 3-1/2" chamber, 24" barrel with Extra-Full Turkey choke tube, Hi-Viz front sight. Completely covered with Mossy Oak Breakup camouflage. Introduced 1999. Imported by Browning.

Price: $929.00
Price: Turkey/Waterfowl Stalker (black stock and metal) $949.00

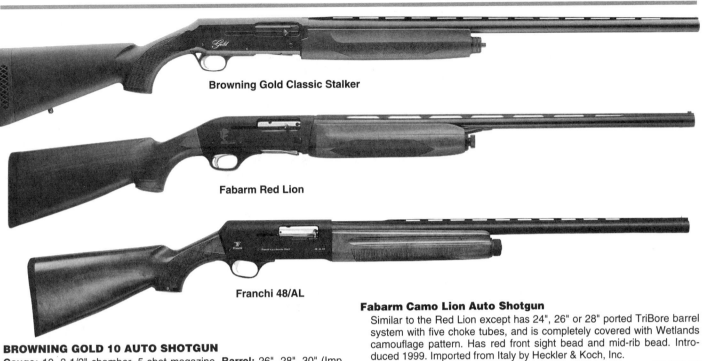

Browning Gold Classic Stalker

Fabarm Red Lion

Franchi 48/AL

BROWNING GOLD 10 AUTO SHOTGUN

Gauge: 10, 3-1/2" chamber, 5-shot magazine. **Barrel:** 26", 28", 30" (Imp. Cyl., Mod., Full standard Invector). **Weight:** 10 lbs. 7 oz. (28" barrel). **Stock:** 14-3/8"x1-1/2"x2-3/8". Select walnut with gloss finish, cut checkering, recoil pad. **Features:** Short-stroke, gas-operated action, cross-bolt safety. Forged steel receiver with polished blue finish. Introduced 1993. Imported by Browning.
Price: **$1,007.95**
Price: Extra barrel. **$276.00**

Browning Gold 10 gauge Auto Combo

Similar to the Gold 10 except comes with 24" and 26" barrels with Imp. Cyl., Mod., Full Invector choke tubes. Introduced 1999. Imported by Browning.
Price: **$1,059.00**

EAA/BAIKAL MP-153 AUTO SHOTGUN

Gauge: 12, 3-1/2" chamber. **Barrel:** 18-1/2", 20", 24", 26", 28"; imp., mod. and full choke tubes. **Weight:** 7.8 lbs. **Stock:** Walnut. **Features:** Gas-operated action with automatic gas-adjustment valve allows use of light and heavy loads interchangeably; 4-round magazine; rubber recoil pad. Introduced 2000. Imported by European American Armory.
Price: MP-153 (blued finish, walnut stock and forend) **$459.00**

FABARM RED LION AUTO SHOTGUN

Gauge: 12, 3" chamber. **Barrel:** 24", 26", 28", choke tubes. **Weight:** 7 lbs. **Length:** 45.5" overall. **Stock:** European walnut with gloss finish. **Features:** TriBore barrel, reversible safety; nickel-plated trigger and carrier release button; leather-covered rubber recoil pad. Introduced 1998. Imported from Italy by Heckler & Koch, Inc.
Price: **$820.00**
Price: Gold Lion (as above except gold-plated trigger, carrier release button, olive wood gripcap). **$915.00**

Fabarm Sporting Clays Lion Auto Shotgun

Similar to the Red Lion except has 28" TriBore ported barrel with interchangeable colored front-sight beads, mid-rib bead, 10mm channeled vent rib, oil-finished walnut stock and forend with olive wood grip-cap. Stock dimensions are 14.58"x1.58"x2.44". Has distinctive gold-colored receiver logo. Available in 12 gauge only, 3" chamber. Introduced 1999. Imported from Italy by Heckler & Koch, Inc.
Price: **$959.00**

Fabarm Sporting Clays Extra

Same as Sporting Clays Lion Auto but has carbon fiber finish.
Price: **$1,249.00**

Fabarm Camo Lion Auto Shotgun

Similar to the Red Lion except has 24", 26" or 28" ported TriBore barrel system with five choke tubes, and is completely covered with Wetlands camouflage pattern. Has red front sight bead and mid-rib bead. Introduced 1999. Imported from Italy by Heckler & Koch, Inc.
Price: **$1,019.00**

FRANCHI AL 48 SHOTGUN

Gauge: 12, 20 or 28, 2-3/4" chamber. **Barrel:** 24", 26", 28" (Franchoke cyl. imp. cyl., mod., choke tubes). **Weight:** 5.5 lbs. (20 gauge). **Length:** NA **Stock:** 14-1/4"x1-5/8"x2-1/2". Walnut with checkered grip and forend. **Features:** Recoil-operated action. Chrome-lined bore; cross-bolt safety. Imported from Italy by Benelli U.S.A.
Price: 12 ga. **$630.00**
Price: 20 ga. **$613.00**
Price: 28 ga. **$680.00**

Franchi AL 48 Deluxe Shotgun

Similar to AL 48 but with select walnut stock and forend and high-polish blue finish. Introduced 2000.
Price: (20 gauge, 26" barrel) **$710.00**
Price: (28 gauge, 26" barrel) **$680.00**

Franchi AL 48 Short Stock Shotgun

Similar to AL 48 but with stock shortened to 12 1/2 " length of pull.
Price: (20 gauge, 26" barrel) **$594.00**

FRANCHI VARIOPRESS 612 SHOTGUN

Gauge: 12, 3" chamber. **Barrel:** 24", 26", 28", Franchoke tubes. **Weight:** 7 lbs., 2 oz. **Length:** 47-1/2" overall. **Stock:** 14-1/4"x1-1/2"x2-1/2". European walnut. **Features:** Alloy frame with matte black finish; gas-operated with Variopress System; four-lug rotating bolt; loaded chamber indicator. Introduced 1996. Imported from Italy by Benelli U.S.A.
Price: **$595.00**
Price: Camo (Advantage camo). **$657.00**
Price: Synthetic (black synthetic stock, forend) **$579.00**
Price: (20 gauge, 24", 26", 28") **$595.00**
Price: Variopress 620 (Advantage camo). **$657.00**

Franchi Variopress 612 Defense Shotgun

Similar to Variopress 612 except has 18 1/2 ", cylinder-bore barrel with black, synthetic stock. Available in 12 gauge, 3" chamber only. Weighs 6-1/2 pounds. Introduced 2000.
Price: **$520.00**

Franchi Variopress 612 Sporting Shotgun

Similar to Variopress 612 except has 30" ported barrel to reduce muzzle jump. Available in 12 gauge, 3" chamber only. Introduced 2000.
Price: **$900.00**

SHOTGUNS

SHOTGUNS — AUTOLOADERS

Mossberg Model 9200 Trophy

Mossberg 9200 Viking

Remington Model 11-87 Premier

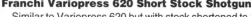

Franchi Variopress 620 Short Stock Shotgun
Similar to Variopress 620 but with stock shortened to 12 1/2 "length of pull for smaller shooters. Introduced 2000.
Price: (20 gauge, 26" barrel) $605.00

LUGER ULTRA LIGHT SEMI-AUTOMATIC SHOTGUNS
Gauge: 12, 3" and 3-1/2" chambers. **Barrel:** 26", 28"; imp. cyl., mod. and full choke tubes. **Weight:** 6-1/2 lbs. **Length:** 48" overall (28" barrel) **Stock:** Gloss-finish European walnut, checkered grip and forend. **Features:** Gas-operated action handles 2-3/4" and 3" loads; chrome-line barrel handles steel shot; blued finish. Introduced 2000. From Stoeger Industries.
Price: $479.00

MOSSBERG MODEL 9200 CROWN GRADE AUTO SHOTGUN
Gauge: 12, 3" chamber. **Barrel:** 24" (rifled bore), 24", 28" (Accu-Choke tubes); vent. rib. **Weight:** About 7.5 lbs. **Length:** 48" overall (28" bbl.). **Stock:** Walnut with high-gloss finish, cut checkering. **Features:** Shoots all 2-3/4" or 3" loads without adjustment. Alloy receiver, ambidextrous top safety. Introduced 1992.
Price: 28", vent. rib $574.00
Price: Trophy, 24" with scope base, rifled bore, Dual-Comb stock $552.00
Price: 24", Fiber Optic or standard rifle sights, rifled bore $517.00

Mossberg Model 9200 Viking
Similar to the Model 9200 Crown Grade except has black matte metal finish, moss-green synthetic stock and forend; 28" Accu-Choke vent. rib barrel with Imp. Cyl., Full and Mod. tubes. Made in U.S. by Mossberg. Introduced 1996.
Price: $556.00

Mossberg Model 9200 Camo Shotgun
Same as the Model 9200 Crown Grade except completely covered with Mossy Oak Tree Stand, Mossy Oak Shadowbranch, Realtree AP gray or OFM camouflage finish. Available with 24" barrel with Accu-Choke tubes. Has synthetic stock and forend. Introduced 1993.
Price: Turkey, 24" vent. rib, Mossy Oak or Realtree finish $538.00
Price: 28" vent. rib, Accu-Chokes, Woodlands camo finish $556.00

Mossberg Model 9200 Special Hunter
Similar to the Model 9200 Crown Grade except with 28" vent rib barrel with Accu choke set, Parkerized finish, black synthetic stock and forend, and sling and swivels. Introduced 1998. Made in U.S. by Mossberg.
Price: $491.00

Mossberg Model 9200 Custom Grade Sporting Shotgun
Same as the Model 9200 Crown Grade except has custom engraved receiver. Comes with 28" vent. rib barrel with Accu-Choke tubes (including Skeet), cut-checkered walnut stock and forend. Introduced 1993.
Price: $590.00

Mossberg Model 9200 Bantam
Same as the Model 9200 Crown Grade except has 1" shorter stock, 22" vent. rib barrel with three Accu-Choke tubes. Made in U.S. by Mossberg. Introduced 1996.
Price: $574.00

REMINGTON MODEL 11-87 PREMIER SHOTGUN
Gauge: 12, 20, 3" chamber. **Barrel:** 26", 28", 30" Rem Choke tubes. Light Contour barrel. **Weight:** About 7-3/4 lbs. **Length:** 46" overall (26" bbl.). **Stock:** Walnut with satin or high-gloss finish; cut checkering; solid brown buttpad; no white spacers. **Sights:** Bradley-type white-faced front, metal bead middle. **Features:** Pressure compensating gas system allows shooting 2-3/4" or 3" loads interchangeably with no adjustments. Stainless magazine tube; redesigned feed latch, barrel support ring on operating bars; pinned forend. Introduced 1987.
Price: $756.00
Price: Left-hand $809.00
Price: Premier Cantilever Deer Barrel, sling, swivels, Monte Carlo stock $836.00

Remington Model 11-87 Special Purpose Magnum
Similar to the 11-87 Premier except has dull stock finish, Parkerized exposed metal surfaces. Bolt and carrier have dull blackened coloring. Comes with 26" or 28" barrel with Rem Chokes, padded Cordura nylon sling and quick detachable swivels. Introduced 1987.
Price: $756.00
Price: With synthetic stock and forend (SPS) $756.00

Remington Model 11-87 SPS Special Purpose Synthetic Camo
Similar to the 11-87 Special Purpose Magnum except has synthetic stock and all metal (except bolt and trigger guard) and stock covered with Mossy Oak Break-Up camo finish. In 12 gauge only, 26", Rem Choke. Comes with camo sling, swivels. Introduced 1992.
Price: $869.00

Remington Model 11-87 SPS Camo

Remington Model 11-87 SPS-T Turkey Camo

Remington Model 11-87 SC NP

Remington Model 1100 Youth Turkey Camo

Remington Model 11-87 SPS-T Turkey Camo

Similar to the 11-87 Special Purpose Magnum except with synthetic stock, 21" vent. rib barrel with Rem choke tube. Completely covered with Mossy Oak Break-Up Brown camouflage. Bolt body, trigger guard and recoil pad are non-reflective black.

Price: **$869.00**
Price: Model 11-87 SPS-T RS/TG (TruGlo fiber optics sights). . . . **$808.00**
Price: Model 11-87 SPS-T Camo CL/RD (Leupold/Gilmore
red dot sight) **$1,193.00**

Remington Model 11-87 SPS-Deer Shotgun

Similar to the 11-87 Special Purpose Camo except has fully-rifled 21" barrel with rifle sights, black non-reflective, synthetic stock and forend, black carrying sling. Introduced 1993.

Price: **$789.00**
Price: With wood stock (Model 11-87 SP Deer gun) Rem choke, 21" barrel
w/rifle sights **$736.00**

Remington Model 11-87 SPS Cantilever Shotgun

Similar to the 11-87 SPS except has fully rifled barrel; synthetic stock with Monte Carlo comb; cantilever scope mount deer barrel. Comes with sling and swivels. Introduced 1994.

Price: **$836.00**

Remington Model 11-87 SC NP Shotgun

Similar to the Model 11-87 Sporting Clays except has low-luster nickel-plated receiver with fine-line engraving, and ported 28" or 30" Rem choke barrel with matte finish. Tournament-grade American walnut stock measures 14-3/16"x2-1/4"x1-1/2". Sporting Clays choke tubes have knurled extensions. Introduced 1997. Made in U.S. by Remington.

Price: **$948.00**

Remington Model 11-87 SP and SPS Super Magnum Shotguns

Similar to Model 11-87 Special Purpose Magnum except has 3-1/2" chamber. Available in flat-finish American walnut or black synthetic stock, 26" or 28" black-matte finished barrel and receiver; imp. cyl., modified and full Rem Choke tubes. Overall length 45-3/4", weighs 8 lbs., 2 oz. Introduced 2000. From Remington Arms Co.

Price: 11-87 SP Super Magnum (walnut stock) **$852.00**
Price: 11-87 SPS Super Magnum (synthetic stock) **$852.00**

Remington Model 11-87 Upland Special Shotgun

Similar to 11-87 Premier except has 23" ventilated rib barrel with straight-grip, English-style walnut stock. Available in 12 or 20 gauge. Overall length 43-1/2", weighs 7-1/4 lbs. (6-1/2 lbs. in 20 ga.). Comes with imp. cyl., modified and full choke tubes. Introduced 2000. From Remington Arms Co.

Price: 12 or 20 gauge **$756.00**

REMINGTON MODEL 1100 SYNTHETIC LT-20

Gauge: 20. Barrel: 26" Rem Chokes. Weight: 6-3/4 lbs. Stock: 14"x1-1/2"x2-1/2". Black synthetic, checkered pistol grip and forend. Features: Matted receiver top with scroll work on both sides of receiver.

Price: **$540.00**
Price: Youth Gun LT-20 (21" Rem Choke) **$540.00**

Remington Model 1100 Synthetic

12 gauge, and has black synthetic stock; vent. rib 28" barrel on 12 gauge, both with Mod. Rem Choke tube. Weighs about 7-1/2 lbs. Introduced 1996.

Price: **$540.00**

Remington Model 1100 Youth Synthetic Turkey Camo

Similar to the Model 1100 LT-20 except has 1" shorter stock, 21" vent rib barrel with Full Rem Choke tube; 3" chamber; synthetic stock and forend are covered with RealTree Advantage camo, and barrel and receiver have non-reflective, black matte finish. Introduced 1999.

Price: **$603.00**

SHOTGUNS — AUTOLOADERS

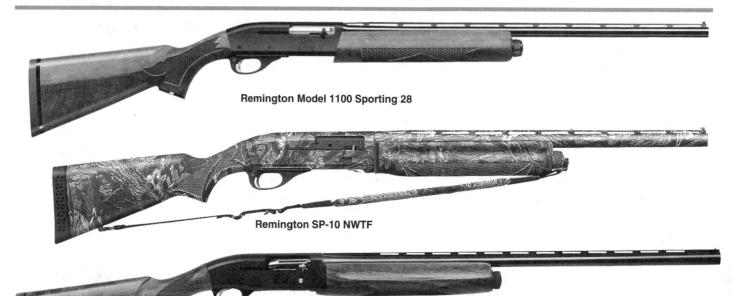

Remington Model 1100 Sporting 28

Remington SP-10 NWTF

Weatherby SAS

Remington Model 1100 LT-20 Synthetic FR RS Shotgun
Similar to the Model 1100 LT-20 except has 21" fully rifled barrel with rifle sights, 2-3/4" chamber, and fiberglass-reinforced synthetic stock. Introduced 1997. Made in U.S. by Remington.
Price: **$573.00**

Remington Model 1100 Sporting 28
Similar to the 1100 LT-20 except in 28 gauge with 25" barrel; comes with Skeet, Imp. Cyl., Light Mod., Mod. Rem Choke tube. Semi-Fancy walnut with gloss finish, Sporting rubber butt pad. Made in U.S. by Remington. Introduced 1996.
Price: **$859.00**

Remington Model 1100 Sporting 20 Shotgun
Similar to the Model 1100 LT-20 except has tournament-grade American walnut stock with gloss finish and sporting-style recoil pad, 28" Rem-Choke barrel for Skeet, Imp. Cyl., Light Modified and Modified. Introduced 1998.
Price: **$859.00**

Remington Model 1100 Classic Trap Shotgun
Similar to Standard Model 1100 except 12 gauge with 30", low-profile barrel, semi-fancy American walnut stock and high-polish blued receiver with engraving and gold eagle inlay. Comes with singles, mid handicap and long handicap choke tubes. Overall length 50-1/2", weighs 8 lbs., 4 oz. Introduced 2000. From Remington Arms Co.
Price: **$885.00**

Remington Model 1100 Sporting 12 Shotgun
Similar to Model 1100 Sporting 20 Shotgun except in 12 gauge, has 28" ventilated barrel with semi-fancy American walnut stock, gold-plated trigger. Overall length 49", weighs 8 lbs. Introduced 2000. From Remington Arms Co.
Price: **$859.00**

Remington Model 1100 Synthetic FR CL Shotgun
Similar to the Model 1100 LT-20 except 12 gauge, has 21" fully rifled barrel with cantilever scope mount and fiberglass-reinforced synthetic stock with Monte Carlo comb. Introduced 1997. Made in U.S. by Remington.
Price: **$620.00**

REMINGTON MODEL SP-10 MAGNUM SHOTGUN
Gauge: 10, 3-1/2" chamber, 2-shot magazine. **Barrel:** 26", 30" (Full and Mod. Rem Chokes). **Weight:** 10-3/4 to 11 lbs. **Length:** 47-1/2" overall (26" barrel). **Stock:** Walnut with satin finish or black synthetic. Checkered grip and forend. **Sights:** Twin bead. **Features:** Stainless steel gas system with moving cylinder; 3/8" ventilated rib. Receiver and barrel have matte finish. Brown recoil pad. Comes with padded Cordura nylon sling. Introduced 1989.
Price: **$1,199.00**
Price: SP-10 Magnum Turkey Camo (23" vent rib barrel, Turkey Extra-Full Rem Choke tube) Mossy Oak Break-up.................. **$1,319.00**

Remington Model SP-10 Magnum Camo Shotgun
Similar to the SP-10 Magnum except buttstock, forend, receiver, barrel and magazine cap are covered with Mossy Oak Break-Up camo finish; bolt body and trigger guard have matte black finish. Rem Choke tube, 26" vent. rib barrel with mid-rib bead and Bradley-style front sight, swivel studs and quick-detachable swivels, and a non-slip Cordura carrying sling in the same camo pattern. Introduced 1993.
Price: **$1,319.00**
Price: SP-10 Magnum Synthetic **$1,199.00**

SARSILMAZ SEMI-AUTOMATIC SHOTGUN
Gauge: 12, 3" chamber. **Barrel:** 26" or 28"; fixed chokes. **Weight:** N/A. **Length:** N/A. **Stock:** Walnut or synthetic. **Features:** Handles 2-3/4" or 3" magnum loads. Introduced 2000. Imported from Turkey by Armsport Inc.
Price: With walnut stock................................ **$969.95**
Price: With synthetic stock.............................. **$919.95**

WEATHERBY SAS AUTO SHOTGUN
Gauge: 12, 20, 2-3/4" or 3" chamber. **Barrel:** 26", 28" (20 ga.); 26", 28", 30" (12 ga.); Briley Multi-Choke tubes. **Weight:** 6-3/4 to 7-3/4 lbs. **Stock:** 14-1/4"x2-1/4"x1-1/2". Claro walnut. **Features:** Alloy receiver with matte finish; gold-plated trigger; magazine cut-off. Introduced 1999. Imported by Weatherby.
Price: 12 or 20 ga. **$899.00**

WINCHESTER SUPER X2 AUTO SHOTGUN
Gauge: 12, 3", 3-1/2" chamber. **Barrel:** 24", 26", 28"; Invector Plus choke tubes. **Weight:** 7-1/4 to 7-1/2 lbs. **Stock:** 14-1/4"x1-3/4"x2". Walnut or black synthetic. **Features:** Gas-operated action shoots all loads without adjustment; vent. rib barrels. Introduced 1999. Made in U.S. by U.S. Repeating Arms Co.
Price: Field, walnut or synthetic stock, 3"................... **$799.00**
Price: Camo Waterfowl, 3-1/2", Mossy Oak Shadow Grass.... **$1,033.00**
Price: Turkey, 3-1/2", synthetic stock, 24" **$955.00**
Price: Magnum, 3-1/2", synthetic stock **$941.00**

NEW!

NEW!

Includes a wide variety of sporting guns and guns suitable for competitive shooting.

Armscor M-30F Field

Benelli Nova Pump

Benelli Nova Pump Rifled Slug

Browning BPS 10 gauge

ARMSCOR M-30F FIELD PUMP SHOTGUN

Gauge: 12, 3" chamber. **Barrel:** 28" fixed Mod., or with Mod. and Full choke tubes. **Weight:** 7.6 lbs. **Stock:** Walnut-finished hardwood. **Features:** Double action slide bars; blued steel receiver; damascened bolt. Introduced 1996. Imported from the Philippines by K.B.I., Inc.
Price: With fixed choke $239.00
Price: With choke tubes $269.00

BENELLI NOVA PUMP SHOTGUN

Gauge: 12, 3-1/2" chamber. **Barrel:** 24", 26", 28"; chrome lined, vent rib; choke tubes. **Weight:** 8 lbs. **Length:** 47.5" overall. **Stock:** Black polymer. **Features:** Montefeltro rotating bolt design with dual action bars; magazine cut-off; synthetic trigger assembly. Four-shot magazine Introduced 1999. Imported from Italy by Benelli USA.
Price: With black stock $390.00
Price: With Camo finish $456.00

Benelli Nova Pump Slug Gun

Similar to the Nova except has 18.5" barrel with adjustable rifle-type or ghost ring sights; weighs 7.2 lbs.; black synthetic stock. Introduced 1999. Imported from Italy by Benelli USA.
Price: With rifle sights $320.00
Price: With ghost-ring sights $355.00

Benelli Nova Pump Rifled Slug Gun

Similar to Nova Pump Slug Gun except has 24" barrel and rifled bore; open rifle sights; synthetic stock; weighs 8.1 pounds.
Price: $544.00

BROWNING BPS PUMP SHOTGUN

Gauge: 10, 12, 3-1/2" chamber; 12 or 20, 3" chamber (2-3/4" in target guns), 28, 2-3/4" chamber, 5-shot magazine, 410 ga., 3" chamber. **Barrel:** 10 ga.—24" Buck Special, 28", 30", 32" Invector; 12, 20 ga.—22", 24", 26", 28", 30", 32" (Imp. Cyl., mod. or full). 410 ga.—26" barrel. (Imp. Cyl., mod. and full choke tubes.) Also available with Invector choke tubes, 12 or 20 ga.; Upland Special has 22" barrel with Invector tubes. BPS 3" and 3-1/2" have back-bored barrel. **Weight:** 7 lbs., 8 oz. (28" barrel). **Length:** 48-3/4" overall (28" barrel). **Stock:** 14-1/4"x1-1/2"x2-1/2". Select walnut, semi-beavertail forend, full pistol grip stock. **Features:** All 12 gauge 3" guns except Buck Special and game guns have back-bored barrels with Invector Plus choke tubes. Bottom feeding and ejection, receiver top safety, high post vent. rib. Double action bars eliminate binding. Vent. rib barrels only. All 12 and 20 gauge guns with 3" chamber available with fully engraved receiver flats at no extra cost. Each gauge has its own unique game scene. Introduced 1977. Imported from Japan by Browning.
Price: 10 ga., Hunting, Invector $532.00
Price: 12 ga., 3-1/2" Mag., Hunting, Invector Plus $532.00
Price: 12, 20 ga., Hunting, Invector Plus $444.00
Price: 12 ga. Buck Special $408.00
Price: 28 ga., Hunting, Invector $444.00
Price: 410 ga., Hunting, Invector . . . . NA

Browning BPS 10 gauge Turkey

Similar to the BPS Hunter except has 24" barrel with Hi-Viz front sight for turkey hunting. Available with either walnut or black composite stock and forend. Introduced 1999. Imported by Browning.
Price: Hunter (walnut) $532.00
Price: Stalker (composite) $532.00

Browning BPS 10 gauge Camo Pump

Similar to the BPS 10 gauge Hunter except completely covered with Mossy Oak Shadow Grass camouflage. Available with 24", 26", 28" barrel. Introduced 1999. Imported by Browning.
Price: $602.00

SHOTGUNS — SLIDE ACTIONS

Browning BPS Stalker

Ithaca Model 37 Turkeyslayer

Browning BPS Waterfowl Camo Pump Shotgun

Similar to the BPS Hunter except completely covered with Mossy Oak Shadow Grass camouflage. Available in 12 gauge, with 24", 26" or 28" barrel, 3" chamber. Introduced 1999. Imported by Browning.
Price: **$514.00**

Browning BPS Game Gun Deer Special

Similar to the standard BPS except has newly designed receiver/magazine tube/barrel mounting system to eliminate play, heavy 20.5" barrel with rifle-type sights with adjustable rear, solid receiver scope mount, "rifle" stock dimensions for scope or open sights, sling swivel studs. Gloss or matte finished wood with checkering, polished blue metal. Introduced 1992.
Price: **$516.00**

Browning BPS Game Gun Turkey Special

Similar to the standard BPS except has satin-finished walnut stock and dull-finished barrel and receiver. Receiver is drilled and tapped for scope mounting. Rifle-style stock dimensions and swivel studs. Has Extra-Full Turkey choke tube. Introduced 1992.
Price: **$482.00**

Browning BPS Stalker Pump Shotgun

Same gun as the standard BPS except all exposed metal parts have a matte blued finish and the stock has a durable black finish with a black recoil pad. Available in 10 ga. (3-1/2") and 12 ga. with 3" or 3-1/2" chamber, 22", 28", 30" barrel with Invector choke system. Introduced 1987.
Price: 12 ga., 3" chamber, Invector Plus **$444.00**
Price: 10, 12 ga., 3-1/2" chamber. **$532.00**

Browning BPS Micro Pump Shotgun

Same as BPS Upland Special except 20 ga. only, 22" Invector barrel, stock has pistol grip with recoil pad. Length of pull is 13-1/4". Introduced 1986.
Price: **$444.00**

EAA/BAIKAL IZH-81 PUMP SHOTGUN

NEW! **Gauge:** 12, 3" chamber. **Barrel:** 18-1/2", 20", 22", 24", 26", 28"; imp., mod. and full choke tubes. **Weight:** N/A. **Stock:** Hardwood. **Features:** Hammer-forged barrel; machined receiver; push-button, trigger-block safety; 5-round, detachable steel magazine; two, opposing extractors for sure ejection. Introduced 2000. Imported by European American Armory.
Price: IZH-81 (blued finish, hardwood stock) **$269.00**

EAA/BAIKAL MP-133 PUMP SHOTGUN

NEW! **Gauge:** 12, 3-1/2" chamber. **Barrel:** 18-1/2", 20", 24", 26", 28"; imp., mod. and full choke tubes. **Weight:** N/A. **Stock:** Walnut; checkered grip and grooved forearm. **Features:** Hammer-forged, chrome-lined barrel with ventilated rib; machined steel parts; dual action bars; trigger-block safety; 4-shot magazine tube; handles 2-3/4" through 3-1/2" shells. Introduced 2000. Imported by European American Armory.
Price: MP-133 (blued finish, walnut stock and forend) **$299.00**

ITHACA MODEL 37 DELUXE PUMP SHOTGUN

Gauge: 12, 16, 20, 3" chamber. **Barrel:** 26", 28", 30" (12 gauge), 26", 28" (16 and 20 gauge), choke tubes. **Weight:** 7 lbs. **Stock:** Walnut with cut-checkered grip and forend. **Features:** Steel receiver; bottom ejection; brushed blue finish, vent rib barrels. Reintroduced 1996. Made in U.S. by Ithaca Gun Co.
Price: **$545.95**
Price: With straight English-style stock **$545.95**
Price: Model 37 New Classic (ringtail forend, sunburst recoil pad, hand-finished walnut stock, 26" or 28" barrel) **$695.95**

Ithaca Model 37 Waterfowler

Similar to the Model 37 Deluxe except in 12 gauge only with 28" barrel, special extended steel shot choke tube system. Complete coverage of Advantage Wetlands couflage. Introduced 1999. Made in U.S. by Ithaca Gun Co.
Price: **$595.00**

Ithaca Model 37 Turkeyslayer Pump Shotgun

Similar to the Model 37 Deluxe except has 22" barrel with rifle sights, extended ported choke tube and full-coverage, Realtree Advantage, Realtree All-Purpose Brown, All-Purpose Grey, or Xtra Brown camouflage finish. Introduced 1996. Made in U.S. by Ithaca Gun Co.
Price: 12 ga. only **$569.95**
Price: Youth Turkeyslayer (20 gauge, 6.5 lbs., shorter stock) **$569.95**

ITHACA MODEL 37 DEERSLAYER II PUMP SHOTGUN

Gauge: 12, 20, 3" chamber. **Barrel:** 20", 25", fully rifled. **Weight:** 7 lbs. **Stock:** Cut-checkered American walnut with Monte Carlo comb. **Sights:** Rifle-type. **Features:** Integral barrel and receiver. Bottom ejection. Brushed blue finish. Reintroduced 1997. Made in U.S. by Ithaca Gun Co.
Price: **$565.95**
Price: Smooth Bore Deluxe **$515.95**
Price: Rifled Deluxe **$515.95**

Ithaca Model 37 Hardwoods 20/2000 Deerslayer

Similar to the Model 37 Deerslayer II except has synthetic stock and forend, and has the Truglo Fibre Optic sight system. Drilled and tapped for scope mounting. Complete coverage of RealTree 20/2000 Hardwoods camouflage. Introduced 1999. Made in U.S. by Ithaca Gun Co.
Price: **$565.95**

Ithaca Model 37 Hardwoods 20/2000 Turkeyslayer

Similar to the Model 37 Turkeyslayer except has synthetic stock and forend, Extra-Full extended and ported choke tube, long forcing cone, and Truglo Fibre Optic sight system. Complete coverage of RealTree Hardwoods 20/2000 camouflage. Introduced 1999. Made in U.S. by Ithaca Gun Co.
Price: **$565.95**

MOSSBERG MODEL 835 CROWN GRADE ULTI-MAG PUMP

Gauge: 12, 3-1/2" chamber. **Barrel:** Ported 24" rifled bore, 24", 28", Accu-Mag choke tubes for steel or lead shot. **Weight:** 7-3/4 lbs. **Length:** 48-1/2"

SHOTGUNS — SLIDE ACTIONS

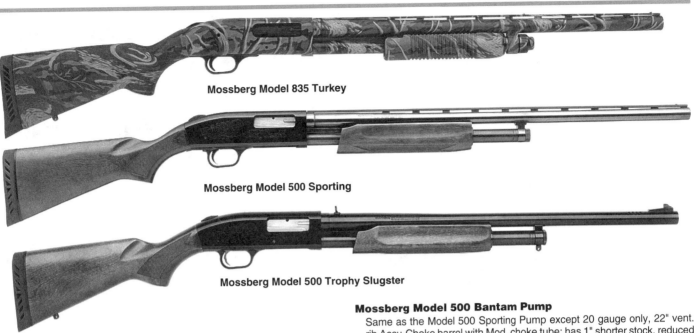

Mossberg Model 835 Turkey

Mossberg Model 500 Sporting

Mossberg Model 500 Trophy Slugster

overall. **Stock:** 14"x1-1/2"x2-1/2". Dual Comb. Cut-checkered hardwood or camo synthetic; both have recoil pad. **Sights:** White bead front, brass mid-bead; Fiber Optic. **Features:** Shoots 2-3/4", 3" or 3-1/2" shells. Back-bored and ported barrel to reduce recoil, improve patterns. Ambidextrous thumb safety, twin extractors, dual slide bars. Mossberg Cablelock included. Introduced 1988.
Price: 28" vent. rib, hardwood stock...................... $361.00
Price: Combo, 24" rifled bore, rifle sights, 28" vent. rib, Accu-Mag choke tubes Woodlands camo finish .... NA
Price: RealTree or Mossy Oak Camo Turkey, 24" vent. rib, Accu-Mag Extra-Full tube, synthetic stock...................... NA
Price: RealTree Camo, 28" vent. rib, Accu-Mag tubes, synthetic stock...................... $571.00
Price: RealTree Camo Combo, 24" rifled bore, rifle sights, 24" vent. rib, Accu-Mag choke tubes, synthetic stock, hard case $561.00
Price: OFM Camo, 28" vent. rib, Accu-Mag tubes, synthetic stock...................... NA
Price: OFM Camo Combo, 24" rifled bore, rifle sights, 28" vent. rib, Accu-Mag tubes, synthetic stock .... NA

Mossberg American Field Model 835 Pump Shotgun
Same as the Model 835 Crown Grade except has walnut-stained hardwood stock and comes only with Modified choke tube, 28" barrel. Introduced 1992.
Price: $331.00

Mossberg Model 835 Special Hunter
Similar to the Model 835 Crown Grade except with 24" or 28" ported barrel with Accu-Mag Mod. choke tube, Parkerized finish, black synthetic stock and forend; comes with sling and swivels. Introduced 1998. Made in U.S. by Mossberg.
Price: $363.00

MOSSBERG MODEL 500 SPORTING PUMP
Gauge: 12, 20, 410, 3" chamber. **Barrel:** 18-1/2" to 28" with fixed or Accu-Choke, plain or vent. rib. **Weight:** 6-1/4 lbs. (410), 7-1/4 lbs. (12). **Length:** 48" overall (28" barrel). **Stock:** 14"x1-1/2"x2-1/2". Walnut-stained hardwood. Cut-checkered grip and forend. **Sights:** White bead front, brass mid-bead; Fiber Optic. **Features:** Ambidextrous thumb safety, twin extractors, disconnecting safety, dual action bars. Quiet Carry forend. Many barrels are ported. Mossberg Cablelock included. From Mossberg.
Price: From about...................... $322.00
Price: Sporting Combos (field barrel and Slugster barrel), from.. $382.00

Mossberg Model 500 Bantam Pump
Same as the Model 500 Sporting Pump except 20 gauge only, 22" vent. rib Accu-Choke barrel with Mod. choke tube; has 1" shorter stock, reduced length from pistol grip to trigger, reduced forend reach. Introduced 1992.
Price: $336.00
Price: With full Woodlands camouflage finish $376.00

Mossberg Model 500 Camo Pump
Same as the Model 500 Sporting Pump except 12 gauge only and entire gun is covered with special camouflage finish. Receiver drilled and tapped for scope mounting. Comes with quick detachable swivel studs, swivels, camouflage sling, Mossberg Cablelock.
Price: From about...................... $346.00
Price: Camo Combo (as above with extra Slugster barrel), from about...................... $422.00

Mossberg Model 500 Persuader/Cruiser Shotguns
Similar to Mossberg Model 500 except has 18-1/2" or 20" barrel with cylinder bore choke, synthetic stock and blue or parkerized finish. Available in 12, 20 and 410 gauge with bead or ghost ring sights, 6- or 8-shot magazines. From Mossberg.
Price: 12 gauge, 20" barrel, bead sight. $294.00
Price: 20 or 410 gauge, 18-1/2" barrel, bead sight $305.00
Price: 12 gauge, parkerized finish, 18-1/2" barrel, ghost ring sights $416.00
Price: Home Security 410 (410 gauge, 18-1/2" barrel with spreader choke) $319.00

Mossberg Model 590 Special Purpose Shotguns
Similar to Model 500 except has parkerized or Marinecote finish, 9-shot magazine and black synthetic stock (some models feature Speed Feed. Available in 12 gauge only with 20", cylinder bore barrel. Weighs 7-1/4 lbs. From Mossberg.
Price: Bead sight, heat shield over barrel $370.00
Price: Ghost ring sight, Speed Feed stock. $519.00

MOSSBERG MODEL 500 SLUGSTER
Gauge: 12, 20, 3" chamber. **Barrel:** 24", ported rifled bore. Integral scope mount. **Weight:** 7-1/4 lbs. **Length:** 44" overall. **Stock:** 14" pull, 1-3/8" drop at heel. Walnut; Dual Comb design for proper eye positioning with or without scoped barrels. Recoil pad and swivel studs. **Features:** Ambidextrous thumb safety, twin extractors, dual slide bars. Comes with scope mount. Mossberg Cablelock included. Introduced 1988.
Price: Rifled bore, with integral scope mount, Dual-Comb stock, 12 or 20 .... $367.00
Price: Fiber Optic, rifle sights $398.00
Price: Rifled bore, rifle sights $398.00
Price: 20 ga., Standard or Bantam, from $367.00

SHOTGUNS

Remington 870 Wingmaster

Remington Model 870 Express Super Magnum

Remington Model 870 Express Rifle-Sighted Deer Gun

REMINGTON MODEL 870 WINGMASTER
Gauge: 12, 3" chamber. **Barrel:** 26", 28", 30" (Rem Chokes). Light Contour barrel. **Weight:** 7-1/4 lbs. **Length:** 46-1/2" overall (26" bbl.). **Stock:** 14"x2-1/2"x1". American walnut with satin or high-gloss finish, cut-checkered pistol grip and forend. Rubber butt pad. **Sights:** Ivory bead front, metal mid-bead. **Features:** Double action bars; cross-bolt safety; blue finish. Introduced 1986.
Price: $569.00
Price: 870 Wingmaster Super Magnum $649.00

Remington Model 870 50th Anniversary Classic Trap Shotgun
Similar to Model 870 TC Wingmaster except has 30" ventilated rib with singles, mid handicap and long handicap choke tubes, semi-fancy American walnut stock and high-polish blued receiver with engraving and gold shield inlay. From Remington Arms Co.
Price: $775.00

Remington Model 870 Marine Magnum
Similar to the 870 Wingmaster except all metal is plated with electroless nickel and has black synthetic stock and forend. Has 18" plain barrel (Cyl.), bead front sight, 7-shot magazine. Introduced 1992.
Price: $545.00

Remington Model 870 Wingmaster LW 20 ga.
Similar to the Model 870 Wingmaster except in 28 gauge and 410-bore only, 25" vent rib barrel with Rem Choke tubes, high-gloss wood finish. 26" & 28" barrels-20 ga.
Price: 20 gauge $569.00
Price: 410-bore................................. $596.00
Price: 28 gauge $649.00

Remington Model 870 Express
Similar to the 870 Wingmaster except has a walnut-toned hardwood stock with solid, black recoil pad and pressed checkering on grip and forend. Outside metal surfaces have a black oxide finish. Comes with 26" or 28" vent rib barrel with a Mod. Rem Choke tube. Introduced 1987.
Price: 12 or 20 .... $329.00
Price: Express Combo, 12 ga., 26" vent rib with Mod. Rem Choke and 20" fully rifled barrel with rifle sights $436.00
Price: Express 20 ga., 26" or 28" with Mod. Rem Choke tubes .. $329.00
Price: Express L-H (left-hand), 12 ga., 28" vent rib with Mod. Rem Choke tube.. $356.00
Price: Express Synthetic, 12-ga, 26" or 28" $329.00
Price: Express Combo (20 ga.) with extra Deer rifled barrel $436.00

Remington Model 870 Express Super Magnum
Similar to the 870 Express except has 28" vent. rib barrel with 3-1/2" chamber, vented recoil pad. Introduced 1998.
Price: $369.00
Price: Super Magnum Synthetic............................ $376.00
Price: Super Magnum Turkey Camo (Turkey Extra Full Rem Choke, full-coverage RealTree Advantage camo) $500.00
Price: Super Magnum Combo (26" with Mod. Rem Choke and 20" fully rifled deer barrel with 3" chamber and rifle sights; wood stock) $516.00
Price: Super Magnum Synthetic Turkey (black) $389.00

Remington Model 870 Wingmaster Super Magnum Shotgun
Similar to Model 870 Express Super Magnum except has high-polish blued finish, 28" ventilated barrel with imp. cyl., modified and full choke tubes, checkered high-gloss walnut stock. Overall length 48", weighs 7-1/2 lbs. Introduced 2000.
Price: $649.00

Remington Model 870 Express Youth Gun
Same as the Model 870 Express except comes with 13" length of pull, 21" barrel with Mod. Rem Choke tube. Hardwood stock with low-luster finish. Introduced 1991.
Price: 20 ga. Express Youth (1" shorter stock), from $329.00
Price: 20 ga. Youth Deer 20" FR/RS $363.00

Remington Model 870 Express Rifle-Sighted Deer Gun
Same as the Model 870 Express except comes with 20" barrel with fixed Imp. Cyl. choke, open iron sights, Monte Carlo stock. Introduced 1991.
Price: $329.00
Price: With fully rifled barrel $363.00
Price: Express Synthetic Deer (black synthetic stock, black matte metal).. $369.00

Remington Model 870 Express Turkey
Same as the Model 870 Express except comes with 3" chamber, 21" vent. rib turkey barrel and Extra-Full Rem Choke Turkey tube; 12 ga. only. Introduced 1991.
Price: $343.00
Price: Express Turkey Camo stock has RealTree Advantage camo, matte black metal.. $396.00
Price: Express Youth Turkey camo (as above with 1" shorter length of pull).. $396.00

Remington Model 870 Express Synthetic HD Home Defense
Similar to the 870 Express with 18" barrel except has synthetic stock and forend. Introduced 1994.
Price: $316.00

SHOTGUNS — SLIDE ACTIONS

Remington 870 SPS Super Slug Deer Gun

Winchester 1300 Black Shadow Field Gun

Winchester 1300 Ranger

Remington Model 870 SPS Super Slug Deer Gun

Similar to the Model 870 Express Synthetic except has 23" rifled, modified contour barrel with cantilever scope mount. Comes with black synthetic stock and forend with swivel studs, black Cordura nylon sling. Introduced 1999. Fully rifled centilever barrel.

Price: $555.00

Remington Model 870 SPS Super Magnum Camo

Has synthetic stock and all metal (except bolt and trigger guard) and stock covered with Mossy Oak Break-Up camo finish In 12 gauge 3-1/2", 26" vent. rib, Rem Choke. Comes with camo sling, swivels.

Price: $569.00
Price: Model 870 SPS-T Super Magnum Camo (3-1/2" chamber). $569.00
Price: Model 870 SPS-T RS/TG (TruGlo fiber optics sights) $544.00
Price: Model 870 SPS-T Super Mag Camo CL/RD (Leupold/Gilmore dot sight). $889.00

SARSILMAZ PUMP SHOTGUN

Gauge: 12, 3" chamber. **Barrel:** 26" or 28". **Weight:** N/A. **Length:** N/A. **Stocks:** Oil-finished hardwood. **Features:** Includes extra pistol-grip stock. Introduced 2000. Imported from Turkey by Armsport Inc.

Price: With pistol-grip stock $299.95
Price: With metal stock.................................... $349.95

TRISTAR MODEL 1887 LEVER-ACTION SHOTGUN

Gauge: 12, 2-3/4" chamber, 5-shot magazine. **Barrel:** 30" (Full). **Weight:** 8 lbs. **Length:** 48" overall. **Stocks:** 12-3/4" pull. Rounded-knob pistol grip; walnut with oil finish; blued, checkered steel buttplate. Dimensions duplicate original WRA Co. specifications. **Sights:** Brass, bead front. **Features:** Recreation of Browning's original 1885 patents and design as made by Winchester Repeating Arms. External hammer with half- and full-cock positions; has original-type WRA Co. logo on left side of receiver; two-piece walnut forend. Announced 1997. Imported by Tristar Sporting Arms.

Price: .... NA

WINCHESTER MODEL 1300 WALNUT PUMP

Gauge: 12, 20, 3" chamber, 5-shot capacity. **Barrel:** 26", 28", vent. rib, with Full, Mod., Imp. Cyl. Winchoke tubes. **Weight:** 6-3/8 lbs. **Length:** 42-5/8" overall. **Stock:** American walnut, with deep cut checkering on pistol grip, traditional ribbed forend; high luster finish. **Sights:** Metal bead front. **Features:** Twin action slide bars; front-locking rotary bolt; roll-engraved receiver; blued, highly polished metal; cross-bolt safety with red indicator. Introduced 1984. From U.S. Repeating Arms Co., Inc.

Price: $391.00

Winchester Model 1300 Upland Special Pump Gun

Similar to the Model 1300 Walnut except has straight-grip stock, 24" barrel. Introduced 1999. Made in U.S. by U.S. Repeating Arms Co.

Price: $391.00

Winchester Model 1300 Black Shadow Field Gun

Similar to the Model 1300 Walnut except has black composite stock and forend, matte black finish. Has vent. rib 26" or 28" barrel, 3" chamber, comes with Mod. Winchoke tube. Introduced 1995. From U.S. Repeating Arms Co., Inc.

Price: 12 or 20 gauge.................................. $330.00

Winchester Model 1300 Black Shadow Deer Gun

Similar to the Model 1300 Black Shadow Turkey Gun except has ramp-type front sight, fully adjustable rear, drilled and tapped for scope mounting. Black composite stock and forend, matte black metal. Smoothbore 22" barrel with one Imp. Cyl. WinChoke tube; 12 gauge only, 3" chamber. Weighs 7-1/4 lbs. Introduced 1994. From U.S. Repeating Arms Co., Inc.

Price: $329.00
Price: With rifled barrel................................ $353.00

WINCHESTER MODEL 1300 RANGER PUMP GUN

Gauge: 12, 20, 3" chamber, 5-shot magazine. **Barrel:** 26", 28" vent. rib with Full, Mod., Imp. Cyl. Winchoke tubes. **Weight:** 7 to 7-1/4 lbs. **Length:** 48-5/8" to 50-5/8" overall. **Stock:** Walnut-finished hardwood with ribbed forend. **Sights:** Metal bead front. **Features:** Cross-bolt safety, black rubber recoil pad, twin action slide bars, front-locking rotating bolt. From U.S. Repeating Arms Co., Inc.

Price: Vent. rib barrel, Winchoke $344.00
Price: Model 1300 Compact, 20 ga., 22" vent. rib $343.00

Winchester Model 1300 Black Shadow Turkey Gun

Similar to the Model 1300 RealTree® Turkey except synthetic stock and forend are matte black, and all metal surfaces finished matte black. Drilled and tapped for scope mounting. In 12 or 20 gauge, 3" chamber, 22" vent. rib barrel; comes with one Extra-Full Winchoke tube (20 gauge has Full). Introduced 1994. From U.S. Repeating Arms Co., Inc.

Price: $329.00

SHOTGUNS

Includes a variety of game guns and guns for competitive shooting.

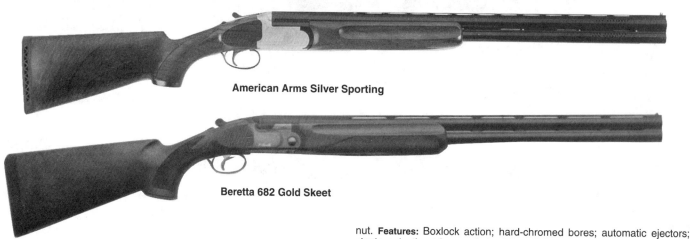

American Arms Silver Sporting

Beretta 682 Gold Skeet

AMERICAN ARMS SILVER I O/U

Gauge: 12, 20, 28, 410, 3" chamber (28 has 2-3/4"). **Barrel:** 26" (Imp. Cyl. & Mod., all gauges), 28" (Mod. & Full, 12, 20). **Weight:** About 6-3/4 lbs. **Stock:** 14-1/8"x1-3/8"x2-3/8". Checkered walnut. **Sights:** Metal bead front. **Features:** Boxlock action with scroll engraving, silver finish. Single selective trigger, extractors. Chrome-lined barrels. Manual safety. Rubber recoil pad. Introduced 1987. Imported from Italy by American Arms, Inc.
Price: 12 or 20 gauge **$649.00**
Price: 28 or 410 . . . . **$679.00**

American Arms Silver II Shotgun

Similar to the Silver I except 26" barrel (Imp. Cyl., Mod., Full choke tubes, 12 and 20 ga.), 28" (Imp. Cyl., Mod., Full choke tubes, 12 ga. only), 26" (Imp. Cyl. & Mod. fixed chokes, 28 and 410), automatic selective ejectors. Weight is about 6 lbs., 15 oz. (12 ga., 26").
Price: **$765.00**
Price: 28, 410 . . . . **$815.00**
Price: Two-barrel sets. **$1,239.00**

AMERICAN ARMS SILVER SPORTING O/U

Gauge: 12, 2-3/4" chambers, 20 3" chambers. **Barrel:** 28", 30" (Skeet, Imp. Cyl., Mod., Full choke tubes). **Weight:** 7-3/8 lbs. **Length:** 45-1/2" overall. **Stock:** 14-3/8"x1-1/2"x2-3/8". Figured walnut, cut checkering; Sporting Clays quick-mount buttpad. **Sights:** Target bead front. **Features:** Boxlock action with single selective mechanical trigger, automatic selective ejectors; special broadway channeled rib; vented barrel rib; chrome bores. Chrome-nickel finish on frame, with engraving. Introduced 1990. Imported from Italy by American Arms, Inc.
Price: **$965.00**

AMERICAN ARMS WS/OU 12, TS/OU 12 SHOTGUNS

Gauge: 12, 3-1/2" chambers. **Barrel:** WS/OU—28" (Imp. Cyl., Mod., Full choke tubes); TS/OU—24" (Imp. Cyl., Mod., Full choke tubes). **Weight:** 6 lbs., 15 oz. **Length:** 46" overall. **Stock:** 14-1/8"x1-1/8"x2-3/8". European walnut with cut checkering, black vented recoil pad, matte finish. **Features:** Boxlock action with single selective trigger, automatic selective ejectors; chrome bores. Matte metal finish. Imported by American Arms, Inc.
Price: **$799.00**
Price: With Mossy Oak Break-Up camo **$885.00**

American Arms WT/OU 10 Shotgun

Similar to the WS/OU 12 except chambered for 10 gauge 3-1/2" shell, 26" (Full & Full, choke tubes) barrel. Single selective trigger, extractors. Non-reflective finish on wood and metal. Imported by American Arms, Inc.
Price: **$995.00**

APOLLO TR AND TT SHOTGUNS

NEW! **Gauge:** 12, 20, 410, 3" chambers; 28 2-3/4" chambers. **Barrel:** 26", 28", 30", 32". **Weight:** 6 to 7-1/4 lbs. **Length:** N/A. **Stock:** Oil-finished European wal-

nut. **Features:** Boxlock action; hard-chromed bores; automatic ejectors; single selective trigger; choke tubes (12 and 20 ga. only). Introduced 2000. From Sigarms.
Price: Apollo TR 30 Field (color casehardened side plates) . . . **$2,240.00**
Price: Apollo TR 40 Gold (gold overlays on game scenes) **$2,675.00**
Price: Apollo TT 25 Competition (wide vent. rib with mid-bead). **$1,995.00**

BERETTA DT 10 TRIDENT SHOTGUNS

Gauge: 12, 2-3/4", 3" chambers. **Barrel:** 28", 30", 32", 34"; competition-style vent rib; fixed or Optima Choke tubes. **Weight:** 7.9 to 9 lbs. **Length:** N/A. **Stock:** High-grade walnut stock with oil finish; hand-checkered grip and forend; adjustable stocks available. **Features:** Detachable, adjustable trigger group; raised and thickened receiver; forend iron has replaceable nut to guarantee wood-to-metal fit; Optima Bore to improve shot pattern and reduce felt recoil. Introduced 2000. Imported from Italy by Beretta USA.
Price: DT 10 Trident Trap (selective, lockable single trigger;
adjustable stock). **$9,450.00**
Price: DT 10 Trident Trap Combo (single and o/u barrels) . . . **$11,995.00**
Price: DT 10 Trident Skeet (skeet stock with rounded recoil
pad, tapered rib).. . . . . **$9,450.00**
Price: DT 10 Trident Sporting (sporting clays stock with
rounded recoil pad).. . . . . **$9,240.00**

BERETTA SERIES S682 GOLD SKEET, TRAP OVER/UNDERS

Gauge: 12, 2-3/4" chambers. **Barrel:** Skeet—28"; trap—30" and 32", Imp. Mod. & Full and Mobilchoke; trap mono shotguns—32" and 34" Mobilchoke; trap top single guns—32" and 34" Full and Mobilchoke; trap combo sets—from 30" O/U, to 32" O/U, 34" top single. **Stock:** Close-grained walnut, hand checkered. **Sights:** White Bradley bead front sight and center bead. **Features:** Receiver has Greystone gunmetal gray finish with gold accents. Trap Monte Carlo stock has deluxe trap recoil pad. Various grades available; contact Beretta USA for details. Imported from Italy by Beretta USA
Price: S682 Gold Skeet **$2,850.00**
Price: S682 Gold Skeet, adjustable stock **$3,515.00**
Price: S682 Gold Trap **$3,100.00**
Price: S682 Gold Trap Top Combo **$4,085.00**
Price: S682 Gold Trap with adjustable stock **$3,625.00**
Price: S686 Silver Pigeon Trap **$1,850.00**
Price: S686 Silver Pigeon Trap Top Mono. **$1,850.00**
Price: S686 Silver Pigeon Skeet (28") **$1,760.00**
Price: S687 EELL Diamond Pigeon Trap **$4,815.00**
Price: S687 EELL Diamond Pigeon Skeet **$4,790.00**
Price: S687 EELL Diamond Pigeon Skeet, adjustable stock . . . **$5,810.00**
Price: S687 EELL Diamond Pigeon Trap Top
Mono. . . . . **$5,055.00** to **$5,105.00**
Price: ASE Gold Skeet **$12,060.00**
Price: ASE Gold Trap **$12,145.00**
Price: ASE Gold Trap Combo **$16,055.00**

SHOTGUNS — OVER/UNDERS

Beretta 682 Gold Sporting

Beretta Over/Under Field Shotgun

BERETTA MODEL S686 WHITEWING O/U

Gauge: 12, 3" chambers. **Barrel:** 26", 28", Mobilchoke tubes (Imp. Cyl., Mod., Full). **Weight:** 6.7 lbs. **Length:** 45.7" overall (28" barrels). **Stock:** 14.5"x2.2"x1.4". American walnut; radiused black buttplate. **Features:** Matte chrome finish on receiver, matte blue barrels; hard-chrome bores; low-profile receiver with dual conical locking lugs; single selective trigger, ejectors. Introduced 1999. Imported from Italy by Beretta U.S.A.
Price: **$1,295.00**

BERETTA S686 ONYX SPORTING O/U SHOTGUN

Gauge: 12, 3" chambers. **Barrel:** 28", 30" (Mobilchoke tubes). **Weight:** 7.7 lbs. **Stock:** Checkered American walnut. **Features:** Intended for the beginning Sporting Clays shooter. Has wide, vented 12.5mm target rib, radiused recoil pad. Polished black finish on receiver and barrels. Introduced 1993. Imported from Italy by Beretta U.S.A.
Price: **$1,575.00**

BERETTA ULTRALIGHT OVER/UNDER

Gauge: 12, 2-3/4" chambers. **Barrel:** 26", 28", Mobilchoke choke tubes. **Weight:** About 5 lbs., 13 oz. **Stock:** Select American walnut with checkered grip and forend. **Features:** Low-profile aluminum alloy receiver with titanium breech face insert. Electroless nickel receiver with game scene engraving. Single selective trigger; automatic safety. Introduced 1992. Imported from Italy by Beretta U.S.A.
Price: **$1,795.00**

Beretta Ultralight Deluxe Over/Under Shotgun

Similar to the Ultralight except has matte electroless nickel finish receiver with gold game scene engraving; matte oil-finished, select walnut stock and forend. Introduced 1999. Imported from Italy by Beretta U.S.A.
Price: **$1,985.00**

BERETTA OVER/UNDER FIELD SHOTGUNS

Gauge: 12, 20, 28, and 410 bore, 2-3/4", 3" and 3-1/2" chambers. **Barrel:** 26" and 28" (Mobilchoke tubes). **Stock:** Close-grained walnut. **Features:** Highly-figured, American walnut stocks and forends, and a unique, weather-resistant finish on barrels. The S686 Onyx bears a gold P. Beretta signature on each side of the receiver. Silver designates standard 686, 687 models with silver receivers; 686 Silver Pigeon has enhanced engraving pattern, Schnabel forend; 686 Silver Essential has matte chrome finish; Gold indicates higher grade 686EL, 687EL models with full sideplates; Diamond is for 687EELL models with highest grade wood, engraving. Case provided with Gold and Diamond grades. Silver Gold, Diamond grades introduced 1994. Imported from Italy by Beretta U.S.A.
Price: S686 Onyx **$1,565.00**
Price: S686 Silver Pigeon two-bbl. set **$2,560.00**
Price: S686 Silver Pigeon **$1,850.00**
Price: S687 Silver Pigeon **$2,255.00**
Price: S687 Silver Pigeon II (deep relief game scene engraving, oil finish wood, 12 ga. only) **$2,110.00**
Price: S687EL Gold Pigeon (gold inlays, sideplates) **$3,935.00**
Price: S687EL Gold Pigeon, 410, 26"; 28 ga., 28" **$4,230.00**

Price: S687EELL Diamond Pigeon (engraved sideplates)..... **$5,540.00**
Price: S687EELL Diamond Pigeon Combo, 20 and 28 ga., 26". **$6,180.00**

BERETTA MODEL SO5, SO6, SO9 SHOTGUNS

Gauge: 12, 2-3/4" chambers. **Barrel:** To customer specs. **Stock:** To customer specs. **Features:** SO5—Trap, Skeet and Sporting Clays models SO5; SO6—SO6 and SO6 EELL are field models. SO6 has a case-hardened or silver receiver with contour hand engraving. SO6 EELL has hand-engraved receiver in a fine floral or "fine English" pattern or game scene, with bas-relief chisel work and gold inlays. SO6 and SO6 EELL are available with sidelocks removable by hand. Imported from Italy by Beretta U.S.A.
Price: SO5 Trap, Skeet, Sporting **$13,000.00**
Price: SO6 Trap, Skeet, Sporting **$17,500.00**
Price: SO6 EELL Field, custom specs **$28,000.00**
Price: SO9 (12, 20, 28, 410, 26", 28", 30", any choke) **$31,000.00**

BERETTA SPORTING CLAYS SHOTGUNS

Gauge: 12 and 20, 2-3/4" and 3" chambers. **Barrel:** 28", 30", 32" Mobilchoke. **Stock:** Close-grained walnut. **Features:** Equipped with Beretta Mobilchoke flush-mounted screw-in choke tube system. Dual-purpose O/U for hunting and Sporting Clays.12 or 20 gauge, 28", 30" Mobilchoke tubes (four, Skeet, Imp. Cyl., Mod., Full). Wide 12.5mm top rib with 2.5mm center groove; 686 Silver Pigeon has silver receiver with scroll engraving; 687 Silver Pigeon Sporting has silver receiver, highly figured walnut; 687 EL Pigeon Sporting has game scene engraving with gold inlaid animals on full sideplate. Introduced 1994. Imported from Italy by Beretta USA.
Price: 682 Gold Sporting, 28", 30", 31" (with case) **$3,100.00**
Price: 682 Gold Sporting, 28", 30", ported, adj. l.o.p......... **$3,230.00**
Price: 686 Silver Pigeon Sporting........................ **$1,915.00**
Price: 686 Silver Pigeon Sporting (20 gauge) **$1,915.00**
Price: 687 Silver Pigeon Sporting........................ **$2,270.00**
Price: 687 Silver Pigeon Sporting (20 gauge) **$2,270.00**
Price: 687 Diamond Pigeon EELL Sporter (hand engraved sideplates, deluxe wood) **$5,515.00**
Price: ASE Gold Sporting Clay........................... **$12,145.00**

Beretta S687EL Gold Pigeon Sporting O/U

Similar to the S687 Silver Pigeon Sporting except has sideplates with gold inlay game scene, vent. side and top ribs, bright orange front sight. Stock and forend are of high grade walnut with fine-line checkering. Available in 12 gauge only with 28" or 30" barrels and Mobilchoke tubes. Weight is 6 lbs., 13 oz. Introduced 1993. Imported from Italy by Beretta USA.
Price: **$4,015.00**

BRNO ZH 300 OVER/UNDER SHOTGUN

Gauge: 12, 2-3/4" chambers. **Barrel:** 26", 27-1/2", 29" (Skeet, Imp. Cyl., Mod., Full). **Weight:** 7 lbs. **Length:** 44.4" overall. **Stock:** European walnut. **Features:** Double triggers; automatic safety; polished blue finish engraved receiver. Announced 1998. Imported from the Czech Republic by Euro-Imports.
Price: ZH 301, field..................................... **$594.00**
Price: ZH 302, Skeet **$608.00**
Price: ZH 303, 12 ga. trap **$608.00**
Price: ZH 321, 16 ga. **$595.00**

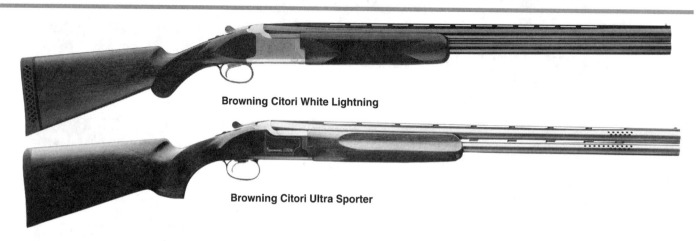

Browning Citori White Lightning

Browning Citori Ultra Sporter

BRNO 501.2 OVER/UNDER SHOTGUN

Gauge: 12, 2-3/4" chambers. **Barrel:** 27.5" (Full & Mod.). **Weight:** 7 lbs. **Length:** 44" overall. **Stock:** European walnut. **Features:** Boxlock action with double triggers, ejectors; automatic safety; hand-cut checkering. Announced 1998. Imported from The Czech Republic by Euro-Imports.
Price: **$850.00**

BROWNING CITORI O/U SHOTGUN

Gauge: 12, 20, 28 and 410. **Barrel:** 26", 28" in 28 and 410. Offered with Invector choke tubes. All 12 and 20 gauge models have back-bored barrels and Invector Plus choke system. **Weight:** 6 lbs., 8 oz. (26" 410) to 7 lbs., 13 oz. (30" 12 ga.). **Length:** 43" overall (26" bbl.). **Stock:** Dense walnut, hand checkered, full pistol grip, beavertail forend. Field-type recoil pad on 12 ga. field guns and trap and Skeet models. **Sights:** Medium raised beads, German nickel silver. **Features:** Barrel selector integral with safety, automatic ejectors, three-piece takedown. Imported from Japan by Browning. Contact Browning for complete list of models and prices.
Price: Grade I, Hunting, Invector, 12 and 20 . . . . **$1,388.00**
Price: Grade I, Lightning, 28 and 410, Invector **$1,489.00**
Price: Grade III, Lightning, 28 and 410, Invector **$2,377.00**
Price: Grade VI, 28 and 410 Lightning, Invector. **$3,344.00**
Price: Grade I, Lightning, Invector Plus, 12, 20 . . . . **$1,432.00**
Price: Grade I, Hunting, 28", 30" only, 3-1/2", Invector Plus. . . . **$1,489.00**
Price: Grade III, Lightning, Invector, 12, 20 . . . . **$2,127.00**
Price: Grade VI, Lightning, Invector, 12, 20 . . . . **$3,095.00**
Price: Gran Lightning, 26", 28", Invector, 12, 20 . . . . **$1,963.00**
Price: Gran Lightning, 28, 410 . . . . **$2,068.00**
Price: White Lightning (silver nitride receiver with engraved scroll and rosette, 12 ga., 26", 28"). **$1,478.00**
Price: Citori Satin Hunter (12 ga., satin-finished wood, matte-finished barrels and receiver) 3" chambers **$1,318.00**
Price: As above, 3-1/2" chambers **$1,420.00**

Browning Superlight Citori Over/Under

Similar to the standard Citori except available in 12, 20 with 24", 26" or 28" Invector barrels, 28 or 410 with 26" barrels choked Imp. Cyl. & Mod. or 28" choked Mod. & Full. Has straight grip stock, Schnabel forend tip. Superlight 12 weighs 6 lbs., 9 oz. (26" barrels); Superlight 20, 5 lbs., 12 oz. (26" barrels). Introduced 1982.
Price: Grade I only, 28 or 410, Invector **$1,511.00**
Price: Grade III, Invector, 12. . . . . **$2,127.00**
Price: Grade VI, Invector, 12 or 20, gray or blue **$3,095.00**
Price: Grade VI, 28 or 410, Invector, gray or blue **$3,334.00**
Price: Grade I Invector, 12 or 20 . . . . **$1,442.00**
Price: Grade I Invector, Upland Special (24" bbls.), 12 or 20. . . **$1,442.00**
Price: Citori Superlight Feather (12 ga., alloy receiver, 6 lbs. 6 oz.) **$1,592.00**

Browning Citori O/U Special Skeet

Similar to standard Citori except 26", 28" barrels, ventilated side ribs, Invector choke tubes; stock dimensions of 14-3/8"x1-1/2"x2", fitted with

Skeet-style recoil pad; conventional target rib and high post target rib.
Price: Grade I Invector, 12, 20 ga., Invector Plus (high post rib)
. . . . **$1,658.00**
Price: Grade I, 28 and 410 (high post rib) **$1,627.00**
Price: Grade III, 28, 410 (high post rib) **$2,316.00**
Price: Golden Clays,12, 20. . . . . **$3,434.00**
Price: Golden Clays, 28, 410 . . . . **$3,356.00**
Price: Grade III, 12, 20, Invector Plus **$2,310.00**
Price: Adjustable comb stock, add **$210.00**

Browning Citori Special Trap Models

Similar to standard Citori except 12 gauge only; 30", 32" ported or nonported (Invector Plus); Monte Carlo cheekpiece (14-3/8"x1-3/8"x1-3/8"x2"); fitted with trap-style recoil pad; high post target rib, ventilated side ribs.
Price: Grade I, Invector Plus, ported bbls. **$1,658.00**
Price: Grade III, Invector Plus Ported. **$2,310.00**
Price: Golden Clays **$3,434.00**
Price: Grade I, adjustable stock **$1,878.00**
Price: Grade III, adjustable stock **$2,530.00**
Price: Golden Clays, adjustable stock **$3,654.00**

Browning Citori XT Trap Over/Under

Similar to the Citori Special Trap except has engraved silver nitride receiver with gold highlights, vented side barrel rib. Available in 12 gauge with 30" or 32" barrels, Invector-Plus choke tubes. Introduced 1999. Imported by Browning.
Price: **$1,834.00**
Price: With adjustable-comb stock **$2,054.00**

Browning Micro Citori Lightning

Similar to the standard Citori 20 ga. Lightning except scaled down for smaller shooter. Comes with 24" Invector Plus back-bored barrels, 13-3/4" length of pull. Weighs about 6 lbs., 3 oz. Introduced 1991.
Price: Grade I. **$1,486.00**

Browning Citori Lightning Feather O/U

Similar to the 12 gauge Citori Grade I except has 2-3/4" chambers, rounded pistol grip, Lightning-style forend, and lighweight alloy receiver. Weighs 7 lbs. 9 oz. with 26" barrels. Silvered, engraved receiver. Introduced 1999. Imported by Browning.
Price: **$1,582.00**

Browning Citori Ultra Sporter

Similar to the Citori Hunting except has slightly grooved, semi-beavertail forend, satin-finish stock, radiused rubber butt pad. Has three interchangeable trigger shoes, trigger has three length of pull adjustments. Ventilated rib tapers from 13mm to 10mm, 28" or 30" barrels (ported or non-ported) with Invector Plus choke tubes. Ventilated side ribs. Introduced 1989.
Price: With ported barrels, gray or blue receiver **$1,800.00**
Price: Golden Clays **$3,396.00**

**Browning 425
Sporting Clays**

Browning Citori Sporting Hunter

Similar to the Citori Hunting I except has Sporting Clays stock dimensions, a Superposed-style forend, and Sporting Clays butt pad. Available in 12 gauge with 3" chambers, back-bored 26", 28", all with Invector Plus choke tube system. Introduced 1998. Imported from Japan by Browning.
Price: 12 gauge, 3-1/2" **$1,595.00**
Price: 12, 20 gauge, 3" **$1,500.00**

Browning Citori Ultra XS Skeet

Similar to other Citori Ultra models except features a semi-beavertail forearm with deep finger grooves, ported barrels and triple system. Adjustable comb is optional. Introduced 2000.
Price: 28" or 30" barrel **$2,059.00**

Browning Citori Feather XS Shotguns

Similar to the standard Citori except has lightweight alloy receiver, silver nitrade Nitex receiver, Schnabel forearm, ventilated side rib and Hi-Viz Comp fiber optics sight. Available in 12, 20, 28 and 410 gauges. Introduced 2000.
Price: 28" or 30" barrel . . . . **$2,200.00** to **$2,270.00**

Browning Citori High Grade Shotguns

Similar to standard Citori except has full sideplates with engraved hunting scenes and gold inlays, highgrade, hand-oiled walnut stock and forearm. Introduced 2000. From Browning.
Price: Citori Privilege (fully embellished sideplates) **$5,120.00**
Price: Citori BG VI Lightning (gold inlays of ducks and pheasants)
. . . . **from $3,340.00**
Price: Citori BG III Superlight (scroll engraving on grayed receiver,
gold inlays) **$2,190.00**

Browning Nitra Citori XS Sporting Clays

Similar to the Citori Grade I except has silver nitride receiver with gold accents, stock dimensions of 14-3/4"x1-1/2"x2-1/4" with satin finish, right-hand palm swell, Schnabel forend. Comes with Modified, Imp. Cyl. and Skeet Invector-Plus choke tubes. Back-bored barrels; vented side ribs. Introduced 1999. Imported by Browning.
Price: 12, 20 ga. **$2,011.00**
Price: 28 ga., 410-bore **$2,077.00**

Browning Special Sporting Clays

Similar to the Citori Ultra Sporter except has full pistol grip stock with palm swell, gloss finish, 28", 30" or 32" barrels with back-bored Invector Plus chokes (ported or non-ported); high post tapered rib. Also available as 28" and 30" two-barrel set. Introduced 1989.
Price: With ported barrels **$1,636.00**
Price: As above, adjustable comb **$1,856.00**

Browning Lightning Sporting Clays

Similar to the Citori Lightning with rounded pistol grip and classic forend. Has high post tapered rib or lower hunting-style rib with 30" back-bored Invector Plus barrels, ported or non-ported, 3" chambers. Gloss stock finish, radiused recoil pad. Has "Lightning Sporting Clays Edition" engraved and gold filled on receiver. Introduced 1989.
Price: Low-rib, ported **$1,564.00**
Price: High-rib, ported **$1,636.00**

BROWNING LIGHT SPORTING 802 ES O/U

Gauge: 12, 2-3/4" chambers. **Barrel:** 28", back-bored Invector Plus. Comes with flush-mounted Imp. Cyl. and Skeet; 2" extended Imp. Cyl. and Mod.; and 4" extended Imp. Cyl. and Mod. tubes. **Weight:** 7 lbs., 5 oz. **Length:** 45" overall. **Stock:** 14-3/8" x 1/8" x 1-9/16" x 1-3/4". Select walnut with ra-diused solid recoil pad, Schnabel-type forend. **Features:** Trigger adjustable for length of pull; narrow 6.2mm ventilated rib; ventilated barrel side rib; blued receiver. Introduced 1996. Imported from Japan from Browning.
Price: **$1,965.00**

BROWNING 425 SPORTING CLAYS

Gauge: 12, 20, 2-3/4" chambers. **Barrel:** 12 ga.—28", 30", 32" (Invector Plus tubes), back-bored; 20 ga.—28", 30" (Invector Plus tubes). **Weight:** 7 lbs., 13 oz. (12 ga., 28"). **Stock:** 14-13/16" (1/8")x1-7/16"x2-3/16" (12 ga.). Select walnut with gloss finish, cut checkering, Schnabel forend. **Features:** Grayed receiver with engraving, blued barrels. Barrels are ported on 12 gauge guns. Has low 10mm wide vent rib. Comes with three interchangeable trigger shoes to adjust length of pull. Introduced in U.S. 1993. Imported by Browning.
Price: Grade I, 12, 20 ga., Invector Plus **$1,855.00**
Price: Golden Clays, 12, 20 ga., Invector Plus **$3,507.00**
Price: With adjustable comb stock, add **$2,075.00**

Browning 425 WSSF Shotgun

Similar to the 425 Sporting Clays except in 12 gauge only, 28" barrels, has stock dimensions specifically tailored to women shooters (14-1/4"x1-1/2"x1-1/2"); top lever and takedown lever are easier to operate. Stock and forend have teal-colored finish or natural walnut with Women's Shooting Sports Foundation logo. Weighs 7 lbs., 4 oz. Introduced 1995. Imported by Browning.
Price: **$1,855.00**

CHARLES DALY SUPERIOR TRAP AE MC

Gauge: 12, 2-3/4" chambers. **Barrel:** 30" choke tubes. **Weight:** About 7 lbs. **Stock:** Checkered walnut; pistol grip, semi-beavertail forend. **Features:** Silver engraved receiver, chrome moly steel barrels; gold single selective trigger; automatic safety; automatic ejectors; red bead front sight, metal bead center; recoil pad. Introduced 1997. Imported from Italy by K.B.I., Inc.
Price: **$1,219.00**

CHARLES DALY FIELD HUNTER OVER/UNDER SHOTGUN

Gauge: 12, 20, 28 and 410 bore (3" chambers, 28 ga. has 2-3/4"). **Barrel:** 28" Mod & Full, 26" Imp. Cyl. & Mod (410 is Full & Full). **Weight:** About 7 lbs. **Length:** NA. **Stock:** Checkered walnut pistol grip and forend. **Features:** Blued engraved receiver, chrome moly steel barrels; gold single selective trigger; automatic safety; extractors; gold bead front sight. Introduced 1997. Imported from Italy by K.B.I., Inc.
Price: 12 or 20 ga. **$749.00**
Price: 28 ga. **$809.00**
Price: 410 bore **$849.00**

Charles Daly Field Hunter AE Shotgun

Similar to the Field Hunter except 28 gauge and 410-bore only; 26" (Imp. Cyl. & Mod., 28 gauge), 26" (Full & Full, 410); automatic; ejectors. Introduced 1997. Imported from Italy by K.B.I., Inc.
Price: 28 . . . . **$889.00**
Price: 410 . . . . **$929.00**

Charles Daly Superior Hunter AE Shotgun

Similar to the Field Hunter AE except has silvered, engraved receiver. Introduced 1997. Imported from Italy by F.B.I., Inc.
Price: 28 ga. **$1,059.00**
Price: 410 bore **$1,099.00**

Charles Daly Field Hunter AE-MC

Similar to the Field Hunter except in 12 or 20 only, 26" or 28" barrels with five multichoke tubes; automatic ejectors. Introduced 1997. Imported from Italy by K.B.I., Inc.
Price: 12 or 20 . . . . **$979.95**

SHOTGUNS

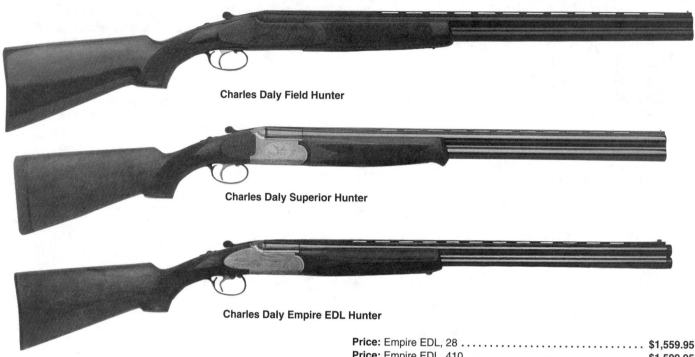

Charles Daly Field Hunter

Charles Daly Superior Hunter

Charles Daly Empire EDL Hunter

Charles Daly Superior Sporting O/U

Similar to the Field Hunter AE-MC except 28" or 30" barrels; silvered, engraved receiver; five choke tubes; ported barrels; red bead front sight. Introduced 1997. Imported from Italy by K.B.I., Inc.

Price: **$1,259.95**

CHARLES DALY EMPIRE TRAP AE MC

Gauge: 12, 2-3/4" chambers. **Barrel:** 30" choke tubes. **Weight:** About 7 lbs. **Stock:** Checkered walnut; pistol grip, semi-beavertail forend. **Features:** Silvered, engraved, reinforced receiver; chrome moly steel barrels; gold single selective trigger; automatic safety, automatic ejector; red bead front sight, metal bead center; recoil pad. Introduced 1997. Imported from Italy by K.B.I., Inc.

Price: **$1,539.95**

CHARLES DALY DIAMOND REGENT GTX DL HUNTER O/U

Gauge: 12, 20, 410, 3" chambers, 28, 2-3/4" chambers. **Barrel:** 26", 28", 30" (choke tubes), 26" (Imp. Cyl. & Mod. in 28, 26" (Full & Full) in 410. **Weight:** About 7 lbs. **Stock:** Extra select fancy European walnut with 24" hand checkering, hand rubbed oil finish. **Features:** Boss-type action with internal side lumps. Deep cut hand-engraved scrollwork and game scene set in full sideplates. GTX detachable single selective trigger system with coil springs; chrome moly steel barrels; automatic safety; automatic ejectors, white bead front sight, metal bead center sight. Introduced 1997. Imported from Italy by K.B.I., Inc.

Price: 12 or 20 . . . . **$22,299.00**
Price: 28 . . . . **$22,369.00**
Price: 410 . . . . **$22,419.00**
Price: Diamond Regent GTX EDL Hunter (as above with engraved scroll and birds, 10 gold inlays), 12 or 20 . . . . **$26,249.00**
Price: As above, 28 . . . . **$26,499.00**
Price: As above, 410 . . . . **$26,549.00**

CHARLES DALY EMPIRE EDL HUNTER O/U

Gauge: 12, 20, 410, 3" chambers, 28 ga., 2-3/4". **Barrel:** 26", 28" (12, 20, choke tubes), 26" (Imp. Cyl. & Mod., 28 ga.), 26" (Full & Full, 410). **Weight:** About 7 lbs. **Stocks:** Checkered walnut pistol grip buttstock, semi-beavertail forend; recoil pad. **Features:** Silvered, engraved receiver; chrome moly barrels; gold single selective trigger; automatic safety; automatic ejectors; red bead front sight, metal bead middle sight. Introduced 1997. Imported from Italy by K.B.I., Inc.

Price: Empire EDL (dummy sideplates) 12 or 20 . . . . **$1,559.95**

Price: Empire EDL, 28 . . . . **$1,559.95**
Price: Empire EDL, 410 . . . . **$1,599.95**

Charles Daly Empire Sporting O/U

Similar to the Empire EDL Hunter except 12 or 20 gauge only, 28", 30" barrels with choke tubes; ported barrels; special stock dimensions. Introduced 1997. Imported from Italy by K.B.I., Inc.

Price: **$1,499.95**

CHARLES DALY DIAMOND GTX SPORTING O/U SHOTGUN

Gauge: 12, 20, 3" chambers. **Barrel:** 28", 30" with choke tubes. **Weight:** About 8.5 lbs. **Stock:** Checkered deluxe walnut; Sporting clays dimensions. Pistol grip; semi-beavertail forend; hand rubbed oil finish. **Features:** Chromed, hand-engraved receiver; chrome moly steel barrels; GTX detachable single selective trigger system with coil springs, automatic safety; automatic ejectors; red bead front sight; ported barrels. Introduced 1997. Imported from Italy by K.B.I., Inc.

Price: **$5,804.95**

CHARLES DALY DIAMOND GTX TRAP AE-MC O/U SHOTGUN

Gauge: 12, 2-3/4" chambers. **Barrel:** 30" (Full & Full). **Weight:** About 8.5 lbs. **Stock:** Checkered deluxe walnut; pistol grip; trap dimensions; semi-beavertail forend; hand-rubbed oil finish. **Features:** Silvered, hand-engraved receiver; chrome moly steel barrels; GTX detachable single selective trigger system with coil springs, automatic safety; automatic-ejectors, red bead front sight, metal bead middle; recoil pad. Introduced 1997. Imported from Italy by K.B.I., Inc.

Price: **$5,804.95**

CHARLES DALY DIAMOND GTX DL HUNTER O/U

Gauge: 12, 20, 410, 3" chambers, 28, 2-3/4" chambers. **Barrel:** 26, 28", choke tubes in 12 and 20 ga., 26" (Imp. Cyl. & Mod.), 26" (Full & Full) in 410-bore. **Weight:** About 8.5 lbs. **Stock:** Select fancy European walnut stock, with 24 lpi hand checkering; hand-rubbed oil finish. **Features:** Boss-type action with internal side lugs, hand-engraved scrollwork and game scene. GTX detachable single selective trigger system with coil springs; chrome moly steel barrels, automatic safety, automatic ejectors, red bead front sight, recoil pad. Introduced 1997. Imported from Italy by K.B.I., Inc.

Price: 12 or 20 . . . . **$12,399.00**
Price: 28 . . . . **$12,489.00**
Price: 410 . . . . **$12,529.00**
Price: GTX EDL Hunter (with gold inlays), 12, 20 . . . . **$15,999.00**
Price: As above, 28 . . . . **$16,179.00**
Price: As above, 410 . . . . **$16,219.00**

CZ 581 Solo

Fabarm Max Lion

Franchi Alcione

CZ 581 SOLO OVER/UNDER SHOTGUN

Gauge: 12, 2-3/4" chambers. **Barrel:** 27.6" (Mod. & Full). **Weight:** 7.37 lbs. **Length:** 44.5" overall. **Stock:** Circassian walnut. **Features:** Automatic ejectors; double triggers; Kersten-style double lump locking system. Imported from the Czech Republic by CZ-USA.
Price: **$799.00**

EAA/BAIKAL MP-233 OVER/UNDER SHOTGUN

Gauge: 12, 3" chambers. **Barrel:** 26", 28", 30"; imp., mod. and full choke tubes. **Weight:** 7.28 lbs. **Stock:** Walnut; checkered forearm and grip. **Features:** Hammer-forged barrels; chrome-lined bores; removable trigger assembly (optional single selective trigger or double trigger); ejectors. Introduced 2000. Imported by European American Armory.
Price: MP-233.. **$879.00**

EAA/BAIKAL IZH-27 OVER/UNDER SHOTGUN

Gauge: 12 (3" chambers), 16 (2-3/4" chambers), 20 (3" chambers), 28 (2-3/4" chambers), 410 (3"). **Barrel:** 26-1/2", 28-1/2" (imp., mod. and full choke tubes for 12 and 20 gauges; improved cylinder and modified for 16 and 28 gauges; improved modified and full for 410; 16 also offered in mod. and full). **Weight:** N/A. **Stock:** Walnut, checkered forearm and grip. Imported by European American Armory.
Price: IZH-27 (12, 16 and 20 gauge) **$459.00**
Price: IZH-27 (28 and 410 gauge) **$499.00**

FABARM MAX LION OVER/UNDER SHOTGUNS

Gauge: 12, 3" chambers, 20, 3" chambers. **Barrel:** 26", 28", 30" (12 ga.); 26", 28" (20 ga.), choke tubes. **Weight:** 7.4 lbs. **Length:** 47.5" overall (26" barrel). **Stock:** European walnut; leather-covered recoil pad. **Features:** TriBore barrel, boxlock action with single selective trigger, manual safety, automatic ejectors; chrome-lined barrels; adjustable trigger. Silvered, engraved receiver. Comes with locking, fitted luggage case. Introduced 1998. Imported from Italy by Heckler & Koch, Inc.
Price: 12 or 20 .... **$1,939.00**

FABARM ULTRA MAG LION O/U SHOTGUN

Gauge: 12, 3-1/2" chambers. **Barrel:** 28" (Cyl., Imp. Cyl., Mod., Imp. Mod., Full, SS-Mod., SS-Full choke tubes). **Weight:** 7.9 lbs. **Length:** 50" overall. **Stock:** Black-colored walnut. **Features:** TriBore barrel, matte finished metal surfaces; single selective trigger; non-auto ejectors; leather-covered recoil pad. Comes with locking hard plastic case. Introduced 1998. Imported from Italy by Heckler & Koch, Inc.
Price: **$1,229.00**

Fabarm Ultra Camo Mag Lion O/U Shotgun

Similar to the Ultra Mag Lion except completely covered with Wetlands camouflage pattern, has the ported TriBore barrel system, and a mid-rib bead. Chambered for 3-1/2" shells. Stock and forend are walnut. Introduced 1999. Imported from Italy by Heckler & Koch, Inc.
Price: **$1,329.00**

FABARM SILVER LION OVER/UNDER SHOTGUNS

Gauge: 12, 3" chambers, 20, 3" chambers. **Barrel:** 26", 28", 30" (12 ga.); 26", 28" (20 ga.), choke tubes. **Weight:** 7.2 lbs. **Length:** 47.5" overall (26" barrels). **Stock:** Walnut; leather-covered recoil pad. **Features:** TriBore barrel, boxlock action with single selective trigger; silvered receiver with engraving; automatic ejectors. Comes with locking hard plastic case. Introduced 1998. Imported from Italy by Heckler & Koch, Inc.
Price: 12 or 20 .... **$1,299.00**
Price: Super Light Lion (12 ga. only, 24" barrels, weighs 6.5 lbs.)...................................... **$1,159.00**

Fabarm Silver Lion Cub Model O/U

Similar to the Silver Lion except has 12.5" length of pull, is in 20 gauge only (3-1/2" chambers), and comes with 24" TriBore barrel system. Weight is 6 lbs. Introduced 1999. Imported from Italy by Heckler & Koch, Inc.
Price: **$1,379.00**
Price: Super Light Lion Cub (12 ga. only, 6 lbs., blued receiver) **$1,099.00**

FABARM CAMO TURKEY MAG O/U SHOTGUN

Gauge: 12, 3-1/2" chambers. **Barrel:** 20" TriBore (Ultra-Full ported tubes). **Weight:** 7.5 lbs. **Length:** 46" overall. **Stock:** 14.5"x1.5"x2.29". Walnut. **Sights:** Front bar, Picatinny rail scope base. **Features:** Completely covered with Xtra Brown camouflage finish. Unported barrels. Introduced 1999. Imported from Italy by Heckler & Koch, Inc.
Price: **$1,339.00**

FABARM SPORTING CLAYS COMPETITION LION O/U

Gauge: 12, 20, 3" chambers. **Barrel:** 12 ga. has 30", 20 ga. has 28"; ported TriBore barrel system with five tubes. **Weight:** 7 to 7.8 lbs. **Length:** 49.6" overall (20 ga.). **Stock:** 14.50"x1.38"x2.17" (20 ga.); deluxe walnut; leather-covered recoil pad. **Features:** Single selective trigger, auto ejectors; recoil reducer installed in buttstock; 10mm channeled rib; silvered, engraved receiver. Introduced 1999. Imported from Italy by Heckler & Koch, Inc.
Price: **$1,419.00**

Fabarm Sporting Clays Competition Extra

Same as Sporting Clays Competition Lion O/U but has carbon fiber finish.
Price: **$1,750.00**

FRANCHI ALCIONE FIELD OVER/UNDER SHOTGUN

Gauge: 12, 3" chambers. **Barrel:** 26", 28"; Franchoke tubes. **Weight:** 7.5 lbs. **Length:** 43" overall with 26" barrels. **Stock:** European walnut. **Features:**

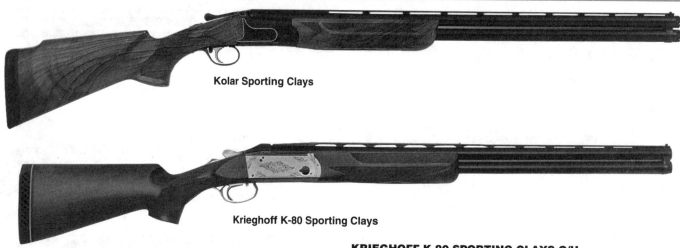

Kolar Sporting Clays

Krieghoff K-80 Sporting Clays

Boxlock action with ejectors; barrel selector is mounted on the trigger; silvered, engraved receiver; vent center rib; automatic safety. Imported from Italy by Benelli USA. Hard case included.
Price: $993.00
Price: (20 gauge barrel set) $336.00

Franchi Alcione Sport O/U Shotgun
Similar to the Alcione except has 2-3/4" chambers, elongated forcing cones and porting for Sporting Clays shooting. 10mm vent rib, tightly curved pistol grip, manual safety, removeable sideplates. Imported from Italy by Benelli USA.
Price: $1,300.00

Franchi Alcione Light Field (LF) Shotgun
Similar to Alcione Field except features alloy frame, weighs 6.8 pounds (12 gauge) or 6.7 pounds (20 gauge). Both frames accept either the 2 3/4"-chamber 12 gauge or 3"-chamber 20 gauge barrel sets.
Price: $1,100.00

KOLAR SPORTING CLAYS O/U SHOTGUN
Gauge: 12, 2-3/4" chambers. **Barrel:** 28", 30", 32"; extended choke tubes. **Stock:** 14-5/8"x2-1/2"x1-7/8"x1-3/8". French walnut. **Features:** Single selective trigger, detachable, adjustable for length; overbored barrels with long forcing cones; flat tramline rib; matte blue finish. Made in U.S. by Kolar.
Price: Standard............................... $7,250.00
Price: Elite $10,050.00
Price: Elite Gold $11,545.00
Price: Legend $13,045.00
Price: Custom Gold $24,750.00

Kolar AAA Competition Trap Over/Under Shotgun
Similar to the Sporting Clays gun except has 32" O/U / 34" Unsingle or 30" O/U / 34" Unsingle barrels as an over/under, unsingle, or combination set. Stock dimensions are 14-1/2"x2-1/2"x1-1/2"; American or French walnut; step parallel rib standard. Contact maker for full listings. Made in U.S. by Kolar.
Price: Over/under, choke tubes, Standard $7,025.00
Price: Unsingle, choke tubes, Standard $7,775.00
Price: Combo (30"/34", 32"/34"), Standard............... $10,170.00

Kolar AAA Competition Skeet Over/Under Shotgun
Similar to the Sporting Clays gun except has 28" or 30" barrels with Kolarite AAA sub gauge tubes; stock of American or French walnut with matte finish; flat tramline rib; under barrel adjustable for point of impact. Many options available. Contact maker for complete listing. Made in U.S. by Kolar.
Price: Standard, choke tubes $8,645.00
Price: Standard, choke tubes, two-barrel set $10,710.00

KRIEGHOFF K-80 SPORTING CLAYS O/U
Gauge: 12. **Barrel:** 28", 30" or 32" with choke tubes. **Weight:** About 8 lbs. **Stock:** #3 Sporting stock designed for gun-down shooting. **Features:** Choice of standard or lightweight receiver with satin nickel finish and classic scroll engraving. Selective mechanical trigger adjustable for position. Choice of tapered flat or 8mm parallel flat barrel rib. Free-floating barrels. Aluminum case. Imported from Germany by Krieghoff International, Inc.
Price: Standard grade with five choke tubes, from.......... $8,150.00

KRIEGHOFF K-80 SKEET SHOTGUN
Gauge: 12, 2-3/4" chambers. **Barrel:** 28" (Skeet & Skeet, optional Tula or choke tubes). **Weight:** About 7-3/4 lbs. **Stock:** American Skeet or straight Skeet stocks, with palm-swell grips. Walnut. **Features:** Satin gray receiver finish. Selective mechanical trigger adjustable for position. Choice of ventilated 8mm parallel flat rib or ventilated 8-12mm tapered flat rib. Introduced 1980. Imported from Germany by Krieghoff International, Inc.
Price: Standard, Skeet chokes........................ $6,900.00
Price: As above, Tula chokes........................ $7,825.00
Price: Lightweight model (weighs 7 lbs.), Standard $6,900.00
Price: Two-Barrel Set (tube concept), 12 ga., Standard...... $11,840.00
Price: Skeet Special (28", tapered flat rib, Skeet & Skeet choke tubes) $7,575.00

Krieghoff K-80 Four-Barrel Skeet Set
Similar to the Standard Skeet except comes with barrels for 12, 20, 28, 410. Comes with fitted aluminum case.
Price: Standard grade $16,950.00

Krieghoff K-80 International Skeet
Similar to the Standard Skeet except has 1/2" ventilated Broadway-style rib, special Tula chokes with gas release holes at muzzle. International Skeet stock. Comes in fitted aluminum case.
Price: Standard grade $7,825.00

KRIEGHOFF K-80 O/U TRAP SHOTGUN
Gauge: 12, 2-3/4" chambers. **Barrel:** 30", 32" (Imp. Mod. & Full or choke tubes). **Weight:** About 8-1/2 lbs. **Stock:** Four stock dimensions or adjustable stock available; all have palm swell grips. Checkered European walnut. **Features:** Satin nickel receiver. Selective mechanical trigger, adjustable for position. Ventilated step rib. Introduced 1980. Imported from Germany by Krieghoff International, Inc.
Price: K-80 O/U (30", 32", Imp. Mod. & Full), from.......... $7,375.00
Price: K-80 Unsingle (32", 34", Full), Standard, from........ $7,950.00
Price: K-80 Combo (two-barrel set), Standard, from $9,975.00
Price: $1,310.00

LEBEAU - COURALLY BOSS-VEREES O/U
Gauge: 12, 20, 2-3/4" chambers. **Barrel:** 25" to 32". **Weight:** To customer specifications. **Stock:** Exhibition-quality French walnut. **Features:** Boss-type sidelock with automatic ejectors; single or double triggers; chopper lump barrels. A custom gun built to customer specifications. Imported from Belgium by Wm. Larkin Moore.
Price: From....................................... $81,000.00

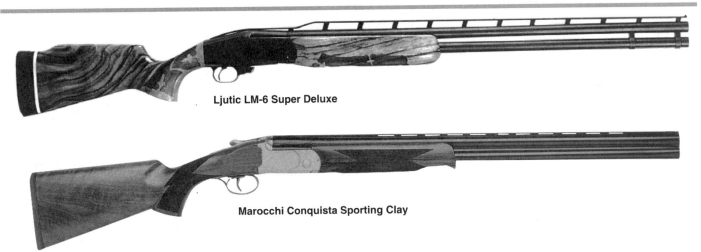

Ljutic LM-6 Super Deluxe

Marocchi Conquista Sporting Clay

LJUTIC LM-6 SUPER DELUXE O/U SHOTGUN

Gauge: 12. **Barrel:** 28" to 34", choked to customer specs for live birds, trap, International Trap. **Weight:** To customer specs. **Stock:** To customer specs. Oil finish, hand checkered. **Features:** Custom-made gun. Hollow-milled rib, pull or release trigger, pushbutton opener in front of trigger guard. From Ljutic Industries.
Price: Super Deluxe LM-6 O/U $17,995.00
Price: Over/under Combo (interchangeable single barrel, two trigger guards, one for single trigger, one for doubles) $24,995.00
Price: Extra over/under barrel sets, 29"-32" $5,995.00

LUGER CLASSIC O/U SHOTGUNS

Gauge: 12, 3" and 3-1/2" chambers. **Barrel:** 26", 28", 30"; imp. cyl. mod. and full choke tubes. **Weight:** 7-1/2 lbs. **Length:** 45" overall (28" barrel) **Stock:** Select-grade European walnut, hand-checkered grip and forend. **Features:** Gold, single selective trigger; automatic ejectors. Introduced 2000. From Stoeger Industries.
Price: Classic (26", 28" or 30" barrel; 3-1/2" chambers) $919.00
Price: Classic Sporting (30" barrel; 3" chambers) $964.00

MAROCCHI CONQUISTA SPORTING CLAYS O/U SHOTGUNS

Gauge: 12, 2-3/4" chambers. **Barrel:** 28", 30", 32" (ContreChoke tubes); 10mm concave vent. rib. **Weight:** About 8 lbs. **Stock:** 14-1/2"-14-7/8"x2-3/16"x1-7/16"; American walnut with checkered grip and forend; Sporting Clays butt pad. **Sights:** 16mm luminescent front. **Features:** Has lower monoblock and frame profile. Fast lock time. Ergonomically-shaped trigger is adjustable for pull length. Automatic selective ejectors. Coin-finished receiver, blued barrels. Comes with five choke tubes, hard case. Also available as true left-hand model—opening lever operates from left to right; stock has left-hand cast. Introduced 1994. Imported from Italy by Precision Sales International.
Price: Grade I, right-hand $1,995.00
Price: Grade I, left-hand $2,120.00
Price: Grade II, right-hand $2,330.00
Price: Grade II, left-hand $2,685.00
Price: Grade III, right-hand, from $3,599.00
Price: Grade III, left-hand, from $3,995.00

Marocchi Lady Sport O/U Shotgun

Ergonomically designed specifically for women shooters. Similar to the Conquista Sporting Clays model except has 28" or 30" barrels with five Contrechoke tubes, stock dimensions of 13-7/8"-14-1/4"x1-11/32"x2-9/32"; weighs about 7-1/2 lbs. Also available as left-hand model—opening lever operates from left to right; stock has left-hand cast. Also available with colored graphics finish on frame and opening lever. Introduced 1995. Imported from Italy by Precision Sales International.
Price: Grade I, right-hand $2,120.00
Price: Left-hand, add (all grades) $101.00
Price: Lady Sport Spectrum (colored receiver panel) $2,199.00
Price: Lady Sport Spectrum, left-hand $2,300.00

Marocchi Conquista Trap Over/Under Shotgun

Similar to the Conquista Sporting Clays model except has 30" or 32" barrels choked Full & Full, stock dimensions of 14-1/2"- 14-7/8"x1-11/16"x1-9/32"; weighs about 8-1/4 lbs. Introduced 1994. Imported from Italy by Precision Sales International.
Price: Grade I, right-hand $1,995.00
Price: Grade II, right-hand $2,330.00
Price: Grade III, right-hand, from $3,599.00

Marocchi Conquista Skeet Over/Under Shotgun

Similar to the Conquista Sporting Clays except has 28" (Skeet & Skeet) barrels, stock dimensions of 14-3/8"- 14-3/4"x2-3/16"x1-1/2". Weighs about 7-3/4 lbs. Introduced 1994. Imported from Italy by Precision Sales International.
Price: Grade I, right-hand $1,995.00
Price: Grade II, right-hand $2,330.00
Price: Grade III, right-hand, from $3,599.00

MAROCCHI CLASSIC DOUBLES
MODEL 92 SPORTING CLAYS O/U SHOTGUN

Gauge: 12, 3" chambers. **Barrel:** 30"; back-bored, ported (ContreChoke Plus tubes); 10 mm concave ventilated top rib, ventilated middle rib. **Weight:** 8 lbs. 2 oz. **Stock:** 14-1/4"- 14-5/8"x 2-1/8"x1-3/8"; American walnut with checkered grip and forend; Sporting Clays butt pad. **Features:** Low profile frame; fast lock time; automatic selective ejectors; blued receiver and barrels. Comes with three choke tubes. Ergonomically shaped trigger adjustable for pull length without tools. Barrels are back-bored and ported. Introduced 1996. Imported from Italy by Precision Sales International.
Price: $1,598.00

MERKEL MODEL 2001EL O/U SHOTGUN

Gauge: 12, 20, 3" chambers, 28, 2-3/4" chambers. **Barrel:** 12—28"; 20, 28 ga.—26-3/4". **Weight:** About 7 lbs. (12 ga.). **Stock:** Oil-finished walnut; English or pistol grip. **Features:** Self-cocking Blitz boxlock action with cocking indicators; Kersten double cross-bolt lock; silver-grayed receiver with engraved hunting scenes; coil spring ejectors; single selective or double triggers. Imported from Germany by GSI, Inc.
Price: 12, 20 . . . . $6,495.00
Price: 28 ga. $6,495.00
Price: Model 2000EL (scroll engraving, 12 or 20) $5,195.00

Merkel Model 303EL O/U Shotgun

Similar to the Model 2001 EL except has Holland & Holland-style sidelock action with cocking indicators; English-style Arabesque engraving. Available in 12, 20 gauge. Imported from Germany by GSI, Inc.
Price: $19,995.00

Merkel Model 2002 EL O/U Shotgun

Similar to the Model 2001 EL except has dummy sideplates, Arabesque engraving with hunting scenes; 12, 20 gauge. Imported from Germany by GSI, Inc.
Price: $9,995.00

SHOTGUNS

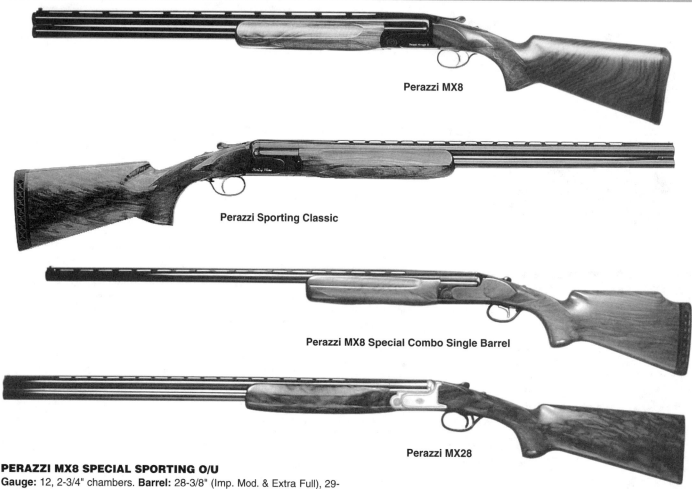

Perazzi MX8

Perazzi Sporting Classic

Perazzi MX8 Special Combo Single Barrel

Perazzi MX28

PERAZZI MX8 SPECIAL SPORTING O/U

Gauge: 12, 2-3/4" chambers. **Barrel:** 28-3/8" (Imp. Mod. & Extra Full), 29-1/2" (choke tubes). **Weight:** 7 lbs., 12 oz. **Stock:** Special specifications. **Features:** Has single selective trigger; flat 7/16"x5/16" vent. rib. Many options available. Imported from Italy by Perazzi U.S.A., Inc.
Price: $9,790.00

Perazzi Sporting Classic O/U

Same as the Special Sporting except is deluxe version with select wood and engraving, Available with flush mount choke tubes, 29.5" barrels. Introduced 1993.
Price: From $11,160.00

PERAZZI MX12 HUNTING OVER/UNDER

Gauge: 12, 2-3/4" chambers. **Barrel:** 26", 27-5/8", 28-3/8", 29-1/2" (Mod. & Full); choke tubes available in 27-5/8", 29-1/2" only (MX12C). **Weight:** 7 lbs., 4 oz. **Stock:** To customer specs; Interchangeable. **Features:** Single selective trigger; coil springs used in action; Schnabel forend tip. Imported from Italy by Perazzi U.S.A., Inc.
Price: From $8,840.00
Price: MX12C (with choke tubes), from $9,460.00

Perazzi MX20 Hunting Over/Under

Similar to the MX12 except 20 ga. frame size. Available in 20, 28, 410 with 2-3/4" or 3" chambers. 26" standard, and choked Mod. & Full. Weight is 6 lbs., 6 oz.
Price: From $8,840.00
Price: MX20C (as above, 20 ga. only, choke tubes), from $9,460.00

PERAZZI MX8/MX8 SPECIAL TRAP, SKEET

Gauge: 12, 2-3/4" chambers. **Barrel:** Trap—29-1/2" (Imp. Mod. & Extra Full), 31-1/2" (Full & Extra Full). Choke tubes optional. Skeet—27-5/8" (Skeet & Skeet). **Weight:** About 8-1/2 lbs. (Trap); 7 lbs., 15 oz. (Skeet). **Stock:** Interchangeable and custom made to customer specs. **Features:** Has detachable and interchangeable trigger group with flat V springs. Flat

7/16" ventilated rib. Many options available. Imported from Italy by Perazzi U.S.A., Inc.
Price: From $8,840.00
Price: MX8 Special (adj. four-position trigger), from $9,350.00
Price: MX8 Special Combo (o/u and single barrel sets), from . $12,340.00

Perazzi MX8 Special Skeet Over/Under

Similar to the MX8 Skeet except has adjustable four-position trigger, Skeet stock dimensions.
Price: From $9,350.00

Perazzi MX8/20 Over/Under Shotgun

Similar to the MX8 except has smaller frame and has a removable trigger mechanism. Available in trap, Skeet, sporting or game models with fixed chokes or choke tubes. Stock is made to customer specifications. Introduced 1993.
Price: From $9,790.00

PERAZZI MX10 OVER/UNDER SHOTGUN

Gauge: 12, 2-3/4" chambers. **Barrel:** 29.5", 31.5" (fixed chokes). **Weight:** NA. **Stock:** Walnut; cheekpiece adjustable for elevation and cast. **Features:** Adjustable rib; vent. side rib. Externally selective trigger. Available in single barrel, combo, over/under trap, Skeet, pigeon and sporting models. Introduced 1993. Imported from Italy by Perazzi U.S.A., Inc.
Price: From $11,030.00

PERAZZI MX28, MX410 GAME O/U SHOTGUNS

Gauge: 28, 2-3/4" chambers, 410, 3" chambers. **Barrel:** 26" (Imp. Cyl. & Full). **Weight:** NA. **Stock:** To customer specifications. **Features:** Made on scaled-down frames proportioned to the gauge. Introduced 1993. Imported from Italy by Perazzi U.S.A., Inc.
Price: From $17,670.00

Piotti Boss

Rizzini S790 Emel

Ruger Woodside

PIOTTI BOSS OVER/UNDER SHOTGUN

Gauge: 12, 20. **Barrel:** 26" to 32", chokes as specified. **Weight:** 6.5 to 8 lbs. **Stock:** Dimensions to customer specs. Best quality figured walnut. **Features:** Essentially a custom-made gun with many options. Introduced 1993. Imported from Italy by Wm. Larkin Moore.

Price: From **$39,200.00**

REMINGTON MODEL 300 IDEAL O/U SHOTGUN

Gauge: 12, 3" chambers. **Barrel:** 26", 28", 30" (imp. cyl., mod. and full Rem Choke tubes). **Weight:** 7 lbs. 6 oz. to 7 lbs. 14 oz. **Length:** 42-3/4" overall (26" brl.) **Stock:** Satin-finished American walnut; checkered forearm and grip; rubber recoil pad. **Features:** Low-profile rib; mid-bead and ivory front bead; fine-line engraved receiver with high-polish blued finish; automatic ejectors. Introduced 2000. From Remington Arms Co.

Price: **$1,999.00**

RIZZINI S790 EMEL OVER/UNDER SHOTGUN

Gauge: 20, 28, 410. **Barrel:** 26", 27.5" (Imp. Cyl. & Imp. Mod.). **Weight:** About 6 lbs. **Stock:** 14"x1-1/2"x2-1/8". Extra-fancy select walnut. **Features:** Boxlock action with profuse engraving; automatic ejectors; single selective trigger; silvered receiver. Comes with Nizzoli leather case. Introduced 1996. Imported from Italy by Wm. Larkin Moore & Co.

Price: From **$9,600.00**

Rizzini S792 EMEL Over/Under Shotgun

Similar to the S790 EMEL except has dummy sideplates with extensive engraving coverage. Comes with Nizzoli leather case. Introduced 1996. Imported from Italy by Wm. Larkin Moore & Co.

Price: From **$9,400.00**

RIZZINI S790 SPORTING EL OVER/UNDER

Gauge: 12, 2-3/4" chambers. **Barrel:** 28", 29.5", Imp. Mod., Mod., Full choke tubes. **Weight:** 8.1 lbs. **Stock:** 14-1/2"x1-1/2"x2-1/4". Extra-fancy select walnut. **Features:** Boxlock action; automatic ejectors; single selective trigger; 10mm top rib. Comes with case. Introduced 1996. Imported from Italy by Wm. Larkin Moore & Co.

Price: **$6,250.00**

RIZZINI UPLAND EL OVER/UNDER SHOTGUN

Gauge: 12, 16, 20, 28, 410. **Barrel:** 26", 27-1/2", Mod. & Full, Imp. Cyl. & Imp. Mod. choke tubes. **Weight:** About 6.6 lbs. **Stock:** 14-1/2"x1-1/2"x2-1/4". **Features:** Boxlock action; single selective trigger; ejectors; profuse engraving on silvered receiver. Comes with fitted case. Introduced 1996. Imported from Italy by Wm. Larkin Moore & Co.

Price: From **$3,500.00**

RIZZINI ARTEMIS OVER/UNDER SHOTGUN

Same as the Upland EL model except has dummy sideplates with extensive game scene engraving. Fancy European walnut stock. Comes with fitted case. Introduced 1996. Imported from Italy by Wm. Larkin Moore & Co.

Price: From **$2,375.00**

RIZZINI S782 EMEL OVER/UNDER SHOTGUN

Gauge: 12, 2-3/4" chambers. **Barrel:** 26", 27.5" (Imp. Cyl. & Imp. Mod.). **Weight:** About 6.75 lbs. **Stock:** 14-1/2"x1-1/2"x2-1/4". Extra fancy select walnut. **Features:** Boxlock action with dummy sideplates; extensive engraving with gold inlaid game birds; silvered receiver; automatic ejectors; single selective trigger. Comes with Nizzoli leather case. Introduced 1996. Imported from Italy by Wm. Larkin Moore & Co.

Price: From **$12,250.00**

ROTTWEIL PARAGON OVER/UNDER

Gauge: 12, 2-3/4" chambers. **Barrel:** 28", 30", five choke tubes. **Weight:** 7 lbs. **Stock:** 14-1/2"x1-1/2"x2-1/2"; European walnut. **Features:** Boxlock action. Detachable trigger assembly; ejectors can be deactivated; convertible top lever for right- or left-hand use; trigger adjustable for position. Imported from Germany by Dynamit Nobel-RWS, Inc.

Price: **$5,995.00**

RUGER WOODSIDE OVER/UNDER SHOTGUN

Gauge: 12, 3" chambers. **Barrel:** 26", 28", 30" (Full, Mod., Imp. Cyl. and two Skeet tubes). **Weight:** 7-1/2 to 8 lbs. **Stock:** 14-1/8"x1-1/2"x2-1/2". Select Circassian walnut; pistol grip or straight English grip. **Features:** Has a newly patented Ruger cocking mechanism for easier, smoother opening. Buttstock extends forward into action as two side panels. Single selective mechanical trigger; selective automatic ejectors; serrated free-floating rib; back-bored barrels with stainless steel choke tubes. Blued barrels, stainless steel receiver. Engraved action available. Introduced 1995. Made in U.S. by Sturm, Ruger & Co.

Price: **$1,849.00**
Price: Woodside Sporting Clays (30" barrels) **$1,849.00**

RUGER RED LABEL O/U SHOTGUN

Gauge: 12, 20, 3" chambers; 28 2-3/4" chambers. **Barrel:** 26", 28" (Skeet [two], Imp. Cyl., Full, Mod. screw-in choke tubes). Proved for steel shot. **Weight:** About 7 lbs. (20 ga.); 7-1/2 lbs. (12 ga.). **Length:** 43" overall (26" barrels). **Stock:** 14"x1-1/2"x2-1/2". Straight grain American walnut or black synthetic. Checkered pistol grip and forend, rubber butt pad. **Features:** Stainless steel receiver. Single selective mechanical trigger, selective automatic ejectors; serrated free-floating vent. rib. Comes with two Skeet, one Imp. Cyl., one Mod., one Full choke tube and wrench. Made in U.S. by Sturm, Ruger & Co.

Price: Red Label with pistol grip stock **$1,369.00**
Price: English Field with straight-grip stock **$1,369.00**
Price: All-Weather Red Label with black synthetic stock **$1,369.00**
Price: Factory engraved All-Weather models . . . . **$1,575.00** to **$1,650.00**

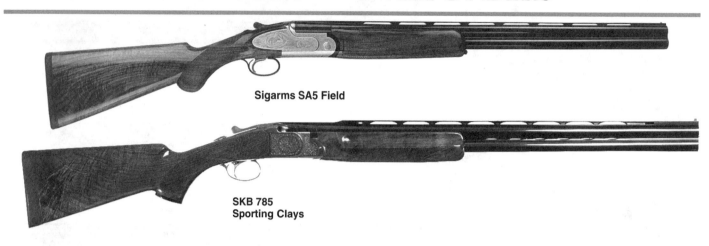

Sigarms SA5 Field

SKB 785
Sporting Clays

Ruger Engraved Red Label O/U Shotguns

Similar to Red Label except has scroll engraved receiver with 24-carat gold game bird (pheasant in 12 gauge, grouse in 20 gauge, woodcock in 28 gauge, duck on All-Weather 12 gauge). Introduced 2000.

Price: Engraved Red Label (12 gauge, 30" barrel) $1,650.00
Price: Engraved Red Label (12, 20 and 28 gauge in 26" and 28" barrels) $1,575.00
Price: Engraved Red Label, All-Weather (synthetic stock, 12 gauge only; 26" and 28" brls.) $1,575.00
Price: Engraved Red Label, All-Weather (synthetic stock, 12 gauge only, 30" barrel) $1,650.00

Ruger Sporting Clays O/U Shotgun

Similar to the Red Label except 30" back-bored barrels, stainless steel choke tubes. Weighs 7.75 lbs., overall length 47". Stock dimensions of 14-1/8"x1-1/2"x2-1/2". Free-floating serrated vent. rib with brass front and mid-rib beads. No barrel side spacers. Comes with two Skeet, one Imp. Cyl., one Mod. + Full choke tubes. 12 ga. introduced 1992, 20 ga. introduced 1994.

Price: 12 or 20 .... $1,443.00
Price: All-Weather with black synthetic stock $1,443.00

SARSILMAZ OVER/UNDER SHOTGUN

Gauge: 12, 3" chambers. **Barrel:** 26", 28"; fixed chokes or choke tubes. **Weight:** N/A. **Length:** N/A. **Stock:** Oil-finished hardwood. **Features:** Double or single selective trigger; wide ventilated rib; chrome-plated parts; blued finish. Introduced 2000. Imported from Turkey by Armsport Inc.

Price: Double triggers; mod. and full or imp. cyl. and mod. fixed chokes $499.95
Price: Single selective trigger; imp. cyl. and mod. or mod. and full fixed chokes $575.00
Price: Single selective trigger; five choke tubes and wrench $695.00

SIGARMS SA5 OVER/UNDER SHOTGUN

Gauge: 12, 20, 3" chamber. **Barrel:** 26-1/2", 27" (Full, Imp. Mod., Mod., Imp. Cyl., Cyl. choke tubes). **Weight:** 6.9 lbs. (12 gauge), 5.9 lbs. (20 gauge). **Stock:** 14-1/2" x 1-1/2" x 2-1/2". Select grade walnut; checkered 20 l.p.i. at grip and forend. **Features:** Single selective trigger; automatic ejectors; hand-engraved detachable sideplated; matte nickel receiver, rest blued; tapered bolt lock-up. Introduced 1997. Imported by Sigarms, Inc.

Price: Field, 12 gauge................................. $2,670.00
Price: Sporting Clays $2,800.00
Price: Field 20 gauge $2,670.00

SKB Model 505 Shotguns

Similar to the Model 585 except blued receiver, standard bore diameter, standard Inter-Choke system on 12, 20, 28, different receiver engraving. Imported from Japan by G.U. Inc.

Price: Field, 12 (26", 28"), 20 (26", 28") $1,049.00
Price: Sporting Clays, 12 (28", 30") $1,149.00

SKB Model 585 Gold Package

Similar to the Model 585 Field except has gold-plated trigger, two gold-plated game inlays, and Schnabel forend. Silver or blue receiver. Introduced 1998. Imported from Japan by G.U. Inc.

Price: 12, 20 ga. $1,489.00
Price: 28, 410 .... $1,539.00

SKB MODEL 785 OVER/UNDER SHOTGUN

Gauge: 12, 20, 3"; 28, 2-3/4"; 410, 3". **Barrel:** 26", 28", 30", 32" (Inter-Choke tubes). **Weight:** 6 lbs., 10 oz. to 8 lbs. **Stock:** 14-1/8"x1-1/2"x2-3/16" (Field). Hand-checkered American black walnut with high-gloss finish; semi-beavertail forend. Target stocks available in standard or Monte Carlo styles. **Sights:** Metal bead front (Field), target style on Skeet, trap, Sporting Clays models. **Features:** Boxlock action with Greener-style cross bolt; single selective chrome-plated trigger, chrome-plated selective ejectors; manual safety. Chrome-plated, over-size, back-bored barrels with lengthened forcing cones. Introduced 1995. Imported from Japan by G.U. Inc.

Price: Field, 12 or 20 .... $1,949.00
Price: Field, 28 or 410 .... $2,029.00
Price: Field set, 12 and 20 .... $2,829.00
Price: Field set, 20 and 28 or 28 and 410 .... $2,929.00
Price: Sporting Clays, 12 or 20........................ $2,099.00
Price: Sporting Clays, 28 .... $2,169.00
Price: Sporting Clays set, 12 and 20 .... $2,999.00
Price: Skeet, 12 or 20................................ $2,029.00
Price: Skeet, 28 or 410. .... $2,069.00
Price: Skeet, three-barrel set, 20, 28, 410 .... $4,089.00
Price: Trap, standard or Monte Carlo.................... $2,029.00
Price: Trap combo, standard or Monte Carlo.............. $2,829.00

SKB MODEL 585 OVER/UNDER SHOTGUN

Gauge: 12 or 20, 3"; 28, 2-3/4"; 410, 3". **Barrel:** 12 ga.—26", 28", 30", 32", 34" (Inter-Choke tube); 20 ga.—26", 28" (Inter-Choke tube); 28—26", 28" (Inter-Choke tube); 410—26", 28" (Imp. Cyl. & Mod., Mod. & Full). Ventilated side ribs. **Weight:** 6.6 to 8.5 lbs. **Length:** 43" to 51-3/8" overall. **Stock:** 14-1/8"x1-1/2"x2-3/16". Hand checkered walnut with high-gloss finish. Target stocks available in standard and Monte Carlo. **Sights:** Metal bead front (field), target style on Skeet, trap, Sporting Clays. **Features:** Boxlock action; silver nitride finish with Field or Target pattern engraving; manual safety, automatic ejectors, single selective trigger. All 12 gauge barrels are back-bored, have lengthened forcing cones and longer choke tube system. Sporting Clays models in 12 gauge with 28" or 30" barrels available with optional 3/8" step-up target-style rib, matte finish, nickel center bead, white front bead. Introduced 1992. Imported from Japan by G.U., Inc.

Price: Field $1,329.00
Price: Two-barrel Field Set, 12 & 20 .... $2,129.00
Price: Two-barrel Field Set, 20 & 28 or 28 & 410. .... $2,179.00
Price: Trap, Skeet. $1,429.00
Price: Two-barrel trap combo. $2,129.00
Price: Sporting Clays model .... $1,149.00 to $1,529.00
Price: Skeet Set (20, 28, 410) $3,329.00

SHOTGUNS

NEW!

SHOTGUNS — OVER/UNDERS

Tristar-TR-SC

STOEGER/IGA CONDOR I OVER/UNDER SHOTGUN
Gauge: 12, 20, 3" chambers. **Barrel:** 26" (Imp. Cyl. & Mod. choke tubes), 28" (Mod. & Full choke tubes). **Weight:** 6-3/4 to 7 lbs. **Stock:** 14-1/2"x1-1/2"x2-1/2". Oil-finished hardwood with checkered pistol grip and forend. **Features:** Manual safety, single trigger, extractors only, ventilated top rib. Introduced 1983. Imported from Brazil by Stoeger Industries.
Price: With choke tubes **$559.00**
Price: Condor Supreme (same as Condor I with single trigger, choke tubes, but with auto. ejectors), 12 or 20 ga., 26", 28" . . . **$674.00**

Stoeger/IGA Condor Waterfowl O/U
Similar to the Condor I except has Advantage camouflage on the barrels, stock and forend; all other metal has matte black finish. Comes only with 30" choke tube barrels, 3" chambers, automatic ejectors, single trigger and manual safety. Designed for steel shot. Introduced 1997. Imported from Brazil by Stoeger.
Price: **$729.00**

Stoeger/IGA Turkey Model O/U
Similar to the Condor I model except has Advantage camouflage on the barrels stock and forend. All exposed metal and recoil pad are matte black. Has 26" (Full & Full) barrels, single trigger, manual safety, 3" chambers. Introduced 1997. Imported from Brazil by Stoeger.
Price: **$729.00**

TRISTAR-TR-SC "EMILLIO RIZZINI" OVER/UNDER
Gauge: 12, 20, 2-3/4" chambers. **Barrel:** 28", 30" (Imp. Cyl., Mod., Full choke tubes). **Weight:** 7-1/2 lbs. **Length:** 46" overall (28" barrel). **Stock:** 1-1/2"x2-3/8"x14-3/8". Semi-fancy walnut; pistol grip with palm swell; semi-beavertail forend; black Sporting Clays recoil pad. **Features:** Silvered boxlock action with Four Locks locking system, auto ejectors, single selective (inertia) trigger, auto safety. Hard chrome bores. Vent. 10mm rib with target-style front and mid-rib beads, vent. spacer rib. Introduced 1998. Imported from Italy by Tristar Sporting Arms, Ltd.
Price: **$949.00**
Price: 20 ga. **$1,022.00**

Tristar TR-Royal Emillio Rizzini Over/Under
Similar to the TR-SC except has special parallel stock dimensions (1-1/2"x1-5/8"x14-3/8") to give low felt recoil; Rhino ported, extended choke tubes; solid barrel spacer; has "TR-Royal" gold engraved on the silvered receiver. Available in 12 gauge (28", 30") 20 and 28 gauge (28" only). Introduced 1999. Imported from Italy by Tristar Sporting Arms, Ltd.
Price: 12 ga. **$1,277.00**
Price: 20, 28 ga. **$1,345.00**

Tristar-TR-L "Emillio Rizzinni" Over/Under
Similar to the TR-SC except has stock dimensions designed for female shooters (1-1/2" x 3" x 13-1/2"). Standard grade walnut. Introduced 1998. Imported from Italy by Tristar Sporting Arms, Ltd.
Price: **$966.00**

TRISTAR-TR-I, II "EMILLIO RIZZINI" OVER/UNDERS
Gauge: 12, 20, 3" chambers (TR-I); 12, 16, 20, 28, 410 3" chambers (except 28, 2-3/4"). **Barrel:** 12 ga., 26" (Imp. Cyl. & Mod.), 28" (Mod. & Full); 20 ga., 26" (Imp. Cyl. & Mod.), fixed chokes. **Weight:** 7-1/2 lbs. **Stock:** 1-1/2"x2-3/8"x14-3/8". Walnut with palm swell pistol grip, hand checkering, semi-beavertail forend, black recoil pad. **Features:** Boxlock action with blued finish, Four Locks® locking system, gold single selective (inertia) trigger system, automatic safety, extractors. Introduced 1998. Imported from Italy by Tristar Sporting Arms, Ltd.

Price: TR-I **$654.00**
Price: TR-II (automatic ejectors, choke tubes) 12, 16 ga. **$852.00**
Price: 20, 28 ga., 410. . . . . **$880.00**

Tristar-TR-MAG "Emillio Rizzini" Over/Under
Similar to the TR-I except 12 gauge, 3-1/2" chambers; choke tubes; 24" or 28" barrels with three choke tubes; extractors; auto safety. Matte blue finish on all metal, non-reflective wood finish. Introduced 1998. Imported from Italy by Tristar Sporting Arms, Ltd.
Price: **$728.00**

TRISTAR TR-CLASS SL EMILLIO RIZZINI O/U
Gauge: 12, 2-3/4" chambers. **Barrel:** 28", 30", (Imp. Cyl., Mod., Full choke tubes). **Weight:** 7-1/2-7-3/4 lbs. **Stock:** 1-1/2"x1-3/8"x14-1/4". Fancy walnut with palm swell, hand checkering, semi-beavertail forend, black recoil pad, gloss finish. **Features:** Boxlock action with silvered, engraved sideplates; Four Lock locking system; automatic ejectors; hard chrome bores; vent tapered 7mm rib with target-style front bead. hand-fitted gun. Introduced 1999. Imported from Italy by Tristar Sporting Arms, Ltd.
Price: **$1,690.00**

VERONA LX501 HUNTING O/U SHOTGUNS
Gauge: 12, 20, (3" chambers), 28, 410 (2-3/4"). **Barrel:** 28"; 12, 20 ga. have Interchoke tubes, 28 ga. and 410 have fixed Full & Mod. **Weight:** 6-7 lbs. **Stock:** Matte-finished walnut with machine-cut checkering. **Features:** Gold-plated single-selective trigger; ejectors; engraved, blued receiver, non-automatic safety; coil spring-operated firing pins. Introduced 1999. Imported from Italy by B.C. Outdoors.
Price: 12 and 20 ga. **$720.00**
Price: 28 ga. and 410 . . . . **$755.00**

Verona LX692 Gold Hunting Over/Under Shotguns
Similar to tthe Verona LX501 except has engraved, silvered receiver with false sideplates showing gold-inlaid bird hunting scenes on three sides; Schnabel forend tip; hand-cut checkering; black rubber butt pad. Available in 12 and 20 gauge only, with five InterChoke tubes. Introduced 1999. Imported from Italy by B.C. Outdoors.
Price: **$1,295.00**

Verona LX680 Sporting Over/Under Shotguns
Similar to the Verona LX501 except has engraved, silvered receiver; ventilated middle rib; beavertail forend; hand-cut checkering; available in 12 or 20 gauge only with 2-3/4" chambers. Introduced 1999. Imported from Italy by B.C. Outdoors.
Price: **$1,020.00**

Verona LX680 Skeet/Sporting, Trap O/U Shotguns
Similar to the Verona LX501 except with Skeet or trap stock dimensions; beavertail forend, palm swell on pistol grip; ventilated center barrel rib. Introduced 1999. Imported from Italy by B.C. Outdoors.
Price: **$1,130.00**
Price: Gold Competition (false sideplates with gold-inlaid hunting scenes) **$1,500.00**

Verona LX692 Gold Sporting Over/Under Shotguns
Similar to the Verona LX680 except with false sideplates that have gold-inlaid bird hunting scenes on three sides; red high-visibility front sight. Introduced 1999. Imported from Italy by B.C. Outdoors.
Price: **$1,365.00**

WEATHERBY ATHENA GRADE IV O/U SHOTGUNS
Gauge: 12, 20, 3" chambers. **Action:** Boxlock (simulated sidelock) top lever break-open. Selective auto ejectors, single selective trigger (selector inside trigger guard). **Barrel:** 26", 28", IMC Multi-Choke tubes. **Weight:** 12 ga., 7-3/8 lbs.; 20 ga. 6-7/8 lbs. **Stock:** American walnut, checkered pistol grip and forend (14-1/4"x1-1/2"x2-1/2"). **Features:** Mechanically operated trigger. Top tang safety, Greener cross bolt, fully engraved receiver, recoil pad installed. IMC models furnished with three interchangeable flush-fitting choke tubes. Imported from Japan by Weatherby. Introduced 1982.

SHOTGUNS

SHOTGUNS — OVER/UNDERS

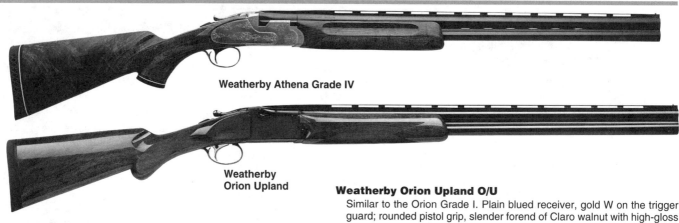

Weatherby Athena Grade IV

Weatherby Orion Upland

Price: 12 ga., IMC, 26", 28" $2,399.00
Price: 20 ga., IMC, 26", 28" $2,399.00

Weatherby Athena Grade V Classic Field O/U
Similar to the Athena Grade IV except has rounded pistol grip, slender forend, oil-finished Claro walnut stock with fine-line checkering, Old English recoil pad. Sideplate receiver has rose and scroll engraving. Available in 12 gauge, 26", 28", 20 gauge, 26", 28", all with 3" chambers. Introduced 1993.
Price: $2,799.00

WEATHERBY ORION GRADE III FIELD O/U SHOTGUNS
Gauge: 12, 20, 3" chambers. **Barrel:** 26", 28", IMC Multi-Choke tubes. **Weight:** 6-1/2 to 9 lbs. **Stock:** 14-1/4"x1-1/2"x2-1/2". American walnut, checkered grip and forend. Rubber recoil pad. **Features:** Selective automatic ejectors, single selective inertia trigger. Top tang safety, Greener cross bolt. Has silver-gray receiver with engraving and gold duck/pheasant. Imported from Japan by Weatherby.
Price: Orion III, Field, 12, IMC, 26", 28" $1,799.00
Price: Orion III, Field, 20, IMC, 26", 28" $1,799.00

Weatherby Orion Grade III Classic Field O/U
Similar to the Orion III Field except the stock has a rounded pistol grip, satin oil finish, slender forend, Old English recoil pad. Introduced 1993. Imported from Japan by Weatherby.
Price: $1,799.00

Weatherby Orion Grade II Classic Field O/U
Similar to the Orion III Classic Field except stock has high-gloss finish, and the bird on the receiver is not gold. Available in 12 gauge, 26", 28", 30" barrels, 20 gauge, 26" 28", both with 3" chambers, 28 gauge, 26", 2-3/4" chambers. All have IMC choke tubes. Imported from Japan by Weatherby.
Price: $1,499.00

Weatherby Athena III Classic Field O/U
Has Grade III Claro walnut with oil finish, rounded pistol grip, slender forend; silver nitride/gray receiver has rose and scroll engraving with gold-overlay upland game scenes. Introduced 1999. Imported from Japan by Weatherby.
Price: $1,999.00

Weatherby Orion Grade I Field O/U
Similar to the Orion Grade III Field except has blued receiver with engraving, and the bird is not gold. Available in 12 gauge, 26", 28", 30", 20 gauge, 20", 28", both with 3" chambers and IMC choke tubes. Imported from Japan by Weatherby.
Price: $1,449.00

Weatherby Orion Upland O/U
Similar to the Orion Grade I. Plain blued receiver, gold W on the trigger guard; rounded pistol grip, slender forend of Claro walnut with high-gloss finish; black butt pad. Available in 12 and 20 gauge with 26" and 28" barrels. Introduced 1999. Imported from Japan by Weatherby.
Price: $1,199.00

WEATHERBY ORION SSC OVER/UNDER SHOTGUN
Gauge: 12, 3" chambers. **Barrel:** 28", 30", 32" (Skeet, SC1, Imp. Cyl., SC2, Mod. IMC choke tubes). **Weight:** About 8 lbs. **Stock:** 14-3/4"x2-1/4"x1-1/2". Claro walnut with satin oil finish; Schnabel forend tip; Sporter-style pistol grip; Pachmayr Decelerator recoil pad. **Features:** Designed for Sporting Clays competition. Has lengthened forcing cones and back-boring; ported barrels with 12mm grooved rib with mid-bead sight; mechanical trigger is adjustable for length of pull. Introduced 1998. Imported from Japan by Weatherby.
Price: $1,899.00

Weatherby Orion III English Field O/U
Similar to the Orion III Classic Field except has straight grip English-style stock. Available in 12 gauge (28"), 20 gauge (26", 28") with IMC Multi-Choke tubes. Silver/gray nitride receiver is engraved and has gold-plate overlay. Introduced 1997. Imported from Japan by Weatherby.
Price: $1,879.00

Weatherby Orion Grade II Classic Sporting O/U
Similar to the Orion II Classic Field except in 12 gauge only with (3" chambers), 28", 30" barrels with Skeet, SC1, SC2 Imp. Cyl., Mod. chokes. Weighs 7.5-8 lbs. Competition center vent rib; middle bead and enlarged front beads. Rounded grip; high gloss stock. Radiused heel recoil pad. Receiver finished in silver nitride with acid-etched, gold-plate clay pigeon monogram. Barrels have lengthened forcing cones. Introduced 1993. Imported by Weatherby.
Price: $1,649.00

Weatherby Orion Grade II Sporting Clays
Similar to the Orion II Classic Sporting except has traditional pistol grip with diamond inlay, and standard full-size forend. Available in 12 gauge only, 28", 30" barrels with Skeet, Imp. Cyl., SC2, Mod. Has lengthened forcing cones, back-boring, stepped competition rib, radius heel recoil pad, hand-engraved, silver/nitride receiver. Introduced 1992. Imported by Weatherby.
Price: $1,649.00

WINCHESTER SUPREME O/U SHOTGUNS
Gauge: 12, 2-3/4", 3" chambers. **Barrel:** 28", 30", Invector Plus choke tubes. **Weight:** 7 lbs. 6 oz. to 7 lbs. 12. oz. **Length:** 45" overall (28" barrel). **Stock:** Checkered walnut stock. **Features:** Chrome-plated chambers; back-bored barrels; tang barrel selector/safety; deep-blued finish. Introduced 2000. From U.S. Repeating Arms. Co.
Price: Supreme Field (28" barrel, 6mm ventilated rib) $1,324.00
Price: Supreme Sporting (28" or 30" barrel, 10mm rib,
adj. trigger) $1,485.00

SHOTGUNS

Variety of models for utility and sporting use, including some competitive shooting.

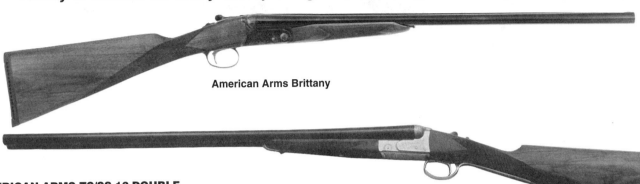

American Arms Brittany

**Beretta Model 470
Silver Hawk**

AMERICAN ARMS TS/SS 12 DOUBLE

Gauge: 12, 3-1/2" chambers. **Barrel:** 26", choke tubes; solid raised rib. **Weight:** 7 lbs., 6 oz. **Stock:** Walnut; cut-checked grip and forend. **Features:** Non-reflective metal and wood finishes; boxlock action; single trigger; extractors. Imported by American Arms, Inc.
Price: $799.00

AMERICAN ARMS WT/SS 10 DOUBLE

Gauge: 10, 3-1/2" chambers. **Barrel:** 28", choke tubes. **Weight:** 10 lbs., 3 oz. **Length:** 45" overall. **Stock:** 14-1/4"x1-1/8"x2-3/8"; walnut. **Features:** Boxlock action with extractors; single selective trigger; non-reflective wood and metal finishes. Imported by American Arms, Inc.
Price: $860.00

AMERICAN ARMS GENTRY DOUBLE SHOTGUN

Gauge: 12, 20, 410, 3" chambers; 28 ga. 2-3/4" chambers. **Barrel:** 26" (Imp. Cyl. & Mod., all gauges), 28" (Mod., & Full, 12 and 20 gauges). **Weight:** 6-1/4 to 6-3/4 lbs. **Stock:** 14-1/8"x1-3/8"x2-3/8". Hand-checkered walnut with semi-gloss finish. **Sights:** Metal bead front. **Features:** Boxlock action with English-style scroll engraving, color case-hardened finish. Single trigger, extractors. Independent floating firing pins. Manual safety. Five-year warranty. Introduced 1987. Imported from Spain by American Arms, Inc.
Price: 12 or 20 .... $750.00
Price: 28 or 410 .... $795.00

AMERICAN ARMS BRITTANY SHOTGUN

Gauge: 12, 20, 3" chambers. **Barrel:** 12 ga.—27"; 20 ga.—25" (Imp. Cyl., Mod., Full choke tubes). **Weight:** 6 lbs., 7 oz. (20 ga.). **Stock:** 14-1/8"x1-3/8"x2-3/8". Hand-checkered walnut with oil finish, straight English-style with semi-beavertail forend. **Features:** Boxlock action with case-color finish, engraving; single selective trigger, automatic selective ejectors; rubber recoil pad. Introduced 1989. Imported from Spain by American Arms, Inc.
Price: $885.00

ARRIETA SIDELOCK DOUBLE SHOTGUNS

Gauge: 12, 16, 20, 28, 410. **Barrel:** Length and chokes to customer specs. **Weight:** To customer specs. **Stock:** 14-1/2"x1-1/2"x2-1/2 (standard dimensions), or to customer specs. Straight English with checkered butt (standard), or pistol grip. Select European walnut with oil finish. **Features:** Essentially a custom gun with myriad options. Holland & Holland-pattern hand-detachable sidelocks, selective automatic ejectors, double triggers (hinged front) standard. Some have self-opening action. Finish and engraving to customer specs. Imported from Spain by Wingshooting Adventures.
Price: Model 557, auto ejectors, from................ $2,750.00
Price: Model 570, auto ejectors, from................ $3,380.00
Price: Model 578, auto ejectors, from................ $3,740.00
Price: Model 600 Imperial, self-opening, from $4,990.00
Price: Model 601 Imperial Tiro, self-opening, from.......... $5,750.00
Price: Model 801, from...................... $7,950.00
Price: Model 802, from...................... $7,950.00
Price: Model 803, from...................... $5,850.00
Price: Model 871, auto ejectors, from............ $4,290.00
Price: Model 872, self-opening, from $9,790.00
Price: Model 873, self-opening, from $6,850.00

Price: Model 874, self-opening, from $7,950.00
Price: Model 875, self-opening, from $12,950.00

BERETTA MODEL 470 SILVER HAWK SHOTGUN

Gauge: 12, 20, 3" chambers. **Barrel:** 26" (Imp. Cyl. & Imp. Mod.), 28" (Mod. & Full). **Weight:** 5.9 lbs. (20 gauge). **Stock:** Select European walnut, straight English grip. **Features:** Boxlock action with single selective trigger; selector provides automatic ejection or extraction; silver-chrome action and forend iron with fine engraving; top lever highlighted with gold inlaid hawk's head. Comes with ABS case. Introduced 1997. Imported from Italy by Beretta U.S.A.
Price: 12 ga. $3,630.00
Price: 20 ga. $3,755.00

CHARLES DALY SUPERIOR HUNTER DOUBLE SHOTGUN

Gauge: 12, 20, 3" chambers, 28, 2-3/4" chambers. **Barrel:** 28" (Mod. & Full) 26" (Imp. Cyl. & Mod.). **Weight:** About 7 lbs. **Stock:** Checkered walnut pistol grip buttstock, splinter forend. **Features:** Silvered, engraved receiver; chrome-lined barrels; gold single trigger; automatic safety; extractors; gold bead front sight. Introduced 1997. Imported from Italy by K.B.I., Inc.
Price: $1,179.95
Price: 28 ga., 26" $1,094.95

Charles Daly Empire Hunter Double Shotgun

Similar to the Superior Hunter except has deluxe wood, game scene engraving, automatic ejectors. Introduced 1997. Imported from Italy by K.B.I., Inc.
Price: 12 or 20 .... $1,595.95

CHARLES DALY DIAMOND REGENT DL DOUBLE SHOTGUN

Gauge: 12, 20, 410, 3" chambers, 28, 2-3/4" chambers. **Barrel:** 28" (Mod. & Full), 26" (Imp. Cyl. & Mod.), 26" (Full & Full, 410). **Weight:** About 5-7 lbs. **Stock:** Special select fancy European walnut, English-style butt, splinter forend; hand-checkered; hand-rubbed oil finish. **Features:** Drop-forged action with gas escape valves; demiblock barrels of chrome-nickel steel with concave rib; selective automatic-ejectors; hand-detachable, double-safety H&H sidelocks with demi-relief hand engraving; H&H pattern easy-opening feature; hinged trigger; coin finished action. Introduced 1997. Imported from Spain by K.B.I., Inc.
Price: 12 or 20 .... $19,999.00
Price: 28 .... $20,499.00
Price: 410 .... $20,499.00

CHARLES DALY FIELD HUNTER DOUBLE SHOTGUN

Gauge: 10, 12, 20, 28, 410 (3" chambers; 28 has 2-3/4"). **Barrel:** 32" (Mod. & Mod.), 28, 30" (Mod. & Full) 26" (Imp. Cyl. & Mod.) 410 (Full & Full). **Weight:** 6 lbs. to 11.4 lbs. **Stock:** Checkered walnut pistol grip and forend. **Features:** Silvered, engraved receiver; gold single selective trigger in 10-, 12, and 20 ga.; double triggers in 28 and 410; automatic safety; extractors; gold bead front sight. Introduced 1997. Imported from Spain by K.B.I., Inc.

Charles Daly Field Hunter

Fabarm Classic Lion

A.H. Fox DE Grade

Price: 10 ga. **$984.95**
Price: 12 or 20 ga. **$809.95**
Price: 28 ga. **$854.95**
Price: 410-bore. **$854.95**
Price: As above, 12 or 20 AE. MC **$939.95**

CHARLES DALY DIAMOND DL DOUBLE SHOTGUN

Gauge: 12, 20, 410, 3" chambers, 28, 2-3/4" chambers. **Barrel:** 28" (Mod. & Full), 26" (Imp. Cyl. & Mod.), 26" (Full & Full, 410). **Weight:** About 5-7 lbs. **Stock:** Select fancy European walnut, English-style butt, beavertail forend; hand-checkered, hand-rubbed oil finish. **Features:** Drop-forged action with gas escape valves; demiblock barrels with concave rib; selective automatic ejectors; hand-detachable double safety sidelocks with hand-engraved rose and scrollwork. Hinged front trigger. Color case-hardened receiver. Introduced 1997. Imported from Spain by K.B.I., Inc.
Price: 12 or 20 . . . . **$6,959.95**
Price: 28 . . . . **$7,274.95**
Price: 410 . . . . **$7,274.95**

DAKOTA PREMIER GRADE SHOTGUNS

Gauge: 12, 16, 20, 28, 410. **Barrel:** 27". **Weight:** N/A. **Length:** N/A. **Stock:** Exhibition-grade English walnut, hand-rubbed oil finish with straight grip and splinter forend. **Features:** French grey finish; 50 percent coverage engraving; double triggers; selective ejectors. Finished to customer specifications. Made in U.S. by Dakota Arms.
Price: 12, 16, 20 gauge **$12,950.00**
Price: 28 and 410 gauge. **$14,245.00**

Dakota The Dakota Legend Shotguns

Similar to Premier Grade except has special selection English walnut, full-coverage scroll engraving, oak and leather case. Made in U.S. by Dakota Arms.
Price: 12, 16, 20 gauge **$18,000.00**
Price: 28 and 410 gauge 19,800.00

NEW! EAA/BAIKAL BOUNTY HUNTER IZH-43K SHOTGUN

Gauge: 12 (2-3/4", 3" chambers), 20 (3" chambers), 28 (2-3/4" chambers), 410 (3" chambers). **Barrel:** 18-1/2", 20", 24", 26", 28", three choke tubes. **Weight:** 7.28 lbs. Overall **length:** N/A. **Stock:** Walnut, checkered forearm and grip. **Features:** Machined receiver; hammer-forged barrels with chrome-line bores; external hammers; double triggers (single, selective trigger available); rifle barrel inserts optional. Imported by European American Armory.
Price: IZH-43K (12 gauge) **$439.00**
Price: IZH-43K (20, 28 and 410 gauge) **$469.00**

EAA/BAIKAL IZH-43 SHOTGUN

Gauge: 12 (2-3/4", 3" chambers), 16 (2-3/4" chambers), 20 (2-3/4" and 3" chambers). **Barrel:** 20", 24", 26", 28"; imp., mod. and full choke tubes. **Weight:** N/A. **Stock:** Hardwood or walnut; checkered forend and grip. **Features:** Hammer forged barrel; internal hammers; extractors; engraved receiver; automatic tang safety; non-glare rib. Imported by European American Armory.
Price: IZH-43 Bounty Hunter (12 gauge, 2-3/4" chambers, 20" brl., dbl. triggers) **$269.00**
Price: IZH-43 Bounty Hunter (12 or 20 gauge, 2-3/4" chambers, 20" brl., dbl. triggers) **$309.00**
Price: IZH-43 (12 gauge, single selective trigger, walnut stock) . . **$339.00**
Price: IZH-43 (16 or 20 gauge). **$399.00**
Price: IZH-43 (20/28 gauge two-barrel set) **$579.00**

EAA/BAIKAL MP-213 SHOTGUN

Gauge: 12, 3" chambers. **Barrel:** 24", 26", 28"; imp., mod. and full choke tubes. **Weight:** 7.28 lbs. **Stock:** Walnut, checkered forearm and grip; rubber butt pad. **Features:** Hammer-forged barrels; chrome-lined bores; machined receiver; double trigger (each trigger fires both barrels independently); ejectors. Introduced 2000. Imported by European American Armory.
Price: IZH-213 . . . . **$879.00**

EAA/BAIKAL BOUNTY HUNTER MP-213 COACH GUN

Gauge: 12, 3" chamber. **Barrel:** 18.5", 20", 24", 26", 28", imp., mod. and full choke tubes. **Weight:** 7 lbs. **Stock:** Walnut, checkered forend and grip. **Features:** Selective double trigger with removable assembly (single trigger and varied pull weights available); ejectors; engraved receiver. Imported by European American Armory.
Price: MP-213. . . . . **$879.00**

FABARM CLASSIC LION DOUBLE SHOTGUN

Gauge: 12, 3" chambers. **Barrel:** 26" (Cyl., Imp. Cyl., Mod., Imp. Mod., Full choke tubes). **Weight:** 7.2 lbs. **Length:** 47.6" overall. **Stock:** Oil-finished European walnut. **Features:** Boxlock action with single selective trigger, automatic ejectors, automatic safety. Introduced 1998. Imported from Italy by Heckler & Koch, Inc.
Price: Grade I. **$1,488.00**
Price: Grade II (sidelock action) **$2,110.00**

A.H. FOX SIDE-BY-SIDE SHOTGUNS

Gauge: 16, 20, 28, 410. **Barrel:** Length and chokes to customer specifications. Rust-blued Chromox or Krupp steel. **Weight:** 5-1/2 to 6-3/4 lbs. **Stock:** Dimensions to customer specifications. Hand-checkered Turkish Circassian walnut with hand-rubbed oil finish. Straight, semi- or full pistol grip; splinter, Schnabel or beavertail forend; traditional pad, hard rubber buttplate or skeleton butt. **Features:** Boxlock action with automatic ejectors; double or Fox single selective trigger. Scalloped, rebated and color case-hardened receiver; hand finished and hand-engraved. Grades differ in engraving, inlays, grade of wood, amount of hand finishing. Add $1,000 for 28 or 410-bore. Introduced 1993. Made in U.S. by Connecticut Shotgun Mfg.

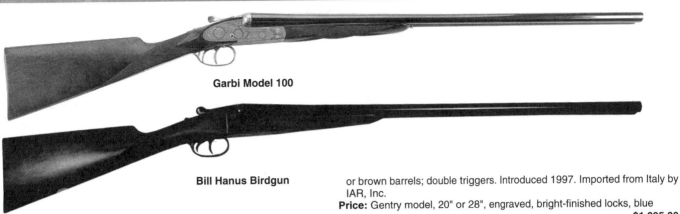

Garbi Model 100

Bill Hanus Birdgun

Price: CE Grade	$9,500.00
Price: XE Grade	$11,000.00
Price: DE Grade	$13,500.00
Price: FE Grade	$18,500.00
Price: Exhibition Grade	$26,000.00
Price: 28/410 CE Grade	$8,200.00
Price: 28/410 XE Grade	$9,700.00
Price: 28/410 DE Grade	$13,800.00
Price: 28/410 FE Grade	$14,700.00
Price: 28/410 Exhibition Grade	$26,000.00

GARBI MODEL 100 DOUBLE

Gauge: 12, 16, 20, 28. **Barrel:** 26", 28", choked to customer specs. **Weight:** 5-1/2 to 7-1/2 lbs. **Stock:** 14-1/2"x2-1/4"x1-1/2". European walnut. Straight grip, checkered butt, classic forend. **Features:** Sidelock action, automatic ejectors, double triggers standard. Color case-hardened action, coin finish optional. Single trigger; beavertail forend, etc. optional. Five other models are available. Imported from Spain by Wm. Larkin Moore.
Price: From **$4,600.00**

Garbi Model 200 Side-by-Side

Similar to the Garbi Model 100 except has heavy-duty locks, magnum proofed. Very fine Continental-style floral and scroll engraving, well figured walnut stock. Other mechanical features remain the same. Imported from Spain by Wm. Larkin Moore.
Price: **$10,000.00**

Garbi Model 101 Side-by-Side

Similar to the Garbi Model 100 except is hand engraved with scroll engraving, select walnut stock. Better overall quality than the Model 100. Imported from Spain by Wm. Larkin Moore.
Price: From **$5,950.00**

Garbi Model 103A, B Side-by-Side

Similar to the Garbi Model 100 except has Purdey-type fine scroll and rosette engraving. Better overall quality than the Model 101. Model 103B has nickel-chrome steel barrels, H&H-type easy opening mechanism; other mechanical details remain the same. Imported from Spain by Wm. Larkin Moore.
Price: Model 103A, from **$7,400.00**
Price: Model 103B, from **$10,400.00**

BILL HANUS BIRDGUN

Gauge: 16, 20, 28. **Barrel:** 27", 20 and 28 ga.; 28", 16 ga. (Skeet 1 & Skeet 2). **Weight:** 5 lbs., 4 oz. to 6 lbs., 4 oz. **Stock:** 14-3/8"x1-1/2"x2-3/8", with 1/4" cast-off. Select walnut. **Features:** Boxlock action with ejectors; splinter forend, straight English grip; checkered butt; English leather-covered handguard included. Made by AYA. Introduced 1998. Imported from Spain by Bill Hanus Birdguns.
Price: **$1,895.00**

IAR COWBOY SHOTGUNS

Gauge: 12. **Barrel:** 20", 28". **Weight:** 7 lbs. (20" barrel). **Length:** 36-7/8" overall (20" barrel). **Stock:** Walnut. **Features:** Exposed hammers; blued or brown barrels; double triggers. Introduced 1997. Imported from Italy by IAR, Inc.
Price: Gentry model, 20" or 28", engraved, bright-finished locks, blue barrels **$1,895.00**
Price: Cowboy model, 20" or 28", no engraving on color case-hardened locks, brown patina barrels **$1,895.00**

ITHACA CLASSIC DOUBLES SPECIAL FIELD GRADE SxS

Gauge: 20, 28, 2-3/4" chambers, 410, 3". **Barrel:** 26", 28", 30", fixed chokes. **Weight:** 5 lbs., 14 oz. (20 gauge). **Stock:** 14-1/2"x2-1/4"x1-3/8". High-grade American black walnut, hand-rubbed oil finish; splinter or beavertail forend, straight or pistol grip. **Features:** Double triggers, ejectors; color case-hardened, engraved action body with matted top surfaces. Introduced 1999. Made in U.S. by Ithaca Classic Doubles.
Price: From **$3,150.00**

Ithaca Classic Doubles Grade 4E SxS Shotgun

Similar to the Special Field Grade except has gold-plated triggers, jeweled barrel flats and hand-turned locks. Feather crotch and flame-grained black walnut is hand-checkered 28 lpi with fleur de lis pattern. Action body is engraved with three game scenes and bank note scroll, and color case-hardened. Introduced 1999. Made in U.S. by Ithaca Classic Doubles.
Price: From **$4,199.00**

Ithaca Classic Doubles Grade 7E SxS Shotgun

Similar to the Special Field Grade except engraved with bank note scroll and flat 24k gold game scenes: gold setter and gold pointer on opposite action sides, and an American bald eagle is inlaid on the bottom plate. Hand-timed, polished, jeweled ejectors and locks. Exhibition grade American black walnut stock and forend with eight-panel fleur de lis borders. Introduced 1999. Made in U.S. by Itaca Classic Doubles.
Price: From **$8,399.00**

LEBEAU - COURALLY BOXLOCK SxS SHOTGUN

Gauge: 12, 16, 20, 28, 410-bore. **Barrel:** 25" to 32". **Weight:** To customer specifications. **Stock:** French walnut. **Features:** Anson & Deely-type action with automatic ejectors; single or double triggers. Essentially a custom gun built to customer specifications. Imported from Belgium by Wm. Larkin Moore.
Price: From **$23,000.00**

LEBEAU - COURALLY SIDELOCK SxS SHOTGUN

Gauge: 12, 16, 20, 28, 410-bore. **Barrel:** 25" to 32". **Weight:** To customer specifications. **Stock:** Fancy French walnut. **Features:** Holland & Holland-type action with automatic ejectors; single or double triggers. Essentially a custom gun built to customer specifications. Imported from Belgium by Wm. Larkin Moore.
Price: From **$47,000.00**

MERKEL MODEL 47E, 147E SIDE-BY-SIDE SHOTGUNS

Gauge: 12, 3" chambers, 16, 2-3/4" chambers, 20, 3" chambers. **Barrel:** 12, 16 ga.—28"; 20 ga.—26-3/4" (Imp. Cyl. & Mod., Mod. & Full). **Weight:** About 6-3/4 lbs. (12 ga.). **Stock:** Oil-finished walnut; straight English or pistol grip. **Features:** Anson & Deeley-type boxlock action with single selective or double triggers, automatic safety, cocking indicators. Color case-hardened receiver with standard Arabesque engraving. Imported from Germany by GSI.
Price: Model 47E (H&H ejectors) **$2,795.00**
Price: Model 147E (as above with ejectors) **$3,395.00**

SHOTGUNS

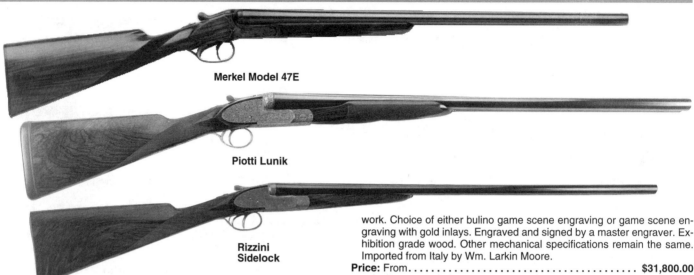

Merkel Model 47E

Piotti Lunik

Rizzini Sidelock

Merkel Model 47SL, 147SL Side-by-Sides

Similar to the Model 122 except with Holland & Holland-style sidelock action with cocking indicators, ejectors. Silver-grayed receiver and sideplates have Arabesque engraving, engraved border and screws (Model 47S), or fine hunting scene engraving (Model 147S). Imported from Germany by GSI.

Price: Model 47SL **$5,395.00**
Price: Model 147SL **$6,995.00**
Price: Model 247SL (English-style engraving, large scrolls) ... **$6,995.00**
Price: Model 447SL (English-style engraving, small scrolls) ... **$8,995.00**

Merkel Model 280EL and 360EL Shotguns

Similar to Model 47E except has smaller frame. Greener cross bolt with double under-barrel locking lugs, fine engraved hunting scenes on silver-grayed receiver, luxury-grade wood, Anson and Deely box-lock action. Holland & Holland ejectors, single-selective or double triggers. Introduced 2000. From Merkel.

Price: Model 280EL (28 gauge, 28" barrel, imp. cyl. and
mod. chokes) 4 mod. chokes).. .... **$4,995.00**
Price: Model 360EL (410 gauge, 28" barrel, mod. and
full chokes). **$4,995.00**
Price: Model 280/360EL two-barrel set (28 and 410 gauge
as above) **$7,495.00**

Merkel Model 280SL and 360SL Shotguns

Similar to Model 280EL and 360EL except has sidelock action, double triggers, English-style Arabesque engraving. Introduced 2000. From Merkel.

Price: Model 280SL (28 gauge, 28" barrel, imp. cyl. and
mod. chokes) **$7,495.00**
Price: Model 360SL (410 gauge, 28" barrel, mod. and
full chokes) **$7,495.00**
Price: Model 280/360SL two-barrel set **$10,995.00**

PIOTTI KING NO. 1 SIDE-BY-SIDE

Gauge: 12, 16, 20, 28, 410. **Barrel:** 25" to 30" (12 ga.), 25" to 28" (16, 20, 28, 410). To customer specs. Chokes as specified. **Weight:** 6-1/2 lbs. to 8 lbs. (12 ga. to customer specs.). **Stock:** Dimensions to customer specs. Finely figured walnut; straight grip with checkered butt with classic splinter forend and hand-rubbed oil finish standard. Pistol grip, beavertail forend, satin luster finish optional. **Features:** Holland & Holland pattern sidelock action, automatic ejectors. Double trigger with front trigger hinged standard; non-selective single trigger optional. Coin finish standard; color case-hardened optional. Top rib; level, file-cut standard; concave, ventilated optional. Very fine, full coverage scroll engraving with small floral bouquets, gold crown in top lever, name in gold, and gold crest in forend. Imported from Italy by Wm. Larkin Moore.

Price: From. **$25,600.00**

Piotti King Extra Side-by-Side

Similar to the Piotti King No. 1 except highest quality wood and metal work. Choice of either bulino game scene engraving or game scene engraving with gold inlays. Engraved and signed by a master engraver. Exhibition grade wood. Other mechanical specifications remain the same. Imported from Italy by Wm. Larkin Moore.

Price: From. **$31,800.00**

Piotti Lunik Side-by-Side

Similar to the Piotti King No. 1 in overall quality. Has Renaissance-style large scroll engraving in relief, gold crown in top lever. Best quality Holland & Holland-pattern sidelock ejector double with chopper lump (demi-bloc) barrels. Other mechanical specifications remain the same. Imported from Italy by Wm. Larkin Moore.

Price: From. **$27,500.00**

PIOTTI PIUMA SIDE-BY-SIDE

Gauge: 12, 16, 20, 28, 410. **Barrel:** 25" to 30" (12 ga.), 25" to 28" (16, 20, 28, 410). **Weight:** 5-1/2 to 6-1/4 lbs. (20 ga.). **Stock:** Dimensions to customer specs. Straight grip stock with walnut checkered butt, classic splinter forend, hand-rubbed oil finish are standard; pistol grip, beavertail forend, satin luster finish optional. **Features:** Anson & Deeley boxlock ejector double with chopper lump barrels. Level, file-cut rib, light scroll and rosette engraving, scalloped frame. Double triggers with hinged front standard, single non-selective optional. Coin finish standard, color case-hardened optional. Imported from Italy by Wm. Larkin Moore.

Price: From. **$13,400.00**

RIZZINI SIDELOCK SIDE-BY-SIDE

Gauge: 12, 16, 20, 28, 410. **Barrel:** 25" to 30" (12, 16, 20 ga.), 25" to 28" (28, 410). To customer specs. Chokes as specified. **Weight:** 6-1/2 lbs. to 8 lbs. (12 ga. to customer specs). **Stock:** Dimensions to customer specs. Finely figured walnut; straight grip with checkered butt with classic splinter forend and hand-rubbed oil finish standard. Pistol grip, beavertail forend, satin luster finish optional. **Features:** Holland & Holland pattern sidelock action, auto ejectors. Double triggers with front trigger hinged optional; non-selective single trigger standard. Coin finish standard. Top rib level, file cut standard; concave optional. Imported from Italy by Wm. Larkin Moore.

Price: 12, 20 ga., from **$45,000.00**
Price: 28, 410 bore, from **$50,000.00**

SKB Model 385 Sporting Clays

Similar to the Field Model 385 except 12 gauge only; 28" barrel with choke tubes; raised ventilated rib with metal middle bead and white front. Stock dimensions 14-1/4"x1-7/16"x1-7/8". Introduced 1998. Imported from Japan by G.U. Inc.

Price: **$1,899.00**
Price: Sporting Clays set, 20, 28 ga. **$2,699.00**

SKB MODEL 385 SIDE-BY-SIDE

Gauge: 12, 20, 3" chambers; 28, 2-3/4" chambers. **Barrel:** 26" (Imp. Cyl., Mod., Skeet choke tubes). **Weight:** 6-3/4 lbs. **Length:** 42-1/2" overall. **Stock:** 14-1/8"x1-1/2"x2-1/2" American walnut with straight or pistol grip stock, semi-beavertail forend. **Features:** Boxlock action. Silver nitrided receiver with engraving; solid barrel rib; single selective trigger, selective automatic ejectors, automatic safety. Introduced 1996. Imported from Japan by G.U. Inc.

Price: **$1,799.00**
Price: Field Set, 20, 28 ga., 26" or 28", English or pistol grip... **$2,579.00**

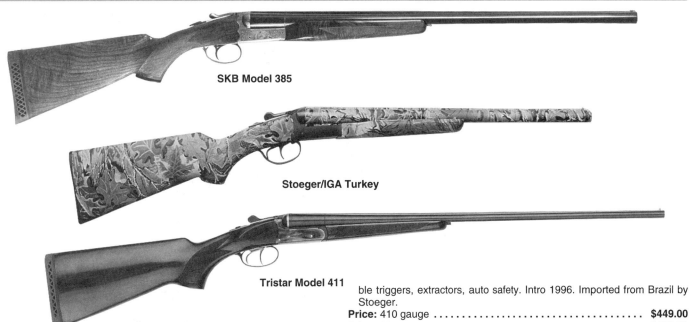

SKB Model 385

Stoeger/IGA Turkey

Tristar Model 411

SKB Model 485 Side-by-Side

Similar to the Model 385 except has dummy sideplates, raised ventilated rib with metal middle bead and white front, extensive upland game scene engraving, semi-fancy American walnut English or pistol grip stock. Imported from Japan by G.U. Inc.
Price: $2,439.00
Price: Field set, 20, 28 ga., 26" $3,479.00

STOEGER/IGA UPLANDER SIDE-BY-SIDE SHOTGUN

Gauge: 12, 20, 28, 2-3/4" chambers; 410, 3" chambers. **Barrel:** 26" (Full & Full, 410 only, Imp. Cyl. & Mod.), 28" (Mod. & Full). **Weight:** 6-3/4 to 7 lbs. **Stock:** 14-1/2"x1-1/2"x2-1/2". Oil-finished hardwood. Checkered pistol grip and forend. **Features:** Automatic safety, extractors only, solid matted barrel rib. Double triggers only. Introduced 1983. Imported from Brazil by Stoeger Industries.
Price: $437.00
Price: With choke tubes $477.00
Price: Coach Gun, 12, 20, 410, 20" bbls. $415.00
Price: Coach Gun, nickel finish, black stock. $464.00
Price: Coach Gun, engraved stock. $479.00

Stoeger/IGA Ladies Side-by-Side

Similar to the Uplander except in 20 ga. only with 24" barrels (Imp. Cyl. & Mod. choke tubes), 13" length of pull, ventilated rubber recoil pad. Has extractors, double triggers, automatic safety. Introduced 1996. Imported from Brazil by Stoeger.
Price: $489.00

Stoeger/IGA Turkey Side-by-Side

Similar to the Uplander Model except has Advantage camouflage on stock, forend and barrels; 12 gauge only with 3" chambers, and has 24" choke tube barrels. Overall length 40". Introduced 1997. Imported from Brazil by Stoeger.
Price: $559.00

Stoeger/IGA English Stock Side-by-Side

Similar to the Uplander except in 410 or 20 ga. only with 24" barrels, straight English stock and beavertail forend. Has automatic safety, extractors, double triggers. Intro 1996. Imported from Brazil by Stoeger.
Price: 410 ga (mod. and mod. chokes). $437.00
Price: 20 ga (imp. cyl and mod. choke tubes) $477.00

Stoeger/IGA Youth Side-by-Side

Similar to the Uplander except in 410-bore with 24" barrels (Mod.), or 20 ga. (imp. cyl. and mod.), 13" length of pull, ventilated recoil pad. Has dou-

ble triggers, extractors, auto safety. Intro 1996. Imported from Brazil by Stoeger.
Price: 410 gauge $449.00
Price: 20 gauge $449.00

Stoeger/IGA Coach and Deluxe Coach Gun

Similar to the Uplander except 12, 20 or 410 gauges, 20" barrels, choked Imp. Cyl. & Mod., 3" chambers; hardwood pistol grip stock with checkering; double triggers; extractors. Introduced 1997. Imported form Brazil by Stoeger.
Price: Coach Gun. $415.00
Price: Deluxe Coach Gun (engraved stagecoach on stock). $415.00

Stoeger/IGA Uplander Shotgun

Gauge: 12, 20, 410 (3" chambers); 28 (2-3/4" chambers). **Barrel:** 24", 26", 28". **Weight:** 6-3/4 lbs. **Length:** 40" to 44" overall. **Stock:** Brazilian hardwood; checkered grip and forearm. **Features:** Automatic safety; extractors; handles steel shot. Introduced 1997. Imported from Brazil by Stoeger.
Price: With chokes tubes $477.00

Stoeger/IGA Deluxe Uplander Supreme Shotgun

Similar to the Uplander except with semi-fancy American walnut with thin black Pachmayr rubber recoil pad, matte lacquer finish. Choke tubes and 3" chambers standard 12 and 20 gauge; 28 gauge has 26", 3" chokes, fixed Mod. & Full. Double gold plated triggers; extractors. Introduced 1997. Imported from Brazil by Stoeger.
Price: 12, 20. . . . . $599.00

TRISTAR MODEL 411 SIDE-BY-SIDE

Gauge: 12, 16, 20, 410, 3" chambers; 28, 2-3/4". **Barrel:** 12 ga., 26", 28"; 16, 20, 28 ga., 410-bore, 26"; 12 and 20 ga. have three choke tubes, 16, 28 (Imp. Cyl. & Mod.), 410 (Mod. & Full) fixed chokes. **Weight:** 6-6-3/4 lbs. **Stock:** 14-3/8" l.o.p. Standard walnut with pistol grip, splinter-style forend; hand checkered. **Features:** Engraved, color case-hardened boxlock action; double triggers, extractors; solid barrel rib. Introduced 1998. Imported from Italy by Tristar Sporting Arms, Ltd.
Price: $808.00

Tristar Model 411D Side-by-Side

Similar to the model 411 except has automatic ejectors, straight English-style stock, single trigger. Solid barrel rib with matted surface; chrome bores; color case-hardened frame; splinter forend. Introduced 1999. Imported from Italy by Tristar Sporting Arms, Ltd.
Price: $1,057.00

Tristar Model 411R Coach Gun Side-by-Side

Similar to the Model 411 except in 12 or 20 gauge only with 20" barrels and fixed chokes (Cyl. & Cyl.). Has double triggers, extractors, choke tubes. Introduced 1999. Imported from Italy by Tristar Sporting Arms, Ltd.
Price: $705.00

SHOTGUNS

Variety of designs for utility and sporting purposes, as well as for competitive shooting.

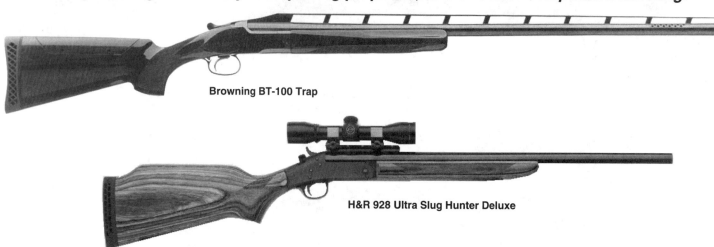

Browning BT-100 Trap

H&R 928 Ultra Slug Hunter Deluxe

BERETTA DT 10 TRIDENT TRAP TOP SINGLE SHOTGUN

Gauge: 12, 3" chamber. **Barrel:** 34"; five Optima Choke tubes (full, full, imp. modified, mod. and imp. cyl.). **Weight:** 8.8 lbs. **Length:** N/A. **Stock:** High-grade walnut; adjustable. **Features:** Detachable, adjustable trigger group; Optima Bore for improved shot pattern and reduced recoil; slim Optima Choke tubes; raised and thickened receiver for long life. Introduced 2000. Imported from Italy by Beretta USA.
Price: **$9,450.00**

BRNO ZBK 100 SINGLE BARREL SHOTGUN

Gauge: 12 or 20. **Barrel:** 27.5". **Weight:** 5.5 lbs. **Length:** 44" overall. **Stock:** Beech. **Features:** Polished blue finish; sling swivels. Announced 1998. Imported from The Czech Republic by Euro-Imports.
Price: **$185.00**

BROWNING BT-100 TRAP SHOTGUN

Gauge: 12, 2-3/4" chamber. **Barrel:** 32", 34" (Invector Plus); back-bored; also with fixed Full choke. **Weight:** 8 lbs., 9 oz. **Length:** 48-1/2" overall (32" barrel). **Stock:** 14-3/8"x1-9/16"x1-7/16x2" (Monte Carlo); 14-3/8"x1-3/4"x1-1/4"x2-1/8" (thumbhole). Walnut with high gloss finish; cut checkering. Wedge-shaped forend with finger groove. **Features:** Available in stainless steel or blue. Has drop-out trigger adjustable for weight of pull from 3-1/2 to 5-1/2 lbs., and for three length postions; Ejector-Selector allows ejection or extraction of shells. Available with adjustable comb stock and thumbhole style. Introduced 1995. Imported from Japan by Browning.
Price: Grade I, blue, Monte Carlo, Invector Plus **$2,095.00**
Price: As above, fixed Full choke **$2,046.00**
Price: With low-luster wood **$1,667.00**
Price: Stainless steel, Monte Carlo, Invector Plus **$2,536.00**
Price: As above, fixed Full choke **$2,487.00**
Price: Thumbhole stock, blue, Invector Plus **$2,384.00**
Price: Thumbhole stock, stainless, Invector Plus **$2,825.00**
Price: Thumbhole stock, blue, fixed choke **$2,337.00**
Price: Thumbhole stock, stainless, fixed choke **$2,778.00**
Price: BT-100 Satin (no ejector-selector, satin finish wood, metal) **$1,667.00**

EAA/BAIKAL IZH-18 SINGLE BARREL SHOTGUN

Gauge: 12 (2-3/4" and 3" chambers), 20 (2-3/4" and 3"), 16 (2-3/4"), 410 (3"). **Barrel:** 26-1/2", 28-1/2"; modified or full choke (12 and 20 gauge); full only (16 gauge), improved cylinder (20 gauge) and full or improved modified (410). **Weight:** N/A. **Stock:** Walnut-stained hardwood; rubber recoil pad. **Features:** Hammer-forged steel barrel; machined receiver; cross-block safety; cocking lever with external cocking indicator; optional automatic ejector, screw-in chokes and rifle barrel. Imported by European American Armory.
Price: IZH-18 (12, 16, 20 or 410) **$95.00**
Price: IZH-18 (20 gauge with imp. cyl. or 410 with imp. mod.) **$109.00**

HARRINGTON & RICHARDSON SB2-980 ULTRA SLUG

Gauge: 12, 20, 3" chamber. **Barrel:** 22" (20 ga. Youth) 24", fully rifled. **Weight:** 9 lbs. **Length:** NA. **Stock:** Walnut-stained hardwood. **Sights:** None furnished; comes with scope mount. **Features:** Uses the H&R 10 gauge action with heavy-wall barrel. Monte Carlo stock has sling swivels; comes with black nylon sling. Introduced 1995. Made in U.S. by H&R 1871, Inc.
Price: **$209.95**

Harrington & Richardson Model 928 Ultra Slug Hunter Deluxe

Similar to the SB2-980 Ultra Slug except uses 12 gauge action and 12 gauge barrel blank bored to 20 gauge, then fully rifled with 1:35" twist. Has hand-checkered camo laminate Monte Carlo stock and forend. Comes with Weaver-style scope base, offset hammer extension, ventilated recoil pad, sling swivels and camo nylon sling. Introduced 1997. Made in U.S. by H&R 1871 Inc.
Price: **$239.95**

HARRINGTON & RICHARDSON TAMER SHOTGUN

Gauge: 410, 3" chamber. **Barrel:** 19-1/2" (Full). **Weight:** 5-6 lbs. **Length:** 33" overall. **Stock:** Thumbhole grip of high density black polymer. **Features:** Uses H&R Topper action with matte electroless nickel finish. Stock holds four spare shotshells. Introduced 1994. From H&R 1871, Inc.
Price: **$124.95**

HARRINGTON & RICHARDSON TOPPER MODEL 098

Gauge: 12, 16, 20, 28 (2-3/4"), 410, 3" chamber. **Barrel:** 12 ga.—28" (Mod., Full); 16 ga.— 28" (Mod.); 20 ga.—26" (Mod.); 28 ga.—26" (Mod.); 410 bore—26" (Full). **Weight:** 5-6 lbs. **Stock:** Black-finish hardwood with full pistol grip; semi-beavertail forend. **Sights:** Gold bead front. **Features:** Break-open action with side-lever release, automatic ejector. Satin nickel frame, blued barrel. Reintroduced 1992. From H&R 1871, Inc.
Price: **$114.95**
Price: Topper Junior 098 (as above except 22" barrel, 20 ga. (Mod.), 410-bore (Full), 12-1/2" length of pull) **$119.95**

Harrington & Richardson Topper Deluxe Model 098

Similar to the standard Topper 098 except 12 gauge only with 3-1/2" chamber, 28" barrel with choke tube (comes with Mod. tube, others optional). Satin nickel frame, blued barrel, black-finished wood. Introduced 1992. From H&R 1871, Inc.
Price: **$134.95**

Harrington & Richardson Topper Junior Classic Shotgun

Similar to the Topper Junior 098 except available in 20 gauge (3", Mod.), 410-bore (Full) with 3" chamber; 28 gauge, 2-3/4" chamber (Mod.); all have 22" barrel. Stock is American black walnut with cut-checkered pistol grip and forend. Ventilated rubber recoil pad with white line spacers. Blued barrel, blued frame. Introduced 1992. From H&R 1871, Inc.
Price: **$144.95**

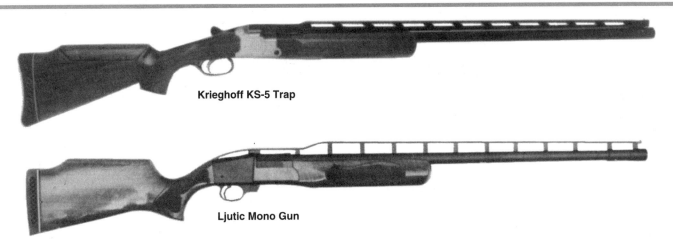

Krieghoff KS-5 Trap

Ljutic Mono Gun

Harrington & Richardson Topper Deluxe Rifled Slug Gun

Similar to the 12 gauge Topper Model 098 except has fully rifled and ported barrel, ramp front sight and fully adjustable rear. Barrel twist is 1:35". Nickel-plated frame, blued barrel, black-finished stock and forend. Introduced 1995. Made in U.S. by H&R 1871, Inc.

Price: **$169.95**

KRIEGHOFF K-80 SINGLE BARREL TRAP GUN

Gauge: 12, 2-3/4" chamber. **Barrel:** 32" or 34" Unsingle; 34" Top Single. Fixed Full or choke tubes. **Weight:** About 8-3/4 lbs. **Stock:** Four stock dimensions or adjustable stock available. All hand-checkered European walnut. **Features:** Satin nickel finish with K-80 logo. Selective mechanical trigger adjustable for finger position. Tapered step vent. rib. Adjustable point of impact on Unsingle.

Price: Standard grade full Unsingle, from................. **$7,950.00**
Price: Standard grade full Top Single combo (special order),
from **$9,975.00**
Price: RT (removable trigger) option, add **$1,000.00**

KRIEGHOFF KS-5 TRAP GUN

Gauge: 12, 2-3/4" chamber. **Barrel:** 32", 34"; Full choke or choke tubes. **Weight:** About 8-1/2 lbs. **Stock:** Choice of high Monte Carlo (1-1/2"), low Monte Carlo (1-3/8") or factory adjustable stock. European walnut. **Features:** Ventilated tapered step rib. Adjustable trigger or optional release trigger. Satin gray electroless nickel receiver. Comes with fitted aluminum case. Introduced 1988. Imported from Germany by Krieghoff International, Inc.

Price: Fixed choke, cased **$3,695.00**
Price: With choke tubes **$4,120.00**

Krieghoff KS-5 Special

Same as the KS-5 except the barrel has a fully adjustable rib and adjustable stock. Rib allows shooter to adjust point of impact from 50%/50% to nearly 90%/10%. Introduced 1990.

Price: **$4,695.00**

LJUTIC MONO GUN SINGLE BARREL

Gauge: 12 only. **Barrel:** 34", choked to customer specs; hollow-milled rib, 35-1/2" sight plane. **Weight:** Approx. 9 lbs. **Stock:** To customer specs. Oil finish, hand checkered. **Features:** Totally custom made. Pull or release trigger; removable trigger guard contains trigger and hammer mechanism; Ljutic pushbutton opener on front of trigger guard. From Ljutic Industries.

Price: With standard, medium or Olympic rib, custom 32"-34" bbls., and
fixed choke. **$5,795.00**
Price: As above with screw-in choke barrel **$6,095.00**
Price: Stainless steel mono gun........................ **$6,795.00**

Ljutic LTX PRO 3 Deluxe Mono Gun

Deluxe light weight version of the Mono Gun with high quality wood, upgrade checkering, special rib height, screw in chokes, ported and cased.

Price: **$8,995.00**
Price: Stainless steel model **$9,995.00**

MARLIN MODEL 55GDL GOOSE GUN
BOLT-ACTION SHOTGUN

Gauge: 12 only, 2-3/4" or 3" chamber. **Action:** Bolt action, thumb safety, detachable two-shot clip. Red cocking indicator. **Barrel:** 36" (Full) with burnished bore for lead or steel shot. **Weight:** 8 lbs. **Length:** 56-3/4" overall. **Stock:** Black fiberglass-filled synthetic with moulded-in checkering and swivel studs; ventilated recoil pad. **Sights:** Brass bead front, U-groove rear. **Features:** Brushed blue finish; thumb safety; red cocking indicator; 2-shot detachable box magazine. Introduced 1997. Made in U.S. by Marlin Firearms Co.

Price: **$396.00**

MARLIN MODEL 25MG GARDEN GUN SHOTGUN

Gauge: 22 WMR shotshell, 7-shot magazine. **Barrel:** 22" smoothbore. **Weight:** 6 lbs. **Length:** 41" overall. **Stock:** Press-checkered hardwood. **Sights:** High-visibility bead front. **Features:** Bolt action; thumb safety; red cocking indicator. Introduced 1999. Made in U.S. by Marlin.

Price: **$231.00**

MARLIN MODEL 512P SLUGMASTER SHOTGUN

Gauge: 12, 3" chamber; 2-shot detachable box magazine. **Barrel:** 21", rifled (1:28" twist). **Weight:** 8 lbs. **Length:** 41-3/4" overall. **Stock:** Black fiberglass-filled synthetic stock with moulded-in checkering, swivel studs; ventilated recoil pad; padded black nylon sling. **Sights:** Ramp front with brass bead and removable Wide-Scan hood and fiber-optic inserts, adjustable fiber-optic rear. Drilled and tapped for scope mounting. **Features:** Uses Model 55 action with thumb safety. Designed for shooting saboted slugs. Comes with special Weaver scope mount. Introduced 1997. Made in U.S. by Marlin Firearms Co.

Price: **$377.00**

Marlin Model 512P Slugmaster Shotgun

Similar to the Model 512 except has black fiberglass-filled synthetic stock with moulded-in checkering, swivel studs; ventilated recoil pad; padded black nylon sling. Has 21" fully rifled and ported barrel with 1:28" rifling twist. Introduced 1997. Made in U.S. by Marlin Firearms Co.

Price: **$377.00**

MOSSBERG MODEL 695 SLUGSTER

Gauge: 12, 3" chamber. **Barrel:** 22"; fully rifled, ported. **Weight:** 7-1/2 lbs. **Stock:** Black synthetic, with swivel studs and rubber recoil pad. **Sights:** Blade front, folding rifle-style leaf rear; Fiber Optic. Comes with Weaver-style scope bases. **Features:** Matte metal finish; rotating thumb safety; detachable 2-shot magazine. Mossberg Cablelock. Made in U.S. by Mossberg. Introduced 1996.

Price: **$345.00**
Price: With Fiber Optic rifle sights **$367.00**
Price: Scope Combo Model includes Protecto case and Bushnell
1.5-4.5x scope .... **NA**
Price: With woodlands camo stock, Fiber Optic sights......... **$397.00**

Mossberg 695

New England Firearms Camo Turkey

Ruger KTS-1234-BRE

MOSSBERG SSi-ONE 12 GAUGE SLUG SHOTGUN

NEW! Gauge: 12, 3" chamber. **Barrel:** 24", fully rifled. **Weight:** 8 pounds. **Length:** 40" overall. **Stock:** Walnut, fluted and cut checkered; sling-swivel studs; drilled and tapped for scope base. **Sights:** None (scope base supplied). **Features:** Frame accepts interchangeable rifle barrels (see Mossberg SSi-One rifle listing); lever-opening, break-action design; ambidextrous, top-tang safety; internal eject/extract selector. Introduced 2000. From Mossberg.
Price: **$400.00**

NEW ENGLAND FIREARMS CAMO TURKEY SHOTGUN

NEW! Gauge: 10, 3 1/2 "chamber. **Barrel:** 24"; extra-full, screw-in choke tube. **Weight:** N/A. **Stock:** American hardwood, green and black camouflage finish with sling swivels and ventilated recoil pad. **Sights:** Bead front. **Features:** Matte metal finish; stock counterweight to reduce recoil; patented transfer bar system for hammer-down safety; includes camo sling and trigger lock. Accepts other factory-fitted barrels. Introduced 2000. From New England Firearms.
Price: $205.95

NEW ENGLAND FIREARMS TRACKER SLUG GUN

Gauge: 12, 20, 3" chamber. **Barrel:** 24" (Cyl.). **Weight:** 5-1/4 lbs. **Length:** 40" overall. **Stock:** Walnut-finished hardwood with full pistol grip, recoil pad. **Sights:** Blade front, fully adjustable rifle-type rear. **Features:** Break-open action with side-lever release; blued barrel, color case-hardened frame. Introduced 1992. From New England Firearms.
Price: Tracker **$129.95**
Price: Tracker II (as above except fully rifled bore) **$139.95**

NEW ENGLAND FIREARMS SPECIAL PURPOSE SHOTGUNS

Gauge: 10, 3-1/2" chamber. **Barrel:** 28" (Full), 32" (Mod.). **Weight:** 9.5 lbs. **Length:** 44" overall (28" barrel). **Stock:** American hardwood with walnut or matte camo finish; ventilated rubber recoil pad. **Sights:** Bead front. **Features:** Break-open action with side-lever release; ejector. Matte finish on metal. Introduced 1992. From New England Firearms.
Price: Walnut-finish wood sling and swivels................. **$149.95**
Price: Camo finish, sling and swivels **$159.95**
Price: Camo finish, 32", sling and swivels **$179.95**
Price: Black matte finish, 24", Turkey Full choke tube, sling and swivels
.... **$184.95**

NEW ENGLAND FIREARMS SURVIVOR

Gauge: 12, 20, 410/45 Colt, 3" chamber. **Barrel:** 22" (Mod.); 20" (410/45 Colt, rifled barrel, choke tube). **Weight:** 6 lbs. **Length:** 36 overall. **Stock:** Black polymer with thumbhole/pistol grip, sling swivels; beavertail forend. **Sights:** Bead front. **Features:** Buttplate removes to expose storage for extra ammunition; forend also holds extra ammunition. Black or nickel finish. Introduced 1993. From New England Firearms.

Price: Black **$129.95**
Price: Nickel... **$145.95**
Price: 410/45 Colt, black **$145.95**
Price: 410/45 Colt, nickel **$164.95**

NEW ENGLAND FIREARMS STANDARD PARDNER

Gauge: 12, 20, 410, 3" chamber; 16, 28, 2-3/4" chamber. **Barrel:** 12 ga.—28" (Full, Mod.), 32" (Full); 16 ga.—28" (Full), 32" (Full); 20 ga.—26" (Full, Mod.); 28 ga.—26" (Mod.); 410-bore—26" (Full). **Weight:** 5-6 lbs. **Length:** 43" overall (28" barrel). **Stock:** Walnut-finished hardwood with full pistol grip. **Sights:** Bead front. **Features:** Transfer bar ignition; break-open action with side-lever release. Introduced 1987. From New England Firearms.
Price: **$99.95**
Price: Youth model (12, 20, 28 ga., 410, 22" barrel, recoil pad).. **$109.95**
Price: 12 ga., 32" (Full)................................. **$104.95**

RUGER KTS-1234-BRE TRAP MODEL
SINGLE-BARREL SHOTGUN

Gauge: 12, 2 3/4" chamber. **Barrel:** 34". **Weight:** 9 lbs. **Length:** 50 1/2" overall. **Stock:** Select walnut checkered; adjustable pull length 13 -15". **Features:** Fully adjustable rib for pattern position; adjustable stock comb cast for right- or left-handed shooters; straight grooves the length of barrel to keep wad from rotating for pattern improvement. Full and modified choke tubes supplied. Gold inlaid eagle and Ruger name on receiver. Introduced 2000. From Sturm Ruger & Co.
Price: **$2,850.00**

ROSSI MODEL 12-G SHOTGUN

Gauge: 12, 20, 2-3/4" chamber; 410, 3" chamber. **Barrel:** 28". **Weight:** 5 lbs. **Length:** NA. **Stock:** Stained hardwood. **Features:** Spur hammer; intregral safety; ejector; spur hammer. Imported from Brazil by BrazTech.
Price: **$119.00**
Price: Youth (shorter stock, 22" barrel) **$119.00**

Tar-Hunt Mountaineer

SAVAGE MODEL 210F MASTER SHOT SLUG GUN

Gauge: 12, 3" chamber; 2-shot magazine. **Barrel:** 24" 1:35" rifling twist. **Weight:** 7-1/2 lbs. **Length:** 43.5" overall. **Stock:** Glass-filled polymer with positive checkering. **Features:** Based on the Savage Model 110 action; 60 bolt lift; controlled round feed; comes with scope mount. Introduced 1996. Made in U.S. by Savage Arms.
Price: $402.00

Savage Model 210FT Master Shot Shotgun

Similar to the Model 210F except has smoothbore barrel threaded for Winchoke-style choke tubes (comes with one Full tube); Advantage camo pattern covers the stock; pillar-bedded synthetic stock; bead front sight, U-notch rear. Introduced 1997. Made in U.S. by Savage Arms, Inc.
Price: $466.00

SNAKE CHARMER II SHOTGUN

Gauge: 410, 3" chamber. **Barrel:** 18-1/4". **Weight:** About 3-1/2 lbs. **Length:** 28-5/8" overall. **Stock:** ABS grade impact resistant plastic. **Features:** Thumbhole-type stock holds four extra rounds. Stainless steel barrel and frame. Reintroduced 1989. From Sporting Arms Mfg., Inc.
Price: $149.00
Price: Snake Charmer II Field Gun (as above except has conventional wood buttstock with 14" length of pull, 24" barrel 410 or 28 ga.) $160.00
Price: New Generation Snake Charmer (as above except with black carbon steel bbl.) $139.00

TAR-HUNT RSG-12 PROFESSIONAL RIFLED SLUG GUN

Gauge: 12, 2-3/4" chamber, 1-shot magazine. **Barrel:** 21-1/2"; fully rifled, with muzzle brake. **Weight:** 7-3/4 lbs. **Length:** 41-1/2" overall. **Stock:** Matte black McMillan fiberglass with Pachmayr Decelerator pad. **Sights:** None furnished; comes with Leupold windage bases only. **Features:** Uses rifle-style action with two locking lugs; two-position safety; Shaw barrel; single-stage, trigger; muzzle brake. Many options available. Right- and left-hand models at same prices. Introduced 1991. Made in U.S. by Tar-Hunt Custom Rifles, Inc.
Price: Professional model, right- or left hand $1,395.00
Price: Matchless model (400-grit gloss metal finish, McMillan
Fibergrain stock), right- or left-hand $1,873.00
Price: Peerless model NP-3 nickel/Teflon metal finish, McMillan
Fibergrain stock, right- or left-hand. $2,072.00

Tar-Hunt RSG-20 Mountaineer Slug Gun

Similar to the RSG-12 Professional except chambered for 20 gauge (2-3/4") shells; 21" Shaw rifled barrel, with muzzle brake; two-lug bolt; one-shot blind magazine; matte black finish; McMillan fiberglass stock with Pachmayr Decelerator pad; receiver drilled and tapped for Rem. 700 bases. Weighs 6-1/2 lbs. Introduced 1997. Made in U.S. by Tar-Hunt Custom Rifles, Inc.
Price: $1,295.00

THOMPSON/CENTER ENCORE RIFLED SLUG GUN

Gauge: 20, 3" chamber. **Barrel:** 26", fully rifled. **Weight:** About 7 pounds. **Length:** 40-1/2" overall. **Stock:** Walnut with walnut forearm. **Sights:** Steel, click-adjustable rear and ramp-style front, both with fiber optics. **Features:** Encore system features a variety of rifle, shotgun and muzzle-loading rifle barrels interchangeable with the same frame. Break-open design operates by pulling up and back on trigger guard spur. Composite stock and forearm available. Introduced 2000.
Price: $612.48

WESSON & HARRINGTON LONG TOM CLASSIC SHOTGUN

Gauge: 12, 3" chamber. **Barrel:** 32", (Full). **Weight:** 7-1/2 lbs. **Length:** 46" overall. **Stock:** 14"x1-3/4"x2-5/8". American black walnut with hand-checkered grip and forend. **Features:** Color case-hardened receiver and crescent steel buttplate, blued barrel. Receiver engraved with the National Wild Turkey Federation logo. Introduced 1998. Made in U.S. by H&R 1871, Inc.
Price: $349.95

Designs for utility, suitable for and adaptable to competitions and other sporting purposes.

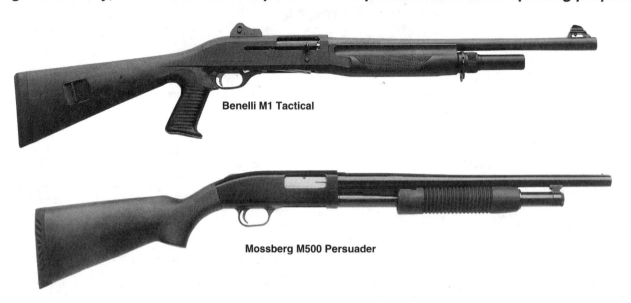

Benelli M1 Tactical

Mossberg M500 Persuader

AMERICAN ARMS PHANTOM HP AUTO SHOTGUN
Gauge: 12, 3" chamber. **Barrel:** 19"; threaded for external choke tubes. **Stock:** Black synthetic. **Sights:** Bead front. **Features:** Gas-operated action; blue/black finish; five-shot extended magazine tube. Imported by American Arms, Inc.
Price: .... **NA**

BENELLI M3 CONVERTIBLE SHOTGUN
Gauge: 12, 3" chamber, 5-shot magazine. **Barrel:** 19-3/4" (Cyl.). **Weight:** 7 lbs., 8 oz. **Length:** 41" overall. **Stock:** High-impact polymer with sling loop in side of butt; rubberized pistol grip on stock. **Sights:** Post front, buckhorn rear adjustable for windage. Ghost ring system available. **Features:** Combination pump/auto action. Alloy receiver with inertia recoil rotating locking lug bolt; matte finish; automatic shell release lever. Introduced 1989. Imported by Benelli USA.
Price: With standard stock, open rifle sights............... **$1,060.00**
Price: With ghost ring sight system, standard stock.......... **$1,100.00**
Price: With ghost ring sights, pistol grip stock **$1,120.00**

BENELLI M1 TACTICAL SHOTGUN
Gauge: 12, 3", 5-shot magazine. **Barrel:** 18.5", choke tubes. **Weight:** 6.5 lbs. **Length:** 39.75" overall. **Stock:** Black polymer. **Sights:** Rifle type with Ghost Ring system, tritium night sights optional. **Features:** Semi-auto intertia recoil action. Cross-bolt safety; bolt release button; matte-finish metal. Introduced 1993. Imported from Italy by Benelli USA.
Price: With rifle sights, standard stock **$890.00**
Price: With ghost ring rifle sights, standard stock............ **$960.00**
Price: With ghost ring sights, pistol grip stock **$970.00**
Price: With rifle sights, pistol grip stock **$910.00**

Benelli M1 Practical
Similar to M1 Field Shotgun, but with Picatinny receiver rail for scope mounting, nine-round magazine, 26" compensated barrel and ghost-ring sights. Designed for IPSC competition.
Price: **$1,200.00**

BENELLI M4 SUPER 90 JOINT SERVICE COMBAT SHOTGUN
NEW! **Gauge:** 12, 3" chamber. **Barrel:** 18.5". **Weight:** 8.4 pounds. **Length:** 39.8 inches. **Stock:** Synthetic, modular. **Sights:** Ghost-ring style, rear adjustable for windage and elevation using cartridge rim. **Features:** Auto-regulating, gas-operated (ARGO) action. Integral, Picatinny rail on receiver for sight mounting. Black matte finish. Improved cylinder. Can be reconfigured without tools with three buttstocks and two barrels. Introduced 2000. Imported from Italy by Benelli USA.
Price: .... **NA**

BERETTA MODEL 1201FP GHOST RING AUTO SHOTGUN
Gauge: 12, 3" chamber. **Barrel:** 18" (Cyl.). **Weight:** 6.3 lbs. **Stock:** Special strengthened technopolymer, matte black finish. **Stock:** Fixed rifle type. **Features:** Has 5-shot magazine. Adjustable Ghost Ring rear sight, tritium front. Introduced 1988. Imported from Italy by Beretta U.S.A.
Price: **$860.00**

CROSSFIRE SHOTGUN/RIFLE
Gauge/Caliber: 12, 2-3/4" chamber 4-shot/223 Rem. (5-shot). **Barrel:** 20" (shotgun), 18" (rifle). **Weight:** About 8.6 lbs. **Length:** 40" overall. **Stock:** Composite. **Sights:** Meprolight night sights. Integral Weaver-style scope rail. **Features:** Combination pump-action shotgun, rifle; single selector, single trigger; dual action bars for both upper and lower actions; ambidextrous selector and safety. Introduced 1997. Made in U.S. From Hesco.
Price: About **$1,895.00**
Price: With camo finish................................. **$1,995.00**

FABARM FP6 PUMP SHOTGUN
Gauge: 12, 3" chamber. **Barrel:** 20" (Cyl.); accepts choke tubes. **Weight:** 6.6 lbs. **Length:** 41.25" overall. **Stock:** Black polymer with textured grip, grooved slide handle. **Sights:** Blade front. **Features:** Twin action bars; anodized finish; free carrier for smooth reloading. Introduced 1998. Imported from Italy by Heckler & Koch, Inc.
Price: **$499.00**
Price: With flip-up front sight, Picatinny rail with rear sight, oversize safety button **$499.00**

MOSSBERG MODEL 500 PERSUADER SECURITY SHOTGUNS
Gauge: 12, 20, 410, 3" chamber. **Barrel:** 18-1/2", 20" (Cyl.). **Weight:** 7 lbs. **Stock:** Walnut-finished hardwood or black synthetic. **Sights:** Metal bead front. **Features:** Available in 6- or 8-shot models. Top-mounted safety, double action slide bars, swivel studs, rubber recoil pad. Blue, Parkerized, Marinecote finishes. Mossberg Cablelock included. From Mossberg.
Price: 12 or 20 ga., 18-1/2", blue, wood or synthetic stock, 6-shot **$307.00**
Price: Cruiser, 12 or 20 ga., 18-1/2", blue, pistol grip, heat shield .... **$298.00** to **$307.00**
Price: As above, 410-bore **$305.00**

Mossberg Model 500, 590 Mariner Pump
Similar to the Model 500 or 590 Security except all metal parts finished with Marinecote metal finish to resist rust and corrosion. Synthetic field stock; pistol grip kit included. Mossberg Cablelock included.
Price: 6-shot, 18-1/2" barrel **$416.00**
Price: 9-shot, 20" barrel **$370.00**

SHOTGUNS

Tactical Response TR-870

Winchester Model 1300 Defender

Mossberg Model HS410 Shotgun

Similar to the Model 500 Security pump except chambered for 20 gauge or 410 with 3" chamber; has pistol grip forend, thick recoil pad, muzzle brake and has special spreader choke on the 18.5" barrel. Overall length is 37.5", weight is 6.25 lbs. Blue finish; synthetic field stock. Mossberg Cablelock and video included. Introduced 1990.

Price: HS 410 . . . . **$319.00**

Mossberg Model 500, 590 Ghost-Ring Shotguns

Similar to the Model 500 Security except has adjustable blade front, adjustable Ghost-Ring rear sight with protective "ears." Model 500 has 18.5" (Cyl.) barrel, 6-shot capacity; Model 590 has 20" (Cyl.) barrel, 9-shot capacity. Both have synthetic field stock. Mossberg Cablelock included. Introduced 1990. From Mossberg.

Price: Model 500, blue **$307.00**
Price: As above, Parkerized **$416.00**
Price: Model 590, blue **$370.00**
Price: As above, Parkerized **$425.00**
Price: Parkerized Speedfeed stock . . . . **$462.00 to $519.00**

MOSSBERG MODEL 9200A1 JUNGLE GUN

Gauge: 12, 2-3/4" chamber; 5-shot magazine. **Barrel:** 18" (Cyl.). **Weight:** About 7 lbs. **Length:** 38-1/2" overall. **Stock:** Black synthetic. **Sights:** Bead front. **Features:** Designed to function only with 2-3/4" 00 Buck loads; Parkerized finish; mil-spec heavy wall barrel; military metal trigger housing; ambidextrous metal tang safety. Introduced 1998. Made in U.S. by Mossberg.

Price: **$704.00**

MOSSBERG MODEL 590 SHOTGUN

Gauge: 12, 3" chamber. **Barrel:** 20" (Cyl.). **Weight:** 7-1/4 lbs. **Stock:** Synthetic field or Speedfeed. **Sights:** Metal bead front. **Features:** Top-mounted safety, double slide action bars. Comes with heat shield, bayonet lug, swivel studs, rubber recoil pad. Blue, Parkerized or Marinecote finish. Mossberg Cablelock included. From Mossberg.

Price: Blue, synthetic stock. **$370.00**
Price: Parkerized, synthetic stock. **$425.00**
Price: Parkerized, Speedfeed stock **$450.00**

Mossberg 590DA Double-Action Pump Shotgun

Similar to Model 590 except trigger requires a long stroke for each shot, duplicating the trigger pull of double-action-only pistols and revolvers. Available in 12 gauge only with black synthetic stock and parkerized finish with 14" (law enforcement only), 18 1/2 "and 20" barrels. Six-shot magazine tube (nine-shot for 20" barrel). Front bead or ghost ring sights. Weighs 7 pounds (18 1/2" barrel). Introduced 2000. From Mossberg.

Price: Bead sight, 6-shot magazine **$510.00**
Price: Ghost ring sights, 6-shot magazine **$558.00**
Price: Bead sight, 9-shot magazine **$541.00**
Price: Ghost ring sights, 9-shot magazine **$597.00**

TACTICAL RESPONSE TR-870 STANDARD MODEL SHOTGUN

Gauge: 12, 3" chamber, 7-shot magazine. **Barrel:** 18" (Cyl.). **Weight:** 9 lbs. **Length:** 38" overall. **Stock:** Fiberglass-filled polypropolene with non-snag recoil absorbing butt pad. Nylon tactical forend houses flashlight. **Sights:** Trak-Lock ghost ring sight system. Front sight has tritium insert. **Features:** Highly modified Remington 870P with Parkerized finish. Comes with nylon three-way adjustable sling, high visibility non-binding follower, high performance magazine spring, Jumbo Head safety, and Side Saddle extended 6-shot shell carrier on left side of receiver. Introduced 1991. From Scattergun Technologies, Inc.

Price: Standard model **$815.00**
Price: FBI model. **$770.00**
Price: Patrol model. **$595.00**
Price: Border Patrol model **$605.00**
Price: K-9 model (Rem. 11-87 action) **$995.00**
Price: Urban Sniper, Rem. 11-87 action. **$1,290.00**
Price: Louis Awerbuck model **$705.00**
Price: Practical Turkey model. **$725.00**
Price: Expert model **$1,350.00**
Price: Professional model. **$815.00**
Price: Entry model **$840.00**
Price: Compact model **$635.00**
Price: SWAT model **$1,195.00**

WINCHESTER MODEL 1300 DEFENDER PUMP GUN

Gauge: 12, 20, 3" chamber, 5- or 8-shot capacity. **Barrel:** 18" (Cyl.). **Weight:** 6-3/4 lbs. **Length:** 38-5/8" overall. **Stock:** Walnut-finished hardwood stock and ribbed forend, or synthetic; or pistol grip. **Sights:** Metal bead front. **Features:** Cross-bolt safety, front-locking rotary bolt, twin action slide bars. Black rubber butt pad. From U.S. Repeating Arms Co.

Price: 8-shot, wood or synthetic stock **$321.00**

Winchester 8-Shot Pistol Grip Pump Security Shotgun

Same as regular Defender Pump but with pistol grip and forend of high-impact resistant ABS plastic with non-glare black finish. Introduced 1984.

Price: Pistol Grip Defender. **$321.00**

Winchester Model 1300 Stainless Marine Pump Gun

Same as the Defender except has bright chrome finish, stainless steel barrel, rifle-type sights only. Phosphate coated receiver for corrosion resistance. Pistol grip optional.

Price: **$511.00**

SHOTGUNS

| CVA Hawken | Dixie Pennsylvania | Harper's Ferry | Kentucky | Le Page |

CVA HAWKEN PISTOL

Caliber: 50. **Barrel:** 9-3/4"; 15/16" flats. **Weight:** 50 oz. **Length:** 16-1/2" overall. **Stocks:** Select hardwood. **Sights:** Beaded blade front, fully adjustable open rear. **Features:** Color case-hardened lock, polished brass wedge plate, instep, ramrod thimble, trigger guard, grip cap. Imported by CVA.

Price: **$149.95**
Price: Kit **$119.95**

DIXIE PENNSYLVANIA PISTOL

Caliber: 44 (.430" round ball). **Barrel:** 10", (7/8" octagon). **Weight:** 2-1/2 labs. **Stocks:** Walnut-stained hardwood. **Sights:** Blade front, open rear drift-adjustable for windage; brass. **Features:** Available in flint only. Brass trigger guard, thimbles, instep, wedge plates; high-luster blue barrel. Imported from Italy by Dixie Gun Works.

Price: Finished **$195.00**
Price: Kit **$185.00**

FRENCH-STYLE DUELING PISTOL

Caliber: 44. **Barrel:** 10". **Weight:** 35 oz. **Length:** 15-3/4" overall. **Stocks:** Carved walnut. **Sights:** Fixed. **Features:** Comes with velvet-lined case and accessories. Imported by Mandall Shooting Supplies.

Price: **$295.00**

HARPER'S FERRY 1806 PISTOL

Caliber: 58 (.570" round ball). **Barrel:** 10". **Weight:** 40 oz. **Length:** 16" overall. **Stocks:** Walnut. **Sights:** Fixed. **Features:** Case-hardened lock, brass-mounted browned barrel. Replica of the first U.S. Gov't.-made flint-lock pistol. Imported by Navy Arms, Dixie Gun Works.

Price: .... **$275.00** to **$405.00**
Price: Kit (Dixie) **$249.00**

KENTUCKY FLINTLOCK PISTOL

Caliber: 44, 45. **Barrel:** 10-1/8". **Weight:** 32 oz. **Length:** 15-1/2" overall. **Stocks:** Walnut. **Sights:** Fixed. **Features:** Specifications, including caliber, weight and length may vary with importer. Case-hardened lock, blued barrel; available also as brass barrel flint Model 1821. Imported by Navy Arms, The Armoury.

Price: .... **$145.00** to **$235.00**
Price: In kit form, from .... **$90.00** to **$112.00**
Price: Single cased set (Navy Arms) **$360.00**
Price: Double cased set (Navy Arms) **$590.00**

Kentucky Percussion Pistol

Similar to flint version but percussion lock. Imported by The Armoury, Navy Arms, CVA (50-cal.).

Price: .... **$129.95** to **$225.00**
Price: Steel barrel (Armoury) **$179.00**
Price: Single cased set (Navy Arms) **$355.00**
Price: Double cased set (Navy Arms) **$600.00**

LE PAGE PERCUSSION DUELING PISTOL

Caliber: 44. **Barrel:** 10", rifled. **Weight:** 40 oz. **Length:** 16" overall. **Stocks:** Walnut, fluted butt. **Sights:** Blade front, notch rear. **Features:** Double-set triggers. Blued barrel; trigger guard and buttcap are polished silver. Imported by Dixie Gun Works.

Price: **$259.95**

LYMAN PLAINS PISTOL

Caliber: 50 or 54. **Barrel:** 8"; 1:30" twist, both calibers. **Weight:** 50 oz. **Length:** 15" overall. **Stocks:** Walnut half-stock. **Sights:** Blade front, square notch rear adjustable for windage. **Features:** Polished brass trigger guard and ramrod tip, color case-hardened coil spring lock, spring-loaded trigger, stainless steel nipple, blackened iron furniture. Hooked patent breech, detachable belt hook. Introduced 1981. From Lyman Products.

Price: Finished **$229.95**
Price: Kit **$184.95**

BLACKPOWDER

Lyman Plains Pistol   **Pedersoli Mang**   **Queen Anne**   **Traditions Pioneer**   **Traditions William Parker**

Traditions Buckhunter Pro

PEDERSOLI MANG TARGET PISTOL

Caliber: 38. **Barrel:** 10.5", octagonal; 1:15" twist, **Weight:** 2.5 lbs. **Length:** 17.25" overall. **Stocks:** Walnut with fluted grip. **Sights:** Blade front, open rear adjustable for windage.
Features: Browned barrel, polished breech plug, rest color case-hardened. Imported from Italy by Dixie Gun Works.
Price: $786.00

QUEEN ANNE FLINTLOCK PISTOL

Caliber: 50 (.490" round ball). **Barrel:** 7-1/2", smoothbore. **Stocks:** Walnut. **Sights:** None. **Features:** Browned steel barrel, fluted brass trigger guard, brass mask on butt. Lockplate left in the white. Made by Pedersoli in Italy. Introduced 1983. Imported by Dixie Gun Works.
Price: $225.00
Price: Kit $175.00

THOMPSON/CENTER ENCORE 209x50 MAGNUM PISTOL

Caliber: 50. **Barrel:** 15"; 1:20" twist. **Weight:** About 4 lbs. **Grips:** American walnut grip and forend. **Sights:** Click-adjustable, steel rear, ramp front. **Features:** Uses 209 shotgun primer for closed-breech ignition; accepts charges up to 110 grains of FFg black powder or two, 50-grain Pyrodex pellets. Introduced 2000.
Price: $569.47

TRADITIONS BUCKHUNTER PRO IN-LINE PISTOL

Caliber: 50, 54. **Barrel:** 9-1/2", round. **Weight:** 48 oz. **Length:** 14" overall. **Stocks:** Smooth walnut or black epoxy coated grip and forend. **Sights:** Beaded blade front, folding adjustable rear. **Features:** Thumb safety; removable stainless steel breech plug; adjustable trigger, barrel drilled and tapped for scope mounting. From Traditions.
Price: With walnut grip $219.00
Price: Nickel with black grip $234.00
Price: With walnut grip and 12-1/2" barrel $234.00

TRADITIONS KENTUCKY PISTOL

Caliber: 50. **Barrel:** 10"; octagon with 7/8" flats; 1:20" twist. **Weight:** 40 oz. **Length:** 15" overall. **Stocks:** Stained beech. **Sights:** Blade front, fixed rear. **Features:** Birds-head grip; brass thimbles; color case-hardened lock. Percussion only. Introduced 1995. From Traditions.
Price: Finished $138.00
Price: Kit.. $109.00

TRADITIONS PIONEER PISTOL

Caliber: 45. **Barrel:** 9-5/8"; 13/16" flats, 1:16" twist. **Weight:** 31 oz. **Length:** 15" overall. **Stocks:** Beech. **Sights:** Blade front, fixed rear. **Features:** V-type mainspring. Single trigger. German silver furniture, blackened hardware. From Traditions.
Price: $140.00
Price: Kit.. $116.00

TRADITIONS TRAPPER PISTOL

Caliber: 50. **Barrel:** 9-3/4"; 7/8" flats; 1:20" twist. **Weight:** 2-3/4 lbs. **Length:** 16" overall. **Stocks:** Beech. **Sights:** Blade front, adjustable rear. **Features:** Double-set triggers; brass buttcap, trigger guard, wedge plate, forend tip, thimble. From Traditions.
Price: Percussion $189.00
Price: Flintlock $204.00
Price: Kit.. $145.00

TRADITIONS WILLIAM PARKER PISTOL

Caliber: 50. **Barrel:** 10-3/8"; 15/16" flats; polished steel. **Weight:** 37 oz. **Length:** 17-1/2" overall. **Stocks:** Walnut with checkered grip. **Sights:** Brass blade front, fixed rear. **Features:** Replica dueling pistol with 1:20" twist, hooked breech. Brass wedge plate, trigger guard, cap guard; separate ramrod. Double-set triggers. Polished steel barrel, lock. Imported by Traditions.
Price: $262.00

Army 1860

Colt 1860 Army

Baby Dragoon 1848

ARMY 1851 PERCUSSION REVOLVER

Caliber: 44, 6-shot. **Barrel:** 7-1/2". **Weight:** 45 oz. **Length:** 13" overall. **Stocks:** Walnut finish. **Sights:** Fixed. **Features:** 44-caliber version of the 1851 Navy. Imported by The Armoury, Armsport.
Price: **$129.00**

ARMY 1860 PERCUSSION REVOLVER

Caliber: 44, 6-shot. **Barrel:** 8". **Weight:** 40 oz. **Length:** 13-5/8" overall. **Stocks:** Walnut. **Sights:** Fixed. **Features:** Engraved Navy scene on cylinder; brass trigger guard; case-hardened frame, loading lever and hammer. Some importers supply pistol cut for detachable shoulder stock, have accessory stock available. Imported by Cabela's (1860 Lawman), E.M.F., Navy Arms, The Armoury, Cimarron, Dixie Gun Works (half-fluted cylinder, not roll engraved), Euroarms of America (brass or steel model), Armsport, Traditions (brass or steel), Uberti U.S.A. Inc., United States Patent Fire-Arms.
Price: About .... **$92.95 to $395.00**
Price: Hartford model, steel frame, German silver trim,
 cartouches (E.M.F.) **$215.00**
Price: Single cased set (Navy Arms) **$300.00**
Price: Double cased set (Navy Arms). **$490.00**
Price: 1861 Navy: Same as Army except 36-cal., 7-1/2" bbl., weighs 41 oz., cut for shoulder stock; round cylinder (fluted available), from Cabela's, CVA (brass frame, 44-cal.), United States Patent Fire-Arms
 .... **$99.95 to $385.00**
Price: Steel frame kit (E.M.F., Euroarms). .... **$125.00 to $216.25**
Price: Colt Army Police, fluted cyl., 5-1/2", 36-cal. (Cabela's) ... **$124.95**
Price: With nickeled frame, barrel and backstrap, gold-tone fluted cylinder, trigger and hammer, simulated ivory grips (Traditions) **$199.00**

BABY DRAGOON 1848, 1849 POCKET, WELLS FARGO

Caliber: 31. **Barrel:** 3", 4", 5", 6"; seven-groove; RH twist. **Weight:** About 21 oz. **Stocks:** Varnished walnut. **Sights:** Brass pin front, hammer notch rear. **Features:** No loading lever on Baby Dragoon or Wells Fargo models. Unfluted cylinder with stagecoach holdup scene; cupped cylinder pin; no grease grooves; one safety pin on cylinder and slot in hammer face; straight (flat) mainspring. From Armsport, Cimarron F.A. Co., Dixie Gun Works, Uberti U.S.A. Inc.
Price: 6" barrel, with loading lever (Dixie Gun Works) **$254.95**
Price: 4" (Uberti USA Inc.) **$335.00**

CABELA'S STARR PERCUSSION REVOLVERS

NEW! **Caliber:** 44. **Barrel:** 6", 8". **Weight:** N/A. **Length:** N/A. **Grips:** Walnut. **Sights:** Blade front. **Features:** Replicas of government-contract revolvers made by Ebenezer T. Starr. Knurled knob allows quick removal and replacement of cylinder. Introduced 2000. From Cabela's.
Price: Starr 1858 Army double action, 6" barrel. **$349.99**
Price: Starr 1863 Army single action, 8" barrel **$349.99**

COLT 1860 ARMY PERCUSSION REVOLVER

Caliber: 44. **Barrel:** 8", 7-groove, left-hand twist. **Weight:** 42 oz. **Stocks:** One-piece walnut. **Sights:** German silver front sight, hammer notch rear. **Features:** Steel backstrap cut for shoulder stock; brass trigger guard. Cylinder has Navy scene. Color case-hardened frame, hammer, loading lever. Reproduction of original gun with all original markings. From Colt Blackpowder Arms Co.
Price: **$449.95**

COLT 1848 BABY DRAGOON REVOLVER

Caliber: 31, 5-shot. **Barrel:** 4". **Weight:** About 21 oz. **Stocks:** Smooth walnut. **Sights:** Brass pin front, hammer notch rear. **Features:** Color case-hardened frame; no loading lever; square-back trigger guard; round bolt cuts; octagonal barrel; engraved cylinder scene. Imported by Colt Blackpowder Arms Co.
Price: **$429.95**

Colt 1860 "Cavalry Model" Percussion Revolver

Similar to the 1860 Army except has fluted cylinder. Color case-hardened frame, hammer, loading lever and plunger; blued barrel, backstrap and cylinder, brass trigger guard. Has four-screw frame cut for optional shoulder stock. From Colt Blackpowder Arms Co.
Price: **$399.95**

COLT 1851 NAVY PERCUSSION REVOLVER

Caliber: 36. **Barrel:** 7-1/2", octagonal; 7-groove left-hand twist. **Weight:** 40-1/2 oz. **Stocks:** One-piece oiled American walnut. **Sights:** Brass pin front, hammer notch rear. **Features:** Faithful reproduction of the original gun. Color case-hardened frame, loading lever, plunger, hammer and latch. Blue cylinder, trigger, barrel, screws, wedge. Silver-plated brass backstrap and square-back trigger guard. From Colt Blackpowder Arms Co.
Price: **$449.95**

COLT 1861 NAVY PERCUSSION REVOLVER

Caliber: 36. **Barrel:** 7-1/2". **Weight:** 42 oz. **Length:** 13-1/8" overall. **Stocks:** One-piece walnut. **Sights:** Blade front, hammer notch rear. **Features:** Color case-hardened frame, loading lever, plunger; blued barrel, backstrap, trigger guard; roll-engraved cylinder and barrel. From Colt Blackpowder Arms Co.
Price: **$449.95**

COLT 1849 POCKET DRAGOON REVOLVER

Caliber: 31. **Barrel:** 4". **Weight:** 24 oz. **Length:** 9-1/2" overall. **Stocks:** One-piece walnut. **Sights:** Fixed. Brass pin front, hammer notch rear. **Features:** Color case-hardened frame. No loading lever. Unfluted cylinder with engraved scene. Exact reproduction of original. From Colt Blackpowder Arms Co.
Price: **$429.95**

COLT 1862 POCKET POLICE "TRAPPER MODEL" REVOLVER

Caliber: 36. **Barrel:** 3-1/2". **Weight:** 20 oz. **Length:** 8-1/2" overall. **Stocks:** One-piece walnut. **Sights:** Blade front, hammer notch rear. **Features:** Has separate 4-5/8" brass ramrod. Color case-hardened frame and hammer; silver-plated backstrap and trigger guard; blued semi-fluted cylinder, blued barrel. From Colt Blackpowder Arms Co.
Price: **$429.95**

BLACKPOWDER REVOLVERS

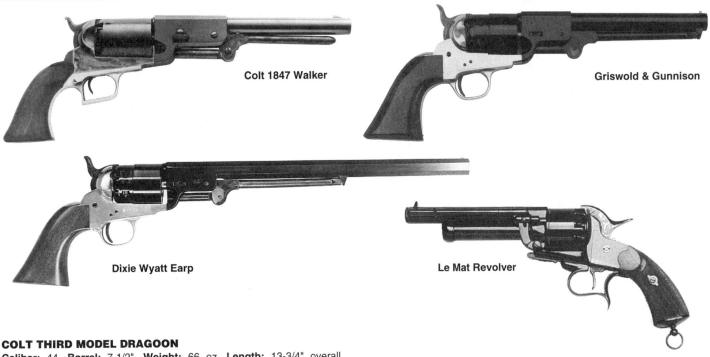

Colt 1847 Walker

Griswold & Gunnison

Dixie Wyatt Earp

Le Mat Revolver

COLT THIRD MODEL DRAGOON
Caliber: 44. **Barrel:** 7-1/2". **Weight:** 66 oz. **Length:** 13-3/4" overall. **Stocks:** One-piece walnut. **Sights:** Blade front, hammer notch rear. **Features:** Color case-hardened frame, hammer, lever and plunger; round trigger guard; flat mainspring; hammer roller; rectangular bolt cuts. From Colt Blackpowder Arms Co.
Price: Three-screw frame with brass grip straps $499.95
Price: First Dragoon (oval bolt cuts in cylinder, square-back
trigger guard) $499.95
Price: Second Dragoon (rectangular bolt cuts in cylinder,
square-back trigger guard) $499.95

Colt Walker 150th Anniversary Revolver
Similar to the standard Walker except has original-type "A Company No. 1" markings embellished in gold. Serial numbers begin with 221, a continuation of A Company numbers. Imported by Colt Blackpowder Arms Co.
Price: $699.95

COLT 1847 WALKER PERCUSSION REVOLVER
Caliber: 44. **Barrel:** 9", 7-groove; right-hand twist. **Weight:** 73 oz. **Stocks:** One-piece walnut. **Sights:** German silver front sight, hammer notch rear. **Features:** Made in U.S. Faithful reproduction of the original gun, including markings. Color case-hardened frame, hammer, loading lever and plunger. Blue steel backstrap, brass square-back trigger guard. Blue barrel, cylinder, trigger and wedge. From Colt Blackpowder Arms Co.
Price: $499.95

DIXIE WYATT EARP REVOLVER
Caliber: 44. **Barrel:** 12", octagon. **Weight:** 46 oz. **Length:** 18" overall. **Stocks:** Two-piece walnut. **Sights:** Fixed. **Features:** Highly polished brass frame, backstrap and trigger guard; blued barrel and cylinder; case-hardened hammer, trigger and loading lever. Navy-size shoulder stock ($45) will fit with minor fitting. From Dixie Gun Works.
Price: $150.00

GRISWOLD & GUNNISON PERCUSSION REVOLVER
Caliber: 36 or 44, 6-shot. **Barrel:** 7-1/2". **Weight:** 44 oz. (36-cal.). **Length:** 13" overall. **Stocks:** Walnut. **Sights:** Fixed. **Features:** Replica of famous Confederate pistol. Brass frame, backstrap and trigger guard; case-hardened loading lever; rebated cylinder (44-cal. only). Rounded Dragoon-type barrel. Imported by Navy Arms as Reb Model 1860.
Price: $115.00
Price: Kit.. $90.00
Price: Single cased set.............................. $235.00
Price: Double cased set.............................. $365.00

LE MAT REVOLVER
Caliber: 44/65. **Barrel:** 6-3/4" (revolver); 4-7/8" (single shot). **Weight:** 3 lbs., 7 oz. **Stocks:** Hand-checkered walnut. **Sights:** Post front, hammer notch rear. **Features:** Exact reproduction with all-steel construction; 44-cal. 9-shot cylinder, 65-cal. single barrel; color case-hardened hammer with selector; spur trigger guard; ring at butt; lever-type barrel release. From Navy Arms.
Price: Cavalry model (lanyard ring, spur trigger guard) $595.00
Price: Army model (round trigger guard, pin-type barrel release) $595.00
Price: Naval-style (thumb selector on hammer) $595.00
Price: Engraved 18th Georgia cased set $795.00
Price: Engraved Beauregard cased set $1,000.00

NAVY ARMS NEW MODEL POCKET REVOLVER
Caliber: 31, 5-shot. **Barrel:** 3-1/2", octagon. **Weight:** 15 oz. **Length:** 7-3/4". **Stocks:** Two-piece walnut. **Sights:** Fixed. **Features:** Replica of the Remington New Model Pocket. Available with polishd brass frame or nickel plated finish. Introduced 2000. Imported by Navy Arms.
Price: Brass frame $165.00
Price: Nickel plated $175.00

NAVY ARMS DELUXE 1858 REMINGTON-STYLE REVOLVER
Caliber: 44. **Barrel:** 6". **Weight:** 3 lbs. **Length:** 11-3/4". **Stocks:** Smooth walnut. **Sights:** Blade front, notch rear. **Features:** Replica of the famous percussion double action revolver. Polished blue finish. Introduced 1999. Imported by Navy Arms.
Price: $355.00

NAVY ARMS STARR SINGLE ACTION MODEL 1863 ARMY REVOLVER
Caliber: 44. **Barrel:** 8". **Weight:** 3 lbs. **Length:** 13-3/4". **Stocks:** Smooth walnut. **Sights:** Blade front, notch rear. **Features:** Replica of the third most popular revolver used by Union forces during the Civil War. Polished blue finish. Introduced 1999. Imported by Navy Arms.
Price: $355.00

NAVY ARMS STARR DOUBLE ACTION MODEL 1858 ARMY REVOLVER
Caliber: 44. **Barrel:** 8". **Weight:** 2 lbs., 13 oz. **Stocks:** Smooth walnut. **Sights:** Dovetailed blade front. **Features:** First exact reproduction—correct in size and weight to the original, with progressive rifling; highly polished with blue finish. From Navy Arms.
Price: Deluxe model $415.00

BLACKPOWDER

BLACKPOWDER REVOLVERS

Uberti 1858

North American Companion

Ruger Old Army

Rogers & Spencer

Pocket Police 1862

NAVY MODEL 1851 PERCUSSION REVOLVER

Caliber: 36, 44, 6-shot. **Barrel:** 7-1/2". **Weight:** 44 oz. **Length:** 13" overall. **Stocks:** Walnut finish. **Sights:** Post front, hammer notch rear. **Features:** Brass backstrap and trigger guard; some have 1st Model squareback trigger guard, engraved cylinder with navy battle scene; case-hardened frame, hammer, loading lever. Imported by The Armoury, Cabela's, Cimarron F.A. Co., Navy Arms, E.M.F., Dixie Gun Works, Euroarms of America, Armsport, CVA (44-cal. only), Traditions (44 only), Uberti U.S.A. Inc., United States Patent Fire-Arms.

Price: Brass frame .... $99.95 to $385.00
Price: Steel frame.......................... $130.00 to $285.00
Price: Kit form................................ $110.00 to $123.95
Price: Engraved model (Dixie Gun Works)................. $159.95
Price: Single cased set, steel frame (Navy Arms) $280.00
Price: Double cased set, steel frame (Navy Arms)........... $455.00
Price: Confederate Navy (Cabela's)...................... $89.99
Price: Hartford model, steel frame, German silver trim,
  cartouche (E.M.F.) $190.00

NEW MODEL 1858 ARMY PERCUSSION REVOLVER

Caliber: 36 or 44, 6-shot. **Barrel:** 6-1/2" or 8". **Weight:** 38 oz. **Length:** 13-1/2" overall. **Stocks:** Walnut. **Sights:** Blade front, groove-in-frame rear. **Features:** Replica of Remington Model 1858. Also available from some importers as Army Model Belt Revolver in 36-cal., a shortened and lightened version of the 44. Target Model (Uberti U.S.A. Inc., Navy Arms) has fully adjustable target rear sight, target front, 36 or 44. Imported by Cabela's, Cimarron F.A. Co., CVA (as 1858 Army, brass frame, 44 only), Dixie Gun Works, Navy Arms, The Armoury, E.M.F., Euroarms of America (engraved, stainless and plain), Armsport, Traditions (44 only), Uberti U.S.A. Inc.

Price: Steel frame, about .... $99.95 to $280.00
Price: Steel frame kit (Euroarms, Navy Arms) ...... $115.95 to $150.00
Price: Single cased set (Navy Arms) $290.00
Price: Double cased set (Navy Arms)...................... $480.00
Price: Stainless steel Model 1858 (Euroarms, Uberti U.S.A. Inc., Cabela's, Navy Arms, Armsport, Traditions) .... $169.95 to $380.00
Price: Target Model, adjustable rear sight (Cabela's, Euroarms, Uberti U.S.A. Inc., Stone Mountain Arms)............... $95.95 to $399.00
Price: Brass frame (CVA, Cabela's, Traditions, Navy Arms) .... $79.95 to $144.95
Price: As above, kit (Dixie Gun Works, Navy Arms).. $145.00 to $188.95

Price: Buffalo model, 44-cal. (Cabela's).................... $119.99
Price: Hartford model, steel frame, German silver trim,
  cartouche (E.M.F.)..................................... $215.00

NORTH AMERICAN COMPANION PERCUSSION REVOLVER

Caliber: 22. **Barrel:** 1-1/8". **Weight:** 5.1 oz. **Length:** 4-5/10" overall. **Stocks:** Laminated wood. **Sights:** Blade front, notch fixed rear. **Features:** All stainless steel construction. Uses standard #11 percussion caps. Comes with bullets, powder measure, bullet seater, leather clip holster, gun rug. Long Rifle or Magnum frame size. Introduced 1996. Made in U.S. by North American Arms.

Price: Long Rifle frame.................................. $191.00

North American Magnum Companion Percussion Revolver

Similar to the Companion except has larger frame. Weighs 7.2 oz., has 1-5/8" barrel, measures 5-7/16" overall. Comes with bullets, powder measure, bullet seater, leather clip holster, gun rag. Introduced 1996. Made in U.S. by North American Arms.

Price: $209.00

POCKET POLICE 1862 PERCUSSION REVOLVER

Caliber: 36, 5-shot. **Barrel:** 4-1/2", 5-1/2", 6-1/2", 7-1/2". **Weight:** 26 oz. **Length:** 12" overall (6-1/2" bbl.). **Stocks:** Walnut. **Sights:** Fixed. **Features:** Round tapered barrel; half-fluted and rebated cylinder; case-hardened frame, loading lever and hammer; silver or brass trigger guard and backstrap. Imported by Dixie Gun Works, Navy Arms (5-1/2" only), Uberti U.S.A. Inc. (5-1/2", 6-1/2" only), United States Patent Fire-Arms and Cimarron F.A. Co.

Price: About .... $139.95 to $335.00
Price: Single cased set with accessories (Navy Arms) $365.00
Price: Hartford model, steel frame, German silver trim,
  cartouche (E.M.F.).................................... $215.00

ROGERS & SPENCER PERCUSSION REVOLVER

Caliber: 44. **Barrel:** 7-1/2". **Weight:** 47 oz. **Length:** 13-3/4" overall. **Stocks:** Walnut. **Sights:** Cone front, integral groove in frame for rear. **Features:** Accurate reproduction of a Civil War design. Solid frame; extra large nipple cut-out on rear of cylinder; loading lever and cylinder easily removed for cleaning. From Dixie Gun Works, Euroarms of America (standard blue, engraved, burnished, target models), Navy Arms.

Price: .... $160.00 to $299.95
Price: Nickel-plated $215.00

BLACKPOWDER REVOLVERS

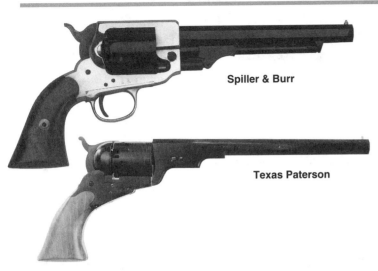

Spiller & Burr

Texas Paterson

Walker

Price: Engraved (Euroarms)............................ $287.00
Price: Kit version.............................. $245.00 to $252.00
Price: Target version (Euroarms) .... $239.00 to $270.00
Price: Burnished London Gray (Euroarms) .... $245.00 to $270.00

RUGER OLD ARMY PERCUSSION REVOLVER

Caliber: 45, 6-shot. Uses .457" dia. lead bullets. **Barrel:** 7-1/2" (6-groove; 16" twist). **Weight:** 46 oz. **Length:** 13-3/4" overall. **Stocks:** Smooth walnut. **Sights:** Ramp front, rear adjustable for windage and elevation; or fixed (groove). **Features:** Stainless steel; standard size nipples, chrome-moly steel cylinder and frame, same lockwork as in original Super Blackhawk. Also available in stainless steel. Made in USA. From Sturm, Ruger & Co.
Price: Stainless steel (Model KBP-7) $499.00
Price: Blued steel (Model BP-7) $478.00
Price: Blued steel, fixed sight (BP-7F) $478.00
Price: Stainless steel, fixed sight (KBP-7F) $499.00

SHERIFF MODEL 1851 PERCUSSION REVOLVER

Caliber: 36, 44, 6-shot. **Barrel:** 5". **Weight:** 40 oz. **Length:** 10-1/2" overall. **Stocks:** Walnut. **Sights:** Fixed. **Features:** Brass backstrap and trigger guard; engraved navy scene; case-hardened frame, hammer, loading lever. Imported by E.M.F.
Price: Steel frame.................................... $172.00
Price: Brass frame $140.00

SPILLER & BURR REVOLVER

Caliber: 36 (.375" round ball). **Barrel:** 7", octagon. **Weight:** 2-1/2 lbs. **Length:** 12-1/2" overall. **Stocks:** Two-piece walnut. **Sights:** Fixed. **Features:** Reproduction of the C.S.A. revolver. Brass frame and trigger guard. Also available as a kit. From Dixie Gun Works, Navy Arms.
Price: $145.00
Price: Kit form (Dixie) $149.95
Price: Single cased set (Navy Arms) $270.00
Price: Double cased set (Navy Arms)................. $430.00

TEXAS PATERSON 1836 REVOLVER

Caliber: 36 (.375" round ball). **Barrel:** 7-1/2". **Weight:** 42 oz. **Stocks:** One-piece walnut. **Sights:** Fixed. **Features:** Copy of Sam Colt's first commercially-made revolving pistol. Has no loading lever but comes with loading tool. From Cimarron F.A. Co., Dixie Gun Works, Navy Arms, Uberti U.S.A. Inc.
Price: About .... $310.00 to $395.00
Price: With loading lever (Uberti U.S.A. Inc.) $450.00
Price: Engraved (Navy Arms)........................... $485.00

Uberti 1861 Navy Percussion Revolver

Similar to Colt 1851 Navy except has round 7-1/2" barrel, rounded trigger guard, German silver blade front sight, "creeping" loading lever. Available with fluted or round cylinder. Imported by Uberti U.S.A. Inc.
Price: Steel backstrap, trigger guard, cut for stock........... $300.00

1ST U.S. MODEL DRAGOON

Caliber: 44. **Barrel:** 7-1/2", part round, part octagon. **Weight:** 64 oz. **Stocks:** One-piece walnut. **Sights:** German silver blade front, hammer notch rear. **Features:** First model has oval bolt cuts in cylinder, square-back flared trigger guard, V-type mainspring, short trigger. Ranger and Indian scene roll-engraved on cylinder. Color case-hardened frame, loading lever, plunger and hammer; blue barrel, cylinder, trigger and wedge. Available with old-time charcoal blue or standard blue-black finish. Polished brass backstrap and trigger guard. From Cimarron F.A. Co., Uberti U.S.A. Inc., United States Patent Fire-Arms, Navy Arms.
Price: .... $325.00 to $435.00

2nd U.S. Model Dragoon Revolver

Similar to the 1st Model except distinguished by rectangular bolt cuts in the cylinder. From Cimarron F.A. Co., Uberti U.S.A. Inc., United States Patent Fire-Arms, Navy Arms.
Price: .... $325.00 to $435.00

3rd U.S. Model Dragoon Revolver

Similar to the 2nd Model except for oval trigger guard, long trigger, modifications to the loading lever and latch. Imported by Cimarron F.A. Co., Uberti U.S.A. Inc., United States Patent Fire-Arms.
Price: Military model (frame cut for shoulder stock, steel backstrap) .... $330.00 to $435.00
Price: Civilian (brass backstrap, trigger guard) $325.00

1862 POCKET NAVY PERCUSSION REVOLVER

Caliber: 36, 5-shot. **Barrel:** 5-1/2", 6-1/2", octagonal, 7-groove, LH twist. **Weight:** 27 oz. (5-1/2" barrel). **Length:** 10-1/2" overall (5-1/2" bbl.). **Stocks:** One-piece varnished walnut. **Sights:** Brass pin front, hammer notch rear. **Features:** Rebated cylinder, hinged loading lever, brass or silver-plated backstrap and trigger guard, color-cased frame, hammer, loading lever, plunger and latch, rest blued. Has original-type markings. From Cimarron F.A. Co. and Uberti U.S.A. Inc.
Price: With brass backstrap, trigger guard.................. $310.00

1861 Navy Percussion Revolver

Similar to Colt 1851 Navy except has round 7-1/2" barrel, rounded trigger guard, German silver blade front sight, "creeping" loading lever. Fluted or round cylinder. Imported by Cimarron F.A. Co., Uberti U.S.A. Inc.
Price: Steel backstrap, trigger guard, cut for stock........... $300.00

U.S. PATENT FIRE-ARMS 1862 POCKET NAVY

Caliber: 36. **Barrel:** 4-1/2", 5-1/2", 6-1/2". **Weight:** 27 oz. (5-1/2" barrel). **Length:** 10-1/2" overall (5-1/2" barrel). **Stocks:** Smooth walnut. **Sights:** Brass pin front, hammer notch rear. **Features:** Blued barrel and cylinder, color case-hardened frame, hammer, lever; silver-plated backstrap and trigger guard. Imported from Italy; available from United States Patent Fire-Arms Mfg. Co.
Price: $335.00

WALKER 1847 PERCUSSION REVOLVER

Caliber: 44, 6-shot. **Barrel:** 9". **Weight:** 84 oz. **Length:** 15-1/2" overall. **Stocks:** Walnut. **Sights:** Fixed. **Features:** Case-hardened frame, loading lever and hammer; iron backstrap; brass trigger guard; engraved cylinder. Imported by Cabela's, Cimarron F.A. Co., Navy Arms, Dixie Gun Works, Uberti U.S.A. Inc., E.M.F., Cimarron, Traditions, United States Patent Fire-Arms.
Price: About .... $225.00 to $445.00
Price: Single cased set (Navy Arms) $405.00
Price: Deluxe Walker with French fitted case (Navy Arms) $540.00
Price: Hartford model, steel frame, German silver trim, cartouche (E.M.F.) $295.00

Armoury R140 Hawken

Cabela's Blue Ridge

Cabela's Traditional Hawken

Cabela's Lightning Fire Fluted

ARMOURY R140 HAWKEN RIFLE

Caliber: 45, 50 or 54. **Barrel:** 29". **Weight:** 8-3/4 to 9 lbs. **Length:** 45-3/4" overall. **Stock:** Walnut, with cheekpiece. **Sights:** Dovetail front, fully adjustable rear. **Features:** Octagon barrel, removable breech plug; double set triggers; blued barrel, brass stock fittings, color case-hardened percussion lock. From Armsport, The Armoury.
Price: .... $225.00 to $245.00

AUSTIN & HALLECK MODEL 420 LR IN-LINE RIFLE

Caliber: 50. **Barrel:** 26", 1" octagon to 3/4" round; 1:28" twist. **Weight:** 7-7/8 lbs. **Length:** 47-1/2" overall. **Stock:** Lightly figured maple in Classic or Monte Carlo style. **Sights:** Ramp front, fully adjustable rear. **Features:** Blue or electroless nickel finish; in-line percussion action with removable weather shroud; Timney adjustable target trigger with sear block safety. Introduced 1998. Made in U.S. by Austin & Halleck.
Price: Blue $459.00
Price: Stainless steel $520.00
Price: Blue, hand-select highly figured wood $737.00

Austin & Halleck Model 320 LR In-Line Rifle

Similar to the Model 420 LR except has black resin synthetic stock with checkered grip and forend. Introduced 1998. Made in U.S. by Austin & Halleck.
Price: Blue $380.00
Price: Stainless steel $446.00

AUSTIN & HALLECK MOUNTAIN RIFLE

Caliber: 50. **Barrel:** 32"; 1:66" twist; 1" flats. **Weight:** 7-1/2 lbs. **Length:** 49" overall. **Stock:** Curly maple. **Sights:** Silver blade front, buckhorn rear. **Features:** Available in percussion or flintlock; double throw adjustable set triggers; rust brown finish. Made in U.S. by Austin & Halleck.
Price: Flintlock $539.00
Price: Percussion $578.00
Price: Fancy wood $592.00

BOSTONIAN PERCUSSION RIFLE

Caliber: 45. **Barrel:** 30", octagonal. **Weight:** 7-1/4 lbs. **Length:** 46" overall. **Stock:** Walnut. **Sights:** Blade front, fixed notch rear. **Features:** Color case-hardened lock, brass trigger guard, buttplate, patchbox. Imported from Italy by E.M.F.
Price: $285.00

CABELA'S TRADITIONAL HAWKEN

Caliber: 50, 54. **Barrel:** 29". **Weight:** About 9 lbs. **Stock:** Walnut. **Sights:** Blade front, open adjustable rear. **Features:** Flintlock or percussion. Adjustable double-set triggers. Polished brass furniture, color case-hardened lock. Imported by Cabela's.
Price: Percussion, right-hand $189.99
Price: Percussion, left-hand $199.99
Price: Flintlock, right-hand $224.99

CABELA'S BLUE RIDGE RIFLE

Caliber: 32, 36, 45, 50. **Barrel:** 39", octagonal. **Weight:** About 7-3/4 lbs. **Length:** 55" overall. **Stock:** American black walnut. **Sights:** Blade front, rear drift adjustable for windage. **Features:** Color case-hardened lockplate and cock/hammer, brass trigger guard and buttplate, double set, double-phased triggers. From Cabela's.
Price: Percussion $379.99
Price: Flintlock $399.99

CABELA'S LIGHTNING FIRE FLUTED RIFLE

Caliber: 50. **Barrel:** 24", fluted; 1:32" twist; muzzle brake. **Weight:** 7 lbs. **Length:** NA. **Stock:** Black synthetic or laminated wood. **Sights:** Blade front, open fully adjustable rear. **Features:** Bolt-action in-line ignition uses musket caps. Introduced 1999. From Cabela's.
Price: Stainless, laminated stock $299.99
Price: Nickel barrel with muzzle brake, black stock $279.99

BLACKPOWDER MUSKETS & RIFLES

Cabela's Timber Ridge

Cabela's Lightning Fire Sidelock

Cook & Brother

CABELA'S KODIAK EXPRESS DOUBLE RIFLE
Caliber: 50, 54, 58, 72. **Barrel:** Length n/a; 1:48" twist. **Weight:** 9.3 lbs. **Length:** 45-1/4" overall. **Stock:** European walnut, oil finish. **Sights:** Fully adjustable double folding-leaf rear, ramp front. **Features:** Percussion. Barrels regulated to point of aim at 75 yards; polished and engraved lock, top tang and trigger guard. From Cabela's.
Price: 50, 54, 58 calibers $649.99
Price: 72 caliber $679.99

CABELA'S LEGACY IN-LINE RIFLE
Caliber: 50. **Barrel:** 22"; 1:28" twist. **Weight:** 9-2/3 lbs. **Length:** 40-1/2" overall. **Stock:** Walnut-stained hardwood with rubber recoil pad. **Sights:** Adjustable rear, ramp front. **Features:** In-line ignition; double safety system; removable breech plug; drilled and tapped for scope mount. Introduced 2000. From Cabela's.
Price: $99.99

CABELA'S LIGHTNING FIRE SIDELOCK RIFLE
Caliber: 50. **Barrel:** 28-3/4"; 1:32" twist. **Weight:** 7.85 lbs. **Length:** NA. **Stock:** Walnut-stained hardwood. **Sights:** Fiber optic front and rear. **Features:** Uses musket cap ignition. Comes with sling swivels, rubber recoil pad, color case-hardened lock. Introduced 1999. From Cabela's.
Price: $219.99

CABELA'S TIMBER RIDGE RIFLE
Caliber: 50, 54. **Barrel:** 24"; 1:32" twist (50-cal.), 1:48" twist (54-cal.). **Weight:** 7-1/2 lbs. **Length:** 42" overall. **Stock:** Composite; black or Advantage camo. **Sights:** Bead on ramp front, open adjustable rear. **Features:** In-line ignition system; sling swivel studs; synthetic ramrod; stainless steel breech plug. Introduced 1999. From Cabela's.
Price: Black stock. $129.99
Price: Advantage camo stock. $159.99

Cabela's Sporterized Hawken Hunter Rifle
Similar to the Traditional Hawken's except has more modern stock style with rubber recoil pad, blued furniture, sling swivels. Percussion only, in 50- or 54-caliber.
Price: Carbine or rifle, right-hand $219.99

COLT MODEL 1861 MUSKET
Caliber: 58. **Barrel:** 40". **Weight:** 9 lbs., 3 oz. **Length:** 56" overall. **Stock:** Oil-finished walnut. **Sight:** Blade front, adjustable folding leaf rear. **Features:** Made to original specifications and has authentic Civil War Colt markings. Bright-finished metal, blued nipple and rear sight. Bayonet and accessories available. From Colt Blackpowder Arms Co.
Price: $799.95

COOK & BROTHER CONFEDERATE CARBINE
Caliber: 58. **Barrel:** 24". **Weight:** 7-1/2 lbs. **Length:** 40-1/2" overall. **Stock:** Select walnut. **Features:** Recreation of the 1861 New Orleans-made artillery carbine. Color case-hardened lock, browned barrel. Buttplate, trigger guard, barrel bands, sling swivels and nosecap of polished brass. From Euroarms of America.
Price: $447.00
Price: Cook & Brother rifle (33" barrel) $480.00

CUMBERLAND MOUNTAIN BLACKPOWDER RIFLE
Caliber: 50. **Barrel:** 26", round. **Weight:** 9-1/2 lbs. **Length:** 43" overall. **Stock:** American walnut. **Sights:** Bead front, open rear adjustable for windage. **Features:** Falling block action fires with shotshell primer. Blued receiver and barrel. Introduced 1993. Made in U.S. by Cumberland Mountain Arms, Inc.
Price: $931.50

CVA COLORADO MUSKET MAG 100 RIFLE
Caliber: 50, 54 **Barrel:** 26"; 1:32" twist. **Weight:** 7-1/2 lbs. **Length:** 42" overall. **Stock:** Synthetic; black, Hardwoods or X-Tra Brown camo. **Sights:** Illuminator front and rear. **Features:** Sidelock action uses musket caps for ignition. Introduced 1999. From CVA.
Price: With black stock. $184.95
Price: With camo stock. $219.95

CVA YOUTH HUNTER RIFLE
Caliber: 50. **Barrel:** 24"; 1:48" twist, octagonal. **Weight:** 5-1/2 lbs. **Length:** 38" overall. **Stock:** Stained hardwood. **Sights:** Bead front, Williams adjustable rear. **Features:** Oversize trigger guard; wooden ramrod. Introduced 1999. From CVA.
Price: $129.95

BLACKPOWDER

BLACKPOWDER MUSKETS & RIFLES

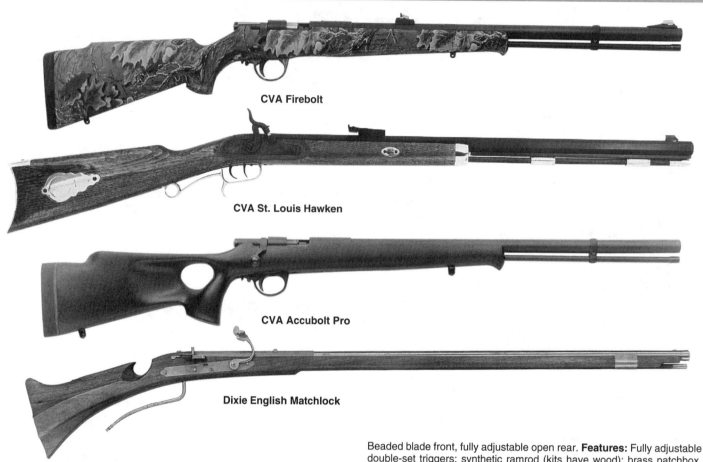

CVA Firebolt

CVA St. Louis Hawken

CVA Accubolt Pro

Dixie English Matchlock

CVA BOBCAT RIFLE
Caliber: 50 and 54. **Barrel:** 26"; 1:48" twist. **Weight:** 6-1/2 lbs. **Length:** 40" overall. **Stock:** Dura-Grip synthetic. **Sights:** Blade front, open rear. **Features:** Oversize trigger guard; wood ramrod; matte black finish. Introduced 1995. From CVA.
Price: $125.95

CVA ECLIPSE IN-LINE RIFLE
Caliber: 50, 54. **Barrel:** 24" round; 1:32" rifling. **Weight:** 7 lbs. **Length:** 42" overall. **Stock:** Black Advantage camo synthetic. **Sights:** Illuminator Fiber Optic Sight System; drilled and tapped for scope mounting. **Features:** In-line action uses modern trigger with automatic safety; stainless percussion bolt; swivel studs. Three-way ignition system (No. 11, musket or No. 209 shotgun primers). From CVA.
Price: 50 or 54, blue, black stock $159.95
Price: 50 or 54, blue, Advantage Brown camo stock $199.95
Price: 50 or 54, Hardwoods camo $199.95

CVA Staghorn Rifle
Similar to the Eclipse except has standard open sights, manual safety, black DuraGrip stock and ramrod. From CVA.
Price: 50 or 54 .... $134.95

CVA MOUNTAIN RIFLE
Caliber: 50. **Barrel:** 32"; 1:66" rifling. **Weight:** 8-1/2 lbs. **Length:** NA **Stock:** American hard maple. **Sights:** Blade front, buckhorn rear. **Features:** Browned steel furniture; German silver wedge plates; patchbox. Made in U.S. From CVA.
Price: $379.95

CVA ST. LOUIS HAWKEN RIFLE
Caliber: 50, 54. **Barrel:** 28", octagon; 15/16" across flats; 1:48" twist. **Weight:** 8 lbs. **Length:** 44" overall. **Stock:** Select hardwood. **Sights:**

Beaded blade front, fully adjustable open rear. **Features:** Fully adjustable double-set triggers; synthetic ramrod (kits have wood); brass patchbox, wedge plates, nosecap, thimbles, trigger guard and buttplate; blued barrel; color case-hardened, engraved lockplate. V-type mainspring. Button breech. Introduced 1981. From CVA.
Price: St. Louis Hawken, finished (50- , 54-cal.) $194.95
Price: Left-hand, percussion......................... $234.95
Price: Flintlock, 50-cal. only $234.95
Price: Percussion kit (50-cal., blued, wood ramrod).......... $169.95

CVA HunterBolt MusketMag Rifle
Similar to the Firebolt except has standard open sights, black DuraGrip synthetic stock. Available in camo X-Tra Brown and Hardwoods camo. Three-way ignition system. From CVA.
Price: 50 or 54 .... $184.95 to $239.95

CVA FIREBOLT MUSKETMAG BOLT-ACTION IN-LINE RIFLES
Caliber: 50, 54. **Barrel:** 24". **Weight:** 7 lbs. **Length:** NA. **Stock:** DuraGrip synthetic; thumbhole, traditional, camo. **Sights:** CVA Illuminator Fiber Optic Sight System. **Features:** Bolt-action, in-line ignition system. Stainless steel or matte blue barrel; removable breech plug; trigger-block safety. Introduced 1997. Three-way ignition system. From CVA.
Price: Stainless barrel, traditional stock $299.95
Price: Matte blue barrel, camo stock $279.95
Price: Matte blue barrel, traditional stock $239.95
Price: With Teflon finish, black stock $279.95
Price: As above, synthetic Sniper stock $299.95
Price: As above, synthetic Advantage camo stock............. $299.95

DIXIE ENGLISH MATCHLOCK MUSKET
Caliber: 72. **Barrel:** 44". **Weight:** 8 lbs. **Length:** 57.75" overall. **Stock:** Walnut with satin oil finish. **Sights:** Blade front, open rear adjustable for windage. **Features:** Replica of circa 1600-1680 English matchlock. Getz barrel with 11" octagonal area at rear, rest is round with cannon-type muzzle. All steel finished in the white. Imported by Dixie Gun Works.
Price: $895.00

BLACKPOWDER MUSKETS & RIFLES

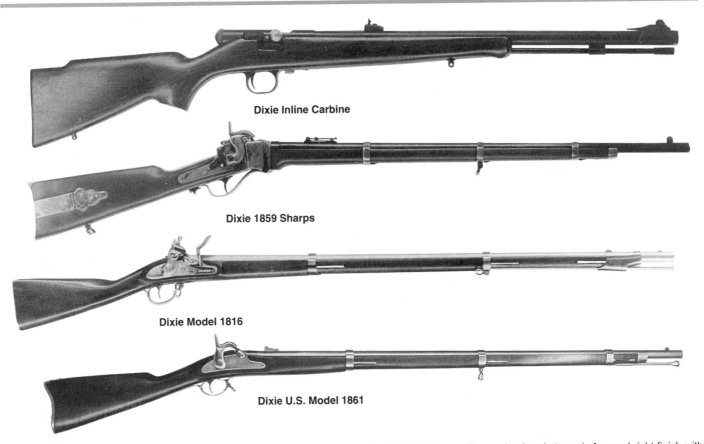

Dixie Inline Carbine

Dixie 1859 Sharps

Dixie Model 1816

Dixie U.S. Model 1861

DIXIE EARLY AMERICAN JAEGER RIFLE

Caliber: 54. **Barrel:** 27-1/2" octagonal; 1:24" twist. **Weight:** 8-1/4 lbs. **Length:** 43-1/2" overall. **Stock:** American walnut; sliding wooden patchbox on on butt. **Sights:** Notch rear, blade front. **Features:** Flintlock or percussion. Browned steel furniture. Introduced 2000. Imported from Italy by Dixie Gun Works.
Price: Flintlock or percussion **$695.00**

DIXIE DELUXE CUB RIFLE

Caliber: 40. **Barrel:** 28". **Weight:** 6-1/2 lbs. **Stock:** Walnut. **Sights:** Fixed.**Features:** Short rifle for small game and beginning shooters. Brass patchbox and furniture. Flint or percussion. From Dixie Gun Works.
Price: Finished **$415.00**
Price: Kit **$375.00**
Price: Super Cub (50-caliber) **$367.00**

DIXIE 1863 SPRINGFIELD MUSKET

Caliber: 58 (.570" patched ball or .575" Minie). **Barrel:** 50", rifled. **Stock:** Walnut stained. **Sights:** Blade front, adjustable ladder-type rear. **Features:** Bright-finish lock, barrel, furniture. Reproduction of the last of the regulation muzzleloaders. Imported from Japan by Dixie Gun Works.
Price: Finished **$595.00**
Price: Kit **$525.00**

DIXIE INLINE CARBINE

Caliber: 50, 54. **Barrel:** 24"; 1:32" twist. **Weight:** 6.5 lbs. **Length:** 41" overall. **Stock:** Walnut-finished hardwood with Monte Carlo comb. **Sights:** Ramp front with red insert, open fully adjustable rear. **Features:** Sliding "bolt" fully encloses cap and nipple. Fully adjustable trigger, automatic safety. Aluminum ramrod. Imported from Italy by Dixie Gun Works.
Price: **$349.95**

DIXIE PEDERSOLI 1857 MAUSER RIFLE

Caliber: 54. **Barrel:** 39-3/8". **Weight:** N/A. **Length:** 52" overall. **Stock:** European walnut with oil finish, sling swivels. **Sights:** Fully adjustable rear,

lug front. **Features:** Percussion (musket caps). Armory bright finish with color case-hardened lock and barrel tang, engraved lockplate, steel ramrod. Introduced 2000. Imported from Italy by Dixie Gun Works.
Price: **$895.00**

DIXIE PEDERSOLI 1766 CHARLEVILLE MUSKET

Caliber: 69. **Barrel:** 44-3/4". **Weight:** 10-1/2 lbs. **Length:** 57-1/2" overall. **Stock:** European walnut with oil finish. **Sights:** Fixed rear, lug front. **Features:** Smoothbore flintlock. Armory bright finish with steel furniture and ramrod. Introduced 2000. Imported from Italy by Dixie Gun Works.
Price: **$795.00**

DIXIE SHARPS NEW MODEL 1859 MILITARY RIFLE

Caliber: 54. **Barrel:** 30", 6-groove; 1:48" twist. **Weight:** 9 lbs. **Length:** 45-1/2" overall. **Stock:** Oiled walnut. **Sights:** Blade front, ladder-style rear. **Features:** Blued barrel, color case-hardened barrel bands, receiver, hammer, nosecap, lever, patchbox cover and buttplate. Introduced 1995. Imported from Italy by Dixie Gun Works.
Price: **$895.00**

DIXIE U.S. MODEL 1816 FLINTLOCK MUSKET

Caliber: 69. **Barrel:** 42", smoothbore. **Weight:** 9.75 lbs. **Length:** 56.5" overall. **Stock:** Walnut with oil finish. **Sights:** Blade front. **Features:** All metal finished "National Armory Bright"; three barrel bands with springs; steel ramrod with button-shaped head. Imported by Dixie Gun Works.
Price: **$725.00**

DIXIE U.S. MODEL 1861 SPRINGFIELD

Caliber: 58. **Barrel:** 40". **Weight:** About 8 lbs. **Length:** 55-13/16" overall. **Stock:** Oil-finished walnut. **Sights:** Blade front, step adjustable rear. **Features:** Exact recreation of original rifle. Sling swivels attached to trigger guard bow and middle barrel band. Lockplate marked "1861" with eagle motif and "U.S. Springfield" in front of hammer; "U.S." stamped on top of buttplate. From Dixie Gun Works.
Price: **$595.00**
Price: From Stone Mountain Arms **$599.00**
Price: Kit **$525.00**

BLACKPOWDER

Euroarms Volunteer

Euroarms 1861

Gonic Model 93 Thumbhole

Great American Sporting

E.M.F. 1863 SHARPS MILITARY CARBINE

Caliber: 54. **Barrel:** 22", round. **Weight:** 8 lbs. **Length:** 39" overall. **Stock:** Oiled walnut. **Sights:** Blade front, military ladder-type rear. **Features:** Color or case-hardened lock, rest blued. Imported by E.M.F.
Price: $600.00

EUROARMS VOLUNTEER TARGET RIFLE

Caliber: .451. **Barrel:** 33" (two-band), 36" (three-band). **Weight:** 11 lbs. (two-band). **Length:** 48.75" overall (two-band). **Stock:** European walnut with checkered wrist and forend. **Sights:** Hooded bead front, adjustable rear with interchangeable leaves. **Features:** Alexander Henry-type rifling with 1:20" twist. Color case-hardened hammer and lockplate, brass trigger guard and nosecap, rest blued. Imported by Euroarms of America.
Price: Two-band $720.00
Price: Three-band $773.00

EUROARMS 1861 SPRINGFIELD RIFLE

Caliber: 58. **Barrel:** 40". **Weight:** About 10 lbs. **Length:** 55.5" overall. **Stock:** European walnut. **Sights:** Blade front, three-leaf military rear. **Features:** Reproduction of the original three-band rifle. Lockplate marked "1861" with eagle and "U.S. Springfield." Metal left in the white. Imported by Euroarms of America.
Price: $530.00

GONIC MODEL 93 M/L RIFLE

Caliber: 45, 50. **Barrel:** 26"; 1:24" twist. **Weight:** 6-1/2 to 7 lbs. **Length:** 43" overall. **Stock:** American hardwood with black finish. **Sights:** Adjustable or aperture rear, hooded post front. **Features:** Adjustable trigger with side safety; unbreakable ram rod; comes with A. Z. scope bases installed. Introduced 1993. Made in U.S. by Gonic Arms, Inc.
Price: Model 93 Standard (blued barrel) $686.00
Price: Model 93 Standard (stainless brl., 50 cal. only) $745.00

Gonic Model 93 Deluxe M/L Rifle

Similar to the Model 93 except has classic-style walnut or gray laminated wood stock. Introduced 1998. Made in U.S. by Gonic Arms, Inc.
Price: Blue barrel, sights, scope base, choice of stock $859.00
Price: Stainless barrel, sights, scope base, choice of stock
(50 cal. only) $918.00
Price: Blue barrel, peep sight, scope bases, choice of stock $869.00
Price: Stainless barrel, peep sight, scope base, choice of stock
(50 cal. only) $928.00

Gonic Model 93 Mountain Thumbhole M/L Rifles

Similar to the Model 93 except has high-grade walnut or gray laminate stock with extensive hand-checkered panels, Monte Carlo cheekpiece and beavertail forend; integral muzzle brake. Introduced 1998. Made in U.S. by Gonic Arms, Inc.
Price: Blue or stainless $2,500.00

Gonic Model 93 Deluxe Rifle

Price: Blue or stainless barrel, walnut or gray laminate stock .. $1,612.00

GREAT AMERICAN SPORTING RIFLE

Caliber: 69. **Barrel:** 28", 1-1/4" octagon to 1-1/8" round. **Weight:** 10 lbs. **Length:** NA **Stock:** Walnut. **Sights:** Silver blade front, adjustable semi-buckhorn rear. **Features:** Hooked, patent Manton-style breech plug; iron furniture; bedded barrel; brown finish. Made in U.S. by October Country Muzzleloading, Inc.
Price: $1,495.00

HARPER'S FERRY 1803 FLINTLOCK RIFLE

Caliber: 54 or 58. **Barrel:** 35". **Weight:** 9 lbs. **Length:** 59-1/2" overall. **Stock:** Walnut with cheekpiece. **Sights:** Brass blade front, fixed steel rear. **Features:** Brass trigger guard, sideplate, buttplate; steel patchbox. Imported by Euroarms of America, Navy Arms (54-cal. only), Cabela's.
Price: .... $495.95 to $729.00
Price: 54-cal. (Navy Arms) $625.00
Price: 54-caliber (Cabela's) $599.99

BLACKPOWDER

BLACKPOWDER MUSKETS & RIFLES

Harper's Ferry 1803

J.P. Murray

Kentucky Flintlock

Knight T-Bolt M/L

HAWKEN RIFLE

Caliber: 45, 50, 54 or 58. **Barrel:** 28", blued, 6-groove rifling. **Weight:** 8-3/4 lbs. **Length:** 44" overall. **Stock:** Walnut with cheekpiece. **Sights:** Blade front, fully adjustable rear. **Features:** Coil mainspring, double-set triggers, polished brass furniture. From Armsport, Navy Arms, E.M.F.
Price: . . . . $220.00 to $345.00

J.P. MURRAY 1862-1864 CAVALRY CARBINE

Caliber: 58 (.577" Minie). **Barrel:** 23". **Weight:** 7 lbs., 9 oz. **Length:** 39" overall. **Stock:** Walnut. **Sights:** Blade front, rear drift adjustable for windage. **Features:** Browned barrel, color case-hardened lock, blued swivel and band springs, polished brass buttplate, trigger guard, barrel bands. From Navy Arms, Euroarms of America.
Price: . . . . $405.00 to $453.00

J.P. HENRY TRADE RIFLE

Caliber: 54. **Barrel:** 34"; 1" flats. **Weight:** 8-1/2 lbs. **Length:** 45" overall. **Stock:** Premium curly maple. **Sights:** Silver blade front, fixed buckhorn rear. **Features:** Brass buttplate, side plate, trigger guard and nosecap; browned barrel and lock; L&R Large English percussion lock; single trigger. Made in U.S. by J.P. Gunstocks, Inc.
Price: $965.50

KENTUCKIAN RIFLE

Caliber: 44. **Barrel:** 35". **Weight:** 7 lbs. (Rifle), 5-1/2 lbs. (Carbine). **Length:** 51" overall (Rifle), 43" (Carbine). **Stock:** Walnut stain. **Sights:** Brass blade front, steel V-ramp rear. **Features:** Octagon barrel, case-hardened and engraved lockplates. Brass furniture. Imported by Dixie Gun Works.
Price: Flintlock $269.95
Price: Percussion $259.95

KENTUCKY FLINTLOCK RIFLE

Caliber: 44, 45, or 50. **Barrel:** 35". **Weight:** 7 lbs. **Length:** 50" overall. **Stock:** Walnut stained, brass fittings. **Sights:** Fixed. **Features:** Available in carbine model also, 28" bbl. Some variations in detail, finish. Kits also available from some importers. Imported by Navy Arms, The Armoury.
Price: About . . . . $217.95 to $345.00
Price: Flintlock, 45 or 50-cal. (Navy Arms) $435.00

Kentucky Percussion Rifle

Similar to flintlock except percussion lock. Finish and features vary with importer. Imported by Navy Arms, The Armoury, CVA.
Price: About $259.95
Price: 45- or 50-cal. (Navy Arms) $425.00
Price: Kit, 50-cal. (CVA) $189.95

KNIGHT T-BOLT IN-LINE RIFLE

Caliber: 50. **Barrel:** 22", 26"; 1:28" twist. **Weight:** 6 lbs. **Length:** 41" overall. **Stock:** Composite black, Mossy Oak Break-Up or Advantage camo. **Sights:** Bead on ramp front, fully adjustable rear; drilled and tapped for scope mounts. **Features:** Straight-pull T-Bolt action with double-safety system, removable hammer, removable stainless steel breech plug; adjustable trigger. Introduced 1998. Made in U.S. by Knight Rifles.
Price: Blue or stainless . . . . $399.95 to $519.95

KNIGHT DISC IN-LINE RIFLE

Caliber: 50. **Barrel:** 24", 26". **Weight:** 7 lbs., 14 oz. **Length:** 43" overall (24" barrel). **Stock:** Checkered synthetic with palm swell grip, rubber recoil pad, swivel studs; black, Advantage or Mossy Oak Break-Up camouflage. **Sights:** Bead on ramp front, fully adjustable open rear. **Features:** Bolt-action in-line system uses #209 shotshell primer for ignition; primer is held in plastic drop-in Primer Disc. Available in blued or stainless steel. Made in U.S. by Knight Rifles.
Price: . . . . $449.95 to $569.95

BLACKPOWDER

Knight Disc M/L

Knight Bighorn In/Line

Knight LK-93 Wolverine

Knight Wolverine II

Features: Patented double safety; Sure-Fire in-line percussion ignition; Timney Featherweight adjustable trigger; aluminum ramrod; receiver drilled and tapped for scope bases. Made in U.S. by Knight Rifles.
Price: Hunter, walnut stock. **$549.95**
Price: Stalker, laminated or composite stock **$569.95**
Price: Predator (stainless steel), laminated or composite stock . . **$649.95**
Price: Knight Hawk, stainless, composite thumbhole stock **$769.95**

KNIGHT LK-93 WOLVERINE RIFLE
Caliber: 50, 54. **Barrel:** 22", blued. **Weight:** 6 lbs. **Stock:** Black Advantage; Mossy Oak Break-Up camo. **Sights:** Bead front on ramp, open adjustable rear. **Features:** Patented double safety system; removable breech plug; Sure-Fire in-line percussion ignition system. Made in U.S. by Knight Rifles.
Price: From. **$269.95**
Price: LK-93 Stainless, from. **$339.95**
Price: LK-93 Thumbhole, from **$309.95**
Price: Youth model, blued, 50-cal. only **$279.95**

Knight Wolverine II In-Line Rifle
Similar to Wolverine except features solid composite stock in black, Advantage Timber, Mossy Oak Break-Up or Realtree Hardwoods camo patterns; adjustable trigger; blued or stainless steel; 50 or 54 caliber. Length 41" overall, weighs 6 lbs., 11 oz. Introduced 2000. Made in U.S. by Knight Rifles.
Price: Blued finish, black composite stock **$269.95**

LONDON ARMORY 2-BAND 1858 ENFIELD
Caliber: .577" Minie, .575" round ball. **Barrel:** 33". **Weight:** 10 lbs. **Length:** 49" overall. **Stock:** Walnut. **Sights:** Folding leaf rear adjustable for elevation. **Features:** Blued barrel, color case-hardened lock and hammer, polished brass buttplate, trigger guard, nosecap. From Navy Arms, Euroarms of America, Dixie Gun Works.
Price: . . . . **$385.00 to $531.00**

Knight Master Hunter Disc In-Line Rifle
Similar to Knight Disc rifle except features premier, wood laminated two-tone stock, gold-plated trigger and engraved trigger guard, jeweled bolt and fluted, air-gauged Green Mountain 26" barrel. Length 45" overall, weighs 7 lbs., 7 oz. Includes black composite thumbhole stock. Introduced 2000. Made in U.S. by Knight Rifles.
Price: **$999.95**

KNIGHT BIGHORN IN-LINE RIFLE
Caliber: 50. **Barrel:** 22", 26"; 1:28" twist. **Weight:** 7 lbs. **Length:** 41" overall (22" barrel). **Stock:** Synthetic; black Advantage or Mossy Oak Break-Up camouflage. Black rubber recoil pad. **Sights:** Bead on ramp front, full adjustable open rear. **Features:** Patented double safety system; adjustable trigger; comes with #11 Red Hot Nipple. Available in blue or stainless steel. Made in U.S. by Knight Rifles.
Price: . . . . **$329.95 to $439.95**

KNIGHT AMERICAN KNIGHT M/L RIFLE
Caliber: 50. **Barrel:** 22"; 1:28" twist. **Weight:** 6 lbs. **Length:** 41" overall. **Stock:** Black composite. **Sights:** Bead on ramp front, open fully adjustable rear. **Features:** Double safety system; one-piece removable hammer assembly; drilled and tapped for scope mounting. Introduced 1998. Made in U.S. by Knight Rifles.
Price: **$199.95**

KNIGHT MK-85 RIFLE
Caliber: 50, 54. **Barrel:** 24". **Weight:** 6-3/4 lbs. **Stock:** Walnut, laminated or composite. **Sights:** Hooded blade front on ramp, open adjustable rear.

London Armory 1861

Lyman Cougar In/Line

Lyman Trade

Lyman Deerstalker

LONDON ARMORY 1861 ENFIELD MUSKETOON

Caliber: 58, Minie ball. **Barrel:** 24", round. **Weight:** 7 - 7-1/2 lbs. **Length:** 40-1/2" overall. **Stock:** Walnut, with sling swivels. **Sights:** Blade front, graduated military-leaf rear. **Features:** Brass trigger guard, nosecap, buttplate; blued barrel, bands, lockplate, swivels. Imported by Euroarms of America, Navy Arms.

Price: . . . . $300.00 to $427.00
Price: Kit . . . . $365.00 to $373.00

LONDON ARMORY 3-BAND 1853 ENFIELD

Caliber: 58 (.577" Minie, .575" round ball, .580" maxi ball). **Barrel:** 39". **Weight:** 9-1/2 lbs. **Length:** 54" overall. **Stock:** European walnut. **Sights:** Inverted "V" front, traditional Enfield folding ladder rear. **Features:** Recreation of the famed London Armory Company Pattern 1853 Enfield Musket. One-piece walnut stock, brass buttplate, trigger guard and nosecap. Lockplate marked "London Armoury Co." and with a British crown. Blued Baddeley barrel bands. From Dixie Gun Works, Euroarms of America, Navy Arms.

Price: About . . . . $350.00 to $495.00
Price: Assembled kit (Dixie, Euroarms of America) . . $425.00 to $431.00

LYMAN COUGAR IN-LINE RIFLE

Caliber: 50 or 54. **Barrel:** 22"; 1:24" twist. **Weight:** NA. **Length:** NA. **Stock:** Smooth walnut; swivel studs. **Sights:** Bead on ramp front, folding adjustable rear. Drilled and tapped for Lyman 57WTR receiver sight and Weaver scope bases. **Features:** Blued barrel and receiver. Has bolt safety notch and trigger safety. Rubber recoil pad. Delrin ramrod. Introduced 1996. From Lyman.

Price: $249.95
Price: Stainless steel $299.95

LYMAN TRADE RIFLE

Caliber: 50, 54. **Barrel:** 28" octagon;1:48" twist. **Weight:** 8-3/4 lbs. **Length:** 45" overall. **Stock:** European walnut. **Sights:** Blade front, open rear adjustable for windage or optional fixed sights. **Features:** Fast twist rifling for conical bullets. Polished brass furniture with blue steel parts, stainless steel nipple. Hook breech, single trigger, coil spring percussion lock. Steel barrel rib and ramrod ferrules. Introduced 1980. From Lyman.

Price: Percussion $299.95
Price: Flintlock $324.95

LYMAN DEERSTALKER RIFLE

Caliber: 50, 54. **Barrel:** 24", octagonal; 1:48" rifling. **Weight:** 7-1/2 lbs. **Stock:** Walnut with black rubber buttpad. **Sights:** Lyman #37MA beaded front, fully adjustable fold-down Lyman #16A rear. **Features:** Stock has less drop for quick sighting. All metal parts are blackened, with color case-hardened lock; single trigger. Comes with sling and swivels. Available in flint or percussion. Introduced 1990. From Lyman.

Price: 50- or 54-cal., percussion. $304.95
Price: 50- or 54-cal., flintlock $334.95
Price: 50- or 54-cal., percussion, left-hand. $319.95
Price: 50-cal., flintlock, left-hand $349.95
Price: Stainless steel $384.95

LYMAN GREAT PLAINS RIFLE

Caliber: 50- or 54-cal. **Barrel:** 32"; 1:60" twist. **Weight:** 9 lbs. **Stock:** Walnut. **Sights:** Steel blade front, buckhorn rear adjustable for windage and elevation and fixed notch primitive sight included. **Features:** Blued steel furniture. Stainless steel nipple. Coil spring lock, Hawken-style trigger guard and double-set triggers. Round thimbles recessed and sweated into rib. Steel wedge plates and toe plate. Introduced 1979. From Lyman.

Price: Percussion $434.95
Price: Flintlock $459.95
Price: Percussion kit. $349.95
Price: Flintlock kit $374.95
Price: Left-hand percussion $444.95
Price: Left-hand flintlock. $469.95

BLACKPOWDER

Lyman Great Plains

Markesbery Black Bear

Markesbery KM Colorado

Markesbery KM Grizzly Bear

Lyman Great Plains Hunter Rifle
Similar to the Great Plains model except has 1:32" twist shallow-groove barrel and comes drilled and tapped for the Lyman 57GPR peep sight.
Price: . . . . **$434.95 to $459.95**

MARKESBERY KM BLACK BEAR M/L RIFLE
Caliber: 36, 45, 50, 54. **Barrel:** 24"; 1:26" twist. **Weight:** 6-1/2 lbs. **Length:** 38-1/2" overall. **Stock:** Two-piece American hardwood, walnut, black laminate, green laminate, black composition, X-Tra or Mossy Oak Break-Up camouflage. **Sights:** Bead front, open fully adjustable rear. **Features:** Interchangeable barrels; exposed hammer; Outer-Line Magnum ignition system uses small rifle primer or standard No. 11 cap and nipple. Blue, black matte, or stainless. Made in U.S. by Markesbery Muzzle Loaders.
Price: American hardwood walnut, blue finish $536.63
Price: American hardwood walnut, stainless $553.09
Price: Black laminate, blue finish $539.67
Price: Camouflage stock, blue finish $556.46
Price: Black composite, blue finish. $532.65

MARKESBERY KM COLORADO ROCKY MOUNTAIN M/L RIFLE
Caliber: 36, 45, 50, 54. **Barrel:** 24"; 1:26" twist. **Weight:** 6-1/2 lbs. **Length:** 38-1/2" overall. **Stock:** American hardwood walnut, green or black laminate. **Sights:** Firesight bead on ramp front, fully adjustable open rear. **Features:** Replicates Reed/Watson rifle of 1851. Straight grip stock with or without two barrel bands, rubber recoil pad, large-spur hammer. Made in U.S. by Markesbery Muzzle Loaders, Inc.
Price: American hardwood walnut, blue finish $545.92
Price: Black or green laminate, blue finish $548.30
Price: American hardwood walnut, stainless $563.17
Price: Black or green laminate, stainless $566.34

Markesbery KM Brown Bear M/L Rifle
Similar to the KM Black Bear except has one-piece thumbhole stock with Monte Carlo comb. Stock available in Crotch Walnut composite, green or black laminate, black composite or X-Tra or Mossy Oak Break-Up camouflage. Contact maker for complete price listing. Made in U.S. by Markesbery Muzzle Loaders, Inc.
Price: Black composite, blue finish. $658.83
Price: Crotch Walnut composite, stainless $676.11
Price: Green laminate, stainless. $680.07

Markesbery KM Grizzly Bear M/L Rifle
Similar to the KM Black Bear except has thumbhole buttstock with Monte Carlo comb. Stock available in Crotch Walnut composite, green or black laminate, black composite or X-Tra or Mossy Oak Break-Up camouflage. Contact maker for complete price listing. Made in U.S. by Markesbery Muzzle Loaders, Inc.
Price: Black composite, blue finish. $642.96
Price: Crotch Walnut composite, stainless $660.98
Price: Camouflage composite, blue finish $666.67

Markesbery KM Polar Bear M/L Rifle
Similar to the KM Black Bear except has one-piece stock with Monte Carlo comb. Stock available in American Hardwood walnut, green or black laminate, black composite, or X-Tra or Mossy Oak Break-Up camouflage. Has interchangeable barrel system, Outer-Line ignition system, crossbolt double safety. Available in 36, 45, 50, 54 caliber. Contact maker for full price listing. Made in U.S. by Markesbery Muzzle Loaders, Inc.
Price: American Hardwood walnut , blue finish $539.01
Price: Black composite, blue finish. $536.63
Price: Black laminate, blue finish $541.17
Price: Camouflage, stainless $573.94

BLACKPOWDER

Markesbery KM Brown Bear

Mississippi 1841

Navy Arms 1763

Navy Arms 1859 Sharps

Navy Arms Berdan

Mississippi 1841 Percussion Rifle
Similar to Zouave rifle but patterned after U.S. Model 1841. Imported by Dixie Gun Works, Euroarms of America, Navy Arms.
Price: About .... $430.00 to $500.00

NAVY ARMS HAWKEN HUNTER RIFLE/CARBINE
Caliber: 50, 54, 58. **Barrel:** 22-1/2" or 28"; 1:48" twist. **Weight:** 6 lbs., 12 oz. **Length:** 39" overall. **Stock:** Walnut with cheekpiece. **Sights:** Blade front, fully adjustable rear. **Features:** Double-set triggers; all metal has matte black finish; rubber recoil pad; detachable sling swivels. Imported by Navy Arms.
Price: Rifle or Carbine $240.00

NAVY ARMS 1763 CHARLEVILLE
Caliber: 69. **Barrel:** 44-5/8". **Weight:** 8 lbs., 12 oz. **Length:** 59-3/8" overall. **Stock:** Walnut. **Sights:** Brass blade front. **Features:** Replica of the French musket used by American troops during the Revolution. Imported by Navy Arms.
Price: $925.00

NAVY ARMS PARKER-HALE VOLUNTEER RIFLE
Caliber: .451. **Barrel:** 32". **Weight:** 9-1/2 lbs. **Length:** 49" overall. **Stock:** Walnut, checkered wrist and forend. **Sights:** Globe front, adjustable ladder-type rear. **Features:** Recreation of the type of gun issued to volunteer regiments during the 1860s. Rigby-pattern rifling, patent breech, detented lock. Stock is glass bedded for accuracy. Imported by Navy Arms.
Price: $850.00

NAVY ARMS 1859 SHARPS CAVALRY CARBINE
Caliber: 54. **Barrel:** 22". **Weight:** 7-3/4 lbs. **Length:** 39" overall. **Stock:** Walnut. **Sights:** Blade front, military ladder-type rear. **Features:** Color case-hardened action, blued barrel. Has saddle ring. Introduced 1991. Imported from Navy Arms.
Price: $940.00

NAVY ARMS BERDAN 1859 SHARPS RIFLE
Caliber: 54. **Barrel:** 30". **Weight:** 8 lbs., 8 oz. **Length:** 46-3/4" overall. **Stock:** Walnut. **Sights:** Blade front, folding military ladder-type rear. **Features:** Replica of the Union sniper rifle used by Berdan's 1st and 2nd Sharpshooter regiments. Color case-hardened receiver, patchbox, furniture. Double-set triggers. Imported by Navy Arms.
Price: $1,095.00
Price: 1859 Sharps Infantry Rifle (three-band). $1,030.00

NAVY ARMS PENNSYLVANIA LONG RIFLE
Caliber: 32, 45. **Barrel:** 40-1/2". **Weight:** 7-1/2 lbs. **Length:** 56-1/2" overall. **Stock:** Walnut. **Sights:** Blade front, fully adjustable rear. **Features:** Browned barrel, brass furniture, polished lock with double-set triggers. Imported by Navy Arms.
Price: Percussion $490.00
Price: Flintlock $505.00

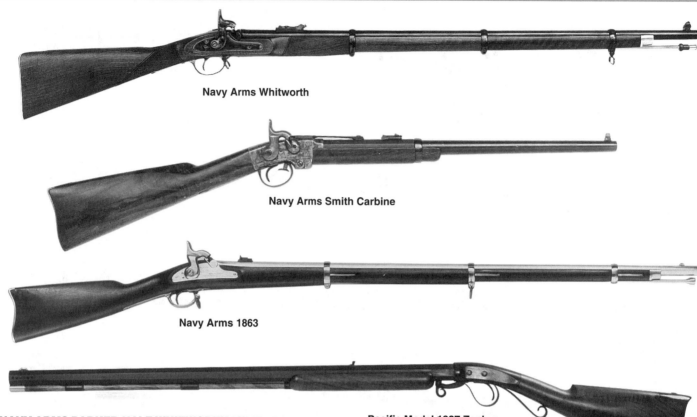

Navy Arms Whitworth

Navy Arms Smith Carbine

Navy Arms 1863

Pacific Model 1837 Zephyr

NAVY ARMS PARKER-HALE WHITWORTH MILITARY TARGET RIFLE

Caliber: 45. **Barrel:** 36". **Weight:** 9-1/4 lbs. **Length:** 52-1/2" overall. **Stock:** Walnut. Checkered at wrist and forend. **Sights:** Hooded post front, open step-adjustable rear. **Features:** Faithful reproduction of the Whitworth rifle, only bored for 45-cal. Trigger has a detented lock, capable of being adjusted very finely without risk of the sear nose catching on the half-cock bent and damaging both parts. Introduced 1978. Imported by Navy Arms.
Price: $875.00

NAVY ARMS SMITH CARBINE

Caliber: 50. **Barrel:** 21-1/2". **Weight:** 7-3/4 lbs. **Length:** 39" overall. **Stock:** American walnut. **Sights:** Brass blade front, folding ladder-type rear. **Features:** Replica of the breech-loading Civil War carbine. Color case-hardened receiver, rest blued. Cavalry model has saddle ring and bar, Artillery model has sling swivels. Imported by Navy Arms.
Price: Cavalry model $600.00
Price: Artillery model.................................... $600.00

NAVY ARMS 1863 C.S. RICHMOND RIFLE

Caliber: 58. **Barrel:** 40". **Weight:** 10 lbs. **Length:** NA. **Stocks:** Walnut. **Sights:** Blade front, adjustable rear. **Features:** Copy of the three-band rifle musket made at Richmond Armory for the Confederacy. All steel polished bright. Imported by Navy Arms.
Price: $550.00

NAVY ARMS 1863 SPRINGFIELD

Caliber: 58, uses .575 Minie. **Barrel:** 40", rifled. **Weight:** 9-1/2 lbs. **Length:** 56" overall. **Stock:** Walnut. **Sights:** Open rear adjustable for elevation. **Features:** Full-size, three-band musket. Polished bright metal, including lock. From Navy Arms.
Price: Finished rifle.................................... $550.00

NAVY ARMS 1861 SPRINGFIELD RIFLE

Caliber: 58. **Barrel:** 40" **Weight:** 10 lbs., 4 oz. **Length:** 56" overall. **Stock:** Walnut. **Sights:** Blade front, military leaf rear. **Features:** Steel barrel, lock and all furniture have polished bright finish. Has 1855-style hammer. Imported by Navy Arms.
Price: $550.00

PACIFIC RIFLE MODEL 1837 ZEPHYR

Caliber: 62. **Barrel:** 30", tapered octagon. **Weight:** 7-3/4 lbs. **Length:** NA. **Stock:** Oil-finished fancy walnut. **Sights:** German silver blade front, semi-buckhorn rear. Options available. **Features:** Improved underhammer action. First production rifle to offer Forsyth rifle, with narrow lands and shallow rifling with 1:144" pitch for high-velocity round balls. Metal finish is slow rust brown with nitre blue accents. Optional sights, finishes and integral muzzle brake available. Introduced 1995. Made in U.S. by Pacific Rifle Co.
Price: From... $995.00

Pacific Rifle Big Bore, African Rifles

Similar to the 1837 Zephyr except in 72-caliber and 8-bore. The 72-caliber is available in standard form with 28" barrel, or as the African with flat buttplate, checkered upgraded wood; weight is 9 lbs. The 8-bore African has dual-cap ignition, 24" barrel, weighs 12 lbs., checkered English walnut, engraving, gold inlays. Introduced 1998. Made in U.S. by Pacific Rifle Co.
Price: 72-caliber, from $1,150.00
Price: 8-bore from.................................... $2,500.00

PEIFER MODEL TS-93 RIFLE

Caliber: 45, 50. **Barrel:** 24" Douglas premium; 1:20" twist in 45; 1:28" in 50. **Weight:** 7 lbs. **Length:** 43-1/4" overall. **Stock:** Bell & Carlson solid composite, with recoil pad, swivel studs. **Sights:** Williams bead front on ramp, fully adjustable open rear. Drilled and tapped for Weaver scope mounts with dovetail for rear peep. **Features:** In-line ignition uses #209 shotshell primer; extremely fast lock time; fully enclosed breech; adjustable trigger; automatic safety; removable primer holder. Blue or stainless. Made in U.S. by Peifer Rifle Co. Introduced 1996.

BLACKPOWDER MUSKETS & RIFLES

Peifer TS-93

Remington Model 700 ML

C.S. Richmond 1863

Ruger K77/50RSBBZ

Price: Blue, black stock $730.00
Price: Blue, wood or camouflage composite stock, or stainless
with black composite stock............................. $803.00
Price: Stainless, wood or camouflage composite stock $876.00

PRAIRIE RIVER ARMS PRA CLASSIC RIFLE

Caliber: 50, 54. **Barrel:** 26"; 1:28" twist. **Weight:** 7-1/2 lbs. **Length:** 40-1/2"
overall. **Stock:** Hardwood or black all-weather. **Sights:** Blade front, open
adjustable rear. **Features:** Patented internal percussion ignition system.
Drilled and tapped for scope mount. Introduced 1995. Made in U.S. by
Prairie River Arms, Ltd.
Price: 4140 alloy barrel, hardwood stock $375.00
Price: As above, stainless barrel $425.00
Price: 4140 alloy barrel, black all-weather stock $390.00
Price: As above, stainless barrel $440.00

PRAIRIE RIVER ARMS PRA BULLPUP RIFLE

Caliber: 50, 54. **Barrel:** 28"; 1:28" twist. **Weight:** 7-1/2 lbs. **Length:** 31-1/2"
overall. **Stock:** Hardwood or black all-weather. **Sights:** Blade front, open
adjustable rear. **Features:** Bullpup design thumbhole stock. Patented internal percussion ignition system. Left-hand model available. Dovetailed
for scope mount. Introduced 1995. Made in U.S. by Prairie River Arms, Ltd.
Price: 4140 alloy barrel, hardwood stock $375.00
Price: As above, black stock.............................. $390.00
Price: Stainless barrel, hardwood stock $425.00
Price: As above, black stock.............................. $440.00

REMINGTON MODEL 700 ML, MLS RIFLES

Caliber: 50, 54. **Barrel:** 24"; 1:28" twist. **Weight:** 7-3/4 lbs. **Length:** 44-1/2"
overall. **Stock:** Black fiberglass-reinforced synthetic with checkered grip
and forend; magnum-style buttpad. **Sights:** Ramped bead front, open fully
adjustable rear. Drilled and tapped for scope mounts. **Features:** Uses the
Remington 700 bolt action, stock design, safety and trigger mechanisms;
removable stainelss steel breech plug, No. 11 nipple; solid aluminum ram-
rod. Comes with cleaning tools and accessories.
Price: ML, blued, 50-caliber only $396.00
Price: MLS, stainless, 50- or 54-caliber $496.00
Price: ML, blued, Mossy Oak Break-Up camo stock $439.00
Price: MLS, stainless, Mossy Oak Break-Up camo stock $532.00
Price: ML Youth (12-3/8" length of pull, 21" barrel) $396.00

C.S. RICHMOND 1863 MUSKET

Caliber: 58. **Barrel:** 40". **Weight:** 11 lbs. **Length:** 56-1/4" overall. **Stock:**
European walnut with oil finish. **Sights:** Blade front, adjustable folding leaf
rear. **Features:** Reproduction of the three-band Civil War musket. Sling
swivels attached to trigger guard and middle barrel band. Lockplate
marked "1863" and "C.S. Richmond." All metal left in the white. Brass buttplate and forend cap. Imported by Euroarms of America, Navy Arms.
Price: .... NA

RUGER 77/50 IN-LINE PERCUSSION RIFLE

Caliber: 50. **Barrel:** 22"; 1:28" twist. **Weight:** 6-1/2 lbs. **Length:** 41-1/2"
overall. **Stock:** Birch with rubber buttpad and swivel studs. **Sights:** Gold
bead front, folding leaf rear. Comes with Ruger scope mounts. **Features:**
Shares design features with the Ruger 77/22 rifle. Stainless steel bolt and
nipple/breech plug; uses #11 caps; three-position safety; blued steel ramrod. Introduced 1997. Made in U.S. by Sturm, Ruger & Co.
Price: 77/50RS... $434.00
Price: 77/50RSO Officer's (straight-grip checkered walnut stock,
blued) $555.00
Price: K77/50RSBBZ (stainless steel, black laminated stock) $601.00
Price: K77/50RSP All-Weather (stainless steel,
synthetic stock)....................................... $580.00

BLACKPOWDER MUSKETS & RIFLES

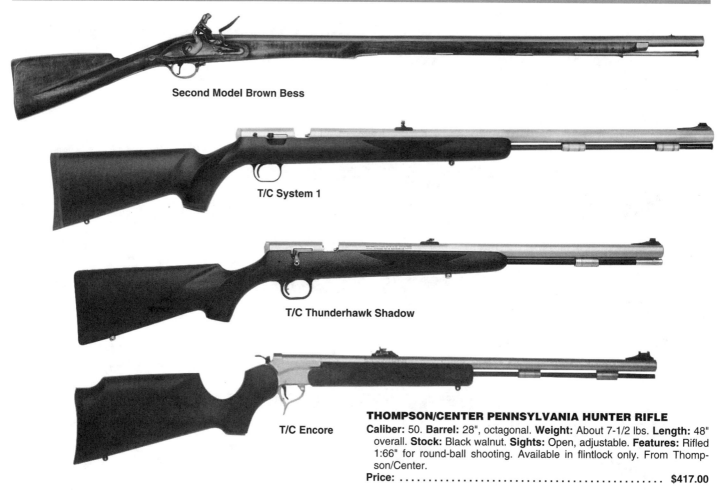

Second Model Brown Bess

T/C System 1

T/C Thunderhawk Shadow

T/C Encore

SECOND MODEL BROWN BESS MUSKET

Caliber: 75, uses .735" round ball. **Barrel:** 42", smoothbore. **Weight:** 9-1/2 lbs. **Length:** 59" overall. **Stock:** Walnut (Navy); walnut-stained hardwood (Dixie). **Sights:** Fixed. **Features:** Polished barrel and lock with brass trigger guard and buttplate. Bayonet and scabbard available. From Navy Arms, Dixie Gun Works, Cabela's.

Price: Finished . . . . $475.00 to $850.00
Price: Kit (Dixie Gun Works, Navy Arms) . . . . $575.00 to $625.00
Price: Carbine (Navy Arms) $835.00

THOMPSON/CENTER BLACK MOUNTAIN MAGNUM RIFLE

Caliber: 50, 54. **Barrel:** 26"; 1:28" twist. **Weight:** 7 lbs. **Length:** 4-3/4" overall. **Stock:** American Walnut or black composite. **Sights:** Ramp front with Tru-Glo fiber optic inseat, click adjustable open rear with Tru-Glo fiber optic inserts. **Features:** Side lock percussion with breeech designed for Pyrodex Pellets, loose blackpowder and Pyrodex. blued steel. Uses QLA muzzle system. Introduced 1999. Made in U.S. by Thompson/Center Arms.

Price: Blue, composite stock, 50-cal. $353.52
Price: Blue, walnut stock, 50- or 54-cal. (westraner) $387.16

THOMPSON/CENTER FIRE STORM RIFLE

Caliber: 50. **Barrel:** 26"; 1:28" twist. **Weight:** 7 lbs. **Length:** 41-3/4" overall. **Stock:** Black synthetic with rubber recoil pad, swivel studs. **Sights:** Click-adjustable steel rear and ramp-style front, both with fiber optic inserts. **Features:** Side hammer lock is the first designed for up to three 50-grain Pyrodex pellets; patented Pyrodex Pyramid breech directs ignition fire 360 degrees around base of pellet; uses 209 shotgun primers; Quick Load Accurizor Muzzle System; aluminum ramrod. Introduced 2000. Made in U.S. by Thomson/Center Arms.

Price: Blue finish, percussion model. $391.00
Price: Blue finish, flintlock model with 1:48" twist for round balls, conicals. $391.00

THOMPSON/CENTER PENNSYLVANIA HUNTER RIFLE

Caliber: 50. **Barrel:** 28", octagonal. **Weight:** About 7-1/2 lbs. **Length:** 48" overall. **Stock:** Black walnut. **Sights:** Open, adjustable. **Features:** Rifled 1:66" for round-ball shooting. Available in flintlock only. From Thompson/Center.

Price: $417.00

Thompson/Center Pennsylvania Hunter Carbine

Similar to the Pennsylvania Hunter except has 21" barrel, weighs 6.5 lbs., and has an overall length of 38". Designed for shooting patched round balls. Available in flintlock only. Introduced 1992. From Thompson/Center.

Price: $438.00

THOMPSON/CENTER SYSTEM 1 IN-LINE RIFLE

Caliber: 32, 50, 54, 58; 12-gauge. **Barrel:** 26" round; 1:38" twist. **Weight:** About 7-1/2lbs. **Length:** 44" overall. **Stock:** American black walnut or composite. **Sights:** Ramp front with white bead, adjustable leaf rear. **Features:** In-line ignition. Interchangeable barrels; removable breech plug allows cleaning from the breech; fully adjustable trigger; sliding thumb safety; QLA muzzle system; rubber recoil pad; sling swivel studs. Introduced 1997. Made in U.S. by Thompson/Center Arms.

Price: Blue, walnut stock $396.00
Price: Stainless, composite stock, 50-, 54-caliber $440.00
Price: Stainless, camo composite stock, 50-caliber $479.00
Price: Extra barrels, blue $176.00
Price: Extra barrels, stainless, 50-, 54-caliber $220.00

THOMPSON/CENTER ENCORE 209x50 MAGNUM

Caliber: 50. **Barrel:** 26"; interchangeable with centerfire calibers. **Weight:** 7 lbs. **Length:** 40-1/2" overall. **Stock:** American walnut butt and forend, or black composite. **Sights:** Tru-Glo Fiber Optic front, Tru-Glo Fiber Optic rear. **Features:** Blue or stainless steel. Uses the stock, frame and forend of the Encore centerfire pistol; break-open design using trigger guard spur; stainless steel universal breech plug; uses #209 shotshell primers. Introduced 1998. Made in U.S. by Thompson/Center Arms.

Price: $590.03
Price: Blue, walnut stock and forend $590.03
Price: Blue, composite stock and forend $590.03
Price: Stainless, composite stock and forend. $665.91

BLACKPOWDER MUSKETS & RIFLES

T/C Black Diamond

T/C Hawken

Traditions Buckhunter Pro In-Line

Traditions Buckhunter

THOMPSON/CENTER THUNDERHAWK SHADOW

Caliber: 50, 54. **Barrel:** 24"; 1:38" twist. **Weight:** 7 lbs. **Length:** 41-3/4" overall. **Stock:** American walnut or black composite with rubber recoil pad. **Sights:** Bead on ramp front, adjustable leaf rear. **Features:** Uses modern in-line ignition system, adjustable trigger. Knurled striker handle indicators for Safe and Fire. Black wood ramrod, Drilled and tapped for T/C scope mounts. Introduced 1996. From Thompson/Center Arms.
Price: Blued $294.00

THOMPSON/CENTER BLACK DIAMOND RIFLE

Caliber: 50. **Barrel:** 22-1/2" with QLA; 1:28" twist. **Weight:** 6 lbs., 9 oz. **Length:** 41-1/2" overall. **Stock:** Black Rynite with moulded-in checkering and grip cap, or walnut. **Sights:** Tru-Glo Fiber Optic ramp-style front, Tru-Glo Fiber Optic open rear. **Features:** In-line ignition system for musket cap, No. 11 cap, or 209 shotshell primer; removable universal breech plug; stainless steel construction. Introduced 1998. Made in U.S. by Thompson/Center Arms.
Price: $312.87
Price: With walnut stock $353.32

THOMPSON/CENTER HAWKEN RIFLE

Caliber: 45, 50 or 54. **Barrel:** 28" octagon, hooked breech. **Stock:** American walnut. **Sights:** Blade front, rear adjustable for windage and elevation. **Features:** Solid brass furniture, double-set triggers, button rifled barrel, coil-type mainspring. From Thompson/Center Arms.
Price: Percussion model (45-, 50- or 54-cal.) $489.35
Price: Flintlock model (50-cal.) $501.14

TRADITIONS BUCKHUNTER PRO IN-LINE RIFLES

Caliber: 50 (1:32" twist); 54 (1:48" twist). **Barrel:** 24" tapered round. **Weight:** 7-1/2 lbs. **Length:** 42" overall. **Stock:** Composite or thumbhole available in black, Break-Up or camouflage. **Sights:** Beaded blade front, fully adjustable open rear. Drilled and tapped for scope mounting. **Features:** In-line percussion ignition system; adjustable trigger; manual thumb safety; removable stainless steel breech plug. Eleven models available. Introduced 1996. From Traditions.
Price: . . . . $169.00 to $219.00

TRADITIONS BUCKSKINNER CARBINE

Caliber: 50. **Barrel:** 21"; 15/16" flats, half octagon, half round; 1:20" or 1:66" twist. **Weight:** 6 lbs. **Length:** 37" overall. **Stock:** Beech or black laminated. **Sights:** Beaded blade front, fiber optic open rear click adjustable for windage and elevation or fiber optics. **Features:** Uses V-type mainspring, single trigger. Non-glare hardware. From Traditions.
Price: Flintlock $218.00
Price: Flintlock, laminated stock $292.00

TRADITIONS IN-LINE BUCKHUNTER SERIES RIFLES

Caliber: 50, 54. **Barrel:** 24", round; 1:32" (50); 1:48" (54) twist. **Weight:** 7 lbs., 6 oz. to 8 lbs. **Length:** 41" overall. **Stock:** All-Weather black or camo composite. **Sights:** Fiber Optic blade front, click adjustable rear. Drilled and tapped for scope mounting. **Features:** Removable breech plug; PVC ramrod; sling swivels. Introduced 1995. From Traditions.
Price: $175.00
Price: With RS Redi-Pak (powder measure, powder flask, two fast loaders, 5-in-1 loader, capper, ball starter, ball puller, cleaning jag, nipple wrench, bullets) 50- and 54-caliber. $199.00
Price: Pro Model (fiber optics front & rear sights) . . . . $169.00 to $219.00

TRADITIONS DEERHUNTER RIFLE SERIES

Caliber: 32, 50 or 54. **Barrel:** 24", octagonal; 15/16" flats; 1:48" or 1:66" twist. **Weight:** 6 lbs. **Length:** 40" overall. **Stock:** Stained hardwood or All-Weather composite with rubber buttpad, sling swivels. **Sights:** Blade front, fixed rear or adjustable fiber optics. **Features:** Flint or percussion with color case-hardened lock. Hooked breech, oversized trigger guard, blackened furniture, PVC ramrod. All-Weather has composite stock and C-Nickel barrel. Drilled and tapped for scope mounting. Imported by Traditions, Inc.
Price: Percussion, 50 or 54; 1:48" twist $161.00
Price: Flintlock, 50-caliber only; 1:66" twist $183.00
Price: Flintlock, All-Weather, 50-cal. $161.00
Price: Percussion, All-Weather, 50 or 54 . . . . $152.00

BLACKPOWDER MUSKETS & RIFLES

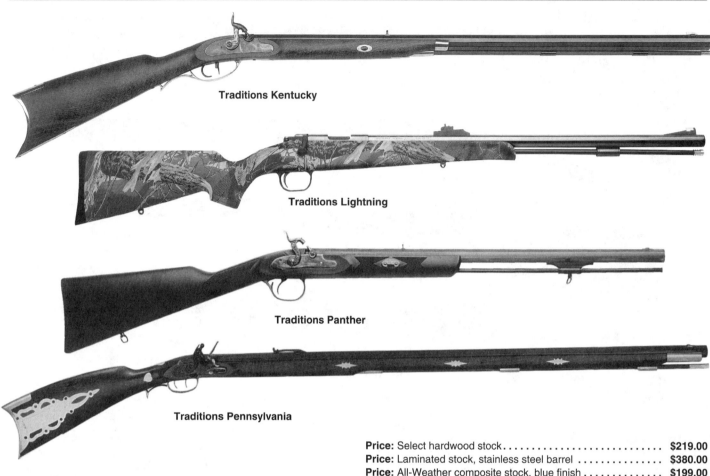

Traditions Kentucky

Traditions Lightning

Traditions Panther

Traditions Pennsylvania

Traditions Deerhunter All-Weather Composite Stock Rifle

Black composite stock with checkered grip and forend. Blued barrel, C-Nickel or Advantage camouflage finish, 50-caliber flintlock. Introduced 1996. Imported by Traditions.

Price: Blued, flintlock, 50-cal. **$160.00**
Price: Blued or Hardwoods, 50-cal. **$175.00**

TRADITIONS HAWKEN WOODSMAN RIFLE

Caliber: 50 and 54. **Barrel:** 28"; 15/16" flats. **Weight:** 7 lbs., 11 oz. **Length:** 44-1/2" overall. **Stock:** Walnut-stained hardwood. **Sights:** Beaded blade front, hunting-style open rear adjustable for windage and elevation. **Features:** Percussion only. Brass patchbox and furniture. Double triggers. From Traditions.

Price: 50 or 54 . . . . **$219.00**
Price: 50-cal., left-hand. **$233.00**
Price: 50-caliber, flintlock **$248.00**

TRADITIONS KENTUCKY RIFLE

Caliber: 50. **Barrel:** 33-1/2"; 7/8" flats; 1:66" twist. **Weight:** 7 lbs. **Length:** 49" overall. **Stock:** Beech; inletted toe plate. **Sights:** Blade front, fixed rear. **Features:** Full-length, two-piece stock; brass furniture; color case-hardened lock. Introduced 1995. From Traditions.

Price: Finished **$226.00**
Price: Kit. **$175.00**

TRADITIONS LIGHTNING BOLT-ACTION MUZZLELOADER

Caliber: 50, 54. **Barrel:** 24" round; blued, stainless, C-Nickel or Ultra Coat. **Weight:** 7 lbs. **Length:** 43" overall. **Stock:** Brown laminated, All-Weather composite, Advantage, or Break-Up camouflage. **Sights:** Fiber Optic blade front, fully adjustable open rear. **Features:** Twenty-one variations available. Field-removable stainless steel bolt; silent thumb safety; adjustable trigger; drilled and tapped for scope mounting. Lightning Fire System allows use of No. 11 or musket caps. Introduced 1997. Imported by Traditions.

Price: Select hardwood stock. **$219.00**
Price: Laminated stock, stainless steel barrel **$380.00**
Price: All-Weather composite stock, blue finish **$199.00**
Price: All-Weather composite, stainless steel **$279.00**
Price: Camouflage composite **$307.00**
Price: All-Weather composite **$307.00**
Price: Camouflage composite **$351.00**
Price: Composite, with muzzle brake **$249.00**
Price: Composite, with muzzle brake, stainless, fluted barrel **$376.00**

Traditions Lightning Lightweight Bolt-Action Rifles

Similar to Lightning except features 22" lightweight, fluted barrel and Spi-der Web-pattern black composite stock. Overall length 41", weighs 6 lb., 5 oz. Introduced 2000. From Traditions.

Price: Blued finish. **$239.00**
Price: C-Nickel finish. **$249.00**
Price: Stainless **$289.00**

TRADITIONS PANTHER RIFLE

Caliber: 50. **Barrel:** 24" octagon (1:48" twist); 15/16" flats. **Weight:** 6 lbs. **Length:** 40" overall. **Stock:** All-Weather composite. **Sights:** Brass blade front, fixed rear. **Features:** Percussion only; color case-hardened lock; blackened furniture; sling swivels; PVC ramrod. Introduced 1996. Imported by Traditions.

Price: **$116.00**
Price: With RS Redi-Pak (powder measure, flask, fast loaders, 5-in-1 loader, capper, ball starter, ball puller, cleaning jag, nipple wrench). **$169.00**

TRADITIONS PENNSYLVANIA RIFLE

Caliber: 50. **Barrel:** 40-1/4"; 7/8" flats; 1:66" twist, octagon. **Weight:** 9 lbs. **Length:** 57-1/2" overall. **Stock:** Walnut. **Sights:** Blade front, adjustable rear. **Features:** Brass patchbox and ornamentation. Double-set triggers. From Traditions.

Price: Flintlock **$474.00**
Price: Percussion **$467.00**

BLACKPOWDER

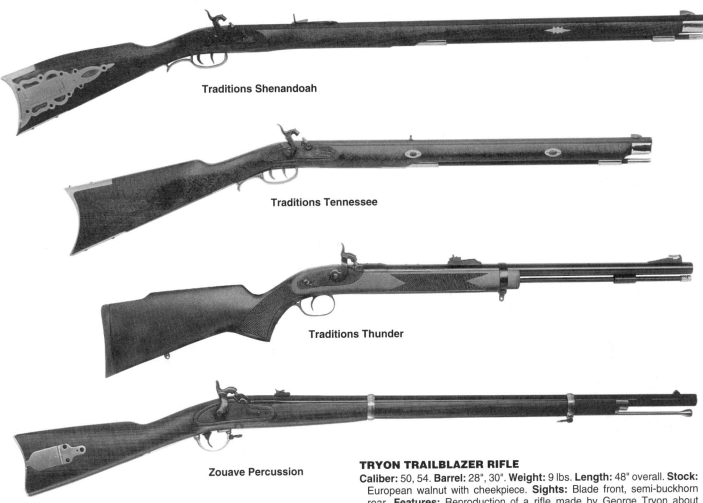

Traditions Shenandoah

Traditions Tennessee

Traditions Thunder

Zouave Percussion

TRADITIONS SHENANDOAH RIFLE

Caliber: 50. **Barrel:** 33-1/2" octagon; 1:66" twist. **Weight:** 7 lbs., 3 oz. **Length:** 49-1/2" overall. **Stock:** Walnut. **Sights:** Blade front, buckhorn rear. **Features:** V-type mainspring; double-set trigger; solid brass buttplate, patchbox, nosecap, thimbles, trigger guard. Introduced 1996. From Traditions.

Price: Flintlock **$365.00**
Price: Percussion **$350.00**

TRADITIONS TENNESSEE RIFLE

Caliber: 50. **Barrel:** 24", octagon; 15/16" flats; 1:66" twist. **Weight:** 6 lbs. **Length:** 40-1/2" overall. **Stock:** Stained beech. **Sights:** Blade front, fixed rear. **Features:** One-piece stock has inletted brass furniture, cheekpiece; double-set trigger; V-type mainspring. Flint or percussion. Introduced 1995. From Traditions.

Price: Percussion **$270.00**
Price: Flintlock **$284.00**

TRADITIONS THUNDER MAGNUM RIFLE

Caliber: 50. **Barrel:** 24"; 1:32" twist. **Weight:** 7 lbs., 9 oz. **Length:** 42-1/2" overall. **Stock:** Hardwood or composite. **Sights:** Fiber optic front, adjustable rear. **Features:** Sidelock action with thumb-activated safety. Introduced 1999. From Traditions.

Price: Hardwood. **$349.00**
Price: Composite **$339.00**
Price: Composite, C-Nickel. **$359.00**

TRYON TRAILBLAZER RIFLE

Caliber: 50, 54. **Barrel:** 28", 30". **Weight:** 9 lbs. **Length:** 48" overall. **Stock:** European walnut with cheekpiece. **Sights:** Blade front, semi-buckhorn rear. **Features:** Reproduction of a rifle made by George Tryon about 1820. Double-set triggers, back action lock, hooked breech with long tang. From Armsport.

Price: About **$825.00**

WHITE MODEL 97 WHITETAIL HUNTER RIFLE

Caliber: 45, 50. **Barrel:** 22", 1:24" twist (50 cal.). **Weight:** 7.6 lbs. **Length:** 39-7/8" overall. **Stock:** Black laminated wood or black composite with swivel studs. **Sights:** Marble fully adjustable, steel rear with white diamond; red-bead front with high-visibility inserts. **Features:** In-line ignition with FlashFire one-piece nipple and breech plug that uses standard or magnum No. 11 caps; fully adjustable trigger; double safety system; aluminum ramrod; drilled and tapped for scope. Includes hard gun case. Introduced 2000. Made in U.S. by Muzzleloading Technologies Inc.

Price: Laminated wood stock **$549.95**
Price: Black composite stock **$549.95**

White Model 98 Elite Hunter Rifle

Similar to Model 97 but features 24" barrel with longer action for extended sight radius. Overall length 43-5/16", weighs 8.2 lbs. Choice of black laminated or black hardwood stock. From Muzzleloading Technologies Inc.

Price: Black laminated stock (45 or 50 cal.) **$699.95**
Price: Black hardwood stock (45 or 50 cal.) **$699.95**

ZOUAVE PERCUSSION RIFLE

Caliber: 58, 59. **Barrel:** 32-1/2". **Weight:** 9-1/2 lbs. **Length:** 48-1/2" overall. **Stock:** Walnut finish, brass patchbox and buttplate. **Sights:** Fixed front, rear adjustable for elevation. **Features:** Color case-hardened lockplate, blued barrel. From Navy Arms, Dixie Gun Works, E.M.F., Cabela's.

Price: About . . . . **$325.00** to **$465.00**

BLACKPOWDER SHOTGUNS

Cabela's 12-Gauge

Dixie Magnum

Knight TK2000

Traditions
Buckhunter Pro

CABELA'S BLACKPOWDER SHOTGUNS
Gauge: 10, 12, 20. **Barrel:** 10-ga., 30"; 12-ga., 28-1/2" (Extra-Full, Mod., Imp. Cyl. choke tubes); 20-ga., 27-1/2" (Imp. Cyl. & Mod. fixed chokes). **Weight:** 6-1/2 to 7 lbs. **Length:** 45" overall (28-1/2" barrel). **Stock:** American walnut with checkered grip; 12- and 20-gauge have straight stock, 10-gauge has pistol grip. **Features:** Blued barrels, engraved, color case-hardened locks and hammers, brass ramrod tip. From Cabela's.
Price: 10-gauge $499.99
Price: 12-gauge $449.99
Price: 20-gauge $429.99

CVA TRAPPER PERCUSSION
Gauge: 12. **Barrel:** 28". **Weight:** 6 lbs. **Length:** 46" overall. **Stock:** English-style checkered straight grip of walnut-finished hardwood. **Sights:** Brass bead front. **Features:** Single-blued barrel; color case-hardened lockplate and hammer; screw adjustable sear engagements, V-type mainspring; brass wedge plates; color case-hardened and engraved trigger guard and tang. From CVA.
Price: Finished $239.95

DIXIE MAGNUM PERCUSSION SHOTGUN
Gauge: 10, 12, 20. **Barrel:** 30" (Imp. Cyl. & Mod.) in 10-gauge; 28" in 12-gauge. **Weight:** 6-1/4 lbs. **Length:** 45" overall. **Stock:** Hand-checkered walnut, 14" pull. **Features:** Double triggers; light hand engraving; case-hardened locks in 12-gauge, polished steel in 10-gauge; sling swivels. From Dixie Gun Works.
Price: Upland $449.00
Price: 12-ga. kit. $375.00
Price: 20-ga. $495.00
Price: 10-ga. $495.00
Price: 10-ga. kit. $395.00

KNIGHT TK2000 MUZZLELOADING SHOTGUN
Gauge: 12. **Barrel:** 26", extra-full choke tube. **Weight:** 7 lbs., 9 oz. **Length:** 45" overall. **Stock:** Synthetic black or Realtree X-tra Brown; recoil pad; swivel studs. **Sights:** Fully adjustable rear, blade front with fiber optics. **Features:** Receiver drilled and tapped for scope mount; in-line ignition; adjustable trigger; removable breech plug; double safety system; imp. cyl. choke tube available. Introduced 2000. Made in U.S. by Knight Rifles.
Price: $349.95

NAVY ARMS STEEL SHOT MAGNUM SHOTGUN
Gauge: 10. **Barrel:** 28" (Cyl. & Cyl.). **Weight:** 7 lbs., 9 oz. **Length:** 45-1/2" overall. **Stock:** Walnut, with cheekpiece. **Features:** Designed specifically for steel shot. Engraved, polished locks; sling swivels; blued barrels. Imported by Navy Arms.
Price: $605.00

NAVY ARMS T&T SHOTGUN
Gauge: 12. **Barrel:** 28" (Full & Full). **Weight:** 7-1/2 lbs. **Stock:** Walnut. **Sights:** Bead front. **Features:** Color case-hardened locks, double triggers; blued steel furniture. From Navy Arms.
Price: $580.00

TRADITIONS BUCKHUNTER PRO SHOTGUN
Gauge: 12. **Barrel:** 24", choke tube. **Weight:** 6 lbs., 4 oz. **Length:** 43" overall. **Stock:** Composite matte black, Break-Up or Advantage camouflage. **Features:** In-line action with removable stainless steel breech plug; thumb safety; adjustable trigger; rubber buttpad. Introduced 1996. From Traditions.
Price: $248.00
Price: With Advantage, Shadow Branch, or Break-Up camouflage stock $292.00

THOMPSON/CENTER
BLACK MOUNTAIN MAGNUM SHOTGUN
Gauge: 12. **Barrel:** 27" screw-in Turkey choke tube. **Weight:** 7 lbs. **Length:** 41-3/4" overall. **Stock:** Black composite. **Sights:** Bead front. **Features:** Sidelock percussion action. Polished blue finish. Introduced in 1999. Made in U.S. by Thompson/Center Arms.
Price: $387.16

Beeman P1

Beeman/FWB P30

Beeman/FWB C55

Beeman/Feinwerkbau 103

Benjamin Sheridan CO2

BEEMAN P1 MAGNUM AIR PISTOL

Caliber: 177, 5mm, single shot. **Barrel:** 8.4". **Weight:** 2.5 lbs. **Length:** 11" overall. **Power:** Top lever cocking; spring-piston. **Stocks:** Checkered walnut. **Sights:** Blade front, square notch rear with click micrometer adjustments for windage and elevation. Grooved for scope mounting. **Features:** Dual power for 177 and 20-cal.: low setting gives 350-400 fps; high setting 500-600 fps. Rearward expanding mainspring simulates firearm recoil. All Colt 45 auto grips fit gun. Dry-firing feature for practice. Optional wooden shoulder stock. Introduced 1985. Imported by Beeman.
Price: 177, 5mm **$415.00**

Beeman P2 Match Air Pistol

Similar to the Beeman P1 Magnum except shoots only 177 pellets; completely recoilless single-stroke pnuematic action. Weighs 2.2 lbs. Choice of thumbrest match grips or standard style. Introduced 1990.
Price: 177, 5mm, standard grip **$385.00**
Price: 177, match grip **$455.00**

BEEMAN P3 AIR PISTOL

Caliber: 177 pellet, single shot. **Barrel:** N/A. **Weight:** 1.7 lbs. **Length:** 9.6" overall. **Power:** Single-stroke pneumatic; overlever barrel cocking. **Grips:** Reinforced polymer. **Sights:** Adjustable rear, blade front. **Features:** Velocity 410 fps. Polymer frame; automatic safety; two-stage trigger; built-in muzzle brake. Introduced 1999 by Beeman.
Price: **$159.00**

BEEMAN/FEINWERKBAU 65 MKII AIR PISTOL

Caliber: 177, single shot. **Barrel:** 6.1", removable bbl. wgt. available. **Weight:** 42 oz. **Length:** 13.3" overall. **Power:** Spring, sidelever cocking. **Stocks:** Walnut, stippled thumbrest; adjustable or fixed. **Sights:** Front, interchangeable post element system, open rear, click adjustable for windage and elevation and for sighting notch width. Scope mount available. **Features:** New shorter barrel for better balance and control. Cocking effort 9 lbs. Two-stage trigger, four adjustments. Quiet firing, 525 fps. Programs instantly for recoil or recoilless operation. Permanently lubricated. Steel piston ring. Imported by Beeman.
Price: Right-hand **$1,070.00**

BEEMAN/FEINWERKBAU 103 PISTOL

Caliber: 177, single shot. **Barrel:** 10.1", 12-groove rifling. **Weight:** 2.5 lbs. **Length:** 16.5" overall. **Power:** Single-stroke pneumatic, underlever cocking. **Stocks:** Stippled walnut with adjustable palm shelf. **Sights:** Blade front, open rear adjustable for windage and elevation. Notch size adjustable for width. Interchangeable front blades. **Features:** Velocity 510 fps. Fully adjustable trigger. Cocking effort of 2 lbs. Imported by Beeman.
Price: Right-hand **$1,195.00**
Price: Left-hand **$1,235.00**

BEEMAN/FWB P30 MATCH AIR PISTOL

Caliber: 177, single shot. **Barrel:** 10-5/16", with muzzlebrake. **Weight:** 2.4 lbs. **Length:** 16.5" overall. **Power:** Pre-charged pneumatic. **Stocks:** Stippled walnut; adjustable match type. **Sights:** Undercut blade front, fully adjustable match rear. **Features:** Velocity to 525 fps; up to 200 shots per CO2 cartridge. Fully adjustable trigger; built-in muzzlebrake. Introduced 1995. Imported from Germany by Beeman.
Price: Right-hand **$1,275.00**
Price: Left-hand **$1,350.00**

BEEMAN/FWB C55 CO₂ RAPID FIRE PISTOL

Caliber: 177, single shot or 5-shot magazine. **Barrel:** 7.3". **Weight:** 2.5 lbs. **Length:** 15" overall. **Power:** Special CO2 cylinder. **Stocks:** Anatomical, adjustable. **Sights:** Interchangeable front, fully adjustable open micro-click rear with adjustable notch size. **Features:** Velocity 510 fps. Has 11.75" sight radius. Built-in muzzlebrake. Introduced 1993. Imported by Beeman Precision Airguns.
Price: Right-hand **$1,460.00**
Price: Left-hand **$1,520.00**

BEEMAN HW70A AIR PISTOL

Caliber: 177, single shot. **Barrel:** 6-1/4", rifled. **Weight:** 38 oz. **Length:** 12-3/4" overall. **Power:** Spring, barrel cocking. **Stocks:** Plastic, with thumbrest. **Sights:** Hooded post front, square notch rear adjustable for windage and elevation. Comes with scope base. **Features:** Adjustable trigger, 31-lb. cocking effort, 440 fps MV; automatic barrel safety. Imported by Beeman.
Price: **$185.00**
Price: HW70S, black grip, silver finish **$210.00**

BEEMAN/WEBLEY TEMPEST AIR PISTOL

Caliber: 177, 22, single shot. **Barrel:** 6-7/8". **Weight:** 32 oz. **Length:** 8.9" overall. **Power:** Spring-piston, break barrel. **Stocks:** Checkered black plastic with thumbrest. **Sights:** Blade front, adjustable rear. **Features:** Velocity to 500 fps (177), 400 fps (22). Aluminum frame; black epoxy finish; manual safety. Imported from England by Beeman.
Price: **$180.00**

Beeman/Webley Hurricane Air Pistol

Similar to the Tempest except has extended frame in the rear for a click-adjustable rear sight; hooded front sight; comes with scope mount. Imported from England by Beeman.
Price: **$225.00**

BENJAMIN SHERIDAN CO₂ PELLET PISTOLS

Caliber: 177, 20, 22, single shot. **Barrel:** 6-3/8", rifled brass. **Weight:** 29 oz. **Length:** 9.8" overall. **Power:** 12-gram CO2 cylinder. **Stocks:** Walnut. **Sights:** High ramp front, fully adjustable notch rear. **Features:** Velocity to 500 fps. Turn-bolt action with cross-bolt safety. Gives about 40 shots per CO2 cylinder. Black or nickel finish. Made in U.S. by Benjamin Sheridan Co.
Price: Black finish, EB17 (177), EB20 (20), about **$115.23**

AIRGUNS

AIRGUNS—HANDGUNS

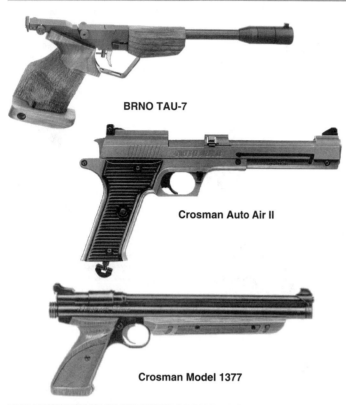

BRNO TAU-7

Crosman Auto Air II

Crosman Model 1377

Daisy/Power Line 717

BENJAMIN SHERIDAN PNEUMATIC PELLET PISTOLS
Caliber: 177, 20, 22, single shot. **Barrel:** 9-3/8", rifled brass. **Weight:** 38 oz. **Length:**13-1/8" overall. **Power:** Underlever pnuematic, hand pumped. **Stocks:** Walnut stocks and pump handle. **Sights:** High ramp front, fully adjustable notch rear. **Features:** Velocity to 525 fps (variable). Bolt action with cross-bolt safety. Choice of black or nickel finish. Made in U.S. by Benjamin Sheridan Co.
Price: Black finish, HB17 (177), HB20 (20), HB22 (22), about $129.50

 NEW!

BERETTA 92 FS/CO2 AIR PISTOLS
Caliber: 177 pellet, 8-shot magazine. **Barrel:** 4.9". **Weight:** 44.4 oz. **Length:** 8.2" (10.2" with compensator). Power: CO2 cartridge. **Grips:** plastic or wood. **Sights:** Adjustable rear, blade front. **Features:** Velocity to 375 fps. Replica of Beretta 92 FS pistol. Single- and double-action trigger; ambidextrous safety; black or nickel-plated finish. Made by Umarex for Beretta USA.
Price: Starting at $200.00

BRNO TAU-7 CO2 MATCH PISTOL
Caliber: 177. **Barrel:** 10.24". **Weight:** 37 oz. **Length:** 15.75" overall. **Power:** 12.5-gram CO2 cartridge. **Stocks:** Stippled hardwood with adjustable palm rest. **Sights:** Blade front, open fully adjustable rear. **Features:** Comes with extra seals and counterweight. Blue finish. Imported by Great Lakes Airguns.
Price: About $299.50

BSA 240 MAGNUM AIR PISTOL
Caliber: 177, 22, single shot. **Barrel:** 6". **Weight:** 2 lbs. **Length:** 9" overall. **Power:** Spring-air, top-lever cocking. **Stocks:** Walnut. **Sights:** Blade front, micrometer adjustable rear. **Features:** Velocity 510 fps (177), 420 fps (22); crossbolt safety. Combat autoloader styling. Imported from U.K. by Precision Sales International, Inc.
Price: $259.99

COLT GOVERNMENT 1911 A1 AIR PISTOL
Caliber: 177, 8-shot cylinder magazine. **Barrel:** 5", rifled. **Weight:** 38 oz. **Length:** 8-1/2" overall. **Power:** CO2 cylinder. **Stocks:** Checkered black plastic or smooth wood. **Sights:** Post front, adjustable rear. **Features:** Velocity to 393 fps. Quick-loading cylinder magazine; single and double action; black or silver finish. Introduced 1998. Imported by Colt's Mfg. Co., Inc.
Price: Black finish $199.00
Price: Silver finish $209.00

CROSMAN BLACK VENOM PISTOL
Caliber: 177 pellets, BB, 17-shot magazine; darts, single shot. **Barrel:** 4.75" smoothbore. **Weight:** 16 oz. **Length:** 10.8" overall. **Power:** Spring. **Stocks:** Checkered. **Sights:** Blade front, adjustable rear. **Features:** Velocity to 270 fps (BBs), 250 fps (pellets). Spring-fed magazine; cross-bolt safety. Introduced 1996. Made in U.S. by Crosman Corp.
Price: About $20.00

CROSMAN BLACK FANG PISTOL
Caliber: 177 BB, 17-shot magazine. **Barrel:** 4.75" smoothbore. **Weight:** 10 oz. **Length:** 10.8" overall. **Power:** Spring. **Stocks:** Checkered. **Sights:** Blade front, fixed notch rear. **Features:** Velocity to 250 fps. Spring-fed magazine; cross-bolt safety. Introduced 1996. Made in U.S. by Crosman Corp.
Price: About $16.00

CROSMAN MODEL 1322, 1377 AIR PISTOLS
Caliber: 177 (M1377), 22 (M1322), single shot. **Barrel:** 8", rifled steel. **Weight:** 39 oz. **Length:** 13-5/8". **Power:** Hand pumped. **Sights:** Blade front, rear adjustable for windage and elevation. **Features:** Bolt action moulded plastic grip, hand size pump forearm. Cross-bolt safety. From Crosman.
Price: About $60.00

CROSMAN AUTO AIR II PISTOL
Caliber: BB, 17-shot magazine, 177 pellet, single shot. **Barrel:** 8-5/8" steel, smoothbore. **Weight:** 13 oz. **Length:** 10-3/4" overall. **Power:** CO2 cartridge. **Stocks:** Grooved plastic. **Sights:** Blade front, adjustable rear; highlighted system. **Features:** Velocity to 480 fps (BBs), 430 fps (pellets). Semi-automatic action with BBs, single shot with pellets. Silvered finish. Introduced 1991. From Crosman.
Price: About $38.00

CROSMAN MODEL 357 SERIES AIR PISTOL
Caliber: 177 10-shot pellet clips. **Barrel:** 4" (Model 3574GT), 6" (Model 3576GT). **Weight:** 32 oz. (6"). **Length:** 11-3/8" overall (357-6). **Power:** CO2 Powerlet. **Stocks:** Grip, wrap-around style. **Sights:** Ramp front, fully adjustable rear. **Features:** Average 430 fps (Model 3574GT). Break-open barrel for easy loading. Single or double action. Vent. rib barrel. Wide, smooth trigger. Two cylinders come with each gun. Black finish. From Crosman.
Price: 4" or 6", about $65.00

CROSMAN MODEL 1008 REPEAT AIR
Caliber: 177, 8-shot pellet clip. **Barrel:** 4.25", rifled steel. **Weight:** 17 oz. **Length:** 8.625" overall. **Power:** CO2 Powerlet. **Stocks:** Checkered black plastic. **Sights:** Post front, adjustable rear. **Features:** Velocity about 430 fps. Break-open barrel for easy loading; single or double semi-automatic action; two 8-shot clips included. Optional carrying case available. Introduced 1992. From Crosman.
Price: About $60.00
Price: With case, about $70.00
Price: Model 1008SB (silver and black finish), about $60.00

DAISY MODEL 2003 PELLET PISTOL
Caliber: 177 pellet, 35-shot clip. **Barrel:** Rifled steel. **Weight:** 2.2 lbs. **Length:** 11.7" overall. **Power:** CO2. **Stocks:** Checkered plastic. **Sights:** Blade front, open rear. **Features:** Velocity to 400 fps. Crossbolt trigger-block safety. Made in U.S. by Daisy Mfg. Co.
Price: About $67.95

DAISY MODEL 454 AIR PISTOL
Caliber: 177 BB, 20-shot clip. **Barrel:** Smoothbore steel. **Weight:** 1.6 lbs. **Length:** 10.4" overall. **Power:** CO2. **Stocks:** Moulded black, ribbed composition. **Sights:** Blade front, fixed rear. **Features:** Velocity to 420 fps. Semi-automatic action; cross-bolt safety; black finish. Introduced 1998. Made in U.S. by Dairy Mfg. Co.
Price: $61.95

DAISY/POWERLINE 717 PELLET PISTOL
Caliber: 177, single shot. **Barrel:** 9.61". **Weight:** 2.25 lbs. **Length:** 13-1/2" overall. **Stocks:** Moulded wood-grain plastic, with thumbrest. **Sights:** Blade and ramp front, micro-adjustable notch rear. **Features:** Single pump pneumatic pistol. Rifled steel barrel. Cross-bolt trigger block. Muzzle velocity 385 fps. From Daisy Mfg. Co. Introduced 1979.
Price: About $71.95

Daisy/PowerLine 747 Pistol
Similar to the 717 pistol except has a 12-groove rifled steel barrel by Lothar Walther, and adjustable trigger pull weight. Velocity of 360 fps. Manual cross-bolt safety.
Price: About $140.00

AIRGUNS

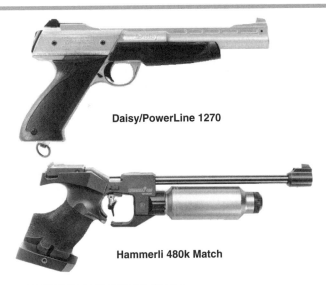

Daisy/PowerLine 1270

Hammerli 480k Match

Marksman 2005 Laserhawk

DAISY/POWERLINE 1140 PELLET PISTOL
Caliber: 177, single shot. **Barrel:** Rifled steel. **Weight:** 1.3 lbs. **Length:** 11.7" overall. **Power:** Single-stroke barrel cocking. **Stocks:** Checkered resin. **Sights:** Hooded post front, open adjustable rear. **Features:** Velocity to 325 fps. Made of black lightweight engineering resin. Introduced 1995. From Daisy.
Price: About $38.95

DAISY/POWERLINE 44 REVOLVER
Caliber: 177 pellets, 6-shot. **Barrel:** 6", rifled steel; interchangeable 4" and 8". **Weight:** 2.7 lbs. **Length:** 13.1" overall. **Power:** CO_2. **Stocks:** Moulded plastic with checkering. **Sights:** Blade on ramp front, fully adjustable notch rear. **Features:** Velocity up to 400 fps. Replica of 44 Magnum revolver. Has swingout cylinder and interchangeable barrels. Introduced 1987. From Daisy Mfg. Co.
Price: $59.95

DAISY/POWERLINE 1270 CO_2 AIR PISTOL
Caliber: BB, 60-shot magazine. **Barrel:** Smoothbore steel. **Weight:** 17 oz. **Length:** 11.1" overall. **Power:** CO_2 pump action. **Stocks:** Moulded black polymer. **Sights:** Blade on ramp front, adjustable rear. **Features:** Velocity to 420 fps. Crossbolt trigger block safety; plated finish. Introduced 1997. Made in U.S. by Daisy Mfg. Co.
Price: About $39.95

EAA/BAIKAL IZH-46 TARGET AIR PISTOL
Caliber: 177, single shot. **Barrel:** 11.02". **Weight:** 2.87 lbs. **Length:** 16.54" overall. **Power:** Underlever single-stroke pneumatic. **Grips:** Adjustable wooden target. **Sights:** Micrometer fully adjustable rear, blade front. **Features:** Velocity about 420 fps. Hammer-forged, rifled barrel. Imported from Russia by European American Armory.
Price: $275.00

EAA/BAIKAL MP-654K AIR PISTOL
Caliber: 177 BB, detachable 13-shot magazine. **Barrel:** 3.75". **Weight:** 1.6 lbs. **Length:** 6.34". **Power:** CO2 cartridge. **Grips:** Black checkered plastic. **Sights:** Notch rear, blade front. **Features:** Velocity about 380 fps. Double-action trigger; slide safety; metal slide and frame. Replica of Makarov pistol. Imported from Russia by European American Armory.
Price: $110.00

EAA/BAIKAL MP-651K AIR PISTOL/RIFLE
Caliber: 177 pellet (8-shot magazine); 177 BB (23-shot). **Barrel:** 5.9" (17.25" with rifle attachment). **Weight:** 1.54 lbs. (3.3 lbs. with rifle attachment). **Length:** 9.4" (31.3" with rifle attachment) **Power:** CO2 cartridge, semi-automatic. **Stock:** Plastic. **Sights:** Notch rear/blade front (pistol); periscopic sighting system (rifle). **Features:** Velocity 328 fps. Unique pistol/rifle combination allows the pistol to be inserted into the rifle shell. Imported from Russia by European American Armory.
Price: $95.00

"GAT" AIR PISTOL
Caliber: 177, single shot. **Barrel:** 7-1/2" cocked, 9-1/2" extended. **Weight:** 22 oz. **Power:** Spring-piston. **Stocks:** Cast checkered metal. **Sights:** Fixed. **Features:** Shoots pellets, corks or darts. Matte black finish. Imported from England by Stone Enterprises, Inc.
Price: $24.95

HAMMERLI 480 MATCH AIR PISTOL
Caliber: 177, single shot. **Barrel:** 9.8". **Weight:** 37 oz. **Length:** 16.5" overall. **Power:** Air or CO_2. **Stocks:** Walnut with 7-degree rake adjustment. Stippled grip area. **Sights:** Undercut blade front, fully adjustable open match rear. **Features:** Underbarrel cannister charges with air or CO_2 for power supply; gives 320 shots per filling.

Trigger adjustable for position. Introduced 1994. Imported from Switzerland by Hammerli Pistols U.S.A.
Price: $1,325.00

Hammerli 480K2 Match Air Pistol
Similar to the 480 except has a short, detachable aluminum air cylinder for use only with compressed air; can be filled while on the gun or off; special adjustable barrel weights. Muzzle velocity of 470 fps, gives about 180 shots. Has stippled black composition grip with adjustable palm shelf and rake angle. Comes with air pressure gauge. Introduced 1996. Imported from Switzerland by SIGARMS, Inc.
Price: $1,112.50

MARKSMAN 1010 REPEATER PISTOL
Caliber: 177, 18-shot BB repeater. **Barrel:** 2-1/2", smoothbore. **Weight:** 24 oz. **Length:** 8-1/4" overall. **Power:** Spring. **Features:** Velocity to 200 fps. Thumb safety. Black finish. Uses BBs, darts, bolts or pellets. Repeats with BBs only. From Marksman Products.
Price: Matte black finish $26.00
Price: Model 2000 (as above except silver-chrome finish) $27.00

MARKSMAN 2005 LASERHAWK SPECIAL EDITION AIR PISTOL
Caliber: 177, 24-shot magazine. **Barrel:** 3.8", smoothbore. **Weight:** 22 oz. **Length:** 10.3" overall. **Power:** Spring-air. **Stocks:** Checkered. **Sights:** Fixed fiber optic front sight. **Features:** Velocity to 300 fps with Hyper-Velocity pellets. Square trigger guard with skeletonized trigger; extended barrel for greater velocity and accuracy. Shoots BBs, pellets, darts or bolts. Made in the U.S. From Marksman Products.
Price: $32.00

MORINI 162E MATCH AIR PISTOL
Caliber: 177, single shot. **Barrel:** 9.4". **Weight:** 32 oz. **Length:** 16.1" overall. **Power:** Scuba air. **Stocks:** Adjustable match type. **Sights:** Interchangeable blade front, fully adjustable match-type rear. **Features:** Power mechanism shuts down when pressure drops to a pre-set level. Adjustable electronic trigger. Introduced 1995. Imported from Switzerland by Nygord Precision Products.
Price: $995.00

PARDINI K58 MATCH AIR PISTOL
Caliber: 177, single shot. **Barrel:** 9.0". **Weight:** 37.7 oz. **Length:** 15.5" overall. **Power:** Pre-charged compressed air; single-stroke cocking. **Stocks:** Adjustable match type; stippled walnut. **Sights:** Interchangeable post front, fully adjustable match rear. **Features:** Fully adjustable trigger. Introduced 1995. Imported from Italy by Nygord Precision Products.
Price: $750.00
Price: K2 model, precharged air pistol, introduced in 1998 . . . . $895.00

RWS/DIANA MODEL 5G AIR PISTOL
Caliber: 177, single shot. **Barrel:** 7". **Weight:** 2-3/4 lbs. **Length:** 15" overall. **Power:** Spring-air, barrel cocking. **Stocks:** Plastic, thumbrest design. **Sights:** Tunnel front, micro-click open rear. **Features:** Velocity of 450 fps. Adjustable two-stage trigger with automatic safety. Imported from Germany by Dynamit Nobel-RWS, Inc.
Price: $260.00

RWS C-225 AIR PISTOLS
Caliber: 177, 8-shot rotary magazine. **Barrel:** 4", 6". **Weight:** NA. **Length:** NA. **Power:** CO_2. **Stocks:** Checkered black plastic. **Sights:** Post front, rear adjustable for windage. **Features:** Velocity to 385 fps. Semi-automatic fire; decocking lever. Imported from Germany by Dynamit Nobel-RWS.
Price: 4", blue $210.00
Price: 4", nickel $220.00
Price: 6", blue $220.00
Price: 6", nickel $245.00

STEYR LP 5CP MATCH AIR PISTOL
Caliber: 177, 5-shot magazine. **Barrel:** NA. **Weight:** 40.7 oz. **Length:** 15.2" overall. **Power:** Pre-charged air cylinder. **Stocks:** Adjustable match type. **Sights:** Interchangeable blade front, fully adjustable match rear. **Features:** Adjustable sight radius; fully adjustable trigger. Has barrel compensator. Introduced 1995. Imported from Austria by Nygord Precision Products.
Price: $1,150.00

AIRGUNS

STEYR LP10P MATCH PISTOL
Caliber: 177, single shot. **Barrel:** 9". **Weight:** 38.7 oz. **Length:** 15.3" overall. **Power:** Scuba air. **Stocks:** Fully adjustable Morini match with palm shelf; stippled walnut. **Sights:** Interchangeable blade in 4mm, 4.5mm or 5mm widths, fully adjustable open rear with interchangeable 3.5mm or 4mm leaves. **Features:** Velocity about 500 fps. Adjustable trigger, adjustable sight radius from 12.4" to 13.2". With compensator. Imported from Austria by Nygord Precision Products.
Price: $1,195.00

TECH FORCE SS2 OLYMPIC COMPETITION AIR PISTOL
Caliber: 177 pellet, single shot. **Barrel:** 7.4". **Weight:** 2.8 lbs. **Length:** 16.5" overall. **Power:** Spring piston, sidelever. **Grips:** Hardwood. **Sights:** Extended adjustable rear, blade front accepts inserts. **Features:** Velocity 520 fps. Recoilless design; adjustments allow duplication of a firearm's feel. Match-grade, adjustable trigger; includes carrying case. Imported from China by Compasseco Inc.
Price: $295.00

TECH FORCE 35 AIR PISTOL
Caliber: 177 pellet, single shot. **Barrel:** N/A. **Weight:** 2.86 lbs. **Length:** 14.9" overall. **Power:** Spring piston, underlever. **Grips:** Hardwood. **Sights:** Micrometer adjustable rear, blade front. **Features:** Velocity 400 fps. Grooved for scope mount; trigger safety. Imported from China by Compasseco Inc.
Price: $49.95

Tech Force 8 Air Pistol
Similar to Tech Force 35, but with break-barrel action, ambidextrous polymer grips. From Compasseco Inc.
Price: $59.95

Tech Force S2-1 Air Pistol
Similar to Tech Force 8, but more basic grips and sights for plinking. From Compasseco Inc.
Price: $29.95

WALTHER CP88 PELLET PISTOL
Caliber: 177, 8-shot rotary magazine. **Barrel:** 4", 6". **Weight:** 37 oz. (4" barrel) **Length:** 7" (4" barrel). **Power:** CO_2. **Stocks:** Checkered plastic. **Sights:** Blade front, fully adjustable rear. **Features:** Faithfully replicates size, weight and trigger pull of the 9mm Walther P88 compact pistol. Has SA/DA trigger mechanism; ambidextrous safety, levers. Comes with two magazines, 500 pellets, one CO_2 cartridge. Introduced 1997. Imported from Germany by Interarms.
Price: Blue $179.00
Price: Nickel $189.00

WALTHER LP20I MATCH PISTOL
Caliber: 177, single shot. **Barrel:** 8.66". **Weight:** NA. **Length:** 15.1" overall. **Power:** Scuba air. **Stocks:** Orthopaedic target type. **Sights:** Undercut blade front, open match rear fully adjustable for windage and elevation. **Features:** Adjustable velocity; matte finish. Introduced 1995. Imported from Germany by Nygord Precision Products.
Price: $1,095.00

Walther CP88

Walther CP88 Competition Pellet Pistol
Similar to the standard CP88 except has 6" match-grade barrel, muzzle weight, wood or plastic stocks. Weighs 41 oz., has overall length of 9". Introduced 1997. Imported from Germany by Interarms.
Price: Blue, plastic grips $170.00
Price: Nickel, plastic grips $195.00
Price: Blue, wood grips $205.00
Price: Nickel, wood grips $232.00

WALTHER CP99 AIR PISTOL
Caliber: 177 pellet, 8-shot rotary magazine. **Barrel:** 3". **Weight:** 26 oz. **Length:** 7.1" overall. **Power:** CO2 cartridge. **Grip:** Polymer. **Sights:** Drift-adjustable rear, blade front. **Features:** Velocity 320 fps. Replica of Walther P99 pistol. Trigger allows single and double action; ambidextrous magazine release; interchangeable backstraps to fit variety of hand sizes. Introduced 2000. From Walther USA.
Price: . . . . NA

WALTHER PPK/S AIR PISTOL
Caliber: 177 BB. **Barrel:** N/A. **Weight:** 20 oz. **Length:** 6.3" overall. **Power:** CO2 cartridge. **Grip:** Plastic. **Sights:** Fixed rear, blade front. **Features:** Replica of Walther PPK pistol. Blow back system moves slide when fired; trigger allows single and double action. Introduced 2000. From Walther USA.
Price: . . . . NA

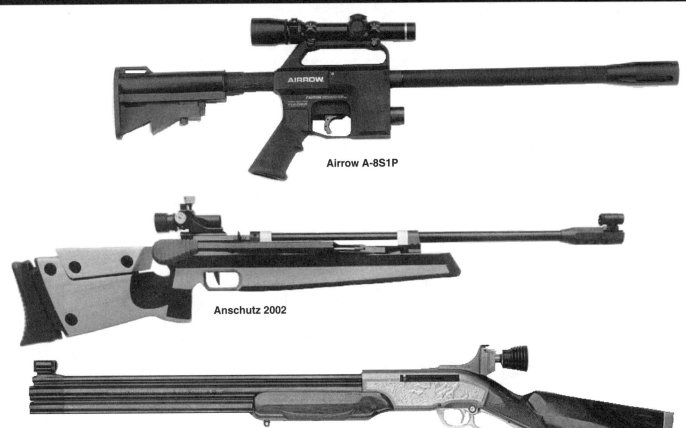

Airrow A-8S1P

Anschutz 2002

ARS/Career 707

AIRROW MODEL A-8SRB STEALTH AIR GUN
Caliber: 177, 22, 25, 38, 9-shot. **Barrel:** 19.7"; rifled. **Weight:** 6 lbs. **Length:** 34" overall. **Power:** CO_2 or compressed air; variable power. **Stock:** Telescoping CAR-15-type. **Sights:** Variable 3.5-10x scope. **Features:** Velocity 1100 fps in all calibers. Pneumatic air trigger. All aircraft aluminum and stainless steel construction. Mil-spec materials and finishes. Introduced 1992. From Swivel Machine Works, Inc.
Price: About $2,599.00

AIRROW MODEL A-8S1P STEALTH AIR GUN
Caliber: #2512 16" arrow. **Barrel:** 16". **Weight:** 4.4 lbs. **Length:** 30.1" overall. **Power:** CO_2 or compressed air; variable power. **Stock:** Telescoping CAR-15-type. **Sights:** Scope rings only. **Features:** Velocity to 650 fps with 260-grain arrow. Pneumatic air trigger. All aircraft aluminum and stainless steel construction. Mil-spec materials and finishes. Waterproof case. Introduced 1991. From Swivel Machine Works, Inc.
Price: About $1,699.00

ANSCHUTZ 2002 MATCH AIR RIFLE
Caliber: 177, single shot. **Barrel:** 25.2". **Weight:** 10.4 lbs. **Length:** 44.5" overall. **Stock:** European walnut, blonde hardwood or colored laminated hardwood; stippled grip and forend. Also available with flat-forend walnut stock for benchrest shooting and aluminum. **Sights:** Optional sight set #6834. **Features:** Muzzle velocity 575 fps. Balance, weight match the 1907 ISU smallbore rifle. Uses #5021 match trigger. Recoil and vibration free. Fully adjustable cheekpiece and buttplate; accessory rail under forend. Available in Pneumatic and Compressed Air versions. Introduced 1988. Imported from Germany by Gunsmithing, Inc., Accuracy International, Champion's Choice.
Price: Right-hand, blonde hardwood stock, with sights $1,275.00
Price: Right-hand, walnut stock $1,275.00
Price: Right-hand, color laminate stock $1,300.00
Price: Right-hand, aluminum stock, butt plate $1,495.00
Price: Left-hand, color laminate stock $1,595.00
Price: Model 2002D-RT Running Target, right-hand, no sights $1,248.90
Price: #6834 Sight Set $227.10

ARS/KING HUNTING MASTER AIR RIFLE
Caliber: 22, 5-shot repeater. **Barrel:** 22-3/4". **Weight:** 7-3/4 lbs. **Length:** 42" overall. **Power:** Pre-compressed air from 3000 psi diving tank. **Stock:** Indonesian walnut with checkered grip and forend; rubber buttpad. **Sights:** Blade front, fully adjustable open rear. Receiver grooved for scope mounting. **Features:** Velocity over 1000 fps with 32-grain pellet. High and low power switch for hunting or target velocities. Side lever cocks action and inserts pellet. Rotary magazine. Imported from Korea by Air Rifle Specialists.
Price: $580.00
Price: Hunting Master 900 (9mm, limited production) $1,000.00

ARS/Magnum 6 Air Rifle
Similar to the King Hunting Master except is 6-shot repeater with 23-3/4" barrel, weighs 8-1/4 lbs. Stock is walnut-stained hardwood with checkered grip and forend; rubber buttpad. Velocity of 1000+ fps with 32-grain pellet. Imported from Korea by Air Rifle Specialists.
Price: $500.00

ARS HUNTING MASTER AR6 AIR RIFLE
Caliber: 22, 6-shot repeater. **Barrel:** 25-1/2". **Weight:** 7 lbs. **Length:** 41-1/4" overall. **Power:** Pre-compressed air from 3000 psi diving tank. **Stock:** Indonesian walnut with checkered grip; rubber buttpad. **Sights:** Blade front, adjustable peep rear. **Features:** Velocity over 1000 fps with 32-grain pellet. Receiver grooved for scope mounting. Has 6-shot rotary magazine. Imported by Air Rifle Specialists.
Price: $580.00

ARS/CAREER 707 AIR RIFLE
Caliber: 22, 6-shot repeater. **Barrel:** 23". **Weight:** 7.75 lbs. **Length:** 40.5" overall. **Power:** Pre-compressed air; variable power. **Stock:** Indonesian walnut with checkered grip, gloss finish. **Sights:** Hooded post front with interchangeable inserts, fully adjustable diopter rear. **Features:** Velocity to 1000 fps. Lever-action with straight feed magazine; pressure gauge in lower front air reservoir; scope mounting rail included. Introduced 1996. Imported from the Philippines by Air Rifle Specialists.
Price: $580.00

ARS/FARCO FP SURVIVAL AIR RIFLE
Caliber: 22, 25, single shot. **Barrel:** 22-3/4". **Weight:** 5-3/4 lbs. **Length:** 42-3/4" overall. **Power:** Multi-pump foot pump. **Stock:** Philippine hardwood. **Sights:** Blade front, fixed rear. **Features:** Velocity to 850 fps (22 or 25). Receiver grooved for scope mounting. Imported from the Philippines by Air Rifle Specialists.
Price: $295.00

ARS/FARCO CO_2 AIR SHOTGUN
Caliber: 51 (28-gauge). **Barrel:** 30". **Weight:** 7 lbs. **Length:** 48-1/2" overall. **Power:** 10-oz. refillable CO_2 tank. **Stock:** Hardwood. **Sights:** Blade front, fixed rear. **Features:** Gives over 100 ft. lbs. energy for taking small game. Imported from the Philippines by Air Rifle Specialists.
Price: $460.00

AIRGUNS

Beeman Kodiak

Beeman Mako

Beeman R1 Rifle

Beeman R1 Laser Mk II

ARS/Farco CO₂ Stainless Steel Air Rifle

Similar to the ARS/Farco CO₂ shotgun except in 22- or 25-caliber with 21-1/2" barrel; weighs 6-3/4 lbs., 42-1/2" overall; Philippine hardwood stock with stippled grip and forend; blade front sight, adjustable rear, grooved for scope mount. Uses 10-oz. refillable CO₂ cylinder. Made of stainless steel. Imported from the Philippines by Air Rifle Specialists.
Price: Including CO₂ cylinder $460.00

ARS/QB77 DELUXE AIR RIFLE

Caliber: 177, 22, single shot. **Barrel:** 21-1/2". **Weight:** 5-1/2 lbs. **Length:** 40" overall. **Power:** Two 12-oz. CO₂ cylinders. **Stock:** Walnut-stained hardwood. **Sights:** Blade front, adjustable rear. **Features:** Velocity to 625 fps (22), 725 fps (177). Receiver grooved for scope mounting. Comes with bulk-fill valve. Imported by Air Rifle Specialists.
Price: $195.00

BEEMAN BEARCUB AIR RIFLE

Caliber: 177, single shot. **Barrel:** 13". **Weight:** 7.2 lbs. **Length:** 37.8" overall. **Power:** Spring-piston, barrel cocking. **Stock:** Stained hardwood. **Sights:** Hooded post front, open fully adjustable rear. **Features:** Velocity to 915 fps. Polished blue finish; receiver dovetailed for scope mounting. Imported from England by Beeman Precision Airguns.
Price: $325.00

BEEMAN CROW MAGNUM AIR RIFLE

Caliber: 20, 22, 25, single shot. **Barrel:** 16"; 10-groove rifling. **Weight:** 8.5 lbs. **Length:** 46" overall. **Power:** Gas-spring; adjustable power to 32 foot pounds muzzle energy. Barrel-cocking. **Stock:** Classic-style hardwood; hand checkered. **Sights:** For scope use only; built-in base and 1" rings included. **Features:** Adjustable two-stage trigger. Automatic safety. Also available in 22-caliber on special order. Introduced 1992. Imported by Beeman.
Price: $1,220.00

BEEMAN KODIAK AIR RIFLE

Caliber: 25, single shot. **Barrel:** 17.6". **Weight:** 9 lbs. **Length:** 45.6" overall. **Power:** Spring-piston, barrel cocking. **Stock:** Stained hardwood. **Sights:** Blade front, open fully adjustable rear. **Features:** Velocity to 820 fps. Up to 30 foot pounds muzzle energy. Introduced 1993. Imported by Beeman.
Price: $625.00

BEEMAN MAKO AIR RIFLE

Caliber: 177, single shot. **Barrel:** 20", with compensator. **Weight:** 7.3 lbs. **Length:** 38.5" overall. **Power:** Pre-charged pneumatic. **Stock:** Stained beech; Monte Carlo cheekpiece; checkered grip. **Sights:** None furnished. **Features:** Velocity to 930 fps. Gives over 50 shots per charge. Manual safety; brass trigger blade; vented rubber butt pad. Requires scuba tank for air. Introduced 1994. Imported from England by Beeman.
Price: $1,000.00
Price: Mako FT (thumbhole stock) $1,350.00

BEEMAN R1 AIR RIFLE

Caliber: 177, 20 or 22, single shot. **Barrel:** 19.6", 12-groove rifling. **Weight:** 8.5 lbs. **Length:** 45.2" overall. **Power:** Spring-piston, barrel cocking. **Stock:** Walnut-stained beech; cut-checkered pistol grip; Monte Carlo comb and cheekpiece; rubber buttpad. **Sights:** Tunnel front with interchangeable inserts, open rear click-adjustable for windage and elevation. Grooved for scope mounting. **Features:** Velocity of 940-1000 fps (177), 860 fps (20), 800 fps (22). Non-drying nylon piston and breech seals. Adjustable metal trigger. Milled steel safety. Right- or left-hand stock. Available with adjustable cheekpiece and buttplate at extra cost. Custom and Super Laser versions available. Imported by Beeman.
Price: Right-hand, 177, 20, 22 . . . . $540.00
Price: Left-hand, 177, 20, 22 . . . . $575.00

BEEMAN R1 LASER MK II AIR RIFLE

Caliber: 177, 20, 22, 25, single shot. **Barrel:** 16.1" or 19.6". **Weight:** 8.4 lbs. **Length:** 41.7" overall. **Power:** Spring-piston, barrel cocking. **Stock:** Laminated wood with high cheekpiece, ventilated recoil pad. **Sights:** Tunnel front with interchangeable inserts, open adjustable rear; receiver grooved for scope mounting. **Features:** Velocity to 1150 fps (177). Special powerplant components. Built from the Beeman R1 rifle by Beeman.
Price: $895.00

BEEMAN R6 AIR RIFLE

Caliber: 177, single shot. **Barrel:** NA. **Weight:** 7.1 lbs. **Length:** 41.8" overall. **Power:** Spring-piston, barrel cocking. **Stock:** Stained hardwood. **Sights:** Tunnel post front, open fully adjustable rear. **Features:** Velocity to 815 fps. Two-stage Rekord adjustable trigger; receiver dovetailed for scope mounting; automatic safety. Introduced 1996. Imported from Germany by Beeman Precision Airguns.
Price: $285.00

AIRGUNS

Beeman R6 Rifle

Beeman R9 Deluxe

Beeman R11

Beeman Super 12

BEEMAN R7 AIR RIFLE
Caliber: 177, 20, single shot. **Barrel:** 17". **Weight:** 6.1 lbs. **Length:** 40.2" overall. **Power:** Spring piston. **Stock:** Stained beech. **Sights:** Hooded front, fully adjustable micrometer click open rear. **Features:** Velocity to 700 fps (177), 620 fps (20). Receiver grooved for scope mounting; double-jointed cocking lever; fully adjustable trigger; checkered grip. Imported by Beeman.
Price: **$280.00**

BEEMAN R9 AIR RIFLE
Caliber: 177, 20, single shot. **Barrel:** NA. **Weight:** 7.3 lbs. **Length:** 43" overall. **Power:** Spring-piston, barrel cocking. **Stock:** Stained hardwood. **Sights:** Tunnel post front, fully adjustable open rear. **Features:** Velocity to 1000 fps (177), 800 fps (20). Adjustable Rekord trigger; automatic safety; receiver dovetailed for scope mounting. Introduced 1996. Imported from Germany by Beeman Precision Airguns.
Price: **$320.00**

Beeman R9 Deluxe Air Rifle
Same as the R9 except has an extended forend stock, checkered pistol grip, grip cap, carved Monte Carlo cheekpiece. Globe front sight with inserts. Introduced 1997. Imported by Beeman.
Price: **$370.00**

BEEMAN R11 AIR RIFLE
Caliber: 177, single shot. **Barrel:** 19.6". **Weight:** 8.8 lbs. **Length:** 47" overall. **Power:** Spring-piston, barrel cocking. **Stock:** Walnut-stained beech; adjustable buttplate and cheekpiece. **Sights:** None furnished. Has dovetail for scope mounting. **Features:** Velocity 910-940 fps. All-steel barrel sleeve. Imported by Beeman.
Price: **$530.00**

BEEMAN SUPER 12 AIR RIFLE
Caliber: 22, 25, 12-shot magazine. **Barrel:** 19", 12-groove rifling. **Weight:** 7.8 lbs. **Length:** 41.7" overall. **Power:** Pre-charged pneumatic; external air reservoir. **Stock:** European walnut. **Sights:** None furnished; drilled and tapped for scope mounting; scope mount included. **Features:** Velocity to 850 fps (25-caliber). Adjustable power setting gives 30-70 shots per 400 cc air bottle. Requires scuba tank for air. Introduced 1995. Imported by Beeman.
Price: **$1,675.00**

BEEMAN S1 MAGNUM AIR RIFLE
Caliber: 177, single shot. **Barrel:** 19". **Weight:** 7.1 lbs. **Length:** 45.5" overall. **Power:** Spring-piston, barrel cocking. **Stock:** Stained beech with Monte Carlo cheekpiece; checkered grip. **Sights:** Hooded post front, fully adjustable micrometer click rear. **Features:** Velocity to 900 fps. Automatic safety; receiver grooved for scope mounting; two-stage adjustable trigger; curved rubber buttpad. Introduced 1995. Imported by Beeman.
Price: **$210.00**

BEEMAN RX-1 GAS-SPRING MAGNUM AIR RIFLE
Caliber: 177, 20, 22, 25, single shot. **Barrel:** 19.6", 12-groove rifling. **Weight:** 8.8 lbs. **Power:** Gas-spring piston air; single stroke barrel cocking. **Stock:** Walnut-finished hardwood, hand checkered, with cheekpiece. Adjustable cheekpiece and buttplate. **Sights:** Tunnel front, click-adjustable rear. **Features:** Velocity adjustable to about 1200 fps. Uses special sealed chamber of air as a mainspring. Gas-spring cannot take a set. Introduced 1990. Imported by Beeman.
Price: 177, 20, 22 or 25 regular, right-hand **$590.00**
Price: 177, 20, 22, 25, left-hand **$625.00**

BEEMAN R1 CARBINE
Caliber: 177, 20, 22, 25, single shot. **Barrel:** 16.1". **Weight:** 8.6 lbs. **Length:** 41.7" overall. **Power:** Spring-piston, barrel cocking. **Stock:** Stained beech; Monte Carlo comb and checkpiece; cut checkered pistol grip; rubber buttpad. **Sights:** Tunnel front with interchangeable inserts, open adjustable rear; receiver grooved for scope mounting. **Features:** Velocity up to 1000 fps (177). Non-drying nylon piston and breech seals. Adjustable metal trigger. Machined steel receiver end cap and safety. Right- or left-hand stock. Imported by Beeman.
Price: 177, 20, 22, 25, right-hand............................... **$540.00**
Price: As above, left-hand **$575.00**
Price: R1-AW (synthetic stock, nickel plating) **$650.00**

BEEMAN/FEINWERKBAU 300-S SERIES MATCH RIFLE
Caliber: 177, single shot. **Barrel:** 19.9", fixed solid with receiver. **Weight:** Approx. 10 lbs. with optional bbl. sleeve. **Length:** 42.8" overall. **Power:** Spring-piston, single stroke sidelever. **Stock:** Match model—walnut, deep forend, adjustable buttplate. **Sights:** Globe front with interchangeable inserts. Click micro. adjustable match aperture rear. Front and rear sights move as a single unit. **Features:** Recoilless, vibration free. Five-way adjustable match trigger. Grooved for scope mounts. Permanent lubrication, steel piston ring. Cocking effort 9 lbs. Optional 10-oz. barrel sleeve. Available from Beeman.
Price: Right-hand **$1,235.00**
Price: Left-hand **$1,370.00**

AIRGUNS

Beeman/Feinwerkbau 300-S

Beeman/Feinwerkbau 603

Benjamin Sheridan Pneumatic

BEEMAN/FEINWERKBAU 603 AIR RIFLE
Caliber: 177, single shot. **Barrel:** 16.6". **Weight:** 10.8 lbs. **Length:** 43" overall. **Power:** Single stroke pneumatic. **Stock:** Special laminated hardwoods and hard rubber for stability. Multi-colored stock also available. **Sights:** Tunnel front with interchangeable inserts, click micrometer match aperture rear. **Features:** Velocity to 570 fps. Recoilless action; double supported barrel; special, short rifled area frees pellet form barrel faster so shooter's motion has minimum effect on accuracy. Fully adjustable match trigger with separately adjustable trigger and trigger slack weight. Trigger and sights blocked when loading latch is open. Introduced 1997. Imported by Beeman.
Price: Right-hand **$1,625.00**
Price: Left-hand **$1,775.00**

BEEMAN/FEINWERKBAU 300-S MINI-MATCH
Caliber: 177, single shot. **Barrel:** 17-1/8". **Weight:** 8.8 lbs. **Length:** 40" overall. **Power:** Spring-piston, single stroke sidelever cocking. **Stock:** Walnut. Stippled grip, adjustable buttplate. Scaled-down for youthful or slightly built shooters. **Sights:** Globe front with interchangeable inserts, micro. adjustable rear. Front and rear sights move as a single unit. **Features:** Recoilless, vibration free. Grooved for scope mounts. Steel piston ring. Cocking effort about 9-1/2 lbs. Barrel sleeve optional. Left-hand model available. Introduced 1978. Imported by Beeman.
Price: Right-hand **$1,270.00**
Price: Left-hand **$1,370.00**

BEEMAN/FEINWERKBAU P70 AIR RIFLE
Caliber: 177, single shot. **Barrel:** 16.6". **Weight:** 10.6 lbs. **Length:** 42.6" overall. **Power:** Precharged pneumatic. **Stock:** Laminated hardwoods and hard rubber for stability. Multi-colored stock also available. **Sights:** Tunnel front with interchangeable inserts, click micormeter match aperture rear. **Features:** Velocity to 570 fps. Recoilless action; double supported barrel; special short rifled area frees pellet from barrel faster so shooter's motion has minimum effect on accuracy. Fully adjustable match trigger with separately adjustable trigger and trigger slack weight. Trigger and sights blocked when loading latch is open. Introduced 1997. Imported by Beeman.
Price: P70, pre-charged, right-hand **$1,545.00**
Price: P70, pre-charged, left-hand **$1,640.00**
Price: P70, pre-charged, right-hand, multi **$1,645.00**
Price: P70, pre-charged, left-hand, multi **$1,745.00**

BEEMAN/HW 97 AIR RIFLE
Caliber: 177, 20, single shot. **Barrel:** 17.75". **Weight:** 9.2 lbs. **Length:** 44.1" overall. **Power:** Spring-piston, underlever cocking. **Stock:** Walnut-stained beech; rubber buttpad. **Sights:** None. Receiver grooved for scope mounting. **Features:** Velocity 830 fps (177). Fixed barrel with fully opening, direct loading breech. Adjustable trigger. Introduced 1994. Imported by Beeman Precision Airguns.
Price: Right-hand only **$530.00**

BENJAMIN SHERIDAN PNEUMATIC (PUMP-UP) AIR RIFLES
Caliber: 177 or 22, single shot. **Barrel:** 19-3/8", rifled brass. **Weight:** 5-1/2 lbs. **Length:** 36-1/4" overall. **Power:** Underlever pneumatic, hand pumped. **Stock:** American walnut stock and forend. **Sights:** High ramp front, fully adjustable notch rear. **Features:** Variable velocity to 800 fps. Bolt action with ambidextrous push-pull safety. Black or nickel finish. Introduced 1991. Made in the U.S. by Benjamin Sheridan Co.
Price: Black finish, Model 397 (177), Model 392 (22), about **$140.00**
Price: Nickel finish, Model S397 (177), Model S392 (22), about **$150.00**

BENJAMIN SHERIDAN W.F. AIR RIFLE
Caliber: 177 single-shot. **Barrel:** 19-3/8", rifled brass. **Weight:** 5 lbs. **Length:** 36-1/2" overall. Power 12-gram CO_2 cylinder. **Stocks:** American walnut with buttplate. **Sights:** High ramp front, fully adjustable notch rear. **Features:** Velocity to 680 fps (177). Bolt action with ambidextrous push-pull safety. Gives about 40 shots per cylinder. Black finish. Introduced 1991. Made in the U.S. by Benjamin Sheridan Co.
Price: Black finish, Model G397 (177) **$140.00**

BRNO TAU-200 AIR RIFLE
Caliber: 177, single shot. **Barrel:** 19", rifled. **Weight:** 7-1/2 lbs. **Length:** 42" overall. **Power:** 6-oz. CO_2 cartridge. **Stock:** Wood match style with adjustable comb and buttplate. **Sights:** Globe front with interchangeable inserts, fully adjustable open rear. **Features:** Adjustable trigger. Comes with extra seals, large CO_2 bottle, counterweight. Introduced 1993. Imported by Century International Arms, Great Lakes Airguns. Available in Standard Universal, Deluxe Universal, International and Target Sporter versions.
Price: Standard Universal (ambidex. stock with buttstock extender, adj. cheekpiece). **$349.50**
Price: Deluxe Universal (as above but with micro-adj. aperture sight) **$449.50**
Price: International (like Deluxe Universal but with right- or left-hand stock) **$454.50**
Price: Target Sporter (like Std. Universal but with 4X scope, no sights) **$412.50**

BSA MAGNUM SUPERSTAR™ MK2 MAGNUM AIR RIFLE, CARBINE
Caliber: 177, 22, 25, single shot. **Barrel:** 18". **Weight:** 8 lbs., 8 oz. **Length:** 43" overall. **Power:** Spring-air, underlever cocking. **Stock:** Oil-finished hardwood; Monte Carlo with cheekpiece, checkered at grip; recoil pad. **Sights:** Ramp front, micrometer adjustable rear. Maxi-Grip scope rail. **Features:** Velocity 1020 fps (177), 800 fps (22), 675 fps (25). Patented rotating breech design. Maxi-Grip scope rail protects optics from recoil; automatic anti-beartrap plus manual safety. Imported from U.K. by Precision Sales International, Inc.
Price: **$479.99**
Price: MKII Carbine (14" barrel, 39-1/2" overall) **$479.99**

AIRGUNS

BRNO Tau-200

BRNO TAU-200 Sporter

BSA Magnum Gold Star

Crosman Model 760

BSA MAGNUM SUPERSPORT™ AIR RIFLE

Caliber: 177, 22, 25, single shot. **Barrel:** 18". **Weight:** 6 lbs., 8 oz. **Length:** 41" overall. **Power:** Spring-air, barrel cocking. **Stock:** Oil-finished hardwood; Monte Carlo with cheekpiece, recoil pad. **Sights:** Ramp front, micrometer adjustable rear. Maxi-Grip scope rail. **Features:** Velocity 1020 fps (177), 800 fps (22), 675 fps (25). Patented Maxi-Grip scope rail protects optics from recoil; automatic anti-beartrap plus manual tang safety. Muzzle brake standard. Imported for U.K. by Precision Sales International, Inc.
Price: $279.99
Price: Carbine, 14" barrel, muzzle brake $299.99

BSA MAGNUM GOLDSTAR MAGNUM AIR RIFLE

Caliber: 177, 22, 10-shot repeater. **Barrel:** 18". **Weight:** 8 lbs., 8 oz. **Length:** 42.5" overall. **Power:** Spring-air, underlever cocking. **Stock:** Oil-finished hardwood; Monte Carlo with cheekpiece, checkered at grip; recoil pad. **Sights:** Ramp front, micrometer adjustable rear; comes with Maxi-Grip scope rail. **Features:** Velocity 1020 fps (177), 800 fps (22). Patented 10-shot indexing magazine; Maxi-Grip scope rail protects optics from recoil; automatic anti-beartrap plus manual safety; muzzlebrake standard. Imported from U.K. by Precision Sales International, Inc.
Price: $699.99

BSA MAGNUM SUPERTEN AIR RIFLE

Caliber: 177, 22 10-shot repeater. **Barrel:** 17-1/2". **Weight:** 7 lbs., 8 oz. **Length:** 37" overall. **Power:** Precharged pneumatic via buddy bottle. **Stock:** Oil-finished hardwood; Monte Carlo with cheekpiece, cut checkering at grip; adjustable recoil pad. **Sights:** No sights; intended for scope use. **Features:** Velocity 1300+ fps (177), 1000+ fps (22). Patented 10-shot indexing magazine, bolt-action loading. Left-hand version also available. Imported from U.K. by Precision Sales International, Inc.
Price: $879.99
Price: Left-hand $1,069.00

BSA METEOR MK6 AIR RIFLE

Caliber: 177, 22, single shot. **Barrel:** 18". **Weight:** 6 lbs. **Length:** 41" overall. **Power:** Spring-air, barrel cocking. **Stock:** Oil-finished hardwood. **Sights:** Ramp front, micrometer adjustable rear. **Features:** Velocity 650 fps (177), 500 fps (22). Automatic anti-beartrap; manual tang safety. Receiver grooved for scope mounting. Imported from U.K. by Precision Sales International, Inc.
Price: Rifle $199.99
Price: Carbine $219.99

COPPERHEAD BLACK SERPENT RIFLE

Caliber: 177 pellets, 5-shot, on BB, 195-shot magazine. **Barrel:** 19-1/2" smoothbore steel. **Weight:** 2 lbs., 14 oz. **Length:** 35-7/8" overall. **Power:** Pneumatic, single pump. **Stock:** Textured plastic. **Sights:** Blade front, open adjustable rear. **Features:** Velocity to 405 fps. Introduced 1996. Made in U.S. by Crosman Corp.
Price: About $48.00

CROSMAN MODEL 66 POWERMASTER

Caliber: 177 (single shot pellet) or BB, 200-shot reservoir. **Barrel:** 20", rifled steel. **Weight:** 3 lbs. **Length:** 38-1/2" overall. **Power:** Pneumatic; hand pumped. **Stock:** Wood-grained ABS plastic; checkered pistol grip and forend. **Sights:** Ramp front, fully adjustable open rear. **Features:** Velocity about 645 fps. Bolt action, cross-bolt safety. Introduced 1983. From Crosman.
Price: About $60.00
Price: Model 664X (as above, with 4x scope) $70.00
Price: Model 664SB (as above with silver and black finish), about $75.00
Price: Model 664GT (black and gold finish, 4x scope) about.............. $73.00

CROSMAN MODEL 760 PUMPMASTER

Caliber: 177 pellets (single shot) or BB (200-shot reservoir). **Barrel:** 19-1/2", rifled steel. **Weight:** 2 lbs., 12 oz. **Length:** 33.5" overall. **Power:** Pneumatic, hand pumped. **Stock:** Walnut-finished ABS plastic stock and forend. **Features:** Velocity to 590 fps (BBs, 10 pumps). Short stroke, power determined by number of strokes. Post front sight and adjustable rear sight. Cross-bolt safety. Introduced 1966. From Crosman.
Price: About $40.00
Price: Model 760SB (silver and black finish), about.................... $55.00

AIRGUNS

AIRGUNS—LONG GUNS

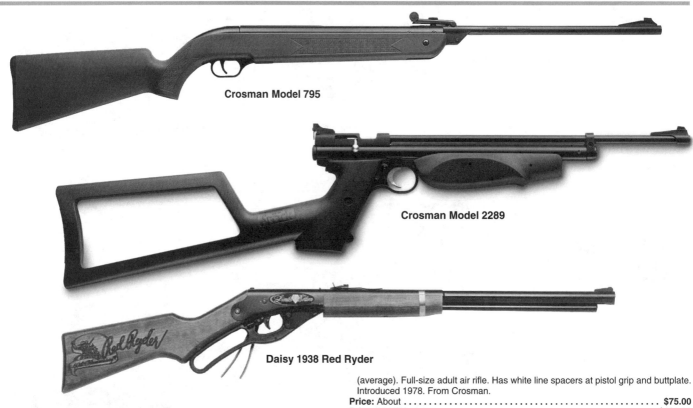

Crosman Model 795

Crosman Model 2289

Daisy 1938 Red Ryder

CROSMAN MODEL 782 BLACK DIAMOND AIR RIFLE
Caliber: 177 pellets (5-shot clip) or BB (195-shot reservoir). **Barrel:** 18", rifled steel. **Weight:** 3 lbs. **Power:** CO$_2$ Powerlet. **Stock:** Wood-grained ABS plastic; checkered grip and forend. **Sights:** Blade front, open adjustable rear. **Features:** Velocity up to 595 fps (pellets), 650 fps (BB). Black finish with white diamonds. Introduced 1990. From Crosman.
Price: About $63.00

CROSMAN MODEL 795 SPRING MASTER RIFLE
Caliber: 177, single shot. **Barrel:** Rifled steel. **Weight:** 4 lbs., 8 oz. **Length:** 42" overall. **Power:** Spring-piston. **Stock:** Black synthetic. **Sights:** Hooded front, fully adjustable rear. **Features:** Velocity about 550 fps. Introduced 1995. From Crosman.
Price: About $90.00

CROSMAN MODEL 1077 REPEATAIR RIFLE
Caliber: 177 pellets, 12-shot clip. **Barrel:** 20.3", rifled steel. **Weight:** 3 lbs., 11 oz. **Length:** 38.8" overall. **Power:** CO$_2$ Powerlet. **Stock:** Textured synthetic or American walnut. **Sights:** Blade front, fully adjustable rear. **Features:** Velocity 590 fps. Removable 12-shot clip. True semi-automatic action. Introduced 1993. From Crosman.
Price: About $75.00
Price: 1077W (walnut stock) $110.00

CROSMAN MODEL 2289 RIFLE
Caliber: .22, single shot. **Barrel:** 14.625", rifled steel. **Weight:** 3 lbs. 3 oz. **Length:** 31" overall. **Power:** Hand pumped, pneumatic. **Stock:** Composition, skeletal type. **Sights:** Blade front, rear adjustable for windage and elevation. **Features:** Velocity to 575 fps. Detachable stock. Metal parts blued. From Crosman.
Price: About $73.00

CROSMAN MODEL 2100 CLASSIC AIR RIFLE
Caliber: 177 pellets (single shot), or BB (200-shot BB reservoir). **Barrel:** 21", rifled. **Weight:** 4 lbs., 13 oz. **Length:** 39-3/4" overall. **Power:** Pump-up, pneumatic. **Stock:** Wood-grained checkered ABS plastic. **Features:** Three pumps give about 450 fps, 10 pumps about 755 fps (BBs). Cross-bolt safety; concealed reservoir holds over 200 BBs. From Crosman.
Price: About $75.00
Price: Model 2104GT (black and gold finish, 4x scope), about $95.00
Price: Model 2100W (walnut stock, pellets only), about $120.00

CROSMAN MODEL 2200 MAGNUM AIR RIFLE
Caliber: 22, single shot. **Barrel:** 19", rifled steel. **Weight:** 4 lbs., 12 oz. **Length:** 39" overall. **Stock:** Full-size, wood-grained ABS plastic with checkered grip and forend or American walnut. **Sights:** Ramp front, open step-adjustable rear. **Features:** Variable pump power—three pumps give 395 fps, six pumps 530 fps, 10 pumps 595 fps

(average). Full-size adult air rifle. Has white line spacers at pistol grip and buttplate. Introduced 1978. From Crosman.
Price: About $75.00
Price: 2200W, about $120.00

DAISY MODEL 840
Caliber: 177 pellet single shot; or BB 350-shot. **Barrel:** 19", smoothbore, steel. **Weight:** 2.7 lbs. **Length:** 36.8" overall. **Power:** Pneumatic, single pump. **Stock:** Moulded wood-grain stock and forend. **Sights:** Ramp front, open, adjustable rear. **Features:** Muzzle velocity 335 fps (BB), 300 fps (pellet). Steel buttplate; straight pull bolt action; cross-bolt safety. Forend forms pump lever. Introduced 1978. From Daisy Mfg. Co.
Price: About $32.95

DAISY/POWERLINE 853
Caliber: 177 pellets. **Barrel:** 20.9"; 12-groove rifling, high-grade solid steel by Lothar Waltherô, precision crowned; bore size for precision match pellets. **Weight:** 5.08 lbs. **Length:** 38.9" overall. **Power:** Single-pump pneumatic. **Stock:** Full-length, select American hardwood, stained and finished; black buttplate with white spacers. **Sights:** Globe front with four aperture inserts; precision micrometer adjustable rear peep sight mounted on a standard 3/8" dovetail receiver mount. **Features:** Single shot. From Daisy Mfg. Co.
Price: About $225.00

DAISY/POWERLINE 856 PUMP-UP AIRGUN
Caliber: 177 pellets (single shot) or BB (100-shot reservoir). **Barrel:** Rifled steel with shroud. **Weight:** 2.7 lbs. **Length:** 37.4" overall. **Power:** Pneumatic pump-up. **Stock:** Moulded wood-grain with Monte Carlo cheekpiece. **Sights:** Ramp and blade front, open rear adjustable for elevation. **Features:** Velocity from 315 fps (two pumps) to 650 fps (10 pumps). Shoots BBs or pellets. Heavy die-cast metal receiver. Cross-bolt trigger-block safety. Introduced 1984. From Daisy Mfg. Co.
Price: About $39.95

DAISY MODEL 990 DUAL-POWER AIR RIFLE
Caliber: 177 pellets (single shot) or BB (100-shot magazine). **Barrel:** Rifled steel. **Weight:** 4.1 lbs. **Length:** 37.4" overall. **Power:** Pneumatic pump-up and 12-gram CO$_2$. **Stock:** Moulded woodgrain. **Sights:** Ramp and blade front, adjustable open rear. **Features:** Velocity to 650 fps (BB), 630 fps (pellet). Choice of pump or CO$_2$ power. Shoots BBs or pellets. Heavy die-cast receiver dovetailed for scope mount. Cross-bolt trigger block safety. Introduced 1993. From Daisy Mfg. Co.
Price: About $58.95

DAISY 1938 RED RYDER 60th ANNIVERSARY CLASSIC
Caliber: BB, 650-shot repeating action. **Barrel:** Smoothbore steel with shroud. **Weight:** 2.2 lbs. **Length:** 35.4" overall. **Stock:** Walnut stock burned with Red Ryder lariat signature. **Sights:** Post front, adjustable V-slot rear. **Features:** Walnut forend. Saddle ring with leather thong. Lever cocking. Gravity feed. Controlled velocity. One of Daisy's most popular guns. From Daisy Mfg. Co.
Price: About $39.95

AIRGUNS

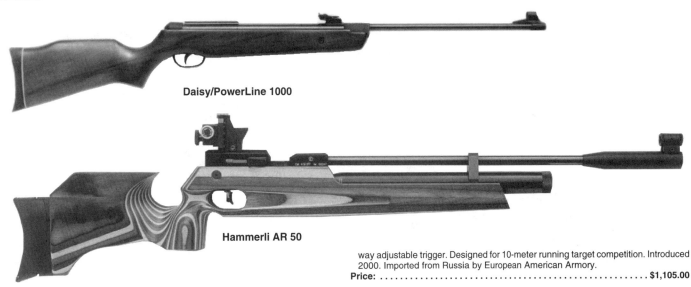

Daisy/PowerLine 1000

Hammerli AR 50

DAISY/POWERLINE 1170 PELLET RIFLE

Caliber: 177, single shot. **Barrel:** Rifled steel. **Weight:** 5.5 lbs. **Length:** 42.5" overall. **Power:** Spring-air, barrel cocking. **Stock:** Hardwood. **Sights:** Hooded post front, micrometer adjustable open rear. **Features:** Velocity to 800 fps. Monte Carlo comb. Introduced 1995. From Daisy Mfg. Co.
Price: About **$129.95**
Price: Model 131 (velocity to 600 fps) **$117.95**
Price: Model 1150 (black copolymer stock, velocity to 600 fps). **$77.95**

DAISY/POWERLINE EAGLE 7856 PUMP-UP AIRGUN

Caliber: 177 (pellets), BB, 100-shot BB magazine. **Barrel:** Rifled steel with shroud. **Weight:** 3.3 lbs. **Length:** 37.4" overall. **Power:** Pneumatic pump-up. **Stock:** Moulded wood-grain plastic. **Sights:** Ramp and blade front, open rear adjustable for elevation. **Features:** Velocity from 315 fps (two pumps) to 650 fps (10 pumps). Finger grooved forend. Cross-bolt trigger-block safety. Introduced 1985. From Daisy Mfg. Co.
Price: With 4x scope, about **$49.95**

DAISY/POWERLINE 880

Caliber: 177 or BB, 50-shot BB magazine, single shot for pellets. **Barrel:** Rifled steel. **Weight:** 3.7 lbs. **Length:** 37.6" overall. **Power:** Multi-pump pneumatic. **Stock:** Moulded wood grain; Monte Carlo comb. **Sights:** Hooded front, adjustable rear. **Features:** Velocity to 685 fps. (BB). Variable power (velocity and range) increase with pump strokes; resin receiver with dovetail scope mount. Introduced 1997. Made in U.S. by Daisy Mfg. Co.
Price: About **$50.95**
Price: Model 4880 with Glo-Point fiber optic sight **$57.95**

DAISY/POWERLINE 1000 AIR RIFLE

Caliber: 177, single shot. **Barrel:** NA. **Weight:** 6.15 lbs. **Length:** 43" overall. **Power:** Spring-air, barrel cocking. **Stock:** Stained hardwood. **Sights:** Hooded blade front on ramp, fully adjustable micrometer rear. **Features:** Velocity to 1000 fps. Blued finish; trigger block safety. Introduced 1997. From Daisy Mfg. Co.
Price: About **$208.95**

DAISY/YOUTHLINE MODEL 105 AIR RIFLE

Caliber: BB, 400-shot magazine. **Barrel:** 13-1/2". **Weight:** 1.6 lbs. **Length:** 29.8" overall. **Power:** Spring. **Stock:** Moulded woodgrain. **Sights:** Blade on ramp front, fixed rear. **Features:** Velocity to 275 fps. Blue finish. Cross-bolt trigger block safety. Made in U.S. by Daisy Mfg. Co.
Price: **$28.95**

DAISY/YOUTHLINE MODEL 95 AIR RIFLE

Caliber: BB, 700-shot magazine. **Barrel:** 18". **Weight:** 2.4 lbs. **Length:** 35.2" overall. **Power:** Spring. **Stock:** Stained hardwood. **Sights:** Blade on ramp front, open adjustable rear. **Features:** Velocity to 325 fps. Cross-bolt trigger block safety. Made in U.S. by Daisy Mfg. Co.
Price: **$38.95**

EAA/BAIKAL IZH-32BK AIR RIFLE

Caliber: 177 pellet, single shot. **Barrel:** 11.68". **Weight:** 12.13 lbs. **Length:** 47.24" overall. **Power:** Single-stroke pneumatic. **Stock:** Walnut with full pistol grip, adjustable cheek piece and butt stock. **Sights:** None; integral rail for scope mount. **Features:** Velocity 541 fps. Side-cocking mechanism; hammer-forged, rifled barrel; five-

way adjustable trigger. Designed for 10-meter running target competition. Introduced 2000. Imported from Russia by European American Armory.
Price: **$1,105.00**

EAA/BAIKAL IZH-61 AIR RIFLE

Caliber: 177 pellet, 5-shot magazine. **Barrel:** 17.75". **Weight:** 6.39 lbs. **Length:** 30.98" overall. **Power:** Spring piston, side-cocking lever. **Stock:** Black plastic. **Sights:** Adjustable rear, fully hooded front. **Features:** Velocity 490 fps. Futuristic design with adjustable stock. Imported from Russia by European American Armory.
Price: **$85.00**

EAA/BAIKAL MP-512 AIR RIFLE

Caliber: 177 or 22 pellet, single shot. **Barrel:** 17.7". **Weight:** 6.17 lbs. **Length:** 41.34" overall. **Power:** Spring-piston, single stroke. **Stock:** Black synthetic. **Sights:** Adjustable rear, hooded front. **Features:** Velocity 490 fps. Hammer-forged, rifled barrel; automatic safety; scope mount rail. Introduced 2000. Imported from Russia by European American Armory.
Price: 177 caliber **$50.00**
Price: 22 caliber **$63.00**

EAA/BAIKAL MP-532 AIR RIFLE

Caliber: 177 pellet, single shot. **Barrel:** 15.75". **Weight:** 9.26 lbs. **Length:** 46.06" overall. **Power:** Single-stroke pneumatic. **Stock:** One- or two-piece competition-style stock with adjustable butt pad, pistol grip. **Sights:** Fully adjustable rear, hooded front. **Features:** Velocity 460 fps. Five-way adjustable trigger. Introduced 2000. Imported from Russia by European American Armory.
Price: **$595.00**

HAMMERLI AR 50 AIR RIFLE

Caliber: 177. **Barrel:** 19.8". **Weight:** 10 lbs. **Length:** 43.2" overall. **Power:** Compressed air. **Stock:** Anatomically-shaped universal and right-hand; match style; multi-colored laminated wood. **Sights:** Interchangeable element tunnel front, fully adjustable Hammerli peep rear. **Features:** Vibration-free firing release; fully adjustable match trigger and trigger stop; stainless air tank, built-in pressure gauge. Gives 270 shots per filling. Introduced 1998. Imported from Switzerland by Sigarms, Inc.
Price: . . . . **$1,062.50 to $1,400.00**

HAMMERLI MODEL 450 MATCH AIR RIFLE

Caliber: 177, single shot. **Barrel:** 19.5". **Weight:** 9.8 lbs. **Length:** 43.3" overall. **Power:** Pneumatic. **Stock:** Match style with stippled grip, rubber buttpad. Beach or walnut. **Sights:** Match tunnel front, Hammerli diopter rear. **Features:** Velocity about 560 fps. Removable sights; forend sling rail; adjustable trigger; adjustable comb. Introduced 1994. Imported from Switzerland by Sigarms, Inc.
Price: Beech stock **$1,355.00**
Price: Walnut stock. **$1,395.00**

MARKSMAN BB BUDDY AIR RIFLE

Caliber: 177, 20-shot magazine. **Barrel:** 10.5" smoothbore. **Weight:** 1.6 lbs. **Length:** 33" overall. **Power:** Spring-air. **Stock:** Moulded composition. **Sights:** Blade on ramp front, adjustable V-slot rear. **Features:** Velocity 275 fps. Positive feed; automatic safety. Youth-sized lightweight design. Introduced 1998. Made in U.S. From Marksman Products.
Price: **$27.95**

MARKSMAN 1798 COMPETITION TRAINER AIR RIFLE

Caliber: 177, single shot. **Barrel:** 15", rifled. **Weight:** 4.7 lbs. **Power:** Spring-air, barrel cocking. **Stock:** Synthetic. **Sights:** Laserhawk fiber optic front, match-style diopter rear. **Features:** Velocity about 495 fps. Automatic safety. Introduced 1998. Made in U.S. From Marksman Products.
Price: **$70.00**

AIRGUNS

Marksman 1790

RWS Model 24C

Savage Model 600F

MARKSMAN 1745 BB REPEATER AIR RIFLE
Caliber: 177 BB or pellet, 18-shot BB reservoir. **Barrel:** 15-1/2", rifled. **Weight:** 4.75 lbs. **Length:** 36" overall. **Power:** Spring-air. **Stock:** Moulded composition with ambidextrous Monte Carlo cheekpiece and rubber recoil pad. **Sights:** Hooded front, adjustable rear. **Features:** Velocity about 450 fps. Break-barrel action; automatic safety. Uses BBs, pellets, darts or bolts. Introduced 1997. Made in the U.S. From Marksman Products.
Price: $58.00
Price: Model 1745S (same as above except comes with #1804 4x20 scope). $73.00

MARKSMAN 1790 BIATHLON TRAINER
Caliber: 177, single shot. **Barrel:** 15", rifled. **Weight:** 4.7 lbs. **Power:** Spring-air, barrel cocking. **Stock:** Synthetic. **Sights:** Hooded front, match-style diopter rear. **Features:** Velocity of 450 fps. Endorsed by the U.S. Shooting Team. Introduced 1989. From Marksman Products.
Price: $70.00

MARKSMAN 2015 LASERHAWK™ BB REPEATER AIR RIFLE
Caliber: 177 BB, 20-shot magazine. **Barrel:** 10.5" smoothbore. **Weight:** 1.6 lbs. **Length:** Adjustable to 33", 34" or 35" overall. **Power:** Spring-air. **Stock:** Moulded composition. **Sights:** Fixed fiber optic front sight, adjustable elevation V-slot rear. **Features:** Velocity about 275 fps. Positive feed; automatic safety. Adjustable stock. Introduced 1997. Made in the U.S. From Marksman Products.
Price: $33.00

RWS/DIANA MODEL 24 AIR RIFLE
Caliber: 177, 22, single shot. **Barrel:** 17", rifled. **Weight:** 6 lbs. **Length:** 42" overall. **Power:** Spring-air, barrel cocking. **Stock:** Beech. **Sights:** Hooded front, adjustable rear. **Features:** Velocity of 700 fps (177). Easy cocking effort; blue finish. Imported from Germany by Dynamit Nobel-RWS, Inc.
Price: $215.00
Price: Model 24C $215.00

RWS/Diana Model 34 Air Rifle
Similar to the Model 24 except has 19" barrel, weighs 7.5 lbs. Gives velocity of 1000 fps (177), 800 fps (22). Adjustable trigger, synthetic seals. Comes with scope rail.
Price: 177 or 22 .... $290.00
Price: Model 34N (nickel-plated metal, black epoxy-coated wood stock) ... $350.00
Price: Model 34BC (matte black metal, black stock, 4x32 scope, mounts) .. $510.00

RWS/DIANA MODEL 36 AIR RIFLE
Caliber: 177, 22, single shot. **Barrel:** 19", rifled. **Weight:** 8 lbs. **Length:** 45" overall. **Power:** Spring-air, barrel cocking. **Stock:** Beech. **Sights:** Hooded front (interchangeable inserts available), adjustable rear. **Features:** Velocity of 1000 fps (177-cal.). Comes with scope mount; two-stage adjustable trigger. Imported from Germany by Dynamit Nobel-RWS, Inc.
Price: $435.00
Price: Model 36 Carbine (same as Model 36 rifle except has 15" barrel) ... $435.00

RWS/DIANA MODEL 52 AIR RIFLE
Caliber: 177, 22, single shot. **Barrel:** 17", rifled. **Weight:** 8-1/2 lbs. **Length:** 43" overall. **Power:** Spring-air, sidelever cocking. **Stock:** Beech, with Monte Carlo, cheekpiece, checkered grip and forend. **Sights:** Ramp front, adjustable rear. **Features:** Velocity of 1100 fps (177). Blue finish. Solid rubber buttpad. Imported from Germany by Dynamit Nobel-RWS, Inc.
Price: $565.00
Price: Model 52 Deluxe (select walnut stock, rosewood grip and forend caps, palm swell grip) $810.00
Price: Model 48B (as above except matte black metal, black stock) $535.00
Price: Model 48 (same as Model 52 except no Monte Carlo, cheekpiece or checkering) $510.00

RWS/DIANA MODEL 45 AIR RIFLE
Caliber: 177, single shot. **Weight:** 8 lbs. **Length:** 45" overall. **Power:** Spring-air, barrel cocking. **Stock:** Walnut-finished hardwood with rubber recoil pad. **Sights:** Globe front with interchangeable inserts, micro. click open rear with four-way blade. **Features:** Velocity of 820 fps. Dovetail base for either micrometer peep sight or scope mounting. Automatic safety. Imported from Germany by Dynamit Nobel-RWS, Inc.
Price: $350.00

RWS/DIANA MODEL 54 AIR KING RIFLE
Caliber: 177, 22, single shot. **Barrel:** 17". **Weight:** 9 lbs. **Length:** 43" overall. **Power:** Spring-air, sidelever cocking. **Stock:** Walnut with Monte Carlo cheekpiece, checkered grip and forend. **Sights:** Ramp front, fully adjustable rear. **Features:** Velocity to 1000 fps (177), 900 fps (22). Totally recoilless system; floating action absorbs recoil. Imported from Germany by Dynamit Nobel-RWS, Inc.
Price: $785.00

SAVAGE MODEL 1000G AIR RIFLE
Caliber: 177 pellet, single shot. **Barrel:** 18". **Weight:** 7.25 lbs. **Length:** 45.3" overall. **Power:** Spring piston, break-barrel action. **Stock:** Walnut-finished hardwood with recoil pad. **Sights:** Adjustable rear notch, hooded front post. **Features:** Velocity 1,000 fps. Also available with 2.5-power scope. Introduced 2000. From Savage Arms.
Price: $181.00

SAVAGE MODEL 600F AIR RIFLE
Caliber: 177 pellet, 25-shot tubular magazine. **Barrel:** 18" polymer-coated steel. **Weight:** 6 lbs. **Length:** 40" overall. **Power:** spring piston, break-barrel action. **Stock:** Black polymer stock with lacquer finish. **Sights:** Adjustable rear notch, hooded front post. **Features:** Velocity 600 fps. Repeating action. Also available with 2.5-power scope. Introduced 2000. From Savage Arms.
Price: $126.00

Savage Model 560F

Steyr LG1P

Whiscombe JW70 FB

SAVAGE MODEL 560F AIR RIFLE
Caliber: 177 pellet, single shot. **Barrel:** 18" polymer-coated steel. **Weight:** 5.5 lbs. **Length:** 39" overall. **Power:** Spring piston, break-barrel action. **Stock:** Metallic-black finished polymer stock. **Sights:** Adjustable notch rear, post front. **Features:** Velocity 560 fps. Introduced 2000. From Savage Arms.
Price: $92.00

STEYR LG1P AIR RIFLE
Caliber: 177, single shot. **Barrel:** 23.75", (13.75" rifled). **Weight:** 10.5 lbs. **Length:** 51.7" overall. **Power:** Precharged air. **Stock:** Match. Laminated wood. Adjustable buttplate and cheekpiece. **Sights:** Precision diopter. **Features:** Velocity 577 fps. Air cylinders are refillable; about 320 shots per cylinder. Designed for 10-meter shooting. Introduced 1996. Imported from Austria by Nygord Precision Products.
Price: About $1,295.00
Price: Left-hand, about $1,350.00

TECH FORCE BS4 OLYMPIC COMPETITION AIR RIFLE
Caliber: 177 pellet, single shot. **Barrel:** N/A. **Weight:** 10.8 lbs. **Length:** 43.3" overall. **Power:** Spring piston, sidelever action. **Stock:** Wood with semi-pistol grip, adjustable butt plate. **Sights:** Micro-adjustable competition rear, hooded front. **Features:** Velocity 640 fps. Recoilless action; adjustable trigger. Includes carrying case. Imported from China by Compasseco Inc.
Price: $595.00
Price: Optional diopter rear sight. $79.95

TECH FORCE 6 AIR RIFLE
Caliber: 177 pellet, single shot. **Barrel:** 14". **Weight:** 6 lbs. **Length:** 35.5" overall. **Power:** Sspring piston, sidelever action. **Stock:** Paratrooper-style folding, full pistol grip. **Sights:** Adjustable rear, hooded front. **Features:** Velocity 800 fps. All-metal construction; grooved for scope mounting. Imported from China by Compasseco Inc.
Price: $69.95

Tech Force 51 Air Rifle
Similar to Tech Force 6, but with break-barrel cocking mechanism and folding stock fitted with recoil pad. Overall length, 36". Weighs 6 lbs. From Compasseco Inc.
Price: $69.95

TECH FORCE 25 AIR RIFLE
Caliber: 177, 22 pellet; single shot. **Barrel:** N/A. **Weight:** 7.5 lbs. **Length:** 46.2" overall. **Power:** Spring piston, break-action barrel. **Stock:** Oil-finished wood; Monte Carlo stock with recoil pad. **Sights:** Adjustable rear, hooded front with insert. **Features:** Velocity 1,000 fps (177); grooved receiver and scope stop for scope mounting; adjustable trigger; trigger safety. Imported from China by Compasseco Inc.
Price: 177 or 22 caliber $125.00
Price: Includes rifle and Tech Force 96 red dot point sight $164.95

TECH FORCE 36 AIR RIFLE
Caliber: 177 pellet, single shot. **Barrel:** N/A. **Weight:** 7.4 lbs. **Length:** 43" overall. **Power:** Spring piston, underlever cocking. **Stock:** Monte Carlo hardwood stock; recoil pad. **Sights:** Adjustable rear, hooded front. **Features:** Velocity 900 fps; grooved receiver and scope stop for scope mounting; auto-reset safety. Imported from China by Compasseco Inc.
Price: $89.95

WHISCOMBE JW SERIES AIR RIFLES
Caliber: 177, 20, 22, 25, single shot. **Barrel:** 15", Lothar Walther. Polygonal rifling. **Weight:** 9 lbs., 8 oz. **Length:** 39" overall. **Power:** Dual spring-piston, multi-stroke; underlever cocking. **Stock:** Walnut with adjustable buttplate and cheekpiece. **Sights:** None furnished; grooved scope rail. **Features:** Velocity 660-1000 (JW80) fps (22-caliber, fixed barrel) depending upon model. Interchangeable barrels; automatic safety; muzzle weight; semi-floating action; twin opposed pistons with counter-wound springs; adjustable trigger. All models include H.O.T. System (Harmonic Optimization Tunable System). Introduced 1995. Imported from England by Pelaire Products.
Price: JW50, MKII fixed barrel only $1,895.00
Price: JW60, MKII fixed barrel only $1,895.00
Price: JW70, MKII fixed barrel only $1,950.00
Price: JW80, MKII. $1,995.00

AIRGUNS

MANUFACTURER'S DIRECTORY

A

A Zone Bullets, 2039 Walter Rd., Billings, MT 59105 / 800-252-3111; FAX: 406-248-1961
A&B Industries,Inc (See Top-Line USA Inc)
A&M Waterfowl,Inc., P.O. Box 102, Ripley, TN 38063 / 901-635-4003; FAX: 901-635-2320
A&W Repair, 2930 Schneider Dr., Arnold, MO 63010 / 314-287-3725
A-Square Co.,Inc., One Industrial Park, Bedford, KY 40006-9667 / 502-255-7456; FAX: 502-255-7657
A-Tech Corp., P.O. Box 1281, Cottage Grove, OR 97424
A.A. Arms, Inc., 4811 Persimmont Ct., Monroe, NC 28110 / 704-289-5356 or 800-935-1119; FAX: 704-289-5859
A.B.S. III, 9238 St. Morritz Dr., Fern Creek, KY 40291
A.G. Russell Knives,Inc., 1705 Hwy. 71B North, Springdale, AR 72764 / 501-751-7341
A.R.M.S., Inc., 230 W. Center St., West Bridgewater, MA 02379-1620 / 508-584-7816; FAX: 508-588-8045
A.W. Peterson Gun Shop, Inc., 4255 W. Old U.S. 441, Mt. Dora, FL 32757-3299 / 352-383-4258; FAX: 352-735-1001
ABO (USA) Inc, 615 SW 2nd Avenue, Miami, FL 33130 / 305-859-2010 FAX: 305-859-2099
AC Dyna-tite Corp., 155 Kelly St., P.O. Box 0984, Elk Grove Village, IL 60007 / 847-593-5566; FAX: 847-593-1304
Acadian Ballistic Specialties, P.O. Box 787, folsom, LA 70437 / 504-796-0078 gunsmith@neasolft.com
Accu-Tek, 4510 Carter Ct, Chino, CA 91710
Accupro Gun Care, 15512-109 Ave., Surrey, BC U3R 7E8 CANADA / 604-583-7807
Accura-Site (See All's, The Jim Tembelis Co., Inc.)
Accuracy Innovations, Inc., P.O. Box 376, New Paris, PA 15554 / 814-839-4517; FAX: 814-839-2601
Accuracy Int'l. North America, Inc., PO Box 5267, Oak Ridge, TN 37831 / 423-482-0330; FAX: 423-482-0336
Accuracy International, 9115 Trooper Trail, P.O. Box 2019, Bozeman, MT 59715 / 406-587-7922; FAX: 406-585-9434
Accuracy Internationl Precision Rifles (See U.S. Importer-Gunsite Custom Shop; Gunsite Training Center)
Accuracy Unlimited, 16036 N. 49 Ave., Glendale, AZ 85306 / 602-978-9089; FAX: 602-978-9089
Accuracy Unlimited, 7479 S. DePew St., Littleton, CO 80123
Accurate Arms Co., Inc., 5891 Hwy. 230 West, McEwen, TN 37101 / 800-416-3006 FAX: 931-729-4211
Accuright, RR 2 Box 397, Sebeka, MN 56477 / 218-472-3383
Ace Custom 45's, Inc., 1880 1/2 Upper Turtle Creek Rd., Kerrville, TX 78028 / 830-257-4290; FAX: 830-257-5724
Ace Sportswear, Inc., 700 Quality Rd., Fayetteville, NC 28306 / 919-323-1223; FAX: 919-323-5392
Ackerman & Co., Box 133 US Highway Rt. 7, Pownal, VT 05261 / 802-823-9874 muskets@togsther.net
Ackerman, Bill (See Optical Services Co)
Acra-Bond Laminates, 134 Zimmerman Rd., Kalispell, MT 59901 / 406-257-9003; FAX: 406-257-9003
Action Bullets & Alloy Inc, RR 1, P.O. Box 189, Quinter, KS 67752 / 913-754-3609; FAX: 913-754-3629
Action Direct, Inc., P.O. Box 830760, Miami, FL 33283 / 305-559-4652; FAX: 305-559-4652 action-direct.com
Action Products, Inc., 22 N. Mulberry St., Hagerstown, MD 21740 / 301-797-1414; FAX: 301-733-2073
Action Target, Inc., P.O. Box 636, Provo, UT 84603 / 801-377-8033; FAX: 801-377-8096
Actions by "T" Teddy Jacobson, 16315 Redwood Forest Ct., Sugar Land, TX 77478 / 281-277-4008
AcuSport Corporation, 1 Hunter Place, Bellefontaine, OH 43311-3001 / 513-593-7010 FAX: 513-592-5625
Ad Hominem, 3130 Gun Club Lane, RR, Orillia, ON L3V 6H3 CANADA / 705-689-5303; FAX: 705-689-5303
Adair Custom Shop, Bill, 2886 Westridge, Carrollton, TX 75006
Adams & Son Engravers, John J, 87 Acorn Rd, Dennis, MA 02638 / 508-385-7971
Adams Jr., John J., 87 Acorn Rd., Dennis, MA 02638 / 508-385-7971
ADCO Sales, Inc., 4 Draper St. #A, Woburn, MA 01801 / 781-935-1799; FAX: 781-935-1011
Adkins, Luther, 1292 E. McKay Rd., Shelbyville, IN 46176-8706 / 317-392-3795
Advance Car Mover Co., Rowell Div., P.O. Box 1, 240 N. Depot St., Juneau, WI 53039 / 414-386-4464; FAX: 414-386-4416
Adventure 16, Inc., 4620 Alvarado Canyon Rd., San Diego, CA 92120 / 619-283-6314
Adventure Game Calls, R.D. 1, Leonard Rd., Spencer, NY 14883 / 607-589-4611
Adventurer's Outpost, P.O. Box 547, Cottonwood, AZ 86326-0547 / 800-762-7471; FAX: 602-634-8781
Aero Peltor, 90 Mechanic St, Southbridge, MA 01550 / 508-764-5500; FAX: 508-764-0188
African Import Co., 22 Goodwin Rd, Plymouth, MA 02360 / 508-746-8552 FAX: 508-746-0404
AFSCO Ammunition, 731 W. Third St., P.O. Box L, Owen, WI 54460 / 715-229-2516
Ahlman Guns, 9525 W. 230th St., Morristown, MN 55052 / 507-685-4243; FAX: 507-685-4280
Ahrends, Kim (See Custom Firearms, Inc), Box 203, Clarion, IA 50525 / 515-532-3449; FAX: 515-532-3926
Aimpoint c/o Springfield, Inc., 420 W. Main St, Geneseo, IL 61254 / 309-944-1702
Aimtech Mount Systems, P.O. Box 223, Thomasville, GA 31799-1638 / 912-226-4313; FAX: 912-227-0222 aimtech@surfsouth.com www.aimtech-mounts.com
Air Arms, Hailsham Industrial Park, Diplocks Way, Hailsham, E. Sussex, BN27 3JF ENGLAND / 011-0323-845853
Air Rifle Specialists, P.O. Box 138, 130 Holden Rd., Pine City, NY 14871-0138 / 607-734-7340; FAX: 607-733-3261
Air Venture Airguns, 9752 E. Flower St., Bellflower, CA 90706 / 310-867-6355
Airgun Repair Centre, 3227 Garden Meadows, Lawrenceburg, IN 47025 / 812-637-1463; FAX: 812-637-1463
Airrow, 11 Monitor Hill Rd, Newtown, CT 06470 / 203-270-6343
Aitor-Cuchilleria Del Norte S.A., Izelaieta, 17, 48260, Ermua, S SPAIN / 43-17-08-50
Ajax Custom Grips, Inc., 9130 Viscount Row, Dallas, TX 75247 / 214-630-8893; FAX: 214-630-4942
Aker International, Inc., 2248 Main St., Suite 6, Chula Vista, CA 91911 / 619-423-5182; FAX: 619-423-1363
Al Lind Custom Guns, 7821 76th Ave. SW, Tacoma, WA 98498 / 206-584-6361
Alana Cupp Custom Engraver, P.O. Box 207, Annabella, UT 84711 / 801-896-4834
Alaska Bullet Works, Inc., 9978 Crazy Horse Drive, Juneau, AK 99801 / 907-789-3834; FAX: 907-789-3433
Alco Carrying Cases, 601 W. 26th St., New York, NY 10001 / 212-675-5820; FAX: 212-691-5935
Aldis Gunsmithing & Shooting Supply, 502 S. Montezuma St., Prescott, AZ 86303 / 602-445-6723; FAX: 602-445-6763
Alessi Holsters, Inc., 2465 Niagara Falls Blvd., Amherst, NY 14228-3527 / 716-691-5615
Alex, Inc., Box 3034, Bozeman, MT 59772 / 406-282-7396; FAX: 406-282-7396
Alfano, Sam, 36180 Henry Gaines Rd., Pearl River, LA 70452 / 504-863-3364; FAX: 504-863-7715
All American Lead Shot Corp., P.O. Box 224566, Dallas, TX 75062
All Rite Products, Inc., 5752 N. Silverstone Circle, Mountain Green, UT 84050 / 801-876-3330; FAX: 801-876-2216
All's, The Jim J. Tembelis Co., Inc., 216 Loper Ct., Neenah, WI 54956 / 920-725-5251; FAX: 920-725-5251
Allard, Gary/Creek Side Metal & Woodcrafters, Fishers Hill, VA 22626 / 703-465-3903
Allen Co., Bob, 214 SW Jackson, P.O. Box 477, Des Moines, IA 50315 / 515-283-2191 or 800-685-7020; FAX: 515-283-0779
Allen Co., Inc., 525 Burbank St., Broomfield, CO 80020 / 303-469-1857 or 800-876-8600; FAX: 303-466-7437
Allen Firearm Engraving, 339 Grove Ave., Prescott, AZ 86301 / 520-778-1237
Allen Mfg., 6449 Hodgson Rd., Circle Pines, MN 55014 / 612-429-8231
Allen Sportswear, Bob (See Allen Co., Bob)
Alley Supply Co., P.O. Box 848, Gardnerville, NV 89410 / 702-782-3800
Alliant Techsystems Smokeless Powder Group, 200 Valley Rd., Suite 305, Mt. Arlington, NJ 07856 / 800-276-9337; FAX: 201-770-2528
Allred Bullet Co., 932 Evergreen Drive, Logan, UT 84321 / 435-752-6983; FAX: 435-752-6983
Alpec Team, Inc., 201 Ricken Backer Cir., Livermore, CA 94550 / 510-606-8245; FAX: 510-606-4279
Alpha 1 Drop Zone, 2121 N. Tyler, Wichita, KS 67212 / 316-729-0800
Alpha Gunsmith Division, 1629 Via Monserate, Fallbrook, CA 92028 / 619-723-9279 or 619-728-2663
Alpha LaFranck Enterprises, P.O. Box 81072, Lincoln, NE 68501 / 402-466-3193
Alpha Precision, Inc., 2765-B Preston Rd. NE, Good Hope, GA 30641 / 770-267-6163
Alpine Indoor Shooting Range, 2401 Government Way, Coeur d'Alene, ID 83814 / 208-676-8824 FAX: 208-676-8824
Altamont Co., 901 N. Church St., P.O. Box 309, Thomasboro, IL 61878 / 217-643-3125 or 800-626-5774; FAX: 217-643-7973
Alumna Sport by Dee Zee, 1572 NE 58th Ave., P.O. Box 3090, Des Moines, IA 50316 / 800-798-9899
Amadeo Rossi S.A., Rua: Amadeo Rossi, 143, Sao Leopoldo, RS 93030-220 BRAZIL / 051-592-5566
AmBr Software Group Ltd., P.O. Box 301, Reistertown, MD 21136-0301 / 800-888-1917; FAX: 410-526-7212
American Ammunition, 3545 NW 71st St., Miami, FL 33147 / 305-835-7400; FAX: 305-694-0037
American Arms Inc., 2604 NE Industrial Dr, N. Kansas City, MO 64116 / 816-474-3161; FAX: 816-474-1225
American Bullet, 1512 W Chester Pike #298, West Chester, PA 19382-7754 / 610-399-6584
American Custom Gunmakers Guild, PO Box 812, Burlington, IA 52601 / 318-752-6114; FAX: 319-752-6114 acgg@acgg.org acgg.org
American Derringer Corp., 127 N. Lacy Dr., Waco, TX 76705 / 800-642-7817 or 817-799-9111; FAX: 817-799-7935
American Display Co., 55 Cromwell St., Providence, RI 02907 / 401-331-2464; FAX: 401-421-1264
American Frontier Firearms Mfg., Inc, PO Box 744, Aguanga, CA 92536 / 909-763-0014; FAX: 909-763-0014
American Gas & Chemical Co., Ltd, 220 Pegasus Ave, Northvale, NJ 07647 / 201-767-7300
American Gripcraft, 3230 S Dodge 2, Tucson, AZ 85713 / 602-790-1222
American Gunsmithing Institute, 1325 Imola Ave #504, Napa, CA 94559 / 707-253-0462; FAX: 707-253-7149
American Handgunner Magazine, 591 Camino de la Reina, Ste 200, San Diego, CA 92108 / 619-297-5350; FAX: 619-297-5353
American Pioneer Video, PO Box 50049, Bowling Green, KY 42102-2649 / 800-743-4675
American Products, Inc., 14729 Spring Valley Road, Morrison, IL 61270 / 815-772-3336; FAX: 815-772-8046
American Safe Arms, Inc., 1240 Riverview Dr., Garland, UT 84312 / 801-257-7472; FAX: 801-785-8156
American Sales & Kirkpatrick Mfg. Co., P.O. Box 677, Laredo, TX 78042 / 210-723-6893; FAX: 210-725-0672
American Sales & Mfg. Co., PO Box 677, Laredo, TX 78042 / 956-723-6893; FAX: 956-725-0672 holsters@kirkpatrickleather.com http://kirkpatrickleather.com
American Security Products Co., 11925 Pacific Ave., Fontana, CA 92337 / 909-685-9680 or 800-421-6142; FAX: 909-685-9685
American Small Arms Academy, P.O. Box 12111, Prescott, AZ 86304 / 602-778-5623
American Target, 1328 S. Jason St., Denver, CO 80223 / 303-733-0433; FAX: 303-777-0311
American Target Knives, 1030 Brownwood NW, Grand Rapids, MI 49504 / 616-453-1998
American Western Arms, Inc., 1450 S.W. 10th St., Suite 3B, Delray Beach, FL 33444 / 877-292-4867; FAX: 561-330-0881
American Whitetail Target Systems, P.O. Box 41, 106 S. Church St., Tennyson, IN 47637 / 812-567-4527
Americase, P.O. Box 271, 1610 E. Main, Waxahachie, TX 75165 / 800-880-3629; FAX: 214-937-8373
Ames Metal Products, 4323 S. Western Blvd., Chicago, IL 60609 / 773-523-3230; or 800-255-6937 FAX: 773-523-3854
Amherst Arms, P.O. Box 1457, Englewood, FL 34295 / 941-475-2020; FAX: 941-473-1212
Ammo Load, Inc., 1560 E. Edinger, Suite G, Santa Ana, CA 92705 / 714-558-8858; FAX: 714-569-0319
Amrine's Gun Shop, 937 La Luna, Ojai, CA 93023 / 805-646-2376
Amsec, 11925 Pacific Ave., Fontana, CA 92337
Amtec 2000, Inc., 84 Industrial Rowe, Gardner, MA 01440 / 508-632-9608; FAX: 508-632-2300
Analog Devices, Box 9106, Norwood, MA 02062
Andela Tool & Machine, Inc., RD3, Box 246, Richfield Springs, NY 13439
Anderson Manufacturing Co., Inc., 22602 53rd Ave. SE, Bothell, WA 98021 / 206-481-1858; FAX: 206-481-7839
Andres & Dworsky, Bergstrasse 18, A-3822 Karlstein, Thaya, AUSTRIA / 0 28 44-285
Angel Arms, Inc., 1825 Addison Way, Haywood, CA 94545 / 510-783-7122
Angelo & Little Custom Gun Stock Blanks, P.O. Box 240046, Dell, MT 59724-0046
Anics Firm Inc3 Commerce Park Square, 23200 Chagrin Blvd., Suite 240, Beechwood, OH 44122 / 800-556-1582; FAX: 216-292-2588
Anschutz GmbH, Postfach 1128, D-89001 Ulm, Donau, GERMANY / 731-40120
Answer Products Co., 1519 Westbury Drive, Davison, MI 48423 / 810-653-2911
Anthony and George Ltd., Rt. 1, P.O. Box 45, Evington, VA 24550 / 804-821-8117
Antique American Firearms, P.O. Box 71035, Dept. GD, Des Moines, IA 50325 / 515-224-6552
Antique Arms Co., 1110 Cleveland Ave., Monett, MO 65708 / 417-235-6501
Apel GmbH, Ernst, Am Kirschberg 3, D-97218, Gerbrunn, GERMANY / 0 (931) 707192
Aplan Antiques & Art, James O., James O., HC 80, Box 793-25, Piedmont, SD 57769 / 605-347-5016
AR-7 Industries, LLC, 998 N. Colony Rd., Meriden, CT 06450 / 203-630-3536; FAX: 203-630-3637
Arco Powder, HC-Rt. 1 P.O. Box 102, County Rd. 357, Mayo, FL 32066 / 904-294-3882; FAX: 904-294-1498

Arizona Ammunition, Inc., 21421 No. 14th Ave., Suite E, Phoenix, AZ 85027 / 623-516-9004; FAX: 623-516-9012 azammo.com

Arkansas Mallard Duck Calls, Rt. Box 182, England, AR 72046 / 501-842-3597

ArmaLite, Inc., P.O. Box 299, Geneseo, IL 61254 / 309-944-6939; FAX: 309-944-6949

Armament Gunsmithing Co., Inc., 525 Rt. 22, Hillside, NJ 07205 / 908-686-0960 FAX: 718-738-5019

Armas Kemen S. A. (See U.S. Importers)

Armas Urki Garbi, 12-14 20.600, Eibar (Guipuzcoa), / 43-11 38 73

Armfield Custom Bullets, 4775 Caroline Drive, San Diego, CA 92115 / 619-582-7188; FAX: 619-287-3238

Armi Perazzi S.p.A., Via Fontanelle 1/3, 1-25080, Botticino Mattina, / 030-2692591; FAX: 030 2692594+

Armi San Marco (See U.S. Importers-Taylor's & Co I

Armi San Paolo, 172-A, I-25062, via Europa, ITALY / 030-2751725

Armi Sport (See U.S. Importers-Cape Outfitters)

Armite Laboratories, 1845 Randolph St., Los Angeles, CA 90001 / 213-587-7768; FAX: 213-587-5075

Armoloy Co. of Ft. Worth, 204 E. Daggett St., Fort Worth, TX 76104 / 817-332-5604; FAX: 817-335-6517

Armor (See Buck Stop Lure Co., Inc.)

Armor Metal Products, P.O. Box 4609, Helena, MT 59604 / 406-442-5560; FAX: 406-442-5650

Armory Publications, 17171 Bothall Way NE, #276, Seattle, WA 98155 / 208-664-5061; FAX: 208-664-9906 armorypub@aol.com www.grocities.com/armorypub

Arms & Armour Press, Wellington House, 125 Strand, London, WC2R 0BB ENGLAND / 0171-420-5555; FAX: 0171-240-7265

Arms Corporation of the Philippines, Bo. Parang Marikina, Metro Manila, PHILIPPINES / 632-941-6243 or 632-941-6244; FAX: 632-942-0682

Arms Craft Gunsmithing, 1106 Linda Dr., Arroyo Grande, CA 93420 / 805-481-2830

Arms Ingenuity Co., P.O. Box 1, 51 Canal St., Weatogue, CT 06089 / 203-658-5624

Arms Software, P.O. Box 1526, Lake Oswego, OR 97035 / 800-366-5559 or 503-697-0533; FAX: 503-697-3337

Arms, Programming Solutions (See Arms Software)

Armscorp USA, Inc., 4424 John Ave., Baltimore, MD 21227 / 410-247-6200; FAX: 410-247-6205 armscorp_md@yahoo.com

Armsport, Inc., 3950 NW 49th St., Miami, FL 33142 / 305-635-7850; FAX: 305-633-2877

Arnold Arms Co., Inc., P.O. Box 1011, Arlington, WA 98223 / 800-371-1011 or 360-435-1011; FAX: 360-435-7304

Aro-Tek Ltd., 206 Frontage Rd. North, Suite C, Pacific, WA 98047 / 206-351-2984; FAX: 206-833-4483

Arratoonian, Andy (See Horseshoe Leather Products)

Arrieta S.L., Morkaiko 5, 20870, Elgoibar, SPAIN / 34-43-743150; FAX: 34-43-743154+

Art Jewel Enterprises Ltd., Eagle Business Ctr., 460 Randy Rd., Carol Stream, IL 60188 / 708-260-0400

Art's Gun & Sport Shop, Inc., 6008 Hwy. Y, Hillsboro, MO 63050

Artistry in Wood, 134 Zimmerman Rd., Kalispell, MT 59901 / 406-257-9003

Arundel Arms & Ammunition, Inc., A., 24A Defense St., Annapolis, MD 21401 / 410-224-8683

Arvo Ojala Holsters, P.O. Box 98, N. Hollywood, CA 91603 / 818-222-9700; FAX: 818-222-0401

Ashby Turkey Calls, P.O. Box 1466, Ava, MO 65608-1466 / 417-967-3787

Ashley Outdoors, Inc, 2401 Ludelle St, Fort Worth, TX 76105 / 888-744-4880; FAX: 800-734-7939

Aspen Outfitting Co, Jon Hollinger, 9 Dean St, Aspen, CO 81611 / 970-925-3406

Astra Sport, S.A., Apartado 3, 48300 Guernica, Espagne, SPAIN / 34-4-6250100; FAX: 34-4-6255186+

Atamec-Bretton, 19 rue Victor Grignard, F-42026, St.-Etienne (Cedex 1, / 77-93-54-69; FAX: 33-77-93-57-98+

Atlanta Cutlery Corp., 2143 Gees Mill Rd., Box 839 CIS, Conyers, GA 30207 / 800-883-0300; FAX: 404-388-0246

Atlantic Mills, Inc., 1295 Towbin Ave., Lakewood, NJ 08701-5934 / 800-242-7374

Atlantic Rose, Inc., P.O. Box 10717, Bradenton, FL 34282-0717

Atsko/Sno-Seal, Inc., 2664 Russell St., Orangeburg, SC 29115 / 803-531-1820; FAX: 803-531-2139

Auguste Francotte & Cie S.A., rue du Trois Juin 109, 4400 Herstal-Liege, BELGIUM / 32-4-248-13-18; FAX: 32-4-948-11-79

Austin & Halleck, 1099 Welt, Weston, MO 64098 / 816-386-2176; FAX: 816-386-2177

Austin Sheridan USA, Inc., P.O. Box 577, 36 Haddam Quarter Rd., Durham, CT 06422 / 860-349-1772; FAX: 860-349-1771 swalzer@palm.net

Autauga Arms, Inc., Pratt Plaza Mall No. 13, Prattville, AL 36067 / 800-262-9563; FAX: 334-361-2961

Auto Arms, 738 Clearview, San Antonio, TX 78228 / 512-434-5450

Auto-Ordnance Corp., PO Box 220, Blauvelt, NY 10913 / 914-353-7770

Automatic Equipment Sales, 627 E. Railroad Ave., Salesburg, MD 21801

Autumn Sales, Inc. (Blaser), 1320 Lake St., Fort Worth, TX 76102 / 817-335-1634; FAX: 817-338-0119

Avnda Otaola Norica, 16 Apartado 68, 20600, Eibar,

AWC Systems Technology, P.O. Box 41938, Phoenix, AZ 85080-1938 / 602-780-1050 FAX: 602-780-2967

AYA (See U.S. Importer-New England Custom Gun Service)

B

B & P America, 12321 Brittany Cir, Dallas, TX 75230 / 972-726-9069

B&D Trading Co., Inc., 3935 Fair Hill Rd., Fair Oaks, CA 95628 / 800-334-3790 or 916-967-9366; FAX: 916-967-4873

B-Square Company, Inc., ;, P.O. Box 11281, 2708 St. Louis Ave., Ft. Worth, TX 76110 / 817-923-0964 or 800-433-2909 FAX: 817-926-7012

B-West Imports, Inc., 2425 N. Huachuca Dr., Tucson, AZ 85745-1201 / 602-628-1990; FAX: 602-628-3602

B.B. Walker Co., PO Box 1167, 414 E Dixie Dr, Asheboro, NC 27203 / 910-625-1380; FAX: 910-625-8125

B.C. Outdoors, Larry McGhee, PO Box 61497, Boulder City, NV 89006 / 702-294-0025

B.M.F. Activator, Inc., 12145 Mill Creek Run, Plantersville, TX 77363 / 936-894-2397 or 800-527-2881 FAX: 936-894-2397

Badger Shooters Supply, Inc., P.O. Box 397, Owen, WI 54460 / 800-424-9069; FAX: 715-229-2332

Baekgaard Ltd., 1855 Janke Dr., Northbrook, IL 60062 / 708-498-3040; FAX: 708-493-3106

Baelder, Harry, Alte Goennebeker Strasse 5, 24635, Rickling, GERMANY / 04328-722732; FAX: 04328-722733

Baer Custom, Inc, Les, 29601 34th Ave, Hillsdale, IL 61257 / 309-658-2716; FAX: 309-658-2610

Baer's Hollows, P.O. Box 284, Eads, CO 81036 / 719-438-5718

Bagmaster Mfg., Inc., 2731 Sutton Ave., St. Louis, MO 63143 / 314-781-8002; FAX: 314-781-3363

Bain & Davis, Inc., 307 E. Valley Blvd., San Gabriel, CA 91776-3522 / 818-573-4241 or 213-283-7449 caindavis@aol.com

Baker, Stan, 10000 Lake City Way, Seattle, WA 98125 / 206-522-4575

Baker's Leather Goods, Roy, PO Box 893, Magnolia, AR 71753 / 501-234-0344

Balance Co., 340-39 Ave., S.E., Box 505, Calgary, AB T2G 1X6 CANADA

Bald Eagle Precision Machine Co., 101-A Allison St., Lock Haven, PA 17745 / 570-748-6772; FAX: 570-748-4443

Balickie, Joe, 408 Trelawney Lane, Apex, NC 27502 / 919-362-5185

Ballard Industries, 10271 Lockwood Dr., Suite B, Cupertino, CA 95014 / 408-996-0957; FAX: 408-257-6828

Ballard Rifle & Cartridge Co., LLC, 113 W Yellowstone Ave, Cody, WY 82414 / 307-587-4914; FAX: 307-527-6097

Ballisti-Cast, Inc., 6347 49th St. NW, Plaza, ND 58771 / 701-497-3333; FAX: 701-497-3335

Ballistic Engineering & Software, Inc., 185 N. Park Blvd., Suite 330, Lake Orion, MI 48362 / 313-391-1074

Ballistic Product, Inc., 20015 75th Ave. North, Corcoran, MN 55340-9456 / 612-494-9237; FAX: 612-494-9236 info@ballisticproducts.com www.ballisticproducts.com

Ballistic Research, 1108 W. May Ave., McHenry, IL 60050 / 815-385-0037

Bandcor Industries, Div. of Man-Sew Corp., 6108 Sherwin Dr., Port Richey, FL 34668 / 813-848-0432

Bang-Bang Boutique (See Holster Shop, The)

Banks, Ed, 2762 Hwy. 41 N., Ft. Valley, GA 31030 / 912-987-4665

Bansner's Gunsmithing Specialties, 261 East Main St. Box VH, Adamstown, PA 19501 / 800-368-2379; FAX: 717-484-0523

Bar-Sto Precision Machine, 73377 Sullivan Rd., P.O. Box 1838, Twentynine Palms, CA 92277 / 760-367-2747; FAX: 760-367-2407

Barbour, Inc., 55 Meadowbrook Dr., Milford, NH 03055 / 603-673-1313; FAX: 603-673-6510

Barnes, 110 Borner St S, Prescott, WI 54021-1149 / 608-897-8416

Barnes Bullets, Inc., P.O. Box 215, American Fork, UT 84003 / 801-756-4222 or 800-574-9200; FAX: 801-756-2465 email@barnesbullets.com barnesbullets.com

Baron Technology, 62 Spring Hill Rd., Trumbull, CT 06611 / 203-452-0515; FAX: 203-452-0663

Barraclough, John K., 55 Merit Park Dr., Gardena, CA 90247 / 310-324-2574

Barramundi Corp., P.O. Drawer 4259, Homosassa Springs, FL 32687 / 904-628-0200

Barrett Firearms Manufacturer, Inc., P.O. Box 1077, Murfreesboro, TN 37133 / 615-896-2938; FAX: 615-896-7313

Barry Lee Hands Engraving, 26192 E. Shore Route, Bigfork, MT 59911 / 406-837-0035

Barta's Gunsmithing, 10231 US Hwy. 10, Cato, WI 54206 / 920-732-4472

Barteaux Machete, 1916 SE 50th Ave., Portland, OR 97215-3238 / 503-233-5880

Bartlett Engineering, 40 South 200 East, Smithfield, UT 84335-1645 / 801-563-5910

Basics Information Systems, Inc., 1141 Georgia Ave., Suite 515, Wheaton, MD 20902 / 301-949-1070; FAX: 301-949-5326

Bates Engraving, Billy, 2302 Winthrop Dr, Decatur, AL 35603 / 256-355-3690

Bauer, Eddie, 15010 NE 36th St., Redmond, WA 98052

Baumgartner Bullets, 3011 S. Alane St., W. Valley City, UT 84120

Bauska Barrels, 105 9th Ave. W., Kalispell, MT 59901 / 406-752-7706

Bear Archery, RR 4, 4600 Southwest 41st Blvd., Gainesville, FL 32601 / 904-376-2327

Bear Arms, 121 Rhodes St., Jackson, SC 29831 / 803-471-9859

Bear Hug Grip, Inc., P.O. Box 16649, Colorado Springs, CO 80935-6649 / 800-232-7710

Bear Mountain Gun & Tool, 120 N. Plymouth, New Plymouth, ID 83655 / 208-278-5221; FAX: 208-278-5221

Beartooth Bullets, P.O. Box 491, Dept. HLD, Dover, ID 83825-0491 / 208-448-1865 beartooth@trasport.com

Beaver Lodge (See Fellowes, Ted)

Beaver Park Product, Inc., 840 J St., Penrose, CO 81240 / 719-372-6744

BEC, Inc., 1227 W. Valley Blvd., Suite 204, Alhambra, CA 91803 / 626-281-5751; FAX: 626-293-7073

Beeline Custom Bullets Limited, P.O. Box 85, Yarmouth, NS B5A 4B1 CANADA / 902-648-3494; FAX: 902-648-0253

Beeman Precision Airguns, 5454 Argosy Dr., Huntington Beach, CA 92649 / 714-890-4800; FAX: 714-890-4808

Behlert Precision, Inc., P.O. Box 288, 7067 Easton Rd., Pipersville, PA 18947 / 215-766-8681 or 215-766-7301; FAX: 215-766-8681

Beitzinger, George, 116-20 Atlantic Ave., Richmond Hill, NY 11419 / 718-847-7661

Belding's Custom Gun Shop, 10691 Sayers Rd., Munith, MI 49259 / 517-596-2388

Bell & Carlson, Inc., Dodge City Industrial Park, 101 Allen Rd., Dodge City, KS 67801 / 800-634-8586 or 316-225-6688; FAX: 316-225-9095

Bell Reloading, Inc., 1725 Harlin Lane Rd., Villa Rica, GA 30180

Bell's Gun & Sport Shop, 3309-19 Mannheim Rd, Franklin Park, IL 60131

Bell's Legendary Country Wear, 22 Circle Dr., Bellmore, NY 11710 / 516-679-1158

Bellm Contenders, P.O. Box 459, Cleveland, UT 84518 / 801-653-2530

Belltown Ltd., 11 Camps Rd., Kent, CT 06757 / 860-354-5750 FAX: 860-354-6764

Ben William's Gun Shop, 1151 S. Cedar Ridge, Duncanville, TX 75137 / 214-780-1807

Ben's Machines, 1151 S. Cedar Ridge, Duncanville, TX 75137 / 214-780-1807 FAX: 214-780-0316

Benchmark Guns, 12593 S. Ave. 5 East, Yuma, AZ 85365

Benchmark Knives (See Gerber Legendary Blades)

Benelli Armi S.p.A., Via della Stazione, 61029, Urbino, ITALY / 39-722-307-1; FAX: 39-722-327427+

Benelli USA Corp, 17603 Indian Head Hwy, Accokeek, MD 20607 / 301-283-6981; FAX: 301-283-6988 benelliusa.com

Bengtson Arms Co., L., 6345-B E. Akron St., Mesa, AZ 85205 / 602-981-6375

Benjamin/Sheridan Co., Crossman, Rts. 5 and 20, E. Bloomfield, NY 14443 / 716-657-6161; FAX: 716-657-5405

Bentley, John, 128-D Watson Dr., Turtle Creek, PA 15145

Beomat of America, Inc., 300 Railway Ave., Campbell, CA 95008 / 408-379-4829

Beretta S.p.A., Pietro, Via Beretta, 18-25063, Gardone V.T., ITALY / 39-30-8341-1 FAX: 39-30-8341-421

Beretta U.S.A. Corp., 17601 Beretta Drive, Accokeek, MD 20607 / 301-283-2191; FAX: 301-283-0435

Berger Bullets Ltd., 5342 W. Camelback Rd., Suite 200, Glendale, AZ 85301 / 602-842-4001; FAX: 602-934-9083

Bernardelli S.p.A., Vincenzo, 125 Via Matteotti, PO Box 74, Brescia, ITALY / 39-30-8912851-2-3; FAX: 39-30-8910249

Berry's Mfg., Inc., 401 North 3050 East St., St. George, UT 84770 / 435-634-1682; FAX: 435-634-1683 sales@berrysmfg.com www.berrysmfg.com

MANUFACTURER'S DIRECTORY

Bersa S.A., Gonzales Castillo 312, 1704, Ramos Mejia, ARGENTINA / 541-656-2377; FAX: 541-656-2093+
Bert Johanssons Vapentillbehor, S-430 20 Veddige, SWEDEN,
Bertuzzi (See U.S. Importer-New England Arms Co)
Better Concepts Co., 663 New Castle Rd., Butler, PA 16001 / 412-285-9000
Beverly, Mary, 3201 Horseshoe Trail, Tallahassee, FL 32312
Bianchi International, Inc., 100 Calle Cortez, Temecula, CA 92590 / 909-676-5621; FAX: 909-676-6777
Biesen, Al, 5021 Rosewood, Spokane, WA 99208 / 509-328-9340
Biesen, Roger, 5021 W. Rosewood, Spokane, WA 99208 / 509-328-9340
Big Bear Arms & Sporting Goods, Inc., 1112 Milam Way, Carrollton, TX 75006 / 972-416-8051 or 800-400-BEAR; FAX: 972-416-0771
Big Bore Bullets of Alaska, P.O. Box 872785, Wasilla, AK 99687 / 907-373-2673; FAX: 907-373-2673 doug@mta-online.net ww.awloo.com/bbb/index.
Big Bore Express, 7154 W. State St., Boise, ID 83703 / 800-376-4010; FAX: 208-376-4020
Big Sky Racks, Inc., P.O. Box 729, Bozeman, MT 59771-0729 / 406-586-9393; FAX: 406-585-7378
Big Spring Enterprises "Bore Stores", P.O. Box 1115, Big Spring Rd., Yellville, AR 72687 / 870-449-5297; FAX: 870-449-4446
Bilal, Mustafa, 908 NW 50th St., Seattle, WA 98107-3634 / 206-782-4164
Bilinski, Bryan. See: FIELDSPORT LTD
Bill Austin's Calls, Box 284, Kaycee, WY 82639 / 307-738-2552
Bill Adair Custom Shop, 2886 Westridge, Carrollton, TX 75006 / 972-418-0950
Bill Hanus Birdguns LLC, P.O. Box 533, Newport, OR 97365 / 541-265-7433; FAX: 541-265-7400
Bill Johns Master Engraver, 7927 Ranch Roach 965, Fredericksburg, TX 78624-9545 / 830-997-6795
Bill Wiseman and Co., P.O. Box 3427, Bryan, TX 77805 / 409-690-3456; FAX: 409-690-0156
Bill's Custom Cases, P.O. Box 2, Dunsmuir, CA 96025 / 530-235-0177; FAX: 530-235-4959
Bill's Gun Repair, 1007 Burlington St., Mendota, IL 61342 / 815-539-5786
Billeb, Stephen L., 1101 N. 7th St., Burlington, IA 52601 / 319-753-2110
Billings Gunsmiths Inc., 1841 Grand Ave., Billings, MT 59102 / 406-256-8390
Billingsley & Brownell, P.O. Box 25, Dayton, WY 82836 / 307-655-9344
Billy Bates Engraving, 2302 Winthrop Dr., Decatur, AL 35603 / 205-355-3690
Birchwood Casey, 7900 Fuller Rd., Eden Prairie, MN 55344 / 800-328-6156 or 612-937-7933; FAX: 612-937-7979
Birdsong & Assoc, W. E., 1435 Monterey Rd, Florence, MS 39073-9748 / 601-366-8270
Bismuth Cartridge Co., 3500 Maple Ave., Suite 1650, Dallas, TX 75219 / 214-521-5880; FAX: 214-521-9035
Bison Studios, 1409 South Commerce St., Las Vegas, NV 89102 / 702-388-2891; FAX: 702-383-9967
Bitterroot Bullet Co., PO Box 412, Lewiston, ID 83501-0412 / 208-743-5635 FAX: 208-743-5635
BKL Technologies, PO Box 5237, Brownsville, TX 78523
Black Belt Bullets (See Big Bore Express)
Black Hills Ammunition, Inc., P.O. Box 3090, Rapid City, SD 57709-3090 / 605-348-5150; FAX: 605-348-9827
Black Hills Shooters Supply, P.O. Box 4220, Rapid City, SD 57709 / 800-289-2506
Black Powder Products, 67 Township Rd. 1411, Chesapeake, OH 45619 / 614-867-8047
Black Sheep Brand, 3220 W. Gentry Parkway, Tyler, TX 75702 / 903-592-3853; FAX: 903-592-0527
Blackhawk East, Box 2274, Loves Park, IL 61131
Blacksmith Corp., PO Box 280, North Hampton, OH 45349 / 800-531-2665; FAX: 937-969-8399 bcbooks@glassci-ty.net
BlackStar AccuMax Barrels, 11501 Brittmoore Park Drive, Houston, TX 77041 / 281-721-6040; FAX: 281-721-6041
BlackStar Barrel Accurizing (See BlackStar AccuMax Barrels)
Blacktail Mountain Books, 42 First Ave. W., Kalispell, MT 59901 / 406-257-5573
Blair Engraving, J. R., PO Box 64, Glenrock, WY 82637 / 307-436-8115
Blammo Ammo, P.O. Box 1677, Seneca, SC 29679 / 803-882-1768
Blaser Jagdwaffen GmbH, D-88316, Isny Im Allgau, GERMANY
Bleile, C. Roger, 5040 Ralph Ave., Cincinnati, OH 45238 / 513-251-0249
Blount, Inc., Sporting Equipment Div., 2299 Snake River Ave., P.O. Box 856, Lewiston, ID 83501 / 800-627-3640 or 208-746-2351; FAX: 208-799-3904
Blue and Gray Products Inc (See Ox-Yoke Originals, Inc.)
Blue Book Publications, Inc., One Appletree Square, 8009 34th Ave. S. Suite 175, Minneapolis, MN 55425 / 800-877-4867 or 612-854-5229; FAX: 612-853-1486
Blue Mountain Bullets, HCR 77, P.O. Box 231, John Day, OR 97845 / 541-820-4594
Blue Ridge Machinery & Tools, Inc., P.O. Box 536-GD, Hurricane, WV 25526 / 800-872-6500; FAX: 304-562-5311
BMC Supply, Inc., 26051 - 179th Ave. S.E., Kent, WA 98042
Bo-Mar Tool & Mfg. Co., Rt. 8, Box 405, Longview, TX 75604 / 903-759-4784; FAX: 903-759-9141
Bob Allen Co.214 SW Jackson, P.O. Box 477, Des Moines, IA 50315 / 800-685-7020 FAX: 515-283-0779
Bob Rogers Gunsmithing, P.O. Box 305, 344 S. Walnut St., Franklin Grove, IL 61031 / 815-456-2685; FAX: 815-288-7142
Bob Schrimsher's Custom Knifemaker's Supply, P.O. Box 308, Emory, TX 75440 / 903-473-3330; FAX: 903-473-2235
Bob's Gun Shop, P.O. Box 200, Royal, AR 71968 / 501-767-1970; FAX: 501-767-1970
Bob's Tactical Indoor Shooting Range & Gun Shop, 90 Lafayette Rd., Salisbury, MA 01952 / 508-465-5561
Boessler, Erich, Am Vogeltal 3, 97702, Munnerstadt, GERMANY
Bohemia Arms Co., 17101 Los Modelos St., Fountain Valley, CA 92708 / 619-442-7005; FAX: 619-442-7005
Boker USA, Inc., 1550 Balsam Street, Lakewood, CO 80215 / 303-462-0662; FAX: 303-462-0668 bokerusa@world-net.att.net bokerusa.com
Boltin, John M., P.O. Box 644, Estill, SC 29918 / 803-625-2185
Bonanza (See Forster Products), 310 E Lanark Ave, Lanark, IL 61046 / 815-493-6360; FAX: 815-493-2371
Bond Arms, Inc., P.O. Box 1296, Granbury, TX 76048 / 817-573-4445; FAX: 817-573-5636
Bond Custom Firearms, 8954 N. Lewis Ln., Bloomington, IN 47408 / 812-332-4519
Bondini Paolo, Via Sorrento 345, San Carlo di Cesena, ITALY / 0547-663-240; FAX: 0547-663-780
Bone Engraving, Ralph, 718 N Atlanta, Owasso, OK 74055 / 918-272-9745
Boone Trading Co., Inc., P.O. Box BB, Brinnan, WA 98320
Boone's Custom Ivory Grips, Inc., 562 Coyote Rd., Brinnon, WA 98320 / 206-796-4330
Boonie Packer Products, P.O. Box 12204, Salem, OR 97309 / 800-477-3244 or 503-581-3244; FAX: 503-581-3191
Borden Ridges Rimrock Stocks, RR 1 Box 250 BC, Springville, PA 18844 / 570-965-2505 FAX: 570-965-2328
Borden Rifles Inc, RD 1, Box 250BC, Springville, PA 18844 / 717-965-2505; FAX: 717-965-2328
Border Barrels Ltd., Riccarton Farm, Newcastleton, SCOTLAND UK
Borovnik KG, Ludwig, 9170 Ferlach, Bahnhofstrasse 7, AUSTRIA / 042 27 24 42; FAX: 042 26 43 49
Bosis (See U.S. Importer-New England Arms Co.)
Boss Manufacturing Co., 221 W. First St., Kewanee, IL 61443 / 309-852-2131 or 800-447-4581; FAX: 309-852-0848
Bostick Wildlife Calls, Inc., P.O. Box 728, Estill, SC 29918 / 803-625-2210 or 803-625-4512
Bowen Classic Arms Corp., P.O. Box 67, Louisville, TN 37777 / 865-984-3583 bowsarms.com
Bowen Knife Co., Inc., P.O. Box 590, Blackshear, GA 31516 / 912-449-4794
Bowerly, Kent, 710 Golden Pheasant Dr, Redmond, OR 97756 / 541-595-6028
Boyds' Gunstock Industries, Inc., 25376 403RD AVE, MITCHELL, SD 57301 / 605-996-5011; FAX: 605-996-9878
Brace, Larry D., 771 Blackfoot Ave., Eugene, OR 97404 / 541-688-1278; FAX: 541-607-5833
Bradley Gunsight Co., P.O. Box 340, Plymouth, VT 05056 / 860-589-0531; FAX: 860-582-6294
Brass Eagle, Inc., 7050A Bramalea Rd., Unit 19, Mississauga,, ON L4Z 1C7 CANADA / 416-848-4844
Bratcher, Dan, 311 Belle Air Pl., Carthage, MO 64836 / 417-358-1518
Brauer Bros. Mfg. Co., 2020 Delman Blvd., St. Louis, MO 63103 / 314-231-2864; FAX: 314-249-4952
Break-Free, Inc., P.O. Box 25020, Santa Ana, CA 92799 / 714-953-1900; FAX: 714-953-0402
Brenneke KG, Wilhelm, Ilmenauweg 2, 30851 Langenhagen, GERMANY / 0511-97262-0; FAX: 0511-97262-62
Brian Perazone-Gunsmith, Cold Spring Rd., Roxbury, NY 12474 / 607-326-4088; FAX: 607-326-3140
Bridgeman Products, Harry Jaffin, 153 B Cross Slope Court, Englishtown, NJ 07726 / 732-536-3604; FAX: 732-972-1004
Bridgers Best, P.O. Box 1410, Berthoud, CO 80513
Briese Bullet Co., Inc., RR1, Box 108, Tappen, ND 58487 / 701-327-4578; FAX: 701-327-4579
Brigade Quartermasters, 1025 Cobb International Blvd., Dept. VH, Kennesaw, GA 30144-4300 / 404-428-1248 or 800-241-3125; FAX: 404-426-7726
Briganti, A.J., 512 Rt. 32, Highland Mills, NY 10930 / 914-928-9573
Briley Mfg. Inc., 1230 Lumpkin, Houston, TX 77043 / 800-331-5718 or 713-932-6995; FAX: 713-932-1043
British Antiques, P.O. Box 35369, Tucson, AZ 85740 / 520-575-9063 britishantiques@hotmail.com
British Sporting Arms, RR1, Box 130, Millbrook, NY 12545 / 914-677-8303
BRNO (See U.S. Importers-Bohemia Arms Co.)
Broad Creek Rifle Works, Ltd., 120 Horsey Ave., Laurel, DE 19956 / 302-875-5446; FAX: 302-875-1449 bcqw4guns@aol.com
Brockman's Custom Gunsmithing, P.O. Box 357, Gooding, ID 83330 / 208-934-5050
Brocock Ltd., 43 River Street, Digbeth, Birmingham, B5 5SA ENGLAND / 011-021-773-1200
Broken Gun Ranch, 10739 126 Rd., Spearville, KS 67876 / 316-385-2587; FAX: 316-385-2597
Brolin Arms, 2755 Thompson Creek Rd., Pomona, CA 91767 / 909-392-7822; FAX: 909-392-7824
Brooker, Dennis, Rt. 1, Box 12A, Derby, IA 50068 / 515-533-2103
Brooks Tactical Systems, 279-C Shorewood Ct., Fox Island, WA 98333 / 253-549-2866 FAX: 253-549-2703 brooks@brookstactical.com www.brookstactical.com
Brown, H. R. (See Silhouette Leathers)
Brown Co, E. Arthur, 3404 Pawnee Dr, Alexandria, MN 56308 / 320-762-8847
Brown Dog Ent., 2200 Calle Camelia, 1000 Oaks, CA 91360 / 805-497-2318; FAX: 805-497-1618
Brown Manufacturing, P.O. Box 9219, Akron, OH 44305 / 800-837-GUNS
Brown Precision,Inc., 7786 Molinos Ave., Los Molinos, CA 96055 FAX: 916-384-1638
Brown Products, Inc., Ed, 43825 Muldrow Trail, Perry, MO 63462 / 573-565-3261; FAX: 573-565-2791
Brownells, Inc., 200 S. Front St., Montezuma, IA 50171 / 515-623-5401; FAX: 515-623-3896
Browning Arms Co., One Browning Place, Morgan, UT 84050 / 801-876-2711; FAX: 801-876-3331
Browning Arms Co. (Parts & Service), 3005 Arnold Tenbrook Rd., Arnold, MO 63010 / 314-287-6800; FAX: 314-287-9751
BRP, Inc. High Performance Cast Bullets, 1210 Alexander Rd., Colorado Springs, CO 80909 / 719-633-0658
Brunton U.S.A., 620 E. Monroe Ave., Riverton, WY 82501 / 307-856-6559; FAX: 307-856-1840
Bryan & Assoc, R D Sauls, PO Box 5772, Anderson, SC 29623-5772 / 864-261-6810
Brynin, Milton, P.O. Box 383, Yonkers, NY 10710 / 914-779-4333
BSA Guns Ltd., Armoury Rd. Small Heath, Birmingham, ENGLAND / 011-021-772-8543; FAX: 011-021-773-084
BSA Optics, 3911 SW 47th Ave #914, Ft Lauderdale, FL 33314 / 954-581-2144 FAX: 954-581-3165
Bucheimer, J. (See JUMBO SPORTS PRODUCTS)
Bucheimer, J. M. (See Jumbo Sports Products), 721 N 20th St, St Louis, MO 63103 / 314-241-1020
Buck Knives, Inc., 1900 Weld Blvd., P.O. Box 1267, El Cajon, CA 92020 / 619-449-1100 or 800-326-2825; FAX: 619-562-5774 8
Buck Stix--SOS Products Co., Box 3, Neenah, WI 54956
Buck Stop Lure Co., Inc., 3600 Grow Rd. NW, P.O. Box 636, Stanton, MI 48888 / 517-762-5091; FAX: 517-762-5124
Buckeye Custom Bullets, 6490 Stewart Rd., Elida, OH 45807 / 419-641-4463
Buckhorn Gun Works, 8109 Woodland Dr., Black Hawk, SD 57718 / 605-787-6472
Buckskin Bullet Co., P.O. Box 1893, Cedar City, UT 84721 / 435-586-3286
Buckskin Machine Works, A. Hunkeler, 3235 S. 358th St., Auburn, WA 98001 / 206-927-5412
Budin, Dave, Main St., Margaretville, NY 12455 / 914-568-4103; FAX: 914-586-4105
Buenger Enterprises/Goldenrod Dehumidifier, 3600 S. Harbor Blvd., Oxnard, CA 93035 / 800-451-6797 or 805-985-5828; FAX: 805-985-1534
Buffalo Arms Co., 99 Raven Ridge, Samuels, ID 83864 / 208-263-6953; FAX: 208-265-2096
Buffalo Bullet Co., Inc.., 12637 Los Nietos Rd., Unit A., Santa Fe Springs, CA 90670 FAX: 562-944-5054
Buffalo Rock Shooters Supply, R.R. 1, Ottawa, IL 61350 / 815-433-2471
Buffer Technologies, P.O. Box 104930, Jefferson City, MO 65110 / 573-634-8529; FAX: 573-634-8522
Bull Mountain Rifle Co., 6327 Golden West Terrace, Billings, MT 59106 / 406-656-0778
Bull-X, Inc., 520 N. Main, Farmer City, IL 61842 / 309-928-2574 or 800-248-3845; FAX: 309-928-2130
Bullberry Barrel Works, Ltd., 2430 W. Bullberry Ln. 67-5, Hurricane, UT 84737 / 435-635-9866; FAX: 435-635-0348
Bullet Metals, P.O. Box 1238, Sierra Vista, AZ 85636 / 520-458-5321; FAX: 520-458-1421 alloymetal-smith@theriver.com

MANUFACTURER'S DIRECTORY

Bullet Swaging Supply Inc., P.O. Box 1056, 303 McMillan Rd, West Monroe, LA 71291 / 318-387-3266; FAX: 318-387-7779

Bullet'n Press, 19 Key St., Eastport, ME 04631 / 207-853-4116 www.nemaine.com/bnpress

Bullet, Inc., 3745 Hiram Alworth Rd., Dallas, GA 30132

Bullseye Bullets, 8100 E Broadway Ave #A, Tampa, FL 33619-2223 / 813-630-9186 bbullets8100@aol.com

Burgess, Byron, PO Box 6853, Los Osos, CA 93412 / 805-528-1005

Burkhart Gunsmithing, Don, P.O. Box 852, Rawlins, WY 82301 / 307-324-6007

Burnham Bros., P.O. Box 1148, Menard, TX 78659 / 915-396-4572; FAX: 915-396-4574

Burris Co., Inc., P.O. Box 1747, 331 E. 8th St., Greeley, CO 80631 / 970-356-1670; FAX: 970-356-8702

Bushmann Hunters & Safaris, P.O. Box 293088, Lewisville, TX 75029 / 214-317-0768

Bushmaster Firearms (See Quality Parts Co/Bushmaster Firearms)

Bushmaster Hunting & Fishing, 451 Alliance Ave., Toronto, ON M6N 2J1 Canada / 416-763-4040; FAX: 416-763-0623

Bushnell Sports Optics Worldwide, 9200 Cody, Overland Park, KS 66214 / 913-752-3400 or 800-423-3537; FAX: 913-752-3550

Bushwacker Backpack & Supply Co (See Counter Assault)

Bustani, Leo, P.O. Box 8125, W. Palm Beach, FL 33410 / 305-622-2710

Buster's Custom Knives, P.O. Box 214, Richfield, UT 84701 / 801-896-5319

Butler Creek Corp., 290 Arden Dr., Belgrade, MT 59714 / 800-423-8327 or 406-388-1356; FAX: 406-388-7204

Butler Enterprises, 834 Oberting Rd., Lawrenceburg, IN 47025 / 812-537-3584

Butterfield & Butterfield, 220 San Bruno Ave., San Francisco, CA 94103 / 415-861-7500

Buzztail Brass (See Grayback Wildcats)

Byron Burgess, P.O. Box 6853, Los Osos, CA 93412 / 805-528-1005

C

C&D Special Products (See Claybuster Wads & Harvester Bullets)

C&H Research, 115 Sunnyside Dr., Box 351, Lewis, KS 67552 / 316-324-5445 www.09.net(chr)

C-More Systems, P.O. Box 1750, 7553 Gary Rd., Manassas, VA 20108 / 703-361-2663; FAX: 703-361-5881

C. Palmer Manufacturing Co., Inc., P.O. Box 220, West Newton, PA 15089 / 412-872-8200; FAX: 412-872-8302

C. Sharps Arms Co. Inc., 100 Centennial, Box 885, Big Timber, MT 59011 / 406-932-4353; FAX: 406-932-4443

C.S. Van Gorden & Son, Inc., 1815 Main St., Bloomer, WI 54724 / 715-568-2612

C.W. Erickson's Mfg. Inc., 530 Garrison Ave NE, PO Box 522, Buffalo, MN 55313 / 612-682-3665; FAX: 612-682-4328

Cabanas (See U.S. Importer-Mandall Shooting Supplies, Inc.)

Cabela's, 812-13th Ave., Sidney, NE 69160 / 308-254-6644 or 800-237-4444; FAX: 308-254-6745

Cabinet Mtn. Outfitters Scents & Lures, P.O. Box 766, Plains, MT 59859 / 406-826-3970

Cache La Poudre Rifleworks, 140 N. College, Ft. Collins, CO 80524 / 303-482-6913

Cali'co Hardwoods, Inc., 3580 Westwind Blvd., Santa Rosa, CA 95403 / 707-546-4045; FAX: 707-546-4027 calicohardwoods@msn.com

Calibre Press, Inc., 666 Dundee Rd., Suite 1607, Northbrook, IL 60062 / 800-323-0037; FAX: 708-498-6869

Calico Light Weapon Systems, 1489 Greg St., Sparks, NV 89431

California Sights (See Fautheree, Andy)

Cambos Outdoorsman, 532 E. Idaho Ave., Ontario, OR 97914 / 541-889-3138 FAX: 541-889-2633

Camdex, Inc., 2330 Alger, Troy, ML 48083 / 810-528-2300; FAX: 810-528-0989

Cameron's, 16690 W. 11th Ave., Golden, CO 80401 / 303-279-7365; FAX: 303-628-5413

Camilli, Lou, 600 Sandtree Dr., Suite 212, Lake Park, FL 33403

Camillus Cutlery Co., 54 Main St., Camillus, NY 13031 / 315-672-8111; FAX: 315-672-8832

Camp-Cap Products, P.O. Box 3805, Chesterfield, MO 63006 / 314-532-4340; FAX: 314-532-4340

Campbell, Dick, 20000 Silver Ranch Rd., Conifer, CO 80433 / 303-697-0150; FAX: 303-697-0150

Cannon, Andy. (See CANNON'S)

Cannon Safe, Inc., 9358 Stephens St., Pico Rivera, CA 90660 / 310-692-0636 or 800-242-1055; FAX: 310-692-7252

Cannon's, Andy Cannon, Box 1026, 320 Main St., Polson, MT 59860 / 406-887-2048

Canons Delcour, Rue J.B. Cools, B-4040, Herstal, BELGIUM / +32.(0)42.40.61.40; FAX: +32(0)42.40.22.88

Canyon Cartridge Corp., P.O. Box 152, Albertson, NY 11507 FAX: 516-294-8946

Cape Outfitters, 599 County Rd. 206, Cape Girardeau, MO 63701 / 573-335-4103; FAX: 573-335-1555

Caraville Manufacturing, P.O. Box 4545, Thousand Oaks, CA 91359 / 805-499-1234

Carbide Checkering Tools (See J&R Engineering)

Carbide Die & Mfg. Co., Inc., 15615 E. Arrow Hwy., Irwindale, CA 91706 / 626-337-2518

Carhartt,Inc., P.O. Box 600, 3 Parklane Blvd., Dearborn, MI 48121 / 800-358-3825 or 313-271-8460; FAX: 313-271-3455

Carl Walther GmbH, B.P. 4325, D-89033, Ulm, GERMANY

Carl Walther USA, PO Box 208, Ten Prince St, Alexandria, VA 22313 / 703-548-1400; FAX: 703-549-7826

Carl Zeiss Inc, 13017 N Kingston Ave, Chester, VA 23836-2743 / 804-861-0033 or 800-388-2984; FAX: 804-733-4024

Carlson, Douglas R, Antique American Firearms, PO Box 71035, Dept GD, Des Moines, IA 50315 / 515-224-6552

Carnahan Bullets, 17645 110th Ave. SE, Renton, WA 98055

Carolina Precision Rifles, 1200 Old Jackson Hwy., Jackson, SC 29831 / 803-827-2069

Carrell's Precision Firearms, 643 Clark Ave., Billings, MT 59101-1614 / 406-962-3593

Carry-Lite, Inc., 5203 W. Clinton Ave., Milwaukee, WI 53223 / 414-355-3520; FAX: 414-355-4775

Carter's Gun Shop, 225 G St., Penrose, CO 81240 / 719-372-6240

Cartridge Transfer Group, Pete de Coux, 235 Oak St., Butler, PA 16001 / 412-282-3426

Cascade Bullet Co., Inc., 2355 South 6th St., Klamath Falls, OR 97601 / 503-884-9316

Cascade Shooters, 2155 N.W. 12th St., Redwood, OR 97756

Case & Sons Cutlery Co., W R, Owens Way, Bradford, PA 16701 / 814-368-4123 or 800-523-6350; FAX: 814-768-5369

Case Sorting System, 12695 Cobblestone Creek Rd., Poway, CA 92064 / 619-486-9340

Cash Mfg. Co., Inc., P.O. Box 130, 201 S. Klein Dr., Waunakee, WI 53597-0130 / 608-849-5664; FAX: 608-849-5664

Caspian Arms, Ltd., 14 North Main St., Hardwick, VT 05843 / 802-472-6454; FAX: 802-472-6709

Cast Performance Bullet Company, 113 Riggs Rd, Shoshoni, WY 82649 / 307-856-4347

Casull Arms Corp., P.O. Box 1629, Afton, WY 83110 / 307-886-0200

Caswell Detroit Armor Companies, 1221 Marshall St. NE, Minneapolis, MN 55413-1055 / 612-379-2000; FAX: 612-379-2367

Catco-Ambush, Inc., P.O.Box 300, Corte Madera, CA 94926

Cathey Enterprises, Inc., P.O. Box 2202, Brownwood, TX 76804 / 915-643-2553; FAX: 915-643-3653

Cation, 2341 Alger St., Troy, MI 48083 / 810-689-0658; FAX: 810-689-7558

Caywood, Shane J., P.O. Box 321, Minocqua, WI 54548 / 715-277-3866

CBC, Avenida Humberto de Campos 3220, 09400-000, Ribeirao Pires, SP, BRAZIL / 55-11-742-7500; FAX: 55-11-459-7385

CBC-BRAZIL, 2 Cuckoo Lane, Honley, Yorkshire HD7 2BR, ENGLAND / 44-1484-661062; FAX: 44-1484-663709

CCG Enterprises, 5217 E. Belknap St., Halton City, TX 76117 / 800-819-7464

CCI Div. of Blount, Inc., Sporting Equipment Div.2299 Sn, P.O. Box 856, Lewiston, ID 83501 / 800-627-3640 or 208-746-2351; FAX: 208-746-2915

CCL Security Products, 199 Whiting St, New Britain, CT 06051 / 800-733-8588

Cedar Hill Game Calls Inc., 238 Vic Allen Rd, Downsville, LA 71234 / 318-982-5632; FAX: 318-368-2245

Celestron International, P.O. Box 3578, 2835 Columbia St., Torrance, CA 90503 / 310-328-9560; FAX: 310-212-5835

Centaur Systems, Inc., 1602 Foothill Rd., Kalispell, MT 59901 / 406-755-8609; FAX: 406-755-8609

Center Lock Scope Rings, 9901 France Ct., Lakeville, MN 55044 / 612-461-2114

Central Specialties Ltd (See Trigger Lock Division/Central Specialties Ltd.)

Century Gun Dist. Inc., 1467 Jason Rd., Greenfield, IN 46140 / 317-462-4524

Century International Arms, Inc., 1161 Holland Dr, Boca Raton, FL 33487

CFVentures, 509 Harvey Dr., Bloomington, IN 47403-1715

CH Tool & Die Co (See 4-D Custom Die Co), 711 N Sandusky St, PO Box 889, Mt Vernon, OH 43050-0889 / 740-397-7214; FAX: 740-397-6600

Chace Leather Products, 507 Alden St., Fall River, MA 02722 / 508-678-7556; FAX: 508-675-9666

Chadick's Ltd., P.O. Box 100, Terrell, TX 75160 / 214-563-7577

Chambers Flintlocks Ltd., Jim, 116 Sams Branch Rd, Candler, NC 28715 / 828-667-8361 FAX: 828-665-0852

Champion Shooters' Supply, P.O. Box 303, New Albany, OH 43054 / 614-855-1603; FAX: 614-855-1209

Champion Target Co., 232 Industrial Parkway, Richmond, IN 47374 / 800-441-4971

Champion's Choice, Inc., 201 International Blvd., LaVergne, TN 37086 / 615-793-4066; FAX: 615-793-4070

Champlin Firearms, Inc., P.O. Box 3191, Woodring Airport, Enid, OK 73701 / 580-237-7388; FAX: 580-242-6922

Chapman Academy of Practical Shooting, 4350 Academy Rd., Hallsville, MO 65255 / 573-696-5544 or 573-696-2266

Chapman, J Ken. (See OLD WEST BULLET MOULDS J ken Champman)

Chapman Manufacturing Co., 471 New Haven Rd., P.O. Box 250, Durham, CT 06422 / 860-349-9228; FAX: 860-349-0084

Chapuis Armes, 21 La Gravoux, BP15, 42380, St. Bonnet-le-Chatea, FRANCE / (33)77.50.06.96+

Chapuis USA, 416 Business Park, Bedford, KY 40006

Charter 2000, 273 Canal St, Shelton, CT 06484 / 203-922-1652

Checkmate Refinishing, 370 Champion Dr., Brooksville, FL 34601 / 352-799-5774 FAX: 352-799-2986

Cheddite France S.A., 99 Route de Lyon, F-26501, Bourg-les-Valence, FRANCE / 33-75-56-4545; FAX: 33-75-56-3587

Chelsea Gun Club of New York City Inc., 237 Ovington Ave., Apt. D53, Brooklyn, NY 11209 / 718-836-9422 or 718-833-2704

Chem-Pak Inc., PO Box 2058, Winchester, VA 22604-1258 / 800-336-9828 or 703-667-1341 FAX: 703-722-3993

Cherry Creek State Park Shooting Center, 12500 E. Belleview Ave., Englewood, CO 80111 / 303-693-1765

Chet Fulmer's Antique Firearms, P.O. Box 792, Rt. 2 Buffalo Lake, Detroit Lakes, MN 56501 / 218-847-7712

CheVron Bullets, RR1, Ottawa, IL 61350 / 815-433-2471

Cheyenne Pioneer Products, PO Box 28425, Kansas City, MO 64188 / 816-413-9196 FAX: 816-455-2859 cheyennepp@aol.com www.cartridgeboxes.com

Chicago Cutlery Co., 1536 Beech St., Terre Haute, IN 47804 / 800-457-2665

Chicasaw Gun Works, 4 Mi. Mkr., Pluto Rd. Box 868, Shady Spring, WV 25918-0868 / 304-763-2848 FAX: 304-763-3725

Chipmunk (See Oregon Arms, Inc.)

Choate Machine & Tool Co., Inc., P.O. Box 218, 116 Lovers Ln., Bald Knob, AR 72010 / 501-724-6193 or 800-972-6390; FAX: 501-724-5873

Chopie Mfg.,Inc., 700 Copeland Ave., LaCrosse, WI 54603 / 608-784-0926

Christensen Arms, 385 N. 3050 E., St. George, UT 84790 / 435-624-9535; FAX: 435-674-9293

Christie's East, 219 E. 67th St., New York, NY 10021 / 212-606-0400

Chu Tani Ind., Inc., P.O. Box 2064, Cody, WY 82414-2064

Chuck's Gun Shop, P.O. Box 597, Waldo, FL 32694 / 904-468-2264

Churchill (See U.S. Importer-Ellett Bros)

Churchill, Winston, Twenty Mile Stream Rd., RFD P.O. Box 29B, Proctorsville, VT 05153 / 802-226-7772

Churchill Glove Co., James, PO Box 298, Centralia, WA 98531 / 360-736-2816 FAX: 360-330-0151

CIDCO, 21480 Pacific Blvd., Sterling, VA 22170 / 703-444-5353

Ciener Inc., Jonathan Arthur, 8700 Commerce St., Cape Canaveral, FL 32920 / 407-868-2200; FAX: 407-868-2201

Cimarron F.A. Co., P.O. Box 906, Fredericksburg, TX 78624-0906 / 210-997-9090; FAX: 210-997-0802

Cincinnati Swaging, 2605 Marlington Ave., Cincinnati, OH 45208

Clark Custom Guns, Inc., 336 Shootout Lane, Princeton, LA 71067 / 318-949-9884; FAX: 318-949-9829

Clark Firearms Engraving, P.O. Box 80746, San Marino, CA 91118 / 818-287-1652

Clarkfield Enterprises, Inc., 1032 10th Ave., Clarkfield, MN 56223 / 612-669-7140

Claro Walnut Gunstock Co., 1235 Stanley Ave., Chico, CA 95928 / 530-342-5188; FAX: 530-342-5199

Classic Arms Company, Rt 1 Box 120F, Burnet, TX 78611 / 512-756-4001

Classic Arms Corp., P.O. Box 106, Dunsmuir, CA 96025-0106 / 530-235-2000

Classic Guns, Inc., Frank S. Wood, 3230 Medlock Bridge Rd., Suite 110, Norcross, GA 30092 / 404-242-7944

Classic Old West Styles, 1060 Doniphan Park Circle C, El Paso, TX 79936 / 915-587-0684

Claybuster Wads & Harvester Bullets, 309 Sequoya Dr., Hopkinsville, KY 42240 / 800-922-6287 or 800-284-1746; FAX: 502-885-8088 50

Clean Shot Technologies, 21218 St. Andrews Blvd. Ste 504, Boca Raton, FL 33433 / 888-866-2532

Clear Creek Outdoors, Pat LaBoone, 2550 Hwy 23, Wrenshall, MN 55797 / 218-384-3670

Clearview Mfg. Co., Inc., 413 S. Oakley St., Fordyce, AR 71742 / 501-352-8557; FAX: 501-352-7120

Clearview Products, 3021 N. Portland, Oklahoma City, OK 73107

Cleland's Outdoor World, Inc, 10306 Airport Hwy., Swanton, OH 43558 / 419-865-4713; FAX: 419-865-5865

Clements' Custom Leathercraft, Chas, 1741 Dallas St., Aurora, CO 80010-2018 / 303-364-0403; FAX: 303-739-9824

Clenzoil Corp., P.O. Box 80226, Sta. C, Canton, OH 44708-0226 / 330-833-9758; FAX: 330-833-4724

Clift Mfg., L. R., 3821 hammonton Rd, Marysville, CA 95901 / 916-755-3390; FAX: 916-755-3393

Clift Welding Supply & Cases, 1332-A Colusa Hwy., Yuba City, CA 95993 / 916-755-3390 FAX: 916-755-3393

Cloward's Gun Shop, 4023 Aurora Ave. N, Seattle, WA 98103 / 206-632-2072

Clymer Manufacturing Co. Inc., 1645 W. Hamlin Rd., Rochester Hills, MI 48309-3312 / 248-853-5555; FAX: 248-853-1530

Cobalt Mfg., Inc., 4020 Mcewen Rd Ste 180, Dallas, TX 75244-5090 / 817-382-8986 FAX: 817-383-4281

Cobra Sport S.r.l., Via Caduti Nei Lager No. 1, 56020 San Romano, Montopoli v/Arno (Pi, ITALY / 0039-571-450490; FAX: 0039-571-450492

Coffin, Charles H., 3719 Scarlet Ave., Odessa, TX 79762 / 915-366-4729 FAX: 915-366-4729

Coffin, Jim (See Working Guns)

Coffin, Jim. See: WORKING GUNS

Cogar's Gunsmithing, P.O. Box 755, Houghton Lake, MI 48629 / 517-422-4591

Coghlan's Ltd., 121 Irene St., Winnipeg, MB R3T 4C7 CANADA / 204-284-9550; FAX: 204-475-4127

Cold Steel Inc., 2128-D Knoll Dr., Ventura, CA 93003 / 800-255-4716 or 800-624-2363 FAX: 805-642-9727

Cole's Gun Works, Old Bank Building, Rt. 4 Box 250, Moyock, NC 27958 / 919-435-2345

Cole-Grip, 16135 Cohasset St., Van Nuys, CA 91406 / 818-782-4424

Coleman Co., Inc., 250 N. St. Francis, Wichita, KS 67201

Coleman's Custom Repair, 4035 N. 20th Rd., Arlington, VA 22207 / 703-528-4486

Collectors Firearms Etc, P.O. Box 62, Minnesota City, MN 55959 / 507-689-2925

Collings, Ronald, 1006 Cielta Linda, Vista, CA 92083

Colonial Arms, Inc., P.O. Box 636, Selma, AL 36702-0636 / 334-872-9455; FAX: 334-872-9540 colonialarms@mind-spring.com www.colonialarms.com

Colonial Knife Co., Inc., P.O. Box 3327, Providence, RI 02909 / 401-421-1600; FAX: 401-421-2047

Colonial Repair, 47 NAVARRE ST, ROSLINDALE, MA 02131-4725 / 617-469-4951

Colorado Gunsmithing Academy, 27533 Highway 287 South, Lamar, CO 81052 / 719-336-4099 or 800-754-2046; FAX: 719-336-9642

Colorado School of Trades, 1575 Hoyt St., Lakewood, CO 80215 / 800-234-4594; FAX: 303-233-4723

Colorado Sutlers Arsenal (See Cumberland States Arsenal)

Colt Blackpowder Arms Co., 110 8th Street, Brooklyn, NY 11215 / 212-925-2159; FAX: 212-966-4986

Colt's Mfg. Co. Inc., P.O. Box 1868, Hartford, CT 06144-1868 / 800-962-COLT or 860-236-6311; FAX: 860-244-1449

Compass Industries, Inc., 104 East 25th St., New York, NY 10010 / 212-473-2614 or 800-221-9904; FAX: 212-353-0826

Compasseco, Ltd., 151 Atkinson Hill Ave., Bardtown, KY 40004 / 502-349-0910

Competition Electronics, Inc., 3469 Precision Dr., Rockford, IL 61109 / 815-874-8001; FAX: 815-874-8181

Competitor Corp. Inc., Appleton Business Center, 30 Tricnit Road Unit 16, New Ipswich, NH 03071 / 603-878-3891; FAX: 603-878-3950

Component Concepts, Inc., 530 S Springbrook Dr, Newberg, OR 97132-7056 / 503-554-8095 FAX: 503-554-9370

Concept Development Corp., 14715 N. 78th Way, Suite 300, Scottsdale, AZ 85260 / 800-472-4405; FAX: 602-948-7560

Conetrol Scope Mounts, 10225 Hwy. 123 S., Seguin, TX 78155 / 210-379-3030 or 800-CONETROL; FAX: 210-379-3030

CONKKO, P.O. Box 40, Broomall, PA 19008 / 215-356-0711

Connecticut Shotgun Mfg. Co., P.O. Box 1692, 35 Woodland St., New Britain, CT 06051 / 860-225-6581; FAX: 860-832-8707

Connecticut Valley Classics (See CVC)

Conrad, C. A., 3964 Ebert St., Winston-Salem, NC 27127 / 919-788-5469

Cook Engineering Service, 891 Highbury Rd., Vict, 3133 AUSTRALIA

Coonan Arms (JS Worldwide DBA), 1745 Hwy. 36 E., Maplewood, MN 55109 / 612-777-3156; FAX: 612-777-3683

Cooper Arms, P.O. Box 114, Stevensville, MT 59870 / 406-777-5534; FAX: 406-777-5228

Cooper-Woodward, 3800 Pelican Rd., Helena, MT 59602 / 406-458-3800

Cor-Bon Bullet & Ammo Co., 1311 Industry Rd., Sturgis, SD 57785 / 800-626-7266; FAX: 800-923-2666

Corbin Mfg. & Supply, Inc., 600 Industrial Circle, P.O. Box 2659, White City, OR 97503 / 541-826-5211; FAX: 541-826-8669

Corkys Gun Clinic, 4401 Hot Springs Dr., Greeley, CO 80634-9226 / 970-330-0516

Corry, John, 861 Princeton Ct., Neshanic Station, NJ 08853 / 908-369-8019

Cosmi Americo & Figlio s.n.c., Via Flaminia 307, Ancona, ITALY / 071-888208; FAX: 39-071-887008+

Coulston Products, Inc., P.O. Box 30, 201 Ferry St. Suite 212, Easton, PA 18044-0030 / 215-253-0167 or 800-445-9927; FAX: 215-252-1511

Counter Assault, Box 4721, Missoula, MT 59806 / 406-728-6241 FAX: 406-728-8800

Cousin Bob's Mountain Products, 7119 Ohio River Blvd., Ben Avon, PA 15202 / 412-766-5114 FAX: 412-766-5114

Cox, Ed. C., RD 2, Box 192, Prosperity, PA 15329 / 412-228-4984

CP Bullets, 1310 Industrial Hwy #5-6, South Hampton, PA 18966 / 215-953-7264; FAX: 215-953-7275

CQB Training, P.O. Box 1739, Manchester, MO 63011

Craftguard, 3624 Logan Ave., Waterloo, IA 50703 / 319-232-2959 FAX: 319-234-0804

Craig, Spegel, P.O. Box 3108, Bay City, OR 97107 / 503-377-2697

Craig Custom Ltd., Research & Development, 629 E. 10th, Hutchinson, KS 67501 / 316-669-0601

Crandall Tool & Machine Co., 19163 21 Mile Rd., Tustin, MI 49688 / 616-829-4430

Creative Concepts USA, Inc., P.O. Box 1705, Dickson, TN 37056 / 615-446-8346 or 800-874-6965 FAX: 615-446-0646

Creedmoor Sports, Inc., P.O. Box 1040, Oceanside, CA 92051 / 619-757-5529

Creek Side Metal & Woodcrafters, Fishers Hill, VA 22626 / 703-465-3903

Creekside Gun Shop Inc., Main St., Holcomb, NY 14469 / 716-657-6338 FAX: 716-657-7900

Creighton Audette, 19 Highland Circle, Springfield, VT 05156 / 802-885-2331

Crimson Trace Lasers, 1433 N.W. Quimby, Portland, OR 97209 / 503-295-2406; FAX: 503-295-2225

Crit'R Call (See Rocky Mountain Wildlife Products)

Crosman Airguns, Rts. 5 and 20, E. Bloomfield, NY 14443 / 716-657-6161 FAX: 716-657-5405

Crosman Blades (See Coleman Co., Inc.)

Crosman Products of Canada Ltd., 1173 N. Service Rd. West, Oakville, ON L6M 2V9 CANADA / 905-827-1822

Crossfire, L.L.C., 2169 Greenville Rd., La Grange, GA 30241 / 706-882-8070 FAX: 706-882-9050

Crouse's Country Cover, P.O. Box 160, Storrs, CT 06268 / 860-423-8736

CRR, Inc./Marble's Inc., 420 Industrial Park, P.O. Box 111, Gladstone, MI 49837 / 906-428-3710; FAX: 906-428-3711

Crucelegui, Hermanos (See U.S. Importer-Mandall Shooting Supplies Inc.)

Cryo-Accurizing, 2250 N. 1500 West, Ogden, UT 84404/ 801-395-2796 or 888-279-6266

Cubic Shot Shell Co., Inc., 98 Fatima Dr., Campbell, OH 44405 / 330-755-0349

Cullity Restoration, 209 Old Country Rd., East Sandwich, MA 02537 / 508-888-1147

Cumberland Arms, 514 Shafer Road, Manchester, TN 37355 / 800-797-8414

Cumberland Mountain Arms, P.O. Box 710, Winchester, TN 37398 / 615-967-8414; FAX: 615-967-9199

Cumberland States Arsenal, 1124 Palmyra Road, Clarksville, TN 37040

Cummings Bullets, 1417 Esperanza Way, Escondido, CA 92027

Cupp, Alana, Custom Engraver, PO Box 207, Annabella, UT 84711 / 801-896-4834

Curly Maple Stock Blanks (See Tiger-Hunt)

Curtis Cast Bullets, 527 W. Babcock St., Bozeman, MT 59715 / 406-587-8117; FAX: 406-587-8117

Curtis Custom Shop, RR1, Box 193A, Wallingford, KY 41093 / 703-659-4265

Curtis Gun Shop (See Curtis Cast Bullets)

Custom Bullets by Hoffman, 2604 Peconic Ave., Seaford, NY 11783

Custom Calls, 607 N. 5th St., Burlington, IA 52601 / 319-752-4465

Custom Checkering Service, Kathy Forster, 2124 SE Yamhill St., Portland, OR 97214 / 503-236-5874

Custom Chronograph, Inc., 5305 Reese Hill Rd., Sumas, WA 98295 / 360-988-7801

Custom Firearms (See Ahrends, Kim)

Custom Gun Products, 5021 W. Rosewood, Spokane, WA 99208 / 509-328-9340

Custom Gun Stocks, 3062 Turners Bend Rd, McMinnville, TN 37110 / 615-668-3912

Custom Products (See Jones Custom Products)

Custom Quality Products, Inc., 345 W. Girard Ave., P.O. Box 71129, Madison Heights, MI 48071 / 810-585-1616; FAX: 810-585-0644

Custom Riflestocks, Inc., Michael M. Kokolus, 7005 Herber Rd., New Tripoli, PA 18066 / 610-298-3013

Custom Tackle and Ammo, P.O. Box 1886, Farmington, NM 87499 / 505-632-3539

Cutco Cutlery, P.O. Box 810, Olean, NY 14760 / 716-372-3111

CVA, 5988 Peachtree Corners East, Norcross, GA 30071 / 800-251-9412; FAX: 404-242-8546

CVC, 5988 Peachtree Crns East, Norcross, GA 30071

Cylinder & Slide, Inc., William R. Laughridge, 245 E. 4th St., Fremont, NE 68025 / 402-721-4277; FAX: 402-721-0263

CZ USA, PO Box 171073, Kansas City, KS 66117 / 913-321-1811; FAX: 913-321-4901

D

D&D Gunsmiths, Ltd., 363 E. Elmwood, Troy, MI 48083 / 810-583-1512; FAX: 810-583-1524

D&G Precision Duplicators (See Greene Precision Du

D&H Precision Tooling, 7522 Barnard Mill Rd., Ringwood, IL 60072 / 815-653-4011

D&H Prods. Co., Inc., 465 Denny Rd., Valencia, PA 16059 / 412-898-2840 or 800-776-0281; FAX: 412-898-2013

D&J Bullet Co. & Custom Gun Shop, Inc., 426 Ferry St., Russell, KY 41169 / 606-836-2663; FAX: 606-836-2663

D&L Industries (See D.J. Marketing)

D&L Sports, P.O. Box 651, Gillette, WY 82717 / 307-686-4008

D&R Distributing, 308 S.E. Valley St., Myrtle Creek, OR 97457 / 503-863-6850

D-Boone Ent., Inc., 5900 Colwyn Dr., Harrisburg, PA 17109

D.C.C. Enterprises, 259 Wynburn Ave., Athens, GA 30601

D.D. Custom Stocks, R.H. "Dick" Devereaux, 5240 Mule Deer Dr., Colorado Springs, CO 80919 / 719-548-8468

D.J. Marketing, 10602 Horton Ave., Downey, CA 90241 / 310-806-0891; FAX: 310-806-6231

Da-Mar Gunsmith's Inc., 102 1st St., Solvay, NY 13209

Dade Screw Machine Products, 2319 NW 7th Ave., Miami, FL 33127 / 305-573-5050

Daewoo Precision Industries Ltd., 34-3 Yeoeuido-Dong, Yeongdeungoo-GU 15th Fl., Seoul, KOREA

Daisy Mfg. Co., PO Box 220, Rogers, AR 72757 / 501-621-4210; FAX: 501-636-0573

Dakota (See U.S. Importer-EMF Co., Inc.)

Dakota Arms, Inc., HC 55, Box 326, Sturgis, SD 57785 / 605-347-4686; FAX: 605-347-4459

Dakota Corp., 77 Wales St., P.O. Box 543, Rutland, VT 05701 / 802-775-6062 or 800-451-4167; FAX: 802-773-3919

DAMASCUS-U.S.A., 149 Deans Farm Rd., Tyner, NC 27980 / 252-221-2010; FAX: 252-221-2009

DAN WESSON FIREARMS, 119 Kemper Lane, Norwich, NY 13815 / 607-336-1174; FAX: FAX:607-336-2730

Dan's Whetstone Co., Inc., 130 Timbs Place, Hot Springs, AR 71913 / 501-767-1616; FAX: 501-767-9598

Danforth, Mikael. (See VEKTOR USA, Mikael Danforth)

Dangler, Homer L., Box 254, Addison, MI 49220 / 517-547-6745

Danner Shoe Mfg. Co., 12722 NE Airport Way, Portland, OR 97230 / 503-251-1100 or 800-345-0430; FAX: 503-251-1119

Danuser Machine Co., 550 E. Third St., P.O. Box 368, Fulton, MO 65251 / 573-642-2246; FAX: 573-642-2240

Dara-Nes, Inc. (See Nesci Enterprises, Inc.)

Darlington Gun Works, Inc., P.O. Box 698, 516 S. 52 Bypass, Darlington, SC 29532 / 803-393-3931

Darwin Hensley Gunmaker, P.O. Box 329, Brightwood, OR 97011 / 503-622-5411

Data Tech Software Systems, 19312 East Eldorado Drive, Aurora, CO 80013

Datumtech Corp., 2275 Wehrle Dr., Buffalo, NY 14221

Dave Norin Schrank's Smoke & Gun, 2010 Washington St., Waukegan, IL 60085 / 708-662-4034

Dave's Gun Shop, 555 Wood Street, Powell, WY 82435 / 307-754-9724

David Clark Co., Inc., PO Box 15054, Worcester, MA 01615-0054 / 508-756-6216; FAX: 508-753-5827

David Condon, Inc., 109 E. Washington St., Middleburg, VA 22117 / 703-687-5642

David Miller Co., 3131 E Greenlee Rd, Tucson, AZ 85716 / 520-326-3117

David R. Chicoine, 19 Key St., Eastport, ME 04631 / 207-853-4116 gnpress@nemaine.com

David W. Schwartz Custom Guns, 2505 Waller St, Eau Claire, WI 54703 / 715-832-1735

Davide Pedersoli and Co., Via Artigiani 57, Gardone VT, Brescia 25063, ITALY / 030-8912402; FAX: 030-8911019

Davidson, Jere, Rt. 1, Box 132, Rustburg, VA 24588 / 804-821-3637

Davis, Don, 1619 Heights, Katy, TX 77493 / 713-391-3090

Davis Industries, 15150 Sierra Bonita Ln., Chino, CA 91710 / 909-597-4726; FAX: 909-393-9771

Davis Products, Mike, 643 Loop Dr., Moses Lake, WA 98837 / 509-765-6178 or 509-766-7281

Daystate Ltd., Birch House Lanee, Cotes Heath Staffs, ST15.022, ENGLAND / 01782-791755; FAX: 01782-791617

Dayton Traister, 4778 N. Monkey Hill Rd., P.O. Box 593, Oak Harbor, WA 98277 / 360-679-4657; FAX: 360-675-1114

DBI Books Division of Krause Publications 700 E State St, Iola, WI 54990-0001 / 630-759-1229

de Coux, Pete (See Cartridge Transfer Group)

Dead Eye's Sport Center, RD 1, 76 Baer Rd, Shickshinny, PA 18655 / 570-256-7432

Decker Shooting Products, 1729 Laguna Ave., Schofield, WI 54476 / 715-359-5873

Deepeeka Exports Pvt. Ltd., D-78, Saket, Meerut-250-006, INDIA / 011-91-121-512889 or 011-91-121-545363; FAX: 011-91-121-542988

Deer Me Products Co., Box 34, 1208 Park St., Anoka, MN 55303 / 612-421-8971; FAX: 612-422-0526

Defense Training International, Inc., 749 S. Lemay, Ste. A3-337, Ft. Collins, CO 80524 / 303-482-2520; FAX: 303-482-0548

Degen Inc. (See Aristocrat Knives)

deHaas Barrels, RR 3, Box 77, Ridgeway, MO 64481 / 816-872-6308

Del Rey Products, P.O. Box 5134, Playa Del Rey, CA 90296-5134 / 213-823-0494

Del-Sports, Inc., Box 685, Main St., Margaretville, NY 12455 / 914-586-4103; FAX: 914-586-4105

Delhi Gun House, 1374 Kashmere Gate, Delhi, 0110 006 INDIA FAX: 91-11-2917344

Delorge, Ed, 6734 W. Main, Houma, LA 70360 / 504-223-0206

Delta Arms Ltd., P.O. Box 1000, Delta, VT 84624-1000

Delta Enterprises, 284 Hagemann Drive, Livermore, CA 94550

Delta Frangible Ammunition LLC, P.O. Box 2350, Stafford, VA 22555-2350 / 540-720-5778 or 800-339-1933; FAX: 540-720-5667

Dem-Bart Checkering Tools, Inc., 6807 Bickford Ave., Old Hwy. 2, Snohomish, WA 98290 / 360-568-7356; FAX: 360-568-1798

Denver Instrument Co., 6542 Fig St., Arvada, CO 80004 / 800-321-1135 or 303-431-7255; FAX: 303-423-4831

DeSantis Holster & Leather Goods, Inc., P.O. Box 2039, 149 Denton Ave., New Hyde Park, NY 11040-0701 / 516-354-8000; FAX: 516-354-7501

Desert Mountain Mfg., P.O. Box 130184, Coram, MT 59913 / 800-477-0762 or 406-387-5361; FAX: 406-387-5361

Detroit-Armor Corp., 720 Industrial Dr. No. 112, Cary, IL 60013 / 708-639-7666; FAX: 708-639-7694

Dever Co., Jack, 8590 NW 90, Oklahoma City, OK 73132 / 405-721-6393

Devereaux, R.H. "Dick" (See D.D. Custom Stocks, R.H. "Dick Devereaux)

Dewey Mfg. Co., Inc., J., P.O. Box 2014, Southbury, CT 06488 / 203-264-3064; FAX: 203-262-6907 deweyrods@world-net.att.net www.deweyrods.com

DGR Custom Rifles, 4191 37th Ave SE, Tappen, ND 58487 / 701-327-8135

DGS, Inc., Dale A. Storey, 1117 E. 12th, Casper, WY 82601 / 307-237-2414 FAX: 307-237-2414 dalest@trib.com www.dgsrifle.com

DHB Products, P.O. Box 3092, Alexandria, VA 22302 / 703-836-2648

Diamond Machining Technology, Inc. (See DMT)

Diamond Mfg. Co., P.O. Box 174, Wyoming, PA 18644 / 800-233-9601

Diana (See U.S. Importer - Dynamit Nobel-RWS, Inc., 81 Ruckman Rd., Closter, NJ 07624 / 201-767-7971; (FAX: 201-767-1589)

Dibble, Derek A., 555 John Downey Dr., New Britain, CT 06051 / 203-224-2630

Dick Marple & Associates, 21 Dartmouth St, Hooksett, NH 03106 / 603-627-1837; FAX: 603-627-1837

Dietz Gun Shop & Range, Inc., 421 Range Rd., New Braunfels, TX 78132 / 210-885-4662

Dilliott Gunsmithing, Inc., 657 Scarlett Rd., Dandridge, TN 37725 / 865-397-9204 gunsmithd@aol.com dilliottgunsmithing.com

Dillon, Ed, 1035 War Eagle Dr. N., Colorado Springs, CO 80919 / 719-598-4929; FAX: 719-598-4929

Dillon Precision Products, Inc., 8009 East Dillon's Way, Scottsdale, AZ 85260 / 602-948-8009 or 800-762-3845; FAX: 602-998-2786

Dina Arms Corporation, P.O. Box 46, Royersford, PA 19468 / 610-287-0266; FAX: 610-287-0266

Division Lead Co., 7742 W. 61st Pl., Summit, IL 60502

Dixie Gun Works, Inc., Hwy. 51 South, Union City, TN 38261 / order 800-238-6785;

Dixon Muzzleloading Shop, Inc., 9952 Kunkels Mill Rd., Kempton, PA 19529 / 610-756-6271

DKT, Inc., 14623 Vera Drive, Union, MI 49130-9744 / 800-741-7083 orders; FAX: 616-641-2015

DLO Mfg., 10807 SE Foster Ave., Arcadia, FL 33821-7304

DMT--Diamond Machining Technology Inc., 85 Hayes Memorial Dr., Marlborough, MA 01752 FAX: 508-485-3924

Doctor Optic Technologies, Inc., 4685 Boulder Highway, Suite A, Las Vegas, NV 89121 / 800-290-3634 or 702-898-7161; FAX: 702-898-3737

Dohring Bullets, 100 W. 8 Mile Rd., Ferndale, MI 48220

Dolbare, Elizabeth, P.O. Box 222, Sunburst, MT 59482-0222

Domino, PO Box 108, 20019 Settimo Milanese, Milano, ITALY / 1-39-2-33512040; FAX: 1-39-2-33511587

Donnelly, C. P., 405 Kubli Rd., Grants Pass, OR 97527 / 541-846-6604

Doskocil Mfg. Co., Inc., P.O. Box 1246, 4209 Barnett, Arlington, TX 76017 / 817-467-5116; FAX: 817-472-9810

Double A Ltd., P.O. Box 11306, Minneapolis, MN 55411 / 612-522-0306

Douglas Barrels Inc., 5504 Big Tyler Rd., Charleston, WV 25313-1398 / 304-776-1341; FAX: 304-776-8560

Downsizer Corp., P.O. Box 710316, Santee, CA 92072-0316 / 619-448-5510; FAX: 619-448-5780 www.downsizer.com

Dr. O's Products Ltd., P.O. Box 111, Niverville, NY 12130 / 518-784-3333; FAX: 518-784-2800

Drain, Mark, SE 3211 Kamilche Point Rd., Shelton, WA 98584 / 206-426-5452

Dremel Mfg. Co., 4915-21st St., Racine, WI 53406

Dressel Jr., Paul G., 209 N. 92nd Ave., Yakima, WA 98908 / 509-966-9233; FAX: 509-966-3365

Dri-Slide, Inc., 411 N. Darling, Fremont, MI 49412 / 616-924-3950

Dropkick, 1460 Washington Blvd., Williamsport, PA 17701 / 717-326-6561; FAX: 717-326-4950

DTM International, Inc., 40 Joslyn Rd., P.O. Box 5, Lake Orion, MI 48362 / 313-693-6670

Du-Lite Corp., 171 River Rd., Middletown, CT 06457 / 203-347-2505; FAX: 203-347-9404

Duane A. Hobbie Gunsmithing, 2412 Pattie Ave, Wichita, KS 67216 / 316-264-8266

Duane's Gun Repair (See DGR Custom Rifles)

Dubber, Michael W., P.O. Box 312, Evansville, IN 47702 / 812-424-9000; FAX: 812-424-6551

Duck Call Specialists, P.O. Box 124, Jerseyville, IL 62052 / 618-498-9855

Duffy, Charles E (See Guns Antique & Modern DBA), Williams Lane, PO Box 2, West Hurley, NY 12491 / 914-679-2997

Dumoulin, Ernest, Rue Florent Boclinville 8-10, 13-4041, Votten, BELGIUM / 41 27 78 92

Duncan's Gun Works, Inc., 1619 Grand Ave., San Marcos, CA 92069 / 619-727-0515

Dunham Boots, 1 Keuka business Park #300, Penn Yan, NY 14527-8995 / 802-254-2316

Duofold, Inc., RD 3 Rt. 309, Valley Square Mall, Tamaqua, PA 18252 / 717-386-2666; FAX: 717-386-3652

Dybala Gun Shop, P.O. Box 1024, FM 3156, Bay City, TX 77414 / 409-245-0866

Dykstra, Doug, 411 N. Darling, Fremont, MI 49412 / 616-924-3950

Dynalite Products, Inc., 215 S. Washington St., Greenfield, OH 45123 / 513-981-2124

Dynamit Nobel-RWS, Inc., 81 Ruckman Rd., Closter, NJ 07624 / 201-767-7971; FAX: 201-767-1589

E

E&L Mfg., Inc., 4177 Riddle By Pass Rd., Riddle, OR 97469 / 541-874-2137; FAX: 541-874-3107

E-A-R, Inc., Div. of Cabot Safety Corp., 5457 W. 79th St., Indianapolis, IN 46268 / 800-327-3431; FAX: 800-488-8007

E-Z-Way Systems, P.O. Box 4310, Newark, OH 43058-4310 / 614-345-6645 or 800-848-2072; FAX: 614-345-6600

E. Arthur Brown Co., 3404 Pawnee Dr., Alexandria, MN 56308 / 320-762-8847

E.A.A. Corp., P.O. Box 1299, Sharpes, FL 32959 / 407-639-4842 or 800-536-4442; FAX: 407-639-7006

Eagan, Donald V., P.O. Box 196, Benton, PA 17814 / 717-925-6134

Eagle Arms, Inc. (See ArmaLite, Inc.)

Eagle Grips, Eagle Business Center, 460 Randy Rd., Carol Stream, IL 60188 / 800-323-6144 or 708-260-0400; FAX: 708-260-0486

Eagle Imports, Inc., 1750 Brielle Ave., Unit B1, Wanamassa, NJ 07712 / 908-493-0333

EAW (See U.S. Importer-New England Custom Gun Service)

Echols & Co., D'Arcy, 164 W. 580 S., Providence, UT 84332 / 801-753-2367

Eckelman Gunsmithing, 3125 133rd St. SW, Fort Ripley, MN 56449 / 218-829-3176

Eclectic Technologies, Inc., 45 Grandview Dr., Suite A, Farmington, CT 06034

Ed~ Brown Products, Inc., 43825 Muldrow Trail, Perry, MO 63462 / 573-565-3261; FAX: 573-565-2791

Eddie Salter Calls, Inc., Hwy. 31 South-Brewton Industrial, Park, Brewton, AL 36426 / 205-867-2584; FAX: 206-867-9005

Edenpine, Inc. c/o Six Enterprises, Inc., 320 D Turtle Creek Ct., San Jose, CA 95125 / 408-999-0201; FAX: 408-999-0216

EdgeCraft Corp., S. Weiner, 825 Southwood Road, Avondale, PA 19311 / 610-268-0500 or 800-342-3255; FAX: 610-268-3545 www.chefschoice.com

Edmisten Co., P.O. Box 1293, Boone, NC 28607

Edmund Scientific Co., 101 E. Gloucester Pike, Barrington, NJ 08033 / 609-543-6250

Ednar, Inc., 2-4-8 Kayabacho, Nihonbashi Chuo-ku, Tokyo, JAPAN / 81(Japan)-3-3667-1651; FAX: 81-3-3661-8113

Eezox, Inc., P.O. Box 772, Waterford, CT 06385-0772 / 800-462-3331; FAX: 860-447-3484

Effebi SNC-Dr. Franco Beretta, via Rossa, 4, 25062, ITALY / 030-2751955; FAX: 030-2180414

Efficient Machinery Co, 12878 NE 15th Pl, Bellevue, WA 98005

Eggleston, Jere D., 400 Saluda Ave., Columbia, SC 29205 / 803-799-3402

EGW Evolution Gun Works, 4050 B-8 Skyron Dr., Doylestown, PA 18901 / 215-348-9892; FAX: 215-348-1056

Eichelberger Bullets, Wm, 158 Crossfield Rd., King Of Prussia, PA 19406

Ekol Leather Care, P.O. Box 2652, West Lafayette, IN 47906 / 317-463-2250; FAX: 317-463-7004

El Dorado Leather (c/o Dill), P.O. Box 566, Benson, AZ 85602 / 520-586-4791; FAX: 520-586-4791

El Paso Saddlery Co., P.O. Box 27194, El Paso, TX 79926 / 915-544-2233; FAX: 915-544-2535

Eldorado Cartridge Corp (See PMC/Eldorado Cartridge Corp.)

Electro Prismatic Collimators, Inc., 1441 Manatt St., Lincoln, NE 68521

Electronic Shooters Protection, Inc., 11997 West 85th Place, Arvada, CO 80005 / 800-797-7791; FAX: 303-456-7179

Electronic Trigger Systems, Inc., P.O. Box 13, 230 Main St. S., Hector, MN 55342 / 320-848-2760; FAX: 320-848-2760

Eley Ltd., P.O. Box 705, Witton, Birmingham, B6 7UT ENGLAND / 021-356-8899; FAX: 021-331-4173

Elite Ammunition, P.O. Box 3251, Oakbrook, IL 60522 / 708-366-9006

Elk River, Inc., 1225 Paonia St., Colorado Springs, CO 80915 / 719-574-4407

Elkhorn Bullets, P.O. Box 5293, Central Point, OR 97502 / 541-826-7440

Ellett Bros., 267 Columbia Ave., P.O. Box 128, Chapin, SC 29036 / 803-345-3751 or 800-845-3711; FAX: 803-345-1820

Ellicott Arms, Inc./Woods Pistolsmithing, 3840 Dahlgren Ct., Ellicott City, MD 21042 / 410-465-7979

Elliott Inc., G. W., 514 Burnside Ave, East Hartford, CT 06108 / 203-289-5741; FAX: 203-289-3137

Elsen Inc., Pete, 1523 S 113th St, West Allis, WI 53214

Emerging Technologies, Inc. (See Laseraim Technologies, Inc.)

Emap USA, 6420 Wilshire Blvd., Los Angeles, CA 90048 / 213-782-2000; FAX: 213-782-2867

EMF Co., Inc., 1900 E. Warner Ave., Suite 1-D, Santa Ana, CA 92705 / 714-261-6611; FAX: 714-756-0133

Empire Cutlery Corp., 12 Kruger Ct., Clifton, NJ 07013 / 201-472-5155; FAX: 201-779-0759

English, Inc., A.G., 708 S. 12th St., Broken Arrow, OK 74012 / 918-251-3399

Engraving Artistry, 36 Alto Rd., RFD 2, Burlington, CT 06013 / 203-673-6837

Enguix Import-Export, Alpujarras 58, Alzira, Valencia, SPAIN / (96) 241 43 95; FAX: (96) (241 43 95

Enhanced Presentations, Inc., 5929 Market St., Wilmington, NC 28405 / 910-799-1622; FAX: 910-799-5004

Enlow, Charles, 895 Box, Beaver, OK 73932 / 405-625-4487

Entre'prise Arms, Inc., 15861 Business Center Dr., Irwindale, CA 91706

EPC, 1441 Manatt St., Lincoln, NE 68521 / 402-476-3946

Epps, Ellwood (See "Gramps" Antique, Box 341, Washago, ON L0K 2B0 CANADA / 705-689-5348

Erhardt, Dennis, 3280 Green Meadow Dr., Helena, MT 59601 / 406-442-4533

Erma Werke GmbH, Johan Ziegler St., 13/15/FeldiglSt., D-8060 Dachau, GERMANY

Eskridge Rifles, Steven Eskridge, 218 N. Emerson, Mart, TX 76664 / 817-876-3544

Eskridge, Steven. (See ESKRIDGE RIFLES)

Essex Arms, P.O. Box 363, Island Pond, VT 05846 / 802-723-6203 FAX: 802-723-6203

Essex Metals, 1000 Brighton St., Union, NJ 07083 / 800-282-8369

Estate Cartridge, Inc., 12161 FM 830, Willis, TX 77378 / 409-856-7277; FAX: 409-856-5486

MANUFACTURER'S DIRECTORY

Euber Bullets, No. Orwell Rd., Orwell, VT 05760 / 802-948-2621

Euro-Imports, 905 West Main St Ste E, El Cajon, CA 92020 / 619-442-7005; FAX: 619-442-7005

Euroarms of America, Inc., P.O. Box 3277, Winchester, VA 22604 / 540-662-1863; FAX: 540-662-4464

European American Armory Corp (See E.A.A. Corp)

Evans, Andrew, 2325 NW Squire St., Albany, OR 97321 / 541-928-3190; FAX: 541-928-4128

Evans Engraving, Robert, 332 Vine St, Oregon City, OR 97045 / 503-656-5693

Evans Gunsmithing (See Evans, Andrew)

Eversull Co., Inc., K., 1 Tracemont, Boyce, LA 71409 / 318-793-8728; FAX: 318-793-5483

Excalibur Electro Optics Inc, P.O. Box 400, Fogelsville, PA 18051-0400 / 610-391-9105; FAX: 610-391-9220

Excel Industries Inc., 4510 Carter Ct., Chino, CA 91710 / 909-627-2404; FAX: 909-627-7817

Executive Protection Institute, PO Box 802, Berryville, VA 22611 / 540-955-1128

Eyster Heritage Gunsmiths, Inc., Ken, 6441 Bishop Rd., Centerburg, OH 43011 / 614-625-6131

Eze-Lap Diamond Prods., P.O. Box 2229, 15164 West State St., Westminster, CA 92683 / 714-847-1555; FAX: 714-897-0280

F

F&A Inc. (See ShurKatch Corporation)

F.A.I.R. Techni-Mec s.n.c. di Isidoro Rizzini & C., Via Gitti, 41 Zona Industrial, 25060 Marcheno (Bres, ITALY / 030/861162-8610344; FAX: 030/8610179

Fabarm S.p.A., Via Averolda 31, 25039 Travagliato, Brescia, ITALY / 030-6863629; FAX: 030-6863684

Fagan & Co.Inc, 22952 15 Mile Rd, Clinton Township, MI 48035 / 810-465-4637; FAX: 810-792-6996

Fair Game International, P.O. Box 77234-34053, Houston, TX 77234 / 713-941-6269

Faith Associates, Inc., PO Box 549, Flat Rock, NC 28731-0549 / 828-692-1916; FAX: 828-697-6827

Fanzoj GmbH, Griesgasse 1, 9170 Ferlach, 9170 AUSTRIA / (43) 04227-2283; FAX: (43) 04227-2867

Far North Outfitters, Box 1252, Bethel, AK 99559

Farm Form Decoys, Inc., 1602 Biovu, P.O. Box 748, Galveston, TX 77553 / 409-744-0762 or 409-765-6361; FAX: 409-765-8513

Farmer-Dressel, Sharon, 209 N. 92nd Ave., Yakima, WA 98908 / 509-966-9233; FAX: 509-966-3365

Farr Studio,Inc., 1231 Robinhood Rd., Greeneville, TN 37743 / 615-638-8825

Farrar Tool Co., Inc., 12150 Bloomfield Ave., Suite E, Santa Fe Springs, CA 90670 / 310-863-4367; FAX: 310-863-5123

Faulhaber Wildlocker, Dipl.-Ing. Norbert Wittasek, Seilergasse 2, A-1010 Wien, AUSTRIA / OM-43-1-5137001; FAX: OM-43-1-5137001

Faulk's Game Call Co., Inc., 616 18th St., Lake Charles, LA 70601 / 318-436-9726 FAX: 318-494-7205

Faust Inc., T. G., 544 minor St, Reading, PA 19602 / 610-375-8549; FAX: 610-375-4488

Fausti Cav. Stefano & Figlie snc, Via Martiri Dell Indipendenza, 70, Marcheno, 25060 ITALY

Fautheree, Andy, P.O. Box 4607, Pagosa Springs, CO 81157 / 970-731-5003; FAX: 970-731-5009

Feather, Flex Decoys, 1655 Swan Lake Rd., Bossier City, LA 71111 / 318-746-8596; FAX: 318-742-4815

Federal Arms Corp. of America, 7928 University Ave, Fridley, MN 55432 / 612-780-8780; FAX: 612-780-8780

Federal Cartridge Co., 900 Ehlen Dr., Anoka, MN 55303 / 612-323-2300; FAX: 612-323-2506

Federal Champion Target Co., 232 Industrial Parkway, Richmond, IN 47374 / 800-441-4971; FAX: 317-966-7747

Federated-Fry (See Fry Metals)

FEG, Budapest, Soroksariut 158, H-1095, HUNGARY

Feken, Dennis, Rt. 2, Box 124, Perry, OK 73077 / 405-336-5611

Felk, Inc., 2121 Castlebridge Rd., Midlothian, VA 23113 / 804-794-3744

Fellowes, Ted, Beaver Lodge, 9245 16th Ave. SW, Seattle, WA 98106 / 206-763-1698

Feminine Protection, Inc., 949 W. Kearney Ste. 100, Mesquite, TX 75149 / 972-289-8997 FAX: 972-289-4410

Ferguson, Bill, P.O. Box 1238, Sierra Vista, AZ 85636 / 520-458-5321; FAX: 520-458-9125

FERLIB, Via Costa 46, 25063, Gardone V.T., ITALY / 30-89-12-586; FAX: 30-89-12-586

Ferris Firearms, 7110 F.M. 1863, Bulverde, TX 78163 / 210-980-4424

Fibron Products, Inc., P.O. Box 430, Buffalo, NY 14209-0430 / 716-886-2378; FAX: 716-886-2394

Fieldsport Ltd, Bryan Bilinski, 3313 W South Airport Rd, Traverse Vity, MI 49684 / 616-933-0767

Fiocchi Munizioni S.p.A. (See U.S. Importer-Fiocchi of America, Inc.)

Fiocchi of America Inc., 5030 Fremont Rd., Ozark, MO 65721 / 417-725-4118 or 800-721-2666 FAX: 417-725-1039

Firearms Co Ltd/Alpine (See U.S. Importer-Mandall Shooting Supplies, Inc.)

Firearms Engraver's Guild of America, 332 Vine St., Oregon City, OR 97045 / 503-656-5693

Firearms International, 5709 Hartsdale, Houston, TX 77036 / 713-460-2447

First Inc, Jack, 1201 Turbine Dr., Rapid City, SD 57701 / 605-343-9544; FAX: 605-343-9420

Fish Mfg. Gunsmith Sptg. Co., Marshall F, Rd. Box 2439, Rt. 22 N, Westport, NY 12993 / 518-962-4897 FAX: 518-962-4897

Fisher, Jerry A., 553 Crane Mt. Rd., Big Fork, MT 59911 / 406-837-2722

Fisher Custom Firearms, 2199 S. Kittredge Way, Aurora, CO 80013 / 303-755-3710

Fisher Enterprises, Inc., 1071 4th Ave. S., Suite 303, Edmonds, WA 98020-4143 / 206-771-5382

Fisher, R. Kermit (See Fisher Enterprises, Inc), 1071 4th Ave S Ste 303, Edmonds, WA 98020-4143 / 206-771-5382

Fitz Pistol Grip Co., P.O. Box 744, LEWISTON, CA 96052-0744 / 916-778-0240

Flambeau Products Corp., 15981 Valplast Rd., Middlefield, OH 44062 / 216-632-1631; FAX: 216-632-1581

Flannery Engraving Co., Jeff W, 11034 Riddles Run Rd, Union, KY 41091 / 606-384-3127

Flashette Co., 4725 S. Kolin Ave., Chicago, IL 60632 FAX: 773-927-3083

Flayderman & Co., Inc., PO Box 2446, Ft Lauderdale, FL 33303 / 954-761-8855

Fleming Firearms, 7720 E 126th St. N, Collinsville, OK 74021-7016 / 918-665-3624

Flents Products Co., Inc., P.O. Box 2109, Norwalk, CT 06852 / 203-866-2581; FAX: 203-854-9322

Flintlocks Etc., 160 Rositter Rd, Richmond, MA 01254 / 413-698-3822

Flintlocks, Etc, 160 Rossiter Rd., P.O. Box 181, Richmond, MA 01254 / 413-698-3822; FAX: 413-698-3866 flintetc@vgernet.net pedersoli

Flitz International Ltd., 821 Mohr Ave., Waterford, WI 53185 / 414-534-5898; FAX: 414-534-2991

Flores Publications Inc, J (See Action Direct Inc), PO Box 830760, Miami, FL 33283 / 305-559-4652; FAX: 305-559-4652

Fluoramics, Inc., 18 Industrial Ave., Mahwah, NJ 07430 / 800-922-0075; FAX: 201-825-7035

Flynn's Custom Guns, P.O. Box 7461, Alexandria, LA 71306 / 318-455-7130

FN Herstal, Voie de Liege 33, Herstal, 4040 Belgium / (32)41.40.82.83; FAX: (32)41.40.86.79

Fobus International Ltd., P.O. Box 64, Kfar Hess, 40692 ISRAEL / 972-9-7964170; FAX: 972-9-7964169

Folks, Donald E., 205 W. Lincoln St., Pontiac, IL 61764 / 815-844-7901

Foothills Video Productions, Inc., P.O. Box 651, Spartanburg, SC 29304 / 803-573-7023 or 800-782-5358

Foredom Electric Co., Rt. 6, 16 Stony Hill Rd., Bethel, CT 06801 / 203-792-8622

Forgett Jr., Valmore J., 689 Bergen Blvd., Ridgefield, NJ 07657 / 201-945-2500; FAX: 201-945-6859

Forgreens Tool Mfg., Inc., P.O. Box 990, 723 Austin St., Robert Lee, TX 76945 / 915-453-2800; FAX: 915-453-2460

Forkin, Ben (See Belt MTN Arms)

Forkin Arms, 205 10th Ave SW, White Sulphur Spring, MT 59645 / 406-547-2344; FAX: 406-547-2456

Forrest Inc., Tom, PO Box 326, Lakeside, CA 92040 / 619-561-5800; FAX: 619-561-0227

Forrest Tool Co., P.O. Box 768, 44380 Gordon Lane, Mendocino, CA 95460 / 707-937-2141; FAX: 717-937-1817

Forster, Kathy (See Custom Checkering Service, Kathy Forster)

Forster, Larry L., P.O. Box 212, 220 First St. NE, Gwinner, ND 58040-0212 / 701-678-2475

Forster Products, 310 E Lanark Ave, Lanark, IL 61046 / 815-493-6360; FAX: 815-493-2371

Fort Hill Gunstocks, 12807 Fort Hill Rd., Hillsboro, OH 45133 / 513-466-2763

Fort Knox Security Products, 1051 N. Industrial Park Rd., Orem, UT 84057 / 801-224-7233 or 800-821-5216; FAX: 801-226-5493

Fort Worth Firearms, 2006-B, Martin Luther King Fwy., Ft. Worth, TX 76104-6303 / 817-536-0718; FAX: 817-535-0290

Forthofer's Gunsmithing & Knifemaking, 5535 U.S. Hwy 93S, Whitefish, MT 59937-8411 / 406-862-2674

Fortune Products, Inc., HC04, Box 303, Marble Falls, TX 78654 / 210-693-6111; FAX: 210-693-6394

Forty Five Ranch Enterprises, Box 1080, Miami, OK 74355-1080 / 918-542-5875

Fountain Products, 492 Prospect Ave., West Springfield, MA 01089 / 413-781-4651; FAX: 413-733-8217

4-D Custom Die Co., 711 N. Sandusky St., P.O. Box 889, Mt. Vernon, OH 43050-0889 / 740-397-7214; FAX: 740-397-6600

Fowler Bullets, 806 Dogwood Dr., Gastonia, NC 28054 / 704-867-3259

Fowler, Bob (See Black Powder Products)

Fox River Mills, Inc., P.O. Box 298, 227 Poplar St., Osage, IA 50461 / 515-732-3798; FAX: 515-732-5128

Foy Custom Bullets, 104 Wells Ave., Daleville, AL 36322

Francesca, Inc., 3115 Old Ranch Rd., San Antonio, TX 78217 / 512-826-2584; FAX: 512-826-8211

Franchi S.p.A., Via del Serpente 12, 25131, Brescia, ITALY / 030-3581833; FAX: 030-3581554

Francotte & Cie S.A. Auguste, rue de Trois Juin 109, 4400 Herstal-Liege, BELGIUM / 32-4-248-13-18; FAX: 32-4-948-11-79

Frank Custom Classic Arms, Ron, 7131 Richland Rd, Ft Worth, TX 76118 / 817-284-9300; FAX: 817-284-9300

Frank E. Hendricks Master Engravers, Inc., HC03, Box 434, Dripping Springs, TX 78620 / 512-858-7828

Frank Knives, 13868 NW Keleka Pl., Seal Rock, OR 97376 / 541-563-3041; FAX: 541-563-3041

Frank Mittermeier, Inc., P.O. Box 2G, 3577 E. Tremont Ave., Bronx, NY 10465 / 718-828-3843

Frankonia Jagd Hofmann & Co., D-97064 Wurzburg, Wurzburg, GERMANY / 09302-200; FAX: 09302-20200

Franzen International,Inc (U.S. Importer for Peters Stahl GmbH)

Fred F. Wells/Wells Sport Store, 110 N Summit St, Prescott, AZ 86301 / 520-445-3655

Freedom Arms, Inc., P.O. Box 150, Freedom, WY 83120 / 307-883-2468 or 800-833-4432; FAX: 307-883-2005

Freeman Animal Targets, 5519 East County Road, 100 South, Plainsfield, IN 46168 / 317-272-2663; FAX: 317-272-2674

Fremont Tool Works, 1214 Prairie, Ford, KS 67842 / 316-369-2327

French, Artistic Engraving, J. R., 1712 Creek Ridge Ct, Irving, TX 75060 / 214-254-2654

Frielich Police Equipment, 211 East 21st St., New York, NY 10010 / 212-254-3045

Front Sight Firearms Training Institute, P.O. Box 2619, Aptos, CA 95001 / 800-987-7719; FAX: 408-684-2137

Frontier, 2910 San Bernardo, Laredo, TX 78040 / 956-723-5409; FAX: 956-723-1774

Frontier Arms Co.,Inc., 401 W. Rio Santa Cruz, Green Valley, AZ 85614-3932

Frontier Products Co., 2401 Walker Rd, Roswell, NM 88201-8950 / 614-262-9357

Frontier Safe Co., 3201 S. Clinton St., Fort Wayne, IN 46806 / 219-744-7233; FAX: 219-744-6678

Frost Cutlery Co., P.O. Box 22636, Chattanooga, TN 37422 / 615-894-6079; FAX: 615-894-9576

Fry Metals, 4100 6th Ave., Altoona, PA 16602 / 814-946-1611

Fujinon, Inc., 10 High Point Dr., Wayne, NJ 07470 / 201-633-5600; FAX: 201-633-5216

Fullmer, Geo. M., 2499 Mavis St., Oakland, CA 94601 / 510-533-4193

Fulmer's Antique Firearms, Chet, PO Box 792, Rt 2 Buffalo Lake, Detroit Lakes, MN 56501 / 218-847-7712

Fulton Armory, 8725 Bollman Place No. 1, Savage, MD 20763 / 301-490-9485; FAX: 301-490-9547

Furr Arms, 91 N. 970 W., Orem, UT 84057 / 801-226-3877; FAX: 801-226-3877

Fusilier Bullets, 10010 N. 6000 W., Highland, UT 84003 / 801-756-6813

FWB, Neckarstrasse 43, 78727, Oberndorf a. N., GERMANY / 07423-814-0; FAX: 07423-814-89

G

G&H Decoys,Inc., P.O. Box 1208, Hwy. 75 North, Henryetta, OK 74437 / 918-652-3314; FAX: 918-652-3400

G.C.C.T., 4455 Torrance Blvd., Ste. 453, Torrance, CA 90503-4398

G.G. & G., 3602 E. 42nd Stravenue, Tucson, AZ 85713 / 520-748-7167; FAX: 520-748-7583

G.H. Enterprises Ltd., Bag 10, Okotoks, AB T0L 1T0 CANADA / 403-938-6070

G.U. Inc (See U.S. Importer for New SKB Arms Co)

G.W. Elliott, Inc., 514 Burnside Ave., East Hartford, CT 06108 / 203-289-5741; FAX: 203-289-3137

G96 Products Co., Inc., 85 5th Ave, Bldg #6, Paterson, NJ 07544 / 973-684-4050 FAX: 973-684-4050

Gage Manufacturing, 663 W. 7th St., A, San Pedro, CA 90731 / 310-832-3546

Gaillard Barrels, P.O. Box 21, Pathlow, SK S0K 3B0 CANADA / 306-752-3769; FAX: 306-752-5969

Gain Twist Barrel Co. Rifle Works and Armory, 707 12th Street, Cody, WY 82414 / 307-587-4919; FAX: 307-527-6097

Galati International, PO Box 10, Wesco, MO 65586 / 314-257-4837; FAX: 314-257-2268

Galaxy Imports Ltd.,Inc., P.O. Box 3361, Victoria, TX 77903 / 361-573-4867; FAX: 361-576-9622 galaxy@tisd.net

GALCO International Ltd., 2019 W. Quail Ave., Phoenix, AZ 85027 / 602-258-8295 or 800-874-2526; FAX: 602-582-6854

Galena Industries AMT, 3551 Mayer Ave., Sturgis, SD 57785 / 605-423-4105

Gamba S.p.A. Societa Armi Bresciane Srl, Renato, Via Artigiani 93, ITALY / 30-8911640; FAX: 30-8911648

Gamba, USA, P.O. Box 60452, Colorado Springs, CO 80960 / 719-578-1145; FAX: 719-444-0731

Game Haven Gunstocks, 13750 Shire Rd., Wolverine, MI 49799 / 616-525-8257

Game Winner, Inc., 2625 Cumberland Parkway, Suite 220, Atlanta, GA 30339 / 770-434-9210; FAX: 770-434-9215

Gamebore Division, Polywad Inc, PO Box 7916, Macon, GA 31209 / 912-477-0669

Gamo (See U.S. Importers-Arms United Corp, Daisy Mfg. Co.,)

Gamo USA, Inc., 3911 SW 47th Ave., Suite 914, Ft. Lauderdale, FL 33314 / 954-581-5822; FAX: 954-581-3165

Gander Mountain, Inc., 12400 Fox River Rd., Wilmont, WI 53192 / 414-862-6848

GAR, 590 McBride Avenue, West Paterson, NJ 07424 / 973-754-1114; FAX: 973-754-1114

Garbi, Armas Urki, 12-14 20.600 Eibar, Guipuzcoa, SPAIN

Garcia National Gun Traders, Inc., 225 SW 22nd Ave., Miami, FL 33135 / 305-642-2355

Garrett Cartridges, Inc., P.O. Box 178, Chehalis, WA 98532 / 360-736-0702

Garthwaite Pistolsmith, Inc., Jim, Rt 2 Box 310, Watsontown, PA 17777 / 570-538-1566; FAX: 570-538-2965

Gary Goudy Classic Stocks, 263 Hedge Rd., Menlo Park, CA 94025-1711 / 415-322-1338

Gary Reeder Custom Guns, 2710 N Steves Blvd. #22, Flagstaff, AZ 86004 / 520-526-3313; FAX: 520-527-0840 gary@reedercustomguns.com www.reedercustomguns.com

Gary Schneider Rifle Barrels Inc., 12202 N. 62nd Pl., Scottsdale, AZ 85254 / 602-948-2525

Gator Guns & Repair, 6255 Spur Hwy., Kenai, AK 99611 / 907-283-7947

Gaucher Armes, S.A., 46 rue Desjoyaux, 42000, Saint-Etienne, FRANCE / 04-77-33-38-92; FAX: 04-77-61-95-72

GDL Enterprises, 409 Le Gardeur, Slidell, LA 70460 / 504-649-0693

Gehmann, Walter (See Huntington Die Specialties)

Genco, P.O. Box 5704, Asheville, NC 28803

Gene's Custom Guns, P.O. Box 10534, White Bear Lake, MN 55110 / 612-429-5105

Genecco Gun Works, K, 10512 Lower Sacramento Rd., Stockton, CA 95210 / 209-951-0706 FAX: 209-931-3872

Gentex Corp., 5 Tinkham Ave., Derry, NH 03038 / 603-434-0311; FAX: 603-434-3002 sales@derry.gentexcorp.com www.derry.gentexcorp.com

Gentner Bullets, 109 Woodlawn Ave., Upper Darby, PA 19082 / 610-352-9396

Gentry Custom Gunmaker, David, 314 N Hoffman, Belgrade, MT 59714 / 406-388-GUNS

George & Roy's, PO Box 2125, Sisters, OR 97759-2125 / 503-228-5424 or 800-553-3022; FAX: 503-225-9409

George, Tim, Rt. 1, P.O. Box 45, Evington, VA 24550 / 804-821-8117

George E. Mathews & Son, Inc., 10224 S. Paramount Blvd., Downey, CA 90241 / 562-862-6719; FAX: 562-862-6719

George Hoenig (Sheffield) Ltd., 25-31 Allen St., Sheffield, S3 7AW ENGLAND / 0114-2766123; FAX: 0114-2738465

Gerald Pettinger Books, see Pettinger Books, G, Rt. 2, Box 125, Russell, IA 50238 / 515-535-2239

Gerber Legendary Blades, 14200 SW 72nd Ave., Portland, OR 97223 / 503-639-6161 or 800-950-6161; FAX: 503-684-7008

Gervais, Mike, 3804 S. Cruise Dr., Salt Lake City, UT 84109 / 801-277-7729

Getz Barrel Co., P.O. Box 88, Beavertown, PA 17813 / 717-658-7263

Giacomo Sporting USA, 6234 Stokes Lee Center Rd., Lee Center, NY 13363

Gibbs Rifle Co., Inc., 211 Lawn St, Martinsburg, WV 25401 / 304-262-1651; FAX: 304-262-1658

Gil Hebard Guns, 125-129 Public Square, Knoxville, IL 61448 / 309-289-2700 FAX: 309-289-2233

Gilbert Equipment Co., Inc., 960 Downtowner Rd., Mobile, AL 36609 / 205-344-3322

Gilkes, Anthony W., 26574 HILLMAN HWY, MEADOWVIEW, VA 24361-3142 / 303-657-1873; FAX: 303-657-1885

Gillmann, Edwin, 33 Valley View Dr., Hanover, PA 17331 / 717-632-1662

Gilman-Mayfield, Inc., 3279 E. Shields, Fresno, CA 93703 / 209-221-9415; FAX: 209-221-9419

Gilmore Sports Concepts, 5949 S. Garnett, Tulsa, OK 74146 / 918-250-3810; FAX: 918-250-3845 gilmore@web-zone.net www.gilmoresports.com

Giron, Robert E., 1328 Pocono St., Pittsburgh, PA 15218 / 412-731-6041

Glacier Glove, 4890 Aircenter Circle, Suite 210, Reno, NV 89502 / 702-825-8225; FAX: 702-825-6544

Glaser Safety Slug, Inc., P.O. Box 8223, Foster City, CA 94404 / 800-221-3489; FAX: 510-785-6685 safetyslug.com

Glass, Herb, P.O. Box 25, Bullville, NY 10915 / 914-361-3021

Glimm, Jerome C., 19 S. Maryland, Conrad, MT 59425 / 406-278-3574

Glock GmbH, P.O. Box 50, A-2232, Deutsch Wagram, AUSTRIA

Glock, Inc., PO Box 369, Smyrna, GA 30081 / 770-432-1202; FAX: 770-433-8719

Glynn Scobey Duck & Goose Calls, Rt. 3, Box 37, Newbern, TN 38059 / 901-643-6241

GML Products, Inc., 394 Laredo Dr., Birmingham, AL 35226 / 205-979-4867

Gner's Hard Cast Bullets, 1107 11th St., LaGrande, OR 97850 / 503-963-8796

Goens, Dale W., P.O. Box 224, Cedar Crest, NM 87008 / 505-281-5419

Goergen's Gun Shop, Inc., 17985 538th Ave, Austin, MN 55912 / 507-433-9280 FAX: 507-433-9280

GOEX Inc., PO Box 659, Doyline, LA 71023-0659 / 318-382-9300; FAX: 318-382-9303

Golden Age Arms Co., 115 E. High St., Ashley, OH 43003 / 614-747-2488

Golden Bear Bullets, 3065 Fairfax Ave., San Jose, CA 95148 / 408-238-9515

Gonic Arms/North American Arm, 134 Flagg Rd., Gonic, NH 03839 / 603-332-8456 or 603-332-8457

Gonzalez Guns, Ramon B, PO Box 370, 93 St. Joseph's Hill Rd, Monticello, NY 12701 / 914-794-4515

Goodling's Gunsmithing, R.D. 1, Box 1097, Spring Grove, PA 17362 / 717-225-3350

Goodwin, Fred, Silver Ridge Gun Shop, Sherman Mills, ME 04776 / 207-365-4451

Gordie's Gun Shop, 1401 Fulton St., Streator, IL 61364 / 815-672-7202

Gordon Wm. Davis Leather Co., P.O. Box 2270, Walnut, CA 91788 / 909-598-5620

Gotz Bullets, 7313 Rogers St., Rockford, IL 61111

Gould & Goodrich, 709 E. McNeil, Lillington, NC 27546 / 910-893-2071; FAX: 910-893-4742

Gournet, Geoffroy, 820 Paxinosa Ave., Easton, PA 18042 / 610-559-0710

Gozon Corp. U.S.A., P.O. Box 6278, Folson, CA 95763 / 916-983-2026; FAX: 916-983-9500

Grace, Charles E., 1305 Arizona Ave., Trinidad, CO 81082 / 719-846-9435

Grace Metal Products, P.O. Box 67, Elk Rapids, MI 49629 / 616-264-8133

Graf & Sons, 4050 S Clark St, Mexico, MO 65265 / 573-581-2266 FAX: 573-581-2875

"Gramps" Antique Cartridges, Box 341, Washago, ON L0K 2B0 CANADA / 705-689-5348

Granite Mountain Arms, Inc, 3145 W Hidden Acres Trail, Prescott, AZ 86305 / 520-541-9758; FAX: 520-445-6826

Grant, Howard V., Hiawatha 15, Woodruff, WI 54568 / 715-356-7146

Graphics Direct, P.O. Box 372421, Reseda, CA 91337-2421 / 818-344-9002

Graves Co., 1800 Andrews Ave., Pompano Beach, FL 33069 / 800-327-9103; FAX: 305-960-0301

Grayback Wildcats, 5306 Bryant Ave., Klamath Falls, OR 97603 / 541-884-1072

Graybill's Gun Shop, 1035 Ironville Pike, Columbia, PA 17512 / 717-684-2739

GrE-Tan Rifles, 29742 W.C.R. 50, Kersey, CO 80644 / 970-353-6176; FAX: 970-356-9133

Great American Gunstock Co., 3420 Industrial Drive, Yuba City, CA 95993 / 530-671-4570; FAX: 530-671-3906

Great Lakes Airguns, 6175 S. Park Ave, New York, NY 14075 / 716-648-6666; FAX: 716-648-5279

Green, Arthur S., 485 S. Robertson Blvd., Beverly Hills, CA 90211 / 310-274-1283

Green, Roger M., P.O. Box 984, 435 E. Birch, Glenrock, WY 82637 / 307-436-9804

Green Genie, Box 114, Cusseta, GA 31805

Green Head Game Call Co., RR 1, Box 33, Lacon, IL 61540 / 309-246-2155

Green Mountain Rifle Barrel Co., Inc., P.O. Box 2670, 153 West Main St., Conway, NH 03818 / 603-447-1095; FAX: 603-447-1099

Greenwood Precision, P.O. Box 468, Nixa, MO 65714-0468 / 417-725-2330

Greg Gunsmithing Repair, 3732 26th Ave. North, Robbinsdale, MN 55422 / 612-529-8103

Greg's Superior Products, P.O. Box 46219, Seattle, WA 98146

Greider Precision, 431 Santa Marina Ct., Escondido, CA 92029 / 619-480-8892; FAX: 619-480-9800

Gremmel Enterprises, 2111 Carriage Drive, Eugene, OR 97408-7537 / 541-302-3000

Grier's Hard Cast Bullets, 1107 11th St., LaGrande, OR 97850 / 503-963-8796

Griffin & Howe, Inc., 36 W. 44th St., Suite 1011, New York, NY 10036 / 212-921-0980

Griffin & Howe, Inc., 33 Claremont Rd., Bernardsville, NJ 07924 / 908-766-2287

Grifon, Inc., 58 Guinam St., Waltham, MS 02154

Groenewold, John, P.O. Box 830, Mundelein, IL 60060 / 847-566-2365

GRS Corp., Glendo, P.O. Box 1153, 900 Overlander St., Emporia, KS 66801 / 316-343-1084 or 800-835-3519

Grulla Armes, Apartado 453, Avda Otaloa 12, Eiber, SPAIN

Gruning Precision Inc, 7101 Jurupa Ave., No. 12, Riverside, CA 92504 / 909-689-6692 FAX: 909-689-7791

GSI, Inc., 7661 Commerce Ln., Trussville, AL 35173 / 205-655-8299

GTB, 482 Comerwood Court, San Francisco, CA 94080 / 650-583-1550

Guarasi, Robert. (See WILCOX INDUSTRIES CORP)

Guardsman Products, 411 N. Darling, Fremont, MI 49412 / 616-924-3950

Gun Accessories (See Glaser Safety Slug, Inc.), PO Box 8223, Foster City, CA 94404 / 800-221-3489; FAX: 510-785-6685

Gun City, 212 W. Main Ave., Bismarck, ND 58501 / 701-223-2304

Gun Hunter Books (See Gun Hunter Trading Co), 5075 Heisig St, Beaumont, TX 77705 / 409-835-3006

Gun Hunter Trading Co., 5075 Heisig St., Beaumont, TX 77705 / 409-835-3006

Gun Leather Limited, 116 Lipscomb, Ft. Worth, TX 76104 / 817-334-0225; FAX: 800-247-0609

Gun List (See Krause Publications), 700 E State St, Iola, WI 54945 / 715-445-2214; FAX: 715-445-4087

Gun Locker Div. of Airmold W.R. Grace & Co.-Conn., Becker Farms Ind. Park, P.O. Box 610, Roanoke Rapids, NC 27870 / 800-344-5716; FAX: 919-536-2201

Gun South, Inc. (See GSI, Inc.)

Gun Vault, 7339 E Acoma Dr., Ste. 7, Scottsdale, AZ 85260 / 602-951-6855

Gun-Alert, 1010 N. Maclay Ave., San Fernando, CA 91340 / 818-365-0864; FAX: 818-365-1308

Gun-Ho Sports Cases, 110 E. 10th St., St. Paul, MN 55101 / 612-224-9491

Guncraft Books (See Guncraft Sports Inc), 10737 Dutchtown Rd, Knoxville, TN 37932 / 423-966-4545; FAX: 423-966-4500

Guncraft Sports Inc., 10737 Dutchtown Rd., Knoxville, TN 37932 / 423-966-4545; FAX: 423-966-4500

Gunfitters, P.O. 426, Cambridge, WI 53523-0426 / 608-764-8128 gunfitters@aol.com www.gunfitters.com

Gunline Tools, 2950 Saturn St., "O", Brea, CA 92821 / 714-993-5100; FAX: 714-572-4128

Gunnerman Books, P.O. Box 217, Owosso, MI 48867 / 517-729-7018; FAX: 517-725-9391

Guns, 81 E. Streetsboro St., Hudson, OH 44236 / 330-650-4563

Guns Antique & Modern DBA/Charles E. Duffy, Williams Lane, West Hurley, NY 12491 / 914-679-2997

Guns Div. of D.C. Engineering, Inc., 8633 Southfield Fwy., Detroit, MI 48228 / 313-271-7111 or 800-886-7623; FAX: 313-271-7112

GUNS Magazine, 591 Camino de la Reina, Suite 200, San Diego, CA 92108 / 619-297-5350 FAX: 619-297-5353

Gunsite Custom Shop, P.O. Box 451, Paulden, AZ 86334 / 520-636-4104; FAX: 520-636-1236

Gunsite Gunsmithy (See Gunsite Custom Shop)

Gunsite Training Center, P.O. Box 700, Paulden, AZ 86334 / 520-636-4565; FAX: 520-636-1236

Gunsmithing Ltd., 57 Unquowa Rd., Fairfield, CT 06430 / 203-254-0436; FAX: 203-254-1535

Gunsmithing, Inc., 208 West Buchanan St., Colorado Springs, CO 80907 / 719-632-3795; FAX: 719-632-3493

Gurney, F. R., Box 13, Sooke, BC V0S 1N0 CANADA / 604-642-5282; FAX: 604-642-7859

Gwinnell, Bryson J., P.O. Box 248C, Maple Hill Rd., Rochester, VT 05767 / 802-767-3664

H

H&B Forge Co., Rt. 2, Geisinger Rd., Shiloh, OH 44878 / 419-895-1856

H&P Publishing, 7174 Hoffman Rd., San Angelo, TX 76905 / 915-655-5953

H&R 1871, Inc., 60 Industrial Rowe, Gardner, MA 01440 / 978-632-9393; FAX: 978-632-2300

H&S Liner Service, 515 E. 8th, Odessa, TX 79761 / 915-332-1021

MANUFACTURER'S DIRECTORY

H-S Precision, Inc., 1301 Turbine Dr., Rapid City, SD 57701 / 605-341-3006; FAX: 605-342-8964

H. Krieghoff Gun Co., Boschstrasse 22, D-89079, Ulm, GERMANY / 731-401820; FAX: 731-4018270

H.K.S. Products, 7841 Founion Dr., Florence, KY 41042 / 606-342-7841 or 800-354-9814; FAX: 606-342-5865

H.P. White Laboratory, Inc., 3114 Scarboro Rd., Street, MD 21154 / 410-838-6550; FAX: 410-838-2802

Hafner World Wide, Inc., P.O. Box 1987, Lake City, FL 32055 / 904-755-6481; FAX: 904-755-6595

Hagn Rifles & Actions, Martin, PO Box 444, Cranbrook, BC V1C 4H9 CANADA / 604-489-4861

Hakko Co. Ltd., 1-13-12, Narimasu, Itabashiku Tokyo, JAPAN / 03-5997-7870/2; FAX: 81-3-5997-7840

Hale, Engraver, Peter, 800 E Canyon Rd., Spanish Fork, UT 84660 / 801-798-8215

Half Moon Rifle Shop, 490 Halfmoon Rd., Columbia Falls, MT 59912 / 406-892-4409

Hall Manufacturing, 142 CR 406, Clanton, AL 35045 / 205-755-4094

Hall Plastics, Inc., John, P.O. Box 1526, Alvin, TX 77512 / 713-489-8709

Hallberg Gunsmith, Fritz, 532 E. Idaho Ave, Ontario, OR 97914 / 541-889-3135; FAX: 541-889-2633

Hallowell & Co., PO Box 1445, Livingston, MT 59047 / 406-222-4770 FAX: 406-222-4792 morris@hallowellco.com www.hallowellco.com

Hally Caller, 443 Wells Rd., Doylestown, PA 18901 / 215-345-6354

Halstead, Rick, 313 TURF ST, CARL JUNCTION, MO 64834-9658 / 918-540-0933

Hamilton, Jim, Rte. 5, Box 278, Guthrie, OK 73044 / 405-282-3634

Hamilton, Alex B (See Ten-Ring Precision, Inc)

Hammans, Charles E., P.O. Box 788, 2022 McCracken, Stuttgart, AR 72106 / 870-673-1388

Hammerli Ltd., Seonerstrasse 37, CH-5600, SWITZERLAND / 064-50 11 44; FAX: 064-51 38 27

Hammerli USA, 19296 Oak Grove Circle, Groveland, CA 95321 FAX: 209-962-5311

Hammets VLD Bullets, P.O. Box 479, Rayville, LA 71269 / 318-728-2019

Hammond Custom Guns Ltd., 619 S. Pandora, Gilbert, AZ 85234 / 602-892-3437

Hammonds Rifles, RD 4, Box 504, Red Lion, PA 17356 / 717-244-7879

HandCrafts Unltd (See Clements' Custom Leathercraft, Chas,), 1741 Dallas St, Aurora, CO 80010-2018 / 303-364-0403; FAX: 303-739-9824

Handgun Press, P.O. Box 406, Glenview, IL 60025 / 847-657-6500; FAX: 847-724-8831 jschroed@inter-access.com

Hands Engraving, Barry Lee, 26192 E Shore Route, Bigfork, MT 59911 / 406-837-0035

Hank's Gun Shop, Box 370, 50 West 100 South, Monroe, UT 84754 / 801-527-4456

Hanned Precision (See Hanned Line, The)

Hansen & Co. (See Hansen Cartridge Co.), 244-246 Old Post Rd, Southport, CT 06490 / 203-259-6222; FAX: 203-254-3832

Hanson's Gun Center, Dick, 233 Everett Dr, Colorado Springs, CO 80911

Hanus Birdguns Bill, PO Box 533, Newport, OR 97365 / 541-265-7433; FAX: 541-265-7400

Hanusin, John, 3306 Commercial, Northbrook, IL 60062 / 708-564-2706

Hardin Specialty Dist., P.O. Box 338, Radcliff, KY 40159-0338 / 502-351-6649

Harford (See U.S. Importer-EMF Co. Inc.)

Harper's Custom Stocks, 928 Lombrano St., San Antonio, TX 78207 / 210-732-5780

Harrell's Precision, 5756 Hickory Dr., Salem, VA 24133 / 703-380-2683

Harrington & Richardson (See H&R 1871, Inc.)

Harris Engineering Inc., Dept GD54, Barlow, KY 42024 / 502-334-3633 FAX: 502-334-3000

Harris Enterprises, P.O. Box 105, Bly, OR 97622 / 503-353-2625

Harris Gunworks, 20813 N. 19th Ave., PO Box 9249, Phoenix, AZ 85067 / 602-582-9627; FAX: 602-582-5178

Harris Hand Engraving, Paul A., 113 Rusty Ln., Boerne, TX 78006-5746 / 512-391-5121

Harris Publications, 1115 Broadway, New York, NY 10010 / 212-807-7100 FAX: 212-627-4678

Harrison Bullets, 6437 E. Hobart St., Mesa, AZ 85205

Harry Lawson Co., 3328 N. Richey Blvd., Tucson, AZ 85716 / 520-326-1117

Hart & Son, Inc., Robert W., 401 Montgomery St, Nescopeck, PA 18635 / 717-752-3655; FAX: 717-752-1088

Hart Rifle Barrels,Inc., P.O. Box 182, 1690 Apulia Rd., Lafayette, NY 13084 / 315-677-9841; FAX: 315-677-9610 hartrb@aol.com hartbarrels.com

Hartford (See U.S. Importer-EMF Co. Inc.)

Hartmann & Weiss GmbH, Rahlstedter Bahnhofstr. 47, 22143, Hamburg, GERMANY / (40) 677 55 85; FAX: (40) 677 55 92

Harvey, Frank, 218 Nightfall, Terrace, NV 89015 / 702-558-6998

Harwood, Jack O., 1191 S. Pendlebury Lane, Blackfoot, ID 83221 / 208-785-5368

Hastings Barrels, 320 Court St., Clay Center, KS 67432 / 913-632-3169; FAX: 913-632-6554

Hatfield Gun, 224 N. 4th St., St. Joseph, MO 64501

Hawk Laboratories, Inc. (See Hawk, Inc.), 849 Hawks Bridge Rd, Salem, NJ 08079 / 609-299-2700; FAX: 609-299-2800

Hawk, Inc., 849 Hawks Bridge Rd., Salem, NJ 08079 / 609-299-2700; FAX: 609-299-2800

Hawken Shop, The (See Dayton Traister)

Haydel's Game Calls, Inc., 5018 Hazel Jones Rd., Bossier City, LA 71111 / 800-HAYDELS; FAX: 318-746-3711

Haydon Shooters Supply, Russ, 15018 Goodrich Dr NW, Gig Harbor, WA 98329-9738 / 253-857-7557; FAX: 253-857-7884

Heatbath Corp., P.O. Box 2978, Springfield, MA 01101 / 413-543-3381

Hebard Guns, Gil, 125-129 Public Square, Knoxville, IL 61448

HEBB Resources, P.O. Box 999, Mead, WA 99021-0999 / 509-466-1292

Hecht, Hubert J, Waffen-Hecht, PO Box 2635, Fair Oaks, CA 95628 / 916-966-1020

Heckler & Koch GmbH, P.O. Box 1329, 78722 Oberndorf, Neckar, GERMANY / 49-7423179-0; FAX: 49-7423179-2406

Heckler & Koch, Inc., 21480 Pacific Blvd., Sterling, VA 20166-8900 / 703-450-1900; FAX: 703-450-8160

Hege Jagd-u. Sporthandels GmbH, P.O. Box 101461, W-7770, Ueberlingen a. Boden, GERMANY

Heidenstrom Bullets, Urdngt 1, 3937 Heroya, NORWAY,

Heilmann, Stephen, P.O. Box 657, Grass Valley, CA 95945 / 530-272-8758

Heinie Specialty Products, 301 Oak St., Quincy, IL 62301-2500 / 217-228-9500; FAX: 217-228-9502 rheinie@heinie.com www.heinie.com

Hellweg Ltd., 40356 Oak Park Way, Suite W, Oakhurst, CA 93644 / 209-683-3030; FAX: 209-683-3422

Helwan (See U.S. Importer-Interarms)

Hendricks, Frank E. Inc., Master Engravers, HC 03, Box 434, Dripping Springs, TX 78620 / 512-858-7828

Henigson & Associates, Steve, PO Box 2726, Culver City, CA 90231 / 310-305-8288; FAX: 310-305-1905

Henriksen Tool Co., Inc., 8515 Wagner Creek Rd., Talent, OR 97540 / 541-535-2309 FAX: 541-535-2309

Henry Repeating Arms Co., 110 8th St., Brooklyn, NY 11215 / 718-499-5600

Hensley, Gunmaker, Darwin, PO Box 329, Brightwood, OR 97011 / 503-622-5411

Heppler, Keith. (See KEITH'S CUSTOM GUNSTOCKS)

Heppler's Machining, 2240 Calle Del Mundo, Santa Clara, CA 95054 / 408-748-9166; FAX: 408-988-7711

Heppler, Keith M, Keith's Custom Gunstocks, 540 Banyan Cir, Walnut Creek, CA 94598 / 510-934-3509; FAX: 510-934-3143

Hercules, Inc. (See Alliant Techsystems, Smokeless Powder Group)

Heritage Firearms (See Heritage Mfg., Inc.)

Heritage Manufacturing, Inc., 4600 NW 135th St., Opa Locka, FL 33054 or 305-685-5966; FAX: 305-687-6721

Heritage Wildlife Carvings, 2145 Wagner Hollow Rd., Fort Plain, NY 13339 / 518-993-3983

Heritage/VSP Gun Books, P.O. Box 887, McCall, ID 83638 / 208-634-4104; FAX: 208-634-3101

Herrett's Stocks, Inc., P.O. Box 741, Twin Falls, ID 83303 / 208-733-1498

Hertel & Reuss, Werk fr Optik und Feinmechanik GmbH, Quellhofstrasse 67, 34 127, GERMANY / 0561-83006; FAX: 0561-893308

Herter's Manufacturing, Inc., 111 E. Burnett St., P.O. Box 518, Beaver Dam, WI 53916 / 414-887-1765; FAX: 414-887-8444

Hesco-Meprolight, 2139 Greenville Rd., LaGrange, GA 30241 / 706-884-7967; FAX: 706-882-4683

Heydenberk, Warren R., 1059 W. Sawmill Rd., Quakertown, PA 18951 / 215-538-2682

Hi-Grade Imports, 8655 Monterey Rd., Gilroy, CA 95021 / 408-842-9301; FAX: 408-842-2374

Hi-Performance Ammunition Company, 484 State Route 366, Apollo, PA 15613 / 412-327-8100

Hi-Point Firearms, 5990 Philadelphia Dr., Dayton, OH 45415 / 513-275-4991; FAX: 513-522-8330

Hickman, Jaclyn, Box 1900, Glenrock, WY 82637

Hidalgo, Tony, 12701 SW 9th Pl., Davie, FL 33325 / 954-476-7645

High Bridge Arms, Inc, 3185 Mission St., San Francisco, CA 94110 / 415-282-8358

High North Products, Inc., P.O. Box 2, Antigo, WI 54409 / 715-627-2331 FAX: 715-623-5451

High Performance International, 5734 W. Florist Ave., Milwaukee, WI 53218 / 414-466-9040

High Standard Mfg. Co., Inc., 10606 Hempstead Hwy., Suite 116, Houston, TX 77092 / 713-462-4200, 800-467-2228

High Tech Specialties, Inc., P.O. Box 387R, Adamstown, PA 19501 / 215-484-0405 or 800-231-9385

Highline Machine Co., Randall Thompson, 654 Lela Place, Grand Junction, CO 81504 / 970-434-4971

Hill, Loring F., 304 Cedar Rd., Elkins Park, PA 19027

Hill Speed Leather, Ernie, 4507 N 195th Ave, Litchfield Park, AZ 85340 / 602-853-9222; FAX: 602-853-9235

Hines Co, S C, PO Box 423, Tijeras, NM 87059 / 505-281-3783

Hinman Outfitters, Bob, 107 N Sanderson Ave, Bartonville, IL 61607-1839 / 309-691-8132

HIP-GRIP Barami Corp., 6689 Orchard Lake Rd. No. 148, West Bloomfield, MI 48322 / 248-738-0462; FAX: 248-738-2542

Hiptmayer, Armurier, RR 112 750, P.O. Box 136, Eastman, PQ J0E 1P0 CANADA / 514-297-2492

Hiptmayer, Heidemarie, RR 112 750, P.O. Box 136, Eastman, PQ J0E 1P0 CANADA / 514-297-2492

Hiptmayer, Klaus, RR 112 750, P.O. Box 136, Eastman, PQ J0E 1P0 CANADA / 514-297-2492

Hirtenberger Aktiengesellschaft, Leobersdorferstrasse 31, A-2552, Hirtenberg, / 43(0)2256 81184; FAX: 43(0)2256 81807

HiTek International, 484 El Camino Real, Redwood City, CA 94063 / 415-363-1404 or 800-54-NIGHT FAX: 415-363-1408

Hiti-Schuch, Atelier Wilma, A-8863 Predlitz, Pirming, Y1 AUSTRIA / 0353418278

HJS Arms, Inc., P.O. Box 3711, Brownsville, TX 78523-3711 / 800-453-2767; FAX: 210-542-2767

Hoag, James W., 8523 Canoga Ave., Suite C, Canoga Park, CA 91304 / 818-998-1510

Hobson Precision Mfg. Co., 210 Big Oak Ln, Brent, AL 35034 / 205-926-4662 FAX: 205-926-3193 cahobbob@dbtech.net

Hoch Custom Bullet Moulds (See Colorado Shooter's

Hodgdon Powder Co., 6231 Robinson, Shawnee Mission, KS 66202 / 913-362-9455; FAX: 913-362-1307

Hodgman, Inc., 1750 Orchard Rd., Montgomery, IL 60538 / 708-897-7555; FAX: 708-897-7558

Hodgson, Richard, 9081 Tahoe Lane, Boulder, CO 80301

Hoehn Sales, Inc., 2045 Kohn Road, Wright City, MO 63390 / 636-745-8144; FAX: 636-745-7868 hoehnsal@usmo.com benchrestcentral.com

Hoelscher, Virgil, 8230 Hillrose St, Sunland, CA 91040-2404 / 310-631-8545

Hoenig & Rodman, 6521 Morton Dr., Boise, ID 83704 / 208-375-1116

Hofer Jagdwaffen, P., Buchsenmachermeister, Kirchgasse 24, A-9170 Ferlach, AUSTRIA

Hoffman New Ideas, 821 Northmoor Rd., Lake Forest, IL 60045 / 312-234-4075

Hogue Grips, P.O. Box 1138, Paso Robles, CA 93447 / 800-438-4747 or 805-239-1440; FAX: 805-239-2553

Holland & Holland Ltd., 33 Bruton St., London, ENGLAND / 44-171-499-4411; FAX: 44-171-408-7962

Holland's Gunsmithing, P.O. Box 69, Powers, OR 97466 / 541-439-5155; FAX: 541-439-5155

Hollinger, Jon. (See ASPEN OUTFITTING CO)

Hollis Gun Shop, 917 Rex St., Carlsbad, NM 88220 / 505-885-3782

Hollywood Engineering, 10642 Arminta St., Sun Valley, CA 91352 / 818-842-8376

Homak, 5151 W. 73rd St., Chicago, IL 60638-6613 / 312-523-3100; FAX: 312-523-9455

Home Shop Machinist The Village Press Publications, P.O. Box 1810, Traverse City, MI 49685 / 800-447-7367; FAX: 616-946-3289

Hondo Ind., 510 S. 52nd St., I04, Tempe, AZ 85281

Hoover, Harvey, 5750 Pearl Dr., Paradise, CA 95969-4829

Hoppe's Div. Penguin Industries, Inc., Airport Industrial Mall, Coatesville, PA 19320 / 610-384-6000

Horizons Unlimited, P.O. Box 426, Warm Springs, GA 31830 / 706-655-3603; FAX: 706-655-3603

Hornady Mfg. Co., P.O. Box 1848, Grand Island, NE 68802 / 800-338-3220 or 308-382-1390; FAX: 308-382-5761

Horseshoe Leather Products, Andy Arratoonian, The Cottage Sharow, Ripon, ENGLAND / 44-1765-605858

Houtz & Barwick, P.O. Box 435, W. Church St., Elizabeth City, NC 27909 / 800-775-0337 or 919-335-4191; FAX: 919-335-1152

Howa Machinery, Ltd., Sukaguchi, Shinkawa-cho Nishikasugai-gun, Aichi 452, JAPAN

Howell Machine, 815 1/2 D St., Lewiston, ID 83501 / 208-743-7418

Hoyt Holster Co., Inc., P.O. Box 69, Coupeville, WA 98239-0069 / 360-678-6640; FAX: 360-678-6549

HT Bullets, 244 Belleville Rd., New Bedford, MA 02745 / 508-999-3338

Hubert J. Hecht Waffen-Hecht, P.O. Box 2635, Fair Oaks, CA 95628 / 916-966-1020

Hubertus Schneidwarenfabrik, P.O. Box 180 106, D-42626, Solingen, GERMANY / 01149-212-59-19-94; FAX: 01149-212-59-19-92

Huebner, Corey O., P.O. Box 2074, Missoula, MT 59806-2074 / 406-721-7168

Huey Gun Cases, P.O. Box 22456, Kansas City, MO 64113 / 816-444-1637; FAX: 816-444-1637

Hugger Hooks Co., 3900 Easley Way, Golden, CO 80403 / 303-279-0600

Hughes, Steven Dodd, P.O. Box 545, Livingston, MT 59047 / 406-222-9377; FAX: 406-222-9377

Hume, Don, P.O. Box 351, Miami, OK 74355 / 800-331-2686 FAX: 918-542-4340

Hungry Horse Books, 4605 Hwy. 93 South, Whitefish, MT 59937 / 406-862-7997

Hunkeler, A (See Buckskin Machine Works, A. Hunkeler) 3235 S 358th St., Auburn, WA 98001 / 206-927-5412

Hunter Co., Inc., 3300 W. 71st Ave., Westminster, CO 80030 / 303-427-4626; FAX: 303-428-3980

Hunter's Specialties Inc., 6000 Huntington Ct. NE, Cedar Rapids, IA 52402-1268 / 319-395-0321; FAX: 319-395-0326

Hunterjohn, P.O. Box 771457, St. Louis, MO 63177 / 314-531-7250

Hunters Supply, Inc., PO Box 313, Tioga, TX 76271 / 940-437-2458; FAX: 940-437-2228 hunterssupply@hot-mail.com hunterssupply.net

Hunting Classics Ltd., P.O. Box 2089, Gastonia, NC 28053 / 704-867-1307; FAX: 704-867-0491

Huntington Die Specialties, 601 Oro Dam Blvd., Oroville, CA 95965 / 530-534-1210; FAX: 530-534-1212

Hutton Rifle Ranch, P.O. Box 45236, Boise, ID 83711 / 208-345-8781

Hydrosorbent Products, P.O. Box 437, Ashley Falls, MA 01222 / 413-229-2967; or 800-229-8743 FAX: 413-229-8743 orders@dehumidify.com www.dehumidify.com

Hyper-Single, Inc., 520 E. Beaver, Jenks, OK 74037 / 918-299-2391

I

I.A.B. (See U.S. Importer-Taylor's & Co. Inc.)

I.D.S.A. Books, 1324 Stratford Drive, Piqua, OH 45356 / 937-773-4203; FAX: 937-778-1922

I.N.C. Inc (See Kick Eez)

I.S.S., P.O. Box 185234, Ft. Worth, TX 76181 / 817-595-2090

I.S.W., 106 E. Cairo Dr., Tempe, AZ 85282

IAR Inc., 33171 Camino Capistrano, San Juan Capistrano, CA 92675 / 949-443-3642; FAX: 949-443-3647

IGA (See U.S. Importer-Stoeger Industries)

Ignacio Ugartechea S.A., Chonta 26, Eibar, 20600 SPAIN / 43-121257; FAX: 43-121669

Illinois Lead Shop, 7742 W. 61st Place, Summit, IL 60501

Image Ind. Inc., 382 Balm Court, Wood Dale, IL 60191 / 630-766-2402; FAX: 630-766-7373

IMI, P.O. Box 1044, Ramat Hasharon, 47100 ISRAEL / 972-3-5485617; FAX: 972-3-5406908

IMI Services USA, Inc., 2 Wisconsin Circle, Suite 420, Chevy Chase, MD 20815 / 301-215-4800; FAX: 301-657-1446

Impact Case Co., P.O. Box 9912, Spokane, WA 99209-0912 / 800-262-3322 or 509-467-3303; FAX: 509-326-5436 kkair.com

Imperial (See E-Z-Way Systems), PO Box 4310, Newark, OH 43058-4310 / 614-345-6645; FAX: 614-345-6600

Imperial Magnum Corp., P.O. Box 249, Oroville, WA 98844 / 604-495-3131; FAX: 604-495-2816

Imperial Miniature Armory, 10547 S. Post Oak, Houston, TX 77035 / 713-729-8428 FAX: 713-729-2274

Imperial Schrade Corp., 7 Schrade Ct., Box 7000, Ellenville, NY 12428 / 914-647-7601; FAX: 914-647-8701

Import Sports Inc., 1750 Brielle Ave., Unit B1, Wanamassa, NJ 07712 / 908-493-0302; FAX: 908-493-0301

IMR Powder Co., 1080 Military Turnpike, Suite 2, Plattsburgh, NY 12901 / 518-563-2253; FAX: 518-563-6916

Info-Arm, P.O. Box 1262, Champlain, NY 12919 / 514-955-0355; FAX: 514-955-0357

Ingle, Ralph W., Engraver, 112 Manchester Ct., Centerville, GA 31028 / 912-953-5824

Innovative Weaponry Inc., 2513 E. Loop 820 N., Fort Worth, TX 76118 / 817-284-0099; or 800-334-3573

Innovision Enterprises, 728 Skinner Dr., Kalamazoo, MI 49001 / 616-382-1681 FAX: 616-382-1830

INTEC International, Inc., P.O. Box 5708, Scottsdale, AZ 85261 / 602-483-1708

Inter Ordnance of America LP, 3305 Westwood Industrial Dr, Monroe, NC 28110-5204 / 704-821-8337; FAX: 704-821-8523

Interarms/Howa, PO Box 208, Ten Prince St, Alexandria, VA 22313 / 703-548-1400; FAX: 703-549-7826

Intercontinental Distributors, Ltd., PO Box 815, Beulah, ND 58523

Intrac Arms International, 5005 Chapman Hwy., Knoxville, TN 37920

Intratec, 12405 SW 130th St., Miami, FL 33186-6224 / 305-232-1821; FAX: 305-253-7207

Ion Industries, Inc, 3508 E Allerton Ave, Cudahy, WI 53110 / 414-486-2007; FAX: 414-486-2017

Iosso Products, 1485 Lively Blvd., Elk Grove Village, IL 60007 / 847-437-8400; FAX: 847-437-8478

Iron Bench, 12619 Bailey Rd., Redding, CA 96003 / 916-241-4623

Ironside International Publishers, Inc., P.O. Box 55, 800 Slaters Lane, Alexandria, VA 22313 / 703-684-6111; FAX: 703-683-5486

Ironsighter Co., P.O. Box 85070, Westland, MI 48185 / 734-326-8731; FAX: 734-326-3378

Irwin, Campbell H., 140 Hartland Blvd., East Hartland, CT 06027 / 203-653-3901

Island Pond Gun Shop, Cross St., Island Pond, VT 05846 / 802-723-4546

Israel Arms International, Inc., 5709 Hartsdale, Houston, TX 77036 / 713-789-0745; FAX: 713-789-7513

Israel Military Industries Ltd. (See IMI), PO Box 1044, Ramat Hasharon, ISRAEL / 972-3-5485617; FAX: 972-3-5406908

Ithaca Classic Doubles, Stephen Lamboy, PO Box 665, Mendon, NY 14506 / 706-569-6760; FAX: 706-561-9248

Ithaca Gun Co. LLC, 891 Route 34-B, King Ferry, NY 13081 / 888-9ITHACA; FAX: 315-364-5134

Ivanoff, Thomas G (See Tom's Gun Repair)

J

J J Roberts Firearm Engraver, 7808 Lake Dr, Manassas, VA 20111 / 703-330-0448 FAX: 703-264-8600

J Martin Inc, PO Drawer AP, Beckley, WV 25802 / 304-255-4073; FAX: 304-255-4077

J&D Components, 75 East 350 North, Orem, UT 84057-4719 / 801-225-7007

J&J Products, Inc., 9240 Whitmore, El Monte, CA 91731 / 818-571-5228; FAX: 800-927-8361

J&J Sales, 1501 21st Ave. S., Great Falls, MT 59405 / 406-453-7549

J&L Superior Bullets (See Huntington Die Specialties)

J&R Engineering, P.O. Box 77, 200 Lyons Hill Rd., Athol, MA 01331 / 508-249-9241

J&R Enterprises, 4550 Scotts Valley Rd., Lakeport, CA 95453

J&S Heat Treat, 803 S. 16th St., Blue Springs, MO 64015 / 816-229-2149; FAX: 816-228-1135

J-4 Inc., 1700 Via Burton, Anaheim, CA 92806 / 714-254-8315; FAX: 714-956-4421

J-Gar Co., 183 Turnpike Rd., Dept. 3, Petersham, MA 01366-9604

J. Dewey Mfg. Co., Inc., P.O. Box 2014, Southbury, CT 06488 / 203-264-3064; FAX: 203-262-6907

J. Korzinek Riflesmith, RD 2, Box 73D, Canton, PA 17724 / 717-673-8512

J.A. Blades, Inc. (See Christopher Firearms Co.,)

J.A. Henckels Zwillingswerk Inc., 9 Skyline Dr., Hawthorne, NY 10532 / 914-592-7370

J.G. Dapkus Co., Inc., Commerce Circle, P.O. Box 293, Durham, CT 06422

J.I.T. Ltd., P.O. Box 230, Freedom, WY 83120 / 708-494-0937

J.J. Roberts/Engraver, 7808 Lake Dr., Manassas, VA 22111 / 703-330-0448

J.M. Bucheimer Jumbo Sports Products, 721 N. 20th St., St. Louis, MO 63103 / 314-241-1020

J.P. Enterprises Inc., P.O. Box 26324, Shoreview, MN 55126 / 612-486-9064; FAX: 612-482-0970

J.P. Gunstocks, Inc., 4508 San Miguel Ave., North Las Vegas, NV 89030 / 702-645-0718

J.R. Blair Engraving, P.O. Box 64, Glenrock, WY 82637 / 307-436-8115

J.R. Williams Bullet Co., 2008 Tucker Rd., Perry, GA 31069 / 912-987-0274

J.W. Morrison Custom Rifles, 4015 W. Sharon, Phoenix, AZ 85029 / 602-978-3754

J/B Adventures & Safaris Inc., 2275 E. Arapahoe Rd., Ste. 109, Littleton, CO 80122-1521 / 303-771-0977

Jack Dever Co., 8590 NW 90, Oklahoma City, OK 73132 / 405-721-6393

Jack A. Rosenberg & Sons, 12229 Cox Ln., Dallas, TX 75234 / 214-241-6302

Jack First, Inc., 1201 Turbine Dr., Rapid City, SD 57701 / 605-343-9544; FAX: 605-343-9420

Jackalope Gun Shop, 1048 S. 5th St., Douglas, WY 82633 / 307-358-3441

Jaffin, Harry. (See BRIDGEMAN PRODUCTS)

Jagdwaffen, P. Hofer, Buchsenmachermeister, Kirchgasse 24 A-9170, Ferlach, AUSTRIA / 04227-3683

James Calhoon Varmint Bullets, Shambo Rt., 304, Havre, MT 59501 / 406-395-4079

James Churchill Glove Co., P.O. Box 298, Centralia, WA 98531

James Calhoon Mfg., Rt. 304, Havre, MT 59501 / 406-395-4079

James Wayne Firearms for Collectors and Investors, 2608 N. Laurent, Victoria, TX 77901 / 512-578-1258; FAX: 512-578-3559

Jamison's Forge Works, 4527 Rd. 6.5 NE, Moses Lake, WA 98837 / 509-762-2659

Jantz Supply, P.O. Box 584-GD, Davis, OK 73030-0584 / 580-369-2316; FAX: 580-369-3082

Jarrett Rifles, Inc., 383 Brown Rd., Jackson, SC 29831 / 803-471-3616

Jarvis, Inc., 1123 Cherry Orchard Lane, Hamilton, MT 59840 / 406-961-4392

JAS, Inc., P.O. Box 0, Rosemount, MN 55068 / 612-890-7631

Javelina Lube Products, P.O. Box 337, San Bernardino, CA 92402 / 714-882-5847; FAX: 714-434-6937

JB Custom, P.O. Box 6912, Leawood, KS 66206 / 913-381-2329

Jeff W. Flannery Engraving Co., 11034 Riddles Run Rd., Union, KY 41091 / 606-384-3127

Jeffredo Gunsight, P.O. Box 669, San Marcos, CA 92079 / 619-728-2695

Jena Eur, PO Box 319, Dunmore, PA 18512

Jenco Sales, Inc., P.O. Box 1000, Manchaca, TX 78652 / 800-531-5301 FAX: 800-266-2373

Jenkins Recoil Pads, Inc., 5438 E. Frontage Ln., Olney, IL 62450 / 618-395-3416

Jensen Bullets, 86 North, 400 West, Blackfoot, ID 83221 / 208-785-5590

Jensen's Custom Ammunition, 5146 E. Pima, Tucson, AZ 85712 / 602-325-3346 FAX: 602-322-5704

Jensen's Firearms Academy, 1280 W. Prince, Tucson, AZ 85705 / 602-293-8516

Jericho Tool & Die Co., Inc., RD 3 Box 70, Route 7, Bainbridge, NY 13733-9496 / 607-563-8222; FAX: 607-563-8560

Jerry Phillips Optics, P.O. Box L632, Langhorne, PA 19047 / 215-757-5037 FAX: 215-757-7097

Jesse W. Smith Saddlery, 16909 E. Jackson Road, Elk, WA 99009-9600 / 509-325-0622

Jester Bullets, Rt. 1 Box 27, Orienta, OK 73737

Jewell Triggers, Inc., 3620 Hwy. 123, San Marcos, TX 78666 / 512-353-2999

JGS Precision Tool Mfg., 100 Main Sumner, Coos Bay, OR 97420 / 541-267-4331 FAX: 541-267-5996

Jim Chambers Flintlocks Ltd., Rt. 1, Box 513-A, Candler, NC 28715 / 704-667-8361

Jim Garthwaite Pistolsmith, Inc., Rt. 2 Box 310, Watsontown, PA 17777 / 717-538-1566

Jim Noble Co., 1305 Columbia St, Vancouver, WA 98660 / 360-695-1309; FAX: 360-695-6835 jnobleco@aol.com

Jim Norman Custom Gunstocks, 14281 Cane Rd, Valley Center, CA 92082 / 619-749-6252

Jim's Gun Shop (See Spradlin's)

Jim's Precision, Jim Ketchum, 1725 Moclips Dr., Petaluma, CA 94952 / 707-762-3014

JLK Bullets, 414 Turner Rd., Dover, AR 72837 / 501-331-4194

Johanssons Vapentillbehor, Bert, S-430 20, Veddige, SWEDEN

John Hall Plastics, Inc., Inc., P.O. Box 1526, Alvin, TX 77512 / 713-489-8709

John J. Adams & Son Engravers, PO Box 66, Vershire, VT 05079 / 802-685-0019

John Masen Co. Inc., 1305 Jelmak, Grand Prairie, TX 75050 / 817-430-8732; FAX: 817-430-1715

John Norrell Arms, 2608 Grist Mill Rd, Little Rock, AR 72207 / 501-225-7864

John Partridge Sales Ltd., Trent Meadows Rugeley, Staffordshire, WS15 2HS ENGLAND

John Rigby & Co., 1317 Spring St., Paso Robles, CA 93446 / 805-227-4236; FAX: 805-227-4723

John Uvertl Optical Co., Inc., 308-310 Clay Ave., Mars, PA 16046-0818 / 724-625-3810

John's Custom Leather, 523 S. Liberty St., Blairsville, PA 15717 / 412-459-6802

Johnny Stewart Game Calls, Inc., P.O. Box 7954, 5100 Fort Ave., Waco, TX 76714 / 817-772-3261; FAX: 817-772-3670

Johnson Wood Products, 34968 Crystal Road, Strawberry Point, IA 52076 / 319-933-4930

Johnson's Gunsmithing, Inc, Neal, 208 W Buchanan St, Ste B, Colorado Springs, CO 80907 / 800-284-8671; FAX: 719-632-3493

Johnston Bros. (See C&T Corp. TA Johnson Brothers)

Johnston, James (See North Fork Custom Gunsmithing, James Johnston)

Jonad Corp., 2091 Lakeland Ave., Lakewood, OH 44107 / 216-226-3161

Jonathan Arthur Ciener, Inc., 8700 Commerce St., Cape Canaveral, FL 32920 / 407-868-2200; FAX: 407-868-2201

MANUFACTURER'S DIRECTORY

Jones Co., Dale, 680 Hoffman Draw, Kila, MT 59920 / 406-755-4684

Jones Custom Products, Neil A., 17217 Brookhouser Rd., Saegertown, PA 16433 / 814-763-2769; FAX: 814-763-4228

Jones Moulds, Paul, 4901 Telegraph Rd, Los Angeles, CA 90022 / 213-262-1510

Jones, J.D./SSK Industries, 590 Woodvue Ln., Wintersville, OH 43953 / 740-264-0176; FAX: 740-264-2257

JP Sales, Box 307, Anderson, TX 77830

JRP Custom Bullets, RR2 2233 Carlton Rd., Whitehall, NY 12887 / 518-282-0084 or 802-438-5548

JS Worldwide DBA (See Coonan Arms)

JSL Ltd (See U.S. Importer-Specialty Shooters Supply, Inc.)

Juenke, Vern, 25 Bitterbush Rd., Reno, NV 89523 / 702-345-0225

Jumbo Sports Products, J. M. Bucheimer, 721 N. 20th St., St. Louis, MO 63103 / 314-241-1020

Jungkind, Reeves C., 5001 Buckskin Pass, Austin, TX 78745-2841 / 512-442-1094

Jurras, L. E., P.O. Box 680, Washington, IN 47501 / 812-254-7698

Justin Phillippi Custom Bullets, P.O. Box 773, Ligonier, PA 15658 / 412-238-9671

▬▬ K ▬▬

K&M Industries, Inc., Box 66, 510 S. Main, Troy, ID 83871 / 208-835-2281; FAX: 208-835-5211

K&M Services, 5430 Salmon Run Rd., Dover, PA 17315 / 717-292-3175; FAX: 717-292-3175

K-D, Inc., Box 459, 585 N. Hwy. 155, Cleveland, UT 84518 / 801-653-2530

K-Sports Imports Inc., 2755 Thompson Creek Rd., Pomona, CA 91767 / 909-392-2345 FAX: 909-392-2354

K. Eversull Co., Inc., 1 Tracemont, Boyce, LA 71409 / 318-793-8728

K.B.I. Inc, PO Box 6625, Harrisburg, PA 17112 / 717-540-8518; FAX: 717-540-8567

K.K. Arms Co., Star Route Box 671, Kerrville, TX 78028 / 210-257-4718 FAX: 210-257-4891

K.L. Null Holsters Ltd., 161 School St. NW, Hill City Station, Resaca, GA 30735 / 706-625-5643; FAX: 706-625-9392

Ka Pu Kapili, P.O. Box 745, Honokaa, HI 96727 / 808-776-1644; FAX: 808-776-1731

KA-BAR Knives, 1116 E. State St., Olean, NY 14760 / 800-282-0130; FAX: 716-373-6245

Kahles A Swarovski Company, 1 Wholesale Way, Cranston, RI 02920-5540 / 401-946-2220; FAX: 401-946-2587

Kahr Arms, P.O. Box 220, 630 Route 303, Blauvelt, NY 10913 / 914-353-5996; FAX: 914-353-7833

Kalispel Case Line, P.O. Box 267, Cusick, WA 99119 / 509-445-1121

Kamik Outdoor Footwear, 554 Montee de Liesse, Montreal, PQ H4T 1P1 CANADA / 514-341-3950; FAX: 514-341-1861

Kamyk Engraving Co., Steve, 9 Grandview Dr, Westfield, MA 01085-1810 / 413-568-0457

Kane, Edward, P.O. Box 385, Ukiah, CA 95482 / 707-462-2937

Kane Products, Inc., 5572 Brecksville Rd., Cleveland, OH 44131 / 216-524-9962

Kapro Mfg.Co. Inc. (See R.E.I.)

Kasenit Co., Inc., 13 Park Ave., Highland Mills, NY 10930 / 914-928-9595; FAX: 914-928-7292

Kasmarsik Bullets, 4016 7th Ave. SW, Puyallup, WA 98373

Kaswer Custom, Inc., 13 Surrey Drive, Brookfield, CT 06804 / 203-775-0564; FAX: 203-775-6872

KDF, Inc., 2485 Hwy. 46 N., Seguin, TX 78155 / 210-379-8141; FAX: 210-379-5420

KeeCo Impressions, Inc., 346 Wood Ave., North Brunswick, NJ 08902 / 800-468-0546

Keeler, R. H., 817 "N" St., Port Angeles, WA 98362 / 206-457-4702

Kehr, Roger, 2131 Agate Ct. SE, Lacy, WA 98503 / 360-456-0831

Keith's Bullets, 942 Twisted Oak, Algonquin, IL 60102 / 708-658-3520

Keith's Custom Gunstocks (See Heppler, Keith M)

Keith's Custom Gunstocks, Keith M Heppler, 540 Banyan Circle, Walnut Creek, CA 94598 / 925-934-3509; FAX: 925-934-3143

Kel-Tec CNC Industries, Inc., P.O. Box 3427, Cocoa, FL 32924 / 407-631-0068; FAX: 407-631-1169

Kelbly, Inc., 7222 Dalton Fox Lake Rd., North Lawrence, OH 44666 / 216-683-4674; FAX: 216-683-7349

Kelley's, P.O. Box 125, Woburn, MA 01801 / 617-935-3389

Kellogg's Professional Products, 325 Pearl St., Sandusky, OH 44870 / 419-625-6551; FAX: 419-625-6167

Kelly, Lance, 1723 Willow Oak Dr., Edgewater, FL 32132 / 904-423-4933

Kemen America, 2550 Hwy. 23, Wrenshall, MN 55797

Ken Eyster Heritage Gunsmiths, Inc., 6441 Bishop Rd., Centerburg, OH 43011 / 614-625-6131

Ken Starnes Gunmaker, 15940 SW Holly Hill Rd, Hillsboro, OR 97123-9033 / 503-628-0705; FAX: 503-628-6005

Ken's Gun Specialties, Rt. 1, Box 147, Lakeview, AR 72642 / 501-431-5606

Ken's Kustom Kartridges, 331 Jacobs Rd., Hubbard, OH 44425 / 216-534-4595

Ken's Rifle Blanks, Ken McCullough, Rt. 2, P.O. Box 85B, Weston, OR 97886 / 503-566-3879

Keng's Firearms Specialty, Inc./US Tactical Systems, 875 Wharton Dr., P.O. Box 44405, Atlanta, GA 30336-1405 / 404-691-7611; FAX: 404-505-8445

Kennebec Journal, 274 Western Ave., Augusta, ME 04330 / 207-622-6288

Kennedy Firearms, 10 N. Market St., Muncy, PA 17756 / 717-546-6695

Kenneth W. Warren Engraver, P.O. Box 2842, Wenatchee, WA 98807 / 509-663-6123 FAX: 509-665-6123

KenPatable Ent., Inc., P.O. Box 19422, Louisville, KY 40259 / 502-239-5447

Kent Cartridge America, Inc, PO Box 849, 1000 Zigor Rd, Kearneysville, WV 25430

Kent Cartridge Mfg. Co. Ltd., Unit 16 Branbridges Industrial Esta, Tonbridge, Kent, ENGLAND / 622-872255; FAX: 622-872645

Keowee Game Calls, 608 Hwy. 25 North, Travelers Rest, SC 29690 / 864-834-7204; FAX: 864-834-7831

Kershaw Knives, 25300 SW Parkway Ave., Wilsonville, OR 97070 / 503-682-1966 or 800-325-2891; FAX: 503-682-7168

Kesselring Gun Shop, 400 Hwy. 99 North, Burlington, WA 98233 / 206-724-3113; FAX: 206-724-7003

Ketchum, Jim (See Jim's Precision)

Kickeez Inc, 301 Industrial Dr, Carl Junction, MO 64834-8806 / 419-649-2100; FAX: 417-649-2200 kickey@ipa.net

Kilham & Co., Main St., P.O. Box 37, Lyme, NH 03768 / 603-795-4112

Kim Ahrends Custom Firearms, Inc., Box 203, Clarion, IA 50525 / 515-532-3449; FAX: 515-532-3926

Kimar (See U.S. Importer-IAR,Inc)

Kimball, Gary, 1526 N. Circle Dr., Colorado Springs, CO 80909 / 719-634-1274

Kimber of America, Inc., 1 Lawton St., Yonkers, NY 10705 / 800-880-2418; FAX: 914-964-9340

King & Co., P.O. Box 1242, Bloomington, IL 61702 / 309-473-2161

King's Gun Works, 1837 W. Glenoaks Blvd., Glendale, CA 91201 / 818-956-6010; FAX: 818-548-8606

Kingyon, Paul L. (See Custom Calls)

Kirkpatrick Leather Co., PO Box 677, Laredo, TX 78040 / 956-723-6631; FAX: 956-725-0672

KK Air International (See Impact Case Co.)

KLA Enterprises, P.O. Box 2028, Eaton Park, FL 33840 / 941-682-2829 FAX: 941-682-2829

Kleen-Bore,Inc., 16 Industrial Pkwy., Easthampton, MA 01027 / 413-527-0300; FAX: 413-527-2522 info@kleen-bore.com www.kleen-bore.com

Klein Custom Guns, Don, 433 Murray Park Dr, Ripon, WI 54971 / 920-748-2931

Kleinendorst, K. W., RR 1, Box 1500, Hop Bottom, PA 18824 / 717-289-4687

Klingler Woodcarving, P.O. Box 141, Thistle Hill, Cabot, VT 05647 / 802-426-3811

Kmount, P.O. Box 19422, Louisville, KY 40259 / 502-239-5447

Kneiper, James, P.O. Box 1516, Basalt, CO 81621-1516 / 303-963-9880

Knife Importers, Inc., P.O. Box 1000, Manchaca, TX 78652 / 512-282-6860

Knight & Hale Game Calls, Box 468, Industrial Park, Cadiz, KY 42211 / 502-924-1755; FAX: 502-924-1763

Knight Rifles, 21852 hwy j46, P.O. Box 130, Centerville, IA 52544 / 515-856-2626; FAX: 515-856-2628

Knight Rifles (See Modern Muzzle Loading, Inc.)

Knight's Mfg. Co., 7750 9th St. SW, Vero Beach, FL 32968 / 561-562-5697; FAX: 561-569-2955

Knippel, Richard, 500 Gayle Ave Apt 213, Modesto, CA 95350-4241 / 209-869-1469

Knock on Wood Antiques, 355 Post Rd., Darien, CT 06820 / 203-655-9031

Knoell, Doug, 9737 McCardle Way, Santee, CA 92071

Koevenig's Engraving Service, Box 55 Rabbit Gulch, Hill City, SD 57745 / 605-574-2239

KOGOT, 410 College, Trinidad, CO 81082 / 719-846-9406 FAX: 719-846-9406

Kokolus, Michael M. (See Custom Riflestocks, Inc., Michael M. Kokolus)

Kolar, 1925 Roosevelt Ave, Racine, WI 53406 / 414-554-0800; FAX: 414-554-9093

Kolpin Mfg., Inc., P.O. Box 107, 205 Depot St., Fox Lake, WI 53933 / 414-928-3118; FAX: 414-928-3687

Korth, Robert-Bosch-Str. 4, PO Box 1320, 23909 Ratzeburg, GERMANY / 451-4991497; FAX: 451-4993230

Korzinek Riflesmith, J, RD 2 Box 73D, Canton, PA 17724 / 717-673-8512

Koval Knives, 5819 Zarley St., Suite A, New Albany, OH 43054 / 614-855-0777; FAX: 614-855-0945

Kowa Optimed, Inc., 20001 S. Vermont Ave., Torrance, CA 90502 / 310-327-1913; FAX: 310-327-4177

Kramer Designs, P.O. Box 129, Clancy, MT 59634 / 406-933-8658; FAX: 406-933-8658

Kramer Handgun Leather, P.O. Box 112154, Tacoma, WA 98411 / 206-564-6652; FAX: 206-564-1214

Krause Publications, Inc., 700 E. State St., Iola, WI 54990 / 715-445-2214; FAX: 715-445-4087

Krico Jagd-und Sportwaffen GmbH, Nurnbergerstrasse 6, D-90602, Pyrbaum, GERMANY / 09180-2780; FAX: 09180-2661

Krieger Barrels, Inc., N114 W18697 Clinton Dr., Germantown, WI 53022 / 414-255-9593; FAX: 414-255-9586

Krieghoff Gun Co., H., Boschstrasse 22, D-89079 Elm, GERMANY or 731-4018270

Krieghoff International,Inc., 7528 Easton Rd., Ottsville, PA 18942 / 610-847-5173; FAX: 610-847-8691

Kris Mounts, 108 Lehigh St., Johnstown, PA 15905 / 814-539-9751

KSN Industries Ltd (See U.S. Importer-Israel Arms International, Inc.,)

Kudlas, John M., 622 14th St. SE, Rochester, MN 55904 / 507-288-5579

Kulis Freeze Dry Taxidermy, 725 Broadway Ave., Bedford, OH 44146 / 216-232-8352; FAX: 216-232-7305 jkulis@kastaway.com

KVH Industries, Inc., 110 Enterprise Center, Middletown, RI 02842 / 401-847-3327; FAX: 401-849-0045

Kwik Mount Corp., P.O. Box 19422, Louisville, KY 40259 / 502-239-5447

Kwik-Site Co., 5555 Treadwell, Wayne, MI 48184 / 734-326-1500; FAX: 734-326-4120

▬▬ L ▬▬

L&R Lock Co., 1137 Pocalla Rd., Sumter, SC 29150 / 803-775-6127 FAX: 803-775-5171

L&S Technologies Inc (See Aimtech Mount Systems)

L. Bengtson Arms Co., 6345-B E. Akron St., Mesa, AZ 85205 / 602-981-6375

L.A.R. Mfg., Inc., 4133 W. Farm Rd., West Jordan, UT 84088 / 801-280-3505; FAX: 801-280-1972

L.E. Wilson, Inc., Box 324, 404 Pioneer Ave., Cashmere, WA 98815 / 509-782-1328; FAX: 509-782-7200

L.L. Bean, Inc., Freeport, ME 04032 / 207-865-4761; FAX: 207-552-2802

L.P.A. Snc, Via Alfieri 26, Gardone V.T., Brescia, ITALY / 30-891-14-81; FAX: 30-891-09-51

L.R. Clift Mfg., 3821 Hammonton Rd., Marysville, CA 95901 / 916-755-3390; FAX: 916-755-3393

L.S. Starrett Co., 121 Crescent St., Athol, MA 01331 / 617-249-3551

L.W. Seecamp Co., Inc., P.O. Box 255, New Haven, CT 06502 / 203-877-3429

La Clinique du .45, 1432 Rougemont, Chambly,, PQ J3L 2L8 CANADA / 514-658-1144

Labanu, Inc., 2201-F Fifth Ave., Ronkonkoma, NY 11779 / 516-467-6197; FAX: 516-981-4112

LaBoone, Pat. (See CLEAR CREEK OUTDOORS)

LaBounty Precision Reboring, Inc, 7968 Silver Lake Rd., PO Box 186, Maple Falls, WA 98266 / 360-599-2047 FAX: 360-599-3018

LaCrosse Footwear, Inc., P.O. Box 1328, La Crosse, WI 54602 / 608-782-3020 or 800-323-2668; FAX: 800-658-9444

LaFrance Specialties, P.O. Box 87933, San Diego, CA 92138-7933 / 619-293-3373; FAX: 619-293-7087

Lage Uniwad, P.O. Box 2302, Davenport, IA 52809 / 319-388-LAGE; FAX: 319-388-LAGE

Lair, Sam, 520 E. Beaver, Jenks, OK 74037 / 918-299-2391

Lake Center, P.O. Box 38, St. Charles, MO 63302 / 314-946-7500

Lakefield Arms Ltd (See Savage Arms Inc)

Lakewood Products LLC, 275 June St., Berlin, WI 54923 / 800-872-8458; FAX: 920-361-7719

Lamboy, Stephen. (See ITHACA CLASSIC DOUBLES)

Lampert, Ron, Rt. 1, Box 177, Guthrie, MN 56461 / 218-854-7345

Lamson & Goodnow Mfg. Co., 45 Conway St., Shelburne Falls, MA 03170 / 413-625-6564; or 800-872-6564 FAX: 413-625-9816 www.lamsonsharp.com

Lanber Armas, S.A., Zubiaurre 5, Zaldibar, 48250 SPAIN / 34-4-6827702; FAX: 34-4-6827999

Langenberg Hat Co., P.O. Box 1860, Washington, MO 63090 / 800-428-1860; FAX: 314-239-3151

Lanphert, Paul, P.O. Box 1985, Wenatchee, WA 98807

Lansky Levine, Arthur. (See LANSKY SHARPENERS)

Lansky Sharpeners, Arthur Lansky Levine, PO Box 50830, Las Vegas, NV 89016 / 702-361-7511; FAX: 702-896-9511

Lapua Ltd., P.O. Box 5, Lapua, FINLAND / 6-310111; FAX: 6-4388991

LaRocca Gun Works, 51 Union Place, Worcester, MA 01608 / 508-754-2887; FAX: 508-754-2887

Larry Lyons Gunworks, 110 Hamilton St., Dowagiac, MI 49047 / 616-782-9478

Laser Devices, Inc., 2 Harris Ct. A-4, Monterey, CA 93940 / 408-373-0701; FAX: 408-373-0903

Laseraim Technologies, Inc., P.O. Box 3548, Little Rock, AR 72203 / 501-375-2227

LaserMax, Inc., 3495 Winton Place, Bldg. B, Rochester, NY 14623-2807 / 800-527-3703 FAX: 716-272-5427

Lassen Community College, Gunsmithing Dept., P.O. Box 3000, Hwy. 139, Susanville, CA 96130 / 916-251-8800; FAX: 916-251-8838

Lathrop's, Inc., Inc., 5146 E. Pima, Tucson, AZ 85712 / 520-881-0266 or 800-875-4867; FAX: 520-322-5704

Laughridge, William R (See Cylinder & Slide Inc)

Laurel Mountain Forge, P.O. Box 52, Crown Point, IN 48065 / 219-548-2950; FAX: 219-548-2950

Laurona Armas Eibar, S.A.L., Avenida de Otaola 25, P.O. Box 260, Eibar 20600, SPAIN / 34-43-700600; FAX: 34-43-700616

Lawrence Brand Shot (See Precision Reloading, Inc.)

Lawrence Leather Co., P.O. Box 1479, Lillington, NC 27546 / 910-893-2071; FAX: 910-893-4742

Lawson Co., Harry, 3328 N Richey Blvd., Tucson, AZ 85716 / 520-326-1117 FAX: 520-326-1117

Lawson, John. (See THE SIGHT SHOP)

Lawson, John G (See Sight Shop, The)

Lazzeroni Arms Co., PO Box 26696, Tucson, AZ 85726 / 888-492-7247; FAX: 520-624-4250

LBT, HCR 62, Box 145, Moyie Springs, ID 83845 / 208-267-3588

Le Clear Industries (See E-Z-Way Systems), PO Box 4310, Newark, OH 43058-4310 / 614-345-6645; FAX: 614-345-6600

Lea Mfg. Co., 237 E. Aurora St., Waterbury, CT 06720 / 203-753-5116

Leapers, Inc., 7675 Five Mile Rd., Northville, MI 48167 / 248-486-1231; FAX: 248-486-1430

Leatherman Tool Group, Inc., 12106 NE Ainsworth Cir., P.O. Box 20595, Portland, OR 97294 / 503-253-7826; FAX: 503-253-7830

Lebeau-Courally, Rue St. Gilles, 386 4000, Liege, BELGIUM / 042-52-48-43; FAX: 32-042-52-20-08

Leckie Professional Gunsmithing, 546 Quarry Rd., Ottsville, PA 18942 / 215-847-8594

Lectro Science, Inc., 6410 W. Ridge Rd., Erie, PA 16506 / 814-833-6487; FAX: 814-833-0447

Ledbetter Airguns, Riley, 1804 E Sprague St, Winston Salem, NC 27107-3521 / 919-784-0676

Lee Co., T. K., 1282 Branchwater Ln, Birmingham, AL 35216 / 205-913-5222

Lee Precision, Inc., 4275 Hwy. U, Hartford, WI 53027 / 414-673-3075; FAX: 414-673-9273 leeprecision.com

Lee Supplies, Mark, 9901 France Ct., Lakeville, MN 55044 / 612-461-2114

Lee's Red Ramps, 4 Kristine Ln., Silver City, NM 88061 / 505-538-8529

LeFever Arms Co., Inc., 6234 Stokes, Lee Center Rd., Lee Center, NY 13363 / 315-337-6722; FAX: 315-337-1543

Legacy Sports International, 10 Prince St., Alexandria, VA 22314

Legend Products Corp., 21218 Saint Andrews Blvd., Boca Raton, FL 33433-2435

Leibowitz, Leonard, 1205 Murrayhill Ave., Pittsburgh, PA 15217 / 412-361-5455

Leica USA, Inc., 156 Ludlow Ave., Northvale, NJ 07647 / 201-767-7500; FAX: 201-767-8666

LEM Gun Specialties Inc. The Lewis Lead Remover, P.O. Box 2855, Peachtree City, GA 30269-2024

Leonard Day, 6 Linseed Rd Box 1, West Hatfield, MA 01088-7505 / 413-337-8369

Les Baer Custom,Inc., 29601 34th Ave., Hillsdale, IL 61257 / 309-658-2716; FAX: 309-658-2610

Lestrom Laboratories, Inc., P.O. Box 628, Mexico, NY 13114-0628 / 315-343-3076; FAX: 315-592-3370

Lethal Force Institute (See Police Bookshelf), PO Box 122, Concord, NH 03301 / 603-224-6814; FAX: 603-226-3554

Lett Custom Grips, 672 Currier Rd., Hopkinton, NH 03229-2652 / 800-421-5388 FAX: 603-226-4580

Leupold & Stevens, Inc., 14400 NW Greenbrier Pky., Beaverton, OR 97006 / 503-646-9171; FAX: 503-526-1455

Lever Arms Service Ltd., 2131 Burrard St., Vancouver, BC V6J 3H7 CANADA / 604-736-2711; FAX: 604-738-3503

Lew Horton Dist. Co., Inc., 15 Walkup Dr., Westboro, MA 01581 / 508-366-7400; FAX: 508-366-5332

Liberty Metals, 2233 East 16th St., Los Angeles, CA 90021 / 213-581-9171; FAX: 213-581-9351

Liberty Safe, 1060 N. Spring Creek Pl., Springville, UT 84663 / 800-247-5625; FAX: 801-489-6409

Liberty Shooting Supplies, P.O. Box 357, Hillsboro, OR 97123 / 503-640-5518; FAX: 503-640-5518

Liberty Trouser Co., 3500 6 Ave S., Birmingham, AL 35222-2406 / 205-251-9143

Lightfield Ammunition Corp. (See Slug Group, Inc.), PO Box 376, New Paris, PA 15554 / 814-839-4517; FAX: 814-839-2601

Lightforce U.S.A. Inc., 19226 66th Ave. So., L-103, Kent, WA 98032 / 206-656-1577; FAX: 206-656-1578

Lightning Performance Innovations, Inc., RD1 Box 555, Mohawk, NY 13407 / 800-242-5873; FAX: 315-866-1578

Lilja Precision Rifle Barrels, P.O. Box 372, Plains, MT 59859 / 406-826-3084; FAX: 406-826-3083 lilja@riflebarrels.com www.riflebarrel.com

Lincoln, Dean, Box 1886, Farmington, NM 87401

Lind Custom Guns, Al, 7821 76th Ave SW, Tacoma, WA 98498 / 253-584-6361 lindcustguns@worldnot.att.net

Linder Solingen Knives, 4401 Sentry Dr., Tucker, GA 30084 / 770-939-6915; FAX: 770-939-6738

Lindsay, Steve, RR 2 Cedar Hills, Kearney, NE 68847 / 308-236-7885

Lindsley Arms Cartridge Co., P.O. Box 757, 20 College Hill Rd., Henniker, NH 03242 / 603-428-3127

Linebaugh Custom Sixguns, Route 2, Box 100, Maryville, MO 64468 / 660-562-3031 sixgunner.com

Lion Country Supply, P.O. Box 480, Port Matilda, PA 16870

List Precision Engineering, Unit 1 Ingley Works, 13 River Road, Barking, ENGLAND / 011-081-594-1686

Lithi Bee Bullet Lube, 1728 Carr Rd., Muskegon, MI 49442 / 616-788-4479

"Little John's" Antique Arms, 1740 W. Laveta, Orange, CA 92668

Little Trees Ramble (See Scott Pilkington, Little

Littler Sales Co., 20815 W. Chicago, Detroit, MI 48228 / 313-273-6888; FAX: 313-273-1099

Littleton, J. F., 275 Pinedale Ave., Oroville, CA 95966 / 916-533-6084

Ljutic Industries, Inc., 732 N. 16th Ave., Suite 22, Yakima, WA 98907 / 509-248-0476; FAX: 509-576-8233

Llama Gabilondo Y Cia, Apartado 290, E-01080, Victoria, spain SPAIN

Loch Leven Industries, P.O. Box 2751, Santa Rosa, CA 95405 / 707-573-8735; FAX: 707-573-0369

Lock's Philadelphia Gun Exchange, 6700 Rowland Ave., Philadelphia, PA 19149 / 215-332-6225; FAX: 215-332-4800

Lodewick, Walter H., 2816 NE Halsey St., Portland, OR 97232 / 503-284-2554

Log Cabin Sport Shop, 8010 Lafayette Rd., Lodi, OH 44254 / 330-948-1082; FAX: 330-948-4307

Logan, Harry M., Box 745, Honokaa, HI 96727 / 808-776-1644

Lohman Mfg. Co., Inc., 4500 Doniphan Dr., P.O. Box 220, Neosho, MO 64850 / 417-451-4438; FAX: 417-451-2576

Lomont Precision Bullets, RR 1, Box 34, Salmon, ID 83467 / 208-756-6819; FAX: 208-756-6824

London Guns Ltd., Box 3750, Santa Barbara, CA 93130 / 805-683-4141; FAX: 805-683-1712

Lone Star Gunleather, 1301 Brushy Bend Dr., Round Rock, TX 78681 / 512-255-1805

Lone Star Rifle Company, 11231 Rose Road, Conroe, TX 77303 / 409-856-3363

Long, George F., 1500 Rogue River Hwy., Ste. F, Grants Pass, OR 97527 / 541-476-7552

Lortone Inc., 2856 NW Market St., Seattle, WA 98107

Lothar Walther Precision Tool Inc., 3425 Hutchinson Rd., Cumming, GA 30040 / 770-889-9998; FAX: 770-889-4918 lotharwalther@mindspring.com www.lothar-walther.com

Loweth, Richard H.R., 29 Hedgegrow Lane, Kirby Muxloe, Leics, LE9 2BN ENGLAND / (0) 116 238 6295

LPS Laboratories, Inc., 4647 Hugh Howell Rd., P.O. Box 3050, Tucker, GA 30084 / 404-934-7800

Lucas, Edward E, 32 Garfield Ave., East Brunswick, NJ 08816 / 201-251-5526

Lucas, Mike, 1631 Jessamine Rd., Lexington, SC 29073

Lupton, Keith. (See PAWLING MOUNTAIN CLUB)

Lutz Engraving, Ron E., E1998 Smokey Valley Rd, Scandinavia, WI 54977 / 715-467-2674

Lyman Instant Targets, Inc. (See Lyman Products, Corp.)

Lyman Products Corp., 475 Smith Street, Middletown, CT 06457-1541 / 860-632-2020 or 800-22-LYMAN FAX: 860-632-1699

Lyman Products Corporation, 475 Smith Street, Middletown, CT 06457-1529 / 800-22-LYMAN or 860-632-2020; FAX: 860-632-1699

Lyte Optronics (See TracStar Industries Inc)

M

M. Thys (See U.S. Importer-Champlin Firearms Inc)

M.H. Canjar Co., 500 E. 45th Ave., Denver, CO 80216 / 303-295-2638; FAX: 303-295-2638

M.O.A. Corp., 2451 Old Camden Pike, Eaton, OH 45320 / 937-456-3669

MA Systems, P.O. Box 1143, Chouteau, OK 74337 / 918-479-6378

Mac-1 Airgun Distributors, 13974 Van Ness Ave., Gardena, CA 90249 / 310-327-3581; FAX: 310-327-0238 mac1@concentric.net mac1airgun.com

Macbean, Stan, 754 North 1200 West, Orem, UT 84057 / 801-224-6446

Madis, George, P.O. Box 545, Brownsboro, TX 75756 / 903-852-6480

Madis Books, 2453 West Five Mile Pkwy., Dallas, TX 75233 / 214-330-7168

MAG Instrument, Inc., 1635 S. Sacramento Ave., Ontario, CA 91761 / 909-947-1006; FAX: 909-947-3116

Mag-Na-Port International, Inc., 41302 Executive Dr., Harrison Twp., MI 48045-1306 / 810-469-6727; FAX: 810-469-0425

Mag-Pack Corp., P.O. Box 846, Chesterland, OH 44026

Magma Engineering Co., P.O. Box 161, 20955 E. Ocotillo Rd., Queen Creek, AZ 85242 / 602-987-9008 FAX: 602-987-0148

Magnolia Sports,Inc., 211 W. Main, Magnolia, AR 71753 / 501-234-8410 or 800-530-7816; FAX: 501-234-8117

Magnum Power Products, Inc., P.O. Box 17768, Fountain Hills, AZ 85268

Magnum Research, Inc., 7110 University Ave. NE, Minneapolis, MN 55432 / 800-772-6168 or 612-574-1868; FAX: 612-574-0109 magnumresearch.com

Magnus Bullets, P.O. Box 239, Toney, AL 35773 / 256-420-8359; FAX: 256-420-8360

MagSafe Ammo Co., 4700 S US Highway 17/92, Casselberry, FL 32707-3814 / 407-834-9966; FAX: 407-834-8185

Magtech Ammunition Co. Inc., 837 Boston Rd #12, Madison, CT 06443 / 203-245-8983; FAX: 203-245-2883 rfinemtek@aol.com

Mahony, Philip Bruce, 67 White Hollow Rd., Lime Rock, CT 06039-2418 / 203-435-9341

Mahovsky's Metalife, R.D. 1, Box 149a Eureka Road, Grand Valley, PA 16420 / 814-436-7747

Maine Custom Bullets, RFD 1, Box 1755, Brooks, ME 04921

Maionchi-L.M.I., Via Di Coselli-Zona, Industriale Di Guamo 55060, Lucca, ITALY / 011 39-583 94291

Makinson, Nicholas, RR 3, Komoka, ON N0L 1R0 CANADA / 519-471-5462

Malcolm Enterprises, 1023 E. Prien Lake Rd., Lake Charles, LA 70601

Mallardtone Game Calls, 2901 16th St., Moline, IL 61265 / 309-762-8089

Mandall Shooting Supplies Inc., 3616 N. Scottsdale Rd., Scottsdale, AZ 85252 / 480-945-2553; FAX: 480-949-0734

Marathon Rubber Prods. Co., Inc., 1009 3rd St, Wausau, WI 54403-4765 / 715-845-6255

Marble Arms (See CRR, Inc./Marble's Inc.)

Marchmon Bullets, 8191 Woodland Shore Dr., Brighton, MI 48116

Marent, Rudolf, 9711 Tiltree St., Houston, TX 77075 / 713-946-7028

Mark Lee Supplies, 9901 France Ct., Lakeville, MN 55044 / 612-461-2114

Markell,Inc., 422 Larkfield Center 235, Santa Rosa, CA 95403 / 707-573-0792; FAX: 707-573-9867

Markesbery Muzzle Loaders, Inc., 7785 Foundation Dr., Ste. 6, Florence, KY 41042 / 606-342-5553; or 606-342-2380

Marksman Products, 5482 Argosy Dr., Huntington Beach, CA 92649 / 714-898-7535 or 800-822-8005; FAX: 714-891-0782

Marlin Firearms Co., 100 Kenna Dr., North Haven, CT 06473 / 203-239-5621; FAX: 203-234-7991

MarMik, Inc., 2116 S. Woodland Ave., Michigan City, IN 46360 / 219-872-7231; FAX: 219-872-7231

Marocchi F.lli S.p.A, Via Galileo Galilei 8, I-25068 Zanano, ITALY

Marquart Precision Co., (See Morrison Precision)

Marsh, Johnny, 1007 Drummond Dr., Nashville, TN 37211 / 615-833-3259

Marsh, Mike, Croft Cottage, Main St., Derbyshire, DE4 2BY ENGLAND / 01629 650 669

Marshall Enterprises, 792 Canyon Rd., Redwood City, CA 94062

Marshall F. Fish Mfg. Gunsmith Sptg. Co., Rd. Box 2439, Rt. 22 North, Westport, NY 12993 / 518-962-4897 FAX: 518-962-4897

Martin B. Retting Inc., 11029 Washington, Culver City, CA 90232 / 213-837-2412

Martin Hagn Rifles & Actions, P.O. Box 444, Cranbrook, BC V1C 4H9 CANADA / 604-489-4861

Martin's Gun Shop, 937 S. Sheridan Blvd., Lakewood, CO 80226 / 303-922-2184

Martz, John V., 8060 Lakeview Lane, Lincoln, CA 95648 FAX: 916-645-3815

Marvel, Alan, 3922 Madonna Rd., Jarretsville, MD 21084 / 301-557-6545

MANUFACTURER'S DIRECTORY

Marx, Harry (See U.S. Importer for FERLIB)

Maryland Paintball Supply, 8507 Harford Rd., Parkville, MD 21234 / 410-882-5607

MAST Technology, 4350 S. Arville, Suite 3, Las Vegas, NV 89103 / 702-362-5043; FAX: 702-362-9554

Master Engravers, Inc. (See Hendricks, Frank E)

Master Lock Co., 2600 N. 32nd St., Milwaukee, WI 53245 / 414-444-2800

Match Prep--Doyle Gracey, P.O. Box 155, Tehachapi, CA 93581 / 661-822-5383; FAX: 661-823-8680

Matco, Inc., 1003-2nd St., N. Manchester, IN 46962 / 219-982-8282

Mathews & Son, Inc., George E., 10224 S Paramount Blvd, Downey, CA 90241 / 562-862-6719; FAX: 562-862-6719

Matthews Cutlery, 4401 Sentry Dr., Tucker, GA 30084 / 770-939-6915

Mauser Werke Oberndorf Waffensysteme GmbH, Postfach 1349, 78722, Oberndorf/N., GERMANY

Maverick Arms, Inc., 7 Grasso Ave., P.O. Box 497, North Haven, CT 06473 / 203-230-5300; FAX: 203-230-5420

Maxi-Mount, P.O. Box 291, Willoughby Hills, OH 44094-0291 / 216-944-9456; FAX: 216-944-9456

Maximum Security Corp., 32841 Calle Perfecto, San Juan Capistrano, CA 92675 / 714-493-3684; FAX: 714-496-7733

Mayville Engineering Co. (See MEC, Inc.)

Mazur Restoration, Pete, 13083 Drummer Way, Grass Valley, CA 95949 / 530-268-2412

McBros Rifle Co., P.O. Box 86549, Phoenix, AZ 85080 / 602-582-3713; FAX: 602-581-3825

McCament, Jay, 1730-134th St. Ct. S., Tacoma, WA 98444 / 253-531-8832

McCann Industries, P.O. Box 641, Spanaway, WA 98387 / 253-537-6919; FAX: 253-537-6919 mccann.machine@att.net www.mccannindustries.com

McCann's Machine & Gun Shop, P.O. Box 641, Spanaway, WA 98387 / 253-537-6919; FAX: 253-537-6993 mccann.machine@att.net www.mccannindustries.com

McCann's Muzzle-Gun Works, 14 Walton Dr., New Hope, PA 18938 / 215-862-2728

McCluskey Precision Rifles, 10502 14th Ave. NW, Seattle, WA 98177 / 206-781-2776

McCombs, Leo, 1862 White Cemetery Rd., Patriot, OH 45658 / 614-256-1714

McCormick Corp., Chip, 1825 Fortview Rd Ste 115, Austin, TX 78704 / 800-328-CHIP; FAX: 512-462-0009

McCullough, Ken. (See KEN'S RIFLE BLANKS)

McDonald, Dennis, 8359 Brady St., Peosta, IA 52068 / 319-556-7940

McFarland, Stan, 2221 Idella Ct., Grand Junction, CO 81505 / 970-243-4704

McGhee, Larry. (See B.C. OUTDOORS)

McGowen Rifle Barrels, 5961 Spruce Lane, St. Anne, IL 60964 / 815-937-9816; FAX: 815-937-4024

McGuire, Bill, 1600 N. Eastmont Ave., East Wenatchee, WA 98802 / 509-884-6021

Mchalik, Gary. (See ROSSI FIREARMS, BRAZTECH)

McKenzie, Lynton, 6940 N. Alvernon Way, Tucson, AZ 85718 / 520-299-5090

McKillen & Heyer, Inc., 35535 Euclid Ave., Suite 11, Willoughby, OH 44094 / 216-942-2044

McKinney, R.P. (See Schuetzen Gun Co.)

McMillan Fiberglass Stocks, Inc., 21421 N. 14th Ave., Suite B, Phoenix, AZ 85027 / 602-582-9635; FAX: 602-581-3825

McMillan Optical Gunsight Co., 28638 N. 42nd St., Cave Creek, AZ 85331 / 602-585-7868; FAX: 602-585-7872

McMillan Rifle Barrels, P.O. Box 3427, Bryan, TX 77805 / 409-690-3456; FAX: 409-690-0156

McMurdo, Lynn (See Specialty Gunsmithing), PO Box 404, Afton, WY 83110 / 307-886-5535

MCRW Associates Shooting Supplies, R.R. 1, Box 1425, Sweet Valley, PA 18656 / 717-864-3967; FAX: 717-864-2669

MCS, Inc., 34 Delmar Dr., Brookfield, CT 06804 / 203-775-1013; FAX: 203-775-9462

McWelco Products, 6730 Santa Fe Ave., Hesperia, CA 92345 / 619-244-8876; FAX: 619-244-9398

MDS, P.O. Box 1441, Brandon, FL 33509-1441 / 813-653-1180; FAX: 813-684-5953

Meadow Industries, 24 Club Lane, Palmyra, VA 22963 / 804-589-7672; FAX: 804-589-7672

Measurement Group Inc., Box 27777, Raleigh, NC 27611

Measures, Leon. (See SHOOT WHERE YOU LOOK)

MEC, Inc., 715 South St., Mayville, WI 53050 / 414-387-4500; FAX: 414-387-5802 reloaders@mayul.com www.mayvl.com

MEC-Gar S.r.l., Via Madonnina 64, Gardone V.T. Brescia, ITALY / 39-30-8912687; FAX: 39-30-8910065

MEC-Gar U.S.A., Inc., Box 112, 500B Monroe Turnpike, Monroe, CT 06468 / 203-635-8662; FAX: 203-635-8662

Mech-Tech Systems, Inc., 1602 Foothill Rd., Kalispell, MT 59901 / 406-755-8055

Meister Bullets (See Gander Mountain)

Mele, Frank, 201 S. Wellow Ave., Cookeville, TN 38501 / 615-526-4860

Melton Shirt Co., Inc., 56 Harvester Ave., Batavia, NY 14020 / 716-343-8750; FAX: 716-343-6887

Men-Metallwerk Elisenhuette GmbH, P.O. Box 1263, Nassau/Lahn, D-56372 GERMANY / 2604-7819

Menck, Gunsmith Inc., T.W., 5703 S 77th St, Ralston, NE 68127

Mendez, John A., P.O. Box 620984, Orlando, FL 32862 / 407-344-2791

Meprolight (See Hesco-Meprolight)

Mercer Custom Stocks, R. M., 216 S Whitewater Ave, Jefferson, WI 53549 / 920-674-3839

Merit Corp., Box 9044, Schenectady, NY 12309 / 518-346-1420

Merkel Freres, Strasse 7 October, 10, Suhl, GERMANY

Merkuria Ltd., Argentinska 38, 17005, Praha 7 CZECH, REPUBLIC / 422-875117; FAX: 422-809152

Metal Merchants, PO Box 186, Walled Lake, MI 48390-0186

Metalife Industries (See Mahovsky's Metalife)

Metaloy, Inc., Rt. 5, Box 595, Berryville, AR 72616 / 501-545-3611

Metals Hand Engraver/European Hand Engraving, Ste. 216, 12 South First St., San Jose, CA 95113 / 408-293-6559

MI-TE Bullets, 1396 Ave. K, Ellsworth, KS 67439 / 785-472-4575; FAX: 785-472-5579

Michael's Antiques, Box 591, Waldoboro, ME 04572

Michaels Of Oregon, 1710 Red Soils Ct., Oregon City, OR 97045

Micro Sight Co., 242 Harbor Blvd., Belmont, CA 94002 / 415-591-0769; FAX: 415-591-7531

Microfusion Alfa S.A., Paseo San Andres N8, P.O. Box 271, Eibar, 20600 SPAIN / 34-43-11-89-16; FAX: 34-43-11-40-38

Mid-America Guns and Ammo, 1205 W. Jefferson, Suite E, Effingham, IL 62401 / 800-820-5177

Mid-America Recreation, Inc., 1328 5th Ave., Moline, IL 61265 / 309-764-5089; FAX: 309-764-2722

Middlebrooks Custom Shop, 7366 Colonial Trail East, Surry, VA 23883 / 757-357-0881; FAX: 757-365-0442

Midway Arms, Inc., 5875 W. Van Horn Tavern Rd., Columbia, MO 65203 / 800-243-3220 or 573-445-6363; FAX: 573-446-1018

Midwest Gun Sport, 1108 Herbert Dr., Zebulon, NC 27597 / 919-269-5570

Midwest Sport Distributors, Box 129, Fayette, MO 65248

Mike Davis Products, 643 Loop Dr., Moses Lake, WA 98837 / 509-765-6178 or 509-766-7281

Milberry House Publishing, PO Box 575, Corydon, IN 47112 / 888-738-1567; FAX: 888-738-1567

Military Armament Corp., P.O. Box 120, Mt. Zion Rd., Lingleville, TX 76461 / 817-965-3253

Millennium Designed Muzzleloaders, PO Box 536, Routes 11 & 25, Limington, ME 04049 / 207-637-2316

Miller Arms, Inc., P.O. Box 260 Purl St., St. Onge, SD 57779 / 605-642-5160; FAX: 605-642-5160

Miller Custom, 210 E. Julia, Clinton, IL 61727 / 217-935-9362

Miller Single Trigger Mfg. Co., Rt. 209, Box 1275, Millersburg, PA 17061 / 717-692-3704

Millett Sights, 7275 Murdy Circle, Adm. Office, Huntington Beach, CA 92647 / 714-842-5575 or 800-645-5388; FAX: 714-843-5707

Mills Jr., Hugh B., 3615 Canterbury Rd., New Bern, NC 28560 / 919-637-4631

Milstor Corp., 80-975 Indio Blvd., Indio, CA 92201 / 760-775-9998; FAX: 760-775-5229 milstor@webtv.net

Miltex, Inc., 700 S Lee St, Alexandria, VA 22314-4332 / 888-642-9123; FAX: 301-645-1430

Minute Man High Tech Industries, 10611 Canyon Rd. E., Suite 151, Puyallup, WA 98373 / 800-233-2734

Mirador Optical Corp., P.O. Box 11614, Marina Del Rey, CA 90295-7614 / 310-821-5587; FAX: 310-305-0386

Miroku, B C/Daly, Charles (See U.S. Importer-Bell's)

Mitchell, Jack, c/o Geoff Gaebe, Addieville East Farm, 200 Pheasant Dr, Mapleville, RI 02839 / 401-568-3185

Mitchell Bullets, R.F., 430 Walnut St, Westernport, MD 21562

Mitchell Optics, Inc., 2072 CR 1100 N, Sidney, IL 61877 / 217-688-2219 or 217-621-3018; FAX: 217-688-2505

Mitchell's Accuracy Shop, 68 Greenridge Dr., Stafford, VA 22554 / 703-659-0165

Mittermeier, Inc., Frank, PO Box 2G, 3577 E Tremont Ave, Bronx, NY 10465 / 718-828-3843

Mixson Corp., 7635 W. 28th Ave., Hialeah, FL 33016 / 305-821-5190 or 800-327-0078; FAX: 305-558-9318

MJK Gunsmithing, Inc., 417 N. Huber Ct., E. Wenatchee, WA 98802 / 509-884-7683

MJM Mfg., 3283 Rocky Water Ln., Suite B, San Jose, CA 95148 / 408-270-4207

MKS Supply, Inc. (See Hi-Point Firearms)

MMC, 2513 East Loop 820 North, Ft. Worth, TX 76118 / 817-595-0404; FAX: 817-595-3074

MMP, Rt. 6, Box 384, Harrison, AR 72601 / 501-741-5019; FAX: 501-741-3104

Mo's Competitor Supplies (See MCS Inc)

Modern Gun Repair School, P.O. Box 92577, Southlake, TX 76092 / 800-493-4114; FAX: 800-556-5112

Modern Muzzleloading, Inc, PO Box 130, Centerville, IA 52544 / 515-856-2626

Moeller, Steve, 1213 4th St., Fulton, IL 61252 / 815-589-2300

Molin Industries, Tru-Nord Division, P.O. Box 365, 204 North 9th St., Brainerd, MN 56401 / 218-829-2870

Monell Custom Guns, 228 Red Mills Rd., Pine Bush, NY 12566 / 914-744-3021

Moneymaker Guncraft Corp., 1420 Military Ave., Omaha, NE 68131 / 402-556-0226

Montana Armory, Inc (See C. Sharps Arms Co. Inc.), 100 Centennial, Box 885, Big Timber, MT 59011 / 406-932-4353

Montana Outfitters, Lewis E. Yearout, 308 Riverview Dr. E., Great Falls, MT 59404 / 406-761-0859

Montana Precision Swaging, P.O. Box 4746, Butte, MT 59702 / 406-782-7502

Montana Vintage Arms, 2354 Bear Canyon Rd., Bozeman, MT 59715

Montgomery Community College, P.O. Box 787-GD, Troy, NC 27371 / 910-576-6222 or 800-839-6222; FAX: 910-576-2176

Morini (See U.S. Importers-Mandall Shooting Supplies, Inc.,)

Morrison Custom Rifles, J. W., 4015 W Sharon, Phoenix, AZ 85029 / 602-978-3754

Morrison Precision, 6719 Calle Mango, Hereford, AZ 85615 / 520-378-6207 / morprec@c2i2.com (e-mail)

Morrow, Bud, 11 Hillside Lane, Sheridan, WY 82801-9729 / 307-674-8360

Morton Booth Co., P.O. Box 123, Joplin, MO 64802 / 417-673-1962; FAX: 417-673-3642

Moss Double Tone, Inc., P.O. Box 1112, 2101 S. Kentucky, Sedalia, MO 65301 / 816-827-0827

Mountain Hollow Game Calls, Box 121, Cascade, MD 21719 / 301-241-3282

Mountain Plains, Inc., 244 Glass Hollow Rd., Alton, VA 22920 / 800-687-3000

Mountain Rifles, Inc., P.O. Box 2789, Palmer, AK 99645 / 907-373-4194; FAX: 907-373-4195

Mountain South, P.O. Box 381, Barnwell, SC 29812 / FAX: 803-259-3227

Mountain State Muzzleloading Supplies, Inc., Box 154-1, Rt. 2, Williamstown, WV 26187 / 304-375-7842; FAX: 304-375-3737

Mountain View Sports, Inc., Box 188, Troy, NH 03465 / 603-357-9690; FAX: 603-357-9691

Mowrey Gun Works, P.O. Box 246, Waldron, IN 46182 / 317-525-6181; FAX: 317-525-9595

Mowrey's Guns & Gunsmithing, 119 Fredericks St., Canajoharie, NY 13317 / 518-673-3483

MPC, P.O. Box 450, McMinnville, TN 37110-0450 / 615-473-5513; FAX: 615-473-5516

MPI Stocks, PO Box 83266, Portland, OR 97283 / 503-226-1215; FAX: 503-226-2661

MSC Industrial Supply Co., 151 Sunnyside Blvd., Plainview, NY 11803-9915 / 516-349-0330

MSR Targets, P.O. Box 1042, West Covina, CA 91793 / 818-331-7840

Mt. Alto Outdoor Products, Rt. 735, Howardsville, VA 24562

Mt. Baldy Bullet Co., 12981 Old Hill City Rd., Keystone, SD 57751-6623 / 605-666-4725

MTM Molded Products Co., Inc., 3370 Obco Ct., Dayton, OH 45414 / 937-890-7461; FAX: 937-890-1747

Mulberry House Publishing (See Milberry)

Mulhern, Rick, Rt. 5, Box 152, Rayville, LA 71269 / 318-728-2688

Mullins Ammunition, Rt. 2, Box 304K, Clintwood, VA 24228 / 540-926-6772; FAX: 540-926-6092

Mullis Guncraft, 3523 Lawyers Road E., Monroe, NC 28110 / 704-283-6683

Multi-Scale Charge Ltd., 3269 Niagara Falls Blvd., N. Tonawanda, NY 14120 / 905-566-1255; FAX: 905-276-6295

Multiplex International, 26 S. Main St., Concord, NH 03301 / FAX: 603-796-2223

Multipropulseurs, La Bertrandiere, 42580, FRANCE / 77 74 01 30; FAX: 77 93 19 34

Mundy, Thomas A., 69 Robbins Road, Somerville, NJ 08876 / 201-722-2199

Murmur Corp., 2823 N. Westmoreland Ave., Dallas, TX 75222 / 214-630-5400

Murray State College, 1 Murray Campus St., Tishomingo, OK 73460 / 508-371-2371

Muscle Products Corp., 112 Fennell Dr., Butler, PA 16001 / 800-227-7049 or 412-283-0567; FAX: 412-283-8310

Museum of Historical Arms, Inc., 2750 Coral Way, Suite 204, Miami, FL 33145 / 305-444-9199

Mushroom Express Bullet Co., 601 W. 6th St., Greenfield, IN 46140-1728 / 317-462-6332

MANUFACTURER'S DIRECTORY

Muzzleloaders Etcetera, Inc., 9901 Lyndale Ave. S., Bloomington, MN 55420 / 612-884-1161 muzzleloaders-etcetera.com
Muzzleloading Technologies, Inc, 25 E. Hwy. 40, Suite 330-12, Roosevelt, UT 84066 / 801-722-5996; FAX: 801-722-5909
MWG Co., P.O. Box 971202, Miami, FL 33197 / 800-428-9394 or 305-253-8393; FAX: 305-232-1247

N

N&J Sales, Lime Kiln Rd., Northford, CT 06472 / 203-484-0247
N.B.B., Inc., 24 Elliot Rd., Sterling, MA 01564 / 508-422-7538 or 800-942-9444
N.C. Ordnance Co., P.O. Box 3254, Wilson, NC 27895 / 919-237-2440; FAX: 919-243-9845
Nagel's Custom Bullets, 100 Scott St., Baytown, TX 77520-2849
Nalpak, 1937-C Friendship Drive, El Cajon, CA 92020 / 619-258-1200
Nastoff's 45 Shop, Inc., Steve, 12288 Mahoning Ave, PO Box 446, North Jackson, OH 44451 / 330-538-2977
National Bullet Co., 1585 E. 361 St., Eastlake, OH 44095 / 216-951-1854; FAX: 216-951-7761
National Target Co., 4690 Wyaconda Rd., Rockville, MD 20852 / 800-827-7060 or 301-770-7060; FAX: 301-770-7892
Naval Ordnance Works, Rt. 2, Box 919, Sheperdstown, WV 25443 / 304-876-0998
Navy Arms Co., 689 Bergen Blvd., Ridgefield, NJ 07657 / 201-945-2500; FAX: 201-945-6859
NCP Products, Inc., 3500 12th St. N.W., Canton, OH 44708 / 330-456-5130; FAX: 330-456-5234
Neal Johnson's Gunsmithing, Inc., 208 W. Buchanan St., Suite B, Colorado Springs, CO 80907 / 800-284-8671; FAX: 719-632-3493
Necessary Concepts, Inc., P.O. Box 571, Deer Park, NY 11729 / 516-667-8509; FAX: 516-667-8588
Necromancer Industries, Inc., 14 Communications Way, West Newton, PA 15089 / 412-872-8722
NEI Handtools, Inc., 51583 Columbia River Hwy., Scappoose, OR 97056 / 503-543-6776; FAX: 503-543-6799
Neil A. Jones Custom Products, 17217 Brookhouser Road, Saegertown, PA 16433 / 814-763-2769; FAX: 814-763-4228
Nelson, Gary K., 975 Terrace Dr., Oakdale, CA 95361 / 209-847-4590
Nelson, Stephen, 7365 NW Spring Creek Dr., Corvallis, OR 97330 / 541-745-5232
Nelson/Weather-Rite, Inc., 14760 Santa Fe Trail Dr., Lenexa, KS 66215 / 913-492-3200; FAX: 913-492-8749
Nesci Enterprises Inc., P.O. Box 119, Summit St., East Hampton, CT 06424 / 203-267-2588
Nesika Bay Precision, 22239 Big Valley Rd., Poulsbo, WA 98370 / 206-697-3830
Nettestad Gun Works, RR 1, Box 160, Pelican Rapids, MN 56572 / 218-863-4301
Neumann GmbH, Am Galgenberg 6, 90575, GERMANY / 09101/8258; FAX: 09101/6356
Nevada Pistol Academy, Inc., 4610 Blue Diamond Rd., Las Vegas, NV 89139 / 702-897-1100
New England Ammunition Co., 1771 Post Rd. East, Suite 223, Westport, CT 06880 / 203-254-8048
New England Arms Co., Box 278, Lawrence Lane, Kittery Point, ME 03905 / 207-439-0593; FAX: 207-439-0525 info@newenglandarms.com www.newenglandarms.com
New England Custom Gun Service, 438 Willow Brook Rd., Plainfield, NH 03781 / 603-469-3450; FAX: 603-469-3471
New England Firearms, 60 Industrial Rowe, Gardner, MA 01440 / 508-632-9393; FAX: 508-632-2300
New Orleans Jewelers Supply Co., 206 Charters St., New Orleans, LA 70130 / 504-523-3839; FAX: 504-523-3836
New SKB Arms Co., C.P.O. Box 1401, Tokyo, JAPAN / 81-3-3943-9550; FAX: 81-3-3943-0695
New Win Publishing, Inc., 186 Center St., Clinton, NJ 08809 / 908-735-9701; FAX: 908-735-9703
Newark Electronics, 4801 N. Ravenswood Ave., Chicago, IL 60640
Newell, Robert H., 55 Coyote, Los Alamos, NM 87544 / 505-662-7135
Newman Gunshop, 119 Miller Rd., Agency, IA 52530 / 515-937-5775
Nicholson Custom, 17285 Thornlay Road, Hughesville, MO 65334 / 816-826-8746
Nickels, Paul R., 4789 Summerhill Rd., Las Vegas, NV 89121 / 702-435-5318
Nicklas, Ted, 5504 Hegel Rd., Goodrich, MI 48438 / 810-797-4493
Niemi Engineering, W. B., Box 126 Center Rd, Greensboro, VT 05841 / 802-533-7180; FAX: 802-533-7141
Nightforce (See Lightforce USA Inc)
Nikolai leather, 15451 Electronic In, Huntington Beach, CA 92649 / 714-373-2721 FAX: 714-373-2723

Nikon, Inc., 1300 Walt Whitman Rd., Melville, NY 11747 / 516-547-8623; FAX: 516-547-0309
Nitex, Inc., P.O. Box 1706, Uvalde, TX 78801 / 888-543-8843
No-Sho Mfg. Co., 10727 Glenfield Ct., Houston, TX 77096 / 713-723-5332
Noreen, Peter H., 5075 Buena Vista Dr., Belgrade, MT 59714 / 406-586-7383
Norica, Avnda Otaola, 16 Apartado 68, Eibar, SPAIN
Norinco, 7A Yun Tan N, Beijing, CHINA
Norincoptics (See BEC, Inc.)
Norma Precision AB (See U.S. Importers-Dynamit Nobel-RWS, Inc.,)
Normark Corp., 10395 Yellow Circle Dr., Minnetonka, MN 55343-9101 / 612-933-7060 FAX: 612-933-0046
North American Arms, Inc., 2150 South 950 East, Provo, UT 84606-6285 / 800-821-5783 or 801-374-9990; FAX: 801-374-9998
North American Correspondence Schools The Gun Pro, Oak & Pawney St., Scranton, PA 18515 / 717-342-7701
North American Shooting Systems, P.O. Box 306, Osoyoos, BC V0H 1V0 CANADA / 604-495-3131; FAX: 604-495-2816
North Devon Firearms Services, 3 North St., Braunton, EX33 1AJ ENGLAND / 01271 813624; FAX: 01271 813624
North Fork Custom Gunsmithing, James Johnston, 428 Del Rio Rd., Roseburg, OR 97470 / 503-673-4467
North Mountain Pine Training Center (See Executive Protection Institute)
North Pass, 425 South Bowen St., Ste. 6, Longmount, CO 80501 / 303-682-4315; FAX: 303-678-7109
North Specialty Products, 2664-B Saturn St., Brea, CA 92621 / 714-524-1665
North Star West, P.O. Box 488, Glencoe, CA 95232 / 209-293-7010
North Wind Decoy Co., 1005 N. Tower Rd., Fergus Falls, MN 56537 / 218-736-4378; FAX: 218-736-7060
Northern Precision Custom Swaged Bullets, 329 S. James St., Carthage, NY 13619 / 315-493-1711
Northlake Outdoor Footwear, P.O. Box 10, Franklin, TN 37065-0010 / 615-794-1556; FAX: 615-790-8005
Northside Gun Shop, 2725 NW 109th, Oklahoma City, OK 73120 / 405-840-2353
Northwest Arms, 26884 Pearl Rd., Parma, ID 83660 / 208-722-6771; FAX: 208-722-1062
Nosler, Inc., P.O. Box 671, Bend, OR 97709 / 800-285-3701 or 541-382-3921; FAX: 541-388-4667
Novak's Inc., 1206 1/2 30th St., P.O. Box 4045, Parkersburg, WV 26101 / 304-485-9295; FAX: 304-428-6722
Now Products, Inc., PO Box 27608, Tempe, AZ 85285 / 800-662-6063; FAX: 480-966-0890
Nowlin Mfg. Co., 20622 S 4092 Rd, Claremore, OK 74017 / 918-342-0689; FAX: 918-342-0624
NRI Gunsmith School, 4401 Connecticut Ave. NW, Washington, DC 20008
Nu-Line Guns,Inc., 1053 Caulks Hill Rd., Harvester, MO 63304 / 314-441-4500 or 314-447-4501; FAX: 314-447-5018
Null Holsters Ltd. K.L., 161 School St NW, Resaca, GA 30735 / 706-625-5643; FAX: 706-625-9392
Numrich Arms Corp., 203 Broadway, W. Hurley, NY 12491
NW Sinker and Tackle, 380 Valley Dr., Myrtle Creek, OR 97457-9717
Nygord Precision Products, P.O. Box 12578, Prescott, AZ 86304 / 520-717-2315; FAX: 520-717-2198

O

O.F. Mossberg & Sons,Inc., 7 Grasso Ave., North Haven, CT 06473 / 203-230-5300; FAX: 203-230-5420
Oakland Custom Arms,Inc., 4690 W. Walton Blvd., Waterford, MI 48329 / 810-674-8261
Oakman Turkey Calls, RD 1, Box 825, Harrisonville, PA 17228 / 717-485-4620
Obermeyer Rifled Barrels, 23122 60th St., Bristol, WI 53104 / 262-843-3537; FAX: 262-843-2129
October Country Muzzleloading, P.O. Box 969, Dept. GD, Hayden, ID 83835 / 208-772-2068; FAX: 208-772-9230 octobercountry.com
Oehler Research,Inc., P.O. Box 9135, Austin, TX 78766 / 512-327-6900 or 800-531-5125; FAX: 512-327-6903
Oil Rod and Gun Shop, 69 Oak St., East Douglas, MA 01516 / 508-476-3687
Ojala Holsters, Arvo, PO Box 98, N Hollywood, CA 91603 / 503-669-1404
OK Weber,Inc., P.O. Box 7485, Eugene, OR 97401 / 541-747-0458; FAX: 541-747-5927
Oker's Engraving, 365 Bell Rd., P.O. Box 126, Shawnee, CO 80475 / 303-838-6042
Oklahoma Ammunition Co., 3701A S. Harvard Ave., No. 367, Tulsa, OK 74135-2265 / 918-396-3187; FAX: 918-396-4270
Oklahoma Leather Products,Inc., 500 26th NW, Miami, OK 74354 / 918-542-6651; FAX: 918-542-6653

Old Wagon Bullets, 32 Old Wagon Rd., Wilton, CT 06897
Old West Bullet Moulds, J Ken Chapman, P.O. Box 519, Flora Vista, NM 87415 / 505-334-6970
Old West Reproductions,Inc. R.M. Bachman, 446 Florence S. Loop, Florence, MT 59833 / 406-273-2615; FAX: 406-273-2615
Old Western Scrounger,Inc., 12924 Hwy. A-l2, Montague, CA 96064 / 916-459-5445; FAX: 916-459-3944
Old World Gunsmithing, 2901 SE 122nd St., Portland, OR 97236 / 503-760-7681
Old World Oil Products, 3827 Queen Ave. N., Minneapolis, MN 55412 / 612-522-5037
Ole Frontier Gunsmith Shop, 2617 Hwy. 29 S., Cantonment, FL 32533 / 904-477-8074
Olson, Myron, 989 W. Kemp, Watertown, SD 57201 / 605-886-9787
Olson, Vic, 5002 Countryside Dr., Imperial, MO 63052 / 314-296-8086
Olympic Arms Inc., 620-626 Old Pacific Hwy. SE, Olympia, WA 98513 / 360-491-3447; FAX: 360-491-3447
Olympic Optical Co., P.O. Box 752377, Memphis, TN 38175-2377 / 901-794-3890 or 800-238-7120; FAX: 901-794-0676 80
Omark Industries,Div. of Blount,Inc., 2299 Snake River Ave., P.O. Box 856, Lewiston, ID 83501 / 800-627-3640 or 208-746-2351
Omega Sales, P.O. Box 1066, Mt. Clemens, MI 48043 / 810-469-7323; FAX: 810-469-0425
One Of A Kind, 15610 Purple Sage, San Antonio, TX 78255 / 512-695-3364
Op-Tec, P.O. Box L632, Langhorn, PA 19047 / 215-757-5037
Optical Services Co., P.O. Box 1174, Santa Teresa, NM 88008-1174 / 505-589-3833
Orchard Park Enterprise, P.O. Box 563, Orchard Park, NY 14227 / 616-656-0356
Oregon Arms, Inc. (See Rogue Rifle Co., Inc.)
Oregon Trail Bullet Company, P.O. Box 529, Dept. P, Baker City, OR 97814 / 800-811-0548; FAX: 514-523-1803
Original Box, nc., 700 Linden Ave., York, PA 17404 / 717-854-2897; FAX: 717-845-4276
Original Mink Oil,Inc., 10652 NE Holman, Portland, OR 97220 / 503-255-2814 or 800-547-5895; FAX: 503-255-2487
Orion Rifle Barrel Co., RR2, 137 Cobler Village, Kalispell, MT 59901 / 406-257-5649
Otis Technology, Inc, RR 1 Box 84, Boonville, NY 13309 / 315-942-3320
Ottmar, Maurice, Box 657, 113 E. Fir, Coulee City, WA 99115 / 509-632-5717
Outa-Site Gun Carriers, 219 Market St., Laredo, TX 78040 / 210-722-4678 or 800-880-9715; FAX: 210-726-4858
Outdoor Edge Cutlery Corp., 2888 Bluff St., Suite 130, Boulder, CO 80301 / 303-652-8212; FAX: 303-652-8238
Outdoor Enthusiast, 3784 W. Woodland, Springfield, MO 65807 / 417-883-9841
Outdoor Sports Headquarters,Inc., 967 Watertower Ln., West Carrollton, OH 45449 / 513-865-5855; FAX: 513-865-5962
Outers Laboratories Div. of Blount, Inc.Sporting E, Route 2, P.O. Box 39, Onalaska, WI 54650 / 608-781-5800; FAX: 608-781-0368
Ox-Yoke Originals, Inc., 34 Main St., Milo, ME 04463 / 800-231-8313 or 207-943-7351; FAX: 207-943-2416
Ozark Gun Works, 11830 Cemetery Rd., Rogers, AR 72756 / 501-631-6944; FAX: 501-631-6944 ogw@hotmail.com http://members.tripod.com~ozarkw1

P

P&M Sales and Service, 5724 Gainsborough Pl., Oak Forest, IL 60452 / 708-687-7149
P.A.C.T., Inc., P.O. Box 531525, Grand Prairie, TX 75053 / 214-641-0049
P.M. Enterprises, Inc., 146 Curtis Hill Rd., Chehalis, WA 98532 / 360-748-3743; FAX: 360-748-1802
P.S.M.G. Gun Co., 10 Park Ave., Arlington, MA 02174 / 617-646-8845; FAX: 617-646-2133
Pac-Nor Barreling, 99299 Overlook Rd., P.O. Box 6188, Brookings, OR 97415 / 503-469-7330; FAX: 503-469-7331
Pace Marketing, Inc., P.O. Box 2039, Stuart, FL 34995 / 561-871-9682; FAX: 561-871-6552
Pachmayr Div. Lyman Products, 1875 S. Mountain Ave., Monrovia, CA 91016 / 626-357-7771
Pacific Cartridge, Inc., 2425 Salashan Loop Road, Ferndale, WA 98248 / 360-366-4444; FAX: 360-366-4445
Pacific Research Laboratories, Inc. (See Rimrock R
Pacific Rifle Co., PO Box 1473, Lake Oswego, OR 97035 / 503-538-7437
Paco's (See Small Custom Mould & Bullet Co)
Page Custom Bullets, P.O. Box 25, Port Moresby, NEW GUINEA
Pagel Gun Works, Inc., 1407 4th St. NW, Grand Rapids, MN 55744 / 218-326-3003

Manufacturer's Directory

Pager Pal, 200 W Pleasantview, Hurst, TX 76054 / 800-561-1603 FAX: 817-285-8769 www.pagerpal.com
Paintball Games International Magazine (Aceville Publications, Castle House) 97 High St., Essex, ENGLAND / 011-44-206-564840
Palmer Security Products, 2930 N. Campbell Ave., Chicago, IL 60618 / 800-788-7725; FAX: 773-267-8080
Palsa Outdoor Products, P.O. Box 81336, Lincoln, NE 68501 / 402-488-5288; FAX: 402-488-2321
Para-Ordnance Mfg., Inc., 980 Tapscott Rd., Scarborough, ON M1X 1E7 CANADA / 416-297-7855; FAX: 416-297-1289
Para-Ordnance, Inc., 1919 NE 45th St., Ste 215, Ft. Lauderdale, FL 33308
Paragon Sales & Services, Inc., 2501 Theodore St, Crest Hill, IL 60435-1613 / 815-725-9212; FAX: 815-725-8974
Pardini Armi Srl, Via Italica 154, 55043, Lido Di Camaiore Lu, ITALY / 584-90121; FAX: 584-90122
Paris, Frank J., 17417 Pershing St., Livonia, MI 48152-3822
Parker & Sons Shooting Supply, 9337 Smoky Row Rd, Straw Plains, TN 97871-1257
Parker Gun Finishes, 9337 Smokey Row Rd., Strawberry Plains, TN 37871 / 423-933-3286
Parker Reproductions, 124 River Rd., Middlesex, NJ 08846 / 908-469-0100 FAX: 908-469-9692
Parsons Optical Mfg. Co., P.O. Box 192, Ross, OH 45061 / 513-867-0820; FAX: 513-867-8380
Partridge Sales Ltd., John, Trent Meadows, Rugeley, ENGLAND
Parts & Surplus, P.O. Box 22074, Memphis, TN 38122 / 901-683-4007
Pasadena Gun Center, 206 E. Shaw, Pasadena, TX 77506 / 713-472-0417; FAX: 713-472-1322
Passive Bullet Traps, Inc. (See Savage Range Systems, Inc.)
PAST Sporting Goods,Inc., P.O. Box 1035, Columbia, MO 65205 / 314-445-9200; FAX: 314-446-6606
Paterson Gunsmithing, 438 Main St., Paterson, NJ 07502 / 201-345-4100
Pathfinder Sports Leather, 2920 E. Chambers St., Phoenix, AZ 85040 / 602-276-0016
Patrick Bullets, P.O. Box 172, Warwick, QSLD, 4370 AUSTRALIA
Patrick W. Price Bullets, 16520 Worthley Drive, San Lorenzo, CA 94580 / 510-278-1547
Pattern Control, 114 N. Third St., P.O. Box 462105, Garland, TX 75046 / 214-494-3551; FAX: 214-272-8447
Paul A. Harris Hand Engraving, 113 Rusty Lane, Boerne, TX 78006-5746 / 512-391-5121
Paul D. Hillmer Custom Gunstocks, 7251 Hudson Heights, Hudson, IA 50643 / 319-988-3941
Paul Jones Moulds, 4901 Telegraph Rd., Los Angeles, CA 90022 / 213-262-1510
Paulsen Gunstocks, Rt. 71, Box 11, Chinook, MT 59523 / 406-357-3403
Pawling Mountain Club, Keith Lupton, PO Box 573, Pawling, NY 12564 / 914-855-3825
Paxton Quigley's Personal Protection Strategies, 9903 Santa Monica Blvd., 300, Beverly Hills, CA 90212 / 310-281-1762 www.defend-net.com/paxton
Payne Photography, Robert, Robert, P.O. Box 141471, Austin, TX 78714 / 512-272-4554
PC Co., 5942 Secor Rd., Toledo, OH 43623 / 419-472-6222
Peacemaker Specialists, P.O. Box 157, Whitmore, CA 96096 / 916-472-3438
Pearce Grip, Inc., P.O. Box 187, Bothell, WA 98041-0187 / 206-485-5488; FAX: 206-488-9497
Pease Accuracy, Bob, P.O. Box 310787, New Braunfels, TX 78131 / 210-625-1342
Pease International, 53 Durham St, Portsmouth, NH 03801 / 603-431-1331; FAX: 603-431-1221
PECAR Herbert Schwarz GmbH, Kreuzbergstrasse 6, 10965, Berlin, GERMANY / 004930-785-7383; FAX: 004930-785-1934
Pecatonica River Longrifle, 5205 Nottingham Dr., Rockford, IL 61111 / 815-968-1995 FAX: 815-968-1996
Pedersen, C. R., 2717 S. Pere Marquette Hwy., Ludington, MI 49431 / 616-843-2061
Pedersen, Rex C., 2717 S. Pere Marquette Hwy., Ludington, MI 49431 / 616-843-2061
Peerless Alloy, Inc., 1445 Osage St., Denver, CO 80204-2439 / 303-825-6394 or 800-253-1278
Peet Shoe Dryer, Inc., 130 S. 5th St., P.O. Box 618, St. Maries, ID 83861 / 208-245-2095 or 800-222-PEET; FAX: 208-245-5441
Peifer Rifle Co., P.O. Box 192, Nokomis, IL 62075-0192 / 217-563-7050; FAX: 217-563-7060
Pejsa Ballistics, 2120 Kenwood Pkwy., Minneapolis, MN 55405 / 612-374-3337; FAX: 612-374-5383
Pelaire Products, 5346 Bonky Ct., W. Palm Beach, FL 33415 / 561-439-0691; FAX: 561-967-0052
Pell, John T. (See KOGOT)
Peltor, Inc. (See Aero Peltor)
PEM's Mfg. Co., 5063 Waterloo Rd., Atwater, OH 44201 / 216-947-3721
Pence Precision Barrels, 7567 E. 900 S., S. Whitley, IN 46787 / 219-839-4745
Pendleton Royal, c/o Swingler Buckland Ltd., 4/7 Highgate St., Birmingham, ENGLAND / 44 121 440 3060 or 44 121 446 5898; FAX: 44 121 446 4165
Pendleton Woolen Mills, P.O. Box 3030, 220 N.W. Broadway, Portland, OR 97208 / 503-226-4801
Penn Bullets, P.O. Box 756, Indianola, PA 15051
Penn's Woods Products, Inc., 19 W. Pittsburgh St., Delmont, PA 15626 / 412-468-8311; FAX: 412-468-8975
Pennsylvania Gun Parts Inc, PO Box 665, 300 Third St, East Berlin, PA 17316-0665 / 717-259-8010; FAX: 717-259-0057
Pennsylvania Gunsmith School, 812 Ohio River Blvd., Avalon, Pittsburgh, PA 15202 / 412-766-1812 FAX: 412-766-0855 pgs@pagunsmith.com www.pagunsmith.com
Penrod Precision, 312 College Ave., P.O. Box 307, N. Manchester, IN 46962 / 219-982-8385
Pentax Corp., 35 Inverness Dr. E., Englewood, CO 80112 / 303-799-8000; FAX: 303-790-1131
Pentheny de Pentheny, 108 Petaluma Ave #202, Sebastopol, CA 95472-4220 / 707-573-1390; FAX: 707-573-1390
Perazone-Gunsmith, Brian, Cold Spring Rd, Roxbury, NY 12474 / 607-326-4088; FAX: 607-326-3140
Perazzi USA, Inc., 1207 S. Shamrock Ave., Monrovia, CA 91016 / 626-303-0068; FAX: 626-303-2081
Performance Specialists, 308 Eanes School Rd., Austin, TX 78746 / 512-327-0119
Perugini Visini & Co. S.r.l., Via Camprelle, 126, 25080 Nuvolera, ITALY / 30-6897535; FAX: 30-6897821
Pete Elsen, Inc., 1529 S. 113th St., West Allis, WI 53214
Pete Mazur Restoration, 13083 Drummer Way, Grass Valley, CA 95949 / 916-268-2412
Pete Rickard, Inc., 115 Roy Walsh Rd, Cobleskill, NY 12043 / 518-234-2731: FAX: 518-234-2454 rickard@telenet.net peterickard.com
Peter Dyson & Son Ltd., 3 Cuckoo Lane, Honley Huddersfield, Yorkshire, HD7 2BR ENGLAND / 44-1484-661062; FAX: 44-1484-663709
Peter Hale/Engraver, 800 E. Canyon Rd., Spanish Fork, UT 84660 / 801-798-8215
Peters Stahl GmbH, Stettiner Strasse 42, D-33106, Paderborn, / 05251-750025; FAX: 05251-75611
Petersen Publishing Co., (See Emap USA)
Peterson Gun Shop, Inc., A.W., 4255 W. Old U.S. 441, Mt. Dora, FL 32757-3299 / 352-383-4258; FAX: 352-735-1001
Petro-Explo Inc., 7650 U.S. Hwy. 287, Suite 100, Arlington, TX 76017 / 817-478-8888
Pettinger Books, Gerald, Rt. 2, Box 125, Russell, IA 50238 / 515-535-2239
Pflumm Mfg. Co., 10662 Widmer Rd., Lenexa, KS 66215 / 800-888-4867; FAX: 913-451-7857
PFRB Co., P.O. Box 1242, Bloomington, IL 61702 / 309-473-3964; FAX: 309-473-2161
Philip S. Olt Co., P.O. Box 550, 12662 Fifth St., Pekin, IL 61554 / 309-348-3633; FAX: 309-348-3300
Phillippi Custom Bullets, Justin, P.O. Box 773, Ligonier, PA 15658 / 724-238-2962; FAX: 724-238-9671 jrp@wpa.net http://www.wpa.net~jrphil
Phillips & Rogers, Inc., 100 Hilbig #C, Conroe, TX 77301 / 409-435-0011
Phoenix Arms, 1420 S. Archibald Ave., Ontario, CA 91761 / 909-947-4843; FAX: 909-947-6798
Photronic Systems Engineering Company, 6731 Via De La Reina, Bonsall, CA 92003 / 619-758-8000
Piedmont Community College, P.O. Box 1197, Roxboro, NC 27573 / 336-599-1181 FAX: 336-597-3817 www.piedmont.cc.nc.us
Pierce Pistols, 55 Sorrellwood Lane, Sharpsburg, GA 30277-9523 / 404-253-8192
Pietta (See U.S. Importers-Navy Arms Co, Taylor's & Co.,)
Pilgrim Pewter,Inc. (See Bell Originals Inc. Sid)
Pilkington, Scott (See Little Trees Ramble)
Pine Technical College, 1100 4th St., Pine City, MN 55063 / 800-521-7463; FAX: 612-629-6766
Pinetree Bullets, 133 Skeena St., Kitimat, BC V8C 1Z1 CANADA / 604-632-3768; FAX: 604-632-3768
Pioneer Arms Co., 355 Lawrence Rd., Broomall, PA 19008 / 215-356-5203
Piotti (See U.S. Importer-Moore & Co, Wm. Larkin)
Piquette, Paul R., 80 Bradford Dr., Feeding Hills, MA 01030 / 413-786-8118; or 413-789-4582
Plaxco, J. Michael, Rt. 1, P.O. Box 203, Roland, AR 72135 / 501-868-9787
Plaza Cutlery, Inc., 3333 Bristol, 161 South Coast Plaza, Costa Mesa, CA 92626 / 714-549-3932
Plum City Ballistic Range, N2162 80th St., Plum City, WI 54761 / 715-647-2539
PlumFire Press, Inc., 30-A Grove Ave., Patchogue, NY 11772-4112 / 800-695-7246; FAX: 516-758-4071
PMC/Eldorado Cartridge Corp., P.O. Box 62508, 12801 U.S. Hwy. 95 S., Boulder City, NV 89005 / 702-294-0025; FAX: 702-294-0121
Poburka, Philip (See Bison Studios)
Pohl, Henry A. (See Great American Gun Co.
Pointing Dog Journal, Village Press Publications, P.O. Box 968, Dept. PGD, Traverse City, MI 49685 / 800-272-3246; FAX: 616-946-3289
Police Bookshelf, P.O. Box 122, Concord, NH 03301 / 603-224-6814; FAX: 603-226-3554
Polywad, Inc., P.O. Box 7916, Macon, GA 31209 / 912-477-0669 polywadmpb@aol.com www.polywad.com
Pomeroy, Robert, RR1, Box 50, E. Corinth, ME 04427 / 207-285-7721
Ponsness/Warren, P.O. Box 8, Rathdrum, ID 83858 / 208-687-2231; FAX: 208-687-2233
Pony Express Reloaders, 608 E. Co. Rd. D, Suite 3, St. Paul, MN 55117 / 612-483-9406; FAX: 612-483-9884
Pony Express Sport Shop, 16606 Schoenborn St., North Hills, CA 91343 / 818-895-1231
Potts, Wayne E., 912 Poplar St., Denver, CO 80220 / 303-355-5462
Powder Horn Antiques, P.O. Box 4196, Ft. Lauderdale, FL 33338 / 305-565-6060
Powell & Son (Gunmakers) Ltd., William, 35-37 Carrs Lane, Birmingham, B4 7SX ENGLAND / 121-643-0689; FAX: 121-631-3504
Powell Agency, William, 22 Circle Dr., Bellmore, NY 11710 / 516-679-1158
Power Custom, Inc., 29739 Hwy. J, Gravois Mills, MO 65037 / 513-372-5684; FAX: 573-372-5799 pwpowers@laurie.net www.powercustom.com
Power Plus Enterprises, Inc., PO Box 38, Warm Springs, GA 31830 / 706-655-2132
Powley Computer (See Hutton Rifle Ranch)
Practical Tools, Inc., 7067 Easton Rd., P.O. Box 133, Pipersville, PA 18947 / 215-766-7301; FAX: 215-766-8681
Prairie Gun Works, 1-761 Marion St., Winnipeq, MB R2J 0K6 Canada / 204-231-2976; FAX: 204-231-8566
Prairie River Arms, 1220 N. Sixth St., Princeton, IL 61356 / 815-875-1616 or 800-445-1541; FAX: 815-875-1402
Pranger, Ed G., 1414 7th St., Anacortes, WA 98221 / 206-293-3488
Pre-Winchester 92-90-62 Parts Co., P.O. Box 8125, W. Palm Beach, FL 33407
Precise Metalsmithing Enterprises, 146 Curtis Hill Rd., Chehalis, WA 98532 / 206-748-3743; FAX: 206-748-8102
Precision Airgun Sales, Inc., 5247 Warrensville Ctr Rd, Maple Hts., OH 44137 / 216-587-5005 FAX: 216-587-5005
Precision Cartridge, 176 Eastside Rd., Deer Lodge, MT 59722 / 800-397-3901 or 406-846-3900
Precision Cast Bullets, 101 Mud Creek Lane, Ronan, MT 59864 / 406-676-5135
Precision Castings & Equipment, P.O. Box 326, Jasper, IN 47547-0135 / 812-634-9167
Precision Components, 3177 Sunrise Lake, Milford, PA 18337 / 570-686-4414
Precision Components and Guns, Rt. 55, P.O. Box 337, Pawling, NY 12564 / 914-855-3040
Precision Delta Corp., P.O. Box 128, Ruleville, MS 38771 / 601-756-2810; FAX: 601-756-2590
Precision Gun Works, 104 Sierra Rd Dept. GD, Kerrville, TX 78028 / 830-367-4587
Precision Munitions, Inc., P.O. Box 326, Jasper, IN 47547
Precision Reloading, Inc., P.O. Box 122, Stafford Springs, CT 06076 / 860-684-5680 FAX: 860-684-6788
Precision Sales International, Inc., P.O. Box 1776, Westfield, MA 01086 / 413-562-5055; FAX: 413-562-5056
Precision Shooting,Inc., 222 McKee St., Manchester, CT 06040 / 860-645-8776; FAX: 860-643-8215
Precision Small Arms, 9777 Wilshire Blvd., Suite 1005, Beverly Hills, CA 90212 / 310-859-4867; FAX: 310-859-2868
Precision Small Arms Inc, 9272 Jeronimo Rd, Ste 121, Irvine, CA 92618 / 800-554-5515; FAX: 949-768-4808 www.tcbebe.com
Precision Specialties, 131 Hendom Dr., Feeding Hills, MA 01030 / 413-786-3365; FAX: 413-786-3365
Precision Sport Optics, 15571 Producer Lane, Unit G, Huntington Beach, CA 92649 / 714-891-1309; FAX: 714-892-6920
Premier Reticles, 920 Breckinridge Lane, Winchester, VA 22601-6707 / 540-722-0601; FAX: 540-722-3522
Prescott Projectile Co., 1808 Meadowbrook Road, Prescott, AZ 86303
Preslik's Gunstocks, 4245 Keith Ln., Chico, CA 95926 / 916-891-8236
Price Bullets, Patrick W., 16520 Worthley Dr., San Lorenzo, CA 94580 / 510-278-1547
Prime Reloading, 30 Chiswick End, Meldreth, ROYSTON UK / 0763-260636
Primos, Inc., P.O. Box 12785, Jackson, MS 39236-2785 / 601-366-1288; FAX: 601-362-3274

PRL Bullets, c/o Blackburn Enterprises, 114 Stuart Rd., Ste. 110, Cleveland, TN 37312 / 423-559-0340

Pro Load Ammunition, Inc., 5180 E. Seltice Way, Post Falls, ID 83854 / 208-773-9444; FAX: 208-773-9441

Pro-Mark Div. of Wells Lamont, 6640 W. Touhy, Chicago, IL 60648 / 312-647-8200

Pro-Port Ltd., 41302 Executive Dr., Harrison Twp., MI 48045-1306 / 810-469-6727 FAX: 810-469-0425

Pro-Shot Products, Inc., P.O. Box 763, Taylorville, IL 62568 / 217-824-9133; FAX: 217-824-8861

Professional Gunsmiths of America,Inc., Route 1, Box 224F, Lexington, MO 64067 / 816-259-2636

Professional Hunter Supplies (See Star Custom Bullets,) PO Box 608, 468 Main St, Ferndale, CA 95536 / 707-786-9140; FAX: 707-786-9117

Professional Ordnance, Inc., 1215 E. Airport Dr., Box 182, Ontario, CA 91761 / 909-923-5559; FAX: 909-923-0899

Prolixr Lubricants, P.O. Box 1348, Victorville, CA 92393 / 800-248-5823 or 760-243-3129; FAX: 760-241-0148

Proofmark Corp., P.O. Box 610, Burgess, VA 22432 / 804-453-4337; FAX: 804-453-4337 proofmark@rivnet.net

Protektor Model, 1-11 Bridge St., Galeton, PA 16922 / 814-435-2442

Prototech Industries, Inc., Rt. 1, Box 81, Delia, KS 66418 / 913-771-3571; FAX: 913-771-2531

ProWare, Inc., 15847 NE Hancock St., Portland, OR 97230 / 503-239-0159

PWL Gunleather, P.O. Box 450432, Atlanta, GA 31145 / 770-822-1640; FAX: 770-822-1704 covert@pwlusa.com www.pwlusa.com

Pyromid, Inc., 3292 S. Highway 97, Redmond, OR 97756 / 503-548-1041; FAX: 503-923-1004

Q

Quack Decoy & Sporting Clays, 4 Ann & Hope Way, P.O. Box 98, Cumberland, RI 02864 / 401-723-8202; FAX: 401-722-5910

Quaker Boy, Inc., 5455 Webster Rd., Orchard Parks, NY 14127 / 716-662-3979; FAX: 716-662-9426

Quality Arms, Inc., Box 19477, Dept. GD, Houston, TX 77224 / 281-870-8377; FAX: 281-870-8524 arrieta2@excite.com www.gunshop.com

Quality Firearms of Idaho, Inc., 659 Harmon Way, Middleton, ID 83644-3065 / 208-466-1631

Quality Parts Co./Bushmaster Firearms, 999 Roosevelt Trail Bldg. 3, Windham, ME 04062 / 207-892-2005; FAX: 207-892-8068

Quarton USA, Ltd. Co., 7042 Alamo Downs Pkwy., Suite 370, San Antonio, TX 78238-4518 / 800-520-8435 or 210-520-8430; FAX: 210-520-8433

Que Industries, Inc., P.O. Box 2471, Everett, WA 98203 / 800-769-6930 or 206-347-9843; FAX: 206-514-3266

Queen Cutlery Co., P.O. Box 500, Franklinville, NY 14737 / 800-222-5233; FAX: 800-299-2618

R

R&C Knives & Such, 2136 CANDY CANE WALK, Manteca, CA 95336-9501 / 209-239-3722; FAX: 209-825-6947

R&D Gun Repair, Kenny Howell, RR1 Box 283, Beloit, WI 53511

R&J Gun Shop, 337 S Humbolt St, Canyon City, OR 97820 / 541-575-2130 rjgunshop@highdestertnet.com

R&S Industries Corp., 8255 Brentwood Industrial Dr., St. Louis, MO 63144 / 314-781-5400 polishingcloth.com

R. Murphy Co., Inc., 13 Groton-Harvard Rd., P.O. Box 376, Ayer, MA 01432 / 617-772-3481

R.A. Wells Custom Gunsmith, 3452 1st Ave., Racine, WI 53402 / 414-639-5223

R.E. Seebeck Assoc., P.O. Box 59752, Dallas, TX 75229

R.E.I., P.O. Box 88, Tallevast, FL 34270 / 813-755-0085

R.E.T. Enterprises, 2608 S. Chestnut, Broken Arrow, OK 74012 / 918-251-GUNS; FAX: 918-251-0587

R.F. Mitchell Bullets, 430 Walnut St., Westernport, MD 21562

R.I.S. Co., Inc., 718 Timberlake Circle, Richardson, TX 75080 / 214-235-0933

R.M. Precision, P.O. Box 210, LaVerkin, UT 84745 / 801-635-4656; FAX: 801-635-4430

R.T. Eastman Products, P.O. Box 1531, Jackson, WY 83001 / 307-733-3217 or 800-624-4311

Rabeno, Martin, 92 Spook Hole Rd., Ellenville, NY 12428 / 914-647-4567; FAX: 914-647-2129

Radack Photography, Lauren, 21140 Jib Court L-12, Aventura, FL 33180 / 305-931-3110

Radiator Specialty Co., 1900 Wilkinson Blvd., P.O. Box 34689, Charlotte, NC 28234 / 800-438-6947; FAX: 800-421-9525

Radical Concepts, P.O. Box 1473, Lake Grove, OR 97035 / 503-538-7437

Rainier Ballistics Corp., 4500 15th St. East, Tacoma, WA 98424 / 800-638-8722 or 206-922-7589; FAX: 206-922-7854

Ralph Bone Engraving, 718 N. Atlanta, Owasso, OK 74055 / 918-272-9745

Ram-Line Blount, Inc., P.O. Box 39, Onalaska, WI 54650

Ramon B. Gonzalez Guns, P.O. Box 370, 93 St. Joseph's Hill Road, Monticello, NY 12701 / 914-794-4515

Rampart International, 2781 W. MacArthur Blvd., B-283, Santa Ana, CA 92704 / 800-976-7240 or 714-557-6405

Ranch Products, P.O. Box 145, Malinta, OH 43535 / 313-277-3118; FAX: 313-565-8536

Randall-Made Knives, P.O. Box 1988, Orlando, FL 32802 / 407-855-8075

Randco UK, 286 Gipsy Rd., Welling, DA16 1JJ ENGLAND / 44 81 303 4118

Randolph Engineering, Inc., 26 Thomas Patten Dr., Randolph, MA 02368 / 800-541-1405; FAX: 800-875-4200

Randy Duane Custom Stocks, 110 W. North Ave., Winchester, VA 22601 / 703-667-9461; FAX: 703-722-3993

Range Brass Products Company, P.O. Box 218, Rockport, TX 78381

Ranger Products, 2623 Grand Blvd., Suite 209, Holiday, FL 34609 / 813-942-4652 or 800-407-7007; FAX: 813-942-6221

Ranger Shooting Glasses, 26 Thomas Patten Dr., Randolph, MA 02368 / 800-541-1405; FAX: 617-986-0337

Ranging, Inc., Routes 5 & 20, East Bloomfield, NY 14443 / 716-657-6161; FAX: 716-657-5405

Ransom International Corp., 1027 Spire Dr, Prescott, AZ 86302 / 520-778-7899; FAX: 520-778-7993 ransom@primenet.com www.ransom-intl.com

Rapine Bullet Mould Mfg. Co., 9503 Landis Lane, East Greenville, PA 18041 / 215-679-5413; FAX: 215-679-9795

Raptor Arms Co., Inc., 273 Canal St, #179, Shelton, CT 06484 / 203-924-7618; FAX: 203-924-7624

Ravell Ltd., 289 Diputacion St., 08009, Barcelona, SPAIN / 34(3) 4874486; FAX: 34(3) 4881394

Ray Riling Arms Books Co., 6844 Gorsten St., P.O. Box 18925, Philadelphia, PA 19119 / 215-438-2456; FAX: 215-438-5395

Ray's Gunsmith Shop, 3199 Elm Ave., Grand Junction, CO 81504 / 970-434-6162; FAX: 970-434-6162

Raytech Div. of Lyman Products Corp., 475 Smith Street, Middletown, CT 06457-1541 / 860-632-2020; FAX: 860-632-1699

RCBS Div. of Blount, 605 Oro Dam Blvd., Oroville, CA 95965 / 800-533-5000 or 916-533-5191; FAX: 916-533-1647 www.rcbs.com

Reagent Chemical & Research, Inc. (See Calico Hardwoods, Inc.)

Reardon Products, P.O. Box 126, Morrison, IL 61270 / 815-772-3155

Red Diamond Dist. Co., 1304 Snowdon Dr., Knoxville, TN 37912

Redding Reloading Equipment, 1089 Starr Rd., Cortland, NY 13045 / 607-753-3331; FAX: 607-756-8445

Redfield Media Resource Center, 4607 N.E. Cedar Creek Rd., Woodland, WA 98674 / 360-225-5000 FAX: 360-225-7616

Redfield, Inc., 5800 E Jewell Ave, Denver, CO 80224 / 303-757-6411; FAX: 303-756-2338

Redfield/Blount, PO Box 39, Onalaska, WI 54650 / 800-635-7656

Redman's Rifling & Reboring, 189 Nichols Rd., Omak, WA 98841 / 509-826-5512

Redwood Bullet Works, 3559 Bay Rd., Redwood City, CA 94063 / 415-367-6741

Reed, Dave, Rt. 1, Box 374, Minnesota City, MN 55959 / 507-689-2944

Reiswig, Wallace E. (See Claro Walnut Gunstock Co.,)

Reloaders Equipment Co., 4680 High St., Ecorse, MI 48229

Reloading Specialties, Inc., Box 1130, Pine Island, MN 55463 / 507-356-8500; FAX: 507-356-8800

Remington Arms Co., Inc., 870 Remington Drive, P.O. Box 700, Madison, NC 27025-0700 / 800-243-9700; FAX: 910-548-8700

Remington Double Shotguns, 7885 Cyd Dr., Denver, CO 80221 / 303-429-6947

Renato Gamba S.p.A.-Societa Armi Bresciane Srl., Via Artigiani 93, 25063 Gardone, Val Trompia (BS), ITALY / 30-8911640; FAX: 30-8911648

Renegade, P.O. Box 31546, Phoenix, AZ 85046 / 602-482-6777; FAX: 602-482-1952

Renfrew Guns & Supplies, R.R. 4, Renfrew, ON K7V 3Z7 CANADA / 613-432-7080

Reno, Wayne, 2808 Stagestop Rd, Jefferson, CO 80456 / 719-836-3452

Republic Arms, Inc., 15167 Sierra Bonita Lane, Chino, CA 91710 / 909-597-3873; FAX: 909-597-2612

Retting, Inc., Martin B, 11029 Washington, Culver City, CA 90232 / 213-837-2412

RG-G, Inc., PO Box 935, Trinidad, CO 81082 / 719-845-1436

Rhino, P.O. Box 787, Locust, NC 28097 / 704-753-2198

Rhodeside, Inc., 1704 Commerce Dr., Piqua, OH 45356 / 513-773-5781

Rice, Keith (See White Rock Tool & Die)

Richard H.R. Loweth (Firearms), 29 Hedgegrow Lane, Kirby Muxloe, Leics. LE9 2BN, ENGLAND

Richards Micro-Fit Stocks, 8331 N. San Fernando Ave., Sun Valley, CA 91352 / 818-767-6097; FAX: 818-767-7121

Rickard, Inc., Pete, RD 1, Box 292, Cobleskill, NY 12043 / 800-282-5663; FAX: 518-234-2454

Ridgeline, Inc, Bruce Sheldon, PO Box 930, Dewey, AZ 86327-0930 / 800-632-5900; FAX: 520-632-5900

Ridgetop Sporting Goods, P.O. Box 306, 42907 Hilligoss Ln. East, Eatonville, WA 98328 / 360-832-6422; FAX: 360-832-6422

Ries, Chuck, 415 Ridgecrest Dr., Grants Pass, OR 97527 / 503-476-5623

Rifles, Inc., 873 W. 5400 N., Cedar City, UT 84720 / 801-586-5996; FAX: 801-586-5996

Rigby & Co., John, 66 Great Suffolk St, London, ENGLAND / 0171-620-0690; FAX: 0171-928-9205

Riggs, Jim, 206 Azalea, Boerne, TX 78006 / 210-249-8567

Riley Ledbetter Airguns, 1804 E. Sprague St., Winston Salem, NC 27107-3521 / 919-784-0676

Riling Arms Books Co., Ray, 6844 Gorsten St, PO Box 18925, Philadelphia, PA 19119 / 215-438-2456; FAX: 215-438-5395

Rim Pac Sports, Inc., 1034 N. Soldano Ave., Azusa, CA 91702-2135

Ringler Custom Leather Co., 31 Shining Mtn. Rd., Powell, WY 82435 / 307-645-3255

Ripley Rifles, 42 Fletcher Street, Ripley, Derbyshire, DE5 3LP ENGLAND / 011-0773-748353

River Road Sporting Clays, Bruce Barsotti, P.O. Box 3016, Gonzales, CA 93926 / 408-675-2473

Rizzini F.lli (See U.S. Importers-Moore & C England)

Rizzini SNC, Via 2 Giugno, 7/7Bis-25060, Marcheno (Brescia), ITALY

RLCM Enterprises, 110 Hill Crest Drive, Burleson, TX 76028

RMS Custom Gunsmithing, 4120 N. Bitterwell, Prescott Valley, AZ 86314 / 520-772-7626

Robert Evans Engraving, 332 Vine St., Oregon City, OR 97045 / 503-656-5693

Robert Valade Engraving, 931 3rd Ave., Seaside, OR 97138 / 503-738-7672

Roberts Products, 25328 SE Iss. Beaver Lk. Rd., Issaquah, WA 98029 / 206-392-8172

Robinett, R. G., P.O. Box 72, Madrid, IA 50156 / 515-795-2906

Robinson, Don, Pennsylvaia Hse, 36 Fairfax Crescent, W Yorkshire, ENGLAND / 0422-364458

Robinson Firearms Mfg. Ltd., 1699 Blondeaux Crescent, Kelowna, BC V1Y 4J8 CANADA / 604-868-9596

Robinson H.V. Bullets, 3145 Church St., Zachary, LA 70791 / 504-654-4029

Rochester Lead Works, 76 Anderson Ave., Rochester, NY 14607 / 716-442-8500; FAX: 716-442-4712

Rock River Arms, 101 Noble St., Cleveland, IL 61241

Rockwood Corp., Speedwell Division, 136 Lincoln Blvd., Middlesex, NJ 08846 / 800-243-8274; FAX: 980-560-7475

Rocky Mountain Arms, Inc., 1813 Sunset Pl, Unit D, Longmont, CO 80501 / 800-375-0846; FAX: 303-678-8766

Rocky Mountain High Sports Glasses, 8121 N. Central Park Ave., Skokie, IL 60076 / 847-679-1012 or 800-323-1418; FAX: 847-679-0184

Rocky Mountain Rifle Works Ltd., 1707 14th St., Boulder, CO 80302 / 303-443-9189

Rocky Mountain Target Co., 3 Aloe Way, Leesburg, FL 34788 / 352-365-9598

Rocky Mountain Wildlife Products, P.O. Box 999, La Porte, CO 80535 / 970-484-2768; FAX: 970-484-0807

Rocky Shoes & Boots, 294 Harper St., Nelsonville, OH 45764 / 800-848-9452 or 614-753-1951; FAX: 614-753-4024

Rodgers & Sons Ltd., Joseph (See George Ibberson (Sheffield) Ltd.,)

Rogue Rifle Co., Inc., P.O. Box 20, Prospect, OR 97536 / 541-560-4040; FAX: 541-560-4041

Rogue River Rifleworks, 1317 Spring St., Paso Robles, CA 93446 / 805-227-4706; FAX: FAX:805-227-4723

Rohner, Hans, 1148 Twin Sisters Ranch Rd., Nederland, CO 80466-9600

Rohner, John, 186 Virginia Ave, Asheville, NC 28806 / 303-444-3841

Romain's Custom Guns, Inc., RD 1, Whetstone Rd., Brockport, PA 15823 / 814-265-1948

Ron Frank Custom Classic Arms, 7131 Richland Rd., Ft. Worth, TX 76118 / 817-284-9300; FAX: 817-284-9300

Ron Lutz Engraving, E. 1998 Smokey Valley Rd., Scandinavia, WI 54977 / 715-467-2674

Rooster Laboratories, P.O. Box 412514, Kansas City, MO 64141 / 816-474-1622; FAX: 816-474-1307

Rorschach Precision Products, P.O. Box 151613, Irving, TX 75015 / 214-790-3487

Manufacturer's Directory

Rosenberg & Son, Jack A, 12229 Cox Ln, Dallas, TX 75234 / 214-241-6302

Rosenthal, Brad and Sallie, 19303 Ossenfort Ct., St. Louis, MO 63038 / 314-273-5159; FAX: 314-273-5149

Ross, Don, 12813 West 83 Terrace, Lenexa, KS 66215 / 913-492-6982

Rosser, Bob, 1824 29th Ave., Suite 214, Birmingham, AL 35209 / 205-870-4422; FAX: 205-870-4421

Rossi Firearms, Braztech, Gary Mchalik, 16175 NW 49th Ave, Miami, FL 33014-6314 / 305-474-0401

Roto Carve, 2754 Garden Ave., Janesville, IA 50647

Rottweil Compe, 1330 Glassell, Orange, CA 92667

Round Edge, Inc., P.O. Box 723, Lansdale, PA 19446 / 215-361-0859

Roy Baker's Leather Goods, P.O. Box 893, Magnolia, AR 71753 / 501-234-0344

Roy's Custom Grips, Rt. 3, Box 174-E, Lynchburg, VA 24504 / 804-993-3470

Royal Arms Gunstocks, 919 8th Ave. NW, Great Falls, MT 59404 / 406-453-1149 FAX: 406-453-1194 royalarms@lmt.net lmt.net/~royalarms

RPM, 15481 N. Twin Lakes Dr., Tucson, AZ 85739 / 520-825-1233; FAX: 520-825-3333

Rubright Bullets, 1008 S. Quince Rd., Walnutport, PA 18088 / 215-767-1339

Rucker Dist. Inc., P.O. Box 479, Terrell, TX 75160 / 214-563-2094

Ruger (See Sturm, Ruger & Co., Inc.)

Rumanya Inc., 11513 Piney Lodge Rd, Gaithersburg, MD 20878-2443 / 281-345-2077; FAX: 281-345-2005

Rundell's Gun Shop, 6198 Frances Rd., Clio, MI 48420 / 313-687-0559

Runge, Robert P., 94 Grove St., Ilion, NY 13357 / 315-894-3036

Rupert's Gun Shop, 2202 Dick Rd., Suite B, Fenwick, MI 48834 / 517-248-3252

Russ Haydon Shooters' Supply, 15018 Goodrich Dr. NW, Gig Harbor, WA 98329 / 253-857-7557; FAX: 253-857-7884

Russ Trading Post, William A. Russ, 23 William St., Addison, NY 14801-1326 / 607-359-3896

Russ, William. (See RUSS TRADING POST)

Rustreprufe Laboratories, 1319 Jefferson Ave., Sparta, WI 54656 / 608-269-4144

Rusty Duck Premium Gun Care Products, 7785 Foundation Dr., Suite 6, Florence, KY 41042 / 606-342-5553; FAX: 606-342-5556

Rutgers Book Center, 127 Raritan Ave., Highland Park, NJ 08904 / 732-545-4344 FAX: 732-545-6686

Rutten (See U.S. Importer-Labanu Inc)

RWS (See U.S. Importer-Dynamit Nobel-RWS, Inc.), 81 Ruckman Rd, Closter, NJ 07624 / 201-767-7971; FAX: 201-767-1589

Ryan, Chad L., RR 3, Box 72, Cresco, IA 52136 / 319-547-4384

S

S&B Industries, 11238 McKinley Rd., Montrose, MI 48457 / 810-639-5491

S&K Mfg. Co., P.O. Box 247, Pittsfield, PA 16340 / 814-563-7808; FAX: 814-563-4067

S&S Firearms, 74-11 Myrtle Ave., Glendale, NY 11385 / 718-497-1100; FAX: 718-497-1105

S.A.R.L. G. Granger, 66 cours Fauriel, 42100, Saint Etienne, FRANCE / 04 77 25 14 73; FAX: 04 77 38 66 99

S.C.R.C., P.O. Box 660, Katy, TX 77492-0660 FAX: 713-578-2124

S.D. Meacham, 1070 Angel Ridge, Peck, ID 83545

S.G.S. Sporting Guns Srl., Via Della Resistenza, 37 20090, Buccinasco, ITALY / 2-45702446; FAX: 2-45702464

S.I.A.C.E. (See U.S. Importer-IAR Inc)

S.L.A.P. Industries, P.O. Box 1121, Parklands, 02121 SOUTH AFRICA / 27-11-788-0030; FAX: 27-11-788-0030

Sabatti S.r.l., via Alessandro Volta 90, 25063 Gardone V.T., Brescia, ITALY / 030-8912207-831312; FAX: 030-8912059

SAECO (See Redding Reloading Equipment)

Saf-T-Lok, 5713 Corporate Way, Suite 100, W. Palm Beach, FL 33407

Safari Outfitters Ltd., 71 Ethan Allan Hwy., Ridgefield, CT 06877 / 203-544-9505

Safari Press, Inc., 15621 Chemical Lane B, Huntington Beach, CA 92649 / 714-894-9080; FAX: 714-894-4949

Safariland Ltd., Inc., 3120 E. Mission Blvd., P.O. Box 51478, Ontario, CA 91761 / 909-923-7300; FAX: 909-923-7400

SAFE, P.O. Box 864, Post Falls, ID 83854 / 208-773-3624 FAX: 208-773-6819 staysafe@safe-llc.com www.safe-llc.com

Safety Speed Holster, Inc., 910 S. Vail Ave., Montebello, CA 90640 / 323-723-4140; FAX: 323-726-6973

Sako Ltd (See U.S. Importer-Stoeger Industries)

Samco Global Arms, Inc., 6995 NW 43rd St., Miami, FL 33166 / 305-593-9782 FAX: 305-593-1014

Sampson, Roger, 2316 Mahogany St., Mora, MN 55051 / 612-679-4868

San Francisco Gun Exchange, 124 Second St., San Francisco, CA 94105 / 415-982-6097

San Marco (See U.S. Importers-Cape Outfitters-EMF)

Sanders Custom Gun Service, 2358 Tyler Lane, Louisville, KY 40205 / 502-454-3338; FAX: 502-451-8857

Sanders Gun and Machine Shop, 145 Delhi Road, Manchester, IA 52057

Sandia Die & Cartridge Co., 37 Atancacio Rd. NE, Auquerque, NM 87123 / 505-298-5729

Sarco, Inc., 323 Union St., Stirling, NJ 07980 / 908-647-3800; FAX: 908-647-9413

Sauer (See U.S. Importers-Paul Co., The, Sigarms Inc.,)

Sauls, R. (See BRYAN & ASSOC)

Saunders Gun & Machine Shop, R.R. 2, Delhi Road, Manchester, IA 52057

Savage Arms (Canada), Inc., 248 Water St., P.O. Box 1240, Lakefield, ON K0L 2H0 CANADA / 705-652-8000; FAX: 705-652-8431

Savage Arms, Inc., 100 Springdale Rd., Westfield, MA 01085 / 413-568-7001; FAX: 413-562-7764

Savage Range Systems, Inc., 100 Springdale RD., Westfield, MA 01085 / 413-568-7001; FAX: 413-562-1152

Saville Iron Co. (See Greenwood Precision)

Savino, Barbara J., P.O. Box 51, West Burke, VT 05871-0051

Scanco Environmental Systems, 5000 Highlands Parkway, Suite 180, Atlanta, GA 30082 / 770-431-0025; FAX: 770-431-0028

Scansport, Inc., P.O. Box 700, Enfield, NH 03748 / 603-632-7654

Scattergun Technologies, Inc., 620 8th Ave. South, Nashville, TN 37203 / 615-254-1441; FAX: 615-254-1449

Sceery Game Calls, P.O. Box 6520, Sante Fe, NM 87502 / 505-471-9110; FAX: 505-471-3476

Schaefer Shooting Sports, P.O. Box 1515, Melville, NY 11747-0515 / 516-643-5466 FAX: 516-643-2426 rschaefe@optonline.net www.schaefershooting.com

Scharch Mfg., Inc., 10325 CR 120, Salida, CO 81201 / 719-539-7242 or 800-836-4683; FAX: 719-539-3021

Scherer, Box 250, Ewing, VA 24240 / 615-733-2615; FAX: 615-733-2073

Schiffman, Curt, 3017 Kevin Cr., Idaho Falls, ID 83402 / 208-524-4684

Schiffman, Mike, 8233 S. Crystal Springs, McCammon, ID 83250 / 208-254-9114

Schiffman, Norman, 3017 Kevin Cr., Idaho Falls, ID 83402 / 208-524-4684

Schmidt & Bender, Inc., 438 Willow Brook Rd., Meriden, NH 03770 / 800-468-3450 or 800-468-3450; FAX: 603-469-3471

Schmidtke Group, 17050 W. Salentine Dr., New Berlin, WI 53151-7349

Schmidtman Custom Ammunition, 6 Gilbert Court, Cotati, CA 94931

Schneider Bullets, 3655 West 214th St., Fairview Park, OH 44126

Schneider Rifle Barrels, Inc, Gary, 12202 N 62nd Pl, Scottsdale, AZ 85254 / 602-948-2525

Schroeder Bullets, 1421 Thermal Ave., San Diego, CA 92154 / 619-423-3523; FAX: 619-423-8124

Schuetzen Pistol Works, 620-626 Old Pacific Hwy. SE, Olympia, WA 98513 / 360-459-3471; FAX: 360-491-3447

Schulz Industries, 16247 Minnesota Ave., Paramount, CA 90723 / 213-439-5903

Schumakers Gun Shop, 512 Prouty Corner Lp. A, Colville, WA 99114 / 509-684-4848

Scope Control, Inc., 5775 Co. Rd. 23 SE, Alexandria, MN 56308 / 612-762-7295

ScopLevel, 151 Lindbergh Ave., Suite C, Livermore, CA 94550 / 925-449-5052; FAX: 925-373-0861

Score High Gunsmithing, 9812-A, Cochiti SE, Albuquerque, NM 087123 / 800-326-5632 or 505-292-5532; FAX: 505-292-2592

Scot Powder, Rt.1 Box 167, McEwen, TN 37101 / 800-416-3006; FAX: 615-729-4211

Scot Powder Co. of Ohio, Inc., Box GD96, Only, TN 37140 / 615-729-4207 or 800-416-3006; FAX: 615-729-4217

Scott, Dwight, 23089 Englehardt St., Clair Shores, MI 48080 / 313-779-4735

Scott Fine Guns Inc., Thad, PO Box 412, Indianola, MS 38751 / 601-887-5929

Scott McDougall & Associates, 7950 Redwood Dr., Suite 13, Cotati, CA 94931 / 707-546-2264; FAX: 707-795-1911 www.colt380.com

Searcy Enterprises, PO Box 584, Boron, CA 93596 / 760-762-6771 FAX: 760-762-0191

Second Chance Body Armor, P.O. Box 578, Central Lake, MI 49622 / 616-544-5721; FAX: 616-544-9824

Seebeck Assoc., R.E., P. O. Box 59752, Dallas, TX 75229

Seecamp Co. Inc., L. W., PO Box 255, New Haven, CT 06502 / 203-877-3429

Segway Industries, P.O. Box 783, Suffern, NY 10901-0783 / 914-357-5510

Seligman Shooting Products, Box 133, Seligman, AZ 86337 / 602-422-3607

Sellier & Bellot, USA Inc, PO Box 27006, Shawnee Mission, KS 66225 / 913-685-0916; FAX: 913-685-0917

Selsi Co., Inc., P.O. Box 10, Midland Park, NJ 07432-0010 / 201-935-0388; FAX: 201-935-5851

Semmer, Charles (See Remington Double Shotguns), 7885 Cyd Dr, Denver, CO 80221 / 303-429-6947

Sentinel Arms, P.O. Box 57, Detroit, MI 48231 / 313-331-1951; FAX: 313-331-1456

Service Armament, 689 Bergen Blvd., Ridgefield, NJ 07657

Servus Footwear Co., 1136 2nd St., Rock Island, IL 61204 / 309-786-7741; FAX: 309-786-9808

Shappy Bullets, 76 Milldale Ave., Plantsville, CT 06479 / 203-621-3704

Sharp Shooter Supply, 4970 Lehman Road, Delphos, OH 45833 / 419-695-3179

Sharps Arms Co., Inc., C., 100 Centennial, Box 885, Big Timber, MT 59011 / 406-932-4353

Shaw, Inc., E. R. (See Small Arms Mfg. Co.)

Shay's Gunsmithing, 931 Marvin Ave., Lebanon, PA 17042

Sheffield Knifemakers Supply, Inc., P.O. Box 741107, Orange City, FL 32774-1107 / 904-775-6453; FAX: 904-774-5754

Sheldon, Bruce. (See RIDGELINE, INC)

Shepherd Enterprises, Inc., Box 189, Waterloo, NE 68069 / 402-779-2424; FAX: 402-779-4010 sshepherd@shepherdscopes.com www.shepherdscopes.com

Sherwood, George, 46 N. River Dr., Roseburg, OR 97470 / 541-672-3159

Shilen, Inc., 205 Metro Park Blvd., Ennis, TX 75119 / 972-875-5318; FAX: 972-875-5402

Shiloh Creek, Box 357, Cottleville, MO 63338 / 314-925-1842; FAX: 314-925-1842

Shiloh Rifle Mfg., 201 Centennial Dr., Big Timber, MT 59011 / 406-932-4454; FAX: 406-932-5627

Shockley, Harold H., 204 E. Farmington Rd., Hanna City, IL 61536 / 309-565-4524

Shoemaker & Sons Inc., Tex, 714 W Cienega Ave, San Dimas, CA 91773 / 909-592-2071; FAX: 909-592-2378

Shoot Where You Look, Leon Measures, Dept GD, 408 Fair, Livingston, TX 77351

Shoot-N-C Targets (See Birchwood Casey)

Shooter's Choice, 16770 Hilltop Park Place, Chagrin Falls, OH 44023 / 216-543-8808; FAX: 216-543-8811

Shooter's Edge Inc., P.O.Box 769, Trinidad, CO 81082

Shooter's World, 3828 N. 28th Ave., Phoenix, AZ 85017 / 602-266-0170

Shooters Supply, 1120 Tieton Dr., Yakima, WA 98902 / 509-452-1181

Shootin' Accessories, Ltd., P.O. Box 6810, Auburn, CA 95604 / 916-889-2220

Shootin' Shack, Inc., 1065 Silver Beach Rd., Riviera Beach, FL 33403 / 561-842-0990

Shooting Chrony, Inc., 3269 Niagara Falls Blvd., N. Tonawanda, NY 14120 / 905-276-6292; FAX: 416-276-6295

Shooting Specialties (See Titus, Daniel)

Shooting Star, 1715 FM 1626 Ste 105, Manchaca, TX 78652 / 512-462-0009

Shotgun Sports, PO Box 6810, Auburn, CA 95604 / 530-889-2220; FAX: 530-889-9106

Shotguns Unlimited, 2307 Fon Du Lac Rd., Richmond, VA 23229 / 804-752-7115

ShurKatch Corporation, PO Box 850, Richfield Springs, NY 13439 / 315-858-1470; FAX: 315-858-2969

Siegrist Gun Shop, 8752 Turtle Road, Whittemore, MI 48770

Sierra Bullets, 1400 W. Henry St., Sedalia, MO 65301 / 816-827-6300; FAX: 816-827-6300

Sierra Specialty Prod. Co., 1344 Oakhurst Ave., Los Altos, CA 94024 FAX: 415-965-1536

SIG, CH-8212 Neuhausen, SWITZERLAND

SIG-Sauer (See U.S. Importer-Sigarms Inc.)

Sigarms, Inc., Corporate Park, Exeter, NH 03833 / 603-772-2302; FAX: 603-772-9082

Sightron, Inc., 1672B Hwy. 96, Franklinton, NC 27525 / 919-528-8783; FAX: 919-528-0995

Signet Metal Corp., 551 Stewart Ave., Brooklyn, NY 11222 / 718-384-5400; FAX: 718-388-7488

Sile Distributors, Inc., 7 Centre Market Pl., New York, NY 10013 / 212-925-4111; FAX: 212-925-3149

Silencio/Safety Direct, 56 Coney Island Dr., Sparks, NV 89431 / 800-648-1812 or 702-354-4451; FAX: 702-359-1074

Silent Hunter, 1100 Newton Ave., W. Collingswood, NJ 08107 / 609-854-3276

Silhouette Leathers, P.O. Box 1161, Gunnison, CO 81230 / 303-641-6639

Silver Eagle Machining, 18007 N. 69th Ave., Glendale, AZ 85308

Silver Ridge Gun Shop (See Goodwin, Fred)

Simmons, Jerry, 715 Middlebury St., Goshen, IN 46526 / 219-533-8546

MANUFACTURER'S DIRECTORY

Simmons Gun Repair, Inc., 700 S. Rogers Rd., Olathe, KS 66062 / 913-782-3131; FAX: 913-782-4189
Simmons Outdoor Corp., PO Box 217, Heflin, AL 36264
Sinclair International, Inc., 2330 Wayne Haven St., Fort Wayne, IN 46803 / 219-493-1858; FAX: 219-493-2530
Singletary, Kent, 2915 W. Ross, Phoenix, AZ 85027 / 602-582-4900
Sipes Gun Shop, 7415 Asher Ave., Little Rock, AR 72204 / 501-565-8480
Siskiyou Gun Works (See Donnelly, C. P.)
Six Enterprises, 320-D Turtle Creek Ct., San Jose, CA 95125 / 408-999-0201; FAX: 408-999-0216
SKAN A.R., 4 St. Catherines Road, Long Melford, Suffolk, O10 9JU ENGLAND / 011-0787-312942
SKB Shotguns, 4325 S. 120th St., Omaha, NE 68137 / 800-752-2767; FAX: 402-330-8029
Skeoch, Brian R., P.O. Box 279, Glenrock, WY 82637 / 307-436-9655 FAX: 307-436-9034
Skip's Machine, 364 29 Road, Grand Junction, CO 81501 / 303-245-5417
Sklany's Machine Shop, 566 Birch Grove Dr., Kalispell, MT 59901 / 406-755-4257
Slezak, Jerome F., 1290 Marlowe, Lakewood (Cleveland), OH 44107 / 216-221-1668
Slug Group, Inc., P.O. Box 376, New Paris, PA 15554 / 814-839-4517; FAX: 814-839-2601
Slug Site, Ozark Wilds, 21300 Hwy. 5, Versailles, MO 65084 / 573-378-6430 john.ebeling.com
Small Arms Mfg. Co., 5312 Thoms Run Rd., Bridgeville, PA 15017 / 412-221-4343; FAX: 412-221-4303
Small Arms Specialists, 443 Firchburg Rd, Mason, NH 03048 / 603-878-0427 FAX: 603-878-3905 miniguns@empire.net miniguns.com
Small Custom Mould & Bullet Co., Box 17211, Tucson, AZ 85731
Smart Parts, 1203 Spring St., Latrobe, PA 15650 / 412-539-2660; FAX: 412-539-2298
Smires, C. L., 5222 Windmill Lane, Columbia, MD 21044-1328
Smith & Wesson, 2100 Roosevelt Ave., Springfield, MA 01104 / 413-781-8300; FAX: 413-731-8980
Smith, Art, 230 Main St. S., Hector, MN 55342 / 320-848-2760; FAX: 320-848-2760
Smith, Mark A., P.O. Box 182, Sinclair, WY 82334 / 307-324-7929
Smith, Michael, 620 Nye Circle, Chattanooga, TN 37405 / 615-267-8341
Smith, Ron, 5869 Straley, Ft. Worth, TX 76114 / 817-732-6768
Smith, Sharmon, 4545 Speas Rd., Fruitland, ID 83619 / 208-452-6329
Smith Abrasives, Inc., 1700 Sleepy Valley Rd., P.O. Box 5095, Hot Springs, AR 71902-5095 / 501-321-2244; FAX: 501-321-9232
Smith Saddlery, Jesse W., 16909 E Jackson Rd, Elk, WA 99009-9600 / 509-325-0622
Smokey Valley Rifles (See Lutz Engraving, Ron E)
Snapp's Gunshop, 6911 E. Washington Rd., Clare, MI 48617 / 517-386-9226
Sno-Seal, Inc. (See Atsko/Sno-Seal)
Societa Armi Bresciane Srl (See U.S. Importer-Cape Outfitters)
SOS Products Co. (See Buck Stix-SOS Products Co.), Box 3, Neenah, WI 54956
Sotheby's, 1334 York Ave. at 72nd St., New York, NY 10021 / 212-606-7260
Sound Technology, Box 391, Pelham, AL 35124 / 205-664-5860 or 907-486-2825
South Bend Replicas, Inc., 61650 Oak Rd.., South Bend, IN 46614 / 219-289-4500
Southeastern Community College, 1015 S. Gear Ave., West Burlington, IA 52655 / 319-752-2731
Southern Ammunition Co., Inc., 4232 Meadow St., Loris, SC 29569-3124 / 803-756-3262; FAX: 803-756-3583
Southern Bloomer Mfg. Co., P.O. Box 1621, Bristol, TN 37620 / 615-878-6660; FAX: 615-878-8761
Southern Security, 1700 Oak Hills Dr., Kingston, TN 37763 / 423-376-6297; FAX: 800-251-9992
Southwind Sanctions, P.O. Box 445, Aledo, TX 76008 / 817-441-8917
Sparks, Milt, 605 E. 44th St. No. 2, Boise, ID 83714-4800
Spartan-Realtree Products, Inc., 1390 Box Circle, Columbus, GA 31907 / 706-569-9101; FAX: 706-569-0042
Specialty Gunsmithing, Lynn McMurdo, P.O. Box 404, Afton, WY 83110 / 307-886-5535
Specialty Shooters Supply, Inc., 3325 Griffin Rd., Suite 9mm, Fort Lauderdale, FL 33317
Speedfeed Inc., PO Box 1146, Rocklin, CA 95677 / 916-630-7720; FAX: 916-630-7719
Speer Products Div. of Blount Inc. Sporting Equipm, P.O. Box 856, Lewiston, ID 83501 / 208-746-2351; FAX: 208-746-2915
Spegel, Craig, PO Box 387, Nehalem, OR 97131 / 503-368-5653

Speiser, Fred D., 2229 Dearborn, Missoula, MT 59801 / 406-549-8133
Spencer Reblue Service, 1820 Tupelo Trail, Holt, MI 48842 / 517-694-7474
Spencer's Custom Guns, 4107 Jacobs Creek Dr, Scottsville, VA 24590 / 804-293-6836 FAX: 804-293-6836
SPG LLC, P.O. Box 1625, Cody, WY 82414 / 307-587-7621; FAX: 307-587-7695
Sphinx Engineering SA, Ch. des Grandex-Vies 2, CH-2900, Porrentruy, SWITZERLAND FAX: 41 66 66 30 90
Spokhandguns, Inc., 1206 Fig St., Benton City, WA 99320 / 509-588-5255
Sport Flite Manufacturing Co., P.O. Box 1082, Bloomfield Hills, MI 48303 / 248-647-3747
Sporting Arms Mfg., Inc., 801 Hall Ave., Littlefield, TX 79339 / 806-385-5665; FAX: 806-385-3394
Sporting Clays Of America, 9257 Bluckeye Rd, Sugar Grove, OH 43155-9632 / 740-746-8334; FAX: 740-746-8605
Sports Innovations Inc., P.O. Box 5181, 8505 Jacksboro Hwy., Wichita Falls, TX 76307 / 817-723-6015
Sportsman Safe Mfg. Co., 6309-6311 Paramount Blvd., Long Beach, CA 90805 / 800-266-7150 or 310-984-5445
Sportsman Supply Co., 714 E. Eastwood, P.O. Box 650, Marshall, MO 65340 / 816-886-9393
Sportsman's Communicators, 588 Radcliffe Ave., Pacific Palisades, CA 90272 / 800-538-3752
Sportsmatch U.K. Ltd., 16 Summer St., Leighton Buzzard, Bedfordshire, LU7 8HT ENGLAND / 01525-381638; FAX: 01525-851236
Sportsmen's Exchange & Western Gun Traders, Inc., 560 S. C St., Oxnard, CA 93030 / 805-483-1917
Spradlin's, 457 Shannon Rd, Texos Creek, CO 81223 / 719-275-7105 FAX: 719-275-3852 spradlins@prodigt.net jimspradlin.com
Springfield Sporters, Inc., RD 1, Penn Run, PA 15765 / 412-254-2626; FAX: 412-254-9173
Springfield, Inc., 420 W. Main St., Geneseo, IL 61254 / 309-944-5631; FAX: 309-944-3676
Spyderco, Inc., 4565 N. Hwy. 93, P.O. Box 800, Golden, CO 80403 / 303-279-8383 or 800-525-7770; FAX: 303-278-2229
SSK Industries, 590 Woodvue Lane, Wintersville, OH 43953 / 740-264-0176; FAX: 740-264-2257
Stackpole Books, 5067 Ritter Rd., Mechanicsburg, PA 17055-6921 / 717-796-0411; FAX: 717-796-0412
Stalker, Inc., P.O. Box 21, Fishermans Wharf Rd., Malakoff, TX 75148 / 903-489-1010
Stalwart Corporation, 76 Imperial, Unit A, Evanston, WY 82930 / 307-789-7687; FAX: 307-789-7688
Stan De Treville & Co., 4129 Normal St., San Diego, CA 92103 / 619-298-3393
Stanley Bullets, 2085 Heatheridge Ln., Reno, NV 89509
Stanley Scruggs' Game Calls, Rt. 1, Hwy. 661, Cullen, VA 23934 / 804-542-4241 or 800-323-4828
Star Ammunition, Inc., 5520 Rock Hampton Ct., Indianapolis, IN 46268 / 800-221-5927; FAX: 317-872-5847
Star Bonifacio Echeverria S.A., Torrekva 3, Eibar, 20600 SPAIN / 43-107340; FAX: 43-101524
Star Custom Bullets, P.O. Box 608, 468 Main St., Ferndale, CA 95536 / 707-786-9140; FAX: 707-786-9117
Star Machine Works, PO Box 1872, Pioneer, CA 95666 / 209-295-5000
Stark's Bullet Mfg., 2580 Monroe St., Eugene, OR 97405
Starke Bullet Company, P.O. Box 400, 605 6th St. NW, Cooperstown, ND 58425 / 888-797-3431
Starkey Labs, 6700 Washington Ave. S., Eden Prairie, MN 55344
Starkey's Gun Shop, 9430 McCombs, El Paso, TX 79924 / 915-751-3030
Starlight Training Center, Inc., Rt. 1, P.O. Box 88, Bronaugh, MO 64728 / 417-843-3555
Starline, Inc., 1300 W. Henry St., Sedalia, MO 65301 / 660-827-6640 FAX: 660-827-6650 bjhayden@starline-bra.com http://www.starlinebrass.com
Starr Trading Co., Jedediah, P.O. Box 2007, Farmington Hills, MI 48333 / 810-683-4343; FAX: 810-683-3282
Starrett Co., L. S., 121 Crescent St, Athol, MA 01331 / 978-249-3551 FAX: 978-249-8495
State Arms Gun Co., 815 S. Division St., Waunakee, WI 53597 / 608-849-5800
Steelman's Gun Shop, 10465 Beers Rd., Swartz Creek, MI 48473 / 810-735-4884
Steffens, Ron, 18396 Mariposa Creek Rd., Willits, CA 95490 / 707-485-0873
Stegall, James B., 26 Forest Rd., Wallkill, NY 12589
Steger, James R., 1131 Dorsey Pl., Plainfield, NJ 07062
Steve Henigson & Associates, P.O. Box 2726, Culver City, CA 90231 / 310-305-8288; FAX: 310-305-1905
Steve Kamyk Engraver, 9 Grandview Dr., Westfield, MA 01085-1810 / 413-568-0457
Steve Nastoff's 45 Shop, Inc., 12288 Mahoning Ave., P.O. Box 446, North Jackson, OH 44451 / 330-538-2977

Steves House of Guns, Rt. 1, Minnesota City, MN 55959 / 507-689-2573
Stewart Game Calls, Inc., Johnny, PO Box 7954, 5100 Fort Ave, Waco, TX 76714 / 817-772-3261; FAX: 817-772-3670
Stewart's Gunsmithing, P.O. Box 5854, Pietersburg North 0750, Transvaal, SOUTH AFRICA / 01521-89401
Steyr Mannlicher AG & CO KG, Mannlicherstrasse 1, A-4400, Steyr, AUSTRIA / 0043-7252-78621; FAX: 0043-7252-68621
STI International, 114 Halmar Cove, Georgetown, TX 78628 / 800-959-8201; FAX: 512-819-0465
Stiles Custom Guns, 76 Cherry Run Rd, Box 1605, Homer City, PA 15748 / 712-479-9945
Stillwell, Robert, 421 Judith Ann Dr., Schertz, TX 78154
Stoeger Industries, 5 Mansard Ct., Wayne, NJ 07470 / 201-872-9500 or 800-631-0722; FAX: 201-872-2230
Stoeger Publishing Co. (See Stoeger Industries)
Stone Enterprises Ltd., Rt. 609, P.O. Box 335, Wicomico Church, VA 22579 / 804-580-5114; FAX: 804-580-8421
Stone Mountain Arms, 5988 Peachtree Corners E., Norcross, GA 30071 / 800-251-9412
Stoney Point Products, Inc., PO Box 234, 1822 N Minnesota St, New Ulm, MN 56073-0234 / 507-354-3360; FAX: 507-354-7236 stoney@newulmtel.net www.stoney-point.com
Storage Tech, 1254 Morris Ave., N. Huntingdon, PA 15642 / 800-437-9393
Storey, Dale A. (See DGS Inc.)
Storm, Gary, P.O. Box 5211, Richardson, TX 75083 / 214-385-0862
Stott's Creek Armory, Inc., 2526 S. 475W, Morgantown, IN 46160 / 317-878-5489; FAX: 317-878-9489 www.sccalendar.com
Stratco, Inc., P.O. Box 2270, Kalispell, MT 59901 / 406-755-1221; FAX: 406-755-1226
Strawbridge, Victor W., 6 Pineview Dr., Dover, NH 03820 / 603-742-0013
Strayer, Sandy. (See STRAYER-VOIGT, INC)
Strayer-Voigt, Inc, Sandy Strayer, 3435 Ray Orr Blvd, Grand Prairie, TX 75050 / 972-513-0575
Streamlight, Inc., 1030 W. Germantown Pike, Norristown, PA 19403 / 215-631-0600; FAX: 610-631-0712
Strong Holster Co., 39 Grove St., Gloucester, MA 01930 / 508-281-3300; FAX: 508-281-6321
Strutz Rifle Barrels, Inc., W. C., PO Box 611, Eagle River, WI 54521 / 715-479-4766
Stuart, V. Pat, Rt.1, Box 447-S, Greenville, VA 24440 / 804-556-3845
Sturgeon Valley Sporters, K. Ide, P.O. Box 283, Vanderbilt, MI 49795 / 517-983-4338
Sturm Ruger & Co. Inc., 200 Ruger Rd., Prescott, AZ 86301 / 520-541-8820; FAX: 520-541-8850
Sullivan, David S .(See Westwind Rifles Inc.)
Summit Specialties, Inc., P.O. Box 786, Decatur, AL 35602 / 205-353-0634; FAX: 205-353-9818
Sun Welding Safe Co., 290 Easy St. No.3, Simi Valley, CA 93065 / 805-584-6678 or 800-729-SAFE FAX: 805-584-6169
Sunny Hill Enterprises, Inc., W1790 Cty. HHH, Malone, WI 53049 / 920-795-4722 FAX: 920-795-4822
"Su-Press-On",Inc., P.O. Box 09161, Detroit, MI 48209 / 313-842-4222
Sure-Shot Game Calls, Inc., P.O. Box 816, 6835 Capitol, Groves, TX 77619 / 409-962-1636; FAX: 409-962-5465
Survival Arms, Inc., 273 Canal St., Shelton, CT 06484-3173 / 203-924-6533; FAX: 203-924-2581
Svon Corp., 280 Eliot St., Ashland, MA 01721 / 508-881-8852
Swann, D. J., 5 Orsova Close, Eltham North Vic., 3095 AUSTRALIA / 03-431-0323
Swanndri New Zealand, 152 Elm Ave., Burlingame, CA 94010 / 415-347-6158
SwaroSports, Inc. (See JagerSport Ltd, One Wholesale Way, Cranston, RI 02920 / 800-962-4867; FAX: 401-946-2587
Swarovski Optik North America Ltd., 2 Slater Rd., Cranston, RI 02920 / 401-946-2220 or 800-426-3089 FAX: 401-946-2587
Sweet Home, Inc., P.O. Box 900, Orrville, OH 44667-0900
Swenson's 45 Shop, A. D., 3839 Ladera Vista Rd, Fallbrook, CA 92028-9431
Swift Bullet Co., P.O. Box 27, 201 Main St., Quinter, KS 67752 / 913-754-3959; FAX: 913-754-2359
Swift Instruments, Inc., 952 Dorchester Ave., Boston, MA 02125 / 617-436-2960; FAX: 617-436-3232
Swift River Gunworks, 450 State St., Belchertown, MA 01007 / 413-323-4052
Szweda, Robert (See RMS Custom Gunsmithing)

T

T&S Industries, Inc., 1027 Skyview Dr., W. Carrollton, OH 45449 / 513-859-8414

MANUFACTURER'S DIRECTORY

T.F.C. S.p.A., Via G. Marconi 118, B, Villa Carcina 25069, ITALY / 030-881271; FAX: 030-881826
T.G. Faust, Inc., 544 Minor St., Reading, PA 19602 / 610-375-8549; FAX: 610-375-4488
T.H.U. Enterprises, Inc., P.O. Box 418, Lederach, PA 19450 / 215-256-1665; FAX: 215-256-9718
T.K. Lee Co., 1282 Branchwater Ln., Birmingham, AL 35216 / 205-913-5222
T.W. Menck Gunsmith Inc., 5703 S. 77th St., Ralston, NE 68127
Tabler Marketing, 2554 Lincoln Blvd., Suite 555, Marina Del Rey, CA 90291 / 818-755-4565; FAX: 818-755-0972
Taconic Firearms Ltd., Perry Lane, PO Box 553, Cambridge, NY 12816 / 518-677-2704; FAX: 518-677-5974
TacStar, PO Box 547, Cottonwood, AZ 86326-0547 / 602-639-0072; FAX: 602-634-8781
TacTell, Inc., P.O. Box 5654, Maryville, TN 37802 / 615-982-7855; FAX: 615-558-8294
Tactical Defense Institute, 574 Miami Bluff Ct., Loveland, OH 45140 / 513-677-8229 FAX: 513-677-0447
Talley, Dave, P.O. Box 821, Glenrock, WY 82637 / 307-436-8724 or 307-436-9315
Talmage, William G., 10208 N. County Rd. 425 W., Brazil, IN 47834 / 812-442-0804
Talon Mfg. Co., Inc., 621 W. King St., Martinsburg, WV 25401 / 304-264-9714; FAX: 304-264-9725
Tamarack Products, Inc., P.O. Box 625, Wauconda, IL 60084 / 708-526-9333; FAX: 708-526-9353
Tanfoglio Fratelli S.r.l., via Valtrompia 39, 41, Brescia, ITALY / 30-8910361; FAX: 30-8910183
Tanglefree Industries, 1261 Heavenly Dr., Martinez, CA 94553 / 800-982-4868; FAX: 510-825-3874
Tank's Rifle Shop, P.O. Box 474, Fremont, NE 68026-0474 / 402-727-1317; FAX: 402-721-2573
Tanner (See U.S. Importer-Mandall Shooting Supplies Inc.,)
Tar-Hunt Custom Rifles, Inc., RR3, P.O. Box 572, Bloomsburg, PA 17815-9351 / 717-784-6368; FAX: 717-784-6368
Taracorp Industries, Inc., 1200 Sixteenth St., Granite City, IL 62040 / 618-451-4400
Target Shooting, Inc., PO Box 773, Watertown, SD 57201 / 605-882-6955; FAX: 605-882-8840
Tarnhelm Supply Co., Inc., 431 High St., Boscawen, NH 03303 / 603-796-2551; FAX: 603-796-2918
Tasco Sales, Inc., 2889 Commerce Pky., Miramar, FL 33025
Taurus International Firearms, Inc., 16175 NW 49th Ave., Miami, FL 33014 / 305-624-1115; FAX: 305-623-7506
Taurus S.A. Forjas, Avenida Do Forte 511, Porto Alegre, RS BRAZIL 91360 / 55-51-347-4050; FAX: 55-51-347-3065
Taylor & Robbins, P.O. Box 164, Rixford, PA 16745 / 814-966-3233
Taylor's & Co., Inc., 304 Lenoir Dr., Winchester, VA 22603 / 540-722-2017; FAX: 540-722-2018
TCCI, P.O. Box 302, Phoenix, AZ 85001 / 602-237-3823; FAX: 602-237-3858
TCSR, 3998 Hoffman Rd., White Bear Lake, MN 55110-4626 / 800-328-5323; FAX: 612-429-0526
TDP Industries, Inc., 606 Airport Blvd., Doylestown, PA 18901 / 215-345-8687; FAX: 215-345-6057
Techno Arms (See U.S. Importer- Auto-Ordnance Corp.)
Tecnolegno S.p.A., Via A. Locatelli, 6 10, 24019 Zogno, I ITALY / 0345-55111; FAX: 0345-55155
Ted Blocker Holsters, Inc., Clackamas Business Park Bldg A, 14787 SE 82nd Dr, Clackamas, OR 97015 / 503-557-7757; FAX: 503-557-3771
Tele-Optics, 630 E. Rockland Rd., PO Box 6313, Libertyville, IL 60048 / 847-362-7757
Ten-Ring Precision, Inc., Alex B. Hamilton, 1449 Blue Crest Lane, San Antonio, TX 78232 / 210-494-3063; FAX: 210-494-3066
TEN-X Products Group, 1905 N Main St, Suite 133, Cleburne, TX 76031-1305 / 972-243-4016 or 800-433-2225; FAX: 972-243-4112
Tennessee Valley Mfg., P.O. Box 1175, Corinth, MS 38834 / 601-286-5014
Tepeco, P.O. Box 342, Friendswood, TX 77546 / 713-482-2702
Terry K. Kopp Professional Gunsmithing, Rt 1 Box 224F, Lexington, MO 64067 / 816-259-2636
Testing Systems, Inc., 220 Pegasus Ave., Northvale, NJ 07647
Teton Arms, Inc., P.O. Box 411, Wilson, WY 83014 / 307-733-3395
Tetra Gun Lubricants (See FTI, Inc.)
Tex Shoemaker & Sons, Inc., 714 W. Cienega Ave., San Dimas, CA 91773 / 909-592-2071; FAX: 909-592-2378
Texas Armory (See Bond Arms, Inc.)
Texas Platers Supply Co., 2453 W. Five Mile Parkway, Dallas, TX 75233 / 214-330-7168
Thad Rybka Custom Leather Equipment, 134 Havilah Hill, Odenville, AL 35120
Thad Scott Fine Guns, Inc., P.O. Box 412, Indianola, MS 38751 / 601-887-5929
The Accuracy Den, 25 Bitterbrush Rd., Reno, NV 89523 / 702-345-0225
The Armoury, Inc., Rt. 202, Box 2340, New Preston, CT 06777 / 860-868-0001; FAX: 860-868-2919
The Ballistic Program Co., Inc., 2417 N. Patterson St., Thomasville, GA 31792 / 912-228-5739 or 800-368-0835
The BulletMakers Workshop, RFD 1 Box 1755, Brooks, ME 04921
The Competitive Pistol Shop, 5233 Palmer Dr., Ft. Worth, TX 76117-2433 / 817-834-8479
The Country Armourer, P.O. Box 308, Ashby, MA 01431-0308 / 508-827-6797; FAX: 508-827-4845
The Creative Craftsman, Inc., 95 Highway 29 North, P.O. Box 331, Lawrenceville, GA 30246 / 404-963-2112; FAX: 404-513-9488
The Custom Shop, 890 Cochrane Crescent, Peterborough, ON K9H 5N3 CANADA / 705-742-6693
The Dutchman's Firearms, Inc., 4143 Taylor Blvd., Louisville, KY 40215 / 502-366-0555
The Ensign-Bickford Co., 660 Hopmeadow St., Simsbury, CT 06070
The Eutaw Co., Inc., P.O. Box 608, U.S. Hwy. 176 West, Holly Hill, SC 29059 / 803-496-3341
The Firearm Training Center, 9555 Blandville Rd., West Paducah, KY 42086 / 502-554-5886
The Fouling Shot, 6465 Parfet St., Arvada, CO 80004
The Gun Doctor, 435 East Maple, Roselle, IL 60172 / 708-894-0668
The Gun Doctor, P.O. Box 39242, Downey, CA 90242 / 310-862-3158
The Gun Parts Corp., 226 Williams Lane, West Hurley, NY 12491 / 914-679-2417; FAX: 914-679-5849
The Gun Room, 1121 Burlington, Muncie, IN 47302 / 765-282-9073; FAX: 765-282-5270 bshstleguns@aol.com
The Gun Room Press, 127 Raritan Ave., Highland Park, NJ 08904 / 732-545-4344; FAX: 732-545-4344
The Gun Shop, 62778 Spring Creek Rd., Montrose, CO 81401
The Gun Shop, 5550 S. 900 East, Salt Lake City, UT 84117 / 801-263-3633
The Gun Shop, 716-A South Rogers Road, Olathe, KS 66062
The Gun Works, 247 S. 2nd, Springfield, OR 97477 / 541-741-4118; FAX: 541-988-1097 gunworks@worldnet.att.net www.thegunworks.com
The Gunsight, 1712 North Placentia Ave., Fullerton, CA 92631
The Gunsmith in Elk River, 14021 Victoria Lane, Elk River, MN 55330 / 612-441-7761
The Hanned Line, P.O. Box 2387, Cupertino, CA 95015-2387 smith@hanned.com www.hanned.com
The Holster Shop, 720 N. Flagler Dr., Ft. Lauderdale, FL 33304 / 305-463-7910; FAX: 305-761-1483
The House of Muskets, Inc., P.O. Box 4640, Pagosa Springs, CO 81157 / 970-731-2295
The Keller Co., 4215 McEwen Rd., Dallas, TX 75244 / 214-770-8585
The Lewis Lead Remover (See LEM Gun Specialties Inc.)
The NgraveR Co., 67 Wawecus Hill Rd., Bozrah, CT 06334 / 860-823-1533
The Ordnance Works, 2969 Pidgeon Point Road, Eureka, CA 95501 / 707-443-3252
The Orvis Co., Rt. 7, Manchester, VT 05254 / 802-362-3622; FAX: 802-362-3525
The Outdoor Connection,Inc., 201 Cotton Dr., P.O. Box 7751, Waco, TX 76714-7751 / 800-533-6076 or 817-772-5575; FAX: 817-776-3553
The Outdoorsman's Bookstore, Llangorse, Brecon, LD3 7UE U.K. / 44-1874-658-660; FAX: 44-1874-658-650
The Park Rifle Co., Ltd., Unit 6a Dartford Trade Park, Power Mill Lane, Dartford DA7 7NX, ENGLAND / 011-0322-222512
The Paul Co., 27385 Pressonville Rd., Wellsville, KS 66092 / 785-883-4444; FAX: 785-883-2525
The Powder Horn, Inc., P.O. Box 114 Patty Drive, Cusseta, GA 31805 / 404-989-3257
The Protector Mfg. Co., Inc., 443 Ashwood Place, Boca Raton, FL 33431 / 407-394-6011
The Robar Co.'s, Inc., 21438 N. 7th Ave., Suite B, Phoenix, AZ 85027 / 602-581-2648; FAX: 602-582-0059
The School of Gunsmithing, 6065 Roswell Rd., Atlanta, GA 30328 / 800-223-4542
The Shooting Gallery, 8070 Southern Blvd., Boardman, OH 44512 / 216-726-7788
The Sight Shop, John G. Lawson, 1802 E. Columbia Ave., Tacoma, WA 98404 / 206-474-5465
The Southern Armory, 25 Millstone Road, Woodlawn, VA 24381 / 703-238-1343; FAX: 703-238-1453
The Surecase Co., 233 Wilshire Blvd., Ste. 900, Santa Monica, CA 90401 / 800-92ARMLOC
The Swampfire Shop (See Peterson Gun Shop, Inc.)
The Walnut Factory, 235 West Rd. No. 1, Portsmouth, NH 03801 / 603-436-2225; FAX: 603-433-7003
The Wilson Arms Co., 63 Leetes Island Rd., Branford, CT 06405 / 203-488-7297; FAX: 203-488-0135
Theis, Terry, HC 63 Box 213, Harper, TX 78631 / 830-864-4438
Theoben Engineering, Stephenson Road, St. Ives Huntingdon, Cambs., PE17 4WJ ENGLAND / 011-0480-461718
Thiewes, George W., 14329 W. Parada Dr., Sun City West, AZ 85375
Things Unlimited, 235 N. Kimbau, Casper, WY 82601 / 307-234-5277
Thirion Gun Engraving, Denise, PO Box 408, Graton, CA 95444 / 707-829-1876
Thomas, Charles C., 2600 S. First St., Springfield, IL 62794 / 217-789-8980; FAX: 217-789-9130
Thompson, Norm, 18905 NW Thurman St., Portland, OR 97209
Thompson Bullet Lube Co., P.O. Box 472343, Garland, TX 75047-2343 / 972-271-8063; FAX: 972-840-6743 thomlube@flash.net www.thompsonbulletlube.com
Thompson Precision, 110 Mary St., P.O. Box 251, Warren, IL 61087 / 815-745-3625
Thompson, Randall. (See HIGHLINE MACHINE CO.)
Thompson Target Technology, 618 Roslyn Ave., SW, Canton, OH 44710 / 216-453-7707; FAX: 216-478-4723
Thompson, Randall (See Highline Machine Co.)
Thompson/Center Arms, P.O. Box 5002, Rochester, NH 03867 / 603-332-2394; FAX: 603-332-5133
3-D Ammunition & Bullets, PO Box 433, Doniphan, NE 68832 / 402-845-2285 or 800-255-6712; FAX: 402-845-6546
3-Ten Corp., P.O. Box 269, Feeding Hills, MA 01030 / 413-789-2086; FAX: 413-789-1549
300 Below Services (See Cryo-Accurizing)
Thunden Ranch, HCR 1, Box 53, Mt. Home, TX 78058 / 830-640-3138
Thunder Mountain Arms, P.O. Box 593, Oak Harbor, WA 98277 / 206-679-4657; FAX: 206-675-1114
Thurston Sports, Inc., RD 3 Donovan Rd., Auburn, NY 13021 / 315-253-0966
Tiger-Hunt Gunstocks, Box 379, Beaverdale, PA 15921 / 814-472-5161 tigerhunt4@aol.com www.gunstockwood.com
Tikka (See U.S. Importer-Stoeger Industries)
Timber Heirloom Products, 618 Roslyn Ave. SW, Canton, OH 44710 / 216-453-7707; FAX: 216-478-4723
Time Precision, Inc., 640 Federal Rd., Brookfield, CT 06804 / 203-775-8343
Tink's Safariland Hunting Corp., P.O. Box 244, 1140 Monticello Rd., Madison, GA 30650 / 706-342-4915; FAX: 706-342-7568
Tinks & Ben Lee Hunting Products (See Wellington Outdoors)
Tioga Engineering Co., Inc., P.O. Box 913, 13 Cone St., Wellsboro, PA 16901 / 717-724-3533; FAX: 717-662-3347
Tippman Pneumatics, Inc., 3518 Adams Center Rd., Fort Wayne, IN 46806 / 219-749-6022; FAX: 219-749-6619
Tirelli, Snc Di Tirelli Primo E.C., Via Matteotti No. 359, Gardone V.T. Brescia, I ITALY / 030-8912819; FAX: 030-832240
TM Stockworks, 6355 Maplecrest Rd., Fort Wayne, IN 46835 / 219-485-5389
TMI Products (See Haselbauer Products, Jerry)
Tom Forrest, Inc., P.O. Box 326, Lakeside, CA 92040 / 619-561-5800; FAX: 619-561-0227
Tom's Gun Repair, Thomas G. Ivanoff, 76-6 Rt. Southfork Rd., Cody, WY 82414 / 307-587-6949
Tom's Gunshop, 3601 Central Ave., Hot Springs, AR 71913 / 501-624-3856
Tombstone Smoke'n' Deals, 3218 East Bell Road, Phoenix, AZ 85032 / 602-905-7013; FAX: 602-443-1998
Tonoloway Tack Drives, HCR 81, Box 100, Needmore, PA 17238
Tooley Custom Rifles, 516 Creek Meadow Dr., Gastonia, NC 28054 / 704-864-7525
Top-Line USA, Inc., 7920-28 Hamilton Ave., Cincinnati, OH 45231 / 513-522-2992 or 800-346-6699; FAX: 513-522-0916
Torel, Inc., 1708 N. South St., P.O. Box 592, Yoakum, TX 77995 / 512-293-2341; FAX: 512-293-3413
TOZ (See U.S. Importer-Nygord Precision Products)
Track of the Wolf, Inc., P.O. Box 6, Osseo, MN 55369-0006 / 612-424-2500; FAX: 612-424-9860
TracStar Industries, Inc., 218 Justin Dr., Cottonwood, AZ 86326 / 520-639-0072; FAX: 520-634-8781
Tradewinds, Inc., P.O. Box 1191, 2339-41 Tacoma Ave. S., Tacoma, WA 98401 / 206-272-4887
Traditions Performance Firearms, P.O. Box 776, 1375 Boston Post Rd., Old Saybrook, CT 06475 / 860-388-4656; FAX: 860-388-4657 trad@ctz.nai.net www.traditionsmuzzle.com
Trafalgar Square, P.O. Box 257, N. Pomfret, VT 05053 / 802-457-1911
Traft Gunshop, P.O. Box 1078, Buena Vista, CO 81211
Trail Visions, 5800 N. Ames Terrace, Glendale, WI 53209 / 414-228-1328
Trammco, 839 Gold Run Rd., Boulder, CO 80302
Trax America, Inc., P.O. Box 898, 1150 Eldridge, Forrest City, AR 72335 / 870-633-0410 or 800-232-2327; FAX: 870-633-4788

DIRECTORY

Treadlok Gun Safe, Inc., 1764 Granby St. NE, Roanoke, VA 24012 / 800-729-8732 or 703-982-6881; FAX: 703-982-1059

Treemaster, P.O. Box 247, Guntersville, AL 35976 / 205-878-3597

Treso, Inc., P.O. Box 4640, Pagosa Springs, CO 81157 / 303-731-2295

Trevallion Gunstocks, 9 Old Mountain Rd., Cape Neddick, ME 03902 / 207-361-1130

Trico Plastics, 590 S. Vincent Ave., Azusa, CA 91702

Trigger Lock Division/Central Specialties Ltd., 1122 Silver Lake Road, Cary, IL 60013 / 847-639-3900; FAX: 847-639-3972

Trijicon, Inc., 49385 Shafer Ave., P.O. Box 930059, Wixom, MI 48393-0059 / 810-960-7700; FAX: 810-960-7725

Trilux, Inc., P.O. Box 24608, Winston-Salem, NC 27114 / 910-659-9438; FAX: 910-768-7720

Trinidad St. Jr Col Gunsmith Dept, 600 Prospect St., Trinidad, CO 81082 / 719-846-5631; FAX: 719-846-5667

Triple-K Mfg. Co., Inc., 2222 Commercial St., San Diego, CA 92113 / 619-232-2066; FAX: 619-232-7675

Tristar Sporting Arms, Ltd., 1814-16 Linn St., P.O. Box 7496, N. Kansas City, MO 64116 / 816-421-1400; FAX: 816-421-4182

Trius Traps, Inc., P.O. Box 471, 221 S. Miami Ave., Cleves, OH 45002 / 513-941-5682; FAX: 513-941-7970

Trooper Walsh, 2393 N Edgewood St, Arlington, VA 22207

Trophy Bonded Bullets, Inc., 900 S. Loop W., Suite 190, Houston, TX 77054 / 713-645-4499 or 888-308-3006; FAX: 713-741-6393

Trotman, Ken, 135 Ditton Walk, Unit 11, Cambridge, CB5 8PY ENGLAND / 01223-211030; FAX: 01223-212317

Tru-Balance Knife Co., P.O. Box 140555, Grand Rapids, MI 49514 / 616-453-3679

Tru-Square Metal Prods., Inc., 640 First St. SW, P.O. Box 585, Auburn, WA 98071 / 206-833-2310; FAX: 206-833-2349

True Flight Bullet Co., 5581 Roosevelt St., Whitehall, PA 18052 / 610-262-7630; FAX: 610-262-7806

Truglo, Inc, PO Box 1612, McKinna, TX 75070 / 972-774-0300 FAX: 972-774-0323 www.truglosights.com

Trulock Tool, Broad St., Whigham, GA 31797 / 912-762-4678

TTM, 1550 Solomon Rd., Santa Maria, CA 93455 / 805-934-1281

Tucker, James C., P.O. Box 1212, Paso Robles, CA 93447-1212

Tucson Mold, Inc., 930 S. Plumer Ave., Tucson, AZ 85719 / 520-792-1075; FAX: 520-792-1075

Turkish Firearms Corp., 522 W. Maple St., Allentown, PA 18101 / 610-821-8660; FAX: 610-821-9049

Turnbull Restoration, Doug, 6680 Rt 58 & 20 Dept. SM 2000, PO Box 471, Bloomfield, NY 14469 / 716-657-6338

Tuttle, Dale, 4046 Russell Rd., Muskegon, MI 49445 / 616-766-2250

Tyler Manufacturing & Distributing, 3804 S. Eastern, Oklahoma City, OK 73129 / 405-677-1487 or 800-654-8415

U

U.S. Fire-Arms Mfg. Co. Inc., 55 Van Dyke Ave., Hartford, CT 06106 / 877-227-6901; FAX: 860-724-6809 sales @ us-firearms.com; www.usfirearms.com

U.S. Importer-Wm. Larkin Moore, 8430 E. Raintree Ste. B-7, Scottsdale, AZ 85260

U.S. Repeating Arms Co., Inc., 275 Winchester Ave., Morgan, UT 84050-9333 / 801-876-3440; FAX: 801-876-3737

U.S. Tactical Systems (See Keng's Firearms Specialty)

U.S.A. Magazines, Inc., P.O. Box 39115, Downey, CA 90241 / 800-872-2577

Uberti, Aldo, Casella Postale 43, I-25063 Gardone V.T., ITALY

Uberti USA, Inc., P.O. Box 469, Lakeville, CT 06039 / 860-435-8068; FAX: 860-435-8146

UFA, Inc., 6927 E. Grandview Dr., Scottsdale, AZ 85254 / 800-616-2776

Ugartechea S. A., Ignacio, Chonta 26, Eibar, SPAIN / 43-121257; FAX: 43-121669

Ultimate Accuracy, 121 John Shelton Rd., Jacksonville, AR 72076 / 501-985-2530

Ultra Dot Distribution, 2316 N.E. 8th Rd., Ocala, FL 34470

Ultra Light Arms, Inc., P.O. Box 1270, 214 Price St., Granville, WV 26505 / 304-599-5687; FAX: 304-599-5687

Ultralux (See U.S. Importer-Keng's Firearms Specia

UltraSport Arms, Inc., 1955 Norwood Ct., Racine, WI 53403 / 414-554-3237; FAX: 414-554-9731

Uncle Bud's, HCR 81, Box 100, Needmore, PA 17238 / 717-294-6000; FAX: 717-294-6005

Uncle Mike's (See Michaels of Oregon Co)

Unertl Optical Co. Inc., John, 308 Clay Ave, PO Box 818, Mars, PA 16046-0818 / 412-625-3810

Unique/M.A.P.F., 10 Les Allees, 64700, Hendaye, FRANCE / 33-59 20 71 93

UniTec, 1250 Bedford SW, Canton, OH 44710 / 216-452-4017

United Binocular Co., 9043 S. Western Ave., Chicago, IL 60620

United Cutlery Corp., 1425 United Blvd., Sevierville, TN 37876 / 865-428-2532 or 800-548-0835 FAX: 865-428-2267

United States Optics Technologies, Inc., 5900 Dale St., Buena Park, CA 90621 / 714-994-4901; FAX: 714-994-4904

United States Products Co., 518 Melwood Ave., Pittsburgh, PA 15213 / 412-621-2130; FAX: 412-621-8740

Universal Sports, P.O. Box 532, Vincennes, IN 47591 / 812-882-8680; FAX: 812-882-8680

Unmussig Bullets, D. L., 7862 Brentford Dr., Richmond, VA 23225 / 804-320-1165

Upper Missouri Trading Co., 304 Harold St., Crofton, NE 68730 / 402-388-4844

USAC, 4500-15th St. East, Tacoma, WA 98424 / 206-922-7589

Utica Cutlery Co., 820 Noyes St., Utica, NY 13503 / 315-733-4663; FAX: 315-733-6602

V

V.H. Blackinton & Co., Inc., 221 John L. Dietsch, Attleboro Falls, MA 02763-0300 / 508-699-4436; FAX: 508-695-5349

Valade Engraving, Robert, 931 3rd Ave, Seaside, OR 97138 / 503-738-7672

Valor Corp., 5555 NW 36th Ave., Miami, FL 33142 / 305-633-0127; FAX: 305-634-4536

Valtro USA, Inc, 1281 Andersen Dr., San Rafael, CA 94901 / 415-256-2575; FAX: 415-256-2576

VAM Distribution Co LLC, 1141-B Mechanicsburg Rd., Wooster, OH 44691 www.rex10.com

Van Gorden & Son Inc., C. S., 1815 Main St., Bloomer, WI 54724 / 715-568-2612

Van Horn, Gil, P.O. Box 207, Llano, CA 93544

Van Patten, J. W., P.O. Box 145, Foster Hill, Milford, PA 18337 / 717-296-7069

Van's Gunsmith Service, 224 Route 69-A, Parish, NY 13131 / 315-625-7251

Vancini, Carl (See Bestload, Inc.)

Vann Custom Bullets, 330 Grandview Ave., Novato, CA 94947

Varmint Masters, LLC, Rick Vecqueray, PO Box 6724, Bend, OR 97708 / 541-318-7306; FAX: 541-318-7306 varmint-masters@bendnet.com

Vecqueray, Rick. (See VARMINT MASTERS, LLC)

Vega Tool Co., c/o T.R. Ross, 4865 Tanglewood Ct., Boulder, CO 80301 / 303-530-0174

Vektor USA, Mikael Danforth, 5139 Stanart St, Norfolk, VA 23502 / 888-740-0837; or 757-455-8895; FAX: 757-461-9155

Venco Industries, Inc. (See Shooter's Choice)

Venus Industries, P.O. Box 246, Sialkot-1, PAKISTAN FAX: 92 432 85579

Verney-Carron, B.P. 72, 54 Boulevard Thiers, 42002, FRANCE / 33-477791500; FAX: 33-477790702

Vest, John, P.O. Box 1552, Susanville, CA 96130 / 916-257-7228

Vibra-Tek Co., 1844 Arroya Rd., Colorado Springs, CO 80906 / 719-634-8611; FAX: 719-634-6886

VibraShine, Inc., P.O. Box 577, Taylorsville, MS 39168 / 601-785-9854; FAX: 601-785-9874

Vic's Gun Refinishing, 6 Pineview Dr., Dover, NH 03820-6422 / 603-742-0013

Victory Ammunition, PO Box 1022, Milford, PA 18337 / 717-296-5768; FAX: 717-296-9298

Victory USA, P.O. Box 1021, Pine Bush, NY 12566 / 914-744-2060; FAX: 914-744-5181

Vihtavuori Oy, FIN-41330 Vihtavuori, FINLAND / 358-41-3779211; FAX: 358-41-3771643

Vihtavuori Oy/Kaltron-Pettibone, 1241 Ellis St., Bensenville, IL 60106 / 708-350-1116; FAX: 708-350-1606

Viking Video Productions, P.O. Box 251, Roseburg, OR 97470

Vincent's Shop, 210 Antoinette, Fairbanks, AK 99701

Vincenzo Bernardelli S.p.A., 125 Via Matteotti, P.O. Box 74, Gardone V.T., Bresci, 25063 ITALY / 39-30-8912851-2-3; FAX: 39-30-8910249+

Vintage Arms, Inc., 6003 Saddle Horse, Fairfax, VA 22030 / 703-968-0779; FAX: 703-968-0780

Vintage Industries, Inc., 781 Big Tree Dr., Longwood, FL 32750 / 407-831-8949; FAX: 407-831-5346

Viper Bullet and Brass Works, 11 Brock St., Box 582, Norwich, ON N0J 1P0 CANADA

Viramontez, Ray, 601 Springfield Dr., Albany, GA 31707 / 912-432-9683

Virgin Valley Custom Guns, 450 E 800 N #20, Hurricane, UT 84737 / 435-635-8941; FAX: 435-635-8943 vvcguns@in-fowest.com www.virginvalleyguns.com

Visible Impact Targets, Rts. 5 & 20, E. Bloomfield, NY 14443 / 716-657-6161; FAX: 716-657-5405

Vitt/Boos, 2178 Nichols Ave., Stratford, CT 06614 / 203-375-6859

Voere-KGH m.b.H., P.O. Box 416, A-6333 Kufstein, Tirol, AUSTRIA / 0043-5372-62547; FAX: 0043-5372-65752

Volquartsen Custom Ltd., 24276 240th Street, P.O. Box 397, Carroll, IA 51401 / 712-792-4238; FAX: 712-792-2542

Vom Hoffe (See Old Western Scrounger, Inc., The), 12924 Hwy A-12, Montague, CA 96064 / 916-459-5445; FAX: 916-459-3944

Vorhes, David, 3042 Beecham St., Napa, CA 94558 / 707-226-9116

Vortek Products, Inc., P.O. Box 871181, Canton, MI 48187-6181 / 313-397-5656; FAX: 313-397-5656

VSP Publishers (See Heritage/VSP Gun Books), PO Box 887, McCall, ID 83638 / 208-634-4104; FAX: 208-634-3101

Vulpes Ventures, Inc. Fox Cartridge Division, P.O. Box 1363, Bolingbrook, IL 60440-7363 / 630-759-1229; FAX: 815-439-3945

W

W. Square Enterprises, 9826 Sagedale, Houston, TX 77089 / 713-484-0935; FAX: 281-484-0935

W. Square Enterprises, Load From A Disk, 9826 Sagedale, Houston, TX 77089 / 713-484-0935; FAX: 281-484-0935

W. Waller & Son, Inc., 2221 Stoney Brook Rd., Grantham, NH 03753-7706 / 603-863-4177

W.B. Niemi Engineering, Box 126 Center Road, Greensboro, VT 05841 / 802-533-7180 or 802-533-7141

W.C. Strutz Rifle Barrels, Inc., P.O. Box 611, Eagle River, WI 54521 / 715-479-4766

W.C. Wolff Co., PO Box 458, Newtown Square, PA 19073 / 610-359-9600; FAX: 610-359-9496

W.E. Birdsong & Assoc., 1435 Monterey Rd., Florence, MS 39073-9748 / 601-366-8270

W.E. Brownell Checkering Tools, 9390 Twin Mountain Cir, San Diego, CA 92126 / 619-695-2479; FAX: 619-695-2479

W.J. Riebe Co., 3434 Tucker Rd., Boise, ID 83703

W.R. Case & Sons Cutlery Co., Owens Way, Bradford, PA 16701 / 814-368-4123 or 800-523-6350; FAX: 814-768-5369

Wagoner, Vernon G., 2325 E. Encanto, Mesa, AZ 85213 / 602-835-1307

Wakina by Pic, 24813 Alderbrook Dr., Santa Clarita, CA 91321 / 800-295-8194

Waldron, Herman, Box 475, 80 N. 17th St., Pomeroy, WA 99347 / 509-843-1404

Walker Arms Co., Inc., 499 County Rd. 820, Selma, AL 36701 / 334-872-6231; FAX: 334-872-6262

Walker Mfg., Inc., 8296 S. Channel, Harsen's Island, ML 48028

Wallace, Terry, 385 San Marino, Vallejo, CA 94589 / 707-642-7041

Walls Industries, Inc., P.O. Box 98, 1905 N. Main, Cleburne, TX 76031 / 817-645-4366; FAX: 817-645-7946

Walt's Custom Leather, Walt Whinnery, 1947 Meadow Creek Dr., Louisville, KY 40218 / 502-458-4361

Walters, John, 500 N. Avery Dr., Moore, OK 73160 / 405-799-0376

Walters Industries, 6226 Park Lane, Dallas, TX 75225 / 214-691-6973

Walther GmbH, Carl, B.P. 4325, D-89033 Ulm, GERMANY

WAMCO, Inc., Mingo Loop, P.O. Box 337, Oquossoc, ME 04964-0337 / 207-864-3344

WAMCO--New Mexico, P.O. Box 205, Peralta, NM 87042-0205 / 505-869-0826

Ward & Van Valkenburg, 114 32nd Ave. N., Fargo, ND 58102 / 701-232-2351

Ward Machine, 5620 Lexington Rd., Corpus Christi, TX 78412 / 512-992-1221

Wardell Precision Handguns Ltd., 48851 N. Fig Springs Rd., New River, AZ 85027-8513 / 602-465-7995

Warenski, Julie, 590 E. 500 N., Richfield, UT 84701 / 801-896-5319; FAX: 801-896-5319

Warne Manufacturing Co., 9039 SE Jannsen Rd., Clackamas, OR 97015 / 503-657-5590 or 800-683-5590; FAX: 503-657-5695

Warren & Sweat Mfg. Co., P.O. Box 350440, Grand Island, FL 32784 / 904-669-3166; FAX: 904-669-7272

Warren Muzzleloading Co., Inc., Hwy. 21 North, P.O. Box 100, Ozone, AR 72854 / 501-292-3268

Warren, Kenneth W. (See Mountain States Engraving)

Washita Mountain Whetstone Co., P.O. Box 378, Lake Hamilton, AR 71951 / 501-525-3914

Wasmundt, Jim, P.O. Box 511, Fossil, OR 97830

WASP Shooting Systems, Rt. 1, Box 147, Lakeview, AR 72642 / 501-431-5606

Waterfield Sports, Inc., 13611 Country Lane, Burnsville, MN 55337 / 612-435-8339

Watson Bros., 39 Redcross Way, London Bridge, LONDON U.K. FAX: 44-171-403-336

Watson Trophy Match Bullets, 2404 Wade Hampton Blvd., Greenville, SC 29615 / 864-244-7948 or 941-635-7948

Wayne E. Schwartz Custom Guns, 970 E. Britton Rd., Morrice, MI 48857 / 517-625-4079

Wayne Firearms for Collectors and Investors, James, 2608 N. Laurent, Victoria, TX 77901 / 512-578-1258; FAX: 512-578-3559

Wayne Reno, 2808 Stagestop Rd., Jefferson, CO 80456 / 719-836-3452

MANUFACTURER'S DIRECTORY

Wayne Specialty Services, 260 Waterford Drive, Florissant, MO 63033 / 413-831-7083

WD-40 Co., 1061 Cudahy Pl., San Diego, CA 92110 / 619-275-1400; FAX: 619-275-5823

Weatherby, Inc., 3100 El Camino Real, Atascadero, CA 93422 / 805-466-1767 or 800-227-2016; FAX: 805-466-2527

Weaver Arms Corp. Gun Shop, RR 3, P.O. Box 266, Bloomfield, MO 63825-9528

Weaver Products, P.O. Box 39, Onalaska, WI 54650 / 800-648-9624 or 608-781-5800; FAX: 608-781-0368

Weaver Scope Repair Service, 1121 Larry Mahan Dr., Suite B, El Paso, TX 79925 / 915-593-1005

Webb, Bill, 6504 North Bellefontaine, Kansas City, MO 64119 / 816-453-7431

Weber & Markin Custom Gunsmiths, 4-1691 Powick Rd., Kelowna, BC V1X 4L1 CANADA / 250-762-7575; FAX: 250-861-3655

Weber Jr., Rudolf, P.O. Box 160106, D-5650, GERMANY / 0212-592136

Webley and Scott Ltd., Frankley Industrial Park, Tay Rd., Birmingham, B45 0PA ENGLAND / 011-021-453-1864; FAX: 021-457-7846

Webster Scale Mfg. Co., P.O. Box 188, Sebring, FL 33870 / 813-385-6362

Weems, Cecil, 510 W Hubbard St, Mineral Wells, TX 76067-4847 / 817-325-1462

Weigand Combat Handguns, Inc., 685 South Main Rd., Mountain Top, PA 18707 / 570-868-8358; FAX: 570-868-5218 sales@jackweigand.com www.jackweigand.com

Weihrauch KG, Hermann, Industriestrasse 11, 8744 Mellrichstadt, Mellrichstadt, GERMANY

Weisz Parts, P.O. Box 20038, Columbus, OH 43220-0038 / 614-45-70-500; FAX: 614-846-8585

Welch, Sam, CVSR 2110, Moab, UT 84532 / 801-259-8131

Wellington Outdoors, P.O. Box 244, 1140 Monticello Rd., Madison, GA 30650 / 706-342-4915; FAX: 706-342-7568

Wells, Rachel, 110 N. Summit St., Prescott, AZ 86301 / 520-445-3655

Wells Creek Knife & Gun Works, 32956 State Hwy. 38, Scottsburg, OR 97473 / 541-587-4202; FAX: 541-587-4223

Welsh, Bud, 80 New Road, E. Amherst, NY 14051 / 716-688-6344

Wenger North America/Precise Int'l., 15 Corporate Dr., Orangeburg, NY 10962 / 800-431-2996 FAX: 914-425-4700

Wenig Custom Gunstocks, 103 N. Market St., P.O. Box 249, Lincoln, MO 65338 / 816-547-3334; FAX: 816-547-2881 gunstock@wenig.com www.wenig.com

Werth, T. W., 1203 Woodlawn Rd., Lincoln, IL 62656 / 217-732-1300

Wescombe, Bill (See North Star West)

Wessinger Custom Guns & Engraving, 268 Limestone Rd., Chapin, SC 29036 / 803-345-5677

West, Jack L., 1220 W. Fifth, P.O. Box 427, Arlington, OR 97812

Western Cutlery (See Camillus Cutlery Co.)

Western Design (See Alpha Gunsmith Division)

Western Gunstock Mfg. Co., 550 Valencia School Rd., Aptos, CA 95003 / 408-688-5884

Western Missouri Shooters Alliance, P.O. Box 11144, Kansas City, MO 64119 / 816-597-3950; FAX: 816-229-7350

Western Nevada West Coast Bullets, PO BOX 2270, DAYTON, NV 89403-2270 / 702-246-3941; FAX: 702-246-0836

Westley Richards & Co., 40 Grange Rd., Birmingham, ENGLAND / 010-214722953

Westley Richards Agency USA (See U.S. Importer for Westley Richards & Co.,)

Westrom, John (See Precision Metal Finishing)

Westwind Rifles, Inc., David S. Sullivan, P.O. Box 261, 640 Briggs St., Erie, CO 80516 / 303-828-3823

Weyer International, 2740 Nebraska Ave., Toledo, OH 43607 / 419-534-2020; FAX: 419-534-2697

Whildin & Sons Ltd, E.H., RR 2 Box 119, Tamaqua, PA 18252 / 717-668-6743; FAX: 717-668-6745

Whinnery, Walt (See Walt's Custom Leather)

Whiscombe (See U.S. Importer-Pelaire Products)

White Barn Workshop, 431 County Road, Broadlands, IL 61816

White Flyer Targets, 124 River Road, Middlesex, NJ 08846 / 908 469 0100 or 602-972-7528 FAX: 908-469-9692

White Owl Enterprises, 2583 Flag Rd., Abilene, KS 67410 / 913-263-2613; FAX: 913-263-2613

White Pine Photographic Services, Hwy. 60, General Delivery, Wilno, ON K0J 2N0 CANADA / 613-756-3452

White Rock Tool & Die, 6400 N. Brighton Ave., Kansas City, MO 64119 / 816-454-0478

White Shooting Systems, Inc. (See White Muzzleloading)

Whitestone Lumber Corp., 148-02 14th Ave., Whitestone, NY 11357 / 718-746-4400; FAX: 718-767-1748

Whitetail Design & Engineering Ltd., 9421 E. Mannsiding Rd., Clare, MI 48617 / 517-386-3932

Wichita Arms, Inc., 923 E. Gilbert, P.O. Box 11371, Wichita, KS 67211 / 316-265-0661; FAX: 316-265-0760

Wick, David E., 1504 Michigan Ave., Columbus, IN 47201 / 812-376-6960

Widener's Reloading & Shooting Supply, Inc., P.O. Box 3009 CRS, Johnson City, TN 37602 / 615-282-6786; FAX: 615-282-6651

Wideview Scope Mount Corp., 13535 S. Hwy. 16, Rapid City, SD 57701 / 605-341-3220; FAX: 605-341-9142 wv-don@rapidnet.net

Wiebe, Duane, 846 Holly WYA, Placerville, CA 95667-3415

Wiest, M. C., 10737 Dutchtown Rd., Knoxville, TN 37932 / 423-966-4545

Wilcox All-Pro Tools & Supply, 4880 147th St., Montezuma, IA 50171 / 515-623-3138; FAX: 515-623-3104

Wilcox Industries Corp, Robert F Guarasi, 53 Durham St, Portsmouth, NH 03801 / 603-431-1331; FAX: 603-431-1221

Wild Bill's Originals, P.O. Box 13037, Burton, WA 98013 / 206-463-5738; FAX: 206-465-5925

Wild West Guns, 7521 Old Seward Hwy, Unit A, Anchorage, AK 99518 / 800-992-4570 or 907-344-4500; FAX: 907-344-4005

Wilderness Sound Products Ltd., 4015 Main St. A, Springfield, OR 97478 / 503-741-0263 or 800-437-0006; FAX: 503-741-7648

Wildey, Inc., 45 Angevine Rd, Warren, CT 06754-1818 / 203-355-9000; FAX: 203-354-7759

Wildlife Research Center, Inc., 1050 McKinley St., Anoka, MN 55303 / 612-427-3350 or 800-USE-LURE; FAX: 612-427-8354

Wilhelm Brenneke KG, Ilmenauweg 2, 30851, Langenhagen, GERMANY / 0511/97262-0; FAX: 0511/97262-62

Will-Burt Co., 169 S. Main, Orrville, OH 44667

William Fagan & Co., 22952 15 Mile Rd., Clinton Township, MI 48035 / 810-465-4637; FAX: 810-792-6996

William Powell & Son (Gunmakers) Ltd., 35-37 Carrs Lane, Birmingham, B4 7SX ENGLAND / 121-643-0689; FAX: 121-631-3504

William Powell Agency, 22 Circle Dr., Bellmore, NY 11710 / 516-679-1158

Williams Gun Sight Co., 7389 Lapeer Rd., Box 329, Davison, MI 48423 / 810-653-2131 or 800-530-9028; FAX: 810-658-2140 williamsgunsight.com

Williams Mfg. of Oregon, 110 East B St., Drain, OR 97435 / 503-836-7461; FAX: 503-836-7245

Williams Shootin' Iron Service, The Lynx-Line, Rt 2 Box 223A, Mountain Grove, MO 65711 / 417-948-0902 FAX: 417-948-0902

Williamson Precision Gunsmithing, 117 W. Pipeline, Hurst, TX 76053 / 817-285-0064; FAX: 817-280-0044

Willow Bend, P.O. Box 203, Chelmsford, MA 01824 / 978-256-8508; FAX: 978-256-8508

Willson Safety Prods. Div., PO Box 622, Reading, PA 19603-0622 / 610-376-6161; FAX: 610-371-7725

Wilson Case, Inc., P.O. Box 1106, Hastings, NE 68902-1106 / 800-322-5493; FAX: 402-463-5276 sales@wilsoncase.com www.wilsoncase.com

Wilson Gun Shop, 2234 County Road 719, Berryville, AR 72616 / 870-545-3618; FAX: 870-545-3310

Winchester Div. Olin Corp., 427 N. Shamrock, E. Alton, IL 62024 / 618-258-3566; FAX: 618-258-3599

Winchester Press (See New Win Publishing, Inc.), 186 Center St, Clinton, NJ 08809 / 908-735-9701; FAX: 908-735-9703

Winchester Sutler, Inc., The, 270 Shadow Brook Lane, Winchester, VA 22603 / 540-888-3595; FAX: 540-888-4632

Windish, Jim, 2510 Dawn Dr., Alexandria, VA 22306 / 703-765-1994

Windjammer Tournament Wads Inc., 750 W. Hampden Ave., Suite 170, Englewood, CO 80110 / 303-781-6329

Wingshooting Adventures, 0-1845 W. Leonard, Grand Rapids, MI 49544 / 616-677-1980; FAX: 616-677-1986

Winkle Bullets, R.R. 1, Box 316, Heyworth, IL 61745

Winter, Robert M., P.O. Box 484, 42975-287th St., Menno, SD 57045 / 605-387-5322

Wise Custom Guns, 1402 Blanco Rd, San Antonio, TX 78212-2716 / 210-828-3388

Wise Guns, Dale, 333 W Olmos Dr, San Antonio, TX 78212 / 210-828-3388

Wiseman and Co., Bill, PO Box 3427, Dryan, TX 77805 / 409-690-3456; FAX: 409-690-0156

Wisners Inc/Twin Pine Armory, P.O. Box 58, Hwy. 6, Adna, WA 98522 / 360-748-4590; FAX: 360-748-1802

Wolf (See J.R. Distributing)

Wolf's Western Traders, 40 E. Works, No. 3F, Sheridan, WY 82801 / 307-674-5352 patwolf@wavecom.net

Wolfe Publishing Co., 6471 Airpark Dr., Prescott, AZ 86301 / 520-445-7810 or 800-899-7810; FAX: 520-778-5124

Wolverine Footwear Group, 9341 Courtland Dr. NE, Rockford, MI 49351 / 616-866-5500; FAX: 616-866-5658

Wood, Mel, P.O. Box 1255, Sierra Vista, AZ 85636 / 602-455-5541

Wood, Frank (See Classic Guns, Inc.), 3230 Medlock Bridge Rd, Ste 110, Norcross, GA 30092 / 404-242-7944

Woodleigh (See Huntington Die Specialties)

Woods Wise Products, P.O. Box 681552, 2200 Bowman Rd., Franklin, TN 37068 / 800-735-8182; FAX: 615-726-2637

Woodstream, P.O. Box 327, Lititz, PA 17543 / 717-626-2125 FAX: 717-626-1912

Woodworker's Supply, 1108 North Glenn Rd., Casper, WY 82601 / 307-237-5354

Woolrich, Inc., Mill St., Woolrich, PA 17701 / 800-995-1299; FAX: 717-769-6234/6259

Working Guns, Jim Coffin, 1224 NW Fernwood Cir, Corvallis, OR 97330-2909 / 541-928-4391

World Class Airguns, 2736 Morningstar Dr., Indianapolis, IN 46229 / 317-897-5548

World of Targets (See Birchwood Casey)

World Trek, Inc., 7170 Turkey Creek Rd., Pueblo, CO 81007-1046 / 719-546-2121; FAX: 719-543-6886

Worthy Products, Inc., RR 1, P.O. Box 213, Martville, NY 13111 / 315-324-5298

Wosenitz VHP, Inc., Box 741, Dania, FL 33004 / 305-923-3748; FAX: 305-925-2217

Wostenholm (See Ibberson [Sheffield] Ltd., George)

Wright's Hardwood Gunstock Blanks, 8540 SE Kane Rd., Gresham, OR 97080 / 503-666-1705

WTA Manufacturing, P.O. Box 164, Kit Carson, CO 80825 / 800-700-3054; FAX: 719-962-3570

Wyant Bullets, Gen. Del., Swan Lake, MT 59911

Wyant's Outdoor Products, Inc., P.O. Box 9, Broadway, VA 22815

Wyoming Bonded Bullets, Box 91, Sheridan, WY 82801 / 307-674-8091

Wyoming Custom Bullets, 1626 21st St., Cody, WY 82414

Wyoming Knife Corp., 101 Commerce Dr., Ft. Collins, CO 80524 / 303-224-3454

X

X-Spand Target Systems, 26-10th St. SE, Medicine Hat, AB T1A 1P7 CANADA / 403-526-7997; FAX: 403-528-2362

Y

Yankee Gunsmith, 2901 Deer Flat Dr., Copperas Cove, TX 76522 / 817-547-8433

Yavapai College, 1100 E. Sheldon St., Prescott, AZ 86301 / 520-776-2353 FAX: 520-776-2355

Yavapai Firearms Academy Ltd., P.O. Box 27290, Prescott Valley, AZ 86312 / 520-772-8262

Yearout, Lewis E. (See Montana Outfitters), 308 Riverview Dr E, Great Falls, MT 59404 / 406-761-0859

Yee, Mike, 29927 56 Pl. S., Auburn, WA 98001 / 206-839-3991

Yellowstone Wilderness Supply, P.O. Box 129, W. Yellowstone, MT 59758 / 406-646-7613

Yesteryear Armory & Supply, P.O. Box 408, Carthage, TN 37030

York M-1 Conversions, 803 Mill Creek Run, Plantersville, TX 77363 / 800-527-2881 or 713-477-8442

Young Country Arms, William, 1409 Kuehner Dr #13, Simi Valley, CA 93063-4478

Yukon Arms Classic Ammunition, 1916 Brooks, P.O. Box 223, Missoula, MT 59801 / 406-543-9614

Z

Z's Metal Targets & Frames, P.O. Box 78, South Newbury, NH 03255 / 603-938-2826

Z-M Weapons, 203 South St., Bernardston, MA 01337 / 413-648-9501; FAX: 413-648-0219

Zabala Hermanos S.A., P.O. Box 97, Eibar, 20600 SPAIN / 43-768085 or 43-768076; FAX: 34-43-768201

Zander's Sporting Goods, 7525 Hwy 154 West, Baldwin, IL 62217-9706 / 800-851-4373 FAX: 618-785-2320

Zanoletti, Pietro, Via Monte Gugielpo, 4, I-25063 Gardone V.T., ITALY

Zanotti Armor, Inc., 123 W. Lone Tree Rd., Cedar Falls, IA 50613 / 319-232-9650

ZDF Import Export, Inc., 2975 South 300 West, Salt Lake City, UT 84115 / 801 485-1012; FAX: 801-484-4363

Zeeryp, Russ, 1601 Foard Dr., Lynn Ross Manor, Morristown, TN 37814 / 615-586-2357

Zero Ammunition Co., Inc., 1601 22nd St. SE, P.O. Box 1188, Cullman, AL 35056-1188 / 800-545-9376; FAX: 205-739-4683

Ziegel Engineering, 2108 Lomina Ave., Long Beach, CA 90815 / 562-596-9481; FAX: 562-598-4734 ziegel@aol.com www.ziegelerg.com

Zim's, Inc., 4370 S. 3rd West, Salt Lake City, UT 84107 / 801-268-2505

Zoli, Antonio, Via Zanardelli 39, Casier Postal 21, I-25063 Gardone V.T., ITALY

Ziny's Metal Targets (See Z's Metal Targets & Frames)

Zufall, Joseph F., P.O. Box 304, Golden, CO 80402-0304

MUST-HAVE REFERENCES

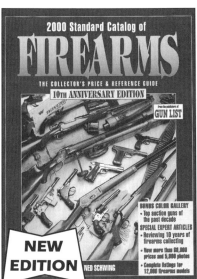

2000 Standard Catalog™ of Firearms
The Collector's Price & Reference Guide,
10th Anniversary Edition
by Ned Schwing
Packed with more than 80,000 real-world prices and over 5,000 photos, this is the must-have resource for every gun collector. This year's 10th Anniversary Edition boasts two first-time special features: A full-color gallery of some of the world's most rare and beautiful firearms; and an insightful look at the firearms industry over the last 10 years. In addition, several sections have been updated and expanded, offering comprehensive coverage on 12,000 different firearm models.
Softcover • 8-1/2 x 11
1,312 pages
5,000+ b&w photos • 40 color photos
Item # GG10 • $32.95

The Gun Digest Book of Assault Weapons
5th Edition
by Jack Lewis & David E. Steele
Here's the latest information (specifications, applications, etc.) on the world's assault weapons, reported in-depth by retired Marine Jack Lewis. Exclusive, detailed coverage of today's military and police weaponry from France, Germany, Russia, South Africa and the USA. Broad coverage of rifles, submachine guns, crew-served machine guns, combat shotguns - plus an educated look into the 21st century.
Softcover • 8-1/2 x 11
256 pages
500 b&w photos
Item # AW5 • $21.95

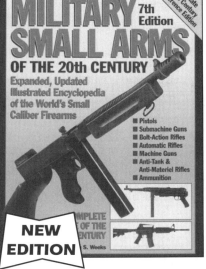

Military Small Arms of the 20th Century
7th Edition
by Ian V. Hogg and John S. Weeks
This is the complete and ultimate small arms reference by Ian Hogg, international military arms authority. Now expanded and updated to include every arm in service from 1900 to 2000; complete with specifications, history and insightful commentary on performance and effectiveness. There is no comparable book.
Softcover • 8-1/2 x 11
416 pages
800+ b&w photos
Item # MSA7 • $24.95

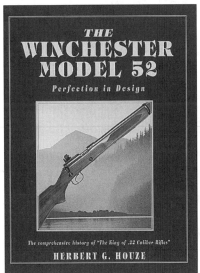

Mauser Military Rifles of the World
2nd Edition
by Robert W. D. Ball
Learn how to identify every Mauser model from 1871 to 1945 while looking over production figures and the relative rarity of each model. This updated edition of a collector's classic unveils 100 new photos of rare guns and the men who used them. Whether your interest is in collecting or military history, this book gives you all the details you won't find anywhere else.
Hardcover • 8-1/2 x 11
304 pages • 1,000 b&w photos
48-page color section
Item # FCM02 • $44.95

Standard Catalog™ of Winchester
Edited by David D. Kowalski
From 1886 to 1929 the Winchester Repeating Arms Company put its name on everything from garden tools to washing machines. Now there is a single price and identification guide covering the full gamut of the company's products. The Standard Catalog of Winchester identifies and values 2,500 collectibles, including firearms, cartridges, shotshells, fishing tackle, sporting goods, tools and pocket knives, plus provides unsurpassed coverage of the company's popular calendars, advertising materials and packaging. You will be amazed at the 2,500 photographs, including hundreds of rarely seen items and a gorgeous four-color gallery of the best Winchester offered.
Softcover • 8-1/2 x 11 • 704 pages
2,500 b&w photos • 75 color photos
Item # SCW1 • $39.95

The Winchester Model 52
Perfection In Design
by Herbert G. Houze
Historical arms enthusiast Herbert Houze unravels the mysteries surrounding the development of what many consider the most perfect rifle ever made. The book covers the rifle's improvements through five modifications. Users, collectors and marksmen will appreciate each variation's history, serial number sequences and authentic photos.
Hardcover • 8-1/2 x 11
192 pages
190 b&w photos
Item # WIN • $34.95

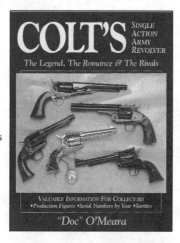
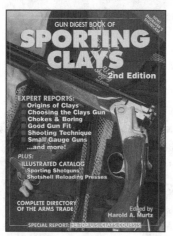

2001 GUNS ILLUSTRATED READER INTEREST SURVEY

1. Check all that apply: In which of the following shooting activities are you currently active?

- ☐ Handgunning
- ☐ Shotgunning
- ☐ Muzzleloading
- ☐ Airgunning
- ☐ Handloading
- ☐ Riflery
- ☐ Precision shooting
- ☐ None of these

2. Check all that apply: Which of the following are you interested in as they relate to *today's* firearms?

- ☐ Handguns—autoloading pistols
- ☐ Handguns—revolvers
- ☐ Handguns—single shot, misc.
- ☐ Handguns—rimfire models
- ☐ Handguns—centerfire models
- ☐ RIFLES—autoloading
- ☐ RIFLES—lever/pump-action
- ☐ RIFLES—bolt-action
- ☐ RIFLES—single shot
- ☐ RIFLES—rimfire models
- ☐ RIFLES—centerfire models
- ☐ Shotguns—autoloading
- ☐ Shotguns—pump-action

- ☐ Shotguns—twin-barrel
- ☐ Shotguns—bolt-action, single shot
- ☐ MUZZLELOADERS—traditional rifles & muskets
- ☐ MUZZLELOADERS—in-line rifles
- ☐ MUZZLELOADERS—handguns
- ☐ Accessories
- ☐ Ammunition—handgun
- ☐ Ammunition—rifle
- ☐ Ammunition—shotgun
- ☐ VINTAGE/SURPLUS ARMS
- ☐ USED GUNS
- ☐ CUSTOMIZED GUNS

3. Check all that apply: Which of the following shooting publications do you read regularly, that is, at least three out of every four issues?

- ☐ American Handgunner
- ☐ Shooting Sportsman
- ☐ Guns & Ammo
- ☐ Guns Magazine
- ☐ Shooting Times
- ☐ Other:_____

4. Check all that apply: Which of the following *gun books* do you regularly purchase?

- ☐ Gun Digest
- ☐ Handguns
- ☐ Shooter's Bible
- ☐ Handloader's Digest
- ☐ Others:_____
- _____

5. Check all that apply: Which of the following did you read in this year's edition of GUNS ILLUSTRATED?

- ☐ FEATURE ARTICLES

NEW PRODUCT EDITORS REPORTS

- ☐ Handgun News: Revolvers, Single-Shots & Others
- ☐ Handgun News: Autoloading Pistols
- ☐ Rifle Report!
- ☐ Shotgun Update
- ☐ Muzzleloader News
- ☐ Ammo Update!

CATALOG SECTIONS:

NEW! SEMI-CUSTOM ARMS
- ☐ Handguns
- ☐ Rifles
- ☐ Shotguns

COMMERCIAL ARMS
- ☐ Handguns
- ☐ Rifles
- ☐ Shotguns
- ☐ Airguns

REFERENCE SECTION:

- ☐ Directory of the Arms Trade

6. ADDITIONAL COMMENTS?_____
_____
_____
_____

Thank you for filling out the 2001 GUNS ILLUSTRATED Reader Interest Survey. Please return your completed survey no later than August 3, 2001. This offer expires on August 3, 2001.

WHICH ONE OF THESE WOULD YOU LIKE FOR TAKING THE TIME TO COMPLETE OUR SURVEY? **

☐ 4 free issues of GUN LIST magazine (a retail value of $22.00). GUN LIST is the leading national newspaper for people who buy and sell quality firearms.

- OR -

☐ 2 free issues of BLADE magazine (a retail value of $9.90). BLADE is the world's #1 knife publication. It is the largest and most comprehensive knife magazine available today.

Name: ☐☐☐☐☐☐☐☐☐☐☐☐☐☐☐☐☐☐☐☐☐☐☐☐☐☐

Address: ☐☐☐☐☐☐☐☐☐☐☐☐☐☐☐☐☐☐☐☐☐☐☐☐☐☐

City: ☐☐☐☐☐☐☐☐☐☐☐☐☐☐☐☐☐☐☐☐☐☐☐☐☐

State: ☐☐ Zip Code: ☐☐☐☐☐ Phone: ☐☐☐–☐☐☐–☐☐☐☐

** PLEASE NOTE: You must complete all of the survey questions and return this by August 3, 2001 to qualify to receive a free gift (4 issues of GUN LIST or 2 issues of BLADE).

ABAZFD

Tape Here

Tape Here

BUSINESS REPLY MAIL

FIRST-CLASS MAIL PERMIT NO. 12 IOLA, WI

POSTAGE WILL BE PAID BY ADDRESSEE

KRAUSE PUBLICATIONS
MARKETING RESEARCH DEPT
700 E STATE ST
IOLA WI   54945-9989

NO POSTAGE
NECESSARY IF
MAILED IN
THE UNITED
STATES